FIRESIDE

HOW TO DESIGN, BUILD, REMODEL AND MAINTAIN YOUR HOME

Joseph D. Falcone, a.i.a., b.a.

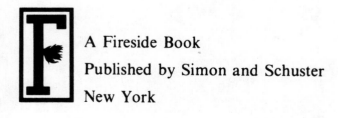
A Fireside Book
Published by Simon and Schuster
New York

DEDICATION

TO MY WIFE AND CHILDREN FOR THEIR RELENT-
LESS PATIENCE IN THE TIME NECESSARY FOR THE
WRITING OF THIS BOOK.

First Fireside Edition, 1980
Published by Simon & Schuster, Inc.
Simon & Schuster Building
Rockefeller Center
1230 Avenue of the Americas
New York, New York 10020
Published by arrangement with John Wiley & Sons, Inc.
FIRESIDE and colophon are registered trademarks
of Simon & Schuster, Inc.

Manufactured in the United States of America

19 18 17 16 15 14 13

Library of Congress Cataloging in Publication Data

Falcone, Joseph D
   How to design, build, remodel, and maintain your
home.

   (A Fireside book)
   Bibliography: p.
   Includes index.
   1. House construction. 2. Dwellings—Remodeling
3. Dwellings—Maintenance and repair.   I. Title.
TH4811.F34   1980   690'.8   80-12951
ISBN 0-671-25617-3

acknowledgments

Grateful appreciation is extended to the following for their generous cooperation and information contained in this book.

Stephen M. Brown
Michael E. Hayes
Eugene A. Liberati
Cynthia Saccoccia
Alcoa Building Products Inc. , Pittsburgh, PA
Allyn & Bacon Publishing Co., Inc., Boston, MA
Alsco Anconda, Akron, OH
American Institute of Architects, Washington, D.C.
American Olean Tile Company, Lansdale, PA
American Parquet Association, Inc., Little Rock, AR
American Plywood Association, Tacoma, WA
American Society of Heating, Refrigerating and Air-Conditioning
 Engineers, Inc., NY, NY
American Technical Society, Chicago, IL
Am-Fin Sauna, Red Hill, PA
Andersen Corporation, Bayport, MN
Architectural Woodwork Institute, Arlington, VA
Armstrong Cork Company, Lancaster, PA
Atlas Minerals & Chemicals Division ESB Inc., Mertztown, PA
Brick Institue of America, McLean, VA
Brockway Smith, Andover, MA
Buckingham Virginia Slate Corporation, Richmond, VA
California Redwood Association, San Francisco, CA
Champion Building Products, Stamford, CT
Congoleum Corp., Kearny, NJ
Create Center, Williamsburg, VA
Dallas Ceramic Company, Dallas, TX
Daystar Corporation, Burlington, MA
Eno Foundation For Transportation Inc., Westport, CT
Factory Mutual System, Norwood, MA
Florida Tile, Lakeland, FL
Frederick Post Co., Englewood, NJ
General Felt Industries, Inc., Los Angeles, CA
Georgia Pacific, Portland, OR
Gold Bond.Buffalo, NY
Greater Providence Board of Realtors, Providence, RI
Harvey Hubble, Inc., Bridgewater, CT
Hilltop Slate Co., Middle Granville, NY

Home Crest Corp., Goshen, IN
John Wiley & Sons Inc., New York, NY
Johns Manville Sales Corporation, Denver, CO
Johnson Rubber Co., Middlefield, OH
Koppers Company Inc., Pittsburg, PA
Lasco Industries, Houston, TX
Lead Industries Association, Inc. New York, NY
Lord & Burnham, Irvington On The Hudson, NY
Ludowici Celadon Company, Chicago, IL
Masonite Corporation, Chicago, IL
Maze, W. H. Co., Peru, IL
Minnesota Lathing & Plastering Bureau, St. Paul, MN
William T. Morgan
Monsanto Textiles Company, Atlanta, GA
Multi-Housing News, New York, NY
National Forest Products Association, Washington, D.C.
National Oak Flooring Manufacturers Association, Inc. Memphis, TN
National Rolling Mills Co., Malvern, PA
Owens Corning Fiberglas, Toledo, OH
Park Avenue Cement Block, Cranston, RI
Plasticrete Corporation, North Haven, CT
Portland Cement Association, Skokie, IL
PPG Industries, Pittsburg, PA
Prentice Hall Inc., Englewood Cliffs, NJ
Providence Journal, Providence, RI
Raynor Manufacturing Co., Dixon, IL
Red Cedar Shingle & Handsplit Shake Bureau, Bellevue, WA
Rheem Manufacturing Co., Chicago, IL
Simmons Broadman Publishing Corp., New York, NY
Stanley Works, New Britain, CT
Supradar Manufacturing Corporation, New York, NY
Theodore Audel & Co., Indianapolis, IN
Tile Council of America, Princeton, NJ
United States Gypsum, Chicago, IL
United States Steel Corporation, Pittsburg, PA
Walter Kidde & Co., Inc. Belleville, NY
Westmoreland Tubular Products Manufacturing Co., Jamica, NY
Weyerhaeuser Forest Products, St. Paul, MN

ABOUT THIS BOOK

Before any project is undertaken, the entire book should be read for the feel of construction methods and techniques. The book is arranged by chapters in order of construction practices and the work described in each chapter should be completed before any subsequent chapter or order of sequence is attempted.

The successful completion of any project will depend upon careful planning, analysis and work accuracy. It has been written for ease in understanding both in text and illustrations and, if followed carefully, should present no problem. Construction is so varied and diversified that only a general description can be written. Each project, large or small has its own characteristics and information can only be applied through a general fashion by the use of this text book.

This book has not been written alone for the **DO-IT-YOUR-SELF** project, but also for general knowledge of construction techniques which can be applied to any type of wood frame building.

ABOUT THE AUTHOR

Joseph D. Falcone, A.I.A. is an architect, educator, city planner and author. He is head of an architectural firm with a permanent staff of architects and engineers, served as Chairman of City Plan Commission for 18 years and has taught and is currently teaching at Secondary, College and University levels.

He is listed in WHO'S WHO IN THE EAST for the past five years for outstanding design in construction and has won a national award in design by the American Association of School Administrators. He has been elected to the International Registry of WHO'S WHO.

Mr. Falcone is considered an expert in all types of building design and construction and has a proven track record of optimum combination of creativity, logic, soundness and economy.

contents

INTRODUCTION

The days of unpredictable high construction costs are here to stay. Labor and material costs have soared to an almost unreachable,unaffordable high and labor unions have almost outpriced themselves from the construction market. Home-owners are almost compelled to do their own home building, repairing, remodeling and maintenance.

If you have outgrown the size of your home, if you are planning to build or buy a home or if you are planning to alter your home, this book will show you **"HOW TO"** from the selection of site to moving-in. You will learn how to select, buy and use building materials, and in doing so, you will learn how to save as much as 70% of the cost of the project. You will learn how to use and become familiar with local building codes and ordinances, how to apply for a building permit, how to prepare necessary documents for exemption to Zoning Laws, how to design the mechanical system at no cost: (Plumbing, Heating, Electrical, Air-Conditioning and Ventilation). You will learn how to converse intelligently with trades men using building trade terms.

On the other hand, if you are planning to hire a building contractor, this book will teach you how to do your own construction supervision and to see that you get what you pay for. It will show you what legal contracts to use and for what purpose. You will also learn how to be your own contractor and how to sub-let various phases of construction to sub-contractors.

This book will teach you how to read plans and specifications and to make changes in plans during construction periods. You will learn how to prepare documents for a change in construction contracts, and if you wish to construct only a part of your home yourself, this book will show you how to avoid the time and expense of litigation.

It will show you the proper scale and design so that your project will be pleasing to the average eye. You will learn what tools to use and for what purpose. If you have limited mechanical abilities, it will show you how to perform certain jobs yourself while contractors are working on other parts of the project at the same time.

The decision to remodel has produced a boom in home improvements. U.S. spending on home repairs totals nearly $30 Billion annually. Sociologists predict that families who economize and maintain a home, center their leisure time activities more on **DO-IT-YOURSELF** projects. With more home centered lives, home owners are increasingly remodeling their home tailored to their tastes and to also increase the resale value.

Two thirds of U.S. families own their home and the proportion is rising steadily. In spite of inflation, high mortgage rates and taxes, home ownership is still the best, safest and the wisest investment a family can make and the only way you can avoid becoming house-poor is to **DO-IT-YOURSELF**: you can do it, all you need do is try.

BASIC TOOLS and USE

CARPENTERS' LEVEL

COMBINATION SQUARE

HACK SAW

PUTTY KNIFE

COMPASS SAW

CROSS CUT SAW

COPING SAW

BIT BRACE

AUGER BIT

KNIVES

MITRE BOXE

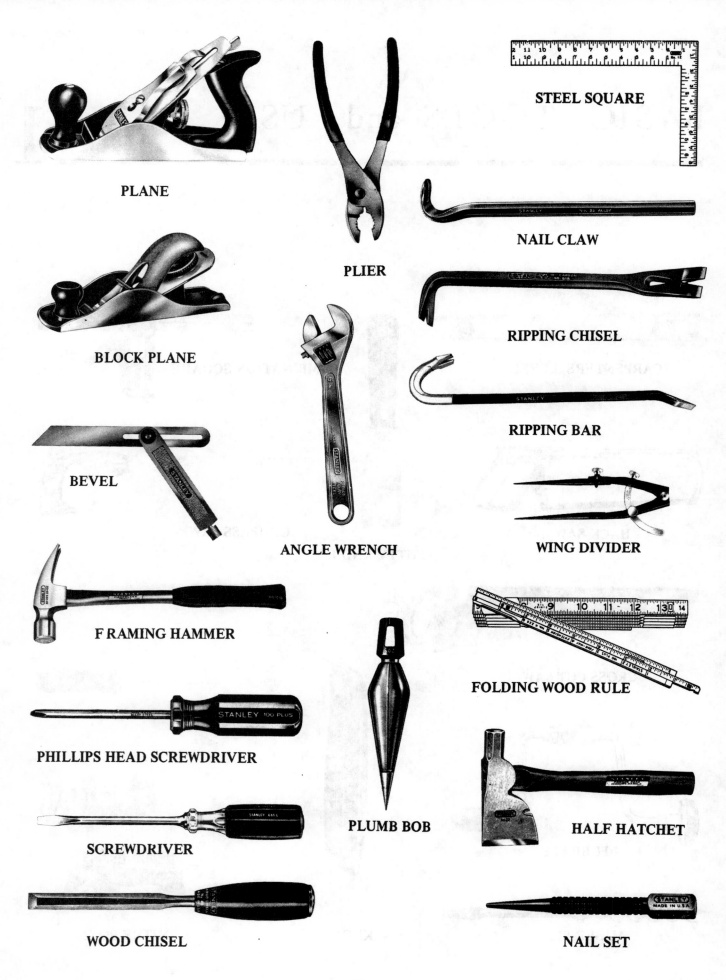

PLANE

PLIER

STEEL SQUARE

NAIL CLAW

BLOCK PLANE

RIPPING CHISEL

RIPPING BAR

BEVEL

ANGLE WRENCH

WING DIVIDER

FRAMING HAMMER

FOLDING WOOD RULE

PHILLIPS HEAD SCREWDRIVER

PLUMB BOB

HALF HATCHET

SCREWDRIVER

WOOD CHISEL

NAIL SET

USING BASIC TOOLS

HAMMER

A medium weight (12-13 ounce) claw hammer is good for general purposes.

- Hold a hammer near the end of the handle for more hitting power. To start a nail, hold it in place and tap it gently a few times until it is firmly set. Hit straight in. (Fig. 1)

- To avoid hammer marks on the wood, use a nail set (Fig. 2) or another nail to drive a nail the last one-eighth inch into the wood.

- To remove a nail use claw end of hammer. Place a small block of wood under the head of the hammer to avoid marking the wood. (Fig. 3)

SCREWDRIVER

You need two types of screwdrivers for household repairs:

Straight blade (Fig. 4), and **Phillips** (Fig. 5). Both come in various sizes. The blade of the screwdriver should fit the slot in the screw. (Fig. 6)

- When using the screwdriver, push against the head of the screw as you turn it. (Fig. 7)

- It's easier to put a screw into wood if you make a hole first with a nail or drill. (Fig. 8). Rub wax or soap on the screw threads to make it go in easier.

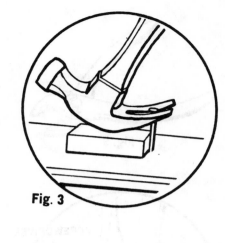

Fig. 3

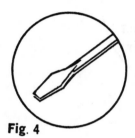

Fig. 4

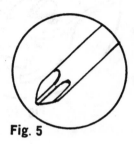

Fig. 5

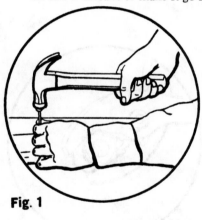

Fig. 1

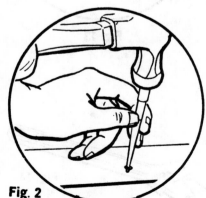

Fig. 2

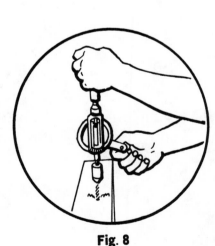

Fig. 8

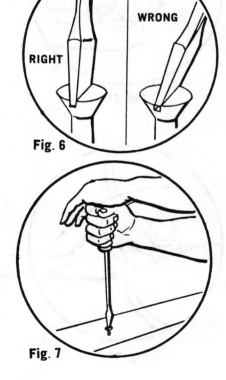

Fig. 6

RIGHT   WRONG

Fig. 7

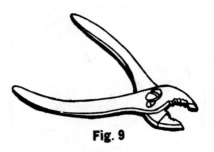

Fig. 9

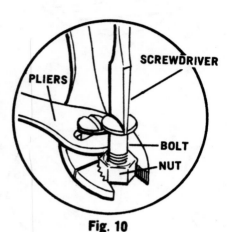

Fig. 10

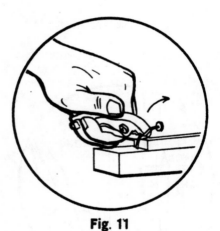

Fig. 11

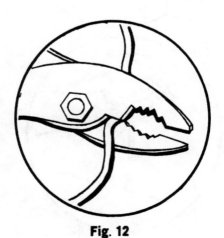

Fig. 12

PLIERS

A **slip joint pliers** can be used for many jobs around the house. (Fig. 9)

- Use pliers to hold a nut while you turn a bolt with a screwdriver. (Fig. 10)

- Use it to remove nails or brads. Pull the nail out at the same angle it was driven in. Use small blocks under the pliers if you need leverage. (Fig. 11)

- Use it to bend or cut wire or to straighten a bent nail. (Fig. 12)

- Use it to turn nuts. Wrap tape or cloth around the nut to avoid scratching it. (Fig. 13)

An **adjustable wrench** (Fig. 14) is adjustable to fit different sizes of nuts. If a nut is hard to loosen, apply a few drops of penetrating oil or kerosene. (Fig. 15). Let it soak a couple of hours or overnight. If the wrench has a tendency to slip off, try turning it over.

HANDSAW

A handsaw (Fig. 16) with about 10 teeth to the inch is good for most household work. (Fig. 17)

Mark where you want to cut. Pull the saw back and forth several times to start a groove. Let the weight of the saw do the cutting at first. If you are sawing a board, it will be easier if you support it and hold it firmly near where you're cutting. (Fig. 18)

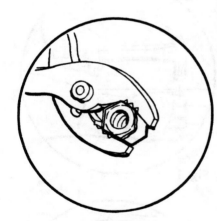

Fig. 13

Fig. 14

4

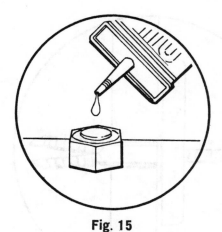

Fig. 15

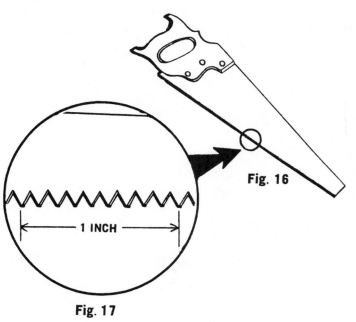

Fig. 16

Fig. 17

1 INCH

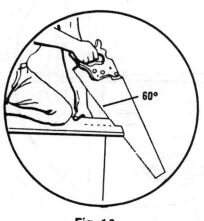

60°

Fig. 18

NAILS, SCREWS, AND BOLTS

Nails, screws, and bolts each have special uses. Keep them on hand for household repairs.

NAILS come in two shapes.

> **Box nails** have large heads. Use them for rough work when appearance doesn't matter. (Fig. 1)

> **Finishing nails** have only very small heads. You can drive them below the surface with a nail set or another nail, and cover them. Use them where looks are important, as in putting up panelling or building shelves. (Fig. 2)

SCREWS are best where holding strength is important. (Fig. 3). Use them to install towel bars, curtain rods, to repair drawers, or to mount hinges. Where screws work loose, you can refill the holes with matchsticks or wood putty and replace them.

> Use **molly screws** or **toggle bolts** on a plastered wall where strength is needed to hold heavy pictures, mirrors, towel bars, etc.

> **Molly screws** have two parts (Fig. 4). To install, first make a small hole in the plaster and drive the casing in even with the wall surface. Tighten screw to spread casing in the back. Remove screw and put it through the item you are hanging, into casing, and tighten.

> **Toggle bolts.** (Fig. 5). Drill a hole in the plaster large enough for the folded toggle to go through. Remove toggle. Put bolt through towel bar or whatever you are hanging. Replace toggle. Push toggle through the wall and tighten with a screwdriver.

> **Plastic anchor screws** (Fig. 6) should be used where you want to attach something to a concrete wall. To install, first make a small hole in the wall and drive casing in even with the wall surface. Put screw through item and into the casing, and tighten.

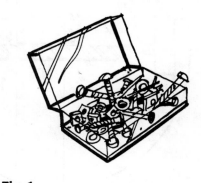

Fig. 1

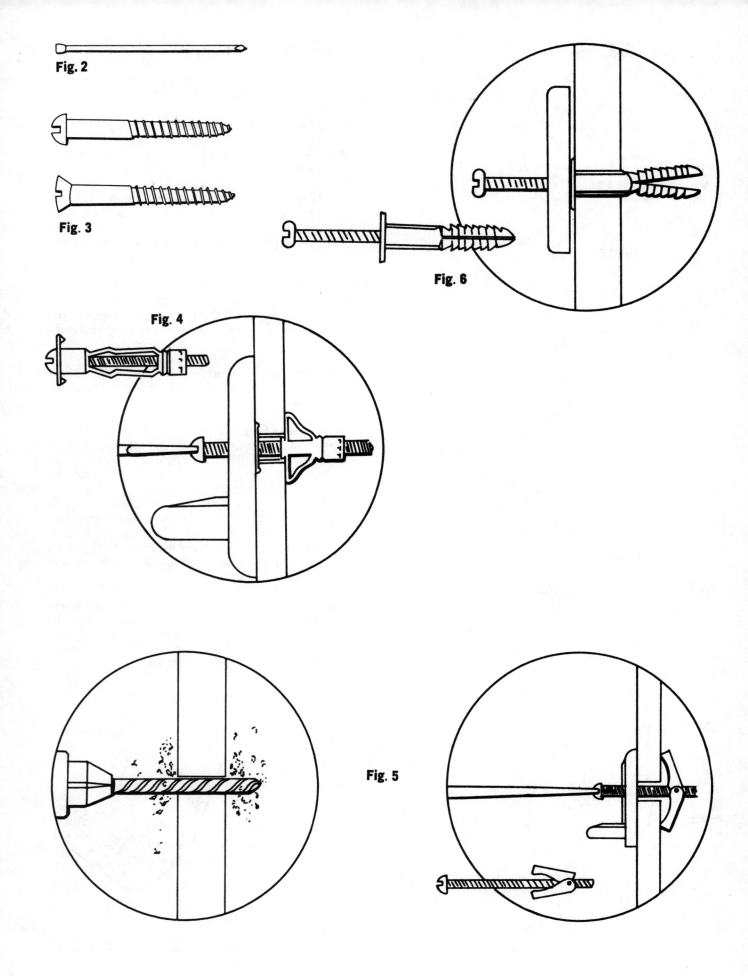

Fig. 2

Fig. 3

Fig. 6

Fig. 4

Fig. 5

6

SITE SELECTION
2

All buildings start with an idea. That idea is later developed on paper and then finally becomes a reality. When you plan your home, the first thought will be, where to build. Only you can answer that question and the experts can only advise you. With that in mind let's try to answer that question with a question. Where would you like to live? In the city? Maybe you would prefer the country or perhaps the woods, a farm or the suburbs? You might consider the ocean or lake front for a house. If you have one or more cars in your family and are not within the proximity of a public transportation system, location may not be a problem. If on the other hand you have school age children or elderly people living in your home, you may want to be close to the conveniences of the city. The distance and time it will take to get to and from work will be another deciding factor.

Once you have selected a site, your next decision is how much land is needed. This question may be answered by law because in some communities, the minimum lot area, where there is no water or sewer, is 80,000 square feet or almost two acres of land. The reason is to prevent wells and cesspools from marrying.

If you tend to be lazy and don't like to cut grass or plow snow or rake leaves or plant a garden, you will be looking for a minimum size lot. This may be as small as 40' x 80'. The minimum sized lot is based on the Zoning laws of your community. If, on the other hand, you are ambitious and enjoy working around the house, you may be looking for a larger lot. If you prefer space without feeling crowded by neighbors, again you may be looking for an even larger parcel. The determining factor of the size house lot is based on what you can afford and your personal living habits.

It is important to choose a neighborhood for its convenience and accessibility to schools. Neighborhood living is important in terms of daily habits for convenience, shopping, church, work. Schools should be about one to two miles away from home unless the school department provides transportation. Shopping areas should be about one to four miles away and church, about four miles. Travel to work should be limited to about 40 minutes by car or public transportation.

By walking through the neighborhood, you can tell if the houses are well kept and attractive, if they are architecturally pleasing and compatible and also if the neighborhood is new and not yet established. This last point will have an effect on the value of your house. If the area has a fast turnover of people moving in and out, this will also affect the value.

Other points to check are: 1. proximity to airports, 2. industrial complexes which will generate heavy traffic, smoke, soot, dirt and noise and 3. further construction of roads and superhighways. Check further for home owners association dues, garbage removal services, police and fire protection, neighborhood affect on automobile insurance, crime rate of area, emergency facilities such as first aid stations and hospitals, ambulance response, parks and playgrounds, recreational facilities such as swimming pools, golf courses, tennis courts, libraries and the reputation of the school system.

Now that you have decided where and how much, your first order of business, after you have agreed on a selling price, (the market value may not be as important as the value to you as a buyer) secure an option to buy with a minimum of down payment with the understanding in the sales agreement that the deposit will be refunded if certain conditions are not met:

1.   You must have a clear title. I suggest the services of a title attorney or a title company. In addition insist upon a title insurance policy.

2.   Check the building and zoning restrictions at the town or city hall. Be sure you are not on the fringe of a residential and non-residential zoning because your neighbor may be a factory or a warehouse.

3.   Check the location of all utilities on the street and the depth below the street or the elevation.

4.   Check for any easements on the property.

5.   Check the exact dimensions of the property.

6. Check for Plat restrictions contained in the deed. This may tell you such things as whether you are allowed to keep domestic animals or how high you can build a fence.

7. Check the location of adjacent wells and cesspools.

8. If there is no sidewalk or curb you may be required to install them.

9. Check site for outcrop of ledge or rock.

10. Have a percolation test made (amount of water ground will absorb for waste disposal system).

When you have satisfied these conditions you may now proceed with the closing. However, careful thought must be given to title ownership. There are several ways of taking ownership:

1. Tenants by the Entirety

Husband and wife take title jointly. This is perhaps the more secure against law suits in that the property can not be forcibly sold to satisfy a judgement against one of you. It can however if both of you signed the obligation.

2. Joint Tenants

Two or more people take title in such a manner that they have one and the same interest. In joint tenancy, there is the right of survivorship, which means that if one of the owners dies, the survivors become the owners.

3. Tenants in Common

Both tenants enjoy joint possession of the property but have separate interests and distinct titles. Each tenant can separately sell his interest.

4. Tenancy in Partnership

Property purchased through partnership funds.

5. Trusts

Described according to purpose for which they are created.

6. Corporate Real Estate

Property owned by a Corporation.

When you have decided on title ownership you must still be aware of the following possibilities which you may inherit:

1. License

Right granted by one party to another permitting use of property for a specific time.

2. Lease

Voluntary alienation of property for period of lease.

3. Descent

Owner dies without a will or property is not willed at time of death.

4. Involuntary Alienation

Transfer of property without owners consent such as tax sale, judgement liens or bankruptcy.

5. Adverse Possession

A statute of limitations that bars the true owner from asserting his claim to the land where he has remained silent and has done nothing to stop the adverse occupant during the statutory period varying from seven to thirty years.

6. Squatters Rights

People who settle on land without a claim-if permitted for more than the statutory period. They could obtain an easement by prescription.

7. Erosion

Wearing away of land through processes of nature-could possibly lose title to land.

8. Eminent Domain

Taking of land by government for public use.

9. Escheat

When an owner dies and leaves no heir or legal claimant, his property reverts to the state under the doctrine of escheat.

10. Confiscation

In times of war, powers granted to the government to take over property of enemy aliens.

Now that you own the property and have a guaranteed title, your next move will be to have the property surveyed. This is necessary to establish the exact property lines. This will show the dimensions and angles of the perimeter of the property. You should instruct the surveyor to install permanent markers because sometimes wooden stakes are used which eventually will rot away. While the surveyor is on site it would be good to have him do a topographical survey which will give us the contour or shape on the surface of the land. This is necessary to establish the level of the floors of the building in relation to the level of the ground. This will also tell where we will cut and/or fill to reshape the land to suit our convenience. The topographical survey will show the following:

1. Shape of land.

2. Location of all trees and sizes.

3. Location of any ledge or rock on the surface of the land.

4. Location of any buildings.

5. Width of sidewalk and street.

6. Compass bearing.

7. Location size and depth of all existing utilities public and private.

8. Location of any easements.

9. Lot and Plat no.

(All property is divided into plats and each plat is again divided into lots, all of which have numbers and all of which is recorded at the town or city hall).

10. Any and all underground services showing location and size. If there are no public improvements on your land and if the authorities are planning such improvements, you will be assessed the cost of these improvements based on the size of the street dimension of your property. The total cost of these improvements is divided by the number of property owners and the length of the street dimension of the property. You will pay for these improvements whether you use them or not.

BUILDING and ZONING LAWS 3

Whether you plan to build a tool shed or another Empire State Building, you will be bound to certain rules and regulations known as Building Laws or Codes. All Communities have adopted such laws in either creating their own codes or adopting state or national codes. In planning of your home you must comply with the laws of your community and these laws apply to the mechanical as well as physical part of the building.

The codes are broken down by classification, such as building type or use and also by Fire Districts and occupancy requirements. These codes are revised from time to time so be certain you are using the latest edition for your community. The purpose of these codes is to provide for minimum building standards to make buildings safe for occupancy. These codes also will apply to existing buildings being altered or added to. If you occupy a building that is pre-code dated, you need not comply unless you alter the building. What you will find in the code is maximum lot coverage, minimum side, rear and front yard dimensions, height restrictions and minimum lot dimensions and a host of other information. If you live in a residential development you also may be subjected to **PLAT RESTRICTIONS**. This you will find in your deed. You may find items such as kinds and height of fences, boarding of animals, etc.

If your plans do not comply with the building codes you have a choice of either changing your plans to comply or file an application with your local **ZONING BOARD OF REVIEW** seeking an exception to the law or code. If you decide to seek an exception it envolves a little work in the form of evidence, such as applications and drawings which must be presented to the Board.

The documents which are necessary are as follows:

1. Radius Plan showing your lot and all lots within a radius of 200' from the corners of your property.

2. All buildings upon all lots shown.

3. Names and addresses of all property owners within the 200' radius.

4. A plan of what you intend to build along with elevations.

5. Plot Plan showing your project on your lot and all existing buildings thereon.

6. Application which will ask what it is you are asking an exception for or to.

This information will be collected by the Secretary of the Zoning Board who will notify all owners within the 200' radius by registered mail of a scheduled meeting to be held by the Zoning Board of Review, upon which your petition will be heard in public and all present will be given a chance to be heard for or against your petition. At the close of the meeting, the Board will render a decision based on all evidence and testimony heard at the meeting and you will be notified. If the decision is in your favor you may go ahead through normal procedures. If your petition is denied, you have recourse through the Courts who MAY reverse the decision of the Zoning Board. It is important to note that no Government Agency can deny a land owner use of his property. If you show good cause, chances are you may be granted an exception.

On the other hand, another course of action is to apply for a complete rezoning of your property. This would be the responsibility of your City Council and there isn't much you can do except start the machinery by contacting your Government Agent representing your District.

All properties are divided into PLATS and LOTS indexed by letters or numbers. Each Lot has a PLAT and LOT No. which is recorded at the Town or City Hall. These in turn are separated by Zones reserving certain areas for RESIDENTIAL, BUSINESS, MANUFACTURING, INDUSTRIAL etc. RESIDENTIAL zones are again separated into Single Family, Two Family and Multi-Family units. It is important to know what your lot is Zoned for. Each Zone has specific Building requirements with which you must comply to receive a building permit. If you do not comply then we go back to the mechanics of the Zoning Board as discussed earlier. You can also find your lot and plat no., by the street address which is a cross reference.

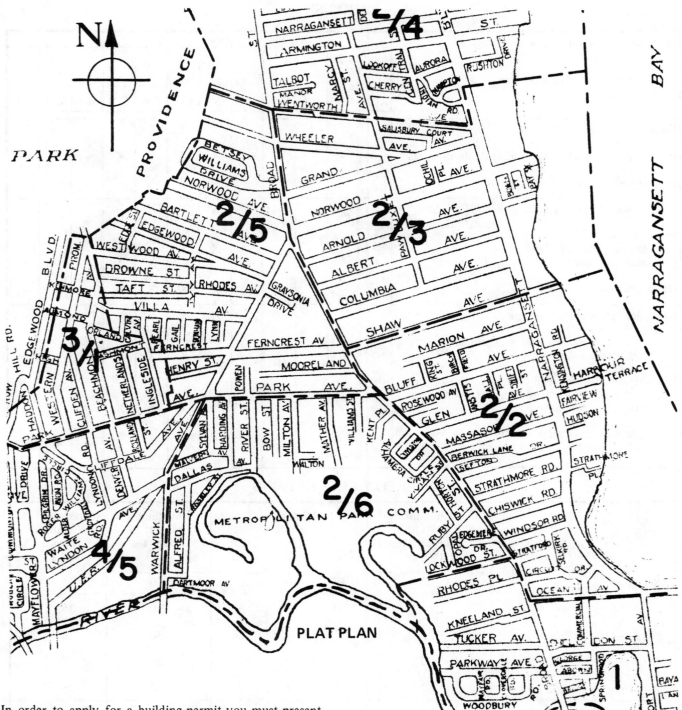

PLAT PLAN

In order to apply for a building permit you must present the plans to the local building department at which time they will be reviewed for compliance with all local and national codes having jurisdiction in your community. If the plans conform, a building permit will be issued for a fee. This permit must be displayed in a conspicuous place for any authority to examine.

In most cases the project must be started within one year from the date of the permit, otherwise you must re-apply. It is recommended that you purchase a copy of the local codes and ordinances before you do any planning. While at the city hall, you will find, as a matter of record, any and all utilities, size of pipe, depth of pipes and location that is within the proximity of your lot, including a granite bound which is a square stone of granite which measures about 4" square with a drill hole in the top center. This is a fixed permanent point in locating your property lines used by surveyors. While on the subject of building inspectors, if your property does not meet the minimum property standards and you refuse to bring it up to standard, the building inspector has the power to condemn your home if he rules it to be a danger to life at which point it must be demolished.

If you violate any provisions of the Zoning or Building laws, or fail to comply with said laws, and are convicted, you may be fined as much as $100 for each penalty or violation.

LAND USE

• = special permit X = Permitted − = prohibited Principal Use	Districts											
	A-80	A-20 A-12 A-8 A-6	B-1	B-2	C-1	C-2	C-3	C-4	C-5	M-1	M-2	S-1
Food stores, delicatessen	−	−	−	−	−	X	X	X	−	−	−	−
Bakery, provided all baked goods sold on premises	−	−	−	−	−	X	X	X	−	−	−	−
Drug store, newstand, variety and notice stores	−	−	−	−	−	X	X	X	−	−	−	−
Book, stationery, and gift shops	−	−	−	−	−	X	X	X	−	−	−	−
Florist shops 1. excluding greenhouse	−	−	−	−	−	X	X	−	−	−	−	−
2. including greenhouse	−	−	−	−	−	−	−	X	X	−	−	−
Hardware stores	−	−	−	−	−	X	X	X	X	−	−	−
Banks and financial institutions	−	−	−	−	X	X	X	X	X	•	•	−
Barber shops and beauty parlors; tailor and custom dressmaking shops	−	−	−	−	−	X	X	X	−	−	−	−
Laundry, dry cleaning, and pressing establishments 1. 5 employees or less working at any one time within the establishment	−	−	−	−	−	X	X	X	X	−	−	−
2. 6 employees or more working at any one time within the establishment	−	−	−	−	−	−	−	−	X	X	X	−

INTENSITY REGULATIONS

District	Minimum Lot Area (sq. ft.)	Minimum Lot Width and Frontage (ft.)	Minimum Yards (ft.)			Maximum Lot Coverage (%)	Maximum Building Height (ft.)
			Front	Rear	Side		
S-1, A-80	20,000	200	40	100	20	10	35
A-20	20,000	125	30	30	15	20	35
A-12	12,000	100	25	20	10	30	35
A-8	8,000	80	25	20	10	30	35
A-6	6,000	60	25	20	8	30	35
B-1	6,000	60	25	20	8	35	35
B-2	6,000	60	25	20	8	50	- -
C-1	6,000	60	25	20	8	60	- -
C-2	6,000	60	25	20	8	60	30
C-3	6,000	60	0	20	0	100	35
C-4	12,000	120	60	20	8	50	35
C-5	10,000	80	30	20	8	60	35
M-1	30,000	150	40	30	20	60	- -
M-2	60,000	200	40	30	25	60	- -

ZONING

Districts	Intended Primarily for the Use of
Residential A-80	Single-family dwellings on lots not served by public water and of minimum areas of 80,000 square feet
Residential A-20	Single-family dwellings on lots of minimum areas of 20,000 square feet
Residential A-12	Single-family dwellings on lots of minimum areas of 12,000 square feet
Residential A-8	Single-family dwellings on lots of minimum areas of 8,000 square feet
Residential A-6	Single-family dwellings on lots of minimum areas of 6,000 square feet
Residential B-1	Single-family and two-family dwellings
Residential B-2	Single-, two- and multi-family dwellings
Commercial C-1	Office business
Commercial C-2	Neighborhood business
Commercial C-3	General business
Commercial C-4	Highway business
Commercial C-5	Heavy business, industry
Industrial M-1	Restricted industry
Industrial M-2	General industry
Open Space S-1	Uses containing high proportion of open space or natural character
Planned districts	Uses in buildings arranged in an efficient, harmonious and convenient manner on sites

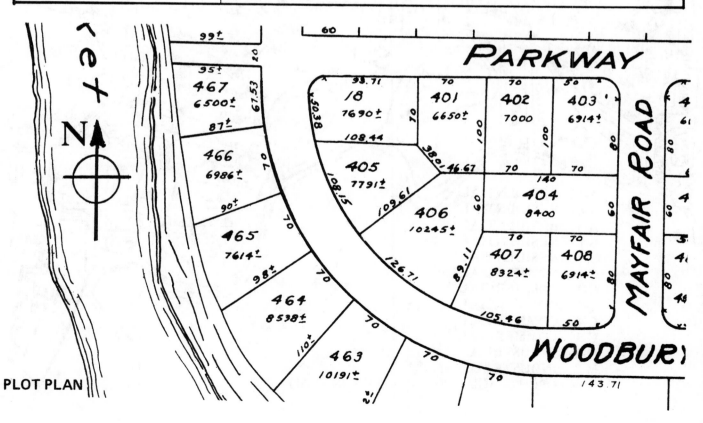

PLOT PLAN

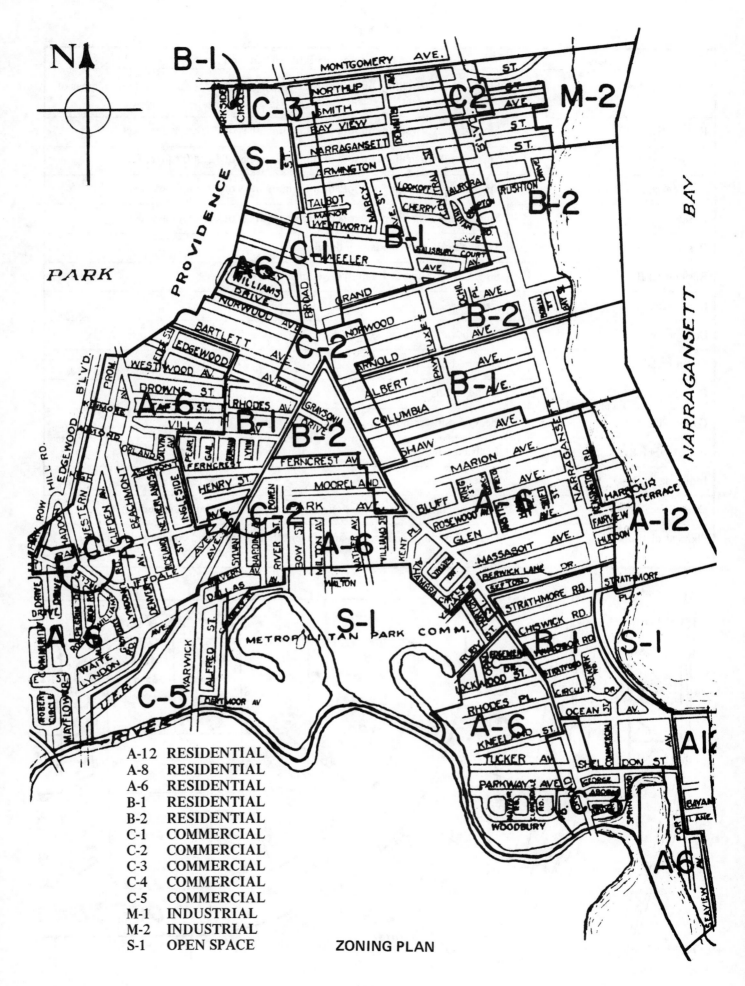

N

A-12 RESIDENTIAL
A-8 RESIDENTIAL
A-6 RESIDENTIAL
B-1 RESIDENTIAL
B-2 RESIDENTIAL
C-1 COMMERCIAL
C-2 COMMERCIAL
C-3 COMMERCIAL
C-4 COMMERCIAL
C-5 COMMERCIAL
M-1 INDUSTRIAL
M-2 INDUSTRIAL
S-1 OPEN SPACE

ZONING PLAN

14

HOW TO READ PLANS

4

A set of building plans is nothing more than a graphic message, like a painting or a photograph, of an idea from the designer to the builder. This graphic message is communicated by way of lines and symbols and once you have learned to recognize these symbols you will be able to read not only a set of house plans but a set of plans for any building. These symbols have been universally accepted so that no matter who the designer of the building is, the reading is the same.

Basically, we will be looking at three (3) kinds of drawings. First will be the *plan* of the building and this is a horizontal plane. If you cut a building mid point at window height, remove the upper portion and look down on the remaining portion, that will be the plan of the building. In this plan you will see all the doors, direction of door swing, location, type and size of doors, location and size of all windows, location of all walls or partitions, location of stairs, fireplace, kitchen cabinets, book shelves, toilet fixtures. All on a single sheet of paper of convenient size, you will see the entire building together and intact drawn at a scale less than full size.

A second kind of drawing is known as *elevations*. This is a vertical picture of one plane only and only one side of the house at a time is shown. It may be the entire outside of one side of the house. It may also be any interior wall of any room of the building or a part of a wall. As you see a wall in looking at it, so you will see it on paper; this too, drawn at a scale less than full size.

A third kind of drawing is known as *sections or details.* This is drawn in a vertical plane showing a wall completely through with all parts not visible when the wall is completed. Also parts of a construction detail are shown to clear up any possible doubt as to how the wall is to be constructed. In other words, if we cut a wall vertically, remove a section and look head on, this is a section of that wall and you will see how it is made.

All of these drawings are drawn to a small scale otherwise the paper would have to be as large as the house; we select a scale small enough to fit on a convenient size sheet of paper and large enough to show details. The most popular scales are 1/8"=1'-0", 1/2"=1'-0", 1/4"=1'-0", 3/8"=1'-0", 3/4"=1'-0", 1-1/2"=1-0", 3"=1-0" and at times' full size scale. In all cases, the scale will be noted on the drawings. If for example we were reading a drawing done at 1/2"= 1'-0" it means that every 1/2" in actual measurement on the drawing is 1'-0" full size, so that if we measured 1" on the drawing, the actual full size dimension is 2'-0"

A complete set of plans will consist of several sheets usually in order of sequence of building or construction. The first sheet will be the PLOT PLAN which will show the size of the building lot, the location of the building on the lot, contour elevations or the level or terrain of the lot including trees, location of all utilities, curb and compass bearing, dimension of property lines including angles, street name, lot and plat numbers.

It is for this drawing that we see why the topographical survey is important because we now have to establish the level of the floor of the house in relation to the level of the ground and the contour elevations will tell us if we need to cut or fill the ground and change the shape to suit our needs for function and also tell us how deep we must excavate below the ground level for the level of the basement we have established. This level of floors may not give us much choice in relation to the level of the sewer line buried in the street. Once we have established this level, which is a matter of record at the city hall, we must have a minimum of 1/8" per foot pitch for the sewer pipe from the house to the connection at the sewer main in the street. If we have plumbing fixtures in the basement, they must be high enough to establish this minimum pitch for proper drainage. An alternative will be to have an electric pump attached to the fixture to pump the waste up into the drain line and then into the sewer. If you do not have sewers in your community you must then build a private sewage disposal system and you may be faced with minimum standards in your local code or health department. This is another reason why you must be familiar with all local laws or codes before any planning is done. It becomes much too expensive to make changes after you have begun construction because not only will you have paid to have it done the first time, you must pay again to undo the error and pay for the third time to do it right, not even to mention the time lost in correcting the error.

If there is no domestic water in your area a well of some kind will be necessary. You may have either a surface well which is dug, or an artesian well which is drilled. In any event, the well should be a minimum of 100' away from a private sewage disposal system and on high ground, or the well and sewage system will marry and you have contaminated drinking water. This theory is very simple. Water has a natural tendency to flow down hill in the easiest possible course. If the well is lower than the disposal system, the water from the sewage disposal system will run into the well.

This PLOT PLAN then should give you all the information you need to know about the site or lot.

Because of the amount of information and size of objects shown, this sheet may be drawn at a different scale as discussed earlier. Usually 1"=10' or 1"=20' because the entire lot must be shown and it may be 100' or more in any one dimension and all sheets within the complete set should be of the same size.

The next sheet in order of sequence will be the foundation plan or basement floor plan which is still the foundation. Remember, we said that a plan is a horizontal cut or view and in the case of a basement plan we are cutting the building about halfway up the windows, removing the portion of the building above that point and looking down on the remainder. Here we will see the size of the foundation by way of dimensions on the outer perimeter of the plan as well as the locations of the windows in the basement usually shown at the center of the windows. Also we will see the size of the main beam which supports the floor above, which in turn is supported by columns. We will see not only the size of the columns, but also the spacing of the columns. The main beam will support what are called floor joists. These will be 2' in width and anywhere from 8" to 12" in height. They will be noted on the plans as 2"x8"-16" O.C. This means that the floor joists are 2" thick and 8" wide spaced 16" on center or 16" apart and are placed in a vertical position with the larger dimension up. One end of these floor joists are supported by the main beam and the other end is supported by the outer foundation wall. This is what holds up the floor. We will also see the chimney, stairs, heating unit, partitions, if

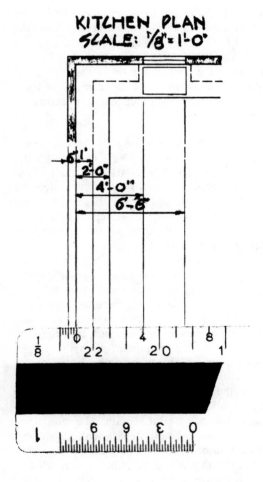

ARCHITECTURAL SCALE

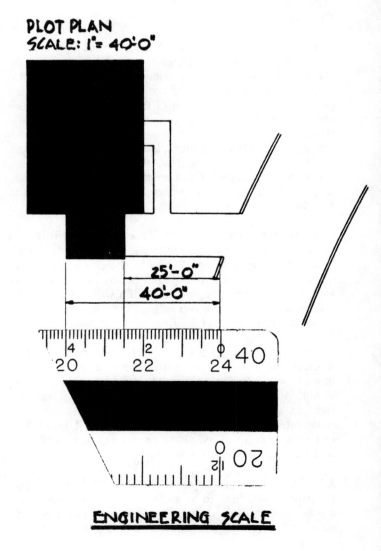

ENGINEERING SCALE

there are any, laundry sinks, the thickness of the concrete floor, bulkhead, if any, and all mechanical parts of the house. Bear in mind that this plan will give us only horizontal dimensions and not vertical dimensions. If there is no basement we then simply read a foundation plan, which will show a wall with no other information. This plan is usually drawn at ¼"=1'-0" scale.

Next in line will be the first floor plan which is read the same way as the basement plan with the same horizontal cut through the windows. This will show all the rooms at this level and the labels. We will see the bath and all the plumbing fixtures, the kitchen will show the location, shape and size of the cabinets with upper and lower units, sink, refrigerator, range, dish-washer, windows and closets. This plan will show all the doors, and the size of the doors as well as the direction of the door swing. All the walls or partitions will be seen including all the windows, fireplace, stairs; you will see dimensions locating all partitions or walls within the building. If you have a garage it will show on this plan including the size, location of doors and windows; porches will also be seen on the first floor plan. Now would be a good time to try this house on for size by simply

measuring your furniture and draw a series of squares and rectangles at the same scale as the floor plan and place the furniture within the rooms to establish the correct size or to make any changes in the floor plan.

If there is a second floor, it will be next in sequence and is read as we did the first floor. It, too, shows all the windows, stairs, doors, partitions, closets, bedrooms and bath.

With the exception of details and sections, this completes our floor plans within the entire project and now we will look for elevations, or vertical drawings and we will see a separate drawing for each of the four sides of the exterior of the house. They will be labeled EAST ELEVATION, NORTH ELEVATION, WEST ELEVATION & SOUTH ELEVATION again drawn at ¼"=1'-0" scale.

Or FRONT ELEVATION, REAR ELEVATION, LEFT SIDE ELEVATION & RIGHT SIDE ELEVATION. By examining this drawing you will see the entire side from the basement up to and including the roof. The floor lines are shown by a dot-dash line and will be labeled by the respective floor such as Basement Floor, First

ARCHITECTURAL SYMBOLS

Symbol	Name	Symbol	Name	Symbol	Name
	EARTH		COMMON BRICK		STRUCTURAL IRON
	GRAVEL		FACE BRICK		CERAMIC TILE
	PLASTER		FIRE BRICK		INSULATION
	WOOD-FINISH		CONC. BLOCK		MARBLE
	WOOD-ROUGH		POURED CONCRETE		ROCK
	SOLID INSULAT'N		STONE-RUBBLE		GLASS

APPLICATIONS

Symbol	Name	Symbol	Name	Symbol	Name
	STONE VENEER-W/WOOD FRAME		STONE VENEER W/MASONRY		BRICK VENEER W/BLOCK WALL
	CONC. FURRED		CONC. BLOCK-FURRED		SOLID PLASTER
	BRICK VENEER-W/WOOD FRAME		BRICK-FURRED		PLYWOOD
	8" BRICK CAVITY WALL		STUD		BRICK-PLASTER
	TILE FLOOR		WOOD FLOOR		BRICK FLOOR
	MARBLE FL.		CONCRETE FL.		FLASHING

17

MECHANICAL SYMBOLS

ELECTRICAL

- CEILING OUTLET
- FAN OUTLET
- DROP CORD
- EXIT LIGHT OUTLET
- WALL OUTLET
- TELEPHONE EXTENSION
- WATERPROOF OUTLET
- DUPLEX OUTLET
- SWITCH & DUPLEX OUTLET
- TRIPLEX OUTLET
- RANGE OUTLET

- SPECIAL PURPOSE OUTLET
- SINGLE POLE SWITCH
- DOUBLE POLE SWITCH
- THREE WAY SWITCH
- FOUR WAY SWITCH
- WATERPROOF SWITCH
- FLUORESCENT LIGHT
- OUTSIDE TELEPHONE
- PUSH BUTTON
- BELL
- LIGHTING PANEL

4 WAY SWITCH

3 WAY SWITCH

DUPLEX OUTLET

FLOOD LIGHT

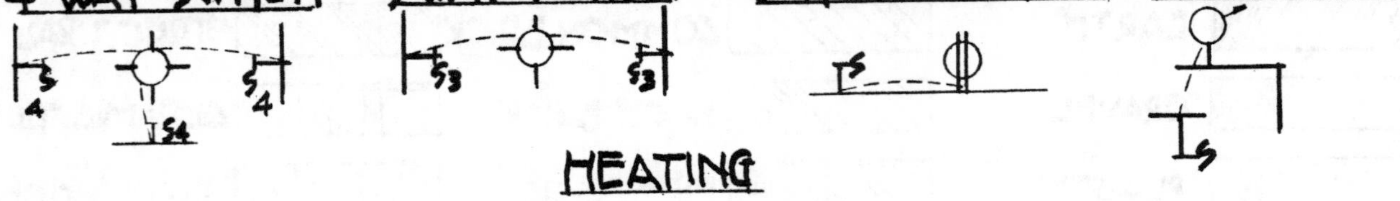

HEATING

- DUCT-PLAN VIEW
- RADIATOR
- SUPPLY LINE
- RETURN LINE
- SUPPLY DUCT
- RETURN DUCT
- CONVECTOR PROJECTING

- CONVECTOR RECESSED
- T CONNECTION
- ELBOW
- RISER
- RETURN
- REGISTER

PLUMBING

- COLD WATER LINE
- HOT WATER LINE
- GAS LINE
- REFRIGERATOR LINE
- FLOOR DRAIN
- CLEANOUT
- WATERCLOSET

- HOT WATER TANK
- SOIL PIPE - FRAME WALL
- PIPE CHASE - BRICK WALL
- LAUNDRY TUB
- KITCHEN SINK
- BATHTUB

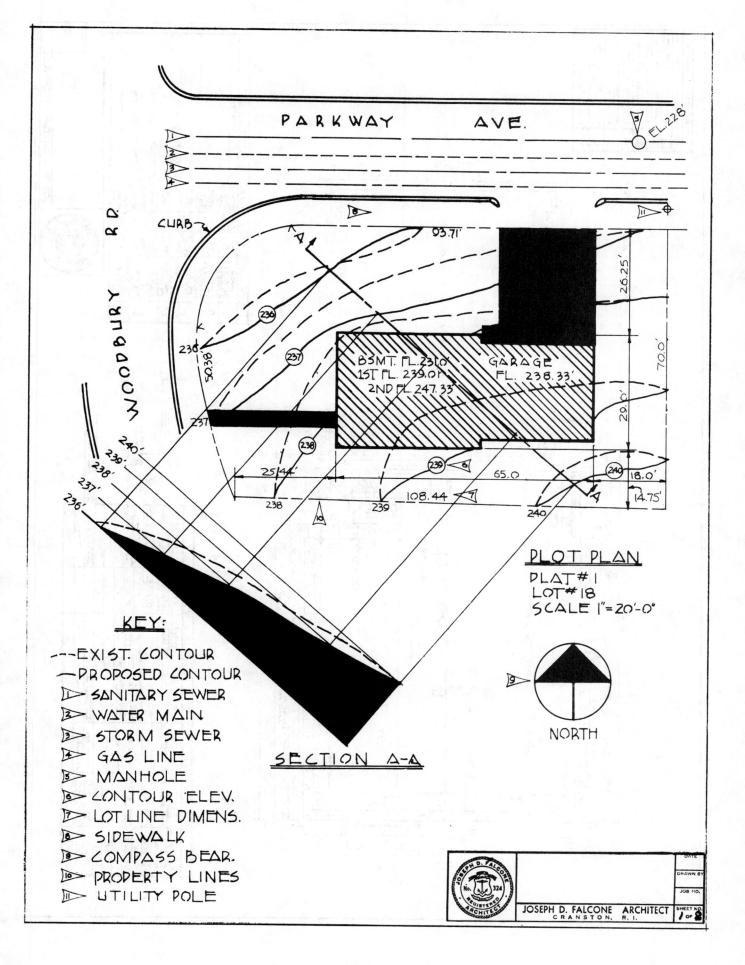

PARKWAY AVE.

EL.228'

WOODBURY RD.

CURB

93.71'

236

230'

237

237'

BSMT. FL. 231.0'
1ST FL. 239.01'
2ND FL. 247.33'

GARAGE
FL. 238.33'

26.25'

70.0'

29.0'

238

240'
239'
238'
237'
236'

25.44'

238

239

108.44

65.0

240

240

18.0'

14.75'

PLOT PLAN
PLAT # 1
LOT # 18
SCALE 1"=20'-0"

KEY:

--- EXIST. CONTOUR

— PROPOSED CONTOUR

1 SANITARY SEWER

2 WATER MAIN

3 STORM SEWER

4 GAS LINE

5 MANHOLE

6 CONTOUR ELEV.

7 LOT LINE DIMENS.

8 SIDEWALK

9 COMPASS BEAR.

10 PROPERTY LINES

11 UTILITY POLE

SECTION A-A

NORTH

JOSEPH D. FALCONE ARCHITECT
CRANSTON, R.I.

JOSEPH D. FALCONE
No. 324
REGISTERED
ARCHITECT

DATE
DRAWN BY
JOB NO.
SHEET NO. 1 OF 8

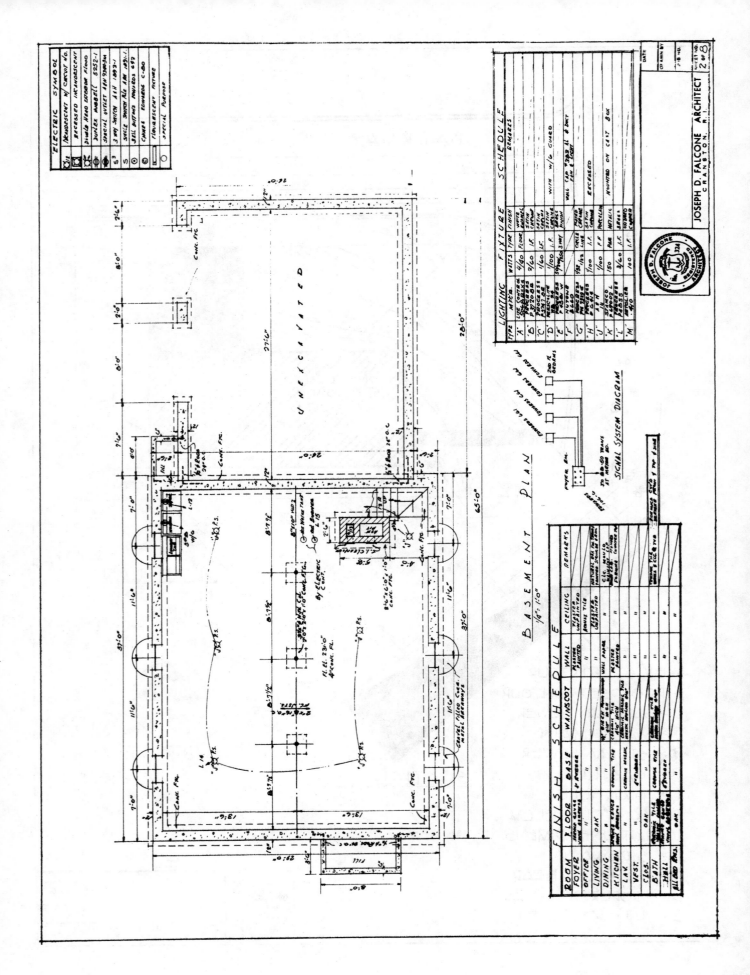

ELECTRIC SYMBOL

Symbol	Description
○ILL	INCANDESCENT W/ CIRCUIT NO.
⊠	RECESSED INCANDESCENT
⊕	DOUBLE HEAD DIAGRAM SIGNS
⊕	DUPLEX HUBBELL 5252-1
⊖	SPECIAL OUTLET #EM 929054M
S³	3 WAY SWITCH AH 1093-I
S	SINGLE SWITCH ALE AH 109-I
⊙	BELL BUTTONS EDWARDS 679
⊡	CHIMES EDWARDS C-80
⊖	FLUORESCENT FIXTURE
○	SPECIAL PURPOSE

LIGHTING FIXTURE SCHEDULE

TYPE	MFR.	WATTS	TYPE	FINISH	REMARKS
"A"	LITE CONTROL PROGRESS	4/40	FLUOR.	WHITE ENAMEL	
"B"	PROGRESS P7700BB	2/40	I.F.	SATIN CHROME	
"C"	PROGRESS RECKLER	1/60	I.F.	SATIN CHROME	
"D"	NO. 24	30/SPECIAL	3 WAY	SATIN CHROME	WITH W/O GUARD
"E"	PROGRESS				
"F"	NUTONE 8160	7/100	I.F.		WALL CAP #303 H ¢ DKT. FEM ¢ LIGHT
"G"	PROGRESS P6118B	198/193	CIRCLE LITE	SATIN CHROME	
"H"	PROGRESS AC44	1/100	I.F.	SATIN CHROME	RECESSED
"J"	1/4		F.F.		
"K"	SEMCOL	1/100	PAR	METALLIC	MOUNTED ON CAST BOX
"L"	PROGRESS P4855	150	I.F.	BRASS	
"M"	PROGRESS P/O	2/60	I.F.	BROWNED COPPER	

U N E X C A V A T E D

CONC. FTG.

BASEMENT PLAN
1/4" = 1'-0"

SIGNAL SYSTEM DIAGRAM

FINISH SCHEDULE

ROOM	FLOOR	BASE	WAINSCOT	WALL	CEILING	REMARKS
FOYER				PLASTER PAINTED	PLASTER UNPAINTED	
OFFICE					ACOUST. TILE	
LIVING	OAK				UNPAINTED	
DINING	OAK			WALL PAPER	"	
KITCHEN				PLASTER PAINTED	"	
LAV.				"	"	
VEST.		OAK		"	"	
CLOS.		OAK		"	"	
BATH				"	"	
HALL				"	"	
ALL BED RMS.	OAK					

JOSEPH D. FALCONE ARCHITECT
CRANSTON, R.I.

SHEET NO. 2 of 8

DRAWN BY

DATE

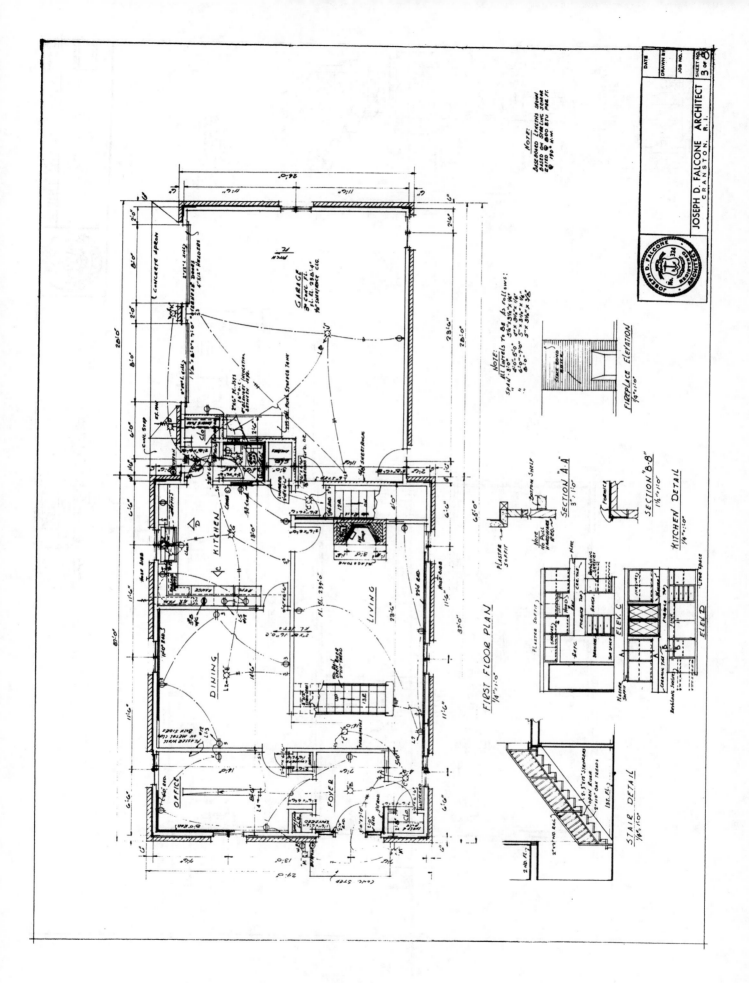

FIRST FLOOR PLAN

1/4"=1'-0"

GARAGE

LIVING

DINING

KITCHEN

OFFICE

FOYER

FIREPLACE ELEVATION
1/4"=1'-0"

SECTION "A-A"
3"=1'-0"

SECTION "B-B"
1/4"=1'-0"

KITCHEN DETAIL
1/4"=1'-0"

ELEV. C

ELEV. D

STAIR DETAIL
1/2"=1'-0"

JOSEPH D. FALCONE ARCHITECT
CRANSTON, R.I.

SHEET NO. 3 OF 8

21

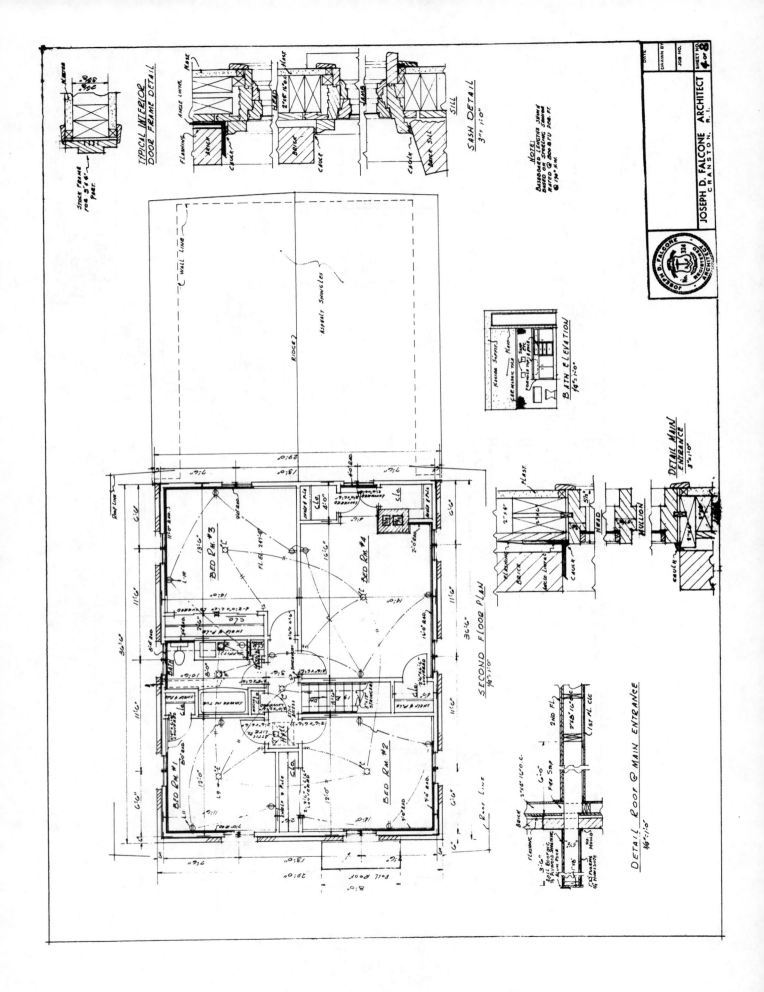

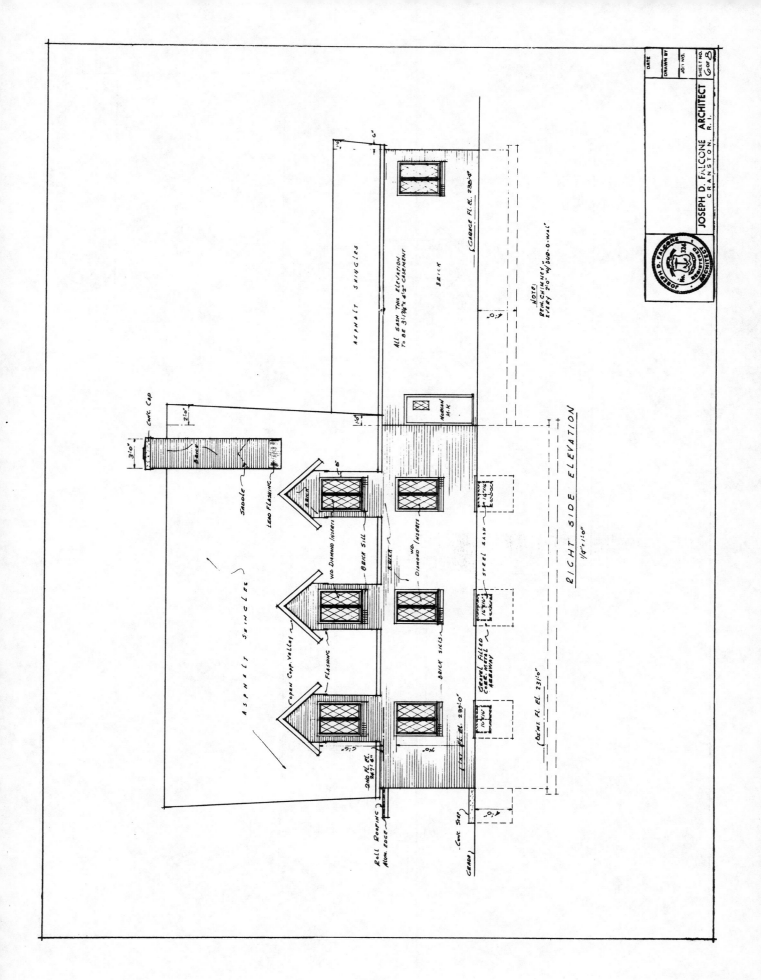

RIGHT SIDE ELEVATION
1/4"=1'-0"

NOTE:
REINF. CHIMNEY
EVERY 2'-0" W/DUR-O-WAL

JOSEPH D. FALCONE ARCHITECT
CRANSTON, R.I.

DATE
DRAWN BY
JOB NO.
SHEET NO. 6 OF 8

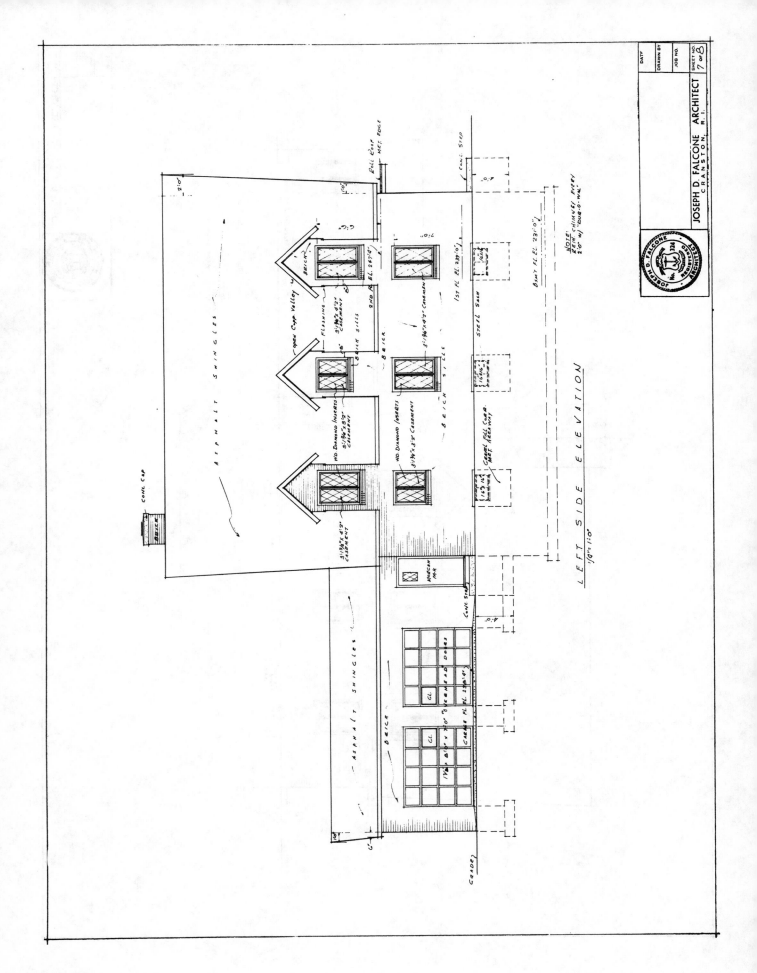

LEFT SIDE ELEVATION
1/4"=1'-0"

ASPHALT SHINGLES

NOTE:
LINE CHIMNEY FLUES
2'-0" W/ 8"x12'-0" WALL

JOSEPH D. FALCONE ARCHITECT
CRANSTON, R.I.

SHEET NO. 7 OF 8

24

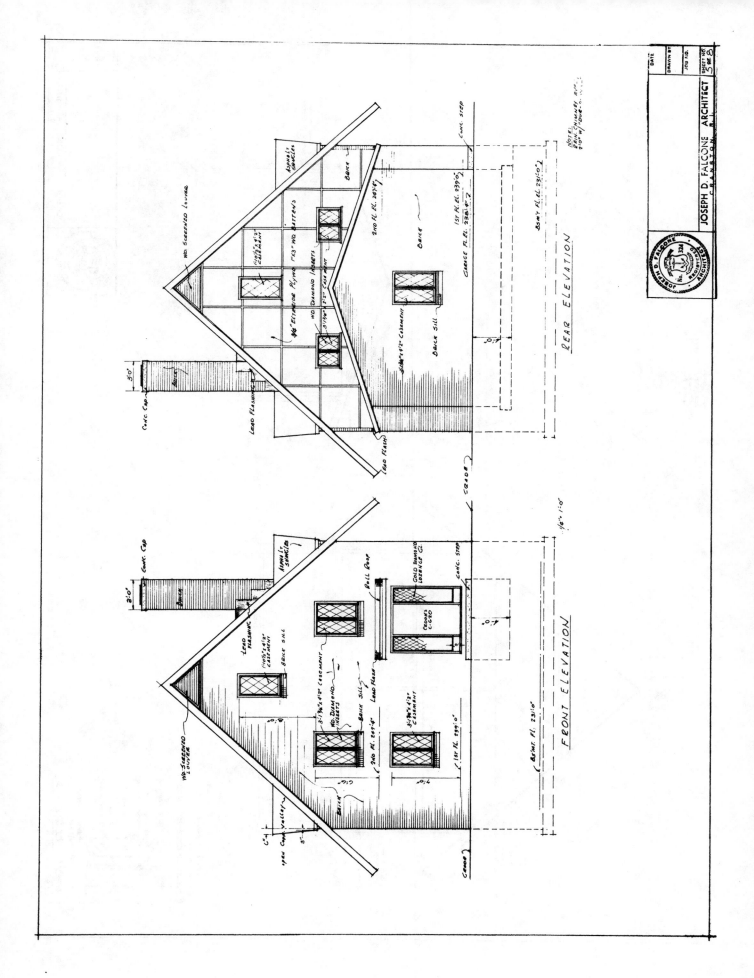

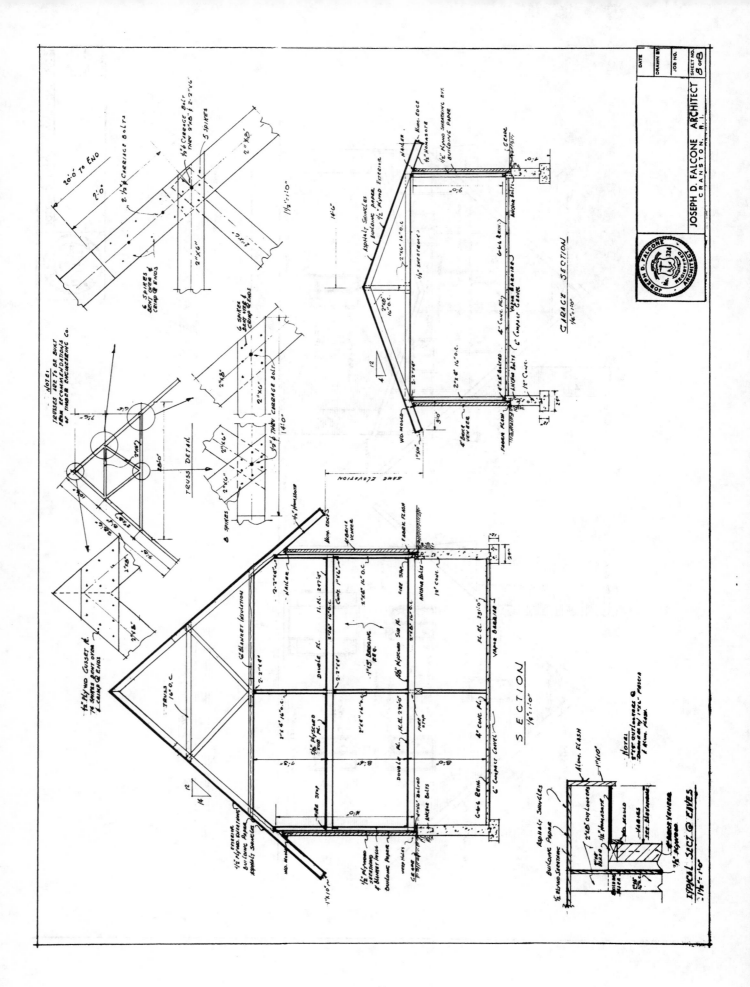

Floor, or Second Floor. The type and size of windows (size meaning height and width of windows are shown on the floor plans). Type meaning style such as double hung, casement, sliding or gliding, awning and vent. You may also find the material of the window such as wood, aluminum, steel or bronze. The configuration of the windows will also be seen as to number of panes of glass and sizes. The design of all exterior doors will be seen on these drawings and the material finish on the exterior such as wood shingles, clapboards, brick etc. This drawing will tell us the distance from the grade to the first floor and the basement. All dotted lines are objects not directly visible. For instance, all information below the ground such as foundation, basement windows, floor of basement bulkhead etc., will be seen dotted because the direct view is obstructed by another object. This drawing will also show us the design of the chimney, including kind, material and height. The ground or finish grade will be seen as corresponding to the finish grade elevations on the PLOT PLAN. This drawing will also tell the kind of gutters and conductors we have as well as the design of the cornice or jet.

Basically that is all there is to reading a set of plans and this will be a good time to explain how a set of plans is produced. There is but one original set which the draftsman has drawn on a special kind of transparent paper using a special kind of pencil determined by the quality of the paper. When the drawings are completed, they are reproduced somewhat like photos from a negative. The original drawings being the negative, are placed over a chemically treated paper, run through a machine which prints by way of a strong light penetrating all but the lines of the drawing. This light transfers the image on to the printing paper, which after leaving the printer is run through a developer using ammonia as a developing agent. The chemical coating on the paper turns white as a direct result of the exposure to the ammonia except the lines on the drawing which are blue. Any number of copies can be made from an original set of drawings. A more popular term for the reproduction is called blueprinting which is obsolete because of new techniques used in reproduction.

There are other processes or ways of printing drawings. By using a different kind of printing paper, copies can be made that will become reproducible or making a negative from a negative. The only way to reproduce a copy of a set of drawings is to photograph them making a negative from the printed copy then making drawings from the negative. This becomes somewhat expensive. We must have a drawing on a transparent sheet of paper in order to copy.

27

PRELIMINARY DESIGN STUDIES 5

Now that we have selected a site and are familiar with all local building and zoning laws, we can begin to plan our home or addition, drawn free hand to scale at ¼"=1'-0". Graph paper will help using ¼" squares both ways and having each square = 12".

Don't be concerned about cost-at least not yet-let your imagination run wild and plan all that you would like to have as though money were no object. To get started, you can collect magazine and newspaper pictures or articles that appeal to you and try to incorporate them into your plans. This stage is the most important and crucial in the entire project. Keep in mind the secret of any plan is the eraser.

Your personal living habits have a direct bearing on your plans. For example, if you do a lot of entertaining, a large formal dining room may be in order or a card or billiard room for after dinner, by a large open fire. If you are an art collector a studio or gallery should be planned keeping in mind that the north is the best natural light and also the coldest exposure. Plan your rooms to have the exposure of your choice but never overlook the possibility of a commanding view from the room of your choice. The number of bedrooms will depend upon the number and sex of people living in your home. If you are planning a garage, how many cars do you have? You may want to make your garage larger to allow space for yard tools such as lawn mower, shovels, rakes, brooms, etc.

If you tend to be lazy and live in the northern climate be careful where you place your house on the lot if you don't want to shovel snow. Northern climate is also conducive to having the garage attached to the house, especially on a cold winter morning. Better still if your lot slopes in either direction, a garage in the basement will be more comfortable. If you are restricted in lot area, you have no choice but to plan a multi-level house. Otherwise a one level house may be your choice.

Esthetics will not play a part in preliminary design but only function should be considered at this time. Try to picture each room furnished and completed. This will help you in your planning stage.

If you are planning to alter or remodel , you must know what you have to work with before you can make any changes. If you do not have a copy of the plans of your house, your builder or bank or building inspector may have a copy. If not, you will need to measure the entire building and draw it on paper to scale. This is a fairly simple procedure. You need only to measure the house as is and transfer the dimensions on paper by way of a plan drawn to scale. Take one room at a time and show all information as if you were drawing the plan to build with.

As you plan your alterations, be careful not to remove any bearing partitions. We are primarily concerned with two kinds of partitions or walls, bearing and non-bearing. A bearing partition or wall is one that is supporting a portion of the building and if removed will create structural damage or cause the collapse of the building. A non-bearing partition is nothing more than a curtain wall and if removed will have no effect on the structural part of the building. Normally a bearing partition is constructed with 2"x4" studs and a non-bearing partition is constructed with 2"x3" studs (more about studs later) which means that a bearing partition is 1" thicker than a non-bearing wall. It is simple to detect a bearing wall by examining the direction of the floor or ceiling joists. We said earlier that the joists are supported on one end by the foundation wall so the other end must be supported by a wall of some kind, hence a bearing wall.

This is not to say that a bearing partition cannot be removed. It does mean that if you elect to remove a bearing partition, you must substitute that wall with another means of supporting the load the wall was designed to support and this means a beam of some kind. To mention a size here would be impossible because many factors are involved in designing the size of a beam. The material of the beam must be known such as wood, steel or concrete. The total loads on the beam must be known and the span or the distance from support to support must also be known. Your local lumber supplier will be happy to tell you what size will be necessary once he has the above information. All exterior walls are bearing partitions and if your house is rectangular in shape, chances are the wall in the center running the entire length of the house is bearing. The bearing partition could be supporting not only the floor but also the roof or both, as well as the ceiling. Be sure you are not removing a bearing partition without taking adequate measures for support. You may wish to remove a portion of a bearing partition, if so the principal as explained earlier will apply.

In your planning try to avoid winders or stairs that turn corners because they tend to be dangerous. Allow a platform at the end of stairs at least three feet deep and put a hand rail on both sides of the stairs. Stairs should be at least three feet wide and the number of stairs is computed by the distance from one floor to the other. If, for example, we establish a distance of 8'-0" from floor to floor and we allowed 12 stairs at 8" each that will give us the required number of stairs. Simply divide the distance between floors by 8" ± and that will give you the number of stairs. It is important to realize that no stair should be higher than 8" which is called the rise or riser and the tread or flat part should be no less than 10". With this information you know how much room the stairs need. By placing all stairs over each other space is saved on each floor.

Keep the same architectural stye if you are adding to your home so that when you have completed your project it will not look like an addition. Maintain the same lines, exterior finish and material. You may vary the floor levels and the roof levels but only after you have made free hand studies to scale to determine the esthetic scale and proportions which will be pleasing to your eye. The entire house should blend together harmoniously.

KITCHEN

Whether you are building new or altering your home, give very careful thought to the kitchen: here is the most expensive and most used room in the house and a functional kitchen is one that requires a minimum amount of steps and this can be accomplished by the following shapes:

U shape
L shape
straight line shape
double straight line shape

With any of the above shapes, all areas should be within arms reach or, as is sometimes referred to, a pivot kitchen. The minimum distance between counters is 4'-0". If you can, put the oven on an outside wall to make it easier to install the exhaust or hood. There are ductless hoods which are effective, but not cheap which work on a principal of a charcoal filter which must be reactivated periodically. Plan counter space on both sides of the refrigerator to make it convenient to open the door by placing parcels on the counto to free your hands without walking across the kitchen floor. The appliances should be arranged as follows in order of use: The refrigerator first because food is removed and washed, which puts the sink next in order of use, after which the food is prepared for cooking; therefore the range will be next in order. A mistake made quite often is to have shelves on the upper cabinets too high for arms reach. This can pose a problem. Plan your shelves so they can be reached without the aid of a ladder or step stool. Lighting is very

important with a minimum of 100 candlepower. (A measurement of light equal to 100 candles). This can be had in either fluorescent or incandescent light. A continuous strip of fluorescent lighting under the upper cabinets by way of indirect lighting will enhance your many hours of kitchen work. There is no rule that says the sink must be under a window, you may plan the sink any place where it will be most convenient and functional for you, including an island counter installation. While on the subject of sinks, there are as many kinds as there are menus in a restaurant. They may be made of stainless steel or porcelain. Both can be had in single compartment, single compartment with single drainboard, single compartment with double drainboard; double compartment, double compartment with single drainboard, double compartment with double drainboard, corner sink with single or double drainboard, flush mounted or raised edge sinks. All of this without considering color or finish. As far as fixtures go, there are many varieties in fittings or faucets including single lever, double lever, hose spray (hose sprays tend to have a problem with leaking and I doubt the need for such a fitting). Before we leave the sink, let's not forget the garbage disposal. If you have a private sewage disposal system, a garbage disposal is not recommended because of the grease interfering with the natural bacteria action of the system and the greater amount of water which is necessary with garbage disposals, thereby overtaxing the sewage system.

Be very careful in your planning of electric outlets because of the number of kitchen appliances available and the electric loads required to operate these units. You should provide a separate electrical circuit for the dishwasher, toaster, broiler, electric frypan, radar oven, garbage disposal, mixer, blender, can openers, and other major appliances you may have. Only this way will you prevent fuses from blowing or circuit breakers from tripping.

Set aside a separate area for baking and put all your supplies and provisions for baking in one place, ususally near the oven. Use normally dead space in the corner cabinets by installing revolving shelves. A flour sifter which pulls out from under side of the upper cabinet shelf is a time saver item and not expensive. Set aside a drawer for bread and pastry using metal liners inserted inside the wooden drawer. A slicing board or block built into the counter will save your counter top from knife wounds and scratches. All cabinet work can be stained, painted or covered with laminated plastic. The easiest to maintain but the most expensive is laminated plastic which comes in a variety of designs. Laminated plastic is nothing more than several sheets of paper fused together with a special kind of adhesive with the finish surface of photographed plastic coating. The photographed surface can be woodgrain, linen, solid colors and on and on and on beyond imagination. The sheets come in 4'x8' and 4'x12' and are applied to wood base or composition base with a special kind of adhesive. Painting the cabinets may be cheaper than stain because you don't have to consider the wood grain. Staining the cabinets merely changes the color of the wood. It does not hide the grain of the wood or any knots or cracks, etc. Because of this, you must be selective in choosing the wood. Hardware plays a great part in kitchen design, so select a hardware style that is compatible with the design of the kitchen. One way to make your cleaning a little easier is not to have any pull hardware on the upper door cabinet. Simply extend the doors about an inch below the bottom of the lower shelf and all you need do is pull from the back of the door to open even with your hands full of flour. The dimensions of the kitchen cabinets are as follows: Counter height is 3'-0", counter depth is 2'-0" space between top of counter and under side of cabinet is from 14" to 18" and the very top shelf should be no higher than 6'-0" from the floor. The depth of the upper cabinet is 12". The finish walls of the kitchen should be of a material that is easy to clean and keep clean and as few seams or joints as possible. Painted plaster is a good finish as is laminated plastic or washable wall paper or vinyl wall covering. Ceramic tile is not recommended on walls above counter nor for counter tops because of the difficulty in cleaning and the dirt finding its way in the joints of the tile and if used on the counter top, should you drop a bottle, you are almost sure to break it. You will be working with acid almost every day which is found in tomato juice, orange juice, lemon juice, lime juice and grapefruit juice so be sure

your selection of finish is acid proof. Vinyl sheet goods is a good product for wall finish. Be sure to allow a toe space on the bottom of the counter at the floor otherwise you would not be able to get close enough to the counter to work comfortably.

Carpet is not recommended for kitchen floors because of spillage; regardless of what the manufacturers tell you, there are some stains that can not be removed from carpets. Sheet goods or Vinyl floor covering is best. Try to avoid any material with joints such as 9"x9" or 12"x12" floor tile again because of the cleaning problem. Under no circumstances should a wood finish floor in the kitchen be used.

Most housewives prefer a kitchen which is not visible from any other room because it is not always possible to keep a tidy kitchen and it can be embarrassing for visitors to see a messy kitchen. The only time you get unexpected visitors is when your house is not in order. Select light and vivid colors for your kitchen, psychologically they will keep you a-wake and alert.

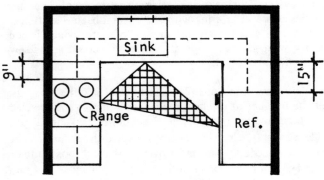

A work triangle is an efficient kitchen arrangement.

MINIMUM DISTANCES FROM APPLIANCES TO INSIDE CORNERS OF BASE CABINETS

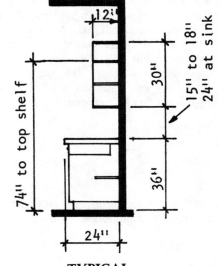

TYPICAL CABINET DIMENSIONS

21" sink counter combined with 36" mixing counter

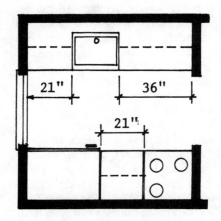

21" range counter combined with 15" refrig counter

KITCHENS FOR 2 BEDROOM UNIT

Sink and range counters combined with 36" mixing counter

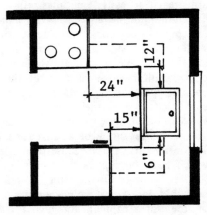

21" sink counter combined with 15" refrig counter

You must select all major appliances before you build your kitchen cabinet work because all cabinets are built around these units, or you must allow space for the units.

Range and oven units can be had in either single or multiple units. A single unit consists of a combination of range top and oven and can be free standing or drop-in type in a variety of sizes and colors. The other alternative is a single built-in oven or ovens with a single built-in surface top again with a variety of combinations. The latter are separate and remote units. A decision must be made in planning your kitchen to provide for your choice of units. Refrigerators also come in a variety of models, sizes and colors including wall hung units similar to a cabinet. Allow at least 40 sq. ft. of cabinet shelf space plus 6 sq. ft. for each person living in the house.

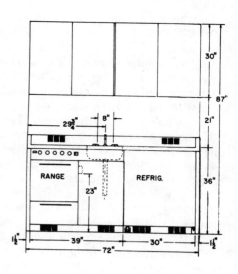

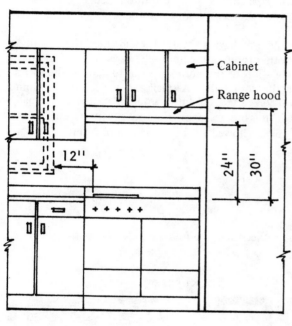

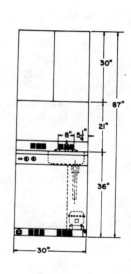

30" clearance to bottom of unprotected wood or metal cabinet. May be reduced to 24" where protection is provided. Protection of underside of cabinet should be at least 1/4" asbestos millboard covered with not less than 28 ga. sheet metal (.015 stainless steel, .024 aluminum, or .020 copper) or construction providing equivalent protection.

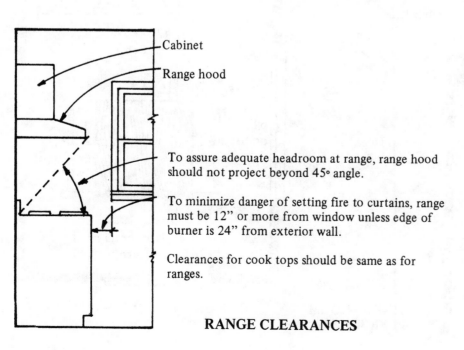

To assure adequate headroom at range, range hood should not project beyond 45° angle.

To minimize danger of setting fire to curtains, range must be 12" or more from window unless edge of burner is 24" from exterior wall.

Clearances for cook tops should be same as for ranges.

RANGE CLEARANCES

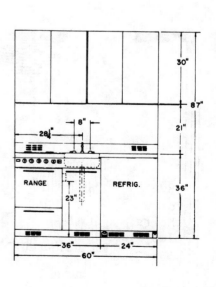

KITCHEN APPLIANCES

DINING ROOM

A decision must be made as to whether you want a formal or informal dining room. An informal dining room is normally used only by the immediate family for every day meals. A formal dining room is used for special occasions such as holidays, as well as every day use. In either case, the minimum size dining room required is 10' x 12', seating about a maximum of 8 people. The number of pieces of dining room furniture will dictate the room size. The dining room should be adjacent to the kitchen with no partition or wall separating, if informal, with a partition or wall separating, if formal. A dbl. swing door is the most practical connection between kitchen and dining area. Give careful thought to choosing window location. Too many windows will restrict placement of furniture. If you have an extension type table, extend the table to full length and allow no less than 4'-0" around perimeter of table for passage. This does not include space needed for chairs or furniture.

If you decide on a fireplace in the dining room, allow enough space between the fire and the person sitting nearest the fireplace. Minimum distance should be about 4' (more about fireplaces later). The decor in the dining room should be bright and cheerful. Neutral wall colors will give you a chance to be more selective in choosing the design of furniture, drapes, dining accessories, floor covering and upholstery. A low hanging ceiling chandelier directly over the center of the dining room table with a dimmer switch can be very dramatic supplemented with candle light. Wall surface should be of a material that is easy to clean, such as painted plaster, paper or vinyl covering, pre-finished plywood or in case of a formal dining room, raised wood panels. If you can not afford raised wood panels a very effective design can be achieved by surface applying wood moulding into panels or a panel designed wall covering will serve the same purpose. Carpeting is appropriate for dining room floors providing there is no color clash with other accessories. Wood floors are not recommended in dining rooms because of permanent damage from spillage of food or beverages. A plastered ceiling or acoustical tile is functional in dining rooms and in some cases, papered ceilings are in order providing it is not overdone. Sound or noise should not be a problem in the dining room because the drapes and carpet will absorb most of the sound. One wall may be set aside for a paper mural with an outdoor scene to break the monotony of the expanse of the room.

You should not have to walk through the dining room to reach another room in the house. Be careful in placing furniture in relation to the door so as not to damage the furniture with the door swing. A small exhaust fan in the dining room will solve the after dinner smoking problem. Normally a closet in the dining room is not necessary because of the storage space allowed in the dining room furniture design.

DINING AREA

Furniture Clearances

To assure adequate space for convenient use of the dining area, not less than the following clearances from the edge of the dining table should be observed.

32" for chairs plus access thereto.
38" for chairs plus access and passage.
42" for serving from behind chair.
24" for passage only.
48" from table to base cabinet (in dining-kitchen)

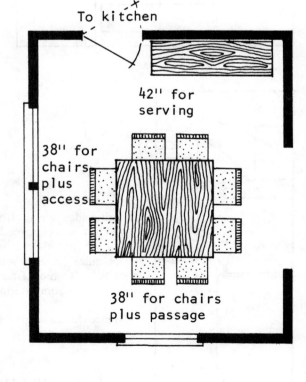

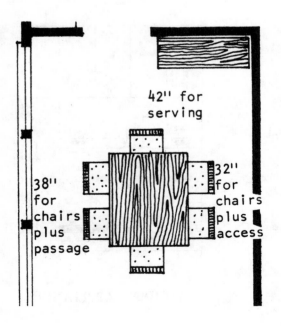

**DINING ROOM
6 PERSONS**

COMBINED SPACES

Often several compatible living functions can be combined advantageously in a single room. Some of the benefits of such arrangements are that less space is used but it is used more intensively, its functions can be changed making it more flexible and serviceable space, it is adaptable to varied furniture arrangements, while visually it can be made more interesting and seem more generous than if the same functions were dispersed into separate rooms.

For adjacent spaces to be considered a combined room, the clear opening between them should permit common use of the spaces. This usually necessitates an opening of at least 8 ft.

COMBINED LIVING-DINING ROOM

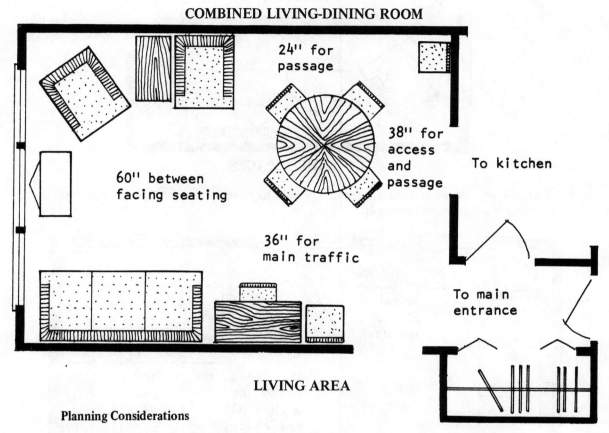

LIVING AREA

Planning Considerations

Thru traffic should be separated from activity centers.

Openings should be located so as to give enough wall space for various furniture arrangements.

Conveninet access should be provided to doors, windows, electric outlets, thermostats and supply grills.

Furniture Clearances

To assure adequate space for convenient use of furniture in the living area, not less than the following clearances should be observed.

60" between facing seating.
24" where circulation occurs between furniture.
30" for use of desk
36" for main traffic.
60" between television set and seating.

Seating arranged around a 10 ft. diameter circle makes a comfortable grouping for conversation.

33

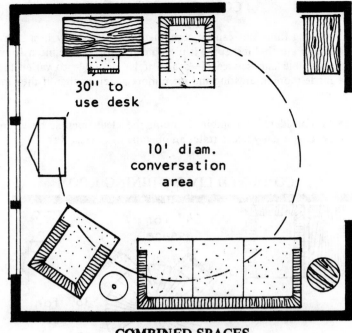

COMBINED SPACES

A bed alcove with natural light and ventilation and which can be screened from the living area is desirable in a 0-bedroom living unit.

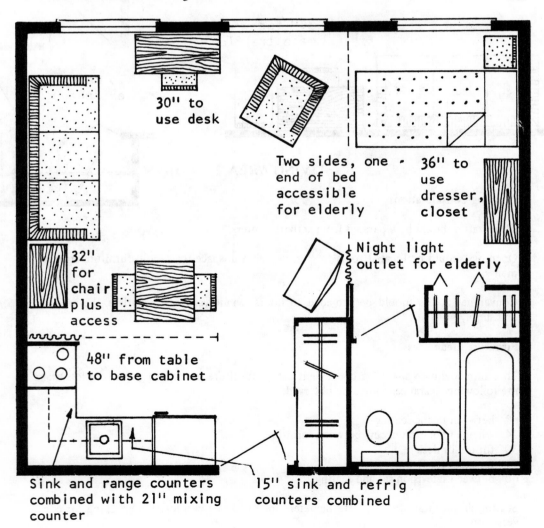

34

KEY TO FURNITURE SIZES

End table
1'-6" x 2'-6"

Television set
1'-4" x 2'-8"

Easy chair
2'-6" x 3'-0"

Chair
1'-6" x 1'-6"

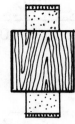

Table for two
2'-6" x 2'-6"

Dresser
1'-6" x 3'-6"
or
1'-6" x 4'-4"

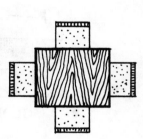

Table for four
2'-6" x 3'-2"

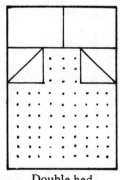

Double bed
4'-6" x 6'-10"

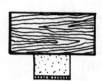

**Desk 1'-8" x 3'-6"
with chair**

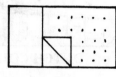

Crib
2'-6" x 4'-6"

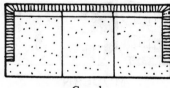

Couch
3'-0" x 6'-10"

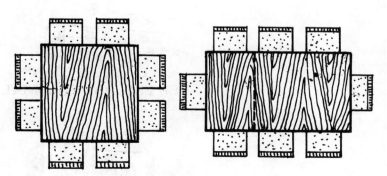

Dining table with chairs for six = 3'-4" x 4'-0"
for eight = 3'-4" x 6'-0" or 4'-0" x 4'-0"

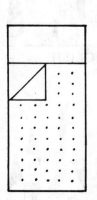 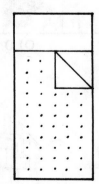

Twin beds
3'-3" x 6'-10"

TUDOR

MONTEREY

EARLY ENGLISH

FRENCH

DUTCH COLONIAL

CAPE COD

DESIGN   STUDIES

MODERN

GEORGIAN

OLD ENGLISH

SOUTHERN COLONIAL

NEW ENGLAND COLONIAL

ELIZABETHAN OR ENGLISH HALF TIMBERED

MEDITERRANEAN

LIVING ROOM

The living room should be the largest single formal room in the house; although the living room is quickly giving way to the family room which is a more informal atmosphere with the same function. It's surprising how many homes have living rooms that become museums or forbidden rooms for any member of the immediate family except on very special occasions. If a room cannot be used, it serves no purpose.

The selection of living room furniture has no limitations on color or design and some designs are very ornate, demanding, overpowering and overupholstered. There is a proverb often used, "In simplicity there is beauty". It is smart to practice that proverb in selecting your living room furniture. All pieces should blend with the entire decor including drapes, wall covering and carpet. A fireplace in the living room can be very inviting and relaxing and the additional cost is well worth the pleasure, comfort and increased value in resale. Do not plan a log storage for the fireplace in the house because of the insects that live and grow within the wood. Plan a storage area for your fireplace wood outdoors under cover as close to the house or room as possible. You have a choice of two types of fireplace dampers, rotary damper and poker damper, both of which are made of cast iron. The poker type is recommended because of the ease in operating—you simply reach in with a poker to adjust the damper. The rotary type has a worm screw mechanism with a rotary handle on the face of the mantle which you turn by hand to adjust the damper. They sometimes become disengaged or become distorted from the high temperatures generated by the fire. Whichever type you prefer, always leave the fireplace damper closed when the fireplace is not in use or the amount of heat lost through the chimney of the fireplace is like an open window and this will increase the fuel consumption of your home. Winged animals, especially bats, will sometimes nest in the warmth of the chimney and later find their way into your home. To prevent this, install screening on the top of your chimney. To prevent rain water from pouring down the chimney install a solid top on top of the chimney with openings on all sides.

The brick in the firebox is not ordinary brick but is instead a special brick called firebrick especially designed to withstand the high amount of heat generated by the fire. Ordinary brick is not designed to absorb this heat without damage, but the firebrick, too, can be damaged by a sudden change in temperature, such as that produced by dousing the fire with water. Let the fire burn out naturally. Protecting the sparks with a fireplace screen. If you are designing and building a fireplace in your home, you may use instead of firebrick in the firebox a fireplace lining made of metal. The only objection to this is the possibility of burning out the metal from prolonged use of the fireplace. Should this happen you will need to rebuild the entire fireplace to replace the unit. Think carefully before you decide on a raised hearth. They can be dangerous and space consuming.

The walls of the living room may be of painted plaster, paper or vinyl wall covering or pre-finished plywood. The colors and textures are much too varied to discuss here and the final decision rests mainly on what you can afford. If you have a long expanse of wall surface you may want to break it up by treating one wall of a different color or material to break up the monotony. The ceiling may be of exposed wood beams and if your living room is alreay built you may still have the effect of exposed wood beams by using styroform simulated beams which are very light in weight and come in a variety of length, size, texture and color. These are glued directly to the ceiling. Another functional ceiling is acoustical tile along with beamed ceiling or used alone. Acoustical tile can be had in many designs, colors, textures and sizes. If your ceiling is old, cracked or in need of repair, it may be less expensive and much simpler to install a suspended acoustical tile ceiling. A sloping wood finish ceiling with exposed beams is very effective but can be had with a single floor only with no floor above the living room. If you are planning such a room allow at least 20' from floor to highest point of roof which will allow enough room to suspend or hang from the roof or ceiling, a balcony accessible by circular stairs. This can be a very dramatic effect used as a library, music room or just to get away someplace alone to relax or meditate.

Carpeting is one of the more functional materials for the floor although a hardwood floor is often used as a finish floor in the living room. If you use a hardwood floor use scatter rugs to add interest to the floor. If you have a piano as part of your living room furniture and if the room is large enough you may use it as a focal point and build a 6" high platform about 4' larger than the overall dimensions of the piano and place the piano on the platform with a carpeted floor to help the acoustics. In any case, the piano should be placed on the coolest wall of the room away from the sun or heating units because heat dries out the wood of the piano, affecting the finish as well as the quality of tuning.

Another very effective plan is to lower the living room floor at least two steps below the main floor of the house. This adds drama and intrigue to the room and house, and will better proportion the height of the ceiling in relation to the length of the room. Anything less than two steps becomes dangerous. Window placement is important in arranging your furniture. The more windows you have, the less wall space you will have for furniture placement.

HALL OR CORRIDOR

A hall is a necessary non-livable area to lead you to your destination without going through another room and should be as confined as possible with a minimum of floor space to serve the purpose. Avoid long runs of hall and they can be avoided with proper planning. The minimum width of a hall should be no less than 36". If you have space, provide for a closet in the hall for general storage. As a rule, halls are inside areas without windows so be sure you plan enough lighting to be functional. Doors should not open into the hall except closet doors because you will restrict the passage. Plan on several electric plugs (duplex convenience outlets) for general purpose. Light colors will open up the area and give the illusion of a better proportioned area. Floors should be of carpet to mute the sound so as not to disturb others in the area.

BEDROOM

The minimum size bedroom is 8' x 10' which allows room for only one single bed and one other piece of furniture. The important thing to remember about planning your bedroom is the location of the windows and the size of the windows. The more windows you plan the less wall space for placement of furniture unless the windows are installed high enough to allow furniture to be placed under the window. Watching TV from bed is a favorite past time and a wall switch within arms reach operating the outlet at the TV will allow you to shut if off without getting out of bed. To help you plan the size of your bedroom, allow at least 30" clearance around the bed for passage. A single bed measures about 3'–0" wide and a double bed is about 4'–6" wide, king and queen beds are larger in width but all are about 6'–6" long. Bedroom furniture varies too greatly to give any sizes but if you cut out your furniture from cardboard to scale, it will allow you to place it in the room on the plans for better design. Be careful of water beds in spite of what the manufacturer tells you. They are heavy when filled with water and your floor may not be able to sustain the concentrated load. Careful planning is the key to a successful function.

Hardwood floors or carpet is best for bedroom floors. Plaster, acoustical tile or drywall construction may be used for the ceiling finish. These finishes are merely suggestions for the variety of selection is too great, and personal choice plays a part in the finished product. If you have the space, a his and hers closet can be very convenient, but the ultimate in bedroom planning is a separate dressing room with a private bath.

The location of doors and windows should permit alternate furniture arrangements.

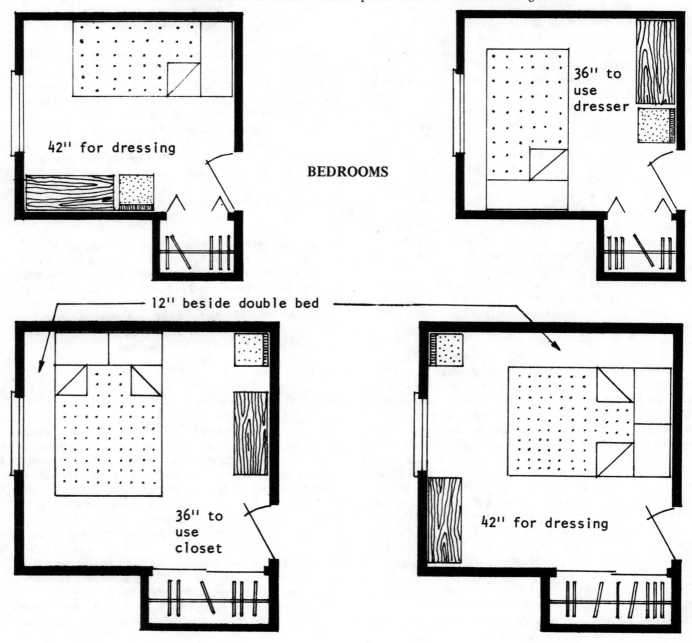

BEDROOMS

BEDROOMS

Furniture Clearances

To assure adequate space for convenient use of furniture in the bedroom, not less than the following clearances should be observed.

42" at one side or foot of bed for dressing.
 6" between side of bed and side of dresser or chest.
36" in front of dresser, closet and chest of drawers.
24" for major circulation path (door to closet, etc.)
22" on one side of bed for circulation.
12" on least used side of double bed. The least used side of a single or twin bed can be placed against the wall except in bedrooms for the elderly.

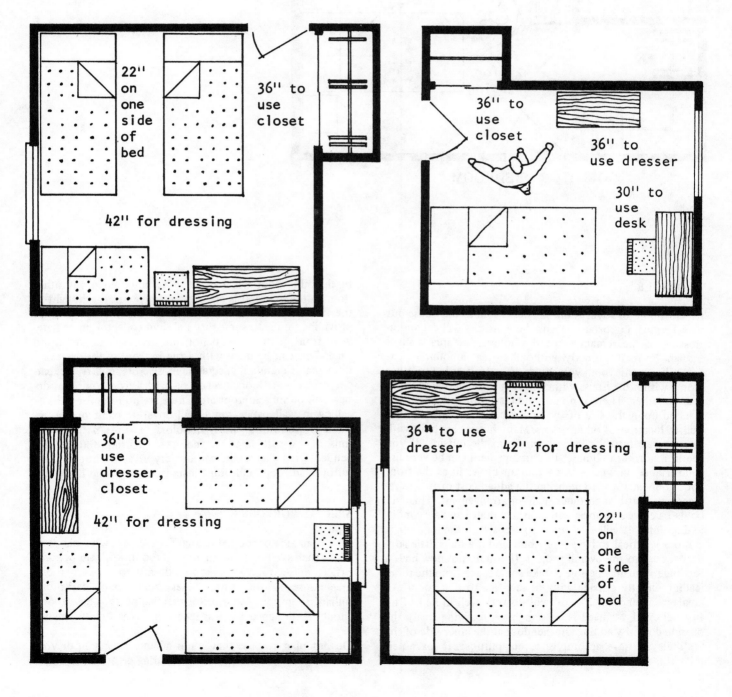

39

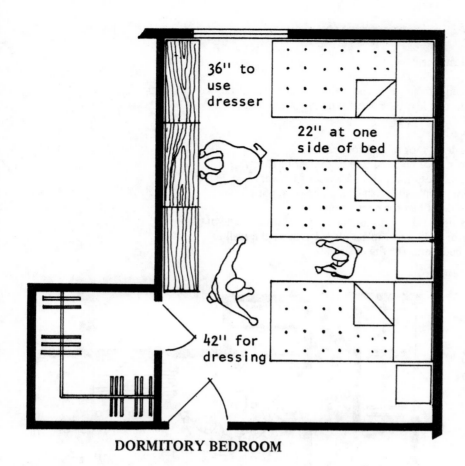

36" to use dresser

22" at one side of bed

42" for dressing

DORMITORY BEDROOM

Where at least two other sleeping spaces are provided, a dormitory is sometimes preferred by larger families.

VESTIBULE

The vestibule or foyer is the smallest room in the house but also the most important because here visitors will get an impression of the remainder of the house. The area is small enough to treat properly without a great amount of expense. From this room you should be guided or led to other rooms within the house without going through one room to reach another. There is no minimum size for this room but is based upon the size of the house and the arrangement as well as location of other rooms. Many houses are built with direct access into the living room from the outside. If you live in a northern climate, this arrangement can be very uncomfortable in winter when cold air blows in as the front door is opened not to mention the added cost of fuel to replace the heat lost through such an arrangement. This fact holds true even in areas with warm climates and air conditioning units. It will save on energy costs. In the long run it is more practical to have a vestibule and it entails little additional cost to the overall project. If you do not now have a vestibule, you may be able to take some space from the room leading directly outside without sacrifice to that room. An area no larger than 3' x 3' will do very well in lieu of no vestibule. All we need is enough space to swing freely the outside door. By adding another door at the inner side of the vestibule we have accomplished our purpose. If space permits, it is most convenient to have a closet in the vestibule.

In that this floor will receive more abuse than any other floor in the house, it is important to give careful thought to the finish of the floor. Wood will make a very beautiful floor providing you have some dirt and sand collector immediately in front of the door, if not, the floor will scratch in no time. This can be done with a rug in front of the door or a floor mat. Ceramic tile, ceramic mosiac tile, quarry tile, carpet or resilient floor covering of bright vivid color and design will be very appropriate. There are no rules for walls or ceiling in wall paper, vinyl wall covering, paint or pre-finished plywood, in a variety of colors, textures, patterns and finishes. A soft large incandescent lighting fixture suspended from the ceiling can be very effective but be careful of head room and don't install a fixture that hangs too low.

SPECIAL PURPOSE ROOMS

This is an area or room designed for your personal habits or needs such as a hobby room, sewing room, work shop, home office, music room, TV room, library room, card room, greenhouse or arboretum, nursery room, pool, darkroom, billiard room, or even a pistol practice range. These rooms should be designed to your special needs and requirements.

Do not plan a house that is not adequate for you or your family unless you make plans for adding on at a later date.

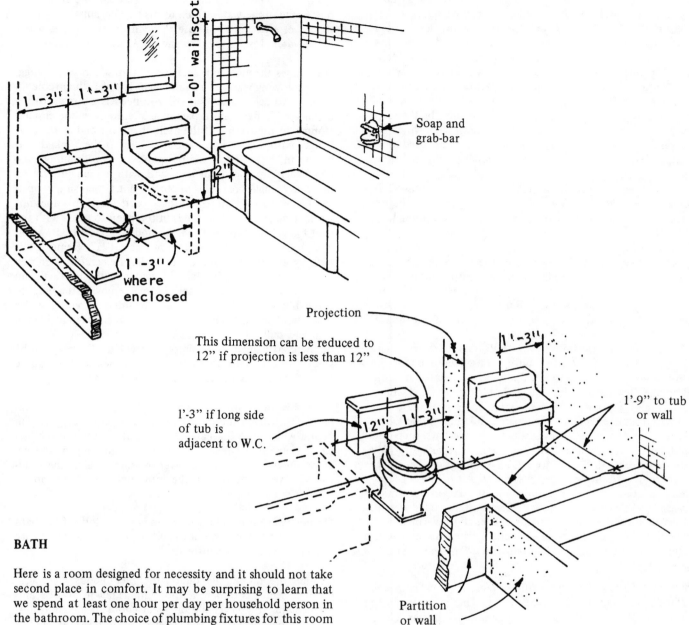

1'-3"   1'-3"

6'-0" wainscot

Soap and
grab-bar

2"

1'-3"
where
enclosed

Projection

This dimension can be reduced to
12" if projection is less than 12"

1'-3" if long side
of tub is
adjacent to W.C.

12"   1'-3"

1'-3"

1'-9" to tub
or wall

Partition
or wall

BATH

Here is a room designed for necessity and it should not take second place in comfort. It may be surprising to learn that we spend at least one hour per day per household person in the bathroom. The choice of plumbing fixtures for this room is unbelievable in color, quality, price and design. What most people commonly call a toilet is in fact a water closet. Many models are built in water closets ranging from the most expensive one piece, quiet flush, positive action, color, water saver to a very simple functional unit with no less than six models in between. These include floor models, wall hung and corner models with water tank covers designed for planters and toilet accessories. All models vary only a few inches in size and require about 30" in width and 2' – 4" in depth with no less than 18" clearance in front of rim of bowl. These fixtures are made of vitreous china and break easily. The cost of this fixture does not include fittings and accessories such as pull handle, piping, valves and seat. The seat also offers many designs, prices, quality, and color ranging from the inexpensive plastic model to the mink upholstered model.

A very common plumbing fixture widespread throughout Europe is the Bidet. A very sanitary functional plumbing fixture which is becoming increasingly popular in private homes in America. The Bidet requires about as much room as the water closet and is available in as many models.

Bathtubs are made of enameled cast iron, enameled formed steel or gel-coat fiberglass. The rectangular models vary in size of 4'–0", 4'–6", 5'–6" and 6'–0" long and about 30" wide varying in height of 12" to 16". These can be had in free standing models, finish one face (built-in) or finish two faces corner models. The square models measure 42" x 37" and 48" x 42" built-in with one finished face. The gel-coated fiberglass models come complete with shower and surrounding wall and ceiling, but a word of caution about gel-coated fiberglass models —— they are not maintenance free as the manufacturers claim them to be. If they are not maintained, they discolor and may become crazed on the surface. This will not affect their use only they can become very unsightly. They must be waxed to preserve the gel-coat finish at least twice a year. If you do not maintain these units, you will not be able to restore the finish and they will have to be painted. These units are not less expensive than the conventional assembly as the manufacturers may lead you to believe they are because, by the time you buy all related accessories and parts and fixtures, the cost may be the same or higher. There is a relatively new style of tub which deserves words of caution, the completely floor recessed models look very pretty with the nude model posing in display ads but there is a danger of falling into them, expecially if you have elderly people or children in your household. In most cases you must use slab on grade type construction (concrete poured directly on the ground) for this model.

Related to the tub or as a separate unit is the shower. The important thing to remember about the shower is the mixing valve, a safety feature well worth the additional cost. This valve maintains the water temperature once you have set it preventing you from receiving burns if someone draws water from another fixture in a different part of the house.

If you plan on a separate shower stall the minimum dimensions should be 30" x 36" with a raised curb under the shower door to prevent flooding should trouble develop with the floor drain. This curb should be about 4" high. The floor of the shower should be flashed. You can also purchase pre-molded metal or gel-coated fiberglass models. The accessories for tub or shower should be grab bars, soap dish and towel bar. When grab bars are installed, make sure they are secured to the wall properly. Too many of them have come loose, resulting in serious injury. All of these accessories can be had in aluminum, stainless steel and ceramics, recessed or surfaced mounted. The curtain rod poses no problem but a shower door or tub enclosure can if it is made of glass and someone slips and falls against the door. Injuries can be minimized if plastic is used instead of glass.

Strangely enough a sink is not found in the bath room—a sink belongs in the kitchen. What is commonly called a sink in the bath room is in fact a lavatory. The lavatory can be free standing or built into a counter called a dresser. These fixtures are made of enameled formed steel, enameled cast iron, vitreous china and stainless steel. They range in shape from square, rectangle, round, corner units and oval in many colors and sizes. They are also cabinet models in many sizes and finishes. Here again, when you buy one of these units it does not include accessories or fittings.

There are many accessories to choose from for this fixture. These include tooth brush holder, tumbler holder, soap dish, although most models have a built-in soap dish by way of a recess in the fixture. These accessories are available in many colors, materials, and design, surface mounted or recessed.

It may be good at this point to mention plumbing traps and their function. All plumbing fixtures must have traps according to code. Normally you don't see the trap because it is hidden under the fixture. They come in a variety of

shapes and finishes but all do the same job. Their operation and function is very simple ——when water runs down the drain of a plumbing fixture it goes through the trap, trapping some of the water which forms a seal against gases from the sewer entering the house through the pipes. The water in the water closet is the trap and no other trap is necessary.

Sometimes through time and use, a trap will become sluggish in allowing waste to run through. If this is the problem - no need to call a plumber. All you need is a screwdriver, a metal coat hanger and a pair of pliers. Remove the circular stopper in the fixture at the drain, bend the end of the coat hanger with a little hook about ½", insert the hooked coat hanger in the drain line and pull gently, this will pull out the hair caught in the drain line, and with a plunger, will remove any smaller particles of obstructions, then simply open the faucet to flush down all loose particles. If this does not work it means the blockage is in too deep to reach with the coat hanger, in this case, on the under side of the trap you will find a plug with a square nut about ½". Remove this plug by unscrewing counter clockwise. Be careful when you have removed this plug, all the water in the trap will run out. Put a pail under the trap before removing the plug, to catch the water. When you remove this plug you'll find a hole about 2" in diameter, large enough to reach inside the trap and pull out the entangled hair or use the hooked end of the coat hanger, then simply screw back the plug but be sure it is tight enough so there are no leaks. This can be tested by opening the faucet to fill the trap again.

A window in a bathroom is not absolutely necessary. An exhaust fan will do the job of ventilation very nicely. If you plan a window in the bath, do not put it over the tub, because you cannot reach it without possible injury and because the water from the shower splashing against the window will eventually rot out the entire unit resulting in an expensive repair project.

Do not plan on installing carpeting on the floor of the bath room because it is a wet area and the carpet will eventually rot out. Use area rugs instead.

Ceramic tile, mosaic tile, quarry tile, sheet goods, are practical. The secret is to have a floor with as few joints or seams as possible. If you decide on sheet goods, install the floor covering before placing the water closet in position. Do not fit the floor covering around the water closet because condensation falling from the water tank of the water closet will find its way under the floor covering. This seepage will cause the floor to come loose and possibly do serious damage to the underfloor which in most cases will be plywood. The plywood will delaminate and the entire floor will have to be replaced, a very expensive job. Avoid any joints at this point in the floor covering. Should you decide on ceramic tile be sure to insist on the non-slip surface type because any clay product is slippery when wet. Paint or ceramic tile walls is very functional for the bathroom and you have many colors and designs to choose from in tile including murals. The entire tub and shower enclosure should be of ceramic tile including the ceiling. One of the best home made remedies for cleaning ceramic tile is half vinegar and half water using a tooth brush to get at the joints of the tile.

The top of dressers or counters should be of laminated plastic without joints or seams. Also available are many accessories including built-in weight scales, tissue dispenser, accessory shelves, waste dispenser, paper towel dispenser, sanitary napkin dispenser, medicine cabinets, soap dispenser, ash tray, newspaper and magazine racks and shower seats. With careful planning, a single bathroom can be designed for two people to use at the same time separating the water closet from the rest of the bath with a partition. It need not extend up to the ceiling but only slightly above eye level. Six feet above the floor will be high enough. Be sure to include a door in the partition such as a shower door or a louvered wood door.

CLOSETS

Closets are not as unimportant as some people may think. Many houses have been rejected from completing sales because of a lack of closets. They too require proper planning for function and useability. The determining factor in designing a closet is the use. A food storage closet requires special planning because of the variety of food container sizes. It should not be more than 12" deep because items become lost deep in the back of the closet.

Shelves at about 12" apart seem to work very well especially for some breakfast cereal packages. The smaller food cans can be stacked one over another two deep. An excellent space saving idea is to attach shelves behind the door, for food storage. These shelves should be about 6" deep and about 8" apart with slatted front and ends. If you plan to store pots and pans, the best solution is to hang them from the handle with the largest one behind the smaller ones for easy access.

Clothes closets should be no less than 24" deep with a shelf and pole no longer than 4'–0" long without intermediate support. The pole should be about 5'–6" above the floor and 12" away from the rear closet wall with the shelf about 2" above the pole. The shelf should be about 12" deep. A shoe rack will make an excellent addition to any closet as will a built-in set of drawers. It does not cost much to install a light in the closet which need be nothing more than a simple pull chain type electric fixture. Doors on a closet should be designed to expose as much of the closet as possible when extended. There are several combination of doors to chose from beginning with single hinge, double hinge, single sliding, double sliding, triple sliding. Bear in mind that a double sliding arrangement will give you only one door wide access and a triple sliding will give you a two door wide opening access. Closet doors should be louvered or undercut 1" at the bottom to afford cross ventilation. By raising the closet floor about 3/4" will prevent dust and dirt from collecting deep inside the closet.

A kitchen should have a closet for storing cleaning utensils such as mops, brooms, vacuum cleaners etc. Several shelves may be installed at about 12" apart in the kitchen closet for storing packaged cleaning agents.

The vestibule should have a closet for guest's clothing with nothing more than a shelf and pole. A rear door closet is handy for removing clothing when coming in through the rear door.

If you have specialty items to be stored in a closet, design the closet around these items for proper storage so you will not be faced with having to ramble through to find what your looking for.

FAMILY ROOM

The family room is fast becoming a general purpose room. This room should be designed for comfortable informal use with a selection of finishes that will withstand abuse and use. Some of the features designed in this room can be a fireplace, built-in hi fi, built-in bar with a sink and shelves for storage of liquor and glasses, library, TV, music, sufficient space for dancing or a home office. For practical purposes, the family room should be within easy access to the kitchen for serving while entertaining. A bath room accessable from the family room is good planning and should also be accessible from a hall or alcove and never from another room to avoid embarrassment to those who will be using the bathroom.

A good quality carpet will take a great deal of abuse. A hardwood floor is not recommended because of possible spillage of alcholic beverages which will permanently stain the finish on the wood floor. Hardwood floors require maintenance at least every six months by waxing to restore the finish. Under no circumstance should you wash wooden floors with water because the water will result in serious damage to the wood. If the floor is waxed every six months, cleaning will not be necessary. Pre-finished plywood or vinyl wall covering is suitable for wall finishes. This room may generate a great deal of noise and a ceiling of acoustical tile, together with drapes and carpeted floors will reduce the noise factor without distrubing the rest of the household. Soft indirect general lighting can be very dramatic in the family room. If you have a Patio as part of your plans, the family room should open up to it.

Throughout this book we have mentioned acoustical tile ceilings frequently and if you have such a ceiling that has become stained because of roof leaks or other reasons, you may be able to salvage the tile by applying white chaulk over the stain.

RECREATION ROOM

As a rule, recreation rooms are built from space already existing in the basement. Therefore, unless you are planning to build a home, space is already defined, and the main concern to guard against is water and moisture. In most cases, this space is below ground and by that fact alone makes the area damp and wet with a minimum of ventilation. All precautions must be taken to correct this condition if it exists before any finish is constructed. If water in the basement is the problem, it must be determined where the water is coming from before the problem can be solved. If it is coming from the walls, there is no solution from the inside treatment of the walls no matter what the products or manufacturer claims. The problem must be solved from the outside and can be expensive. This problem is discussed in a later chapter. If the source of the problem is coming from the floor, it may be a little easier to solve with french drains, sump pump and sump pit. Again, more about this later.

In order to assure dryness after having solved the water problem the solution is simple by installing a separate and independent wall against the interior of the exterior foundation wall. This is done with the addition of 2" x 3" studs placed 16" apart with insulation placed between the studs and the finished wall surface applied to the studs. I do not recommend an expensive wall finish for this room. There are many wall board finishes available made from composition panels that are very attractive and functional. Sheet cork is another finish surface that is very functional for the walls of this room. In most cases, all mechanical equipment is located in the basement of the house, such as heating systems, fuel tanks, hot water tanks, electric panelboards, and well pumps, etc. When these rooms are partitioned off, be sure to allow enough ventilation. Heating burners require oxygen for proper combustion and operation. The solution is simple with the installation of louvered doors within the partition. Carpet on the floor will help the dampness problem but don't put just any carpet. There are carpets manufactured especially for below grade use over concrete floors. The ceiling can be finished with acoustical tile. Give some thought to planning of electric plugs, switches and lights which must be installed before the wall or ceiling finish is applied.

LAUNDRY ROOM

Having a clothes washing machine in the kitchen is not practical, unless you have no other choice. Bacteria from soiled clothing and food do not go well together. A laundry should be a room separate and apart from any other room. If you plan to do ironing in this room, you must then provide for a clothes hamper, a closet for ironed clothes, space for a laundry basket in addition to the washer and dryer, and laundry sink. A door leading directly outdoors is convenient for hanging clothes outside to dry. If you do not have sufficient space for a separate laundry room there are two other solutions. One is the basement or the garage if you do not have a basement and the other solution is the bathroom. One solution to the space problem in the bathroom for laundry is to buy the piggy-back model washer/dryer. One unit fits over the other which is an obvious space saver but in any case, be sure to allow for provisions to connect the machines, be it gas or electric. Most dryers require 220 volts of electricity to operate.

The laundry room is a wet area and you can imagine the damage created if the machine leaks or the drain hose becomes loose from its mooring. The floor should be without seams with a floor drain. Ceramic tile or a plastic product called Seamless Floors will do the job very well. Walls should also be of a water resistant finish such as laminated plastic, ceramic tile, vinyl wall covering or a water proof painted plaster. The ceiling can be of any material of your choice. Be sure to plan for proper lighting, either natural or artificial. The only other space you will need is for storage of laundry supplies such as detergents, bleaches, whiteners, etc.

GARAGE

Garages can be single car or multiple cars, attached, detached or part of the basement. Careful thought should be given to the approach or driveway leading to the garage de-signing it as level as possible even if it means cutting or filling the ground to achieve this design. If the driveway pitches down toward the garage, lower than the street level, surface water may be a problem. If the driveway is pitching up higher than the street this also may be a problem. Either way becomes a two fold problem in reaching the garage in cold climates with freezing rain and or snow and should the brakes of the car accidently become disengaged serious injury or property damage or both could result.

If your garage is to be attached, or part of the basement, you will be subjected to local building codes requiring fireproofing of walls and ceilings. Check your local building codes before any work is performed. Pitch the garage floor towards the door to allow water to run out. Water is brought into the garage by the automobile through melting snow or rain. If floor pitch is not possible, install a floor drain to serve the same purpose. If the wall of your garage is common with the wall of your house, install a curb at the pass door leading from the garage to the house. This curb, which should be at least 4" high, prevents the suction or pulling of air created by the space under the door from the garage to the house taking with it carbon monoxide emitted by the automobile. Carbon monoxide gas is heavier than air causing it to settle on the floor. The raised curb will prevent this action.

The garage is an excellent place for a workshop or storage of rakes, shovels, lawn mowers, snow removal equipment, bicycles, etc. The minimum size garage for a single car is 12' wide by 22' long. To that you must add whatever additional space you need for other purposes.

If your garage is not heated, insulation is not necessary, unless the garage is in the basement — in this case the ceiling will need to be insulated. If you plan to heat the garage it it need be designed no more than to prevent freezing or about 45 degrees. Any heat designed above that would be useless because of the high amount of heat loss through the doors which are almost impossible to design with weatherstripping that is effective enough to prevent greater heat loss. Most garage walls are unfinished inside which adds to the loss factor.

The minimum size for a single car garage door should be no less than 7'-0" wide and 6'-6" high. If the door is hinged it will require two doors each 3'-6" wide opening out. An overhead door rolls up toward the ceiling requiring a minimum of 12" head room above the door height. This will fix the ceiling height of the garage. Overhead doors can be manually operated or electrically operated, including radio control which will allow you to operate the door several feet away. The underside of the roof will make an excellent storage space for seasonal items or seldom used articles. If you plan such a storage be sure to allow for the additional loads in designing the ceiling. The floor should be of concrete at least 4" thick. Window location or number is optional but a pass door in addition to the garage door is almost a necessity. If you plan a workshop in the garage be sure to have at least one electric outlet or plug on a separate circuit for operation of power tools. A three way switch operating the same electric light is most conveninet, one switch at the pass door and another at the garage door.

44

DESIGNING FOR PHYSICALLY

HANDICAPPED

If members of your family are physically handicapped, a thoughtful and careful plan to help make living easier and more comfortable in your home requires little effort or money. Approximately one out of every seven people is handicapped physically. This represents human resources of immeasurable value and great significance. The most common design and construction in homes cause problems for the physically handicapped and these architectural barriers make it very difficult to have access to facilities inside and outside. Our concern is for those who for all practical purposes are confined to a wheelchair, have difficulty in walking requiring braces or crutches, amputees, arthritics, spastics and those suffering with pulmonary and cardiac ills. To offer security to those who are totally blind or impairments affecting sight and those whose deafness or hearing handicap is unable to communicate or hear warning signals. Our purpose is to provide for those with faulty coordination or palsy from brain, spinal or peripheral nerve injury, the aging with reduced mobility, flexibility, coordination and perceptiveness.

The collapsible wheelchair of tublar metal construction with plastic upholstery for back and seat is most commonly used and fall within certain manufacturers limits for design dimensions as follows: Length 42", width when open 25", height of seat above floor 19½", height of armrest above floor 29", height of push handles at the rear from floor 36" and width when collapsed 11". In order for a wheelchair to function properly, the following minimum dimensions are required: turning radius wheel to wheel is 18" and from rear of structure to front of structure is 31½", the average turning space required is 60" x 60", two wheelchairs passing each other requires a space of 60". The person functioning in a wheelchair requires the following dimensions: vertical reach ranges from 54" to 78", working table reach is from 28½" to 33", both arms extended ranges from 54" to 71", the average wall reach is 48" above the floor.

People functioning on crutches require the following dimensions: An average person requires an average of 32" between crutch tips in the normally accepted gait.

SITE WORK

Finish grading should be level and even to attain a normal entrance and make facilities accessible to individuals with physical disabilities. Walks should be at least 48" wide with a slope no greater than 5% and should have a continual common surface without steps or changes in level. If walks cross other walks, they should be of the same level. If a door swings out onto a walk, a platform of at least 3'—0" deep by 5'—0" wide made level should be provided. If ramps are necessary, they should not have a slope greater than 1 foot in 12 feet with a hand rail on at least one side 32" high extending 1'—0" beyond the top and bottom of the ramp. The ramp should have a non-slip surface with a level platform, the ramp should extend at least 1'—0" beyond each side of the doorway. Each ramp should have at least 6'—0" of straight clearance at the bottom.

DOORS

A minimum of 32" wide when open means at least a 34" wide door and shall be operable by a single effort. A pair of doors is not recommended. The floor on both sides of the door should be level for a distance of at least 5'—0" from the door swing. No thresholds should be used and if door closers are used, they should be of the time delay type.

STAIRS

At least one handrail should be installed that extends at least 18" beyond the top and bottom step. Risers should not exceed 7".

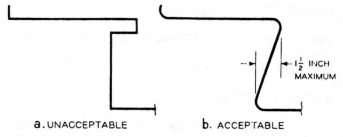

a. UNACCEPTABLE   b. ACCEPTABLE

FLOORS

A non-slip material should be selected for floors and all floors on a given level should be common throughout or be connected by a ramp. There should be no difference in floor levels between hall and bath and dining room.

BATH ROOMS & TOILETS

There should be at least 3'–0" clearance on both sides and in front of the water closet and there should be grab bars on at least one wall. The door leading into the bath or toilet should be no less than 32" wide and should swing out from the room. Hand rails should be installed on the walls at a height of 33" above the floor and parallel to the floor. There should be a clearance of 1½" between the rail and the wall and the rail should be of 1½" dia. securely fastened at the center and ends. The water closet seat should be 20" from the floor. A wall mounted water closet with a narrow understructure that recedes quickly is recommended. If floor mounted, it should not have a front that is wide and perpendicular to the floor at the front of the seat. The bowl should be shallow at the front of the seat and turn backward more than downward to allow a wheelchair to get close to the water closet. Water and drain piping should be insulated under lavatories to prevent people without sensation from self injury by burning. Mirrors above lavatories should be no higher than 40" above the floor measured from the bottom of the mirror. A shelf should be provided under each mirror and the same height as the bottom of the mirror. Towel racks and other dispensers should be no higher than 40" above the floor.

BATHROOM FOR WHEELCHAIR USER

Design Features of the Illustrated Bathroom

Outswinging bathroom door with flush threshold.

Space for both frontal and lateral transfer from wheelchair to water closet.

At least 6" between lavatory and wc to accommodate a toilet chair or toilet mounted side grab bars as per tenant preference.

Standard height toilet seat (1'-3") to permit use of toilet chair (1'-5").

Lavatory with 4" deep undercoated bowl and lever-type faucet, drain at side or rear, any exposed hot water piping to be well insulated, and front edge capable of withstanding 250 lb. load, mounting height 2'-10".

Tilting mirror over lavatory.

Recessed medicine cabinet with unbreakable shelves located near lavatory, mounting height, 5' to top shelf.

All grab bars 1 1/2" outside diameter with 1 1/2" clearance at wall.

Shower with vertical and horizontal grab bars mounted 3' above floor, recessed soap dish and water regulator mounted at 3'-6", regulator accessible from inside and outside the shower, folding seat, no curb, floor sloped to drain.

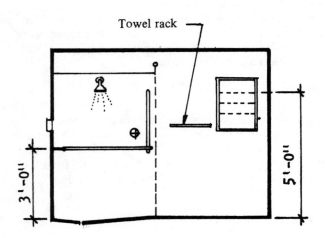

Towel rack

3'-0"   5'-0"

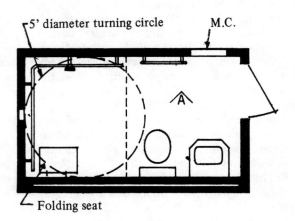

5' diameter turning circle   M.C.

Folding seat

CONTROLS

Switches for controls for lighting, and mechanical control as well as window draperies and fire alarms should be within reach of wheelchair individuals.

WARNING SIGNALS

Audible and visual simultaneous signals should be installed.

ENTRANCE PLATFORMS

Exterior platforms at entrances should provide sufficient space to allow safe standing room while opening a door which swings over it. This means the platform should be at least 3'-6" deep and extend 15" beyond the latch side of the door. Platforms for sliding doors should be at least 3'-6" deep and as wide as the door. The elevation of entrance platforms should be 4" to 6" below the floor of the dwelling at the entrance unless for wheelchair use.

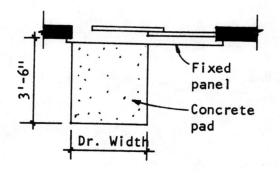

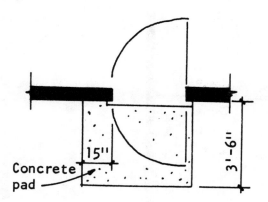

KITCHEN FOR WHEELCHAIR USER

Design Features of the Illustrated Kitchen

Storage cabinet with adjustable shelves, 18" deep plus 6" deep shelves on door, 30" wide, 48" to top shelf.

Work counter, 34" high—usable by person standing or in wheelchair, 29" high knee space to clear wheelchair arms.

Sink with 4" deep undercoated bowl and single lever faucet, drain at side or rear. Any exposed hot water piping to be well insulated.

8" deep wall shelf mounted 12" above work counter.

Standard range with controls at front.

Standard refrigerator.

Outsized cabinet door and drawer pulls.

Not shown—lap or chop boards which rest on a person's lap or on the arms of a wheelchair. If two boards are available, one should have an 8" diam. cutout to receive a mixing bowl.

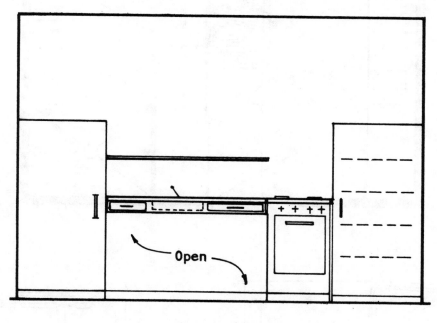

ELEVATION

CENTRAL DINING

Seating for wheelchair users should be on at least 2'-6" centers. Tables should be 3'-6" wide if chair users are to face each other. Wider tables are not recommended because of chair users' restricted reaching ability.

COMBINED SPACES

In housing for the elderly and handicapped, the units suitable for wheelchair users often can be placed advantageously on the ground floor.

COMBINED SPACES

Omission of an easy chair is acceptable to give more space for occupant's wheelchair.

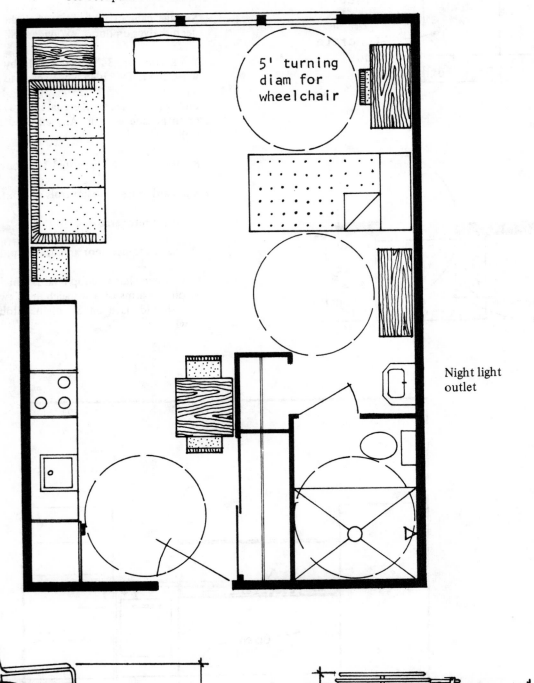

5' turning diam for wheelchair

Night light outlet

THE WHEELCHAIR

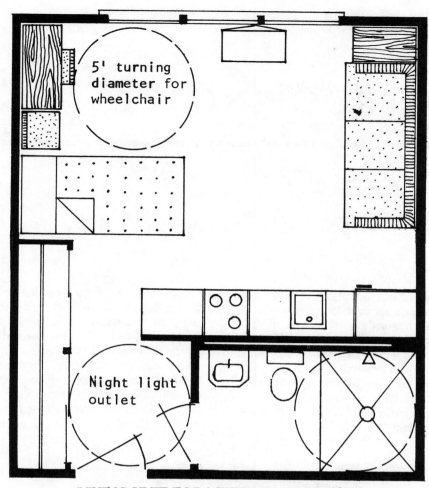

5' turning diameter for wheelchair

Night light outlet

LIVING UNIT FOR WHEELCHAIR USER

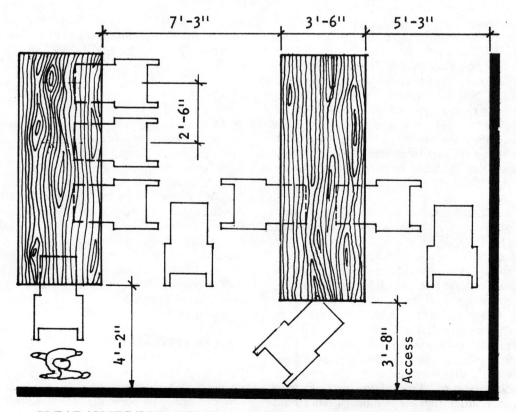

7'-3"   3'-6"   5'-3"

2'-6"

4'-2"

3'-8" Access

CLEARANCES FOR CENTRAL DINING-WHEELCHAIR USERS

DANGERPROOFING

DANGERPROOFING

The home is one of the most dangerous places on earth. Each year thousands of people are accidentally killed in homes, millions are injured and hundreds of thousands of them permanentally. These accidents need not happen, if careful thought and planning is used, unsafe stairways, floors, burns, explosions, fires and poison can be avoided. The dangers lurk in walls, heating systems, stoves and fireplaces. Many people are seriously injured from bumped heads, cracked skin, gouged eyes, crushed fingers, etc. These accidents always happen to someone else, never to you or your family.

STAIRS

The principal source of serious accidents are stairs caused by slippery, elevated, uneven, unsteady and unsuspected surfaces. Poor lighting and non-existent or inadequate safeguards is another danger area. Special attention must be given to stairs. Every tread and riser should be even Sometimes a fraction of an inch difference can cause a bad fall. Stairs should not be too steep, a compatible slope is between 30 degrees and 35 degrees. Spacious intermediate landings should be furnished. Not only will they provide a place to pause on the way up or down, but will also provide a break against any fall. Try to avoid fan shaped or winders. Stairs of less than three steps are dangerous for older people or people with poor vision. Be sure to provide for enough headroom on a stairway. Non-slip finishes are a must on all treads and landings.

Railings lend for physical support and should be properly secured. Every stairway should have a railing including exterior stairs. They should be continuous for the entire length of the stairs and not less than 32" above the riser. Stairs more than 44" wide should have railings on both sides. Balustrades should be thin enough for a child to grab, strong enough not to break, close enough to avoid a child becoming wedged between them. Landings and approaches should be large and well lighted. There should be no less than 30" clearance from all doors swinging at the top and bottom of stairs. The first and last step should be clearly defined with a nosing of contrasting color. Lighting switches should be at the top and bottom of all stairs using three way switches. If householders suffer from sleepwalking, a gate should be provided at the head and foot of all stairs.

BATH

Be sure tubs have a slip-proof flat bottom. Select plumbing fixtures that are of shatter proof material. Hand rails or grab bars should be secured to the wall with no less than two on the tub wall and should be long enough and installed in a vertical position to provide proper support for standing and sitting. One diagonal grab bar may be substituted. Allow enough room between all plumbing fixtures. Install the light switch outside the bath in the hall. Water and electricity do not mix. Use waterproof lighting fixtures in tubs and shower enclosures. Mixing valves at showers will prevent scalding from hot water.

ROOMS AND HALLS

Allow enough space in the rooms for movement of all furniture. Light switches should be located near each bed for access at night. Provide outlets for night lights in halls, especially at stair openings. Do not block line of traffic with furniture. Provide three way electrical switches if more than one door is in the room.

KITCHEN

Avoid sharp edges or corners on all counters, doors and drawers. Provide space for step stool or stepladder to eliminate climbing on chairs. Do not install any shelf higher than 6'–0" above the floor. If possible, use sliding upper cabinet doors to avoid injury when hinged cabinet doors are open. Appliances should be vented. The oven, broiler and cook top should be at least 6" away from an unprotected combustible surface. Do not place gas stoves in front of a window, a breeze could blow out the flame of a gas burner or cause curtains to catch fire. Provide slotted spaces in drawers for knives. Allow a minimum of 2" space between stove and wall or counter. Plan for good lighting and ground all plugs for electrical appliances. A fire extinguisher should be located nearby.

CELLAR AND BASEMENT

Paint projecting or low hanging equipment such as pipes or obstacles a constrasting color. Gas meters must not be near furnaces or boilers nor closer than three feet to any electric meter or appliance. There should be a door leading directly outside from the basement. A fire extinguisher should be placed in the basement and a fire rated ceiling self-closing fire door should be included as protection against fire starting in the basement.

PORCH AND ENTRANCE

Install a toe rail along the outer edge of the porch to prevent miscellaneous items which roll off from accidentally falling on those below. Protect entrances from falling snow or rain. Do not build roof valleys over entrances. Provide snow guards at roof over doorways. Entrances should be recessed and well lighted, especially the steps leading to the entrance.

WINDOWS

Be sure windows can be cleaned from the inside and are equipped with storm sash and screens which can be installed and removed from the inside. Small children have little fear of height and windows in children's rooms should have bars or slats or place the windows high enough above the floor and out of reach of children.

ROOFS AND GUTTERS

If the house is north of the Mason Dixon line, keep the roof design simple and well insulated. Avoid climbing ladders to remove snow and ice accumulation. Provide means of ventilating the attic space.

CHIMNEY AND FIREPLACE

One of the main causes of accidental fire comes from the chimney and fireplace. Be sure flue linings are installed in chimneys, one flue lining for every fire. No woodwork (framing) should be closer than 2" of the chimney. If asbestos insulating board is used the distance may be decreased to ½", if the local building code will permit it. Chimney should set on a firm foundation of concrete and built from the foundation up independent from any support of the building. Do not support chimney on wood shelves. Chimney should extend at least 2'–0" above highest point of roof within a 10'–0" radius. Project the flue lining at least 2" above the brickwork. Cap the chimney to avoid sparks and use screening to avoid winged animals from nesting in the chimney.

Keep the fireplace damper closed when fireplace is not in use. All chimneys should have cleanout doors. Smoke pipes should be at least 18" clear of any framing and should be readily accessible for easy inspection, cleaning and repair or replacement. Faulty, clogged, soot-filled smoke pipes start fires, reduce efficiency and cause deadly gases which when released, can kill the entire family. Improperly designed and constructed fireplaces can result in burnt floors, domestic pets and children. Embers and sparks from the fire can smudge paint, ruin ceilings and walls and can burn the house completely. Correct fireplace dimensions are of prime importance, otherwise efficiency will be lost and sparks may be driven out by down drafts. A damper hinged at the back is a necessity. Brick fireplaces should have walls not less than 8" thick. Stone or concrete block require a minimum

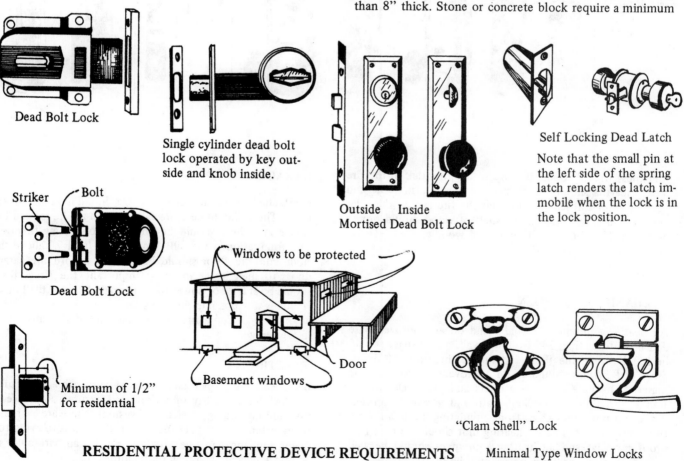

Dead Bolt Lock

Single cylinder dead bolt lock operated by key outside and knob inside.

Striker   Bolt

Dead Bolt Lock

Minimum of 1/2" for residential

Outside   Inside
Mortised Dead Bolt Lock

Self Locking Dead Latch

Note that the small pin at the left side of the spring latch renders the latch immobile when the lock is in the lock position.

Windows to be protected

Door

Basement windows

"Clam Shell" Lock

RESIDENTIAL PROTECTIVE DEVICE REQUIREMENTS   Minimal Type Window Locks

portable and wheeled fire extinguishers

type of agent	regular dry chemical	tri-class dry chemical	pressurized water	Halon 1211	carbon dioxide
Class A fire Paper, wood, cloth etc., where quenching by water or insulating by Tri-Class general purpose dry chemical is effective.	not recommended	yes/excellent Fire-retardant blanket to prevent reflash.	yes/excellent Water saturates material and prevents rekindling.	not recommended	not recommended
Class B fire Gasoline, oils, paints burning liquids, cooking fats, etc., where smothering action is required.	yes/excellent Chemical powder smothers fire. Screen of dry chemical shields operator from heat.	yes/excellent Chemical powder smothers fire. Screen of dry chemical shields operator from heat.	no Water will spread fire, not put it out.	yes/excellent Halon 1211 snuffs out fire, doesn't effect equipment or foodstuffs	yes/excellent Carbon dioxide leaves no residue, does not affect equipment or foodstuffs.
Class C fire Live electrical equipment Fire in motors, switches, appliances, etc. where a non-conducting extinguishing agent is required.	yes/excellent Chemical is a non-conductor; screen of dry chemical shields operator from heat.	yes/excellent Chemical is a non-conductor; screen of dry chemical shields operator from heat.	no Water, a conductor should not be used on live electrical equipment.	yes/excellent Halon 1211 is a non-conductor, leaves no residue, will not damage equipment.	yes/excellent Carbon dioxide is a non-conductor, leaves no residue, will not damage equipment.
How to choose your Extinguishers Determine what type of hazard (class of fire) or hazards you need to protect. Determine the degree of hazard—light, medium heavy, select the extinguisher with appropriate extinguishing agent and rating.					

thickness of 12" walls. Be sure to use firebrick in the fire box. Hearths should be on non-combustible material and should extend at least 8" beyond the fire box at the sides and 20" in front. The mantel shelf of wood should not be less than 12" above the firebox and woodwork at least 8" away from the firebox at the sides.

MECHANICAL EQUIPMENT

All heating equipment should stand on an approved base and be not less than 24" from the wall. An air space should be left between the floor and the heating unit. All ducts, pipes and fittings should be of approved non-combustible material. Insulate all heating ducts and pipes. Do not install return ducts in kitchen, bath and garage to prevent odors and poisonous gases from circulating through the entire house. Ceilings above heating unit should be of a fireproof material and all heating equipment should be well vented. Doors to heater rooms should be fire rated.

GARAGE

If attached to the house, the garage should have a concrete floor. There should be a firewall between the house and the garage and there should be only one connecting firedoor. The foundation wood sill should be at least 7" above the floor and the floor should be pitched toward the garage doors to shed water and more important, the garage floor should be at least 6" lower than the main floor of the house. If this is not possible, build a stepover at least 6" high under the door. Keep a fire extinguisher in an accessible place in the garage.

ELECTRICITY

Be sure of the proper gauge wire, type of cable and insulation or armor, quality of sockets and fixtures, amperage of fuse and grounding of electrical system. These are extremely important to safety. Demand enough circuits to avoid too many appliances in one plug. Do not install bare bulbs in closets which can and may burn clothes.

A lightning rod system will guard against electrical storm damage or injury. If storage batteries are used in your home, there should be a separate room well insulated. Storage batteries under charge generate a great deal of heat and highly explosive hydrogen gas. Never strike a match in a battery room.

Attach a hose type fitting for fighting fires on all floors and keep a garden hose long enough to reach any part of the house connected in the basement. In case of fire, shut off the gas and electricity as well as oil fuel line supplies. Never touch any electrical switch or applicance with wet hands or while standing on a wet or damp floor. Never make any repairs to an electrical device without first turning off the electricity or disconnect the device from the outlet. Never locate switches where they can be reached with wet hands, especially around tubs, showers, sinks and lavatories. Do not use portable electric heaters in the bath room. If you must have one, build it in the wall well out of reach of small children. Avoid long lamp cords that easily become kinked and frayed.

Circuit breaker type electrical panels will eliminate the possibility of using oversized fuses or any substitute because there are no fuses in this type panel. Keep radio antennas well away from high voltage power lines. Never attach them to light or telephone poles.

POISONS

Never run the engine of automobiles in the garage with the door closed. Deadly carbon monoxide can also be generated by incomplete combustion of burning coal. Do not place stove or refrigerators in a room where people sleep. Refrigerator gases can be fatal.

Build out of reach of children a small well-lit medicine cabinet that can be locked. Use it for storing poisonous medicine and cleaning agents.

GENERAL

Security

For increased security, all main entrances should be located on the same (street) side of a building.

To discourage pilferage, mailboxes should be windowless and located in a highly visible part of the lobby.

Housing for the Elderly and Handicapped

An entrance for stretchers should be considered. It should be separate from the main entrance and lobby and should have direct access to an elevator. The building's main entrance should be protected and readily accessible to cars; space for seating near the entrance should be provided.

In housing designed for wheelchair users, an automatic building entrance door should be considered, as well as installation of 6 in. wide view panels extending to within 3 ft. of the floor on the latch side of doors. Vestibules should be at least 6'-6" deep to avoid trapping wheelchairs between the doors.

COST CONTROL

8

An alternate system of framing is spacing all framing lumber 24" o.c. instead of 16" o.c. This system is a way to build for less money without sacrificing quality and it provides for less lumber for floors, walls and roofs and obviously requires less labor.

The system works best with alignment of basic framing members of trusses, studs and joists used in conjunction with plywood for sheathing and sub-floors.

24" framing spacing is recognized by HUD and most building codes; however, check out local codes before planning or construction is begun.

The basic floor assembly consists of a 3/4" T&G plywood over wood joists spaced 24" on center using screw nails for nailing plywood into the joists. The plywood may also be glued to the joists instead of nailed. Studs for walls up to 10'-0" in a single story house with 24" spacing; on a two story house, the studs should be limited to 8'-0" for the first floor. ½" thick plywood can be used for wall sheathing and ½" thick gypsum wallboard is acceptable for interior wall lining.

Roof trusses work best with this type framing.

Comparative cost summary* *16-inch vs. 24-inch o.c. FRAMING*

OPERATION	LABOR COST		MATERIAL COST		TOTAL COST		DIFFERENCE	
	16" o.c.	24" o.c.	16" o.c.	24" o.c.	16" o.c.	24" o.c.	COST	%
1. Frame and erect walls	$451.58	$373.59	$ 794.15	$ 688.65	$1,245.73	$1,062.24	$183.49	14.7
2. Siding	383.17	341.22	386.32	471.76	769.49	812.98	—43.49	—5.6
TOTAL WALLS	$834.75	$714.81	$1,180.47	$1,160.41	$2,015.22	$1,875.22	$140.00	6.9
1. Frame floors	$ 84.91	$ 66.60	$ 315.78	$ 265.10	$ 400.69	$ 331.70	$ 68.99	17.2
2. Subfloors	64.22	57.94	174.30	225.32	238.52	283.26	—44.74	—18.7
TOTAL FLOORS	$149.13	$124.54	$ 490.08	$ 490.42	$ 639.21	$ 614.96	$ 24.25	3.8
GRAND TOTAL WALLS AND FLOORS	$983.88	$839.35	$1,670.55	$1,650.83	$2,654.43	$2,490.18	$164.25	6.2
1. Estimated drywall; hang, tape and spackle	$346.67	$300.00	$ 358.33	$ 357.33	$ 705.00	$ 657.33	$ 47.67	6.8
2. Estimated electrical; drill holes only	32.00	25.07			32.00	25.07	6.93	21.7
TOTAL DRYWALL AND ELECTRICAL	$378.67	$325.07	$ 358.33	$ 357.33	$ 737.00	$ 682.40	$ 54.60	7.4
GRAND TOTALS					$3,391.43	$3,172.58	$218.85	6.45%

*Data by NAHB Research Foundation

Species	Grade	SPAN (feet and inches)							
		2 x 6		2 x 8		2 x 10		2 x 12	
		Nailed*	Glued†	Nailed*	Glued†	Nailed*	Glued†	Nailed*	Glued†
Douglas Fir - Larch	2 & Btr	8-7	8-7	11-3	11-3	14-5	14-5	17-6	17-6
	3	6-7	6-7	8-8	8-8	11-0	11-0	13-5	13-5
Douglas Fir - South	2 & Btr	7-11	8-3	10-6	10-11	13-4	13-10	16-3	16-11
	3	6-4	6-4	8-4	8-4	10-8	10-8	13-0	13-0
Hem-Fir	2 & Btr	7-7	7-7	10-0	10-0	12-10	12-10	15-7	15-7
	3	5-10	5-10	7-8	7-8	9-10	9-10	11-11	11-11
Mountain Hemlock	2 & Btr	7-9	7-9	9-11	10-3	12-8	13-1	15-4	15-11
	3	5-11	5-11	7-10	7-10	10-0	10-0	12-2	12-2
Mountain Hemlock - Hem-Fir	2 & Btr	7-7	7-7	9-11	10-0	12-8	12-10	15-4	15-7
	3	5-10	5-10	7-8	7-8	9-10	9-10	11-11	11-11
Western Hemlock	2 & Btr	7-11	7-11	10-6	10-6	13-4	13-4	16-3	16-3
	3	6-2	6-2	8-1	8-1	10-4	10-4	12-7	12-7
Engelmann Spruce Alpine Fir (Engelmann Spruce - Lodgepole Pine)	2 & Btr	6-10	6-11	9-1	9-1	11-8	11-8	14-2	14-2
	3	5-3	5-3	6-11	6-11	8-10	8-10	10-9	10-9
Lodgepole Pine	2 & Btr	7-3	7-3	9-7	9-7	12-3	12-3	14-11	14-11
	3	5-7	5-7	7-5	7-5	9-5	9-5	11-6	11-6
Ponderosa Pine - Sugar Pine (Ponderosa Pine - Lodgepole Pine)	2 & Btr	7-0	7-0	9-3	9-3	11-9	11-9	14-4	14-4
	3	5-5	5-5	7-1	7-1	9-1	9-1	11-0	11-0
Southern Pine	1 KD	8-10	9-8	11-8	12-9	14-11	16-3	18-1	19-9
	2 KD	8-6	8-8	11-3	11-6	14-4	14-8	17-5	17-9
	3 KD	6-7	6-7	8-8	8-8	11-0	11-0	13-5	13-5
White Woods (Western Woods)	2 & Btr	6-10	6-10	9-0	9-0	11-6	11-6	14-0	14-0
	3	5-3	5-3	6-11	6-11	8-10	8-10	10-9	10-9
Idaho White Pine	2 & Btr	6-10	6-10	9-0	9-0	11-6	11-6	14-0	14-0
	3	5-3	5-3	6-11	6-11	8-10	8-10	10-9	10-9
Western Cedars	2 & Btr	7-3	7-3	9-7	9-7	12-3	12-3	14-11	14-11
	3	5-7	5-7	7-5	7-5	9-5	9-5	11-6	11-6

*Nailed span data provided by Southern Forest Products Association and Western Wood Products Association. Glued span data provided by American Plywood Association.

†23/32" UNDERLAYMENT plywood glued to joist. These spans also apply to double-floor construction due to the stiffening effect of the separate underlayment.

Design Criteria:
   Strength — 10 lbs. per sq. ft. dead load plus 40 lbs. per sq. ft. live load.
   Deflection — Limited to span in inches divided by 360 for live load only.

For the average family, the cost of a home is probably the largest single investment that will ever be made. Don't build a home larger than you need at the present time but make provisions for future additions. By reducing the number of square feet of exterior wall surface, the cost will be reduced. There are no magic formulas or secret plans to residential construction costs.

Seldom will a satisfactory plan work with a square shaped house, so the next least expensive house will be a rectangle which still has only four sides and four corners. Ells project from the main house and if designed with a common wall of the main house, it will help to reduce the cost. The more corners, the higher the cost. If the size of the building lot restricts your planning, a 1½ or 2 story house may be the

High slope rafters* *Spaced 24" o.c.*

SPECIES	GRADE	Slope over 3 in 12 – 20 lbs. per sq. ft. live load. (Light Roof Covering) SPAN (Feet and Inches)		Slope over 3 in 12 – 30 lbs. per sq. ft. live load. (Light Roof Covering) SPAN (Feet and Inches)	
		2 x 4	2 x 6	2 x 4	2 x 6
Douglas Fir - Larch	Const.	7-6		6-2	
	Std.	5-8		4-8	
	1	8-11	14-1	7-10	11-8
	2	8-9	13-0	7-3	10-8
	3	6-7	9-11	5-5	8-2
Douglas Fir South	Const.	7-4		6-0	
	Std.	5-6		4-7	
	1	8-3	12-11	7-2	11-3
	2	8-0	12-7	7-0	10-3
	3	6-5	9-8	5-3	7-11
Hem-Fir	Const.	6-9		5-7	
	Std.	5-1		4-2	
	1	8-5	12-9	7-2	10-6
	2	8-0	11-7	6-7	9-6
	3	5-10	8-11	4-10	7-3
Mountain Hemlock	Const.	6-10		5-8	
	Std.	5-3		4-3	
	1	8-0	12-7	7-0	10-8
	2	7-7	11-10	6-8	9-8
	3	6-1	9-0	4-11	7-5
Mountain Hemlock Hem-Fir	Const.	6-9		5-7	
	Std.	5-1		4-2	
	1	8-0	12-7	7-0	10-6
	2	7-7	11-7	6-7	9-6
	3	5-10	8-11	4-10	7-3
Western Hemlock	Const.	7-1		5-9	
	Std.	5-4		4-4	
	1	8-7	13-5	7-6	11-0
	2	8-3	12-1	6-9	9-11
	3	6-2	9-4	5-0	7-8
Engelmann Spruce - Alpine Fir (Engelmann Spruce - Lodgepole Pine)	Const.	6-2		5-0	
	Std.	4-7		3-9	
	1	8-0	11-7	6-7	9-6
	2	7-3	10-6	5-11	8-8
	3	5-4	8-0	4-4	6-7
Lodgepole Pine	Const.	6-5		5-3	
	Std.	4-10		4-0	
	1	8-0	12-4	6-11	10-1
	2	7-6	11-1	6-2	9-1
	3	5-8	8-6	4-8	7-0
Ponderosa Pine - Sugar Pine (Ponderosa Pine - Lodgepole Pine)	Const.	6-3		5-1	
	Std.	4-7		3-9	
	1	7-10	11-10	6-8	9-8
	2	7-4	10-8	6-0	8-9
	3	5-5	8-2	4-5	6-9
Southern Pine	Const. KD	7-8		6-4	
	Std. KD	5-10		4-9	
	1 KD	8-11	14-0	7-9	12-0
	2 KD	9-2	13-2	7-6	10-9
	3 KD	6-9	9-11	5-6	8-1
Idaho White Pine	Const.	6-1		4-11	
	Std.	4-6		3-8	
	1	7-10	11-4	6-5	9-3
	2	7-1	10-5	5-9	8-6
	3	5-4	8-0	4-4	6-7
Western Cedars	Const.	6-5		5-3	
	Std.	4-10		4-0	
	1	7-7	11-11	6-8	10-1
	2	7-4	11-1	6-2	9-1
	3	5-8	8-6	4-8	7-0
White Woods (Western Woods)	Const.	6-1		4-11	
	Std.	4-6		3-8	
	1	7-7	11-4	6-5	9-3
	2	7-1	10-5	5-4	8-6
	3	5-4	8-0	4-4	6-7

Design Criteria:

Strength — 7 lbs. per sq. ft. dead load plus indicated live load.

Deflection   Limited to span in inches divided by 180.

*Data provided by the Southern Forest Products Association and the Western Wood Products Association.

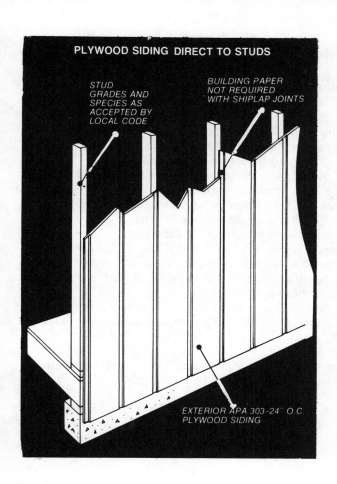

PLYWOOD SIDING DIRECT TO STUDS

STUD GRADES AND SPECIES AS ACCEPTED BY LOCAL CODE

BUILDING PAPER NOT REQUIRED WITH SHIPLAP JOINTS

EXTERIOR APA 303-24" O.C. PLYWOOD SIDING

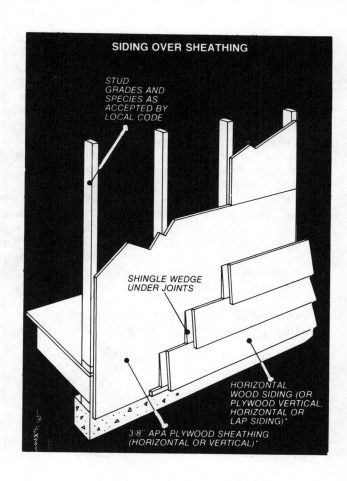

SIDING OVER SHEATHING

STUD GRADES AND SPECIES AS ACCEPTED BY LOCAL CODE

SHINGLE WEDGE UNDER JOINTS

HORIZONTAL WOOD SIDING (OR PLYWOOD VERTICAL, HORIZONTAL OR LAP SIDING)*

3/8" APA PLYWOOD SHEATHING (HORIZONTAL OR VERTICAL)*

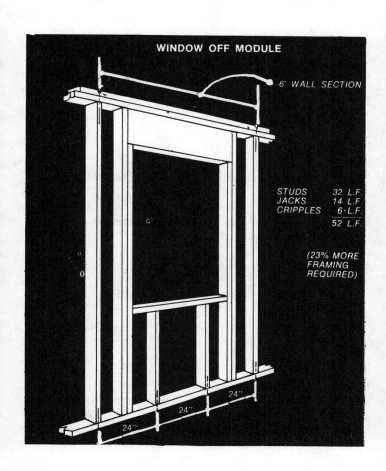

WINDOW OFF MODULE

6' WALL SECTION

STUDS 32 L.F.
JACKS 14 L.F.
CRIPPLES 6 L.F.
52 L.F.

(23% MORE FRAMING REQUIRED)

24" 24" 24"

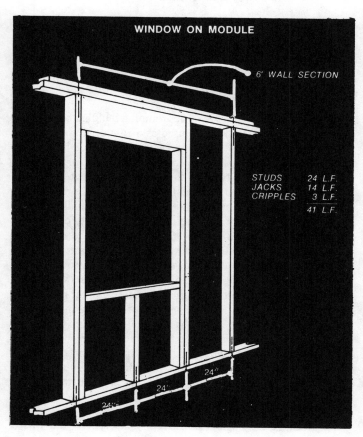

WINDOW ON MODULE

6' WALL SECTION

STUDS 24 L.F.
JACKS 14 L.F.
CRIPPLES 3 L.F.
41 L.F.

24" 24" 24"

answer. This will reduce the foundation and roof areas as well as land area required. Omitting a basement will reduce the cost, but will the savings justify the inconvenience of not having a basement? An attached garage will reduce the cost because of a common wall for house and garage. Short overhangs and flatter roofs will also help the cost factor. If the cubic content can be reduced by a lower ceiling with a minimum of 7'-0", this will help the cost. Keep the house simple in design; elaborate detail is costly. Design the house to be compatible with the neighborhood so as not to restrict the resale value. If the neighborhood has one story houses, try to stay within that style, although a story and a half would not be a drastic change. Locate all equipment requiring a flue in a common position to afford a single chimney with several flues enclosed. If you can wait to build the garage, porch or patio, it will keep down the initial construction cost. The best approach to cost cutting is to stick with your decisions.

Locality will show variation in building material prices. The factors affecting building costs are:

1. quality of construction.

2. size of building.

3. location.

4. season of year.

5. weather.

6. building code requirements.

7. insurance.

8. labor.

9. choice of building material.

There are two methods of determining building costs. They are approximate and only used as a rule of thumb: square foot and cubic foot. These areas do not include basements, garages, porches, patios and attics but are figured on a half area method. The total of these areas is computed, divided by two and added to the living area for a grand total. Square foot method (length times width) is multiplied by the cost per square foot in your area and cubic foot (length times width times height) is multiplied by the cubic foot cost in your area. The cost figures in your area are available from any lumber dealer or home building association, as well as the building inspector. These total costs will not be precise but will provide a guide for budgeting. For alterations, add 25% to the cost because of undoing and redoing. The figures arrived at will be for total approximate cost. Of this total, approximately 30% is building material costs and 70% is the cost of labor, profit, insurance, workmans compensation, etc. The cost must also include about 10% for contingencies. These figures will not include the cost of land.

Scaffolding or stagings will need to be rented and this is part of the total cost. The average rental cost is about $6.00 per month. If a private water or sewage disposal system is necessary, this also must be included in the cost. A local sewage and well contractor will provide these figures. The cost of landscaping varies acccording to plans.

Having brick delivered stacked on pallets will reduce chipping and breakage and will make for faster handling. Do not use first quality lumber if second or third quality will do the job. The location of the site has an influence on the cost factor. The same house can cost or vary several thousands of dollars difference depending on whether it is located in the city or the suburbs. Material costs vary greatly depending upon whether or not the material is native to the region. The cost will be reduced if local building materials can be used. Climate will affect costs. Moderate climates may not require expensive insulation or heating plants or deep frost-free foundations.

Some costs can be saved by taking into account the following:

1. Square or rectangular shaped homes are less expensive to build than irregular shaped homes.

2. A flat or level lot can be less expensive to develop than a sloping lot.

3. The availability of utilities costs less than a site without utilities.

4. Use locally manufactured or produced material.

5. Use stock building material sizes taking advantage of mass produced cost reduction.

6. Use material that can be quickly installed such as prefabricated sections or panels.

7. Use prefinished materials.

8. Use pre-hung doors.

9. Design with a minimum amount of non livable space such as halls.

10. Study local building laws to avoid unnecessary construction changes.

11. Minimize special or custom built items.

12. Design cluster wall plumbing to reduce piping.

13. Dimension building to accommodate stock length lumber.

Accurate prices can be obtained from the source where materials are purchased. Building permit fees must also be included and there may be a charge for hook-up of utilities such as water, gas, sewer, telephone and electricity.

As you plan a list of building materials, there are several ways to avoid overspending. Buy the lowest grade lumber that will do the job; by accurate estimating in quantity, order no more than necessary. For example, if the project requires 12 pieces of 2"x4" 8'-0" long, list the items that way. Don't total the lengths to 96 feet of 2"x4" because the supplier may include a few pieces only 6'-0" long. On the other hand, 6 pieces 16'-0" long will do by cutting them in half.

BOARDS (COMMONS) SIDING, PANELING, SHELVING, SHEATHING, FORM LUMBER	No. 1 Common No. 2 Common No. 3 Common	No. 1 Common board is the best quality for appearance with small knots. No. 2 and No. 3 Common are most used for paneling, siding and shelving available in 1"x2" through 1"x12".
LIGHT FRAMING	Construction Standard Utility	Used where high strength values are not required such as studs, plates, sills, cripples, blocking, etc.
STUDS		For load bearing and non load bearing walls limited to 10'-0" and shorter.
STRUCTURAL LT. FRAMING FOR JOISTS AND PLANKS	Select Structural No. 1 No. 2 No. 3	Used where high strength is needed such as trusses, joists, rafters, and general framing.

All lumber has grade stamps to identify the piece for use intended. Following is the grade stamp for Western Wood Products Association:

A—mark for Western Wood Products Association

B—Mill number

C—Grade name

D—Wood specie

E—Moisture content S—DRY indicates seasoned lumber. S—GREEN indicates unseasoned lumber or green lumber.

Greater serviceability can be achieved if the bark side of the wood is placed to the outside when nailing in place when exposed to the weather. This prevents grain separation and the tendency to splinter. If the surface is to be painted, this technique will diminish checking and cracking and will hold the paint. The outside of the bark is determined by the curvature of the growth rings.

Approximate per cent of cost breakdown:

	ITEM	%
1.	Excavation	1
2.	Foundations	5
3.	Waterproofing	2
4.	Rough Carpentry	18
5.	Masonry	2
6.	Roofing	2
7.	Sheet Metal	1.5
8.	Plumbing	6
9.	Heating Ventilating & Air Conditioning	7
10.	Electrical	7
11.	Insulation	2
12.	Finish Carpentry & Millwork	15
13.	Finish Hardware	2
14.	Drywall or Lath & Plaster	7
15.	Tile work	.5
16.	Acoustical work	2
17.	Finish Floors	3
18.	Painting & Decorating	3
19.	Appliances	2
20.	Specialties	.5
21.	Site Utilities	1
22.	Walks & Driveways	1.5
23.	Site Improvements	1
24.	Landscaping	1
25.	Accessories	1
26.	Miscellaneous Metals	1
27.	Miscellaneous	4
		100%

STAKING OUT

Locating the house on the lot following dimensions on the PLOT PLAN is Staking Out. This can be accomplished with the use of a measuring tape, level and transit (if available). Before this can be done, the lot lines location and dimension must be plotted on the ground because building location dimensions are taken from property lines. Each corner of the house must be located on the lot by dimensions found on the Plot Plan by driving a wooden stake of 2"x4" cut to a point on one end and driven into the ground. This must be done very carefully because from this point on, the entire house is based on these dimensions. A nail is driven into the top of the stake at the EXACT dimension of the house.

Square corners can be achieved without the use of the transit using the 3, 4, 5 method of triangulation. These proportions will establish a right angle of 90°. Once you have established these angles, a double check is accomplished by measuring the diagonals which should have the same dimensions.

BATTER BOARDS

The wood stakes indicating the exact corners of the building are temporary, used only for reference and will be removed after the installation of the batter boards. The points on these wooden stakes will be transferred onto the batter boards which are used to retain these points during excavation and construction. They will not interfere with construction and they should not be disturbed. The batter boards are installed about 4'-0" outside the perimeter of the house. Installation of batter boards consists of driving 2"x4" wood stakes about 3'-0" long with a pointed end into the ground, three for each corner are required. These should be placed about 6'-0" to 8'-0" on each side of the corner stake forming a right angle. 1"x6" board is nailed to the stake in a level horizontal plane all at the same level. Transfer the nail point on the corner stake to the batter board by using a strong string, line or cord stretched across the batter boards at opposite ends of the building located directly over the nail on the corner stake. Use a plumb bob to transfer this point. Repeat this procedure on all corners of the building by driving a nail into the horizontal batter board letting the nail stick-up about ½". These batter boards will remain in position until the foundation is completed. Once these lines are strung, they will be the exact dimensions of the outside foundation line of the house.

In the case of an addition, simply project or extend the sides of the house and square the length using batter boards on two sides only. Heights are already established by transferring the top of the existing foundation to the batter boards of the new addition.

EXCAVATION

The strung building lines are removed during excavation to allow ample space for operating excavating equipment. The top soil is removed first and stock piled on site away from the building location to be used later for finish grading. From the Plot Plan we have established a finish grade elevation as well as existing grade elevations and the Plot Plan also tells us the Basement Floor elevation or level. From this information we can determine how deep we must excavate below the existing grade or ground. Referring to the Plot Plan, the existing grade at the location of the house is about Elevation 241. This is shown by the dash line. The Basement Floor elevation is 231.0 which means we must excavate down 10'-0" below the existing grade plus 1'-0" for the footing, gives us a total depth of 11'-0" below the ground. The Garage, which has no basement, is unexcavated, therefore, the only excavation required is a trench for the foundation of the garage which must be below the prevailing frost line to prevent upheaval when the ground freezes. Excavation should extend about two feet beyond the outside foundation walls. No foundation should be set on filled land without proper compacting. Extend the bottom of the foundation down to the original undisturbed or virgin earth.

If ledge is encountered, leave it and work around it. You will notice that the new grade shown by a solid line is about 237.5 at the location of the house. This tells us that the grade will be cut about 3'-6" to our new grade level.

INTRODUCTION 10

TO CONSTRUCTION

Most homes built in North America are of wood frame construction principally because frame construction costs less than other types of construction, and is easier and cheaper to insulate. Wood is more versatile to shape and form than most other building materials.

A well built wood frame house is one of the most lasting types of construction. To help keep this enduring quality a few simple precautions must be followed when storing lumber on site.

All lumber, framing and finish should be protected from the weather until ready for use. Delivery should be planned only as needed to avoid prolonged exposure. Keep lumber at least 6" above ground and protected with a waterproof cover. Finish lumber is often water repellent pre-treated. If untreated, millwork should receive a water repellent treatment or a coat of paint when delivered. Do not store millwork indoors with wet plaster. It must be allowed to dry before storing millwork such as mouldings, doors, windows, flooring, cabinets, etc.

When trees are felled at the forest and delivered to the lumber mill, the logs are cut to a full dimension such as 2"x4". This green lumber is put into a kiln or oven for drying. This is called seasoning. During the drying process, the lumber shrinks through moisture evaporation and a 2"x4" becomes 1 5/8" x 3 5/8". Lumber lengths are in 2' intervals. So it is with all seasoned lumber, framing and finish, except plywood and composition panels. When you order lumber from your lumber dealer, you are charged for the full 2"x4" because this is how the dealer pays for it. A 1" thick x 12" wide board is 3/4" thick and 11 1/2" wide. The length is not affected. A 12% to 20% moisture content in lumber is allowed for framing lumber and 3% to 8% for interior finish lumber. This drying out process or seasoning causes the wall of fiber cells to shrink. There is a constant movement in wood which varies with the seasons.

In the winter months the heat within the house causes the wood to shrink because the moisture is absorbed by the heat. The summer months has a reverse effect on the wood causing it to absorb the moisture with a swelling effect. The movement can be as much as 1/4".

Decay in wood is caused by fungi which penetrate the wood, feeding upon the cells and breaking down the wood. Four requirements are necessary for fungi growth a) Air, b) moisture, c) food, d) favorable temperature. Remove any one of these and fungi cannot exist and the wood will be preserved for very long periods of time. This system of preservation can be accomplished in several ways. One is to impregnate the wood with poison which is by way of several commercial preservatives such as coal-tar, creosote or zinc chloride. Painting it is another way of preserving wood. Keeping wood constantly submerged in water is another.

Besides decay, there are other defects in wood which affect the acceptability from a standpoint of strength, durability and appearance. These are known as shakes, checks, knots, wane and pitch pockets. All these defects are graded by the National Lumber Manufacturers Association together with the United States Department of Agriculture, into various grades meeting specific requirements regarding strength. This is important because all wood is not of the same strength but varies according to species. This grading, called Stress Grading, will tell us the amount of load the wood will support. For this reason a specific specie of wood or woods is desirable for framing. Grading also separates wood into Yard Lumber which is a general purpose or utility grade, Structural Lumber used primarily for load bearing and Factory or Shop Lumber used for finish work and millwork such as doors, windows, mouldings etc. Lumber is sold by Board Feet. To compute board feet, divide the sectional area in inches by 12 and multiply the length in feet. Ex: 2" x 4", 8'-0" long is $\frac{2x4x8}{12}$ =5 1/3 b/f.

The woods most used for various purposes in building are as follows:

POSTS, GIRDERS, TRUSSES & HEAVY FRAMING

Dense Yellow Pine
Douglas Fir
White Oak
Larch
Spruce

LIGHT FRAMING, STUDS, JOISTS, RAFTERS

Spruce
Hemlock
Common Yellow Pine
Larch

OUTSIDE FINISH

White Pine
Cypress
Redwood
Poplar
Spruce

SHINGLES, CLAPBOARDS

Cedar
Cypress
Redwood

WINDOWS, DOORS, FRAMES

White Pine
Fir

FLOORS

Oak
Maple
Yellow Pine
Birch
Beach

FINISH (Painted)

White Pine
Birch
Gum
Redwood
Poplar

NATURAL FINISH

Oak
Chestnut
Walnut
Mahogany
White Pine
Birch
Redwood
Cedar

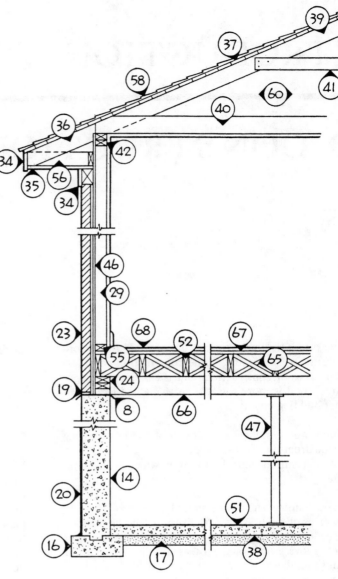

Typical residential terms.

8.	Termite shield	
14.	Foundation wall	41. Collar beam
16.	Foundation wall footing	42. Double plate
17.	Gravel fill	46. Diagonal sheathing or plywood
19.	Weep hole	47. Basement post (lally column)
20.	Waterproofing	51. Concrete floor or slab
23.	Brick veneer	52. Floor joist
24.	Sill	55. Sole plate
29.	Studding	56. Lookout
34.	Fascia	58. Roofing shingles
35.	Soffit	59. Ridge
36.	Rafter overhang	60. Attic space
37.	Roof boards or plywood	65. Cross-bridging
38.	Vapor barrier	66. Girder or beam
39.	Rafter	67. Plywood subflooring
40.	Ceiling joist	68. Finish flooring

Typical residential terms.

1. Chimney flues or pots
2. Chimney
3. Flashing
4. Ridgeboard
5. Collar beam
6. Vent; louver
7. Cornice return
8. Brick veneer
9. End rafter
10. Insulation
11. Top double plate

12. Roof decking
13. Gutter
14. Stud
15. Flooring paper
16. Finish flooring
17. Shutter
18. Corner post
19. Subfloor
20. Lintel; header
21. Porch frieze board
22. Porch post

23. Brick sill
24. Grade line
25. Cinder or gravel fill
26. Drain tile
27. Footing
28. Keyway
29. Foundation wall
30. Waterproofing
31. Knee brace
32. Bridging
33. Floor joists

34. Sill plate
35. Corner brace
36. Steel column
37. Beam; girder
38. Wall sheathing
39. Building paper
40. Stoop
41. Trim pilaster
42. Pediment door trim
43. Double-hung window
44. Windowsill

45. Downspout
46. Rake mold
47. Mullion
48. Basement window
49. Areaway wall
50. Bevel siding
51. Wood window trim
52. Dormer

INTRODUCTION

The modern wood frame house is an economical, long-lasting structure. Few, if any, materials can compare with wood framing in residential construction. To produce an efficient house, however, you must use sound construction methods and select good-quality, suitable materials.

This series of how-to sheets was developed by the American Plywood Association as an elementary guide to wood-frame construction. It is intended as a guide and help to those who have little major-construction experience. The sheets illustrate the basic steps to completing the structural shell of a house.

Each sheet, in nontechnical language, illustrates step-by-step construction of a single-story house with a concrete block foundation, plywood-and-stud walls, and plywood-sheathed gable roof. Each how-to sheet covers one step of construction. Usually the most common and simplest construction methods are described, and no attempt has been made to show the wide variety of alternate methods, although a few are mentioned. For illustrative purposes, an example house 24 x 48 ft. is used through the series, and terms are explained in a glossary.

American Plywood Association	A trade association representing most of the nation's manufacturers of construction plywood. The Association has three main jobs: *research* to improve plywood performance and products; *inspection and testing* to ensure plywood's consistently high quality; and *promotion and information service*.	**Gable**	The triangular portion of the end wall of a house with a pitched roof.
Batten	A thin, narrow piece of board used to cover vertical joints of plywood siding.	**Gusset**	A small piece of wood, plywood, or metal attached to corners or intersections of a frame to add stiffness and strength.
Batter Board	A temporary framework used to assist in locating corners when laying out a foundation.	**Header**	One or more pieces of framing lumber used around openings to support free ends of floor joists, studs, or rafters.
Blocking	Small wood pieces used between structural members to support panel edges.	**Header Joist (ribbon or band joist)**	The horizontal lumber member that is butted against ends of floor joists around the outside of the house to add support to and tie joists together.
Bottom Plate (sole plate)	The lowest horizontal member of a wall or partition which rests on the subflooring. Wall studs are nailed to the bottom plate.	**In-line Joint**	A connection made by butting two pieces of lumber, such as floor joists, end-to-end and fastening them together using an additional splice piece nailed on both sides of the joint.
Chalk Line (snap line)	A long spool-wound cord encased in a container filled with chalk. Chalk-covered string is pulled from the case, pulled taut across a surface, lifted, and snapped directly downward so that it leaves a long straight chalk mark.	**Joist**	One of a series of parallel framing members used to support floor or ceiling loads, and supported in turn by larger beams, girders or bearing walls, or foundation.
Collar Beam	A horizontal tie beam in a gable roof, connecting two opposite rafters at a point considerably above the wall plate.	**Kiln Dried**	Wood seasoned in a humidity and temperature-controlled oven to minimize shrinkage and warping.
Course	A continuous level row of construction units, as a layer of foundation block, shingles, or plywood panels, as in subflooring or roof sheathing.	**Lap Joint**	A connection made by placing two pieces of material side by side and fastening them by nailing, gluing, etc.
Cripple	Any part of a frame which is cut less than full length, as in cripple studs under a window opening.	**o.c.**	On center. A method of indicating the spacing of framing members by stating the measurement from the center of one member to the center of the next.
d	The abbreviation for "penny" in designating nail size; for example 8d nails are 8-penny nails, 2½ in. long.	**Plumb Bob**	A weight attached to a line for testing perpendicular surfaces for trueness.
Dimension Lumber	Lumber 2 to 5 in. thick and up to 12 in. wide. Includes joists, rafters, studs, planks, girders, and posts.	**Rafter**	One of a series of structural members of a roof, designed to support roof loads.
Doubling	To use two like framing members nailed together, such as studs or joists, to add strength to a building.	**Rake**	The overhanging part of a roof at a gable end.
Fascia	Horizontal board that is used as a facing.	**Ridge Board**	Central framing member at the peak, or ridge, of a roof. The roof rafters frame into it from each side.
Fascia Rafter	End rafters at the end of the rake.	**Setback**	Placing of a building a specified distance from street or property lines to comply with building codes and restrictions.
Footing	The concrete (usually) base for foundation walls, posts, chimneys, etc. The footing is wider than the member it supports, and distributes the weight to the ground over a larger area to prevent settling.	**Sill (Mudsill, Sill Plate)**	The lowest framing member of a structure, resting on the foundation and supporting the floor system and the uprights of the frame.

Soffit   Underside of a roof overhang.

Span   The distance between supports of a structural member.

Studs (Wall)   Vertical members (usually 2 x 4's) making up the main framing of a wall.

Subflooring   Bottom layer of plywood in a two-layer floor.

Top Plate   The uppermost horizontal member nailed to the wall or partition studs. Top plate is usually doubled with end joints offset.

Underlayment   Top layer of plywood in a two-layer floor. Provides a smooth base for carpet, tile or sheet flooring.

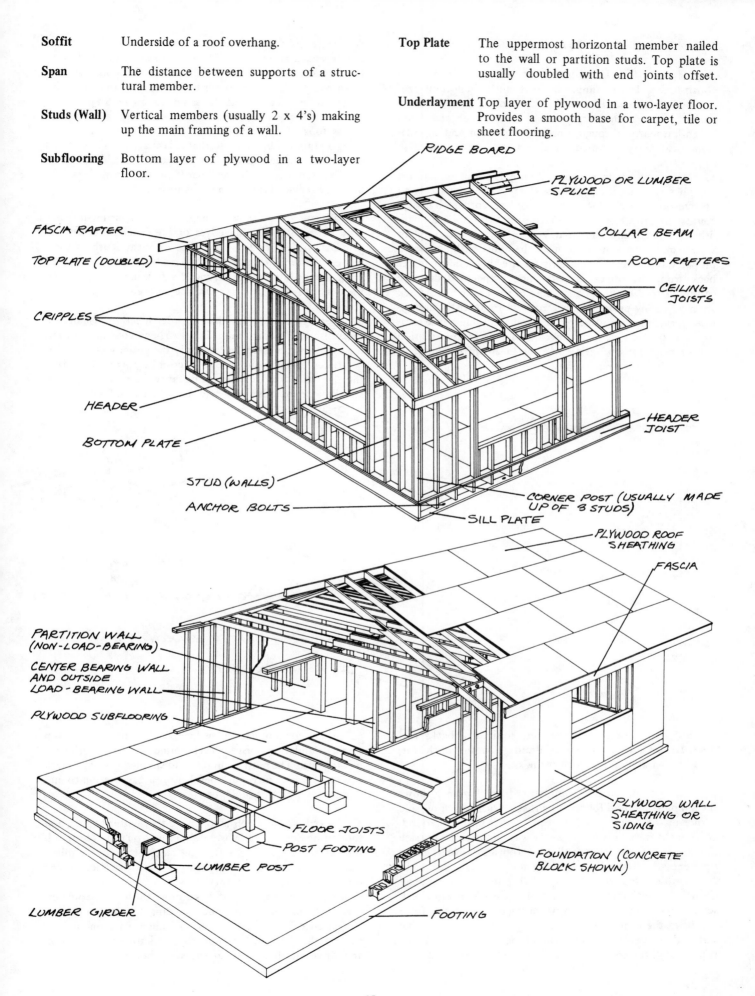

LAYOUT THE FOUNDATION

Laying out a foundation is the critical beginning in house construction. It is a simple but extremely important process and requires careful work. If you make sure the foundation is *square* and *level*, you will find all later jobs—from rough carpentry through finish construction and installation of cabinetry—are made much easier.

1. Make sure your proposed house location on the lot complies with local regulations. If property lines are at all in question, verify location of lot-line corners by city, county, or private surveyor. Once property lines are established, it is equally vital that you review city, county, or state requirements on location of the house with respect to property lines. Most regulations require that a house be set back from the street property line a specified distance (often 25 to 30 ft.) and that sides of the house be set back from adjoining property lines (often 5 to 10 ft.). Carelessness in establishing property lines and allowable house location could result in extending a garage or future addition over a neighbor's property line, or in an infringement of local building-code regulations.

4. After corners are located and squared, drive three 2 x 4 stakes at each corner as shown in Figure 1. Locate these stakes 3 ft. to 4 ft. outside the actual foundation line. Then nail 1 x 6 batter boards horizontally so that their top edges are all level and at the same grade (see Step 6 for a method of checking their levelness). Hold a string-line across tops of opposite batter boards at two corners and, using a plumb bob, adjust so that it is exactly over the tacks in the two corner stakes. Cut saw kerfs ¼ in. deep where the line touches the batter boards so that string-lines may be easily replaced if broken or disturbed.

Cut all saw kerfs the same depth since the string-line not only defines the outside edges of the foundation but will provide a reference line to ensure uniform depth of footing excavation. When you have made similar cuts in all eight batter boards and strung the four lines in position, the outside foundation lines are accurately established.

5. Next, locate the lengthwise girder location, usually on the centerline of the house. Double check your house plans for exact position since occasionally the girder will be slightly off centerline to support an interior bearing wall. To find the line, measure the correct distance from corners. Then install batter boards and locate string-line as in Step 4.

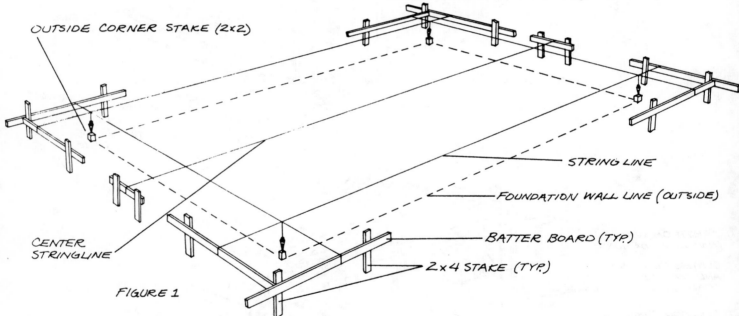

OUTSIDE CORNER STAKE (2x2)

STRING LINE

FOUNDATION WALL LINE (OUTSIDE)

BATTER BOARD (TYP.)

2x4 STAKE (TYP.)

CENTER STRINGLINE

FIGURE 1

2. Set house location, based on required setbacks and other factors such as the natural drainage pattern of the lot; then level or at least rough-clear the site.

3. Lay out the outside foundation lines. Figure 1 shows the simplest method for locating these. Locate each outside corner of the house and drive small stakes into the ground. Drive tacks into tops of these stakes to indicate the outside line of the foundation wall (not footings). Next check squareness of house by measuring the diagonals, corner to corner, to see that they are equal. (If structure is rectangular, all diagonal measurements will equal.) You can check squareness of any corner by measuring down one side for 6 ft., down the other for 8 ft. The length of the diagonal line across these two end points should measure exactly 10 ft. If it doesn't, the corner isn't truly square. See Figure 2.

6. Check for foundation levelness. Remember that the top of the foundation must be level around the entire perimeter of the house. The most accurate—and simplest—way to check this is to use a surveyor's level, if you have access to and familiarity with this tool.

The next best approach is to ensure that batter boards, and thus string-lines, are all absolutely level. You can accomplish this with a 10 ft. to 14 ft. long piece of straight lumber. (Judge its straightness by sighting along the surface.) Using this straightedge in conjunction with a carpenter or masonry level, drive temporary stakes around the house perimeter, spaced a distance apart not exeeding the length of the straightedge lumber (see Figure 3). Then place one end of the straightedge on a batter board, check for exact levelness, and drive another stake to the same height. Each time a stake is driven, the straightedge and level should be reversed end-for-end, which should ensure close accuracy in establishing the height of each stake with reference to the batter board. The final check on overall levelness comes when you level the last stake with the batter board where you began. If the straightedge is level here, then you have a level foundation base line.

During foundation excavation, the corner stakes and temporary leveling stakes will be removed. This stresses the importance of the leveled batter boards and string-line, because corners and foundation levelness must be located using the string-line.

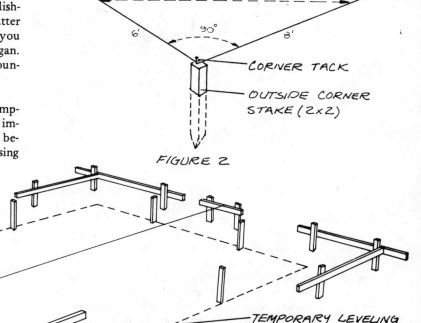

FIGURE 2

FIGURE 3

CONCRETE BLOCK FOUNDATION AND POST FOOT-INGS

Poured concrete footings are most commonly used for house foundations. Footings, properly sized and constructed, prevent settling or cracking of building walls. Footings must be completely level, and must extend at least 12 in. below the frost line and at least 6 in. into undisturbed soil. These requirements dictate the depth at which you place the footings. *Do not place foundations on black top soil.*

Do not pour concrete if the temperature is expected to go below about 40° F within the first week after pour, unless you are prepared to take extensive measures to protect it.

A row of post footings will be located along the centerline of the house. These support posts and girders which, in turn, support the floor joists. Minimum height for post footings should be 8 in. above finish grade in crawl-space foundations. Post footing thickness is determined in Step 3.

FOOTINGS

1. Make preliminary excavation for perimeter footing. The amount of excavation may vary, depending on site conditions. To allow yourself adequate working space, excavate about 2 ft. beyond the outside of the wall. (If you dig too deep, fill with concrete—never soil.)

2. Using a plumb bob from the foundation layout stringline, locate outside corners of the block foundation. Measure about 4 in. beyond corner points to establish footing edge lines (see Figure 1). Outline both outside and inside perimeters of the footing with string. Dig the footing trench to required depth. Install forms of 1/2 inch APA® grade-trademarked plywood or 2 x 8's supported by 2 x 4 stakes driven into the soil about 2 ft. apart (see Figure 2). These stakes should be driven below the top of the formboards, to facilitate leveling the concrete.

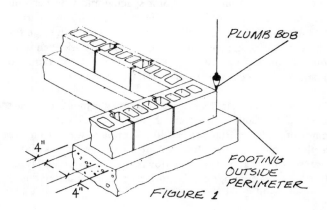

FIGURE 1

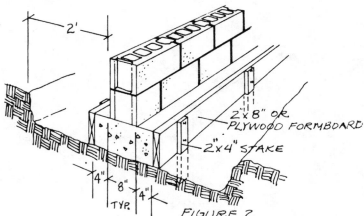

FIGURE 2

3. Using the lengthwise centerline string, mark locations for floor-supporting posts. Post spacing is specified on your house plan, as is post footing size. Post footings are generally about 20 in. square, but may vary in size depending on allowable soil pressure and post spacing. Again, check local building codes. Some require a steel rod extending out the top of the post footing to engage the post and keep it in place. The bottom of the footing should be at the same level as the perimeter footing. Height should be a minimum of 8 inches above ground in a crawl space house. Build forms of 1/2 in. APA grade-trademarked plywood and 2 x 4's. End-post footings may be poured integrally with the perimeter footings.

4. Prepare and place concrete. If ready-mix concrete is available, order a mix with at least 2000 psi 28-day strength. Or you can mix concrete on the site using a 1:3:5 mix (one part by volume of Portland cement; 3 parts clean sand; and 5 parts gravel). Use about 5 1/2 gallons of water per sack of cement if sand is wet, (6 1/4 gallons per sack if sand is dry). Mix concrete thoroughly, and place in forms in thin layers. "Spade" and tamp concrete carefully between pours to prevent air pockets. Top of footings should be smooth and level all around.

5. Cure concrete and strip forms. In warm weather, leave forms in place for three days, sprinkling daily with water so concrete will not dry too quickly. In cool weather, leave forms in place 7 days; in cold weather (below 40°), don't pour.

FOUNDATION WALL

6. As in Step 2, accurately locate outside wall corners on footings, using a plumb bob. (Block walls should be centered on footing.) String a cord tautly between corners to outline outside of block wall and mark with chalk, or use a chalk line. Lay the first course of blocks without mortar all around the perimeter to determine joint spacing and whether you will have to cut any blocks. Space blocks 3/8 in. apart (a 3/8 in. maximum joint is allowable, provided the average for the entire course is no more than 1/2 in.). Mark each joint on the foundation. Check the house plan for any required openings for crawl space vents, drains, utilities, etc.

7. Prepare mortar. Mix 2 parts masonry cement (or 1 part each of Portland cement and hydrated lime) with 4 to 6 parts of damp mortar sand. Add just enough water to make a plastic mortar that clings to the trowel and block but is not so soft that it squeezes down too much when laying block. After mixing, place mortar on a wet mortar board near where blocks will be laid.

8. Lay blocks as shown in Figure 3. All blocks must conform to ASTM C-90, Grade A. Finished height of the foundation wall should be approximately 12 in. above finish grade level. First build each corner up to full height, to establish required thickness of joints. Use corner blocks with one flat end at corners. Build corners up using a mason's level to keep blocks plumb and level. Then stretch line between corners to guide laying additional blocks. For the first course of blocks, place mortar on footings for the full width of the block. For succeeding courses, apply mortar on face shells only.

9. Set anchor bolts for sill plate. Before laying the last two courses, locate and position anchor bolts as shown on plans, or as in Figure 4 if not shown on plans. Be sure to provide at least two bolts per individual sill plate. Fill all cells in the top course, or cover with 4 in. solid masonry units, or use a wood sill plate wide enough to bear on both the inner and outer shells of the blocks. Install fiberglass sill sealer between foundation and wood sill plate.

10. After block wall is completed, wait at least 7 days before placing backfill against wall. Do not backfill until floor sheathing is installed. If a drain is provided, slope soil in crawl space toward drain.

POSTS AND GIRDERS

Posts and girders are the basic structural members that support the floor joists along the centerline of the house. Wood posts are fastened to the girder that rests upon them (see Figure 1).

Posts for an average house are generally 4 x 6 or 6 x 6 solid lumber, cut to proper length as outlined in Step 3. The girders used to support floor joists are generally built up of two or three pieces of 2x dimension lumber. If available, order kiln-dried lumber (and keep it dry) to reduce shrinkage. Your house plans will specify post spacing, girder span lengths, and lumber grades. The long dimension of the house dictates the overall length of the girder. For example, in a 48 ft. long house, three girder sections each approximately 16 ft. long will be needed (see Step 1).

Before ordering material, check local conditions to see if materials must be treated for termite protection. Also check plans to see whether a vapor barrier (a good idea in any case) must be installed in the crawl space.

1. Determine length of girder required. Overall length of the girder is determined by the length of the house. The girder must reach from inside-surface to inside-surface of the foundation wall, minus 1/2 in. clearance on each end. In the example 48 ft. house, the overall girder length is 46 ft. 7 in. (48 ft. less 16 in. to compensate for thickness of both end foundation walls and 1 in. total clearance).

2. Fabricate the girder. For the 48 ft. house, the centerline girder is best fabricated in three 16 ft. sections, with two cut to fit the required length. For built-up girder sections, use three 2 x's nailed together with 20d (4 in. long) common nails 32 in. o.c. in each of two rows, one along the top and one along the bottom of the girder. Stagger top and bottom rows of nails (see Figure 2).

3. Determine length of posts. At each post location, stretch a line from opposite sill plates. Use building twin or heavy nylon fishline, and stretch it tight to eliminate sag. Measure down from the string to the post foundation, then substract the depth of the girder from this dimension and cut post to length. If post footings have protruding lengths of reinforcing bar, drill post bottom so the post can slip over the bar.

4. Install a vapor barrier if required. Use a 6-mil-thick polyethylene film, placed to cover all ground inside the foundation, lapping edges about 6 in. Use sand or gravel to hold edges down.

5. Place the posts on post footings. If a vapor barrier has been stretched across the footings, rest posts directly on the vapor barrier. If no vapor barrier is present, use pieces of 15-pound asphalt-impregnated building felt between concrete post footing and end of post.

6. Once all posts are in place, lift girders and place them on top of posts. Girders should be cut so that butt joints fall over the center line of a supporting post (see Figure 1). Trim the two end girder sections to allow for a 1/2 in. space between foundation and girder (Figure 3). At this point it may be valuable to plumb and brace the posts and girders with 2 x 4's and stakes, until floor joists are installed.

7. Now check the level of the entire girder. Tops of all girders should be level with top of sill plates (Figure 4). Shim if necessary. Once everything is level, nail the posts to the girders. The ends of the girders that butt together should be toenailed with at least six 10d common nails. Firmly attach the girder to each post on the underside with galvanized steel framing anchors or clip angles and lag screws.

Note: The center girders may be solid lumber. If so, they should be placed so that the top of the girder is slightly above the sill plate (about 1/8 in.) to allow for shrinkage.

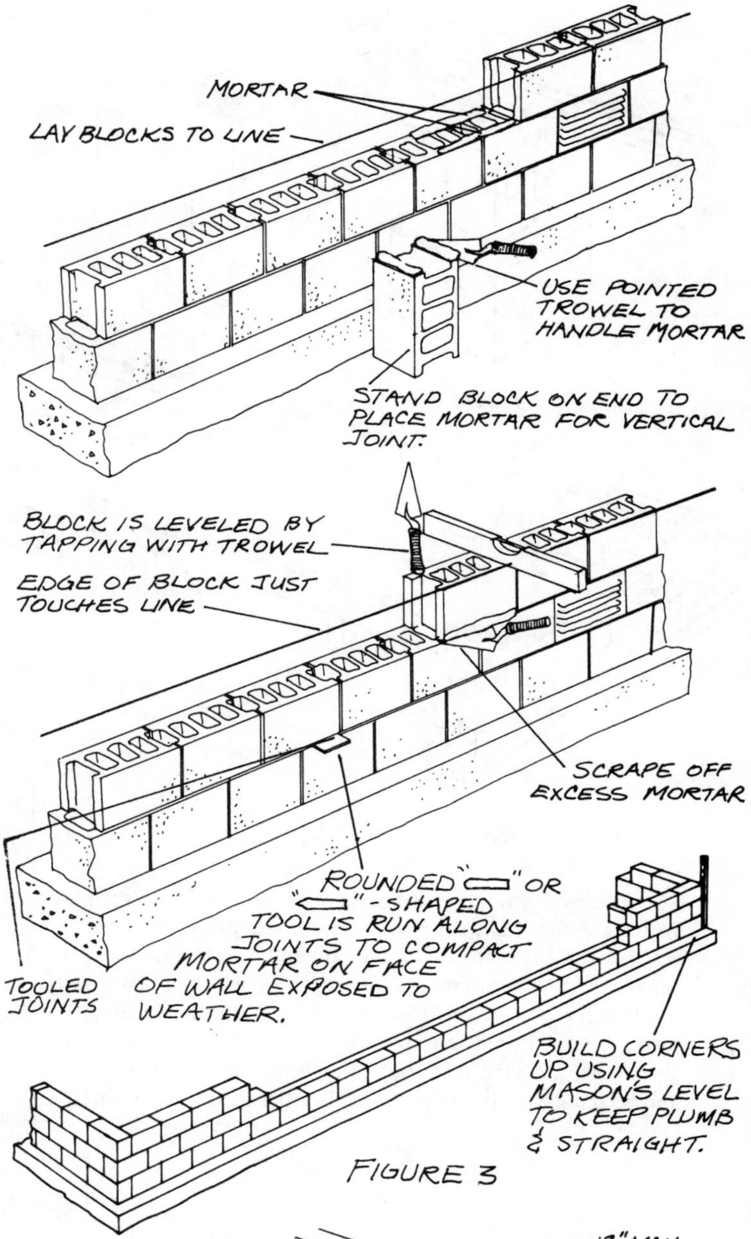

MORTAR

LAY BLOCKS TO LINE

USE POINTED TROWEL TO HANDLE MORTAR

STAND BLOCK ON END TO PLACE MORTAR FOR VERTICAL JOINT.

BLOCK IS LEVELED BY TAPPING WITH TROWEL

EDGE OF BLOCK JUST TOUCHES LINE

SCRAPE OFF EXCESS MORTAR

ROUNDED "⌒" OR "⌴"-SHAPED TOOL IS RUN ALONG JOINTS TO COMPACT MORTAR ON FACE OF WALL EXPOSED TO WEATHER.

TOOLED JOINTS

BUILD CORNERS UP USING MASON'S LEVEL TO KEEP PLUMB & STRAIGHT.

FIGURE 3

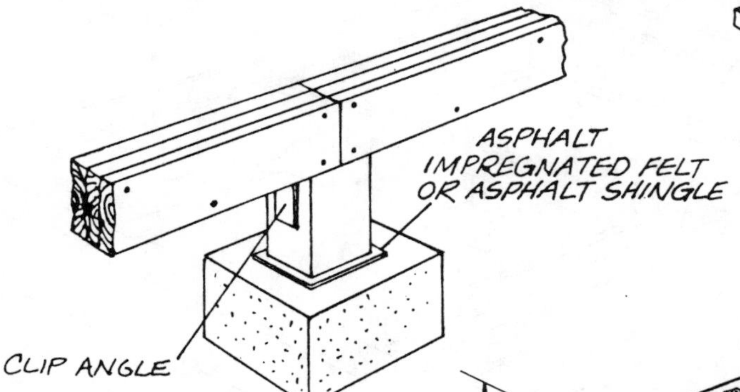

ASPHALT IMPREGNATED FELT OR ASPHALT SHINGLE

CLIP ANGLE

FIGURE 1

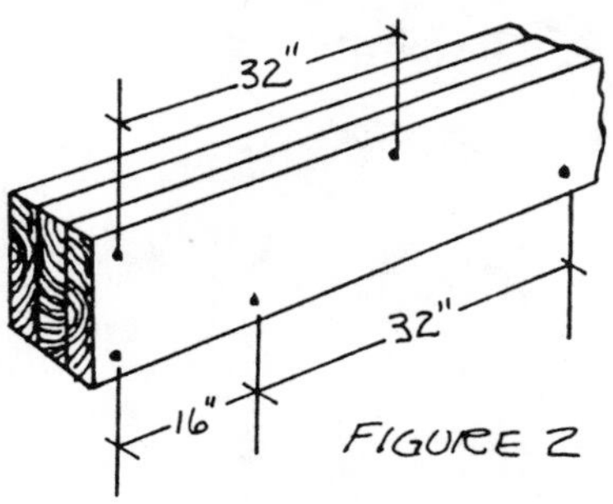

32"

32"

16"

FIGURE 2

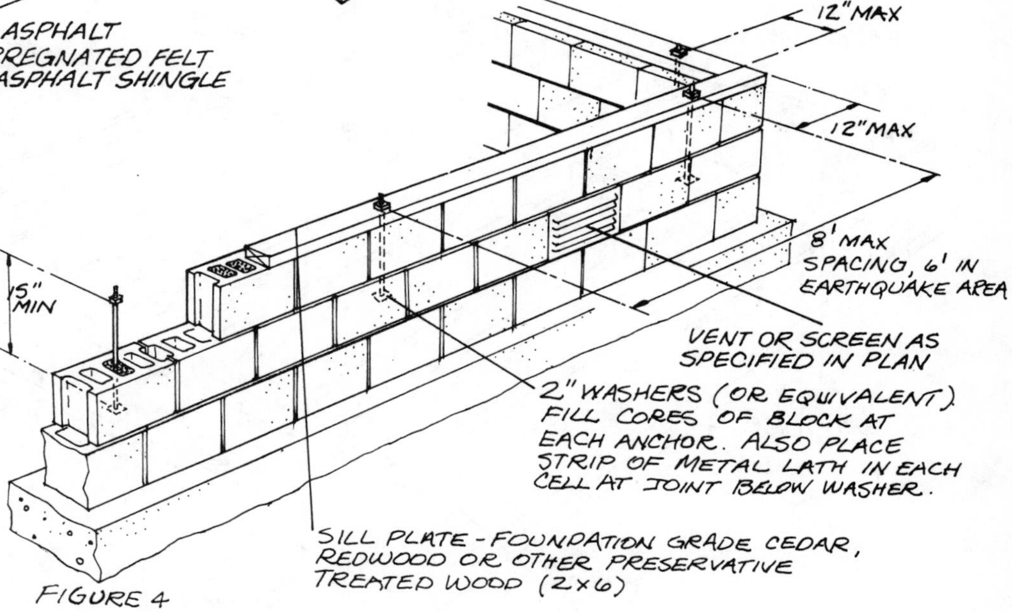

5" MIN

FIGURE 4

12" MAX

12" MAX

8' MAX SPACING, 6' IN EARTHQUAKE AREA

VENT OR SCREEN AS SPECIFIED IN PLAN

2" WASHERS (OR EQUIVALENT) FILL CORES OF BLOCK AT EACH ANCHOR. ALSO PLACE STRIP OF METAL LATH IN EACH CELL AT JOINT BELOW WASHER.

SILL PLATE-FOUNDATION GRADE CEDAR, REDWOOD OR OTHER PRESERVATIVE TREATED WOOD (2x6)

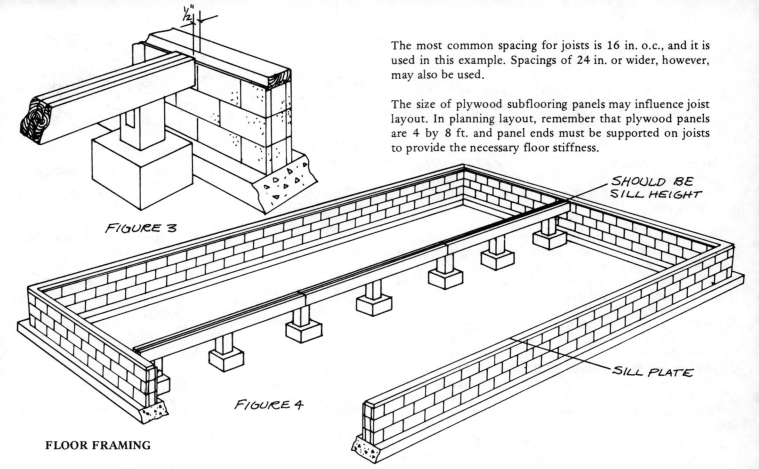

The most common spacing for joists is 16 in. o.c., and it is used in this example. Spacings of 24 in. or wider, however, may also be used.

The size of plywood subflooring panels may influence joist layout. In planning layout, remember that plywood panels are 4 by 8 ft. and panel ends must be supported on joists to provide the necessary floor stiffness.

FIGURE 3

SHOULD BE SILL HEIGHT

SILL PLATE

FIGURE 4

FLOOR FRAMING

See Figure 1 for an overall view of typical floor framing. Joists are the main supporting members of the floor. They rest on the sill plate at the outside end and the girder at the inner end. In residential construction, joists are generally 2x lumber placed on edge. When purchasing lumber for joists, order kiln-dried material if available to minimize shrinkage. Be sure to check your house plans for joist size and spacing and for any special lumber grade requirements.

Any joists having a slight bow edgewise should be placed so that the bow or "crown" is on top. (You can determine if a joist is crowned by sighting along the edge.) A crowned joist will tend to straighten out when subfloor and normal floor loading are applied. Also, with straight joists, the edge having the largest edge knots should be placed on top because, in that position, the joists are stronger.

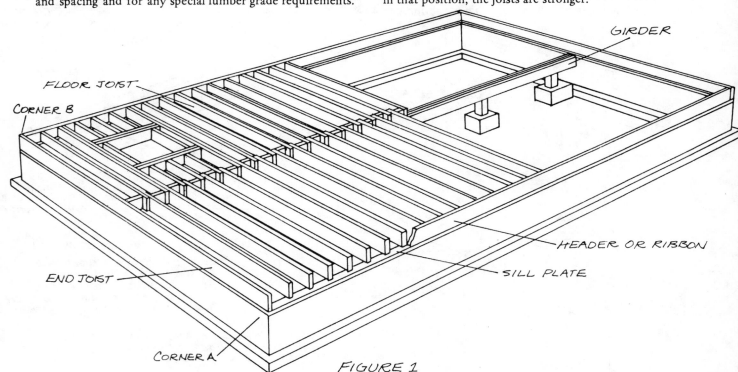

GIRDER

FLOOR JOIST

CORNER B

HEADER OR RIBBON

SILL PLATE

END JOIST

CORNER A

FIGURE 1

JOIST LAYOUT

1. Lay out floor-joist positions. Mark joist locations on the sill plates using two marks, one for each side of the joist (see Figure 2). Mark the end joist location on the sill, even with the outside edge of the sill. Mark the location of the first interior joist, so that spacing between joists is 13 3/4 in. (16 in. from outside of sill to centerline of first interior joist). Mark position of other joists, spacing them 16 in. o.c., continuing to the end of the house. The location of the end joist at this end of the house should also be marked on the sill.

2. Repeat this process on the opposite sill except that spacing between the end and first interior joist is 12 1/4 inches (14 1/2 inches from outside of sill to centerline of first interior joist, to allow for joist overlap at the center of the house). You must start the joist layout from the same end wall as in Step 1, so that all joists are parallel to the outside walls. Also mark joist locations on the girder, to ensure alignment of joists between the sidewalls.

3. Check the floor plan and mark on the sill plates the location of all partitions parallel to the joists. Generally, double joists are required under each partition, and the extra joists must be located and marked on the sill. A regular joist can serve as one of the "doubling" joists (see Figure 3).

4. Also mark location of any openings for crawl-space access, chimney, etc. Regular joists on each side of these openings will be placed with other regular joists, but all special framing should be left out until these regular joists are in. (When locating a floor opening, measure from its center in opposite directions to locate the inside edges. This is necessary to make sure the opening is located properly according to the plans.).

SETTING THE JOISTS

5. Select straight pieces of joist material for headers and end joists. Cut and nail them in place. Use 8d common nails and toenail from the outside lower edge of the header and end joist into the sill, spacing nails about every 16 in. Nail corner joints with three 16d common nails.

6. Using a steel square, mark vertical alignment for each joist on the inside face of header joists. Merely continue the horizontal lines on the sill to the inside face of the header.

7. Cut joists to length, if necessary. Lap of joists over center of the girder should be at least 4 in. and no more than 28 inches. Lay the joists across the sill and girder with all crown edges facing the same direction. This eliminates the need for additional checking when joists are tipped for installation.

NOTE: Floor joists can be butted over the center girder to form in-line joists (instead of being lapped) if joists are spliced with a 24 inch long piece of plywood or lumber, nailed to each joist.

8. Place joists at marks and drive two 16d common nails through the headers into the end of each floor joist. Toenail joists to the girder, using three 8d common nails for each joist. Nail lapped joists together over girder with three 10d common nails.

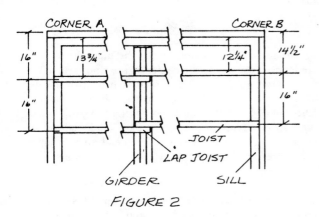

FIGURE 2

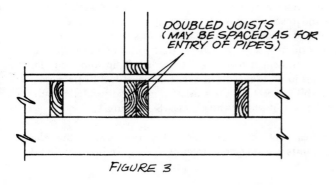

FIGURE 3

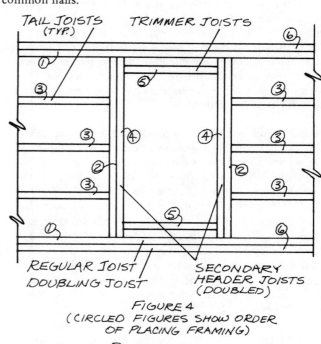

FIGURE 4
(CIRCLED FIGURES SHOW ORDER OF PLACING FRAMING)

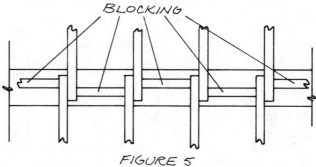

FIGURE 5

FLOOR OPENINGS

9. Frame openings in floor as shown on plans. One such opening is illustrated in Figures 1 and 4. The order of placing members is critical, if you are going to end nail the members. Order of placement is illustrated in Figure 4 for the particular opening shown. If members are placed in the order shown, all but the "trimmers" can be end-nailed.

10. An alternate method to the careful order described above, involves use of "framing anchors," specially made steel angles which will allow placement of members in a more logical, less critical order.

11. Install solid blocking between joists over the girder to help keep the joists parallel and to straighten any that tend to twist. Nail blocking on alternate sides of the girder centerline (see Figure 5). Drive two 16d nails into each end of each piece of blocking. Keep solid blocking flush with the top edges of the joists.

12. Check level of top of all joists, headers, and blocking. Shim up or trim down as needed to provide a firm, level base for plywood subflooring.

PLYWOOD SUBFLOORING

Subflooring is used over floor joists to form a working platform and base for finish flooring. In the example house, a two-layer floor system is assumed; that is, the floor is made up of plywood subflooring and a separate layer of underlayment, plus floor covering (e.g., carpet or resilient tiles), or it consists of subflooring plus hardwood. Plywood provides a smooth, solid, stable base for underlayment or wood strip or block finish flooring.

Plywood can be obtained in a number of grades and thicknesses that are suitable for use as subfloor, but C-D interior grade plywood sheathing is commonly used for this application. Panels of this grade carry an Identification Index marking on the back that give allowable spacing of joists for various thicknesses of plywood. For floor joists 16 in. o.c., for example, you can use APA® grade-trademarked C-D sheathing marked with an Identification Index of 32/16 (the 32 is allowable spacing for roof rafters in inches; the 16 is spacing for floor joists). Be sure to specify exterior glue if construction delays will entail long outside storage or exposure. (Cover and protect subflooring if possible during construction, in this case.)

When applying subflooring, place the plywood on the joists so that the C grade (the better) face is up. C-D grade plywood has C-grade veneer on the face and D-grade on the back. Space plywood panels 1/8 in. apart at edge joints and 1/16 in. apart at end joints over joists. (A copper penny is about 1/16 in. thick.) In wet or humid areas, double these spacings.

SUBFLOOR SHEATHING LAYOUT

1. Begin at the corner of the house where you began the joist layout described on page 71. A little time spent at this

point planning ahead can save time and material in the long run. Review your plans and make trial measurement with your tape to estimate how the first row of panels will come out at the other end of the floor. To ensure proper alignment of the first row, strike a chalk line across the joists (the length of the floor area) 4 ft. 0 in. from the outside edge of the header.

Start the first row with a full-sized 4 x 8 ft. panel set flush with the outside edge of the end joist and the long panel dimension across the joists. Use the chalk marks as a guide for alignment of the first row. Allow 1/16 in. between panel ends. Trim the end of the last panel in the first row flush with the end joist. (Any odd-sized panel sections required to fill in at the end of a row should cover two or more spans. These fill-in panels must be placed with the face grain across supports.)

If the last panel in the first row comes out 1 in. or more short of the inside edge of the end joist (due to an odd building dimension), nail a 2 x 4 "scab" (a block) to the end joist to support the panel end (see Figure 1). Then use a filler strip of scrap material as required. Remember that you can increase the panel end gaps slightly to gain length in a row. (Always maintain a minimum gap of 1/16 in. between panel ends.)

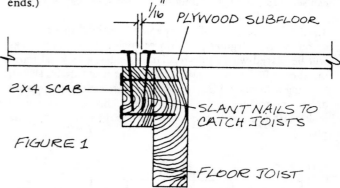

FIGURE 1

2. Lay out the remaining rows up to the place where the joists are lapped (usually at the center of the floor area). To stagger the panel joints, start the second row with a half panel (4 x 4 ft). Leave 1/8 in. gap at the panel edges (between the rows). Start the third row with a full panel once again, and so on. Trim an occasional panel end slightly, if required, as you go down the row to keep end joints roughly centered over the joists. (Usually only one panel per row need be trimmed.)

3. Since floor joists are generally lapped side-by-side over the interior girder, you will need to "step back" your panel layout somewhere near this point. Usually, house dimensions and joist overlap work out so that a joint between rows of panels falls over the joist lap area. If so, you have no problem. You will simply cut the first panel of the next row 1 1/2 inches short to allow for the lap. If, in some unusual case, this joint does not fall over the lap, it will be necessary to "scab" a 2 x 4 on the side of a joist every 8 ft., to support the end of one of the panels. (See Figure 1.)

In any case, begin the second half of the floor so that the panel joints are staggered as indicated above in Steps 1 and 2.

EXAMPLE

Some of the above points can be illustrated by the example subfloor layout in Figure 2. If you simply started from corner A and laid the first row of panels with the recommended 1/16 in. gap, you would probably need to trim the fourth panel (Panel B), since it would force the fifth one too far off centerline of joist. By figuring carefully, or by laying the fifth and sixth panels in place and measuring, you can make just the right amount of cut on only one panel in the row.

where the joists lap at the girder, since rows of nails must jog at that point. Where scabs are required, due to the offset at the overlapped joists over the girder, use 10d nails to attach 2 x 4 scab to the side of the joist to support the panel ends (see Figure 1). The scab should be of sufficient length to provide full support to the panel ends.

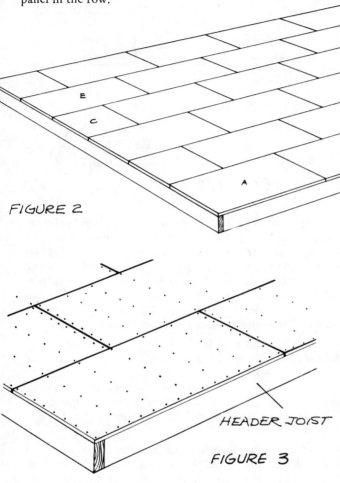

FIGURE 2

HEADER JOIST

FIGURE 3

HEADER JOIST

SUBFLOOR NAILING AND PLACEMENT

Nail panels in place as shown. Use 6d common nails for 1/2 in. plywood or 8d for 5/8 in. or 3/4 in. plywood. Place nails 3/8 in. from edge of plywood panel and space 6 in. apart along the outside perimeter of the house and along plywood end butt joint over interior joists. Drive nails at a slight angle to penetrate floor joists. Space nails 10 in. apart when nailing into joists under panel interior. (With these spacings, 9 nails are required across each end of each panel, 17 nails along an 8-ft. supported panel edge, and 6 nails along each interior joist. See Figure 3.)

Drive subfloor nails accurately so that they all penetrate the joists. Nails that miss joists, or angle out the side of joists, can cause floor squeaks. It is usually worthwhile to snap chalk lines on the plywood showing joist locations, to ensure that nails are driven correctly. NOTE: Take special care

WALL FRAMING

Wall framing is a term that includes the vertical studs and horizontal members (bottom and top plates, window and door headers) of both exterior and interior walls that support the ceiling and roof. Wall framing lumber in conventional house construction is generally of 2 x 4 lumber, with the exception of headers over windows and doors in load-bearing walls, which may be 2 x 6's or larger or two or more 2 x 4's nailed together.

Before selecting or cutting wall framing materials, check house drawings to determine whether dimensions are drawn to the middle or the outside of the stud. Also check dimensions given for roughin-in door and window openings against the millwork manufacturer's installation recommendations.

Wall framing described here is called "platform construction." Wall sections are constructed flat on the subfloor then tilted up into position. Length of exterior wall sections must be determined by the number of helpers you have available to assist you in raising walls. If only two men are on hand, it may be wise to frame sections no longer than about 24 ft.

1.   Lay out and mark on the subfloor, location of all exterior and interior walls. Then select 2 x 4 bottom plates for all exterior walls and cut them to length. Temporarily nail them in place (to the subfloor), with the outside edge of the 2 x 4 flush with the edge of the floor header joist. Use 8d scaffold nails, since they permit easy withdrawal. Next, position the bottom of all interior wall partitions, again tacking in place with 8d scaffold nails. By laying out all walls—both exterior and interior—you can identify all wall intersections and determine special framing required (see Figure 1).

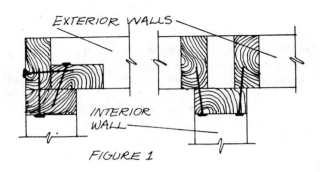

EXTERIOR WALLS

INTERIOR WALL

FIGURE 1

2. While bottom plates are still tacked in place, mark location of all major openings (make sure it's a rough, clear opening) on all plates. Then lay out all stud locations, which are generally 16 in. on center. Start on one exterior corner, and with a tape, measure and mark the location of each stud (Figure 2). Remember that most plywood sheathing and siding panels are 48 in. wide, so the dimension from the outside of the corner to the centerline of the first stud from that corner should be 16 in. Extra studs needed at wall intersections and those required to carry special loads at door openings should also be noted and marked.

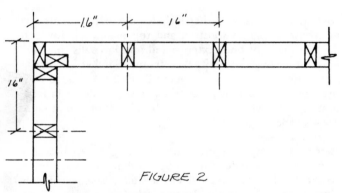

FIGURE 2

3. After all bottom plates are marked, cut a second set of plates and mark them exactly like the bottom plates. These will be the lower member of the doubled top plates.

4. Prepare to cut all wall-height stud framing members. To the floor-to-ceiling height dimension noted on your drawing, add about 1 in. for underlayment and ceiling material thickness and substract about 4 1/2 in. for three 2 x 4 place thicknesses. Measure and cut one stud to the proper length, double-check its length, and mark it as a "stud pattern." Cut all other studs to this pattern to ensure standard stud height for all exterior and interior walls. (Note: precut studs may also be used.) Then cut all cripples, jack studs, and headers, each time checking for proper length. Where several pieces of the same length are required, as in cripples, always use the same member as the pattern.

5. Assemble long-wall exterior wall sections first. Move the interior wall plates and end exterior wall plates out of the way to clear the floor for working space. (Make sure you've marked their location on both plate and subfloor for later reference.) Remove scaffold nails from exterior wall bottom plates. Tip on edge and nail in place with 16d nails driven diagonally through the plate into plywood subfloor (see Figure 3). Nailing the bottom plate to the subfloor will

keep the completed wall section from sliding off the floor deck during tilt-up.) Make sure the 16d nails are not driven into the edge of the 2 x 4 where a stud will be located or into a floor joist. Move the top plate of the same wall parallel to the bottom plate, a stud-height distance apart.

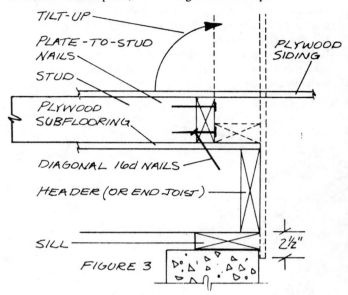

TILT-UP

PLATE-TO-STUD NAILS

STUD

PLYWOOD SUBFLOORING

DIAGONAL 16d NAILS

HEADER (OR END JOIST)

SILL

PLYWOOD SIDING

2½"

FIGURE 3

6. Locate all full-height studs and nail in place by driving nails through the bottom and top plates into the ends of the studs, two 16d nails in each plate at each stud. (You will add another top plate after the wall is erected.) Where special wall-intersection framing is required, as at corners and where interior wall will join, nail it in place. Next nail all cripples in place. Then cut and install all bottom top headers. The following sizes are recommended.

Maximum Span (ft.)	3 1/2	5	6 1/2	8
Header Size (in.)	2 x 6	2 x 8	2 x 10	2 x 12

7. Check the wall for squareness by measuring the diagonals from corner to corner. When the wall is square, the two diagonals will be exactly the same length.

8. Before tipping wall sections in place, cut several 1 x 4 or 1 x 6 diagonal braces so that, once the wall is upright, these braces can be used to attach the wall framing temporarily to the subfloor, to prevent the wall from tipping over (Figure 4).

9. Erect the wall sections; first the long walls. As you tilt the sections into place, the diagonally driven 16d nails (Figure 3) will withdraw gradually from the floor. Use 16d nails spaced 16" on center to secure the wall sections to the floor. Then build and raise the shorter end walls. Nail them to the floor and to the side walls at the corners.

10. Frame interior walls. Interior partitions are laid out exactly like exterior walls except that no sheathing or siding is attached. Interior walls should be braced diagonally during raising and, where necessary, nailed to exterior walls at their intersection. When all walls are in place, apply a second layer of top plates throughout. Make sure that butt joints in the two layers are offset, and that the doubling plates are properly lapped, to tie together all intersection walls (see Figure 5).

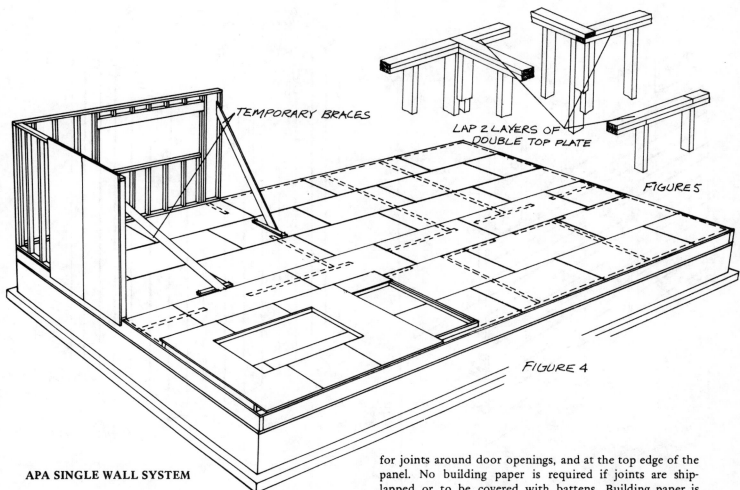

TEMPORARY BRACES

LAP 2 LAYERS OF
DOUBLE TOP PLATE

FIGURE 5

FIGURE 4

APA SINGLE WALL SYSTEM

The APA Single Wall System saves time and money. Plywood panel siding bearing the APA grade-trademark—available in a wide variety of textures and patterns is applied direct to wall framing (Figure 1), thus eliminating the costs of material and labor for installing the sheathing layer of conventional double-wall construction. Single-wall construction meets all requirements for structural performance, as a combination siding and sheathing.

APA grade-trademarked plywood siding comes in panels 3/8 to 3/4 in. thick and 4 ft. by 8,9, or 10 ft. long. (Check your lumber dealer for panel-length availability in your area.)

Normally, panels are installed vertically, with the long dimension running parallel to the studs. However, they may be installed horizontally. Allowable stud spacing is marked on the APA grade-trademark on the back.

Exterior panel may be used on studs 24 in. o.c. when applied with face grain horizontal, subject to your preference on finishing and appearance. No extra corner bracing is needed with panel siding.

Before applying plywood siding, check your house plans to see if there are any special requirements. Panel thickness may be specified, or windows may have to be attached to framing before siding is applied. The plans also may call out particular butt-joint locations or give specific details

for joints around door openings, and at the top edge of the panel. No building paper is required if joints are ship-lapped or to be covered with battens. Building paper is required for unbattened square butt joints in single-wall construction.

Panel the side walls first, then the shorter end walls.

1. See "Wall Framing," Steps 1 through 7, for framing of tilt-up walls; or erect 2 x 4 stud walls in place.

2. Cut siding panels to proper length. See Figure 2 for guide. In determining length, allow for 1 in. lap over top of foundation wall and 1 1/2 in. for covering the second top plate after wall tilt-up.

3. Place the first panel at one end of the wall framing section, making sure the edge of the panel is flush with the outside edge of the corner stud.

4. Apply the panel to the wall framing. Use hot-dip galvanized, aluminum, or other nonstaining nails to prevent staining of the siding from nail weathering and rusting. Use 6d box, siding, or casing nails for plywood siding 1/2 inch or less thick; use 8d nails for thicker panels. Drive nails every 6 in. along panel ends and edges, every 12 in. at intermediate supports. See Figure 3 for nailing ship-lapped panels. All edges of panel siding must be backed by solid lumber framing or blocking.

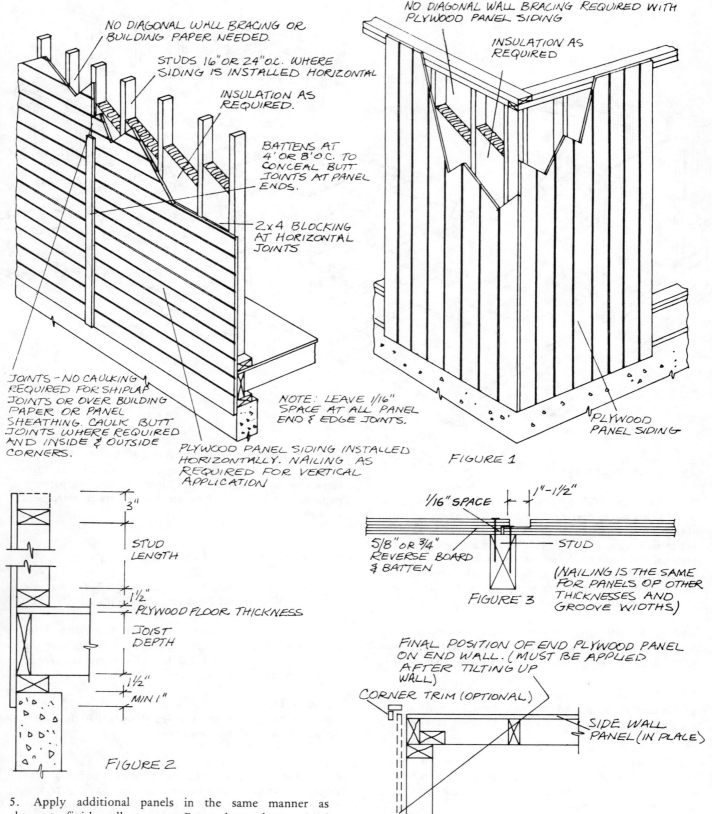

FIGURE 1

FIGURE 2

FIGURE 3

(NAILING IS THE SAME FOR PANELS OF OTHER THICKNESSES AND GROOVE WIDTHS)

FIGURE 4

5. Apply additional panels in the same manner as above, to finish wall coverage. Remember to leave a 1/16 inch space between all ends and edges of panels. This spacing is necessary to ensure that panels will stay flat under all weather conditions.

6. Tilt the side wall into position and fasten it through the subfloor to the sill plate and header joist.

7. When both side walls are completed and in place, apply siding to shorter end walls. Place one panel at the end of each wall and temporarily tack it into position. Allow for overlap of sidewall framing and siding. See Figure 4 for help in figuring the overlap (normally about 3 1/2 in. plus panel thickness). It is usually easier to use corner trim pieces than to try to trim edges to perfect fit. Permanently fasten all remaining panels to wall framing; do not apply panel at the other end of the wall. Remove temporarily fastened panel from wall. The open framing at either end of the walls facilitates tilt-up and attachment to side walls. See Figure 4.

8. Tilt walls into position and nail to side walls at corners with 16d nails. Apply corner siding panels to complete siding application.

9. Caulk joints as required. No caulking is required for shiplapped joints or for joints backed by building paper. Caulk butt joints at all inside and outside wall corners, using any of the various high-performance polyurethane, thiokol, or silicone caulks. In some cases, a foam rod or other type of filler material may be used behind the sealant. Always follow the sealant manufacturer's instructions and recommendations.

10. Apply battens and trim strips as desired for appearance, or as shown on plans. Lap corner trim strip over siding joint as shown in Figure 4, so that there is no continuous joint through corner trim and siding. Where siding is applied with face grain across the studs, apply battens to conceal the vertical butt joints at panel ends. Block behind horizontal joint. Nails through battens must penetrate the studs at least 1 inch.

SIDING OVER SHEATHING

Conventional exterior wall covering consists of a sheathing material overlaid with siding. Plywood used in both places provides strength and stiffness, durability, and distinctive appearance.

APA® grade-trademarked C-D Interior sheathing, 3/8 in. thick, is recommended over studs spaced 16 in. o.c., although 24 in. spacing may be an acceptable alternative in some code areas. Sheathing may be applied vertically with panel face grain parallel to the studs. For extra stiffness, however, apply plywood sheathing horizontally with the face grain across the studs (face grain runs the long way of the panel). Be sure to check local building regulations first to see if horizontal joints must be blocked.

Apply sheathing to tilt-up side walls first, and erect them; then sheath shorter end walls. Before applying sheathing, check your house plans for possible special requirements. The plans may also call out special details at door openings, wall corners, and at the top edge of the panel.

SHEATHING INSTALLATION

1. See page 73, "Wall Framing," Steps 1 through 7, for framing of tilt-up walls; or erect 2 x 4 stud walls in place.

2. For vertical application, position the first plywood sheathing panel at one end of the wall framing section. Make sure the edge of the panel is flush with the outside edge of the corner stud. Allow the sheathing to overlap the top plate by 1½ in. so that the panel will cover the second top plate when installed after the wall is erected. Since most floor-to-ceiling heights are 7 ft.-6 in. to 7 ft.-9 in., the sheathing will also overlap the bottom plate. Do not trim. If sheathing is applied with face grain across the studs, be sure to make the same overlap allowances over the bottom plate.

3. Nail the sheathing to the wall frame. Use 6d box or common nails, spacing them 6 in. o.c. at panel edges and 12 in. o.c. over intermediate studs.

4. Apply the rest of the APA grade-trademarked plywood sheathing to the wall section to finish coverage. Remember to leave a 1/16 in. space between all panel ends and 1/8 in. between panel edges.

5. Tilt the wall into position and fasten the bottom plate to the floor framing with 16d nails. Fasten the overlapped sheathing to the header joist with 6d nails at 6 in. o.c.

6. When both side walls are completed and in place, apply sheathing to shorter end walls. Place one panel at end of wall framing and temporarily tack into place. Allow for overlap of side wall framing and sheathing.

Overlap will be about 3½ in. plus the sheathing thickness. Permanently fasten all remaining panels to wall framing; do not apply last panel at other end of wall. Remove temporarily fastened panel from wall. The open framing at either end of the walls allows the end-wall panels to be tilted up past the side walls.

7. Tilt walls into position and nail to side walls at corners with 16d nails. Attach bottom plate and sheathing to floor framing as in Step 5. Apply corner panels to complete sheathing installation.

8. Add a plywood filler strip, if necessary, below the sheathing to help tie the floor to the sill (see Figure 1). Nail this filler 6 in. o.c. to both header joist and sill.

SIDING INSTALLATION

9. Apply plywood siding to sheathed walls (Figure 2). Texture 1-11, 303-16 in. o.c. sidings, and other Exterior panels under 7/16 in. thick may be applied with face grain parallel to studs 16 in. o.c. Any Exterior panel may be used over studs 24 in. o.c. if face grain is across studs (subject to your preference on finishing and appearance). Use hot-dipped galvanized, aluminum or other nonstaining nails to prevent staining of the siding from nail weathering and rusting. Use 6d box, siding, or casing nails for plywood siding ½ in. or less thick; use 8d nails for thicker panels. Drive nails every 6 in. along panel ends and edges, every 12 in. at intermediate supports. Nails through battens must penetrate studs at least 1 in. or be driven through the plywood sheathing if the joint does not occur over a stud.

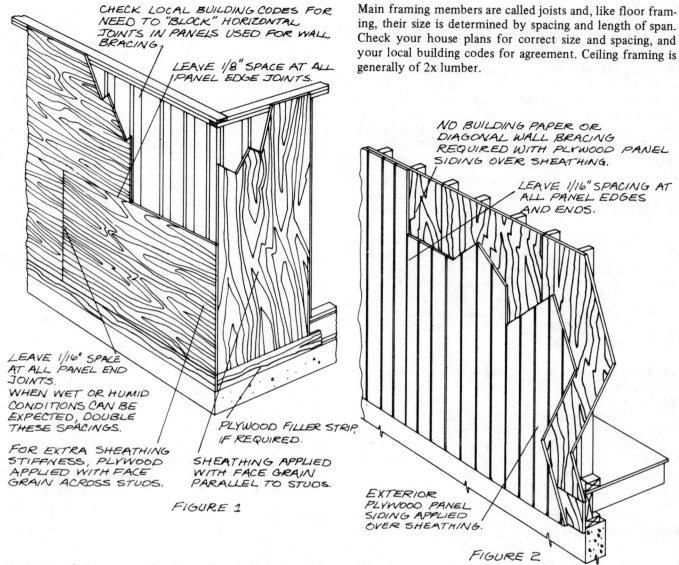

Main framing members are called joists and, like floor framing, their size is determined by spacing and length of span. Check your house plans for correct size and spacing, and your local building codes for agreement. Ceiling framing is generally of 2x lumber.

Figure 1 labels:
CHECK LOCAL BUILDING CODES FOR NEED TO "BLOCK" HORIZONTAL JOINTS IN PANELS USED FOR WALL BRACING.

LEAVE 1/8" SPACE AT ALL PANEL EDGE JOINTS.

LEAVE 1/16" SPACE AT ALL PANEL END JOINTS. WHEN WET OR HUMID CONDITIONS CAN BE EXPECTED, DOUBLE THESE SPACINGS.

FOR EXTRA SHEATHING STIFFNESS, PLYWOOD APPLIED WITH FACE GRAIN ACROSS STUDS.

PLYWOOD FILLER STRIP, IF REQUIRED.

SHEATHING APPLIED WITH FACE GRAIN PARALLEL TO STUDS.

FIGURE 1

Figure 2 labels:
NO BUILDING PAPER OR DIAGONAL WALL BRACING REQUIRED WITH PLYWOOD PANEL SIDING OVER SHEATHING.

LEAVE 1/16" SPACING AT ALL PANEL EDGES AND ENDS.

EXTERIOR PLYWOOD PANEL SIDING APPLIED OVER SHEATHING.

FIGURE 2

10. Leave 1/16 in. space between all ends and edges of siding panels.

11. Caulk square-edged siding butt joints with any of the various high-performance polyurethane, thiokol, or silicone caulks. In some cases, a foam rod or other type filler material may be used behind the sealant. Always follow sealant manufacturer's recommendations. No caulking is needed for ship-lapped joints or for joints covered by battens.

CEILING FRAMING

After exterior and interior walls are erected, plumbed for straightness, braced, and tied together with the second top plates, ceiling framing can be installed. Basic construction of ceiling framing is similar to that of floors, except that header joists are not included.

Ceiling framing does three things. It ties together opposite walls and roof rafters to resist the outward pressure imposed on the walls from the pitched roof. It supports the finished ceiling, and it supports either a second story, or in this example, an attic storage area.

You will want to install your ceiling framing before your roof rafters, to give you a working platform for building the roof. You should lay out both ceiling framing and roof rafters at the same time, however, since the ceiling joists must lap the roof rafters, and be securely nailed to them. Follow your house plans for location of members. It is much easier to space ceiling joists at the same spacing as roof rafters, and that is the method shown here.

With plywood sheathing and siding, and with doubled top plates, ceiling joists and roof rafters need not line up over the wall studs. In fact, wall studs are usually placed at 16 in. o.c., whereas roof rafters and ceiling joists can be placed at 24 in. o.c.

If the load-bearing interior wall is not continuous, a beam will be needed to carry the inside ends of the ceiling joists. Check your house plans to determine type, placement, and size of beam necessary to support the load. The beam may be below the ceiling joists, at the same level as the joists, or may even be above them. If it is at the same level, or above them, it must support the joists with metal hangers.

1. Lay out the position of the ceiling joists and roof rafters in approximately the same manner as was done for floor joists, marking location of each joist and each rafter on both outside plates and the interior bearing wall. Note at this point that the two roof rafters on opposite sides of the house will frame opposite each other at the center, but that the ceiling joists will lap these rafters. The easiest method for making everything line up is to use filler blocks over the interior bearing partition, as shown in Figure 1. Then the two ceiling joists "meeting" over the center partition can be placed one on each side of the roof rafter, with the filler block occupying the space of the roof rafter at the center point.

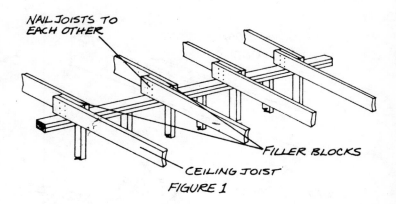

FIGURE 1

2. Begin installing ceiling rafters. Because the end rafter will be placed with its outside face flush with the outside of the wall, the ceiling joist at the end of the house will not lap its rafter (see Figures 2 and 3). For this reason, it is easier to place the end joist after the gable end has been framed. Place your first ceiling joist to lap the first interior roof rafter, which will have its centerline 24 in. from the face of the end wall. Succeeding joists (and rafters) are spaced 24 in. o.c.

3. Trim corners of ceiling joists at outer walls where they must match the rafter slope. (Your house plan will tell you the slope). If only a small amount must be removed, you may saw it off after rafters are in place.

4. Cut ceiling joists to proper length with the outer end flush with the outside of the wall and allowing for at least 4 in. overlap at the center.

5. Install ceiling joists and toenail to the top plate of the exterior walls with two 10d nails on each side. At the center lap, nail the joists to the filler block, and then toenail to the plate of the load-bearing wall or beam (Figure 4). Since the ceiling rafters are supplying the tie across the building, they must be well spiked. For a 24 ft. wide building, with ceiling joists and roof rafters both at 24 in. spacings, four 16d nails are required from each ceiling joist into the filler block. Tie together ceiling joists and the non-bearing walls that run parallel to them, as in Figure 5. As with floor framing, place ceiling joists with the crown up.

6. Cut and frame attic access in the same manner as openings in the floor. Fire regulations and building codes usually list minimum size requirements, and your house plans show locations. If the opening is small (2 to 3 ft. square), doubling of the headers and joists is not necessary.

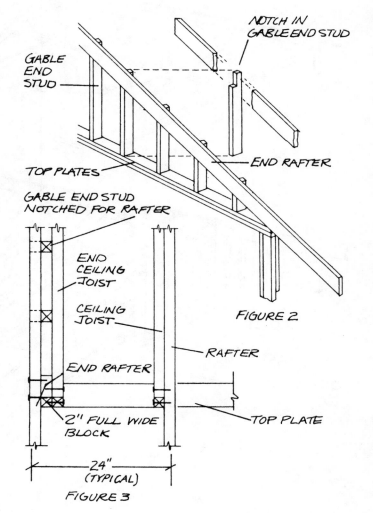

FIGURE 2

FIGURE 3

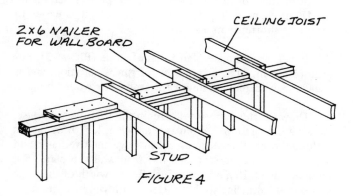

FIGURE 4

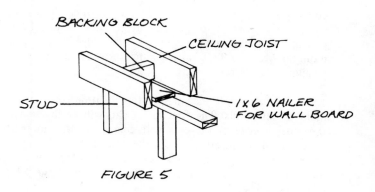

FIGURE 5

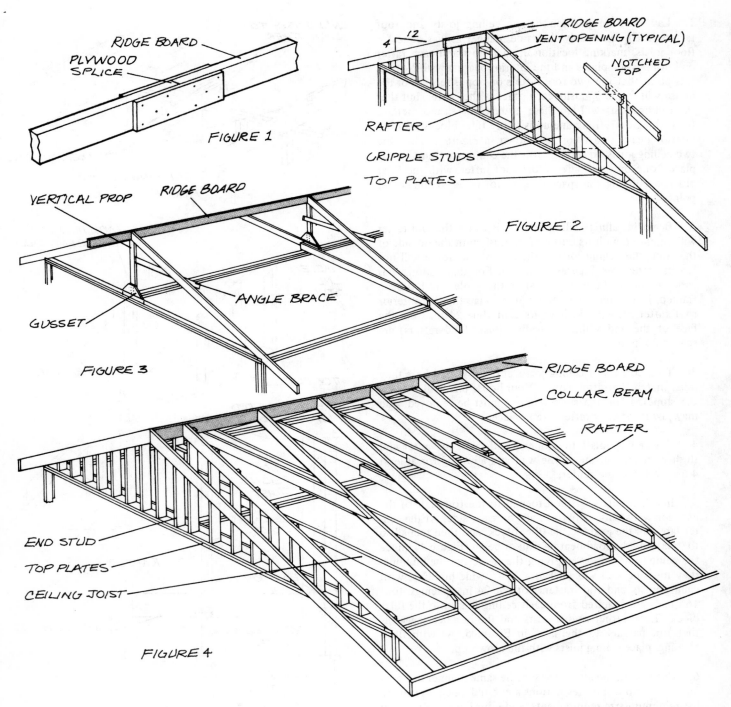

RIDGE BOARD

PLYWOOD SPLICE

FIGURE 1

RIDGE BOARD

VENT OPENING (TYPICAL)

4 12

NOTCHED TOP

RAFTER

CRIPPLE STUDS

TOP PLATES

FIGURE 2

VERTICAL PROP

RIDGE BOARD

ANGLE BRACE

GUSSET

FIGURE 3

RIDGE BOARD

COLLAR BEAM

RAFTER

END STUD

TOP PLATES

CEILING JOIST

FIGURE 4

ROOF FRAMING

Roof framing is the combination of rafters, ridge board, collar beams, and cripple studs. In gable roof construction, all rafters are precut to the same length and pattern. Each pair of rafters is fastened at the top to a ridge board, commonly a 2 x 8 for 2 x 6 rafters, which provides support and a nailing area for rafter ends.

1. If not already done, mark rafter locations on the top plate of side walls. The first rafter pair will be flush with the outside edge of the end wall. Space the first interior rafter at 24 in. measured from the end of the building to the center of the rafter. All succeeding rafter locations are measured 24 in. center to center. They will be at the sides of ceiling-joist ends.

2. Next, mark rafter locations on the ridge board, allowing for specified gable overhang. To achieve required total length of ridge board, you may have to splice it (see Figure 1). Do not splice it yet, however, because it is easier to erect it in shorter sections.

3. Check your house plan for roof slope (Figure 2). For example, 4 in. of rise in 12 in. of run is common, and is usually considered minimum for asphalt or wood shingles.

4. Draw a rafter pattern full-size on the floor of the house, showing actual slope. From this drawing, length of rafters including over all: angle of cut at ridge and overhang, and location of notched seat cut (to fit on wall top plate) can be determined. Remember to include the width of the ridge board in the drawing so that rafter length will be accurate.

5. Lay out the pair of rafters, marking top and bottom angles and seat cut location. Make the cuts and check fit by setting them up at floor level. Once a good fit is achieved, mark this set of rafters for identification and use it as a pattern for the remainder.

6. Cut remaining rafters. For a 48 ft. house with rafters spaced 24 in. o.c., you will need 24 more pairs cut to the pattern (25 total pairs). In addition, you will need two pairs of fascia rafters for the ends of the gable overhang (Figure 4). Since they cover the end of the ridge board, they must be longer than the pattern rafters by half the width of the ridge board. Fascia rafters will have the same cuts at the top and bottom as the regular rafters, but they will not have a seat cut.

Getting started with erection of the roof framing is the most complicated part of framing a house. Plan it carefully, making sure you have all materials on hand and all steps in mind before you begin. It is best to make a "dry run" at ground level. Erection procedure will be much easier if you have at least two helpers. A considerable amount of temporary bracing will be required if the job must be done with only one or two men.

7. Build temporary props of 2 x 4's to hold the rafters and ridge board in place during roof framing installation. The props should be long enough to reach from the top plate to the bottom of the ridge board, and should be fitted with a plywood gusset at the bottom; when installed the plywood gusset is nailed temporarily to the top plate or to a ceiling joist. The props are also diagonally braced from about midpoint in both directions to maintain true vertical (check with a plumb bob).

8. Move ridge board sections and rafters onto the ceiling framing. (Lay plywood panels over the ceiling joists for safer footing.) First erect the ridge board and the rafters nearest its ends, as shown in Figure 3. If the ridge of the house is longer than the individual pieces of ridge board, you'll find it easier to erect each piece separately, rather than splicing the ridge board full length first. Support the ridge board at both ends with the temporary props. Toenail the first rafter pair securely to the ridge board using at least two 8d nails on each side, then nail at wall. Install other end rafter pair in the same manner.

9. Make the ridge board joints, using plywood gussets on each side of the joint and nailing them securely to the ridge board.

10. Check the ridge board for level. Also check for straightness over the centerline of the house.

11. After full length of the ridge board is erected, put up the remaining rafters in pairs, nailing them securely in place. Check occasionally to make sure ridge board remains straight. If all rafters are cut and assembled accurately, the roof should be self-aligning.

12. Toenail the rafters to the wall plate with 10d nails, using at least two per side. Also nail the ceiling joists to the rafters. For a 24 ft. wide house, you will need four 16d nails at each lap. In high wind areas, it's a good idea to add metal-strap fasteners for extra uplift resistance.

13. Cut and install 1 x 6 collar beams at every other pair of rafters (4 ft. o.c.); see Figure 4. Nail each end with four 8d nails. Collar beams should be in the upper third of the attic crawl space. Remove temporary props.

14. Square a line across the end wall plate directly below the ridge board. If a vent is to be installed, measure half its width on each side of the center mark for location of the first stud on each side. Mark positions for remaining studs at 16 in. o.c., then measure and cut studs. Notch the top end to fit under the rafter so that the stud bottom will be flush with the top plate. Cut cripple studs and headers to frame in vent opening (see Figures 2 or 4).

15. Cut and install fascia board to correct length of ridge board. Bevel the top edge to roof slope. Nail the board to rafter ends, then install fascia rafters. Fascia rafters cover the end of the ridge board (see Figure 4). Where nails will be exposed to weather, use hot-dip galvanized or other non-staining nails.

NOTE: Readymade lightweight wood roof trusses may be available at building supply dealers in lengths from 20 to 32 ft. or more. Because they span from one exterior wall to the other, with no interior bearing walls required, they allow greater flexibility in planning interior room arrangement. Trusses are most adaptable to houses with rectangular plans where the constant width requires only one type of truss.

ROOF SHEATHING

Roof sheathing, the covering over rafters or trusses, provides structural strength and rigidity, and makes a solid base for fastening the roofing material. APA® grade-trademarked sheathing is marked with an Identification Index, which tells you the recommended rafter spacing for the plywood thickness. For the example house, with 24 in. spans (distance between rafters), plywood with a marking of 24/0 is adequate. Sheathing panels with this Identification Index are available in 3/8 and 1/2 thickness.

Your house plan will show either "open soffits" (Figure 1) or "closed soffits" (Figure 2). If you have closed soffits, all of your roof sheathing can be APA grade-trademarked C-D INT grade. With open soffits, all panels to be exposed at the overhang, either along the side or at the end of the roof, must be Exterior type, and of high enough appearance grade to permit painting or staining to blend well with the rest of the house. To keep the roofing nails from showing through the underside, these exposed soffit panels must be at least 1/2 in. thick (and you'll have to consider the length of roofing nails as well). Many of the textured-finish plywoods of 1/2 in. and 5/8 in. thickness can be used with the textured side down to provide attractive open soffits.

With either open or boxed soffits, you will need a roof sheathing layout.

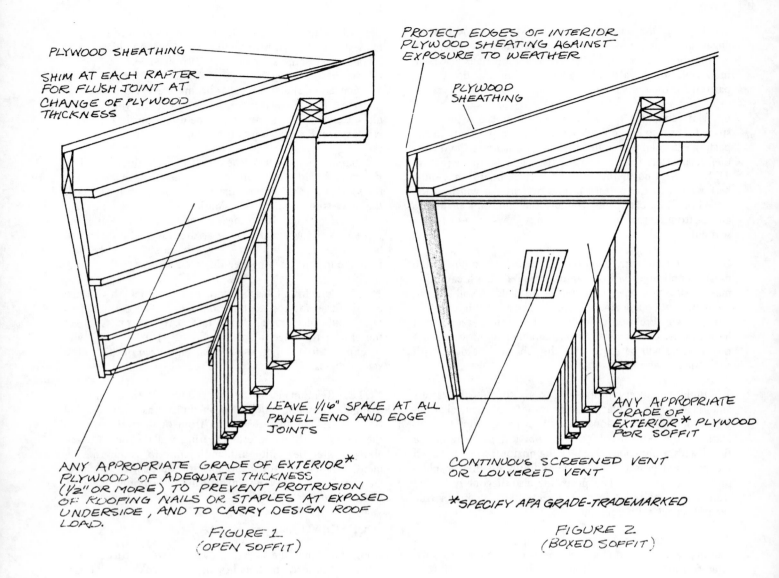

PLYWOOD SHEATHING

SHIM AT EACH RAFTER FOR FLUSH JOINT AT CHANGE OF PLYWOOD THICKNESS

LEAVE 1/16" SPACE AT ALL PANEL END AND EDGE JOINTS

ANY APPROPRIATE GRADE OF EXTERIOR* PLYWOOD OF ADEQUATE THICKNESS (1/2" OR MORE) TO PREVENT PROTRUSION OF ROOFING NAILS OR STAPLES AT EXPOSED UNDERSIDE, AND TO CARRY DESIGN ROOF LOAD.

FIGURE 1
(OPEN SOFFIT)

PROTECT EDGES OF INTERIOR PLYWOOD SHEATING AGAINST EXPOSURE TO WEATHER

PLYWOOD SHEATHING

ANY APPROPRIATE GRADE OF EXTERIOR* PLYWOOD FOR SOFFIT

CONTINUOUS SCREENED VENT OR LOUVERED VENT

*SPECIFY APA GRADE-TRADEMARKED

FIGURE 2
(BOXED SOFFIT)

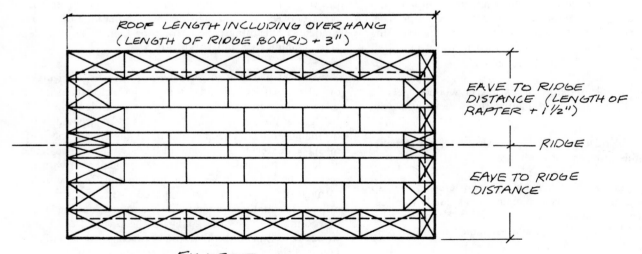

ROOF LENGTH INCLUDING OVERHANG (LENGTH OF RIDGE BOARD + 3")

EAVE TO RIDGE DISTANCE (LENGTH OF RAFTER + 1 1/2")

RIDGE

EAVE TO RIDGE DISTANCE

FIGURE 3
FOR "OPEN SOFFITS" ALL PANELS MARKED WITH X'S MUST BE EXT-DFPA "SOFFIT" PANELS.

1. Draw your layout. It may be a freehand sketch, but should be relatively close to scale. The easiest method is to draw a simple rectangle representing half of the roof. The long side will represent the length of the ridge board. Make the short side equal to the length of your rafters, including overhangs. If you have open soffits, draw a second line (possibly dotted) inside the ends and bottom, to show the area that must be covered by Exterior plywood. Remember that this is only half of the roof, and that any cutting of panels on this side can be planned so that the cutoff portions will be useful on the other. If your eave overhang is less than 2 ft., and you have an open soffit, you may wish to start with a half panel width of soffit plywood. Otherwise, you will probably start with a full 4 x 8 ft. section of plywood at the bottom of the roof, and work upward toward the ridge, where you may have to cut the last row of panels. Stagger panels in succeeding rows.

2. Complete your layout for the whole roof. The layout shows panel size and placement as well as sheathing panel quantities needed (See Figure 3). If your diagram should show that you will have excessive waste in cutting, you may be able to reduce scrap by slightly shortening the rafter overhang at the eave, or the gable overhang.

As shown in Figure 3, for the example house, nearly half of the panels are "soffit" panels. For such a case, rather than shimming to level up soffit and interior sheathing panels (as in Step 7), you may want to use interior sheathing panels of the same thickness as your soffit panels, even though they might then be a little thicker than the minimum required.

3. Cut panels as required, marking cutting lines first to ensure square corners.

4. Begin panel placement at corner of the roof. If you are using special soffit panels, remember to place them best or textured side down.

5. Fasten each panel in the first course (row), in turn, to the roof framing using 6d common smooth, ring shank, or spiral thread nails. Space nails 6 in. o.c. along panel ends and 12 in. o.c. at intermediate supports.

6. Leave 1/16 in. space at panel ends and 1/8 in. at edge joints. In areas of high humidity, double the spacing.

7. Apply the second course, using a soffit half panel in first (overhang) position. If the main sheathing panels are thinner than the soffit sheathing, install small shims to ease the joint transition (Figure 1).

8. Apply remaining courses as above.

NOTE: If your plans show closed soffits, the roof sheathing will be all the same grade and thickness. For applying plywood to the underside of closed soffits, use nonstaining type nails.

NAILS

On any construction job, the cost of nails used is so small, compared with their importance, that they should always be of the best quality. Sizes (length) are indicated by "penny," abbreviated as "d" (as in 8d). Length of all nails will be the same in a particular penny size, regardless of head or shank configuration. Only the diameter changes. Use nonstaining siding or casing nails to prevent siding from discoloring due to nail weathering or rusting.

NAIL SIZE AND NUMBER PER POUND

| | | COMMON | | BOX | |
Size	Length (in.)	Diameter (in.)	No. per Pound	Diameter (in.)	No. Per Pound
4d	1-1/2	.102	316	.083	473
5d	1-3/4	.102	271	.083	406
6d	2	.115	181	.102	236
7d	2-1/4	.115	161	.102	210
8d	2-1/2	.131	106	.115	145
10d	3	.148	69	.127	94
12d	3-1/4	.148	63	.127	88
16d	3-1/2	.165	49	.134	71
20d	4	.203	31	.148	52
30d	4-1/2	.220	24	.148	46
40d	5	.238	18	.165	35

COMMON AND BOX NAILS

Common and box nails are for normal building construction, particularly framing. Smooth box nails of the same penny size will have a smaller diameter than common nails. Since this smaller diameter has less tendency to split the lumber, they are recommended for most uses. You also get more box nails per pounds, as shown on the table.

SCAFFOLD NAILS

Scaffold or "double-headed" nails can save you time and trouble in many operations where the fastener must later be removed—as in scaffolding, bracing, concrete forms, and temporary fastening during framing layout.

CASING AND FINISH NAILS

These are for use when you do not want large nailheads visible, such as in interior and exterior siding applications. To further reduce visibility, both may be driven deeper into the material with a nail-set and the holes filled with wood filler of matching color.

NONSTAINING NAILS

For long service and freedom from staining, use nonstaining nails. They are necessary where exterior exposure is combined with need for good appearance; for example, in siding, fascias, soffits, exterior trim, and wood decks. Galvanizing is the most common nail coating, and offers good protection against staining. Nails also are made of metals or alloys not subject to corrosion, including aluminum, bronze, and stainless steel.

NAILS COMMONLY USED FOR RESIDENTIAL CONSTRUCTION

PENNY (d) SIZES

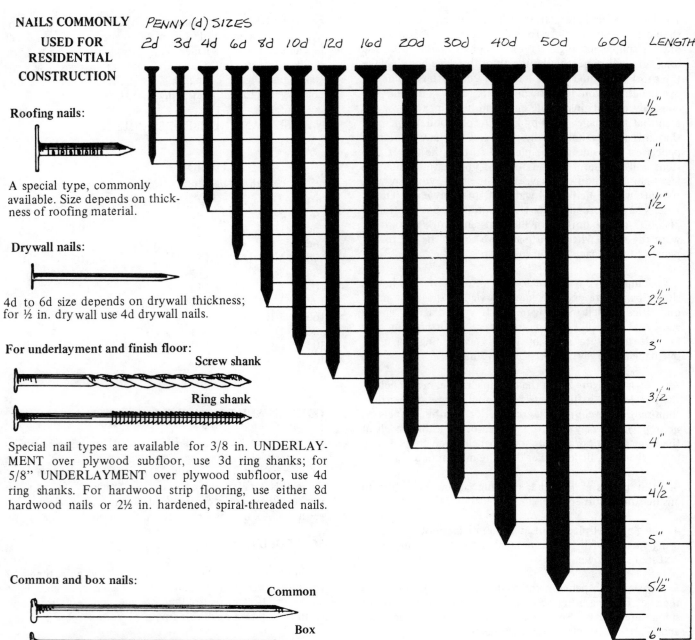

2d 3d 4d 6d 8d 10d 12d 16d 20d 30d 40d 50d 60d   LENGTH

½"
1"
1½"
2"
2½"
3"
3½"
4"
4½"
5"
5½"
6"

Roofing nails:

A special type, commonly available. Size depends on thickness of roofing material.

Drywall nails:

4d to 6d size depends on drywall thickness; for ½ in. drywall use 4d drywall nails.

For underlayment and finish floor:

Screw shank

Ring shank

Special nail types are available for 3/8 in. UNDERLAYMENT over plywood subfloor, use 3d ring shanks; for 5/8" UNDERLAYMENT over plywood subfloor, use 4d ring shanks. For hardwood strip flooring, use either 8d hardwood nails or 2½ in. hardened, spiral-threaded nails.

Common and box nails:

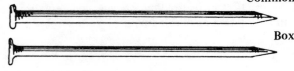

Common

Box

16d for general framing.
8d and 10d for toenailing.
6d and 8d for subfloor, wall sheathing and roof sheathing. Size depends on thickness of plywood sheathing.

Scaffold nails:

8d and 10d most common, for scaffolds, bracing, and any temporary fastening that must be later removed.

Siding nails:

Nonstaining nails of size specified for siding thickness (usually 6d and 8d).

Casing and finish nails:

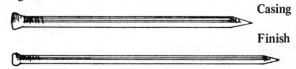

Casing

Finish

4d, 6d, and 8d most common, for exterior and interior trim and paneling where large nailheads should not show. Use casing nails for exterior siding.

DEFORMED-SHANK NAILS

A variety of deformed-shank patterns such as screw shank, ring shank, and barbed are available. These all have greater holding power than smooth nails. Often, you may use a smaller size deformed-shank nail and still do the job satisfactorily.

DESIGN OF WOOD STRUCTURES FOR PERMANENCE

Long service-life in a building or structure is the result of careful planning which begins on the drawing board and continues through the various stages of construction. It means attention to details and conformance with those methods and practices which have been found to be essential to good construction.

All building materials are subject to possible deterioration when exposed to unfavorable conditions. Moisture which may cause decay in wood can be expected to produce rusting or corrosion of metals. This moisture, in freezing, may cause cracks in concrete and masonry. Protection against the damaging effects of moisture should be incorporated into the construction of any building.

Wood structures, when properly designed, will resist damage by moisture and by living organisms. Subterranean termites and fungi, which produce decay, constitute the major problem.

GENERAL RECOMMENDATIONS FOR GOOD CONSTRUCTION

The recommendations included for all buildings will provide basic resistance to decay. Due to climatic conditions, or the geographical location additional control measures may be required in some buildings or structures.

Control of decay or termite attack is accomplished primarily through the application of four fundamental construction practices:

1. Positive site and building drainage.

2. Adequate separation of wood elements from known moisture sources to (a) prevent excessive absorption, (b) allow for periodic inspection, and (c) provide the necessary physical barrier for termite protection.

3. Use of naturally durable or treated wood where indicated.

4. Ventilation and condensation control in enclosed spaces.

These construction practices eliminate the danger of decay or subterranean termite damage. They also serve to control damage from other insects present in limited geographical areas. They are accepted standards of construction.

SITE DRAINAGE AND SANITATION

In all cases the building site should be graded to provide positive drainage away from foundation walls. In determining the height of the foundation, it is important to take into consideration the proposed height of finish grade to assure proper clearance for wood members resting on top of the foundation. Figure 1.

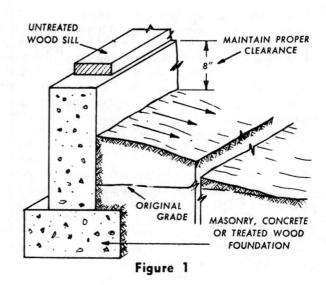

Figure 1

All roots, wood forms and scraps of lumber should be removed from the immediate vicinity of the house before back filling and before placing a floor slab. Particular care should be taken to remove all scraps of lumber from enclosed crawl spaces.

BUILDING DRAINAGE

All exposed wood surfaces, as well as adjoining areas, should be pitched to assure rapid water run-off. Construction details which tend to trap moisture in end grain joints should be avoided.

Foundations: Good foundation drainage and dampproofing of walls below grade are insurance against the development of undesirable moisture conditions in crawl spaces and basements. Figure 2.

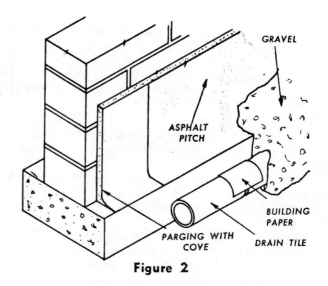

Figure 2

Moisture-proofing of poured concrete walls is accomplished by two coats of asphalt or tar applied from footing to finish grade. Unit masonry walls, require a 1/2-inch layer of portland cement mortar applied from footing to finish grade leaving a cove at the junction of the footing and wall. Mortar should then be mopped with asphalt or tar. Footing drains, connected to a positive outfall should be installed around foundations enclosing habitable spaces below grade. Drain tile may also be needed within a crawl space where excessive moisture prevails. Figure 3.

For slab-on-ground construction and basement floors, earth should be covered with not less than 4 inches of coarse gravel or crushed stone over which a separating membrane is placed before pouring the slab. In slab-on-ground construction and where basements contain living space, this membrane should be a vapor barrier having a permeability not greater than one perm.

Flashing is needed at the following places:

1. Heads of all openings in exterior walls unless protected by overhanging eaves. Figure 4.

2. Under window openings where masonry veneer is used. Figure 5.

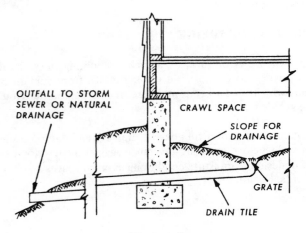

Figure 3

3. Where changes in exterior finish materials occur. Figure 6.

4. Between concrete porch, or patio floors, and wood finish where such floors are above the top of the foundation. Figure 7.

5. At the junction of roof deck and wood siding, at roof valleys and around chimneys and vent stacks. Figure 8.

Siding: Exterior wood siding should extend at least 1 inch below the top of the foundation to provide a drip line protecting the sill from rainwater. Figure 9.

Where the exterior finish is masonry veneer a one-inch space should be allowed between sheathing and the veneer. Weep holes and flashing should be provided at the base of the veneer wall to allow for drainage. Figure 10.

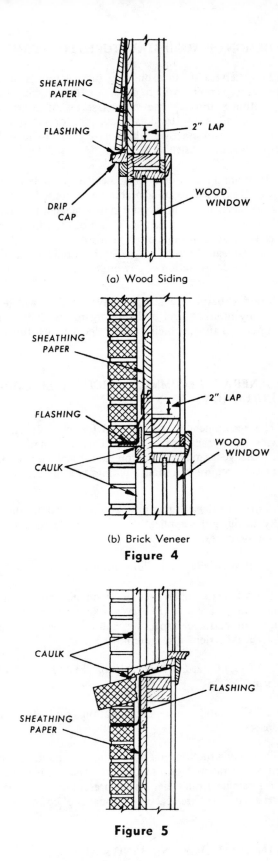

(a) Wood Siding

(b) Brick Veneer
Figure 4

Figure 5

Roofs. Shingles should project at least 1½ inches beyond the roof sheathing to provide a drip line. When asphalt shingles are used, a starting course of wood shingles is desirable. Gutters and down spouts are needed unless eave projection is 24-inches or greater. Roof run-off should be drained away from the structure.

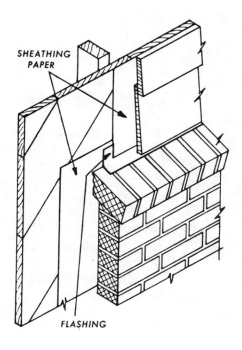

(a) Brick Veneer and Wood Siding

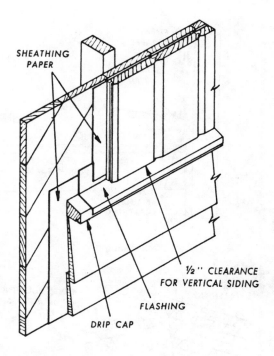

(b) Horizontal and Vertical Wood Siding

Figure 6

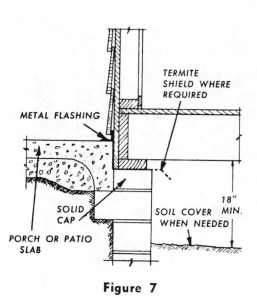

Figure 7

In northern areas melting snow may result in ice dams on roof overhang and gutters to the extent that water may work back under shingles and drip into attic spaces or walls. Protection is provided by the applicationtion of 55-pound roll roofing or 6-mil polyethylene extending over the roof sheathing and behind the gutter. Figure 11.

Exposed Structural Members: Exposed structural members should be designed for drainage away from end joints to allow rapid drying. In instances where proper detailing of such joints may not provide sufficient protection, the designer can specify naturally durable or treated lumber.

SEPARATION OF WOOD ELEMENTS

The separations specified in this section are recommended for all buildings and are those considered necessary to, (a) maintain wood elements in permanent structures at safe moisture contents for decay protection, (b) provide a termite barrier and, (c) facilitate periodic inspection. When it is not possible or practical to comply with the clearance specified the use of naturally durable or treated wood is recommended. However, when termites are known to exist, space must be provided for periodic inspection.

1. In crawl spaces and other unexcavated places, clearance between the bottom of wood joists or structural planks without joists and the ground, should be at least 18 inches. Between the bottom of wood girders or wood posts and the ground, the clearance should be at least 12 inches. Figures 9 & 12.

2. In basements or cellars wood posts which support floor framing should rest on concrete pedestals extending 2 inches above concrete floors and 6 inches above earth floors and separated therefrom by an impervious barrier. Figure 13.

3. Main beams or girders framing into masonry walls should have ½ inch of air space at the top, end and sides. Figure 14.

4. Wood sills which rest on concrete or masonry exterior walls should be at least 8 inches above the exposed earth on the exterior of the building. Figure 9.

5. Wood siding and trim should be at least 6 inches above exposed earth on the exterior of a structure. Figure 9.

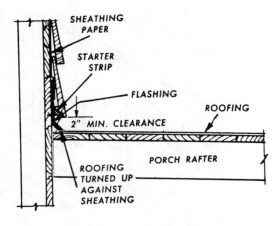

SHEATHING PAPER

STARTER STRIP

FLASHING

ROOFING

2" MIN. CLEARANCE

ROOFING TURNED UP AGAINST SHEATHING

PORCH RAFTER

(a) Wood Siding and Roof

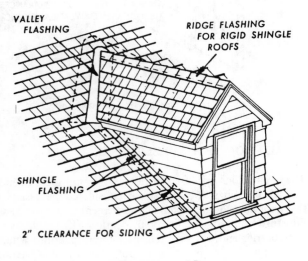

VALLEY FLASHING

RIDGE FLASHING FOR RIGID SHINGLE ROOFS

SHINGLE FLASHING

2" CLEARANCE FOR SIDING

(b) At Valley and Dormer

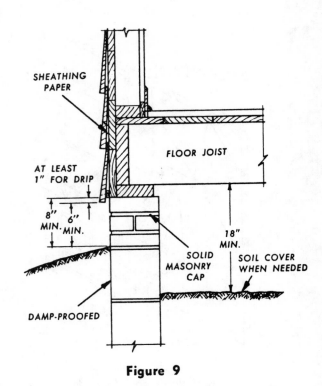

SHEATHING PAPER

FLOOR JOIST

AT LEAST 1" FOR DRIP

8" MIN. 6" MIN.

18" MIN.

SOLID MASONRY CAP

SOIL COVER WHEN NEEDED

DAMP-PROOFED

Figure 9

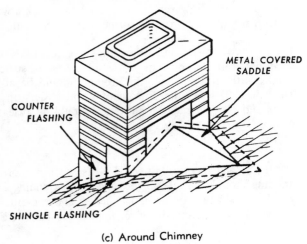

METAL COVERED SADDLE

COUNTER FLASHING

SHINGLE FLASHING

(c) Around Chimney

Figure 8

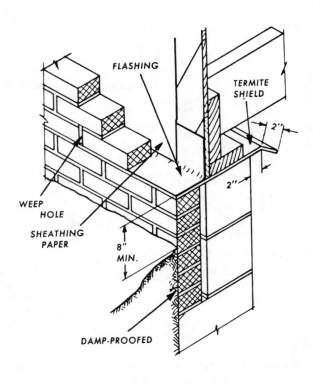

FLASHING

TERMITE SHIELD

2"

WEEP HOLE

SHEATHING PAPER

8" MIN.

2"

DAMP-PROOFED

Figure 10

6.   Fences and similar items should be separated from the main structure by at least 2 inches.

7.   Exterior steps. Structural portions of wood stairs, such as stringers and posts, should be at least 6 inches above the finished grade. Figure 15.

8.   Porches, breezeways and patios: Beams, headers and posts supporting floor framing should be at least 12 inches above the ground. Floor joists should be at least 18 inches above the ground. Posts which rest on wood, concrete or masonry floors should be supported on pedestals extending at least 2 inches above the floor or at least 6 inches above exposed earth. Figures 12 & 13.

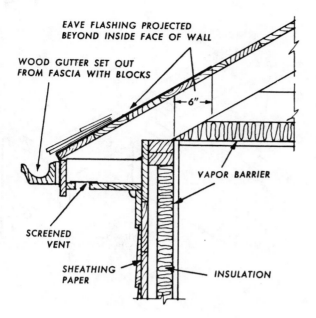

Figure 11

9. Planters, concrete steps, or porch slabs resting on the ground should be below the top of the foundation, or separated from wood in the main structure by at least 2 inches, or otherwise protected from concealed termite penetration.

10. Ends of main structural members exposed to weather and supporting roofs or floors should rest on foundations which provide a clearance of at least 12 inches above the ground or 6 inches above concrete.

11. Shutters, window boxes, and other decorative attachments should be separated from exterior siding to avoid trapping rain water.

VENTILATION AND CONDENSATION CONTROL IN ENCLOSED SPACES

All crawl spaces under houses without basements and other unexcavated spaces under porches, breezeways and patios or other appendages should be ventilated by openings in the foundation walls. Such spaces should be provided with access panels so that they may be easily inspected. The vent openings should have a net area not less than 2 square feet for each 100 linear feet of exterior wall, plus 1/3 square foot for each 100 square feet of crawl space. Openings should be arranged to provide cross ventilation and covered with corrosion resistant wire mesh, not less than 1/4 inch nor more than ½ inch in any dimension. No unventilated, inaccessible spaces should be permitted.

When soil in crawl spaces is noticeably damp it should be covered with a layer of impervious material, such as asphalt saturated felt weighing 55-pounds per square. The ground surface should be leveled and the cover material turned at walls and piers and lapped at least 2 inches, but need not be sealed. If ground cover is used, the net area of vent openings may be reduced to 10 percent of the preceding recommendation.

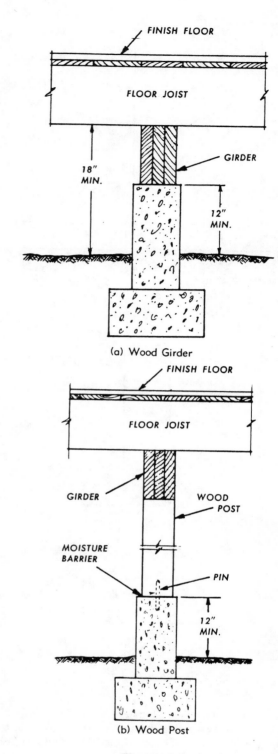

(a) Wood Girder

(b) Wood Post

Figure 12

Attic Spaces: To eliminate the problem of moisture condensation on roof framing in cold weather and to permit the escape of heat in hot weather, ventilation of all spaces is required.

For gable roofs, screened louvers generally are provided and the net area of the opening should be about 1/300 of the area of the ceiling below. When a 3/4-inch slot is provided beneath the eaves, the ventilating area may be reduced to 1/900. Figure 11.

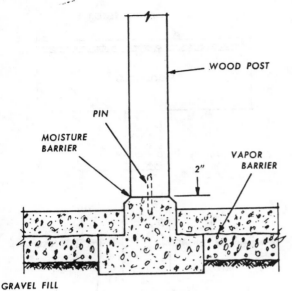

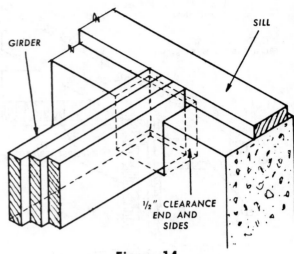

WOOD POST

MOISTURE BARRIER

PIN

2"

VAPOR BARRIER

GRAVEL FILL

(a) Above Concrete Floor

GIRDER

SILL

½" CLEARANCE END AND SIDES

Figure 14

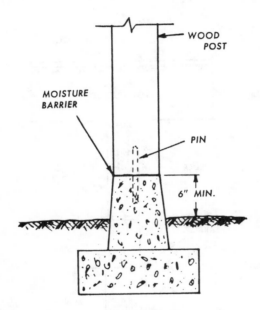

WOOD POST

MOISTURE BARRIER

PIN

6" MIN.

(b) Above Earth Floor

Figure 13

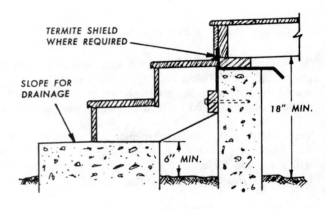

TERMITE SHIELD WHERE REQUIRED

SLOPE FOR DRAINAGE

18" MIN.

6" MIN.

Figure 15
Exterior Wood Steps at Ground

For hip roofs, it is customary to provide a 3/4-inch slot beneath the eaves and a sheet metal ventilator near the peak, in which case the net area of the inlet should be 1/900, and that of the outlet 1/1600 of the area of the ceiling below.

For flat roofs, blocking and bridging should be arranged to prevent interference with movement of air. Such roofs may be ventilated along overhanging eaves on the basis of net area of opening equal to 1/250 of the area of the ceiling below. Figure 16.

Vapor Protection for Walls and Ceilings. In cold climates when winter temperature customarily falls below 0° Farenheit, walls of all dwellings which are insulated to produce a U value of less than 0.25 would have a vapor barrier with a permeability rating no greater than one perm applied to the warm side of the walls. Where a water resistant building paper is used between sheathing and siding, or where a water resistant material is incorporated into the sheathing, it should be a "breathing-type," having a vapor permeability of at least 5 perms.

With the exception of climates where winter temperatures commonly fall below -20° F or where roof slopes are less than 3 in 12, vapor barriers are not considered necessary for ceilings of dwellings.

In occupancies other than dwellings where winter humidities are low or where positive ventilation of the interior is provided, vapor barriers may not be necessary.

Vapor barriers should be carefully installed to provide a complete envelope preventing moisture vapor produced inside the structure from entering enclosed spaces where condensation may occur. The principle of vapor protection is to make the warm side of the wall as vapor tight as possible and the cold side permeable enough to permit the passage of moisture vapor to the outside and yet provide sufficient resistance to cold air infiltration and penetration of wind driven rain.

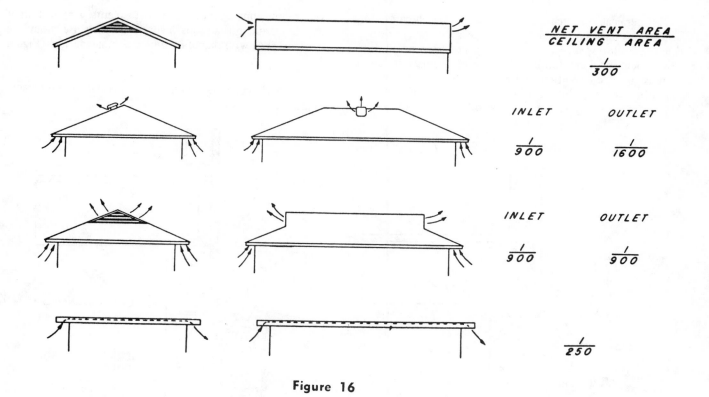

$$\frac{\text{NET VENT AREA}}{\text{CEILING AREA}}$$

$\frac{1}{300}$

INLET $\frac{1}{900}$ OUTLET $\frac{1}{1600}$

INLET $\frac{1}{900}$ OUTLET $\frac{1}{900}$

$\frac{1}{250}$

Figure 16

TERMITE BARRIERS

A termite barrier is considered to be any building material or component which can be made impenetrable to termites and which drives the insect into the open where its activities can be detected and eliminated.

All structures should be designed to provide adequate and accessible clearance between earth and wood in order to permit periodic inspection. When the clearances recommended under the heading, Separation of Wood Elements are provided, no additional protection is required, unless a specific termite hazard is known to exist. However, foundations and piers of hollow units should have solid masonry caps in which all joints or voids are filled with mortar.

Where local experiences indicate that additional protection against termites is required, one or more of the following barriers should be specified depending on the degree of hazard:

1. Preservatively treated lumber for all floor framing up to and including the sub-floor. For this purpose pressure treatment with an approved preservative is recommended.

2. Properly installed termite shields should be of not less than 26 gauge galvanized iron, or other suitable metal of proper thickness, installed in an approved manner on top of all foundation walls and piers, and around all pipes leading from the ground, Figure 17. Longitudinal joints should be locked and soldered. Where masonry veneer is used the shield should extend through the wall to outside face of the veneer. Figure 10.

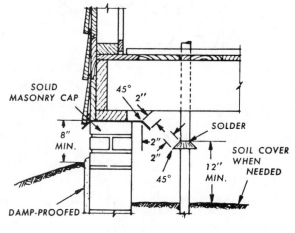

(a) At Exterior Wall

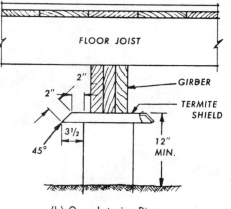

(b) Over Interior Pier

Figure 17

91

3. Chemical soil treatment: The following chemical formulations have been found to be successful and are recommended: aldrin, 0.5 percent in water emulsion or oil solution; benzene hexachloride, 0.8 percent gamma in water emulsion or oil solution; chlordane, 1.0 percent in water emulsion or soil solution; DDT, 8.0 percent in oil; dieldrin, 0.5 percent in water emulsion or oil solution. In general water emulsions are not injurious to plants. Application of chemicals and precautions involved in their use should be in accordance with manufacturers recommendations. Figure 18.

4. Poured concrete foundations, provided no cracks greater than 1/64 inch are present.

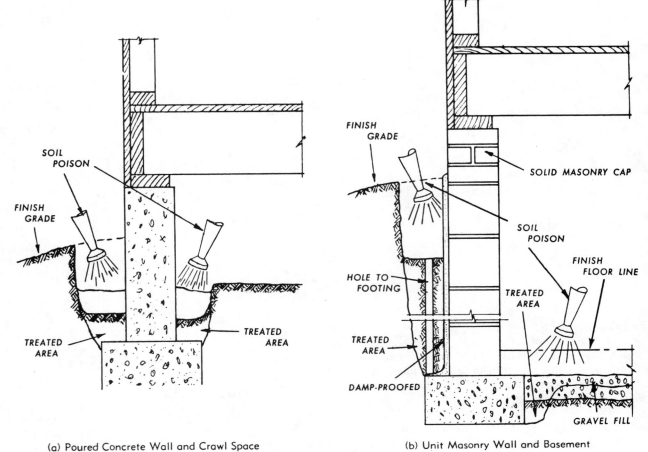

(a) Poured Concrete Wall and Crawl Space

(b) Unit Masonry Wall and Basement

Figure 18

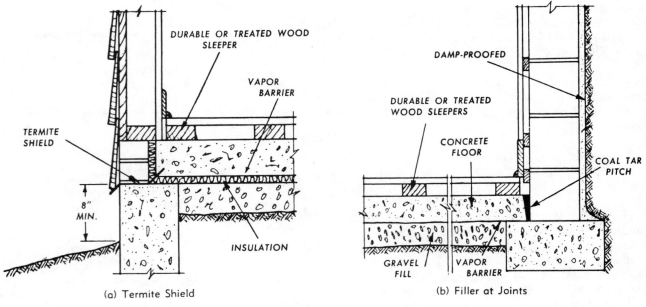

(a) Termite Shield

(b) Filler at Joints

Figure 19

5. Poured reinforced concrete caps, at least 4 inches thick, on unit masonry foundations, provided no cracks greater than 1/64 inch occur.

Any of the barriers mentioned can be installed without major changes in established construction methods. The five types should be considered as alternative methods when additional protection of wood structures is required. It is important to appreciate, however, that periodic inspection is essential to the successful function of any of the barrier types recommended.

Slab-on-Ground Construction requires special consideration in areas where the termite hazard is a significant problem. Concrete slabs vary in their susceptibility to penetration by termites, and cannot be considered to provide adequate protection unless the slab and supporting foundation are poured integrally to avoid cracks or holes through which termites may enter.

Where other types of slab construction are used, termites may penetrate through joints between the slab and wall. They may also enter through expansion joints or openings made for plumbing or conduit. Thus it is necessary to provide a barrier at these points which may be accomplished by the use of termite shields, coal tar pitch, or by chemical soil treatment. Figures 18 & 19.

Masonry veneer in contact with the ground may provide access for termites in infested areas. For this reason the veneer should be kept at least 8 inches above finished grade, unless termite shields are installed in an approved manner or the soil on the exterior has received a chemical treatment. Figure 10.

RECOMMENDATIONS FOR THE USE OF NATURALLY DURABLE OR TREATED WOOD

Approved durable and treated woods are usually recommended for two reasons. First, the location of the member in question may be such that it cannot be maintained at a safe moisture content and second, climatic or site conditions in certain areas may not permit control of decay or termites by construction practices alone.

Where wood is embedded in the ground for the support of permanent structures, it should be of approved pressure-treated wood, except where it is completely below the ground water line or continuously submerged in fresh water.

Wood sleepers and sills resting on a concrete or masonry slab, which is in direct contact with earth, should be of approved durable or treated wood.

Where it is not practical or possible to maintain the clearance between wood and earth previously recommended the appropriate wood framing should be of approved durable or treated wood.

NATURALLY DURABLE HEARTWOOD

Toxic substances deposited by the living tree in the struc-

ture of certain species makes the heartwood of such species resistant to decay or termite attack. Decay resistant commercial species are: Bald Cypress (Tidewater Red), Cedars, Redwood, Black Locust, and Black Walnut. Termite resistant species are: Redwood, Bald Cypress (Tidewater Red), Eastern Red Cedar.

Naturally durable heartwood may be speciied for all conditions of exposure except for members embedded in the ground to support permanent structures. For maximum durability, specifications should require 100 percent heartwood.

TREATED WOOD

The effectiveness of preservative treatment is dependent upon the following factors: (a) type of chemical used, (b) amount of penetration, (c) amount of retention and, (d) uniform distribution of preservative. It is important to select the right preservative and to specify the correct retention for the intended exposure.

Where possible, wood members selected for treatment should be dimensioned and machined prior to preservative application. When such precutting is not feasible, all untreated surfaces exposed by sawing, planing, boring or routing, must be treated with a liberal application of the preservative used in the initial treatment. This is accomplished by brushing, spraying, dipping, or soaking the untreated surfaces with the preservative.

NON-PRESSURE TREATED WOOD

Wood may be preservatively treated by one of the following non-pressure processes: (a) cold soaking or dipping in which the immersion time is dictated by the desired retention and end penetration; and (b) vacuum process or hot-and-cold-bath method using treating cycles designed to produce the desired retention and penetration.

Preservatives used for non-pressure treated wood are of two types:

(1) Water repellent preservative—a solution of light petroleum solvent containing water repellent materials and a minimum of 5% by weight of pentachlorophenol, meeting the standards of the National Woodwork Manufacturers Association. This treatment can be painted.

(2) Oil-borne preservative—a solution of heavier petroleum solvent containing 5% by weight of pentachlorophenol meeting the American Wood-Preservers' Association standard P9. This treatment is not recommended for painting.

These treatments are intended to provide resistance to moderate exposures and, in the case of the water repellant preservative, to retard liquid moisture absorption as well. Their effectiveness is based on the fact that the end grain of wood readily absorbs the preservative to a sufficient depth for adequate protection. Penetration of side grain, however, is usually less than that obtained by pressure treatment.

Moderate exposure implies that the wood is dry most of the time but may be occasionally damp enough to permit decay to occur. In general, the non-pressure treatments are effective for protection where the thinness and dryness of the member permits sufficient penetration and retention.

Non-pressure treatments have been widely used for window sash and doors and their frames, as well as for wood siding and miscellaneous exterior trim. The water repellent preservatives have the extra advantage of providing better paint performance on these items. Other recommended applications include: fence parts not in contact with the ground; ends of joists framed into masonry below grade; and exterior stairs, porch framing and trim. Where wood members are exposed to the weather, ends which abut or are held by fastenings which tend to retain moisture are effectively protected by non-pressure treatment.

MAINTENANCE INSPECTIONS

To supplement the design and construction details recommended, periodic inspections of the structure are necessary. Such inspections should concentrate on three specific areas: (1) foundations, including crawl spaces, (2) attic spaces and roofs, and (3) exterior surfaces, joints and architectural details.

Usually an annual inspection in early spring is sufficient. In warmer climates where termites are more active, semi-annual inspections of foundations and crawl spaces are recommended. It is also advisable to check enclosed spaces during periods of severe prolonged cold weather for evidence of condensation.

Since decay protection is inherent in structures designed according to recommendations previously outlined, the primary function of periodic inspections is to detect evidence of termite activity. When shelter tubes are discovered, they should be destroyed and the ground below should be poisoned. If crawl-space soil is noticeably damp, vents should be checked or a soil cover provided.

It should be emphasized that damage from decay or termites develops slowly. Periodic inspections will provide assurance that proper clearances are being maintained and that termite barriers have not been breached. They will also reveal symptoms which are indicative of moisture penetration or condensation. Once detected by inspection there is ample time to take corrective action before significant damage has occurred.

INTRODUCTION

Nine out of ten homes in this country are of wood frame construction. Many of them are covered with wood siding, others may be covered with wood shingles, composition shingles or siding, brick veneer or stucco. Regardless of the type of exterior covering, these houses are in the general classification of wood frame construction.

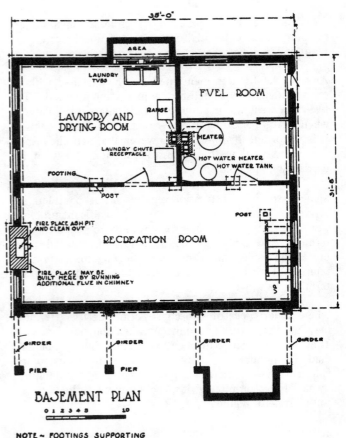

BASEMENT PLAN

0 1 2 3 4 5   10

NOTE ~ FOOTINGS SUPPORTING WOODEN POSTS AND COLUMNS SHOULD EXTEND ABOVE THE FINISH FLOOR. EACH END OF SUCH POST OR COLUMN SHOULD BE GIVEN TWO BRUSH APPLICATIONS OF HOT REFINED CREOSOTE TO PREVENT DECAY.

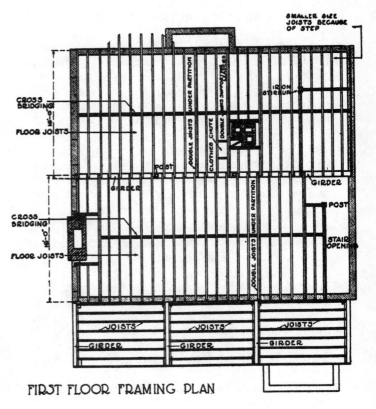

FIRST FLOOR FRAMING PLAN

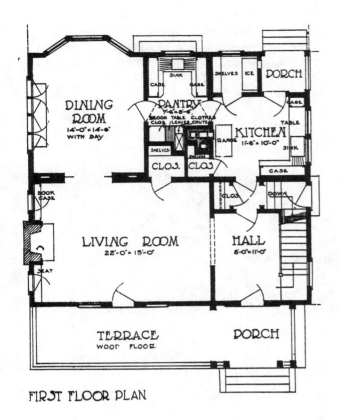

FIRST FLOOR PLAN

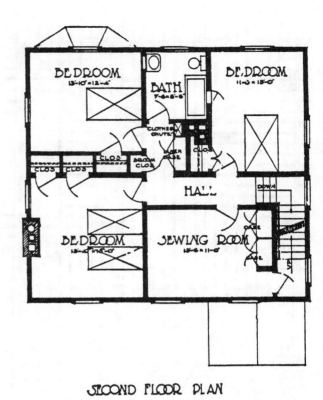

SECOND FLOOR PLAN

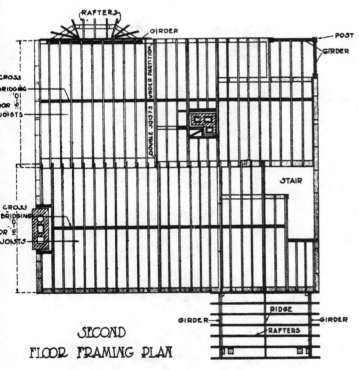

SECOND
FLOOR FRAMING PLAN

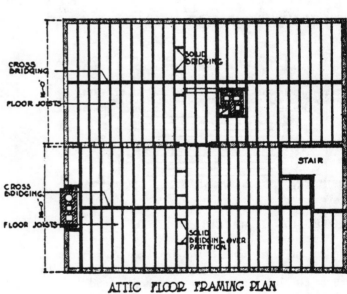

ATTIC FLOOR FRAMING PLAN

Wood framed houses are preferred for a number of important reasons In general, frame construction costs less than other types or provides more house for a given price. It provides better insulation, thereby increasing comfort to the occupants and reducing fuel and air-conditioning bills. The various patterns of exterior wood siding and the range of exterior paints and finishes, compatible with wood, enable architects and builders to produce any architectural style.

A well-built wood frame home is one of the most durable types of structure. Some of the oldest existing buildings in the United States are of this type. Moreover, the flexibility of wood as a building material has assured its continued popularity for the most modern architectural efforts.

With any type of structure, sound construction practices must be followed to assure durability and trouble-free performance. This information provides recommendations and illustrations which will serve as a guide to proper construction with wood.

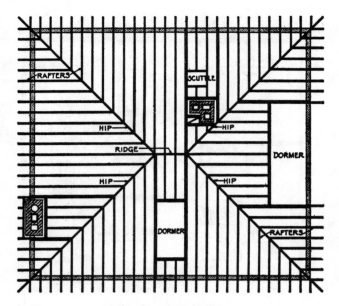

ROOF FRAMING PLAN

NOTES—FRAME BUILDINGS SHOULD BE DESIGNED TO APPLY STANDARD LENGTHS OF LUMBER.
STANDARD LENGTHS ARE MANUFACTURED IN MULTIPLES OF TWO FEET UP TO LENGTH OF TWENTY FOUR FEET.
WHERE GIRDERS OR OTHER MEMBERS ARE BUILT UP, SECTIONS SHOULD BE SECURELY SPIKED TOGETHER.
THE CUTTING OF BEAMS, GIRDERS, JOISTS OR OTHER SUPPORTING TIMBERS SHOULD BE DONE IN SUCH MANNER AS NOT TO REDUCE THE STRENGTH OF SUCH TIMBERS.
ALL JOISTS UNDER PARTITIONS, AROUND LARGE OPENINGS, CHIMNEYS ETC. SHOULD BE DOUBLED.
ALL TIMBER BEARING MEMBERS SHOULD BE LAID CROWN EDGE UP TOPS AND ENDS OF PORCH TIMBERS SHOULD RECEIVE TWO BRUSH APPLICATIONS OF HOT REFINED CREOSOTE, OR OTHER PRESERVATIVE.
STUDS SHOULD BE DOUBLED UNDER ENDS OF ALL DOUBLE JOISTS.
DISTANCE BETWEEN ROWS OF CROSS BRIDGING OR CROSS BRIDGING AND BEARING SHOULD NOT EXCEED EIGHT FEET.

WHEN THE SIZE OF LUMBER IS GIVEN IN WHOLE NUMBERS AMERICAN STANDARD NOMINAL SIZES ARE MEANT. STRESSES SHOULD BE BASED ON THE ACTUAL SIZE OF MATERIAL USED.
THE MINIMUM ACTUAL SIZE OF LUMBER SIGNIFIED BY WHOLE NUMBERS SHALL NOT BE LESS THAN AS FOLLOWS.

NOMINAL SIZE.	ACTUAL FINISHED SIZE.
2 X 4	1⅝ X 3⅝
2 X 6	1⅝ X 5⅝
2 X 8	1⅝ X 7½
2 X 10	1⅝ X 9½
2 X 12	1⅝ X 11½
3 X 4	2⅝ X 3⅝
3 X 6	2⅝ X 5⅝
3 X 8	2⅝ X 7½
3 X 10	2⅝ X 9½
3 X 12	2⅝ X 11½

FOR POSTS 5X5 AND LARGER, AND FOR BEAMS 5X6 AND LARGER THE FINISHED SIZE MAY BE ½" SMALLER IN EACH DIMENSION THAN THE NOMINAL SIZE.

PROTECTION OF MATERIALS AT SITE

Lumber and other items of woodwork should be protected from the weather upon apprival at the building site. It is well to establish a schedule so that lumber and millwork will be delivered only as needed, and to follow these simple rules:

(1) Keep piles of lumber at least six inches above ground and protect them with a waterproof cover. Finish lumber, particularly, should be kept under cover—preferably in-doors—until it is installed.

(2) Store door and window frames, siding and exterior trim inside. Where this is not possible, they should be kept off the ground and covered. These items are often pre-treated when received. Untreated millwork should receive a water repellent treatment or a priming coat of paint when delivered.

(3) Store interior doors, trim, flooring and cabinet work in the building. Wet plaster should be allowed to dry before interior finish, cabinets, flooring or paneling are delivered unless other protected storage is available.

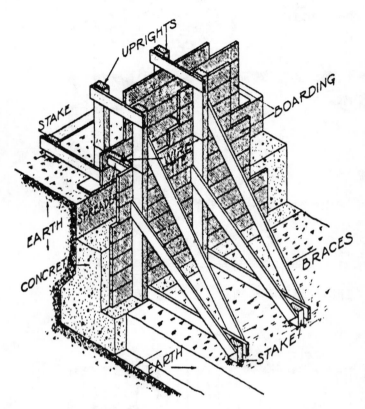

FORMS FOR WALL IN SOLID EARTH

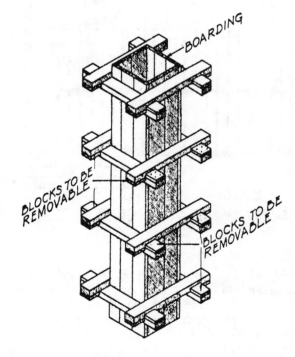

FORMS FOR PIERS

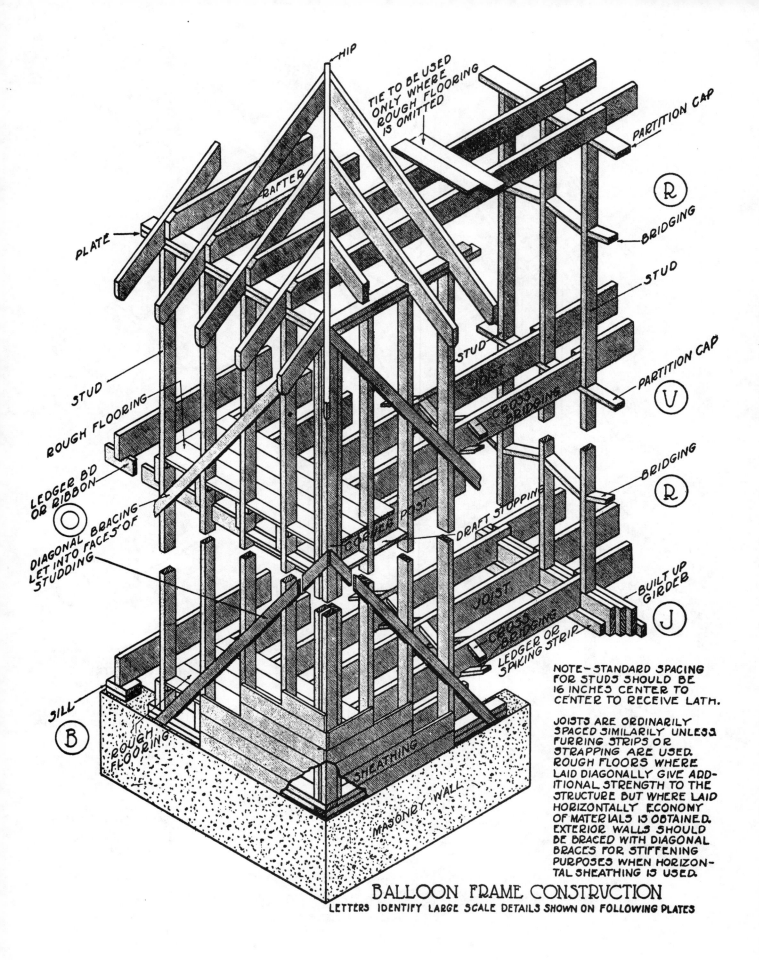

HIP

TIE TO BE USED ONLY WHERE ROUGH FLOORING IS OMITTED

PARTITION CAP

RAFTER

Ⓡ

PLATE

BRIDGING

STUD

STUD

ROUGH FLOORING

JOIST

STUD

PARTITION CAP

Ⓥ

CROSS BRIDGING

LEDGER B'D OR RIBBON

BRIDGING

Ⓞ

DIAGONAL BRACING LET INTO FACES OF STUDDING

CORNER POST

DRAFT STOPPING

Ⓡ

JOIST

BUILT UP GIRDER

CROSS BRIDGING

Ⓙ

LEDGER OR SPIKING STRIP

SILL

NOTE—STANDARD SPACING FOR STUDS SHOULD BE 16 INCHES CENTER TO CENTER TO RECEIVE LATH.

Ⓑ

ROUGH FLOORING

JOISTS ARE ORDINARILY SPACED SIMILARILY UNLESS FURRING STRIPS OR STRAPPING ARE USED. ROUGH FLOORS WHERE LAID DIAGONALLY GIVE ADDITIONAL STRENGTH TO THE STRUCTURE BUT WHERE LAID HORIZONTALLY ECONOMY OF MATERIALS IS OBTAINED. EXTERIOR WALLS SHOULD BE BRACED WITH DIAGONAL BRACES FOR STIFFENING PURPOSES WHEN HORIZONTAL SHEATHING IS USED.

SHEATHING

MASONRY WALL

BALLOON FRAME CONSTRUCTION
LETTERS IDENTIFY LARGE SCALE DETAILS SHOWN ON FOLLOWING PLATES

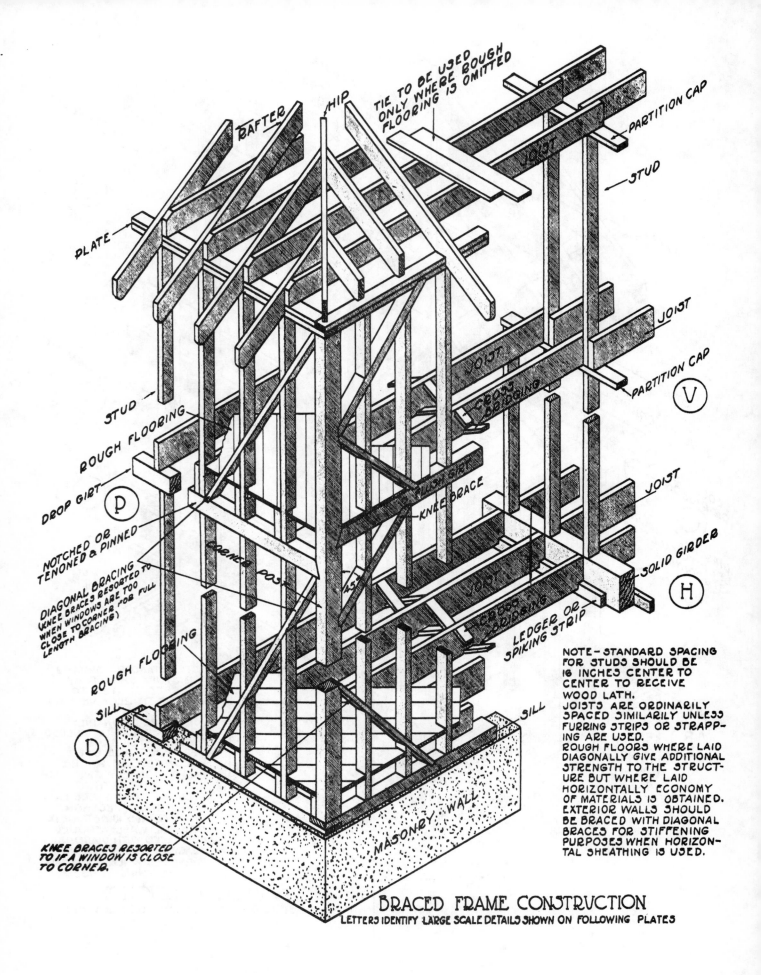

BRACED FRAME CONSTRUCTION
LETTERS IDENTIFY LARGE SCALE DETAILS SHOWN ON FOLLOWING PLATES

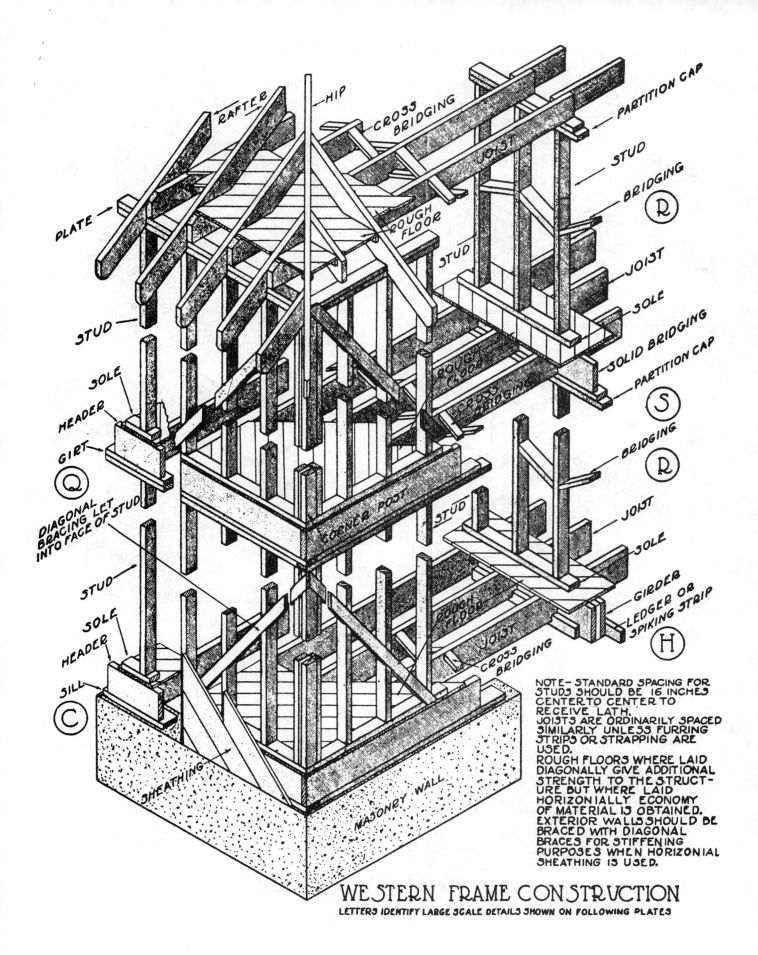

RAFTER — HIP — CROSS BRIDGING — PARTITION CAP

PLATE — ROUGH FLOOR — JOIST

STUD — STUD — BRIDGING — ⓡ

SOLE — ROUGH FLOOR — JOIST

HEADER — CROSS BRIDGING — SOLE

GIRT — SOLID BRIDGING

ⓠ — PARTITION CAP

DIAGONAL BRACING LET INTO FACE OF STUD — ⓢ

CORNER POST — STUD — BRIDGING — ⓡ

STUD — JOIST

SOLE — SOLE

HEADER — ROUGH FLOOR — GIRDER

SILL — JOIST — LEDGER OR SPIKING STRIP

ⓒ — CROSS BRIDGING — ⓗ

SHEATHING

MASONRY WALL

NOTE— STANDARD SPACING FOR STUDS SHOULD BE 16 INCHES CENTER TO CENTER TO RECEIVE LATH.
JOISTS ARE ORDINARILY SPACED SIMILARLY UNLESS FURRING STRIPS OR STRAPPING ARE USED.
ROUGH FLOORS WHERE LAID DIAGONALLY GIVE ADDITIONAL STRENGTH TO THE STRUCTURE BUT WHERE LAID HORIZONIALLY ECONOMY OF MATERIAL IS OBTAINED.
EXTERIOR WALLS SHOULD BE BRACED WITH DIAGONAL BRACES FOR STIFFENING PURPOSES WHEN HORIZONIAL SHEATHING IS USED.

WESTERN FRAME CONSTRUCTION
LETTERS IDENTIFY LARGE SCALE DETAILS SHOWN ON FOLLOWING PLATES

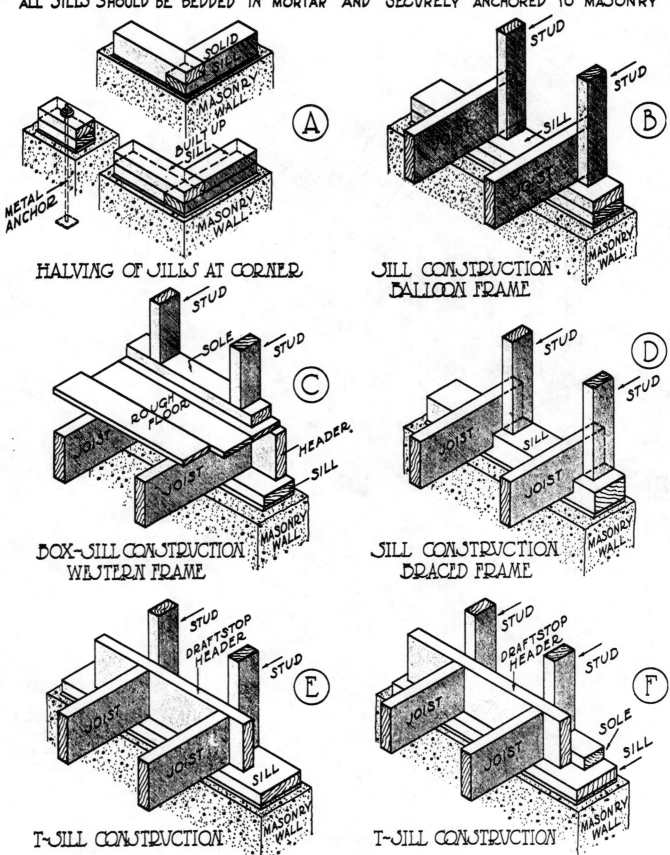

HALVING OF SILLS AT CORNER

SILL CONSTRUCTION
BALLOON FRAME

BOX-SILL CONSTRUCTION
WESTERN FRAME

SILL CONSTRUCTION
BRACED FRAME

T-SILL CONSTRUCTION

T-SILL CONSTRUCTION

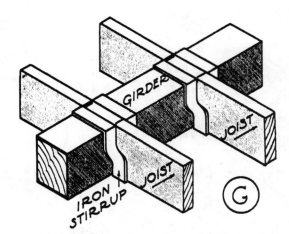

JOISTS HUNG ON GIRDER
WITH IRON STIRRUPS

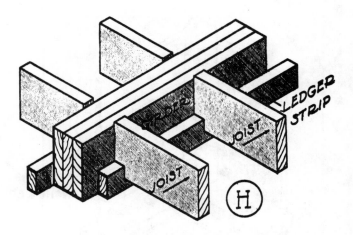

GIRDER CONSTRUCTION TO
EQUALIZE SHRINKAGE
BRACED & WESTERN FRAME

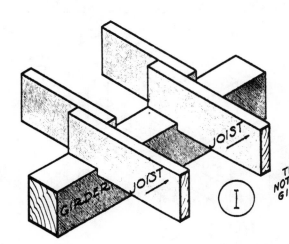

JOISTS SIZED DOWN 1 IN
ON GIRDER WITH LAP

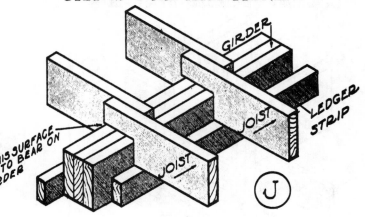

GIRDER CONSTRUCTION TO
EQUALIZE SHRINKAGE
BALLOON FRAME

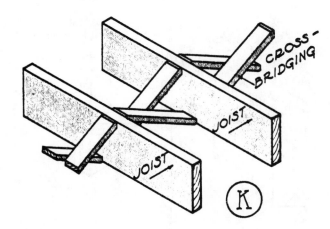

CROSS-BRIDGING BETWEEN JOISTS

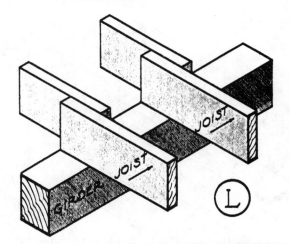

JOISTS LAPPED ON TOP OF GIRDER

DIMINISHED DEPTH OF BEAM AT BEARING POINTS REDUCES CARRYING CAPACITY.

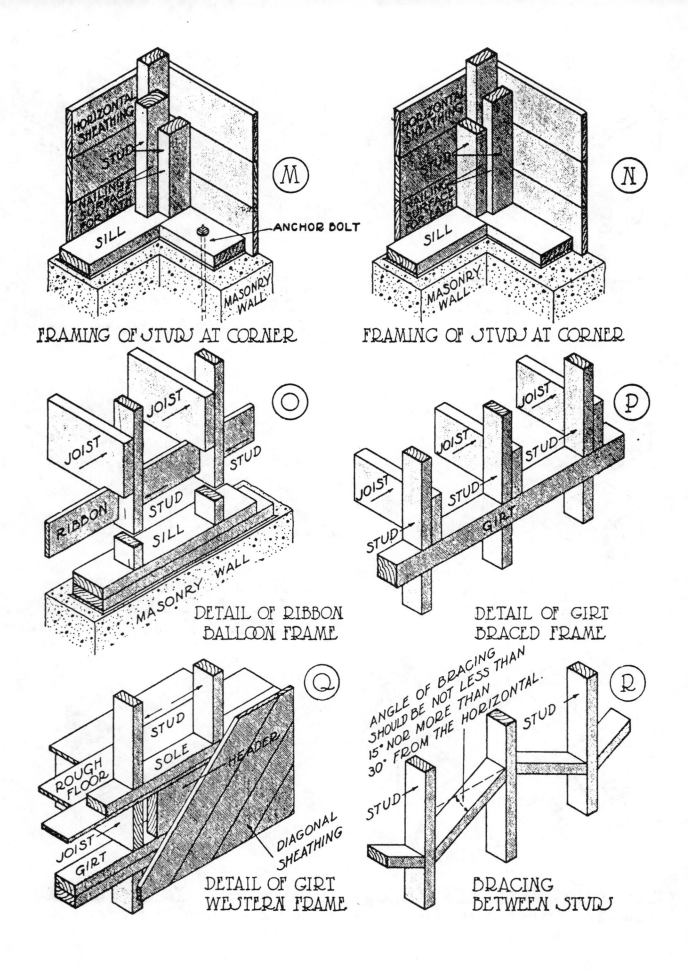

HORIZONTAL SHEATHING

STUD

NAILING SURFACE FOR LATH

SILL

ANCHOR BOLT

MASONRY WALL

Ⓜ

FRAMING OF STUDS AT CORNER

HORIZONTAL SHEATHING

STUD

NAILING SURFACE FOR LATH

SILL

MASONRY WALL

Ⓝ

FRAMING OF STUDS AT CORNER

JOIST

JOIST

STUD

RIBBON

STUD

SILL

MASONRY WALL

Ⓞ

DETAIL OF RIBBON
BALLOON FRAME

JOIST

JOIST

STUD

STUD

GIRT

Ⓟ

DETAIL OF GIRT
BRACED FRAME

STUD

SOLE

ROUGH FLOOR

HEADER

JOIST

GIRT

DIAGONAL SHEATHING

Ⓠ

DETAIL OF GIRT
WESTERN FRAME

ANGLE OF BRACING
SHOULD BE NOT LESS THAN
15° NOR MORE THAN
30° FROM THE HORIZONTAL.

STUD

STUD

STUD

Ⓡ

BRACING
BETWEEN STUDS

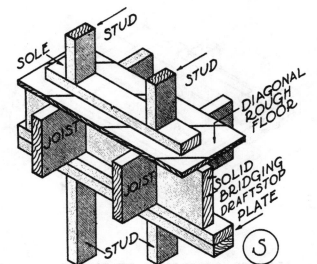

PARTITION AT RIGHT ANGLES TO JOISTS
WESTERN FRAME

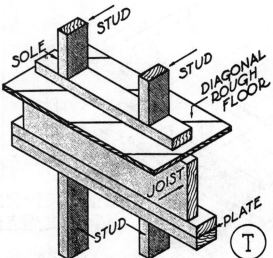

PARTITION PARALLEL WITH JOISTS
WESTERN FRAME

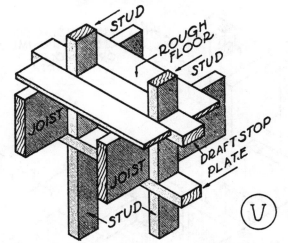

PARTITION AT RIGHT ANGLES TO JOISTS
BALLOON AND
BRACED FRAME

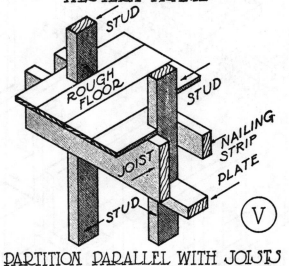

PARTITION PARALLEL WITH JOISTS
BALLOON AND
BRACED FRAME

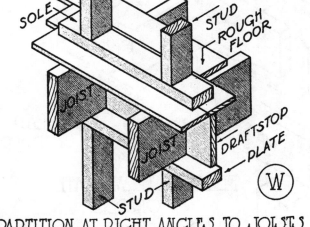

PARTITION AT RIGHT ANGLES TO JOISTS
BALLOON FRAME

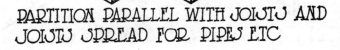

PARTITION PARALLEL WITH JOISTS AND
JOISTS SPREAD FOR PIPES ETC

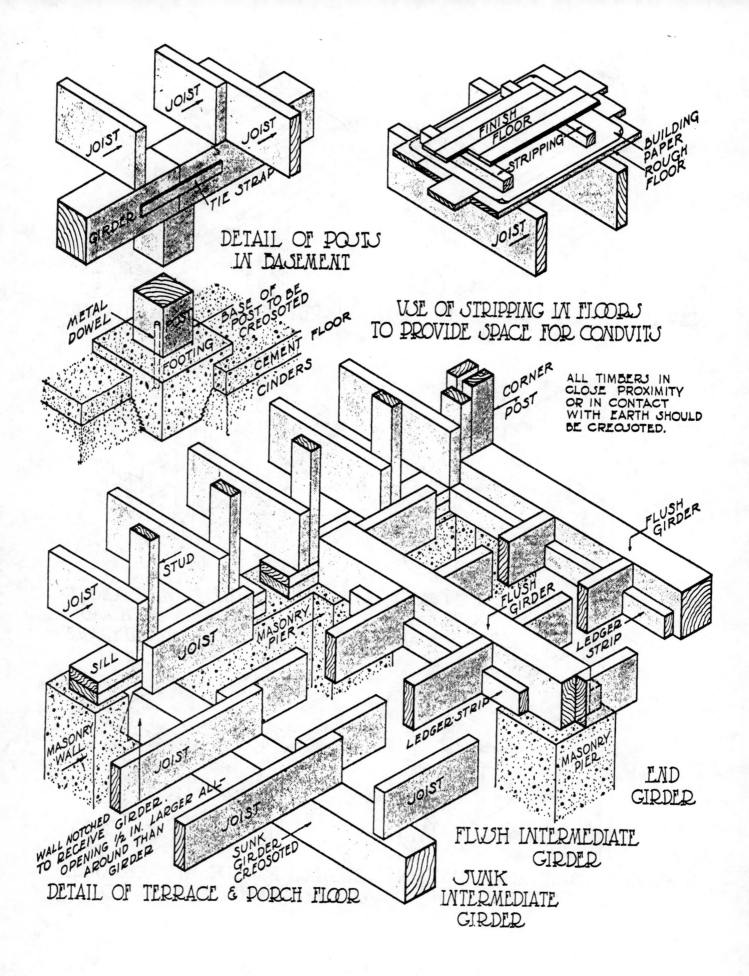

DETAIL OF POSTS
IN BASEMENT

JOIST

JOIST

JOIST

GIRDER

TIE STRAP

FINISH FLOOR

STRIPPING

BUILDING PAPER
ROUGH FLOOR

JOIST

METAL DOWEL

POST

BASE OF POST TO BE CREOSOTED

FOOTING

CEMENT FLOOR

CINDERS

USE OF STRIPPING IN FLOORS
TO PROVIDE SPACE FOR CONDUITS

CORNER POST

ALL TIMBERS IN CLOSE PROXIMITY OR IN CONTACT WITH EARTH SHOULD BE CREOSOTED.

FLUSH GIRDER

STUD

JOIST

JOIST

MASONRY PIER

FLUSH GIRDER

LEDGER STRIP

SILL

MASONRY WALL

JOIST

LEDGER STRIP

JOIST

MASONRY PIER

END GIRDER

WALL NOTCHED TO RECEIVE GIRDER OPENING ½ IN. LARGER ALL AROUND THAN GIRDER

JOIST

SUNK GIRDER CREOSOTED

FLUSH INTERMEDIATE GIRDER

SUNK INTERMEDIATE GIRDER

DETAIL OF TERRACE & PORCH FLOOR

104

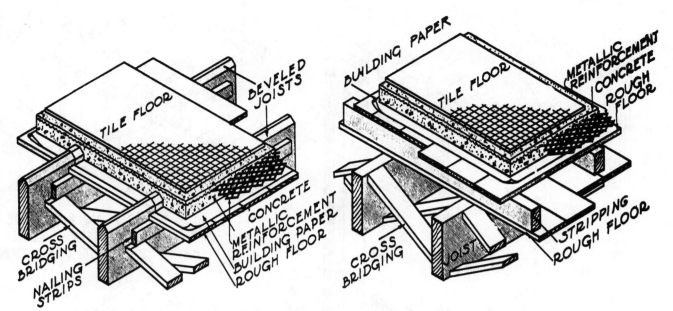

TILE FLOOR FLUSH WITH MAIN FLOOR   TILE FLOOR STEPPED UP
METHODS OF LAYING TILE FLOORS

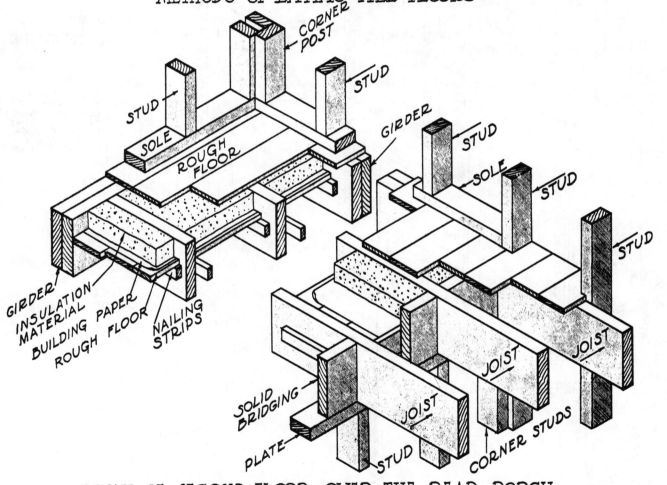

DETAIL OF SECOND FLOOR OVER THE REAR PORCH

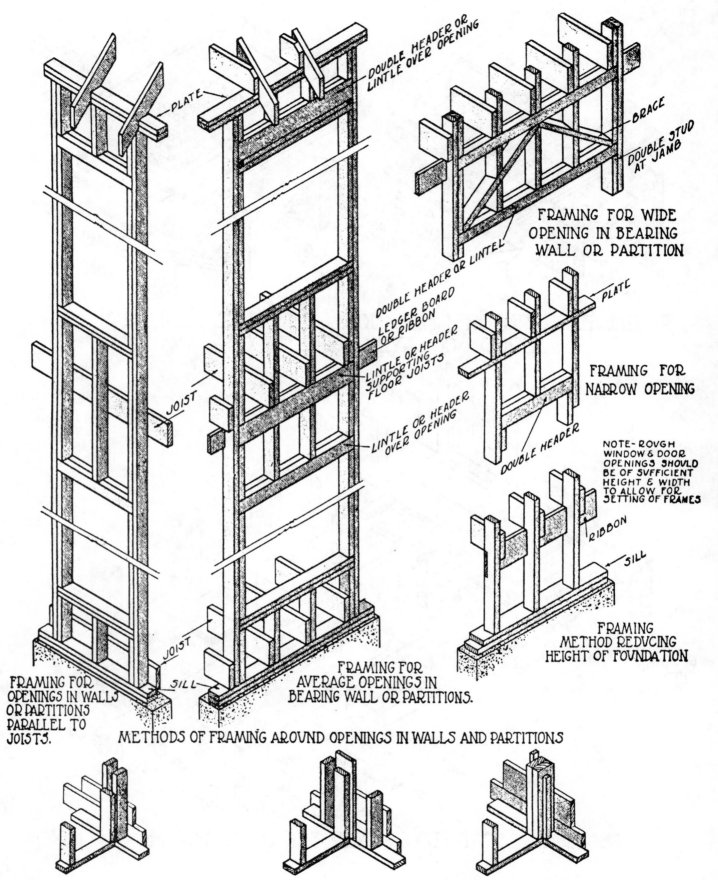

PLATE

DOUBLE HEADER OR LINTLE OVER OPENING

JOIST

JOIST

SILL

FRAMING FOR OPENINGS IN WALLS OR PARTITIONS PARALLEL TO JOISTS.

DOUBLE HEADER OR LINTEL

LEDGER BOARD OR RIBBON

LINTLE OR HEADER SUPPORTING FLOOR JOISTS

LINTLE OR HEADER OVER OPENING

JOIST

SILL

FRAMING FOR AVERAGE OPENINGS IN BEARING WALL OR PARTITIONS.

BRACE

DOUBLE STUD AT JAMB

LINTEL

FRAMING FOR WIDE OPENING IN BEARING WALL OR PARTITION

PLATE

FRAMING FOR NARROW OPENING

DOUBLE HEADER

NOTE- ROUGH WINDOW & DOOR OPENINGS SHOULD BE OF SUFFICIENT HEIGHT & WIDTH TO ALLOW FOR SETTING OF FRAMES

RIBBON

SILL

FRAMING METHOD REDUCING HEIGHT OF FOUNDATION

METHODS OF FRAMING AROUND OPENINGS IN WALLS AND PARTITIONS

METHODS OF FRAMING STUDS AT PARTITION CORNERS

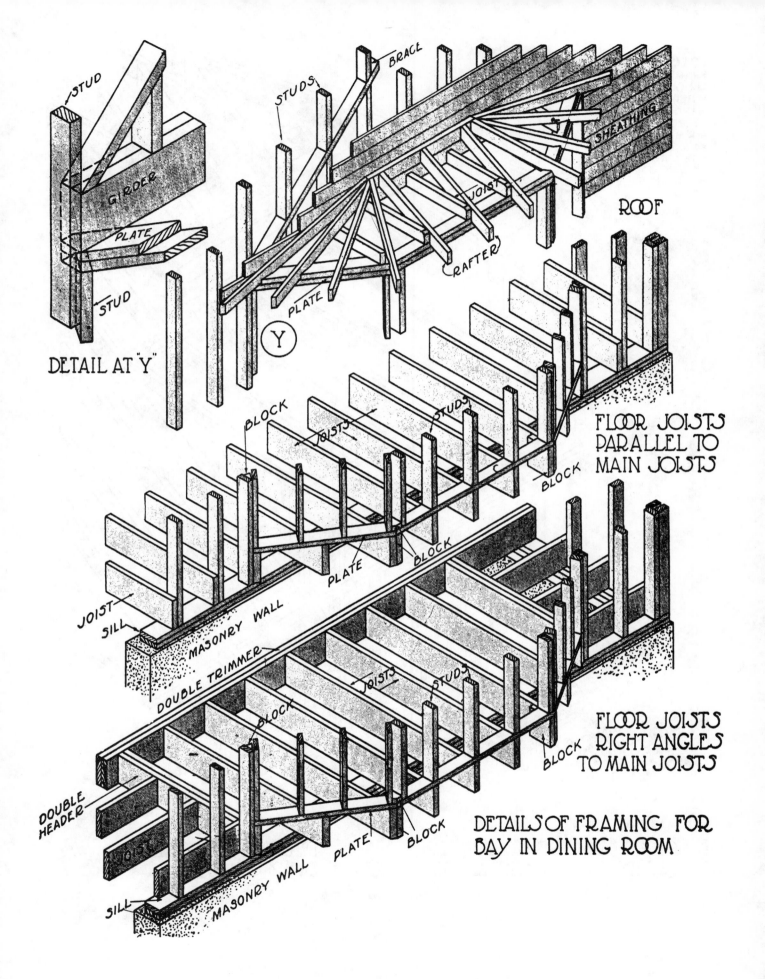

DETAIL AT "Y"

ROOF

FLOOR JOISTS
PARALLEL TO
MAIN JOISTS

FLOOR JOISTS
RIGHT ANGLES
TO MAIN JOISTS

DETAILS OF FRAMING FOR
BAY IN DINING ROOM

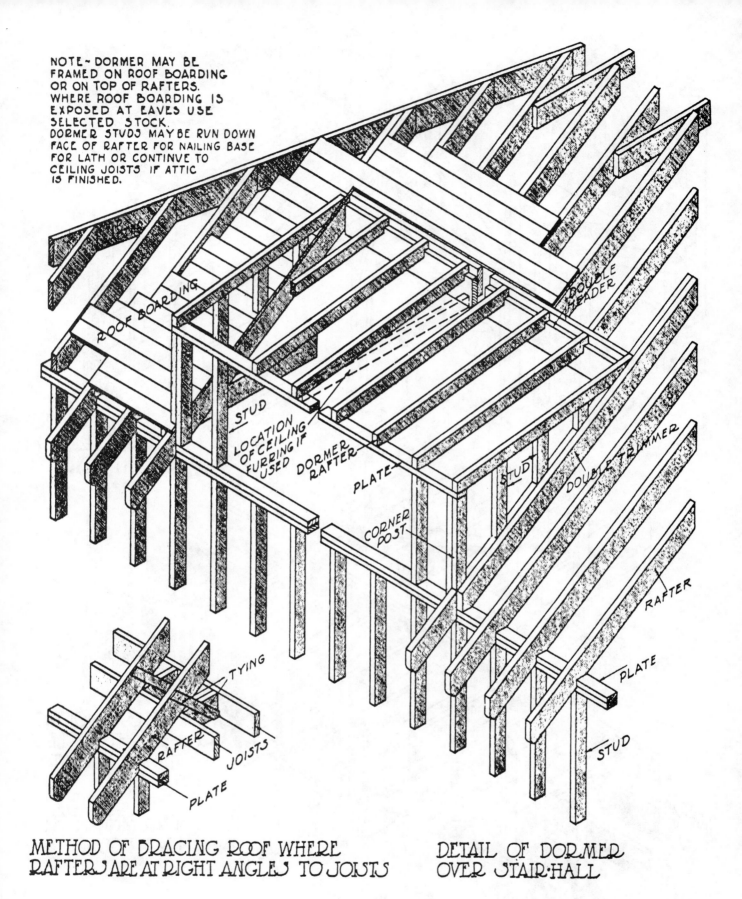

NOTE ~ DORMER MAY BE
FRAMED ON ROOF BOARDING
OR ON TOP OF RAFTERS.
WHERE ROOF BOARDING IS
EXPOSED AT EAVES USE
SELECTED STOCK.
DORMER STUDS MAY BE RUN DOWN
FACE OF RAFTER FOR NAILING BASE
FOR LATH OR CONTINUE TO
CEILING JOISTS IF ATTIC
IS FINISHED.

ROOF BOARDING

DOUBLE HEADER

STUD

LOCATION
OF CEILING
FURRING IF
USED

DORMER
RAFTER

PLATE

STUD

DOUBLE TRIMMER

CORNER
POST

RAFTER

PLATE

STUD

TYING

RAFTER

JOISTS

PLATE

METHOD OF BRACING ROOF WHERE
RAFTERS ARE AT RIGHT ANGLES TO JOISTS

DETAIL OF DORMER
OVER STAIR HALL

108

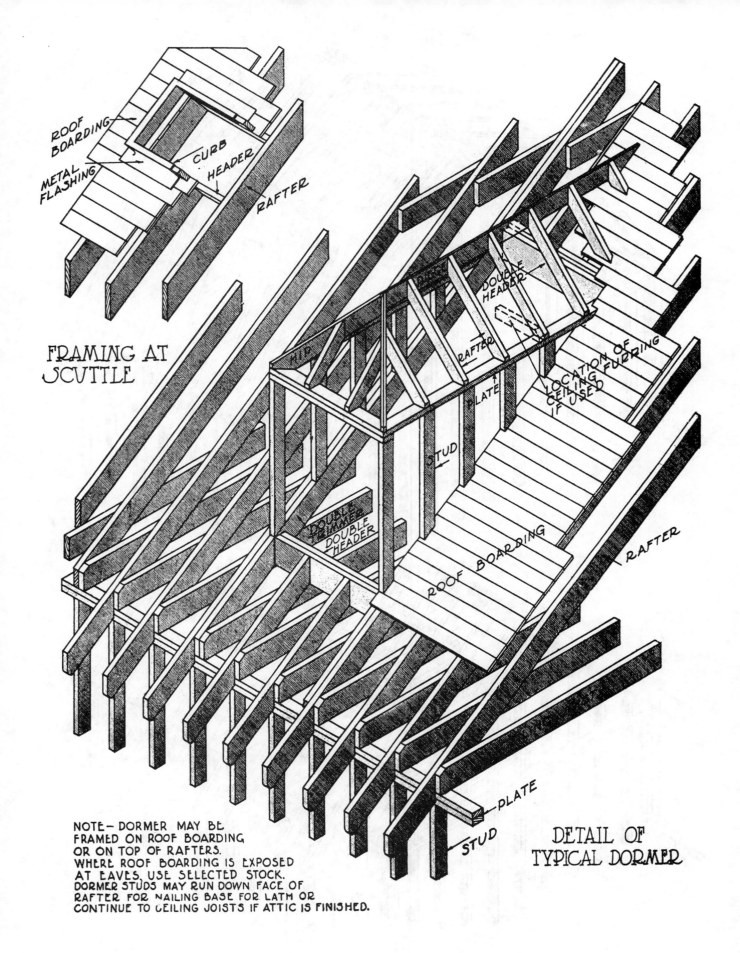

ROOF BOARDING

METAL FLASHING

CURB

HEADER

RAFTER

FRAMING AT SCUTTLE

HIP

DOUBLE HEADER

RAFTER

PLATE

LOCATION OF CEILING FURRING IF USED

STUD

DOUBLE TRIMMER

DOUBLE HEADER

ROOF BOARDING

RAFTER

PLATE

STUD

NOTE— DORMER MAY BE FRAMED ON ROOF BOARDING OR ON TOP OF RAFTERS. WHERE ROOF BOARDING IS EXPOSED AT EAVES, USE SELECTED STOCK. DORMER STUDS MAY RUN DOWN FACE OF RAFTER FOR NAILING BASE FOR LATH OR CONTINUE TO CEILING JOISTS IF ATTIC IS FINISHED.

DETAIL OF TYPICAL DORMER

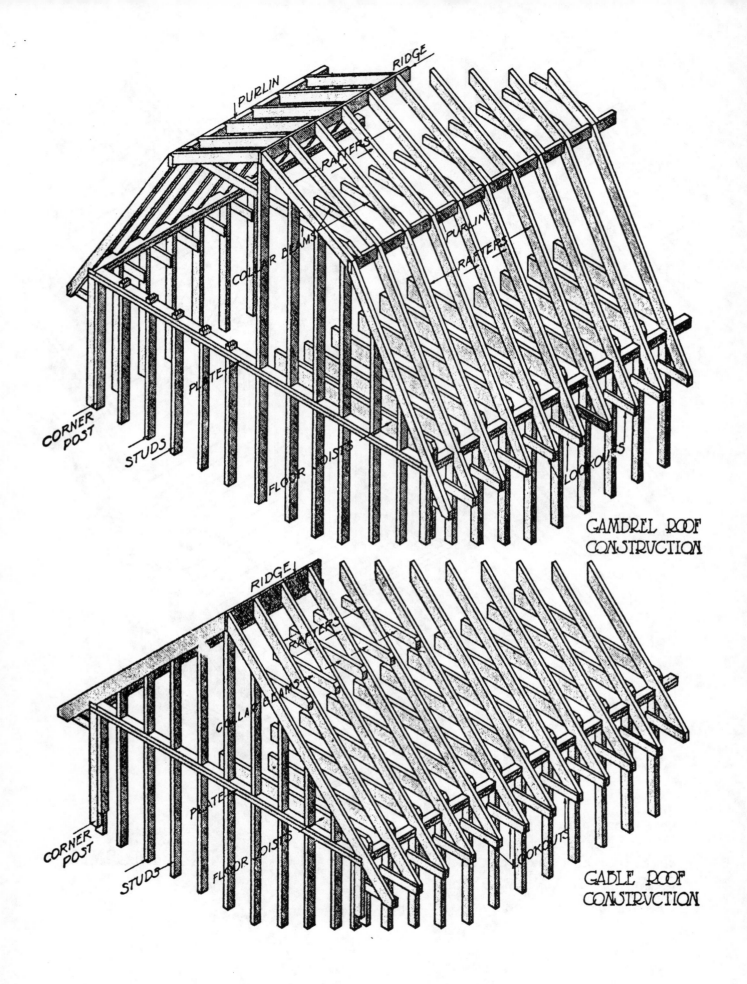

PURLIN   RIDGE

RAFTERS

COLLAR BEAMS

PURLIN

RAFTERS

PLATE

CORNER POST

STUDS

FLOOR JOISTS

LOOKOUTS

GAMBREL ROOF CONSTRUCTION

RIDGE

RAFTERS

COLLAR BEAMS

PLATE

CORNER POST

STUDS

FLOOR JOISTS

LOOKOUTS

GABLE ROOF CONSTRUCTION

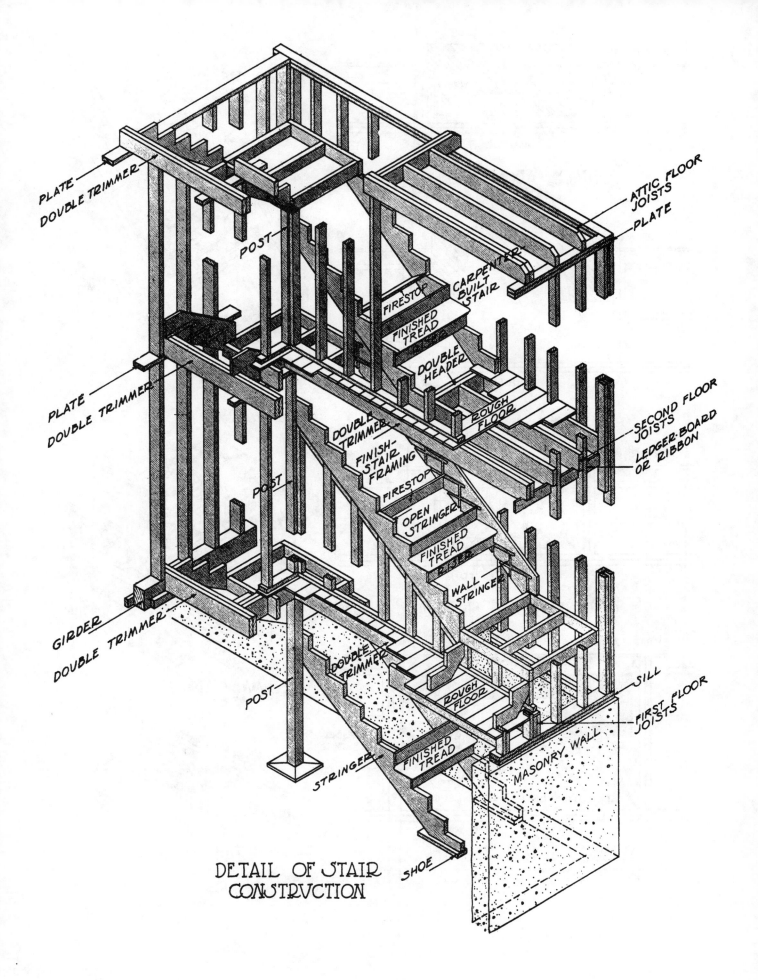

PLATE

DOUBLE TRIMMER

POST

PLATE

DOUBLE TRIMMER

POST

GIRDER

DOUBLE TRIMMER

POST

ATTIC FLOOR JOISTS

PLATE

FIRESTOP

CARPENTER BUILT STAIR

FINISHED TREAD

DOUBLE HEADER

DOUBLE TRIMMER

ROUGH FLOOR

FINISH-STAIR FRAMING

SECOND FLOOR JOISTS

LEDGER-BOARD OR RIBBON

FIRESTOP

OPEN STRINGER

FINISHED TREAD

WALL STRINGER

SILL

FIRST FLOOR JOISTS

DOUBLE TRIMMER

ROUGH FLOOR

FINISHED TREAD

MASONRY WALL

STRINGER

SHOE

DETAIL OF STAIR CONSTRUCTION

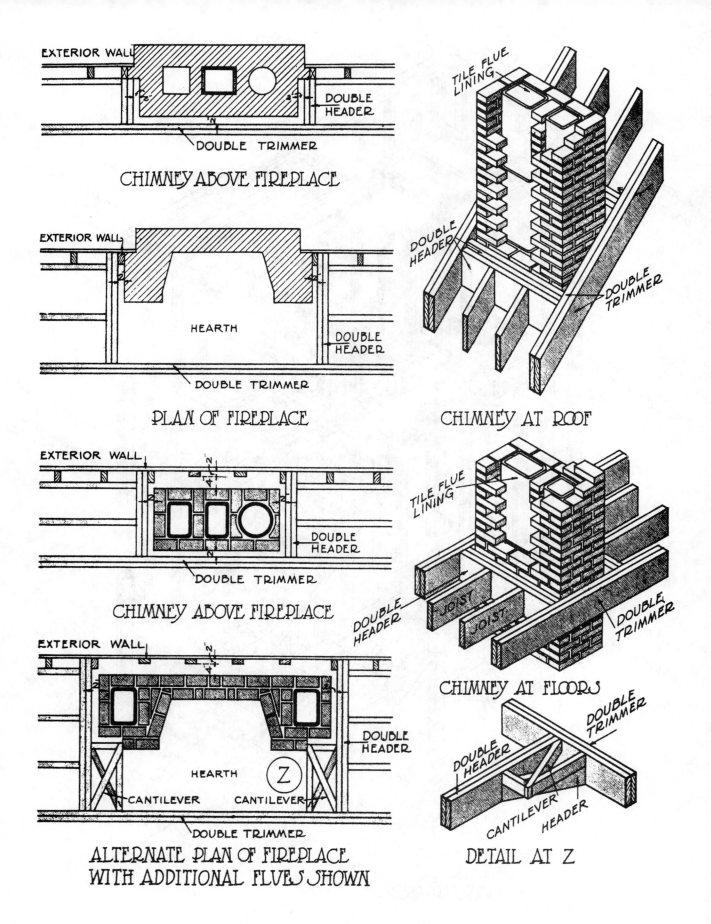

CHIMNEY ABOVE FIREPLACE

EXTERIOR WALL

DOUBLE HEADER

DOUBLE TRIMMER

PLAN OF FIREPLACE

EXTERIOR WALL

HEARTH

DOUBLE HEADER

DOUBLE TRIMMER

CHIMNEY ABOVE FIREPLACE

EXTERIOR WALL

DOUBLE HEADER

DOUBLE TRIMMER

ALTERNATE PLAN OF FIREPLACE
WITH ADDITIONAL FLUES SHOWN

EXTERIOR WALL

HEARTH

Z

CANTILEVER   CANTILEVER

DOUBLE TRIMMER

CHIMNEY AT ROOF

TILE FLUE LINING

DOUBLE HEADER

DOUBLE TRIMMER

CHIMNEY AT FLOORS

TILE FLUE LINING

DOUBLE HEADER

JOIST

JOIST

DOUBLE TRIMMER

DETAIL AT Z

DOUBLE TRIMMER

DOUBLE HEADER

CANTILEVER   HEADER

PLATFORM FRAME CONSTRUCTION

In platform construction, the subfloor extends to the outside edges of the building and provides a platform upon which exterior walls and interior partitions are erected. Platform construction is the type of framing most generally used for one-story houses. It is also used alone or in combination with balloon construction for two-story structures. Building techniques in some parts of the country have been developed almost entirely around the platform system. Figure 1.

Platform construction is easier to erect because it provides a flat surface, at each floor level, on which to work. It is also easily adapted to various methods of prefabrication. With a platform framing system, it is common practice to assemble the wall framing on the floor and then tilt the entire unit into place.

BALLOON FRAME CONSTRUCTION

In balloon frame construction both studs and first-floor joists rest on the anchored sill. The second-floor joists bear on a 1 x 4-inch ribbon strip which has been let into the in-

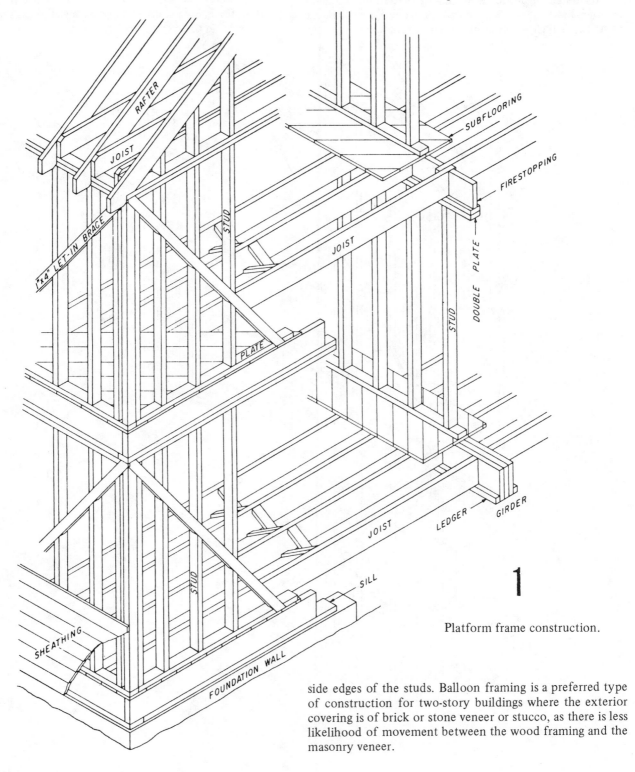

1

Platform frame construction.

side edges of the studs. Balloon framing is a preferred type of construction for two-story buildings where the exterior covering is of brick or stone veneer or stucco, as there is less likelihood of movement between the wood framing and the masonry veneer.

113

Where exterior walls are of solid masonry, it is also desirable to use balloon framing for interior bearing partitions. It eliminates variations in settlement which may occur between exterior walls and interior supports. Figure 2.

FASTENINGS

Nails are used most generally for fastening 1- and 2-inch framing lumber. The minimum recommended schedule for common wire nails is included in Table I. Other types of nails, including those with annular of spiral grooves, have demonstrated higher load-carrying capacities, but their use is often limited to special purposes. They have particular value where high withdrawal resistance is required.

Nailed joints are strongest when the load is acting at right angles to the nails. Joints, where the load is applied parallel to the nail in such way as to cause withdrawal, should be avoided since nails are weakest when loaded in this manner. Figure 3.

Sometimes, the most practical way to fasten wood members is toe-nailing, in which nails are driven at an approximate 30-degree angle with the grain. It is a preferred method for nailing studs to sills where wall sheathing does not serve to tie these members together.

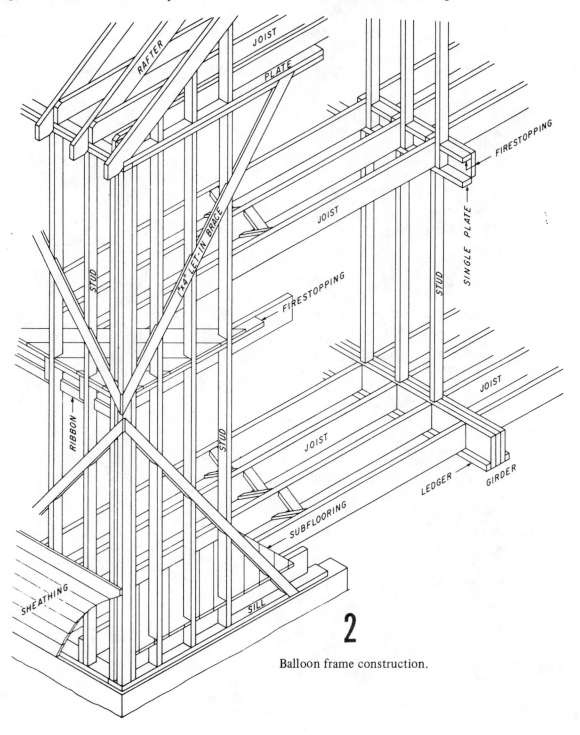

2

Balloon frame construction.

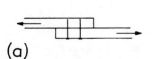

(a) Nail perpendicular to load. (b) Toe nailing. (c) Nail in withdrawal. **3**

Methods of loading nails.

PLANK AND BEAM CONSTRUCTION

In the plank and beam method of framing, beams of adequate size are spaced up to 8 feet apart. They are covered with nominal 2-inch planks which serve as the base for finish flooring or roof covering. Ends of the beams are supported on posts. The covering for exterior walls is attached to supplementary members set between the posts.

FOUNDATIONS

Although the wood frame house is noted for its strength and resilience, adequate and properly installed footings are still as essential as they are for other types of construction. Footings should extend far enough below exterior grade to be free from frost action during winter months. Where roots of trees were removed during excavation, soil should be well compacted before footings are poured, filled ground should be avoided if possible.

Where poor soil conditions exist, satisfactory foundations may be provided by use of treated timber piles capped with wood or concrete sills.

Although the size of the footing will depend upon the local building code, it is good practice, generally, to make the depth of the footing equal to the thickness of the foundation wall it supports. The projection of the footing should be equal to one half the thickness of the foundation wall. Usually, footings are of plain concrete. Sometimes it is necessary to use reinforced concrete where unequal soil conditions cannot be avoided, in which case, engineering analysis of the footings is required.

The foundation wall may be of poured concrete or of masonry units. Where masonry units are used, a ½-inch coat of portland cement mortar should be applied to the exterior of the wall and then covered with two coats of asphalt. Drain tiles should also be installed around the exterior of footings and connected to a positive outfall, Figure 5. These measures will assure a dry basement.

Where basements are not provided, foundations may consist of free-standing piers, piers with curtain walls between them, or piers supporting grade beams. In any of these methods, the piers and their footings must be of sufficient size to carry the weight of the house and its contents. Spacing of the piers will depend upon arrangement of the floor framing and location of load-bearing walls and partitions. A distance in the order of 8 to 12 feet is the usual practice, Figure 6.

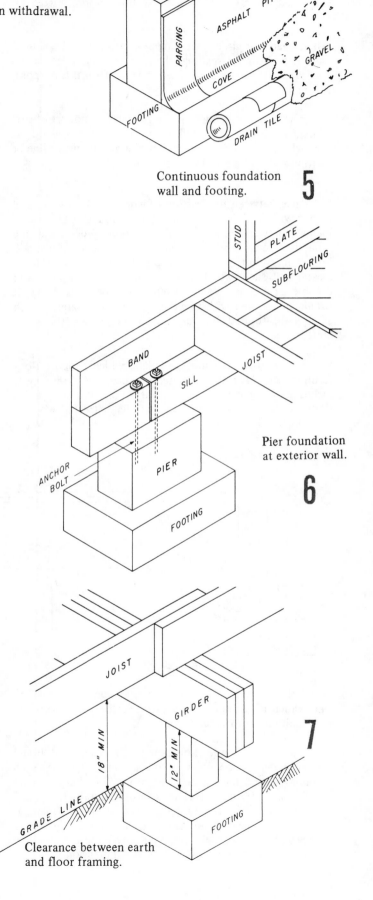

Continuous foundation wall and footing. **5**

Pier foundation at exterior wall. **6**

Clearance between earth and floor framing. **7**

Wood sills, which rest on concrete or masonry exterior walls, should be placed at least 6 inches above the exposed earth on the exterior of the building, or approved durable or treated wood should be used for this purpose, Figure 11, 12.

Wood beams or girders, framing into masonry walls, should have ½ inch of air space at the top, end and sides, unless approved durable or treated wood is used for this purpose, Figure 13.

Where wood is embedded in the ground for support of permanent structures, it should be approved treated wood except where it is completely below the ground water line or continuously submerged in fresh water.

Clearance between the bottom of wood joists, or structural planks without joists, and the ground should be at least 18 inches. Between the bottom of wood girders and the ground, the clearance should be at least 12 inches, Figure 7. Where it is not practical or possible to maintain these clearances, such wood framing should be of approved durable or treated wood. Where the ground is damp, it should be covered with a layer of impervious material, such as asphalt-saturated felt weighing 55 pounds per 108 square feet.

Wood posts, in basements or cellars, which support floor framing, should rest on concrete pedestals extending 2 inches above concrete floors and 6 inches above earth floors, except where approved durable or treated wood is used, Figure 8.

FLOOR FRAMING

Floor framing consists of sills, girders, joists and subflooring, with all members tied together in such a way as to support the loads expected on the floor and to give lateral support to the exterior walls.

Sills which rest on continuous foundation walls usually consist of one thickness of nominal 2-inch lumber set on the walls in such a way as to provide full and even bearing. They should be anchored to foundation walls with 1/2 inch bolts spaced approximately 8 feet apart with at least two bolts in each piece of sill. Bolts should be embedded at least 6 inches in poured concrete walls and at least 15 inches in masonry unit walls, Figures 11, 12, 13, 14.

Sills which rest on free-standing piers should be large enough to carry the loads between supports. They may be solid or built-up members as provided for beams and girders. Sills should be anchored to piers with 1/2-inch bolts embedded at least 6 inches in poured concrete, and 15 inches in masonry, Figure 6.

Usually, beams and girders consist of solid timbers or built-up members in which nominal 2-inch pieces are nailed together with the wide faces vertical. Such pieces should be fastened together by two rows of 20d nails—one row near the top and the other near the bottom edge. Nails in each row are spaced about 32 inches apart with end joints occurring over supports, Figures 9 and 15. Glued-laminated members also are frequently used. Beams and girders that are not continuous should be tied together across supports. A bearing of 4 inches on supports is recommended.

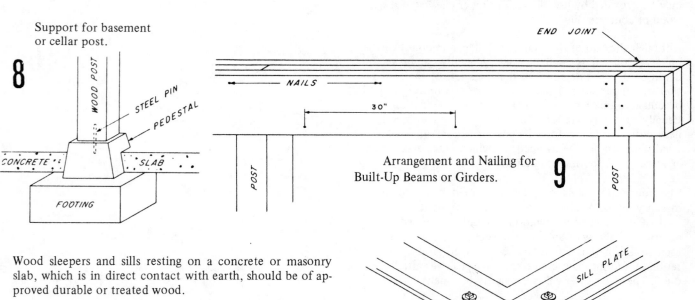

Support for basement or cellar post.

8

Arrangement and Nailing for Built-Up Beams or Girders.

9

Anchorage of sill to continuous foundation wall.

11

Wood sleepers and sills resting on a concrete or masonry slab, which is in direct contact with earth, should be of approved durable or treated wood.

The crawl space, under houses without basements, should be ventilated by openings in the foundation walls. Such openings should have a net area of not less than 2 square feet for each 100 linear feet of exterior wall, plus 1/3 square foot for each 100 square feet of crawl space. Openings should be arranged to provide cross-ventilation and should be covered with corrosion-resistant wire mesh not less than 1/4 inch nor more than 1/2 inch in any dimension.

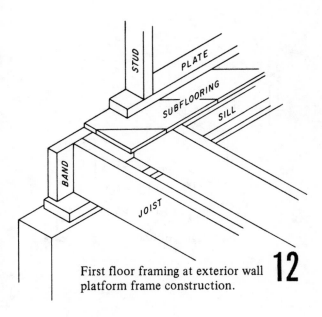

First floor framing at exterior wall platform frame construction. **12**

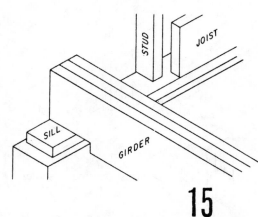

First floor framing at exterior wall balloon frame construction. **15**

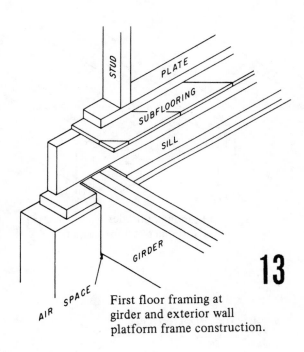

First floor framing at girder and exterior wall platform frame construction. **13**

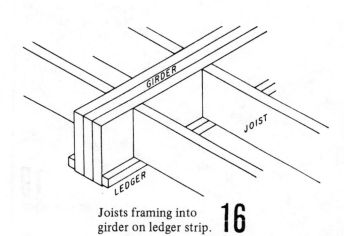

Joists framing into girder on ledger strip. **16**

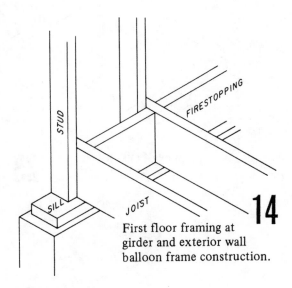

First floor framing at girder and exterior wall balloon frame construction. **14**

Joists framing into girder with framing anchors. **17**

117

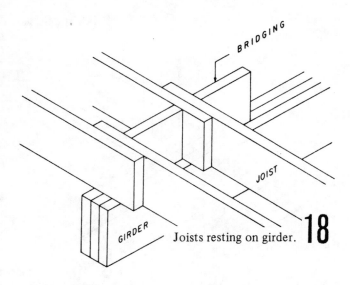

BRIDGING

JOIST

GIRDER

Joists resting on girder. **18**

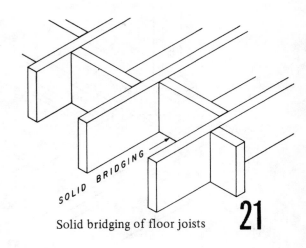

SOLID BRIDGING

Solid bridging of floor joists **21**

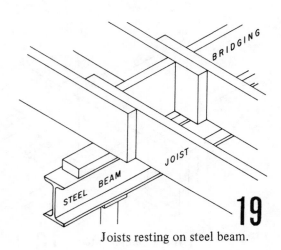

BRIDGING

STEEL BEAM

JOIST

Joists resting on steel beam. **19**

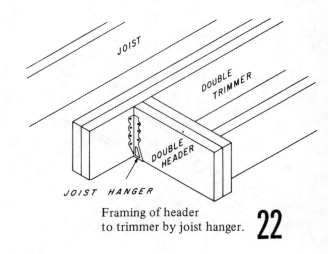

JOIST

DOUBLE TRIMMER

DOUBLE HEADER

JOIST HANGER

Framing of header
to trimmer by joist hanger. **22**

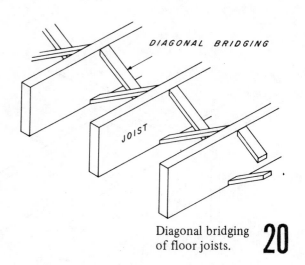

DIAGONAL BRIDGING

JOIST

Diagonal bridging
of floor joists. **20**

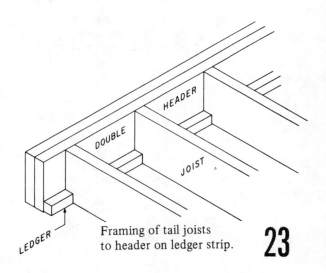

HEADER

DOUBLE

JOIST

LEDGER

Framing of tail joists
to header on ledger strip. **23**

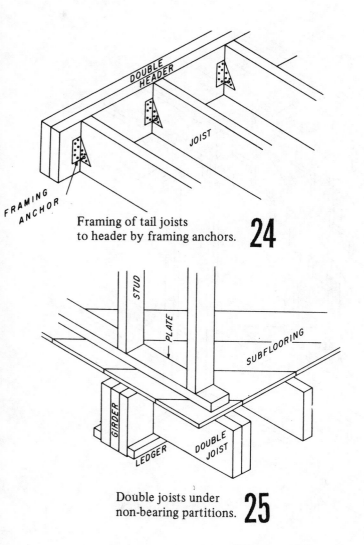

Framing of tail joists
to header by framing anchors. **24**

Double joists under
non-bearing partitions. **25**

Bearing for joists should not be less than 1 1/2 inches on wood or metal, and 3 inches on masonry. Joists should be placed so that the top edge provides an even plane for installation of the subfloor and finished floor. It is better to frame joists into the sides of girders, Figures 16, 17, 18, 19, 20, 21, 22, 23, 24, 25, 26, 27, 28, 29.

Joists should be braced to distribute concentrated loads among several joists and to prevent the joists from buckling under load. To accomplish this, diagonal struts or solid blocks are placed between and at right angles to joists, Figures 20 and 21. Joists should be braced in this manner at the ends and at intervals of not more than 8 feet. Bridging may be omitted at the ends of joists which are nailed to a header or joist band, or which are nailed to adjoining studs, Figures 30, 31, 32, 33.

Proper arrangement of headers, trimmers and tail joists accomplishes framing of openings. Trimmers and headers should be doubled when the span of the header exceeds 4 feet. Headers, more than 6 feet long, should be supported at the ends by joist hangars or framing anchors, unless they are supported on a partition, beam or wall. Tail joists, over 12 feet long, should be supported on framing anchors or on ledger strips not less than nominal 2 x 2 inches, Figures 22, 23 and 24.

Notches for piping, in the top or bottom of joists, should not exceed one sixth the depth of the joists and should not be located in the middle third of the span. Holes bored in joists for piping or electric cables should not be closer than 2 inches to the top or bottom of the joist and the diameter of the hole should not exceed one third of the depth of the joist. Where joists are notched on the ends, the notch should not exceed one fourth the joist depth, Figure 23.

Bearing partitions usually are placed directly over the girders or walls which support the floor framing. They may be offset from such supports if the floor framing is strong enough to carry the added load. In general, bearing partitions running at right angles to joists should not be offset from main girders, or walls, more than the depth of the joist, unless the joists are designed to carry the extra load. When non-bearing partitions run parallel to joists, the joists should be doubled under the partitions, Figures 25, 26, 29, 34.

Second floor joists sometimes project beyond first story walls. When the overhanging wall is at right angles to the joists, the joists may be cantilevered over the supporting wall for the required distance, Figure 35.

Where the overhanging wall is parallel to the supporting joists, a double joist may be used to support lookout joists extending over the wall line below, Figure 36. The double joists should be located a distance of twice the overhang back from the lower wall. Lookout joists may be framed into the double joists by means of a ledger strip, at the upper edge, or by framing anchors.

Wood sub-flooring is preferred because of its resilience and thickness which provide a solid base for installing finish flooring. It usually consists of square-edge or tongued-and-grooved boards. It is better to lay sub-flooring diagonally as this arrangement permits the finish floor to be laid either parallel or at right angles to the joists. Also, diagonal subflooring provides lateral bracing and stiffness to the entire building. Joints in the sub-flooring should be made over the joists unless end-matched boards are used.

FIRESTOPPING

All concealed spaces in wood framing are firestopped with wood blocking, accurately fitted to fill the opening and arranged to prevent drafts from one space to another.

Stud spaces should be firestopped, at each floor level and at the top story ceiling level, with nominal 2-inch blocking. In many instances, sills and plates will serve this purpose but where they are not present, additional blocking is necessary, Figures 30 and 32.

Stud spaces should be firestopped as required for exterior walls, Figures 31 and 33.

Concealed spaces should be firestopped for the full depth of the joists, at the ends and over the supports, with nominal 2-inch blocking, Figures 14, 18, 19 and 31. In many cases, solid bridging will serve as firestopping.

119

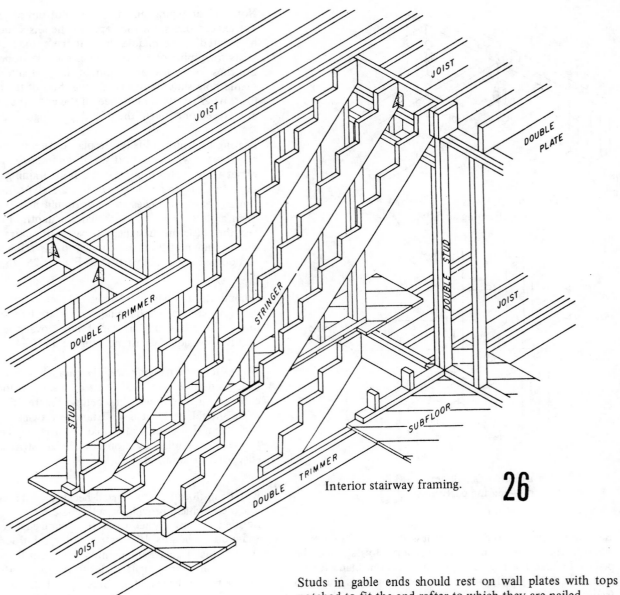

JOIST

JOIST

DOUBLE PLATE

DOUBLE TRIMMER

STRINGER

DOUBLE STUD

JOIST

STUD

SUBFLOOR

DOUBLE TRIMMER

JOIST

Interior stairway framing.

26

Furred spaces on masonry walls should be firestopped at each floor level and at the top ceiling level by wood blocking, of sufficient thickness to fill the space, or by non-combustible material accurately fitted to the space.

Spaces between wood framing, at floors and ceilings, and fireplace and chimney masonry, should be filled with non-combustible material.

EXTERIOR WALL FRAMING

Exterior wall framing should be strong and stiff enough to support the vertical loads from floors and roof. Walls should resist the lateral loads resulting from winds and, in some areas, from earthquakes. Top plates should be doubled and overlapped at wall and bearing partition intersection. This ties the building together into a strong unit.

Studs in gable ends should rest on wall plates with tops notched to fit the end rafter to which they are nailed.

Exterior walls should be braced by suitable sheathing. Additional strength and stiffness may be provided by 1" x 4" members let into the outside face of the studs at an angle of 45 degrees and nailed to top and bottom plates and studs, Figures 1 and 2. Where wood sheathing boards are applied diagonally, let-in braces are not necessary. Sheathing should be nailed to sills, headers, studs, plates or continuous headers and to gable end rafters.

Studs in exterior walls are placed with the wide faces perpendicular to direction of the wall. Studs should be at least nominal 2 x 4 inches for one-and-two-story buildings. In three-story buildings, studs in the bottom story should be at least nominal 2 x 6 inches. In one-story buildings, studs may be spaced 24 inches, on center, unless otherwise limited by the wall covering. In multi-story buildings, spacing should not exceed 16 inches on center. An arrangement of multiple studs is used at the corners to provide for ready attachment of exterior and interior surface materials, Figures 37 and 38.

120

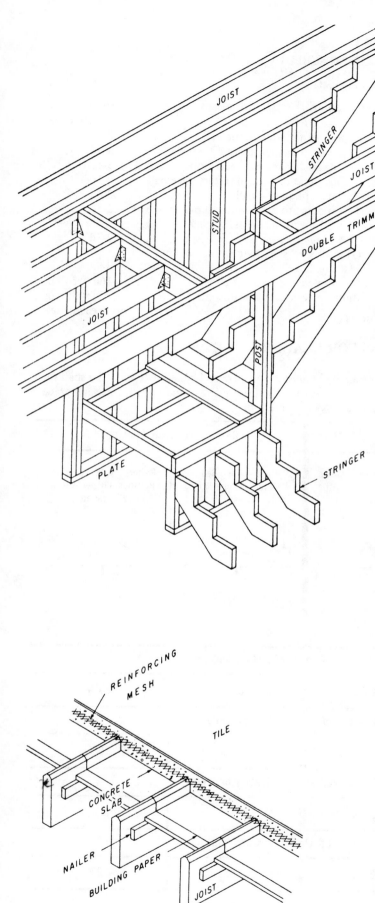

JOIST

STRINGER

JOIST

DOUBLE HEADER

STUD

DOUBLE TRIMMER

JOIST

POST

STRINGER

PLATE

Framing for stairway with a landing.

27

Where doors or windows occur, provision must be made to carry the vertical load across the opening. A header of adequate size is needed, as indicated in Table II. Ends of the header may be supported on studs, Figure 39, or by framing anchors when the span does not exceed 3 feet, Figure 40.

A continuous header consisting of two-inch members set on edge, may be used instead of a double top plate. The depth of the members will be the same as that required to span the largest opening. Joints in individual members should be staggered at least three stud spaces and should not occur over openings. Members are toe-nailed to studs and corners. Intersections, with bearing partitions, should be lapped or tied with metal straps, Figure 41.

Weather-tight walls are provided by sheathing covered on the outside with asphalt saturated felt weighing not less than 15 pounds per 108 square feet, or with other impregnated paper having equivalent water-repellent properties. Sheathing paper must not be of a type which would act as a vapor barrier. Starting at the bottom of the wall, the felt should be lapped 4 inches at horizontal joints and 6 inches at vertical joints. Strips of sheathing paper, about 6 inches wide, are installed behind all exterior trim and around all openings.

INTERIOR PARTITION FRAMING

There are two types of interior partitions—bearing partitions, which support floors, ceilings or roofs, and non-bearing partitions which carry only the weight of the materials in the partition.

Studs should be at least nominal 2 x 4 inches, set with the wide dimension perpendicular to the partitions and capped with two pieces of nominal 2-inch lumber, or by continuous headers which are lapped or tied into exterior walls at points of intersections. Studs supporting floors should be spaced 16 inches on centers; those which support ceilings and roofs may be spaced 24 inches. Where openings occur, loads should be carried across the openings by headers similar to those recommended for exterior walls. Sizes for headers are provided in Table II. Figures 26, 27, 30, 31, 32, 33, 35, 36, 39, 40, 41, 42, 43.

REINFORCING MESH

TILE

CONCRETE SLAB

NAILER

BUILDING PAPER

JOIST

Bathroom floor construction. for ceramic tile covering.

28

Table I

RECOMMENDED NAILING SCHEDULE

Using Common Nails

Joist to sill or girder, toe nail 3-8d
Bridging to joist, toe nail each end 2-8d
Ledge strip 3-16d
                              at each joist
1" x 6" subfloor or less to each joist, face nail 2-8d
Over 1" x 6" subfloor to each joist, face nail .3-8d
2" subfloor to joist or girder, blind and
  face nail 2-16d
Sole plate to joist or blocking, face nail . . . . .16d @ 16" oc
Top plate to stud, end nail 2-16d
Stud to sole plate, toe nail 4-8d
Doubled studs, face nail . . . . .16d @ 24" oc
Doubled top plates, face nail . . . . .16d @ 16" oc
Top plates, laps and intersections, face nail. . .2-16d

Continuous header, two pieces . . . . .16d @ 16" oc
                              along each edge
Ceiling joists to plate, toe nail 3-8d
Continuous header to stud, toe nail. 4-8d
Ceiling joists, laps over partitions, face nail. . .3-16d
Ceiling joists to parallel rafters, face nail 3-16d
Rafter to plate, toe nail 3-8d
1-inch brace to each stud and plate, face nail .2-8d
1" x 8" sheathing or less to each bearing,
  face nail. 2-8d
Over 1" x 8" sheathing to each bearing,
  face nail. 3-8d
Built-up corner studs . . . . .16d @ 24" oc
Built-up girders and beams . . . . .20d @ 32" oc
                              along each edge

Table II

MAXIMUM SPANS FOR HEADERS

In this table, headers consist of two pieces of nominal 2-inch framing lumber set on edge and nailed together. The span for the two pieces is expressed as a percentage of the maximum allowable span for floor joists of the same species and grade spaced 16 inches on centers and subjected to a live load of 40 pounds per square foot.

Exterior Wall Openings			Bearing Partition Openings	
Rafters with Bearing Partition (Slope of 3 in 12 or less) No attic storage	Trussed Rafters (Slope of 3 in 12 or less) No attic storage — Rafters with Bearing Partition (Slope over 3 in 12) Attic storage	Trussed Rafters (Slope over 3 in 12) Attic storage	Rafters with Bearing Partition (Slope of 3 in 12 or less) No attic storage	Rafters with Bearing Partition (Slope over 3 in 12) Attic storage
Buildings up to 26 ft. wide — 1 story or 2nd story of 2-story buildings				
60%	45%	40%	50%	35%
Buildings up to 26 ft. wide — 1st story of 1½ or 2 story buildings				
40%	35%	35%	35%	30%
Buildings 27 to 32 ft. wide — 1 story or 2nd story of 2 story buildings				
55%	40%	35%	45%	35%
Buildings 27 to 32 ft. wide — 1st story of 1½ or 2 story buildings				
35%	35%	35%	35%	30%

Note 1 — Span for a header of two 2 x 4's should not exceed 2'-6" in bearing partitions under attic storage nor 3'-0" elsewhere.

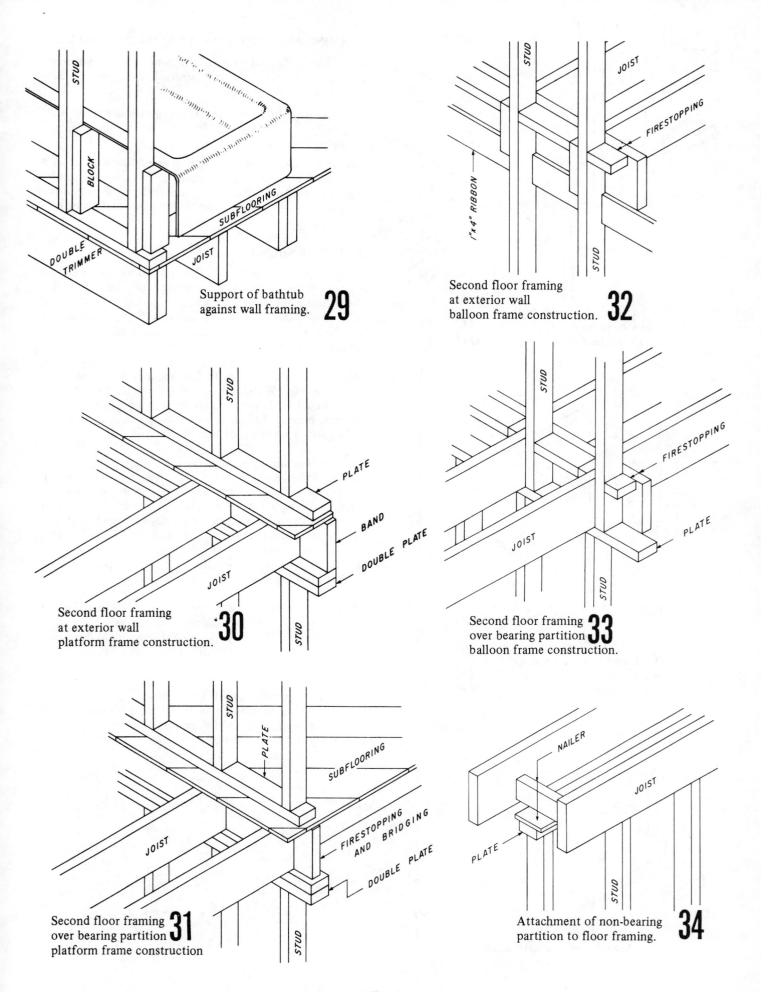

Support of bathtub against wall framing. **29**

Second floor framing at exterior wall balloon frame construction. **32**

Second floor framing at exterior wall platform frame construction. **30**

Second floor framing over bearing partition balloon frame construction. **33**

Second floor framing over bearing partition platform frame construction **31**

Attachment of non-bearing partition to floor framing. **34**

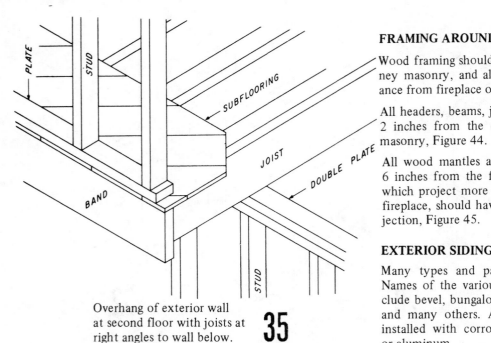

Overhang of exterior wall at second floor with joists at right angles to wall below. **35**

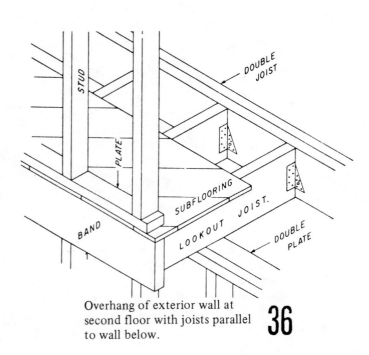

Overhang of exterior wall at second floor with joists parallel to wall below. **36**

FRAMING AROUND CHIMNEYS AND FIREPLACES

Wood framing should be separated from fireplace and chimney masonry, and all wood trim should have proper clearance from fireplace openings.

All headers, beams, joists and studs should be keep at least 2 inches from the outside face of chimney or fireplace masonry, Figure 44.

All wood mantles and similar trim should be kept at least 6 inches from the fireplace opening. Parts of the mantle, which project more than 1 1/2 inches from the face of the fireplace, should have additional clearance equal to the projection, Figure 45.

EXTERIOR SIDING

Many types and patterns of wood siding are available. Names of the various types, varying with the locality, include bevel, bungalow, colonial, rustic, shiplap, drop siding and many others. All siding and exterior trim should be installed with corrosion-resistant nails, usually galvanized or aluminum.

Where wood sheathing is used, siding may be nailed at 24-inch intervals. Where other types of sheathing are used, nails should be driven through the sheathing into the studs at each bearing. Length of nail will vary with thickness of siding and types of sheathing.

Bevel siding and square-edge boards, applied horizontally, should be lapped 1 inch with nails driven just above the lap to permit possible movement due to change in moisture conditions, Figure 47. Preferable spacing of siding is that where the bottom of a piece coincides with the top of trim over door and window openings, Figures 48 and 49. This arrangement requires careful planning by the carpenter before starting to apply the siding. It is good practice to apply a liberal coating of water repellent to the end surfaces.

Corner treatment of siding depends upon the overall house design and may involve corner boards, mitered corners, metal corners, or alternately lapped corners. Mitered corners on the exterior are difficult to make weather tight. Figure 50.

Siding is frequently applied vertically in order to produce a desired architectural effect. Where tongued-and-grooved boards are used, the siding should be blind-nailed to wood sheathing at 24-inch intervals.

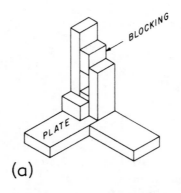

(a)

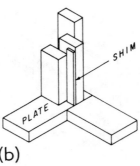

(b)

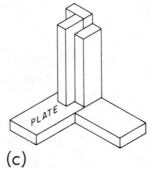

(c)

Assembly of studs at outside corner. **37**

124

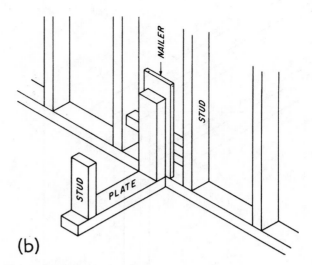

(a)   (b)

Assembly of studs where partition meets wall.   **38**

Where square-edge boards are used with battens, the boards are spaced about ½ inch apart and nailed only at the center. The batten is attached by one nail driven through the center so that it passes between the boards. This arrangement permits movement with change in moisture conditions, Figure 47. Where other than wood sheathing is used, blocking should be provided between studs to permit nailing of the vertical siding.

Shingles, other than shakes, when used as exterior wall covering, should have exposures to the weather as follows for No. 1 Grade:

	Maximum Exposure (Inches)	
Shingle Length	Single Course	Double Course
16-inch	7½	12
18-inch	8½	14
24-inch	11½	16

Where shingles are installed in double courses, the butt of the exposed shingle extends about ½ inch below the under course in order to produce a shadow line.

Shingles should be nailed with corrosion-resistant nails of sufficient length to penetrate the sheathing, using two nails for shingles up to 8 inches wide and three nails for wider shingles. For single coursing, nails should be driven approximately 1 inch above butt line of following course. For double coursing, the under course should be attached to the sheathing with 3d nails or staples and the outer course attached with small headed nails driven approximately 2 inches above the butts and 3/4 inch from edges.

When other than wood sheathing is used, it is necessary to apply 1 x 3-inch horizontal nailing strips over the sheathing spaced to correspond with the weather exposure of the shingles, Figure 49.

Masonry veneer should be supported on the foundation wall and attached to the wood framing with corrosion-resistant metal ties. Ties are spaced 24 inches on centers horizontally and each tie should not support more than 2 square feet of wall area. They should be attached to studs if other than wood sheathing is used. Figure 51.

Framing around exterior wall opening using header and double studs.   **39**

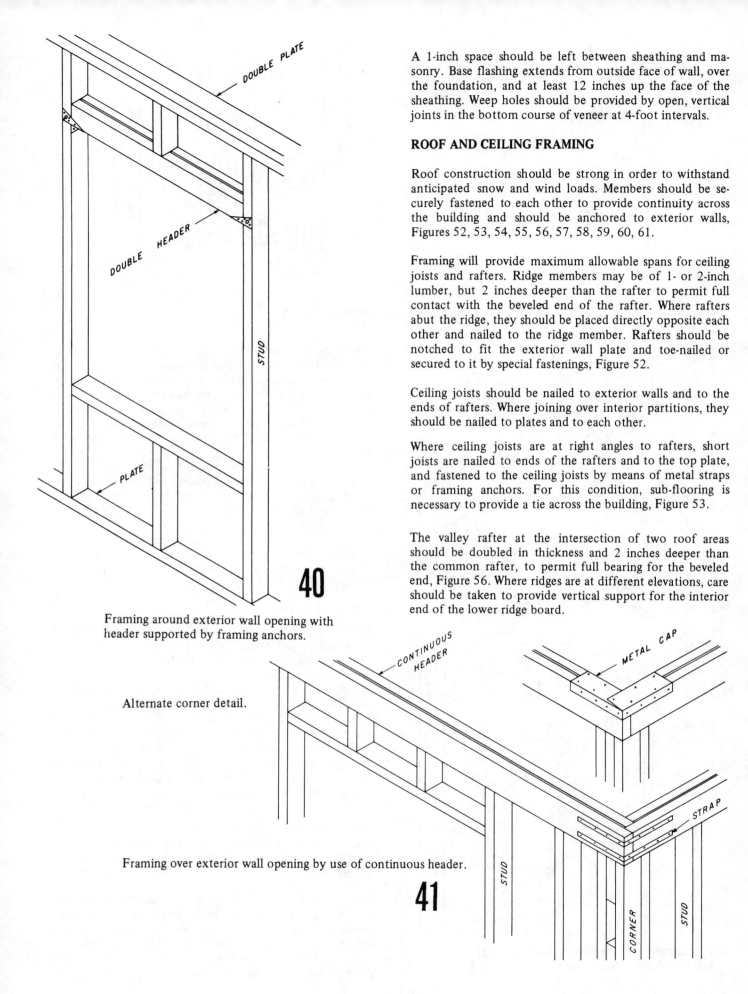

A 1-inch space should be left between sheathing and masonry. Base flashing extends from outside face of wall, over the foundation, and at least 12 inches up the face of the sheathing. Weep holes should be provided by open, vertical joints in the bottom course of veneer at 4-foot intervals.

ROOF AND CEILING FRAMING

Roof construction should be strong in order to withstand anticipated snow and wind loads. Members should be securely fastened to each other to provide continuity across the building and should be anchored to exterior walls, Figures 52, 53, 54, 55, 56, 57, 58, 59, 60, 61.

Framing will provide maximum allowable spans for ceiling joists and rafters. Ridge members may be of 1- or 2-inch lumber, but 2 inches deeper than the rafter to permit full contact with the beveled end of the rafter. Where rafters abut the ridge, they should be placed directly opposite each other and nailed to the ridge member. Rafters should be notched to fit the exterior wall plate and toe-nailed or secured to it by special fastenings, Figure 52.

Ceiling joists should be nailed to exterior walls and to the ends of rafters. Where joining over interior partitions, they should be nailed to plates and to each other.

Where ceiling joists are at right angles to rafters, short joists are nailed to ends of the rafters and to the top plate, and fastened to the ceiling joists by means of metal straps or framing anchors. For this condition, sub-flooring is necessary to provide a tie across the building, Figure 53.

The valley rafter at the intersection of two roof areas should be doubled in thickness and 2 inches deeper than the common rafter, to permit full bearing for the beveled end, Figure 56. Where ridges are at different elevations, care should be taken to provide vertical support for the interior end of the lower ridge board.

40

Framing around exterior wall opening with header supported by framing anchors.

Alternate corner detail.

Framing over exterior wall opening by use of continuous header.

41

126

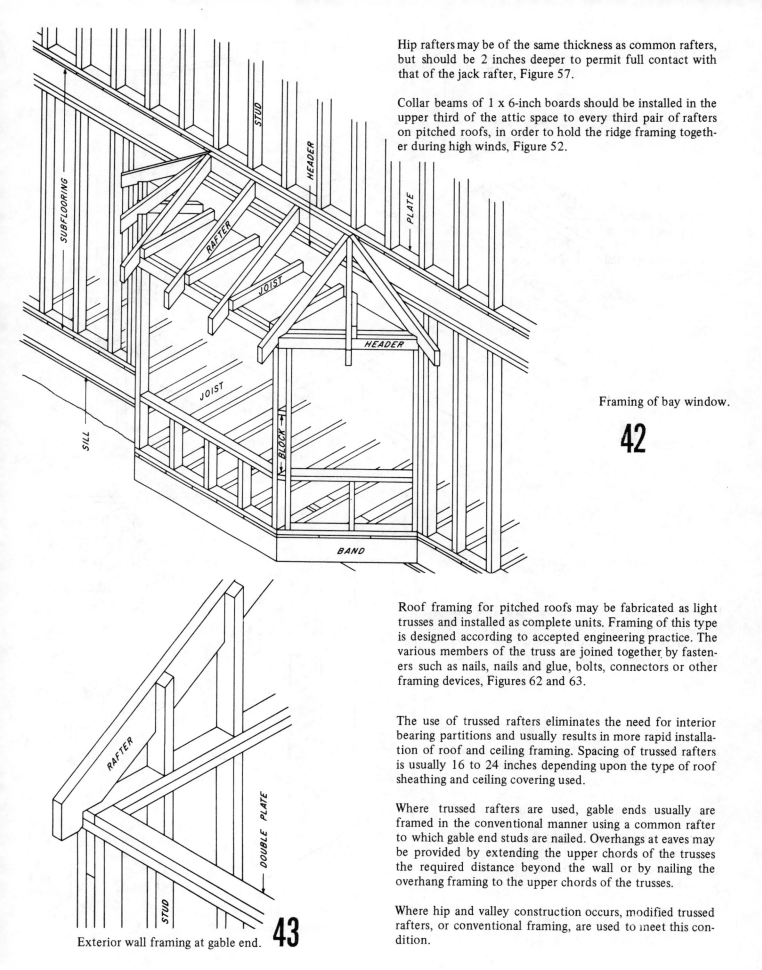

Hip rafters may be of the same thickness as common rafters, but should be 2 inches deeper to permit full contact with that of the jack rafter, Figure 57.

Collar beams of 1 x 6-inch boards should be installed in the upper third of the attic space to every third pair of rafters on pitched roofs, in order to hold the ridge framing together during high winds, Figure 52.

Framing of bay window.

42

Roof framing for pitched roofs may be fabricated as light trusses and installed as complete units. Framing of this type is designed according to accepted engineering practice. The various members of the truss are joined together by fasteners such as nails, nails and glue, bolts, connectors or other framing devices, Figures 62 and 63.

The use of trussed rafters eliminates the need for interior bearing partitions and usually results in more rapid installation of roof and ceiling framing. Spacing of trussed rafters is usually 16 to 24 inches depending upon the type of roof sheathing and ceiling covering used.

Where trussed rafters are used, gable ends usually are framed in the conventional manner using a common rafter to which gable end studs are nailed. Overhangs at eaves may be provided by extending the upper chords of the trusses the required distance beyond the wall or by nailing the overhang framing to the upper chords of the trusses.

Where hip and valley construction occurs, modified trussed rafters, or conventional framing, are used to meet this condition.

Exterior wall framing at gable end. **43**

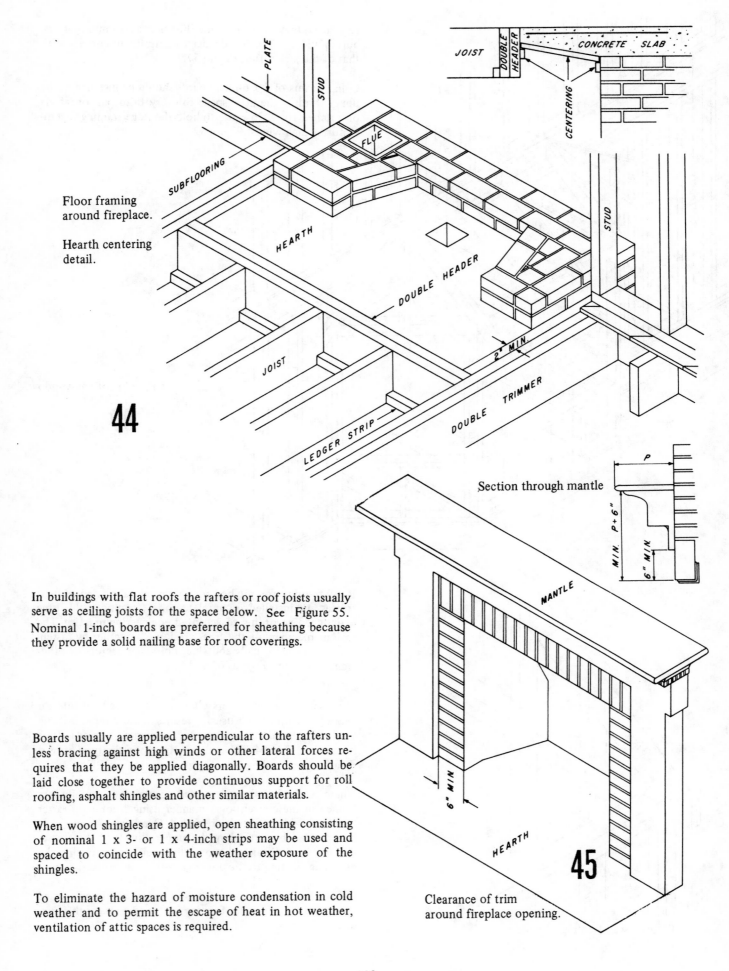

JOIST DOUBLE HEADER CONCRETE SLAB

CENTERING

PLATE

STUD

FLUE

SUBFLOORING

Floor framing
around fireplace.

Hearth centering
detail.

HEARTH

STUD

DOUBLE HEADER

2" MIN.

JOIST

LEDGER STRIP

DOUBLE TRIMMER

44

P

Section through mantle

MIN. P+6"

6" MIN.

MANTLE

In buildings with flat roofs the rafters or roof joists usually
serve as ceiling joists for the space below. See Figure 55.
Nominal 1-inch boards are preferred for sheathing because
they provide a solid nailing base for roof coverings.

Boards usually are applied perpendicular to the rafters unless bracing against high winds or other lateral forces requires that they be applied diagonally. Boards should be
laid close together to provide continuous support for roll
roofing, asphalt shingles and other similar materials.

When wood shingles are applied, open sheathing consisting
of nominal 1 x 3- or 1 x 4-inch strips may be used and
spaced to coincide with the weather exposure of the
shingles.

To eliminate the hazard of moisture condensation in cold
weather and to permit the escape of heat in hot weather,
ventilation of attic spaces is required.

6" MIN

HEARTH

45

Clearance of trim
around fireplace opening.

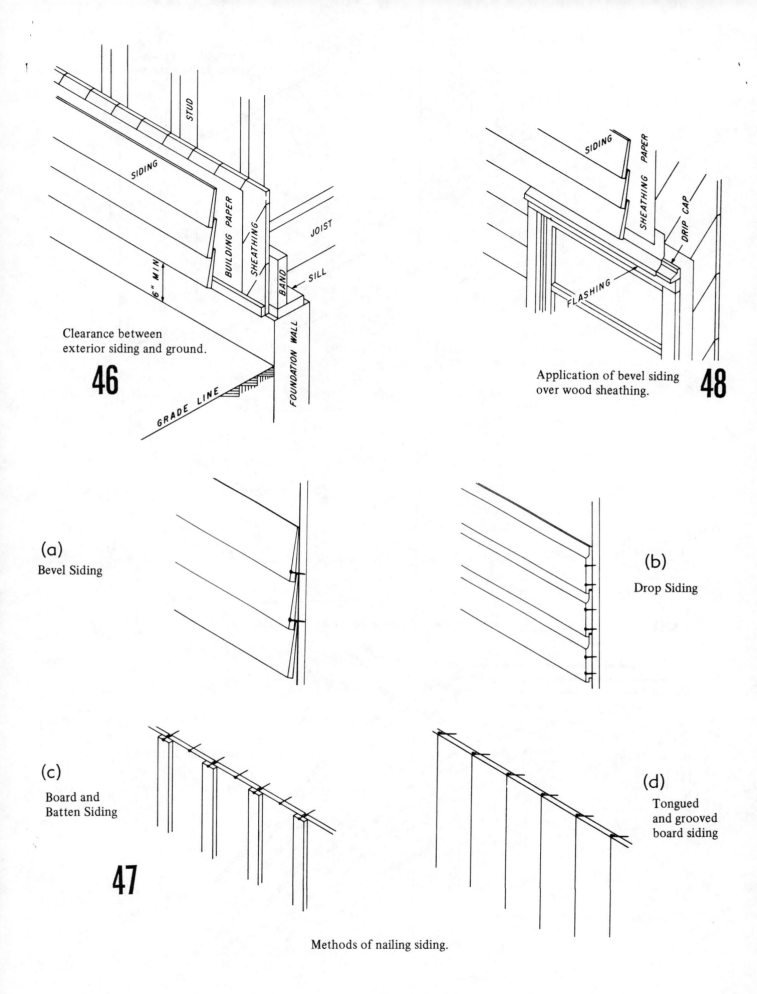

SIDING

STUD

BUILDING PAPER

SHEATHING

JOIST

BAND

SILL

6" MIN.

Clearance between
exterior siding and ground.

46

GRADE LINE

FOUNDATION WALL

SIDING

SHEATHING PAPER

DRIP CAP

FLASHING

Application of bevel siding
over wood sheathing.

48

(a)
Bevel Siding

(b)
Drop Siding

(c)
Board and
Batten Siding

47

(d)
Tongued
and grooved
board siding

Methods of nailing siding.

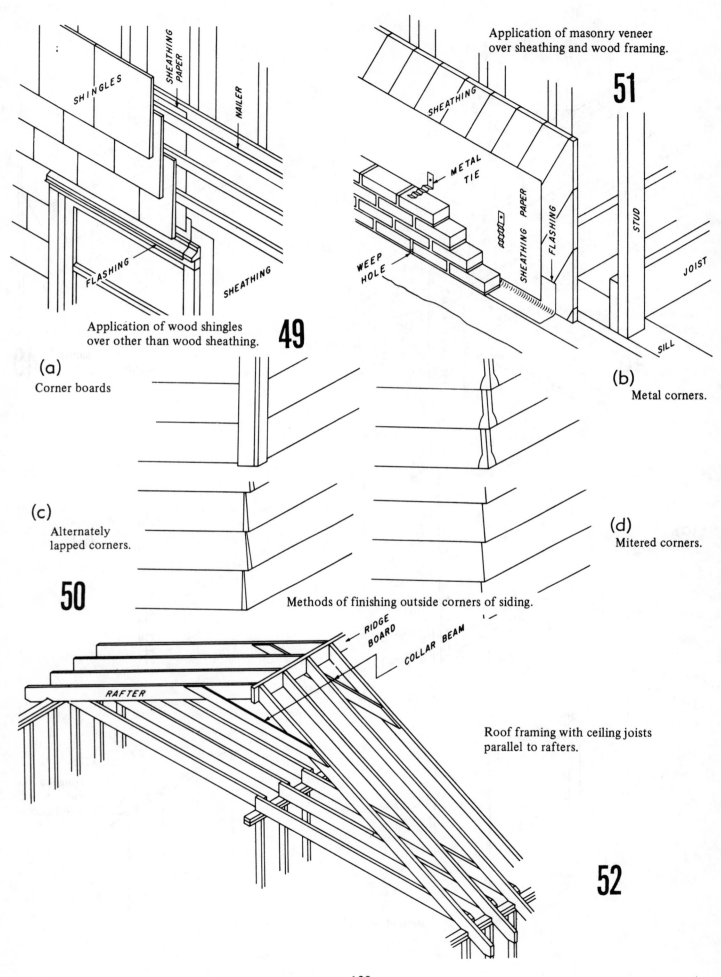

SHINGLES

SHEATHING PAPER

NAILER

FLASHING

SHEATHING

Application of wood shingles over other than wood sheathing. **49**

Application of masonry veneer over sheathing and wood framing.

51

SHEATHING

METAL TIE

WEEP HOLE

SHEATHING PAPER

FLASHING

STUD

JOIST

SILL

(a) Corner boards

(b) Metal corners.

(c) Alternately lapped corners.

(d) Mitered corners.

50

Methods of finishing outside corners of siding.

RIDGE BOARD

COLLAR BEAM

RAFTER

Roof framing with ceiling joists parallel to rafters.

52

130

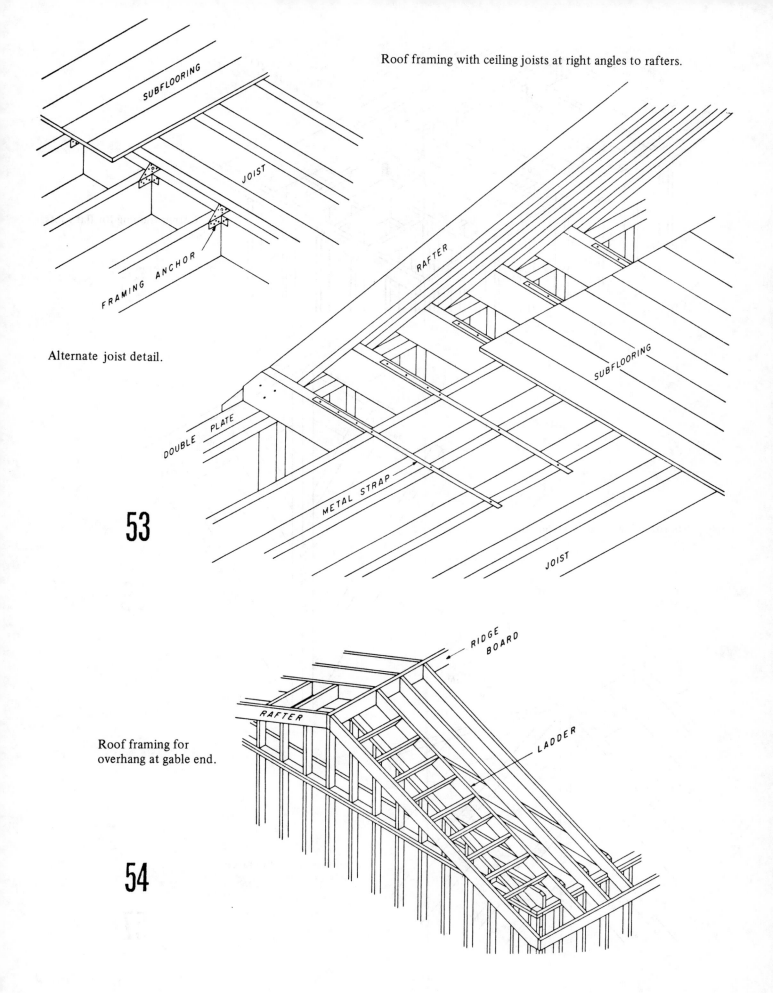

SUBFLOORING

JOIST

FRAMING ANCHOR

Alternate joist detail.

Roof framing with ceiling joists at right angles to rafters.

RAFTER

SUBFLOORING

DOUBLE PLATE

METAL STRAP

JOIST

53

RIDGE BOARD

RAFTER

LADDER

Roof framing for
overhang at gable end.

54

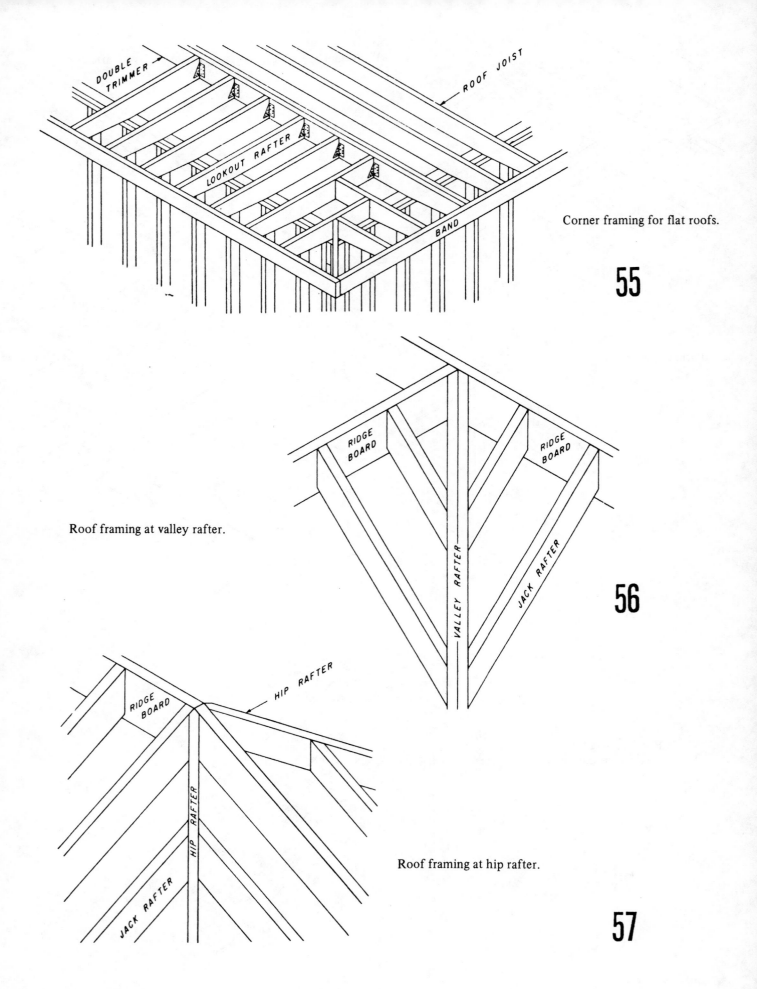

Corner framing for flat roofs.

55

Roof framing at valley rafter.

56

Roof framing at hip rafter.

57

132

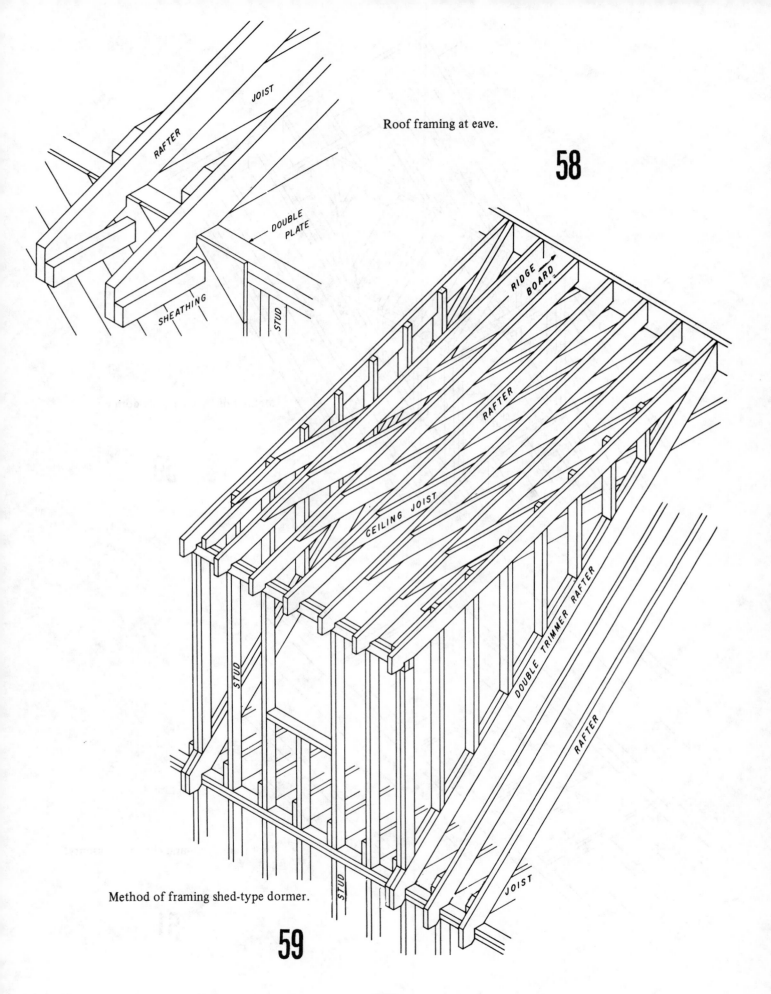

Roof framing at eave.

58

Method of framing shed-type dormer.

59

133

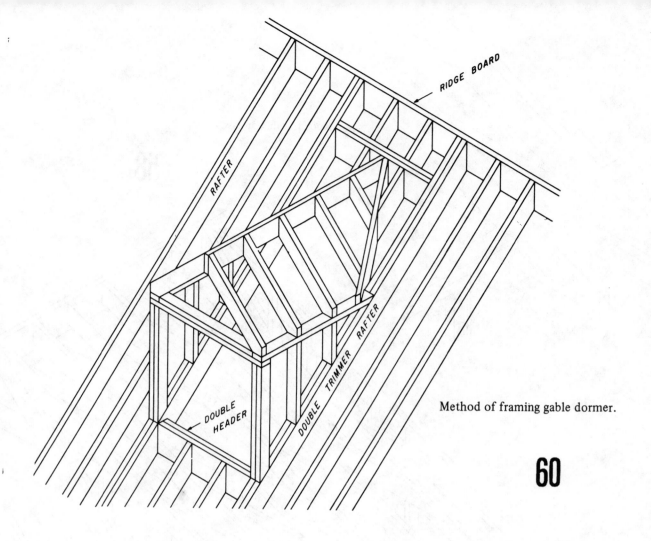

Method of framing gable dormer.

60

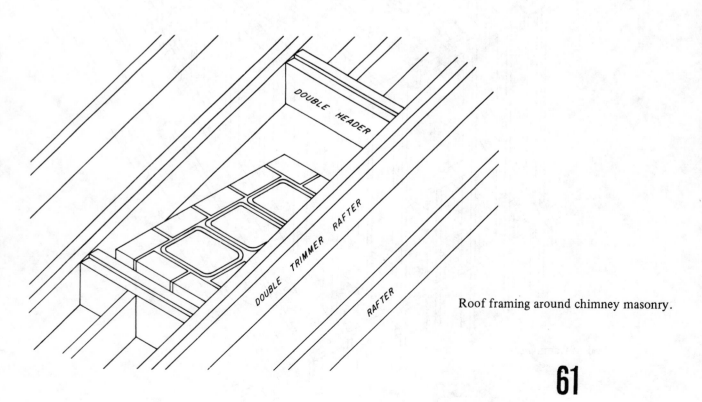

Roof framing around chimney masonry.

61

134

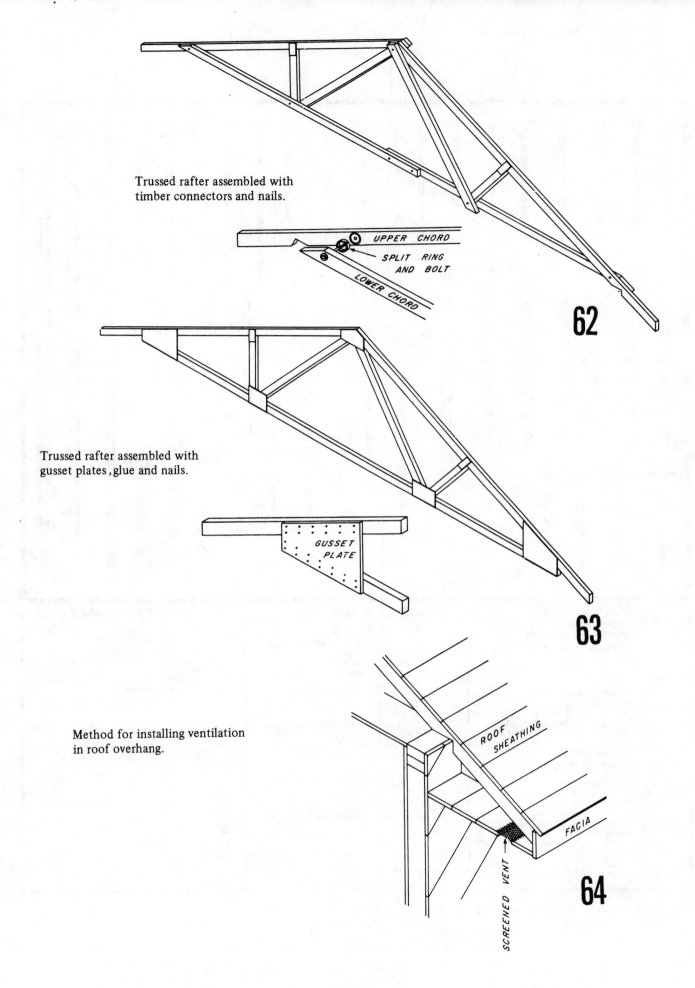

Trussed rafter assembled with
timber connectors and nails.

UPPER CHORD

SPLIT RING
AND BOLT

LOWER CHORD

62

Trussed rafter assembled with
gusset plates, glue and nails.

GUSSET
PLATE

63

Method for installing ventilation
in roof overhang.

ROOF
SHEATHING

FACIA

SCREENED VENT

64

135

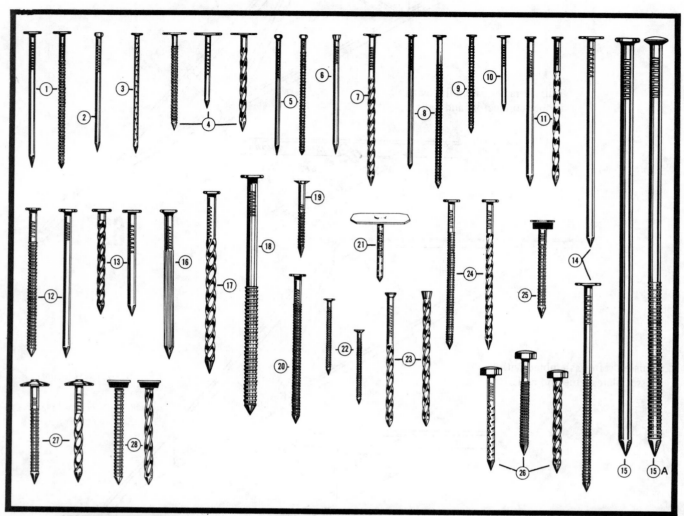

STORMGUARD® NAILS
FOR EXTERIOR APPLICATIONS
(Hot-dipped zinc-coated twice in molten zinc)

1. Wood Siding, Box (Plain & Anchor)
2. Finishing
3. Insulating, Plastic Siding
4. Asphalt Shingle (Anchor, Plain & Screw)
5. Cedar Shake (Plain & Anchor)
6. Casing
7. Cribber
8. "Split-Less" Wood Siding (Plain & Anchor)
9. Asbestos
10. Cedar Shingle
11. Hardboard Siding (Plain & Screw)
12. Common (Anchor & Plain)
13. Aluminum, Steel & Vinyl Siding (Screw & Plain)
14. Insulation Roof Deck (Plain & Anchor)
15. Gutter Spike (Plain)
15 A. Gutter Spike (Anchor)

INTERIOR & OTHER NAILS

16. Masonry
17. Pole Barn, Truss Rafter (Screw)
18. Pole Barn (Anchor)
19. Drywall, GWB-54 Style
20. Underlayment, Plywood (Sub-floor, sheathing, etc.)
21. "Square-Cap" Roofing
22. Underlayment (Flat Head & Countersunk)
23. Spiral Flooring (Casing Head & Countersunk)
24. Pallet (Anchor & Screw)

METAL ROOFING NAILS

25. Rubber Washer (Stormguard, Anchor)
26. Compressed Lead Head (Barbed, Anchor & Screw)
27. Umbrella Head (Stormguard, Anchor & Screw)
28. Lead Washer (Stormguard, Anchor & Screw)

Penny-Wise Nail Lengths

2d	1″	12d	3¼″
3d	1¼″	16d	3½″
4d	1½″	20d	4″
5d	1¾″	30d	4½″
6d	2″	40d	5″
7d	2¼″	50d	5½″
8d	2½″	60d	6″
9d	2¾″	70d	7″
10d	3″	80d	8″

FOUNDATIONS

11

SPREAD FOOTINGS

There are three kinds of foundations: a) Full Basement, b) Crawl Space, c) Slab on Grade. They all require a spread footing. The purpose of a spread footing is to support the load the same way snow shoes support a person walking on snow. Wood forms must be constructed for a poured concrete spread footing of dimensions shown in the illustration. These dimensions are for the average allowable soil-bearing capacities. The total weight of the building is being supported by the ground. It must be clearly understood that soil will support anywhere from ½ ton to 80 tons per square foot, depending upon the type of soil from sand to clay or ledge.

The soil must be firm and level when constructing the wood forms for the spread footing. The foundation must be tied to the footing to avoid sliding or slipping. This is accomplished by a key formed into the footing from a 2" x 4" with both edges beveled to facilitate removing from the form after the concrete has hardened. This key is continuous as is the spread footing around the entire perimeter of the building. ½" diameter reinforcing steel rods should be placed 2" from the bottom and edge of the footing on both sides. These can be placed before the concrete is poured or inserted after the concrete is poured while still wet. These rods prevent the footing from cracking or breaking when the footings are fully loaded. Stepped footings are often required on lots that are sloped. Do not exceed 2'-0" on the vertical dimensions between steps. If concrete blocks are used for foundation, the vertical height should equal an even number of blocks in height. Usually blocks are 8" high. The bottom of the footing should always be level along the horizontal, never inclined. If the foundation or part of is bearing on ledge, no footing is necessary.

During construction, the weight on the footing increases, causing soil compression. This compression creates a slight movement called settlement of the structure. Whenever there are two or more different sub-soils under various parts of the house, a variation in settlement will result in unequal movement. The round steel reinforcing rods in the footing will help to prevent this situation.

MIXING

a) Materials for concrete shall be thoroughly mixed to assure that a uniform distribution of all material has been achieved.

b) Field Mixing. Concrete mixes (field mixing operation) for small jobs where batching and mixing operations are done on the job, concrete mixed in accordance with Table 6-3.2 will provide plain concrete meeting minimum standards provided the amount of water added at the mixer does not make the concrete overwet. These mixes have been determined in accordance with recommended procedures assuming conditions applicable to the average small job for average aggregates.

Concrete is made up of several ingredients: cement, sand, crushed stone and water. The proportion of ingredients determines the strength of the concrete. The average mix generally used is 1: 2½: 5½ which is one part cement, 2½ parts sand and 5 parts crushed stone with just enough water to make the mix a working consistency. The sand must be clean screened and free from organic matter such as loam, the water must be clean and free from any harsh chemicals. Dry mix all the ingredients first, then add the water in small amounts while working the mix. Do not mix or pour concrete in freezing weather. Forms may be stripped or removed the next day. It is recommended that you purchase ready mixed concrete. Tell the supplier what you intend to use the concrete for and they will know the proper mix. Concrete is ordered by the cubic yard.

FOUNDATIONS

The purpose of the foundation is to support the load of the house above and to transmit this load on to the concrete spread footing. Foundations are usually of poured concrete or concrete block 8" to 12" thick. (Check your local building code.) Poured concrete is recommended because the solid mass reduces the problem of water leaks or termites.

If you chose a poured concrete foundation, it is best if you sub-let the job of preparing the concrete including the

TABLE 6-3.2

CONCRETE PROPORTIONS (Field Mixing)

Maximum Size of Coarse Aggregate	Minimum Cement (Sacks Per CY)	Maximum Water Gals Per Sack) (3)	Approximate Proportions (By Volume) Per Sack of Cement (1)		
			Cement	Fine Agg.	Coarse Agg.
3/4 in. ---------	6.0	5	1	2-1/2	2-3/4
1 in. ---------	5.8	5	1	2-1/2	3
1-1/2 in. ---------	5.4	5	1	2-1/2	3-1/2
(2) 2 in. ---------	5.2	5	1	2-1/2	4

Notes: (1) For concrete which will not be subject to freezing and thawing, the above proportions may be varied to use up to 5 percent less cement and 10 percent more fine aggregate. One sack of cement is equal to one cf or 94 lb.

(2) Not recommended for slabs or other thin sections.

(3) Includes moisture in aggregate.

formwork to a firm who specializes in this work. Voids or pockets must be provided in the foundation for underground service such as gas, water or sewer and also a pocket on each end wall to support the main beam. If you plan a house without a basement, the bottom of the footing must be below the frost depth in your area.

A concrete block foundation requires a ½" coat of cement plaster on the outside surface of the wall. This is called parging. The top layer of block must be filled solid with concrete at the core of the block to seal the wall against passage of water. If the height of the block foundation wall is ten times the thickness of the wall or larger, round steel reinforcing rods are required to strengthen the block walls. In poured concrete walls, rods may not be necessary. The majority of concrete block walls are built of 8" high, 16" long, and 8" wide units. The actual thickness is 7-5/8" high, 15-5/8" long and 7-5/8" wide.

For the sake of economy and good construction, care and careful planning should be exercised to avoid cutting concrete block. Wall lengths and heights should be in multiples of 8" to afford an even number of blocks. At beam bearing locations, fill the core of the block solid with concrete. If the block walls are longer than 12'-0" they should be reinforced with pilasters for strength. The mortar joints are the weakest part of the wall and should be laid in a full bed of mortar made up of Portland cement mix. Be sure to lay the block in a lap bond, that is; the vertical joints in every other course are in alignment. Corners should have intersecting block walls bonded by interlocking or lapping of alternate courses. Fill the core with insulation to reduce heat loss. This should be a granule type insulation that can be poured from the package into the block core.

In areas subjected to earth quakes, block walls should not be used for foundations unless they are reinforced with steel rods placed vertically in the block.

Horizontal reinforcing should also be used in the joints or mortar beds. Foundations are not necessary under garage overhead doors because there is no wall to support. Anchor bolts must be set in the top of the foundation to secure the framework to the foundation. These anchor bolts are about 18" long and ½" dia. threaded on one end with washer and nut and hooked or bent on the other end. The hooked end is inserted into the foundation with the threaded end on top. In the case of a poured concrete foundation, the anchor bolts are placed into position while the concrete is still wet with the bolt about 4" or 5" above the top of wall, set 3" back from the outside surface of the wall, placed about 4'-0" apart around the entire perimeter of the foundation. If the bolts are used with Concrete Block foundations, insert the hooked end either between joints of the block or in the core before filling them with concrete. The hooked end should be locked between joints.

In the case of Poured concrete foundation, the basement windows are installed in the forms at locations shown on plans and the concrete is poured around them. Basement windows are installed with the block walls, in either case, the top of the windows should be in line with the top of the foundation. Window sizes should be decided before foundation work is begun and, in the case of a block wall, the sizes should be in modules with block courses without having to cut the block to fit.

BULKHEADS

Outside entrances from the basement are accomplished by the use of Bulkheads. These units can be purchased in a package made of steel or can be built entirely of concrete walls and stairs with metal or wood doors. The size of these units must be established before any foundation work is started because openings must be left in the foundation to receive these units. The number of stairs required in a bulkhead is determined by the vertical distance between the

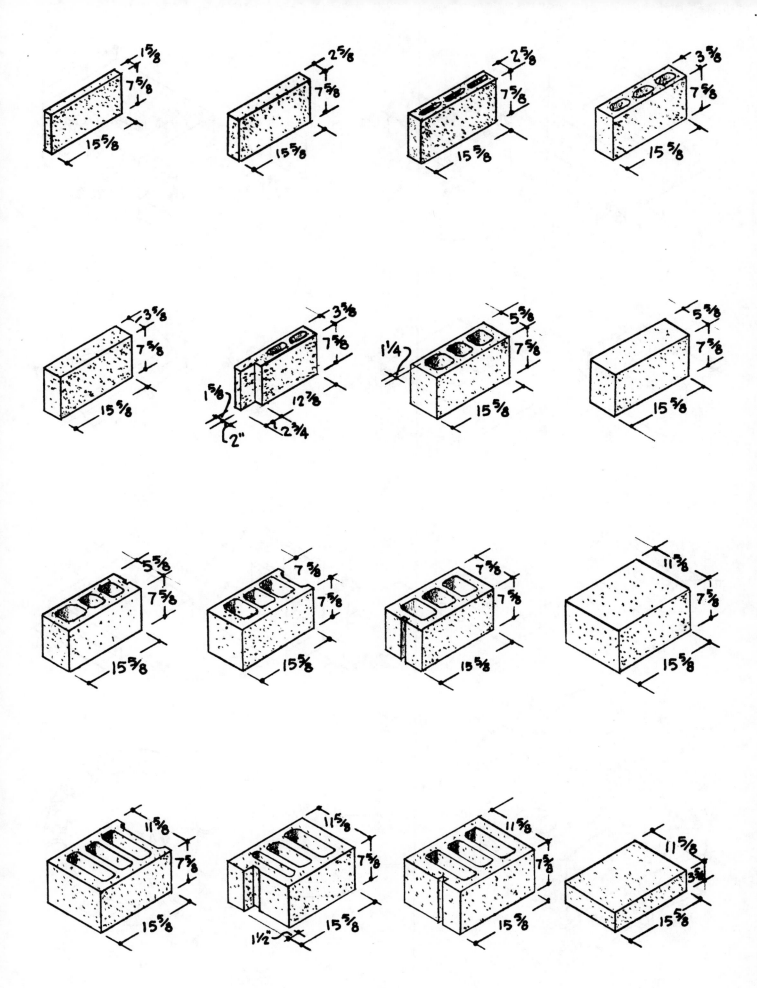

139

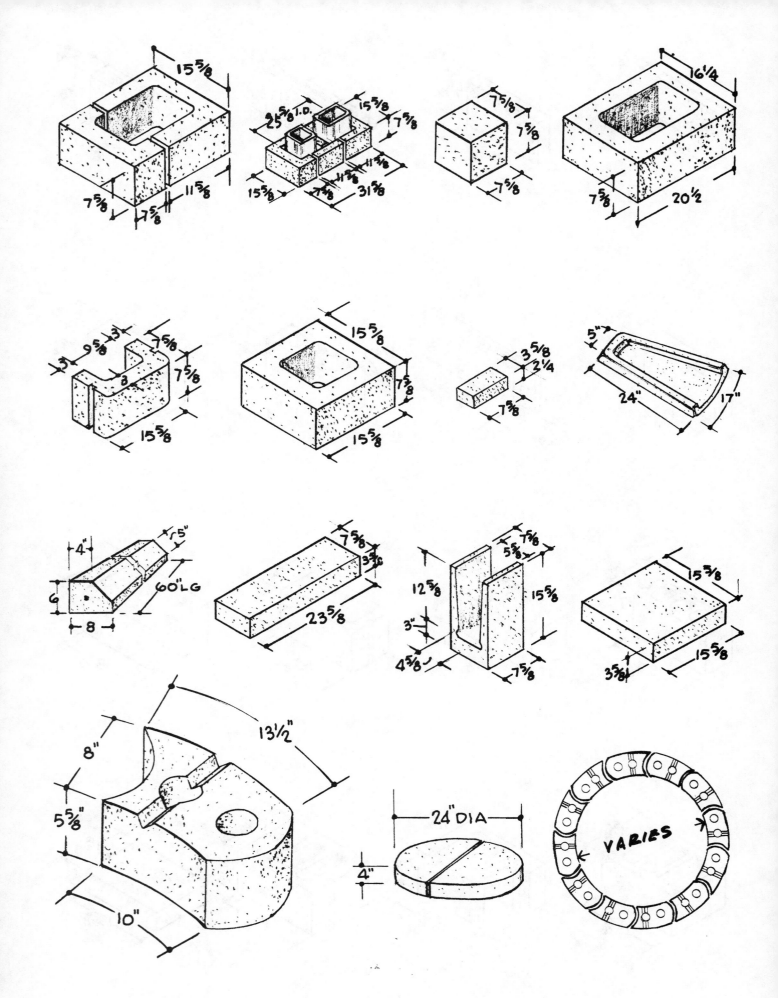

140

finished basement floor and finish grade. Allow about 6" or 8" above the grade for the first step to prevent water from running into the basement. If built of concrete, 8" thick walls can be used reinforced with ½" steel rods. If built of concrete block, 8" thick block can be used. The width of the stair treads should be about 10" wide and the risers should be no more than 8" high.

WATER PROOFING

All foundations whether concrete or block, basement, crawl space or slab on ground should receive one or two coats of asphalt, pitch or any preparation manufactured for this purpose applied on the outside surface of the foundation from the footings up to within a couple inches below the finish grade. In the case of a concrete block foundation, this is applied over the parging. This application will prevent moisture penetration through the wall. It can be applied by brush or spray.

DRAIN TILE

Provisions must be made to prevent water from finding its way into the basement, crawl space or slab on grade. This is accomplished with the installation of a 4" drain line or pipe sometimes called a French Drain. The pipe is laid around the perimeter of the foundation beginning at a high point just above the top of the spread footing, pitching down a minimum of 1/16" per foot to a run-off, catch basin, dry-well or sewer. This pipe is to be laid in a 2'-0" bed of crushed stone using perforated Orangeburg pipe with the perforations on the bottom, or clay pipe with about ¼" open joints covering only the top half of the joint with asphalt paper to prevent clogging the pipe. The asphalt paper can be tied around the pipe with wire. This pipe will direct any water underground into the pipe and away from the building instead of through the wall and into the building.

If the house is already built and you have a similar water problem, the same design can be used. But instead of putting it outside the wall lay the pipe under the basement floor about 12" to 18" away from the wall, collect the water in a pit and use a sump pump to discharge the water through a window outdoors. The pump is electrically operated and is controlled by an automatic float triggered by the height of water in the pit.

FOUNDATION SILL

Not only the first but the most important piece of wood to be used on your home is the foundation sill, because the entire house—floors, walls, ceilings and roof, is directly related to the foundation sill. The sill is also the closest piece of wood to the ground which makes it more vulnerable to termite and insect attack and it is at this point that we make provisions to prevent this from happening. (See Chapter 12 for Termite Protection.)

There are several methods of constructing a foundation sill, Western Framing, Braced Framing, Balloon Framing and variations of all, any of which is acceptable.

The sill consists of a continuous 4" x 6" wood member around the entire perimeter of the top of the foundation. Remove the nuts and washers from the anchor bolts and set the sill along the top of the foundation wall. Set the end of the sill on the outer edge of the foundation wall and transfer the anchor bolt's location onto the sill by drawing a line across the sill on each side of the anchor bolts using a carpenters square. Measure the distance from the outside foundation to the center of the anchor bolt and transfer this dimension onto the sill. Be sure to measure each bolt separately. After transferring the exact position of the anchor bolts onto the wood sill, drill a hole ¼" larger than the diameter of the bolt to allow for adjustment in placing the sill on top of the foundation. Repeat the procedure until all the holes have been marked and drilled. In joining the sills, allow an overlap of about 6" to halve each piece together. Try the sills for size and make any adjustments necessary for proper fitting over the anchor bolts. After all sills are fitted and cut, treat them with a wood preservative. Cover the entire area of the wood, especially the ends which will require more than one coat. The outside of the sill should be in alignment with the outside of the foundation.

FOUNDATION WALLS - REDUCED THICKNESS

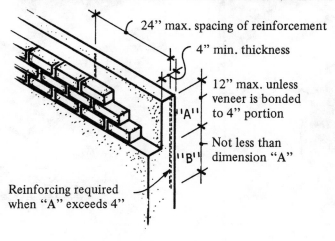

24" max. spacing of reinforcement

4" min. thickness

12" max. unless veneer is bonded to 4" portion

"A"

Not less than dimension "A"

"B"

Reinforcing required when "A" exceeds 4"

STEPPED WALL FOOTINGS

The following sketch indicates construction of stepped wall footings.

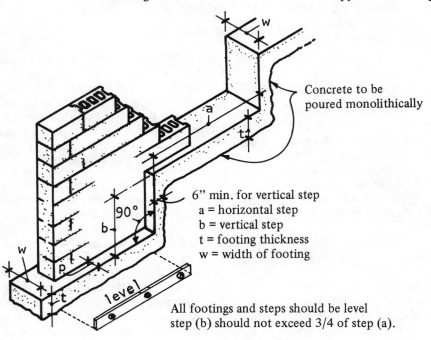

Concrete to be poured monolithically

6" min. for vertical step
a = horizontal step
b = vertical step
t = footing thickness
w = width of footing

All footings and steps should be level
step (b) should not exceed 3/4 of step (a).

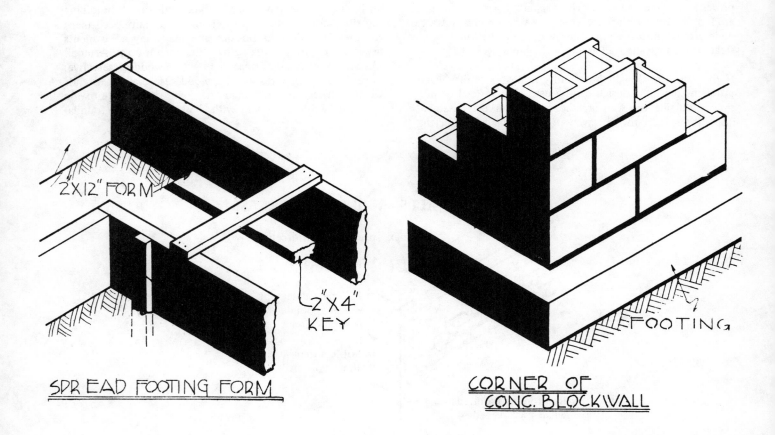

SPREAD FOOTING FORM

2X12" FORM

2"X4" KEY

CORNER OF CONC. BLOCKWALL

FOOTING

TERMITES and

CARPENTER ANTS

12

The home of the termite is in the ground, and is attracted by wood, working its way inside, often leaving no visual sign of its presence. The first indication may be noticed too late to make it worthwhile to correct the damage. These unwanted pests can be found even in the cleanest of homes because they can be brought in with fruits, vegetables and clothing or sometimes even by domestic pets. When they are not able to find enough food (wood) in or on the ground, they will emerge from the soil and attack the wood in buildings taking care to avoid contact with outside air or light. They will gain entrance through any part of the wood structure in contact with the ground through openings in the foundation, around pipes and conduits or through cracks in the foundation. If none of these are available, they will construct tubes made from mud to reach the wood of the building, they work quickly and quietly devouring and destroying all wood in their path from the inside of the wood working their way outside. They will hollow-out a board leaving nothing but the paint. Detection is difficult. They are careful not to eat through the outside surface of the wood even going so far as to block up any surface hole accidentally broken through. Egg laying of termites increases rapidly within two or three years after the colony is established and a colony can consist of several thousands of termites. The worker termite will leave the colony seeking wood because the principal food of termites is cellulose, the main ingredinet of wood.

Here are some danger signs which may be encountered: Swarms of tiny black or dark brown insects with whitish, opaque wings, thick waists and curved antennae. These are reproductive termites which swarm in the spring and fall of the year, then shed their wings and go underground to start their colony. Watch for clusters of discarded wings. Winged termites are often mistaken for winged ants. The ant has a thin, wasplike waist with transparent wings and elbow shaped antennae. Tubes are built in the ground leading from a crack in the foundation to the wood structure of the house. The shelter tubes may be attached to the foundation or they may rise directly upward without support. This is a sure sign of termite infestation.

Good construction details generally eliminate damage to wood structures. However, when such details are ignored, decay or termite damage may occur, unless naturally durable heartwood or preservatively treated wood is used.

DECAY is caused by fungi which are low forms of plant life, some species of which depend upon the digestion of wood for their sustenance. Fungi may attack wood in service only under the combined environmental conditions of: (1) temperature in the range of 41° to 104° F., (2) adequate supply of oxygen, and (3) moisture content in excess of 20 percent.

The foregoing requirements of fungi indicate a method to prevent decay in structures. Temperature, except in arctic climates, is impractical to control. Lack of sufficient oxygen to support decay occurs only when wood is completely below the ground water line or continuously submerged in fresh water. Control of moisture content of wood is a practical and effective method for prevention of decay.

THE SUBTERRANEAN TERMITE is an insect which attacks in colonies and derives its nourishment from cellulosic materials such as wood, fabrics, paper and fiber board. To obtain nourishment the termite may attack wood structures above the ground by means of shelter tubes attached to foundation walls, piers and other members in contact with the ground. However, only under conditions which permit the insect to establish and maintain contact with soil moisture, is a colony able to penetrate and consume wood in service. This requirement indicates that a barrier separating wood from earth, supplemented by inspection, is a practical and effective method for preventing damage by termites.

PRINCIPLES OF GOOD CONSTRUCTION

Protection of wood structures to provide maximum service-life involves three methods of control which can be handled by proper design and construction. One, or more of the following methods may be employed: (1) control moisture content of wood, (2) provide effective termite barriers, (3) use naturally durable or treated wood.

Wood construction maintained at a moisture content of 20 percent or less WILL NOT DECAY. Optimum conditions for decay occur when moisture content is above 25 percent. It should be stressed that when wood is protected from water or from vapor condensation, and exposed to normal atmospheric conditions such as exist inside buildings and outdoors, its moisture content rarely exceeds 15 percent. Therefore, moisture content control by means of accepted design and construction details is a simple and practical method of providing protection against decay.

While control of moisture contributes to the prevention of subterranean termite attack, the primary control method requires the use of effective barriers supplemented by periodic inspection. Termite barriers are provided by the use of accepted construction practices which drive termites into the open where the shelter tubes can be detected by inspection.

Wood structures which are provided with a recognized barrier supplemented by periodic inspection can be PERMANENTLY ENSURED AGAINST SUBTERRANEAN TERMITE ATTACK

When termite shield and wood sill have been prepared for installation, a leveling bed of grout (cement) fine screened sand and water) must be applied to the top of the foundation to provide a firm, level, sealed bed. The thickness of the grout will vary from 1/2" to 1-1/4". When you apply the grout, install the termite shield, then the wood sill over the shield. Install the washers and hand tighten the nuts of the anchor bolts. One entire wall length should be done at a time. Once the sill is in place, drive a nail into each corner of the building and string a line taut. This is used to make the sill straight. Leveling is done with a carpenters level. If the sill has to be raised to level, use wood shingles being careful to apply the tapered end on both sides of the sill. The farther you drive the wood shingles together, the higher the sill will raise. Use this method until the sill is perfectly straight and level, then tighten up the nuts with a wrench. Follow this procedure on all walls and sides of the building. Where the sills are halved, nail them together with 10d nails and remove any excess grout. When you have completed the shield and sill installation, there should be no void or space between the wall and the sill.

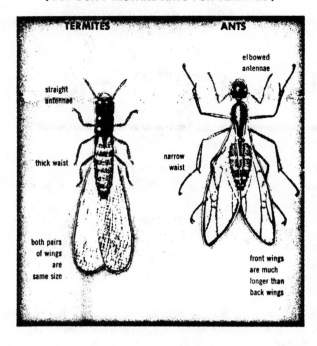

Protection against termites is accomplished by a barrier of toxicant sprayed beneath and around the house which make it impossible for the termites to cross or pass. The termites above the chemical barrier will die for lack of moisture and those below it will die from lack of food. If any damage has affected the structural portion of the house, it should be replaced. This spraying should be done once a year for lasting protection.

To guard against termites, a metal shield of not less than 26 gauge of non-rusting metal such as galvanized sheet metal, copper or aluminum should be placed between the top of the foundation and the bottom of the sill. The metal should be no less than 8" wide extending out beyond the outside foundation about 1" with a 60 degree bend. Be sure to overlap and seal the joints of the metal. The same procedure should be followed in locating the transfer of the anchor bolt holes onto the termite shield as we did the foundation sill. Longitudinal joints should be locked and soldered.

A few simple precautions will help keep your home safe. Keep a clean yard, especially around the house. Remove all scrap lumber in contact with the ground. Have tree stumps removed as soon as possible. Do not use waste lumber or wood of any kind for fill. No portion of the house should be in contact with the ground. Wood posts should be sealed with creosote and bent or damaged termite shields should be repaired. Seal all foundation cracks immediately—termites will pass through a crack 1/64" wide. A chemical spray on the exterior of the foundation on the ground will discourage termites. At least once a year have a trained termite expert inspect your home.

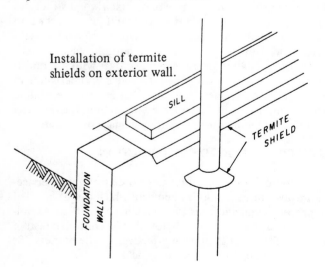

Installation of termite shields on exterior wall.

144

These pests cause close to $350 million worth of damage every year literally eating you out of house and home. The most discouraging fact is that a queen termite may live for over 30 years and keep on producing successively larger batches of eggs. Probing with an ice pick, knife or screwdriver will uncover termites or termite damaged wood. If termites are present during probing they will appear as milk-white plumb bobs. The most likely time is usually on a warm spring day after a rain fall. Termites are found all over the United States with the exception of Alaska. The rate of infestation is extremely high in areas with a mean average temperature of 45 degrees. The farther south, the more prevalent. Termite damage can begin in homes from time of construction to any time thereafter. Termites will also chew rugs, books, clothing, curtains and paper.

Carpenter ants crawl about houses and yard. They can get into food and will excavate galleries for their colony in wood. They can damage or weaken buildings, trees, poles and posts. In the crawling stage these insects are large, black and wingless measuring about 1/4" to 3/8" long indoors or outdoors. They may wander anywhere but sometimes seem to follow a specific trail marked by a visible narrow path clean of any vegetation. In the winged stage a sudden flight of numerous large, black ants with darker wing veins and brownish bodies may be seen. The wings extend beyond the end of the body about half the body length. Sometimes a pile of sawdust or an accumulation of course fibrous "sawdust" will be found near a colony in a building, hollow tree or pole. The ants carry the sawdust out in building their nests and neatly dispose of it. They do not eat wood but will damage the wood in nest building. If infested, the damaged wood will have interconnecting, irregular chambers and tunnels with clean smooth inner walls. You may not see the colonies because the entrance may be hidden but they can be found in any part of the house. They sometimes nest in hollow porch columns, walls etc. Outdoors they live in trees that are partly hollow or decaying, also in stumps, logs, poles and posts. Termites are sometimes confused with carpenter ants. No sawdust is produced with termites because they eat the wood. Ants eat foodstuffs and other insects.

The ants mate during a brief flight after leaving the parent colony. The male soon dies and the female breaks off her wings, digs a small chamber in suitable wood, seals herself in, lays her egss and raises her family of workers. The colony may eventually contain several queens and thousands of workers. After two or three years the colony will produce large, winged males and females who will leave the colony and start the cycle over again. Flights are common in spring and early summer.

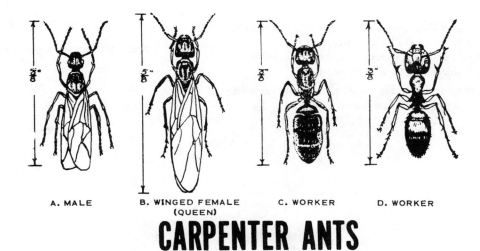

A. MALE   B. WINGED FEMALE (QUEEN)   C. WORKER   D. WORKER

CARPENTER ANTS

TABLE 5-2.1
SOIL POISONS

Chemicals	Concentrations
Aldrin	0.5% Applied in water emulsion
Chlordane	1.0% Applied in water emulsion
Dieldrin	0.5% Applied in water emulsion
Heptachlor	0.5% Applied in water emulsion
Chlordane and Heptachlor	0.5% Chlordane plus 0.25% Heptachlor a 0.75% solution applied in water emulsion

SOIL POISONING

When the soil poisoning method of termite protection is required by the Standard and is permitted by Federal, state or local regulations, the chemicals and concentrations shown in Table 5-2.1 shall be applied.

GEOGRAPHIC DISTRIBUTION OF TERMITE INFESTATION

Region III, termite protection generally not required.

Region IV, (including Alaska) termite protection not required.

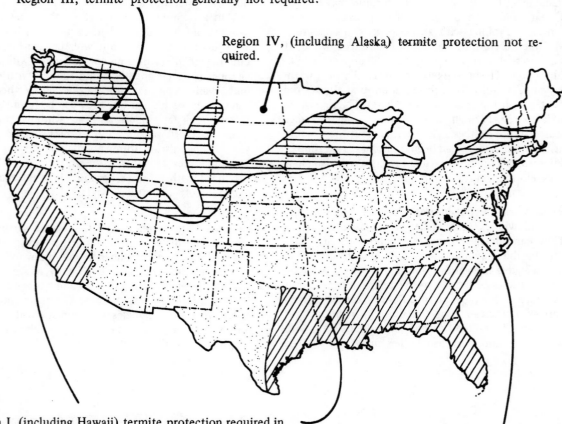

Region I, (including Hawaii) termite protection required in all areas. If construction is of slab-on-ground type a chemical barrier should be used, except that monolithic slab design may be considered as termite protection.

Puerto Rico is an area of severe infestation, all lumber should be pressure treated per AWPI Standards.

Region II, termite protection generally required.

FLOOR FRAMING

13

BEAM & COLUMNS

Once the sill is in position, straight, level and tight, the main beam must be installed. In your planning, if your selection of a beam is wood, the top of the beam is level with the top of the foundation sill. If your selection is steel, a wood nailer is level with the top of the foundation sill. Referring to the Foundation Plans, the distance from foundation wall to foundation wall is 34'-6". Within that distance, the beam must be supported by columns placed about 8'-0" apart. Without these columns, the beam would not support the load without failing. The beam is wood 8" x 10" designed for this house based on codes, loads and distances called spans.

The end of the beam is resting on the foundation wall and must bear at least 4" onto the foundation wall. The size of the end beam pocket within the foundation is determined by the beam size. In this case the width of the pocket is the same as the width of the beam or 8", the depth is a minimum of 4" and the height is the beam height minus the sill (10" for the beam height less 4" for the foundation sill height = 6"). Once the beam is in position, place temporary supports under the beam about 8'-0" apart of 2-2"x4" nailed together. A steel plate of 1/4" thick must be placed under the beam on both ends. The size of the steel plate should be the same size as the pocket-in this case, 8" x 4" x 1/4" There is no need to secure the plates because the weight of the beam will hold them in position. The purpose of the plate is to afford an even, level bearing for the beam. Height adjustments can be made with steel wedges placed under the steel bearing plate which is set in a bed of mortar or grout. If one continuous length of beam is not possible, joints must be made over a column halving the beam as we did the foundation sill and nailed together. Instead of a solid wood beam, your code may allow you to use what is called a built-up beam made up of 4 pieces of 2" x 10" bolted together with broken joints.

Now that the beam is in place, columns must be installed under the beam. Again referring to the Basement Plan of the plans, you will see a note which reads 3 1/2" H. W. Col. which means 3 1/2" diameter heavy weight column spaced 8'-7 1/2" apart supported by 2'-0" square and 1'-0" deep

concrete footings shown dotted under each column. The top of these concrete footings is the same level as the top of the foundation spread footings. Locate these footings following the dimensions indicated on the Basement Plan. 8'-7 1/2" in one direction and 13'-6" in the other direction which is to the center of the footings. The size of the column footing is determined by the load it will be required to support and the bearing capacity of the soil. The column footings indicated on the plans are for an average condition. Check with your local building inspector for assistance.

The forms for the concrete footings are made up of 2" x 12" filled with concrete of the same proportions as the foundation concrete. Once the concrete has hardened, remove the forms and measure the distance between the top of the footing and the bottom of the beam. Subtract 1/2" and this becomes the overall length of the columns; including the bearing plate on the top and on the bottom of the column. These columns are ordered to length through your local building supply dealer. The top steel plate of the column has predrilled holes for securing the column to the beam with screws. Let the bottom hang free and use steel wedges to make up the varying void under the column. Force a concrete mix under the base plate of the column. The basement concrete floor will hold the bottom of the column in position.

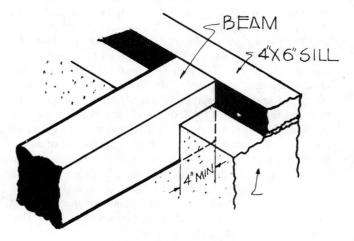

GIRDER POCKET

STEEL COLUMN CAPS AND BASE PLATES

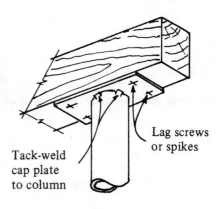

WOOD BEAM AND STEEL COLUMN

Tack-weld cap plate to column

Lag screws or spikes

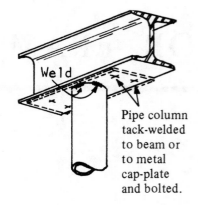

STEEL BEAM AND COLUMN

Weld

Pipe column tack-welded to beam or to metal cap-plate and bolted.

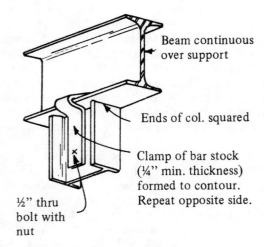

STEEL BEAM AND COLUMN

Beam continuous over support

Ends of col. squared

Clamp of bar stock (¼" min. thickness) formed to contour. Repeat opposite side.

½" thru bolt with nut

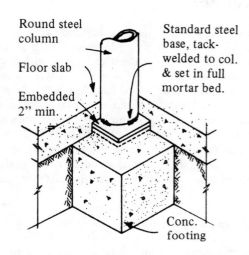

STEEL COLUMN AND FOOTING

Round steel column

Floor slab

Embedded 2" min.

Standard steel base, tack-welded to col. & set in full mortar bed.

Conc. footing

FLOOR JOISTS

The framing members that support the floor are called Floor Joists. The size of floor joists are determined by load, span and spacing. A rule of thumb for sizing floor joists is Span in feet x 1 1/2 depth of joist in inches. Ex: 1.5 x 8 =(12'-0" span) (8" depth joist.) Referring to the Basement Plan, the size of the floor joists are 2" x 8" spaced 16" apart. Joists can be spaced 12", 16" and 24" apart. 16" spacing is the most common. In determing the floor joist size, it is necessary to know the span or distance from the center of the beam to the outside foundation wall, the live load which is the load the joists are expected to carry, ususally about 40 lbs. per sq. foot, the dead load which is the weight of all the building material supported by the joists, including a plastered ceiling under the joist. All of these loads are combined or added to determine the total load being supported by the floor joists. Check your building code for the minimum live load for floor joists. Building Codes usually specify that the maximum bending of floor joists fully loaded, called deflection, is not to exceed 1/360 of the span. This means a span of 15'-0" will allow a minimum of 1/2" bending.

Study the architectural plans carefully, especially the Basement Floor Plan and note the direction of the floor joists indicated by the double arrowed line with the notation 2" x 8"/16" oc. O.C. means on center.

Joists under all partitions which are parallel to the joists must be doubled because of the extra load of the partition carried by the joists. Do not break the continuity of 16" spacing of the joists when laying out the location of the joists on the sill. Provide for all floor openings such as stairs chimneys etc. and double the joists around the perimeter of these openings, which will be found on the First Floor Plan. This doubling is called Header. Under no circumstances should the floor be supported by the chimney. In fact, most codes require a clearance of at least 2" between the chimney and the framing because of the heat generated by the chimney.

Joists are not perfectly straight and by running your eye across one edge of the joist, you will see a high point or crown. When installing the joist, be sure the crown is up.

The end of the joist is in alignment with the outside line of the foundation sill. Nail the joist to the sill on one end and the beam on the other with 8d nails, two each side and one on the end. If a joist falls on an anchor bolt, notch the joist to fit over the bolt. Building codes state that nails should not be closer together than 1/2 their length nor closer to the edge of a framing member than 1/4 their length. After a few joists have been nailed in position, place a piece of plywood over the joists to provide a temporary working platform. You must maintain a high level of accuracy in laying and cutting floor framing. All parts must fit together tightly to maintain the strength of the entire assembly. If your design includes a section of the floor overhanging beyond the foundation, simply use longer joists to the desired length where the overhang is parallel to the joists. If the overhang is perpendicular to the joists, double the joists at a point twice the distance of the overhang and reverse the joist direction at that point.

Looking at the Basement Plan, the distance from the center of the beam to the outside foundation wall is 14'-6". Framing lumber comes in multiples of 2'-0" lengths of even dimenstions. That 14'-6" distance means we have to use 16'-0" long joists with a waste of 1'-6". If that 14'-6" dimension were changed to 14'-0", there would be no waste. The joists parallel to the wall on both ends of the building should be 3 5/8" back from the outside sill line to allow room for the wall above.

After we complete the installation of the floor joists, we are ready for backfilling, because the joists will give the necessary bracing to the foundation. Do not allow any wood or organic material in the backfill. If large rock are used for backfill be careful not to break or crack the foundation with the rock rolling against the wall. Place the rock, do not allow it to roll free. If the foundation is cracked, it must be rebuilt, it may not be possible to repair it without leaking.

BRIDGING

Before the installation of the first of two layers of flooring called sub-flooring, cross bridging is used to stiffen the floor and spread the load over a broader area of floor. This cross bridging is done with 1" x 3" wood called furring. The ends are cut at an angle to fit snugly against the joist and are nailed with 2-6d nails top and bottom, halfway between the beam and the outside wall for the entire length of the bay. Cross or diagonal bridging can be accomplished with metal as well as wood especially designed for that purpose. Another method of bridging is called solid bridging which is done with blocks of wood the same depth as the joists. Any of the described bridging is acceptable but must be nailed in place before the sub-flooring is installed. To install the bridging, snap a chalk line across the tops of the joists. Start two nails into the ends of all the bridging and attach one to each side of the joist. The bottom can be nailed later even after the sub-floor is in place.

DESIGN LIVE LOADS

General

Design live loads shall consist of the weight of all moving and variable loads that may act on the building or other structures including loads on floors, operational loads on roofs and ceiling, but not including wind, snow, earthquake or dead load. The design live loads specified herein are minimum. If local building code requirements are higher than those contained herein, the local code requirements shall be used.

Floor and Ceiling Loads

Design live floor and ceiling loads shall be not less than the uniformly distributed loads shown in Table 6-1.1.

Concentrated Loads

Consideration shall be given to effect of concentrated wheel loads on structures. Floors in garages or portions of buildings used for storage of passenger cars for not more than nine passengers shall be designed for the designated uniform live loads of Table 6-1.1 or 2000 pounds acting on an area of 20 sq. in.

TABLE 6-1-1

FLOOR OR CEILING LIVE LOADS

Location	Live Load (psf)
Dwelling rooms (other than sleeping quarters)	40
Dwelling rooms (sleeping quarters and attic floors)	30
Ceiling joist-attics (served by permanent or disappearing stair)	30
Ceiling joist-attics (limited storage roof slope over 3 in 12)	20
Ceiling joists-attics (without storage roof slope 3 in 12 or less)	10
Stairs	60
Public stairs and corridors (two family dwellings)	60
Garages and carports (passenger cars)	75
Balconies and porches	60
Sidewalks and driveways	250

SUB-FLOORING

The installation of the sub-floor is the final step in completing the floor framing. Plywood, composition panel, or boards may be used for sub-flooring which adds rigidity to the structure and provides a base for the finish floor. If boards are used, they may be laid at a 45 degree diagonal to the joists. This will increase the waste but will provide bracing action and will permit the wood finish floor to be laid in any direction. If you lay the sub-floor boards perpendicular to the joists, the wood finish floor must be laid parallel to the joists. In either case, let the boards extend out over the walls and openings and saw them off after the boards have been nailed in place. Use two 8d nails at each joist for boards 6" in width or under and three nails for widths over 6". The boards are 3/4" thick in random lengths. If plywood is used for sub-flooring, check your local building code for minimum thickness. Usually 1/2" thick plywood over joists spaced 16" on center will meet the minimum requirements. The long dimension, or 8'-0" length should run perpendicular to the joists and joints should be broken in successive courses. Screw nails should be used in nailing plywood sub-flooring spaced 6" apart on every joist otherwise the floors will squeak. All sub-flooring should fall on the center of the joist.

Girders may be solid or built-up of two or more members. Built-up girders should be assembled with nails of sufficient length to penetrate all members and to allow for clinching nail from both sides as follows: two nails at ends of piece and each splice, and two rows of nails in between splices at top and bottom of girder at 32 inches o.c. Stagger nails.

Structural steel to be encased in concrete should not be painted.

Structural steel in weather-tight buildings not subject to condensation or high humidity conditions should receive one shop coat of paint and one coat on abraded surfaces after erection.

Structural steel exposed to weather or located in weathertight buildings subject to condensation or high humity conditions should receive one shop coat of paint, one coat on abraded surfaces after erection and a second coat of paint suitable for the climate and exposure.

FLOORS

Joist Framed Over Beams

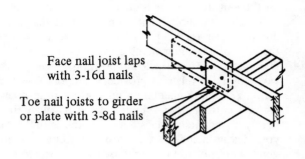

Face nail joist laps with 3-16d nails

Toe nail joists to girder or plate with 3-8d nails

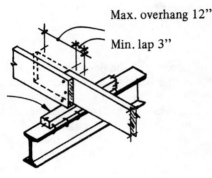

Max. overhang 12"

Min. lap 3"

2" x 4" cont. wood nailer, clinched to beam. (bolted to beam in seismic areas 2 and 3).

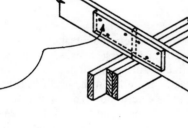

Where bearing is sufficient to provide stresses within limits for the grade and species, tie butted joists with 1" x 6" x 24" wood tie, or 18 ga. 2" x 18" metal tie. 6-8d nails in each tie. (Ties may be omitted when subfloor provides tie across joists).

12" max.

Wood blocking, toe nailed to joist or clinched to beam

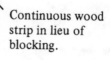

Continuous wood strip in lieu of blocking.

The sketches below indicate three acceptable methods of framing floor joists into the side of wood girders.

18 ga. 3" x 3" x 6"

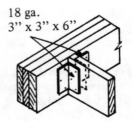

Steel Angle

1 1/2 x 1/4 strap

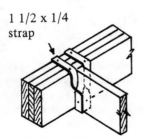

Steel Joist Hanger

Toe nail with 3-10d nails

2" x 2"

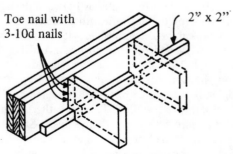

Wood Bearing Strip

STEEL BEAM SPAN

MAXIMUM ALLOWABLE UNIFORM LOADS FOR AMERICAN STANDARD I-BEAMS WITH LATERAL SUPPORT

SPAN IN FEET

SIZE OF BEAM	WEIGHT OF BEAM PER FT.	4	6	8	10	12	14	16	18	20	22	24	26	28	30	32	34	36	38	40
4 x 2 3/4	7.7	10	7	5																
	9.5	11	7	6																
5 x 3	10.0	16	11	8	6															
	11.3	20	13	10	8															
6 x 3 1/8	12.5	24	16	12	10	8														
	17.3	29	19	15	12	10														
7 x 3 3/4	15.3	35	23	17	14	12	10													
	20.0	40	27	20	16	15	13													
8 x 4	18.4	47	32	24	19	16	14	12												
	23.0	53	36	27	21	18	15	13												
10 x 4 3/4	25.4	80	54	41	33	27	23	20	18	16										
	35.0	97	65	49	39	32	28	24	22	20										
12 x 5	31.8	110	80	60	48	40	34	30	27	24	22	20								
	35.0	126	84	63	50	42	36	32	28	25	23	21								
12 x 5 1/4	40.8	144	100	75	60	50	43	37	33	30	27	25								
	50.0	168	112	84	67	56	48	42	37	34	31	28								
15 x 5 1/2	42.9	160	131	98	79	65	56	49	44	39	36	33	30	28	26	25				
	50.0	214	143	107	86	71	61	54	48	43	39	36	33	31	29	27				
18 x 6	54.7		196	147	118	98	84	74	66	59	54	49	45	42	39	37	35	33	31	
	70.0		226	170	136	113	97	85	76	68	62	57	52	49	45	43	40	38	36	
20 x 6 1/4	65.4		260	195	156	130	111	97	87	78	71	65	60	56	52	49	46	43	41	39
	75.0		281	211	169	140	120	105	94	84	77	70	65	60	56	53	50	47	44	42

LOADS ARE IN KIPS. 1 KIP = 1,000 POUNDS

MAXIMUM ALLOWABLE UNIFORM LOADS FOR WIDE FLANGE I-BEAMS WITH LATERAL SUPPORT

SPAN IN FEET

SIZE OF BEAM	WEIGHT OF BEAM PER FT.	4	6	8	9	10	12	14	18	20	22	24	26	28	30	32	34	36	38	40
8 x 5 1/4	17	47	31	24	19	16	13	12												
8 x 6 1/2	24		46	35	28	23	20	17												
8 x 8	31		60	46	37	30	26	23	20	18	16									
10 x 5 1/4	21	62	48	36	29	24	21	18	16	14										
10 x 8	33			74	58	47	39	33	29	26	23									
10 x 10	49				88	73	61	52	46	40	36	33	30	28	26					
12 x 6 1/2	27		74	57	45	38	32	28	25	23	21	19								
12 x 8	40		87	69	58	49	43	38	35	32·	29									
12 x 10	53			108	94	79	67	59	52	47	43	39								
12 x 12	65				117	98	84	73	65	59	53	49	45	42	39					
14 x 6 3/4	30		93	70	56	46	40	35	31	28	25	23	21	20	19					
14 x 8	43			105	84	70	60	52	46	42	38	35	32	30	28					
14 x 10	61				123	102	88	77	68	62	56	51	47	44	41					
14 x 12	78				156	135	115	101	90	81	73	67	62	58	54					
14 x 14 1/2	87					152	132	115	102	92	84	77	71	66	61	57	54	51		
16 x 7	36		124	94	75	63	54	47	42	38	34	31	29	27	25	24	22			
16 x 8 1/2	58			157	126	105	90	78	70	63	57	52	48	45	42	39	37			
16 x 11 1/2	88				202	168	144	126	112	101	92	84	78	72	67	63	59			
18 x 7 1/2	50			148	119	99	85	74	66	59	54	49	46	42	40	37	35	33	31	
18 x 8 3/4	64			188	156	130	111	98	87	78	71	65	60	56	52	49	46	43	41	
18 x 11 3/4	96				224	189	176	154	137	123	112	103	95	88	82	77	72	68	65	
21 x 8 1/4	62			211	169	141	120	105	94	84	77	70	65	60	56	53	50	47	44	42

LOADS ARE IN KIPS. 1 KIP = 1,000 POUNDS

FLOOR JOIST SPAN

SOUTHERN YELLOW PINE – 30 LB. LIVE LOAD

JOIST SIZE (NOMINAL)	SPACING OF JOISTS O.C. IN INCHES	LUMBER GRADES			
		NO. 1 DENSE KILN-DRIED 2" DIM.	NO. 2 DENSE KILN-DRIED 2" DIM.	NO. 1 DENSE 2" DIM.	NO. 2 DENSE 2" DIM.
2 x 6	12	12'-5"	12'-5"	12'-5"	12'-5"
	16	11'-4"	11'-4"	11'-4"	11'-4"
	24	10'-2"	10'-2"	10'-0"	9'-2"
2 x 8	12	16'-1"	16'-1"	16'-1"	16'-1"
	16	14'-9"	14'-9"	14'-9"	14'-9"
	24	13'-1"	13'-1"	13'-1"	12'-4"
2 x 10	12	19'-11"	19'-11"	19'-11"	19'-11"
	16	18'-3"	18'-3"	18'-3"	18'-3"
	24	16'-2"	16'-2"	16'-2"	15'-7"
2 x 12	12	23'-9"	23'-9"	23'-9"	23'-9"
	16	21'-9"	21'-9"	21'-9"	21'-9"
	24	19'-2"	19'-2"	19'-2"	18'-11"

SOUTHERN YELLOW PINE – 40 LB. LIVE LOAD

JOIST SIZE (NOMINAL)	SPACING OF JOISTS O.C. IN INCHES	LUMBER GRADES			
		NO. 1 DENSE KILN-DRIED 2" DIM.	NO. 2 DENSE KILN-DRIED 2" DIM.	NO. 1 DENSE 2" DIM.	NO. 2 DENSE 2" DIM.
2 x 6	12	11'-5"	11'-5"	11'-5"	11'-5"
	16	10'-5"	10'-5"	10'-5"	10'-1"
	24	9'-2"	9'-2"	8'-11"	8'-3"
2 x 8	12	14'-9"	14'-9"	14'-9"	14'-9"
	16	13'-6"	13'-6"	13'-6"	13'-6"
	24	12'-0"	12'-0"	11'-11"	11'-0"
2 x 10	12	18'-3"	18'-3"	18'-3"	18'-3"
	16	16'-9"	16'-9"	16'-9"	16'-9"
	24	14'-10"	14'-10"	14'-10"	14'-10"
2 x 12	12	21'-9"	21'-9"	21'-9"	21'-9"
	16	19'-11"	19'-11"	19'-11"	19'-11"
	24	17'-7"	17'-7"	17'-7"	16'-11"

LARCH AND DOUGLAS FIR – 30 LB. LIVE LOAD

JOIST SIZE (NOMINAL)	SPACING OF JOISTS O.C. IN INCHES	LUMBER GRADES				
		SELECT STRUCTURAL	DENSE CONSTRUCTION	CONSTRUCTION	STANDARD	UTILITY
2 x 6	12	11'-4"	11'-4"	11'-4"	11'-4"	8'-4"
	16	10'-4"	10'-4"	10'-4"	10'-4"	7'-2"
	24	9'-0"	9'-0"	9'-0"	9'-0"	5'-10"
2 x 8	12	15'-4"	15'-4"	15'-4"	15'-4"	12'-4"
	16	14'-0"	14'-0"	14'-0"	14'-0"	10'-8"
	24	12'-4"	12'-4"	12'-4"	12'-4"	8'-8"
2 x 10	12	18'-4"	18'-4"	18'-4"	18'-4"	16'-10"
	16	17'-0"	17'-0"	17'-0"	17'-0"	14'-8"
	24	15'-6"	15'-6"	15'-6"	15'-6"	12'-0"
2 x 12	12	21'-2"	21'-2"	21'-2"	21'-2"	19'-8"
	16	19'-8"	19'-8"	19'-8"	19'-8"	17'-0"
	24	17'-10"	17'-10"	17'-10"	17'-10"	14'-0"

LARCH AND DOUGLAS FIR – 40 LB. LIVE LOAD

JOIST SIZE (NOMINAL)	SPACING OF JOISTS O.C. IN INCHES	LUMBER GRADES				
		SELECT STRUCTURAL	DENSE CONSTRUCTION	CONSTRUCTION	STANDARD	UTILITY
2 x 6	12	10'-6"	10'-6"	10'-6"	10'-6"	7'-4"
	16	9'-8"	9'-8"	9'-8"	9'-8"	6'-4"
	24	8'-4"	8'-4"	8'-4"	8'-2"	5'-2"
2 x 8	12	14'-4"	14'-4"	14'-4"	14'-4"	10'-0"
	16	13'-0"	13'-0"	13'-0"	13'-0"	9'-6"
	24	11'-6"	11'-6"	11'-6"	11'-0"	7'-10"
2 x 10	12	17'-4"	17'-4"	17'-4"	17'-4"	15'-2"
	16	16'-2"	16'-2"	16'-2"	16'-2"	13'-0"
	24	14'-6"	14'-6"	14'-6"	14'-0"	10'-8"
2 x 12	12	20'-0"	20'-0"	20'-0"	20'-0"	17'-8"
	16	18'-8"	18'-8"	18'-8"	18'-8"	15'-4"
	24	16'-10"	16'-10"	16'-10"	16'-10"	12'-6"

WOOD GIRDER

One Story Floor Loads

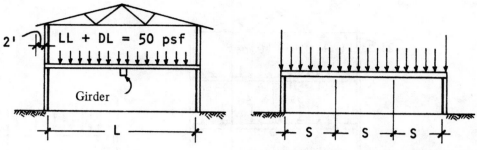

End splits may not exceed the girder depth

In order that stresses not be exceeded, in the following table the girder may not be offset from centerline of house by more than one foot. However, girders may be located to suit design conditions provided unit stresses conform to industry standards for grade and species.

NOMINAL LUMBER SIZES	GIRDER SPANS – S IN FEET					
	HOUSE WIDTHS – L IN FEET					
	22	24	26	28	30	32
LUMBER HAVING AN ALLOWABLE BENDING STRESS NOT LESS THAN 1000 PSI						
2 - 2x6	4'-0"	--	--	--	--	--
3 - 2x6	5'-3"	5'-0"	4'-10"	4'-8"	4'-5"	4'-2"
2 - 2x8	5'-3"	4'-10"	4'-5"	4'-2"	--	--
3 - 2x8	6'-11"	6'-7"	6'-4"	6'-2"	5'-10"	5'-5"
2 - 2x10	6'-9"	6'-2"	5'-8"	5'-3"	4'-11"	4'-8"
3 - 2x10	8'-10"	8'-5"	8'-1"	7'-10"	7'-5"	6'-11"
2 - 2x12	8'-2"	7'-6"	6'-11"	6'-5"	6'-0"	5'-8"
3 - 2x12	10'-9"	10'-3"	9'-10"	9'-6"	9'-0"	8'-5"
LUMBER HAVING AN ALLOWABLE BENDING STRESS NOT LESS THAN 1500 PSI						
2 - 2x6	4'-10"	4'-5"	4'-1"	--	--	--
3 - 2x6	6'-5"	6'-2"	5'-11"	5'-8"	5'-3"	4'-11"
2 - 2x8	6'-4"	5'-10"	5'-4"	5'-0"	4'-8"	4'-4"
3 - 2x8	8'-6"	8'-1"	7'-9"	7'-5"	7'-0"	6'-6"
2 - 2x10	8'-1"	7'-5"	6'-10"	6'-4"	5'-11"	5'-7"
3 - 2x10	10'-10"	10'-4"	9'-11"	9'-6"	8'-11"	8'-4"
2 - 2x12	9'-10"	9'-0"	8'-4"	7'-9"	7'-2"	6'-9"
3 - 2x12	13'-2"	12'-7"	12'-1"	11'-7"	10'-10"	10'-2"

FLOORS

Joists Framed Into Steel Beam

Where subfloor does not provide a lateral tie, locate 18 ga. 1 1/2" x 24" metal tie at top or bottom of every third joist.

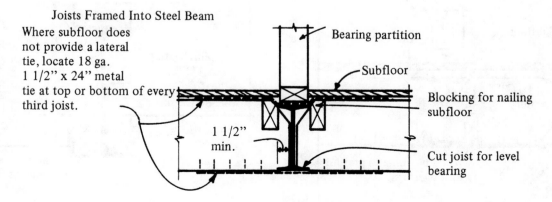

Bearing partition

Subfloor

Blocking for nailing subfloor

1 1/2" min.

Cut joist for level bearing

153

WOOD GIRDER

Two Story Floor Loads

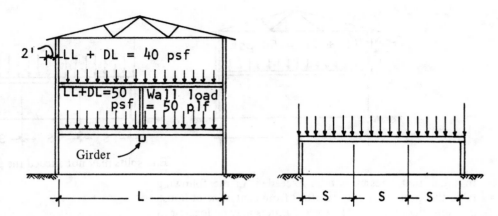

In order that stresses not be exceeded, in the following table the girder may not be offset from centerline of house by more than one foot. However, girders may be located to suit design conditions provided unit stresses conform to industry standards for grade and species.

End splits may not exceed one girder depth

NOMINAL LUMBER SIZES	GIRDER SPANS = S IN FEET					
	HOUSE WIDTHS = L IN FEET					
	22	24	26	28	30	32
LUMBER HAVING AN ALLOWABLE BENDING STRESS NOT LESS THAN 1000 PSI						
3 - 2x8	4'-2"	--	--	--	--	--
2 - 2x12	4'-4"	4'-0"	--	--	--	--
3 - 2x10	5'-4"	4'-11"	4'-7"	4'-3"	4'-0"	--
3 - 2x12	6'-6"	6'-0"	5'-6"	5'-2"	4'-10"	4'-6"
LUMBER HAVING AN ALLOWABLE BENDING STRESS NOT LESS THAN 1500 PSI						
2 - 2x10	4'-3"	--	--	--	--	--
3 - 2x8	5'-0"	4'-7"	4'-3"	--	--	--
2 - 2x12	5'-2"	4'-9"	4'-5"	4'-1"	--	--
2 - 2x10	6'-5"	7'-6"	5'-6"	5'-1"	4'-9"	4'-6"
3 - 2x12	7'-9"	7'-2"	6'-8"	6'-2"	5'-9"	5'-5"

FLOORS

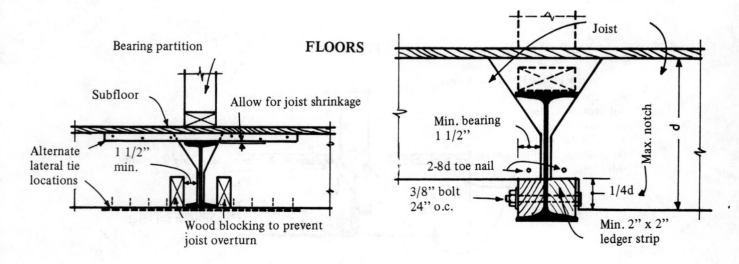

154

WALL FRAMING

14

Platform or Western Frame has become popular throughout the country because of shorter lengths of studs used in framing. It also provides a platform at each floor level for working without the use of stagging or scaffolding as well as having built-in fire stops at critical areas. It is faster to erect by building wall panels on the floor and tilting them into position. The disadvantage to Western Framing is that the shrinkage in a two story house may cause cracking of walls and ceilings.

Ballon Framing is another type of construction more suitable for two or more stories. We will use the best of both techniques, a combination of both, taking the advantages of each.

Lay out and assemble the entire exterior walls, one wall at a time, with 2" x 4" spaced 16" apart from the first floor plan locating all doors and windows centers.

Decisions on doors and windows must be made before any exterior partition work can be accomplished. Door and window manufacturers' catalogs will give the necessary dimensions for rough openings for doors and windows and these dimensions must be adhered to carefully for the units to fit into the walls. (see Chapter 20) Door sizes will be found on the plan and by adding 3" to these sizes for width and height, it will provide the proper rough openings in the walls. The height of the windows above the floor should be the same as the height of the doors. For example, if the door height is 7'-0" plus 3" for the rough opening, the distance from the top of the window to the floor will be 7'-3". The size of the window will determine the sill height above the floor.

In preparing the exterior walls, 8'-0" long 2" x 4" studs, will allow a finished ceiling height of between 7'-2" and 7'-6". If a higher ceiling is preferred, the longer studs will be required. This dimension is average for frame construction and any higher ceiling will serve no function but will add more cubic content, increasing not only the cost of the building but also the cost of the heating. Lay the 2" x 4" studs 8'-0" long on the sub-floor about 16" apart. Use as many studs as necessary to complete the entire wall. In the opposite direction, parallel to the wall length, lay studs end

to end, the longer the studs the better. This is called a plate and eventually this plate will be doubled, but not until this single plate is nailed to the ends of the studs. Use two 10d nails nailed through the plate into the end of the stud. In nailing the studs to the plate, be sure they line up with the 16" spacing of the floor joists falling, not on top of, but along side the joist because these studs will be nailed not only to the foundation sill but also into the side of the floor joists tieing together the sill, floor joists and wall. The outside stud line should be on the same plane as the outside foundation sill. Be sure to double all studs around openings for windows, doors etc. Leave the corner posts off the wall assembly for the time being.

Once the wall has been assembled, lift the wall into position, nail the bottom of the studs into the joist and toenail into the foundation sill. Plumb and brace the wall temporarily with diagonal bracing of 1" x 6". Follow this method on all exterior and bearing walls. The center of bearing partitions should fall over the center of beams. There are several methods of constructing corner posts. By far the strongest is a 4" x 6" with a 2" x 4" nailed together to form an inside corner.

When all the exterior and bearing partitions are plumb,, level and braced, nail the double plate tying the entire assembly together. Cross lap the double plate at corners similar to the foundation sill construction and be sure the joining of the bottom plate falls at a stud center. Break up the joints on the upper plate. Be certain all studs are of the exact length before assembling by cutting one to proper length and use it as a template to measure the others.

Individual members of the studded walls may be nailed one at a time achieving the same results. Follow the same procedure as outlined and install the first of the double plate after all the studs are nailed into position. Plumb brace and install the double plate as outlined. All bearing partitions are designed to support the floor or ceiling above, and the roof. When the continuity of the 16" spacing of the studs is broken, such as over doors and windows, the wall is weakened at that point and provisions must be made to support the loads above. This is accomplished by a header or lintel forming a beam made up of 2 pieces of 2" x 4", 2" x 6", 2" x 8", 2" x 10" or 2" x 12" nailed together. The size of the header is determined by the width of the opening and the loads to be supported. The following table indicated the header size based on the span for average loading:

HEADER SIZE	SPAN
Two 2" x 4"	3'-0"
Two 2" x 6"	4'-0"
Two 2" x 8"	5'-0"
Two 2" x 10"	6'-6"
Two 2" x 12"	8'-0"

These headers are nailed together with 16d nails with a 3/8" spacer between to make the full thickness stud of 3 5/8". If the span is unusually wide or the load especially heavy, a truss may be required. Carefully check the rough openings dimensions in the wall because errors may be difficult to correct after the wall is completed.

In aligning the walls for trueness and straightness, drive a nail in each corner of the wall in line with the outside stud. Let the nail stick out about 1/2", run a line from nail to nail and align the wall along the entire length with the line or chord. Be sure it is tight enough to form a straight line.

Because of the high cost of energy, to allow heavier or thicker wall insulation, exterior studs may be 2" x 6" placed 24"

apart instead of 2" x 4" placed 16" apart. There is little or no initial savings in this type of construction. The savings will result in use of less fuel for heating and cooling. If this system is used 6" thick blanket insulation may be used instead of 4" thick blanket.

Resistance to Racking

For usual one-story construction, second floor of two-story construction, or third floor of three-story frame construction, diagonal sheathing, or corner bracing, or at least one 8-foot or three 4-foot braced wall sections without openings should be provided in each wall.

For usual first floor of two-story construction or first and second floor of three-story frame construction, diagonal sheathing, or corner and intermediate bracing, or at least two 8-foot or five 4-foot braced wall sections without openings should be provided in each wall.

Corner braces may be let into either outside or inside face of studs sole plate and top plate at an angle as near to 45 degrees as is practicable. Brace should be a straight-grain wood, free of knots.

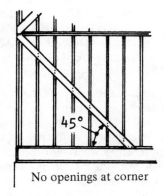

45°

No openings at corner

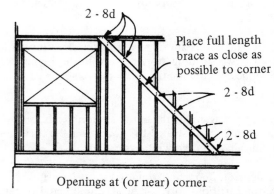

2 - 8d

Place full length brace as close as possible to corner

2 - 8d

2 - 8d

Openings at (or near) corner

Studs are typically toenailed to wall plates with 4-8d or 3-10d nails. End studs of bearing partitions adjacent to masonry walls should be anchored to the wall approximately 24" o.c.

Framing Openings

Double studs should be used at all openings in bearing walls and partitions. The sketch above illustrates a typical double-framed openings. Inner studs are continuous from header to sole plate and sill must not cut into jamb studs more than 1/2 inch.

Studs

When stud size and spacing are not determined by engineering calculations for specific conditions, the following table may be used.

Notes: (1) Except where applied finish material requires lesser spacing
(2) If openings are framed with double jamb studs, stud spacing may be 24" o.c.
(3) Acceptable only when door is not installed, or where folding or sliding door is used.

EXTERIOR WALLS AND BEARING PARTITIONS		
LOADING CONDITIONS	MIN. SIZE	MAX. SIZE
Supporting roof and ceiling	2" x 4"	24" o.c. (1)
Supporting one floor	2" x 4"	16" o.c.
Supporting two floors	2" x 6"	16" o.c.
NON-BEARING PARTITIONS		
SIZE	SPACING	
	PARTITION WITH OPENING	PARTITION WITHOUT OPENING
2" x 3" - 3" way	16" o.c. (2)	24" o.c. (1)
2" x 4" - 2" way	16" o.c. (3)	16" o.c.
2" x 4" - 4" way	24" o.c. (1)	24" o.c.

LINTEL AND HEADER SPANS

NOMINAL LUMBER SIZES	HOUSE WIDTHS = L IN FEET					
	22	24	26	28	30	32
LUMBER WITH A MINIMUM ALLOWABLE BENDING STRESS OF 1000 PSI						
2 - 2x4	2'-0"	--	--	--	--	--
2 - 2x6	3'-2"	2'-11"	2'-9"	2'-7"	2'-5"	2'-3"
1 - 2x8	2'-1"	--	--	--	--	--
2 - 2x8	4'-2"	3'-10"	3'-7"	3'-5"	3'-2"	3'-0"
1 - 2x10	2'-8"	2'-6"	2'-4"	2'-2"	2'-0"	--
2 - 2x10	5'-3"	4'-11"	4'-7"	4'-4"	4'-1"	3'-10"
1 - 2x12	3'-3"	3'-0"	2'-10"	2'-8"	2'-6"	2'-4"
2 - 2x12	6'-5"	6'-0"	5'-7"	5'-3"	4'-11"	4'-8"
LUMBER WITH A MINIMUM ALLOWABLE BENDING STRESS OF 1500 PSI						
2 - 2x4	2'-5"	2'-3"	2'-1"	2'-0"	--	--
2 - 2x6	3'-9"	3'-6"	3'-3"	3'-1"	2'-11"	2'-9"
1 - 2x8	2'-6"	2'-4"	2'-2"	2'-0"	--	--
2 - 2x8	5'-0"	4'-8"	4'-4"	4'-1"	3'-10"	3'-7"
1 - 2x10	3'-2"	2'-11"	2'-9"	2'-7"	2'-5"	2'-4"
2 - 2x10	6'-4"	5'-11"	5'-6"	5'-2"	4'-11"	4'-7"
1 - 2x12	3'-10"	3'-7"	3'-4"	3'-2"	3'-0"	2'-10"
2 - 2x12	7'-9"	7'-2"	6'-9"	6'-4"	5'-11"	5'-7"

Exterior Wall Openings Carrying Roof-Ceiling Plus Story Floor and Wall Loads

LL + DL = 25 psf

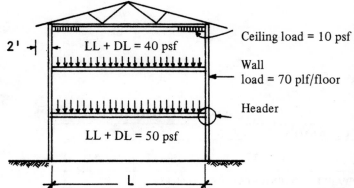

Ceiling load = 10 psf

Wall load = 70 plf/floor

Header

Center support for floor may be offset from centerline of house width up to one foot.

End splits may not exceed header depth

Exterior Wall Openings Carrying Only Roof-Ceiling Loads

LL + DL = 25psf

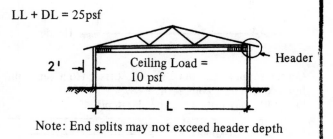

Ceiling Load = 10 psf

Header

Note: End splits may not exceed header depth

LINTEL AND HEADER SPANS

NOMINAL LUMBER SIZES	HOUSE WIDTHS = L IN FEET					
	22	24	26	28	30	32
LUMBER WITH A MINIMUM ALLOWABLE BENDING STRESS OF 1000 PSI						
2 - 2x6	2'-3"	2'-1"	2'-0"	--	--	--
2 - 2x8	3'-0"	2'-9"	2'-7"	2'-6"	2'-4"	2'-2"
1 - 2x10	--	--	--	--	--	--
2 - 2x10	3'-10"	3'-7"	3'-4"	3'-2"	3'-0"	2'-10"
1 - 2x12	2'-4"	2'-2"	2'-0"	--	--	--
2 - 2x12	4'-8"	4'-4"	4'-1"	3'-10"	3'-7"	3'-5"
LUMBER WITH A MINIMUM ALLOWABLE BENDING STRESS OF 1500 PSI						
2 - 2x6	2'-9"	2'-6"	2'-5"	2'-3"	2'-1"	2'-0"
2 - 2x8	3'-7"	3'-4"	3'-2"	2'-11"	2'-9"	2'-8"
1 - 2x10	2'-3"	2'-2"	2'-0"	--	--	--
2 - 2x10	4'-7"	4'-3"	4'-0"	3'-9"	3'-7"	3'-4"
1 - 2x12	2'-9"	2'-7"	2'-5"	2'-4"	2'-2"	2'-1"
2 - 2x12	5'-7"	5'-2"	4'-10"	4'-7"	4'-4"	4'-1"

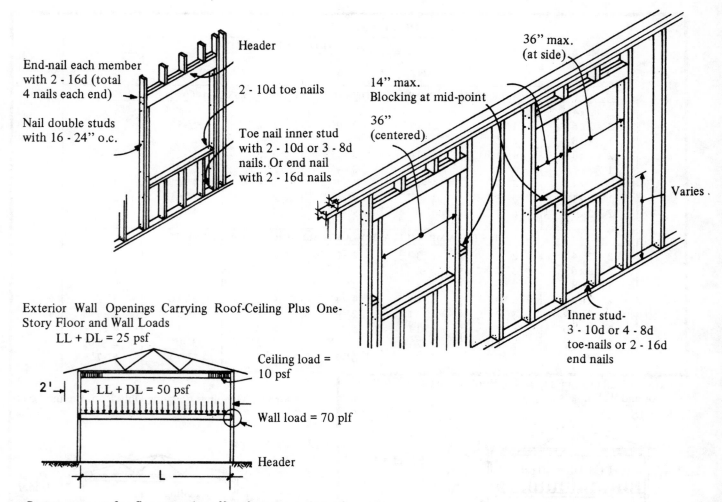

End-nail each member with 2 - 16d (total 4 nails each end)

Nail double studs with 16 - 24" o.c.

Header

2 - 10d toe nails

Toe nail inner stud with 2 - 10d or 3 - 8d nails. Or end nail with 2 - 16d nails

36" max. (at side)

14" max. Blocking at mid-point

36" (centered)

Varies

Inner stud- 3 - 10d or 4 - 8d toe-nails or 2 - 16d end nails

Exterior Wall Openings Carrying Roof-Ceiling Plus One-Story Floor and Wall Loads

LL + DL = 25 psf

2'

LL + DL = 50 psf

Ceiling load = 10 psf

Wall load = 70 plf

Header

L

Center support for floor may be offset from centerline of house width up to one foot.
End splits may not exceed header depth

LINTEL AND HEADER SPANS

NOMINAL LUMBER SIZES	HOUSE WIDTHS = L IN FEET					
	22	24	26	28	30	32
LUMBER WITH A MINIMUM ALLOWABLE BENDING STRESS OF 1000 PSI						
2 - 2x3	2'-4''	2'-3''	2'-2''	2'-1''	2'-0''	--
2 - 2x4	3'-3''	3'-2''	3'-1''	2'-11''	2'-10''	2'-8''
1 - 2x6	2'-11''	2'-8''	2'-6''	2'-4''	2'-2''	2'-1''
2 - 2x6	5'-2''	5'-0''	4'-10''	4'-8''	4'-5''	4'-2''
1 - 2x8	3'-10''	3'-7''	3'-4''	3'-1''	2'-11''	2'-9''
2 - 2x8	6'-10''	6'-7''	6'-4''	6'-1''	5'-10''	5'-6''
1 - 2x10	4'-11''	4'-6''	4'-3''	3'-11''	3'-8''	3'-6''
2 - 2x10	8'-8''	8'-4''	8'-1''	7'-10''	7'-5''	7'-0''
1 - 2x12	5'-11''	5'-6''	5'-1''	4'-10''	4'-6''	4'-3''
2 - 2x12	10'-7''	10'-2''	9'-10''	9'-6''	9'-0''	8'-6''
LUMBER WITH A MINIMUM ALLOWABLE BENDING STRESS OF 1500 PSI						
2 - 2x3	2'-10''	2'-9''	2'-8''	2'-7''	2'-5''	2'-3''
2 - 2x4	4'-0''	3'-10''	3'-9''	3'-7''	3'-4''	3'-2''
1 - 2x6	3'-6''	3'-3''	3'-0''	2'-10''	2'-8''	2'-6''
2 - 2x6	6'-4''	6'-1''	5'-10''	5'-7''	5'-3''	5'-0''
1 - 2x8	4'-7''	4'-3''	4'-0''	3'-8''	3'-6''	3'-3''
2 - 2x8	8'-4''	8'-0''	7'-9''	7'-5''	7'-0''	6'-7''
1 - 2x10	5'-10''	5'-5''	5'-1''	4'-9''	4'-5''	4'-2''
2 - 2x10	10'-8''	10'-3''	9'-10''	9'-5''	8'-11''	8'-4''
1 - 2x12	7'-2''	6'-7''	6'-2''	5'-9''	5'-5''	5'-1''
2 - 2x12	12'-11''	12'-5''	12'-0''	11'-6''	10'-10''	10'-2''

CEILING FRAMING

15

The same procedure is used in installing ceiling joists as described for floor joists. This is the first indication of the walls being put to work. One end of the ceiling joist will rest on the outside wall and the other end will rest on the bearing partition. The roof overhang must be known because the ceiling joists will extend beyond the outside wall or stud line by the dimension established by the overhang of the roof. Use four 8d nails, two on each side of joist toenailed into the double plate. The size of the joist will depend upon the span and load. (see table) The only openings required in the ceiling are for chimneys or attic access panels. The access panels are usually found in the ceiling of a closet measuring about 18" x 24". Double headers must be used in this case just as we did for openings in the floor. Bridging is not necessary in the ceiling joists.

Disappearing stairs may be used instead of access panels.

When ceiling joists are used to provide resistance to rafter thrust, joists should be nailed together with the same number and size of nails used to nail ceiling joists to rafters. Joists should be toenailed to exterior wall plates with three 10d nails and to center bearing partition plates with four 10d nails in each pair of joists.

METHODS OF PROVIDING A FLUSH CEILING OVER OPENINGS

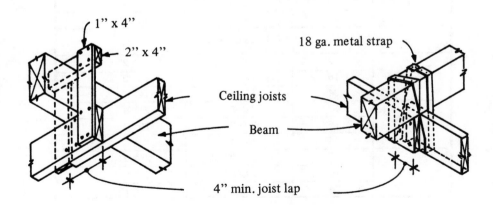

Nailing at lap should be equal to nailing for joist to rafter.

159

CEILING JOIST SPAN

JOIST SIZE	SPACING OF JOISTS O.C.	LUMBER GRADES GRADES	
		NO. 1 KILN-DRIED	NO.2 KILN-DRIED
SOUTHERN YELLOW PINE			
LIMITED ATTIC STORAGE			
2 x 6	12	14'- 4''	14'- 4''
	16	13'- 0''	13'- 0''
	24	11'- 4''	11'- 4''
2 x 8	12	18'- 4''	18'- 4''
	16	17'- 0''	17'- 0''
	24	15'- 4''	15'- 4''
2 x 10	12	21'- 10''	21'- 10''
	16	20'- 4''	20'- 4''
	24	18'- 4''	18'- 4''
NO ATTIC STORAGE			
2 x 6	12	17'- 2''	17'- 2''
	16	16'- 0''	16'- 0''
	24	14'- 4''	14'- 4''
2 x 8	12	21'- 8''	21'- 8''
	16	20'- 2''	20'- 2''
	24	18'- 4''	18'- 4''
2 x 10	12	24'- 0''	24'- 0''
	16	24'- 0''	24'- 0''
	24	21'- 10''	21'- 10''
DOUGLAS FIR AND LARCH			
LIMITED ATTIC STORAGE			
2 x 6	12	14'- 4''	14'- 4''
	16	13'- 0''	13'- 0''
	24	11'- 4''	11'- 4''
2 x 8	12	18'- 4''	18'- 4''
	16	17'- 0''	17'- 0''
	24	15'- 4''	15'-'4''
2 x 10	12	21'- 10''	21'- 10''
	16	20'- 4''	20'- 4''
	24	18'- 4''	18'- 4''
NO ATTIC STORAGE			
2 x 6	12	17'- 2''	17'- 2''
	16	16'- 0''	16'- 0''
	24	14'- 4''	14'- 4''
2 x 8	12	21'- 8''	21'- 8''
	16	20'- 2''	20'- 2''
	24	18'- 4''	18'- 4''
2 x 10	12	24'- 0''	24'- 0''
	16	24'- 0''	24'- 0''
	24	21'- 10''	21'- 10''

160

ROOF FRAMING

Careful workmanship is required to achieve a successful roof. This, however, offers the most difficulty in framing. The choice of design in roofs is varied and the overall appearance of a house is greatly affected by the design of the roof lines.

GABLE ROOF is the most popular and easy to ventilate.

HIP ROOF slightly more difficult to build because all sides are pitched.

FLAT ROOF is the most economical and easiest to construct. A dead level roof is not recommended. So called flat roofs are pitched just enough to shed the water, about 1/8" to 1/4" pitch per foot.

SHED ROOF is similar to a flat roof with a more pronounced pitch.

MANSARD ROOF is of French design gaining in popularity and more difficult to construct.

GAMBREL ROOF provided for additional space on upper level floors.

BUTTERFLY ROOF provides more light and ventilation but may cause a problem in drainage.

"A" FRAME ROOF provides a dual function of walls and roof, adds more cubic content to building and more area to heat.

The members used in roof construction are called roof rafters which are spaced 16" apart. In preparing or cutting the roof rafters to fit, we are concerned with ridge cut or plumb cut which is the high or center portion of the roof, and the heel or seat cut which is at the wall line resting on the double plate. The tail cut is the overhang of the roof. The precise layout of these cuts is determined by the slope or pitch of the roof and the width or span of the building. The rise is the vertical distance from the top of the double wall plate to the top of the roof. The run is half the span or the horizontal distance from the outside wall to the center of the roof. The span is the horizontal distance from the outside wall to the opposite outside wall. The slope or pitch of roof is indicated on drawings $\frac{14}{12}$ which means for every 12" horizontal dimension, the rise is 14".

The basic tool for roof construction and layout is the carpenters square. The larger leg is called the body and the shorter leg is the tongue. The body and tongue come together at the heel forming a right angle or 90 degree. Before you do any cutting, try to visualize the framed roof in place. This will help eliminate errors.

The roof pitch indicated on the plans is 14 on the rise and 12 on the run. Take the steel square and locate number 12 on the tongue and number 14 on the body, move figures 12 and 14 over the width face of the rafter until each figure is over the edge nearest you, mark these lines by drawing a pencil along both edges of the square. Move the steel square over to the right until the figure 14 on the square is over the first mark under the figure 12. Repeat these marks as many times as there are whole feet in the run or 12 times. The run of the rafter is half the span of the rafter, or half the distance the rafter is extended before it meets its mate on the other side. This cut or meeting of its mate is the plumb cut which is the first slanting line made at the first figure 14. In cutting the seat or heel, mark the center of the rafter width, move the square to the right and make a slanting line across the face of the rafter, along the left side of the square or the 14" side. Where this line intersects the center line, it is the seat or heel cut which must fit snugly and firmly on top of the wall double plate. The tail or roof overhang cut can be made later. Before cutting the roof rafters, make a model from a 3/4" thick piece of wood the same width as the rafter. From this model you can mark all the rafters for cutting instead of laying out each rafter separately.

Where the rafters come together at the plumb cut is called the ridge. (top of roof) A ridge board is installed for the entire length of the roof between the plumb cuts. This ridge board is 2" wider than the roof rafters. If, for example, the roof rafters are 2" x 6", the ridge board will be 2" x 8". Select straight pieces of ridge stock and lay out the 16" rafter spacing by marking the top of the wall double plate. Joints in the ridge board should occur at the center of the rafters. Cut the ridge boards and lay them across the ceiling joists. Nail the gable rafter first at the wall double plate, install the opposite rafter while another workman holds the two rafters at the ridge temporarily. Place the ridge board be-

ROOF DESIGNS

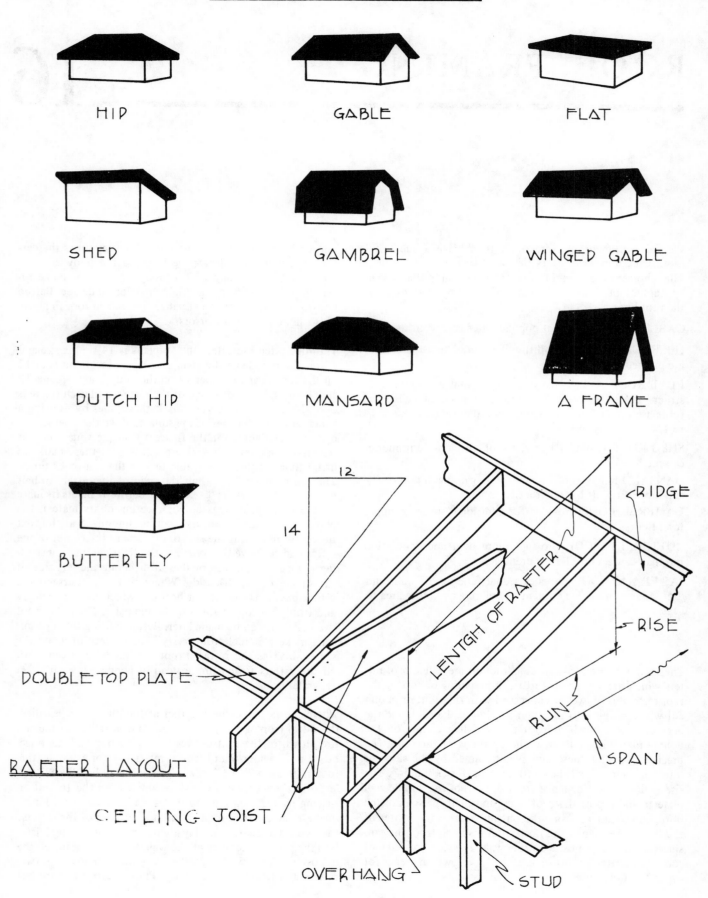

HIP

GABLE

FLAT

SHED

GAMBREL

WINGED GABLE

DUTCH HIP

MANSARD

A FRAME

BUTTERFLY

12

14

RIDGE

LENTGH OF RAFTER

RISE

RUN

SPAN

DOUBLE TOP PLATE

RAFTER LAYOUT

CEILING JOIST

OVERHANG

STUD

162

tween the two rafters with the top of the ridge level with the top of the rafters and nail it temporarily in place. Move about five or six rafters away and install another pair of roof rafters. Plumb the assembly and make any necessary adjustments then nail permanently with 16d nails through the ridge board into one rafter and toenail the opposite rafter into the ridgeboard with 8d nails. Continue the process until all rafters are in place. As with the floor joists, install the roof rafters with the crown or curve turned upward. Use extra care in framing a roof to prevent a fall.

The entire roof assembly must be braced and stiffened by installing collar beams of 1" x 6" at every other rafter. These collar beams are parallel with the ceiling joists attached half way up the run of the roof rafter nailed to two rafters, one on each side of the roof tying them together. To erect a gable end frame, simply construct a 2" x 4" stud wall 16" o.c. from the top of the wall double plate to the under side of the end roof rafters. The length of these studs will diminish in size with the pitch of the roof.

Hip and valley roof rafters are used to join two intersecting roofs together pitching in different directions. Jack rafters are the varied length rafters from the top of the double wall plate to the hip or valley rafter. Use the same pattern cuts as the common rafters; the only difference is the length of the rafters and the plumb cut ,which is at an angle to set apart the hip or valley rafters,both of which act as a ridge on a slant or pitch. Jack rafters should be erected in pairs to prevent pushing the hip or valley out of alignment. Double all roof at openings such as chimney, skylights etc. similar to the floor and ceiling construction. Use a plumb bob to transfer the openings onto the roof from the floor and ceiling. (See table for roof rafter size) Another method of accomplishing the same purpose is to use roof trusses for roof framing. These trusses are pre-engineered assemblies of roof rafters and joists lifted onto the wall and into position. They do not require any interior support and will span from outside wall to outside wall allowing flexibility of interior partition arrangement. Roof trusses are made up of many types and configurations.

DORMERS

A structure projecting above the roof slop with a vertical wall is a dormer. Its chief purpose is to allow light and ventilation, and if a full dormer, more space, and to enhance the aesthetics of the roof. The design of the roof of a dormer can be shed roof, gable roof or hip roof and is constructed much like the main roof. The wall ends of the dormer are resting on the main roof rafters which are doubled at that point.

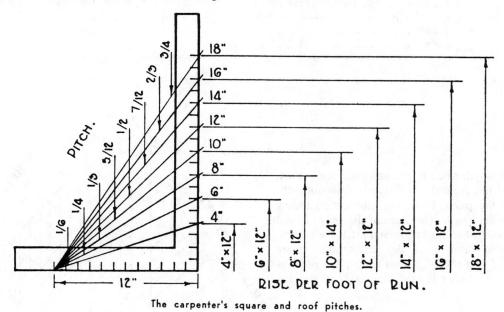

The carpenter's square and roof pitches.

163

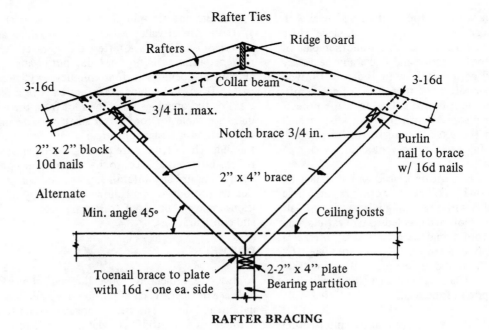

Rafter Ties

Rafters

Ridge board

3-16d

Collar beam

3-16d

3/4 in. max.

Notch brace 3/4 in.

2" x 2" block
10d nails

Purlin
nail to brace
w/ 16d nails

Alternate

2" x 4" brace

Min. angle 45°

Ceiling joists

Toenail brace to plate
with 16d - one ea. side

2-2" x 4" plate
Bearing partition

RAFTER BRACING

BRACE	PURLIN
2 x 4-16" o.c. (Same as rafter spacing)	None required
2 x 4-24" o.c. (Same as rafter spacing)	None required
2 x 4-32" o.c. ---	2 x 4 on edge
2 x 4-48" o.c. ---	2 x 4 on edge
2 x 4-72" o.c. ---	2 x 6 on edge

To find the rafter length when its run and pitch are known, follow the vertical line from the run to its intersection with the radial line of the pitch. From the intersection follow the curved line to the length. The diagram also may be used to determine the run when the length and pitch are known, or to determine the pitch when the length and run are known. Example: For a run of 20 feet and a pitch of 10 in 12, the length of the rafter is read directly from the diagram as 26 feet.

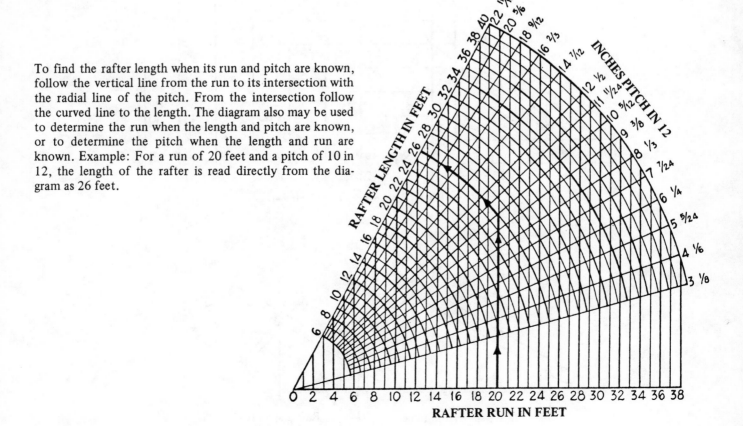

RAFTER LENGTH IN FEET

INCHES PITCH IN 12

RAFTER RUN IN FEET

Rafter Ties

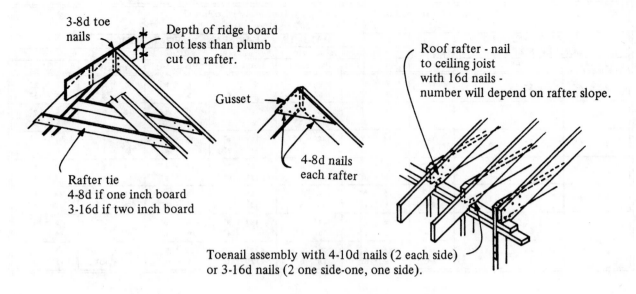

3-8d toe nails

Depth of ridge board not less than plumb cut on rafter.

Gusset

4-8d nails each rafter

Rafter tie
4-8d if one inch board
3-16d if two inch board

Roof rafter - nail to ceiling joist with 16d nails - number will depend on rafter slope.

Toenail assembly with 4-10d nails (2 each side) or 3-16d nails (2 one side-one, one side).

NUMBER OF 16d NAILS REQUIRED TO PROVIDE
TIE FOR UNSUPPORTED RAFTERS AND CEILING JOISTS

SLOPE OF ROOF	RAFTER TIED TO EVERY CEILING JOIST			RAFTER TIED TO CEILING JOIST 4 FT. O.C.	
	SPACING	WIDTH UP TO 26 FT.	WIDTH 26 TO 32 FT.	WIDTH UP TO 26 FT.	WIDTH 26 TO 32 FT.
4 in 12 ------------	16" o.c. --------------	5	7	--	--
	24" o.c. --------------	8	11		
5 in 12 -------------	16" o.c. --------------	4	6	10	--
	24" o.c. --------------	7	9		
6 in 12 -------------	16" o.c. --------------	3	4	8	11
	24" o.c. --------------	5	7		
7 in 12 -------------	16" o.c. --------------	3	3	7	9
8 in 12 -------------	24" o.c. --------------	4	6		
9 in 12 -------------	16" o.c. --------------	3	3	5	6
10 in 12 -------------	24" o.c. --------------	3	4		
11 in 12 -------------	24" o.c. --------------	3	4		
12 in 12 -------------	16" o.c. --------------	3	3	3	4
	24" o.c. --------------	3	3		

MAXIMUM SPANS FOR RAFTERS

Roof Load of 30 Lbs. Per Sq. Ft. Uniformly Distributed For Slopes of 20" or More								
AMERICAN STANDARD LUMBER SIZES		ON CENTER	MAXIMUM CLEAR SPAN - PLATE TO RIDGE					
			SO. PINE & DOUGLAS FIR		WESTERN HEMLOCK		SPRUCE	
NOMINAL	NET		Unplast'd	Plastered	Unplast'd	Plastered	Unplast'd	Plast'd
2" x 4"	1 5/8" x 3 5/8"	16"	7' - 8"	6' - 10"	7' - 4"	6' - 6"	7' - 0"	6' - 2"
		24"	6' - 3"	6' - 0"	6' - 0"	5' - 8"	5' - 9"	5' - 5"
2" x 6"	1 5/8" x 5 5/8"	16"	11' - 9"	10' - 6"	11' - 3"	10' - 1"	10' - 9"	9' - 7"
		24"	9' - 8"	9' - 3"	9' - 3"	8' - 10"	8' - 10"	8' - 5"
3" x 6"	2 5/8" x 5 5/8"	16"	14' - 10"	12' - 3"	14' - 1"	11' - 9"	13' - 6"	11' - 1"
		24"	12' - 3"	10' - 10"	11' - 9"	10' - 4"	11' - 1"	9' - 10"
2" x 8"	1 5/8" x 7 1/2"	16"	15' - 7"	14' - 0"	15' - 0"	13' - 4"	14' - 3"	12' - 9"
		24"	12' - 10"	12' - 3"	12' - 4"	11' - 9"	11' - 9"	11' - 2"
3" x 8"	2 5/8" x 7 1/2"	16"	19' - 5"	16' - 1"	18' - 7"	15' - 5"	17' - 9"	14' - 7"
		24"	16' - 1"	14' - 3"	15' - 5"	13' - 7"	14' - 9"	12' - 11"
2" x 10"	1 5/8" x 9 1/2"	16"	19' - 7"	17' - 6"	18' - 9"	16' - 10"	17' - 11"	16' - 11"
		24"	16' - 3"	15' - 6"	15' - 6"	14' - 10"	14' - 10"	14' - 0"
2" x 12"	1 5/8" x 11 1/2"	16"	23' - 6"	21' - 2"	22' - 6"	20' - 3"	21' - 6"	19' - 3"
		24"	19' - 6"	18' - 8"	17' - 10"	17' - 10"	17' - 10"	17' - 0"

LOW SLOPE ROOF RAFTERS
(Roof Slope 3 in 12 or Less)

		NOT SUPPORTING FINISHED CEILING						SUPPORTING FINISHED CEILING					
2x6	12	14 4	14 4	14 4	14 4	11 4	9 6	13 8	13 8	13 8	13 8	10 6	8 10
	16	13 0	13 0	13 0	12 10	9 8	8 4	12 4	12 4	12 4	11 10	9 0	7 8
	24	11 4	11 4	11 4	10 6	8 0	6 8	10 10	10 8	10 8	9 8	7 4	6 2
2x8	12	18 4	18 4	18 4	18 4	17 6	15 4	17 8	17 8	17 8	17 8	16 2	14 2
	16	17 0	17 0	17 0	17 0	15 0	13 4	16 4	16 4	16 4	16 2	14 0	12 4
	24	15 4	15 4	15 4	14 4	12 4	10 10	14 6	14 6	14 6	13 2	11 4	10 0
2x10	12	21 10	21 10	21 10	21 10	21 10	20 8	21 0	21 0	21 0	21 0	21 0	19 0
	16	20 4	20 4	20 4	20 4	20 4	18 0	19 6	19 6	19 6	19 6	19 2	16 8
	24	18 4	18 4	18 4	18 0	16 6	14 8	17 8	17 8	17 8	16 8	15 8	13 6
2x12	12	24 0	24 0	24 0	24 0	24 0	24 0	24 0	24 0	24 0	24 0	24 0	23 0
	16	23 6	23 6	23 6	23 6	23 6	21 10	22 6	22 6	22 6	22 6	22 6	20 0
	24	21 2	21 2	21 2	21 2	20 0	19 6	20 4	20 4	20 2	20 2	18 6	16 4

RAFTERS
(Roof Slope Over 3 in 12)

		LIGHT ROOFING						HEAVY ROOFING					
2x4	12	10 10	9 6	8 0	7 4	5 8	5 2	9 4	8 2	6 10	6 4	4 10	4 4
	16	10 0	8 4	7 0	6 4	5 0	4 6	8 0	7 2	6 0	5 6	4 2	3 10
	24	7 4	6 10	5 2	5 2	4 0	3 8	6 8	5 10	5 0	4 6	3 6	3 2
2x6	12	16 10	16 10	16 10	16 10	13 4	11 2	15 6	15 6	15 6	14 10	11 4	9 6
	16	15 8	15 8	15 8	15 0	11 6	9 8	14 4	14 0	14 2	12 10	9 8	8 4
	24	13 10	13 6	13 6	12 2	9 4	7 8	12 6	11 6	11 8	10 6	8 0	6 8
2x8	12	21 2	21 2	21 2	21 2	20 10	18 0	19 8	19 8	19 8	19 8	17 6	15 4
	16	19 10	19 10	19 6	19 0	17 8	15 8	18 4	18 4	18 4	17 6	15 0	13 4
	24	17 10	17 10	17 10	16 8	14 4	12 8	16 6	15 8	15 10	14 4	12 4	10 10
2x10	12	24 0	24 0	24 0	24 0	24 0	24 0	23 6	23 6	23 6	23 6	23 0	20 8
	16	23 8	23 8	23 8	23 8	23 8	21 0	21 10	21 10	21 10	21 10	20 4	18 0
	24	21 4	21 4	21 4	21 0	19 8	17 2	19 8	19 8	19 8	18 0	16 2	14 8

PLANK and BEAM FRAMING 17

INTRODUCTION

The plank-and-beam method for framing floors and roofs has been used in heavy timber buildings for many years. The adaptation of this system to residential construction has raised many technical questions from designers and builders concerning details of application , advantages and limitations, construction details and structural requirements for the plank-and-beam method of framing.

GENERAL DESCRIPTION

Whereas conventional framing utilizes joists, rafters and studs spaced 12 to 24 inches on centers, the plank-and-beam method requires fewer and larger sized pieces spaced farther apart. A simple comparison of the two methods is shown in Figure 1.

In plank-and-beam framing, plank subfloors or roofs, usually of 2-inch nominal thickness, are supported on beams spaced up to 8 feet apart. The ends of the beams are supported on posts or piers. Wall spaces between posts are provided with supplementary framing to the extent required for attachment of exterior and interior finish. This supplementary framing and its covering also serve to provide lateral bracing for the building.

PRINCIPLES OF DESIGN

The most successful plank-and-beam houses are those which are designed from the beginning for this method of framing. Such procedure permits the correlation of the structural framework with the exterior dimensions of the house, the location of doors and windows and the location of interior partitions. Proper study of these features in the early stages will contribute much to simplified framing.

The most efficient use of 2-inch plank occurs when it is continuous over more than one span. Where standard lengths of lumber are used, such as 12, 14 or 16 feet, beam spacings of 6, 7 or 8 feet are indicated and this has bearing on the overall dimensions of the house. Where end joints in the plank are allowed to occur between supports, random length planks may be used and the beam spacing adjusted to fit the dimensions of the house.

Windows and doors should be located between posts in exterior walls to eliminate the need for headers over the openings. The wide spacing between posts permits ample opportunity for large glass areas. However, a sufficient amount of solid wall should be present to provide adequate lateral bracing.

Combination of conventional framing with plank-and-beam framing is sometimes used. Where the two adjoin each other on a side-by-side basis, no particular problems are encountered. Where a plank-and-beam floor or roof is supported on a stud wall, a post should be placed under the end of the beam to carry the concentrated load. Where conventional roof framing is used with plank-and-beam construction, a header should be installed to carry the load from the rafters to the posts.

ADVANTAGES OF SYSTEM

There are many advantages to be gained through the use of the plank-and-beam system of framing. Perhaps the most outstanding is the distinctive architectural effect provided by the exposed plank-and-beam ceiling. In many houses the roof plank serves as the ceiling, thereby providing added height to living areas with no increase in cost. Where planks are selected for appearance, no further ceiling treatment is needed except the application of a stain, sealer or paint, and this results in quite a saving in cost.

Well-planned plank-and-beam framing permits substantial savings in labor. The pieces are larger and there are fewer of them than in conventional framing. Cross-bridging of joists is eliminated entirely. Larger and fewer nails are required. All of this adds up to labor saving at the job site.

In plank-and-beam framing, the ceiling height is measured to the underside of the plank, whereas in conventional construction, it is measured to the underside of the joists. The difference between the thickness of the plank and the depth of the joist results in a reduction in the volume of the building. It also reduces the height of the exterior walls. This is illustrated in Figure 2.

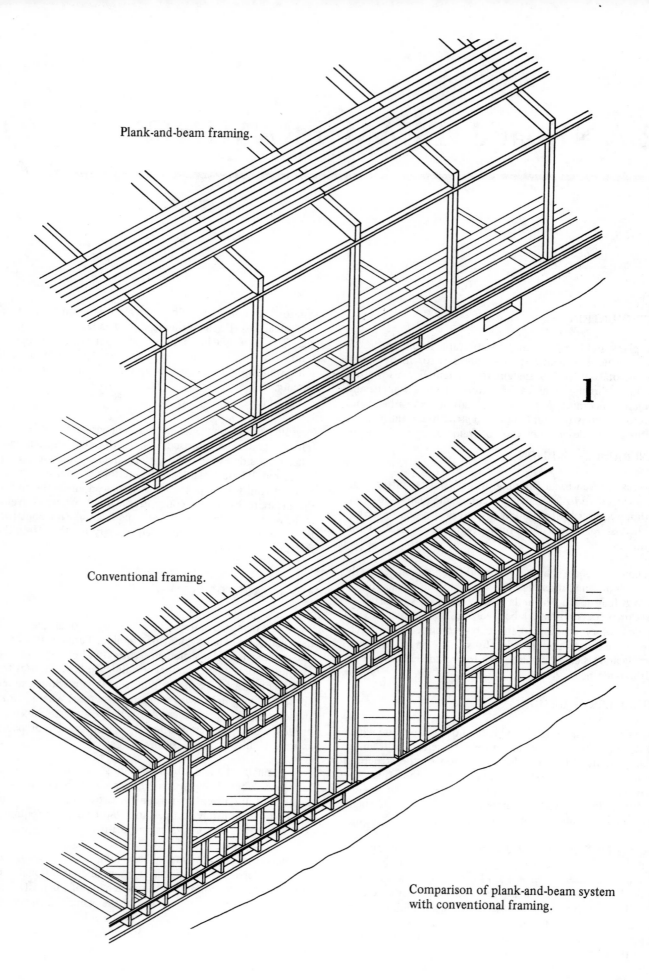

Plank-and-beam framing.

Conventional framing.

Comparison of plank-and-beam system with conventional framing.

1

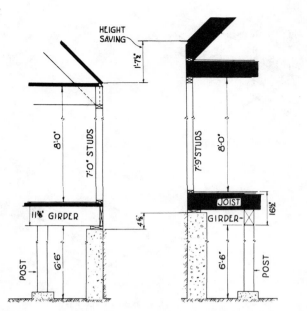

Joisted construction. Plank-and-beam construction.

Comparison of height
of plank-and-beam house with
conventionally framed house.

2

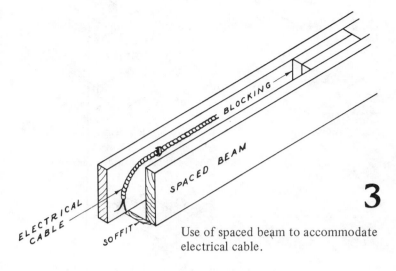

3

Use of spaced beam to accommodate
electrical cable.

LIMITATIONS OF SYSTEM

There are limitations on the use of the plank-and-beam system, but they are readily resolved through careful study in the planning stage. When this is done, the parts of the house fit together very quickly and easily.

The plank floors are designed for moderate uniform loads and are not intended to carry heavy concentrated loads. Where such loads occur as those for bearing partitions, bathtubs, refrigerators, etc., additional framing is needed beneath the planks to transmit the loads to the beams.

In moderate climates, the insulation provided by the nominal 2-inch plank is usually adequate. In colder climates, additional insulation is often desired and this may be installed in the amount needed to meet local conditions. Insulation may be applied to the underside of the planks, in which case its appearance is a factor. The insulation also may be installed on top of the planks where it should be in rigid form. This type is usually laid in mastic and limited to a roof slope of 3-in-12, or lower. A vapor barrier between the wood plank and the insulation is recommended.

Location of the electrical distribution system may present a problem because of the lack of concealed spaces in the ceiling. However, the main supporting beams may be made of several pieces of 2-inch lumber and separated by short blocking, which provides a space to accommodate electrical cable and pipes for other uses. This is illustrated in Figure 3. Solid beams may be routed along their top surfaces for this purpose. Concealed spaces in the supplementary wall framing provide ample space for wall outlets and electrical cable.

CONSTRUCTION DETAILS

The plank-and-beam system is essentially a skeleton framework. Planks are designed to support a moderate load, uniformly distributed. This is carried to the beams which in turn transmit their loads to posts which are supported on the foundation. Where heavy concentrated loads occur in places other than over main beams or posts supplementary beams are needed to carry such loads.

Foundations for plank-and-beam framing may be continuous walls or piers, supported on adequate footings. With posts spaced up to 8 feet apart in exterior walls, this system is well adapted to pier foundations for houses without basements.

Posts should be of adequate size to carry the load and large enough to provide full bearing for the ends of beams. In general, posts should be at least 4 x 4 inches, nominal. Where the ends of beams abut over a post, a dimension of 6 inches parallel to the beams is recommended for the post. The posts may be solid or made up of several pieces of 2 inch lumber well spiked together.

The size of beams will vary with the span and spacing as indicated in the tables included herein. Beams may be solid or glued laminated pieces, or may be built up of several thinner pieces securely nailed to each other or to spacer blocks between them. When built-up beams are used, a cover plate attached to the underside provides the appearance of a solid piece as illustrated in Figure 4. Fastening of beams to posts is accomplished by framing anchors or angle clips.

Since the 2-inch plank floor or roof frequently serves as the finish ceiling for the room below, appearance as well as structural requirements of the plank should be considered. For the purpose of distributing load, tongued-and-grooved or grooved-for-spline lumber is recommended. Methods for making the joint to provide various architectural effects are shown in Figure 5. To provide a pleasing appearance, a reasonably good grade of lumber should be selected and it should be sufficiently seasoned to meet the requirements of service conditions so as to avoid large cracks at the joints.

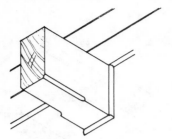
Solid beam.

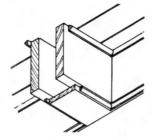
Spaced beam.

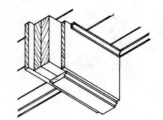
Cased beam.

4

Methods of finishing undersides of beams.

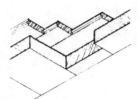
Squared edges with finish flooring at right angles.

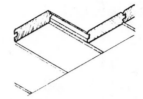
Tongued-and-grooved.

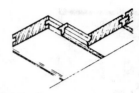
Grooved plank with splined insert moulding.

5

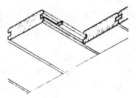
Grooved plank with spline and V-joint.

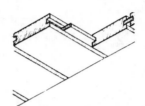
Grooved plank with exposed spline.

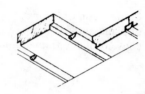
Rabbeted plank with batten insert.

Methods of treating joints in exposed plank ceilings.

In laying the plank, greater advantage can be taken of the strength and stiffness of the material by making the planks continuous over more than one span. For example, using the same span and uniform load in each case, a plank which is continuous over two spans is nearly two and one-half times as stiff as a plank which extends over a single span. This is illustrated in Figure 6. Planks should be nailed to each support with two 16d nails.

The finish floor should be laid at right angles to the plank subfloor, using the same procedure followed in conventional construction. Where the underside of plank is to serve as a ceiling, care is needed to make sure that flooring nails do not penetrate through the plank.

Partitions in the plank-and-beam system usually will be non-bearing. Where bearing partitions occur, they should be placed over beams and the beams enlarged to carry the added load. If this is not possible, supplementary beams must be placed in the floor framing arrangement. Non-bearing partitions, which are parallel to the planks, should have support to carry this load to the beams. This may be accomplished by using two 2 x 4 inch pieces set on edge as the sole plate. Where openings occur in the partition, the two 2 x 4 inch pieces may be placed under the plank floor and supported on the beams by framing anchors. This method is illustrated in Figure 7. Where the non-bearing partition is at right angles to the planks, no supplementary framing is needed since the partition load will be distributed across a number of planks.

As in conventional framing, lateral bracing is required in the exterior walls to provide resistance against wind forces. In plank-and-beam framing, this is accomplished by installing solid panels at appropriate intervals wherein the supplementary wall framing and the posts are all tied together by diagonal bracing or suitable sheathing.

STRUCTURAL REQUIREMENT

Good design requires that all members be properly fastened together in order that the house will act as a unit in resisting external forces. With fewer pieces than in conventional framing, particular care must be given to connections where beams abut each other and where beams join the posts. Where gable roofs are used, provision must be made to absorb the horizontal thrust produced by sloping roof beams. Methods for doing this are shown in the illustrations included herein.

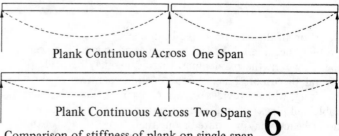
Plank Continuous Across One Span

Plank Continuous Across Two Spans **6**

Comparison of stiffness of plank on single span with plank continuous over two spans.

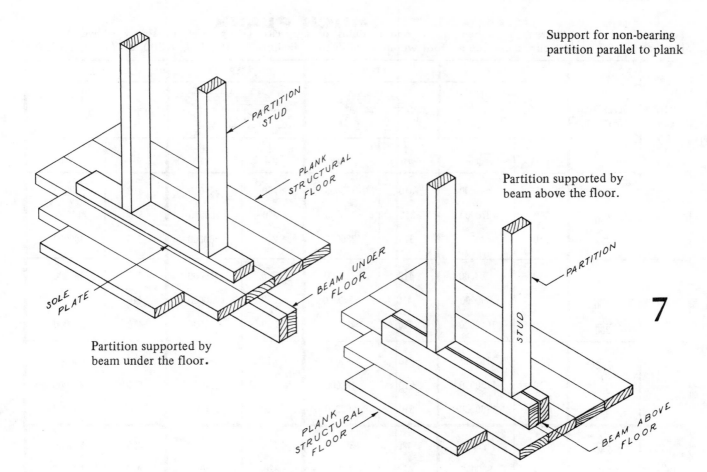

Partition supported by
beam above the floor.

7

Partition supported by
beam under the floor.

In most cases, structural design of the plank-and-beam house will be controlled by the local building code to the extent of specifying design loading requirements. A live load of 40 pounds per square foot is commonly specified for floors. For roofs, some codes specify 20 pounds per square foot and others 30 pounds.

To provide adequate safety, all codes require that framing members be so proportioned that the allowable fiber stress in bending is not exceeded when the member is subjected to full live and dead loads. As a general rule, codes do not place any limits on deflection because it does not have bearing on safety. However, from the standpoint of appearance, most designers and builders prefer to place some limit on the allowable deflection.

Tables indicating allowable loads for planks and beams will be found herein. Allowable loads for posts will be found in Wood Structural Design Data, a publication of the National Lumber Manufacturers Association.

Design data for plank floors and roofs are included in Table 1. Computations for bending are based on the live load indicated, plus 10 pounds per square foot of dead load. Computations for deflection are based on the live load only. The table shows four general arrangements of planks as follows:

Type A—Extending over a single span.
Type B—Continuous over two equal spans.
Type C—Continuous over three equal spans.
Type D—A combination of Types A and B.

To use Table I, first determine the plank arrangement (Types A, B, C or D), the span, the live load to be supported and the deflection limitation. Then select from the table the corresponding required values for fiber stress in bending (f) and modulus of elasticity (E). The plank to be used should be of a grade and species which meets these minimum values. The maximum span for a specific grade and species of plank may be determined by reversing these steps.

For those who prefer to use random length planks (instead of arrangements Type A, B, C or D), similar technical information concerning it is included in Random Length Wood Decking, a publication of the National Lumber Manufacturers Association.

Computations for both bending and deflection were based on the live load indicated plus 10 pounds per square foot of dead load. All beams in the table were designed to extend over a single span.

Design data for beams are included in Table 2

To use the table, first determine the span; then select from the table the proper size of beam with the corresponding required values for fiber stress in bending (f) and modulus of elasticity (E). The beam used should be of a grade and species which meets these minimum values. The maximum span for a beam of specific size, grade and species can be determined by reversing these steps.

171

NOMINAL TWO-INCH PLANK

Required values for fiber stress in bending (f) and modulus of elasticity (E) to support safely a live load of 20, 30 or 40 pounds per square foot within a deflection limitation of $l/240$, $l/300$ or $l/360$. TABLE 1

PLANK SPAN IN FEET	LIVE LOAD psf	DEFLECTION LIMITATION	TYPE A		TYPE B		TYPE C		TYPE D	
			f psi	E psi	f psi	E psi	f psi	E psi	f psi	E psi
6	20	$\frac{l}{240}$	310	450000	310	190000	250	240000	310	320000
		$\frac{l}{300}$	310	570000	310	230000	250	300000	310	400000
		$\frac{l}{360}$	310	680000	310	280000	250	360000	310	480000
	30	$\frac{l}{240}$	410	580000	410	280000	330	360000	410	480000
		$\frac{l}{300}$	410	850000	410	350000	330	450000	410	600000
		$\frac{l}{360}$	410	1020000	410	420000	330	540000	410	720000
	40	$\frac{l}{240}$	510	910000	510	380000	410	480000	510	640000
		$\frac{l}{300}$	510	1130000	510	470000	410	600000	510	800000
		$\frac{l}{360}$	510	1360000	510	560000	410	720000	510	960000
7	20	$\frac{l}{240}$	420	720000	420	300000	330	380000	420	510000
		$\frac{l}{300}$	420	900000	420	370000	330	480000	420	640000
		$\frac{l}{360}$	420	1080000	420	450000	330	570000	420	760000
	30	$\frac{l}{240}$	560	1080000	560	450000	450	570000	560	760000
		$\frac{l}{300}$	560	1350000	560	560000	450	710000	560	950000
		$\frac{l}{360}$	560	1620000	560	670000	450	860000	560	1140000
	40	$\frac{l}{240}$	700	1440000	700	600000	560	760000	700	1020000
		$\frac{l}{300}$	700	1800000	700	750000	560	950000	700	1270000
		$\frac{l}{360}$	700	2160000	700	900000	560	1140000	700	1530000
8	20	$\frac{l}{240}$	543	1070000	543	445000	434	565000	543	757500
		$\frac{l}{300}$	543	1340000	543	557000	434	707000	543	948000
		$\frac{l}{360}$	543	1610000	543	670000	434	850000	543	1140000
	30	$\frac{l}{240}$	724	1610000	724	669000	580	847000	724	1140000
		$\frac{l}{300}$	724	2010000	724	835000	580	1060000	724	1422000
		$\frac{l}{360}$	724	2420000	724	1010000	580	1270000	724	1715000
	40	$\frac{l}{240}$	906	2140000	906	891000	720	1130000	906	1515000
		$\frac{l}{300}$	906	2670000	906	1110000	720	1410000	906	1890000
		$\frac{l}{360}$	906	3220000	906	1340000	720	1700000	906	2280000

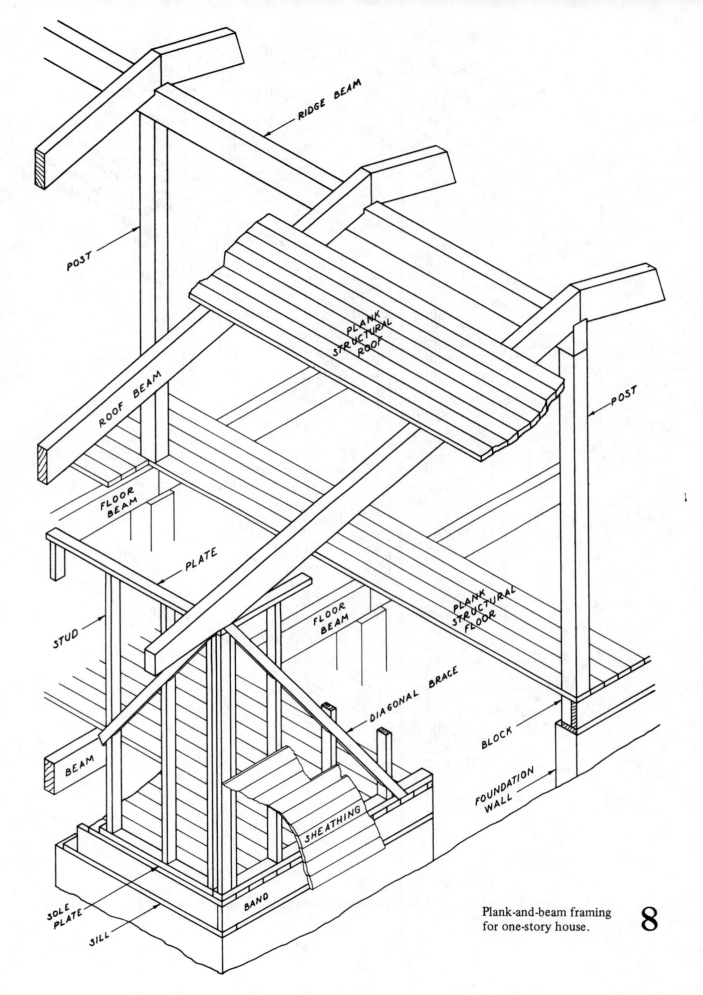

RIDGE BEAM

POST

ROOF BEAM

PLANK STRUCTURAL ROOF

POST

FLOOR BEAM

PLATE

STUD

FLOOR BEAM

PLANK STRUCTURAL FLOOR

DIAGONAL BRACE

BLOCK

BEAM

FOUNDATION WALL

SHEATHING

SOLE PLATE

BAND

SILL

Plank-and-beam framing for one-story house.

8

173

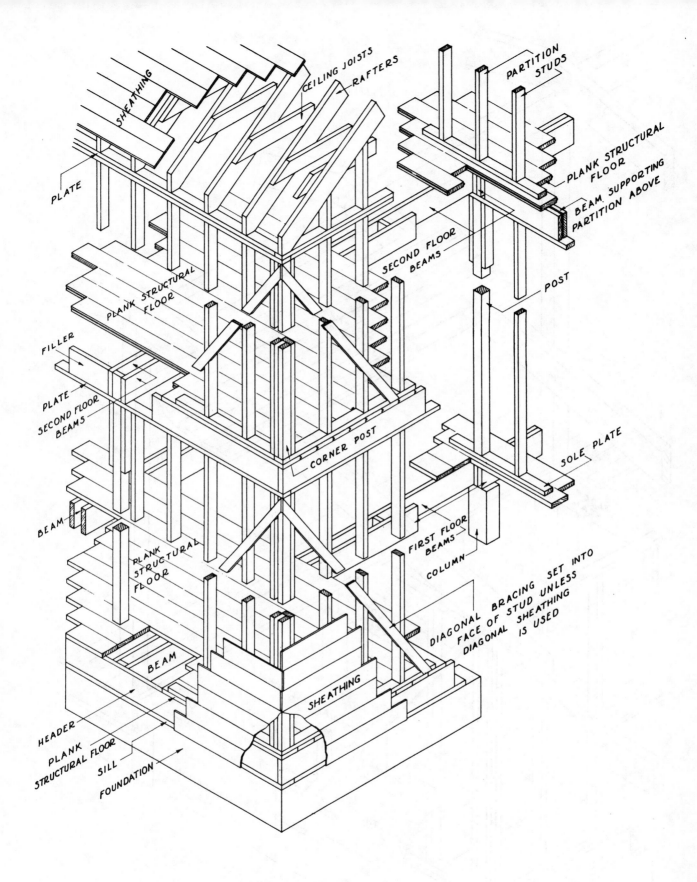

SHEATHING

CEILING JOISTS

RAFTERS

PARTITION STUDS

PLATE

PLANK STRUCTURAL FLOOR

BEAM SUPPORTING PARTITION ABOVE

SECOND FLOOR BEAMS

PLANK STRUCTURAL FLOOR

POST

FILLER

PLATE

SECOND FLOOR BEAMS

CORNER POST

SOLE PLATE

BEAM

FIRST FLOOR BEAMS

COLUMN

PLANK STRUCTURAL FLOOR

DIAGONAL BRACING SET INTO FACE OF STUD UNLESS DIAGONAL SHEATHING IS USED

BEAM

SHEATHING

HEADER

PLANK STRUCTURAL FLOOR

SILL

FOUNDATION

Plank-and-beam framing combined with conventional framing in two-story house. **9**

174

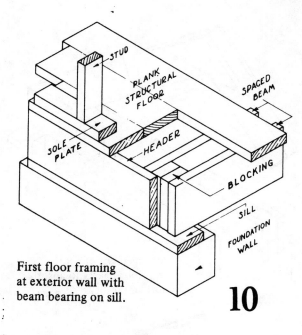

First floor framing
at exterior wall with
beam bearing on sill.

10

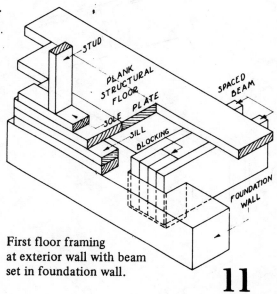

First floor framing
at exterior wall with beam
set in foundation wall.

11

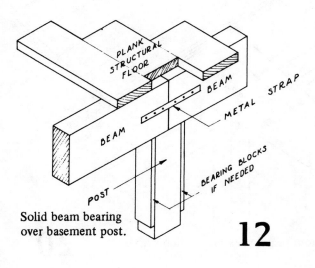

Solid beam bearing
over basement post.

12

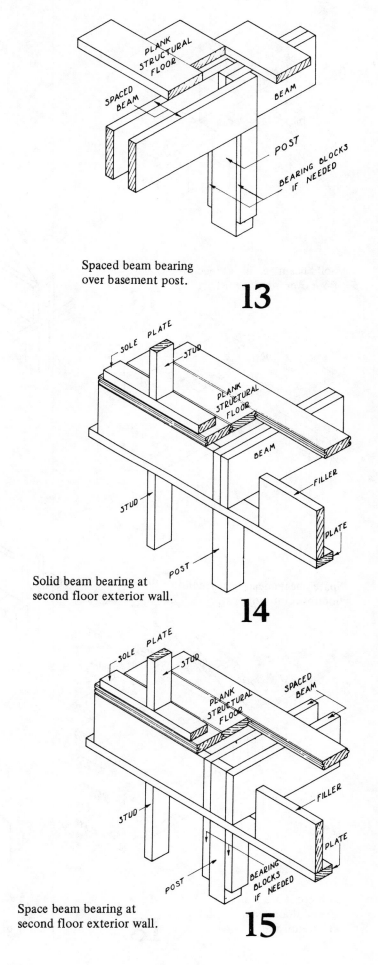

Spaced beam bearing
over basement post.

13

Solid beam bearing at
second floor exterior wall.

14

Space beam bearing at
second floor exterior wall.

15

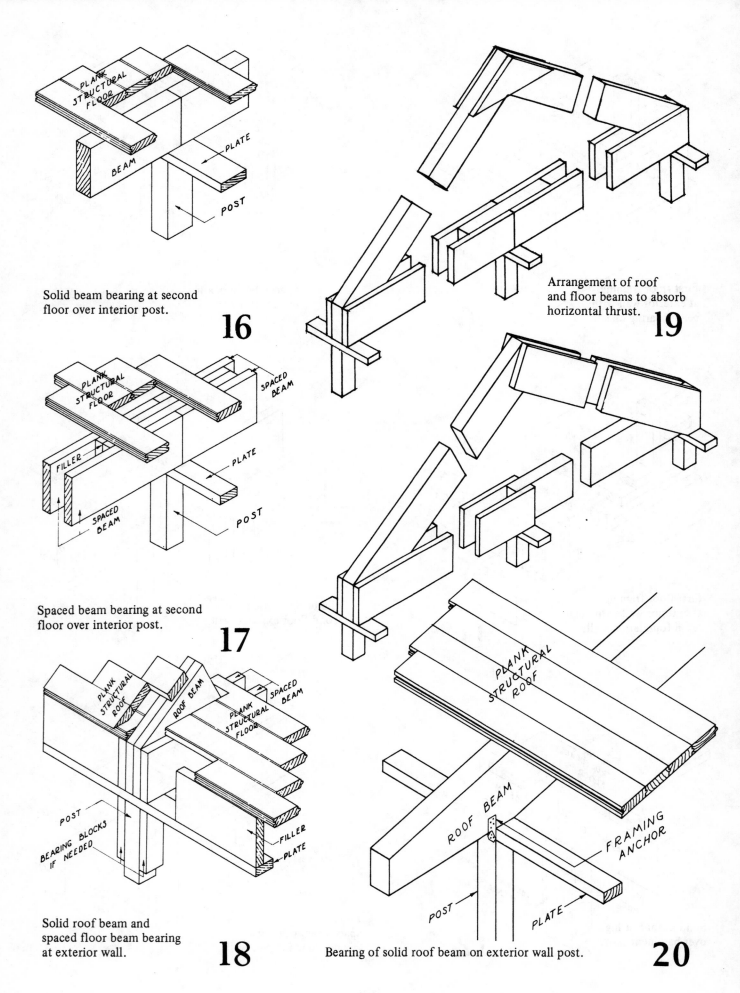

Solid beam bearing at second
floor over interior post.

16

Spaced beam bearing at second
floor over interior post.

17

Solid roof beam and
spaced floor beam bearing
at exterior wall.

18

Arrangement of roof
and floor beams to absorb
horizontal thrust.

19

Bearing of solid roof beam on exterior wall post.

20

176

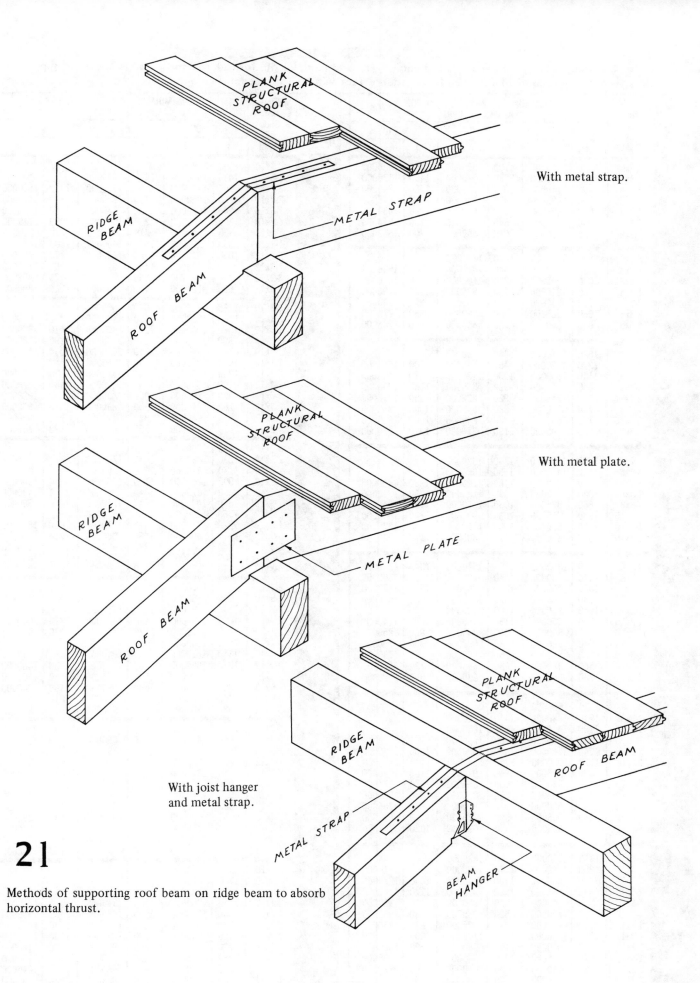

PLANK STRUCTURAL ROOF

RIDGE BEAM

ROOF BEAM

METAL STRAP

With metal strap.

PLANK STRUCTURAL ROOF

RIDGE BEAM

ROOF BEAM

METAL PLATE

With metal plate.

PLANK STRUCTURAL ROOF

RIDGE BEAM

ROOF BEAM

METAL STRAP

BEAM HANGER

With joist hanger and metal strap.

21

Methods of supporting roof beam on ridge beam to absorb horizontal thrust.

FLOOR AND ROOF BEAMS

Required values for fiber stress in bending (f) and modulus of elasticty (E) for the sizes shown to support safely a live load of 20 pounds per square foot within a deflection limitation of $l/360$.

TABLE 2

SPAN	NOMINAL SIZE OF BEAM	6'-0" f	6'-0" E	7'-0" f	7'-0" E	8'-0" f	8'-0" E
10'	2-3x6	1020	1110000	1190	1300000	1360	1480000
	1-3x8	1100	875000	1280	1020000	1460	1170000
	2-2x8	890	710000	1030	825000	1180	940000
	1-4x8	790	635000	920	740000	1050	845000
	3-2x8	590	475000	690	550000	790	630000
	2-3x8	550	440000	640	510000	730	585000
	1-6x8	520	520000	610	490000	700	560000
11'	2-3x6	1230	1480000	1440	1730000		
	1-3x8	1320	1170000	1540	1360000	1760	1550000
	2-2x8	1070	945000	1250	1100000	1430	1260000
	1-4x8	960	845000	1120	985000	1270	1130000
	3-2x8	710	630000	830	735000	950	840000
	2-3x8	660	585000	780	680000	880	775000
	1-6x8	630	560000	740	650000	840	745000
12'	1-3x8	1580	1510000	1840	1760000		
	2-2x8	1270	1220000	1490	1430000	1700	1640000
	1-4x8	1140	1100000	1330	1280000	1510	1460000
	3-2x8	850	815000	990	955000	1130	1090000
	2-3x8	790	755000	920	882000	1050	1010000
	1-6x8	750	720000	880	845000	1000	965000
	2-2x10	790	600000	920	705000	1060	805000
	1-3x10	980	745000	1150	870000	1310	995000
13'	2-2x8	1500	1560000	1740	1820000		
	1-4x8	1340	1400000	1550	1630000		
	3-2x8	990	1040000	1160	1220000	1330	1400000
	2-3x8	920	965000	1080	1130000	1230	1290000
	1-6x8	880	925000	1030	1080000	1180	1240000
	2-2x10	930	770000	1080	900000	1240	1030000
	1-3x10	1150	950000	1350	1110000	1540	1270000
	1-4x10	830	690000	970	805000	1110	920000
14'	3-2x8	1150	1300000	1350	1510000	1540	1730000
	2-3x8	1070	1200000	1250	1400000	1430	1600000
	1-6x8	1030	1150000	1200	1340000	1370	1530000
	1-3x10	1340	1180000	1570	1380000	1780	1580000
	2-2x10	1080	960000	1260	1120000	1440	1280000
	1-4x10	970	860000	1130	1000000	1290	1140000
	3-2x10	720	640000	840	745000	960	855000
	2-3x10	670	590000	780	690000	890	790000
	1-6x10	640	565000	750	660000	850	755000
	4-2x10	540	480000	630	560000	720	640000
	2-2x12	740	540000	870	630000	990	720000
15'	3-2x8	1320	1590000				
	2-3x8	1230	1480000	1440	1720000		
	1-6x8	1180	1410000	1370	1650000		
	1-3x10	1540	1460000	1800	1700000		
	2-2x10	1240	1180000	1450	1380000	1650	1570000
	1-4x10	1110	1050000	1300	1230000	1480	1400000
	3-2x10	820	786000	960	918000	1100	1050000
	2-3x10	770	730000	900	850000	1030	970000
	1-6x10	740	695000	860	810000	980	925000
	4-2x10	620	590000	720	690000	830	785000
	2-2x12	850	665000	990	775000	1140	885000
	1-4x12	760	594000	890	695000	1020	792000
16'	2-2x10	1410	1440000	1650	1670000		
	1-4x10	1260	1280000	1470	1490000	1680	1710000
	3-2x10	940	960000	1100	1110000	1250	1270000
	2-3x10	880	886000	1020	1030000	1170	1180000
	1-6x10	840	845000	970	985000	1110	1130000
	4-2x10	700	720000	820	835000	940	955000
	1-8x10	610	620000	710	725000	810	830000
	1-3x12	1200	1000000	1400	1177000	1600	1330000
	2-2x12	970	810000	1130	940000	1290	1080000
	1-4x12	870	725000	1010	845000	1150	965000
	3-2x12	650	540000	750	630000	860	720000
	2-3x12	600	500000	700	588000	800	665000

SPAN OF BEAM	NOMINAL SIZE OF BEAM	6'-0" f	6'-0" E	7'-0" f	7'-0" E	8'-0" f	8'-0" E
17'	2-2x10	1590	1720000				
	1-4x10	1430	1530000	1670	1790000		
	3-2x10	1060	1140000	1240	1330000	1410	1530000
	2-3x10	990	1060000	1150	1240000	1310	1410000
	1-6x10	940	1010000	1100	1180000	1250	1350000
	4-2x10	790	860000	930	1000000	1060	1140000
	1-8x10	690	740000	810	865000	920	990000
	1-3x12	1350	1200000	1580	1400000	1800	1600000
	2-2x12	1090	970000	1280	1130000	1450	1290000
	1-4x12	980	865000	1140	1010000	1300	1150000
	3-2x12	730	645000	850	740000	970	858000
	2-3x12	680	600000	790	700000	900	800000
18'	3-2x10	1190	1360000	1370	1590000		
	2-3x10	1110	1260000	1300	1470000	1480	1680000
	1-6x10	1060	1200000	1230	1400000	1410	1600000
	4-2x10	890	1020000	1040	1190000	1190	1360000
	1-8x10	780	840000	910	1030000	1030	1180000
	1-3x12	1520	1420000	1780	1660000		
	2-2x12	1230	1150000	1430	1340000	1630	1530000
	1-4x12	1100	1030000	1280	1200000	1460	1370000
	3-2x12	820	765000	960	895000	1090	1020000
	2-3x12	760	710000	890	830000	1010	950000
	1-6x12	720	680000	840	790000	960	900000
	4-2x12	620	575000	720	670000	820	765000
19'	3-2x10	1320	1600000				
	2-3x10	1230	1480000	1440	1730000		
	1-6x10	1170	1410000	1370	1650000		
	4-2x10	990	1200000	1160	1400000	1320	1600000
	2-4x10	890	1070000	1040	1250000	1190	1430000
	1-8x10	860	1040000	1010	1210000	1150	1380000
	2-2x12	1360	1350000	1590	1580000		
	1-4x12	1220	1210000	1430	1410000	1630	1600000
	3-2x12	910	900000	1060	1050000	1210	1200000
	2-3x12	840	835000	980	980000	1130	1110000
	1-6x12	800	800000	940	930000	1070	1060000
	4-2x12	680	675000	790	790000	910	900000
20'	2-3x10	1370	1730000				
	1-6x10	1300	1650000				
	4-2x10	1100	1400000	1280	1630000		
	2-4x10	990	1250000	1150	1460000	1320	1660000
	1-8x10	960	1210000	1120	1410000	1280	1610000
	2-2x12	1510	1580000				
	1-4x12	1350	1410000	1580	1640000		
	3-2x12	1010	1050000	1180	1220000	1350	1400000
	2-3x12	940	975000	1090	1140000	1250	1300000
	1-6x12	890	930000	1040	1090000	1190	1240000
	4-2x12	760	790000	880	920000	1010	1050000
	2-4x12	680	705000	790	820000	900	940000
21'	4-2x10	1210	1620000				
	2-4x10	1090	1450000	1270	1690000		
	1-8x10	1050	1400000	1230	1630000		
	1-4x12	1490	1630000				
	3-2x12	1110	1210000	1300	1420000	1480	1620000
	2-3x12	1030	1130000	1200	1320000	1380	1500000
	1-6x12	970	1070000	1130	1250000	1310	1430000
	4-2x12	830	910000	970	1060000	1110	1210000
	2-4x12	750	815000	870	950000	990	1090000
	3-3x12	690	750000	800	875000	920	1000000
	1-8x12	720	790000	840	920000	960	1050000
	1-10x12	580	620000	660	725000	750	826000
22'	2-4x10	1200	1670000				
	1-8x10	1160	1610000				
	3-2x12	1220	1400000	1420	1630000		
	2-3x12	1130	1300000	1320	1510000	1520	1730000
	1-6x12	1080	1240000	1260	1450000	1450	1650000
	4-2x12	920	1050000	1070	1230000	1230	1400000
	2-4x12	820	940000	960	1090000	1100	1250000
	5-2x12	730	840000	860	980000	980	1120000
	3-3x12	750	865000	880	1010000	1010	1160000
	1-8x12	790	910000	920	1060000	1060	1210000
	1-10x12	620	715000	730	835000	830	955000

RANDOM LENGTH WOOD DECKING
(Two-Inch Nominal Thickness)

FOREWORD The convenience, economy and appearance of timber floor and roof decking are advantages long recognized by architects, engineers and builders. Although nominal 2-inch, standard-length decking is generally available, some waste results where end trimming is necessary to conform with standard arrangement of framing.

Where random-length plank floors are continuous over three or more spans, such decks provide 30 percent more stiffness under uniform load than decks composed of short planks laid in a series of single spans.

GENERAL DISCUSSION

The use of 2-inch planks in standard lengths, for roof decks and floors, is well established. Available publications are concerned principally with plank spans that divide into standard lengths of center-matched, 2-inch lumber. Spans of 6, 7 and 8 feet are most suitable for general use. Nine and ten foot spans offer limited possibilities.

When standard lengths of lumber are used in plank decks, end joints are customarily located over the supporting beam. This construction is desirable from the standpoint of design. A deck so laid is really a beam supported by two or more reactions, as shown in Figure 1. The beam (deck) may be classified as simple, continuous, or a combination of the two. Moments, stresses and deflection can be computed by the standard beam formulas in engineering hand books.

However, standard-length decking does not always fit the dimension of the building. For example, a roof 34 feet long can be accommodated by one 6-foot and four 7- foot spans, or by two 8 -foot and three 6-foot spans. Such non-uniform spacing of beams may complicate the wall design, or the uneven spacing of exposed beams could be undesirable for aesthetic reasons. For a specific purpose, it might be preferable to divide the roof into five spans, each about 6 feet 9 1/2 inches long. Obviously, such beam spacing would not be economical for the use of standard lengths. The cost of trimming the planks to fit and the waste involved could be excessive.

A consideration of the problem of the 34-foot plank roof, supported by evenly spaced beams, suggests the use of plank in random lengths without reference to location of the end joints. In addition to reducing costs, it would speed up construction.

DESIGN CRITERIA

Random-length decking cannot be designed by conventional engineering procedures. The location of end-joints between planks, the lack of continuity from plank to plank, lateral load distribution, and the effectiveness of tongue-and-groove joints, in transferring stress, are among the variables that cannot be evaluated readily.

Investigations at the Oregon Forest Products Laboratory were conducted on 3-span continuous panels of random-length, 2 x 6-inch decking. The planks were end-and center-matched and laid, as shown in Figure 2, in accordance with the following arrangment.

PREMIUM
A select grade with minimum natural growth characteristics. Recommended where the finest appearance is desired. Shown is standard smooth face with "V" groove.

ARCHITECTURAL
A high line commercial grade decking which allows moderate imperfections. Shown is optional textured face with channel pattern.

CALIFORNIA RUSTIC
A low line commercial grade decking. Recommended for applications where a large number of natural imperfections are acceptable -on panel to create rustic appearance. Face is standard textured.

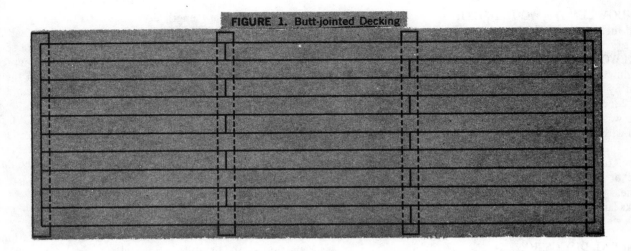

FIGURE 1. Butt-jointed Decking

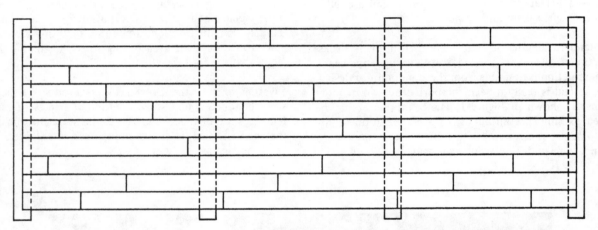

FIGURE 2. Random-length Decking

Distance between joints in adjacent rows of decking must be at least two feet. Joints in rows not directly adjacent must be separated by one foot or by two rows of decking. In any section of a deck less than one foot in length the number of end joints must not exceed one-third of the number of decking courses. There may be only one joint in each plank between supports. A joint on a support shall be considered as a joint in one of the adjacent spans. Joints must all be end-matched. Courses must be slant nailed within one foot of all end-joints. In end spans, one-third of courses must be free of end joints. (Exception may be made where a cantilevered overhang equal to 20% or more of the end span is present, or where end span is shortened to attain equivalent deflection reduction.)

(1) End joints in adjacent plank lines were at least 12 inches apart, and

(2) Each plank rested on at least one support.

Since the strength and stiffness of the end-jointed panels, under discussion, depend upon reasonably full engagement of tongues and grooves, it is important that the planks are seasoned adequately to meet service conditions.

When this type of decking is used as a structural floor, it is recommended that nominal 1-inch strip flooring be applied at right angles to the planks to distribute the loads over the floor system.

End-matched planks may not always be readily available. Square-end planks may be used and the effect of end matching provided by grooving the ends of the planks for metal splines to extend 3/4-inch into the ends of pieces. Such splines will transfer loads as well as conventional end-matching.

Planks should be fastened to supporting beams with two 16d nails at each crossing. One should be driven blind, the other in the face of the plank.

SHEATHING

WALL AND ROOF SHEATHING

When the walls and roof framing are completed, sheathing must be applied over the wall studs and roof rafters. The sheathing provides a rigidity to the frame and also provides a surface for applying the finish roof and walls. Material used for sheathing is 4' x 8' plywood or composition board, (check local codes for minimum thickness) or 3/4" thick 6" wide common boards. Be sure to locate the joints over the center of the stud or rafter and if common boards are used for sheathing, do not join adjacent boards over the same stud or rafter. Fit sheathing carefully at valleys, hips and ridges and nail them securely. Common boards may be nailed diagonally for extra strength but there is also greater waste because of angle cutting.

If plywood sheathing is used, it must be nailed with the face grain perpendicular to the studs or rafters, with end joints directly over the center of a stud or rafter, again breaking up the joints. Be careful in handling plywood, it may slip off the roof, or the wind may throw you and the plywood off balance resulting in serious injury.

Apply sheathing to the walls before the roof is installed to reinforce the frame of the building. Start the first course of wall sheathing about 1/2" below the top of the concrete or block foundation and the roof sheathing 3/4" of an inch past or over the rafter ends or overhang. Work up the roof to the ridge on all sides.

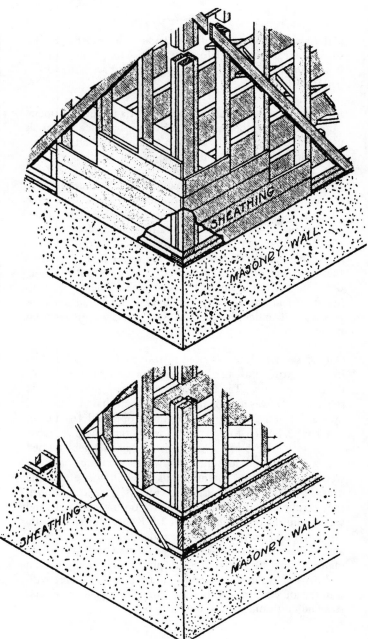

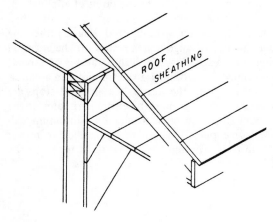

ROOF COVERING

Materials for covering roofs are classified by weight per 100 square feet called a square (100 square feet = one square). For example a 30 lb. roofing paper or felt weights 30 lbs. per 100 square feet.

Roof construction and finish consists of a number of operations which must be followed in proper sequence. Materials used for roofing include Built-up roofing, Asphalt Shingles, Wood shingles, Mineral Fiber Shingles, Slate Shingles, Tile, Roll Roofing, Galvanized Metal, Aluminum, Terne & Copper. The selection of roofing material is influenced by initial cost, maintenance, durability, aesthetics and roof pitch or slope. Local building codes may prohibit certain materials because of fire hazard or wind resistance. Moisture control is an important consideration in avoiding roof failures. Sometimes moisture vapor from the lower floors, rising to the attic, will be chilled below its dew point and will condense on the underside of the roof deck or sheathing, causing the sheathing to warp and buckle. Louvered openings constructed under the eaves in the gables will prevent this problem.

One of several materials used in roofing is Tar, which is a familiar word but has different meanings for different people. To many, Tar is a black adhesive liquid or plastic substance. However, it is much more than that. Tar is a hydrocarbon and an organic compound obtained from coal. The coal is heated to a very high temperature which cracks the molecules into gas. This gas is further distilled, refined and separated into products known as creosote, used for wood preservatives, chemical oils used in manufacturing drugs, dyes, paints, varnishes, cosmetics, plastics and synthetic rubber and pitches used for roofing materials and water proofing compounds. Coal Tar Roofing Pitch has superb water and corrosive resistance qualities as well as being an excellent adhesion for fusing roofing felts. All roofing material must be stored in a dry place prior to application and off the ground, preferably on a platform covered with waterproof coverings. Store rolls of felt and paper on end to avoid deforming or damaging.

a) BUILT-UP roofing or Tar & Gravel is used on a flat roof or a pitch not to exceed $3\frac{}{12}$. It is installed as follows: starting at the low point of the roof, lay one ply thickness of Rosin Sheathing Paper weighing about 5 lbs. per 100 sq. ft. Lap each sheet at least two 2" and nail sufficiently to hold in place until the entire roof is covered. Begin again at the low point and lay one ply of coated base sheet lapping each sheet 4" over the underlayment. Lap ends about 6" and nail along the lap at maximum of 9" spacing, staggering the nails through the center of the sheet at 18" intervals. Again beginning at the low point of the roof, apply a uniform mopping of asphalt approximately 23 lbs. per 100 sq. ft. into which, while still hot, embed three plys or layers of 15 lb. asphalt felt paper. Lap each sheet 24" over the preceeding sheet and mop full width of lap so that felt does not touch felt. Broom each ply to assure complete bondage. Be sure, in overlapping the plys, the top ply is over the bottom ply. Over the entire surface, pour a uniform coat of 400 lb. per sq. ft. of gravel or 300 lb. per square ft. of slag, or crushed rock, which are 1/4" to 5/8" in size. Hot asphalt must be hand or machine mopped at a proper temperature and in proper amounts to eliminate any voids and must flow from the sides of each ply. After each ply is laid in the hot asphalt, it must be broomed with a 36" wide broom to assure proper adhesion and to eliminate any voids in the asphalt and to force any moisture vapor out from between the plies of paper. Do not apply roofing on a wet surface. Asphalt must not be below 350° at the point of application. No more asphalt must be spread or poured at one time than can be immediately covered with gravel or slag. Overheating may cause a chemical change which draws off the essential oils reducing the weathering life. Temperatures of asphalt may be determined by dropping a thermometer in a pail of asphalt just drawn from the kettle. Metal gravel stops are secured to the roof edges around the entire perimeter of the roof. The gravel stops can be such metal as aluminum, galvanized metal or copper. It is not recommended to reroof over a built-up roof. The old roof must be stripped to the sheathing.

BUILT-UP ROOFING

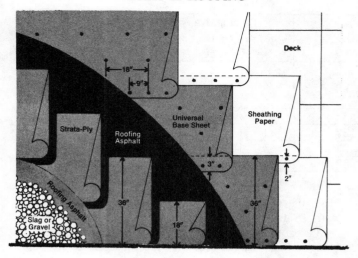

b)   ROLL ROOFING is roofing felts or paper saturated with asphalt surfaced with mineral granules. The rolls are available in 36" width weighing from 15 to 120 lbs. a square. This type roof can be used with any roof pitch including flat roofs.

Lay the base course, as explained in Built-up roofing, beginning at the low point of the roof. Roll roofing is nailed at the top edge with galvanized large head nails about 12" apart. Lap the second roll 2" over the first and seal with mastic roofing cement for the entire length of the overlap over the nails. The ends should lap about 6" again nailing only the under layer. No nails are to be visible in this type roofing. If the Salvage double covering is used, the overlap is 19" with a 17" exposure.

Reroofing over an existing roof is not recommended. Better results will be obtained by removing the old roof and constructing a new one. The heavier the paper, the longer the service of the roof. A common weight for this type roofing is 90 lb. mineral surfaced.

c)   ASPHALT SHINGLES is a saturated felt coated with multi-colored granules manufactured into strips of different shape and size. The most popular is the square butt shingle 12" wide and 36" long with slotted butts to similate indivual shingles. The portion of shingles exposed is termed "to the weather " and the average exposure is about 5". There are many qualities of asphalt shingles which is determined by weight, from 180 lbs. to 380 lbs. sq. Needless to say, the heavier the shingles, the longer the life or service. An average weight is a 235 lb. per square shingle.

The roof pitch or slope must be 4" or greater when using asphalt shingles. Begin at the low part of the roof and lay one course of 14 lb. felt base with 6" lap covering the entire roof surface. Nail the first course of asphalt shingles at the low point of the roof upside down (tabs up) over a course of wooden shingles. A second layer or double course is installed right side up making a total of three courses. Be sure to break up the joints on all courses.

Some shingles are self sealing by means of several spots of asphalt above the tabs. This will allow the shingles to fuse to each other. Nails used on asphalt shingles are 1 1/4" galvanized roofing nails. Drive one nail about 1/2" above each slot on the square butt. The succeeding courses will cover the nails of each course. Three tab shingles require 4 nails per strip. Do not sink the nail into the shingle, simply drive it flush.

In order to get the shingles straight, you may have to snap a line at each course or every other course as a guide. To cover the ridge of the roof, or the hips, cut the strips of shingles at the tab (3 pieces of shingles per strip) and nail them over the ridge in a lapped fashion as installed on the roof. Cover the entire ridge or hip, and the last shingle applied will be with roofing mastic.

It is not necessary to remove old asphalt shingles for reroofing except the ridge and hip. Apply new roofing over the old using longer nails. 20 to 25 years is the average life of an asphalt shingle roof.

ASPHALT SHINGLES

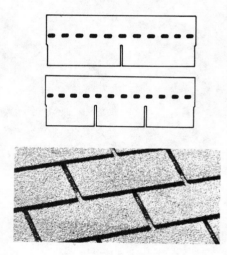

d)   ASBESTOS CEMENT SHINGLES are brittle and break very easily. They are a fireproof product but this offers little comfort if the roof framing is not. These shingles are made with similated wood grain and slate effect. Because these shingles are rigid, specially molded pieces are made for ridges and hips. A minimum of a 5" pitch is recommended for Asbestos Cement Shingles. Nail holes are pre-punched and a galvanized or copper nail must be used. A special cutting tool is required for fitting or a cut can be hand made by using an old chisel punch or hatchet blade by simply scoring along a straight edge and breaking along the score over a solid base.

Cover the roof with 15 lb. felt as with asphalt shingles, and beginning at the low part of the roof, lay the shingles end to end along the row (butted) and overlap the succeeding course breaking up the joints. These shingles will not rust, rot, shrink or scale and will measure about 16" to 30" long, 9" to 14" wide, and 1/4" thick with a 7" exposure, and weigh about 500 lbs. per square.

Type of Application	Size (inches)	Thickness (inches)	Minimum Lap (inches) Head	Size	Maximum Exposure (inches)
Individual Unit	8 x 16	5/32 to 1/4	2	2	7
	9 x 18	1/4	2	2	8
Multiple Unit	14 x 30	5/32	2	-	6
Dutch Lap	16 x 16	5/32	3	4	12 x 13
Ranch Design	24 x 12	5/32	3	4	20 x 9
French	16 x 16	5/32	3	3	13 x 13

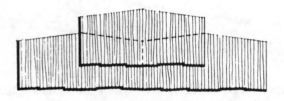

ASBESTOS CEMENT SHINGLES

Beginning at the low point of the roof, cover the entire roof with 15 lb. paper except the first course, which should be 30 lb. paper. This is to prevent water from penetrating the shingles if ice dams occur on the lower part of the roof. Double the first course of shingles and be sure to stagger the joints at least 2". Continue the coursing using 3d galvanized or aluminum nails only 2 per shingle spaced not more than 3/4" from the edge of the shingle and at least 1" above the exposure line. Shingles should be loosely placed to allow for swelling and expansion. No finish is required on wood shingles. However, staining will prolong the life of the shingles and wood shingles will help to insulate the roof. They perform well when exposed to strong winds, hail or snow.

Minimum roof pitch is 3 1/2" and the exposure of wood shingles is depended upon the roof pitch or slope, varying from 3" to 7" exposure. Wood shingles are normally applied in straight single courses but may vary to achieve special effects for thatch, serrated, weave and ocean. Project the first course about 1 1/2" beyond the roof sheathing or overhang. Wood shingles may be applied over old roof in re-roofing.

f) SLATE SHINGLE is a natural quarried rock product split into thin sheets used for roof covering. The marked cleavage of the slate rock lends itself to a natural, irregular and pleasing roof surface with natural color variations from blacks and greys, blues and greens and browns and reds. A slate roof will usually outlast the life of the building. They require a larger or stronger roof framing system because of the weight of the shingles and the roof pitch should be no less than 6".

Beginning at the low point of the roof, lay a 20 lb. paper of felt overlapping at least 6". Build up the first course of slate shingles with a wood strip about 1/2" thick and about 1 1/4" wide. This is called a cant and is used to give the first course the same pitch as the succeeding courses. The first course is applied the long way, parallel with the roof and the second course, over the first, (double course) is laid the conventional way with all joints on both courses staggered. Copper nails are used in the pre-holed slate shingles. Exposure is about 6". Cutting is done by hand or with a special cutting tool. If by hand, score the shingle over a bed of sand until it cuts with a hammer and chisel. Damaged slate shingles are very simple to replace once the roof is completed.

e) WOOD SHINGLES may not be acceptable in certain areas because they may be a fire hazard. Some wood shingles are treated to meet fire safety requirements. There are two types of wood shingles: machine sawed and handsplit, both of which are made from western red cedar, redwood and cyprus, all highly decay-resistant woods. Machine sawed shingles are 16", 18" and 24" long in random widths, tapered with 1/2" to 3/4" thick butts. They are graded No. 1, 2 and 3 according to knots and defects. Handsplit shingles sometimes called shakes vary in thickness with butts ranging from 5/8" to 1 1/4" thick with lengths of 24", 32" and 36" with random widths.

CERTIGRADE RED CEDAR SHINGLES

GRADE	Length	Thickness (at Butt)	No. of Courses Per Bundle	Bdls/Cartons Per Square		Description
No. 1 BLUE LABEL	16" (Fivex) 18" (Perfections) 24" (Royals)	.40" .45" .50"	20/20 18/18 13/14	4 bdls. 4 bdls. 4 bdls.		The premium grade of shingles for roofs and sidewalls. These top-grade shingles are 100% heartwood . . . 100% clear and 100% edge-grain.
No. 2 RED LABEL	16" (Fivex) 18" (Perfections) 24" (Royals)	.40" .45" .50"	20/20 18/18 13/14	4 bdls. 4 bdls. 4 bdls.		A proper grade for some applications. Not less than 10" clear on 16" shingles, 11" clear on 18" shingles and 16" clear on 24" shingles. Flat grain and limited sapwood are permitted in this grade.
No. 3 BLACK LABEL	16" (Fivex) 18" (Perfections) 24" (Royals)	.40" .45" .50"	20/20 18/18 13/14	4 bdls. 4 bdls. 4 bdls.		A utility grade for economy applications and secondary buildings. Not less than 6" clear on 16" and 18" shingles, 10" clear on 24" shingles.
No. 4 UNDER-COURSING	16" (Fivex) 18" (Perfections)	.40" .45"	14/14 or 20/20 14/14 or 18/18	2 bdls. 2 bdls. 2 bdls. 2 bdls.		A utility grade for undercoursing on double-coursed sidewall applications or for interior accent walls.
No. 1 or No. 2 REBUTTED-REJOINTED	16" (Fivex) 18" (Perfections) 24" (Royals)	.40" .45" .50"	33/33 28/28 13/14	1 carton 1 carton 4 bdls.		Same specifications as above for No. 1 and No. 2 grades but machine trimmed for exactly parallel edges with butts sawn at precise right angles. For sidewall application where tightly fitting joints are desired. Also available with smooth sanded face.

| PITCH | Maximum exposure recommended for roofs: | | | | | | | | |
| | NO. 1 BLUE LABEL | | | NO. 2 RED LABEL | | | NO. 3 BLACK LABEL | | |
	16"	18"	24"	16"	18"	24"	16"	18"	24"
3 IN 12 TO 4 IN 12	3¾"	4¼"	5¾"	3½"	4"	5½"	3"	3½"	5"
4 IN 12 AND STEEPER	5"	5½"	7½"	4"	4½"	6½"	3½"	4"	5½"

| LENGTH AND THICKNESS | Approximate coverage of one square (4 bundles) of shingles based on following weather exposures | | | | | | | | | | | | | | | | | | | | | | | | | | |
	3½"	4"	4½"	5"	5½"	6"	6½"	7"	7½"	8"	8½"	9"	9½"	10"	10½"	11"	11½"	12"	12½"	13"	13½"	14"	14½"	15"	15½"	16"
16" x 5/2"	70	80	90	100*	110	120	130	140	150‡	160	170	180	190	200	210	220	230	240†	....	....	....	....	....	....	....	....
18" x 5/2¼"	....	72½	81½	90½	100*	109	118	127	136	145½	154½	163½	172½	181½	191	200	209	218	227	236	245½	254½	....	....	....	....
24" x 4/2"	....	....	....	....	80	86½	93	100*	106½	113	120	126½	133	140	146½	153	160	166½	173	180	186½	193	200	206½	213†	

NOTES: *Maximum exposure recommended for roofs. ‡Maximum exposure recommended for single-coursing No. 1 grades on sidewalls. Reduce exposure for No. 2 grades.
†Maximum exposure recommended for double-coursing No. 1 grades on sidewalls.

CERTI-SPLIT RED CEDAR HANDSPLIT SHAKES

GRADE	Length and Thickness	18" Pack**		Description
		# Courses Per Bdl.	# Bdls. Per Sq.	
No. 1 HANDSPLIT & RESAWN	15" Starter-Finish 18" x ½" Mediums 18" x ¾" Heavies 24" x ⅜" 24" x ½" Mediums 24" x ¾" Heavies	9/9 9/9 9/9 9/9 9/9 9/9	5 5 5 5 5 5	 These shakes have split faces and sawn backs. Cedar logs are first cut into desired lengths. Blanks or boards of proper thickness are split and then run diagonally through a bandsaw to produce two tapered shakes from each blank.
No. 1 TAPERSPLIT	24" x ½"	9/9	5	 Produced largely by hand, using a sharp-bladed steel froe and a wooden mallet. The natural shingle-like taper is achieved by reversing the block, end-for-end, with each split.
No. 1 STRAIGHT-SPLIT	18" x ⅜" True-Edge* 18" x ⅜" 24" x ⅜"	20" Pack 14 Straight 19 Straight 16 Straight	4 5 5	 Produced in the same manner as tapersplit shakes except that by splitting from the same end of the block, the shakes acquire the same thickness throughout.

NOTE: * Exclusively sidewall product, with parallel edges.
** Pack used for majority of shakes.

| SHAKE TYPE, LENGTH AND THICKNESS | Approximate coverage (in sq. ft.) of one square, when shakes are applied with ½" spacing, at following weather exposures, in inches (h): | | | | | | |
	5½	7½	8½	10	11½	16	
18" x ½" Handsplit-and-Resawn Mediums (a)	55(b)	75(c)	85(d)	100	....	....	(a) 5 bundles will cover 100 sq. ft. roof area when used as starter-finish course at 10" weather exposure; 6 bundles will cover 100 sq. ft. wall area at 8½" exposure; 7 bundles will cover 100 sq. ft. roof area at 7½" weather exposure; see footnote (h).
18" x ¾" Handsplit-and-Resawn Heavies (a)	55(b)	75(c)	85(d)	100	....	....	(b) Maximum recommended weather exposure for 3-ply roof construction.
24" x ⅜" Handsplit	....	75(e)	85	100(f)	115(d)	....	(c) Maximum recommended weather exposure for 2-ply roof construction.
24" x ½" Handsplit-and-Resawn Mediums	....	75(b)	85	100(c)	115(d)	....	(d) Maximum recommended weather exposure for single-coursed wall construction.
24" x ¾" Handsplit-and-Resawn Heavies	....	75(b)	85	100(c)	115(d)	....	(e) Maximum recommended weather exposure for application on roof pitches between 4-in-12 and 8-in-12.
24" x ½" Tapersplit	....	75(b)	85	100(c)	115(d)	....	(f) Maximum recommended weather exposure for application on roof pitches of 8-in-12 and steeper.
18" x ⅜" True-Edge Straight-Split	....	....	....	....	....	112(g)	(g) Maximum recommended weather exposure for double-coursed wall construction.
18" x ⅜" Straight-Split	65(b)	90(c)	100(d)	....	....	....	(h) All coverage based on ½" spacing between shakes.
24" x ⅜" Straight-Split	....	75(b)	85	100(c)	115(d)	....	
15" Starter-Finish Course	Use supplementary with shakes applied not over 10" weather exposure.						

● Valleys should extend far enough under the shingles to insure complete drainage, with water-stop as shown if necessary.

● How the recommended modified "Boston" hip is made.

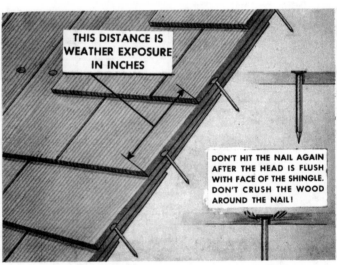

THIS DISTANCE IS WEATHER EXPOSURE IN INCHES

DON'T HIT THE NAIL AGAIN AFTER THE HEAD IS FLUSH WITH FACE OF THE SHINGLE. DON'T CRUSH THE WOOD AROUND THE NAIL!

● Proper weather exposure and nailing will provide a 3-ply roof.

● Drip from gables and the formation of icicles can be prevented by this simple expedient.

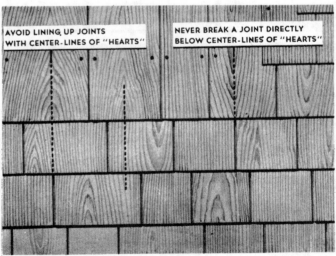

AVOID LINING UP JOINTS WITH CENTER-LINES OF "HEARTS"

NEVER BREAK A JOINT DIRECTLY BELOW CENTER-LINES OF "HEARTS"

● Flat-grain shingles in Red Label and No. 3 Black Label grades should be properly applied as shown above.

● In over-roofing, new flashings should be placed around chimneys without removing the old.

Approximate Number Required, and Weight of Rust-Resistant or Zinc Coated Nails Per Square of Random Width CERTIGRADE Shingles, for Weather Exposures Given.

16-Inch CERTIGRADE	5-Inch Exposure			4½-Inch Exposure			4-Inch Exposure			3½-Inch Exposure		
	Number	Weight Lbs.	Oz.	Number	Weight Lbs.	Oz.	Number	Weight Lbs.	Oz.	Number	Weight Lbs.	Oz.
No. 1 Blue Label Grade	1030	2	0	1144	2	3½	1287	2	8	1471	2	14
Red Label Grade	1310	2	9	1454	2	13½	1637	3	3	1872	3	10
No. 3 Black Label Grade	1545	3	0	1715	3	5	1931	3	12	2206	4	2

18-Inch CERTIGRADE	5½-Inch Exposure			5-Inch Exposure			4½-Inch Exposure			4-Inch Exposure		
No. 1 Blue Label Grade	933	1	13	1030	2	0	1144	2	3½	1287	2	8
Red Label Grade	1190	2	5	1310	2	9	1454	2	13½	1637	3	3
No. 3 Black Label Grade	1348	2	11	1545	3	0	1715	3	5	1931	3	12

24-Inch CERTIGRADE	7½-Inch Exposure			7-Inch Exposure			6½-Inch Exposure			6-Inch Exposure		
No. 1 Blue Label Grade	716	1	14	760	2	0	784	2	1	852	2	4
Red Label Grade	885	2	5	945	2	7½	974	2	9	1060	2	12
No. 3 Black Label Grade	955	2	8	1020	2	10½	1052	2	12	1245	3	0

Note: The above figures are for new roofs, on slat or solid decks. For over-roofing, as larger nails are used, increase weight of nails needed two-thirds for 16-inch and 18-inch shingles and three-fourths for 24-inch shingles. The above table allows a reasonable wastage of nails, and fewer nails may be needed on some jobs.

● **The six simple and easy steps that make a perfect over-roofing job. These are fully described in the text.**

1. Cut away the first course of old shingles at eaves.

2. Cut back old shingles about six inches from gable edges.

3. Nail a strip of lumber along gable edges and eaves to replace the old shingles.

4. Replace old ridge shingles with strip of bevel siding, thin edge downward.

5. Place strip of lumber in each valley to separate old metal from new.

6. Apply the new cedar shingles right over the old, using 5d rust-resistant nails.

FOR NEW ROOF CONSTRUCTION			OVER-ROOFING CONSTRUCTION		DOUBLE-COURSING
3d	3d	4d	5d	6d	5d
FOR 16" AND 18" SHINGLES		FOR 24" SHINGLES	FOR 16" & 18" SHINGLES	FOR 24" SHINGLES	FOR ALL SHINGLES
1¼" LONG	1¼" LONG #14½ GAUGE	1½" LONG #14 GAUGE	1¾" LONG #14 GAUGE	2" LONG #13 GAUGE	1¾" LONG #14 GAUGE
APPROX. 376 NAILS TO LB.	APPROX. 515 NAILS TO LB.	APPROX. 382 NAILS TO LB.	APPROX. 310 NAILS TO LB.	APPROX. 220 NAILS TO LB.	APPROX. 380 NAILS TO LB.

SQUARE CUT NAILS OF SAME LENGTH WILL ALSO GIVE SATISFACTORY SERVICE.

STANDARD "BOX" NAILS OF THE SIZES GIVEN WILL PROVE SATISFACTORY IF PROPERLY ZINC COATED OR MADE RUST-RESISTANT.

HANDSPLIT SHAKES: ROOF SHEATHING—Red cedar handsplit shakes may be applied over open or solid sheathing. When spaced sheathing is used, 1 x 4s (or wider) are spaced on centers equal to the weather exposure at which the shakes are to be laid—but never more than 10 inches. In areas where wind-driven snow conditions prevail, a solid roof deck is recommended.

ROOF PITCH AND EXPOSURES—Proper weather exposure is important. As a general rule, a 7-1/2" exposure is recommended for 18" shakes and 10" exposure for 24"'shakes.

ROOF APPLICATION—A 36-inch wide strip of 30-lb. roofing felt should be laid over sheathing boards at the eave line. The beginning or starter course of shakes should be doubled, for extra texture it can be tripled. The bottom course or courses can be of 15" or 18" shakes—the former being made expressly for this purpose. After applying each course of shakes, an 18" wide strip of 30-lb. roofing felt should be laid over the top portion of the shakes, extending onto the sheathing. Position the bottom edge of the felt above the butt at a distance equal to twice the weather exposure. For example, 24" shakes laid with 10" exposure would have felt applied 20" above the shake butts; thus the felt will cover the top four inches of the shakes, and will extend out 14" onto the sheathing. (See Fig. 5.) When straight-split shakes are used, the "froe-end" (the end from which the shakes have been split and which is smoother) should be laid uppermost, i.e. toward the ridge. Roofing felt interlay is not necessary when straight-split or taper-split shakes are applied in snow-free areas at weather exposures less than one-third the total shake length (3-ply roof).

VALLEYS—Valley and flashing metals that have proved reliable in a particular region should be selected. It is important that valley metals be used whose longevity will match that for which cedar is renowned. Metal valley sheets should be center-crimped, of 20-inch minimum width, and for maximum life should be either underlaid with a strip of 30-lb. roofing felt applied over the sheathing or painted with a good grade metal paint. (See Fig. 6.)

HIPS AND RIDGES—Either site-applied or pre-formed factory-made hip and ridge units may be used. Weather exposures should be the same as roof shakes. Be sure to use longer nails, sufficient to penetrate the underlying sheathing. Advisable to use two 8d nails on each side of shake. (See Fig. 7.)

NAILING—Secure each shake with two (only) rust-resistant nails (hot-dipped zinc or aluminum) driven about one inch from each edge, and one or two inches above the butt line of the course to follow. Adequate nail penetration into sheathing boards is important. The two-inch length (6d) normally is adequate, but longer nails should be used if shake thickness or weather exposure dictates. Do not drive nailheads into shakes.

Roofs Fig. 5

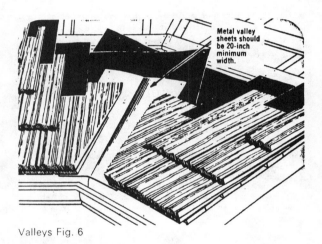

Valleys Fig. 6

Hips and Ridges Fig. 7

WOOD SHAKES

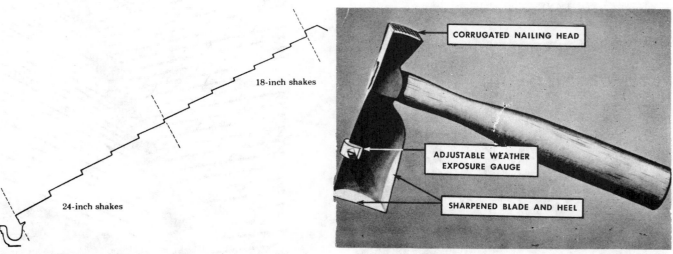

By using two shake sizes and graduating the exposure, you can create a striking dimensional effect.

18-inch shakes

24-inch shakes

CORRUGATED NAILING HEAD

ADJUSTABLE WEATHER EXPOSURE GAUGE

SHARPENED BLADE AND HEEL

● Professional shingle applicators use a special type of shingling hatchet which is designed to speed application.

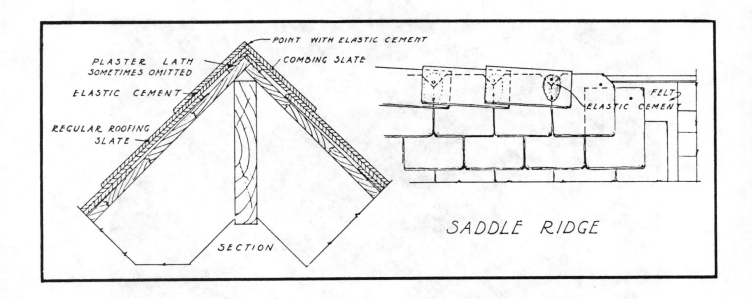

POINT WITH ELASTIC CEMENT

PLASTER LATH SOMETIMES OMITTED

COMBING SLATE

ELASTIC CEMENT

REGULAR ROOFING SLATE

SECTION

FELT

ELASTIC CEMENT

SADDLE RIDGE

LAYING SLATE

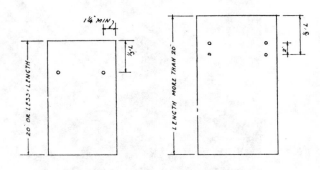

1¼" MIN.

20 OR LESS ÷ LENGTH

LENGTH MORE THAN 20"

LOCATION OF NAIL HOLES

SLATE ROOFING

Smooth and Rough Slates

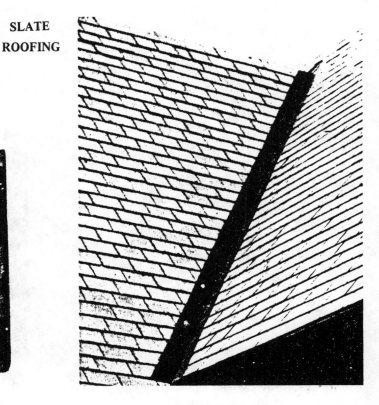

OPEN VALLEY

SLATER'S TOOLS

The tools most commonly used by the slater are the hammer, ripper, and stake. Slater's tools are all drop forged. An approved hammer is forged solid, all in one piece, from crucible cast steel with an unbreakable leather handle to avoid slipping and blistering the hands. One end comes to a sharp point for punching slate and the other forms the hammer head. There is a claw in the center for drawing nails, and on each side of the shank there is a shear edge for cutting slate. The head, point and cutting edge are properly tempered to withstand heavy work.

The ripper is about 24" long and is forged from crucible cast steel. It is used for removing broken slate and making repairs. A hook on the end provides a means of cutting and removing the slating nails. The blade is drawn very thin and the hook end correctly tempered for hard wear.

The stake is about 18" long and T-shaped. The long edge is used as a rest upon which to cut and punch slate or as a straight edge to mark the slat when cutting and fitting around chimneys, hips, and valleys. Slate cutter is used for cutting pieces on the roof and has established itself as a labor-saving device.

MAKING REPAIRS TO SLATE ROOFS

Due to climatic conditions, slates are sometimes broken on the roof. Repairing slate is very easy and can be done by anyone.

First, you must remove both nails with the slate ripper, and remove any remaining slate. Then insert the slate hook half way between the bordering slates and on an even line with those slates; insert your new piece and the job is finished. The new slate will not go left or right because the adjacent slates will hold it in place. The slate hook prevents the slate from sliding out.

This method requires no pieces of flashing to be inserted under the slate. Furthermore, it is an efficient, labor-saving method of repairing slate.

SLATE COVERING

(a) On all surfaces to be covered with slate, furnish and lay genuine asphalt saturated rag felt of an approved equal, not less in weight than that commercially known as "30 pound" felt or equal.

(b) Felt shall be laid in horizontal layers with joins lapped towards the eaves at least 2", and well secured along laps and at ends as necessary to properly hold the felt in place and protect the structure until covered with the slate. All felt shall be preserved unbroken, tight, and whole.
(c) Felt shall lap all hips and ridges at least 12" to form double thickness and shall be lapped 2" over the metal of any valleys or built-in gutters.

SLATE HAMMER

SLATE RIPPER

SLATE CUTTER

SLATE HOOK

SLATE NAIL

NAILS

(a) All slate shall be fastened with two large head slaters' hard copper wire nails, cut copper, cut brass or cut yellow metal slating nails to be inserted as desired of sufficient length to adequately penetrate the roof boarding.

191

TABLE SHOWING THE SIZES OF SLATE

and number of pieces in a square; the exposure to the
weather on the roof laid with standard three-inch lap;
the distance between laths or between rows of nails
and weight per square.

Size of Slate in Inches	Number in Each Square	Exposed when laid; Distance Bet. Laths	*Weight Per Sq. Lbs.	Nails to Sq. 3d Galvd. lbs.—oz.		Size of Slate in Inches	Number in Each Square	Exposed when laid; Distance Bet. Laths	*Weight Per Sq. Lbs.	Nails to Sq. 3d Galvd. lbs.—oz.	
24x14	98	10½ in.	700	1	0	16x12	185	6½ in.	750	1	13
24x12	115	10½ in.	700	1	2	16x10	222	6½ in.	750	2	3
						16x9	247	6½ in.	750	2	7
						16x8	277	6½ in.	750	2	12
22x12	127	9½ in.	710	1	4						
22x11	138	9½ in.	710	1	6	14x12	218	5½ in.	780	2	2
						14x10	262	5½ in.	780	2	9
						14x8	328	5½ in.	780	3	3
20x12	142	8½ in.	725	1	7	14x7	374	5½ in.	780	3	10
20x10	170	8½ in.	725	1	11						
						12x12	267	4½ in.	800	2	9
18x12	160	7½ in.	735	1	9	12x10	320	4½ in.	800	3	3
18x10	192	7½ in.	735	1	14	12x8	400	4½ in.	800	3	15
18x9	214	7½ in.	735	2	1	12x7	457	4½ in.	800	4	8
						12x6	534	4½ in.	800	5	4

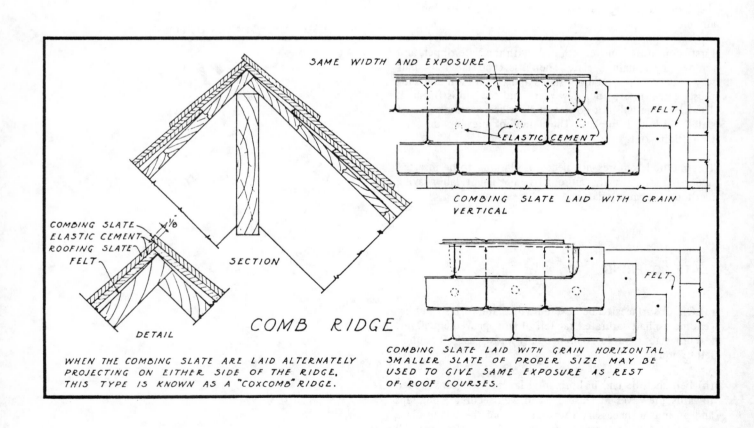

SAME WIDTH AND EXPOSURE

FELT

ELASTIC CEMENT

COMBING SLATE LAID WITH GRAIN VERTICAL

COMBING SLATE
ELASTIC CEMENT
ROOFING SLATE
FELT

⅛

SECTION

FELT

COMB RIDGE

DETAIL

WHEN THE COMBING SLATE ARE LAID ALTERNATELY
PROJECTING ON EITHER SIDE OF THE RIDGE,
THIS TYPE IS KNOWN AS A "COXCOMB" RIDGE.

COMBING SLATE LAID WITH GRAIN HORIZONTAL
SMALLER SLATE OF PROPER SIZE MAY BE
USED TO GIVE SAME EXPOSURE AS REST
OF ROOF COURSES.

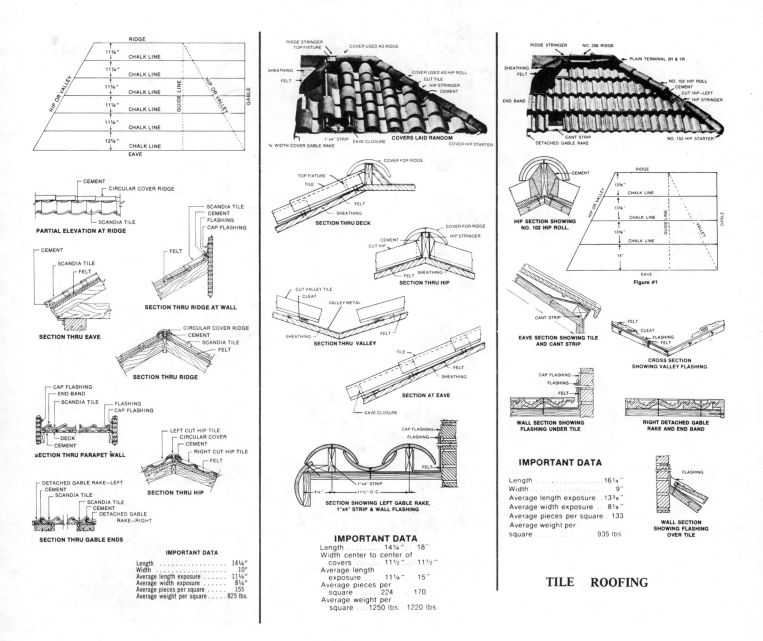

IMPORTANT DATA

Length	14¼"
Width	10"
Average length exposure	11¼"
Average width exposure	8¼"
Average pieces per square	155
Average weight per square	825 lbs.

IMPORTANT DATA

Length	14¼"	18"
Width center to center of covers	11½"	11½"
Average length exposure	11¼"	15"
Average pieces per square	224	170
Average weight per square	1250 lbs.	1220 lbs.

IMPORTANT DATA

Length	16¼"
Width	9"
Average length exposure	13⅜"
Average width exposure	8⅛"
Average pieces per square	133
Average weight per square	935 lbs

TILE ROOFING

g) TILE ROOFING has a Mediterranean and Spanish motif. There are two general catagories of Clay Roofing Tile, (a) flat (b) roll type. The flat type vary from simple pieces to pieces with interlocking sections. Roll type are formed in many shapes from semi-circular to pan shape. All are pre-holed for nailing.

Cover the entire roof with a 40 lb. roofing felt and start with a cant strip similar to the slate shingles. The semi-circular roll type requires wood strips running under the high part of the tile from the eave to the ridge. Like slate, the roof framing must be stronger to support the weight of the tile. Installation of clay tile roofs requires care because there is not much room for tolerance in placing the units. Special shapes are required for valleys, ridges and hips which are set in mastic instead of nails.

h) METAL ROOFING includes a wide choice of material including Copper, Aluminum, Galvanized Iron and Terne. Of the metals used for roofing, Copper is perhaps the most expensive and the most lasting, requiring little maintenance. It will weather to a greenish color called a patina. There are three kinds of joints for copper roofing, a) Batten, b) Flat , c) Standing. Batten seams are formed by nailing 2" x 2" wood strip in the direction of the slope or pitch, about 24" apart. Metal lengths are placed between the battens and bent up along the edge of the wooden batten to form a pan down the slope of the roof. Cleats of the same metal are nailed to the edge of the batten and formed into a lock joint. The flat joints are soldered. A standing seam is formed by turning up one edge 1 1/2" and the adjoining edge 1 1/4". The two are bent and locked together without solder, held to the roof by cleats as in the above method. Flat seams are simply soldered at adjoining pieces. Use a good quality rosin roofing paper for a base sheet.

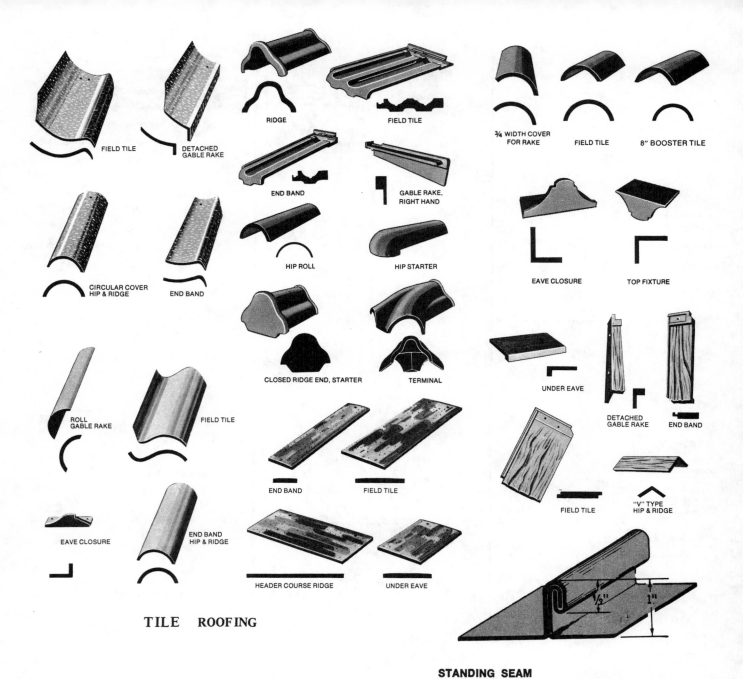

FIELD TILE

DETACHED GABLE RAKE

CIRCULAR COVER HIP & RIDGE

END BAND

ROLL GABLE RAKE

FIELD TILE

EAVE CLOSURE

END BAND HIP & RIDGE

RIDGE

FIELD TILE

END BAND

GABLE RAKE, RIGHT HAND

HIP ROLL

HIP STARTER

CLOSED RIDGE END, STARTER

TERMINAL

END BAND

FIELD TILE

HEADER COURSE RIDGE

UNDER EAVE

¾ WIDTH COVER FOR RAKE

FIELD TILE

8" BOOSTER TILE

EAVE CLOSURE

TOP FIXTURE

UNDER EAVE

DETACHED GABLE RAKE

END BAND

FIELD TILE

"V" TYPE HIP & RIDGE

TILE ROOFING

METAL ROOFING

STANDING SEAM
Standing seams are used to join long dimensions of sheet lead in the direction of roof slope. Sheets should be not more than 16 square feet in area and are usually 3 lb. (3/64 inch thick) in weight.

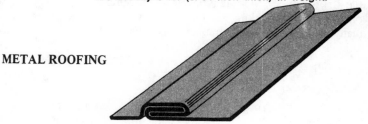

FLAT SEAM
Flat seams are usually auxiliary seams used in conjunction with either standing or batten seams. Their function is to close the cross seams at right angles to the roof slope. They should always be formed in the direction of flow.

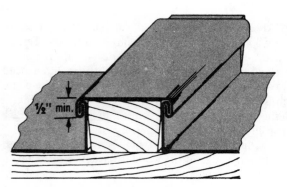

BATTEN SEAM
Batten seams are generally used for large sloping areas and are applicable to the same type of roofing applications as standing seams. They may be used alone or combined with standing seams to create patterns for architectural effect.

194

STRUCTURAL DETAILS

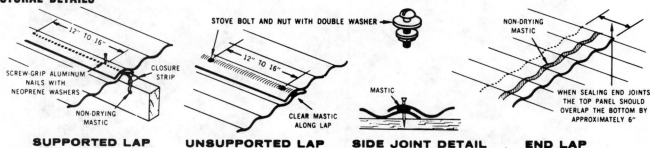

SUPPORTED LAP   **UNSUPPORTED LAP**   **SIDE JOINT DETAIL**   **END LAP**

ALUMINUM ROOFING

SPAN AND LOADING RECOMMENDATIONS

These are maximum allowable spans for uniform loading when panels are fastened as recommended. The spans tabulated below are based on two or more continuous spans (3 or more purlins) and a 2.5 safety factor.

SHAPE	NOMINAL WEIGHT OZ. PR. SQ. FT.	MAXIMUM RECOMMENDED SPANS			
		15 p.s.f.	20 p.s.f.	30 p.s.f.	40 p.s.f.
2½" Corr. (#10)	4 oz.	48"	42"	36"	32"
	5 oz.	54"	48"	42"	36"
	6 oz.	60"	54"	48"	42"
	8 oz.	65"	60"	52"	48"
2.67" Corr. (#9)	5 oz.	58"	54"	48"	42"
	6 oz.	63"	60"	54"	48"
	8 oz.	70"	65"	58"	54"
4.2" Corr. (#8)	6 oz.	65"	62"	56"	50"
	8 oz.	72"	67"	60"	56"
1¼" Corr. (#5)	5 oz.	36"	31"	25"	22"
	6 oz.	40"	34"	28"	25"
2.67" Rib (#72)	5 oz.	54"	48"	42"	36"
	6 oz.	60"	54"	48"	42"
'V' Beam (#41) Reynolds 5.33	6 oz.	76"	72"	66"	60"
	8 oz.	84"	80"	72"	66"
ABCO (#15)	8 oz.	100"	93"	82"	72"

i) ALUMINUM roof is generally made up of corrugated or flutted panels. Aluminum is not recommended in areas of salt water spray. Do not allow aluminum to come in direct contact with other metals because of a chemical action taking place which will break down the metal. Coat both surfaces of unlike metals with heavy asphalt paint or mastic. Use aluminum alloy nails with non-metallic washers between the nail head and the aluminum. Use a good quality rosin roofing paper for a base course.

j) GALVANIZED metal sheets 26 or 28 gauge should be coated with zinc of no less than 2 oz. per sq. ft. End laps should be no less than 8". Lead headed nails or galvanized nails with lead washers should be used. Galvanized metal roofing has a limited life span with an economical cost factor.

k) TERNE metal is made of copper bearing sheet steel. The sheets are dip coated in a mixture of 80% lead and 20% tin. Grades are expressed in terms of weight of coating, the best being 40 lb. A wide variety of widths is available in 50 feet rools. For best results, a Terne metal roof must be painted with an iron oxide linseed oil based primer as a base coat over which any exterior good quality paint may be applied. Use a good quality rosin paper for a base sheet. Seams must be batten or standing.

FLASHING

Any object projecting through the roof such as a chimney, piping, skylight, etc. must be sealed against leakage called flashing. This is accomplished with metal such as lead, aluminum, copper or a fabric reinforced paper or felt. Flashing is also used to join roofs to walls and valleys. Remember that any projection through the roof is a possible problem area and must be properly flashed.

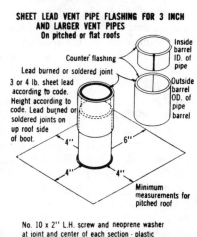

SHEET LEAD VENT PIPE FLASHING FOR 3 INCH AND LARGER VENT PIPES
On pitched or flat roofs

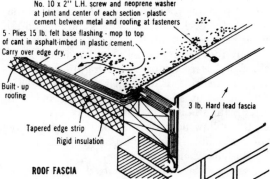

ROOF FASCIA

195

FLASHING

ROOF DECK

Flat roof coverings are not designed for foot traffic and if a deck is designed on a flat roof, special precautions must be taken after the roof is completed. Built-up roofing or tar and gravel is not conducive to decking because the sharp edges of the gravel will puncture the roof. A smooth-cote roof which is a built-up form of roof without the gravel, roll roofing or any type metal roof is best for this purpose.

When roofing is completed, cut strips of roofing paper about 2" wide. Lay these on the roof at 2'-0" apart without cementing. Be sure the paper is in the direction of the roof pitch. Over the paper strips, lay treated 2" x 3" wood flatways again without securing. These 2" x 3" are called sleepers or screeds which act as floor joists. Screw 1" x 4" redwood 3/4" thick to the 2" x 3" countersinking the brass or aluminum headed screws. Do not allow the screw to penetrate through the 2" x 3". Leave a 1/4" space between the redwood to allow roof drainage. This becomes the walking surface of the deck. These 2" x 3"'s and redwood should be built in panels of about 4—0" x 4'-0" allowing removal to make any roof repairs. A rail should be installed around the deck. Wood is recommended using 4" x 4" posts nailed directly to the side of the roof rafters and flashed. The rail should be about 36" high. The flashing and post will be covered with a hollow post built of 1" x 4" x 3/4" wood. Slide the hollow post over the solid post and nail with rust-proof wire nails. Flash the top of the posts before the top rail is installed being careful not to puncture the flashing when securing the top rail. Posts should be spaced about 4'—0" apart.

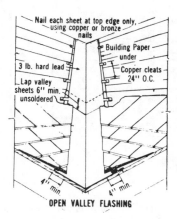

OPEN VALLEY FLASHING

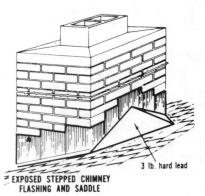

EXPOSED STEPPED CHIMNEY FLASHING AND SADDLE

● Flashings at chimneys must be carefully placed to prevent leakage.

● Flashings and counter flashings are required against brick walls, but for wood walls, flashings in shingle lengths are completely satisfactory.

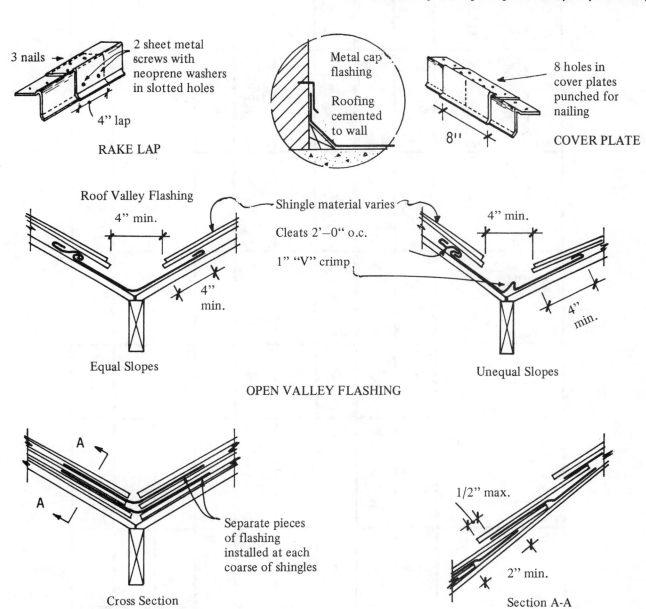

3 nails

2 sheet metal screws with neoprene washers in slotted holes

4" lap

RAKE LAP

Metal cap flashing

Roofing cemented to wall

8 holes in cover plates punched for nailing

8"

COVER PLATE

Roof Valley Flashing

4" min.

Shingle material varies

Cleats 2'-0" o.c.

1" "V" crimp

4" min.

4" min.

4" min.

Equal Slopes

Unequal Slopes

OPEN VALLEY FLASHING

A

A

Separate pieces of flashing installed at each coarse of shingles

Cross Section

1/2" max.

2" min.

Section A-A

CLOSED VALLEY FLASHING FOR ROOFS WITH SLOPES OF 10 IN 12 OR MORE

ASPHALT ROOFING PRODUCTS

PRODUCT	Approx. Shipping Weight Per Square	Packages Per Square	Length	Width	Units Per Square	Side or End Lap	Top Lap	Head Lap	Exposure
Saturated Felt	15 lb. 30 lb.	1/4 1/2	144' 72'	36" 36"		4"to6" 4"to6"	2" 2"		34" 34"
Smooth Roll	65 lb. 50 lb.	1 1	36' 36'	36" 36"		6" 6"	2" 2"		34" 34"
Mineral Surfaced Roll	90 lb. 90 lb. 90 lb.	1.0	36'	36"	1.0 1.075 1.15	6" 6" 6"	2" 3" 4"		34" 33" 32"
Pattern Edge Roll	105 lb. 105 lb.	1 1	42' 48'	36" 32"			2" 2"		16" 14"
19" Selvage Double Coverage	110 lb. to 120 lb.	2	36'	36"			19"	2"	17"
3 Tab Self Sealing Strip Shingle	235 lb. 300 lb.	3 or 4	36" 36"	12" 12"	80 80		7" 7"	2" 2"	5" 5"
2 and 3 Tab Hex Strip	195 lb.	3	36"	11-1/3"	86		2"	2"	5"
Individual Lock Down	145 lb.	2	16"	16"	80	2½"			

198

DOORS and WINDOWS

20

Before any building is begun, selection of doors and windows must be made to provide for proper installation in walls. Window styles are Casement, Bay, Bow, Awning Gliding or Sliding, Double Hung, Picture, Flexivent, Utility or Basement. All of these can be had in Wood, Aluminum, Steel, Bronze, Wood Vinyl Covered, Wood Aluminum Covered with options of single glazing, double glazing, storm sash, screens and safety glass. Window sizes vary with each style.

As a general rule, all tops of windows and doors are in alignment for aesthetics. If you select a 7'–0" high door, the tops of the windows should be 7'–0" above the floor. From that point, work your way down to a window height to establish how high from the floor you want the bottom of the window to fall. Usually in all rooms except kitchens and baths, the height of the windows is 4'–2" or 4'–6". Kitchens and Baths usually require 3'-2" high windows.

Doors usually come in three heights: 6'-6", 6'–8" and 7'–0". Widths vary from 1'–0" up to 3'–0" in increments of 2" widths. All exterior doors are 1 3/4" thick and interior doors are 1 3/8" thick. Door styles are flush panel, wood or glass panels. Flush panel doors are hollow core or solid core with many kinds of finished surfaces in wood veneer. When selecting doors, check your local building code for fire door installation. For example, if you have an attached garage, the building code may require a fire door on the wall between the garage and the house.

For Noise:

1. You can usually stop a door squeak by putting a few drops of oil at the top of each hinge. Move the door back and forth to work the oil into the hinge. If the squeaking does not stop, raise, the pin and add more oil. (Fig. 1).

2. Noisy or squeaking locks should be lubricated with graphite. You can buy this at a hardware store. (Fig. 2)

3. To stop the rattle in the knob, loosen the set-screw on the knob. (Fig. 3) Remove the knob. Put a small piece of putty or modeling clay in the knob. (Fig. 4) Put the knob back on. Push it on as far as possible. Tighten the screw.

FOR STICKING OR DRAGGING DOORS:

1. Tighten screws in the hinges. If screws are not holding, replace them, one at a time, with a longer screw. Or insert a matchstick in the hole and put the old screw back in. (Fig. 5)

2. Look for a shiny spot on the door where it sticks. Open and close the door slowly to find the spot. Sand down the shiny spot. Do not sand too much, or the door will not fit as tight as it should. (Fig. 6)

3. If the door or frame is badly out of shape, you may have to remove the door and plane down the part that drags. (Fig. 7)

NOTE:

Sand edges of the door before painting to prevent a paint build-up. This can cause the door to stick.

LOCKS:

If the lock is tight or won't turn, you may need to lubricate it with graphite.

YOUR PROBLEM

Doors squeak.
Door knob rattles.
Doors stick or drag.
Door may not close because it strikes the frame.
Lock may not catch.

WHAT YOU NEED

Oil
Graphite
Screwdriver
Hammer
Sandpaper
Pliers

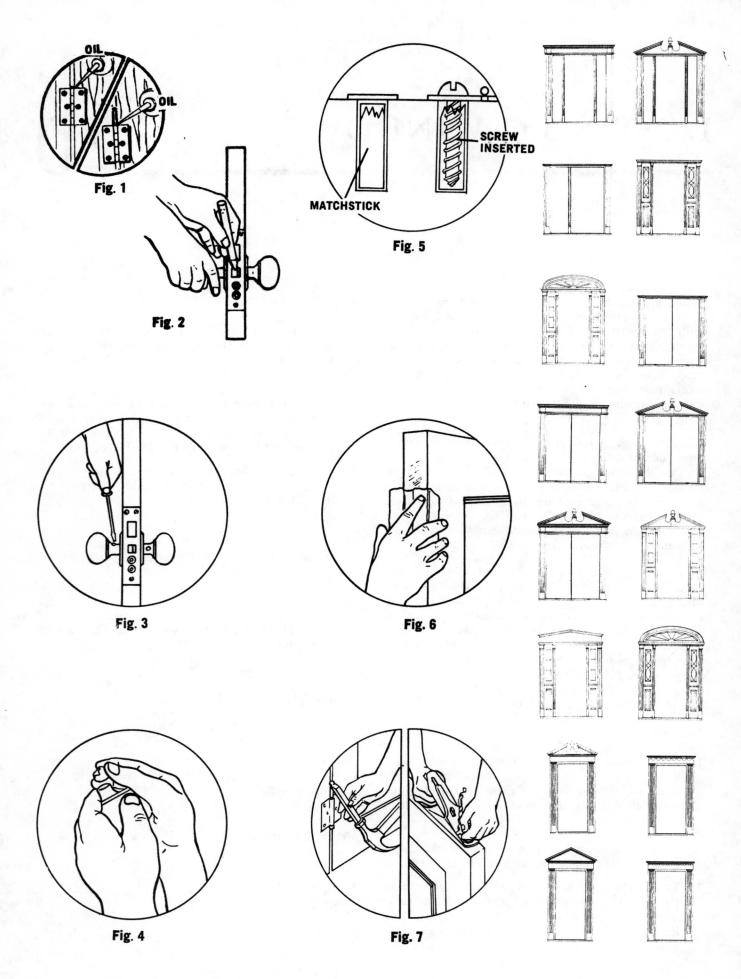

OIL

OIL

Fig. 1

Fig. 2

MATCHSTICK

SCREW INSERTED

Fig. 5

Fig. 3

Fig. 6

Fig. 4

Fig. 7

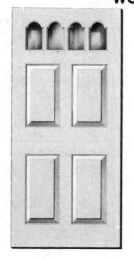

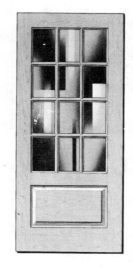

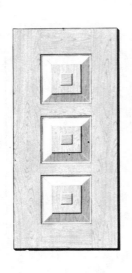
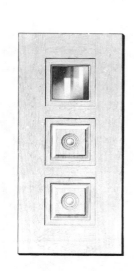

 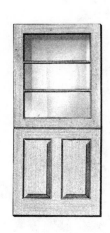  

 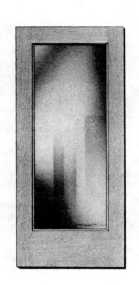 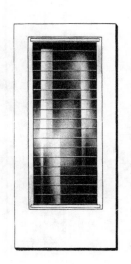 

203

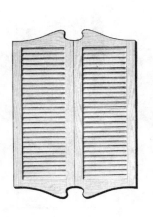
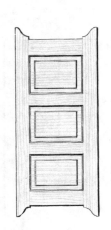
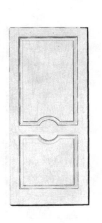

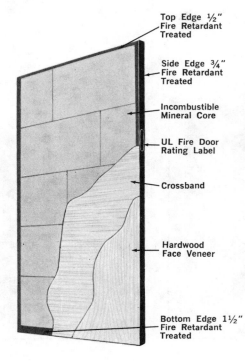

Top Edge ½"
Fire Retardant
Treated

Side Edge ¾"
Fire Retardant
Treated

Incombustible
Mineral Core

UL Fire Door
Rating Label

Crossband

Hardwood
Face Veneer

Bottom Edge 1½"
Fire Retardant
Treated

1 HOUR FIRE DOOR

Fire Doors have been tested and rated by Underwriters' Laboratories, Inc. for fire resistance, heat transmission and structural stability . . . labeled for 1 hour Class "B" openings.

A metal label similar to the one illustrated is secured to the hinge edge of each Class "B" fire door and stipulates 1 hour rating. This metal label is located one-third down from the top edge of door on the hinge stile edge.

INSTALLATION

Maximum clearance for Fire Doors shall be ⅟₁₆" at the sides and top . . . ¼" at the bottom. In fitting door to opening to establish proper width clearance and bevel, plane the lock stile edge only (opposite UL label). The installed door must always have the label on the hinge stile.

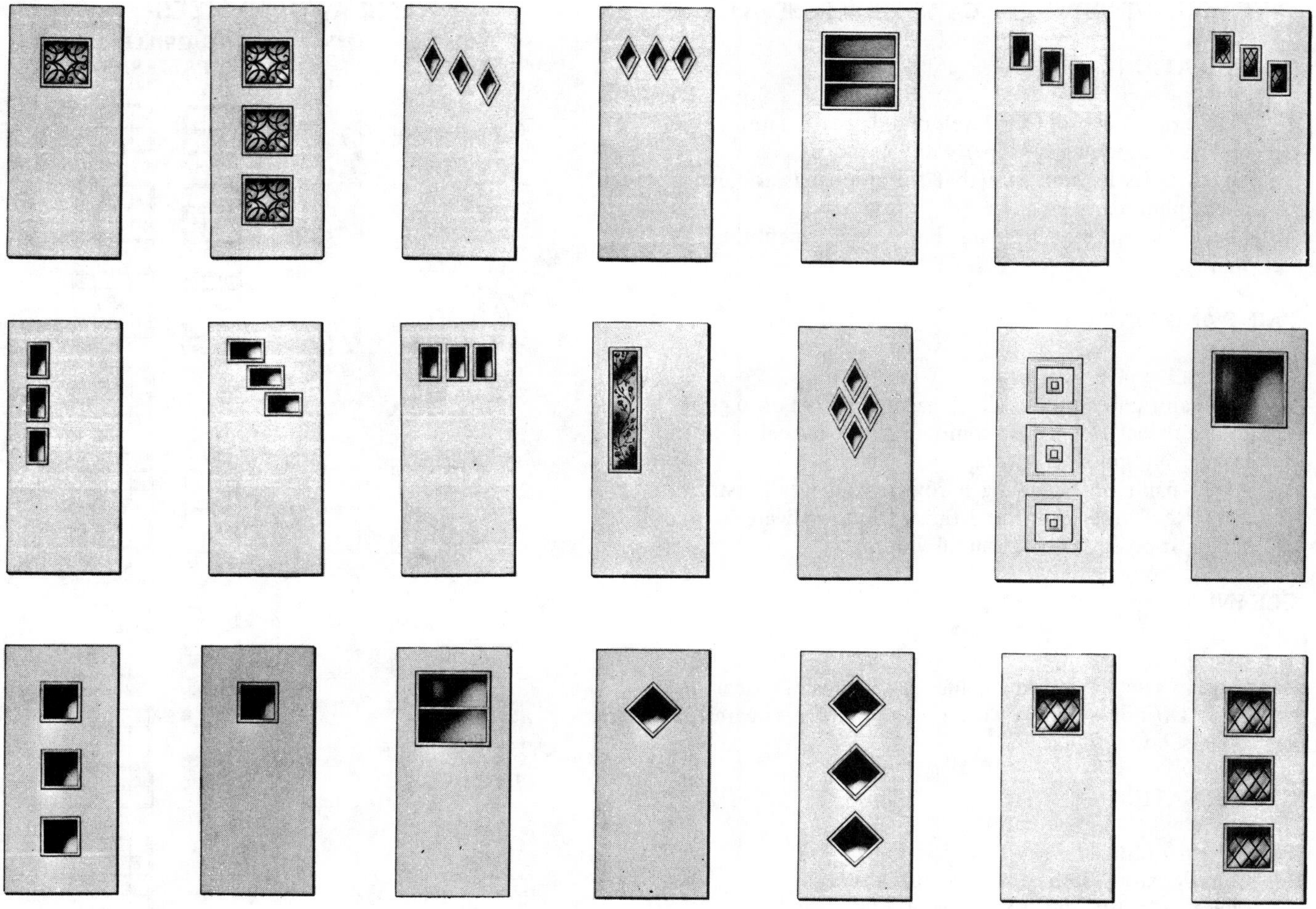

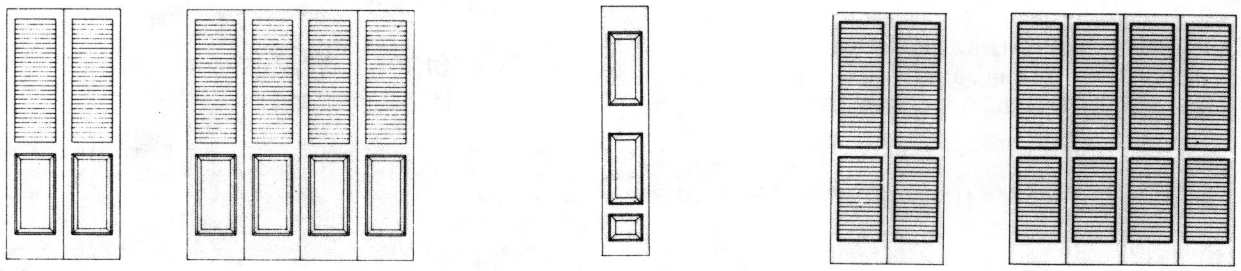

Gliding Doors

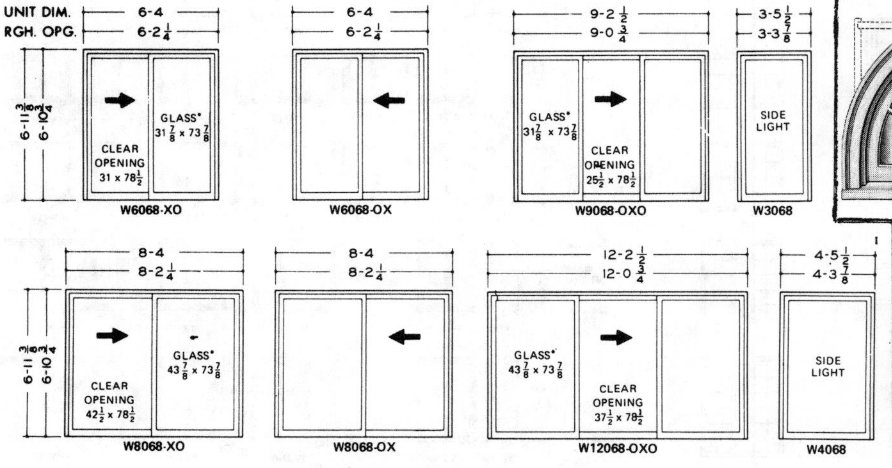
UNIT DIM.
RGH. OPG.
6-4
6-2 1/4
6-11 3/8
6-10 3/4
GLASS* 31 7/8 x 73 7/8
CLEAR OPENING 31 x 78 1/2
W6068-XO
6-4
6-2 1/4
W6068-OX
9-2 1/2
9-0 3/4
GLASS* 31 7/8 x 73 7/8
CLEAR OPENING 25 1/2 x 78 1/2
W9068-OXO
3-5 1/2
3-3 7/8
SIDE LIGHT
W3068
8-4
8-2 1/4
6-11 3/8
6-10 3/4
GLASS* 43 7/8 x 73 7/8
CLEAR OPENING 42 1/2 x 78 1/2
W8068-XO
8-4
8-2 1/4
W8068-OX
12-2 1/2
12-0 3/4
GLASS* 43 7/8 x 73 7/8
CLEAR OPENING 37 1/2 x 78 1/2
W12068-OXO
4-5 1/2
4-3 7/8
SIDE LIGHT
W4068

*Unobstructed Glass Size

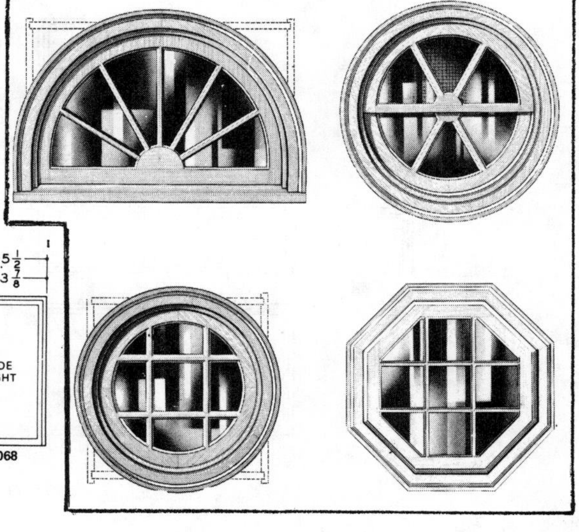

GIVE YOUR WINDOWS THE CARE THEY DESERVE

INSTALLATION

1. Frame opening properly, level, plumb and square.
2. Make sure opening is properly dimensioned.
3. Install units making sure that sill and heads are level, jambs plumb and blocked.
4. Check for squareness of unit before final anchoring in wall.

PAINT AND FINISHING

1. Paint all exposed parts—Face, Tops, Bottoms.
2. Lap paint and clear finish (if natural inside) onto glass to insure seal over glazing compound, and to seal against leakage and possible rotting.
3. Avoid paint on balancing hardware and weatherstripping. Remove all paint and finish from hardware to insure best possible operation of window.

CLEANING

1. Use care in cleaning.
2. If using scraper or razor blade do not break lap seal on glass. Do not cut into glazing compound. Use care to avoid scratching glass.

CONDENSATION

1. If condensation occurs—
Consider storm sash to relieve condition.
Check humidity level to reduce problem.

MAINTENANCE

1. Clean jamb liners and hardware.
2. Brush dirt and dust from outside sill and frame.
3. Do not wash with stream from hose.

BASIC AWNING SIZES

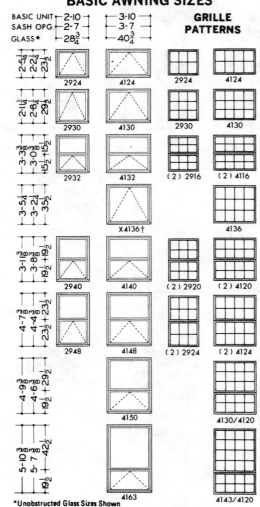

*Unobstructed Glass Sizes Shown

Casement Windows
1'-10½" SASH

BASIC FLEXIVENT® UNITS

GRILLE PATTERNS

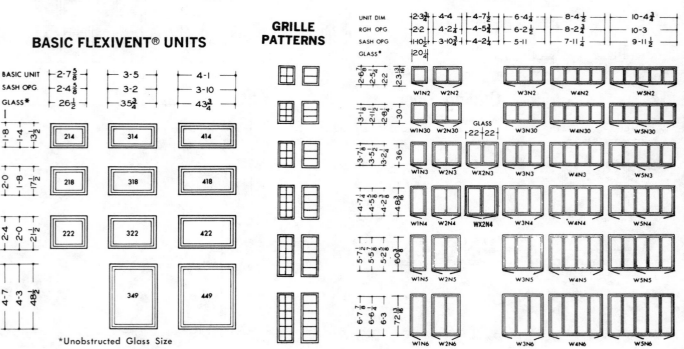

*Unobstructed Glass Size

206

COMBINATIONS

Shutters
TABLE OF SIZES

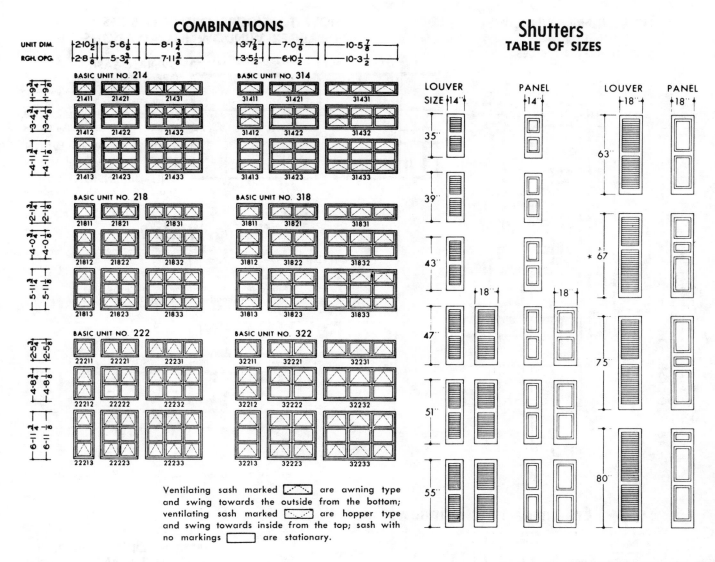

Ventilating sash marked ▱ are awning type and swing towards the outside from the bottom; ventilating sash marked ▱ are hopper type and swing towards inside from the top; sash with no markings ☐ are stationary.

LEADED DIAMOND LIGHTS

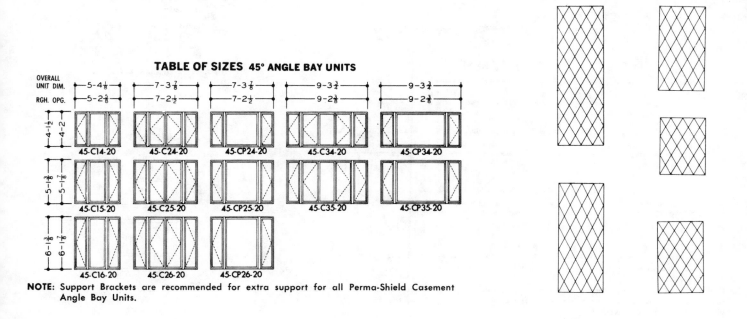

TABLE OF SIZES 45° ANGLE BAY UNITS

NOTE: Support Brackets are recommended for extra support for all Perma-Shield Casement Angle Bay Units.

DOUBLE HUNG WINDOWS

WINDOW UNIT SIZES

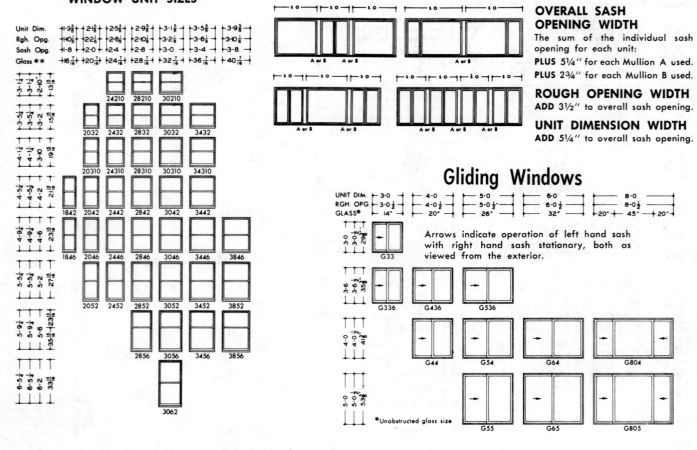

HOW TO FIGURE OPENING SIZES
FOR LARGER WINDOW INSTALLATIONS

OVERALL SASH OPENING WIDTH

The sum of the individual sash opening for each unit:
PLUS 5¼" for each Mullion A used.
PLUS 2¾" for each Mullion B used.

ROUGH OPENING WIDTH

ADD 3½" to overall sash opening.

UNIT DIMENSION WIDTH

ADD 5¼" to overall sash opening.

Gliding Windows

Arrows indicate operation of left hand sash with right hand sash stationary, both as viewed from the exterior.

*Unobstructed glass size.

Casement Bow Windows

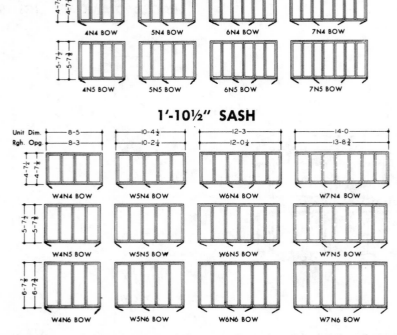

1'-10½" SASH

PATTERNS OF SNAP-IN RIGID VINYL GRILLES AND MUNTINS

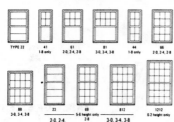

BASEMENT

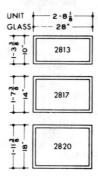

Combinations shown are only suggested layouts and may be subject to change. Ventilating sash are designated as hinged on the Left ⌣ , or hinged on the Right ⌣ , (as viewed from the outside).

EXTERIOR FINISHES

21

CORNICE

The finish at the edge of the roof overhang is called cornice or eave. The purpose is to close the intersection of walls and roof and to carry away from the building water which flows from the roof, preventing it from entering the building. The character of the building is strongly expressed in the design of the cornice which offers a great variety of designs. The projection of the roof may be wide or narrow, exposed or concealed, may reflect a classic or modern design, may have gutters and/or conductors, or not. The construction at the ends of the roof is relatively simple because no water is carried off the roof at that point. The roof sheathing is extended just enough to allow mouldings to be placed under the roof sheathing and rested against the gable. This moulding is called a frieze and crown moulding. The roof overhang is quite a different matter and a little more involved because in addition to several mouldings, a gutter (if used) must be installed. The gutter can be wood, aluminum, copper or galvanized metal, hanging or built-in. The purpose of the gutter is to carry the water away from the building with conductors or downspouts. One square inch of conductor is required for every 150 square feet of roof area.

There are so many ways of constructing a cornice that only a general description can be given in naming the parts. (see illustration). Gutter sizes are 6" x 4" and conductor sizes are 3" x 2". All gutters must pitch ever so slightly toward the conductors to allow water to run off. Gutters can be a trouble spot for most houses, especially for those in colder climates. Ice build-up in the gutters can cause a back up and, if the ice forces itself under the shingles there may be a leak in the walls. The freezing and thawing action causes the water to be forced under the roof because the normal flow of water through the conductors via the gutters is blocked with ice. Hanging the gutters free of the building will help with this problem and a better way is not to install any gutters. No harm will come from allowing the water to fall from the roof onto the ground; at worse, the ground may erode a bit. This can be resolved by placing a row of brick or crushed stone at that point on the ground and with the proper grade pitch away from the building, the water will flow away.

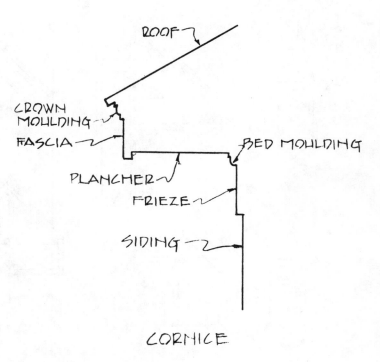

CORNICE

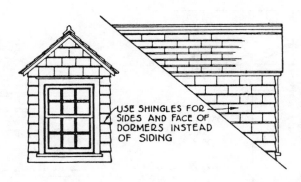

FRONT AND SIDE ELEVATION OF DORMER

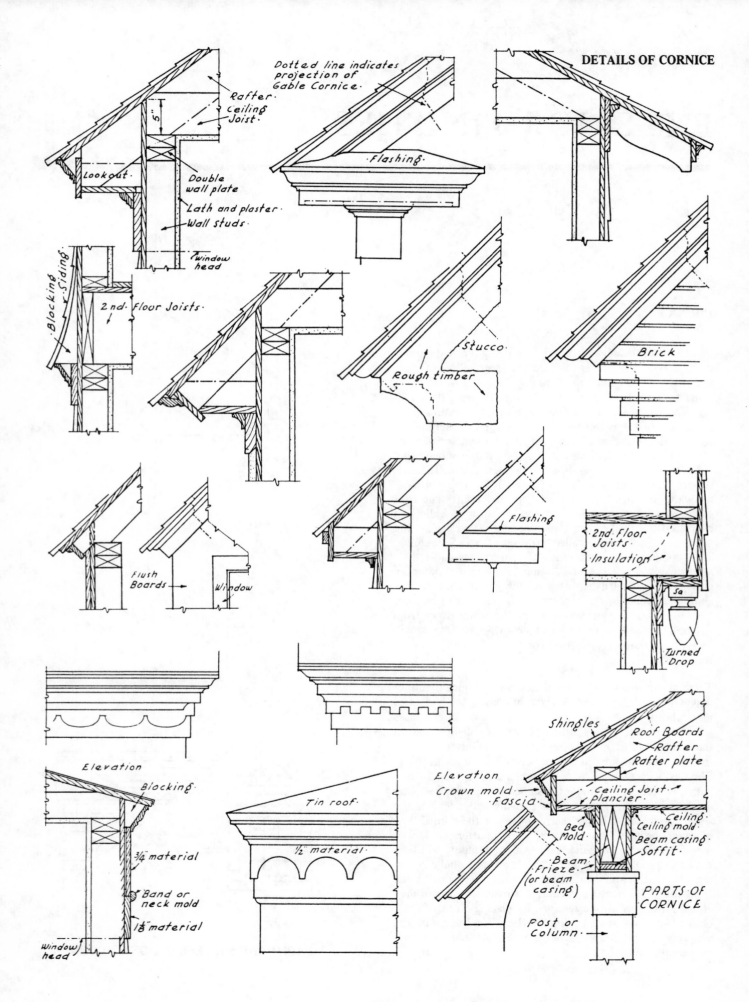

Rafter.

Ceiling Joist.

5"

Lookout.

Double wall plate

Lath and plaster.

Wall studs.

window head

Dotted line indicates projection of Gable Cornice.

Flashing.

Blocking

Siding

2nd. Floor Joists.

Stucco.

Rough timber

Brick

Flush Boards

Window

Flashing

2nd. Floor Joists

Insulation

Sa

Turned Drop

Elevation

Blocking

3/4 material

Band or neck mold

1⅛ material

Window head

Tin roof.

½ material.

Shingles

Roof Boards

Rafter

Rafter plate

Elevation

Crown mold.

Fascia

Ceiling Joist

plancier.

Ceiling

Ceiling mold

Beam casing

Soffit.

Bed Mold

Beam Frieze (or beam casing)

Post or Column.

PARTS OF CORNICE

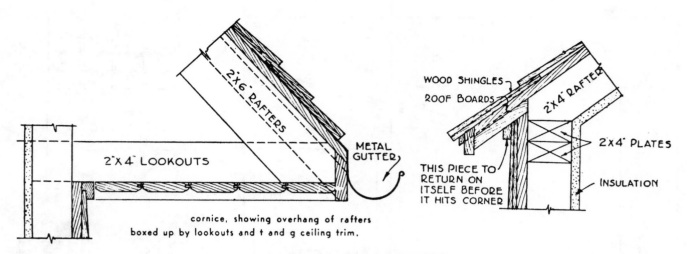

CORNICE CONSTRUCTION DETAIL

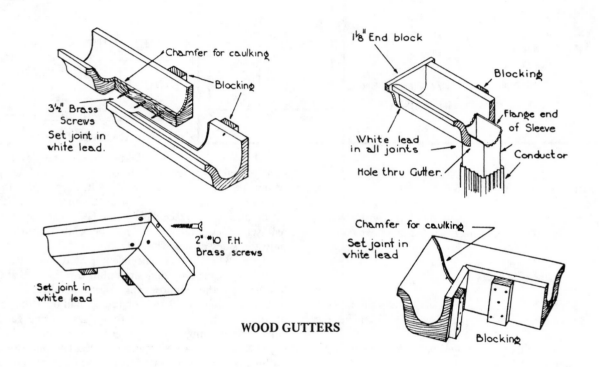

WOOD GUTTERS

RAINFALL DRAINAGE FACTORS FOR DOWNSPOUTS

INTENSITY OF RAINFALL IN INCHES/HOUR LASTING 5 MI.	SQ. FT. OF CALCULATED ROOF DRAINED PER SQ. IN. OF DOWNSPOUT AREA
2	600
3	400
4	300
5	240
6	200
7	175
8	150
9	130
10	120
11	110

Wood Gutters

Install over 1/4 to 1 inch vertical furring strips 24 inches o.c. Install gutters with slight pitch to downspout.

Use continuous sections where possible. When splices are necessary, use a bevel joint with through edges chamfered. Prime and set joint. Fill chamfer with flexible caulking compound.

Downspouts

Hangers may be cast or strap hangers designed for this purpose. Hangers should be of same material as downspout.

Fasten downspouts at top and bottom. In addition, provide at least one hanger for every 6 feet of downspout.

211

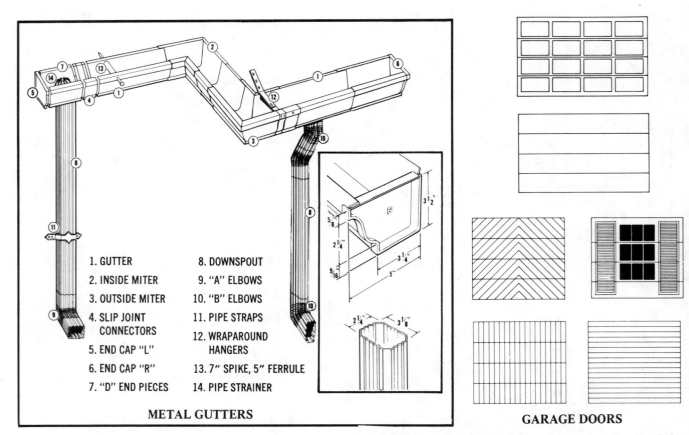

METAL GUTTERS

1. GUTTER
2. INSIDE MITER
3. OUTSIDE MITER
4. SLIP JOINT CONNECTORS
5. END CAP "L"
6. END CAP "R"
7. "D" END PIECES

8. DOWNSPOUT
9. "A" ELBOWS
10. "B" ELBOWS
11. PIPE STRAPS
12. WRAPAROUND HANGERS
13. 7" SPIKE, 5" FERRULE
14. PIPE STRAINER

GARAGE DOORS

Metal Gutters

Install gutters with slight pitch to downspout

Hangers may be cast, strap hangers or spikes (with spacers) designed for this purpose. Hangers should be of same material as gutters.

Maximum spacing of hangers:
Stainless steel . . . . 60 inches o.c.
Galvanized steel . . . . 48 inches o.c.
Copper, aluminum or zinc-copper alloy . . . . 30 inches o.c.

Joints at corners and splices should be soldered or provided with suitable watertight slip joints.

DOOR AND WINDOW INSTALLATION

When exterior door frames and windows are delivered they are complete and intact and require only to be installed. Before installation, cut 6" from a roll of 15 lb. felt paper and nail strips of paper along the entire length of the jambs (sides) of openings for doors and windows using large head galvanized (roofing) nails. This is to ensure a seal between the sheathing and the back of the casings, once the units have been installed, it is impossible to seal. In addition, secure flashing at the sill of window openings using any one of several approved materials, being careful not to nail the flashing where it will cause a leak. If properly installed, this flashing will shed off any water that might find its way under the window sill and leak into the house. Turn the flashing up at the sides about 3" or 4". Nail by turning the flashing over the inside of the stud at the sill. This will avoid breaking the seal. No nails should penetrate the flashing.

Install the window frames taking care to use a level and the same margin of space on both sides of the window opening. Allow the window to rest on the sill, check again for level and drive 8d gal. finish nails into the outer edge of the casing on both sides. Place nails about 12" to 16" apart using a nail set to countersink the nail beyond the surface. Nail only the sides of the windows. Check again to be sure they are level. When this has been completed, nail flashing on top of the window using aluminum cap flashing about 1" longer than the window dimension overall. Using as few nails as possible (only two or three), nail only the very top of the flashing to the sheathing, again using galvanized nails. This flashing should go over the top of the head casing with about 1/4"overhang or drip. The purpose of this flashing is to prevent water from leaking in behind the top of the window. The siding will cover all but the very top of the flashing. The same procedure is followed in the installation of exterior door frames except for the sill. Under the sill, nail three strips of galvanized sheet metal about two inches wide and 6" long using roofing nails. Door frames can not be nailed in place through the sill because they will leak. The only way to secure the sill to the floor is with the straps, when the frame is in place nail the straps to the subfloor. Nail these door frames as you did the window frames being sure they are level. Install the head cap flashing as the windows.

GARAGE DOORS

There are three types of garage doors: hinged, overhead and roll up. All are made of wood, metal or fiberglass with many different designs to blend with the style of architecture. Sizes range from a minimum width of 7'–0" to a maximum of 18'–0"; and a minimum height of 6'–6" up to

8'–0", with thicknesses of 1-3/8". When you prepare the opening of a garage door, use the same process as you did for the other doors. The size of the rough opening is determined by the type of door and manufacturer as well as the size of the door. It would be best to determine a specific model and use the manufacturer's dimensions of rough openings while framing for the garage. Overhead doors require at least 12" minimum headroom above the door height for hardware or track installation. When installing a concrete garage floor be sure to pitch the floor towards the door to allow the water from melting snow or rain brought into the garage to run out. The concrete apron should be about 1/2" lower than the floor with a 2" x 2" x 1/4" continuous steel angle forming a threshold behind the bottom of the door.

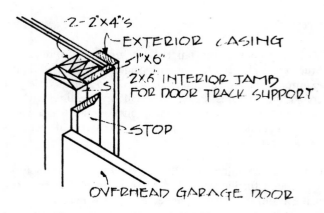

STANDARD FRAME CONSTRUCTION FOR GARAGE DOOR

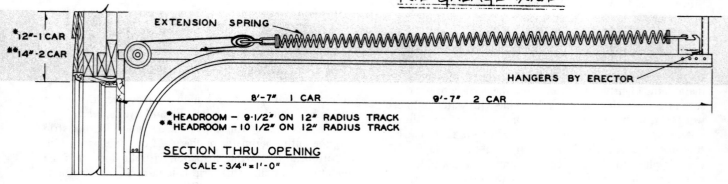

SECTION THRU OPENING
SCALE - 3/4" = 1'-0"

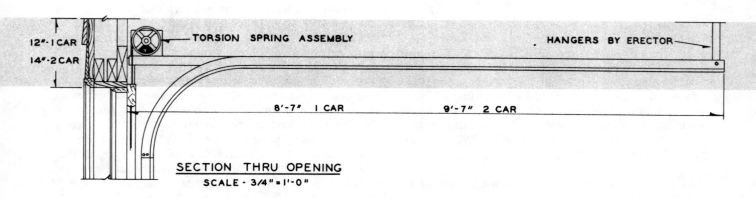

SECTION THRU OPENING
SCALE - 3/4" = 1'-0"

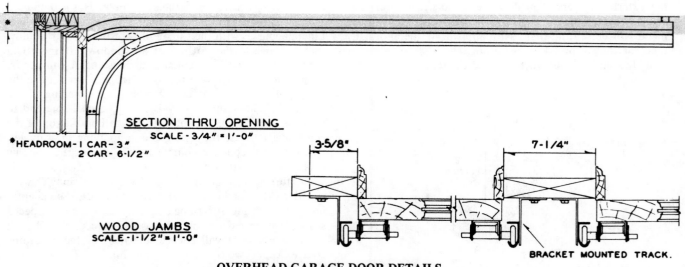

SECTION THRU OPENING
SCALE - 3/4" = 1'-0"

WOOD JAMBS
SCALE - 1-1/2" = 1'-0"

OVERHEAD GARAGE DOOR DETAILS

STUCCO

Many stucco surfaces fail because of faulty application. Stucco is a plaster product with cement added, used on the exterior surface of buildings and comes in a great variety of colors and textures. Properly installed, it requires little or no maintenance. Any movement in the wall upon which stucco is applied will cause cracking. The secret of success is to minimize movement in the walls.

Cover the sheathing with 20 lb. felt. Over the felt apply 1" x 3" wood furring strips 12" apart. Over the furring strips, nail galvanized ribbed expanded metal or wire lath. The furring strips act as a separator between the wall and the stucco and reduce the wall movement.

Stucco should not be applied when the temperature is 32° or colder. It is a three coat application consisting of a scratch coat, which is the first coat; a brown coat, which is the second coat; and the finish or third coat. Mix the stucco according to directions printed on the bag and apply with a trowel of sufficient force to bond the first coat onto the metal lath. Lightly scratch or score the surface to bond the second coat to the base coat. Sprinkle with water and keep wet for at least 48 hours. The second or brown coat should not be applied for at least 5 days after the first coat has thoroughly dried. The brown coat should be at least 1/2" thick applied to the scratch coat and again sprinkle with water and allowed to dry slowly in the same manner. The finish is not applied for at least a week after the brown coat.

The finish coat is what produces the desired texture by smoothing or floating the surface with a wood or metal trowel. Mixtures of sand or crushed stone may be thrown against the surface of the finish coat before it hardens to produce a sand or pebble finish. The coloring in the stucco is pre-mixed at the factory. If you attempt to add color a mottled or blotchy color appearance may result. Proportions in mixing all three coats should be one part cement to three parts sand to which may be added hydraded lime equaling 10% of the weight of the cement.

A rust proof metal bead is applied at the bottom of the stucco wall to act as a stop and metal beads are also used on the exterior corners to protect the corners from breaking. These beads are installed with galvanized wire, wired to the metal lath before the first coat is applied. All metal or nails used for stucco should be rust proof. The bottom of stucco should extend 1/2" below the top of the foundation.

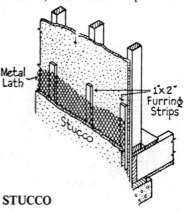

STUCCO

Intersections of Different Materials

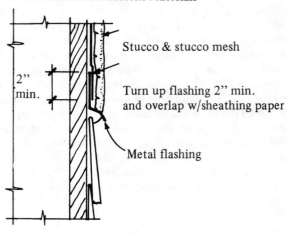

Stucco & stucco mesh

Turn up flashing 2" min. and overlap w/sheathing paper

Metal flashing

2" min.

WOOD SHINGLES OR SHAKES

Apply sheathing paper or building paper over the entire wall surface starting at the bottom and overlap each layer about 2". Nail a continuous 1" x 3" wood furring strip along the entire perimeter of the walls over the paper with the bottom of the furring strip even with the bottom of the foundatin wood sill. This strip is used as a starting course for the shingles to allow the first course to slope. Be sure this starter course is straight and level. Nail two shingles on the ends of a 1"x3" straight wood furring strip of any convenient length. The shingles should be perpendicular to the strip, nailed through the butt end or thick end of the shingles half way across the width of the wood furring strip. Position the top of the furring strip about 1/2" below the top of the foundation and secure by nailing the shingles into the sheathing. This becomes a guide for the first course by sitting the butt of the shingles on top of the furring strip and nailing to the sheathing. Double the first course of wood shingles being careful to break up the joints. Prepare a story pole by marking off the number of courses required to complete the full height of the wall (from the bottom of the first course to the underside of the soffit or cornice or overhang) onto the story pole. This is then used as a guide for all sides allowing all courses to be the same. Line all courses with the top of all door frames and window frames and also the bottom of all windows. If there is a slight difference in the courses' dimensions, it will not be noticeable. The exposure may vary from 5" to 6". Use the story pole to mark the course after the succeeding course is applied. The simplest way is to snap a chalkline and to tack a straight 1" x 3" wood furring to line the top of the chalk line and use this as a guide in applying the shingles. When the first course is completed, simply wedge a fine saw between the bottom of the first course and the top of the wood furring strip at the point of where the shingles were nailed to the furring strip and saw them off. (See chapter on roof covering for shingle quality and grade.) Special shaped galvanized or zinc coated nails are used and each succeeding course will conceal the nails of the preceding course. Apply two or three nails per shingle.

There are several ways of treating corners. Interior corners can be resolved by nailing a 1—1/8" x 1-1/8" finish wood strip in the corner and butting the shingles to it, or by alternating the shingle courses to avoid a straight line joint. A third method is to use rust proof preformed metal corner pieces. Exterior corners can be treated by metal pieces, alternating the joints or by a 1" x 4" corner board.

SIDEWALL APPLICATION—Maximum recommended weather exposure with single-course wall construction is 8-1/2" for 18" shakes and 11-1/2" for 24" shakes. The nailing normally is concealed in single-course applications—that is, nailing points slightly above the butt line of the course to follow. Double-course application requires an underlay of shakes or regular cedar shingles. Weather exposures up to 14" are permissible with 18" handsplit/resawn or tapersplit shakes, and 20" with 24" shakes. If straight-split shakes are used, the double-course exposure may be 16" for 18" shakes and 22" for 24" shakes. Butt nailing of shakes is required with double-course application. Do not drive nailheads into the shake surface.

FINISHES AND WEATHERING QUALITIES—Red cedar shingles, grooved sidewall shakes and handsplit shakes are well equipped by nature to endure without any protective finish or stain. In this state, the wood will eventually weather to a silver or dark gray. The speed of change and final shade depend mainly on atmosphere and climate conditions. Bleaching agents may be applied, in which case the wood will turn an antique silver gray. So-called natural finishes, which are lightly pigmented and maintain the original appearance of the wood, are available commercially. Stains, whether heavy or semi-transparent, are readily "absorbed" by cedar, and paints are most suitable, too. Quality finishes are strongly recommended, and will prove most economical on a long-term basis.

CORNERS—Corners for grooved sidewall shakes should be constructed in the same manner as outlined above for shingle sidewalls. Patented metal corner units also are available.

PAINT/STAIN—Grooved sidewall shakes are marketed in a wide variety of factory-applied colors, ranging from delicate pastels to dark browns and greens. They also are available prime-coated, for finish treatment after they are applied.

GROOVED SIDEWALL SHAKES—Since grooved sidewall shakes are basically a rebutted-rejointed shingle with a machine-grooved surface, many of the requirements for shingle sidewall application apply. But grooved sidewall shakes are always applied double-coursed. This procedure yields a deep shadow line nearly 1" at the butt and greater coverage at lower cost, since extended weather exposures are possible over the undercourse of low-grade shingles. As with shingle sidewalls, the double-course application requires an extra under-course at the foundation line. Grooved sidewall shakes are also available in 4-ft. and 8-ft. wide panels, for even faster application.

SIDEWALL APPLICATION—There are two basic methods of shingle sidewall application—single-course and double-course. In single-coursing (see Fig. 4a) shingles are applied much as in roof construction, but greater weather exposures are permitted. Shingle walls have two layers of shingles at every point, whereas shingle roofs have 3-ply construction. Double-coursing allows for the application of shingles at extended weather exposures over under-coursing-grade shingles. Double-coursing (see Figs. 4b and 4c) gives deep, bold shadow lines. When double-coursed, a shingle wall should be tripled at the foundation line (by using a double underlay). When the wall is single-coursed, the shingles should be doubled at the foundation line.

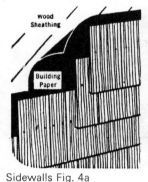 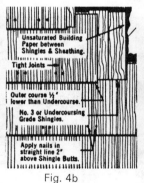  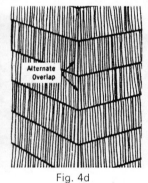 

Sidewalls Fig. 4a   Fig. 4b   Fig. 4c   Fig. 4d   Fig. 4e

As with shingle sidewalls, the double-course application requires an extra under-course at the foundation line. Grooved sidewall shakes are also available in 4-ft. and 8-ft. wide panels, for even faster application.

NAILING—Each outer course grooved shake should be secured with 5d (1-3/4") small-head, rust-resistant nails; these are driven about two inches above the butt, one nail about 3/4" from each edge and additional nails spaced about four inches apart across the shake face. Each undecourse shingle is fastened with staples or one or more nails. Nails that match the factory-applied color and the grooved sidewall shakes are available from some manufacturers.

NAILING—For double-coursing (see Figs. 4b and 4c) each outer course shingle should be secured with two 5d (1-3/4") small-head, rust-resistant nails driven about two inches above the butts, 3/4" in from each side, plus additional nails about four inches apart across the face of the shingle. Single-coursing (see Fig. 4a) involves the same number of nails, but they can be shorter (3d 1-1/4") and should be driven not more than 1" above the butt line of the next course. Never drive the nail so hard that its head crushes the wood.

CORNERS—Outside corners (see Figure 4d) should be constructed with an alternate overlap of shingles between successive courses. Inside corners (see Fig. 4e) should be mitered over a metal flashing, or they may be made by nailing an S4S 1-1/2"- or 2" square strip in the corner, after which the shingles of each course are jointed to the strip.

REBUTTED-AND-REJOINTED SHINGLES—These are shingles whose edges have been machine-trimmed so as to be exactly parallel, and butts retrimmed at precisely right angles. They are used on sidewalls with tight-fitting joints to give a strong horizontal line. Available with the natural "sawed" face, or with one face sanded smooth, they may be applied single or double-coursed.

PAINT/STAIN—Rebutted-rejointed shingles weather beautifully in the natural state. But they are often stained—or painted—with excellent results.

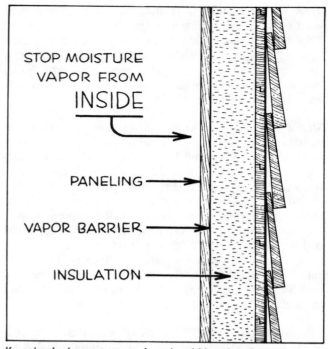

If unchecked, vapor moves from humid interior of house toward colder exterior, condensing with sidewall. This can cause finish problems.

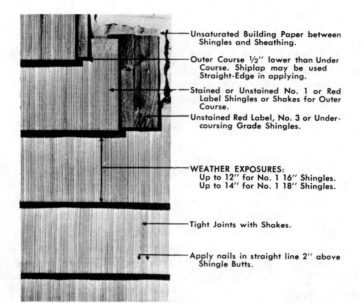

WOOD SHAKES

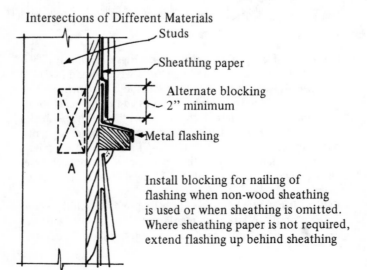

Install blocking for nailing of flashing when non-wood sheathing is used or when sheathing is omitted. Where sheathing paper is not required, extend flashing up behind sheathing

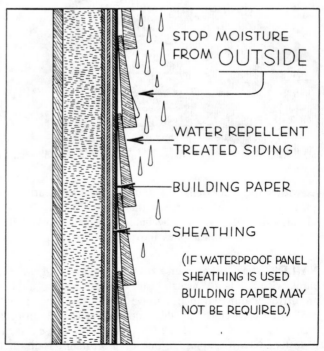

To bar moisture, siding should be treated with a water repellent, and backed up by sheathing covered with water repellent building paper.

216

16-Inch CERTIGRADE	5½-Inch Exposure			6-Inch Exposure			6½-Inch Exposure			7-Inch Exposure			7½-Inch Exposure		
	Number	Weight		Number	Weight		Number	Weight		Number	Weight		Number	Weight	
		Lbs.	Oz.		Lbs.	Oz.		Lbs.	Oz.		Lbs.	Oz.		Lbs.	Oz.
No. 1 Blue Label Grade	933	2	7	852	2	4	784	2	1	735	1	15	680	1	13
Red Label Grade	1190	3	2	1060	2	13	974	2	10	914	2	7	851	2	4
No. 3 Black Label Grade	1348	3	9	1245	3	4	1150	3	0	1044	2	12	945	2	8

18-Inch CERTIGRADE	6-Inch Exposure			6½-Inch Exposure			7-Inch Exposure			7½-Inch Exposure			8-Inch Exposure		
No. 1 Blue Label Grade	852	2	4	784	2	1	735	1	15	680	1	13	628	1	11
Red Label Grade	1060	2	13	974	·2	10	914	2	7	851	2	4	785	2	10
No. 3 Black Label Grade	1245	3	4	1150	3	0	1044	2	12	·945	2	8	845	2	6

24-Inch CERTIGRADE	8-Inch Exposure			9-Inch Exposure			10-Inch Exposure			11-Inch Exposure			12-Inch Exposure		
No. 1 Blue Label Grade	619	1	10	558	1	8	502	1	5	456	1	3	405	1	1
Red Label Grade	745	2	0	692	1	13	620	1	10	565	1	8	515	1	6
No. 3 Black Label Grade	798	2	2	745	2	0	672	1	12	610	1	10	558	1	8

Note: The above figures are for butt-nailing of new double-coursed side walls, using small-headed 5d nails. For the weight of 3d nails to hold the under course in double coursing, one nail per shingle, use one-third of the above weights. For single coursing with 3d nails, subtract one-third from the above weights. For over-walling with 24-inch shingles, add one-half to above weights. Remember that a 12-inch exposure will require half as many nails as a 6-inch exposure, a 14-inch half as many as a 7-inch, and so on.

BRICK OR STONE VENEER

The foundation and foundation wood sill construction will change slightly if masonry veneer is planned. Our previous studies showed the foundatin wood sill flush with the outside of the foundation wall. In this case the foundation wood sill is flush with the inside foundation wall and a 6" shelf is constructed on the outside of the foundation wall to support the veneer. The level of the shelf should be about 6" below the finish grade. The face of the veneer is in line with the outside foundation. Conventional brick is 2" high, 4" deep and 8" long. The 4" dimension is what rests on the shelf. Brick is made of a natural clay product of the dimensions indicated above. This mould is baked in an oven or kiln. The moisture evaporates shrinking the brick to about 1–5/8" high, 3–5/8" deep and 7–5/8" long.

The veneer can be carried to any height on the wall or walls. If carried only part way up, the top of the veneer must be capped to look finished. This is accomplished by turning the brick on end or by using some form of flat stone as a cap. The brick is 3-5/8" deep and the shelf is 6" deep which leaves a cavity of 2–3/8" behind the brick wall or between the back of the brick and the wall sheathing. This cavity or void is important and must be left as such. DO NOT fill the void. It is designed to prevent water from penetrating the wall. Moisture and water will penetrate the veneer and fall behind the veneer into the cavity and carried away through holes in the joints of the brick near the bottom called weep holes. These weep holes are installed in the brick courses at or near the bottom (one row only) by inserting a 1/4" dia. steel rod or short pieces of clothes line rope built into the joints and pulled out before the mortar completely sets. This area is also flashed to prevent the water from entering below the brick coursing. (see illustration). This cavity also acts as insulation. There is no better insulation than a vacuum. While laying brick, be careful to keep the void clean and do not allow mortar to fall into the cavity.

Brick or stone used in this fashion will not support itself laterally without falling over and therefore must be supported by the stud wall. It also serves no structural function but acts only as a curtain wall or veneer. If the veneer were to be removed, the building will remain standing. The veneer must be tied to the stud walls or wood frame with galvanized metal ties. These ties are nailed to the stud wall and bent at a mortar joint and embedded into the mortar locking the veneer to the stud wall. Ties are installed every third course in height spaced about 16" apart. A wood moulding is applied at the doors and windows to seal the space between the brick and the doors and windows. Later this irregular brick line is sealed with caulking compound. Veneer coursing should be planned to line with the tops of all openings. Brick height should not be cut to fit. The window and door sills can be of brick laid on edge with a slope similar to the cap mentioned earlier. The angle of the slope will allow the sill top to line with a course. In estimating brick courses, allow 8" for three courses of brick. If brick is continued above the top of openings, a steel angle or lintel is used to support the brick. Usually a 5" x 3-1/2" x 5/16" (for normal spans angles), bearing at least 4" on both sides of opening is used to support the brick such as over doors, windows or any other type opening. Flashing is installed between the back of the brick and the angle to seal the void, preventing water from entering or leaking through to the inside. Flashing is also required at the sill between the underside of the wood window sill and the joint between the last course and the masonry sill.

Brick is available in many colors, textures and patterns and are sold by lots of 1,000 sometimes using the symbol "M" representing 1,000. Brick takes on a natural clay color but sometimes earth colors are added to the mix to form a blend of colors.

There are two kinds of brick used in construction. The first and most expensive is called face brick. This is the brick used for a finish. The second type is called common brick which is less expensive and is used only as a filler or back-up which is not visible when the wall is completed. Common brick is sometimes moulded from concrete. For veneer purposes, a hard burned moisture resistant brick should be used. Used brick may be an economical way of veneering a home.

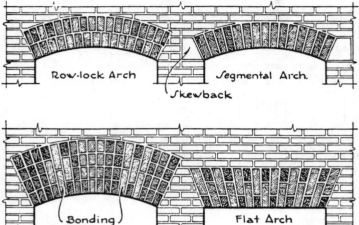

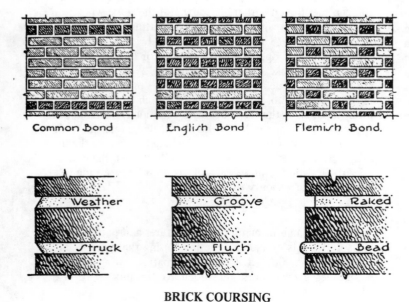

BRICK ARCH DESIGNS

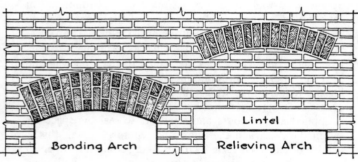

BRICK COURSING

Patterns of brick coursing include Common Bond, English Bond, Flemish Bond and Stack Bond. A stretcher course is a brick laid with the 8" surface exposed; a header course is the 2" surface exposed and a soldier course is a brick on end with the 8" surface in a vertical position. Common Bond consists of five stretcher courses and one header course. The pattern is repeated over and over. English Bond is one header course and one stretched course. Flemish Bond coursing is an alternate of headers and stretchers in the same row. Stack Bond is simply lining up all joints, vertically and horizontally.

Often white stains appear on the surface of the wall. These stains are caused by the water dissolving in sodium lime and magnesium (the mortar), and are called efflorescence. They can be easily removed by washing with diluted muriatic acid and brush. Do not allow this acid to come into contact with any clothing and keep well protected because it will burn clothing and skin. Use a plastic pail in mixing the solution and wear rubber gloves.

Sandstone and Limestone are commonly used for stone veneer. Ready mix mortars are available by simply adding enough water to make the mix a working consistency or mixing by using one part portland cement, three parts sand and 15% by volume of hydrated lime. The installation of brick is similar to block.

Existing homes without shelved foundations can be veneered by installing a continuous 4" x 6" x 3/8" galvanized angle lagged to the foundation just a few courses below the finish grade level. Lag bolts should be galvanized and installed about 4'–0" apart.

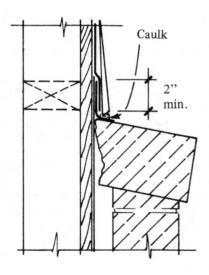

BRICK VENEER SILL
INTERSECTION OF DIFFERENT MATERIALS

Frame Wall with Masonry Veneer Base

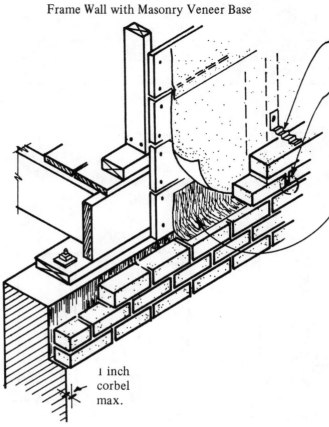

22 ga. galvanized metal anchors fastened to studs

Weep holes 4 ft. o.c. - omit mortar from vertical joints

Extend base flashing (metal or 30 lb. felt) up behind sheathing paper at least 6"

1 inch corbel max.

1/2"

Where sheathing paper is not required, extend base flashing up behind sheathing at least 6 inches.

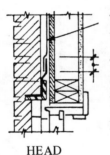

Lap sheathing paper over flashing as shown. Where sheathing paper is not required, extend flashing up behind sheathing.

Turn up flashing 2" minimum.

Extend metal flashing sufficiently at jambs to prevent penetration of water at these points.

HEAD

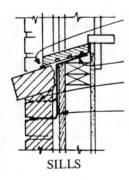

Caulk

Alternate - Flashing may be terminated in rabbet in lieu of methods shown.

Alternate location for flashing

Metal flashing

SILLS

BRICK VENEER
Flashing at Openings

HORIZONTAL SIDING

Several exterior wall surface products are termed horizontal siding. They include clapboards, bevel siding, novelty siding, and lap siding. Redwood, western cedar and cypress require no finish and can be allowed to be exposed and natural. Any other wood specie requires paint or stain. Bevel siding or clapboards are used widely in present day residential construction. Units are cut to varying widths ranging from 4" to 12" and a butt thickness of 1/2" to 3/4" with lapping courses of from 1" to 2". The wider the siding the more exposure the courses. All nails are exposed with this type siding and should be rust proof, if not, rust will bleed to the surface and stain the finish.

When nailing, do not allow the nails to penetrate the preceding course in order to allow room for expansion and movement, otherwise the siding may split. The application is similar to that of wood shingles including the paper starter course and corners. Be sure to snap a line at each course to keep the coursing straight and level. Use the same story pole method for laying out the courses as in applying wood shingles, being sure to line all courses with top and bottoms of doors and windows with minor variations in the exposure if necessary.

Lap siding is similar to beveled siding without the bevel; novelty siding is a tongue and groove siding sometimes used without sheathing (nailing directly to studs) mostly for vacation homes or garages and offers an economical way to cover exterior walls.

VERTICAL SIDING & PLYWOOD

V-joint, Tongue & Groove, Battens and Lap Joint are some of the different designs for vertical siding. The siding may be plain or rough sawed, matched or patterned boards, square edge or plywood, notched or solid boards. Plywood should be sealed at all edges before installation and solid boards should not be more than 8" wide nailed with 2-8d nails about 4'—0" apart. As with other siding, all should extend about 1/2" below the top of the foundation with the

219

starter panel and sheathing covered with paper. Battens are narrow pieces or wood covering the vertical joints of siding, either plywood or wide square edge boards. In nailing battens, nail only to one side of the siding to allow for movement during expansion & contraction. Do not allow any horizontal joints. Carefully plan the design of battens to have some order of semblance and balance especially around doors and windows. Try to avoid a joint half way across a window or door, think of the design in terms of units, planning the parts, not the whole. Be sure to apply paper between the sheathing and the siding and be sure all panels are straight and level. See chapter on Interior Work for Cutting of Plywood.

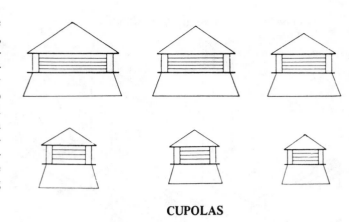

CUPOLAS

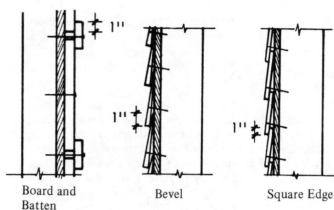

Board and Batten   Bevel   Square Edge   Rabbeted   Ship Lap   T & G

WOOD SIDING

Recommended head lap and nailing pattern for various strip sidings.

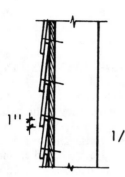
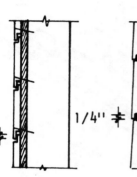

In areas not exposed to wind-driven rain, head lap may be reduced to 1/2" for back-primed siding.

Install wedges under vertical joints at butt ends and corners.

Blind nailing shown. If face nailed, use two nails for widths 8" or more.

Head lap for plywood strip siding may be 3/4".

WEATHERVANES

Horse   Eagle   Rooster   Sailboat

Threaded nails are recommended when sheathing is plywood.

Fill vertical joints in plywood and hard board siding with mastic caulking unless joints are interlapping type. Caulking may be omitted for plywood siding applied over sheathing if edges are treated with water-repellent containing at least 5% pentachlorophenol. Vertical joints in hard board siding should have 1/16" gap.

GABLE LOUVERS

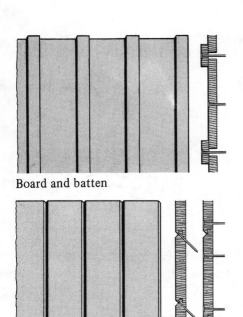

Board and batten

Tongue and groove and shiplap V-joint

Bevel, plain & rabbeted

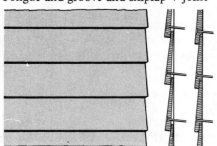

Channel Rustic

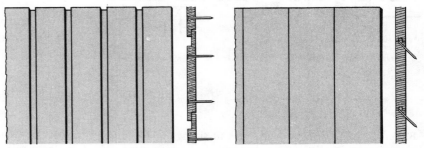

Tongue and groove flush pattern

COMPOSITION SIDING

Hardboard exterior siding is much the same material as interior wall finishes (see chapter on wall finishes). Panels vary from 3/8" to 5/8" thick, up to 4'–0" wide and 9'–0" long made in different patterns as reverse board, battens, V groove, lap, flat, horizontal or vertical. They are available in unpainted, primed or factory finished. Follow the same procedure for installation as with a like wood siding; cutting presents no problem if a fine tooth saw is used, hand or power . 8d hot dipped galvanized nails are used and in some designs, the nails will be exposed.

MINERAL SIDING

Because it is made mainly from asbestos, this siding is brittle and is easily broken. Manufacturers will sell you on the fire safety of these units, but the safeguard against fire is no better than the surface onto which these units are applied. When they become wet, they will appear a much darker color. Painting is not necessary and again, many patterns, color and textures are available.

SIDING SELECTOR

Choosing a siding pattern is a step by step process. First determine whether you want a vertical or a horizontal pattern.

Siding in vertical courses tends to emphasize the vertical lines of a building and make it appear taller; horizontal siding emphasizes the width.

Next choice is between a flush wall surface or one that is more strongly patterned. With a flush wall, the grain and texture of the wood are more pronounced but the total effect may be too strong for a large area.

Bevel, V-joint tongue-and-groove or shiplap, and channel rustic sidings present a detailed surface laid up. The resulting shadow patterns relieve the monotony of a flat plane surface.

Width of the pieces is the next choice. Patterns come in 4, 6, 8, 10, and 12-inch widths. The scale of the building and the special effects desired should help determine what width to use. For example, a narrow horizontal siding will make a structure look taller than a wide horizontal pattern, but less massive. Or, for a wide expanse of wall, a random-width siding might be used for visual relief.

A wood starter course is necessary and the units are preholed at the factory for installation. (See chapter on Roof Shingles for cutting). The units are available in 24" or 48" widths and 12" deep with a 1-1/2" lap, leaving an exposure of 10-1/2". Use the same system for installation as used for roof shingles or similar siding. However, remember that these shingles are more fragile and will crack or break easily. Metal corners are available and installation presents no special problem. If you drive the nail too hard against the panel, it will crack; there is no give with these units.

PANEL SIDING APPLICATION

Panel siding products with shiplap joints may be applied over sheathed or unsheathed walls with studs spaced up to 16" o.c. Panel siding products with butt joints may be applied over sheathed or unsheathed walls with studs spaced up to 24" o.c. These panel sidings applied directly to studs without corner bracing and nailed as recommended, will meet or exceed the racking strength requirements.

All joints and panel edges should fall on center of framing members. If it is necessary to make a joint with a panel that has been field cut and the shiplap removed, use a butt joint, butter edges with caulking and bring to light contact. Do not force or spring panels into place. Leave a slight space where siding butts against trim, and caulk. Allow at least 6" between siding and ground.

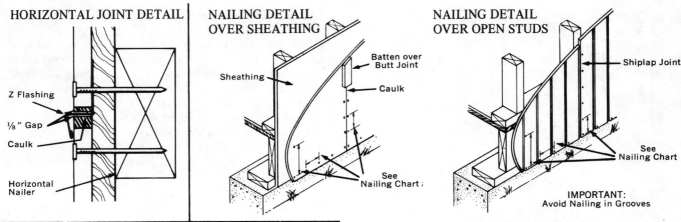

HORIZONTAL JOINT DETAIL

Z Flashing
⅛" Gap
Caulk
Horizontal Nailer

NAILING DETAIL OVER SHEATHING

Sheathing
Batten over Butt Joint
Caulk
See Nailing Chart

NAILING DETAIL OVER OPEN STUDS

Shiplap Joint
See Nailing Chart

IMPORTANT:
Avoid Nailing in Grooves

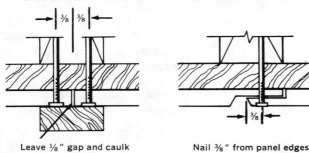

BUTT JOINT DETAIL

⅜ | ⅜

Leave ⅛" gap and caulk

SHIPLAP JOINT DETAIL

⅜

Nail ⅜" from panel edges

Nail and Size Spacing Requirements

6d or 8d galvanized box nail*
3/8" in from edges
4" o.c. along all edges
8" o.c. along intermediate supports
6d or 8d galvanized box nail*
3/8" in from edges
6" o.c. along all edges
12" o.c. along intermediate supports

*Use 6d box nails only for direct panel-to-stud applications or for panel over wood or plywood sheathing applications.

SIDING   APPLICATION

Batten Strips: Use wood or strips of siding cut to desired width. In addition to covering all vertical joints, intermediate batten strips may be installed for design purposes. Batten strips should be installed only at locations where an adequate nailing base is provided.

FINISHING: Siding must be furnished as follows:

Primer: Primecoated panels must be painted within 120 days after installlation. If exposed for a longer period of time, reprime the siding with a good quality exterior grade oil base primer.

Painting: Unprimed panels must be field primed before finish painting. Quality alkyd, oil or latex paints should be used. For all paints, follow the manufacturer's recommendations concerning the use of special primers or undercoats. the rate of spread and application procedures. All exposed areas must be painted.

Coats of Paint Required: Total dry film thickness including prime and topcoat should be a minimum of 4 mils. Proper film thickness may be best obtained by applying two uncut topcoats (2.5 Mils) over the primed surface (1.5 Mils).

Staining: Only quality heavy bodied latex or acrylic latex stains should be used to field finish unprimed or primed textured sidings. Only sidings with woodlike surface textures are suitable for staining.

Coats of Stain Required: This will depend upon the type of stain selected, the trim or siding material being stained and the aesthetic effect desired. All stains should be applied following manufacturer's recommendations for mixing, method of application, rate of spread and number of coats required. All exposed surfaces and edges should be stained.

Prestained Products: Prestained panel sidings do not require field finishing. However, one quart cans of stains are available through local dealers for touching up panel surfaces and for finishing wood trim. When staining trim color effect will vary according to trim material used. Apply a little stain at a time and wipe as necessary until desired effect is obtained.

Non-Vertical Surfaces: Products with wood-like surface textures may be used in mansard roof applications, provided that good construction practices are followed, and that the slope of the surface is no more than 15 degrees from the vertical (45/12) pitch. Do not exceed framing and nail spacing indicated in nailing chart. Plywood or wood board sheathing and building paper are required when siding is applied to non-vertical surfaces.

Residing: Sidings can be used for residing buildings by applying furring strips over old siding or by first removing it and then applying the new siding. In both cases, follow application instrucitons for new construction. A firm and adequate nailing base must be provided.

222

LAP SIDING APPLICATION

Vapor Barriers: A properly installed continuous vapor barrier (1 perm or less rating) such as polyethylene film or foil backed gypsum board, is required on the warm side of the exterior walls in all buildings. This will preclude damaging condensation from occurring within the walls.

Cutting: Whenever possible, cutting and marking of Siding should be done on the back side. If necessary to cut on the finished surface, tools should be clean, and a heavy paper or cardboard should be taped to the under side of the power saw. Use a fine toothed hand saw or a power saw with a combination blade.

Exposed Nails: For exposed nailing, finish nail heads with matching Colorlok touch-up paint or use color-matched nails. Special color-matched nails, caulk and touch-up paint are all available from your lumber dealer. When using the colored nail, use the plastic hammer head cap furnished with the nails.

Care of Finish. The finish is formulated to be long wearing and self cleaning and requires little maintenance. Local conditions may result in heavy dirt accumulation which inhibits the cleaning action, and washing may be desirable for best appearance.

Siding: Can be washed with most liquid household cleaners diluted according to the manufacturer's recommendations. All cleaners should be tested on a small area prior to use to make certain they do not damage the finish. Rinse the surface thoroughly after cleaning.

Coverage: 1150 square feet of 12" Lap Siding is required to cover 1000 surface feet of wall. 1200 square feet of 9" Siding is required to cover 1000 square feet of wall. This figure includes 5% for cutting and waste.

Wall Construction: Lap Siding may be applied over sheathed or unsheathed walls with studs spaced not more than 16" o.c. Adequate bracing of the wall with corner bracing or sheathing is required. For residing walls that have old bevel or shingle siding, removal of the existing siding before installing. Lap Siding is recommended: allow at least 6" between siding and ground.

Building Paper: When Lap Siding is applied directly to studs or over wood sheathing, building paper or felt should be used directly under the siding.

Nails. For siding and outside metal corners use 8d (2 1/2") galvanized box nails. For the metal starter strip and inside metal corner use 6d (2" or longer) galvanized siding, or box nails.

Procedure: Level and install the specially formed metal starter strip along bottom edge of sheathing or sill plate, or up to 1" below, as required by course layout. Install metal inside corner, spacing nails 8" apart along each flange. Install first course of siding so that the mounting strip fastened into the back of the siding fits over the edge of the start-

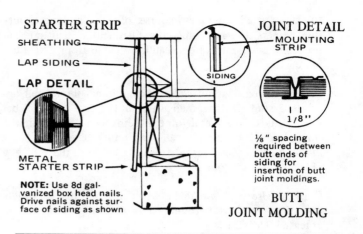

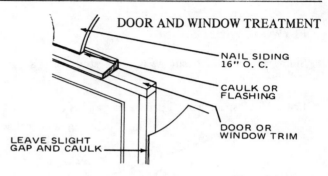

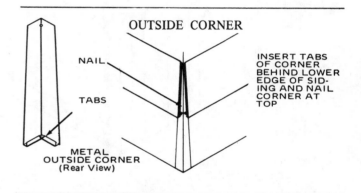

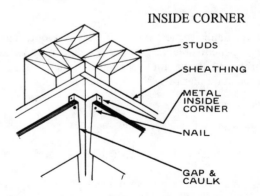

er strip as shown in the starter strip detail. Fasten the siding by nailing along the top edge of each stud location. Hold the siding down firmly and nail. Nail spacing should not exceed 16" o.c. When wood drip cap is not used over door and window opening, provide a nailing shim behind siding. Space nails 16" o.c. along bottom edge of siding over doors and windows. Leave a slight space where the siding butts against the trim, and caulk. Do not force or spring siding in-

223

to place. Install subsequent courses of siding and metal outside corners. Use matching colored touch-up paint and appropriate matching colored caulk available from your lumber dealer.

Joints: On unsheathed walls all butt joints should fall opposite a stud. On sheathed walls, butt joints may fall between studs. The metal joint molding furnished with the siding should be used at all butt joints. The metal joint molding should be inserted from the top into the 1/8" gap at the siding butt joints.

Corners: Use prefinished metal outside and inside corners and trim. Wood trim around doors and windows should be at least 1 1/8" thick.

PLYWOOD PANEL SIDING

Siding joints may occur away from studs with approved nailable sheathing

Leave 1/16" spacing at all panel edges and ends

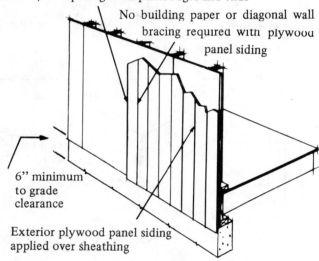

No building paper or diagonal wall bracing required with plywood panel siding

6" minimum to grade clearance

Exterior plywood panel siding applied over sheathing

Note: Caulk vertical joints or treat plywood edges with water repellent unless edges are shiplapped or battened. Nails through battens must penetrate studs at least 1", or through lumber or 1/2" plywood sheathing.

Approved nailable sheathing includes:

1. Nominal 1" boards with studs 16" or 24" o.c.

2. 1/2" 4 or 5 ply, face grain parallel or perpendicular to studs 16" or 24" o.c.

3. 3/8" or 1/2" 3 ply plywood, face grain perpendicular to studs 16" or 24" o.c.; and with face grain parallel or perpendicular to studs 16" o.c.

4. 5/16" plywood, face grain perpendicular to studs 16" o.c.

ASPHALT SIDING

This product is available in two forms, Roll & Shingles. Many are designed to simulate brick or stone. The same general application procedures described for roof shingles can be applied to this siding. Be sure to use the chalk line to align the courses. Special metal trim pieces are installed before the siding; be sure to line courses on all sides. Inside corners should be flashed with a strip of 30 lb. paper extended at least 12" on both sides of the corner. Cutting is no problem with a knife or tin snips.

RE-SIDING

Practically any of the siding described can be used for remodeling or residing over old siding without removing the old siding. The wood trim may have to be modified or built out to accommodate the added wall thickness and additional mouldings may have to be used around doors and windows. The most important factor is that the existing siding is secure and sound. If some of the pieces are rotted, remove and replace them with equal thickness fillers of wood.

Ends of boards that are cut to length while the siding is being fastened in place also should receive treatment with a water repellent.

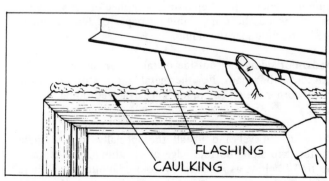

Vulnerable places over door and window frames should be fitted with flashing extended well under the siding. All joints should be caulked.

224

ALUMINUM & VINYL SIDING

For alterations of homes without insulation in the walls, aluminum or vinyl siding offers the best opportunity. There is no need to remove old siding. Over the existing siding, nail either 1/2", or 1" rigid insulation. Some aluminum or vinyl siding has a factory applied insulation sandwiched between the panels. If this is your selection, the additional insulation will not harm anything but will reduce the heat loss of the building. If necessary remove the existing trim from the house such as corner boards, mouldings, fascia, etc. Install the metal corner trim and the metal starter piece, being sure they are straight and level, and begin installing the siding. These units are manufactured in double courses of panels in clapboard design in lengths up to 12'–6". Panels are also available for vertical installation. Either way, there is a wide selection of color and texture all of which are blind nailed. Special shapes are available for trim work and this material can be cut easily with a hack saw or sheet metal shears. Courses are 4" or 8" wide in the horizontal and about 12" wide in the vertical. Special aluminum fasteners must be used with 1-1/2" rust proof nails.

Do not permit water from copper gutters and conductors to drain over aluminum. Do not install aluminum over dissimilar metals without a separation of mastic. To safeguard against the possibility of faulty electrical system, electrical wiring may energize the aluminum siding creating a danger. To avoid such a possibility, aluminum siding should be grounded with No. 8 wire or larger, connected to any convenient place on the siding to a cold water service pipe or an electric service ground. Connectors should be U.L. approved.

One of the disadvantages of aluminum siding is that it dents and scratches easily and cannot be repaired successfully without replacing the panel. Putting a ladder against aluminum siding is difficult without denting and any object thrown against the siding can cause damage.

Vinyl siding is a PVC (poly-vinyl-chloride) product installed in much the same manner as aluminum siding, with all the same accessories, patterns, textures and sizes as aluminum. Like aluminum, these panels require no painting or maintenance. Vinyl will not scratch but ultra violet ray (sunshine), may discolor the finish.

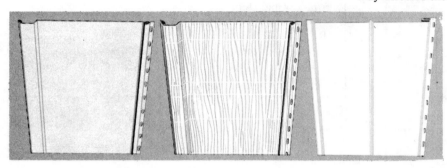

12-INCH VERTICAL　　　　**V-GROOVE**

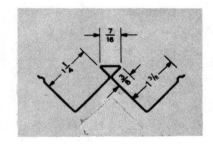

Inside Corner Post

8-INCH HORIZONTAL

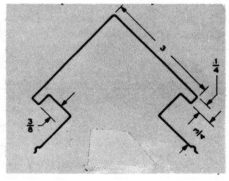

Outside Corner Post

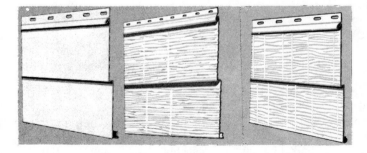

DOUBLE 4-INCH HORIZONTAL

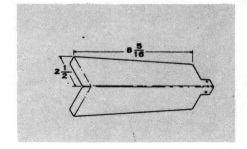

Outside Corner Cap

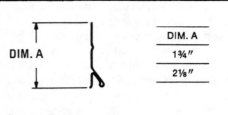

Starter Strip

Used to secure first siding course to wall.

DIM. A
1¾″
2⅛″

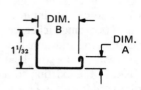

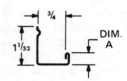

DIM. A	DIM. B
5/16″	1-5/16″
5/16″	9/16″
½″	1-5/16″

DIM. A
5/16″
½″

Window and Door Trim

Receives horizontal and vertical siding on all sides of windows and doors, at rake edges of gables and at hip roof locations. CAUTION: DO NOT NAIL THROUGH ROOF FLASHING.

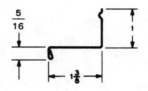

Window Head Flashing

Used as head flashing on windows where no trim exists and as base flashing on vertical siding installations. Nail on 8″ centers.

General Purpose Trim

Use to receive non-insulated horizontal siding over and under windows, at last course of siding and at porch floor locations. May also be used to receive vertical siding at corners and window jambs.

Caulking Compound

For use between windows and side walls. Keep exposed caulking at a minimum and use mineral spirits to clean excesses.

Touch-up Paint

Paint should be thoroughly mixed for best color match. Brush best suited for touching up nicks, while spray should be used on larger areas.

TRIM SHEET AND MISCELLANEOUS PRODUCTS

Trim Sheet

Field formed to cover window and door casings, sills, jambs, leaders, skirt boards, drip edges and frieze boards. May also be used as flashing. Field or shop form with brake. Fasten with color matched aluminum trim nails and conceal wherever possible.

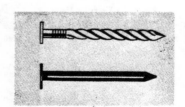

Nails

Always use aluminum fasteners when nailing aluminum.

Back-up Tab

Provides support for non-insulated siding at windows, doors, outside corner cap locations and behind panel overlaps. Install with flat surface out. Nailing not necessary. Average use: 24 tabs per square.

226

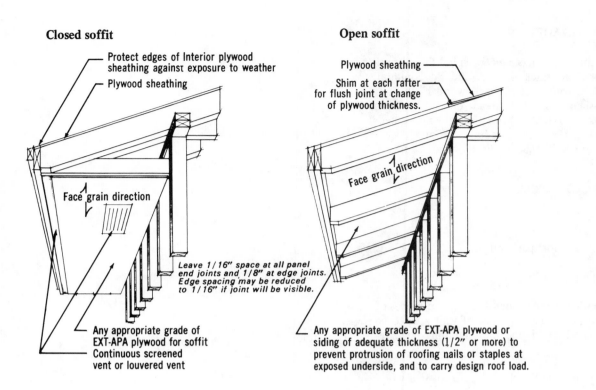

Closed soffit

- Protect edges of Interior plywood sheathing against exposure to weather
- Plywood sheathing

Face grain direction

Leave 1/16" space at all panel end joints and 1/8" at edge joints. Edge spacing may be reduced to 1/16" if joint will be visible.

- Any appropriate grade of EXT-APA plywood for soffit
- Continuous screened vent or louvered vent

Open soffit

- Plywood sheathing
- Shim at each rafter for flush joint at change of plywood thickness.

Face grain direction

- Any appropriate grade of EXT-APA plywood or siding of adequate thickness (1/2" or more) to prevent protrusion of roofing nails or staples at exposed underside, and to carry design roof load.

M.D. OVERLAY

GROUP 2 EXTERIOR PS 1-74 000 (APA)

C-C 24/0 EXTERIOR PS 1-74 000 (APA)

303 SIDING 16 oc

GROUP 3 EXTERIOR PS 1-74 000 (APA)

A-C GROUP 4 EXTERIOR PS 1-74 000 (APA)

A—Plywood for open soffits   (face grain across supports)
(or for combined decking-ceiling)

Max. Span (inches)	Panel Descriptions (Minimum Recommendations)	Species Group
16	7/16" APA 303 Siding	1, 2, 3, 4
	1/2" APA Sanded	1, 2, 3, 4
24	1/2" APA Sanded	1, 2, 3
	19/32" APA 303 Siding (including T1-11)	1
	5/8" APA 303 Siding (including T1-11)	1, 2, 3, 4
	5/8" APA Sanded	1, 2, 3, 4
	3/4" APA 303 Siding	1, 2, 3, 4
32(a)	5/8" APA Sanded	1
	3/4" APA 303 Siding	1
	3/4" APA Sanded	1, 2, 3, 4
48(a)	1⅛" APA Textured(b)	1, 2, 3, 4

(a) Provide adequate blocking, tongue-and-groove edges or other suitable edge supports such as Plyclips.

(b) 1⅛" panels, of Group 2, 3 or 4 species will support 35 psf live load plus 5 psf dead load.

B—Plywood for closed soffits   (face grain across supports)

Nominal Plywood Thickness	Group	Maximum Span (inches), all edges supported
5/16" APA 303 Siding 3/8" APA Sanded		24
7/16" APA 303 Siding 1/2" APA Sanded	1, 2, 3, or 4	32
19/32" or 5/8" APA 303 Siding or APA Sanded		48

227

EXTERIOR PLYWOOD SOFFITS

Use 6d common, smooth, ring-shank, or spiral-thread non-corrosive nails for 1/2" thick or less, and 8d common, smooth, ring-shank or spiral-thread for plywood 1" thick or less. Use 8d ring-shank or spiral-thread, or 10d common smooth shank nails for 1-1/8" textured panels. Space nails 6" at panel edges, and 12" at intermediate supports, except that where spans are 48", space nails 6" at all supports.

SOFFIT SYSTEM AND FASCIA

ACCESSORIES

Channel Molding. To support panel edges.

Divider Strip. For joints.

Vent Strip. For ventilation—provides 17.0 square inches of open area per lineal foot. The amount of vent area to be provided should comply with the local building code requirements.

Aluminum Fascia Cap. 5-1/2" wide, for use over a wood sub-fascia.

Aluminum Roof Edging. Covers the edge of the roof and drops down to cover the top edge of the Fascia Cap. Fascia Cap and Roof Edging may be used with or without the soffit system.

All above accessories available in frost white only.

GENERAL CONSTRUCTION

The Soffit System provides a prefinished soffit compatible with all exterior siding materials. The system is especially suited to soffits two feet or less in width. Spans over two feet require 16" o.c. support. The soffit panels are to be cut from Panel Siding available in 4' x 8' and 4' x 9' Sizes. Whenever face nailing is required, use prefinished nails or galvanized nails and touch-up paint.

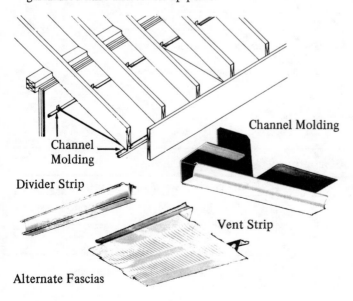

Channel
Molding

Channel Molding

Divider Strip

Vent Strip

Alternate Fascias

228

INTERIOR NON-BEARING

PARTITIONS

Curtain walls or room dividers are partitions not required to support anything except itself. These are called non-bearing partitions and are built of 2" x 3" studs spaced 16" apart. Where these partitions run parallel to the floor joists, the joists were doubled to support the additional load of the partition. If they are perpendicular to the floor joists, no additional support is necessary because the load is distributed over many joists. After the sub-floor is installed, locate the position of all non-bearing partitions following the plans. Over the sub-floor, nail a 2" x 3" flat with 16d spikes or nails. This is called a shoe or sole plate. If the partition is perpendicular to the ceiling joists, simply repeat the process of nailing a 2" x 3" flat against the joists being sure it is level with the 2" x 3" nailed to the sub-floor. Mark off the 16" spacings and nail the 2" x 3" upright studs in place using the same procedure as 2" x 4" studs doubling all openings for doors. These studs are toe nailed into the sole and the plate (upper 2" x 3"). If the partition is parallel to the ceiling joists, simply nail 1" x 3" wood furring strips 16" apart to the ceiling joist being sure to pick-up at least two joists with the furring. Nail the plate to the bottom of the furring and repeat the process as explained. Use 6d nails with 4 at top and bottom on studs. Use studs straight and true. Those studs that are not true can be used for shorter studs around openings. Use two 2" x 3" on edge for headers above openings.

PLANS (Intersecting Walls)

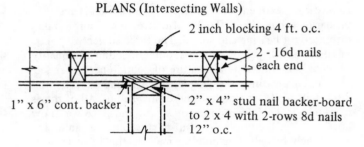

2 inch blocking 4 ft. o.c.

2 - 16d nails each end

1" x 6" cont. backer

2" x 4" stud nail backer-board to 2 x 4 with 2-rows 8d nails 12" o.c.

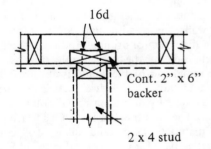

16d

Cont. 2" x 6" backer

2 x 4 stud

SECTION AT CEILING (Non-Bearing Partition)

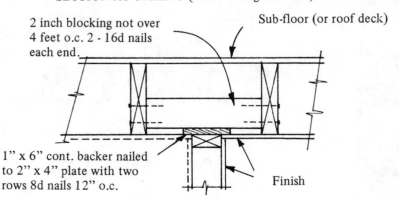

2 inch blocking not over 4 feet o.c. 2 - 16d nails each end.

Sub-floor (or roof deck)

1" x 6" cont. backer nailed to 2" x 4" plate with two rows 8d nails 12" o.c.

Finish

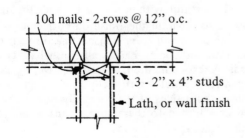

10d nails - 2-rows @ 12" o.c.

3 - 2" x 4" studs

Lath, or wall finish

SOUND PROOFING

Acoustical treatment in residential construction is designed primarily for comfort. To be effective, the comfort takes into account hearing and sound. The three subjective points of sound are degree of loudness, pitch of sound and quality of sound. Loudness is a measure of sound energy per second, pitch measures the frequency of sound or tone and pitch tells us if it is a high sound or low sound. All of this is measured in decibles, or rate of sound, and once we know how many of the noises we want to shut out, we can design accordingly by selecting building material that has been tested for sound absorption. Unwanted noise is unpleasant, it reduces efficiency and can cause fatigue. The kinds of residential noises that can be annoying come from conversation, television, record players, radios, typewriters, musical intruments, vacuum cleaners, dish and clothes washer, washing machine, poorly designed plumbing, heating, and ventilation and air-conditioning, power tools and kitchen appliances. When sound is generated within a room, sound waves strike the walls, floor and ceiling causing these surfaces to vibrate as a diaphram or drum, reproducing these sounds on the opposite side of the room, reflecting back into the room. The remainder of the sound is absorbed by the surfaces. As sound moves through a surface or barrier, its intensity is reduced by an action called Sound Transmission Loss (STL). The transmission loss of a surface will depend upon the material, design and quality of construction. Another system used for rating sound is called Sound Transmission Class (STC). The higher the number rating the better the sound barrier.

WALLS

One of the most effective sound barrier partitions is the double partition with insulation between the studs. The purpose is to separate the finish on both sides of the wall to prevent the sound from transmitting through the partition and into the room. Each wall finish has its own row of studs. A second method, not as effective, is called the spring clip method. Metal spring clips are nailed to a single stud wall on both sides of the studs, Gypsum wallboard is clipped or attached to these spring clips separating the finish wall surface from the studs.

Care must be taken if doors are installed in the partition because the wall treatment is no better than the door treatment for soundproofing. Double rabbetted door frames are used with two solid core doors in the frame. One at each side of the wall. Both doors should be weatherstripped to prevent sound from leaking through. Windows also need to be soundproofed with double glazing. Use a neoprene strip to hold both panes of glass in place.

CONSTRUCTION DETAILS

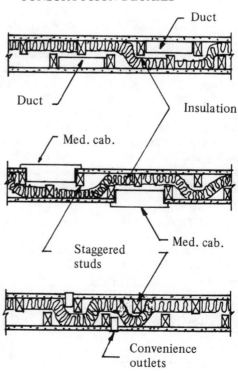

Penetration from opposite side of wall should be separated by one full stud space

FLOORS AND CEILINGS

Wall treatment is not enough. Floors and ceilings must also be treated because sound will telegraph through these surfaces as well. In new construction, the wall should be separated from the floor and ceiling by installing a neoprene gasket between the shoe and the sub-floor and the same gasket between the ceiling and the plate. The partition is literally floating free of the floor and ceiling. Suspended acoustical ceilings, carpeted floor, upholstered furniture, heavy drapes and soft wall finishes such as cork, carpet, acoustical wall panels, drapes, perforated or porous fiberboard and acoustical plaster will help to absorb sound.

An existing room can be soundproofed by floating another floor over the existing floor separating the two with a fiberglass wool blanket. Over the insulation, lay flat 2" x 3" studs called sleepers, but do not nail these to the existing floor. Allow them to rest freely or float over the insulation and lay a new floor over the sleepers being careful not to allow the nail to penetrate through the sleepers into the old floor. The walls can be soundproofed by building a separate second wall as explained above.

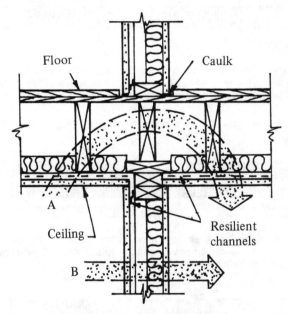

Sound transmission by path A
should not exceed that by path B

STC

30	Loud speech fairly well understood
35	Loud speech audible not intelligible
42	Loud speech audible as a murmur
45	Some loud speech barely audible
48	Hearing strained to note loud speech
50	Loud speech not audible

Double Stud Wall

SEPARATE ROWS 2" X 4" STUDS 16" O.C. ON SEPARATE 2" X 4" PLATES.

⅝" TYPE X GYPSUM BOARD BOTH SIDES

STC · 43	Without Insulation
STC · 55	3½" Fiberglas Insulation*
STC · 59	2 — 3½" Layers of Insulation*

*Faced or Unfaced Insulation gives the same acoustical performance.

Recommended Height Limit — 14 ft.
Thickness — 9¼"
Weight — Approx. 7.1 lbs/sq. ft.

Fire Resistance—1 hour

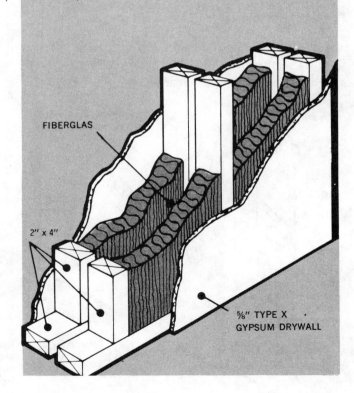

FIBERGLAS

2" x 4"

⅝" TYPE X GYPSUM DRYWALL

231

Check List of Noise Control Precautions

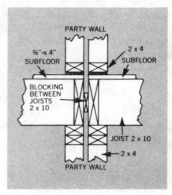

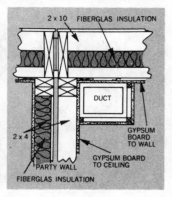

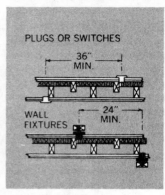

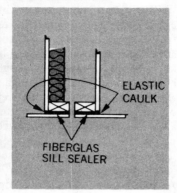

Over Party Walls
Close all open spaces between joists over party walls with blocking to prevent sound travel over walls.

Behind Ducts And Piping
Carry gypsum board wall finish to wall and ceiling line behind ducts before duct is installed and soffit built.

Outlets and Switches
Separate as diagrammed or drop gypsum board wrapped in Fiberglas insulation down between outlets.

At Base Of Walls
Install plates on Fiberglas Sill Sealer. Run wall finish to floor where possible. Caulk air tight on both sides.

Staggered 2" x 4" Wood Studs

⅝" TYPE X GYPSUM BOARD BOTH SIDES

STC · 42	Without Insulation
STC · 49	3½" Fiberglas Insulation*
STC · 52	2 — 3½" Layers of Insulation*

*Faced or Unfaced Insulation gives the same acoustical performance.

Recommended Height Limit — 14 ft.
Thickness — 6⅞"

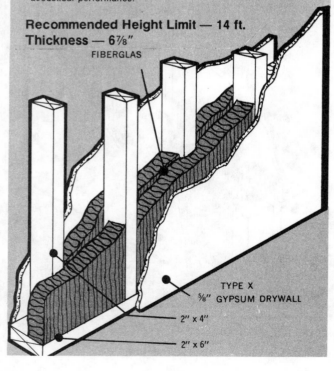

FIBERGLAS

TYPE X
⅝" GYPSUM DRYWALL

2" x 4"

2" x 6"

SOUND CONTROL WITH FIBER GLASS INSULATION

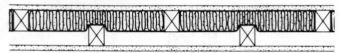

1. Separate the wall faces to break the transmission path. This prevents direct travel of sound energy from one wall surface to the opposite one. Staggered studs may be used to accomplish this purpose.

Use fiber glass insulation to absorb the sound energy within the wall assembly.

2. Another method of breaking direct sound paths is to use a special resilient channel or other resilient attachment of gypsum wallboard to the studs on one side.

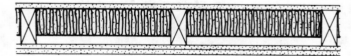

3. Use wall faces of different thicknesses to prevent sympathetic vibration. Faces of the same thickness vibrate at the same frequency, causing resonance of sound in the wall. Different facing thicknesses vibrate at different frequencies, each thereby masking the effect of the other.

Some other ways to reduce sound transmission are:
Use caulking or gaskets at top and bottom of partition and in any area where sound leaks may occur. Avoid back-to-back electrical outlets or fixtures, connecting ducts or any direct carrier of sound from one surface to the other.

Use fiber glass insulation within ceiling and floor assemblies to help reduce sound transmission vertically from room to room.

232

SPRING CLIP

RESILIENT METAL CLIP

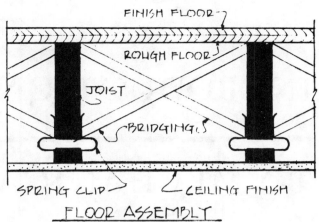

FINISH FLOOR

ROUGH FLOOR

JOIST

BRIDGING

SPRING CLIP

CEILING FINISH

FLOOR ASSEMBLY

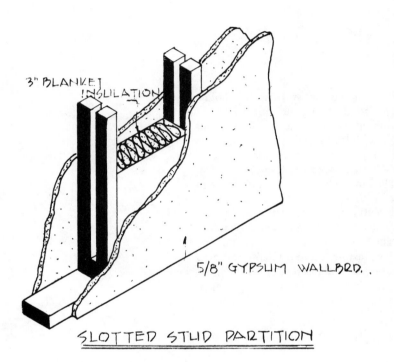

3" BLANKET INSULATION

5/8" GYPSUM WALLBRD.

SLOTTED STUD PARTITION

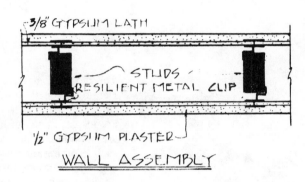

3/8" GYPSUM LATH

STUDS

RESILIENT METAL CLIP

1/2" GYPSUM PLASTER

WALL ASSEMBLY

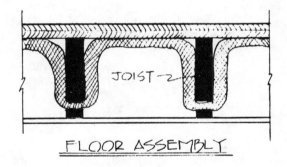

JOIST

FLOOR ASSEMBLY

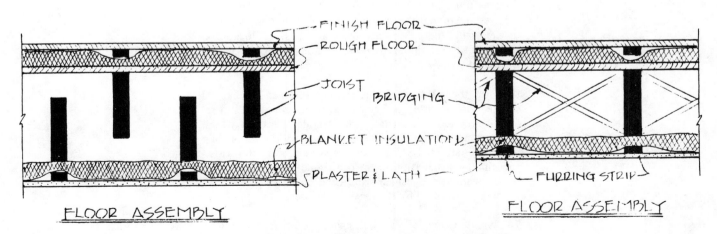

FINISH FLOOR

ROUGH FLOOR

JOIST

BRIDGING

BLANKET INSULATION

PLASTER & LATH

FURRING STRIP

FLOOR ASSEMBLY

FLOOR ASSEMBLY

SOUND INSULATION — CEILINGS, FLOORS & WALLS

INTRODUCTION

24

TO MECHANICAL

The mechanical system of a home consists of the Plumbing, Heating, Ventilation, Air-conditioning and Electrical. At this stage of construction, after all interior stud partitions are in place and before any finish of walls, floors or ceilings are completed, the "roughing-in" of all mechanical facilities such as piping and wiring or duct work to support the mechanical facilities are installed in the partitions where they will be concealed. The finish installation of the mechanical systems such as plumbing fixtures, heating, grills, baseboard, convectors or radiators, lighting fixtures, switches, plugs and plates are not installed until the floors, walls and ceilings are finished. All lines must be tested for leaks or breaks before the finish is completed. Making repairs later will require the finish to be removed in order to expose the problem for correction.

For economy, careful planning in arranging the plumbing fixtures must be employed. Simplification of arrangement dictates clustering of plumbing fixtures on a common wall or wet wall. Where there is more than one story, locate fixtures above each other to use common piping for water, waste and vents.

It is not the purpose of this chapter to teach mechanical engineering because mechanical design is complex and requires experience to install; however, dealers from whom the mechanical equipment is purchased will be more than happy to help in the design of the system and offer assistance in the installation. The local building codes may require licensed tradesmen to install mechanical systems which are inspected by the local authorities.

The chapters that follow are designed to explain the various systems that are available and what is expected of them by way of performance, and to be a guide in choosing a system.

PLUMBING

25

WATER LINES

The cost of installation of a public water supply is less than the cost of installation of a private water supply. In the case of a public water supply, the Town or City Hall will have a record of the water facilities including the size of the water main, depth below the surface and the pressure of the water. All that is required is to run a 3/4" or greater water main from the public supply to the house deep enough to protect the pipe from the frost. This pipe is usually copper. The Utility Company will make the connection from the main street to a shut-off at the property line. From that point into the house becomes the responsibility of the home owner. When the line is brought into the house, the Utility Company will install a water meter and from the meter, the water is distributed throughout the house. In the building of the foundation, a chase or opening was left to receive the water pipe.

If a public water supply is not available, a private water system must be planned. In nature, water is seldom free from impurities. The pure vapor in the atmosphere may collect air-borne bacteria. In percolating through the earth, it filters the water losing most of this bacteria but also picking up salts or gases. Some are harmful and some are not. In some parts of the Central States, methane gas is found in ground water. Calcium and magnesium in the form of sulfates or carbonates as well as iron are common. Earth strata, as well as minerals , vary from one community to another and it is not within the scope of this chapter to recommend directions for locating ground water. Local health officials, State geologists and colleges and universities can help.

Water containing large amounts of calcium and magnesium salts is called hard water and sudsing from soaps is difficult. Rain water is soft and suds easily. A glass of water which looks clear may contain millions of dangerous organisms. Contaminated water can cause typhoid fever, dysentery, diarrhea and intestinal disorders as well as several varieties of intestinal worms. Sand, soft sandstone or sand and gravel substrata as a rule will yield safe water.

The important requirement is to keep at least 100' away from any private sewerage system and preferably to locate the well on high ground (check local code). All well water should be analyzed for chemical content and purity. This will dictate which kind of treatment to use. As a rule, this analysis will be done by local health officials. New wells must be disinfected and kept sealed. If a water softener is necessary, there are several complete packages on the market. The most satisfactory method is to pass the water through zeolite which is a special kind of sand. Another product for filtering water is charcoal. The water should be filtered. There is no way to determine the amount of water a well will yield, but there are certain minimum requirements which are necessary. The minimum amount of water should be 50 gallons per day per person for domestic use only. If water is used for other purposes such as fire fighting, than more water will be required. In addition to the well, a water pump is necessary. These fall into 5 categories: Plunger or Reciprocating type, Turbine, Centrifugal, Rotary and Ejector. These pumps not only push or pull the water from the well into the house, but also provide pressure to allow the water to flow through the pipes within the house. In most cases, a storage water tank is included in the package and these tanks can cause a problem with condensation. One solution is to set the tank over a sand bed to collect the condensation without causing a problem. A hand pump over the well can be very convenient when electric power is lost. If a hand pump is installed, it should be the completely enclosed type.

When the source of water supply is brought into the house, a water main valve must be installed to shut off the water supply within the house to make pipe repairs. From the main water line, a branch is connected to the domestic hot water tank, if the water is not heated as an integral part of the hot water heating system. This tank should be large enough to hold at least a one hour supply of hot water at the rate of 8 gallons per hour per person. All hot water tanks should have a pressure relief valve to prevent excessive pressure due to overheated water throwing off steam inside the tank. Be sure to install the pressure release facing downward and close to the floor.

235

From the main water line, the cold water is carried through piping to all plumbing fixtures requiring cold water and from the hot water source the piping is carried to all plumbing fixtures requiring hot water. All hot and cold water lines should have a valve or water shut-off at all fixtures to make repairs at the fixture without shutting the water off from the entire house. Pipings used for water are: galvanized iron, wrought iron, brass and copper. Hard water will deposit a coating of lime and gypsum on the inside of the pipe and a water softener should be used.

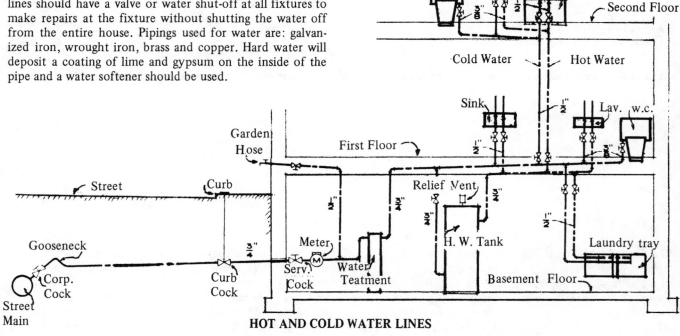

HOT AND COLD WATER LINES

BRANCH WATER SUPPLY PIPING AND   DRAINAGE AND VENT CONNECTORS

Fixture	Branch Hot Water	Branch Cold Water	Soil or Waste Connections	Vent Connections
Water closet	---	1/2 in.	3 in. 4 in.	2 in.
Lavatory	1/2 in.	1/2 in.	1-1/4 in.	1-1/4 in.
Bathtub	1/2 in.	1/2 in.	1-1/2 in.	1-1/4 in.
Sink	1/2 in.	1/2 in.	1-1/2 in.	1-1/4 in.
Laundry tray	1/2 in.	1/2 in.	1-1/2 in.	1-1/4 in.
Sink and tray combination	1/2 in.	1/2 in.	1-1/2 in.	1-1/4 in.
Shower	1/2 in.	1/2 in.	2 in.	1-1/4 in.
Dishwasher	1/2 in.	1/2 in.	1-1/2 in.	1-1/4 in.
Washing machine	1/2 in.	1/2 in.	3 in.	2 in.

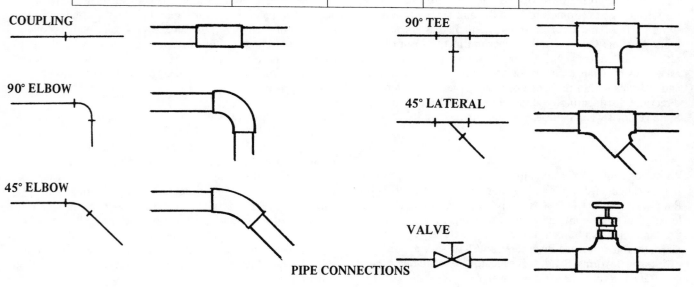

COUPLING

90° ELBOW

45° ELBOW

90° TEE

45° LATERAL

VALVE

PIPE CONNECTIONS

236

Tank Cap. Gal.	Gas and Input in Thousands BTUH				Rec. 60° Rise G.P.H.	Rec. 100° Rise G.P.H.	Approx. Ship. Wt. (lb.)	ROUGHING IN DIMENSIONS (Shown in Inches)							
	Nat.	Mxd.	Mfd.	L.P.				A	B	C	D	E	F	G	H
HIGH-BOY 30	—	—	—	38	53.1	31.9	103	59⅛	55½	13¼	15¾	3	8	2	½
HIGH-BOY 40	—	—	—	38	53.1	31.9	129	59⅝	56	13¼	17¾	3	8	2	½
HIGH-BOY 50	—	—	—	45	63.0	37.8	167	62³⁄₁₆	57⅛	13¼	19¾	4	8	2	½
LOW-BOY 30	—	—	—	36	50.4	30.2	105	48⅞	45¼	13¼	17¾	3	8	2	½
LOW-BOY 40	—	—	—	36	50.4	30.2	139	51⅛	47½	13¼	19¾	3	8	2	½

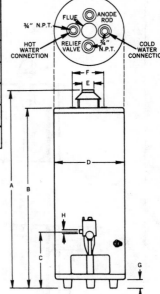

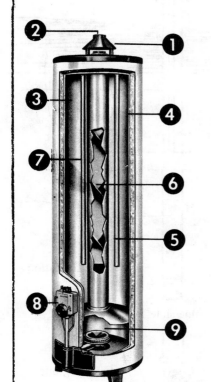

1. Draft Diverter
2. Relief Valve Opening
3. Rheemglas Lining
4. Fiberglas Insulation
5. Dip Tube
6. Flue Baffle
7. Anode Rod
8. Control
9. Burner

GAS HOT WATER HEATER

1. Heat Trap
2. Heating Elements
3. Automatic Temperature Control
4. Relief Valve Opening
5. Cold Water Inlet
6. Electrical Connections
7. Hot Water Outlet
8. Anode Rod
9. Color Styled
10. Fiberglas Insulation
11. Rheemglas Lining
12. Over Temperature Protector

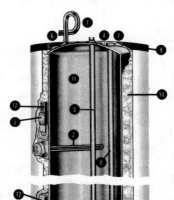

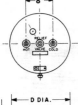

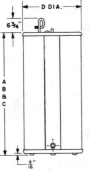

	TANK CAP. GALS.		30	30	40	40	52	52	82	82
	Elements		1	2	1	2	1	2	1	2
A	Hgt. of Heater		38	38	49⅛	49⅛	50½	50½	53⅜	53⅜
B	Hgt. to Water Conn.		38	38	49⅛	49⅛	50½	50½	53⅜	53⅜
C	Hgt. to Junction Box		38	38	49⅛	49⅛	50½	50½	53⅜	53⅜
D	Jacket Dia.		20¼	20¼	20¼	20¼	22¼	22¼	26¼	26¼
HEATING UNIT WATTAGES	N. E. M. A. Standards 230 V. A. C.	Upper		1000		1250		1500		2500
		Lower	1500	600	2000	750	2500	1000	4000	1500
	U.L. Approved 230 V.	Upper		5500		5500		6000		6000
		Lower	5500	5500	5500	5500	6000	6000	6000	6000
	Maximum Wattage Simultaneous Operation			9000		9000		9000		9000
	Approx. Shipping Wt.		91	91	130	130	160	160	250	250

ELECTRIC HOT WATER HEATER

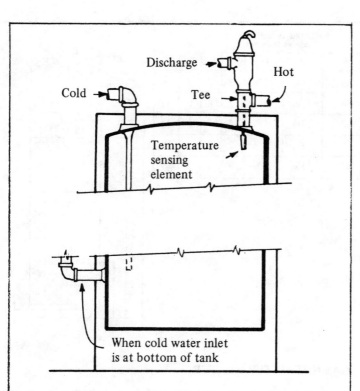

Cold

Discharge

Hot

Tee

Temperature sensing element

When cold water inlet is at bottom of tank

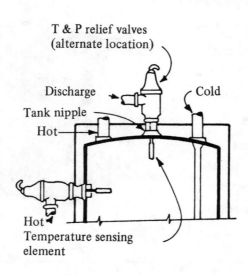

T & P relief valves (alternate location)

Discharge

Cold

Tank nipple

Hot

Hot

Temperature sensing element

Alternate locations for temperature and pressure (T & P) relief valve. Do not install T & P shutoff valve in piping between relief valve and water heater. If necessary, relief valve may be located in hot water discharge pipe from heater.

LOCATION OF RELIEF VALVES ON WATER HEATER

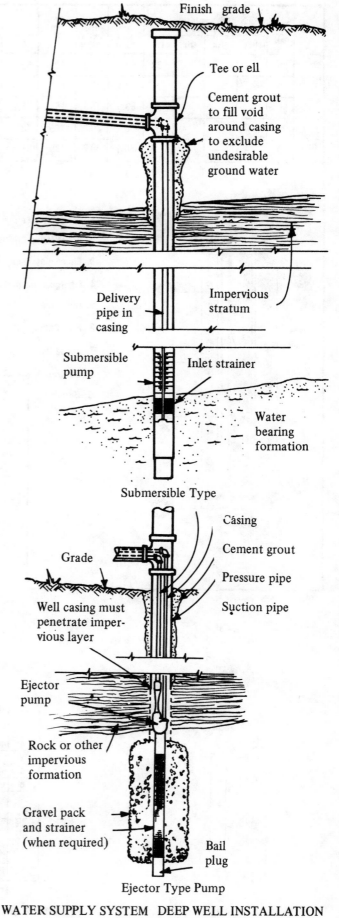

Finish grade

Tee or ell

Cement grout to fill void around casing to exclude undesirable ground water

Delivery pipe in casing

Impervious stratum

Submersible pump

Inlet strainer

Water bearing formation

Submersible Type

Casing

Grade

Cement grout

Pressure pipe

Suction pipe

Well casing must penetrate impervious layer

Ejector pump

Rock or other impervious formation

Gravel pack and strainer (when required)

Bail plug

Ejector Type Pump

WATER SUPPLY SYSTEM DEEP WELL INSTALLATION

SHALLOW WELL INSTALLATION

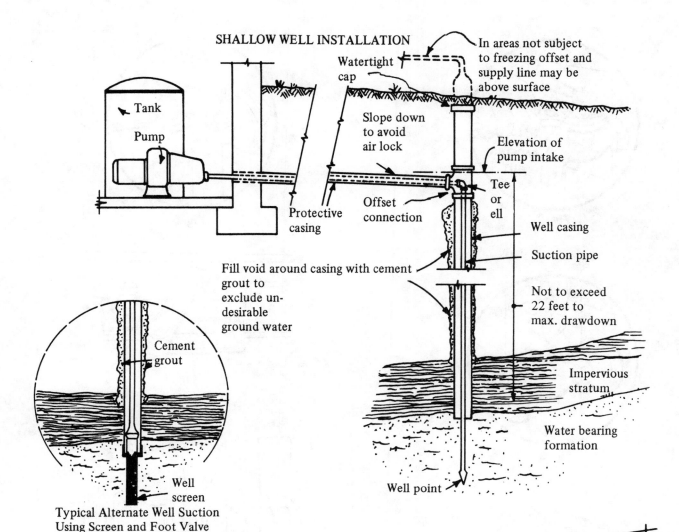

Tank

Pump

Watertight cap

In areas not subject to freezing offset and supply line may be above surface

Slope down to avoid air lock

Elevation of pump intake

Protective casing

Offset connection

Tee or ell

Well casing

Suction pipe

Fill void around casing with cement grout to exclude un-desirable ground water

Not to exceed 22 feet to max. drawdown

Impervious stratum

Water bearing formation

Cement grout

Well screen

Well point

Typical Alternate Well Suction Using Screen and Foot Valve

REPAIR A LEAKING FAUCET

YOUR PROBLEM:

Leaking faucets waste water.
Dripping faucet may cause a spot in the sink.
Constant dripping is annoying

WHAT YOU NEED:

A box of assorted size washers, unless you know the size.

A screwdriver.

An adjustable wrench.

HOW-TO:

1. First turn off the water at the shut-off valve nearest to the faucet you are going to repair. Then turn on the faucet until the water stops flowing. (Fig. 1).

2. Loosen packing nut with wrench (Fig. 2). (Most nuts loosen by turning counter-clockwise.) Use the handle to pull out the valve unit. (Fig. 3)

3. Remove the screw holding the old washer at the bottom of the valve unit. (Fig. 4)

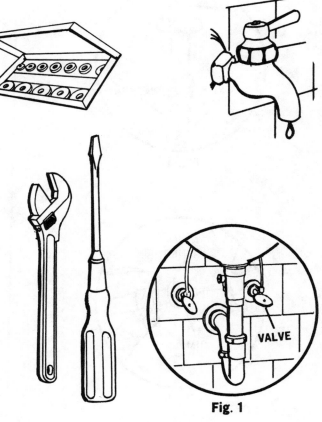

VALVE

Fig. 1

Fig. 2

Fig. 3

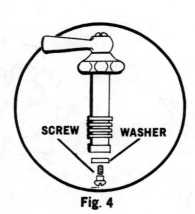

Fig. 4

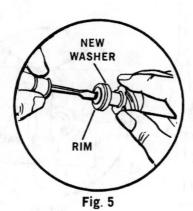

Fig. 5

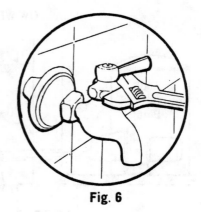

Fig. 6

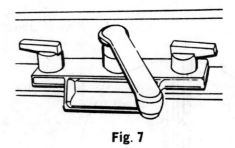

Fig. 7

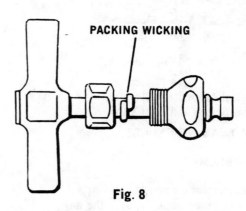

Fig. 8

4. Put in new washer and replace screw. (Fig. 5)

5. Put valve unit back in faucet. Turn handle to the proper position.

6. Tighten the packing nut. (Fig. 6)

7. Turn on the water at the shut-off valve.

Faucets may look different, but they are all built about the same. Mixing faucets, which are used on sinks, laundry tubs, and bathtubs are actually two separate units with the same spout. You'll need to repair each unit separately. (Fig. 7)

Is water leaking around the packing nut? Try tightening the nut. If it still leaks, remove the handle and loosen the packing nut. If there is a washer under it, replace the washer. If there's no washer, you may need to wrap the spindle with "packing wicking". (Fig. 8) Then replace packing nut and handle, and turn water back on at the shut-off valve.

WATER SUPPLY SYSTEM

Advantages	Disadvantages

Plunger type:
    Positive action (force)
    Wide range of speed
    Efficient over wide range of capacity
    Simple construction
    Suitable for hand or power operation
    May be used on almost any depth of well.
    Discharge relatively constant regardless of head

        Discharge pulsates
        Subject to vibration
        Deep-well type must be set directly over well
        Sometimes noisy

Turbine type:
    Simple design
    Discharge steady
    Suitable for direct connection to electric motor
    Practically vibrationless
    Quiet operation
    May be either horizontal or vertical

        Must have very close clearance
        Subject to abrasion damage
        Not suitable for hand operation
        Speed must be relatively constant
        Must be set down near or in water in deep well

Centrifugal type:
    Simple design
    Quiet operation
    Steady discharge
    Efficient when pumping large volumes of water
    Suitable for direct connection to electric motor or for
        belt drive
        May be either horizontal or vertical

        Low efficiency in low capacities
        Low suction-lift (6 to 8 ft.)
        Must be set down near or in water
        Requires relatively large-bore well
        Not suitable for hand operation
        Discharge decreases somewhat as discharge pressure increases

Rotary type:
    Positive action
    Occupies little space
    Wide range of speed
    Steady discharge

        Subject to abrasion
        Likely to get noisy
        Not satisfactory for deep wells

Ejector type:
    Simple construction
    Suitable either for deep or shallow wells
    Need not be set directly over well
    Quiet operation
    Especially suitable for use with pressure system

        Jet nozzle subject to abrasion and clogging
        Limited to wells 120 feet or less in depth
        Discharge decreases somewhat as discharge pressure increases

Chain type:
    Simple
    Easily installed
    Self-priming

        Inefficient
        Limited to shallow wells
        Likely to be unsanitary

Hydraulic ram:
    Simple design
    Low cost
    Uses water for power
    Requires little attention

        Wastes water
        Likely to be noisy
        Not satisfactory for intermittent operation

Siphon:
    Low cost
    Requires no mechanical or hand power except for starting

        Limited to moving water to lower levels
        Requires absolutely airtight pipes

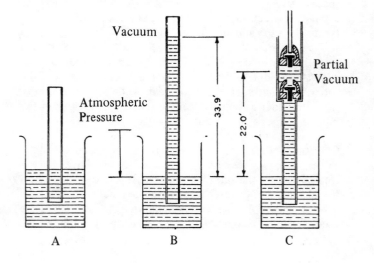

Suction lift caused by atmospheric pressure.
A, No lift or rise inside tube when pressure inside and outside are equal; B, suction lift, with complete vacuum inside tube (theoretical); C, suction lift of pump with partial vacuum inside tube.

Galvanized pipe is mild steel sometimes containing small quantities of copper and molybdenum to increase resistance to corrosion for longer life. Wrought iron is made of puddled iron almost entirely free from impurities which lead to corrosion. This pipe is called "genuine wrought iron" and should be galvanized. Brass piping is available in yellow brass containing 67% copper and 33% zinc. Red brass contains 85% copper and 15% zinc. Yellow brass is used for residential water piping. Copper is available in three types: K, L, & M which is a designation for the thickness of the wall of the pipe. K is designed for underground service and where corrosion conditions are severe. Type L is designed for general plumbing purposes and type M is for use with soldered joints and fittings and is generally used for residential plumbing. Type K & L come in hard or soft tempers, type M is hard only and requires fittings at all turns. Soft copper comes in coils and can be shaped to turn corners but is also easily punctured and damaged.

Cold water lines will condense causing water to drip from the surface of the pipe which may cause damage to the ceiling. To avoid this, the pipe should be covered with insulation. Hot water pipes should also be insulated but for a different reason: to avoid rapid cooling of water which will need to be reheated causing an extra demand on energy.

Fittings required for piping joints include couplings for straight line connection, elbows for 45° turns and 90° turns and tees for branches. Types of fittings are threaded or screwed, flanged, soldered, bronzed, welded or compression. Screw connections are used for pipe up to 4" or more in diameter. Size of pipe is always given in inside dimension. The thread on the outside of the pipe is the male connection and the thread on the inside of the pipe is called the female connection. Flanged connections are fittings with projecting rims or flanges. They are tightened over the pipe by a screwed fitting and bolted to a gasket or seal to prevent leaks. There is also a slip flange connection type of fitting which is a pipe with the end spread out to a larger diameter by a special tool. A nut is slipped over the pipe before enlarging the end and the mate has a flanged screwed connection joining the two together. This type connection is usually done with copper pipe. The soldered joint consists of a fitting which is inserted over the pipe ends joining both ends together. The connection is heated with a torch and solder is applied to the connection. The solder fills the space between the pipe and the fitting and is distributed by capillary attraction over the entire surface of the joint between the pipe and the fitting. When soldering, be sure the surfaces to be soldered are cleaned with emery cloth and soldering paste covers the joints to be soldered. Do not allow the solder to be melted by the direct flame from the torch, it should melt from the heat of the pipe. It is impossible to solder a joint by making repairs with water in the pipe, the pipe must be completely dry.

Control of water through pipes is accomplished with gate valves, check valves and globe valves. Some valves have a small wheel on the side of the handle. If you turn this wheel it will release any water trapped in the pipe but be sure the valve is closed before turning the wheel. Gate valves are used to shut off completely the water supply. Globe valves are used to throttle the flow of water and check valves are used to prevent water from flowing in the opposite direction and also when there is a possibility of water flowing in reverse because of back pressure. Other valves are cock, bibb and faucet. Faucets are used in plumbing fixtures, such as sinks, lavatories and tubs. Valves for connecting to garden hose are called hose bibbs or sill cock.

All piping should be properly supported with pipe hangers. These are brackets attached directly to wood holding the pipe in position. Hangers should be spaced about 10'-0" apart. If you use copper pipe be sure to use copper hangers.

To trace the route of a water supply from the street to the house, the local water utility authority, upon request, will excavate the street to open or expose the water main and install a tap or connection to the property line. A gooseneck type fitting is installed to allow for settlement of the pipe. Two valves, a corporation cock and a curb cock, are located on the line. The curb cock has a long stem reaching up to the level of the ground so that water can be disconnected without entering the home or without excavation. This completes the work of the utility authority, from here on the owner is responsible. From the curb cock a 3/4" copper tubing is installed below the frost line in a trench to the building and, immediately inside the building, a service cock or valve is installed which is used to shut off the water throughout the entire building. Following the service valve is a water meter which measures the amount of water consumed. Following the meter is a drain valve for removing or draining all the water in the piping within the house. If water softeners are used, hose bibbs can be connected without going through the water softener, otherwise the water softener is connected next in line and from there to the source of hot water supply. A 3/4" cold water line is installed in the basement ceiling and 1/2" lines directly to the fixtures. Manufacturers catalogs on selection of plumbing fixtures will tell the spacing and height above the floor for all water lines. Each pipe or riser is installed 2'-0" higher than the fixture with the ends capped to provide an air chamber to reduce knocking or hammering of water lines. Valves are installed under each riser so that repairs can be made without shutting off the water for the entire house.

The hot water system has a 3/4" pipe installed in the basement ceiling and 1/2" lines directly to the fixtures. (Hot water tanks will collect sediment and rust the bottom. Water needs to be drained at least once a year.) The cold water enters the tank, leaving at about 130° F. There is a setting at tank to adjust water temperature.

If water is from a private source, corporation cock, curb cock and water meter are not required. All else remains the same. Keep at least 6" between hot and cold water piping so that the temperature in either pipe is not affected by the other. When installing the riser to the fixtures, the cold water line is always on the right side.

WASTE LINES

Pipes carrying waste are not under pressure and depend upon gravity for removing waste. The minimum pitch or slope of pipe is 1/8" per foot to facilitate even flow. In order to prevent decomposition of waste in the pipe, a circulation of air through the waste piping must be provided. The air circulation dilutes poisonous gases, retards pipe corrosion and maintains a balanced atmospheric pressure in the system. This is accomplished by extending air or vent stacks up through the roof.

Check local codes for plumbing, some require a minimum distance for vents from doors or windows and minimum pipe size, and height above roof. Cleanouts are provided in waste lines to clean out the line if blockage should occur. These are located at the foot of each rise and at the change of direction of pipe. Maximum distance between cleanouts in horizontal lines are about 50'-0". A cleanout is a threaded plug which is removable for pipe access releasing any blockage. Sewer or waste lines produce offensive and harmful gases which would permeate the entire house through the fixtures unless a trap is installed. Traps are nothing more than an offset in the waste pipe designed to retain water which then forms a seal. Traps must be installed under all plumbing fixtures except the water closet. Water in the bowl acts as a built in trap. Vent stacks though the roof discharge gases to the outside.

The main soil pipe in residentail construction is 4" cast iron and the branch waste and vents usually are 1-1/2" or 2". The majority of pipe used for waste lines is asphalt coated cast iron known as soil pipe. It is manufactured in 10'-0" sections with fittings for turns, bends and sweeps. One end of the pipe has a "bell shape forming the female section. Sections are joined with the end of the pipe fitted into the "bell" and they are sealed with a packing called oakum and molten lead joints. All exposed waste piping is chrome coated brass.

For a distance of 5'-0" away from the house outside the building, cast iron pipe must be used. From that point on the sewage piping may be vitrified clay, concrete or fiber piping, except where there are trees, cast iron should be continued to prevent tree roots from blocking the lines. All waste drainage lines should be as straight and direct as possible in order to minimize friction. Changes in direction of drains should be made with easy bends so as not to restrict the flow. Standard plumbing fittings used are : T or 90° bend, Y or 45° bend, TY, 1/6 bend, 1/8 bend, 1/16 bend, and 1/4 bend. T fittings should not be used for waste lines, but can be used for vent lines. Pipes of different sizes are connected by a reducer or increaser fitting.

Flashing of vent line through the roof is accomplished with a pre-formed sheet copper flashing, caulked into the pipe and turned under the roof covering. All joints must be gas and water tight. In addition to cast iron piping, vetrified clay pipe and wrought iron are used. Becoming more popular is polyvinyl chloride (PVC) with sealed slip joints of special mastic. Some codes may prohibit use of PVC.

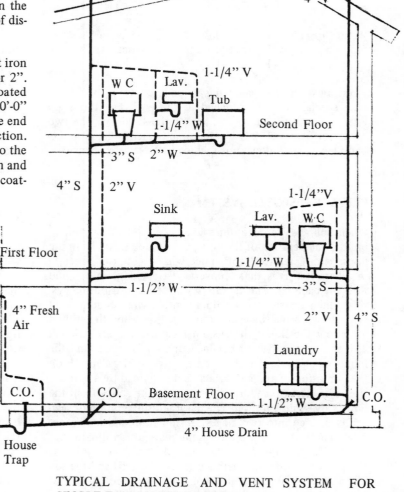

TYPICAL DRAINAGE AND VENT SYSTEM FOR SINGLE FAMILY DWELLINGS

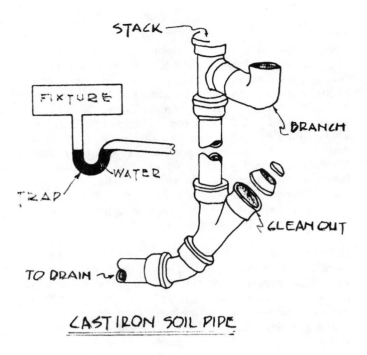

STACK

FIXTURE

BRANCH

WATER

TRAP

CLEAN OUT

TO DRAIN

CAST IRON SOIL PIPE

Plumbing fixtures are classified according to their use as follows:

SOIL	SCULLERY	BATHING
Water Closet	Kitchen Sink	Lavatories
Slop sink	Pantry Sink	Bath Tubs
	Laundry Tray	Showers

Lavatories may be wall hung or pedestal type. Wall hung have special brackets attached to the wall. Lavatories are 32" above the floor to the top of the lavatory. The two models of water closets are siphon jet, which is the more expensive and wash down bowl, which is the less expensive.

PRIVATE DISPOSAL SYSTEM

When public sewers are not available, a private system is built. The operation of the system is simple. Waste from the house is directed to a septic tank, which is built of concrete or fiberglass. This tank converts waste solids into liquid through bacteria. The liquid flows into a distribution system which distributes the liquid into a wide underground area. Between the sun evaporating the liquid and the ground absorbing the liquid, the system becomes very functional. The size of the system depends upon local codes and the number of people it is designed to serve. It also depends on the condition of the soil, which is determined by a percolation test. The procedure is to separate the solids from the liquids by sedimentation. The natural disintegration of sewage is divided into two stages, putrefaction and oxidation. The first stage will produce ammonia, carbon dioxide gas and hydrogen sulphide which causes dark discolorations. As the process continues, methane gas is produced and the solids change to humus and decompose no more. A lack of oxygen causes a slow but continuous decay called anaerobic bacteria. The ammonia is oxidized to nitrates and the sul-

phur compounds to sulphate (plant food). The process than consists of removing the solids to a receptable (septic tank) where they putrefy and then lead the liquid into the soil or drain field where it oxidizes without odor or danger to health. Later, bacteria acts to break down the solids resulting in sludge which needs to be removed from the tank about every three years or more.

The tile lines in the distribution system are placed on a gravel and crushed stone bed and are about 1/4" apart with open joints. These are placed about 16" below the surface of the ground and are sloped about 1/2" per foot. Length of tile and size of tile are determined by local code based on number of occupants and the absorption rate of the soil. Usually from 100' to 300' of tile is required for the average residence.

Detergents will interfere with the bacterial action in the septic tanks. Waste from washing machines should empty into a separate drainage system. Water tight or sealed wells should be at least 100' away from any sewage drainage systems. No structure of any kind or driveways are allowed over a disposal system. Avoid swampy land, muck soil, flowerbeds, vegetable gardens, roadways or pavements in locating disposal systems. Porous soil, in a location where disposal field will not be disturbed, yet may be easily inspected, is most suitable. The system should run in as straight a line as possible in the same direction as the sewer pipe leaving the house. The exception to this is on slopes where it is necessary to run the disposal field across the slope to slow the flow and allow absorption. While laying out the system it is wise to plan for later extension of the disposal field. Depth of tank depends on inlet grade level from house. Grade should be 1" for every 4 feet of pitch. The minimum size tank for any house should be 500 gallons. The larger the tank, the more efficient it is. A tank 50% larger than the minimum will double the time between cleanouts. Depth should be at least 5'-0" regardless of other dimensions. If garbage disposal is used, the tank should be 50% larger than minimum.

To build a concrete tank, either construct a wood form or rent a standard form from county agents, health departments or building material dealers. If a wooden form is built, the hole should be dug so as to use the earth sides of the hole for the outside form. Walls and floor should be 6" thick concrete. Pour the floor of the tank before building the forms. To make sure the tank is the proper depth and in alignment with sewer pipe from the house, make a 2" x 4" frame with inside dimensions equal to the outside dimensions of the tank. Drive stakes around this frame making sure it is level, then nail stakes to the frame. Hang the plywood form inside this frame by nailing planks across the top of form long enough to overlap the sides and hang onto the frame. Center the form inside the frame 6" away from it on all sides and nail the overlapping planks to the frame. Use tees for inlets and outlets before pouring concrete. Tees must be carefully lined up and tied in place before pouring concrete. Join one length of pipe to each tee so that these units may be set into the concrete as part of the tank. The bottom of inlet pipe should be 9" from the top of the tank. The bottom of outlet pipe should be 12" from the top.

Tees should extend 12" or more below flow line. The kinds of pipe used are asphalt impregnated fibre, cast iron, vitrified clay and concrete. 6" pipe is generally used for concrete, tile or clay and 4" pipe for cast iron or fibre. Mortar or bituminous compounds are generally used to join tile pipe, lead and oakum on cast iron. Fibre pipes have a slip joint wedged into position. The sewer line from the house to the tank should be solid (not perforated).

The tank cover can be of reinforced concrete with manholes over the inlet and outlet. Sectional covers of concrete with handles make cleaning easier. These sections should be about 12" wide and as long as the tank is wide overall. A form can be made from 2" x 4" in ladder form. Lay the form over asphalt paper before pouring concrete. When the sections are in place, they can be made water tight by sealing the edges with asphalt or mortar. Distribution box covers can be made in the same manner. Piping from the tank to the distribution box should be solid.

Before building the distribution box, lay the pipe at the proper grade from the tank to the distribution box. The purpose of the distribution box is to direct the effulent flow into all the disposal lines in equal quantity. It can be made in several shapes and sizes. A rectangular shaped box with the long sides running in the same direction as the long sides of the septic tank is most common. If there are many disposal lines in the box, it is better built at right angles to the septic tank. Construct this box of concrete with the inlet and outlet pipe ends set into the concrete. Inlet pipe should be 5" above floor. Set outlets 9" apart. All outlets must be set carefully at exactly the same depth so that each line carries an equal part of the flow. Bricks set on edge in wet concrete floor of the box may be used as baffles to spread the flow as it enters the box from the inlet pipe. Install two or more outlets than are needed to plan for expansion. Plug up these extra outlets until needed. The size of the disposal field will depend upon the rapidity with which the soil can absorb water. A standard percolation test (perc test) is used to determine rate per foot of soil absorption and square footage is tranlated into linear feet. To test the soil, dig a hole one foot square to the depth of the planned trench, usually from 18" to 24" deep. Fill this hole with water and let is seep away so that the earth becomes saturated. Insert a rule in the hole and fill the hole with water to a depth of at least 6". Keep track of the time required for the water to seep entirely away. Divide this time by the number of inches of water poured into the hole. From page 248, estimate the necessary square footage of disposal field trench which is necessary. Add 25% for use of garbage disposal. Do not make this test if the ground is frozen.

Open joints or perforated pipe should be used from the distribution box to the disposal field. The grades of the disposal trenches should be from 2 to 4 inches per 100 feet and no branch should be longer than 100 feet. On steep slopes lines should run across slope. Disposal trenches should be deep enough so that at least 6" of gravel or crushed stone may be laid below the pipe. After pipe is laid, it should be covered with the same coarse gravel to a height of two inches above the crown of the pipe before back fill is added.

Straw or untreated building paper should be laid directly over the gravel to allow back fill to settle above gravel and to prevent it from filtering into gravel and pipe openings. Care in laying disposal lines so that no low spots occur will pay off in many more years of service. Water logged soil will kill the bacteria necessary to purify the effluent.

Tanks should be cleaned when 18 to 20 inches of sludge and scum have accumulated. If chemicals are used, handle them carefully without damaging plumbing fixtures or lines. Lye and caustic soda should never be introduced into the system. In general, length of tanks should not be less than, nor more than 3 times the width. If the entire system is in continuous use, freezing in colder climates is unlikely. An additional tank may be added in series to an existing tank if the system is too small without rebuilding the entire system. Do not allow roof or surface drains to enter the system as this additional water will overload the unit and slow down bacteria action. A cleanout between the house and the tank and between the tank and the distribution box may come in handy should blockage occur. Extend this cleanout with a tee connection to above ground level, tightly capped.

If the system is not properly designed or built, it will become a health hazard causing possible typhoid fever, dysentery, diarrhea, cholera and other diseases. It is poor practice and illegal to discharge wastes into streams, oceans or any body of water. Drainage fields must be located where there are no trees, otherwise the roots will interfere. When inspecting septic tanks for repair or emptying, do not inspect with an open flame because the gases produced by decomposing sewage may explode and cause serious injury.

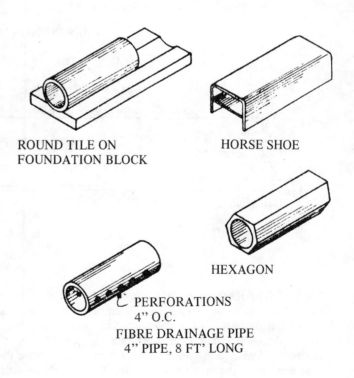

ROUND TILE ON FOUNDATION BLOCK

HORSE SHOE

HEXAGON

PERFORATIONS 4" O.C.
FIBRE DRAINAGE PIPE
4" PIPE, 8 FT' LONG

DRAINAGE TILE

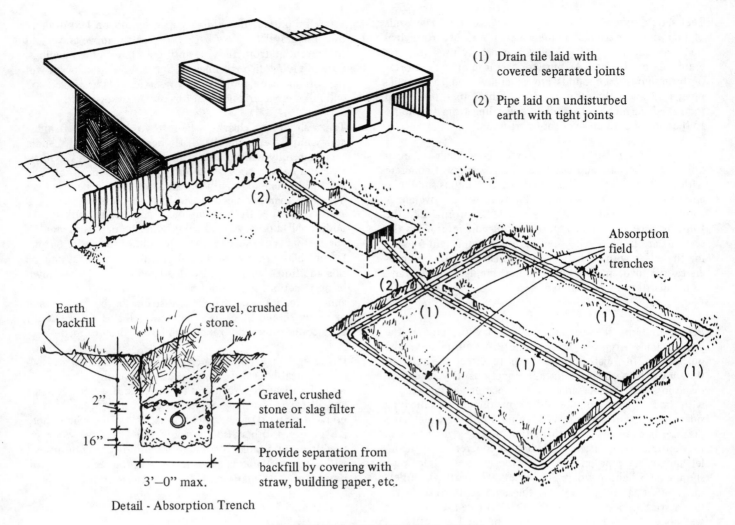

(1) Drain tile laid with covered separated joints

(2) Pipe laid on undisturbed earth with tight joints

Absorption field trenches

Earth backfill

Gravel, crushed stone.

Gravel, crushed stone or slag filter material.

2"

16"

Provide separation from backfill by covering with straw, building paper, etc.

3'–0" max.

Detail - Absorption Trench

ABSORPTION FIELD INSTALLATION

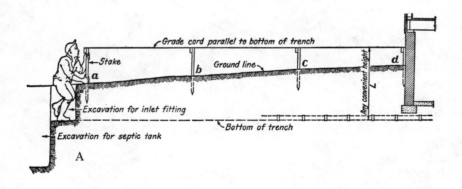

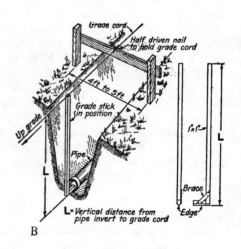

Figure 2.–Establishing grade for sewer. A, 2- by 4-inch stakes are set each side of the trench at convenient distances a, b, c, and d. Then a board is nailed horizontally on the stakes at d, at a convenient height above the bottom of the trench, that is, the bottom of the sewer leaving the house. A board is nailed likewise to the stakes at a, the same height above the inlet to the tank that d is above the bottom of the trench. Similarly, boards are set at b and c by sighting from a to d so the tops of the intermediate boards will be in line. B, The exact grade of the sewer is obtained by measuring from the grade cord with the 1- by 1-inch stick, shown in detail. The length of the stick must equal the height of the board above sewer at d.

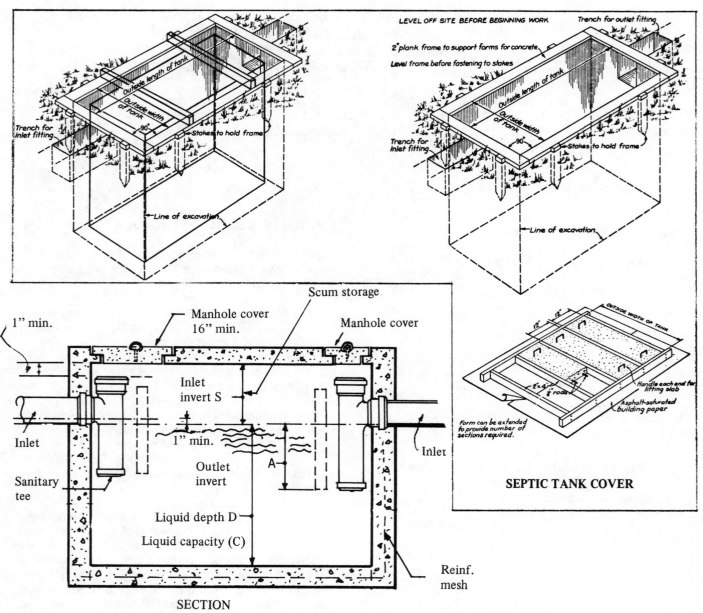

LEVEL OFF SITE BEFORE BEGINNING WORK

2" plank frame to support forms for concrete

Level frame before fastening to stakes

Trench for outlet fitting

Outside length of tank

Outside width of tank

Trench for inlet fitting

Line of excavation

Stakes to hold frame

90°

Trench for inlet fitting

Outside length of tank

Outside width of tank

Line of excavation

Stakes to hold frame

90°

1" min.

Manhole cover 16" min.

Scum storage

Manhole cover

Inlet invert S

1" min.

Inlet

Sanitary tee

Outlet invert

A

Liquid depth D

Liquid capacity (C)

Inlet

Reinf. mesh

SECTION

SEPTIC TANK COVER

OUTSIDE WIDTH OF TANK

12" 12"

2" x 4"

¼ rods

Handle each end for lifting slab

Asphalt-saturated building paper

Form can be extended to provide number of sections required.

A - Approx. 40% of the depth D.

D - Not less than 30" depth. Greater than 6 ft. should not be considered in tank capacity.

S - Not less than 15% of the liquid capacity C.

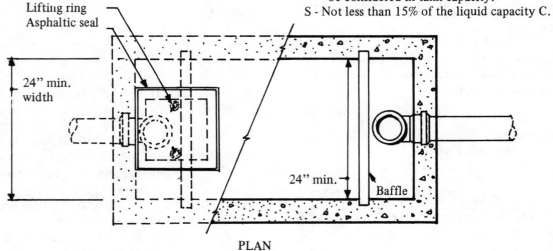

Lifting ring
Asphaltic seal

24" min. width

24" min.

Baffle

PLAN

SINGLE COMPARTMENT SEPTIC TANK

CAPACITIES, DIMENSIONS, AND CONCRETE MATERIALS FOR SEPTIC TANKS SERVING INDIVIDUAL DWELLINGS								
Maximum number of persons served	Liquid capacity of tank in gallons	Recommended inside dimensions				Materials for concrete 1:2½:4 mix		
		Width	Length	Liquid depth	Total depth	Cement sacks	Sand cu. yds.	Gravel cu. yds.
4 or less	500	3'-0"	6'-0"	4'-0"	5'-0"	16	1-1/2	2-1/2
6	600	3'-0"	7'-0"	4'-0"	5'-0"	17	1-3/4	2-3/4
8	750	3'-6"	7'-6"	4'-0"	5'-0"	19	2	3
10	900	3'-6"	8'-6"	4'-0"	5'-0"	21	2-1/4	3-1/4
12	1100	4'-0"	8'-6"	4'-6"	5'-6"	24	2-1/4	3-1/2
14	1200	4'-0"	9'-0"	4'-6"	5'-6"	25	2-1/2	3-3/4
16	1500	4'-6"	10'-0"	4'-6"	5'-6"	28	2-3/4	4-1/4

TABLE I
Minimum Capacities for Septic Tanks

Number of Bedrooms	Min. Liquid Capacity of Tank in Gallons*†
2 or less	500
3	600
4	750
5	900
6	1100
7	1300
8	1500
12	2000

*† Increase minimum liquid capacity by 50% when household garbage grinder discharges into system.

TABLE II

Data for Determining Field Requirement from Percolation Tests

Average time required for water to fall one inch in minutes	Effective absorption area (in bottom of disposal trench) in sq. ft. per bedroom
2 or less	50*
3	60*
4	70*
5	80*
10	100*
15	120*
30	180
60	240
Over 60 unsuitable except for special design with seepage pits	

*Note: A minimum of 150 square feet of effective absorption area (100 lineal feet of 18-inch trench) shall be provided per living unit. See example I.

TABLE III

Size and Minimum Spacing Requirements for Disposal Trenches

Width of at bottom in inches	Depth of in inches	Effective Absorption Area in Sq.Ft. per lin. ft.	Minimum Spacing of lines c to c in feet
18 Min.	18 to 30	1.5	6
24	18 to 30	2.0	6
30	18 to 36	2.5	7.5
36 Max.	24 to 36	3.0	9.0

METHOD OF MAKING PERCOLATION TEST

To provide data on representative soil conditions of site make at least 2 percolation tests at different locations on the disposal field as follows:

a. Dig or bore holes with horizontal dimension of approximately 6 to 12 inches and with straight sides to the estimated depth of the absorption trench.

b. Fill hole with water and allow to seep away. Then fill hole with water to a depth of 12".

c. Record the time, in minutes, required for last 6" of water to completely seep away. Divide the time by 6 to obtain average time for 1 inch of water to seep away.

d. Determine from Table II, seepage area (in square feet) required per bedroom.

Note: Because many seasonal factors affect the results of percolation tests, judgment is required in analyzing these results. If the tests are not conducted during a wet season they should be repeated until the moisture conditions of the soil approach those obtaining during the wet season. In no case shall tests be made in filled or frozen ground. Where fissured rock formations are encountered tests shall be made only under the direction and supervision of the State Department of Health.

EXAMPLE I

Assume: 3-bedroom dwelling
Results of percolation tests:
Test No. 1 - 5 minutes
Test No. 2 - 10 minutes
Average time: 15 − 2 = 7½ minutes

Calculations: From Table I - 600 gal. tank required
From Table II - interpolate between 5 minutes and 10 minutes = 90 sq.ft. per bedroom
90 x 3 = 270 sq.ft. total required for three bedrooms.
From Table III - 2 ft. wide trench = 2 sq.ft. per lin.ft.
270 − 2 = 135 linear feet.

Conclusion:	Use a 600 gal. septic tank
	Use 2 lines 70 ft. long and 24 inches wide spaced 6 ft. apart.
	Note: Other trench widths may be considered where desirable.

EXAMPLE II

Assume:
3-bedroom dwelling
Proposed seepage pit to be 4 feet in dia.
Excavation reveals following soil conditions:
    5 ft. hardpan
    3 ft. sandy clay
    6 ft. tight clay
    unlimited sand and gravel
Inlet to be 3 feet below ground

Calculations:

1   A 4 ft. outside diameter pit will provide:
pi (3.142) x diameter x depth side area of pit, or:
3.142 x 4 ft. x 1 ft. = 12½ sq.ft. of wall area per foot of depth

If total depth were sandy clay then required seepage area would be:

2   3 (bedrooms) x 50 (From Table IV)
    = 150 sq. ft.

Area above sand and gravel actually available for absorption is:

3 ft. above inlet:	= 0
2 ft. hardpan: Unsuitable	= 0
3 ft. sandy clay: 3 x 12½ (from (1) above)	= 37½ sq.ft.
6 ft. tight clay: Unsuitable	= 0
Total wall area above sand and gravel suitable for seepage area	= 37½ sq.ft.

Total seepage area required (from (2) above	= 150 sq.ft.
3 Additional seepage area required: 150 − 37½	= 112½ s.f.

The additional area must be obtained from the sand and gravel below the tight clay. The sand and gravel will provide 50/20 (from Table IV) or 2½ times that of the sandy clay.
Then: Area of sand and gravel required:
    112½ − 2½ (from (3) above)
                      = 45 sq.ft.
Depth into sand and gravel required:
    45 − 12½ (from (1) above)
                      = 3½ ft.

Depth of pit required	5 ft. (hardpan) + 3 ft. (sandy clay) + 6 ft. (tight clay) + 3½ ft. (sand and gravel) = 17½ ft.

GAS PIPING

Since gas is highly dangerous, all joints must be leakproof. Gas is supplied by the Public Utility Company or stored in tanks on the site. The utility is responsible for the piping into the building including the gas meter. From that point it becomes the responsibility of the owner to run the gas piping to the appliance or fixture. If gas is supplied at high pressure, a pressure regulating valve is furnished and installed by the Utility Company. A shut-off valve is placed on the main line to shut off the entire system in addition to each fixture having a valve.

Gas piping should be of best quality, standard, black, wrought iron or steel pipe. The fittings should be of galvanized, malleable iron with cocks and valves of brass. A certain amount of moisture is contained in gas and all pipes should be straight without sags and pitched back so that condensation will flow back into the service pipe or the piping should be dropped. Gas piping should not be bent; change in directions are made with screw couplings and changes in pipe size with reducing fittings. Connections at fixtures should be made with flexible pipe to allow for positioning of fixture or appliance.

HEATING

26

INTRODUCTION

Heat is transferred from warm to cold surfaces by three methods: Radiation, Convection or Conduction. Radiation heat flows through space to a cooler surface in the same way that light travels. The air is not warm but the cooler object it strikes becomes warm. An open fire in a fireplace is an example of Radiation. Convection heat is caused by a warm surface heating the air around it. The warm air rises and the cooler air takes its place causing a convection of current. Hot air registers are an example of convection heat. Conduction heat moves through a solid material. Frying eggs in a pan is an example of conduction heat.

With the three types of heat, you may use either: wet heat, such as hot water or steam, or dry heat, such as electric or air.

Air heat requires a series of metal ducts to distribute the heat throughout the house. If air conditioning is planned, air heat would be the most economical choice of heat because the same metal ducts are used for heating and cooling. If any other type of heating system is used with air conditioning, a separate ducting system will need to be installed in addition to the heating system.

The fuel needed for any heating system is oil, gas, electricity, coal and sun. Insulation plays a very important part in heating and cooling. Heat is measured in BTU (British Thermal Unit), which is the amount of heat required to raise the temperature of one pound of water 1° F. Basically our purpose is to design a heating system to supply the heat lost in a given space and to maintain the required temperature within that space. Heat flows from a high temperature to a low temperature. Warm objects lose heat to cold objects. In the case of a heated house, the warmed air inside is attracted to the cold air outside and that loss must be replaced by the heating system. The ouside wall of the house serves as a barrier between the warm and the cold and heat loss or retention depends on the construction of the external walls. The basic formula for computing heat loss is as follows: area, multiplied by wall effectiveness, multiplied by the degree temperature difference. The area of concern is only the surface of wall exposed to a temperature less than room temperature, such as an exterior wall. By surface is meant wall, glass, doors, floor, roof and wall area exposed to cold temperatures. There is no heat loss between adjacent walls if each room is heated the same temperature. Wall effectiveness is the ability of a certain building material to resist the flow of heat. All building materials have a heat loss factor. Smaller numbers of heat loss indicate good insulation. The heat loss factors are known as heat transmission coefficients, K factors or U factors. Heat transmission coefficients will vary from 0.07 for well insulated walls to 1.13 for glass and doors. Degree temperatue is the difference between the inside room temperature and the coldest temperature likely to occur in a given locality expressed in Fahrenheit. It is common practice to use 70° for inside design temperature. The outside temperature is not the coldest ever recorded, that would be uneconomical. See table for outside temperatures in various parts of the country. The basic rule for heat loss may be stated as follows: A = area, U = heat transmission coefficient, T = temperature difference, (AxUxT). Heating units such as furnaces or boilers are rated in BTU capacity and the results of the heat loss formula will determine the number of BTU or size of heating unit.

Another factor to be considered in designing a system is infiltration, which is amount of heat loss through doors, windows, cracks and fireplaces. In using the heat loss infiltration table, multiply the factor by the cubic content of the room, not the wall area, (cubic content is length x width x height, measured in feet expressed in cubic feet). One more insert must be included to complete all known factors called correction factor (see chart) which is multiplied by the total BTU factor for a total BTU. When the grand total is computed, select the next highest rated BTU heating unit.

The purpose of this formula is to give some insight as to what is involved and how heating systems are calculated. It is not the scope of this chapter to teach the complicated task of sizing or designing a heating system unless one is familiar with the engineering of heating. It is suggested that a heating engineer or a heating contractor be consulted.

CORRECTION FACTOR							
OUTSIDE TEMP.	INSIDE TEMPERATURE						
	50	55	60	65	70	75	80
30	.25	.32	.40	48	57	.67	.77
20	.38	.45	.54	.62	.71	.81	.92
10	.50	.58	.67	.76	.86	.96	1.07
0	.63	.71	.80	.90	1.00	1.11	1.23
-10	.75	.84	.94	1.04	1.14	1.26	1.38
-20	.88	.97	1.07	1.17	1.29	1.41	1.54
-30	1.01	1.10	1.21	1.31	1.43	1.55	1.69

TABLE 1

Outside Design Temperatures in Various Parts of the United States

Connecticut		New York	
Bridgeport	0	New York City	0
Hartford	−5	Albany	−9
New Haven	0	Buffalo	−5
Kansas		Ohio	
Concordia	−10	Cleveland	−2
Dodge City	−11	Columbus	−5
New Jersey		Washington	
Newark	5	Seattle	18
Paterson	−5	Spokane	−15

Although every heating system must be individually designed, there are certain elements common to all. For example, the total heat loss through the walls, ceiling, and floor of each room must be balanced by the heat delivered to each room. The first step, therefore, is to calculate the heat losses.

Heat escapes from a room in two ways:

1. Transmission through walls, ceiling, and floor
2. Infiltration through cracks around windows and doors

Heat loss by transmission will increase in proportion to the area A of the surfaces of the room, the difference between the inside temperature and outside temperature $(t_i - t_o)$, and the coefficient of transmisson U:

$$H = AU (t_i - t_o)$$

Where:
H = Heat loss (Btu/hr.)
A = Area (sq. ft.)
U = Coefficient of transmission (see Table II)
t_i = Inside temperature (70°F is often assumed)
t_o = Outside temperature (assume 15°F above lowest recorded temperature; 0°F is used for New York, Boston, and Philadelphia)

TABLE II
Coefficients of Transmission (U)
(Btu per hour per sq. ft. per degree)

Walls

Wood siding, plastered interior, no insulation	0.26
Wood siding, plastered interior, 2" insulation	0.10
Brick veneer, plastered interior, no insulation	0.26
Brick veneer, plastered interior, 2" insulation	0.10
8" solid brick, no interior finish	0.50
8" solid brick, furred and plastered interior	0.31
12" solid brick, no interior finish	0.36
12" solid brick, furred and plastered interior	0.24
10" cavity brick, no interior finish	0.34
10" cavity brick, furred and plastered interior	0.24

Partitions

Wood frame, plastered, no insulation	0.34
4" solid brick, no finish	0.60
4" solid brick, plastered one side	0.51
4" solid brick, plastered both sides	0.44
6" solid brick, no finish	0.53
8" solid brick, no finish	0.48

Ceilings and Floors

Frame, plastered ceiling, no flooring, no insulation	0.61
Frame, plastered ceiling, no flooring, 2" insulation	0.12
Frame, plastered ceiling, no flooring, 4" insulation	0.06
Frame, no ceiling, wood flooring, no insulation	0.34
Frame, no ceiling, wood flooring, 2" insulation	0.09
Frame, no ceiling, wood flooring, 4" insulation	0.06
Frame, plastered ceiling, wood flooring, no insulation	0.28
Frame, plastered ceiling, wood flooring, 2" insulation	0.09
Frame, plastered ceiling, wood flooring, 4" insulation	0.06
3" bare concrete slab	0.68
3" concrete slab, parquet flooring	0.45
3" concrete slab, wood flooring on sleepers	0.25

Roofs

Asphalt shingled piched roof, no ceiling, no insulation	0.52
Asphalt shingled pitched roof, no ceiling, 2" insulation	0.11
Asphalt shingled pitched roof, plastered ceiling, no insulation	0.31
Asphalt shingled pitched roof, plastered ceiling, 2" insulation	0.10
Built-up flat roof, no ceiling, no insulation	0.49
Built-up roof, no ceiling, 2" board insulation	0.12
Built-up flat roof, plastered ceiling, no insulation	0.31
Built-up flat roof, plastered ceiling, 2" board insulation	0.11

Windows and Doors

Single glazed windows	1.13
Double glazed windows	0.45
Triple glazed windows	0.28
Glass blocks (8" x 8" x 4")	0.56
1 3/4" solid wood doors	0.44
1 3/4" solid wood door with storm door	0.27

TABLE III	
Volume of infiltration (V) (cubic feet per foot of crack per hour)	
Doors not weatherstripped	111
Doors weatherstripped	55
Windows not weatherstripped	39
Windows weatherstripped	24

The coefficient of transmission is a factor which indicates the amount of heat in Btu that will be transmitted through each square foot of surface in one hour for each degree of temperature difference. A poor insulator will have a high U value; a good insulator will have a low U value. U values have been computed by tests for a number of surfaces as shown in Table II.

Air infiltration losses. In addition to the heat which is lost directly through the room surfaces, heat will escape through the cracks between windows and window frames and doors and door frames.

$$H = 0.018LV(t_i - t_o)$$

Where:
H = Heat loss (Btu/hr.)
0.018 = 0.24 x 0.075 (0.24 is specific heat of air in Btu/pound; 0.075 is density of air in pounds/cu.ft.)
L = Length of all cracks (ft.)
V = Volume of air infiltration per foot of crack per hour (see Table III)
t_i = Inside temperature
t_o = Outside temperature

Values for the volume of air infiltration (V) for the average doors and windows are given in Table III.

Humidity control is a contributing factor toward comfort and health in a properly designed heating system. Humidity is the amount of moisture in the air related to the temperature level. The air will hold more water when the temperature is high. A comfortable level is about 50% when the temperature is about 72°. During the winter months, the moisture content indoors is low. If there is no moisture in the air, throat and skin will be irritated and furniture can crack and separate at the joints. Even a higher temperature setting of the thermostat will not provide comfort when the relative humidity is low. In the summer, too much moisture is a problem. Wood will expand and drawers and doors will not operate properly and water is likely to condense. This condition will cause severe damage to woodwork. Humidity is also added to house through bathing, showers and cooking. If too much humidity is present, a dehumidifier will remove water from the air. Warm air heating systems have a built-in controlled humidifier.

Air, unless replaced through circulation will become stale, stagnant and unhealthy. Provisions should be made to provide fresh circulated air throughout the house. Air contains dust and foreign particles and therefor should be filtered. Warm air heating systems have a built-in filtering system. Other systems can have electronic air cleaning grids which will remove 95% of the foreign matter from the air.

Thermostats control the temperature of all types of heating systems and heating systems can be split to provide many separate thermostats controlling certain parts of the house. Thermostats should be located on an inside wall free from cold, air drafts or heat from lamps.

WARM AIR HEAT

Air is heated in a furnace and forced to all parts of the house through ducts called supply ducts by a fan or blower. Air is returned through the return ducts back to the furnace where it is filtered, humidified and reheated and the same process is repeated over again. This heated air provides a quick source of heat. There are three types of warm air heating units: Standard Up-Flow Furnace designed for basement installation with ducts overhead, Counterflow Furnace designed for basement installation with ducts overhead, Counterflow Furnace designed for basementless or main floor installation with ducts below the floor such as crawl spaces and Horizontal Furnace which can be suspended in a crawl space or attic. The metal ducts are designed to fit between the joists and studs. There should be a supply and a return duct in all rooms except kitchen and bath. These rooms need only a supply to prevent odors pulling through the rest of the house. The main and largest duct is called a trunk line and smaller ducts are branched off from the trunk to various rooms in the house. The farther away from the furnace, the smaller the duct size because the amount of air being required to move is less. Ducts can be rectangular or round. The ends of ducts terminate in the room containing a grille or register. The registers are adjustable to control the flow of heat in balancing the system. Sometimes baseboard type registers are used to distribute the heat over a wider area. Warm air heating (not in conjunction with air conditioning) requires the registers to be located close to the floor. If the system is designed for air-conditioning as well as heating, the supply registers are close to the floor and the return registers are close to the ceiling. The theory is that hot air rises and is drawn into the return register for conditioning and recycling.

DUCT SYSTEM FOR WARM AIR HEATING.

High wall register

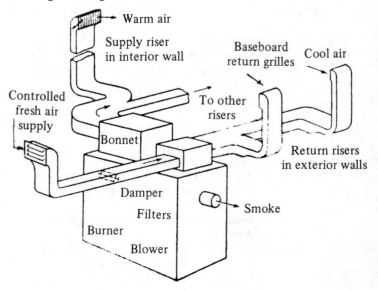

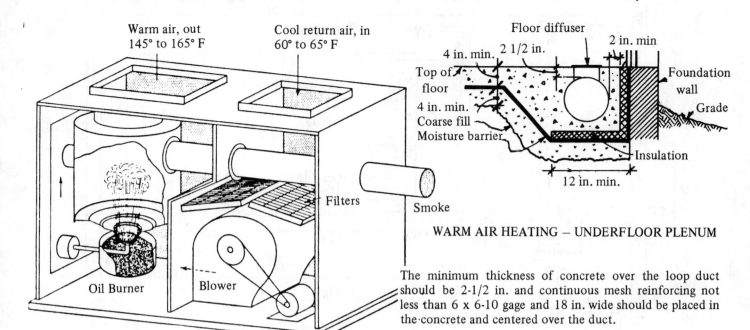

Warm air, out 145° to 165° F   Cool return air, in 60° to 65° F

Filters

Oil Burner   Blower

MECHANICAL WARM-AIR HEATING FURNACE.

Floor diffuser

4 in. min.   2 1/2 in.   2 in. min.

Top of floor

4 in. min.

Coarse fill   Foundation wall   Grade

Moisture barrier

Insulation

Smoke

12 in. min.

WARM AIR HEATING – UNDERFLOOR PLENUM

The minimum thickness of concrete over the loop duct should be 2-1/2 in. and continuous mesh reinforcing not less than 6 x 6-10 gage and 18 in. wide should be placed in the concrete and centered over the duct.

The grade should be sloped away from the house, and the top of the grade should be located below the bottom of the duct.

Where warm air supply outlets are installed low on exterior walls, room air temperatures are largely unaffected by location of the return air intakes. However, returns placed above the occupied space, either high in the inside wall or in the ceiling, are preferred because air motion (drafts) in the occupied zone is then less noticeable. For year-round air conditioning, high returns also reduce stratification of cool air by drawing off the warm air.

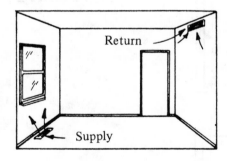

Return

Supply

AIR SUPPLY AND RETURN LOCATION

Underfloor plenum systems are similar to perimeter duct systems with respect to arrangement and location of heating unit and floor supply registers, however, with the omission of the connecting ductwork, the entire crawl space is maintained at furnace air temperatures. Thus, duct costs are reduced somewhat and the entire floor is kept warm, but heat loss by transmission and leakage is increased substantially and musty odors may develop unless the crawl space is moisture proofed. A typical arrangement is shown on the following page.

PERIMETER SYSTEMS

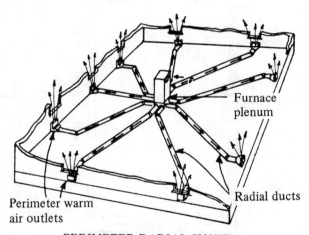

Furnace plenum

Perimeter warm air outlets   Radial ducts

PERIMETER RADIAL SYSTEM

Perimeter system ducts are usually imbedded in concrete as illustrated above. By being imbedded, heat is transmitted from the ducts directly to the concrete, thereby warming the cold concrete floor slab. The ducts also may be installed in a crawl space or in a basement, thereby warming the space under the floor for greater comfort.

Perimeter systems should not be installed in slabs-on-ground located in swales or flat, low-lying areas where there is a possibility of (1) flooding, (2) high ground water after rains, (3) subsurface springs, or excessive moisture in the ground (poor drainage). Drain tiles installed outside the house at the footings will help to alleviate some of these moisture problems provided there is a good outfall or a reliable automatic sump pump system.

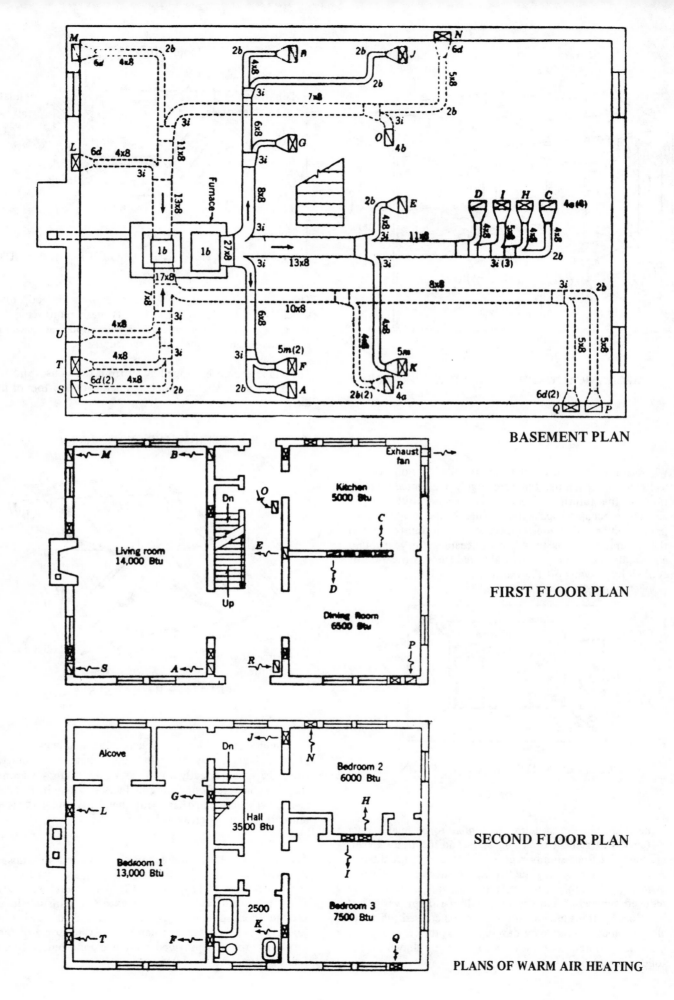

BASEMENT PLAN

FIRST FLOOR PLAN

SECOND FLOOR PLAN

PLANS OF WARM AIR HEATING

254

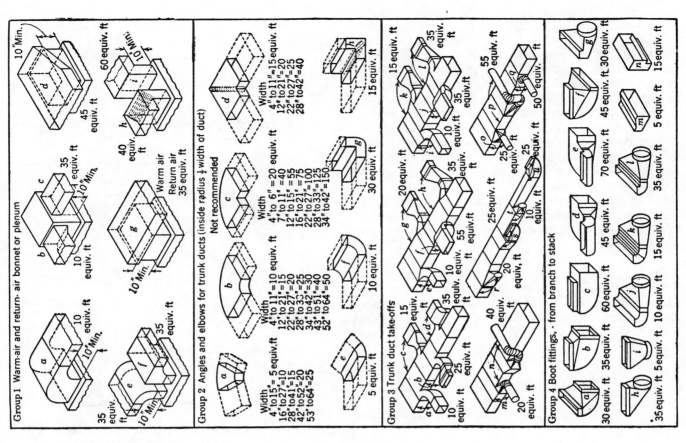

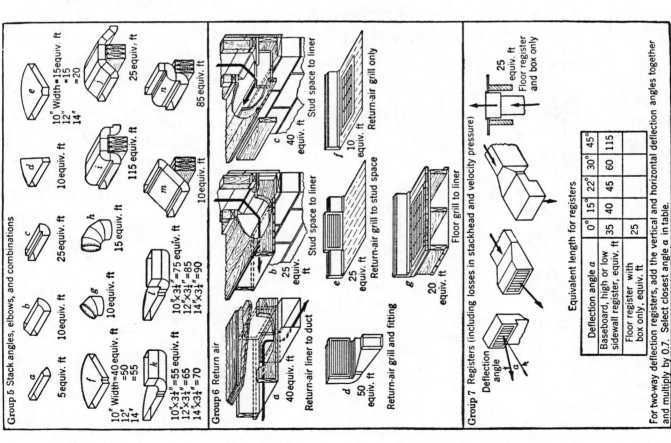

For two-way deflection registers, add the vertical and horizontal deflection angles together and multiply by 0.7. Select closest angle *a* in table.

255

STEAM HEAT

Water is heated to make steam by means of a boiler. The steam is carried through radiators, convectors or baseboard through pipes giving off heat. The steam condenses into water, returns back to the boiler and again is converted into steam. The boiler must be located below the level of the rooms being heated. Valves on radiators control heat and air vent allows air to escape from the radiators while retaining the steam. The steam changes into water in the radiators and gives off heat. All piping must be sloped back toward the boiler to allow the water to return to the boiler. The boiler should be located as near as possible to the center of the house to avoid long runs of piping. Steel and wrought iron pipes are generally used in steam heating with threaded joints.

A one pipe system carries back steam to the radiators and water or condensate back to the boiler in the same pipe. This is the more economical type system. A two pipe system has a separate pipe for condensate or water back to the boiler.

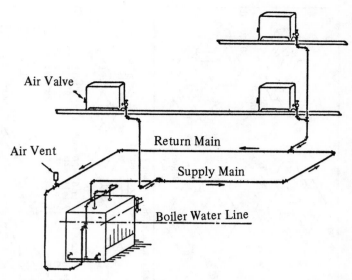

TYPICAL UP-FEED GRAVITY ONE-PIPE AIR-VENT SYSTEM

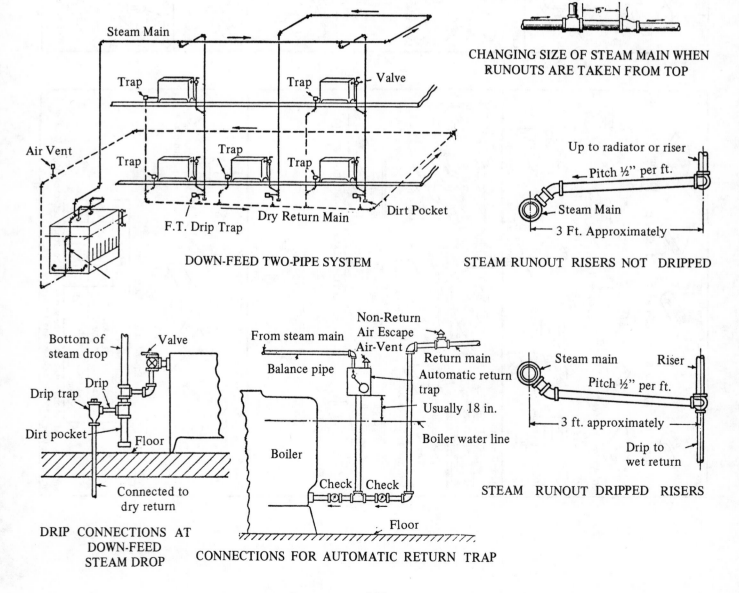

DOWN-FEED TWO-PIPE SYSTEM

CHANGING SIZE OF STEAM MAIN WHEN RUNOUTS ARE TAKEN FROM TOP

STEAM RUNOUT RISERS NOT DRIPPED

DRIP CONNECTIONS AT DOWN-FEED STEAM DROP

CONNECTIONS FOR AUTOMATIC RETURN TRAP

STEAM RUNOUT DRIPPED RISERS

256

HYDRONIC-HOT WATER

Hot water called Hydronic consists of a boiler to heat water to 200° to 215° which then is pumped into pipes carrying the hot water to the radiators, baseboards or convectors. The cooled water is returned to the boiler for reheating. This is known as a one pipe system. A two pipe system of hot water heat is more expensive but more efficient. The principle is the same as the one pipe system except the cooled water is returned back to the boiler through the independent piping system. The boiler is equipped with an expansion tank to compensate for variations of water volume at different temperatures and to relieve air pockets. In addition, each system offers an uninterrupted supply of domestic hot water as a part of the heating system. The piping may be wrought iron, black steel or copper.

In a series-loop forced hot water system, illustrated below, the water flows through each consecutive heating element and individual units cannot be valved. In order to control heat output, each unit should be equipped with a manually adjustable air damper, and each circuit must be equipped with an adjusting cock.

A third system of hot water heat is called Series Loop, which is a single continuous baseboard radiator around the entire exterior wall of the house. Pipes drop under the floor at doors and rise again. There is no individual control with this type heat. Either the entire house is heated or none of it.

In all types of hot water heat, radiators have a large exposed surface to allow the heat to radiate to the room. If convectors are used, they draw in cool air from the bottom, warm the air by contact with the surface of the hot convector and force it out into the room again. Convectors can be wall recessed to increase floor space. Baseboard units may be radiant or convector type. Any system of hot water heating is slow in heating the elements but they cool off more slowly when the heat is turned down or off.

Where radiator, convector, or baseboard enclosures are installed in an outside wall, insulation must be provided to reduce excessive heat loss.

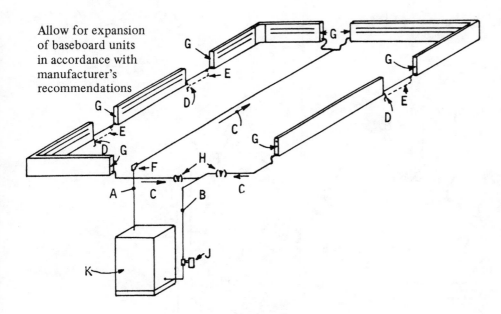

Allow for expansion of baseboard units in accordance with manufacturer's recommendations

A - Supply pipe
B - Return pipe
C - Direction of flow of water
D - Nipple and cap installed in tee to provide for drainage
E - Alternate connection between units when required
F - Flow control valve required if an indirect water heater is used, optional if an indirect water heater is not used
G - Air vent on each unit, if required
H - Balancing cocks
J - Pump or circulator
K - Water boiler

SERIES LOOP BASEBOARD SYSTEM   MULTIPLE CIRCUIT

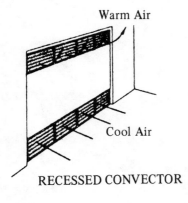

RECESSED CONVECTOR

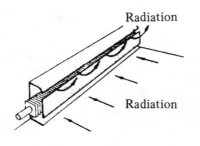

BASEBOARD RADIATOR

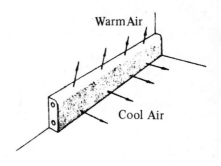

BASEBOARD CONVECTOR

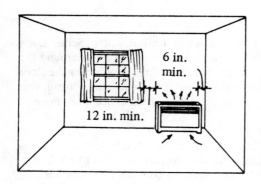

MINIMUM HEATER SPACING
TO WALL AND DRAPERY

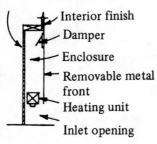

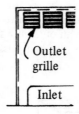

TYPICAL RECESSED CONVECTOR

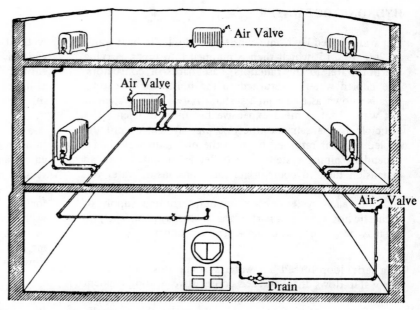

ARRANGEMENT OF PIPING AND RADIATORS IN
"ONE-PIPE CIRCUIT" SYSTEM

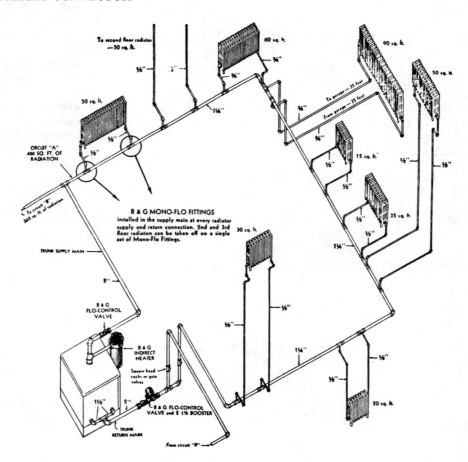

ONE-PIPE HOT-WATER SYSTEM

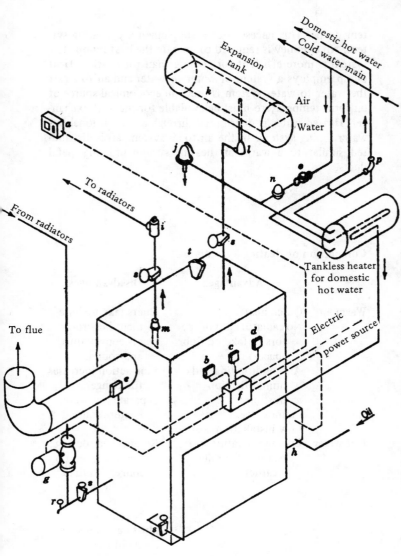

the boiler water is hot enough (above 160° F).

(h) Oil Burner. Reheat may be needed for a number of reasons. From lack of use the boiler water may have cooled below 160° F. The water may have been cooled in making domestic hot water. Finally, when circulation starts, cold radiator water is returned to the boiler and needs to be heated.

(i) Flow-Control Valve   The precise temperature control possible in forced circulation systems is assured by the flow-control valve, which closes when the pump stops, thus preventing gravity circulation which would result in a further rise in room temperature. In principle it is a check valve.

(j) Pressure-Relief Valve   When the pressure in the system exceeds 30 lb. per sq. in., the spring-loaded valve opens, bleeding water out of the pipes and relieving the pressure which might otherwise cause breakage. It should be placed where its discharge will do no damage. With proper system design and adjustment it should not operate except in an emergency.

(k) Expansion Tank. This is sometimes known as a compression tank in closed systems. A cushion of air remains in the top of the tank to adjust for the varying volume of water in the system as the temperature changes.

(l) and (m) Tank and Boiler Air-Control Fittings   Much of the air in the system is eliminated at once by these fittings, which lead the air to the expansion tank. Air accumulating in the boiler cannot leave through the dip tube (m) but finds its way to (l), where it is led to the top of the expansion tank.

(n) Pressure-Reducing Valve   This is the automatic fill valve. It opens when the pressure in the system drops below 12 lb. per sq. in. and closes with a check action against higher pressures. It keeps the system full.

(o) Check Valve. In an emergency where pressure-relief valve (j) did not open and the pressure-reducing valve failed in its checking action, the check valve (o) prevents the boiler from putting the house cold water system under pressure that would be dangerous.

(p) Tempering Valve   This mixing valve operates automatically by a mechanical thermostat to add cold water in sufficient quantities to deliver the domestic hot water at exactly the required temperature.

(q) Tankless Heater. This generates domestic hot water for use in the various plumbing fixtures.

(r) Drain. At this or other low points means of draining the system must be provided.

(s) Gate Valve. The location of gate valves is determined by the need for shutting off sections of the system for repair or servicing without draining the entire water content. Their selection in preference to globe valves is due to the smaller resistance they offer to the passage of water.

(t) Temperature and Pressure Gauge. The operating pressure of the system may be observed as a check on the operation and setting of the pressure-relief valve and on the cushioning effect of the compression tank. Observation of the boiler temperature is a check on the operation of the aquastat which sets this temperature.

CONTROLS — HOT WATER HEATING

(a) House Thermostat. When the room air temperature falls below the setting of the thermostat, the house thermostat turns on the pump and oil burner simultaneously. When satisfied it turns them both off.

(b) Low-Limit Control. This control turns on the oil burner when the boiler water falls below a chosen temperature (about 160° F).

(c) High-Limit Control. "Runaway" performance is prevented by this device, which turns off the oil burner when the boiler water starts to exceed a chosen high temperature (often about 200° F).

(d) Reverse-Acting Control. To prevent the circulation of cold water in the radiators, this control stops the circulating pump when the water falls below 160° F until the burner has had time to raise the temperature again to the desired degree.

(e) Stack-Temperature Control. After the burner starts, the stack-temperature control waits for the resulting rise in the stack temperature. If it does not come in a short time, it turns off the burner which has failed to ignite. This is a safety control.

(f) Junction Box and Relays. This central control station transmits the impulses of the controls previously described.

(g) Circulating Pump   This electrically driven centrifugal pump turns on whenever heat is called for and

RADIANT HEAT

This type of heat can also be called Hydronic. It is similar to hot water heat except instead of radiators, a serpentine endless line or coil of copper tubing is concealed in the floor or ceiling. Radiant heat does not depend upon air movement: it passes directly to the object or person, making it one of the most comfortable types of heating system. Should a leak develop in the lines, it means tearing down the floor or ceiling to make repairs; for that reason the system must be thoroughly tested before any surface is finished. In effect, a radiant heating system acts as one large radiator.

Hot water is circulated through the pipes embedded in the floor or ceiling as in a hot water heating system. This system is primarily but not necessarily used in a house without a basement and is completely concealed.

Electricity may also be employed in radiant heat. Pre-assembled heating panels are designed to be installed in the ceiling under the finish. This type heating is like a giant toaster in the ceiling.

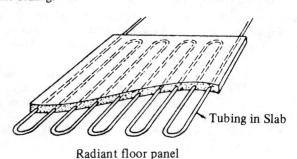

Tubing in Slab

Radiant floor panel

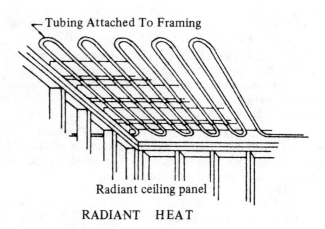

Tubing Attached To Framing

Radiant ceiling panel

RADIANT HEAT

HEAT PUMP

A dual system of heating and cooling is produced by a heat pump. Basically it is a refrigeration unit which pumps natural heat or water to be heated from the outside air. Heat pumps work on the principle that outside air contains heat which is pumped into the house by electricity to heat it and in summer, heat is pumped out to cool it. Heat pump may not be practical for cold climates because when the outside temperature drops below 30° F. the efficiency of the sys-

tem drops. This necessitates a supplementary heating system. No chimney is required to operate the heat pump. The system is more efficient for cooling than for heating. Heat pump employs a system of water to water and air to air. If the water to water system is used, an economical source of uniform temperature must be available for the heat exchanger. Heated water is distributed through a conventional hot water piping system. In the air to air system, air is distributed similar to a warm air heating system utilizing metal ducts.

Comparison of Heating Systems

	Advantages	Disadvantages
Warm air	Quick heat No radiators or convectors to take up floor space Air conditioning and humidification possible Cannot freeze Low installation cost	Ducts take up basement headroom Ducts convey dust and sound Flue action increases fire danger Separate hot water heater required
Hot water	Low temperature heat possible for mild weather	Retains heat during periods when no longer required Slow to heat up Radiators require two lines Must be drained to avoid freezing when not in use
Radiant	No visible heating device Economical operation Good temperature distribution	Slow response to heat needs Air conditioning must be separate unit Repair costly
Steam (one pipe)	Radiators require only one line	Large size pipes required Sloping pipes take up basement headroom Inefficient: time and pressure required to vent air from radiators Water hammer
Electric	No visible heating device Low installation cost Individual room control Clean, silent operation	Operation cost high in many locations Heavy insulation required
Solar	Low operation cost	Supplemental heating system necessary System not fully developed

The heat pump is a packaged unit which can be located outdoors or it may have two cabinets called a remote unit with one inside and one outside. The operation of the heat pump draws outside air or water into the unit, the refrigerant in the evaporator absorbs the heat and a compressor pumps the refrigerant to a high temperature and pressure and the condenser gives off the heat to the outside air creating a heating cycle.

ELECTRIC HEAT

The least expenseive heating system to install is electric heat. It requires no space for boilers or furnaces, nor is a chimney necessary. It has individual room control, it is clean but may not be the least expensive to operate. Proper insulation is the key to an efficient electric heating system. Basically there are 3 kinds of electric heat: Electric Resistance Cable, consisting of covered wire cables heated by electricity and concealed in floor or ceiling. The wires are made in the exact length to provide the necessary wattage. The finish ceiling or floor conceals this system. The second system is Electric Panels. These are pre-fabricated finished ceiling panels with asbestos board covering the entire ceiling. They can be painted, plastered or papered. The third type is Baseboard. These are convector heaters consisting of heating elements enclosed in a metal baseboard. The top and bottom are slotted to allow air to circulate.

The value of electricity converted to heat loss is 1 watt of electricity equals 3.41 BTU.

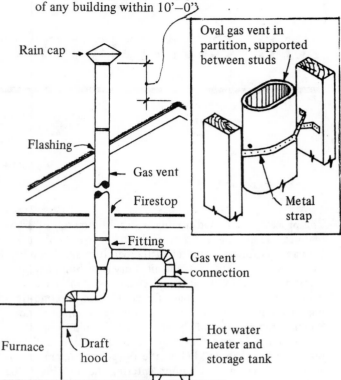

Clearance - Extend at least 3'–0" above the highest point and at least 2'–0" higher than any portion of any building within 10'–0".

Oval gas vent in partition, supported between studs

Rain cap

Flashing

Gas vent

Firestop

Fitting

Gas vent connection

Metal strap

Furnace

Draft hood

Hot water heater and storage tank

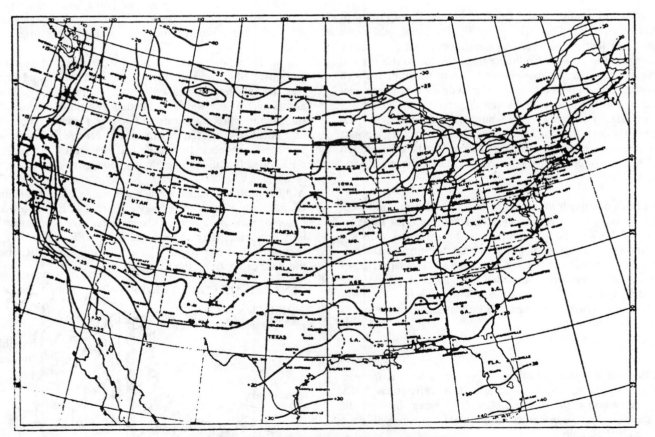

AVERAGE ANNUAL FROST PENETRATION IN INCHES

AIR CONDITIONING

27

The process of air-conditioning is simply a matter of drawing heat from the air and replacing it with cooler air. Human comfort is a matter of temperature and humidity, the two are inseparable. If the air is dry (low humidity) perspiration easily evaporates and cools the skin. Therefore, dehumidification is necessary for comfort in air conditioning. This is what the air-conditioning machinery does. Summer temperature of 75° at a relative humidity of 60% is comfortable. Indoor temperatures in the summer should not be more than 15° below the outdoor temperature to avoid an unpleasant chill upon entering the building or the feeling of intense heat when leaving the building.

Ventilation, humidity and temperature are all important to human comfort. For satisfactory results, air should move about 25 feet per minute. Air conditioners are continually changing the air by introducing fresh air from outdoors and exhausting stale air containing carbon dioxide, reduced oxygen and unpleasant odors. This stale air is not recirculated in the house but discharged directly to the outside. A complete air change every 15 minutes is desirable. Infiltration in homes, in most cases, provides a satisfactory amount of fresh air to make the change. This air needs to be filtered to remove impurities, the dry type filter is the most common.

Warm air heating is most adaptable for central air-conditioning using the same ducts for heating, cooling, and the same filter and blower. Supply ducts must be insulated with air-conditioning because of condensation forming on the surface of the metal and the loss of cooled air. If a separate air-conditioning system is installed, that is, not part of the heating system, all the equipment which is part of a warm air heating system will need to be installed in addition to other equipment.

A hot water or steam heating system can also be employed as air-conditioning by circulating chilled water through the piping system with a water chiller. In this case, blowers are installed on the convectors to circulate the warm air over the chilled air coils.

As winter heat is lost through a building, so summer heat enters by transmission through floors, walls, glass and ceiling in addition to cracks around doors and windows. Latent heat must also be considered. This is heat within the house generated by cooking, which generates about 1,200 BTU per hour, and people, who produce about 300 BTU per hour. Motors from refrigerators, dish washers etc. also generate heat. Lights contribute about 3.5 BTU per hour for each watt of electricity.

Cooling units are rated by tons of refrigeration. Measurement used in amount of refrigeration produced by melting one ton of ice in 24 hours. A ton is equivalent to 12,000 BTU/hr. In sizing a unit, total up all the BTU per hour and divide by 12,000. An average size house will require a 2 or 3 ton unit. A larger house 4 to 6 tons. One horsepower of electricity is required for each ton of air-conditioning.

The mechanical makeup of an air-conditioning system is composed of the evaporator which absorbs heat and vaporizes the refrigerant. This unit must be placed in the house and if part of the warm air heating system, is contained in the plenum directly connected to the furnace. The other unit is called a condenser which gives off the heat and must be placed outdoors. It may be installed inside but must be on an outside wall discharging the heat outdoors.

A dual unit combines heating and cooling and a single unit, cooling only. Check the energy efficiency (EER) of air conditioners you are buying. This measures how efficiently the unit uses electricity. The higher the EER the better. It should be between 7 and 12. To determine the EER, divide the BTU capacity by the wattage.

CENTRAL AIR CONDITIONER

NOISE CONTROL

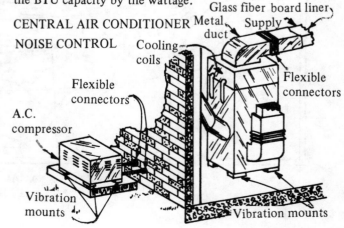

262

ELECTRICITY

28

In planning an electrical system, safety must be of prime concern. Electricity passes through wires creating heat. If undersized wires are used, not only is the system inefficient but the electricity passing through the wire will overload the service, resulting in a breakdown and melting the protective coating or insulation covering the wires and creating a hazard and possible fire. Minimum requirements will be found in local codes and the National Electric Code.

Electrical Terminology:

Ampere: Unit of current to measure the amount of electricity passing through wire.

Circuit: Two or more wires from a source of electrical supply to one or more outlets and return.

Circuit Breaker: A switch which stops or shuts off the flow of electricity at the source of supply.

Conductor: Wire that carries electricity.

Ground: A connection between electricity and earth minimizing danger of electric shock and damage from electrical storm, such as lightning.

Horsepower: A unit of measuring work such as electric motors (one HP=745 watts).

Outlet: Electric plug, switch or light

Receptacle: Electric plug.

Service Entrance: Electric wires from outside building (utility company) to building. Distribution or Electric Panel.

Service Panel: Steel box containing main electric service which distributes electricity through the house containing a fuse or circuit breaker.

Short Circuit: A wrong wire connection.

Volt: Measure or push of electric current.

CIRCUIT BREAKER PANEL

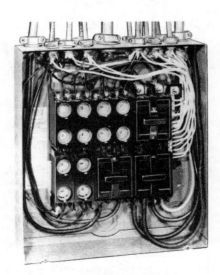

FUSED PANEL

Fuse: A safety device at the source of electrical supply that melts, cutting off the flow of electricity.

Watt: Measure of electric power used by appliance.

Kilowatt: 1,000 watts.

Kilowatt Hour: 1,000 watts per hour. (Utilities charge by Kilowatt hour).

The heart of an electrical system is the distribution panel which is made of metal, attached to the wall or built-in containing a number of fuses or circuit breakers. All electricity must be grounded by running a wire from the panel to a water pipe or a ground terminal. At the point on the house where the wires are attached is an electric meter. From the meter, the wires are attached to the panel inside the house. The wires can be copper or aluminum, overhead or underground. The minimum service required should be 100 amps.

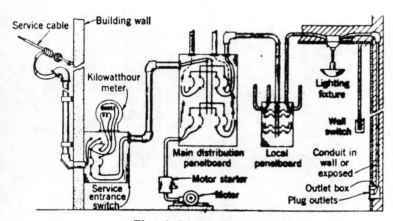

Electric Distribution System

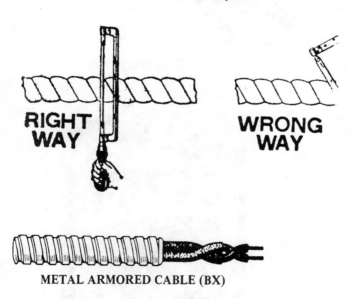

METAL ARMORED CABLE (BX)

NON-METALLIC SHEATH CABLE (ROMAX)

Wires are furnished to the home by the local electric company. These wires supply 240 and 120 volts, single phase, 60 cycles of alternating current and should be at least 10'-0" above the ground at the point of house attachment. The size of the distribution panel is determined by the total electrical load in the house plus any future loads. From the electrical distribution box, branch circuits are extended to various parts of the house all of which are fused either through a circuit breaker or a fuse type panel. Branch circuits carry different electrical loads depending upon the work required to do, ranging from 15 to 50 amperes. The wires used from the distribution panel to the branch circuits are sized according to the service performed. A single cable consists of two or three insulated wires all wrapped into one. These wires have numbers stamped on the wrapping indicating the number of wires in the cable and the diameter of the wire. 12/2 indicates two wires of No. 12 gauge. The larger the wire, the smaller the number. The minimum size wire for residential work is No. 14 gauge. Two kinds of wire covering are available: Non-Metallic Sheath Cable (Romax) which is a flexible cable covering of plastic or fabric, and Metal Armored Cable (BX) which is a steel spiral covering not recommended in damp places.

Do not put all outlets on a single circuit in the same room. Split the circuits to provide some lighting should the fuse blow or the circuit breaker trip. Generally one circuit should take care of about 375 square feet of floor space using No. 12 gauge wire carrying a minimum of 2400 watts, not exceeding 75' in length. A longer run will require a heavier wire.

It is recommended that a separate outlet be installed for the following equipment:

Electric Range
Dish Washer
Clothes Washer
Dryer
Furnace or Boiler
Water Heater
Air Conditioner
Refrigerator
Garbage Disposer
Freezer
Motors

To arrive at the number of lighting circuits required for a house, divide the total square feet of the house by 400 and add the number of separate circuits for equipment.

Wall switches are used to control the flow of electricity to outlet, usually a light. The principle is simple, electricity is running from the distribution panel to the switch called a toggle switch. Within the switch are contacts which break or stop the flow of electricity to the light when the switch is in an off position. When the switch is on, contact is made allowing electricity to flow to the light turning it on. Switches are placed 48" above the floor in a convenient location on the wall. If one switch operates one or more lights, it is called a two way switch. If two switches operate the same lights, it is called a three way switch. Dimmer switches may also be installed to adjust the brightness of a light.

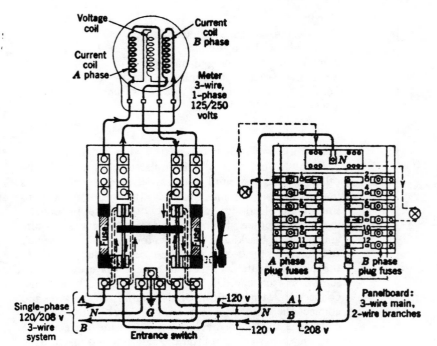

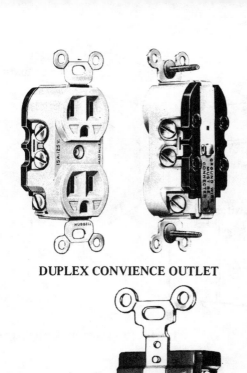

DUPLEX CONVIENCE OUTLET

Service entrance switch, panelboard, and wiring. The arrowheads indicate direction of flow of load currents in the two outside wires A and B, under balanced load. On balanced load no current flows in the neutral wire N.

TOGGLE SWITCH

	Switch Plates
	Duplex Outlet Plates
	Single Outlet Plates
	Blank Wall Plates
	Telephone Plate
	Comb. Switch-Duplex Outlet Plate
	Comb. Switch-Single Outlet Plate
	Comb. 2 Switch—1 Duplex Outlet Plate
	Single Interchangeable Wall Plates (Horizontal)
	One Gang Two Openings Two Gang Four Openings Two Gang Three Openings
	Triple Interchangeable Wall Plates (horizontal)
	Single Interchangeable Wall Plates (vertical)

ELECTRIC WALL PLATES

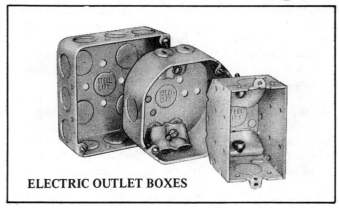

ELECTRIC OUTLET BOXES

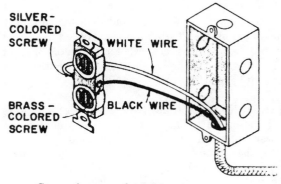

Convenience-outlet wiring

265

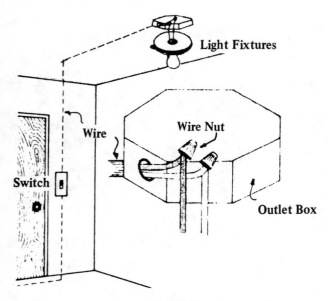

LIGHT FIXTURE WIRING DIAGRAM

Direct-ceiling light shining down only.
Indirect-lamp shining up only.
Semi-direct lamp shining up and down.
Semi-direct-ceiling light shining up and down.
Difused-spread evenly in all directions, such as a hanging globe type fixture.

An electric cable has two insulated wires and sometimes a bare third wire. One of the insulated wires is black, the other, white. The third bare carries no electricity but is used as a ground connection only. It is very important to shut off the electricity before any work is done. In connecting wires together, always match the colors, white to white and black to black. The third or ground wire is connected to a screw on the box or a third connector colored green on the plug or switch. Plugs and switches have one or two screws on each side. Use only the screw on each side for a connection. Strip about 2" of insulation from the wires and connect the white wire to the silver colored screw and the black wire to the brass colored screw on the other side. Be sure the screws are tight after the connection is made. Wrap the wire around the body of the screw and the head of the screw will hold it in place after it is tightened. Leave about 6" of slack wire coiled into the box. When connection is made secure the plug or switch to the box and install the cover plate. If you are installing a lighting fixture, you will see that the fixture will have two wires attached. Connect these two wires to the two wires in the box with wire nuts and attach the fixture to the box. Three way switches require a different formula for attaching wires. The cover of the box containing the switch will have directions for connecting. The wires on the lighting fixtures may not be colored coded with black and white. In that case it will not matter which wire is connected to what color in the box.

If an outlet is to be added, find the nearest outlet box within the location of the new outlet. Remove the cover after shutting off the electricity and detach the plug or switch from the box. Run the new electric cable from the new location to the existing box, connect the like colored wires. If a plug, use the other set of screws (if a four screwed plug) and this will activate the new outlet. If wiring switches, connect the two white wires together and the two black wires to the screws on the switch, one on each side.

Be sure to plan carefully the location of telephone and consult with the telephone office first to determine who will be responsible for wiring.

All outlets, such as lights, switches and plugs must be installed in an electrical box. There are three kinds of electrical boxes: Square, Hexagon and Outlet. The Outlet box is used for switches and plugs which are attached directly to the wall studs flush with the finish wall material. The Hexagon box is generally used for hanging electrical lighting fixtures which are attached directly to the studs or ceiling joists again protruding from the joist or stud the thickness of the finish. The Square box as well as the Hexagon box is used to splice wires together. Under no circumstances should electrical wire be spliced with tape and left exposed. They must be placed into a Square or Hexagon junction box. The two wires to be spliced are held together with a wire nut which locks and twists the two wires together. All wiring is brought into any of these three boxes and the switches, plugs or lighting fixture is connected at or to the box. Plastic boxes are also available.

Thought should be given to the location of electric outlets. Each room should have a minimum of three outlets or plugs spaced about 10'-0" apart, except the kitchen, which should be spaced about every 4'-0" apart. The height of the plugs should be about 18" above the floor except the kitchen, which should be placed between the counter top and the underside of the upper cabinets. All outdoor outlets should be of the waterproof type. The boxes for all the outlets should be secured in place first and then the wire brought to the box from the distribution panel or fed from another outlet box. All wiring is concealed in the floor, wall or ceiling. The same outlet boxes are used for fluorescent or incandescent lighting fixtures.

Fluorescent lighting fixtures require less electricity to operate for a given watt. One foot in length of fluorescent tube = 10 watts of electricity. Light is measured in foot candles which is the amount of light given off by one candle on a square foot of surface one foot away. There are five types of lighting:

RECOMMENDED FOOT CANDLE LEVELS

TV Viewing	5FC
Storage	10FC
Stairway	20FC
Dining	20FC
Bedroom	20FC
Bath	30FC
Living	30FC
Den	30FC
Reading	50FC
Sewing	50FC
Kitchen	50FC
Shop	70FC

TYPICAL APPLIANCE REQUIREMENTS

Appliance or Equipment	Typical Watts	Usual Voltage	Wire Size	Recommended Fuse Size
Electric Range (with oven)	12,000	240	6	50–60 Amp.
Range Top (separate)	5,000	120/240	10	30 Amp.
Range Oven (separate)	5,000	120/240	10	30 Amp.
Refrigerator	300	120	12	20 Amp.
Home Freezer	350	120	12	20 Amp.
Automatic Washer	700	120	12	20 Amp.
Automatic Dryer (elec.)	5,000	120/240	10	30 Amp.
Dishwasher	1,200	120/240	12	20 Amp.
Garbage Disposer	300	120	12	20 Amp.
Roaster	1,400	120	12	20 Amp.
Rotisserie	1,400	120	12	20 Amp.
Furnace	800	120	12	20 Amp.
Dehumidifier	350	120	12	20 Amp.
Waffle Iron	1,000	120	12	20 Amp.
Band Saw	300	120	12	20 Amp.
Table Saw	1,000	120/240	12	20 Amp.
20,000 Btu Air Conditioner	1,200	120/240	12	20 Amp.
Bathroom Heater	2,000	120/240	12	20 Amp.
Ironer	1,500	120	12	20 Amp.
Water Heater	2,000–5,000	120	10	30 Amp.
Television	300	120	12	20 Amp.
Hand Iron	1,100	120	12	20 Amp.
Toaster	1,000	120	12	20 Amp.

RESIDENTIAL LIGHTING CIRCUITS

No. of Sq. Ft.	Number of Lighting Circuits Code Minimum	Recommended
1000	2	3
1200	2	3
1600	3	4
2000	3	5
2400	4	6
2800	5	7

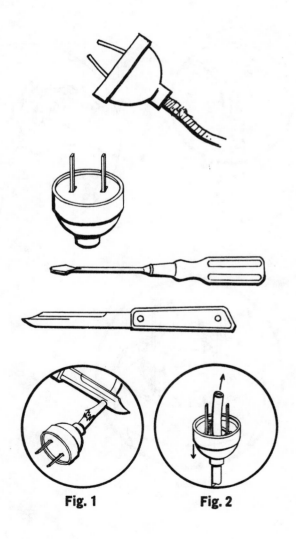

Fig. 1 Fig. 2

ELECTRIC PLUGS—REPAIR OR REPLACE

WHAT YOU NEED

New plug—if your old one cannot be used. (Buy one with a UL label)

Screwdriver

Knife

HOW–TO

1. Cut the cord off at the damaged part. (Fig. 1)

2. Slip the plug back on the cord. (Fig. 2)

3. Clip and separate the cord. (Fig. 3)

4. Tie Underwriters' knot. (Fig. 4)

5. Remove a half-inch of the insulation from the end of the wires. DO NOT CUT ANY OF THE SMALL WIRES (Fig. 5)

6. Twist small wires together, clockwise. (Fig. 6)

7. Pull knot down firmly in the plug. (Fig. 7)

8. Pull one wire around each terminal to the screw. (Fig. 8)

9. Wrap the wire around the screw, clockwise. (Fig. 9)

10. Tighten the screw. Insulation should come to the screw but not under it. (Fig. 10)

11. Place insulation cover back over the plug. (Fig. 11)

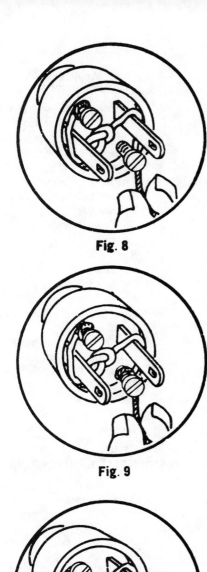

Fig. 8

Fig. 9

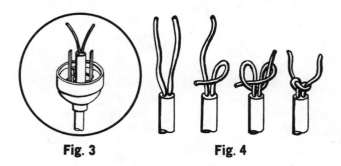

Fig. 3   **Fig. 4**

Fig. 5

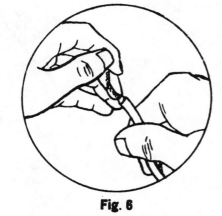

Fig. 6

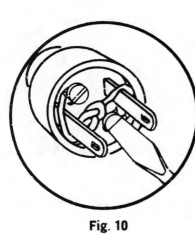

Fig. 10

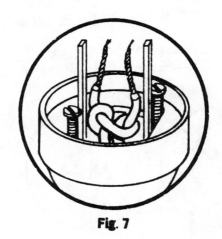

Fig. 7

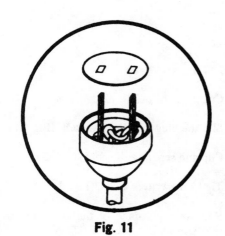

Fig. 11

BURGULAR, SMOKE AND FIRE ALARMS

Burgular, fire or smoke alarms are not difficult to install, but the wiring must be done while the studs are exposed. According to National Fire Protection Association seventy-five percent of dwelling fires start as slow, smoldering fires. Toxic fumes, carbon monoxide, smoke, lack of these, not the flames, are the real danger to life safety. A smoke activated fire warning device can alert residents well before the heat level reaches the 135° needed to activate most heat sensors. Two types of smoke detectors which can provide this kind of advanced warning are available: ionization and photoelectric detectors. The ionization type contains a small amount of radioactive material, usually americium 241, which transforms the air inside the detector chamber into a conductor of electric current. If smoke particles enter the chamber, they mix with the ionized air, slow the ionization process, reduce the current flow—and set off an alarm. The photoelectric detector has a light-sensitive cell as the key component. If smoke enters the chamber, the smoke particles reflect this light beam on the sensitive cell, setting off the alarm. The ionization detector is somewhat faster in detecting flaming fires which may produce little or no visible smoke. The photoelectric detector responds to smoldering fires more quickly.

Don't confuse fire detectors from smoke detectors. A smoke detector will give off a visual or audio alarm only if set off by smoke, the fire alarm will signal only from heat of fire and not smoke.

There are two means of powering detectors: batteries or common house electricity. The ionization detector requires very little current, so they can be effectively run by batteries. The batteries need to be monitered which will require some maintenance, but it must also be understood that the electric current type will not work during power failure. Either kind of detector can be designed to operate on house power and to switch automatically to an internal battery for power if there is a power failure. All units can be interconnected so that when any detector senses smoke, the others in the home also sound an alarm. All battery operated models will sound a warning, an intermittent signal, when the batteries run low. Don't turn off the signal, intending to replace the batteries later. Do it immediately.

LOW VOLTAGE SYSTEM

Another type of electrical system for residential use is called low voltage. This is a 24 volt system controlling switches through a relay. Bell wire can be used for low voltage wiring and there is no danger of electrical shock. All outlets can be controlled from a central station. Lights can be controlled from one or more stations.

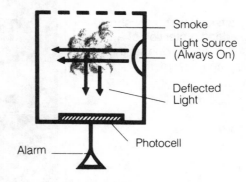

Ionization Detector

Detector Circuit — Alarm — Ionized Air — Positive Electrode — Negative Electrode — Smoke — Radioactive Electrode

Photoelectric Detector

Smoke — Light Source (Always On) — Deflected Light — Photocell — Alarm

Bedrooms at one end of a one-floor house

Install detector alarms between sleeping area and the rest of the house.

One-story house with more than one sleeping area

Bedrooms on second floor of a two-story house

Ideally a two-story house should have the added protection of a detector alarm outside the door at the top of the stairs to the basement.

Bedrooms in attic extension

SOLAR ENERGY

29

Heat generated from the sun is measured in BTU/hr. and is partially lost through the atmosphere. A portion is scattered by contact with air, smoke, moisture, dust and absorbed by water vapor, carbon dioxide and ozone. The remainder of energy striking the earth is called Direct Solar Radiation. When this radiation strikes a surface, part of it is absorbed and part is transmitted through the material or surface. This surface will also radiate heat to the atmosphere. In summation, the energy used for heating comes from the sun but only 40% of this energy is efficient. 60% is lost as described.

The sun is the most practical energy source. It is constant, non-polluting and there is no cost. Its life span is infinite and in every 24 hours the amount of energy reaching the earth from the sun is 5,000 more than the sum of all energy sources on earth. The solar energy which is sometimes intermittent, reaches us in two forms: Direct and Difused radiation. Direct radiation casts a shadow from the sun, Difused radiation is dispersed or reflected and does not cast a shadow. The average intensity of Solar Energy will deliver about 100 to 200 BTU for every square feet of ground. The entire nations energy needs can be filled by the sun.

If and when it comes to pass, solar energy could reduce air pollution by 430,000 tons and solid waste by 20,000,000 tons annually. The simplest form of solar heating is called direct or passive which converts sunlight into thermal energy within the space to be heated. The technique is to install large south facing windows that trap direct solar radiation during the winter daylight hours and store it in the walls, giving it back into the room when the sun sets. The other form of solar heating is the indirect system converting sunlight into thermal energy outside the building. This system requires a means of collecting and storing the heat until ready for distribution. The heat of the indirect system is the solar collection panels which gather the solar radiation and intensifies it to heat water or air which is piped to a conventional system.

There are two types of collectors in the indirect system: concentration and flat plate. The concentration collector consists of a highly reflective curved surface which focuses sunlight on to a radiation absorbing area. The collectors can reach to temperatures of 250° F. They are dish shaped with a tracking system following the sun's rays. Flat plate collectors are more popular because they absorb, diffuse and direct sunlight. In simple terms, these collectors are large flat trays or panels of water or air covered with glass or plastic to create a concentration of heat which in turn heats the water or air. The surface of these panels are coated with an absorbent material to soak up the rays of the sun. The panels are about 4'–0" x 8'–0" and are mounted on a roof or on the ground tilted to capture the most direct radiation. The back side of the panels are insulated. The heated water is carried through the collectors into a storage tank large enough to hold two days supply of heat. The heat is transferred to the rooms by convection circulating the heated water in the storage tank through the conventional heating system of baseboard, convectors or radiators or water coils in a warm air ducting system.

Heat from the air system is stored in large bins of stone. Domestic hot water is preheated by the cold water passing through the storage tank and heating it up to 145° F. In addition to domestic hot water, the system is capable of heating water in swimming pools and whirlpools.

Solar energy can also be used to cool a building. Cooling is designed to drive an absorptive chiller by hot water.

A few guide lines must be kept in mind before a final decision is made to use solar energy.

1. Compare not only the cost of installation but also operating cost of solar energy with conventional fuel. Solar energy is not cheap.

2. The building should be heavily insulated with a factor of at R15 for walls. Doors and windows should be at a minimum of about 12% of the wall perimeter.

3. A well designed solar building needs only about 10 BTU/sq. ft./hr. to keep a comfortable temperature in winter.

4. Climate and location affect the suitability of solar energy. In most parts of the country there is not enough solar radiation to economically heat a home. A

back up system of a conventional heating system must also be installed in addition to the solar system. The Northeast can provide only about 50% of solar heat required to heat a house. The other 50% must be provided by a conventional heating system.

5. Solar systems must be designed according to budget, conventional fuel inflation rate and the component equipment cost. If a system is undersized, solar energy cannot be economically reached because of the cost of equipment that have a minimum size no matter how small the designed system.

6. Collectors are heavy and if roof installed, the roof must be designed to carry the additional load.

7. Collectors work only for a small part of the year.

8. A rule of thumb for engineering calculations is that collectors equal to half the floor space will provide about 70% of the buildings heating load.

9. Installation will cost between $10.00 to $75.00 per sq. ft. of collector with an average of about $20.00 per sq. ft. of collector.

10. About 1% of the building cost will include the increased structural cost for roof supported collectors.

11. Collectors cost about 50% of the cost of solar energy.

12. Solar energy systems that cost more than $25.00 per sq. ft. will not pay for themselves in energy savings for 20 to 30 years.

13. In the near future, with improved design and rising fuel costs, solar heat may be competitive with gas or oil heat.

14. Ask from the manufacturer for proof that the product will perform as advertised. If laboratory tests have been made, ask of a copy of the test.

15. Examine the warranty carefully and know of the limitations.

16. Be sure you know who will service the system should anything go wrong. Not too many people are familiar with solar heating systems.

17. Ask the dealer for a list of previous installations. Talk with these people for advice and guidance.

18. At present, solar domestic hot water is the most effective application because the initial investment is less than solar heating system and hot water is in demand all year.

19. Solar cooling is assisted by heat pumps and has a projected payout of about 10 years because the collector size is small.

20. Water solar systems must be protected by anti-freeze or have an automatic drain system for night time.

21. Initial costs can be high to protect the contractor's lack of experience and contingencies.

22. The legal problem of sun-rights will need to be established before solar energy can be fully accepted.

23. Adding solar energy to an existing building will cost about $10.00 a square foot more than a new building.

24. In an existing building installation, does the building have adequate insulation?

25. Solar heat provides a lower temperature than conventional heating systems and requires larger radiators, ducts, or convectors of heating surface.

26. A water solar energy system is not always compatible with a steam heating system because different radiators are used.

27. Is there a place to store the collectors? If the collectors are stored on the ground be sure the pipes outside are insulated.

28. For domestic hot water solar systems, one square foot of collector is required for every gallon of water.

29. The collectors must face in a southern direction with unobstructed sunlight. If your house is shadowed by large buildings or trees, solar energy is not practical.

30. Find out the amount of usable radiation that will fall in your area during the time you intend to use your solar system.

31. The Federal Energy Administration says that solar energy is not suitable for everyone's home.

32. Solar collector panels must be kept clean in order to absorb the radiation from the sun. If roof mounted make plans for access to the collector panels for periodical cleaning.

USE the SUN to advantage—

1. Remember, solar energy is free.

2. Design your new home with an overhang for windows on the south wall protecting them from summer sun (high in the sky); allowing exposure to winter sun (low in the sky) which will contribute heat by beaming "warm rays" beneath the overhanging eaves and through the windows, flooding rooms with cheerful natural light.

3. Build your home with most of the windows on the southerly exposure, therefore keeping those facing the north to a minimum.

4. Proper location of trees is important. Trees that lose their leaves each fall do not block windows from "warm" winter sunshine.

SOLAR HOT WATER SYSTEM

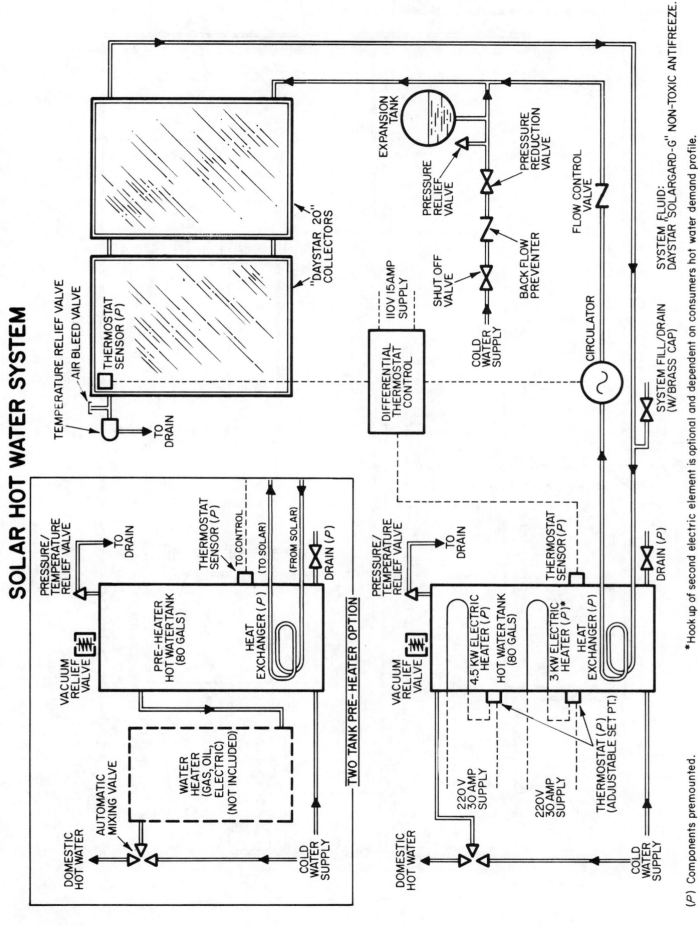

"DAYSTAR 20" COLLECTORS

TEMPERATURE RELIEF VALVE
AIR BLEED VALVE
THERMOSTAT SENSOR (P)
TO DRAIN

EXPANSION TANK
PRESSURE RELIEF VALVE
PRESSURE REDUCTION VALVE
SHUT OFF VALVE
BACK FLOW PREVENTER
FLOW CONTROL VALVE
COLD WATER SUPPLY
110V 15AMP SUPPLY
DIFFERENTIAL THERMOSTAT CONTROL
CIRCULATOR
SYSTEM FILL/DRAIN (W/BRASS CAP)
DRAIN (P)

SYSTEM FLUID: DAYSTAR "SOLARGARD-G" NON-TOXIC ANTIFREEZE.

PRESSURE/TEMPERATURE RELIEF VALVE
TO DRAIN
VACUUM RELIEF VALVE
THERMOSTAT SENSOR (P)
TO CONTROL
(TO SOLAR)
(FROM SOLAR)
DRAIN (P)
PRE-HEATER HOT WATER TANK (80 GALS)
HEAT EXCHANGER (P)
WATER HEATER (GAS, OIL, ELECTRIC) (NOT INCLUDED)
AUTOMATIC MIXING VALVE
DOMESTIC HOT WATER
COLD WATER SUPPLY

TWO TANK PRE-HEATER OPTION

PRESSURE/TEMPERATURE RELIEF VALVE
TO DRAIN
VACUUM RELIEF VALVE
THERMOSTAT SENSOR (P)
4.5 KW ELECTRIC HEATER (P)
HOT WATER TANK (80 GALS)
3 KW ELECTRIC HEATER (P)*
HEAT EXCHANGER (P)
THERMOSTAT (P) (ADJUSTABLE SET PT.)
220V 30 AMP SUPPLY
220V 30 AMP SUPPLY
DRAIN (P)
DOMESTIC HOT WATER
COLD WATER SUPPLY

*Hook up of second electric element is optional and dependent on consumers hot water demand profile.

(P) Components premounted.

273

SOLAR HEATER

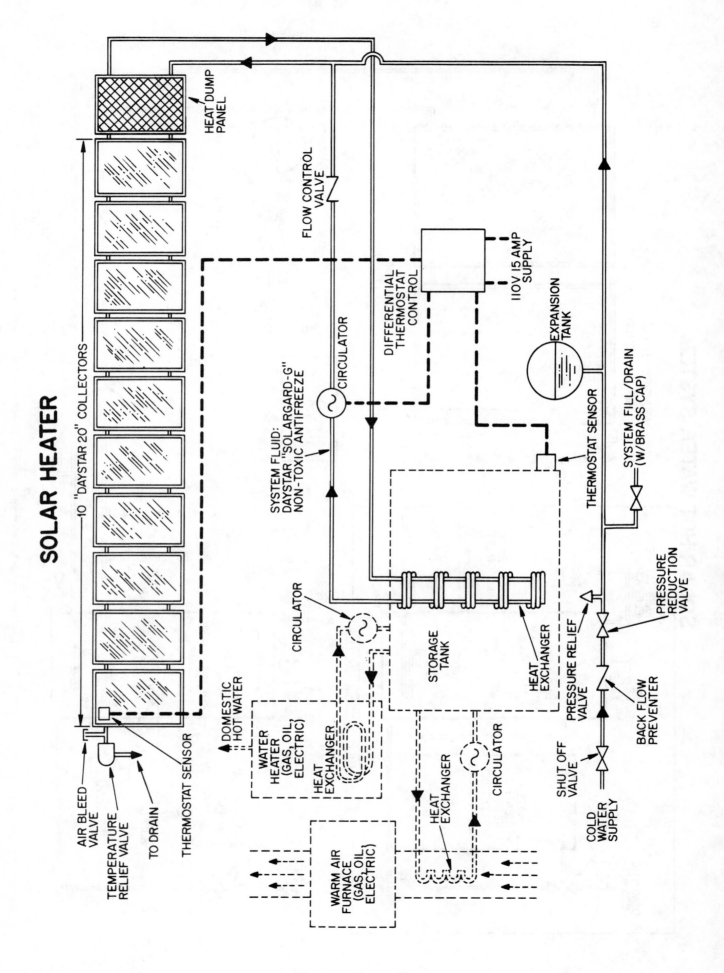

Solar heat is not new, it was the first kind of heat experienced by man. Solar heating will generally provide most of the heat in the spring and fall when the heating load is light and the sun is brightest. Conventional heating systems which are designed to heat a house to 70° F. when the outside temperature is 0° F., work only at about 1/3 capacity during the 10 month heating season. (In some parts of the country.) A solar system designed of smaller capacity than a conventional system will take the heating load for a large percent of the heating time. The number of BTU of heating falling per hour from the sun on one square foot of surface is called Isolation.

Two issues are involved in making solar energy more readily available: Technology and its development and actual process of commercial use. Before solar energy systems become widespread, installers, manufacturers and distributors need to be established and trained, financing needs to be determined, warranties must be developed, building laws and codes must change and be adopted to solar energy.

Tests conducted by New England Electric System showed that solar water heaters will not cover the cost in reduced electric bill for 18 to 20 years. If solar energy is planned, be careful of the rip-off artist.

The following publications are available on solar energy:

SOLAR ENERGY AND YOUR HOME
    Dept. of Housing and Urban Development

BUYING SOLAR
    Office of Consumer Affairs

AMERICAN INSTITUTE OF ARCHITECTS
    1735 New York Avenue, N.W.
    Washington, D.C. 20006

AMERICAN SOCIETY OF HEATING, REFRIGERATING
AND AIR-CONDITIONING ENGINEERS
    345 E. 47th Street
    New York, New York 10017

SOLAR ENERGY INDUSTRIES ASSOCIATION
    1901 Connecticut Avenue, N.W.
    Washington, D.C. 20036

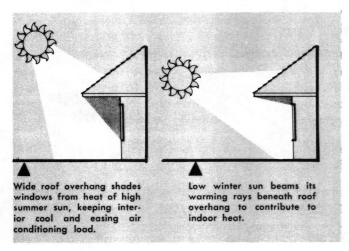

Wide roof overhang shades windows from heat of high summer sun, keeping interior cool and easing air conditioning load.

Low winter sun beams its warming rays beneath roof overhang to contribute to indoor heat.

FIRE STOPS

When the rough mechanical has been completed, but before any insulation is installed in the walls, fire stops are required. (Check local codes.) The spaces between the studs on all bearing partitions form passages concealed from exposure through which a fire may spread rapidly through drafts inside the wall. These fire stops, which are common brick, mineral wool or concrete, are installed between the studs beginning on the top of the foundation wood sill to a height of about 5" above the finish floor. Brick is ideal because the depth of a brick is of the same dimension as the depth of a 2" x 4" stud. The same installation applies on the top of the beam and if more than one story high, the process is repeated at each floor level. If concrete is used, simply nail a 1" x 6" against the studs on the inside and fill the void with concrete. This must be done the entire length of all bearing partitions. Remove the form after the concrete is dry. If brick is used, better spacing will result without cutting the brick if installed on end or soldier coursing.

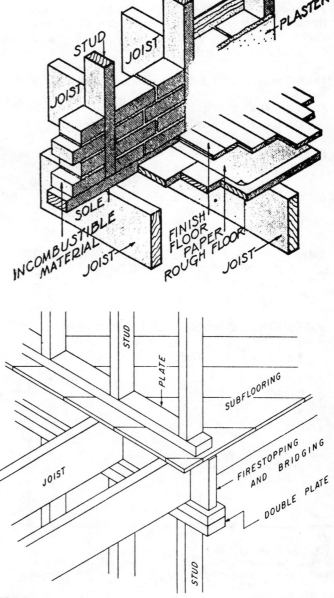

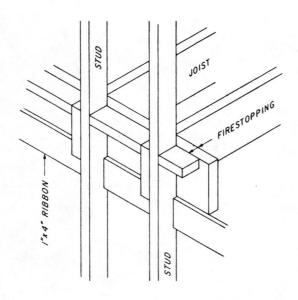

FIRE STOPS

INSULATION and ENERGY

SAVING TECHNIQUES

There is no secret in saving energy and there are limits as to how much energy can be saved in a home, because energy is required for comfort in heating, cooling, lighting and is almost a necessity. Our purpose is to conserve and not use more than is required to meet these needs. The type of energy used in heating and cooling is gas, natural or artificial, oil, and electricity. Fast coming into use is solar energy, but it is still in the experimental stages to be time and field tested, not yet ready for production. Solar energy must have a supplementary back-up system and is not yet designed for a main source of energy.

The amount of heat which is lost through various factors within a house is calculated and the conclusion is a rated heating unit in number of BTU's. This heat loss is determined by area of building, area of glass, area of exterior walls, type and kind of building material used in construction of the walls and heat loss through cracks known as infiltration. All of these factors might require a heating unit rating of about 100,000 BTU's to make up the heat loss. The smaller the BTU capacity, the smaller the unit and consequently the less energy required. The idea is to heat the building to a desired temperature and to sustain or maintain that temperature with a minimum of heat loss and there are several things we can do to reduce this heat loss.

To better understand the theory of heat loss, warm air is attracted to cold air so that when you open the door, the cold air does not come in, but instead the warm air goes out. Our purpose is to reduce, as much as possible, this heat loss by making the building as tight as practical by the use of insulation, weatherstripping, storm windows and doors, etc., in order to hold in as much of the heat as we can.

The basis of computing heat loss in designing a heating unit is to maintain a temperature of 70° fahrenheit inside with a 0° temperature fahrenheit outside except the bathroom which is designed for 75° fahrenheit. These temperatures along with the heat loss calculated, is converted into BTU. What are some of the things we can do to reduce this ener-

gy loss? We can reduce the ratio of exterior wall surface to floor area by carefully dimensioning the overall size of the house. Garages and carports will reduce heat loss. Reducing the ceiling height from 8'–0" to 7'–6" will save about 400 BTU. The following suggestions are based on an average sized house with about 1,200 square feet of floor space. As near a square as possible in house shape can save as much as 600 BTU. Another 1,000 BTU can be gained by avoiding "H", "L" & "T" shaped houses. Reducing the window area to about 10% of the floor area can save about 3,000 BTU. Installing double glazing or storm sash will save another 6,000 BTU. Raising the sill height of the windows will not only provide for better natural light but helps keep the house cooler in the summer because of the roof overhang. The quality of windows affects the heat loss. A poorly fitted window with no weatherstripping can cause as much as five times the infiltration as an average better fitted window. In terms of heat loss, this can be as much as 25,000 BTU. Storm sash alone will save about 3,500 BTU.

Saving energy for air-conditioning must also be considered and the use of storm sash or double glazing is necessary in keeping the heat out, thereby reducing the load on the air-conditioning equipment. A 30" roof overhang is an important part in energy conservation in that it will reduce heat again in the summer and help reduce heat loss in the winter by as much as 1,200 BTU. The average house has two exterior doors and if storm doors were installed as much as another 600 BTU's can be saved and further, if these doors had an interlocking weatherstripping an additional 1,400 BTU's is gained.

In cold climates, by attaching the garage or carport on the northerly exposure and in hot climates on the easterly exposure, will help conserve energy. Trees help by providing shade in the summer and act as a buffer in the winter. Air-conditioning compressors should be located in the shade to help increase the compressor efficiency. If you have a ventilated crawl space, install operating vents which can be closed in the winter and a vapor barrier and perimeter insulation under a concrete floor slab in basementless houses will reduce energy costs. Uninsulated heating ducts in non-livable areas, such as a crawl space, will help keep the area warm by heat loss through the ducts helping the floor above, however, if the ducts were insulated, that heat loss could be saved if you did not want the crawl space heated.

In a full basement house with an average of 2'–0" of basement wall exposure above ground, heat loss through a 12" thick foundation wall would be about 10,000 BTU. By installing 1-1/2" insulation on the interior of the exterior walls, approximately 1,300 BTU's can be saved.

Insulation is rated by thermal factors or "R" value which is the resistance of the material to heat flowing through the insulation. The higher the "R" value, the greater the insulating value. FHA minimum requirements for heated and air-conditioned houses require "R"-19 insulation in ceilings and "R"-11 in walls and floors over uninsulated spaces. The "R" value converted to thickness of insulation is as follows:

An attic fan will reduce the temperature in the summer months. Light colored roof shingles will reflect the sun saving about 600 BTU's.

One of the most direct and initial means of saving energy is not to oversize the mechanical equipment such as heater and air conditioner. This will result in short periods of operation and lower efficiency with greater fuel consumption. Changing filters on the furnace air conditioning unit every season will save fuel. Clogged filters reduce fuel efficiency for heating and cooling. A clock thermostat will automatically control the temperature at a desired setting and if you lower the thermostat 5° at night for 8 hours, you will save about 7% of the annual fuel bill. Setting it back 7° will save about 9% of the annual fuel bill and 10° lower setting will save about 11%. These figures will vary slightly in different parts of the country.

R-VALUES FOR VARIOUS THICKNESS OF INSULATION

	BATTS OR BLANKETS		LOOSE FILL (POURED-IN)			
	Glass Fiber	Rock Wool	Glass Fiber	Rock Wool	Cellulosic Fiber	
R-11	3½" - 4"	3"	5"	4"	3"	R-11
R-13	4"	4½"	6"	4½"	3½"	R-13
R-19	6" - 6½"	5¼"	8" - 9"	6" - 7"	6"	R-19
R-22	8½"	6"	10"	7" - 8"	6"	R-22
R-26	8"	8½"	12"	9"	7" - 7½"	R-26
R-30	9½" - 10½"	9"	13" - 14"	10" - 11"	8"	R-30
R-33	11"	10"	15"	11" - 12"	9"	R-33
R-38	12" - 13"	10½"	17" - 18"	13" - 14"	10" - 11"	R-38

These values vary slightly according to manufacturers.

There is another kind of insulation called Rigid Insulation manufactured in sheets of from 1/2" thick to 4" thick with 1/2" increments in thickness. There are several trade names with varying R values and all will do the same job. Rigid Insulation is used with a solid backing, such as a floor, wall or roof, usually under a concrete floor without a basement, cemented against a concrete or masonry wall behind the finish or on the top side of a roof with exposed planking or beams, under the roof shingles.

In addition, Blanket or Batt Insulation can be had in asphalt impregnated facing paper or foil faced paper or unfaced. The facing forms a vapor barrier for added protection and the installation instructions are clearly marked on the insulation.

In a house with a slab on grade, by using 1" thick rigid insulation along the perimeter of the exterior wall, 24" wide, under the floor, about 4,000 BTU.s can be saved. The "R" values make a difference in savings. For example, R7 value insulation in a house will save about 9,000 BTU's. R11 value will save about 11,000 BTU's. In view of the fact that warm air rises, the ceiling is a very important factor in heat savings. R11 insulation in the ceiling could save about 4,500 BTU's, R19 could save about 12,000 BTU's and R22 may save about 13,000 BTU's.

If you use gas for water heating, a unit with modulating capacities, which is two burners instead of one, gives better overall efficiency. Proper setting of hot water temperature is another means of conserving energy. A setting of 120° is adequate for bathing and washing clothes. Some units are set at between 150° and 180°. The lower setting of 120° could save about from 20% to 25% of the energy required to heat water, which is the second largest energy user in the home.

40% of the hot water load is used for bathing and a low water consumption mixing valve shower head will help save energy.

By installing a humidifier, the humidity can be increased from 20% to 60% offering greater temperature comfort with a reduction of 3° setting on the thermostat saving about 10% of energy heating. Do not use the humidifer during the summer season because it will add to the cooling load.

Providing a recirculating type kitchen range hood in cold climates and an outside exhaust air type in warm climates will also help to conserve energy. A side by side refrigerator/freezer will use about 40% more energy than the conventional over/under refrigerator/freezer. 50% more energy is required for the frostless type unit which amounts to about 200 BTU's. Self cleaning ovens require less energy for cooking but more energy for cleaning. Exhaust fans should have positive shutter closures to prevent large amounts of infiltration when the fan is not in use.

The fourth largest user of energy is lighting. The fluorescent lamps require less energy than incandescent lighting. During the winter months, heat from lighting is regained in the home but in the summer, lighting can add about 800 BTU's in an average home. The use of more special purpose lighting will help conserve energy. Slope the ground outside away from the house to keep the ground next to the foundation dryer and warmer which will reduce the heat load through the foundation walls.

The following are additional recommendations to further conserve energy:

1. Keep the thermostat setting no higher than 68°. The medical profession tells us a cooler house is better for health.

2. If no one will be home for a period of at least six hours or more, turn the thermostat down to 60° before you leave the house and up to 68° when you return. A clock thermost comes in handy for this purpose.

3. Upon retiring, turn the thermostat down to 60°.

4. Check your windows to make sure they are closed tightly with no unreasonable air leaks or broken glass.

5. Turn off all lights when not in use and review the bulb wattages—75 watts may do where you now have 100 watts and 60 watts may do where you now have 75.

6. Clean out the chimney and make sure the top of the chimney is at least 2'-0" above the highest point of the roof for proper efficiency.

7. Keep fireplace dampers closed when not in use.

8. Repair leaking faucets.

9. Use cold water instead of hot whenever possible.

10. Fill, but not overload clothes and dish washing machines.

11. Ventilate attics, one square foot of ventilation for every 150 square feet of space.

12. Caulk around doors, windows and openings.

Most homes built when energy was not expensive did not install enough insulation or any insulation at all. Insulating the attic floor of such a home will do the most good and afford the largest savings. Lay the insulation between the joists with the vapor barrier face down. If some exists, add more to the top of the old. If the old has a vapor barrier, use the unfaced insulation for the new. Do not block the wall vents with insulation, but be sure to start at the wall plate.

When installing insulation in walls, push the insulation in place between the studs so that it touches the inside surface of the sheathing with the vapor barrier on the room side. Make sure there are no gaps. Insulation should touch the wood framing at the top and bottom of each stud space. If more than one piece is required, butt the pieces together snugly. Push insulation behind electrical receptacles, switches, piping and ducts. Stuff all cracks around doors and windows with small pieces of insulation.

To insulate floors over crawl spaces, push the insulation between the floor joists from below with vapor barrier up. Support the insulation by lacing wire back and forth among nails spaced about 2'-0" apart or by stapling chicken wire across the joists.

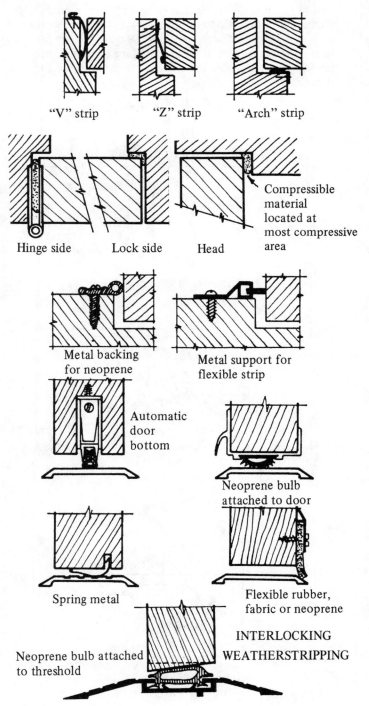

"V" strip   "Z" strip   "Arch" strip

Hinge side   Lock side   Head   Compressible material located at most compressive area

Metal backing for neoprene   Metal support for flexible strip

Automatic door bottom

Neoprene bulb attached to door

Spring metal   Flexible rubber, fabric or neoprene

Neoprene bulb attached to threshold   INTERLOCKING WEATHERSTRIPPING

WEATHERSTRIPPING EXTERIOR DOORS

Weatherstripping seals should be large enough to cope with the allowed tolerances of the various units plus an allowance for distortion which will occur in service. For greater resistance to rain penetration, seals should be placed as far as practicable from the weather face. Where possible, provisions should be made for draining water which passes the weather face before it reaches the weatherstripping. To discourage water from entering peripheral gaps, drip mouldings should be used where practicable.

Door and window units which open outward can often be weatherstripped with a simple compression seal. This is because gusting wind forces tend to move the opening leaf or sash in towards the frame thus closing the unit even tighter. Where doors and windows open inward, adequate weatherstripping is more difficult to achieve because the wind tends to push the unit open. In this case, wiping seals or compression seals with complex locking devices could be used to restrain distortion.

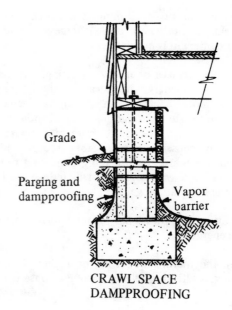

CRAWL SPACE
DAMPPROOFING

When there are no moisture problems traceable to high water table, poor drainage, or rainwater penetration through roofs or exterior walls, the entry of moisture into the crawl space from the soil, with subsequent progress upward into the living areas, may create there a critical relative humidity (condensation) through combination with internally produced moisture. Also decay of wood members in crawl spaces may result from the seepage of moisture into crawl spaces from underlying damp soil.

Crawl spaces should be adequately ventilated and provided with a ground cover.

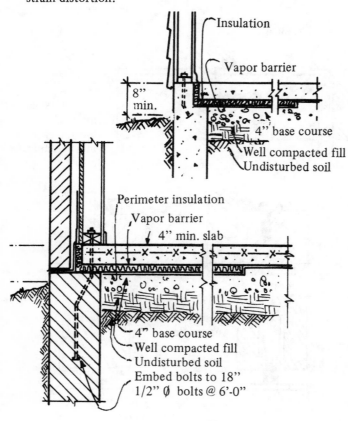

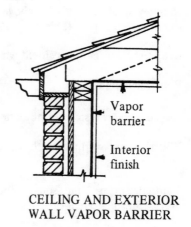

CEILING AND EXTERIOR
WALL VAPOR BARRIER

VAPOR BARRIERS

Walls and Ceilings

Vapor barriers in walls and ceilings protect against the possibility of condensation in winter that could result in paint blistering and peeling or even the rotting of the exterior sheathing and structural members.

Joints in vapor barriers should be lapped over structural members or sealed with tape to provide resistance to vapor transmission.

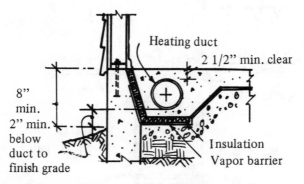

INTERIOR CONCRETE SLABS-ON-GROUND

Here are the new economical levels of insulation recommended by Owens-Corning for six U.S. climatic zones

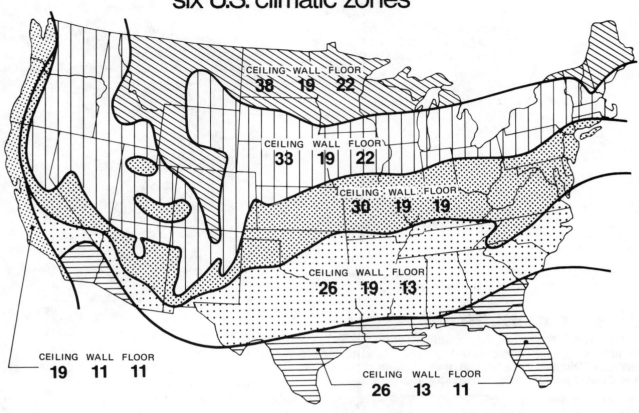

CEILING WALL FLOOR
38 19 22

CEILING WALL FLOOR
33 19 22

CEILING WALL FLOOR
30 19 19

CEILING WALL FLOOR
26 19 13

CEILING WALL FLOOR
19 11 11

CEILING WALL FLOOR
26 13 11

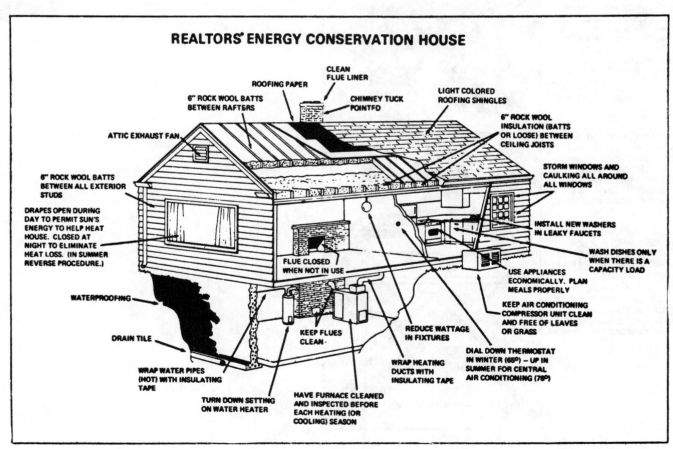

REALTORS' ENERGY CONSERVATION HOUSE

CLEAN FLUE LINER

ROOFING PAPER

6" ROCK WOOL BATTS BETWEEN RAFTERS

CHIMNEY TUCK POINTED

LIGHT COLORED ROOFING SHINGLES

ATTIC EXHAUST FAN

6" ROCK WOOL INSULATION (BATTS OR LOOSE) BETWEEN CEILING JOISTS

6" ROCK WOOL BATTS BETWEEN ALL EXTERIOR STUDS

STORM WINDOWS AND CAULKING ALL AROUND ALL WINDOWS

DRAPES OPEN DURING DAY TO PERMIT SUN'S ENERGY TO HELP HEAT HOUSE. CLOSED AT NIGHT TO ELIMINATE HEAT LOSS. (IN SUMMER REVERSE PROCEDURE.)

INSTALL NEW WASHERS IN LEAKY FAUCETS

WASH DISHES ONLY WHEN THERE IS A CAPACITY LOAD

FLUE CLOSED WHEN NOT IN USE

USE APPLIANCES ECONOMICALLY. PLAN MEALS PROPERLY

WATERPROOFING

KEEP AIR CONDITIONING COMPRESSOR UNIT CLEAN AND FREE OF LEAVES OR GRASS

DRAIN TILE

KEEP FLUES CLEAN

REDUCE WATTAGE IN FIXTURES

DIAL DOWN THERMOSTAT IN WINTER (65°) – UP IN SUMMER FOR CENTRAL AIR CONDITIONING (78°)

WRAP WATER PIPES (HOT) WITH INSULATING TAPE

TURN DOWN SETTING ON WATER HEATER

HAVE FURNACE CLEANED AND INSPECTED BEFORE EACH HEATING (OR COOLING) SEASON

WRAP HEATING DUCTS WITH INSULATING TAPE

1 Pink Fiberglas Batts, with the NAHB Research Foundation label for assured "R-value," installed to Owens-Corning's minimum recommended standards.

2 Double glazed windows, or single glazed with storm sash. Total glass area minimized.

3 Storm door and standard door used in combination, or an insulated door with special seals —to reduce air infiltration.

4 Vapor barriers of 1.0 perm or less—here in walls, and in ceilings and floors, and as ground cover in crawl spaces.

Insulation and moisture

Moisture in your home from cooking, washing dishes, laundering, etc., can cause problems if it reaches a cold surface and condenses within wall or ceiling cavities. Properly applied insulation and good ventilation can help stop this problem.

Vapor barriers such as insulation facings (kraft or foil) or separate vapor barriers (polyethylene or foil-backed gypsum board) should be installed on the warm-in-winter side of walls or ceilings. This will help keep water vapor from reaching a cold surface where it can condense.

To prevent condensation, a positive movement of air out of the attic is essential. Eave vents, openings under the eaves, combined with gable vents or roof vents are effective. As a general rule, one square foot of free vent area should be provided for each 150 square feet of attic floor area when no vapor barrier is used. With a vapor barrier, one square foot of vent area per 300 square feet of floor area is recommended.

Air driven roof vents give an intermediate solution. Power roof or gable vents which are activated by a temperature and humidity control are also used.

5 Perimeter insulation for slab-on-grade construction (placed along edges before slab is poured)—helps keep floors and walls warmer.

Insulation is cheaper than oil. And it can save even more money if it works as part of a total energy-saving system. So, the thermal experts have come up with the system: the Energy-Efficient Home.

It's amazing, for two reasons.

First, thanks to those 10 energy-saving features, it can cut operating costs significantly.

And second, despite those 10 features, it may not cost any more to build than the house without the features!

How can that be possible?

Because there may be major construction trade-offs in an Energy-Efficient Home that offset extra costs, like savings on framing lumber and smaller Heating, Ventilating and Air Conditioning equipment.

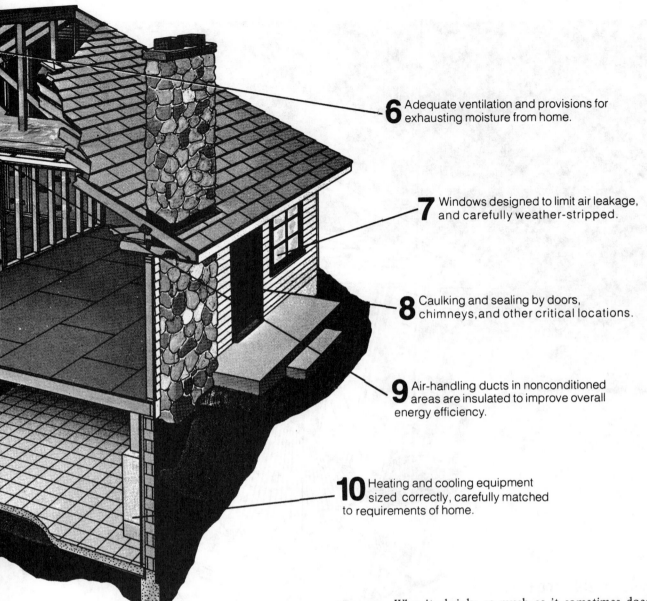

6 Adequate ventilation and provisions for exhausting moisture from home.

7 Windows designed to limit air leakage, and carefully weather-stripped.

8 Caulking and sealing by doors, chimneys, and other critical locations.

9 Air-handling ducts in nonconditioned areas are insulated to improve overall energy efficiency.

10 Heating and cooling equipment sized correctly, carefully matched to requirements of home.

FOAM INSULATION

More and more, government officials are urging home-owners to be cautious about using urea-formaldehyde foam for insulation. If properly applied it can be extremely effective. A string of warnings dealing with the proper application of the foam, which is one of the products blown into existing walls for insulation.

Urea-formeldahyde foam is still considered an acceptable insulator—the Federal Housing Administration will allow it in FHA-insured homes if it meets that agency's standards—but it doesn't deliver the very great amount of thermal protection that originally was expected and claimed.

The foam can shrink more than expected for a longer time than expected, in many if not a majority of cases. That's what reduces its insulating ability. The shrinkage leaves air gaps through which heat passes more readily.

Why it shrinks as much as it sometimes does isn't really understood, particularly because not all foam shrinks by an unacceptable amount. In addition, although urea-formaldahyde foam is basically the same thing no matter who makes it, the formulas vary, and that may have some effect.

Because foaming a wall to insulate it is a process of chemical reaction, it has to be done just right, much as a chemistry lab experiment has to be done just right if you want to get valid results. Potential trouble spots include using ingredients that have degraded because they exceeded their shelf life, mixing ingredients in the wrong proportion, getting the wrong foaming action and putting in the foam when the temperature outside is wrong (under 55 or over 100 degrees Fahrenheit.

Very little research has been done on urea-formeldahyde foam, especially as it acts in a real house wall. What research has been done frequently turns up contradictory results, but it does definitely point to a shrinkage problem. Beyond that, there's confusion and a widely acknowledged need for more research.

THE PROPERLY INSULATED HOME

First, costs plus operating costs have to be considered in the design of homes. Today's typical standard of 6" in ceilings and 3" in walls is no longer adequate. To avoid excessive heating and cooling costs, a home requires a minimum of R-22 for the ceiling, R-13 for floors over unheated spaces and R-13 for exterior walls. Less than this will result in wasted energy, overworked heating/cooling units and high fuel bills. "In some parts of the country," according to the U.S. Department of Commerce's Making the Most of Your Energy Dollars, "when higher priced fuels are used, R-38 insulation (about 12" of mineral fiber batts) in the attic is recommended to give the best results. Even in milder climates, R-30 insulation (about 10") may be economically justified if you use oil or electric heating at current prices."

Here is a home demonstrating the line of energy-conserving insulations and showing the areas requiring thermal protection.

1. Kraft Faced Building Insulation, 2" x 6" studs, 24" o.c. were used in conjunction with R-19 (6") batts to construct this highly efficient wall system.

2. Foil-Faced Building Insulation. To attain additional insulating value from the reflective surface at least a 3/4" air space must be provided.

3. Friction-Fit Building Insulation is an unfaced insulation. Where required, unfaced batts should be covered with a separate vapor barrier such as foil-backed gypsum board or polyethylene film. Sheathing the exterior (3A) with a foam board will increase the overall resistance value of the wall.

4. Sound Control. Multi-family units require building systems to control sound transmission through walls and impact noise in floor/ceiling constructions. Tested systems range from an STC of 34 up to an STC of 63.

5/6. Insulate ceilings to a minimum of R-22 with either blanket insulation or blowing wool. Pictured is R-38, a double layer of R-19 (6") batts, or (6) a combination of blowing wool on top of batt insulation.

7. Fiberglas sill-sealer should cover top of foundation as a barrier to air infiltration.

8. Foundation walls of heated crawl spaces should be insulated with R-11 blanket insulation. A polyethylene vapor barrier should be laid over the ground to prevent moisture build-up in the crawl space area.

9. Floors over unheated crawl spaces, unheated basements and separately heated units should be insulated with Fiberglas batts. The vapor barrier should be placed toward the warm-in-winter side. Where floor vapor barriers are not required unfaced insulation with adequate securement can be used.

10. Walls of below grade living areas should be insulated with Fiberglas masonry wall insulation, or R-8 noise barrier batts where 2" x 3" construction is used to furr out. A separate vapor barrier is normally required.

11. Insulation of slab-on-grade construction is accomplished with rigid Fiberglas perimeter insulation placed along edges of foundation before slab is poured.

Exterior Walls
In room additions, insulate exterior walls with faced insulation stapled in place on warm-in-winter side. Or, unfaced insulation can be used with a separate vapor barrier of either polyethylene or foil-backed gypsum board.

Basement Walls
Insulate basement walls by installing framework of studs or furring strips against masonry walls. Nail bottom plate directly to floor and top plate to joists above. Install pink insulation between studs or furring strips.

Walls Between Heated and Unheated Areas
Insulate walls between heated and unheated areas by placing pink insulation between studs with vapor barrier facing warm-in-winter side. Staple facing at top and hold in place with bowed wire, chicken wire, criss-crossed wires or other methods.

Rips or tears in vapor barriers should be patched after installation. Always install vapor barriers toward the warm-in-winter side of the construction.

Stuff pink insulation in small spaces between studs and in small cracks around doors and window framing to help eliminate heat leaks.

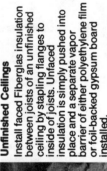

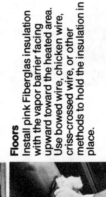

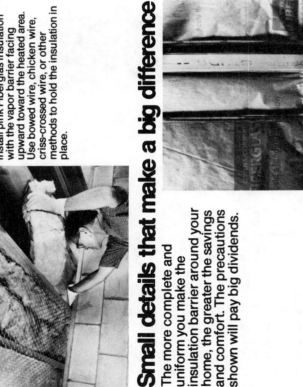

Unfloored Attics
Lay pink Fiberglas insulation between the joists of your attic. If there is no insulation now, use faced insulation with the vapor barrier facing down. If you're adding more insulation, use unfaced Fiberglas insulation. Be sure your insulation covers the top plate but doesn't block any air vents at the eaves.

Unfinished Ceilings
Install faced Fiberglas insulation between joists of an unfinished ceiling by stapling flanges to inside of joists. Unfaced insulation is simply pushed into place and a separate vapor barrier of either polyethylene film or foil-backed gypsum board installed.

Floors
Install pink Fiberglas insulation with the vapor barrier facing upward toward the heated area. Use bowed wire, chicken wire, criss-crossed wire, or other methods to hold the insulation in place.

Small details that make a big difference
The more complete and uniform you make the insulation barrier around your home, the greater the savings and comfort. The precautions shown will pay big dividends.

Insulation installed behind pipes and electrical outlets can help eliminate frozen pipes and drafts around outlets.

CONDENSATION

One of the biggest headaches a homeowner can face is the problem of condensation. The headache can be cured, usually easily and cheaply, by means of vapor barriers and ventilation. But very few people understand the mechanics of vapor barriers, ventilation and condensation.

Paint failure on exterior walls is very often caused by water vapor from inside the home. As excess water builds up indoors during the cold season, it migrates outward and condenses on the cold house siding. It soaks the wood, stains the siding and causes peeling paint. Or the vapor may try to push right on out through the paint, causing blisters.

Excess water vapor migrates to an unheated attic in the winter. There it condenses and forms ice. Over the winter months, the ice builds up. When warm weather comes, the ice melts. It drips down to the ceiling below and causes damage.

Water vapor condenses in a cold wall cavity and soaks the insulation. This makes the insulation less effective. Heating costs rise.

Water vapor migrates outward and condenses on the cold inner face of a brick veneer wall. It then soaks through the bricks, leaching out salts in the bricks and depositing a white powdery stain called efflorescence on the outer face of the wall.

All these problems and others including rot and decay can be eliminated with a proper vapor barrier, and in some cases, minimal ventilation. Ideally, both barrier and ventilation should have been built into the house during construction. That's when the job is easiest. If they weren't however, there are ways to add them later.

A vapor barrier is anything which restricts the passage of water vapor. It may be a plastic film, aluminum foil fastened to insulation batts, special types of paper, even certain kinds of paint.

The primary location for a vapor barrier is between any heated area and the cold area next to it. The important thing to remember is that the barrier always goes on the warm side of that floor, ceiling, or wall, because that stops the migration of the vapor before it can reach a cold surface where it will condense and cause damage.

CELLULOSE INSULATION

The Federal Trade Commission, the State Energy Office and the Cooperative Extension Association are warning homeowners to be wary of a possible fire problem with cellulose insulation.

The energy office said cellulose—generally made of shredded paper—"is an excellent insulating material if properly treated." The office suggests looking for a "flame spread rating"—a commonly accepted measure of flammability—of less than 50, certified by Underwriters Laboratory or the National Cellulose Insulation Manufacturers Association. Also suggested: get written confirmation of the rating from an installer, or be sure it's on the bag if your installing it yourself.

A cooperative extension speaker said that, to be sure, take a sample handful of any cellulose insulation you get and try to set fire to it with a lighter, on a nonflammable surface.

The FTC said consumer deception is most likely in claims about flammability or thermal resistance. It said that, although cellulose insulation may meet standards, it still shouldn't be installed near such a heat source as a recessed ceiling light.

The vent opening for enclosed structural spaces of porch and canopy roofs should equal at least 1/300 of the ceiling area.

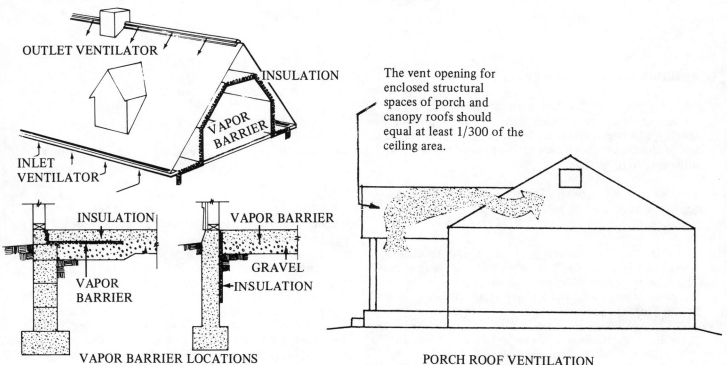

OUTLET VENTILATOR

INSULATION

VAPOR BARRIER

INLET VENTILATOR

INSULATION

VAPOR BARRIER

VAPOR BARRIER

GRAVEL

INSULATION

VAPOR BARRIER LOCATIONS

PORCH ROOF VENTILATION

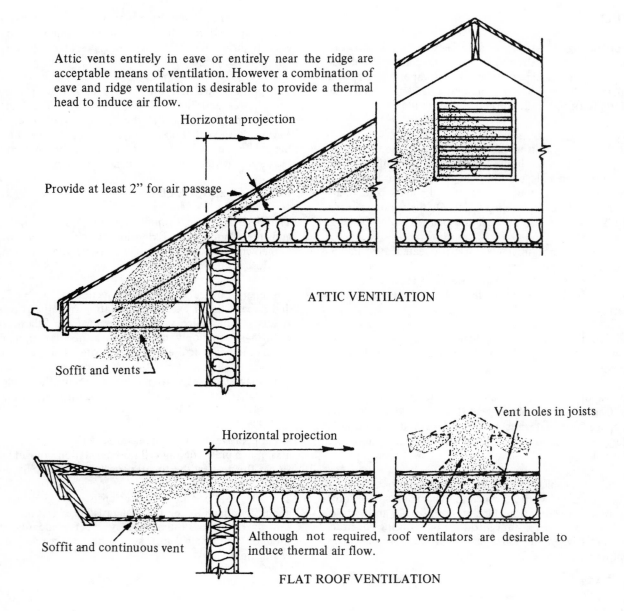

Attic vents entirely in eave or entirely near the ridge are acceptable means of ventilation. However a combination of eave and ridge ventilation is desirable to provide a thermal head to induce air flow.

Horizontal projection

Provide at least 2" for air passage

ATTIC VENTILATION

Soffit and vents

Horizontal projection

Vent holes in joists

Soffit and continuous vent

Although not required, roof ventilators are desirable to induce thermal air flow.

FLAT ROOF VENTILATION

WINDOWS AND ENERGY SAVING

New generations of glass and recent advances in frame design and construction are only some of the factors which have helped bring windows to the point where many wooden and aluminum models now on the market have U values in the 0.40 to 0.60 range.

Windows perform six energy functions. These are solar heating, daylighting, shading, insulation, air tightness, and ventilation.

As a solar collector, window glass can produce substantial savings on fuel bills. The light admitted by a window can substitute for artificial lighting, cutting down on electric energy use. Use of windows for ventilating can ease air conditioning loads in warm months.

These and other functions can be significantly heightened by selection of appropriate materials and designs.

GLASS AS A KEY ELEMENT

There are three basic varieties, of glass:

Plain, clear glass is the least energy efficient type.

Glass that absorbs heat, absorbs the sun's rays and reradiates the energy, chiefly to the outside.

Reflective, or high performance glass, controls the amount of light and heat that passes through it from as low as eight percent to nearly any degree of solar radiation desired. This type can be tinted silver, gold, grey, blue, or bronze on the outside without coloring the light that passes through it to the interior. The colors offer obvious design uses in addition to their primary energy control role.

Multiple glazing improves the efficiency of all three types of glass, since it is essentially a means of providing insulation. Glass is a good conductor of heat, and multiple glazing provides insulating air space to reduce heat losses.

The greatest reduction in U values with the most efficiency takes place when the space between the glass panels is between 3/16 and 5/8 of an inch in width.

Triple glazing is more effective than double glazing with the same overall width. Triple glazing with two quarter-inch air spaces has a U value of 0.47, compared to 0.58 for double glazing with a single half-inch air space.

Even greater efficiency is possible: an uncoated triple glazed window with two half-inch air spaces has a U-value of 0.36.

Time of day and seasons the building is most in use, local climate and type of activity for which the building is needed, determine which design strategies will be most helpful.

Good window orientation to the sun and prevailing winds are primary factors in energy saving site design. Shade trees can control direct heat radiation from the sun on a seasonal basis and ground cover can help control reflected heat radiation to the unit. Planted ground cover also helps moderate air temperatures.

Trees and landscaping, fences, and walls act as effective windbreakers. The best location for a windbreaker tree is at a distance 1½ to 2½ times the height of the building. This deflects the wind over the building. reducing, "pushing action" on the building's "windward" side and "pulling action" on the "leeward" side. (See Figure 1.)

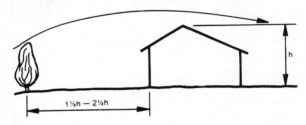

Fig. 1.

A fence or wall windbreaker is most effective, if part of the wind is allowed to penetrate. While heat transmission through windows is reduced by cutting the amount of wind flowing across the glass, a still layer of air at the glass surface helps retard heat flow.

A solid, rather than partially open windbreaker fence creates strong "eddy currents" that erode the still air at the window's surface. This can cancel out the benefits of the windbreak fence by sucking the still layer away. (See Fig. 2 & 3)

Since winter winds come from a different direction than summer winds, it is possible, to place windbreaks so as to divert winter wind without interfering with desirable summer breezes.

Some of the advantages of using windbreaks and landscape cover are:

1. Reduced air infiltration through the cracks around windows.

2. Reduced heat loss through glass by diminished wind erosion of insulating air layer at glass surface.

3. Partial protection from summer sun, east and west, when sun is low in sky.

Disadvantages:

1. Possible need to prune, fertilize, water and spray greenery for insects.

2. Difficulty in finding right spot for windbreak in built-up areas, due to complex wind patterns.

3. Possible decrease of security when windbreak hides units from neighbors' and pedestrians' view.

HOW TO USE SHADE TREES

Deciduous trees provide shade in summer and admit sunlight in winter, while evergreens provide shade in summer and reduce window heat loss in winter.

A tree-shaded, south-facing window receives less solar heat than an unshaded north-facing window.

Trees not only reduce window heat gain by direct blocking but by lowering ground surface temperature.

The winter sky generally, has a much colder temperature than the ground, which retains heat absorbed during the sunlight hours. Therefore, an evergreen planted near a window stands between the colder night air and the window. The tree will reduce the loss of heat from window to night sky.

Some disadvantages of tree use for shade in this manner are the need for maintenance including removing leaves from grounds and rainwater gutters; possible damage to window or building due to lightening or wind-broken tree branches; possible root blockage of underground sewer pipes; winter solar heat gain blocked by evergreens.

The major advantages, in addition to energy savings are aesthetic. Trees change the quality of interior light in the units and surrounding outside area; can unify architectural design; alter visual impact of building on landscape.

Light-colored surfaces will reflect extra sunlight into windows; dark surfaces will absorb sunlight and raise outside temperatures. Planted surfaces absorb sunlight, and lower outside temperature at the same time.

Since light reflected into first floor windows on the sunlit side of a building may account for 10 to 15 percent of total daylight transmitted, choice of ground surface is quite important. White paint, for instance, reflects 75 percent while macadam reflects only 18 percent.

Paved surfaces, light and dark, generally add more heat to units. Light adds more in winter through reflection, black, through air absorption, next to windows. Planted cover is deemed the best for decreasing air conditioning loads in summer because light heat is stored in vegetation, and day and night temperature fluctuate less.

burden. Nothern latitude buildings, to make the most of winter sun heat gain, should concentrate windows on the south (See Figure 4).

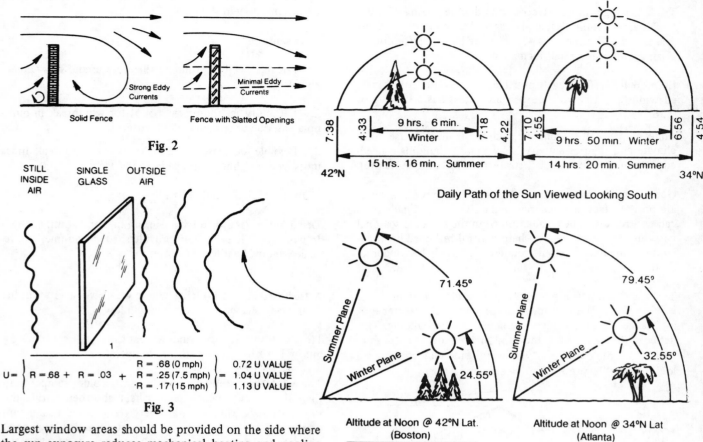

Fig. 2

Fig. 3

Daily Path of the Sun Viewed Looking South

Daily Path of the Sun Viewed Looking East

Fig. 4

Largest window areas should be provided on the side where the sun exposure reduces mechanical heating and cooling needs.

The major benefit of sun transmission through windows is if solar winter heat gain exceeds window heat loss and summer solar heat gain.

The determining factors in heat transmission are angle of sun rays and the number of hours a window receives sunlight. Windows can be tilted to vary light and heat absorption.

The least light is absorbed or reflected when windows are at a 90 degree angle to the light rays. This increases gradually to an angle of 45 degrees. After that, the amount of light absorbed or reflected increases until no light is transmitted.

Since the number of hours a window receives direct sunlight varies with the path of the sun, seasons and latitude, geographical data must be carefully studied.

The further north a site, the more winter sunlight a south exposure permits vs. east and west exposures. The further south a site, the less summer sunlight a south exposure gets compared to east and west exposures.

Therefore, southern latitude locations should have windows mostly on north and south to minimize air conditioning

One possible disadvantage is winter overheating with large south-facing windows in small rooms within lightweight construction buildings.

Cross ventilation can be provided with windows that are out of alignment with wind direction. If window placement on opposite sides of interior space is not possible, the building should be oriented to the direction of the wind.

If placement on adjacent sides is possible then the building should face right into the wind. The object is to create turbulence or air movement within a room. Placement of interior partitions helps develop the proper air movement as well.

Obviously, this reduces the need for mechanical ventilation and air conditioning. There may be a conflict in some buildings between sun, wind and view orientations. It is not suggested in areas of extreme noise or air pollution.

CEILING FINISHES

32

ACOUSTICAL TILE

One of the least expensive ways of finishing a new or old ceiling is with acoustical tile. There are basically three construction methods in doing this: cement to a solid sound surface, apply to 1" x 3" wood furring spaced 12" apart and suspended or lay-in panels by metal suspension system called tees. The selection of texture, color and tile size is varied, 12" x 12", 12" x 24" and 24" x 48" in thickness of 1/2" and 5/8" made of Mineral Fiber, Asbestos or Fiberglass.

If you choose the cemented method, apply 12" x 12" to a solid sound firm surface. If the existing plaster ceiling is cracked but firm and sound you can apply the tile to the surface. The cement is ready to use and is applied to the back side of the tile. Before application, preparation is important to remove loose plaster and scale.

Find the exact center of the room using diagonals and work in all directions radiating from this central point. When you reach the walls, you should have an even margin along the perimeter. If you finish with a tile cut less than half a tile width, begin the first center tile not on the centerline of the tile, but use the centerline of the ceiling as one edge of the first tile. This should be laid out before any cementing is done. When you have carefully planned the room you are now ready for application. Be sure each tile lies perfectly square against the adjacent tile. There is to be no margin for error. If all joints are not in perfect alignment, each tile will creep causing a chain reaction ending in a gross misalignment of tiles.

These tiles are easily cut with a saw. If there is a lighting fixture on the ceiling, remove the fixture exposing the outlet box and snugly fit or cut around it. This is not a difficult job. Simply chalk the edges of the box with carpenters blue chalk, press the tile into position against the box causing the chalk mark to transfer on the back side of the tile which is your cutting line. When the tile is in place, replace the lighting fixture.

If the existing ceiling is badly damaged, it must be furred with 1" x 3" wood furring strips nailed to the ceiling joists spaced 12" apart. The ceiling tile is then nailed to the fur-

ring strips with a special concealed nail. In applying the furring strips, the same theory must be used as the cemented tile to finish with an even perimeter border because the edge of the tile is nailed to half the width of the furring strip. If you prefer, a ceiling moulding may be used along the perimeter of the ceiling against the wall to conceal the cut edge of the tile.

The third method of installation is suspended or drop-in tile. The size of the grid is 24" x 24" or 24" x 48". Use the smaller size for small rooms. The metal suspension system must first be installed by establishing a ceiling height. The minimum working space required when suspending a ceiling below another ceiling is 3". Snap a line on all walls at the level of the new ceiling. Be sure this line is level. A sheet metal angle is nailed along this line. The main suspension beams are then put into place by hanging with wire from the structure above with the ends of the suspension beams resting on the wall angle. Be sure this hanger is straight and level by adjusting the hanging wire. These main carrying beams or tees are 12'-0" long and should span the short dimension of the room. Hang a wire about 4'-0" apart. These main suspension beams are placed 4'-0" apart. When this is completed, simply snap into place the metal cross tees which are designed to fit into the spacing of the main suspension beams and are spaced 2'-0" apart. You now have a 2'-0" x 4'-0" grid and all you need do now is drop the tile into the grid.

In addition to acoustical tile drop-in units, you have a choice of a clear plastic unit with fluorescent lighting above the suspension system illuminating the entire ceiling. Another choice is a plastic egg-crate shape unit with 1/2" square grid used in the same fashion as the plastic unit. In either case a very inexpensive industrial type fluorescent lighting fixture without a shield should be used above the suspension system. The lighting fixtures must be installed before the suspended ceiling.

Acoustical ceilings that are unsatisfactory in appearance are usually the result of poor application. Before ceiling materials are installed, the units should be permitted to reach room temperature and have a stabilized moisture content. They should not be installed in areas where the temperature or humidity vary greatly from the temperatures and conditions that will be normal. Acoustical materials are interior finish products and are designed for installation within the normal expected range of 60° to 85° F. Relative humidity should not be more than 70%. All plastering and other wet work should be complete and dry. All windows and doors should be installed. Heating, Ventilating, Plumbing and Air-conditioning systems should be installed and ready to operate. The temperature of the tile cement and the surface to which the tile is cemented may cause cement failure. Do not cement acoustical tile when room temperatures exceed 100° F. or when the room or cement temperature is below 50° F. Application to a damp plaster or damp room may cause dimensional changes in the tile and failure in the adhesive. Tile cemented to a painted surface will fail if the paint is loose or peeling.

Some ceiling materials are more abuse-resistant than others. It is not good practice to locate acoustical tile or panels on low wall or ceiling surfaces where they might be damaged. Most acoustical ceilings are good thermal insulators. In relatively cold climates where the problem is one of preventing condensation on the underside of cold roof surfaces, it is best to locate vapor-sealed insulation on top of the suspension system.

When selecting lighting, it is best to install the flush recessed fixtures because this will eliminate the shadow problems of side lighting. Lighting fixtures located close to the ceiling will show light grazes across the ceiling and emphasize variations as small as .005 of an inch.

Dust and loose dirt may be easily removed by brushing or with a vacuum cleaner attachment. Be sure to clean in one direction only. Pencil marks, smudges or clinging dirt may be erased with an art gum eraser. A good grade wall cleaner applied with a moist cloth or sponge dampened with as little water as possible, is a good cleaner. After washing, the soapy film should be wiped off.

Acoustical ceilings can be painted by spraying, brushing or rolller without losing any appreciable acoustical efficiency. For best results, panels should be removed, laid flat for painting and allowed to dry throughly while still flat before reinstalling. A good grade paint from a reputable manufacturer should be used.

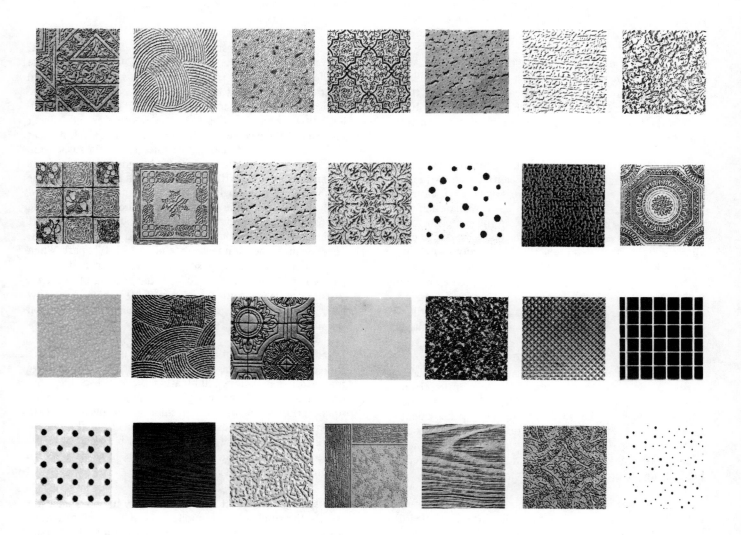

ROOM LENGTH

	8'	9'	10'	11'	12'	13'	14'	15'	16'	17'	18'
8'	2	3	3	3	3	4	4	4	4	5	5
9'	3	3	3	4	4	4	5	5	5	5	5
10'	3	3	3	4	4	4	5	5	5	5	5
11'	3	4	4	4	5	5	5	6	6	6	7
12'	3	4	4	5	5	5	5	6	6	7	7
13'	4	4	4	5	5	6	6	7	7	7	8
14'	4	5	5	5	5	6	6	7	7	8	8
15'	4	5	5	6	6	7	7	7	8	8	9
16'	4	5	5	6	6	7	7	8	8	9	9

ROOM WIDTH (vertical label)

Prepack Estimating Guide—The back of each carton of pre-packaged integrid metal components contains estimating charts to help you determine your material requirements. By locating and cross-referencing your room length and room width, you can quickly arrive at the exact number of prepacks needed to do the job.

i.e.— If your room dimensions are 10' x 15', you would need five integrid prepacks to install the ceiling. Note: When installing Wood Grain Plank or Dark Wood Grain Plank Ceilings, seven additional 4' cross tees are needed for each carton of prepackaged material purchased.

EXPOSED WOOD PLANK

Unlike most conventional ceilings in wood frame construction, this is a system called Plank and Beam Construction whereas the plank or wood ceiling is a structural part of the framing system in conjunction with structural wood beams, all of which are exposed for a finished ceiling. With this type system, no further finish is required on the wood. If you prefer, you may stain the wood but the only thing you will accomplish is the change in the color of of the wood. This system of construction is protected inside the building and needs no further treatment.

GYPSUM BOARD

See wall finishes.

PLASTER

See wall finish.

DRYWALL

See wall finish.

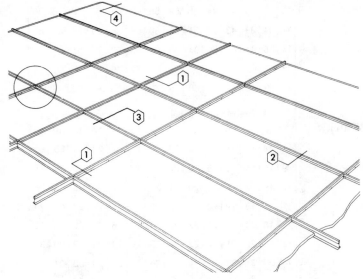

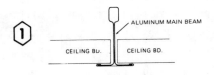

(1) ALUMINUM MAIN BEAM — CEILING BD. | CEILING BD.

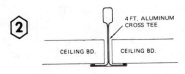

(2) 4 FT. ALUMINUM CROSS TEE — CEILING BD. | CEILING BD.

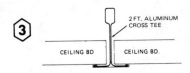

(3) 2 FT. ALUMINUM CROSS TEE — CEILING BD | CEILING BD.

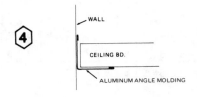

(4) WALL — CEILING BD. — ALUMINUM ANGLE MOLDING

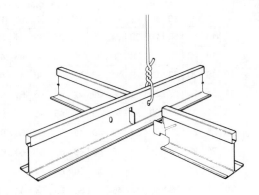

ESTIMATING GUIDE FOR/INTEGRID FURRING CHANNEL SYSTEM

12" x 12" TILES

Room dimension parallel to joist direction (rows) × Room dimension perpendicular to joist direction (columns)

	8'	9'	10'	11'	12'	13'	14'	15'	16'	17'	18'	19'	20'
8'	64	72	80	88	96	104	112	120	128	136	144	152	160
9'	72	81	90	99	108	117	126	135	144	153	162	171	180
10'	80	90	100	110	120	130	140	150	160	170	180	190	200
11'	88	99	110	121	132	143	154	165	176	187	198	209	220
12'	96	108	120	132	144	156	168	180	192	204	216	228	240
13'	104	117	130	143	156	169	182	195	208	221	234	247	260
14'	112	126	140	154	168	182	196	210	224	238	252	266	280
15'	120	135	150	165	180	195	210	225	240	255	270	285	300
16'	128	144	160	176	192	208	224	240	256	272	288	304	320
17'	136	153	170	187	204	221	238	255	272	289	306	323	340
18'	144	162	180	198	216	234	252	270	288	306	324	342	360
19'	152	171	190	209	228	247	266	285	304	323	342	361	380
20'	160	180	200	220	240	260	280	300	320	340	360	380	400

12" x 48" TILES

	8'	9'	10'	11'	12'	13'	14'	15'	16'	17'	18'	19'	20'
8'	16	18	20	22	24	26	28	30	32	34	36	38	40
9'	18	21	23	25	27	30	32	34	36	39	41	43	45
10'	20	23	25	28	30	33	35	38	40	43	45	48	50
11'	22	25	28	31	33	36	39	42	44	47	50	53	55
12'	24	27	30	33	36	39	42	45	48	51	54	57	60
13'	26	30	33	36	39	43	46	49	52	56	59	62	65
14'	28	32	35	39	42	46	49	53	56	60	63	67	70
15'	30	34	38	42	45	49	53	57	60	64	68	72	75
16'	32	36	40	44	48	52	56	60	64	68	72	76	80
17'	34	39	43	47	51	56	60	64	68	73	77	81	85
18'	36	41	45	50	54	59	63	68	72	77	81	86	90
19'	38	43	48	53	57	62	67	72	76	81	86	91	95
20'	40	45	50	55	60	65	70	75	80	85	90	95	100

WALL MOLDING (LIN. FT.)

	8'	9'	10'	11'	12'	13'	14'	15'	16'	17'	18'	19'	20'
8'	32	34	36	38	40	42	44	46	48	50	52	54	56
9'	34	36	38	40	42	44	46	48	50	52	54	56	58
10'	36	38	40	42	44	46	48	50	52	54	56	58	60
11'	38	40	42	44	46	48	50	52	54	56	58	60	62
12'	40	42	44	46	48	50	52	54	56	58	60	62	64
13'	42	44	46	48	50	52	54	56	58	60	62	64	66
14'	44	46	48	50	52	54	56	58	60	62	64	66	68
15'	46	48	50	52	54	56	58	60	62	64	66	68	70
16'	48	50	52	54	56	58	60	62	64	66	68	70	72
17'	50	52	54	56	58	60	62	64	66	68	70	72	74
18'	52	54	56	58	60	62	64	66	68	70	72	74	76
19'	54	56	58	60	62	64	66	68	70	72	74	76	78
20'	56	58	60	62	64	66	68	70	72	74	76	78	80

WALL SPRINGS

	8'	9'	10'	11'	12'	13'	14'	15'	16'	17'	18'	19'	20'
8'	14	15	16	17	18	19	20	21	22	23	24	25	26
9'	15	16	17	18	19	20	21	22	23	24	25	26	27
10'	16	17	18	19	20	21	22	23	24	25	26	27	28
11'	17	18	19	20	21	22	23	24	25	26	27	28	29
12'	18	19	20	21	22	23	24	25	26	27	28	29	30
13'	19	20	21	22	23	24	25	26	27	28	29	30	31
14'	20	21	22	23	24	25	26	27	28	29	30	31	32
15'	21	22	23	24	25	26	27	28	29	30	31	32	33
16'	22	23	24	25	26	27	28	29	30	31	32	33	34
17'	23	24	25	26	27	28	29	30	31	32	33	34	35
18'	24	25	26	27	28	29	30	31	32	33	34	35	36
19'	25	26	27	28	29	30	31	32	33	34	35	36	37
20'	26	27	28	29	30	31	32	33	34	35	36	37	38

CROSS TEES

	8'	9'	10'	11'	12'	13'	14'	15'	16'	17'	18'	19'	20'
8'	14	16	18	20	22	24	26	28	30	32	34	36	38
9'	18	20	23	25	28	30	33	35	38	40	43	45	48
10'	18	20	23	25	28	30	33	35	38	40	43	45	48
11'	21	24	27	30	33	36	39	42	45	48	51	54	57
12'	21	24	27	30	33	36	39	42	45	48	51	54	57
13'	25	28	32	35	39	42	46	49	53	56	60	63	67
14'	25	28	32	35	39	42	46	49	53	56	60	63	67
15'	28	32	36	40	44	48	52	56	60	64	68	72	76
16'	28	32	36	40	44	48	52	56	60	64	68	72	76
17'	32	36	41	45	50	54	59	63	68	72	77	81	86
18'	32	36	41	45	50	54	59	63	68	72	77	81	86
19'	36	40	45	50	55	60	65	70	75	80	85	90	95
20'	36	40	45	50	55	60	65	70	75	80	85	90	95

FURRING CHANNEL 12' LENGTH

	8'	9'	10'	11'	12'	13'	14'	15'	16'	17'	18'	19'	20'
8'	2	2	2	2	2	3	3	3	3	3	3	4	4
9'	2	2	2	2	2	3	3	3	3	3	3	4	4
10'	2	2	2	2	3	3	3	3	3	3	4	4	4
11'	2	3	3	3	3	4	4	4	4	5	5	5	5
12'	2	3	3	3	3	4	4	4	4	5	5	5	5
13'	2	3	3	3	3	4	4	4	4	5	5	5	5
14'	2	3	3	3	3	4	4	4	4	5	5	5	5
15'	3	3	4	4	4	5	5	5	6	6	6	7	7
16'	3	3	4	4	4	5	5	5	6	6	6	7	7
17'	3	3	4	4	4	5	5	5	6	6	6	7	7
18'	3	3	4	4	4	5	5	5	6	6	6	7	7
19'	4	4	5	5	5	6	6	7	7	8	8	8	9
20'	4	4	5	5	5	6	6	7	7	8	8	8	9

2' x 4' PANELS

Room dimension perpendicular to joist direction

Room dimension parallel to joist direction

	8'	10'	12'	14'	16'	18'	20'	22'	24'	26'	28'	30'	32'	34'	36'	38'	40'	42'	44'	46'	48'	50'
8'	8	10	12	14	16	18	20	22	24	26	28	30	32	34	36	38	40	42	44	46	48	50
12'	12	15	18	21	24	27	30	33	36	39	42	45	48	51	54	57	60	63	66	69	72	75
16'	16	20	24	28	32	36	40	44	48	52	56	60	64	68	72	76	80	84	88	92	96	100
20'	20	25	30	35	40	45	50	55	60	65	70	75	80	85	90	95	100	105	110	115	120	125
24'	24	30	36	42	48	54	60	66	72	78	84	90	96	102	108	114	120	126	132	138	144	150
28'	28	35	42	49	56	63	70	77	84	91	98	105	112	119	126	133	140	147	154	161	168	175
32'	32	40	48	56	64	72	80	88	96	104	112	120	128	136	144	152	160	168	176	184	192	200
36'	36	45	54	63	72	81	90	99	108	117	126	135	144	153	162	171	180	189	198	207	216	225
40'	40	50	60	70	80	90	100	100	120	130	140	150	160	170	180	190	200	210	220	230	240	250

12' MAIN RUNNERS

Room dimension perpendicular to joist direction

Room dimension parallel to joist direction

	8'	10'	12'	14'	16'	18'	20'	22'	24'	26'	28'	30'	32'	34'	36'	38'	40'	42'	44'	46'	48'	50'
8'	1	1	1	2	2	2	2	2	3	3	3	3	3	3	4	4	4	4	4	4	4	5
12'	2	2	2	3	3	3	4	4	4	5	5	5	6	6	6	7	7	7	8	8	8	9
16'	2	3	3	4	4	5	5	6	6	7	7	8	8	9	9	10	10	11	11	12	12	13
20'	3	4	4	5	6	6	7	8	8	9	10	10	11	12	12	13	14	14	15	16	16	17
24'	4	5	5	6	7	8	9	10	10	11	12	13	14	15	15	16	17	18	19	20	20	21
28'	4	5	6	7	8	9	10	11	12	13	14	15	16	17	18	19	20	21	22	23	24	25
32'	5	6	7	9	10	11	12	13	14	16	17	18	19	20	21	23	24	25	26	27	28	30
36'	6	7	8	10	11	12	14	15	16	18	19	20	22	23	24	26	27	28	30	31	32	34
40'	6	8	9	11	12	14	15	17	18	20	21	23	24	26	27	29	30	32	33	35	36	38

4' CROSS TEES

Room dimension perpendicular to joist direction

Room dimension parallel to joist direction

	8'	10'	12'	14'	16'	18'	20'	22'	24'	26'	28'	30'	32'	34'	36'	38'	40'	42'	44'	46'	48'	50'
8'	6	8	10	12	14	16	18	20	22	24	26	28	30	32	34	36	38	40	42	44	46	48
12'	9	12	15	16	21	24	27	30	33	36	39	42	45	48	51	54	57	60	63	66	69	72
16'	12	16	20	24	28	32	36	40	44	48	52	56	60	64	68	72	76	80	84	88	92	96
20'	15	20	25	30	35	40	45	50	55	60	65	70	75	80	85	90	95	100	105	110	115	120
24'	18	24	30	36	42	48	54	60	66	72	78	84	90	96	102	108	114	120	126	132	138	144
28'	21	28	35	42	49	56	63	70	77	84	91	98	105	112	119	126	133	140	147	154	161	168
32'	24	32	40	48	56	64	72	80	88	96	104	112	120	128	136	144	152	160	168	176	184	192
36'	27	36	45	54	63	72	81	90	99	108	117	126	135	144	153	162	171	180	189	198	207	216
40'	30	40	50	60	70	80	90	100	110	120	130	140	150	160	170	180	190	200	210	220	230	240

10' WALL MOLDING

Room dimension perpendicular to joist direction

Room dimension parallel to joist direction

	8'	10'	12'	14'	16'	18'	20'	22'	24'	26'	28'	30'	32'	34'	36'	38'	40'	42'	44'	46'	48'	50'
8'	4	4	4	5	5	6	6	6	7	7	8	8	8	9	9	10	10	10	11	11	12	12
12'	4	5	5	6	6	6	7	7	8	8	8	9	9	10	10	10	11	11	12	12	12	13
16'	5	6	6	6	7	7	8	8	8	9	9	10	10	10	11	11	12	12	12	13	13	14
20'	6	6	7	7	8	8	8	9	9	10	10	10	11	11	12	12	12	13	13	14	14	14
24'	7	7	8	8	8	9	9	10	10	10	11	11	12	12	12	13	13	14	14	14	15	15
28'	8	8	8	9	9	10	10	10	11	11	12	12	12	13	13	14	14	14	15	15	16	16
32'	8	9	9	10	10	10	11	11	12	12	12	13	13	14	14	14	15	15	16	16	16	17
36'	9	10	10	10	11	11	12	12	12	13	13	14	14	14	15	15	16	16	16	17	17	18
40'	10	10	11	11	12	12	12	13	13	14	14	14	15	15	16	16	16	17	17	18	18	18

12" x 12" TILES

Room dimension perpendicular to joist direction (columns); Room dimension parallel to joist direction (rows)

	8'	9'	10'	11'	12'	13'	14'	15'	16'	17'	18'	19'	20'
8'	64	72	80	88	96	104	112	120	128	136	144	152	160
9'	72	81	90	99	108	117	126	135	144	153	162	171	180
10'	80	90	100	110	120	130	140	150	160	170	180	190	200
11'	88	99	110	121	132	143	154	165	176	187	198	209	220
12'	96	108	120	132	144	156	168	180	192	204	216	228	240
13'	104	117	130	143	156	169	182	195	208	221	234	247	260
14'	112	126	140	154	168	182	196	210	224	238	252	266	280
15'	120	135	150	165	180	195	210	225	240	255	270	285	300
16'	128	144	160	176	192	208	224	240	256	272	288	304	320
17'	136	153	170	187	204	221	238	255	272	289	306	323	340
18'	144	162	180	198	216	234	252	270	288	306	324	342	360
19'	152	171	190	209	228	247	266	285	304	323	342	361	380
20'	160	180	200	220	240	260	280	300	320	340	360	380	400

12" x 48" TILES

Room dimension perpendicular to joist direction (columns); Room dimension parallel to joist direction (rows)

	8'	9'	10'	11'	12'	13'	14'	15'	16'	17'	18'	19'	20'
8'	16	18	20	22	24	26	28	30	32	34	36	38	40
9'	18	21	23	25	27	30	32	34	36	39	41	43	45
10'	20	23	25	28	30	33	35	38	40	43	45	48	50
11'	22	25	28	31	33	36	39	42	44	47	50	53	55
12'	24	27	30	33	36	39	42	45	48	51	54	57	60
13'	26	30	33	36	39	43	46	49	52	56	59	62	65
14'	28	32	35	39	42	46	49	53	56	60	63	67	70
15'	30	34	38	42	45	49	53	57	60	64	68	72	75
16'	32	36	40	44	48	52	56	60	64	68	72	76	80
17'	34	39	43	47	51	56	60	64	68	73	77	81	85
18'	36	41	45	50	54	59	63	68	72	77	81	86	90
19'	38	43	48	53	57	62	67	72	76	81	86	91	95
20'	40	45	50	55	60	65	70	75	80	85	90	95	100

WALL MOLDING (LIN. FT.)

Room dimension perpendicular to joist direction (columns); Room dimension parallel to joist direction (rows)

	8'	9'	10'	11'	12'	13'	14'	15'	16'	17'	18'	19'	20'
8'	32	34	36	38	40	42	44	46	48	50	52	54	56
9'	34	36	38	40	42	44	46	48	50	52	54	56	58
10'	36	38	40	42	44	46	48	50	52	54	56	58	60
11'	38	40	42	44	46	48	50	52	54	56	58	60	62
12'	40	42	44	46	48	50	52	54	56	58	60	62	64
13'	42	44	46	48	50	52	54	56	58	60	62	64	66
14'	44	46	48	50	52	54	56	58	60	62	64	66	68
15'	46	48	50	52	54	56	58	60	62	64	66	68	70
16'	48	50	52	54	56	58	60	62	64	66	68	70	72
17'	50	52	54	56	58	60	62	64	66	68	70	72	74
18'	52	54	56	58	60	62	64	66	68	70	72	74	76
19'	54	56	58	60	62	64	66	68	70	72	74	76	78
20'	56	58	60	62	64	66	68	70	72	74	76	78	80

WALL SPRINGS

Room dimension perpendicular to joist direction (columns); Room dimension parallel to joist direction (rows)

	8'	9'	10'	11'	12'	13'	14'	15'	16'	17'	18'	19'	20'
8'	14	15	16	17	18	19	20	21	22	23	24	25	26
9'	15	16	17	18	19	20	21	22	23	24	25	26	27
10'	16	17	18	19	20	21	22	23	24	25	26	27	28
11'	17	18	19	20	21	22	23	24	25	26	27	28	29
12'	18	19	20	21	22	23	24	25	26	27	28	29	30
13'	19	20	21	22	23	24	25	26	27	28	29	30	31
14'	20	21	22	23	24	25	26	27	28	29	30	31	32
15'	21	22	23	24	25	26	27	28	29	30	31	32	33
16'	22	23	24	25	26	27	28	29	30	31	32	33	34
17'	23	24	25	26	27	28	29	30	31	32	33	34	35
18'	24	25	26	27	28	29	30	31	32	33	34	35	36
19'	25	26	27	28	29	30	31	32	33	34	35	36	37
20'	26	27	28	29	30	31	32	33	34	35	36	37	38

CROSS TEES

Room dimension perpendicular to joist direction (columns); Room dimension parallel to joist direction (rows)

	8'	9'	10'	11'	12'	13'	14'	15'	16'	17'	18'	19'	20'
8'	14	16	18	20	22	24	26	28	30	32	34	36	38
9'	18	20	23	25	28	30	33	35	38	40	43	45	48
10'	18	20	23	25	28	30	33	35	38	40	43	45	48
11'	21	24	27	30	33	36	39	42	45	48	51	54	57
12'	21	24	27	30	33	36	39	42	45	48	51	54	57
13'	25	28	32	35	39	42	46	49	53	56	60	63	67
14'	25	28	32	35	39	42	46	49	53	56	60	63	67
15'	28	32	36	40	44	48	52	56	60	64	68	72	76
16'	28	32	36	40	44	48	52	56	60	64	68	72	76
17'	32	36	41	45	50	54	59	63	68	72	77	81	86
18'	32	36	41	45	50	54	59	63	68	72	77	81	86
19'	36	40	45	50	55	60	65	70	75	80	85	90	95
20'	36	40	45	50	55	60	65	70	75	80	85	90	95

MAIN RUNNERS 8' LENGTH

Room dimension perpendicular to joist direction (columns); Room dimension parallel to joist direction (rows)

	8'	9'	10'	11'	12'	13'	14'	15'	16'	17'	18'	19'	20'
8'	2	3	3	3	4	4	4	4	5	5	5	5	
9'	2	3	3	3	4	4	4	4	5	5	5	5	
10'	2	3	3	3	4	4	4	4	5	5	5	5	
11'	3	4	4	5	5	6	6	6	7	7	8	8	
12'	3	4	4	5	5	6	6	6	7	7	8	8	
13'	3	4	4	5	5	6	6	6	7	7	8	8	
14'	3	4	4	5	5	6	6	6	7	7	8	8	
15'	4	5	5	6	6	7	7	8	8	9	9	10	10
16'	4	5	5	6	6	7	7	8	8	9	9	10	10
17'	4	5	5	6	6	7	7	8	8	9	9	10	10
18'	4	5	5	6	6	7	7	8	8	9	9	10	10
19'	5	6	7	7	8	9	9	10	10	11	12	12	13
20'	5	6	7	7	8	9	9	10	10	11	12	12	13

12" x 12" TILES

Room dimension perpendicular to joist direction

Room dimension parallel to joist direction

	8'	9'	10'	11'	12'	13'	14'	15'	16'	17'	18'	19'	20'
8'	64	72	80	88	96	104	112	120	128	136	144	152	160
9'	72	81	90	99	108	117	126	135	144	153	162	171	180
10'	80	90	100	110	120	130	140	150	160	170	180	190	200
11'	88	99	110	121	132	143	154	165	176	187	198	209	220
12'	96	108	120	132	144	156	168	180	192	204	216	228	240
13'	104	117	130	143	156	169	182	195	208	221	234	247	260
14'	112	126	140	154	168	182	196	210	224	238	252	266	280
15'	120	135	150	165	180	195	210	225	240	255	270	285	300
16'	128	144	160	176	192	208	224	240	256	272	288	304	320
17'	136	153	170	187	204	221	238	255	272	289	306	323	340
18'	144	162	180	198	216	234	252	270	288	306	324	342	360
19'	152	171	190	209	228	247	266	285	304	323	342	361	380
20'	160	180	200	220	240	260	280	300	320	340	360	380	400

12" x 48" TILES

Room dimension perpendicular to joist direction

Room dimension parallel to joist direction

	8'	9'	10'	11'	12'	13'	14'	15'	16'	17'	18'	19'	20'
8'	16	18	20	22	24	26	28	30	32	34	36	38	40
9'	18	21	23	25	27	30	32	34	36	39	41	43	45
10'	20	23	25	28	30	33	35	38	40	43	45	48	50
11'	22	25	28	31	33	36	39	42	44	47	50	53	55
12'	24	27	30	33	36	39	42	45	48	51	54	57	60
13'	26	30	33	36	39	43	46	49	52	56	59	62	65
14'	28	32	35	39	42	46	49	53	56	60	63	67	70
15'	30	34	38	42	45	49	53	57	60	64	68	72	75
16'	32	36	40	44	48	52	56	60	64	68	72	76	80
17'	34	39	43	47	51	56	60	64	68	73	77	81	85
18'	36	41	45	50	54	59	63	68	72	77	81	86	90
19'	38	43	48	53	57	62	67	72	76	81	86	91	95
20'	40	45	50	55	60	65	70	75	80	85	90	95	100

WALL MOLDING (LIN. FT.)

Room dimension perpendicular to joist direction

Room dimension parallel to joist direction

	8'	9'	10'	11'	12'	13'	14'	15'	16'	17'	18'	19'	20'
8'	32	34	36	38	40	42	44	46	48	50	52	54	56
9'	34	36	38	40	42	44	46	48	50	52	54	56	58
10'	36	38	40	42	44	46	48	50	52	54	56	58	60
11'	38	40	42	44	46	48	50	52	54	56	58	60	62
12'	40	42	44	46	48	50	52	54	56	58	60	62	64
13'	42	44	46	48	50	52	54	56	58	60	62	64	66
14'	44	46	48	50	52	54	56	58	60	62	64	66	68
15'	46	48	50	52	54	56	58	60	62	64	66	68	70
16'	48	50	52	54	56	58	60	62	64	66	68	70	72
17'	50	52	54	56	58	60	62	64	66	68	70	72	74
18'	52	54	56	58	60	62	64	66	68	70	72	74	76
19'	54	56	58	60	62	64	66	68	70	72	74	76	78
20'	56	58	60	62	64	66	68	70	72	74	76	78	80

BRUSH-ON CEMENT QUARTS

Room dimension perpendicular to joist direction

Room dimension parallel to joist direction

	8'	9'	10'	11'	12'	13'	14'	15'	16'	17'	18'	19'	20'
8'	2	2	2	2	2	2	2	3	3	3	3	3	3
9'	2	2	2	2	2	2	3	3	3	3	3	3	3
10'	2	2	2	2	2	3	3	3	3	3	3	3	3
11'	2	2	2	3	3	3	3	3	3	3	3	3	3
12'	2	2	2	3	3	3	3	3	3	3	3	3	4
13'	2	2	3	3	3	3	4	4	4	4	4	4	4
14'	2	3	3	3	3	4	4	4	4	4	5	5	5
15'	2	3	3	3	3	4	4	4	4	5	5	5	6
16'	3	3	3	3	4	4	4	4	5	5	5	6	6
17'	3	3	3	4	4	4	4	5	5	5	6	6	6
18'	3	3	3	4	4	4	5	5	5	6	6	6	6
19'	3	3	4	4	4	5	5	5	6	6	6	7	7
20'	3	3	4	4	4	5	5	5	6	6	6	7	7

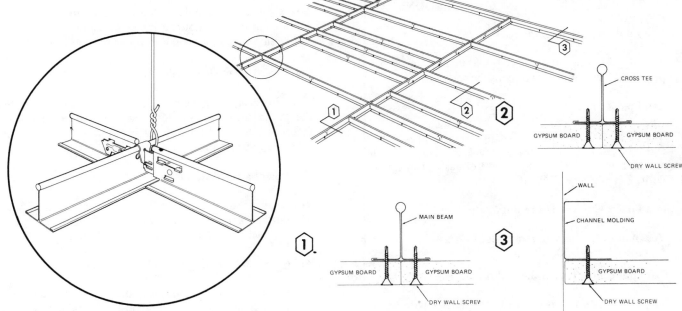

CROSS TEE
GYPSUM BOARD — GYPSUM BOARD
DRY WALL SCREW

MAIN BEAM
GYPSUM BOARD — GYPSUM BOARD
DRY WALL SCREW

WALL
CHANNEL MOLDING
GYPSUM BOARD
DRY WALL SCREW

① ② ③

ESTIMATING GUIDE FOR/STAPLING TO WOOD FURRING STRIPS

12" x 12" TILES

Room dimension perpendicular to joist direction

Room dimension parallel to joist direction

	8'	9'	10'	11'	12'	13'	14'	15'	16'	17'	18'	19'	20'
8'	64	72	80	88	96	104	112	120	128	136	144	152	160
9'	72	81	90	99	108	117	126	135	144	153	162	171	180
10'	80	90	100	110	120	130	140	150	160	170	180	190	200
11'	88	99	110	121	132	143	154	165	176	187	198	209	220
12'	96	108	120	132	144	156	168	180	192	204	216	228	240
13'	104	117	130	143	156	169	182	195	208	221	234	247	260
14'	112	126	140	154	168	182	196	210	224	238	252	266	280
15'	120	135	150	165	180	195	210	225	240	255	270	285	300
16'	128	144	160	176	192	208	224	240	256	272	288	304	320
17'	136	153	170	187	204	221	238	255	272	289	306	323	340
18'	144	162	180	198	216	234	252	270	288	306	324	342	360
19'	152	171	190	209	228	247	266	285	304	323	342	361	380
20'	160	180	200	220	240	260	280	300	320	340	360	380	400

FURRING STRIPS (LIN. FT.)

Room dimension perpendicular to joist direction

Room dimension parallel to joist direction

	8'	9'	10'	11'	12'	13'	14'	15'	16'	17'	18'	19'	20'
8'	72	81	90	99	108	117	126	135	144	153	162	171	180
9'	80	90	100	110	120	130	140	150	160	170	180	190	200
10'	88	99	110	121	132	143	154	165	176	187	198	209	220
11'	96	108	120	132	144	156	168	180	192	204	216	228	240
12'	104	117	130	143	156	169	172	195	208	221	235	247	260
13'	112	126	140	154	168	182	196	210	224	238	252	266	280
14'	120	135	150	165	180	195	210	225	240	255	270	285	300
15'	128	144	160	176	192	208	224	240	256	272	288	304	320
16'	136	153	170	187	204	221	238	255	272	289	306	323	340
17'	144	162	180	198	216	234	252	270	288	306	324	342	360
18'	152	171	190	209	228	247	266	285	304	323	342	361	380
19'	160	180	200	220	240	260	280	300	320	340	360	380	400
20'	168	189	210	231	252	273	294	315	336	357	378	399	420

WALL MOLDING (LIN. FT.)

Room dimension perpendicular to joist direction

Room dimension parallel to joist direction

	8'	9'	10'	11'	12'	13'	14'	15'	16'	17'	18'	19'	20'
8'	32	34	36	38	40	42	44	46	48	50	52	54	56
9'	34	36	38	40	42	44	46	48	50	52	54	56	58
10'	36	38	40	42	44	46	48	50	52	54	56	58	60
11'	38	40	42	44	46	48	50	52	54	56	58	60	62
12'	40	42	44	46	48	50	52	54	56	58	60	62	64
13'	42	44	46	48	50	52	54	56	58	60	62	64	66
14'	44	46	48	50	52	54	56	58	60	62	64	66	68
15'	46	48	50	52	54	56	58	60	62	64	66	68	70
16'	48	50	52	54	56	58	60	62	64	66	68	70	72
17'	50	52	54	56	58	60	62	64	66	68	70	72	74
18'	52	54	56	58	60	62	64	66	68	70	72	74	76
19'	54	56	58	60	62	64	66	68	70	72	74	76	78
20'	56	58	60	62	64	66	68	70	72	74	76	78	80

MOST FREQUENTLY ASKED QUESTIONS ABOUT CEILINGS

Can I put insulation on the back of ceilings?

No. If additional insulation is desired, it must be supported so it is not resting directly on the tile.

Can I paint my ceiling?

Yes. The surface should first be cleaned to remove dust and loose dirt. Scuff marks, scratches, or gouges should be repaired with filler. Apply a water-based paint, such as White Latex Flat Wall Paint.

Can I paint vinyl-coated ceilings?

Yes. After cleaning and repair, use Lo-Lustre Latex Enamel for glossy finish or flat finish.

Can I put ceiling tiles in the bathroom?

Yes, if the bathroom is vented to the outside with a fan.

Can I cement my new ceiling directly over old ceiling tiles?

Its best not to because in many cases, the old ceiling could have deteriorated, and an adequate hold could not be attained. Old ceiling tiles should be removed.

Can I cement my ceiling tiles to any surface?

Yes, any reasonably smooth surface that is structurally sound and free of dirt and grease.

What is the minimum distance that my new suspended ceiling can be lowered from my existing ceiling?

A minimum drop of 3" is required for Integrid or regular suspended ceilings.

Should my ceiling material be allowed to adjust to room conditions prior to installation?

Yes. Ceiling tiles should be unpacked to adjust to normal room conditions 24 hours prior to installation. They should not be installed under conditions of excessive humidity.

Can I paint Chandelier Ceilings?

Yes. However, if Chandelier Ceilings are entirely repainted, the appearance will not look like the delicate two-color factory-made finish. Paint by brushing or spraying—one color only—using any light color.

Can I paint acoustical ceilings?

Yes. Acoustical ceilings can be painted up to three times without appreciable loss of acoustical efficiency, using non-bridging paint which does not cover the holes.

Will grease and dirt clog the holes in acoustical ceilings?

No. Due to the surface tension of the air over the surface of the holes, grease and dirt will not enter the acoustical holes.

STAPLED TO WOOD FURRING STRIPS—

INSTALLATION

Ceiling tiles in this series can be installed by stapling to wood furring strips. This method is satisfactory to cover a cracked, uneven ceiling and still retain the headroom. Furring strips should be straight kiln-dried fir or pine, 1" x 3" or 1" x 4" (nominal dimensions).

STEP 1

Determine Room Layout

Determine location and direction of ceiling joists

Determine width of border tiles

STEP 2

Install Furring Strips

Nail first furring strip flush to ceiling against starting wall at right angles to joists

Nail second furring strip at determined width of border tiles

Install remaining furring strips at 12" intervals

STEP 3

Install Ceiling Tiles

Cut border tiles to size

Staple tiles to furring strips

Repeat across room

STEP 4

Install Wall Molding

Nail standard molding at joint between ceiling and walls

REGULAR SUSPENDED CEILINGS—

INSTALLATION

Suspended ceilings offer an attractive and economical method of lowering high ceilings or finishing off old, unsightly ceilings. A simple metal framework, suspended on wires from above, forms a grid that holds 2' x 4' or 2' x 2' ceiling panels. Recessed or surface-mounted lights can be used, and panels lift out for clening or access to above areas.

STEP 1

Determine Room Layout

Mark desired new ceiling height, using a chalkline.

Determine location and direction of ceiling joists

Determine border panel sizes

STEP 2

Install Wall Molding

Attach wall molding to walls, with bottom of molding in line with level chalk line

STEP 3

Place Hanger Wires and Main Runners

Determine placement of first main runner

Attach screw eyes and hanger wire to joists

Cut and install first main runner

Hang remaining main runners, connecting where necessary

STEP 4

Install Cross Tees and Ceiling Panels

Snap cross tees into main runner

Repeat across room

Measure and cut border panels

Lay in remaining panels

299

INTEGRID MAIN RUNNER SUSPENDED SYSTEM—

INSTALLATION

The Integrid suspension system is designed especially for suspending ceiling tile to any height. It lowers tile ceiling below exposed or low-hanging obstructions and eliminates the impersonal, commercial look of ordinary suspended ceilings by hiding the grid work. No complicated room layout is necessary, and no special tools are required. Recessed or surface-mounted light fixtures can be used.

STEP 1

Install Wall Molding

Mark new ceiling height, using a chalk line

Attach wall molding to walls, with molding lined up with chalk line

STEP 2

Place Hanger Wires and Main Runners

Determine location and direction of ceiling joists, as main runners should run at right angles to joists

Install screw eyes and hanger wires at joists every 48"

Hang main runners from screw eyes

STEP 3

Install Ceiling Tiles and Cross Tees

Determine width of first and last rows of border tiles

Rest four 12" tiles or one 48" tile on wall molding

Snap a cross tee onto the main runner and slide it into the kerf (groove) on the edge of the tiles to lock them tightly in position

Work across the room, installing one row of tiles at a time

Insert a wall spring at the end of each row

CEMENTED TO SOUND, EXISTING CEILING—

INSTALLATION

In many rooms, the existing plaster or drywall ceiling is sound, level condition but is old and unattractive looking. To brighten up these rooms and yet retain headroom ceiling tiles can be installed using Brush-On Ceiling Cement.

Illustrated:

STEP 1

Prepare the Surface

Remove any loose wallpaper or flaking paint

Clean surface of dust, or grease

STEP 2

Determine Room Layout

Measure length and width of room

Establish long-and short-wall border tile sizes

Cut border tiles to size

STEP 3

Install Ceiling Tiles

Apply cement to tiles

Install tiles, inserting tongue into groove

Staple tile to hold until cement dries

STEP 4

Install Wall Molding

Nail standard wall moldings at joint between ceiling and wall

INTERIOR WALL FINISHES

33

PRE-FINISHED PLYWOOD

One of the richest looking and most attractive interior wall finishes is Pre-finished Plywood. It is not necessarily the most expensive if you look for bargains in seconds. The edges may be damaged or the finish slightly marred, which, if you plan carefully, will not be noticeable because the damaged edge can be cut off and the marred surface can be used around doors and windows allowing the cut of the panel to remove the damaged surface. Sometimes the damaged surface is not readily noticeable, unless you look for it.

The sizes of plywood panels are 3/16" and 1/4" thick and width of 4'–0" with lengths of 7'–0" and 8'–0". If your ceiling is less than 8'–0" the excess panel can be used for base and ceiling moulding. One of the advantages of pre-finished plywood is the ease of maintenance which requires an application of paste wax about every 6 months. This material is available in Nutmeg, Oak, Birch, Elm, Pecan, Pine, Cherry, Hickory, Cedar, Cypress, Cottonwood, Teak, Rosewood, Butternut, Redwood, Chestnut, Mahogany, etc., and all these wood species have variations of finishes. Patterns can be had in random width, grooved, V grooved, channel grooved, random scoring and pegged. Finishes range in antique, shadows, plank, tonings and embossed.

The way a log is cut determines the finish surface of the panel: plain sliced will give a subdued grain appearance, whereas, rotary cut will accentuate the grain with a finer grain appearance.

This material can be applied either by nailing or with ready to use adhesive. Before you install the panels, stand them against the finish face exposed and match them for color variation so that the change will be gradual. The wall surface on which these panels are applied must be solid.

In alteration work, if the existing wall is sound and secure, the panels can be applied directly to the wall surface. Should you decide to use adhesive in applying the panels, the ready to use product is applied with a caulking gun by applying a bead around the perimeter of the panel about 1" in from the outer edge, and a large S shape bead along the balance of back side of the panel. The panel should be fitted before applying the adhesive because once contact is made, the panel cannot be readjusted in position. Care should be taken not to get any adhesive on the finish— it will stain the surface. Prefinished plywood is an excellent material applied over badly damaged existing walls providing the wall is sound. The application is no better than the surface on to which the panel is applied.

The second means of application is nailing with matching color nails. The solid backing surface still applies in nailing except you must not lose the stud location in new work. Put a mark on the floor or ceiling at the location of all studs because the panels must be nailed into the studs. In the case of existing walls, finding the studs is not a difficult job. Break away a portion of the existing wall on a horizontal plane until the stud is found, measure 16" from that point and put a temporary mark on the ceiling or floor locating the studs. The small portion of wall which has broken away will be covered by the new panel. Another method is to drive a finish nail into the wall by trial and error until you feel the firmness of the nail indicating the stud location. The V grooves on the panel are random spaced but also spaced at 16" intervals which will also help you to locate the studs once you have found the first one.

The matching color coated nails are driven in the grooves of the panel, never in the face, only this way will the nails be inconspicuous. The grooves then on the surface of the plywood should match the location of the studs. The corner requires a little more time and patience in that the panel must be cut and fitted to the exact configuration of the wall surface, which is seldom perfectly straight and true. Temporarily secure the panel about an inch away from the corner with nails in the groove. Be sure the panel is level. Set the carpenters compass or dividers slightly greater than the greatest distance between the wall and the panel and scribe or transfer the exact configeration of the wall onto the panel. Carefully cut along this mark with a coping saw. If you deviate from the mark, the panel will not fit properly. When you are satisfied with the fit, (you may need to play with the cut or fit with sandpaper to make a perfect fit) you are then ready to apply the panel. The final closure panel may not be a full panel. If cutting is necessary, bevel the edge of the cut with a piece of sandpaper to match the groove and coat with a coloring stick to match. NEVER FIT OR MATCH A PANEL WITH A HORIZONTAL CUT. THERE SHOULD BE NO HORIZONTAL JOINTS WITH-OUT A MOULDING.

Fitting around doors and windows presents no problem. This is one area where money can be saved by not using casings, simply fitting the panel to the position on the door or window where casing would normally terminate. In applying this method, the door or window frame must be on the same plane as the wall finish. The simplest way is to cut the panel to the door or window jamb from floor to ceiling on both sides vertically, and fill in the top and bottom later. Exterior corners require protection against damage from accidental impact. This can be done with a matching color metal moulding or a matching color wood or plastic moulding. Electric box cutouts are done by coating the edge of the box with carpenters blue chalk and positioning the panel. You then press along the box perimeter to transfer the chalk image to the back side of the panel and simply cut along the chalked line.

The important thing to remember is to measure accurately. Mouldings will help cover some errors but measure twice and cut once should be the rule. Before shopping, it will help to make a scaled sketch of the room including furniture placement and colors. Some colors and finishes will rule themselves out right away. Ask to take some sample panels with you. Some rooms may require only an accent wall for a dramatic effect. Others can accomodate four paneled walls and give warmth and charm throughout the entire room.

Be careful of what looks like pre-finished plywood but is not. Manufacturers are doing a pretty good job of simulating wood grain embossed over composition panel. It's easy enough to tell the difference by careful examination and checking the edge of the panels. Plywood will have three layers of wood in alternating grain fused together.

Factory finished or pre-finished paneling is a plywood or processed wood fiber product with a wide almost limitless variety of face treatments. Many paneling faces are, in fact, hardwood or softwood veneers finished to enhance their visual appearance. Other faces are printed to simulate woodgrain and many come very close. Plywood wall paneling is manufactured with a face core and back veneer. The face and back veneer woodgrain run vertically, with the core running horizontally. This gives dimensional strength and stability to the panel. Some natural wood faced panels may be embossed, antiqued or colortoned. They may receive other woodgrain embellishments to achieve a distinctive decor appeal. Processed wood fiber (particleboard, hardboard) wall panels are available with grain-printed vinyl or paper overlays, or printed face surface. Most panels are random grooved falling on 16" centers for nailing over studs. Grooves are cut or embossed into the panel in V-grooves or channel grooves. Less expensive panels have striped groove on the surface.

Plywood is manufactured in flat panels of sheets of wood glued under pressure in alternating the grain. This cross bonding produces great strength in both directions and the wood is split-proof and puncture-proof and is one of the strongest building material, by weight, made. If pieces are to be cut from the same sheet, do not change the saw setting and be sure to allow for the saw kerf or saw blade thickness when mating or matching pieces. If you are cutting with a hand saw, cut into the good face, if using a power saw, cut from the back side.

HOW TO MEASURE, HOW MUCH TO BUY

Provided are the floor and walls of a 16'x20' dining room to make the explanation simple. Each square represents a full twelve inches. Doorways and windows are shown in scale (appropriate size) and in their exact position. By marking off 4' segments along the sketch of each wall, we know how many panels we'll need.

For your own room: First measure and sketch your floor. Measure and sketch each wall in turn. Measure and mark the position and size of doorways and openings. Double-check each and every measurement.

HOW MANY PANELS?

Each panel (when used vertically) covers four feet of wall along the floor. Simply add up the lengths of the walls, and divide by 4. For instance, for a 16'x20' room add 16'+16'+20'+20' to get 72'. Divide by 4 and you find that you need 18 panels. Or, simply count off four-foot segments along the floor on the chart.

As a double-check, show the room sketch to your dealer. He'll always be glad to help.

TOOLS YOU'LL NEED

The only tools it takes are hammer, saw, nailset, carpenter's square and level.

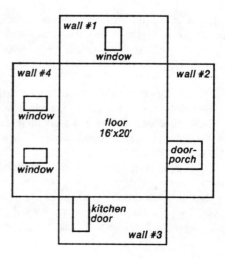

HOW TO INSTALL PANELING

Anyone who can measure, saw and hammer carefully can panel well. Just take your time with measurements. And plan ahead for trouble spots. For at least a couple of days, let air get to all panel faces and backs. Stack the panels, separated by full lengths of furring, in the room you're going to decorate. This will allow panels to condition to room temperature and humidity (Fig. 1). Even though plywood panels are selected at the mill for compatibility of coloring and graining, you'll want to arrange them for a sequence that will be most pleasing to yourself. Line them against the walls in their approximate positions. Number the panels backs with crayon, in the order you want them installed (Fig. 2).

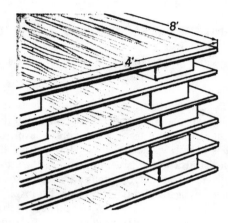

Fig. 1—Stack panels so air washes all surfaces, for a few days.

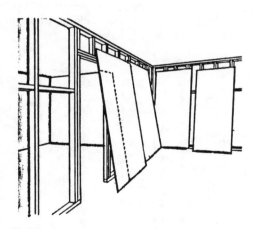

Fig. 2—Arrange panels around the room to show best sequence, in daylight and in artificial light.

NEW CONSTRUCTION

Paneling can be installed directly to smooth studs. Smooth the high spots or shim out low spots if studs aren't perfectly straight. (Building paper, plastic sheeting, or other vapor barrier installed against studs will protect paneling from moisture and provide the insulating benefits of dead air space.)

EXISTING WALLS—PLASTER AND DRY WALLS

Walls are usually constructed of 2x4 studs (verticals) with plates (horizontal) at floor and ceiling. Studs are set every 16" (16" on centers) and at doors and windows. Tap existing wall with a hammer; at a stud the sound will be solid. Nailheads in dry wall or base-boards or chair rails are usually over studs. You'll need these studs, to hold furring and shims that we'll explain later (Fig. 3).

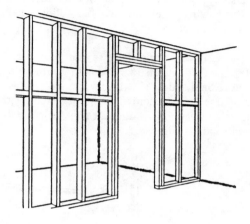

Fig. 3—Studs and plates of partition.

PREPARING A ROOM

Generally there's very little preparation needed. However, if there's loose plaster, tear it out and build out the wall with furring or plywood. If wallboard isn't exactly flat and tight, nail it tight to the studs. Or rip it out, and build out with plywood.

It's best to remove moldings around doors and windows. Do it carefully to avoid splitting, with a wedge or carpenter's pry-bar. Or drive the nails clear through moldings with hammer and nailset.

Should you discover a void in the wall, or if you've removed an electric outlet or are filling in a larger opening (such as to change a window into a smaller pass-through) build out with studding and/or shims to match the vertical plane of the rest of the wall. Build a simple box frame around pipes that you don't want to relocate. Paneling will decorate almost anything. If you're planning built-ins—closets, wall shelving, cabinets—it's best to frame them out before you start to panel.

FURRING

Paneling can be readily installed against any dry, non-masonry wall, but furring is always recommended where wall is old or very uneven. Take the time to check your walls for flatness. Hold a flat length of 2x4 against various areas of the wall. Double-check yourself; use both sides of the 2x4 to be certain (Fig. 4).

303

Check walls vertically. A large carpenter's level is the best way. Or use a good plumb line (a small weight called a plumb-bob, on a cord) if you have one.

Check corners vertically. They can fool you!

If you turn up an unusual condition, mark the wall so you'll be sure to correct it when you're furring and shimming.

Furring strips may be nailed over the old wall, directly into the studs. However, the preferred method of attaching furring strips is with panel adhesive. Just follow label instructions for a secure bond.

Use standard 1x2 furring strips (a size your dealer stocks) or cut strips from sheets of Plyscord (sheathing plywood). Space horizontal furring strips every 16" (measure from center of one strip to center of the next) and vertical furring at least every 48" so that all panel edges will be held tight and solid.

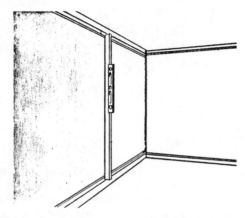

Fig. 4—Check walls for flatness and for true vertical alignment.

Apply additional furring at doors, windows, etc. Don't skimp—use extra furring when in doubt (Fig. 5).

Where necessary, shim out furring to establish even planes—horizontal as well as vertical. Pieces of shingle are ideal for this (Fig. 6). On an uneven wall take special pains to provide a firm, even base for the paneling. If the wall is extraordinarily rough, paneling could be installed over full sheets of 5/16" Plyscord.

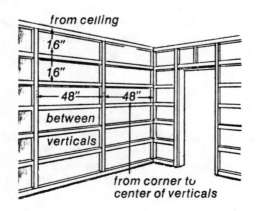

from ceiling

16"
16"
—48"— —48"—
between
verticals

from corner to center of verticals

Fig. 5—Furring placement.

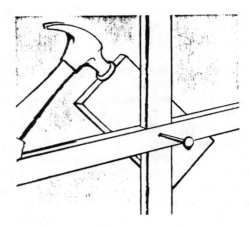

Fig. 6—Shingle used as shim behind furring.

INSTALLING THE PANELING. START AT A CORNER

Most corners are not perfectly true. Usually, panels must be trimmed to fit into the corner.

Here's how: 1. Tap two finishing nails into grooves, at top edge of panel, so that they just protrude through the back. 2. Place panel in corner using a carpenter's level to assure that panel is plumb vertically. When level, drive the nails partially into studs to hold panel in place. 3. Mark the panel edge, parallel to corner. If the walls are irregular or exceptionally rough—as against a brick fireplace, for instance—you might want to scribe (an art compass makes the best tool for this). 4. Cut, plane, file or sand carefully to fit panel into corner (Fig.7).

Note: It might not be necessary to scribe and fit to compensate for slight irregularities or for corners only slightly out of plumb. Especially if you are planning to use inside corner molding. If in doubt, scribe!

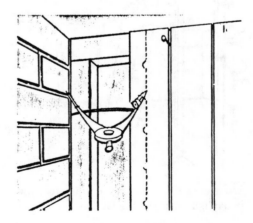

Fig. 7—Scribing at corner with compass.

OVER A MASONRY WALL OR ANY DAMP WALL

Masonry walls, especially when below ground level, pose only one serious problem. They're damp.

First, cure any problems of dampness. (Your dealer can advise on commercial compounds available.) Be sure the paneling you select is appropriate for the location you have in mind.

Second, include a vinyl plastic vapor barrier and insulation in your materials list and use according to manufacturer's instructions.

Third, either (1) attach furring strips to wall with masonry nails, as previously described, or (2) —the preferred —build a suitable frame of 2x3 lumber over the entire wall, as discussed.   (Shim out as necessary.) Fasten the frame directly to the wall with nails or screws into plugs or expansion shields, or fasten with hardened cut nails, bolt anchors, adhesive anchors or adhesive. Or (easiest of all) add spacers between the frame and the masonry wall and wedge and nail the frame tight against the floor and ceiling.

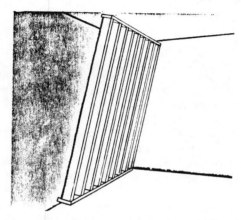

2x3 frame wedged into place against damp or masonry wall.

Fourth, install paneling to frame just as you would over furring. Use same nailing schedule or adhesive method as with furring on a dry wall.

APARTMENT OR OTHER WALL WHERE PANELING MIGHT SOME DAY BE REMOVED

Requires only that you build a frame over the wall and fasten it (nails, screws, bolts or wedges) to the floor or ceiling: or use expandable hollow wall screws or lead plugs to fasten the frame to the wall. Use 2x3 and 1x3 lumber, as with a masonry wall. Shim out where necessary. Use the same nailing or adhesive method as with furring.

Wedges can be used to fasten the frame to the wall.

ADDING A CLOSET

You may want to add a corner closet in an existing room. This is not difficult, but it does require some preliminary planning and framing. Measure the space desired for your closet and mark it out on the floor. Next—cut 2x4's, for your base plates and top plates, as in Fig. 1.

When nailing the base plate to the floor, leave an opening for the door frame. Measure and mark the top and base plates for placement of the studs, which should be toe-nailed 16" on centers. Tilt up wall frame (Fig. 2) and nail to floor and ceiling.

The outside corner is made up from three 2x4's and installed so that it provides inside and outside nailing surfaces that are as thick as the other studs, as shown in Fig. 3.

Now—add drywall to the inside of the closet.

Plywood paneling may be nailed directly to the studs, as in Fig. 4. When the panels are up, install the door frame. Then add your corner molding, cove molding and base molding.

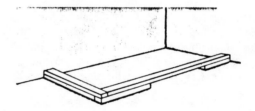

Fig. 1—Base Plate and Top Plate

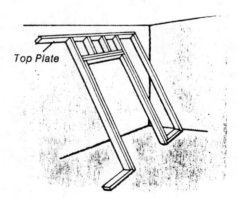

Top Plate

Fig. 2—Wall Section

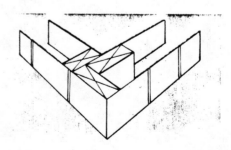

Fig. 3— Inside and Outside Corner Nailing Surfaces

305

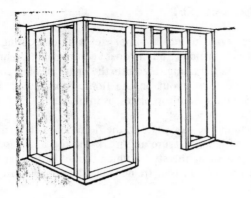

Fig. 4—Structure

NEXT PANELS.

Leave a slight space between panels. The thickness of a dime, or a brad will do. Be sure to maintain a true vertical line, for good alignment at next corner, doorway, etc.

PANELING INTO CORNER

Cut panel slightly oversize at edge going into the room corner, leaving an inch or more excess to permit scribing and/or accurate measuring to compensate for out-of-plumb corner. Keep panel edge exactly parallel with previously installed panel. (Slight irregularities will be concealed by corner molding.)

NAILS, SCHEDULE

Paneling should be nailed to furring, studs, or sheathing with 1" brads or 3d (three-penny, 1 1/4") finishing nails, every 6" along panel edges and every 12" along intermediate furring. Toe-nail (at an angle) at joints through bevels and grooves (Fig. 5). Be careful not to dent or mark the panel face with hammer head. Use nailset. Conceal nail heads with matching putty.

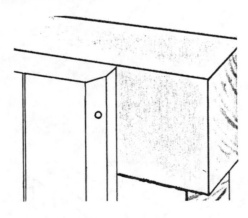

Figure 5

PANEL ADHESIVE

This is the easy, neat method of installation. And it allows time to adjust the panel into the tightest fit before it is locked into place. Follow label directions of the manufacturer.

CUTOUTS FOR DOORS, WINDOWS, OUTLETS, RADIATORS, ETC.

It's always more satisfactory to measure and mark when you visualize the cutout to be made. Even if it should require considerable moving and jockeying of full-size panels back and forth between the room you're paneling and your shop, it's worth the trouble to have the panel handy for marking while you're measuring.

For any irregular shapes or cutouts, wrapping paper may be used for easy, accurate marking. Tape it in position as if it were a panel; then mark off or cut out the opening or shape. Use the sheet as a pattern to transfer the marks onto the panel. Recheck and cut.

CUTTING

Use hand or power saws on paneling, whichever you prefer. Putting masking tape along the line to be cut helps prevent edge splinters and chips.

Handsaw....Use crosscut saw (a rip saw will surely chip the face of the paneling). Have panel face up so saw cuts into face on downstroke. Start cut carefully at edge of paneling. Support cut-off material during final saw strokes.

Power saw....A combination hollow ground blade is recommended for power saws. Blade should cut into the face.

Jig saw....Use a proper blade. It is much easier to cut straight when a simple guide or jig is used to help control the saw movement.

FOR OUTLET BOXES

Measure to edge of adjacent panel. Mark panel to be cut. Drill pilot holes at corners of cutout area for cutting with a jig saw or keyhole saw. Or drill holes close together within cutout area, and press out the scrap piece. Pull outlet flush with panel face.

FOR A DOOR OR WINDOW

Stand the panel next to the opening. Plumb the panel. Measure for cutout and mark the face of the panel with china-marking grease pencil-anything that will be readily seen and will wipe off clean. Extend door jambs to compensate for the thickness of the furring.

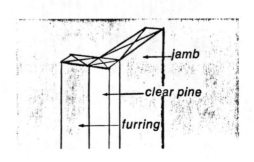

FOR RADIATOR OR CONVECTOR ENCLOSURE

Do it the same as for door and window cutouts. Furring around enclosure provides solid base for paneling.

Additional furring around convector cover.

MOLDINGS

After the paneling is on the walls, you may want to install moldings at corners, ceilings, floors, doors and wndows. Moldings certainly add a finished look to most installations. They also help by covering joints that aren't quite flush and true...even saw cuts that somehow don't always look perfectly accurate.

Your paneling dealer can probably recommend molding shapes in both wood and vinyl, in colors that almost match the paneling tones to match the rest of the wall.

COMPOSITION PANELING

Be very careful in selecting pre-finished wall panel because what looks like plywood may not be plywood but instead a composition or hardboard panel. These panels are made by several manufacturers and can be had in simulated wood grain finish, stone, brick and several designs of deeply dimensional textures. All panels are mirror images with no variation in grain or color. If you alternate the wood grain panels by installing every other panel upside-down this will help break up the monotony and repetition of like panels. These panels are for interior use only and the application is similar to plywood. Be extremely careful in handling these panels, they break easily. They can be used in any dry room.

Hardboard is a man made wood product, also known as pressed wood or board, composition board, fiber board, flakeboard and other descriptive or brand named products. Basically this material is made from wood residue-fiber, chips, flakes, particles and shavings to produce a usable by-product from waste or left over material in processing or manufacturing of lumber and plywood. Hardboard is a smooth panel with knots or grain yet is made almost entirely of natural wood-cellulose for strength. The fibers are re-arranged to provide special properties for hardness and density. Hardboard will not crack or splinter, check craze or

flake and is impact resistant. The panels are available in sizes up to 4'-0" wide and 8'-0" long, in thicknesses from 1/8" to 1/4", surfaced smooth on one or both sides. There are three basic types of hardboard: Service type used for storage areas, closet liners, shelving cabinet backs and drawer bottoms, Standard type for interior paneling, underlayment, screens and wardrobe doors, storage areas, garage liners (perforated) and special prefinished decorative panels used in a variety of patterns and textures; Tempered type is a manufacturing process which introduces oil into the board and is permanently set with a heat process. This gives the board greater strength and moisture resistance.

Particleboard is another engineered wood panel product consisting of wood residues from lumber and plywood manufacturing operations, mainly planer shavings and veneer clippings—processed and bonded by adding synthetic resins and a wax emulsion for moisture resistance. The results is a highly uniform product noted for its smooth surface and strong bond. It has excellent screw and nail holding properties and dimensional stability. Particleboard may be used for shelving, drawers, bookcases, cabinets, counter tops and the like, it will accept stain, varnish paint and lacquer. To minimize warping, both sides should be finished.

Particleboard is worked like natural lumber and although denser, may require carbide tipped blades for extensive cutting. For limited application, regular hand or power tools may be used. Screws are recommended for holding instead of nails. Application is similar to plywood.

Hardboard is easily cut, drilled, routed, planed, sanded, nailed, and glued. It provides an excellent base for paint, varnish, stain and plastic overlay. It can be bent and shaped. For finishing with paint of oil or water base, no special sealer is needed. For enamel, use a pigmented primer-sealer as the base coat. Clear finishes require a transparent filler-sealer, natural paste-wood filler.

WOOD FIBER SUBSTRATE

Processed wood fiber (particleboard, hardboard) wall panels are available with grain-printed vinyl or paper overlays, or printed face surface. These prefinished panels are rigid, appealing and economical. Thicknesses range from 1/8" to 1/4".

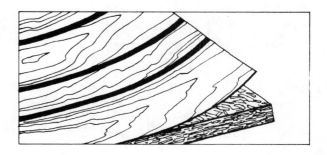

GROOVE TREATMENT

Most vertical wall panelings are "random-grooved" with grooves falling on 16" centers so that nailing over studs will be consistent. A typical random groove pattern may look like this:

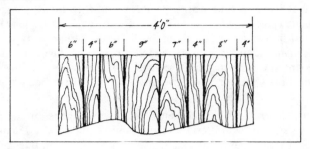

Other groove treatments include uniform spacing (4", 8", 16") and cross-scored grooves randomly spaced to give a "planked effect". Grooves are generally striped darker than the panel surface.

Grooves are cut or embossed into the panel in V-grooves or channel grooves as shown below. Less expensive panels sometimes have a groove just "striped" on the surface.

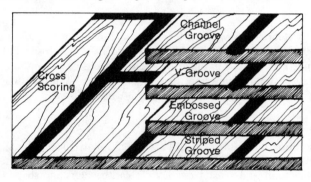

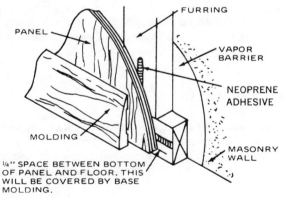

¼" SPACE BETWEEN BOTTOM OF PANEL AND FLOOR. THIS WILL BE COVERED BY BASE MOLDING.

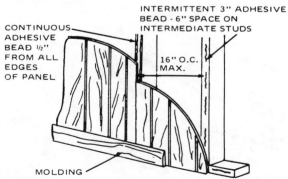

WAINSCOT APPLICATION

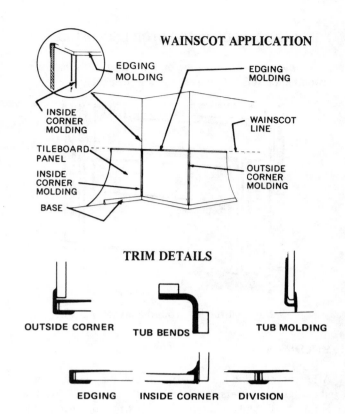

TRIM DETAILS

OUTSIDE CORNER   TUB BENDS   TUB MOLDING

EDGING   INSIDE CORNER   DIVISION

HOW TO BUY AND SPECIFY

Hardboard and particleboard should be specified by intended use, and given the variety of types and thicknesses available it is best to consult your dealer. Figure your requirements carefully to get the most efficient cuts from standard size panels. Many dealers have cut-to-size capabilities and standard shelving widths and lengths.

Hardboard and Particleboard

A wide variety of uses around the home.

Case backs	Card tables
Doors—cabinets & cupboards	Drafting boards
	Typewriter stand
Drawer bottoms	Utility table
Drawer fronts	Ping pong table
Drawer separators	Desktops
End panels	Dressing table
Shelving	Sewing table
Base mouldings, kick plates	Clothes hamper
	Wardrobe cabinets
Bottoms	Flower boxes
Counter fronts	Record cabinets
Counter tops	Bulletin boards
Curved backgrounds	Cutouts for wall decoration
Curved ends	
Shelf dividers	Folding screen
Doors—Sliding	Trays
Playpens	Basketball backstop
Toy chests	Doll houses
Cribs	Playhouses
Table tops	Shuffleboard
Bookcases	Tool chests
Blackboards	Wagons and scooters

How To Panel

1. Step number one is to measure the length, width and height of the area to be paneled. Then draw an outline plan of the area showing the over all dimensions.

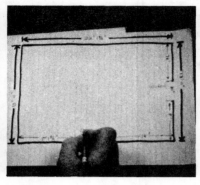

2. Using the outline plan, measure and indicate the locations of the windows, doors, stairways, pipes, ducts and beams.

3. Check the ordinary wood working tools you have. Those shown in the photo above should be all the tools you will need to do a good job of paneling your room.

4. Paneling can be installed on a masonry or concrete block wall.
Two methods can be used . . . a free standing wall or furrings strips.

5. You can install Paneling on plastered or gypsum board walls.

6. Paneling is easy to install on a wall you might wish to build to create or divide a room.

7. Where paneling is installed over a masonry or concrete wall, use a vapor barrier. The material can be either foil or plastic film.

8. FOR FURRING STRIP INSTALLATION, apply strips at the top and bottom of wall and vertically 16" on center. Use concrete nails.

9. As you install the furring strips, check at the side to be sure that all strips are plumb. Do this after the first nail has been driven.

10. Check the flat surface of the furring strip with a level to be sure it is plumb. If shimming is required, use a piece of cedar shingle.

11. A FREE STANDING WALL is assembled on the floor, and tilted into place when completed. Start by placing top and bottom pieces (plates) on the floor.

12. Where the free standing wall fits into a corner, two studs are used. One stud creates a surface for attaching the paneling. The second stud provides a place to tie-in at the corner for the next free standing unit.

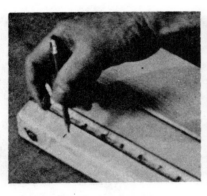 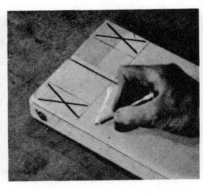 

13. Measure the actual width of one of the 2″ x 4′s, and mark this distance from the end of the plates. Then square a line across the plates.

14. Measure in from opposite edges of the two plates, the thickness of 2″ x 4″, and mark as shown by the heavy black "X's".

15. At right angles from the "X's" shown in "figure 14", mark each plate with an "X" as shown. This establishes the marking points for nailing the corner studs.

16. Starting from the first line you squared across the plates (figure 13), mark at 16″ intervals and square a line. These are your guides for nailing the studs.

17. Layout the marked plates (top and bottom pieces) preparatory to nailing. (Cut studs ½″ less than actual measurement to allow for tilting wall in place).

18. Start nailing at the marked ends of the plates using the "X's" as guides. To set the studs in place, match the ends to the "X's".

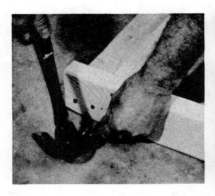

19. Nail the ends, or corner studs, securely. Then move to the 16″ interval marks and nail remaining studs. **Check measurements as you go.**

20. Tilt free standing wall into place. **If you have allowed the one-half inch in height,** wall should move easily into place.

21. Check the wall for approximate plumbness. Do this by pushing the stud wall flush. Move the wall out top or bottom as necessary.

22. Temporarily tack the wall into place at the top to hold it, while you check for true plumbness.

23. When wall is plumb, mark a guide line at the floor. You are now ready to drive special nails through the floor plate.

24. Set the floor plate on the guide line and drive the special nails in and through. **Stop when nail is flush with the plate.**

25. Check wall again for plumbness. At the top, drive narrow points of cedar shingle from opposite ends, to make a holding wedge. Wall can now be nailed upwards.

26. FOR WINDOW OPENING place needed extra studs on each side of opening. Short studs below the opening should not be more than 16″ apart.

27. Line up the level at the window and mark nailing guide lines on the studs which have been placed at each side of the opening.

28. Make a 2" x 4" horizontal member (or sill). Install the sill at the marked points, and nail in place.

29. Electrical wiring and junction boxes should be installed after free-standing wall has been firmly fixed into place.

30. After all wiring has been installed, insulation should be put into place on the exterior walls. Wall is then ready for paneling.

31. AN OPEN STUD WALL is used for dividing areas. This wall can be assembled and tilted into place. **One-half inch of height should be allowed for tilting in.**

32. DOOR OPENINGS are built in same manner as window openings. However, double-studding, for rigidity, is done both at the top and sides of the opening.

33. PLASTERED OR GYPSUM WALLS will form a good base for adhesive installation. Seal new plastered or gypsum walls. Sand painted or plastered walls to remove any glazed finish.

34. UNWRAP PANELS after delivery and stand on long edge in area to be paneled. Do this for at least 48 hours before installation so panels will adjust to room temperature and humidity.

35. MATCH GRAIN AND COLOR, before installation, by standing panels around the walls. This will enable you to find the most pleasing pattern for the room.

36. CIRCULAR SAW CUTTING. When cutting panels with a circular saw, cut from the back side of the panel.

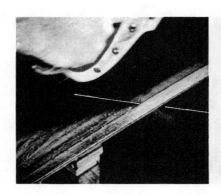

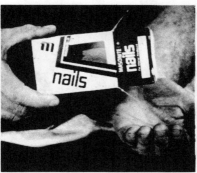

37. HAND SAW CUTTING. **Mark and saw from the surface side of panel when using a hand saw.**

38. NAIL APPLICATION. Paneling can be applied by nailing with Color-Coordinated nails. These nails require no setting or filling.

39. CUTTING AND START-ING. **Deduct one-half inch for the cutting height. Installed panel should be ¼" above floor and below ceiling. START AT CORNER.** One nail will hold panel when testing for plumb.

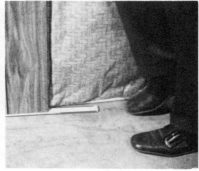

40. Place level on the edge of the panel and find the true plumb. **This is important since the first panel establishes the vertical alignment** for the panels which follow.

41. A piece of cedar shingle placed at the bottom will facilitate moving, as well as holding the panel at a true plumb line.

42. Tack the Paneling at the top to hold in place.
(A black felt pen line on the stud where panels will meet, will prevent show through of stud surface.)

43. Start nailing at corner and move down the stud. **Edge nails should be 4"apart. Intermediate stud nails should be 8" apart.**

44. Measure paneling across to find 16" on center intermediate studs. Remember, intermediate stud nails should be 8" apart. When installing, DO NOT FORCE PANEL. **Panel edges should touch very lightly.**

45. FOR ELECTRICAL OUT-LETS measure from the floor up and from the edge of the previously installed panel. Mark panel to be cut. Be sure to allow for the one-quarter inch that panel will be off the floor.

46. Use as a pattern an actual junction box that matches the one installed in the wall. This will help you avoid incorrect dimensions.

47. Drill holes in the corners of the pattern. To be safe, keep drilled holes within the pattern area. This will avoid overcutting.

48. You can use a key hole saw to cut out the opening. Hole may be cut an eighth of an inch larger than the pattern line since the face plate will cover the area.

49. FOR WINDOW OPENINGS measure from the last installed panel to the edge of the opening and from the floor. Allow one-quarter inch between the floor and panel bottom.

50. Layout and cut panel. **Remember cut on back side when using a circular power saw. Use hand saw when cutting a panel face side.**

51. CHECK PANEL FOR FIT and nail. Follow nailing procedure of 4″ intervals at the edges and 8″ intervals on intermediate studs.

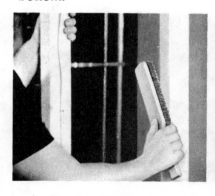

52. WITH ADHESIVE INSTALLATION on a stud or free standing wall, wire brush all stud nailing surfaces. A clean stud surface assures a better adhesive bond.

53. A regular caulking gun is used to apply Panel Adhesive.

54. Trim applying end of the General Purpose Adhesive cartridge to apply · · · · · · · · · · **one-eighth inch continuous strip of adhesive at panel joints and to the top and bottom plate surfaces.**

 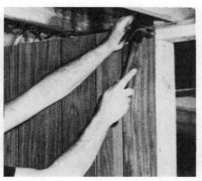 

55. Place three inch (3") long beads of adhesive, six inches (6") apart, on all intermediate studs. Do not skimp. Beads must be at least three inches long.

56. Put panel in place, setting it ¼" from top. Tack at top using Color-Coordinated Nails. Double check to be sure panel is properly placed.

57. Press panel to form a contact with the adhesive. Use a firm, uniform pressure. This will spread the adhesive bead evenly between studs and panel.

58. Grasp bottom of the panel at the edges and slowly pull the panel out and away from the studs. AFTEP TWO MINUTES, repress panel at all stud points.

59. AFTER 20 MINUTES, recheck panel. Go over all intermediate stud areas and edges and apply pressure to assure firm adhesion . . . and even panel surface.

60. WHEN PANELING AROUND DOOR OPENING, follow the same procedure as shown in figure for window openings. Measure dimensions accurately.

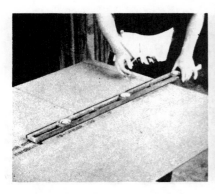 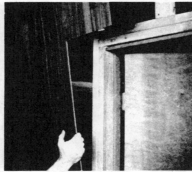 

61. Lay out door opening pattern on the panel. Use hand saw when cutting on the panel face. Use panel back when using power circular saw.

62. After panel is cut, check for fit. Follow recommended procedure for type of installation to be used. (Nails or Adhesive).

63. GYPSUM OR PLASTER WALL installation may be done either with adhesive or nails. Under either method, stand panel against the wall, plumb with level, and mark a line for easier installation.

64. Using the marked line as a guide, place a continuous ribbon of adhesive around the perimeter . . . and three inch (3") long beads every six (6") inches. Use approximately 16 inch spacing.

65. Follow procedure described for stud wall adhesive installation. Tack at top . . . press panel . . . pull out and repress after 2 minutes. Check and reapply pressure after 20 minutes.

66. PANELING AROUND BRICK. Use a compass to measure and scribe. Follow the outline of the brick and mortar joints. Cut carefully with a coping saw.

  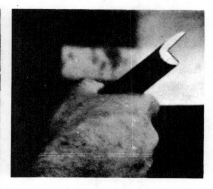

67. Measuring carefully when scribing should result in a perfect fit. Matching an unusually irregular edge may require several "fitting tries" and adjustments.

68. MOLDINGS provide the finishing touch, like the casing shown above. These are Pre-Finished and Color-Coordinated Moldings. No painting or stain-matching required.

69. There's even a molding for outside corners. You just cut this Pre-Finished outside corner and nail it with Color-Coordinated nails.

70. To trim the inside corner, there's a Molding to match. The base of your Paneling installation is easily trimmed with this Molding. Use either the nailing or adhesive method.

71. MATCHING PATTERNED PANELS. Measure the wall and mark the center as a starting point. Set up panels. This will enable you to plan the best end patterns.

72. After pattern arrangement has been achieved, the first panel can be put into place. Remaining panels are then installed.

1/8" HARDBOARD PANELING

These panels, 1/8"-thick hardboard, are designed to perform well when applied to flat interior surfaces, above grade. They should not be used below grade, especially over masonry walls.

To prevent warping, 1/8" hardboard panels must be solidly supported (backed) by plywood, drywall (plaster board), or sound and dry plaster construction. Fastening direct to studs or over furring strips is not recommended.

PRECONDITIONING

All fine woods will expand and contract with changes in humidity. Hardboard panels are no exception. However, proper preparation and precautions will minimize these dimensional changes. To condition panels, expose all sides of the panels indoors for at least 48 hours. Stacking panels on their long edges will assure a full air flow.

PREPARATION OF WALLS

Make sure that walls are sound and all conditions of dampness and seepage have been corrected. Remove existing trim wherever possible. Then either build your framing or apply previously prepared and arranged panels to existing walls.

PANEL ARRANGEMENT

Place all panels against the walls in the order which will give the most attractive color and grain arrangement. Number panel backs and install in numbered order.

MEASURING AND FITTING

Start at the corner of a room and fit the panel loosely into the corner. Scribing to the corner may be helpful on the first panel to plumb the leading edge of the panel. Leave 1/4" clearance at the top and bottom of each panel. The slight opening and gaps at corners, doors, and windows can be concealed by moldings. Use a dime or a #6 finishing nail to establish the proper spacing between panels at vertical joints. Walls behind joints can be stained or painted to prevent obvious show through.

CUTTING

When sawing, the blade should cut into the decorative face. With a hand saw, have decorative face up. (A fine tooth crosscut saw is best). When using a portable power saw, have decorative face down. Carbide tips are recommended. Rough edges can be dressed with a carpenter's plane, rasp, file, or sandpaper.

PANEL INSTALLATION

GLUING: For a fast and visually nail-less installation, use panel adhesive, applied according to package instructions. The only nailing required with this method is at ceiling, and these nails will be covered with moldings.

NAILING: Use 1" brads and nail into the grooves. Space nails 6" apart along all panel edges and 12" apart along intermediates. Toe nails at joints.

FASTENING

Use panel adhesive over surface which is clean and dry, and free with loose dirt, paint, wallpaper or other flaking materials.

A 3/16" bead of adhesive should be applied to the wall around the perimeter of the panel area and vertical zig zag beads 16" apart. Firmly press the panel against the adhesive. Nail the panel at the top and bottom to hold it in position while the adhesive sets. Use brads or finish nails which allow 3/4" penetration into backing and framing. Spacing of nails should not exceed 6" o.c. along top and bottom of panel. Application may also be by finish nails, which allows 3/4" penetration into backing, spaced 4" o.c. around the panel and 8" o.c. at all intermediate supports. Color matched nails should be driven flush or placed in the panel grooves. If uncolored nails are used, set slightly below the panel face to permit a thin fill of matching putty.

FIBERGLASS PANELS

4'-0" x 8'-0" panels simulating brick, stone and wood made of Fiberglass. Panels are fingered for joining, pretrimmed and pre-cut ready for installation with no cutting or sawing except closing. The seams or joints are on the mortar line which are filled with a special compound to match panels. Panels are applied with a special adhesive backing pressed into place and nailed at the mortar joints about 12" apart along every other joint line. Can be used in any room except the kitchen because of the difficulty in cleaning and keeping clean. The surface is rough and food splashing in the joints makes it very difficult to clean.

LAMINATED PLASTIC

Sometimes called Formica which is a manufacturer's registered trade mark. Laminated plastic is made by several companies in all colors and patterns. It is a paper product consisting of several layers of Kraft paper impregnated together with resins fused together in a press at pressures of more than 1,000 lbs. per square inch in temperatures of 250° F. Patterns are printed and protected with a plastic coating. This product is manufactured in four different types. Type I is used for counters and tables. Type II is used for table tops and sink tops. Type III is used for furniture and walls and Type IV is used for paneling and doors. Sheet sizes are 4'-0" x 8'-0" and larger and care must be used in handling because they break very easily.

Laminated Plastic must be applied to a solid backing preferably plywood, with a special adhesive brushed on the back side of the panel. Be careful about proper ventilation in the room when using the adhesive, prolonged exposure will result in harmful health effects. Adhesive must also be applied to the plywood backing. Allow to dry until tacky to the touch and panel must be in alignment before adhesive contacts are made because no readjusting can be made. Once contact is made, apply pressure on the surface to assure total contact. These panels must be fitted before application. There is a special cutting tool for this product but a fine tooth saw will do just as well with filling or sandpaper for final fitting. Metal mouldings are used for interior and exterior corners. Ideally suited for kitchen counter tops and walls.

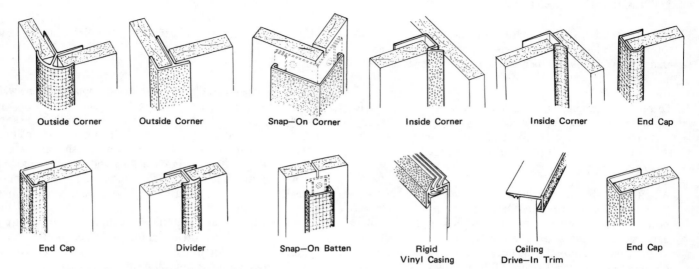

Outside Corner | Outside Corner | Snap—On Corner | Inside Corner | Inside Corner | End Cap

End Cap | Divider | Snap—On Batten | Rigid Vinyl Casing | Ceiling Drive—In Trim | End Cap

FACTORY VINYL SURFACED PLASTER BOARD

A wall covering plaster board with pre-applied vinyl surfacing at the factory in sizes of 1/2" thick and 8, 9 and 10'—0" lengths. Wood grain patterns are square edged, others are beveled edges. There are two basic methods of applying this material over a solid backing. Nailing and adhesive. Nailing is done with color coded nail heads to match the fabric and is nailed along the entire perimeter of the panel at about 12" apart. Adhesive is applied with a caulking gun similar to plywood panels including nailing at top and bottom of panel. The adhesive is special as recommended by the manufacturer. The colors and patterns are as varied as the sheet rolled vinyl, the only difference being factory applied to a plaster board backing. Trim accessories are matching color metal moulding used at exterior corners and trimming around doors and windows, and top and bottom mouldings. Can be used in any room.

VINYL WALLCOVERING AND PAPER

This is a chemical product made into a wall covering with design ranges from plain to prints and embossings. In texture it goes from relatively smooth to deep three dimensional effects. There are three qualities of vinyl wall covering classified as Type 1, light duty, having a minimum of 7 oz. per square yard, for use in areas exposed to normal ordinary wear. Type 11, medium duty, having a minimum weight of 13 oz. per square yard used for walls with better wearing quality with deeper and more attractive embossing. Type 111, heavy duty, with a minimum of 22 oz. per square yard used for walls with heavy traffic, such as lobbies and corridors in public buildings. Vinyl wallcovering generally comes in rolls of 54" widths.

Vinyl wall covering must be applied on a smooth surfaced wall such as plaster or dry wall in sound condition. Masonry block or concrete walls can be used if filled with plaster or cement rubbed smooth. If applying on a painted surface, all loose paint and scale must be removed. If application is over a new plaster or drywall surface, a coat of sizing will be necessary to fill the pores of the wall affording the paste a greater holding power. If sizing is not applied, the paste may be absorbed by the open pores of the new wall surface.

Do not apply vinyl wall covering if temperature is below 60° and store the material at least 24 hours at room temperature to allow the product to acclimatize itself to the area of installation. If the room walls are not level, do not use a vertically striped or geometric pattern. All seams are vertical to match the design of adjacent panel. A special paste is required for application which may be mixed or bought ready to use. Begin behind a door by measuring the total height of the wall and cut a length from the roll about 6" longer than the wall height. All subsequent panels must be cut to match adjacent panel design again allowing a few inches excess for cutting and trimming. Cut all the panels for the entire room and lay them across a makeshift working surface upside-down or design face down. Apply the paste with a brush covering the entire back side of the panel then fold both ends to the middle (paste to paste) with design face up, over fold to make it easier to handle the panel. Position panel against wall and peel away the upper paste to paste fold, taking care to apply the panel level and straight in the corner of the room. Brush away all creases and wrinkles with a dry paper hanger brush and repeat the process with the lower half until the entire panel is secured in place. Trim away the excess top and bottom with a razor sharp knife. You are now ready for the next panel using the same process until all panels are in place. Some designs require that you overlap slightly each panel and some require a butt joint with no overlap. In case of the overlap, cut through both thicknesses of panel with a razor sharp knife for a perfect cut, match and peel away the excess from each panel. Carefully trim around doors and windows. Vinyl wall covering can be used in any room.

ARCHITECTURAL PANELING

A genuine solid wood veneer cut paper thin in widths up to 24" and lengths up to 22'—0" is available in the following wood specie: Afromosia, Ash, Avodire, Benge, Red Birch, White Birch, African Brownwood, Butternut, Camphor Burl, Cherry, Wormey Chestnut, Teak, Ebony, Elm, Red Gum, Koa, Korina, Lacewood, Laurel Mahogony, Makori, Maple, Narra, Oak, Palado, Pecan, Pine, Vera, Redwood, Rosewood, Sapeli, Satinwood, Tigerwood, Walnut and Zebrawood. This product is a wall covering applied similar to vinyl wall covering. The wood finish is raw and requires finishing after installation by sanding slightly. (When sanding wood, always sand in the same direction as the grain of the wood, otherwise you will scratch the surface of the finish). After sanding, finish as you would any wood surface by sealing the grain with lacquer sealer or cut white shellac, lightly sand again and apply two coats of varnish or lacquer again sanding between coats with a final application of paste wax for additional protection. Can be used in any room.

INTERIOR PLANKING

Solid wood 1/2" and 3/4" thick 4" to 12" wide random widths V groove, square edge, channel rustic, spaced boards and finger joined, applied vertically or horizontally in prefinished or unfinished Redwood, Walnut, Oak, Ash, Cypress, Butternut, Cottonwood, Pecan, Cherry and Pine. May be applied directly over studs for new work and over existing wall surface in remodeling with no preparation of existing wall. If applied over an existing wall be sure you locate the studs and nail the planking into the studs. If applied over a concrete or masonry wall the wall must be furred or studded as explained earlier. All planking is tongue and grooved and by nailing into the joints you will conceal the nails. If unfinished, finish same as Architectural Paneling. If finished, apply one coat of paste wax after installation. Can be used in any room.

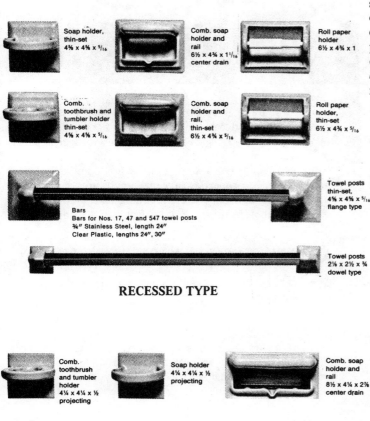

RECESSED TYPE

FLUSH TYPE

CERAMIC TILE

A clay product in thicknesses of 1/4", 5/16", 1/2", 7/16", Ceramic Tile has a variety of finishes including glazed, unglazed, slipproof and mat. Ceramic tile has only a light coating finish, whereas Ceramic Mosaic Tile has the finish through the total thickness of the tile. It is made with a fine grained body impervious to water, stain, dent and frost. Mosiacs are mounted on a prespaced backing sheet in sizes of 12" x 12" ready for application. The size of the tile is 1" x 1", 2" x 1" and 2" x 2". Ceramic Tile on the other hand are larger in size and may or may not be mounted on a backing sheet, depending upon the tile size. In that only the surface is colored, these tiles can break or chip easily. The colors and patterns are unlimited in both, including murals.

A solid wall backing is necessary for the application of ceramic tile. A ready to use adhesive is applied to the wall with a notched trowel. Apply one sheet at a time or one tile at a time taking care to properly space the units for uniformity. Simply press the tile onto the adhesive and slide into position. Apply only a small area at a time. Cutting for fitting is done with a special cutting pliers available at your tile dealer. After the adhesive has set, about 24 hours, a premixed grout, white or gray, which requires only water to a working consistency, is applied with a sponge trowel, covering the entire wall surface working the grout into the joints of the tile. When you are satisfied that all joints are full, allow about one hour for the grout to set, then wipe the tile surface clean with a burlap wiping cloth to remove the excess grout from the face of the tile. Wipe clean with a damp cloth removing all streaks, until surface is clean. Special pieces are available to match the color for trimming around doors, windows, interior and exterior corners and wainscot caps. This product can be used in any room with an ease of maintenance.

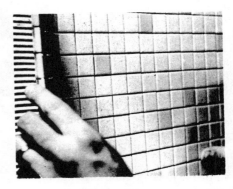

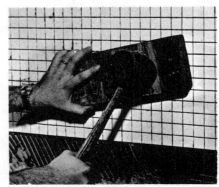

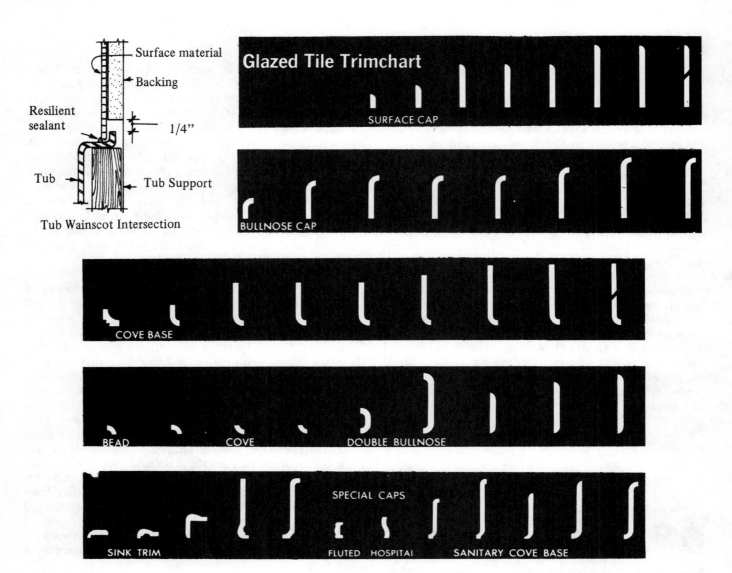

Surface material

Backing

Resilient sealant

1/4"

Tub

Tub Support

Tub Wainscot Intersection

Glazed Tile Trimchart

SURFACE CAP

BULLNOSE CAP

COVE BASE

BEAD   COVE   DOUBLE BULLNOSE

SPECIAL CAPS

SINK TRIM   FLUTED HOSPITAL   SANITARY COVE BASE

DRYWALL

Plaster sandwiched between two layers of heavy paper, also known as plaster board, sheetrock or gypsum board, is a construction technique known as dry wall. The panels are available in thickness of 1/4", 3/8", 1/2", 5/8", and 4'–0" in width. Lengths are 8'–0", 10'–0", 12'–0" and 14'–0", recommended for the following use:

5/8" – Dry wall construction provides resistance to fire exposure and sound transmission.

1/2" – For single layer application in residential construction.

3/8" – Applied principally over wood framing and repair and remodel work.

1/4" – Use over old walls and ceiling surfaces.

TOOLS

Be sure you have the following: Wallboard cutting knife, carpenter's claw hammer, 4' T-square, steel tape measure, keyhole saw, joint finishing knives—4" and 10" blades, plastic pan for joint compound, and medium texture sandpaper.

Gypsum board is an engineered building panel consisting of gypsum (hydrated calcium sulfate, a mineral), fibers, and other ingredients, finished on both sides with special paper to provide smooth surfaces and panel reinforcement. Actually a low density rock, gypsum is non-combustible and non-toxic. The properties that make gypsum board an important part of nearly every building in the country are gypsum's inherent resistance to fire and to the transmission of sound.

ADVANTAGES OF GYPSUM BOARD CONSTRUCTION

Gypsum board walls and ceilings have a number of outstanding advantages:

SOUND ISOLATION

Excellent sound isolation is obtained by separate framing of the two sides of the wall, fastening the wallboard over a sound control material, such as another gypsum board, and including sound absorbing materials in the wall cavity.

DURABILITY

Gypsum board makes strong high-quality walls and ceilings with good dimensional stability. The surfaces may be easily decorated and refinished during their long life.

ECONOMY

Gypsum board products are readily available and relatively easy to apply. They are the least expensive wall surfacing materials availalbe which offer a structurally sound, fire-resistant interior finish.

WORKING WITH GYPSUM BOARD

Refinishing or installing a new drywall partition or ceiling is not difficult if the job is planned ahead of time. As with any building or remodeling job, first make a sketch of the room to scale. Plan on installing the sheets perpendicular to studs and rafters, and buy your sheets in as long a length as you can conveniently handle, to reduce end joints—which must be staggered if they can't be avoided.

CORNERS

Protect outside corner edges with metal corner-bead. Nail it every 5" through the board into the framing.

These panels were designed primarily to reduce costs and time in construction. They take the place of wet plaster and, if properly installed, are very functional and effective. The secret of success in the installation of these panels is the taping of the joints to conceal them making one homogeneous unbroken continuous wall surface for painting or papering. All panels have a tapered edge along the length on both edges of one side designed to receive the paper product tape to conceal the joining of the panels. These panels are nailed to the studs with the nail head ever so slightly countersunk below the surface of the panel. If you drive the nail through the paper and break the surface, the holding power of the nail has been lost. Once the panel is nailed every 6" on all studs, apply a pre-mixed compound to the recessed areas of the panel with a putty knife or spatular, apply the tape over the fill and remove all creases or wrinkles and build up the fill over the tape to the thickness of the panel. At the same time, fill in all the indentations over the nail heads. Allow to dry and sand until smooth and level.

The properties that make gypsum an important building product are its resistance to fire and sound transmission. When gypsum is exposed to fire, the water of crystallization is slowly released as steam which retards heat transfer. Refinishing or installing a new drywall system is not difficult with proper planning. Install the sheets perpendicular to the studs or rafters in as long a length you can conveniently handle in order to reduce joints, which must be staggered. For 3/8" and 1/2" board use 1-5/8" coated type drywall nails, for 5/8" board use 1-7/8" nails. 5-1/2" lbs. of nails are required for every 1,000 square feet of board. For each 500 square feet of board three gallons of ready mix joint compound is needed and a 250 foot roll of wallboard tape.

For ceiling installation of wallboard, make two wood T-braces to hold the panels flat against the ceiling. The T-brace should be a 2" x 4" one inch longer than the floor to the ceiling height. On one end nail a 1" x 4" about 2'–0" long with diagonal cross bracing. Nail the edges of the panel

to the ceiling with nails 6" apart, remove the brace and complete the nailing. Be sure the nails are tight enough to show a dimple in the paper. Protect the outside corners with metal corner beads nailing every 5" into the framing.

When you are ready to tape the joints, apply the ready mix joint compound with a 4" knife fully and evenly to the slight recess at the edges of the panel. Place the wallboard tape centered over the joist and press it firmly into the compound with the knife held at an angle. Allow 24 hours to dry and sand, apply a second coat of compound over the tape, sand after 24 hours, then apply a third coat over the tape. The build-up must be gradual by applying several thin coats. If the compound is applied too heavy, it will crack and shrink. Do not over sand the paper surface. Use the same procedure to cover the dimples over the nail heads, end joints, metal corner beads and inside corners, folding and cutting the tape as necessary. When you have finished, you should have a smooth continuous wall surface ready

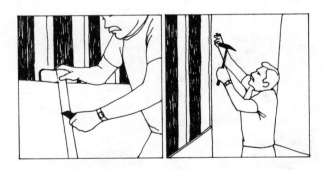

for painting or papering. Cutting drywall panels with a saw is not necessary, you only need to score the surface of the panel where it needs to be cut with a straight edge and snap at the score for a neat, dust free cut. Follow the procedure as explained in plywood panel for cutting around electric outlet boxes. These cuts will need to be cut with a saw. Exterior corners of drywall construction need metal beads to protect the corners from breaking. This bead is applied over the panel and is sealed with the same filler used in taping. If drywall is applied to a masonry or concrete wall, the wall needs to be furred as explained earlier.

SHEETROCK MOLDINGS

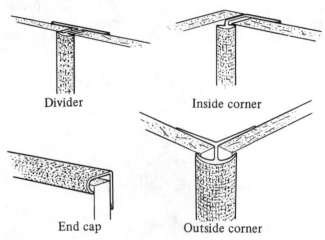

Divider   Inside corner

End cap   Outside corner

REPAIR

Provide for in shape of equilateral triangle around damaged area, cut out plug of wallboard with keyhole saw, slope edges inward at 45°. Cut corresponding plug from sound wallboard, sand edges to exact fit. If necessary, cement extra slat of wallboard to back of face layer to serve as brace. Butter edges (Fig. 3) and finish as a butt joint with joint compound (Fig. 4).

Fig. 3   Fig. 4

PAINT AND STAIN

If you are planning to stain finish wood, you must select a lumber grade free from defects, suitable for staining. Painting will allow you to use a lesser grade because any defects in the finished product will be concealed by the paint. Staining does nothing more than change the color of the natural wood. This will afford you an opportunity to purchase a

less expensive specie of wood and stain it to the color of a more expensive exotic wood specie. Before any painting or staining is done, the surface must be sanded to remove dirt and scratches and if the wood is damaged or dented, a wood filler must be used to make repairs. Stains highlight the variations in wood grain and color, therefore, the surface must be clean, dry and smooth, free of all fingerprints, smudges and pencil marks. Previous coatings and wax must be removed to the bare wood. All surfaces must be wiped with a solvent and tack rag to remove all dust. Open grained woods, such as Mahogany, Oak and Walnut, must be filled with a paste filler and allowed to dry overnight. Close grained woods, such as Birch, Maple or Pine require no filler.

Stain must be thoroughly stirred before use. Try a sample first or apply a sample on an inconspicuous area before staining the entire job because stains vary in color and character with different woods. If lighter color tone or depth is desired, thin the stain with mineral spirits. Apply stain with a brush or rag working it well to a uniform color, allow a few minutes to penetrate and wipe immediately with a soft lint free cloth. Deeper tones can be achieved by allowing the stain to set for a longer time before wiping. Allow to dry at least 4 hours before finishing with one coat or more of clear finish.

Painting will require one coat of primer (for new work) and two coats of the finish of your choice. On old work, sand the surface to allow the paint to adhere to the surface. Latex or water base paint is not recommended over an oil base paint. If you have no idea what the previous coat of paint is, remove a chip of paint and if it is brittle and snaps easily, it's an oil base paint. If, on the other hand, it is soft and stretches, it is a latex base paint. Another tell tale of oil base paint is a sheen or glossy finish. Lead base paints are no longer available for residential use.

Proper brush and brushing is essential to a good quality paint job. As a rule, one gallon of paint will cover between 400 and 500 square feet of surface. Use this as a guide to prevent putting too much or too little paint. A pure bristle brush should be used for oil base paint, a nylon brush for latex paint and a polyester brush for general purpose. The proper brush size is important to a good finish. Latex brush paints can be cleaned with ammoniated water, oil base paint brushes require paint thinner or turpentine to clean. When not in use, brushes should be stored with handle down.

Defective paint surfaces have many causes. Peeling and blistering is caused by a loss of adhesion brought about by moisture getting behind a film of paint and pushing out trying to escape. Protected areas pose more of a problem than open areas because the water is slow to dry and the likelihood of damage is increased. Wood and wood composition is constantly moving, expanding and contracting and this constant movement breaks the film and adhesion of paint causing an opening for water to penetrate and lock in behind the paint resulting in peeling and blistering. If the trapped water freezes it will result in further damage.

Anything that effects the relationship of paint film to the surface it touches will affect adhesion and cause peeling which includes air borne dust, dirt or chemicals not visible to the naked eye. The previous coat of paint has chemical by-products which causes the breakdown of the new coat, especially latex paints. The contact surface of a coat of paint is important. This is why it is difficult to obtain a good coat of paint on a smooth hard surface.

Don't assume a surface to be painted is dry because the sun is shining and it looks dry. Wipe it dry and sand the surface which will remove surface film of degrading paint. Look for trapped moisture forcing its way through old paint. Cut dense planting and heavy shrubs or trees too close to the house blocking good ventilation and air movement. Don't paint when temperatures are expected to drop fast in a few hours or late in the day. The best insurance you can provide to minimize peeling, cracking and blistering is by sanding. This provides a rough surface with more contact points for better adhesion. Sanding will remove dirt, and minute layers of degraded paint. Sand and feather all edges to lessen the chances of lifting or loosening old paint.

HOW TO FINISH PLYWOOD

EXTERIOR FINISHING

CARE AND PREPARATION: Like any good finish material, plywood should be stored and handled with care to avoid damaging exposures before the product has been finished. Storage in a cool, dry place out of the sunlight and weather is best. If left outdoors, straps on plywood packages should be loosened or cut, and plywood stacks should be covered in such a way as to provide good air circulation and ventilation between the panels and protective cover to prevent moisture condensation and possible mold growth.

There is a definite relationship between performance of any finish and the exposure time of raw wood, especially to sunlight and wetting or drying. For best results, then, at least the first coat should be applied as soon as possible.

EDGE SEALING: Since end grain surfaces pick up and lose moisture far more rapidly than side grain, all panels should be edge sealed to minimize possible moisture damage. Both blind and exposed edges should be treated. Sealing is best done when panels are in a stack, but those later cut for application should be resealed.

Siding to be painted should be edge sealed with a liberal brush coat of exterior house paint primer. Generally the same system used on the face of the siding is adequate. Where panels are not to be painted, such as textured siding finished with a stain, best performance is obtained by the liberal application of a good water repellent preservative compatible with the finish to be applied later. Horizontal edges, particularly lower drip edges of siding, should be treated with special care because of their greater wetting exposure.

STAIN FINISHES

Semi-Transparent or Penetrating: Textured plywood sidings are best finished with stains as the resultant appearance satisfies the architectural intent of the rustic siding. High qual-ity oil base or latex emulsion stains are recommended as these penetrate the wood surface and add color without formation of a continuous film, to provide a durable, breathing surface. Where maximum wood color and grain show-through are desired and where color differences in the wood or between the wood and synthetic or wood repairs are not objectionable, a semi-transparent stain may be used. A brush-out test on a sample of the siding, making sure that the sample includes the color-contrasting characteristics, is recommended. If panels do not contain color-contrasting characteristics, a semi-transparent stain may be used directly. One or two coats are applied in accordance with the manufacturer's directions, with two coats providing greater depth of color and longer life.

As is true with most finishes, the method of application generally is as important as the finish material itself. Best performance comes by brushing on the stain which tends to work the material into the wood surface and provides a uniform appearance. Next in order of preference would be application by a long napped roller, which also tends to work the stain into the surface, but is not as effective as brushing. Spray applications are least desired, and if used, should be followed by back brushing or wiping down the surface with a carpet section tacked to a block on a pole handle. To accomplish this, the spray must be applied liberally and the back brushing must be sufficient to work the stain into the surface and under loose particles, particularly on saw textured surfaces. The dry brushing also helps to provide a more uniform appearance. If the spray is fogged onto the surface, too little stain is applied and it rests completely on the extreme surface of any loose particles, dust or fibers which are easily eroded away in the natural weathering process. Care should be taken on windy, dry days to avoid lap marks, especially with the faster drying latex emulsions.

Opaque or Heavy-Bodied Stain: Where masking of all substrate characteristics except texture is desired, oil or latex emulsion opaque or highly pigmented stains should be used. This is particularly applicable where color differences between or within panels is to be obscured and where solid, uniform color is wanted. The opaque stains, properly formulated and correctly applied, penetrate the wood surface and provide a good bond to the panel. Typical shake and shingle paints or stains should be avoided since they form a significant film on the surface and exhibit little penetration into the wood. Typically, they embrittle within a short time, and when cracks appear, water gets underneath to flake away the finish. Such a failed surface is difficult to refinish without removing all the old material. A properly applied stain, in either semi-transparent or opaque type, will weather to a surface that is easily refinished without significant surface preparation. Although checks may appear in the surface, this will in no way affect the integrity of the panel nor the performance of the properly applied stain finish. When restaining is necessary, the checks are then colored to become obscure.

PAINT FINISHES

Primer and Topcoat: Where paint must be used on textured surfaces, or where it is applied to untextured plywood types, top quality acrylic latex exterior house paint systems are recommended. A minimum two coat paint system is essential for wood products, with the primer the more important always. A primer is formulated specifically for controlled penetration, for optimum bond to the substrate and for minimizing extractive staining. Some latex systems are designed to use an oil or alkyd primer, followed by the latex topcoat. Others utilize a specially formulated latex primer, often with emulsified oil included. Some manufacturers recommend two prime coats over extractive-staining woods.

In any case, companion products, preferably made by the same manufacturer to be used together should be specified. Typical shake and shingle paints are NOT recommended due to their characteristics of poor bond and tendency to crack.

Again, brush application is strongly recommended for the first coat in order to form an adequate film with good penetration into the wood surface to provide best performance. To avoid difficulties, use an assured stain resistant primer with a compatible acrylic latex topcoat. Two finish coats give significant improvement in life and performance. Should checks appear, the latex paint system should remain bonded to the substrate with no deterioration.

For most typical paint systems, 5 to 7 mils in total thickness is the maximum film desirable. Thicker films often fail as a result of their own thickness, usually through cracking and loss of bond. This is most noticeable where frequent refinishing adds to the thickness of the paint film faster than erosion can reduce it.

Checking may be expected, particularly on southern exposures, on painted Texture plywood sidings and even with sanded plywood. Checks developed in textured surfaces generally are not objectionable since they blend with the architecturally rough surface. Even where checking occurs, bond and wear characteristics of a good quality latex paint has been found to be completely satisfactory. Where completely smooth and check free surfaces are desired, Medium Density Overlaid plywood should be selected. Similar paint systems to those described above should be used with the overlaid product, including the primer.

Recent government restrictions on use of lead and mercury compounds in finishes have resulted in uncertainties regarding the performance of new paints and stains. In many cases, long-term performance data on lead and mercury substitutes is lacking, and results of tests in progress will not be available for some time.

EXTERIOR CLEAR FINISHES: Clear film finishes on plywood exposed outdoors have been found to be generally unsatisfactory and should be avoided.

INTERIOR FINISHING

PREPARATION OF PANELS: Plywood for interior paneling applications may be of sanded grade, overlaid or any of the several textures. MDO plywood needs no preparation and is finished with conventional paints or enamels for an exceptionally smooth and durable surface. Textured panels may be finished directly with clear sealer, stains or latex paints. Sanded plywood may be finished with paints, enamels or stains. The only sanding required is to smooth filler or spackle applied to any openings in the panel face, or to remove blemishes. To touch-sand, always sand with the grain, using fine sandpaper. Do not paint over dust or spots of oil or glue. All knots, pitch streaks, or sap spots in sanded or textured plywood should be touched up with sealer or shellac before the panels are painted. No other panel preparition is needed.

INTERIOR PAINTS/Flat Finishes

1. OIL BASE. Used where washability, durability and flat appearance are of prime concern. Fingerprints, dirt, crayon and other stains can be scrubbed off repeatedly. Generally, these are alkyd resin base enamels, characterized by good hiding properties. They can be brushed, rolled or sprayed on. Some of them are self priming on wood.

2. WATER BASE. These paints are emulsions of resin (usually polyvinyl acetate, acrylic, or styrene-butadiene latex and water), and have some degree of washability. They are often called latex paints and are easily applied with brush, roller or spray. Color retention is good and they dry quickly. When using these paints, prime plywood surface with primer recommended by the topcoat manufacturer, to prevent grain raise and minimize staining.

Gloss and Semi-Gloss Enamel: These are extremely durable, washable finishes, usually alkyd resin base; also available in acrylic latex water-base type. Use with recommended primer. Their use is primarily in kitchens and bathrooms for trim, cabinets, etc.

INTERIOR NATURAL FINISHES: Smooth or smooth-textured plywood for natural finishes should be carefully selected for pattern and appearance. For the most natural effect, use two coats of clear sealer as a finish to maintain a clean panel surface and avoid soiling.

Plywood's repairs and grain irregularities can be pleasantly subdued with light stain finishes applied in either of two ways.

The sealer is a heavy-bodied non-penetrating type with non-hiding pigments, which preserve natural wood appearance. Tones of light gray, brown or tan go well with wood colors and provide best grain masking.

1. LIGHT STAIN. Another method of applying a natural finish which mellows plywood's grain pattern requires more steps than color toning, but does not require special companion stains and sealers. The panel is first whitened with pigmented resin sealer or interior white undercoat cut "one to one" with thinner. Before it becomes tacky, the sealer is wiped off to permit show of grain. Then, clear resin sealer is applied, allowed to dry, and sandpapered lightly. The color is added with tinted undercoat, thin enamel, pigmented resin sealer or light stain, applied thinly, and wiped to the proper color depth. After drying and light sanding, a coat of satin varnish or brushing lacquer is applied to provide luster and durability.

2. COLOR TONING. Color toning requires companion stains and non-penetrating sealers. These have the advantage of requiring only one step for application of stain and sealer. It is necessary to tint a small amount of sealer with stain until the desired tone is obtained on a sample. Then, enough stain and sealer to do the entire job is mixed in the same proportion and applied by brush or spray. After drying and light sanding, a coat of clear finish is added to give the desired luster and durability.

INTERIOR PAINTS/Flat Finishes

Multicolor Spatter Finish. Spatter finish is usually a lacquer, blending two or more colors of uniform fleck size. When applied by spray equipment, the colors remain separate and distinct, creating an unusal decorative effect. The finish can be applied lightly over a colored background, or fully over a primer, and works well with "V" joints in plywood panels.

Textured Plywood: Textured plywood (rough sawn, patterned surfaces, Texture grades,etc.) may be finished for attractive natural appearance. They should be protected against soiling with two coats of a clear sealer, or, where color is wanted, pigmented stains may be used. If desired, the few repairs and grain irregularities can be subdued by color toning or light stains as described above.

Only semi-gloss or gloss alkyd enamel paint should be used on wood trim. Even if you are using color paint on the walls, a paint store can supply the enamel for a perfect match with the latex paint. A good-quality paint brush must be used on wood. On wide wood surfaces, apply enamel in strips, then spread horizontally. More care is required than for painting walls and ceilings so as to prevent runs that will spoil the appearance.

SPECIAL EFFECTS

Stippled or Textured Finish. This finish may be used along with taping to completely hide joints in plywood paneling. Since the stipple texture paints are usually of latex type, the plywood must be primed with an oil-base or stain-resistant primer. The stipple is then applied as recommended.

A GUIDE TO MOST COMMONLY USED PAINT FINISHING SYSTEMS.

On walls and ceilings, a paint roller does a better job in half the time than a brush. However, you must use a brush to paint a narrow strip at the juncture of walls and ceilings, around windows and doors, and above baseboards, as a roller will not reach these areas.

Paint the ceiling first. Apply the paint in the shape of a "W" to an area about 30 inches square, then spread the paint evenly in both directions. Additional applications are made to unpainted areas and spread to painted areas. Walls are painted in the same manner.

The only thing you need to do to the wood trim is smooth it by sandpapering. A hook scraper does a good job of removing some of the roughness, and an electric finishing sander speeds the work.

Neutral colors such as grays and tans offer the best resistance to fading. Pastel tones, especially yellows, reds, and pinks, give the poorest performances in retaining their colorings under prolonged exposure to the actinic rays of sunlight.

PAINT PEELING

Paint peeling and/or blistering may result from condensation of moisture within the house. Characteristically, the blisters will contain water and the paint peels down to bare wood. (Poor paint, faulty application of paint, and exterior moisture also cause paint troubles, but they are not within the scope of this circular.)

Typically, the moisture in the room penetrates the walls until it reaches the underside of the exterior paint. The building materials through which the water vapor has passed are porous; the paint is not. As a result, the moisture gathers underneath the paint, forms blisters, and eventually the paint peels away from the wood. A membrane vapor barrier eliminates such difficulties by preventing the moisture from entering the walls.

Sometimes this situation can be cured by cold-side venting. Venting each stud space, preferably at the top and the bottom, permits the moisture to escape before it condenses.

This problem sometimes first occurs after an older house has been newly insulated. A combination of factors contributes to the problem — the addition of insulation reduces the amount of leakage through the walls, and usually there is no vapor barrier in older houses.

Whenever possible, a vapor barrier should be installed when an older house is insulated. Absence of a vapor barrier, however, does not always result in a condensation problem; sometimes the moisture levels in the house are so low that no problem arises.

finishing system type	SOLVENT TYPE ALKYD	WATER BASE ALKYD	ALKYD CHLORINATED PARAFFIN- PLASTICIZING OIL	LATEX (WATER-THINNED) VINYL ACRYLIC	LATEX (WATER-THINNED) ACRYLIC EXTERIOR
vehicle/ binder characteristics	Probably most versatile of synthetic resins used in paint chemistry. Available in a full range of sheens for interior and exterior use. Made by combining synthetic materials with various vegetable oils (linseed, soya, tung, etc.) to produce clear, hard resins. Good self-sealing properties on many surfaces, eliminate the need for special primer-sealers or under-coaters. Good weather-resistance and gloss retention for exterior exposure. **LIMITATIONS** Because of their oil content, alkyds tend to darken with age.		Combines positive features of alkyd and plasticizing oil type formulations (when properly pigmented) plus: Excellent color retention in exterior use. Outstanding film resistance to blistering, fumes and dirt collection. Excellent gloss retention and will not stain from rust or copper washdown. Improved flexibility; hence better resistance to cracking. May be used as its own primer on bare spots when repainting wood surfaces.	Excellent adhesion to non-chalky masonry surfaces of all types. Good alkali resistance. Excellent color retention permitting easy touch-up of missed or patched areas at a later date. Good washability, permits easy cleaning. Does not raise "grain" of fibers in the covering used on gypsum wall-board. Excellent self-sealing properties, thus no primer needed except on bare metal surfaces. Fast dry permits application of two coats in one day.	Use as exterior finish on wood or masonry. Outstanding color retention. Excellent for use in repaint work, or properly primed new work. Fast dry.

finishing system type	LATEX (WATER-THINNED) ACRYLIC INTERIOR	POLYESTER-EPOXY SOLVENT THINNED OR ACRYLIC EPOXY WATER-THINNED (TWO COMPONENT)	POLYURETHANE (ONE COMPONENT)	POLYAMIDE-EPOXY (TWO COMPONENT)
vehicle/ binder characteristics	Excellent adhesion to interior surfaces of all types including plaster, wood, and pre-primed metal. Excellent gloss and color retention, with proper preparation. Good flow, easy application, excellent hiding, and self-sealing properties. Exceptional ease of cleaning. Presents no flammability hazard in storage. Fast dry.	Tile-like finishes that can be applied to any firm interior surface. Gloss and Semi-gloss sheens. Two components mixed prior to application. Pot-life is a full working day. Combines the physical toughness, adhesion and chemical resistance of epoxy with the color retention and permanent clarity of polyester or acrylics. Outstanding stain resistance—greater than other coatings. Most stains remain on surface and do not penetrate film. Film is also impervious to moisture.	Outstanding abrasion resistance on wood floors, furniture, paneling, cabinets, etc. Good resistance to normal household materials such as alcohol, water, grease, etc.	Tough, chemical resistant finish with excellent hardness, abrasion resistance and adhesion. Outstanding resistance to alkali and good acid resistance. Excellent for use as a concrete floor finish where heavy traffic wears through an alkyd finish in a short time. **LIMITATIONS** Loses gloss and chalks on prolonged exterior exposure. Film integrity not adversely affected.

EXTERIOR SURFACES — GENERAL PAINTING

As written, the following specifications are applicable to new construction.

However, the same finish coat system will usually apply when re-finishing previously painted surfaces. Some variation may be necessary in use (or non-use) of primers, depending upon the type of existing coating and the condition of the surface to be covered.

Exterior and interior applications are grouped according to the surface to be finished: painted or natural finished wood, masonry, and metal.

Where more than one type of finish is listed, the choice should be made according to specific environmental requirements including, finish, sheen and color desired.

PAINTED WOOD

USE: SURFACE AND REQUIREMENTS	TYPE FINISHING SYSTEM	SHEEN	RECOMMENDATIONS
WOOD SIDING Fume resistant One coat white Extra high hiding	Alkyd Chlorinated Paraffin, Linseed Oil	Gloss	Primer: Exterior Wood Primer Finish: One Coat House Paint
	Acrylic Latex	Flat	Primer: Exterior Wood Primer Finish: One Coat House Paint
WOOD SIDING ABOVE MASONRY To avoid staining Slow chalking Fume resistant Good resistance to color fading	Oil Type Alkyd		Primer: Exterior Wood Primer Finish: House and Trim Paint, Exterior 2 Coats: Finish, White or colors
WOOD SIDING Properly prepared cement-asbestos and rustic wood shakes and shingles	Acrylic Latex	Flat	Primer: Latex House Paint Wood Primer Finish: Latex House Paint 2 Coats: White or colors
		Gloss	Primer: (Same as 2 above) Finish: Latex Gloss House and Trim Paint. White and colors. 2 Coats
WOOD TRIM, SHUTTERS DOORS Accent areas, windows Not for use on large wood areas such as the body of a house.	Alkyd Enamel		Primer: Sun-Proof Universal Primer or Speedhide Ext. Wood Primer Finish: Oil Type House and Trim Color 2 Coats Paints Quick Dry Enamel or Ext.-Int.-Enamel White or colors.
WOOD TRIM, SHUTTERS DOORS, WOOD SIDING OR TRIM (Large or small areas) Accent areas, windows, handrails, etc. only.	Acrylic Latex	Gloss	Primer: Universal Primer or Ext. Wood Primer Finish: Latex Gloss House and trim Paint. White and colors. 2 Coats
WOOD DECKS AND PORCHES Tough, elastic film. Porches, decks, docks, floors, and wood steps Resists abrasive under-foot wear	Alkyd Enamel		Primer: Paints Floor and Deck Enamel reduced with one 1 Coat pint mineral spirits. Paint Thinner per gallon (for wood). For metal use proper inhibitive primers. Finish: Paints Floor and Deck Enamel (full strength). 2 Coats White or colors.

NATURAL OR STAINED WOOD

USE: SURFACE AND REQUIREMENTS	TYPE FINISHING SYSTEM	SHEEN	RECOMMENDATIONS
REDWOOD, CEDAR, ETC. SIDING, WOOD SHINGLE ROOFS. (Stained) To protect, provide color, and retard warping of shakes and shingles. Note: — Not recommended for textured or rough sawn siding.	Latex (for rough or smooth surfaces)	Low Sheen	Primer Solid Color Latex Stain. Many colors. and or Finish: Semi-Transparent Latex Stain 1 or 2 Coats
	Alkyd Stain (for smooth surfaces only)	Flat	Primer: Semi-Transparent Alkyd-Oil Stain. Many colors. and or Finish: Solid Color Alkyd-Oil Stain. Many colors. 2 Coats
HARDWOOD DOORS AND TRIM: Clear, tough, water-resistant hard finish of exceptional depth. Note: — Not recommended for textured or rough sawn siding.	Varnish or Urethane Coating	Gloss	Primer: Clear Sealer-Primer, unreduced, OR Clear Spar Varnish 1 Coat reduced with 1/8 or 1/4 gal. mineral spirits per gal. or Polyurethane-gloss (clear) reduced with 1/8 to 1/4 gal. mineral spirits per gal. OR Polyurethane gloss (clear). Apply freely. Allow one day but no more than two days' drying time before topcoating. Finish: Clear Spar Varnish or Clear Polyurethane-gloss 2 Coats (No reduction for either).

MASONRY

USE: SURFACE AND REQUIREMENTS	TYPE FINISHING SYSTEM	SHEEN	RECOMMENDATIONS
BRICK, STUCCO, AND CONCRETE WALLS: Durable, attractive, and weather-resistant film for use over surfaces free of chalky deposits and efflorescence.	Vinyl Acrylic Latex	Flat	Primer: None required. Finish: Latex Masonry Paint or Emulsion 2 Coats Masonry Paint. (Reduce first coat with one pint water per gallon for porous surfaces.) White and colors.
BRICK, STUCCO, AND CONCRETE WALLS: Durable, attractive, and weather-resistant film for over surfaces free of chalky deposits and efflorescence.	Acrylic Latex	Flat	Primer: Alkali Resistant Primer 1 Coat Finish: Latex House Paint or Exterior Latex 2 Coats Wood Finish. White and colors
		Flat	Primer: Alkali Resistant Primer. 1 Coat Finish: Latex House Paint 1 Coat
		Gloss	Primer: Alkali Resistant Primer. 1 Coat Finish: Latex Gloss and Trim House Paint. White 2 Coats and Colors.
CONCRETE AND CINDER BLOCK WALLS	Vinyl Acrylic Latex	Flat	Primer: Block Filler or Emulsion Masonry 1 Coat Block Filler. Finish: Latex Masonry Paint or Emulsion 2 Coats Masonry Paint. White and Colors.
CEMENT-ASBESTOS SIDING, AND PANELS: Note: — These specifications do not apply to the sandwich-type fiber core insulation boards.	Vinyl Acrylic Latex	Flat	Primer: Alkali Resistant Primer 1 Coat Finish: Latex Masonry Paint or Emulsion 2 Coats Masonry Paint. White and Colors.
COVERED CONCRETE PATIO AND BREEZEWAY FLOORS Durable finish capable of withstanding normal washing but not prolonged soaking.	Vinyl Acrylic Latex	Low Sheen	Primer: Latex Floor and Deck Enamel reduced 1 Coat with one pint water per gallon. Acid etching is not required but will prove adhesion to smooth dense concrete. Finish: Latex Floor and Deck Enamel. White and Colors. 2 Coats (after curing for several days, apply a quality Paste Wax.)
EXTERIOR MASONRY SURFACES Concrete, Block, Brick, Stucco	Sand-textured, Alkyd-Epoxy	Flat	Primer: (No primer needed.) Finish: Textured Masonry Coating 1 Coat Off White and Colors
EXTERIOR CONCRETE ROADS, DRIVEWAYS, ETC.	Alkyd and Chlorinated Rubber	Flat	Primer: None needed. Finish: Traffic and Zone Marking Paint. 2 Coats
NEW EXTERIOR MASONRY SURFACES Concrete, Block, Brick, Stucco. Fill and finish in one application using airless spray	Vinyl Acrylic Latex	Semi-gloss One or Two Coats	Primer: None usually required EXCEPT chalky, weathered exterior surfaces must be sealed prior to application. Use Masonry Sealer. Finish: One coat is usually sufficient using Fill and Finish material in airless spray. After spraying, rollers can be used to release trapped air and minimize pinholing. On exterior applications if pinholes or cracks are noticed, a second coat may be used to insure a good weather seal.

METALS

USE: SURFACE AND REQUIREMENTS	TYPE FINISHING SYSTEM	SHEEN	RECOMMENDATIONS
FERROUS METALS - NORMAL EXPOSURE: Basic inhibitive action. Enamel-like gloss finish with broad range of colors.	Solvent Type Alkyd Enamel	Gloss	Primer: Inhibitive Red or White Primers 1 Coat Finish: Oil Type House and Trim Enamel, or 2 Coats Exterior-Interior Enamel, or Quick Dry Enamel
	Water Base Alkyd Enamel	Gloss	Primer: Inhibitive Red or White Primers 1 Coat Finish: Water Base Gloss Enamel. White and Colors. 2 Coats
FERROUS METALS — NORMAL EXPOSURE: Tough, durable, elastic finish with high light and heat reflecting value.	Metallic Aluminum —Varnish	Alum. Gloss	Primer: Red or White Primers 1 Coat Finish: General-purpose 2 Coats Aluminum Paint.

FERROUS METALS — NORMAL EXPOSURE: Exceptional resistance to corrosive action of normal atmosphere exposures Applicable to metal or wood.	Oleo-resinous Varnish	Gloss	Primer: Inhibitive Red or White Primers. 1 Coat Finish: Bright Chrome Aluminum 2 Coats
FERROUS METALS — HOT SURFACES 450° to 1000° F, STACKS, ETC: DO NOT paint with surface temperature in excess of 140° F Not recommended on surfaces with "in-use" temperature below 450° F (Alum.) or 400° F (Gray). White metal blast cleaning required.	Silicone Resin	Aluminum-Gloss Gray — Semi-Gloss	Primer: Silicone High-Heat Gray. 1 Coat Finish: Silicone High-Heat Resistant Aluminum 1 Thin or Gray. Coat
GALVANIZED METAL — NORMAL EXPOSURE: Surface must be free from grease, dirt, rust, and other contamination. Acid pretreatment is not required. The prime coat performance will be in direct proportion to the surface preparation. Primers (and finish) provide good resistance to normal atmospheric corrosion	Cement-Oil Primer, Oil-Base Finish	Gloss	Primer: Galvanized Steel Primer. 1 Coat Finish: Oil Type House and Trim Paint 2 Coats
	Vinyl Acrylic Latex	Flat	Primer: Solvent clean Naphtha None Required Finish: Latex Masonry Paint or Emulsion
	Cement-Oil Primer, Alkyd-Enamel Finish	Gloss	Primer: Galvanized Steel Primer 1 Coat Finish: Oil Type Trim Color, Exterior-Interior 2 Coats Gloss Enamel, or Quick Dry Enamel, or Water Base Gloss Enamel, White and Colors.
	Aluminum Alkyd — Oil —Resin Finish	Aluminum Gloss	Primer: Galvanized Steel Primer. 1 Coat Finish: General- purpose 2 Coats Aluminum Paint.
ALUMINUM METAL SURFACES: This primer is formulated without lead for use over aluminum. Surface should be free from dirt and grease. Pastel Yellow Color Primer easily hidden by most finish coats	Modified Alkyd	Low Gloss	Primer: Zinc Chromate Primer. 1 Coat Finish: Oil Type House Paint (White and Colors) 2 Coats
	Solvent or Water Base Alkyd Enamel	Gloss	Primer: Chromate Primer 1 Coat Finish: Oil Type House and Trim Color or Exterior-Interior Gloss 2 Coats Enamel or Quick Dry Enamel, or Water Base Gloss Enamel. White and Colors
METAL ROOFS, VENTS, ETC.: When free of surface contamination, prime coat provides excellent resistance to corrosive action. See Specs. Nos. 19,19a,19b and 19c for galvanized surfaces.	Alkyd Enamel	Low or High Gloss	Primer: Inhibitive Red or White Primer. 1 Coat Finish: Paints Red or Green Ranch, Barn and Roof 2 Coats (Low Gloss) Paint or Exterior-Interior Gloss Enamel. (High Gloss) (White and Colors).
VINYL OR COATED ALUMINUM SIDING (Repaint work): Bare, cracked or chipped areas should be primed. All corrosion and mildew must be completely removed See Bulletin F. Adv. 501 for complete details.	Modified Alkyd	Gloss	Primer: Zinc Chromate Primer or Universal 1 Coat Primer. Finish: Oil Type House and Trim Paint. White and Colors. 2 Coats
	Acrylic Latex	Flat	Primer: Zinc Chromate Primer or Univeral 1 Coat Primer. Finish: Latex House Paint 2 Coats White and Colors.
	Acrylic Latex	Gloss	Primer: Zinc Chromate Primer or Universal 1 Coat Primer. Finish: Gloss Latex House and Trim Paint. White and Colors. 2 Coats

FOREWORD: All surfaces should be tested for moisture content before painting. If the moisture meter test indicates a content of less than 8 per cent moisture, regular wall primer-sealer may be safely used. If the content is more than 8 per cent, but not over 12 per cent, an alkali-resistant primer-sealer should be used. If the content is over 12 per cent, painting should not be done.

Before painting new plaster, always remove the water soluble surface salt deposits by dry brushing. If this surface powder is not removed, the finish is likely to appear mottled after drying, especially when using an emulsion system.

PLASTER

USE: SURFACE AND REQUIREMENTS	TYPE FINISHING SYSTEM	SHEEN	RECOMMENDATIONS
PLASTER WALLS AND CEILINGS (Smooth or Sand Finish): Resists yellowing. For general use.	Alkyd-Resin	Flat	Primer: Wall Primer-Sealer 1 Coat Finish: Alkyd Flat or Flat Enamel — Alkyd Type 1 or 2 Coats Flat Dry Fog Spraying Paint. White and Colors.
PLASTER WALLS AND CEILINGS: High resistance to soil and washing. Also suitable for trim, cabinets, other objects and surfaces	Acrylic Latex	Eggshell flat or Semi Gloss	Primer: Wall Primer Sealer. 1 Coat Finish: Latex Flat Enamel or Latex Lo-Lustre Enamel 1 or 2 Coats White and Colors.
PLASTER WALLS AND CEILINGS Dense, hard finish with good resistance to marring; easy to clean. Resists yellowing.	Solvent Type Alkyd-Enamel	Gloss	Primer: Wall Primer 1 Coat Finish: Quick Dry Enamel, or Exterior-Interior Gloss Enamel, or 2 Coats Gloss Dry Fog Spraying Paint. White and Colors.
	Water Base Enamel	Gloss	Primer: Wall Primer Sealer 1 Coat Finish: Water Base Gloss Enamels 2 Coats
PLASTER WALLS AND CEILINGS Exceptional hiding power. Resists yellowing. Durable, tough finish. Easy to clean.	Alkyd Enamel	Satin	Primer: Wall Primer-Sealer. 1 Coat Finish: Lo-Lustre Enamel or Alkyd Interior 2 Coats Lo-Sheen Enamel. White and Colors.
	Acrylic Latex	Semi Gloss	Primer: Wall Primer. 1 Coat Finish: Latex Lo-Lustre Enamel or Latex Semi-Gloss Enamel or 2 Coats Semi-Gloss Dry Fog Spraying Paint. White and Colors.
PLASTER WALLS AND CEILINGS Vinyl emulsion with excellent hiding properties, spreads easily and dries quickly.	Vinyl Acrylic Latex	Velvet Flat	Primer: Wall Primer 1 Coat Finish: Latex Flat or Latex Interior Flat 1 or 2 Coats Wall Paint or Flat Dry Fog Spraying Paint. White and Colors.
PLASTER WALLS AND CEILINGS High build vinyl emulsion with excellent hiding properties Sprays easily and dries quickly. For Spray Application Only.	Spray applied Vinyl Acrylic	Velvet Flat or Textured	Primer: None needed (except metal). Zinc or galvanized — use 1 Coat White Galvanized Steel Primer. Other metals use Zinc Chromate Primer. Finish: High Build Latex Flat Paint. Normal 1 Coat application is 6-10 mils wet. White and Bone White. This product can be tinted. (Textured finishes also available.)
PLASTER WALLS AND CEILINGS Extremely hard-wearing surface for institutional or industrial-commerical areas that require cleaning with strong detergents	Two Component Polyester—Epoxy or Acrylic Epoxy	High Gloss or Semi Gloss	Primer: Dry wall, plaster or concrete — Pigmented Sealer 1 Coat Finish: Gloss or Semi-Gloss Coating. White, Clear, or Colors. 1 or 2 Solvent Type. Coats Water-base Type.
PLASTER WALLS AND CEILINGS Resists yellowing — applicable to properly primed and sealed plaster, brick, cement-masonry composition board, metal, and wood.	Alkyd Resin Enamel	Gloss	Primer: Wall Primer 1 Coat Finish: Exterior-Interior Gloss Enamel, or 1 Coat Quick Dry Enamel or Water Base Gloss Enamels. White and Colors.

MASONRY

USE: SURFACE AND REQUIREMENTS	TYPE FINISHING SYSTEM	SHEEN	RECOMMENDATIONS
CONCRETE AND CINDER BLOCK WALLS (Dense Surface).			Same specifications as those shown above for plaster walls and ceilings except specificaton 27. Select type of paint and sheen desired.
BRICK AND DENSE (POURED) CONCRETE AND MASONRY Exceptionally durable finish for hard-use areas or where repeated washings may be Exceptional resistance to staining; resists yellowing.	Two-Component Polyester-Epoxy or Acrylic Epoxy	High Gloss or Semi Gloss	Primer: Pigmented Sealer. (For protection of natural 1 Coat brick or stone, omit primer above. Instead, apply 2 coats of Gloss or Semi-Gloss Polyester-epoxy or Water Base Acrylic Epoxy.) Finish: Coating in finish and color desired. 1 or 2 Solvent Type Coats Water-base Type
CONCRETE AND CINDER BLOCK WALLS (Porous, Open Face): Exceptional hiding power over interior surfaces. Dries to handling in 30 minutes to one hour.	Acrylic Latex	Flat	Primer: Latex Masonry Block Filler, 1 Coat Block Filler. Finish: Latex Flat (Vinyl Acrylic) or Latex Interior Flat Wall Paint (Acrylic). 1 or 2 White and Colors. Coats
	Acrylic Latex	Semi Gloss	Primer: Latex Masonry Block Filler 1 Coat Finish: Latex Lo-Lustre Enamel or Latex 1 or 2 Semi-Gloss Enamel. Coats
NEW INTERIOR MASONRY SURFACES Concrete, Block, Brick, Stucco Fill and finish in one application using airless spray.	Vinyl Acrylic Latex	Semi Gloss	Primer: None usually required EXCEPT chalky, weathered exterior surfaces must be sealed prior to application. Use Masonry Sealer. Finish: One coat is usually sufficient using Fill and Finish material 1 or 2 in airless spray. After spraying, rollers can be used to release Coats trapped air and minimize pinholing.
CONCRETE AND CINDER BLOCK WALLS (Porous, Open Face): Exceptional hiding power interior surfaces. Dries to handling in 30 minutes to one hour. For Spray Application Only.	Airless Spray applied Vinyl Acrylic Latex	Velvet Flat	Primer: No primer needed on smooth surfaces. For rough surfaces use Block Fillers. Finish: High Build Latex Flat Paint, White and Bone 1 Coat White. This product can be tinted. Normal application is 6-10 mils wet.
CONCRETE AND CINDER BLOCK WALLS: (Porous) Durable and decorative coating system for areas exposed to hard wear that require frequent cleaning with strong detergents and mechanical scrubbers.	Two-Component Polyester-Epoxy or Acrylic Epoxy	High Gloss or Semi Gloss	Primer: Block Filter. 1 or 2 Coats Finish: Gloss or Semi-Gloss. White or Colors. 1 or 2 Solvent Type. Coats Water-base Type.
INTERIOR MASONRY SURFACES — Concrete Block, Brick Stucco and Cement	Sand-textured, Alkyd-Epoxy	Flat	Finish: Textured Masonry Coating. Off-white. 1 Coat It may be tinted.

DRY-WALL

USE: SURFACE AND REQUIREMENTS			
DRY-WALL CONSTRUCTION: Low odor, resists yellowing. For use over interior plaster, wallboard, and wood. Paper-type surfaces must be sealed with an emulsion type sealer before applying finish.	Alkyd-Resin	Flat	Primer: Quick-Drying Emulsion Sealer. 1 Coat Finish: Alkyd Flat. White and Colors. 1 Coat
DRY-WALL CONSTRUCTION: Enamel, high resistance to soil and washing. Wide color selection. Also suitable for trim, cabinets, other objects and surfaces.	Acrylic Latex	Eggshell flat	Primer: Latex Flat Enamel reduced with one pint of water per 1 Coat gallon or Quick-Drying Emulsion Sealer. Finish: Latex Flat Enamel. White and Colors. 1 or 2 Coats

USE: SURFACE AND REQUIREMENTS			
DRY-WALL CONSTRUCTION Low odor, resists yellowing. For use over interior plaster wallboard, and wood Paper-type surfaces must be sealed before applying this finish.	Alkyd Resin	Semi Gloss	Primer: Quick-Drying Emulsion Sealer. 1 Coat Finish: Alkyd Lo-Sheen Enamel 1 Coat
DRY-WALL CONSTRUCTION Latex Enamel, high resistance to soil and washing Wide color selection. Also suitable for trim, cabinets, other objects and surfaces.	Acrylic Latex	Semi Gloss	Primer: Quick-Drying Emulsion Sealer. 1 Coat Finish: Latex Interior Semi-Gloss Enamel 1 or 2 Coats — White and Colors.
DRY-WALL CONSTRUCTION Applicable also to plaster, wallboard, cement-masonry and brick.	Vinyl Acrylic or Latex	Flat	Primer: 2 Coats Acrylic Latex Interior Flat Wall Paint and or One or Two Coats of Vinyl Acrylic Latex Flat Finish: Wall Paint White and Colors.
DRY-WALL CONSTRUCTION Applicable also to plaster, wallboard, cement-masonry and brick. Exceptional hiding power over interior surfaces Dries to handling in 30 minutes to one hour. For Spray Application Only.	Spray applied Vinyl Acrylic Latex	Velvet Flat or Textured	Primer: No primer needed on wallboard or plaster. Finish: High Build Latex Flat Paint. White and Bone White. 1 Coat — This product may be tinted. (Textured finishes also available.)
DRY-WALL CONSTRUCTION Extremely-hard-wearing surface treatment for institutional or industrial-commercial areas that require cleaning with strong detergents and mechanical scrubbers. Provides sanitary surface.	Two-Component Polyester-Epoxy or Acrylic Epoxy	High Gloss or Semi Gloss	Primer: Pigmented Sealer. 1 Coat Finish: Polyester-epoxy, or Water Base 1 or 2 Coats — Gloss or Semi-Gloss Coating. White and Colors.
DRY-WALL CONSTRUCTION To retard flame spread and for short term insulation of structural members in case of fire.	Modified PVA Latex Intumescent Fire Retardant	Flat	Primer: Quick-Drying Emulsion Sealer or 1 Coat — Quick-Dry White Undercoater. Finish: Latex Fire Retardant Paint 2 Coats

WOODWORK & TRIM-PAINTED

USE: SURFACE AND REQUIREMENTS			
WOODWORK AND TRIM (Painted) Resists yellowing. Very high hiding power with exceptional opacity and filling properties. Smooth, brilliant finish is easy to maintain.	Solvent Type Alkyd Enamel	Gloss	Primer: Enamel Undercoater reduced slightly 1 Coat with paint thinner or mineral spirits. Or use Water Base Enamel Undercoater. Finish: Quick-Dry Architectural Gloss White Enamel. 1 or 2 Coats — May be tinted.
	Water Base Alkyd Enamel	Gloss	Primer: Enamel Undercoater reduced slightly 1 Coat with paint thinner or mineral spirits Water Base Enamel Undercoater Finish: Water Base Gloss Enamels. White and Colors. 1 or 2 Coats
WOODWORK AND TRIM (Painted) White. Resists yellowing Very high hiding power. Applicable to interior surfaces where fine rubbed-effect finish is desired.	Alkyd Enamel	Eggshell Flat or Rubbed Effect (Subdued)	Primer: Quick-Dry Enamel Undercoater reduced slightly 1 Coat with paint thinner or mineral spirits or Water Base Enamel Undercoater Finish: Quick-Dry Architectural Eggshell White 1 or 2 Coats Enamel. May be tinted.
WOOD PANELING To retard flame spread and for short term insulation of structural members in case of fire.	Modified PVA Latex Intumescent Fire Retardant	Flat	Primer: Quick-Drying Enamel Undercoater. 1 Coat Finish: Latex Fire Retardant Paint. White and Colors. 2 Coats

USE: SURFACE AND REQUIREMENTS	TYPE FINISHING SYSTEM	SHEEN	RECOMMENDATIONS
WOODWORK AND TRIM (Painted) High gloss finish enamel that resists chalking, yellowing and color fading. Applicalbe to exterior as well as interior surfaces.	Alkyd Enamel (Solvent Type)	Gloss	Primer: Quick-Dry Enamel Undercoater reduced slightly 1 Coat with paint thinner or mineral spirits or Water Base Enamel Undercoater. Finish: Quick-Dry Enamel or Exterior-Interior Gloss Enamel. 1 or 2 White and Colors. Coats
	Alkyd Enamel (Water Base Type)	Gloss	Primer: Quick-Dry Enamel Undercoater reduced slightly 1 Coat with paint thinner or mineral spirits. Or use Finish: Water Base Gloss Enamels. White and Colors. 1 or 2 Coats
WOODWORK AND TRIM (Painted) Resists yellowing, durable finish with exceptional hiding power. Easy to apply over walls as well as trim. Easy to maintain.	Alkyd Enamel	Satin	Primer: Quick-Dry Enamel Undercoater or 1 Coat Water Base White Undercoater. Finish: Lustre Enamel or Alkyd Interior 1 or 2 Lo-Sheen Enamel. White and Colors. Coats
	Acrylic Latex	Semi Gloss	Primer: Quick-Dry Enamel Undercoater or 1 Coat Water Base White Undercoater. Finish: Latex Lo-Lustre Enamel or Latex Semi-Gloss Enamel. 1 or 2 White and Colors. Coats
WOODWORK AND TRIM (Painted) Latex Enamel, high resistance to soil and washing. Wide color selection. Also suitable for trim, cabinets, other objects and surfaces.	Acrylic Latex	Eggshell Flat or Semi Gloss	Primer: Quick-Drying Enamel Undercoater or Water Base White 1 Coat Undercoater. Finish: Latex Flat Enamel or Lo-Lustre 1 or 2 Enamel Designer Bases. White and Colors. Coats
WOODWORK AND TRIM Extremely durable finish for door frames and trim where repeated washings are needed or stains may occur.	Two Component Polyester-Epoxy or Acrylic Epoxy	High Gloss or Semi Gloss	Primer: Quick-Drying Enamel Undercoater or Water 1 Coat Base White Undercoater. Finish: Coating in finish and color desired. White and Colors. 1 or 2 Solvent Type Coats Water-Base Type

WOODWORK & TRIM—NATURAL & STAINED FINISH

USE: SURFACE AND REQUIREMENTS	TYPE FINISHING SYSTEM	SHEEN	RECOMMENDATIONS
WOODWORK AND TRIM Natural finish close-grained woods. Pale finish to preserve natural color of grained wood. Speedhide Q.D. Wood Sealer or Rez Sanding Sealer prime coat preserves the natural color of wood grain by preventing the wetting and darkening effect of clear varnishes; and is quick-drying. For interior use only.	Alkyd or Urethane	Gloss	Primer: Clear Sealer-Primer. 1 Coat Finish: Varnish Gloss-Clear, or Polyurethane Gloss-Clear. 1 or 2 Coats
	Alkyd or Urethane	Satin	Primer: Clear Sealer-Primer, or Clear Wood Sealer. 1 Coat and Finish, or Sanding Sealer. Finish: Varnish Satin-Clear, or Polyurethane Satin Clear, or 1 or 2 Water Base Satin Clear Varnish. Coats
	Alkyd-Vinyl-Toluene Copolymer	Semi Gloss	Primer: Clear Wood Sealer and Finish, or Sanding 2 Coats Sealer. Finish: None needed.
	Urethane	Flat	Primer: Clear Sealer 1 Coat Finish: Polyurethane Flat Clear. 1 or 2 Coats

NOTE: WOODWORK AND TRIM (Natural Finish) Open Grain Woods) To above specifications, indicate the wood is to be filled with Natural Paste Wood Filler before finishing.

LATEX SYSTEMS Latest developments in Latex Wood Staining systems make it practical, and often more economical, to stain and finish bare wood without use of sealer-primer.	Water Base, Alkyd or Urethane	Satin	Primer: No Primer Needed. Finish: Semi-Transparent Interior Latex Stain, or Solid 1 Coat Color Latex Stain FOLLOWED BY 2 coats of Varnish Satin-Clear or Polyurethane or Water Base Satin Clear Varnish.
	Water Base, Alkyd or Urethane	Gloss	Primer: No Primer Needed. Finish: Semi-Transparent Interior Latex Stain, or Solid 1 Coat Color Latex Stain FOLLOWED BY 1 or 2 coats of Varnish Gloss-Clear or Polyurethane Gloss-Clear.

USE: SURFACE AND REQUIREMENTS	TYPE FINISHING SYSTEM	SHEEN	RECOMMENDATIONS
WOODWORK AND TRIM, SOFT WOODS In soft woods, the spongy springwood will absorb much more stain than the denser summerwood. When using Alkyd Stains the application of Rez Sealer - Primer evens up this absorption of stain, resulting in less extreme contrast.	Alkyd or Urethane	Gloss	Primer: 1 Coat Finish: Solid Color Alkyd-Oil Stain. Many colors. 1 Coat OR Semi-Transparent Alkyd-Oil Stain. Many colors. FOLLOWED BY 1 or 2 coats of Varnish Gloss-Clear or Polyurethane Gloss-Clear.
	Alkyd or Urethane	Satin	Primer: Clear Sealer-Primer. 1 Coat Finish: Color tone, or Interior Oil Stain FOLLOWED BY 1 Coat 1 or 2 coats of Varnish Satin-Clear or Polyurethane Satin-Clear or Water Base Satin Clear Varnish.
	Urethane	Flat	Primer: Clear Sealer-Primer 1 Coat Finish: Polyurethane Flat-Clear. 1 Coat
	Alkyd or Urethane	Gloss	Primer: Solid Color Alkyd-Oil Stain. Many colors. 1 Coat OR Semi-Transparent Alkyd-Oil Stain. Many colors. Finish: Varnish Gloss-Clear, or Polyurethane Gloss-Clear 2 Coats
WOODWORK AND TRIM — STAIN AND VARNISH Open grain woods may be stained prior to filling; or stain and fill in one operation by using oil stain as a reducer for the filler.	Alkyd or Urethane	Satin	Primer: Solid Color Alkyd-Oil Stain. Many colors. 1 Coat OR Semi-Transparent Alkyd-Oil Stain. Many colors. Finish: Varnish Satin-Clear, or Polyurethane Satin Clear, or 1 or 2 Water Base Satin Clear Varnish. Coats
	Urethane	Flat	Primer: Solid Color Alkyd-Oil Stain. Many colors. 1 Coat OR Semi-Transparent Alkyd-Oil Stain. Finish: Polyurethane Flat Clear 1 or 2 Coats

WOOD FLOORS

USE: SURFACE AND REQUIREMENTS	TYPE FINISHING SYSTEM	SHEEN	RECOMMENDATIONS
HARDWOOD FLOORS (Natural Finish) Fill pores of open grained woods such as oak, walnut, mahogany, etc. Seal and protect with varnish.	Alkyd	Gloss	Primer: Natural Paste Wood Filler (open grain woods only) 1 Coat FOLLOWED BY 1 coat Sealer-Primer. Finish: Varnish Gloss-Clear 1 or 2 Coats
GYMNASIUM FLOORS Utmost protection on hardwood floors used in all sports. Seals and protects. Rugged and long wearing.	Poly-urethane	Gloss	Primer: Polyurethane Plastic Coating reduced with one quart of 2 Coats paint thinner or mineral spirits per gallon. Rub with steel wool between coats and allow overnight drying. Finish: Polyurethane High Gloss Clear Plastic Coating. 1 Coat
WOOD FLOORS — PAINTED Tough, elastic film with hard finish to resist abrasive underfoot wear.	Alkyd	Gloss	Primer: Floor and Deck Enamel reduced with one 1 Coat pint of paint thinner or mineral spirits per gallon. Finish: Floor and Deck Enamel. White and Colors. 1 or 2 Coats

CONCRETE FLOORS

USE: SURFACE AND REQUIREMENTS	TYPE FINISHING SYSTEM	SHEEN	RECOMMENDATIONS
CONCRETE FLOORS Durable finish, When fully cured, resists alkali and occasional moisture. Withstands normal washing.	Vinyl Acrylic Latex	Low Sheen	Primer: Latex Floor and Deck Enamel Paint, reduced 1 Coat with one pint water per gallon. Finish: Latex Floor and Deck Enamel. White and 2 Coats Colors. Wax after two days' drying for surface sheen.
CONCRETE Aisle and traffic marking paint.	Alkyd and Chlorinated Rubber	Flat	Finish: Traffic and Zone Marking Paint. White or Yellow. 2 Coats
CONCRETE FLOORS — HEAVY DUTY Hard, abrasion and chemical resistant finish with good adhesion Use on laboratory and industrial service floors.	Poly-amide Epoxy (Two Component)	Gloss	Primer: Polyamide-Epoxy. 1 Coat Finish: Polyamide-Epoxy. White and Colors. Mix and 1 Coat apply according to directions.

334

GALVANIZED METAL

USE: SURFACE AND REQUIREMENTS	TYPE FINISHING SYSTEM	SHEEN	RECOMMENDATIONS
GALVANIZED METAL SURFACES Ultimate performance of primer and finish will be in direct proportion to surface preparation. New galvanized steel must be free from dirt, grease, and other surface contamination. All rust must be removed from old galvanized steel. Choice of protective finishes depends on preference for flat, semi-gloss, or gloss.	Alkyd-Resin	Flat	Primer: White Galvanized Steel Primer. 1 Coat Finish: Alkyd Flat Wall Paint or Flat Enamel — 2 Coats Alkyd Type. White and Colors.
	Alkyd-Resin Enamel	Semi Gloss	Primer: White Galvanized Steel Primer. 1 Coat Finish: Semi-Gloss Enamel or Alkyd Interior 2 Coats Lo-Sheen Enamel. White and Colors.
	Solvent Type Alkyd Enamel or Water Base Alkyd Enamel	Gloss	Primer: White Galvanized Steel Primer. 1 Coat Finish: Gloss Enamel or Exterior-Interior 2 Coats Gloss Enamel, or Water Base Gloss Enamel. White and Colors.
	Two-Component Polyester-Epoxy or Acrylic Epoxy	High Gloss or Semi Gloss	Primer: White Galvanized Steel Primer. 1 Coat Finish: Solvent Type Polyester-Epoxy or Water Base 1 or 2 Acrylic-Epoxy in finish and color desired. Coats Solvent Type Water Base Type
EXPOSED GALVANIZED METAL DUCTS After cleaning, all ferrous metal parts, straps, etc., must be primed with inhibitive metal primer; otherwise, rust will occur.	Vinyl Acrylic or Acrylic Latex	Flat	Primer: Solvent Clean Naphtha. 1 Coat Finish: Vinyl Acrylic Latex Flat, or Acrylic Latex Interior Flat Wall Paint 1 or 2 White and Colors. Coats

EXPOSED STRUCTURAL STEEL

USE: SURFACE AND REQUIREMENTS	TYPE FINISHING SYSTEM	SHEEN	RECOMMENDATIONS
EXPOSED STRUCTURAL STEEL COLUMNS ETC. (Normal Exposure) Shop-primed exposed steel can be protected against corrosion and made more attractive by spot-priming all abraded surfaces, followed by a heavy-duty finish coat Eggshell, Semi-Gloss, or Gloss in a range of colors	Alkyd Resin	Eggshell	Primer: Machinery and Equipment Primer or 1 Coat Red or White Inhibitive Primer. (Either solvent base or water base version). Finish: HIgher Hiding Eggshell Wall Paint. 2 Coats
	Vinyl Acrylic Latex	Flat	Primer: Machinery and Equipment Primer or 1 Coat Red or White Inhibitive Primer. (Either solvent base or water base version). Finish: Flat Dry Fog Spraying Paint solvent or water 2 Coats base type. White and Colors.
	Alkyd Resin	Low Semi Gloss	Primer: Machinery and Equipment Primer or 1 Coat Red or White Inhibitive Primer. (Either solvent base or water base version). Finish: Alkyd Interior Lo-Sheen Enamel. 2 Coats Lo-Lustre Enamel.
	Vinyl Acrylic Latex	Semi Gloss	Primer: Machinery and Equipment Primer or 1 Coat Red or White Inhibitive Primer, (Either solvent base or water base version). Finish: Semi-Gloss Dry Fog Spraying Paint solvent 2 Coats or water base type. White and Colors.
	Alkyd-Resin	Gloss	Primer: Machinery and Equipment Primer or 1 Coat Red or White Inhibitive Primer, (Either solvent base or water base version). Finish: Exterior-Interior Gloss Enamel, or 2 Coats Quick Dry Enamel, or Water Base Gloss Enamel

EXPOSED STRUCTURAL STEEL COLUMNS, METAL DOORS, FRAMES BUCKS: METAL WINDOW FRAMES, ETC. Where extra-durable finish is required, due to constant smudging, scuffing, or staining; and where repeated washings are needed for cleanliness.	Two-Component Polyester-Epoxy or Acrylic Epoxy	High Gloss or Semi Gloss	Primer: Zinc Chromate Primer. 1 Coat Finish: Solvent Type Polyester-Epoxy or Water Base 1 or 2 Acrylic-Epoxy in finish and color desired. Coats Solvent Type Water-Base Type

METAL DOORS & TRIM

USE: SURFACE AND REQUIREMENTS	TYPE FINISHING SYSTEM	SHEEN	RECOMMENDATIONS
METAL DOORS AND TRIM (Factory Primed) Enamel for interior-exterior use. Resists chalking and fading. Easy to maintain.	Solvent Type Alkyd Enamel	Gloss	Primer: Machinery and Equipment Primer, or 1 Coat Red or White Inhibitive Primer. (either solvent base or water base version). Finish: Quick-Dry Enamel or Exterior-Interior Gloss Enamel. 2 Coats
	Water Type Alkyd Enamel	Gloss	Primer: Machinery and Equipment Primer, or 1 Coat Red or White Inhibitive Primer. (either solvent base or water base version). Finish: Water Base Gloss Enamel. 2 Coats
METAL DOORS AND TRIM Modified gelled-type low-lustre enamel with good hiding power and sag resistance. Also applicable to plaster, masonry and wood.	Alkyd-Resin Enamel	Semi Gloss	Primer: Machinery and Equipment Primer, or 1 Coat Red or White Inhibitive Primer. (Either solvent base or water base version). Finish: Alkyd Interior Lo-Sheen Enamel, or 2 Coats Lo-Lustre Enamel.
METAL DOORS AND TRIM (Factory Primed)	Two-Component Polyester-Epoxy or Acrylic Epoxy	High Gloss, or Semi Gloss	Primer: Machinery and Equipment Primer, or 1 Coat Red or White Inhibitive Primer. (Either solvent base or water base version). Finish: Coating in finish and color desired. 1 or 2 Solvent Type Coats Water-Base Type

WOOD-DESTROYING WATER   WOOD-DISCOLORING MILDEW   WOOD-ROTTING FUNGI

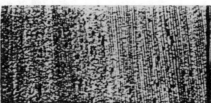

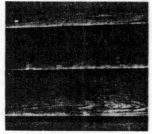

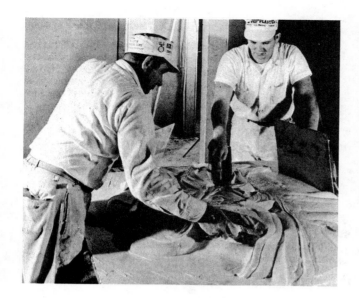

In two coat work, after mixing according to manufacturers direction, apply the plaster with a trowel over the gypsum board the thickness of the plaster grounds, about 3/8" thick. Smooth and level the coat using a darby or long board like wood tool used for uniform thickness, and allow to dry. The finish coat is just a light skim coat affording a smooth white surface.

Three coat is similar except for the first coat which should be applied with enough pressure to assure a locking or bonding to the metal lath to stiffen the wall for succeeding coats. All coats in two or three coat applications can be had prepared ready mix for use by simply adding water to make a working consistency.

PLASTER

Unless you are skilled in working with plaster, except for patching, it is recommended that you contract with a plastering contractor. Plaster is mentioned here only to give you another option for wall construction. Many finishes are available in plaster work including acoustical plaster for sound proofing. Where reduction in noise level is desirable, an acoustical plaster may be used instead of the conventional hard plaster material. A plastered surface is an extremely effective fire barrier. The application of either acoustical or conventional plaster is similar differing only in mix and ingredients.

Two systems are available: plaster over rock lath, or gypsum lath, and metal lath. The rock lath application is a two coat system and the wire or metal lath is a three coat system. Gypsum lath is a factory constructed plaster core with layers of paper on both sides. It is available in 3/8" or 1/2" thickness and in sheet size of 16" x 48". 3/8" thickness is usually applied directly to the studs with metal beads at interior and exterior corners, forming a base for plastering with an additional thickness of 3/8" in two coats making a total finish thickness of 3/4". The first coat is called brown coat and the second coat is finish coat.

The application is similar to stucco requiring three coats, scratch coat, brown coat and finish coat. In order to insure uniform plaster thickness, grounds are installed. These are narrow strips of wood or metal placed around the edges of surfaces and openings. Insulated gypsum lath will add to energy savings if used on interior or exterior walls.

Plaster is available premixed requiring only water to make it of a working consistency. Carefully follow directions printed on the package for mixing. A very light finish coat of plaster can be sprayed over drywall construction making an attractive inexpensive plaster finished surface. Many finishes can be achieved with plaster from smooth to scrolled. If ornamental work is desired, plaster is the best material because it will conform to any shape in finish.

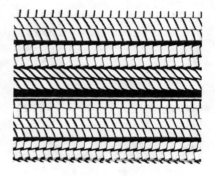

3/8" RIB LATH

Used as combination form and reinforcing for floor slabs over steel joists and plaster base for ceilings below them.

Sheet size 27" x 96" permits faster lathing with less laps. Small 1/8" reverse rib at outer edge simplifies lapping. Furnished in painted, copper alloy steel. Galvanized in 3.4 lb. only. Standard Weights: 3.4 lbs., 4.0 lbs. per square yard.

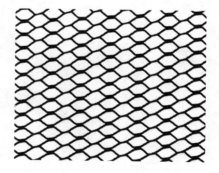

SMALL DIAMOND MESH LATH

Used as a plaster base and reinforcement on almost all types of walls and ceilings, over wood or steel framing. Excellent for flat or curved surfaces. Expanded sheets contain over 11,000 meshes per square yard which reinforce the plaster. Sheets are square and lie perfectly flat against supports. Furnished in painted, copper alloy steel. Galvanized in 3.4 lb. only. Standard Weights: 2.5 lbs., 3.4 lbs. per square yard.

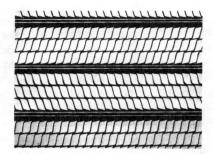

1/8" FLAT RIB LATH

Designed to meet the demand for a more rigid expanded metal lath. Widely used as a plaster base in all types of walls and ceilings over wood or steel framing. Its greatest demand, due to its exceptional rigidity and plaster saving qualities, is in nail-on work over wood framing. Sheets are reversible—either side may face studs. Furnished in painted, copper alloy steel. Standard Weights: 2.75 lbs., 3.4 lbs. per sq.yd.

PLAIN GYPSUM LATH

Standard gypsum plaster base for application to wood or steel framing. May also be applied to furring with Gold Bond clips.
Sizes: 16" x 48", 3/8" or 1/2" thick; 16" x 96", 3/8" thick. Also made 16.2" wide for the West Coast.

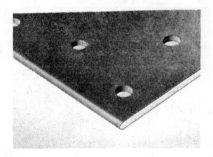

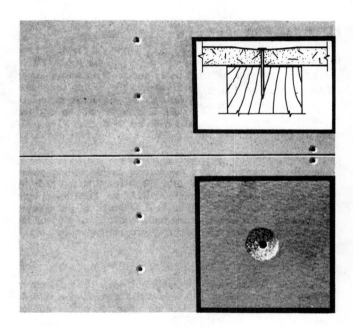

PERFORATED GYPSUM LATH

The 3/4" diameter holes are punched through the lath, spaced one for each 16 square inches of surface. Perforated lath permits high fire ratings by providing a double plaster bond: mechanical and chemical.
Size: 16" x 48", 3/8" thick.

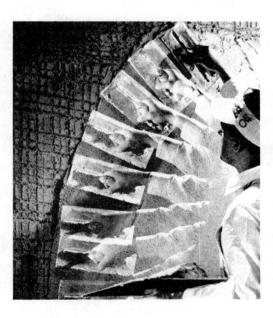

INSULATING GYPSUM LATH

Plain gypsum lath with aluminum foil laminated to back face. It serves as a plaster base, an insulator against heat and cold, and an effective vapor barrier. Cost is approximately two cents per square foot more than plain or perforated gypsum lath.
Size: 16" x 48", 3/8" thick.

1-A Expanded Corner Bead has wide expanded flanges that are easily flexed. Preferred for irregular corners. Provides increased reinforcement close to nose of bead.

4-A Flexible Corner Bead is a general purpose corner bead, economical and most generally used. By snipping flanges, this bead may be bent to any curved design (for archways, telephone niches, etc.).

4-R Expanded Corner Bead is an outstanding new item with small nose and totally expanded 2" wide flanges designed to increase plaster keys and minimize corner cracking. A general purpose bead, suitable for straight or arched corners.

10-A Expanded Bull Nose Corner Bead is a bull nose bead similar to above, but with 2 1/2" wide expanded flanges. Especially suitable on irregular corners.

900 Corner Bead serves dual purpose with either one-or two-coat Imperial Plaster systems. Gives 3/32" grounds, and its 1 1/4" fine-mesh flange can be either stapled or nailed. Provides superior plaster key and eliminates shadowing.

Cornerite and Striplath are strips of painted copper alloy Diamond Mesh lath used as reinforcement. Selv-edge Cornerite, bent lengthwise in the center to form a 100° angle, should be used in all internal plaster angles where metal lath is not lapped or carried around; over non-ferrous lath anchored to the lath; and over internal angles of masonry constructions.

Use is optional in Resilient Rocklath lathing   also used in the "Floating Angle" method of applying gypsum lath to wood framing members in order to reduce plaster cracking. Sizes: 2" x 2" x 96" and 3" x 3" x 96". Striplath is a similar flat strip, used as a plaster reinforcement over joints of non-metallic lathing bases and where dissimilar bases join; also to span pipe chases. Sizes: 4" x 96" and 6" x 96".

6-A Plain Base Screed is a flush type 1/2" ground (job shimmed for 3/4" grounds), used as a straight divider strip between different types of plaster, as between gypsum and portland cement.

8-A Picture Mould provides a concealed mould, attached to lath and plastered flush to the notch opening. Grounds 1/2" (job-shimmed for 3/4" grounds).

Metal Trim   comes in two styles to provide neat edge protection for veneer plastering at cased openings and ceiling or wall intersections. Made of 29-ga. galvanized steel, both have expanded flanges to strengthen the plaster bond. They fit over 1/2" of 5/8" Imperial Plaster Base, and provide 3/32" grounds for Imperial Plasters. No. 701-A is channel-type casing nailed to door or window buck.

P-1 Vinyl Trim   is a channel-shaped rigid trim with flexible vinyl fins which compress on installation to provide a positive acoustical seal comparable in performance to one bead of acoustical sealant. For Imperial Plaster partition perimeters. Length: 8, 9 and 10 ft. Sizes: for 1/2" and 5/8" plaster base.

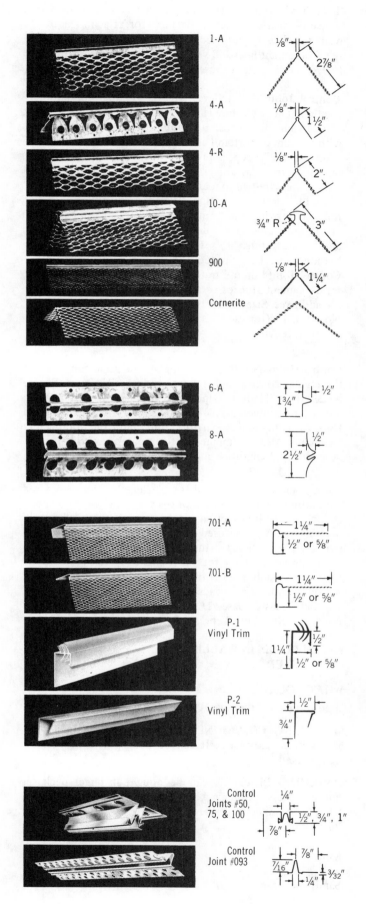

P-2 Vinyl Trim is a channel-shaped vinyl trim with a pressure-sensitive adhesive backing for attachment to the wall at wall-ceiling intersections. Provides positive perimeter relief in radiant heat and veneer plaster systems. Allow 1/8" to 1/4" clear space for insertion. Length' 10 ft.

Control Joint relieves stresses of expansion and contraction in large plastered areas. Made from roll-formed zinc, it is resistant to corrosion in both interior and exterior uses with gypsum or portland cement plaster. An open slot, 1/4" wide and 1/2" deep, is protected with plastic tape which is removed after plastering is completed. The perforated short flanges are wire-tied to metal lath or stapled to gypsum lath. Thus the plaster is key-locked to the control joint, which not only provides plastering grounds but can also be used to create decorative panel designs. Limitations: Where sound and/or fire ratings are prime considerations, adequate protection must be provided behind the control joint. Control Joints should not be used with magnesium oxychloride cement stuccos or stuccos containing calcium chloride additives. Sizes and grounds: No. 50, 1/2" No. 75, 3/4"; No. 100, 1" (for use with exterior stucco curtain walls)—all in 10 ft. lengths.

Control Joint No. 093 applies the same functions of the regular control joint (above) to Imperial Veneer Plaster installations. Made of zinc, with 3/32" ground dimension and a tape-protected 1/4" opening 7/16" deep. Used from floor to ceiling in long partition runs, and from door header to ceiling. Also recommended for repair of existing plastered masonry. Lengths: 8 and 10 ft.

Casing Beads are used as a plaster stop and as exposed trim around window and door openings; also recommended at junction or intersection of plaster and other wall or ceiling finishes. May be used also with metal lath, Rocklath gypsum plaster base, or masonry construction. In order to insure proper grounds for plastering, 3/4" casing beads are recommended for use with metal lath, 5/8" beads with all masonry units, 7/8" beads when the flange is applied under Rocklath plaster base, 1/2" beads when the flange is applied over Rocklath. Lengths: 7, 8 and 10 ft.

PATCH HOLES IN WALLBOARD OR PLASTER

WHAT YOU NEED

Choose one of the two types of patching compounds—

SPACKLING COMPOUND is convenient for small jobs but is more expensive. It can be bought as a powder or ready-mixed.

PATCHING PLASTER can be bought in larger packages and costs less. Both spackling powder and patching plaster need to be mixed with water.

Putty knife.

Knife

Sandpaper—medium grit

Old cloth or a paint brush

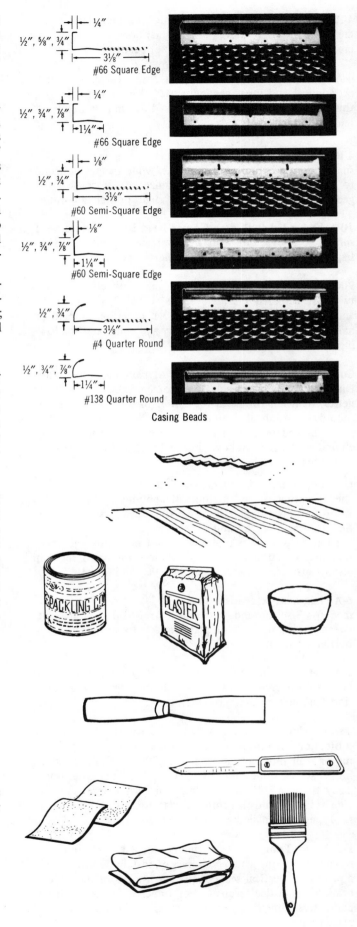

#66 Square Edge
#66 Square Edge
#60 Semi-Square Edge
#60 Semi-Square Edge
#4 Quarter Round
#138 Quarter Round

Casing Beads

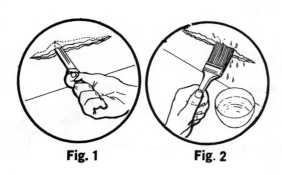

Fig. 1   Fig. 2

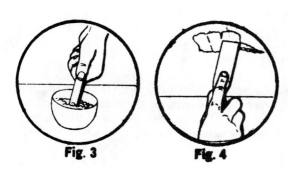

Fig. 3   Fig. 4

Fig. 5

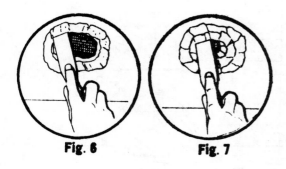

Fig. 6   Fig. 7

Fig. 8

HOW–TO

1. Remove any loose plaster. With a knife, scrape out plaster from the back edges of the crack until the back of the crack is wider than the front surface. (Fig. 1)

2. Thoroughly dampen the surface of the crack with a wet cloth or paint brush. (Fig. 2)

3. Prepare patching compound according to directions on package. Mix only a small amount the first time. (Fig. 3)

4. You can fill small holes with the patching mixture. Be sure to press the mixture until it completely fills the hole. Smooth the surface with the putty knife. (Fig. 4) After the patch has dried, you can sand it. Wrap the sandpaper around a small piece of wood. This makes the surface even. (Fig. 5)

5. Larger holes or cracks should be filled step-by-step. First, partly fill the hole. Let the patch dry. This gives a base for the final fill. Add a second batch of compound. Let dry. Sand until smooth. (Fig. 6)

6. You may need to fill in behind large holes with wadded newspaper. Start patching by working in from all sides. Let dry. Apply another layer around the new edge. Repeat until the hole is filled. After the patch has dried, sand until smooth. (Fig. 7)

NOTE:

If the walls have a textured surface, you'll want to make the patch match it while the plaster is still wet. You might need a sponge or comb to do the texturing. (Fig. 8)

FLOOR FINISHES

34

WOOD PARQUET OR BLOCK FLOORING

A hardwood floor factory finished applied over concrete or wood with ready to use mastic. This floor offers a wide variety of specie and pattern to choose from with ease of maintenance. The units or panels are completely unitized for fast and simple installation. The wood specie available are white oak, red oak, pecan, black walnut, hard maple, cherry, cedar, teak and a variety of other wood.

The sub floor of wood or concrete must be dry, smooth and free of loose paint, wax or dust. Apply ready to use mastic with a notched trowel, a small area at a time. Lay the flooring in freshly spread mastic making sure the first course is laid square with the room and has an even perimeter border. Gently fit the units together to assure a snug fit. Avoid forcing the units into position as this may destroy the squareness or built-in expansion. When completed, roll with a 150 lb. roller within 3 or 4 hours to assure uniform contact. If a roller is not available, walk on each tile to assure contact. A reducer strip can be used at door ways. Carefully lay out the floor before application for an even perimeter border.

PLANK OR STRIP FLOORING

This is a flooring which must be laid one piece at a time. The sizes vary from 2" to 8" wide, 3/8" and 3/4" thick and 1'—0" to 5'—0" long: blind nailed, keyed, pegged or screwed, pre-finished or unfinished with beveled edges in Oak, Maple, Beech, Birch, Pecan, Teak, Walnut and other exotic woods. This flooring can be applied over wood or concrete.

The pegged flooring is pre-drilled with countersunk holes on the top surface of the floor. The flooring is then screwed through the top pre-drilled holes into the sub floor and the holes are plugged with prefitted wood plugs. There is very little waste with this floor. The cut ends can be used by drilling new holes to match and cutting half the thickness of the floor on the back side to mate with the tongue, forming a groove.

COMPUTING FLOORING NEEDS

To ascertain the amount of flooring Strip Oak Flooring requires for a room, first determine the area of the room. Then add one of the following percentages of that figure, depending upon the size of flooring you intend to use:

55% for	3/4 x 1 1/2 inch
42-1/2% for	3/4 x 2 inch
38-1/3% for	3/4 x 2 1/4 inch
38-1/3% for	3/8 x 1 1/2 inch
38-1/3% for	1/2 x 1 1/2 inch
30% for	3/8 x 2 inch
30% for	1/2 x 2 inch
29% for	3/4 x 3 1/4 inch

The added percentages provide an allowance for side-matching, plus another 5 percent for end-matching and normal waste.

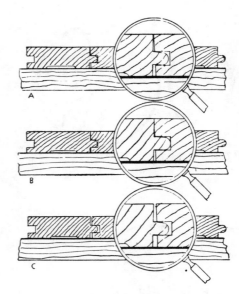

How compression set makes cracks. *A*, Flooring when laid; *B*, the same flooring after it has absorbed moisture as a result of damp conditions in the unfinished house; *C*, the same flooring after subsequent drying. The inverted V-shaped joint is permanently deformed, and there is a wide crack.

	PRODUCT DESCRIPTION AND PATTERN	PANEL SIZE	GRADE	SPECIES	APPROX. WT. (lbs. per m. sq. ft.)
	STANDARD Pattern Unfinished—Paper-Faced	5/16″ x 19″ x 19″ 16 equal alternating squares	Premium Select Rustic	Cherry—Maple Red Oak—White Oak—Cedar—Pecan—Walnut Rhodesian Teak	1250
		5/16″ x 12″ x 12″ 4 equal alternating squares		Angelique (Guiana Teak) Panga-Panga	1250
	STANDARD Pattern Unfinished—WebBack or Mesh-Back	5/16″ x 19″ x 19″ 16 equal alternating squares	Premium Select Rustic	Red Oak—White Oak Pecan	1250
		5/16″ x 11″ x 11″ 4 equal alternating squares	Select & Better (Par & Better) Rustic	Red and White Oak	1250
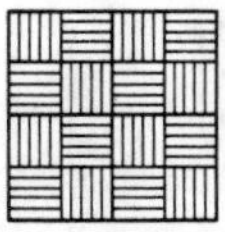	STANDARD Pattern Unfinished—WebBack (For Industrial Use)	5/16″ x 19″ x 19″ 16 equal alternating squares	Select & Better (Par & Better) Select Rustic & Better Rustic	Maple—Red Oak White Oak Pecan	1250 to 2650
		9/16″ x 19″ x 19″ 16 equal alternating squares			
	STANDARD Pattern Unfinished WebBack (For Industrial Use)	11/16″ x 11″ x 11″ 4 equal alternating squares	Select & Better (Par & Better) Industrial & Better (Rustic & Better)	Red Oak—Maple	1250
		¾″ x 12-11/16″ x 12-11/16″ 4 equal alternating squares			
	STANDARD Pattern Factory-Finished (Available in various colors)	5/16″ x 6⅜″ x 6⅜″ 5/16″ x 6½″ x 6½″ individual unit	Choice Natural & Better Natural Cabin	Oak—Walnut Pecan—Maple	1300
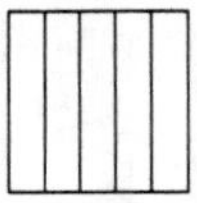	STANDARD Pattern Factory-Finished Foam-Back Tile	5/16″ x 6½″ x 6½″ individual units . . . ⅛″ foam, 2 lb. density	Natural & Better Natural Cabin	Oak—Pecan Maple	1300
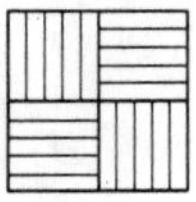	ANTIQUE TEXTURED (Factory-finished and Unfinished)—Kerfsawn Various colors available	5/16″ x 6⅜″ x 6⅜″ individual squares 5/16″ x 6½″ x 6½″ individual squares 5/16″ x 11″ x 11″ 4 equal alternating squares	Select Natural & Better Select & Better (Par & Better)	Red Oak & White Oak Red Oak & White Oak	1250
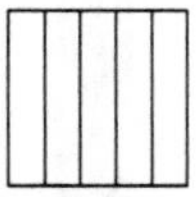	ANTIQUE TEXTURED (Factory-finished and Unfinished)—Wire brushed Various colors available	5/16″ x 6⅜″ x 6⅜″ 5/16″ x 6½″ x 6½″ individual squares	Natural & Better	Oak	1300
	MONTICELLO Pattern Unfinished—Paper-Faced	5/16″ x 13¼″ x 13¼″ 4 equal alternating squares	Select & Better (Par & Better)	Angelique (Guiana Teak) Red Oak—White Oak Panga-Panga—Black Walnut	1250
	HADDON HALL Pattern Unfinished—Paper-Faced	5/16″ x 13¼″ x 13¼″ 4 equal squares	Select & Better (Par & Better)	Angelique (Guiana Teak) Red Oak—White Oak Panga-Panga—Black Walnut	1250
	HERRINGBONE Pattern Unfinished—Paper-Faced	5/16″ x 14⅛″ x 18⅛″ (Approximate overall) 2 - "V" shape courses wide and 11 slats long	Select & Better (Par & Better)	Angelique (Guiana Teak) Red Oak—White Oak Panga-Panga—Black Walnut	1250
	SAXONY Pattern Unfinished—Paper-Faced	5/16″ x 19″ x 19″ 4 equal squares on diagonal and 8 equal half squares	Select & Better (Par & Better)	Angelique (Guiana Teak) Red Oak—White Oak Panga-Panga—Black Walnut	1250
	CANTERBURY Pattern Unfinished—Paper-Faced	5/16″ x 13¼″ x 13¼″ 4 equal alternating squares with diagonal center slats	Select & Better (Par & Better)	Angelique (Guiana Teak) Red Oak—White Oak Panga-Panga—Black Walnut	1250
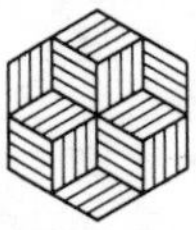	RHOMBS Pattern Unfinished—Paper-Faced	Hexagonal Shape 5/16″ x 15⅛″ x 15⅛″ 12 equal Rhomboids	Select & Better (Par & Better)	Red Oak & White Oak	1250
	BASKET WEAVE Pattern Unfinished—Paper-Faced	5/16″ x 15-1/5″ x 19″ 4 runs of 3 slats and 5 slats alternating	Select & Better (Par & Better)	Angelique (Guiana Teak) Red Oak—White Oak Panga-Panga—Black Walnut	1250
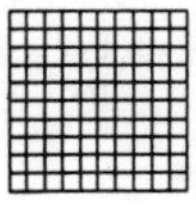	ITALIAN & DOMINO Pattern Unfinished—Paper-Faced	5/16″ x 19″ x 19″ 400 equal size pieces butt-jointed	Premium Par & Select	Black Walnut Angelique (Guiana Teak) Maple—Red Oak White Oak	1250

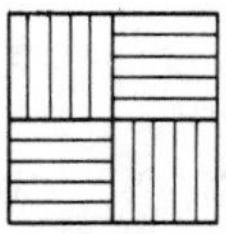

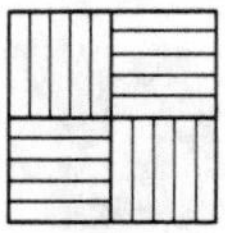

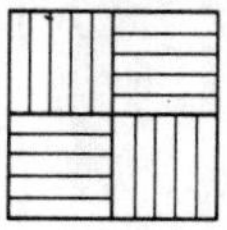

343

Guide to Hardwood Flooring Grades

A brief grade description, for comparison only. NOFMA flooring is bundled by averaging the lengths. A bundle may include pieces from 6 inches under to 6 inches over the nominal length of the bundle. No piece shorter than 9 inches admitted. The percentages under 4 ft. referred to apply on total footage in any one shipment of the item. ¾ inch added to face length when measuring length of each piece.

UNFINISHED OAK FLOORING (Red & White Separated)	BEECH, BIRCH & HARD MAPLE	PECAN FLOORING	PREFINISHED OAK FLOORING (Red & White Separated-graded after finishing)
CLEAR (Plain or Quarter Sawn) Best Appearance Best grade, most uniform color, limited small character marks. Bundles 1¼ ft. and up. Average length 3¾ ft.	***FIRST GRADE WHITE HARD MAPLE** (Spec. Order) Same as FIRST GRADE except face all bright sapwood. ***FIRST GRADE RED BEECH & BIRCH** (Spec. Order) Same as FIRST GRADE except face all red heartwood. **FIRST GRADE** Best Appearance. Natural color variation, limited character marks, unlimited sap. Bdles. 2 ft. & up. 2 & 3 ft. bdles. up to 33% footage.	***FIRST GRADE RED** (Spec. Order) Same as FIRST GRADE except face all heartwood. ***FIRST GRADE WHITE** (Spec. Order) Same as FIRST GRADE except face all bright sapwood. **FIRST GRADE** Excellent Appearance. Natural color variation, limited character marks, unlimited sap Bdles. 2 ft. & up. 2 & 3 ft. Bdles. up to 25% footage.	***PRIME** (Special Order Only) Excellent Appearance Natural color variation, limited character marks, unlimited sap. Bundles 1¼ ft. and up. Average length 3½ ft.
SELECT & BETTER (Special Order) A Combination of Clear and Select grades **SELECT (Plain or Quarter Sawn)** Excellent Appearance Limited character marks, unlimited sound sap. Bundles 1¼ ft. and up. Average length 3¼ ft.	**SECOND & BETTER GRADE** Excellent Appearance. A combination of FIRST and SECOND GRADES. Bdles. 2 ft. & up. 2 & 3 ft. Bdles. up to 40% footage. (NOTE: 5% 1¼ ft. bdles. allowed in SECOND & BETTER jointed flg. only.) **SECOND GRADE** Variegated Appearance. Varying sound wood characteristics of species. Bdles. 2 ft. & up. 2 & 3 ft. Bdles. up to 45% footage.	***SECOND GRADE RED** (Special Order Only) Same as SECOND GRADE except face all heartwood. **SECOND GRADE** Variegated Appearance Varying sound wood characteristics of species. Bundles 1¼ ft. and up. 1¼ ft. to 3 ft. bundles as produced up to 40% footage.	**STANDARD & BETTER GRADE** Combination of STANDARD and PRIME. Bundles 1¼ ft. and up. Average length 3 ft. **STANDARD GRADE** Variegated Appearance Varying sound wood characteristics of species. A sound floor after filling and finishing. Bundles 1¼ ft. and up. Average length 2¾ ft.
NO. 1 COMMON Variegated Appearance Light and dark colors; character marks allowed to provide a variegated appearance, after filling and finishing. Bundles 1¼ ft. and up. Average length 2¾ ft.	**THIRD & BETTER GRADE** A combination of FIRST, SECOND and THIRD GRADES. Bundles 1¼ ft. and up. 1¼ ft. to 3 ft. bundles as produced up to 50% footage. **THIRD GRADE** Rustic Appearance All wood characteristics of species. Serviceable, economical floor after filling. Bundles 1¼ ft. and up. 1¼ ft. to 3 ft. bundles as produced up to 65% footage.	**THIRD GRADE** Rustic Appearance All wood characteristics of species. A serviceable, economical floor after filling. Bundles 1¼ ft. and up. 1¼ ft. to 3 ft. bundles as produced up to 60% footage.	***TAVERN & BETTER GRADE** (Special Order Only) Combination of PRIME, STANDARD and TAVERN. All wood characteristics of species. Bundles 1¼ ft. and up. Average length 3 ft. **TAVERN GRADE** Rustic Appearance All wood characteristics of species. A serviceable, economical floor after filling and finishing. Bundles 1¼ ft. and up. Average length 2¼ ft.
NO. 2 COMMON (Red & White may be mixed) Rustic Appearance All wood characteristics of species. A serviceable, economical floor after filling. Bundles 1¼ ft. and up. Average length 2¼ ft.			

*1¼ FT. SHORTS (Red & White may be mixed)
Unique Variegated Appearance. Lengths 9 inches to 18 inches. Bundles average nominal 1¼ ft. Production limited.

*NO. 1 COMMON & BETTER SHORTS
A combination grade, CLEAR, SELECT, & NO. 1 COMMON 9 inches to 18 inches.

*NO. 2 COMMON SHORTS
Same as No. 2 COMMON, except length 9 inches to 18 inches.

*Check with supplier for grade and species available.
†NESTED FLOORING: Random length tongued and grooved, end-matched flooring is bundled end to end continuously to form 8 ft. long (nominal) bundles. Regular grade requirements apply.
‡NESTED FLOORING: If put up in 8 ft. nested bundles, 9 to 18 inch pieces will be admitted in ¾" x 2¼" as follows in the species of Beech, Birch & Hard Maple: FIRST GRADE, 4 pcs. per bundle; SECOND GRADE, 8 pcs.; THIRD GRADE, as develops. Average lengths: FIRST GRADE, 42 inches; SECOND GRADE, 33 inches; THIRD GRADE, 30 inches.

Publications available on request: Grading information — "Official Flooring Grading Rules"
Installation — "Architect's Specification Manual"

PREFINISHED BEECH & PECAN FLOORING
*TAVERN & BETTER GRADE (Special Order Only)
Combination of PRIME, STANDARD and TAVERN. All wood characteristics of species. Bundles 1¼ ft. and up. Average length 3 ft.

Standard Sizes, Counts & Weights

TONGUE AND GROOVE-END MATCHED			
¾x3¼ in.	¾x3¼ in.	1x4 in.	2210 lbs.
¾x2¼ in.	¾x2¼ in.	1x3 in.	2020 lbs.
¾x2 in.	¾x2 in.	1x2¾ in.	1920 lbs.
¾x1½ in.	¾x1½ in.	1x2¼ in.	1820 lbs.
⅜x2 in.	¹¹⁄₃₂x2 in.	1x2½ in.	1000 lbs.
⅜x1½ in.	¹¹⁄₃₂x1½ in.	1x2 in.	1000 lbs.
½x2 in.	¹⁵⁄₃₂x2 in.	1x2½ in.	1350 lbs.
½x1½ in.	¹⁵⁄₃₂x1½ in.	1x2 in.	1300 lbs.

SQUARE EDGE			
⁵⁄₁₆x2 in.	⁵⁄₁₆x2 in.	face count	1200 lbs.
⁵⁄₁₆x1½ in.	⁵⁄₁₆x1½ in.	face count	1200 lbs.

SPECIAL THICKNESSES (T and G, End Matched)			
¹⁷⁄₁₆x3¼ in.	³³⁄₃₂x3¼ in.	⁵⁄₄x4 in.	2400 lbs.
¹⁷⁄₁₆x2¼ in.	³³⁄₃₂x2¼ in.	⁵⁄₄x3 in.	2250 lbs.
¹⁷⁄₁₆x2 in.	³³⁄₃₂x2 in.	⁵⁄₄x2¾ in.	2250 lbs.

JOINTED FLOORING — i.e., SQUARE EDGE			
¾x2½ in.	¾x2½ in.	1x3¼ in.	2160 lbs.
¾x3¼ in.	¾x3¼ in.	1x4 in.	2300 lbs.
¾x3½ in.	¾x3½ in.	1x4¼ in.	2400 lbs.
¹⁷⁄₁₆x2½ in.	³³⁄₃₂x2½ in.	⁵⁄₄x3¼ in.	2500 lbs.
¹⁷⁄₁₆x3½ in.	³³⁄₃₂x3½ in.	⁵⁄₄x4¼ in.	2600 lbs.

Nail Schedule

Tongue and Groove Flooring Must Be Blind Nailed

¾x1½, 2¼ & 3¼ in.	2 in. machine driven fasteners, 7d or 8d screw or cut nail.	10-12 in. apart*

*If subfloor is ½ inch plywood, fasten into each joist, with additional fastening between.

Following flooring must be laid on a subfloor.

½x1½ & 2 in.	1½ in. machine driven fastener, 5d screw, cut steel or wire casing nail.	10 in. apart
⅜x1½ & 2 in.	1¼ in. machine driven fastener, or 4d bright wire casing nail.	8 in. apart

Square-edge flooring as follows, face-nailed — through top face

⁵⁄₁₆x1½ & 2 in.	1 inch 15 gauge fully barbed flooring brad. 2 nails every 7 inches.	
⁵⁄₁₆x1⅓ in.	1 inch 15 gauge fully barbed flooring brad. 1 nail every 5 inches on alternate sides of strip.	

HOW TO PREVENT FLOOR CRACKS

The cure for cracks in a floor lies wholly in preventing them. See to it that the floor is put down dry, and then see that compression set does not occur afterwards.

1. Assure yourself that the dealer has properly protected the stock while it was in his hands.

2. Do not allow it to be delivered on a rainy day.

3. Make sure that the plaster or masonry walls are dry before the flooring is delivered.

4. Discard all badly crooked boards or use them in inconspicuous places. Cutting them to shorter lengths helps lessen the crook in each piece.

5. Most important, prevent moisture absorption by the flooring after it is delivered to the house.

Air humidity can be lowered, and flooring kept dry, by maintaining some heat in the house from the time the workmen leave until they return on the next workday, even during warm summer weather. Whenever possible, the heating plant should be installed before the interior trim goes in, so as to be available for supplying the necessary heat. Other-

wise, a temporary heating stove should be used. It is good practice to open the bundles and spread the flooring out so that all surfaces are exposed to the air for at least 4 days. This allows time for the flooring to reach a moisture equilibrium with the air in the heated house before it is laid. The temperature inside the house should be maintained at least 15° F. above outdoor temperatures and should not be allowed to cool below about 70° F. during the summer or 62° to 65° F. when the outdoor temperatures are below freezing. Temperatures a little higher than this will do no harm, but severe overheating must be avoided. After the floor receives its protective coat of finish, temperatures should be kept approximately the same as they will be when the house is occupied. Very little heat, of course, is required in warm, dry weather, but spells of damp or cool weather are likely to occur in any month of year.

The recommended temperature conditions will tend to reduce the hazard of carelessness in the preliminary seasoning or storage of the flooring after manufacture.

Another important reason for keeping down moisture in a house nearing completion is that better and smoother floors are obtained with mechanical sanders when the floor and the atmosphere are dry. Furthermore, protecting the flooring in this way also gives protection for other interior woodwork and finish, such as doors, trim, and cabinets.

SQUARE FEET TO BOARD FEET
STRIP FLOORING

**For converting square feet of floor space
to board feet of flooring required.**

SQUARE FEET OF FLOOR SPACE	BOARD FEET REQUIRED (5% Cutting waste included.)				
	3/4 x 2-1/4"	3/4 x 1-1/2"	3/4 x 3-1/4"	1/2 x 2"	3/8 x 1-1/2"
5	7	8	6	7	7
10	14	16	13	13	14
20	28	31	26	26	28
30	42	47	39	39	42
40	55	62	52	52	55
50	69	78	65	65	69
60	83	93	77	78	83
70	97	109	90	91	97
80	111	124	103	104	111
90	125	140	116	117	125
100	138	155	129	130	138
200	277	310	258	260	277
300	415	465	387	390	415
400	553	620	516	520	553
500	692	775	645	650	692
600	830	930	774	780	830
700	968	1085	903	910	968
800	1107	1240	1032	1040	1107
900	1245	1395	1161	1170	1245
1000	1383	1550	1290	1300	1383

CRACKS IN THE MAKING

At the time flooring is delivered, usually the plastering has been finished, most of the trim is up, and the windows and exterior doors have been fitted and are in place.

Sometimes the flooring is delivered on a damp day or even during rain, so that the exposed boards and ends of others in the bundles absorb more or less moisture. If laid in this condition, the flooring will shrink a few months later and show cracks.

Very bad results may also be expected if the flooring is laid or even stored inside the house before plaster or masonry of the walls has had time to dry thoroughly. Moisture evaporates from damp walls into the air within the house. Then some of it will be absorbed by the flooring. It is prudent to accept a delay in completion rather than to have the floor laid while the walls are still damp and thus risk unsatisfactory results.

Another condition that causes flooring to pick up moisture during construction is less obvious but more common. Between the time the floor is laid and the house occupied, the general temperatures within the house both day and night are likely to be lower and the humidities higher than they would be if the house were occupied. At this stage, the house should be heated to keep relative humidity low enough to avoid absorption of moisture by the wood.

COMPRESSION SET

If several days of damp weather occur immediately after the floor is laid in place and before the finish such as varnish, shellac, or floor seal can be applied, the moisture content of the floor is likely to increase greatly. Absorption of moisture is much slower after a floor has received even the first coat of its finish.

Even moderate absorption of moisture from the air can cause boards to press against one another as they swell. Heavy pressure of this sort can result in some crushing of wood fiber. Technically known as compression set moisture. This crushing is the common cause of floor cracks. A relatively narrow margin of each board has to take the brunt of the compression, though the whole board takes up some of it. After a board has once been compressed this way, it never completely recovers.

When the flooring loses moisture after the house is occupied, each board shrinks away from its neighbors surfaces. The width of the crack is roughly equal to the amount of crushing, or "set," the board underwent while at the higher moisture content. The drying and shrinkage are most likely to occur during the winter when the house is heated. The average humidity is then lower than it was during the construction period.

Any subsequent pressure contact between the boards as a result of moisture changes will increase the compression set, and the width of the cracks, when the wood again dries out. Such pressure may occur during a period when the house is unoccupied or unheated for several weeks during cold or damp weather. Foreign matter in the cracks adds to the pressure. A kitchen floor of exposed boards, in which repeated scrubbing cause the cracks to grow wider and wider as the floor grows older, shows the effects of a series of compression sets.

KEY TO OAK FLOORING PERFORMANCE

Hardwood flooring is a quality product precision made from kiln-dried hardwood lumber. Like all kiln-dried products, it requires reasonable care in storage, handling, and installation. Since it has been kiln-dried to a proper moisture content, attention should be given to the following to insure that this moisture content is maintained:

Flooring should not be unloaded or trucked in rain, snow or excessively humid conditions. If the atmosphere is foggy or damp, it should be covered with a tarpaulin.

Flooring should not be delivered until the building has been closed in with outside windows and doors in place and until cement work, plastering, and all other materials are thoroughly dry. In winter construction, the building should be heated prior to delivery of the flooring with heat maintained until the floor is installed and finished.

THE FOLLOWING STEPS ARE ESSENTIAL

1. Check for these conditions and, if they exist, correct them: water or excessive moisture underneath or in the house, insufficient ventilation under the house, walls or concrete not thoroughly dry, green or wet subfloors or joists. A moisture barrier of polyethylene or rolled roofing over crawl spaces is recommended.

2. For best results plywood subfloor, or subfloor boards and joists should be clean, straight and thoroughly dry. Subfloor boards should be 6" wide or less, laid diagonally, and spaced approximately 1/4" apart. Plywood subfloors should be spaced as recommended, and well nailed.

3. PROPER NAILING OF THE SUBFLOOR AND FLOORING IS NECESSARY to insure satisfaction with hardwood floors. Floors, or subfloors, not properly nailed are likely to be loose, and may squeak and buckle. Use the right type and size nail, as shown in the nail schedule.

4. If plywood is used, a minimum of 1/2" thickness with exterior type glue should be used. If 1/2" plywood is used, flooring strips should be nailed through plywood into joists with an additional nail between joists.

5. Areas over heating plant and over uninsulated heating ducts should be insulated with a double-weight of 30-lb. asphalt saturated felt, 30-lb. asbestos felt, or standard insulation board 1/2" thick. Failure to provide proper insulation can cause cracks in floors.

6. Provide adequate expansion space next to all vertical surfaces. Otherwise buckled floors may result.

NAILING SCHEDULE
FOR STRIP HARDWOOD FLOORING

Tongued & Grooved flooring must be blind nailed.

Square-edge flooring must be nailed through top face.

Flooring	Nails	Spacing
Tongued & Grooved		
3/4x1½, 2¼ & 3¼ in.	2 in machine driven fasteners, 7d or 8d screw	10-12 in. apart *
	*If subfloor is 1/2 inch plywood, fasten into each joist, with additional fastening between.	

Following flooring must be laid on a subfloor.

½ x 1½ x 2 in.	1½ in. machine driven driven fastener, 5d screw, cut steel or wire casing nail.	10 in. apart
3/8 x 1½ & 2 in.	1¼ in. machine driven fastener, or 4d bright wire casing nail.	8 in. apart
Square-edge		
5/16 x 1½ & 2 in.	1 in. 15 gauge fully barbed flooring brad. 2 nails every 7 inches.	
5/16 x 1 1/3 in.	1 in. 15 gauge fully barbed flooring brad. 1 nail every 5 inches on alternate sides of strip.	

Oak flooring is like a fine old clock. No matter how perfect the component parts, they must be properly assembled in order to give the expected superior performance.

Emphasis is placed on strip flooring since it is the most extensively used, especially for homes. There is variety in strip flooring. Red and White Oak along with other species are available in various widths and thicknesses. Much of the basic information also applies to other types of flooring. General specifications are included for Plank, Parquet and Block Flooring. Since producers have varying instructions for installation of these products, exact specifications may be obtained from the company whose Plank, Parquet or Block Flooring is used.

OAK—THE FLOOR YOU'LL NEVER WEAR OUT!

In any building it is the floors that receive the greatest wear. They must be strong and long-lasting, and should be of such high quality that replacement or general repair is unnecessary. Floors should remain serviceable throughout the life of the building.

Generations of American home owners have learned that Oak Floors mean lifetime durability. Even after years of hard use and neglect, an Oak Floor can be restored to its original splendor through a simple refinishing process.

Widely used in residential construction as well as in other types of buildings, Oak Flooring may be obtained to harmonize with any architectural design or style of furnishing. The infinite variations in the grain pattern of Oak flooring produce a product that can not be duplicated artificially. With modern finishes that penetrate the pores of the wood and become a part of the wood itself, their beauty is more than skin deep. An Oak Floor has high resistance to wear, and is easily maintained.

SUB-FLOOR CONSTRUCTION

The advantages of a well constructed sub-floor are that it lends bracing strength to a building, and provides a solid base for the finish floor, reducing the possibility of floor sag and squeaks. By acting as a barrier to cold and dampness, it helps keep the building warmer and drier in winter. It provides a safe working surface during erection of the building. This permits deferring application of the finish floor until all plastering and other finishing work have been completed and the building interior has reached normal temperature and humidity levels.

1. SUB-FLOORING OVER WOOD JOISTS—In new buildings subfloors shall be laid over joist construction before the finish flooring is applied. Sub-flooring shall be of kiln-dried or thoroughly air dried, No. 1 Common or No. 2 Common grade lumber of any confinerous species customarily used for sub-flooring or plywood a minimum of 1/2" in thickness bonded with exterior type glue. The boards shall be either 1x4 inches or 1x6 inches (nominal size). Square-edged boards shall be used.

Note—It is best to avoid using boards which have served as forms for concrete work. They may be used only when they are sound, clean, dry and free of warps. Then they should be extra nailed.

Boards 10 to 12 inches wide have been used. This practice has proved extremely unsatisfactory. Use of lumber more than 6 inches wide is not recommended, since expansion and contraction of such boards is out of proportion to that of the narrower finish oak flooring. This condition frequently causes squeaks, buckling and cracks between joints in the finish flooring. With use of 4-inch or 6-inch boards, this danger is averted. Boards wider than 8 inches should never be used.

Square-edged boards, which are more economical, are generally preferred to tongued and grooved boards because the snug jointing of the latter is usually undesirable in sub-flooring. To allow for expansion, boards should be spaced slightly. Square-edge sub flooring is a must for buildings in moist climates and for summer homes which are not heated in winter.

2. DIRECTION OF SUB-FLOORING—Where strip flooring is to be used, the sub-floor boards over joists or sleepers shall be laid diagonally.

Plywood sheets shall be installed with grained outer plies at right angles to joists.

Note—The purpose in laying sub-floors diagonally is two-fold: to lend bracing strength to the building, and to permit the finish flooring to be laid in any direction. This practice is followed also where plank finish flooring is to be used. Where the finish flooring is to be block or parquetry, and sub-flooring is to be nailed on joists or sleepers, sub-floor boards should be laid at right angles to them.

3. NAILING SUB-FLOORS—When applied over joists, square-edge sub-floor boards shall be spaced 1/4 inch apart to allow for expansion. Boards of 4 or 6-inch width shall be face-nailed solidly at every bearing with two 10-penny nails. All butt joints of square-edge boards shall rest on bearings. Plywood shall be nailed every 6 inches along joists with 7-penny or larger nails, with 1/8 inch to 1/4 inch spacing between sheets.

3A. NAILING WIDER BOARDS—When it is necessary to use wider than 6 inches, extra nailing shall be employed at each bearing. Thus, 8-inch boards require three 10-penny nails at each bearing.

Note—It is important that plenty of nails be used in sub-floors. Good nailing keeps the boards rigid, holding them in place and preventing the creeping sometimes caused by shrinkage and expansion in sub-floor lumber. Without adequate nailing, it is impossible to obtain compact, non-squeaking finish floors.

4. FLOOR FURRING—If furring strips are to be used over wood sub-floor construction when electrical conduits and piping are to be laid on top of the sub-floor, such strips shall be of adequate thickness and 1 3/4 inches wide. They shall be nailed through the sub-floor into joists at right angles to the direction in which the finish flooring will be laid. The finish flooring shall be nailed through the furring strips with nails one size larger than those specified in the Nail Schedule for NOFMA Oak Flooring.

5. INSPECTION—Immediately before installation of the finish floors, sub-flooring shall be examined carefully and any defects shall be corrected. Raised nails shall be driven down, loose boards nailed tightly and warped boards replaced if sub-flooring cannot be made level otherwise. The floors shall be swept and cleaned thoroughly. Spots of plaster, mortar and other foreign materials shall be scraped off. Water shall not be used for cleaning.

6. BUILDING PAPER—Good quality building paper shall be laid over all sub-flooring, extending from wall to wall and lapping about 4 inches. The type of building paper known as 15-lb asphalt saturated felt, in rolls, shall be used.

6A. Sub-flooring directly over a heating plant shall be insulated with double weight building paper (30-lb. asphalt felt), 30-lb. asbestos felt or standard insulating board 1/2-inch thick. Such insulation shall be applied either on the basement ceiling or between floor joists of the affected area.

Note—Insulation over the heating plant and over uninsulated heating ducts is considered essential, since it provides protection against excessive heat which might cause cracks in the floor.

7. FLOOR VENTILATION—In basementless joist construction, adequate provision shall be made for the free movement of cross currents of air beneath the building. Air circulation shall be obtained by means of vents or other openings in the foundation walls. The total area of such openings shall be at least 1 1/2 per cent of the first floor area. Ground cover shall be provided to act as a barrier to ground moisture. The cover shall consist of a 4 mill polyethylene film or a 55-lb rolled roofing.

Note—Stagnated and humid air under a structure encourages development of fungus, mold and rot. It is extremely important that adequate circulation be provided.

8. SUB-FLOORS OVER CONCRETE—Oak Flooring may be installed over concrete using 3/4 inch plywood, with an exterior glue line, as a nailing surface. The plywood is installed over a 4 mil polyethelene vapor barrier.

Start with a full panel 1/2 to 3/4-inch from wall line and install long side parallel to longest dimension of room, spacing panels 1/2-inch to 3/4-inch apart. The plywood is then fastened to the slab with powder actuated fasteners spaced 12-inches apart, starting 2-1/2 inches to 3-inches from edges of plywood. Start second course with a part panel or one-half panel to stagger ends.

Sub-flooring then shall be laid diagonally across the sleepers and nailed.

Note—Following is an alternate method, formerly in wide use and still considered satisfactory.

8A. Sleepers shall be embedded in the concrete or shall be attached to it by means of clips or anchors so designed that the sleepers will never loosen. Sleepers shall be spaced 16 inches on centers and laid at right angles to the intended direction of the finish flooring. They shall be wedged up level after being nailed to the anchors. Square-edge sub-flooring boards shall be nailed to the sleepers diagonally.

Note—In the above type installation a moisture barrier should be placed over the fill before the concrete slab is poured.

When clips or anchors are used, sleepers which extend the full room width may be employed. Beveled sleepers which depend on a floor fill to hold them in place are not recommended. They cannot be wedged and leveled, and they seldom are sufficiently tight.

9. SLEEPER LUMBER—Sleepers shall be of a lumber grade equivalent to No. 1 Common or No. 2 Common and shall be impreganted with an approved wood preservative and termite repellent. They shall not be treated with creosote or other preservative material that might bleed through nail holes and stain the finish floor. If laid in mastic they shall be 2 x 4s, 2 x 3s, or 2—1 x 2s. If embedded in the concrete or affixed to it by means of clips or anchors, they shall be 2 x 4s, 2 x 3s or 2 x 2s.

10. OMISSION OF SUB-FLOOR OVER CONCRETE-The hardened slab shall be swept clean and treated with good quality asphalt primer, which shall be allowed to dry thoroughly.

METHOD A.

Apply a damp proofing membrane of polyethylene film or asphalt saturated felt.

a) First apply a coat of mastic of a type designed specifically for bonding wood floors to concrete. If polyethylene (4 mil is most suitable) is to be used, the mastic should be of the cutback type for cold application. If asphalt is to be used, the more economical hot melt mastic can be employed. Follow manufacturers' directions carefully.

b) Polyethylene is embedded in the cold mastic with the edges lapped six inches. Asphalt felt is embedded with the edges butted. In either method allow enough polyethylene or felt to extend up under the baseboards.

Whatever the type of barrier, mastic shall be applied over it to serve as an adhesive for the sleepers which provide a nailing surface for the finish floor. It may cover the entire surface or only predetermined lines where sleepers are to be placed. It shall be 3/32" thick.

Sleepers shall then be embedded in the mastic. They shall consist of flat 2 x 4s ranging from 18 to 30 inches. Laid flat side down, at right angles to the intended direction of the finish flooring, they shall be applied in a staggered pattern with ends lapped at least four inches. Courses shall be 16 inches on centers. It is essential to use random length sleepers in order to effect staggered end joints.

Finish flooring is then nailed directly to the sleepers at each bearing, nailing into both sleepers where they are lapped.

METHOD B.

A more economical, proven method of installing strip flooring over slabs employs two 1 x 2-inch nailing strips with a layer of polyethylene between.

The first course of 1 x 2s shall be of lumber treated with an approved preservative. They shall be adhered to the slab in rivers of mastic supplemented by a 1½-inch concrete nail every 24 inches and shall be laid in courses 16 inches on centers with 1/2" space between ends.

Over the 1 x 2s install a layer of 4 mil polyethylene with edges parallel to the 1 x 2 strips and with joints lapped over them.

Nail second course of 1 x 2s through polyethylene into first course with 4d nails 16 to 24 inches apart.

Install strip flooring at right angles to sleepers by blind nailing to each of them.

Note—In both of the above methods a moisture barrier between the slab and the fill is desirable in most cases. In extremely arid regions a waterproof admixture in the concrete may be used instead of a conventional barrier but the slab must be thoroughly dry before installation of the sleepers.

DIRECTION OF FINISH FLOORING— In new construction, strip flooring in each room shall be laid in the direction of the longest dimension of the building. The flooring shall run continuously between adjoining rooms, and door sills between such rooms shall be omitted.

Note—In some cases it may be desirable to lay the flooring crosswise instead of lengthwise of the building. This is permissible if the rooms are not exceptionally narrow.

USE OF SHORT STRIPS— The shortest pieces of flooring shall be used in closets and in the general floor area. When possible, avoid using short pieces at entrances and doorways. Do not use ripped strips at doors or other places where they may mar appearances.

STARTING TO LAY THE FINISH FLOOR— When tongued and grooved strip flooring is used, the first course shall be laid with the groove edge nearest the wall. A space of about 1 inch, but slightly less than the combined thickness of the baseboard and shoe moulding, shall be left between the flooring and the wall. The baseboard shall be so installed that the lower edge is slightly above the finish floor.

Note—The spaces allow room for expansion of the flooring without ill effects. It is essential that they be no greater than will be covered by the baseboard and shoe moulding. Where the baseboard already has been installed, all the space to be covered by the show moulding should be utilized as expansion space.

NAILING— The groove edge of the first piece of tongued and grooved flooring shall be face-nailed, with the nails driven so that later they will be concealed by the shoe moulding. Then the tongue edge shall be blind-nailed, with the nails driven at an angle of about 50 degrees at the point where the tongue leaves the shoulder. Each strip should be nailed as close to the ends as is practical. In blind-nailing, the head of each nail shall be countersunk with a steel nail set or a nail. After the first piece of flooring has been nailed, begin laying the other pieces, following the above directions regarding spacing and nailing for the first piece along either sidewall. Observe the spacing direction for the first piece nearest the endwall in each course.

Square-edge strip flooring shall be used only over a sub-floor. It shall be face-nailed.

Note—Proper nailing is absolutely essential in the finish floor as well as the sub-floor. Inadequate nailing may easily result in loose or squeaky flooring.

JOINTS— End joints either of tongued and grooved or square-edge strip flooring shall be staggered to avoid having several of them grouped closely together.

Note—It is not necessary that the end joints either of square-edge or tongued and grooved finish flooring occur over joist or sleeper bearing points when a sub-floor is used. Nor is it necessary in use of tongued and grooved flooring when sub-flooring over concrete is omitted.

When a sub-floor is used, nails through the finish floor shall not strike sub-floor joints. Care also shall be taken, when the sub-floor is laid at right angles to the finish floor, ends of flooring do not meet directly over sub-floor joints.

DRAWING UP—   Do not try to hammer each piece of tongued and grooved strip flooring into its final position as soon as it is nailed. After laying three or four pieces, place a short piece of straight-edge hardwood against the tongue of the outside piece and drive the pieces up snugly, taking care not to break the tongue. Repeat this after every three or four pieces have been laid.

NAILING SHOE MOULDING—   The shoe moulding shall be nailed to the baseboard. This shall be done after the entire floor has been laid.

Note—It has been found that nailing to the baseboard is preferable, since this allows freedom for normal expansion of the flooring.

LAYING STRIP FLOORING OVER SLEEPERS—   In general, the flooring shall be applied in the same manner and with observance of the same precautions prescribed for conventional joist construction. The first course, however, shall be laid 1 inch from wall studs or the plaster line. It is not necessary that all joints meet over sleepers, but adjoining strips shall not break over the same sleeper space. The flooring shall be nailed at each bearing point. Wherever a strip passes over lapped sleepers it shall be nailed to both.

LAYING NEW STRIP FLOORING OVER OLD FLOOR—The old floor shall serve as a sub-floor. Examine it carefully and correct any defects . Any existing thresholds shall be removed to allow the new floor to run flush through doorways. Interior doors shall be lifted from their hinges. The base-shoe or moulding strip at the baseboard shall be removed. Building paper shall be laid. Except where cross-wise installation in a narrow room would result, the new flooring shall be installed with the pieces laid at right angles to the old floor boards. In other respects laying and nailing, as well as replacing the moulding, shall be done in the same manner as in new construction. The bottoms of doors shall be planed if this becomes necessary due to the higher level of the new floor.

Note—Ordinarily, the thinner sizes of strip flooring, 3/8 inch, 1/2 inch, or 5/16 inch, are used over an existing finish floor.

PLANK FLOORING—   Plank flooring shall be nailed over wood sub-floors of the type used as a foundation for strip flooring. It shall be laid according to the same general specifications as strip flooring with regard to selection, preparation, time of installation, direction, use of short strips, joints and nailing shoe moulding.   Tongued and grooved plank shall be blind-nailed as in conventional flooring. Additionally, it shall be fastened to the sub-floor with two countersunk screws at each end and other screws at intervals along the length of the plank. The screws shall be covered with wood plugs glued into the holes. Screws and plugs shall be placed at intervals frequent enough to hold the plank securely without marring its appearance. The same types and sizes of nails shall be employed as those used for corresponding thicknesses of strip flooring (See Nail Schedule). The planks shall not be driven tightly together.

Note—Sometimes nails, instead of screws, are used along the length of the plank, although screws are recommended because of their superior holding qualities. If nails are employed, they should be the small-headed type. Driven vertically through the face of the plank, they should be countersunk. The nail holes should be filled with colored putty or plastic wood. The frequency of the fastening lengthwise of the plank is somewhat a matter of individual preference. Some authorities recommend screws or nails at 30-inch intervals.

In specifying that planks shall not be driven tightly together, some manufacturers recommend leaving a slight crack, about the thickness of a putty knife, between planks.

BLOCK AND PARQUET FLOORING—   The styles and types of block and parquet flooring, as well as the recommended procedures for application, vary somewhat among the different manufacturers. It is suggested that detailed installation information be requested from the manufacturer whose product is being used. A few general points are presented, however, as a preliminary guide.

Either the blocks or the individual pieces of parquetry may be nailed or laid in mastic to a wood sub-floor. Nailing is done through the tongues, as in strip flooring application. The mastic method is preferred by many. In this procedure a thin coat of mastic generally is applied over the base, which must be smooth, level and dry. On top of this is placed a layer of 30 lb. asphalt saturated felt. Then asphaltic mastic is troweled on to an average thickness of 3/32 inch. Into this the flooring is embedded. The mastic is applied hot or cold, depending on the manufacturer's recommendations.

When the base is concrete, the mastic method must be used, generally with damp proofing on top the slab. It also is employed in remodeling installations where an old floor of terrazzo or other hard material is to be covered.

Block flooring is available in two major types, unit-blocks and laminated blocks. In unit-blocks, each of which is composed of several short lengths of flooring, the two tongue edges are at right angles to each other. In laminated blocks, made of three plies of hardwood bonded securely with moisture resistant glue, the tongues are on opposed sides.

Installation procedures for the two types are basically the same. In unit-blocks, however, allowance must be made for expansion. There are various means of doing this. Rubber expansion strips often are employed. Generally, no blocks or border strips are laid closer than 1 inch to walls or other vertical surfaces. With laminated blocks, no expansion allowance is necessary.

Both types can be laid either in square or diagonal pattern. The diagonal design is recommended in corridors and in rooms where the length is more than 1½ times the width. In such areas diagonal placement minimizes expansion under high humidity conditions.

To effect a diagonal pattern, installation usually is begun at the center of a room along a line drawn diagonally across the room. The installation is built up by laying succeeding blocks in pyramid order. The room area on one side of the chalk line is completed before the other is begun.

In achieving a square pattern, workmen generally begin at a center point equidistant from the sidewalls, on a chalk line snapped across the width of the room near one end. Succeeding blocks are placed in pyramid order until the large area beyond the chalk line has been completed. The smaller area, which meanwhile has served as a working space and storage for materials, then is completed in the same manner.

WHITE OAK AND RED OAK

In quality and utility there is little if any difference between white oak and red oak, the two groups into which flooring oak varieties are classified.

Even in appearance they are quite similar, both being light in color. White oak has a brownish tinge, while red oak is characterized by a pink cast which usually turns reddish-brown after application of finish.

Generally, the two groups are separated and are ordered by color. In No. 2 Common grade, however, there may be a mixture. The same grading rules apply to both.

FINISHING

A good Oak Flooring may be obtained either unfinished or pre-finished. The unfinished type receives the final finishing on the job after the flooring has been installed.

This section is designed to point out the approved methods of finishing a wood Oak Floor to bring out the full richness and full beauty. Some steps in the finishing operation are similar for all oak flooring, while others may vary with the grade of wood or the type of finish desired, for example, all unfinished wood Oak Flooring must be sanded before any finishing materials are applied. Floors may be finished natural or in a wide range of colors as preferred.

Pre-finished wood Oak Flooring is completely finished at the mill by skilled workmen employing the most modern finishing methods. By means of expert sanding, application of finish materials and buffing, the flooring is given perfect finishing treatment, even to the final polishing. It is ready for service immediately after installation. In saving the time required for finishing the floors after they have been installed, pre-finished flooring hastens completion of a home by several days.

1. WHEN TO BEGIN SURFACING—Sanding shall be done just before application of the final coat of finish to the base moulding and after all other interior work has been completed.

2. PREPARATION—Immediately before the sanding operation is begun, the floor shall be swept clean. Use no water.

3. METHOD—The floor shall be traversed at least three times with an electric sanding machine. A rotary disc sander may be used for the final cut, but other cuts preferably shall be made with a drum type machine. If the latter is employed, the first cut may be made crosswise of the grain or at a 45 degree angle. Succeeding cuts shall be in the direction of the grain. No. 2 sandpaper shall be used for the first traverse, No. ½ for the second, No. 0 for the third.

Note—While three traverses are recommended, acceptable results sometimes are obtained from two. If an especially smooth surface is desired, four or five traverses are recommended, the fourth with No. 00 sandpaper, the fifth with No. 000. After the final machine cut, the floor should receive a buffing by hand with No. 000 sandpaper.

For unusually fine oak floors, where expense is not a primary consideration, manual sanding is recommended. Requiring considerably more time, hand sanding produces a surface even smoother than does machine treatment.

Making the final machine cut with a disc sander is particularly well advised when the floor is of parquet or unit block style.

An electric edger, or hand sander, should be used for surfacing areas near walls, in corners and small closets. Large machines are ineffective in such places. Some spots, such as those around radiator pipes, cannot be adequately surfaced even with an edger. Hand scraping is necessary in such areas.

4. PROTECTING THE SURFACE—After the final sanding or buffing, the floor shall be swept clean. Windows, window sills, doors, door frames and baseboards, as well as the floor itself, then shall be dusted carefully with a painter's tack rag. After the final buffing, the floor shall not be walked on until after the stain, filler or first finish coat has been applied and is dry. Any footmarks that appear shall be wiped off.

5. FINAL SANDING AND FIRST FINISH COAT—The first coat of stain, filler or other finish shall be applied the same day the final sanding and buffing are completed.

Note—If there is a longer interval between the two operations, the grain of the wood will rise perceptibly, causing a rough surface. Observance of the recommended procedure keeps the rising of grain to a minimum.

6. STAIN—Stain, if used, shall be applied before filler or other finish. It shall be an oil stain unless otherwise specified in directions for the finish to be employed. Before application, samples of stain shall be applied to an inconspicuous area or on pieces of scrap flooring. When the desired shade has been achieved, the stain shall be applied to the floor with a flat varnish brush about 3 or 4 inches wide. Application shall proceed lengthwise of the room in courses about 36 inches wide. Stain shall be put on evenly and excess stain wiped off with a soft cloth before it sets.

Note—While stain is used extensively to achieve color effects, pigmented filler has been found more satisfactory. This is especially true of light, medium or dark shades of the natural oak color. Even when an unconventional floor color such as green is preferred, pigmented filler is recommended. In cases such as the latter, however, stain may be used with good results in conjunction with pigmented filler. The objection to use of stain alone is its sensitivity to light, a characteristic which subjects it to fading in spots exposed to brightness. Pigmented filler, on the other hand, is resistant to light.

Only medium or dark stains are recommended for No. 1 Common and No. 2 Common grades. Other grades will take dark tones well, but their beauty of grain shows to better advantage when a light shade is used.

7. WOOD FILLER—One coat of good paste wood filler shall be applied with a short bristled 4-inch flat brush, or as directed by the manufacturer. Brush across the grain first, then with the grain. Care shall be taken to avoid covering too large an area at once. Before the filler in each new area becomes hard, the excess shall be wiped off so that the coat of filler is uniformly even with the surface of the wood. Using excelsior or burlap, wipe across the grain first, then with the grain.

The filler shall be allowed to "set" or dry for 24 hours before other finish materials are applied.

Note—The prime function of filler is to fill the minute crevices in oak, which, like certain other hardwoods, has relatively large pores. Filler aids in imparting a mirror-smooth surface and protects the pores against dirt. Even so, it is more frequently ommitted in today's construction.

Pigmented filler is recommended when a colored floor is desired. When a floor of natural color is preferred, the colorless type should be used.

The proper time for application varies. If stain has been used, filler often is applied after the stain has dried thoroughly. If the floor is not stained and the finish is to be varnish or shellac, filler generally is applied after the final sanding. When used in conjunction with certain kinds of floor seal, filler should be applied after the seal. The manufacturer's directions should be followed.

8. FINISH MATERIALS—Specifications for application of finish materials vary with the manufacturers of the different brands. Care shall be taken that the finish used is applied according to the directions printed on the containers.

Types of Finish—The ideal qualities of a finish for a wood Oak or other hardwood floors are: attractive appearance; durability; ease of maintenance; and capacity for being retouched in worn spots without revealing a patched appearance. Some finishes are transparent, others are not. A transparent type should be used on hardwood flooring to accentuate its natural beauty. The four kinds of finish employed most extensively nowadays are floor seal, varnish, shellac and urethane. Lacquer, too, is sometimes used.

SEALER FINISHES—Floor seal is being used on an increasingly large scale for residential as well as heavy duty flooring. It differs from other finishes in this important respect: instead of forming a surface coating, it penetrates the wood fibers, sealing them together. In effect it becomes a part of the wood itself. It wears only as the wood wears, does not chip or scratch and is practically immune to ordinary stains and spots. While it does not present as shiny an appearance as other finishes, it can be waxed and polished to a pleasing luster. An oak floor finished with seal seldom requires resanding. After years of wear it usually can either be refinished completely after simply cleaning, or it can be retouched in worn spots without revealing lines of demarcation between the old and new finish. Although a complete finish in itself, seal may be used as an undercoat for varnish or shellac. It can be obtain either colorless or in color.

Basically, seals are of two types, normal drying and rapid drying time from approximately 40 minutes to 1½ hours for first coats and from 1 to 3 hours for second coats. Most manufacturers recommend two coats for new oak floors. Some seals, however, produce satisfactory results with one coat. Stated drying times for seal, as well as other finishes, usually presuppose a room temperature of 70 degrees, relative humidity of 50 per cent and adequate ventilation. Variations from those conditions retard or hasten drying.

APPLICATION—Generally, floor seal can be mopped on with a clean string mop or a long-handled applicator equipped with a pad of lamb's wool. It also can be applied with a wide brush or a squeegee. Excess seal is wiped off with clean cloths or a squeegee, except where manufacturer's directions call for rubbing it into the wood. For best results the floor should then be buffed with No. 2 steel wool. An electric buffer makes this task relatively simple. If a power buffer is not available, a sanding machine equipped with steel wool pads may be used; or the buffing may be done by hand. Although one application of seal sometimes is sufficient, a second coat frequently is recommended for new floors or floors that have just been sanded.

SURFACE FINISHES

URETHANE—Also known as polyurethane, this type finish is becoming increasingly popular for residential use. It has been used extensively in commercial and industrial installations and provides an excellent surface with long wearing and low maintenance properties.

There are two basic types of urethane finishes, one of them the so-called moisture curing and the other termed oil-modified. The moisture curing urethane finish is considered to provide better service, but it must be applied under closely controlled conditions. The oil-modified urethane finishes are much simpler to apply and still provide excellent service. The one objection to polyurethane finishes is that, in their natural state, they are rather glossy and a low gloss appearance can be achieved only by an additive, which does affect performance of the finish to some degree.

Most spills and soils can be readily wiped up with a damp cloth, and the entire area can be easily maintained by dry-mopping.

Manufacturer's directions for application must be followed carefully for best performance.

VARNISH—Varnish presents a glossy appearance, is quite durable, fairly resistant to stains and spots, but will show scratches. It is difficult to patch worn spots, however, without leaving lines of demarcation between the old and the new varnish. New types of varnish dry in eight hours or less. Like the other types of finish, it gives satisfactory results if properly waxed and otherwise maintained.

Application—Varnish made especially for floors is preferred. So-called all-purpose varnishes ordinarily are not so durable when used on floors. As a rule, three coats of floor varnish are required when it is applied to bare wood. Two coats usually are adequate, however, when wood filler has been used or when a coat of shellac has been applied first, as is sometimes the case. Cleanliness of both the floor and the applicator is essential to a smooth finish.

LACQUER—Lacquer provides a glossy finish and possesses about the same durability as varnish. One of the advantages of a lacquered floor is that worn spots may be retouched with good results. Lines of demarcation are not noticeable because the new lacquer dissolves the old coat rather than forming an additional layer.

Application—Lacquer is rather difficult to apply, chiefly because it dries so rapidly. It is important to observe rigidly the manufacturer's instructions.

SHELLAC—Two of the chief reasons shellac is so widely used are its quick-drying property and its ease of application. Shellac has moderate resistance to water and other types of stains, but it will spot if liquids remain on it for an extended period. It is transparent, has a high gloss, and does not darken with age as quickly as varnish. If kept waxed and not subjected to extreme wear, it will give satisfactory service. Besides its use as a final finish, shellac may be employed as a one-coat base for varnish.

Application—A wide brush that covers the width of three strip flooring pieces is the most effective and convenient size for application. Strokes should be long and even, with laps joined smoothly. At least two coats are needed and preferably three.

9. WAX—After the final coat of finish has dried thoroughly, the floor shall be treated with a good quality of floor wax recommended for use on hardwood floors, with the possible exception of a urethane treated floor. The wax may be either the paste or liquid type with a spirit base. It shall be applied according to the manufacturer's directions.

Note—Wax not only imparts a lustrous sheen to a floor, but also forms a protective film that prevents dirt from penetrating the wood pores. When it becomes dirty, it is easily removed and new wax applied.

In some cases one coat is sufficient, although in many instances two or three are recommended for best results. One type of approved liquid wax cleans and waxes in a single operation.

Self-polishing liquid wax with a water base is not recommended. Frequent use of water on a hardwood floor will cause the grain to rise, a condition that results in a rough surface. The spirit type of liquid wax is generally considered equal to paste wax when properly applied.

GRADING RULES

STANDARD OAK FLOORING GRADES
QUARTER SAWN

CLEAR—The face shall be practically clear, admitting an average of 3/8 of an inch of bright sap. The question of color shall not be considered. Bundles to be 1 1/4 ft. and up. Average length 3 3/4 ft.

SELECT—The face may contain sap, small streaks, pin worm holes, burls, slight imperfections in working, and small tight knots which do not average more than one to every 3 ft. Bundles to be 1 1/4 ft. and up. Average length 3 1/4 ft.

PLAIN SAWN

CLEAR—The face shall be practically clear, admitting an average of 3/8 of an inch of bright sap. The question of color shall not be considered. Bundles to be 1 1/4 ft. and up. Average length 3 3/4 ft.

SELECT—The face may contain sap, small streaks, pin worm holes, burls, slight imperfections in working, and small tight knots which do not average more than one to every 3 ft. Bundles to be 1 1/4 ft. and up. Average length 3 1/4 ft.

NO. 1 COMMON—Shall be of such nature that will lay a good residential floor and may contain varying wood characteristics, such as flags, heavy streaks and checks, worm holes, knots and minor imperfections in working. Bundles to be 1 1/4 ft. and up. Average length 2 3/4 ft.

NO. 2 COMMON—May contain sound natural variations of the forest product and manufacturing imperfections. The purpose of this grade is to furnish an economical floor suitable for homes, general utility use, or where character marks and contrasting appearance are desired. Bundles to be 1 1/4 ft. and up. Average length 2 1/4 ft.

1 1/4' SHORTS—Pieces 9 to 18 inches long are to be bundled together and designated as 1 1/4' Shorts. Pieces grading No. 1 Common, Select and Clear to be bundled together and designated No. 1 Common & Better with pieces grading No. 2 Common bundled separately and designated as such. Although pieces 6" under and only 3" over the nominal length of the bundle may be included, the pieces must average 1 1/4' which is achieved through the natural preponderance of longer lengths.

The above applies to tongued and grooved strip flooring and, with minor exceptions, to square-edge strip flooring. The points of variance in square-edge are: Clear average length 5 ft.; Select average length 4 ft.; No. 1 Common average length 3 ft.; No. 2 Common average length 2 1/2 ft.

BEECH, BIRCH, HARD MAPLE GRADES

FIRST GRADE—Shall have the face practically free of all defects, but the varying natural color of the wood shall not be considered a defect. Bundles shall be 2 ft. and longer, as the stock will produce; the proportion of 2 and 3 ft. bundles, shall be what the stock will produce up to 33% in footage.

SECOND GRADE—Will admit of tight, sound knots and slight imperfections in dressing, but must lay without waste. Bundles shall be 2 ft. and longer, as the stock will produce; the proportion of 2 and 3 ft. bundles shall be what the stock will produce up to 45% in footage.

THIRD GRADE—Must be of such character as will lay and give a good serviceable floor. Bundles shall be 1 1/4 ft. and longer, as the stock will produce; the proportion of 1 1/4 to 3 ft. bundles shall be what the stock will produce up to 65% in footage.

SPECIAL GRADES—Second and Better Grade is a combination of First and Second Grades developing in the strip without cross-cutting for each grade. The lowest grade pieces admissible shall not be less than standard Second Grade. Standard lengths in this grade shall be in 2-foot bundles and longer, as the stock will produce. Not over 40 percent of the total footage shall be in bundles under 4 ft.

(Note: 5% 1¼-foot bundles allowed in Second and Better Grade-jointed flooring only.)

Third and Better Grade is a combination of First, Second and Third Grades developing in a strip without crosscutting. The lowest grade pieces admissible shall not be less than standard Third Grade. Standard lengths of this grade shall be in 1 1/4-ft. bundles and longer, as the stock will produce. Not over 50 percent of the total footage shall be in bundles under 4 feet.

First Grade White Hard Maple is special stock, selected for uniformity of color. It is almost ivory white and is the finest grade of Hard Maple flooring that can be produced.

First Grade Red Beech and Birch are special grades produced from all red faced stock, and are specially selected for color. The color is rich, being a soft tint which lends to these two woods an individuality found in no other species.

PECAN GRADES

FIRST GRADE—Shall be practically free of defects, but the varying natural color of the wood shall not be considered a defect. Bundles shall be 2 ft. and longer; not over 25% of the footage shall be 2 and 3 feet.

FIRST GRADE RED—Same as First Grade except that face shall be all heartwood.

FIRST GRADE WHITE—Same as First Grade except that face shall be all bright sapwood.

SECOND GRADE—Will admit of tight, sound knots or their equivalent, pin worm holes, streaks, light stains and slight imperfections in working. Shall be of such nature as to lay a sound floor without cutting. Bundles shall be 1 1/4 ft. and longer, as the stock will produce; the proportion of 1 1/4 to 3 ft. bundles shall be what the stock will produce up to 40% in footage.

SECOND GRADE RED—Same as Second Grade except that face shall be all heartwood.

THIRD GRADE—Must be of such character as will give and lay a good serviceable floor. Bundles shall be 1 1/4 ft. and longer, as the stock will produce; the proportion of 1 1/4 to 3 ft. bundles shall be what the stock will produce up to 60% in footage.

3/4 x 2-1/4" NESTED FLOORING

DEFINITION—Nested flooring is random length flooring bundled end to end continuously in 8 foot long bundles.

DESCRIPTION—A bundle with 4 layers of flooring 3 runs wide or 6 layers by 2 runs wide containing a good spread of lengths 9" - 102" nested continuously end to end to make bundles of 8 foot nominal length (7½ - 8½ foot actual length) containing 24 board feet of flooring.

Stock to be bundled by grade as follows:

OAK

In conformance with regular grade requirements.

BEECH, BIRCH, HARD MAPLE AND PECAN

GRADE	MINIMUM AVERAGE LENGTH	MAXIMUM AVERAGE NUMBER of 9-18" Pieces Per Bundle
1st Grade	42"	4
2nd Grade	33"	8
3rd Grade	30"	As Develops

Existing specifications for the different grades, except those pertaining to lengths, are applicable.

PRE-FINISH FLOORING GRADES

OAK

White and Red Oak to be separated in each grade. Grades are established after the flooring has been sanded and finished.

PRIME—Face shall be selected for appearance after finishing, but sapwood and the natural variations of color are permitted. Minimum average length 3 1/2 ft. Bundles 1 1/4 ft. and longer.

STANDARD—May contain sound wood characteristics which are even and smooth after filling and finishing and will lay a sound floor without cutting. Minimum average length 2 3/4 ft. Bundles 1 1/4 ft. and longer.

STANDARD AND BETTER—A combination of Prime and Standard to contain the full product of the board except that no pieces are to be lower than Standard Grade. Minimum average length 3 ft. Bundles 1 1/4 ft. and longer.

TAVERN—Shall be of such nature as will make and lay a serviceable floor without cutting, but purposely containing typical wood characteristics which are to be properly filled and finished.

BEECH AND PECAN

Furnished only in a combination grade of Tavern and Better.

TAVERN AND BETTER—A combination of Prime, Standard and Tavern to contain the full product of the board except that no pieces are to be lower than Tavern Grade. Minimum average length 3 ft. Bundles 1 1/4 ft. and longer.

GENERAL RULES

(All Species Finished & Unfinished)

Hardwood flooring is bundled by averaging the lengths. A bundle may include pieces from 6 inches under to 6 inches over the nominal length of the bundle. No piece shorter than 9 inches admitted.

The percentages under 4 ft. referred to in the grading rules apply on total footage in any one shipment of the item.

3/4-in allowance shall be added to the face length when measuring the length of each piece.

Flooring shall not be considered of standard grade unless the lumber from which the flooring is manufactured has been properly kiln-dried.

RESILIENT FLOORING

This type flooring includes sheet vinyl, vinyl asbestos, linoleum and vinyl composition. Sheet vinyls are among the most popular in todays flooring material. The vinyl content allows them to be extra colorful and adds to the ability to resist wear, grease and alkalis, resists stain, scratches and allows for easy cleaning. This flooring is not recommended for use where excessive hydrostatic pressure is expected. Rolls come in 6'–0" and 12'–0" widths and the thickness of the material is .160 , .090 , .080 , .070, .075, .065 and can be used below or above ground installations. The quality and cost varies from .70 to $1.70 a square foot. The design is not through, but surface only.

INSTALLATION OF VINYL FLOORS

SUBFLOOR PREPARATION

An important part of the success of any floor covering installation and its finished appearance is the subfloor over which it is installed. Subfloors that are rough or uneven will telegraph every irregularity through to the finished flooring

Stagger joints in ashlar fashion.

Fill nail-head depressions level.

Sand high/low joints level.

Fill cracks wider than 1/32".

installation once the adhesive sets up. Your finished flooring installation can look no better than the subfloor over which it is installed.

WOODEN SUBFLOORS

The wood underfloor must be solid, free from movement and have a minimum of 18" of well ventilated air space below it. The subfloor must be clean, dry, smooth and free of wax, grease or other foreign materials or the adhesive will not properly bond to the subfloor. Painted floors must be sanded.

Stripwood subfloors must be of double construction, solid and free from springiness. The width of the boards should be no wider than 3 inches. Rough or uneven boards should be re-nailed to eliminate movement and planed or sanded smooth. Sanding should be done diagonally or with the grain in the wood, not across the grain. The floor covering material should be installed directly to the subfloor with the seams running across the boards. Do not use lining felt. It is not recommended under cushioned vinyl products over any type of subfloor.

Underlayment

The most common type of wooden subfloor that you will encounter is one of the underlayment types. The three most commonly used underlayments are: plywood, hardboard and particleboard (also referred to as chipboard or flakeboard).

The preferred underlayment is 1/4" plywood, DFPA underlayment grade. Any sanded exterior grade plywood may also be used. In areas that are subject to surface moisture for any reason, plywood bonded with exterior glue is recommended. Masonite brand underlayment board installed smooth side down may also be used (minimum thickness, 1/4 inch) in lieu of plywood.

Installation of Underlayment

Stripwood subfloors that are beyond repairing or those with boards over 3 inches should be covered with underlayment. Many consumers prefer to cover stripwood subfloors with underlayment as they often show board joints through the flooring even after meticulous preparation.

Underlayment should be laid out with joints staggered (ashlar fashion) over the surface to which it is being installed. Underlayment joints should fall over joints or the center of a board. The joints in the underlayment should be fitted net without gaps between sheets or excessive tightness.

If the underlayment is being fastened with nails, ring-shanked, resin coated, glue coated or drive screw type nails must be used and should penetrate 1 to 1-1/4" into the joists or subfloor. Nailing should start in the center of the sheet, working toward the edges. Place the nails on 6" centers in the body of the sheet and 4" apart, 3/8" in from the edge around the perimeter of the sheet. The nails must be driven flush with the surface of the underlayment as protruding nailheads will be outlined in the finished flooring. Also, depressions caused by compressing the underlayment with the hammer head if the nail is driven below the surface will telegraph through the finished floor covering. If this occurs, fill the depressions level with latex patching compound.

If a manual or power underlayment stapler is being utilized to fasten the underlayment, divergent type staples should be used, applied the same distance apart as described for

nailing. 18 gauges 3/16 x 7/8" staples are recommended for 1/4" plywood and Masonite underlayment, 16 gauge 3/8 x 1-5/8" for 3/8" plywood. The equipment should be adjusted so that the head of the staple is sunk slightly below the surface of the underlayment. Plywood thicker than 3/8" should be nailed.

Careful inspection should be made of all underlayment joints. If any high-low's exist between sheets, they should be brought to a smooth even plane by sanding or with a hard setting, non-shrinking, non-crumbling, latex floor patching compound applied with a broad bladed wall knife or smooth floor trowel. Any cracks or openings between sheets in the underlayment which are wider than 1/32" should also be filled level with latex patching compound.

REMOVING CUSHIONED VINYL FLOORS FROM SUBFLOORS

Old cushioned vinyl floors require removal from the subfloor before a new floor can be installed. Floor coverings with White Shield backing are easily removed with a minimum of effort and expense.

The wearlayer and foam on the old floor covering should be scored the length of the sheet with a sharp knife approximately every 4" to 12". Start at one end of the room and delaminate a corner of a strip in the backing. Pull gradually, and the wearlayer, foam and one-half of the backing material will pull free leaving a layer of asbestos felt on the subfloor. Occasionally, parts of the foam inner layer will stick to the felt. This condition can often times be eliminated by starting the strips and pulling from the opposite end of the room. A broad, stiff blade putty knife will assist cleavage of wearlayer and foam from the felt if delamination should be difficult.

No further preparation of the felt remaining on the floor is necessary unless there should be loose spots. In this case they can be cut open and recemented. If small areas of asbestos felt come loose from the floor, they can be filled and brought level with a quality latex patching compound.

Under certain conditions it may be necessary to remove asbestos felt from the subfloor such as when a perimeter installation is being removed. In rare instances, it might be necessary to clear an entire subfloor of the asbestos felt. ASBESTOS FELT MUST NOT BE SANDED UNDER ANY CIRCUMSTANCES. INHALATION OF ASBESTOS DUST MAY CAUSE SERIOUS BODILY HARM.

Asbestos felt can be removed from the subfloor by soaking it with a 50-50 solution (equal volumes) of water and denatured alcohol. Isopropyl alcohol or methanol (wood alcohol) can be used in place of denatured alcohol.

CAUTION—THIS SOLUTION IS FLAMMABLE AND ALL PRECAUTIONS NECESSARY TO PREVENT FIRE MUST BE TAKEN. EXTINQUISH ALL FLAMES AND PILOT LIGHTS. DO NOT SMOKE. ADEQUATE VENTILATION MUST BE PROVIDED. ADVISE ALL PEOPLE ON THE PREMISES OF THESE PRECAUTIONARY REQUIREMENTS.

Score old flooring with sharp knife.

Remove in strips.

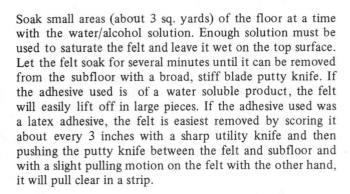
Recement loose spots.

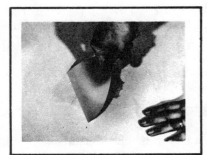
Patch small areas w/felt missing.

Soak about 3 sq. yds. with solution.

Removing felt from latex adhesive.

Soak small areas (about 3 sq. yards) of the floor at a time with the water/alcohol solution. Enough solution must be used to saturate the felt and leave it wet on the top surface. Let the felt soak for several minutes until it can be removed from the subfloor with a broad, stiff blade putty knife. If the adhesive used is of a water soluble product, the felt will easily lift off in large pieces. If the adhesive used was a latex adhesive, the felt is easiest removed by scoring it about every 3 inches with a sharp utility knife and then pushing the putty knife between the felt and subfloor and with a slight pulling motion on the felt with the other hand, it will pull clear in a strip.

Once the felt has been removed, it is not necessary to remove the adhesive residue from the subfloor before installing the new flooring covering, if the same adhesive is to be used.

This solution will work on a great many adhesives and should be tried on a small section of the floor if the adhesive is other than those named. If it does not allow removal of the felt from the adhesive, then the floor can be smoothed with a rubber latex underlayment applied as a skim coat to bring the floor and felt residue level.

MATCHING AND REVERSING

A system, whereby important information for matching and sheet reversal or non-reversal at seams has been embossed into the cut away selvage of flooring products. This will be found on the majority of all permanently installed sheet vinyl floor coverings. Embossed into the cut away selvage are the instructions, "reverse sheets" or "do not reverse", depending on the design.

On those designs with "reverse sheets" in the selvage, one side of the sheet will be imprinted with "C" 's, the opposite edge with "I" 's. Reverse the sheet and align "I" 's or "C" 's.

When aligned, this will be the exact match point of the design. On overall designs where there is no concern for matching, only the words "reverse sheets" will be embossed in the selvage. Most designs will require reversal of sheets at seams.

Some design types will not allow reversing of the sheet and "do not reverse" wording has been imprinted in the selvage. In this case, the sheets are installed side by side. On a few designs in addition to the wording, a small arrow has also been embossed into the selvage. Align the arrows to bring the design to its exact match point.

357

CAUTION—FELT THAT HAS BEEN REMOVED SHOULD IMMEDIATELY BE PLACED IN A CLOSED PLASTIC BAG OR COVERED METAL CONTAINER TO MINIMIZE THE DANGER OF FIRE.

NON-REVERSE DESIGNS

In order to estimate the amount of material needed for matching non-reverse designs, use this method. Allow 3" over the room size for fitting on the first sheet. The next sheet and all succeeding sheets should be cut (consecutively from the roll) to the next multiple of the design repeat over room size.

Example—if the room size is 12' x 13'-9" and you are using 6' wide material and the design being installed has an 18" repeat, cut the first sheet 14' (13'-9" + 3"). The second sheet and succeeding sheets should then be cut 15'-0".

Reverse sheets with C's & I's.

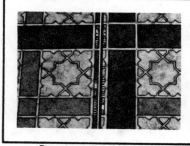

Do not reverse-with arrows.

REVERSE SHEET DESIGNS

When a design requiring sheet reversal is being installed, the first sheet should be cut to room size plus 3" for fitting. The second and all succeeding sheets should have the length of the pattern match added to the room length of the preceding sheet.

Example—if the room size is 12' x 13'-9" and the design being installed is an 18" match, cut the first sheet 14' (13'-9" + 3"). The second sheet should then be cut 15'-3" + 18").

SEAM CUTTING

Cushioned sheet vinyl floor covering products fall into two categories for seam cutting.

A. CUSHIONED VINYL FLOORS

B. BACKED CUSHIONED VINYL FLOORS

There are two distinct techniques required for seam cutting these two product groups.

GROUP A. SEAM CUTTING—CUSHIONED VINYL FLOORS

The first step is to lay out the room and establish where each seam in the flooring material will fall. The following must be taken into consideration: Seams in the floor covering should be placed in the least conspicuous and least traveled areas wherever possible. The flooring seams must fall across the boards on stripwood floors and no closer than 6" to the joints in underlayment.

If the installation is by the Perimeter Adhesion System, seams in the new floor covering must fall as closely as possible to the center of a row of tile on old existing tile floors and be a minimum distance of 6" from seams in existing sheet vinyl floors.

After determining how the sheets of material are to be layed out in the room, snap a chalk line where each seam will fall. Then approximately 8" on both sides of the seam, snap additional parallel chalk lines. The outer chalk lines will act as a guide for adhesive spreading.

The flooring material should be pre-cut allowing sufficient length to acquire a match on the second and successive sheets.

All sheets should be reverse rolled, keeping the diameter the same on each sheet. This relaxes the flooring material and reduces length shrinkage which otherwise might occur.

The first sheet should be fitted to the room. Then turn back one half of the length of the sheet and spread the recommended adhesive on the subfloor up to the first chalk line. On long sheets, cover the adhesive with the flooring material after about 10 lineal feet has been spread on the subfloor. This will prevent the adhesive from filming over because of exposure to the air.

The portion of the sheet where adhesive has been applied to the subfloor should then be thoroughly rolled in both directions with a 100 lb. or heavier, three section steel roller before proceeding further. Following the same procedure as used on the first half of the sheet, apply adhesive to the subfloor on the balance half of the first sheet and roll thoroughly.

Position the second sheet following directions for matching and reversing as described previously in this method. The match should be made at the mid-point of the seam so that any minor run-out will be divided between the opposite ends of the seam.

358

Seam across boards on stripwood.

**Position flooring seams at least 6"
from underlayment joints**

**Seam in middle of tile on perimeter
adhesion system.**

Spread adhesive to 1st line.

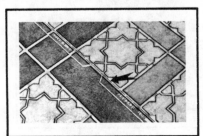

Cover adhesive every 10' on long sheets.

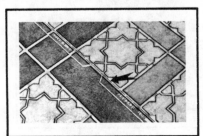

Notch every 6 feet.

In cases where the design allows, seams will fall in embossed mortar joints or lines of the design. The seam should be cut through the center of the mortar joint or line. Do not cut along the edge of the embossings as a high-low seam will result and the seam weld will be poor. A notch about every six feet along the seam, as illustrated, is one way to determine if the mortar joint or line is the proper width. Another way is to accurately determine the exact size of one design unit across the width of the sheet. Then measure two design units across the seam line. This should be done about every 6 feet along the seam.

After matching the design, fit the second sheet to the room, apply adhesive to the subfloor and roll.

The next step is to double cut the seam. A scrap piece of material 2" to 3" wide should now be placed with the White Shield back up directly under the seam area. This piece of scrap serves a dual purpose. One, it adds a slight fullness at the seam area, which is desirable in cushioned flooring products as they are compressable to a degree without buckling. Two, the scrap provides protection for your knife blade against dulling on concrete or nicking on nailheads.

A straight blade utility knife with a sharp blade is recommended for cutting the seam. Use a steel straight edge at the seam line as a guide for the utility knife. Hold the knife straight up/down on a 90° angle and apply enough pressure to cut through both sheets of flooring material with a single cut.

Remove the scrap and you are now ready for adhesive application in the dry zone of the seam area. The 16" wide area will permit the use of a trowel for spreading the adhesive. The most convenient way to keep the sheets apart in this dry zone is to place both knees in this area while spreading adhesive. Care should be taken to avoid excessive adhesive where it meets previously spread adhesive. Even if thoroughly rolled, excessive adhesive could cause a slight ridge to show in some products under certain lighting conditions.

After the adhesive has been spread on the subfloor in the dry zone, embed the sheet which was on top at seam cutting into the wet adhesive and then tuck the other sheet in place by bending the edge of the material slightly as illustrated. Every care should be taken to avoid scraping up adhesive between the sheets as the most inconspicuous seams, particularly in light colored floors, are those that have been kept adhesive free between the two sheets of flooring material. If adhesive oozes up into the seam it is usually because the trowel notches are too wide. A finer notched trowel should be used. If adhesive is accidentally gotten into the seam, it should be cleaned out as it will weaken the sealer weld. Also the seam will eventually darken from the adhesive in the seam.

Roll the seam area with the three section steel rollers and then bring the wearlayers into perfect level with a small steel seam roller. Clean the surface of the flooring with a damp sponge or cloth to remove any adhesive, dry the area and the seam is now ready for seam sealing.

GROUP B. SEAM CUTTING–BACKED CUSHIONED VINYL FLOORS

Backed cushioned vinyl flooring is 12' wide and will cover many areas without seams. Where seams are required, the seaming procedure is to straight edge and butt. A wide trim provides ample selvage for seaming on both overall and geometric patterns.

The first step for installing backed products where seams are necessary is to totally fit the first sheet to the walls and then trim the seam edge.

On overall designs, a chalk line should be snapped parallel to the factory edge, far enough in to eliminate any embossed lettering in the selvage. The seam cut should then be made along the chalk line using a straight edge as a guide with the utility knife held at a 90° angle to the face of the flooring material.

On geometric designs, the seam cut is made from point to point through the design. The exact cutting line will be easily located on all designs. The seam cut, as on overall designs, must be made along a metal straight edge with a utility knife held at a 90° angle to the face of the floor covering material.

All precautions should be taken, realigning the straight edge where necessary to be certain that the seam cut falls in the exact spot on each design unit. On geometric patterns, when they are properly trimmed and butted together, a perfect design repeat results across the seam.

After cutting the seam edge, roll or turn back one half of the sheet at a time and spread adhesive on the subfloor to within 12" of the seam edge. The sheet should be pushed or unrolled slowly into the wet adhesive. This helps to minimize trapped air between the flooring material and the subfloor.

The next step is to trim the seam edge of the second sheet and unless it is an overall design, position it for pattern match. At this point it is not unusual to experience a considerable amount of design run off along the seam. This type of product is very compressible and a sizable design run off can be brought back on to match in the wet adhesive after it has been spread on the subfloor.

Tube back both seam edges and apply adhesive under the 12" area left without the adhesive on the first sheet and approximately 36" wide under the seam edge of the second sheet. Return both seam edges into the wet adhesive immediately after spreading on the subfloor. The 12" of wet adhesive under the first sheet and 36" under the second sheet will allow the design to be adjusted to match exactly, as well as allow for adjusting for a tight fitting seam. Avoid squeezing the adhesive up between the seam as this is undesirable in that it will reduce the seam sealers effectiveness. Any adhesive gotten between the sheets must be cleaned out.

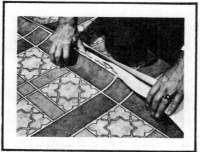
Insert scrap-seam area.

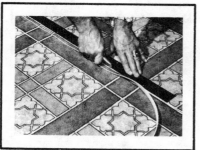
Hold knife at 90° angle.

Apply adhesive to dry zone with trowel.

Tuck sheet in place.

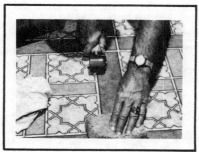
Level sheets with hand roller.

Adjust the design in the middle of the sheet and run a strip of wide tape across the seam to hold it in place until the adhesive sets. Do the same along the seam in both directions, adjusting the design and the seam for tightness placing the tape wherever needed.

Fit the turned up surplus to the walls and the tube back the uncemented portion of the second sheet, spread the adhesive on the subfloor and return the flooring material into the wet adhesive.

Vinyl foam backed material can be installed over existing resilient flooring. However, the existing flooring must be smooth, free of breaks or voids, non-cushioned and firmly bonded to the subfloor. The subfloor can be of either wood or concrete. The existing resilient flooring must be thoroughly prepared in advance of the installation.

SEAM SEALING

The final step, and an extremely important one in the completion of all cushioned vinyl flooring installations is the sealing of seams. All seams in cushioned products require seam sealing. Seam sealing fuses the wearlayer of the seamed sheets together keeping soil and water out and the seam will maintain its original appearance for the life of the floor.

NOZZLE

Just one type of applicator is all that is needed for sealing seams on all cushioned vinyl floors regardless of thickness.

SEAM SEALER APPLICATOR KIT

The Kit includes: 2 cleaning wires and an instruction sheet for using Seam Sealer.

1. Seams must be sealed immediately on completion of the installation. This will prevent foot traffic from soiling and darkening the seam prior to sealing. If traffic must flow across the flooring installation between the time the seam is cut and seam sealed, the seam should be protected from soil by a strip of masking tape.

2. All seams must be dry and free of soil. Any adhesive that may have oozed into the seams must be cleaned out. Otherwise a weak seam sealer weld will result.

3. The seam sealer should not be shaken within about 1/2 hour before using as this will cause air bubbles in the sealer. These air bubbles will transfer through the nozzle onto the seam causing sealer voids.

4. Fill the plastic bottle at least 1/2 full (or fuller, if desired), screw on the nozzle and tighten against leakage. The applicator has one fin with an elongated slot. This fin should be placed into the seam so that the side fins ride on the surface of the floor covering. Excessive downward pressure on the flooring material should be avoided.

Trimming overall design.

Trimming geometric design.

Applying adhesive–1st sheet.

Broom out air.

Align for pattern match.

Applying adhesive to seam area.

Tape seam in place.

5. Start at one end of the seam with continuous light pressure on the plastic bottle, move slowly without interruption down the seam, leaving a bead of sealer at least 1/8" wide centered on the seam. Do not release pressure on the plastic bottle while in the inverted position as air will be sucked into the tip forming air bubbles. The seam sealer should be allowed to dry for at least one hour before traffic of any type is permitted to move over the sealed seam.

6. When all seams have been sealed, pour the remaining in the plastic bottle back into the metal container or glass bottle and rinse the plastic bottle and nozzle with lacquer thinner. Insert the wire into the fin opening. Always store the seam sealer in the original container. If the sealer is allowed to remain in the plastic bottle it will gradually thicken and eventually harden.

Seam Sealers will thicken when exposed to freezing temperatures. This does not harm the seam sealer. Hold container under a warm water tap for a short time and the viscosity will return to normal.

If it should be necessary, small quantities of sealer can be removed after it has dried from the flooring material with lacquer thinner. Wet a clean cloth with lacquer thinner and go over the sealer with light pressure in a circular motion. Turn the cloth regularly using a clean place each time freshly wetted with lacquer thinner until the seam sealer is removed. The flooring surface will be dulled but the lustre can be restored by using Bon Ami Polishing Cleanser on a wet cloth or sponge. Go over the dull spot in a circular motion. Remove the cleanser with clean rinse water, dry the area and buff with a soft cloth to bring up lustre.

ADHESIVE

Directions — Fit the floor covering material to the room. Lay or roll back one half the sheet and expose the subfloor. Apply a band of adhesive around the perimeter of the room and then bands about one foot apart running the length of the room. Lay the flooring material back into the wet adhesive and then use an ordinary push broom to expel all trapped air from under the flooring material and completely flatten it against the subfloor. When applying adhesive to the seam area, apply to both sides of the seam about 3 inches from the seam line. Adhesive cleans up readily with water when still wet. Keep from freezing.

REPAIRING CUSHIONED VINYLS

Occasionally, it may be necessary to repair a cushioned vinyl floor. It is easily done. If at all possible, the material for the repair should come from the original installation.

This will avoid color variation. Many consumers will save the scrap pieces from the original installation which can be used for repair. If not, the repair material can generally be taken from under the refrigerator, stove, or from a closet. The size of the piece needed will be determined by the size of the repair on overall designs; on geometric patterns by the size of the design unit. A virtually invisible repair can be made on geometrics by replacing sections or complete design units.

The repair material should be slightly larger than the damaged spot to be replaced. On geometric designs, position the material for an exact pattern match and then tape firmly in place to avoid movement during cutting. Following a small straight edge or square with a sharp utility knife, apply sufficient pressure to cut through both pieces of material. Remove the damaged flooring wearlayer within the cut area. It will delaminate easily, leaving a layer of White Shield backing on the subfloor. This should not be removed. If the material was a left over scrap, it should be cemented to a piece of underlayment in advance and the removed.

Apply paste with your finger to the back of the repair patch. This will keep surplus adhesive from seeping up through the knife cut. Insert the patch and then roll thoroughly with a small hand roller bringing the wearlayers into level. The repair should then be completely seam sealed.

When making repairs, avoid attempting to follow curved or circular pattern designs, as the cut in the existing floor will usually turn out irregular and a poor repair results.

On overall patterns, a diamond shaped cut will make the least visible repair. First, tape the material to be used for the repair over the damaged area. Then following a small straight edge with a sharp utility knife, cut through both layers of flooring in a diamond shape large enough to remove the damaged spot. Peel out the area to be removed, paste the back of the patch and insert and roll with a hand roller.

After cleaning off excess adhesive and drying the area, all cuts should then be seam sealed.

Roll thoroughly.

Troweling adhesive - perimeter.

Seam Sealer Kit

Bring wearlayers level.

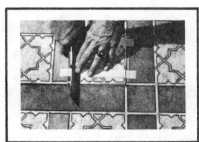

Seam seal all cuts.

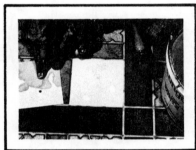

Avoid excessive downward pressure against flooring.

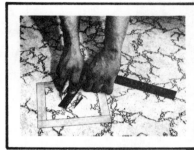

Make diamond cut-overall patterns.

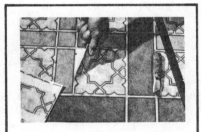

Tape to floor.

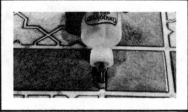

Paste back with finger.

Insert slot into seam.

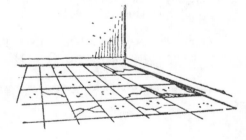

Remove damaged area.

SETTING TILE

YOUR PROBLEM

Tiles have come loose from walls or floor.

Tiles are damaged, need replacing.

WHAT YOU NEED

Something to mix in.

Tile adhesive for the kind of tile you have.

Paint brush or putty knife.

Knife or saw.

New tile (if needed.)

Grout—for ceramic or plastic tile.

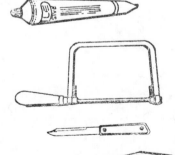

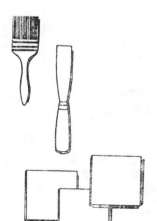

363

HOW-TO—FLEXIBLE TILE

1. Remove loose or damaged tile. A warm iron will help soften the adhesive. (Fig. 1)

2. Scrape off the old adhesive from the floor or wall. Also from the tile if you're to use it again. (Fig. 2)

3. Fit tiles carefully. Some tile can be cut with a knife or shears, others with a saw. Tile is less apt to break if it is warm. (Fig. 3)

4. Spread adhesive on the floor or wall with a paint brush or putty knife. (Fig. 4)

5. Wait until adhesive begins to set before placing the tile. Press tile on firmly. (A rolling pin works well.) (Fig. 5)

FOR CERAMIC OR PLASTIC TILE

1. Scrape off the old adhesive from the floor or wall. Also from old tile if you use it again. (Fig. 6)

2. If you are using new tile and need to fit it, mark it carefully to size. Cut it with a saw. You can make straight cuts on tile by scoring it first. Then it will snap off if you press it on the edge of a hard surface. (Fig. 7)

3. Spread adhesive on the wall or floor and on the back of the tile. Press tile firmly into place. (Fig. 8)

4. Joints on ceramic tile should be filled with grout after the tile has firmly set. Mix grout (powder) with water to form a stiff paste. Press the mixture into the joints with your fingers. Smooth the surface. (Fig. 9)

5. Carefully remove excess grout from the tile surface before it dries. (Fig. 10)

6. Empty excess grout mixture. (Not down the drain!) Clean up surfaces and tools. (Fig. 11)

7. Let grout dry overnight before it gets wet again.

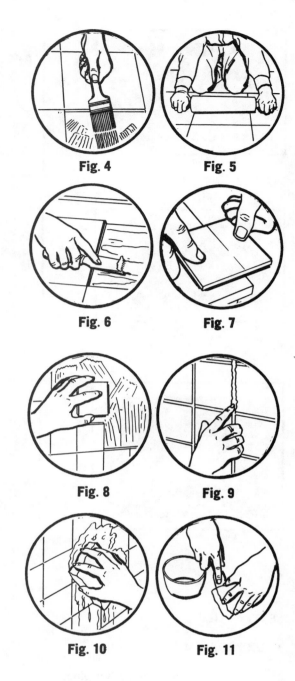

Fig. 4   Fig. 5

Fig. 6   Fig. 7

Fig. 8   Fig. 9

Fig. 10   Fig. 11

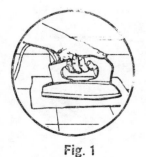

Fig. 1

Fig. 2   Fig. 3

VINYL FLOOR TREATMENTS

HOW TO COPE WITH MAINTENANCE PROBLEMS

PROBLEM	CAUSE	SOLUTION
Dull Appearance	Improper cleaning and rinsing of floor. Wrong finish used.	In areas with very hard water, the rinse water will have to be taken up with a very well "wrung out" mop, then dry floor with absorbent cloth.
	Porous floor.	Clean floor completely and then finish with wax. Apply two thin coats allowing adequate drying time (at least one hour) between coats. Do not use heavy duty (solvent containing) cleaners.
	Too much grit being tracked in.	Protect entryways with mats or scatter rugs. (Avoid rubber backed mats or rugs).
Yellowed film (build-up of wax)	Too many coats of wax in non-traffic areas.	Remove old finish with Floor Cleaner and ammonia following directions on cleaner label. Apply thin coat of Vinyl Dressing. When spot polishing, apply vinyl dressing to dull area.
	Wrong finish.	Remove old finish with Floor Cleaner. Apply thin coat of Vinyl Dressing.
Tacky finish	Too much finish. Wrong finish.	Remove old finish with Floor Cleaner. Apply a thin coat of Vinyl Dressing.
Black Heel Marks	Some rubber heels will mark any flooring.	Rub with wet Bon Ami Polishing Cleanser and rinse thoroughly. Apply Vinyl Dressing.
	Wrong finish.	Clean floor with Floor Cleaner and apply Vinyl Dressing.
Uneven glossy and dull appearance	Uneven finish.	Remove all old finish completely with Floor Cleaner. Then apply Vinyl Dressing evenly as directed.
	Dirty mop or applicator.	
Faded, washed-out appearance	Heavy-duty cleaners crystallizing finishes.	Use Floor Cleaner. Apply Vinyl Dressing.
Traffic paths (yellowing)	Improper maintenance.	Scrub areas with a strong detergent solution. Apply Vinyl Dressing periodically. Renew finish as needed. Check for track-in sources, such as paint, asphalt driveways, oil, concrete, etc.
	Track-in of asphalt, oil soluble pigments or dyes and rubber chemicals.	Yellowing caused by these materials cannot be removed by any practical procedure. They must be avoided, insofar as possible.

REMOVAL OF STUBBORN STAINS

1. Prevention is the most desirable way to avoid staining problems. Products that contain artificial colorants are most likely to cause staining. Items, such as shoe dyes, food dyes, crayons, finger paints and fruit flavored sodas may cause staining unless cleaned up promptly.

2. To avoid loss of gloss, use the least abrasive method of cleaning that is effective for the specific cleaning problem. When a cleanser is required, use Bon Ami Polishing Cleanser only. Remember, most spills "clean up" fast if done promptly.

STAINS AND SPILLS	TREATMENT
1. Acids, Alkalies, Cleansers, Strong Soaps, Alcoholic Beverages, Catsup, Coffee, Food, Dye Markings, Fruit and Fruit Juice, Ink, Iodine, Vegetables, Mercurochrome, Mustard.	1. Wash area with wet cloth or Floor Cleaner. If necessary rub with wet Bon Ami Polishing Cleanser. Rub lightly with a cloth moistened with a 10 to 1 dilution of liquid bleach. Apply Vinyl Dressing when dry, if necessary.
2. Rubber Heel Marks, Shoe Polish, Smudges and Scuffs.	2. Rub lightly with wet Bon Ami Polishing Cleanser then rinse. Apply Vinyl Dressing when dry, if necessary.
3. Lacquer, Nail Polish, Asphalt, Candle Wax, Chewing Gum, Grease, Oil, Tar, Candy, Adhesives, Plaster.	3. Remove excess with a dull kitchen knife. Rub lightly with a solvent such as Carbona, then rinse. Apply Viny Dressing when dry, if necessary.

STAINS AND SPILLS	TREATMENT
4. Rust, Mildew, Dyes, Blood, Grass.	4. Rub lightly with a 10 to 1 dilution of liquid bleach, then rinse. If rust stain does not respond, use a solution of cream of tartar or lemon juice. Apply Vinyl Dressing when dry, if necessary.
5. Oil Base Paints, Solvents, Varnish, Dry Cleaning Fluids.	5. Take up immediately with blotting action. Then rub lightly with a detergent and water and rinse. If dry, try to peel the film from the floor.
6. Shellac.	6. Blot up the excess while wet. If necessary, rub lightly with cloth dipped in alcohol, then rinse. Apply Vinyl Dressing when dry, if necessary.
7. Urine, Excrement.	7. Use Floor Cleaner. If stain is old and does not respond, use 10 to 1 solution of liquid bleach. Apply Vinyl Dressing when dry, if necessary.

COMPARATIVE DATA ON RESILIENT FLOORS

TYPE OF FLOOR AND BASIC COMPONENTS	OVERALL GAUGE	WEAR LAYER	COMMERCIAL	LIGHT COMMERCIAL	RESIDENTIAL	BELOW GRADE	ON GRADE	SUSPENDED	DURABILITY (d)	EASE OF MAINTENANCE	CIGARETTE BURN RESISTANCE (e)	RESILIENCE (f)	QUIETNESS
Vinyl Corlon flooring Vinyl resins with asbestos-fiber back (Hydrocord)	.160"	.035"	•	•	•	•	•	•	E	VG	F	E	E
	.080"	.040"	•	•	•	•	•	•	VG	G	F	F	A
(Quiet Zone II has Cushioncord vinyl-foam backing.)	.090"	.050"	•	•	•	•	•	•	E	VG	F	F	A
	.090"	.050"		•	•	•	•	•	E	VG	F	F	A
	.070"	.030"		•	•	•	•	•	VG	VG	F	F	A
	.065"	.025"			•	•	•	•	G	VG	F	F	A
	.070"	.030"			•	•	•	•	VG	VG	F	F	A
No-wax flooring Exclusive Mirabond surface	.075"	.035"			•	•	•	•	VG	S	P	F	F
	.070"	.030"			•	•	•	•	VG	S	P	F	F
	.065"	.020"			•	•	•	•	VG	S	P	F	F
Cushioned rotovinyl with Mirabond surface	.070"	.010"			•	•	•	•	VG	S	P	G	G
Cushioned vinyl flooring with vinyl backing	.080"	.013"			•	•	•	•	VG	E	P	G	G
Cushioned rotovinyl Foamed-vinyl layer with asbestos-fiber back	.070"	.010"			•	•	•	•	VG	E	P	G	G
Excelon Vinyl-asbestos Vinyl resins and	1/8",3/32"	1/8",3/32"	•	•	•	•	•	•	S,E	E	VG	F	A
	1/8"	1/8"	•	•	•	•	•	•	S	E	VG	F	A
	1/8"	1/8"		•	•	•	•	•	VG	VG	VG	F	A
	3/32"	Surface effects		•	•	•	•	•	G	G	VG	F	A
	Service	not through entire		•	•	•	•	•	G	G	VG	F	A
	Service gauge	thickness		•	•	•	•	•	G	E,G	VG	F	A
	1/8"	1/8" (g)				•	•	•	S	(h)	VG	F	A
Through-grained vinyl composition	1/8"	1/8"	•	•	•	•	•	•	S	E-S	VG	F	A
Vinyl cove base	.080"	.080"	•	•	•	•	•	•					

SUBFLOOR APPLICATION (b)

(b) BELOW GRADE—Partially or completely below the surrounding grade or ground level in direct contact with the ground or a fill which is in direct contact with the ground. ON GRADE—in direct contact with ground. SUSPENDED—Above, on, or below grade level with minimum of 18" of well-ventilated air space below.

(d) Ratings based on abrasion tests to determine surface wear-through or loss of pattern definition, whichever occurred first.

(e) NEMA Method LP-2.204, Modification Time—2 min.

(f) Potential underfoot comfort.

• Ratings are subjective and compare relative qualities of the various flooring materials.

Interpret as follows:
S—Superior
E—Excellent
VG—Very Good
G—Good
F—Fair
A—Acceptable
P—Poor

(g) Recommended only for decorative accent spots, bands, and borders.

(h) Dependent upon the particular flooring used in the floor field.

Where hygiene and decontamination are not absolute requirements, resilient tile floors should not be dismissed as unsanitary. They are also easy to maintain because precision factory cutting assures tight joints and close-fitting edges between each tile.

Moreover, resilient floors in tile form offer distinct advantages—some practical, some aesthetic. Where the floor area is unusually irregular in shape because of juts and recesses, tile floors can sometimes be installed with less waste of material than 6'-wide sheet material. Also, tiles permit an infinite variety of floor designs through placement of two or more contrasting colors of various stylings in custom arrangements of squares, rectangles, bands, and triangles.

FINISHING

After wax stripping, or as often as needed after the light-duty cleaning step, the floor should be finished. It is preferable to apply a thin coat so that the polish film can dry properly in a reasonable length of time.

Polymeric floor finishes should never be applied over waxy finishes because a streaky film may result. However, a waxy finish can be applied over a polymeric finish with satisfactory results.

Paste waxes or liquid solvent waxes, which contain solvents such as naphtha or turpentine, should not be used on resilient floors. Resilient floors should never be treated with lacquers, varnishes, or similar finishes, because they tend to discolor, show foot-traffic lanes, and are difficult to remove.

NO-WAX

CLEANING

Remove loose dirt by sweeping or vacuuming before it can be ground into the surface. In areas where especially gritty dirt, sand, cinders, or small stones are encountered, mats or small rugs should be placed at entrances to reduce the amount tracked in. (CAUTION: Mats with rubber backing should not be used, because they can stain the floor.)

On a regular basis, as needed, the floor should be thoroughly cleaned to remove built-up dirt or film. Use a synthetic general-purpose detergent recommended for floors. Do not use soap-based products which can leave a dulling film.

Rinse thoroughly with clean, warm water. For stubborn dirt, use a nylon cleaning pad. Steel wool and scouring cleansers should not be used.

STAIN RESISTANCE

One of the advantages of resilient flooring is the ease with which accidentally spilled materials can be cleaned up. Whether or not such materials stain the surface of the flooring depends on the nature of the staining agent and how quickly it is removed. All resilient floorings resist staining

or softening by most materials that might normally be spilled on the floor.

Some common materials, including mustard, certain shoe polishes, tincture of Merthiolate, and hair color preparations, will stain resilient flooring. For this reason, special care should be taken to avoid spills.

Some solvents such as aromatic or chlorinated hydrocarbons, ketones, and esters may soften resilient flooring. In cleaning such spills, care must be taken to avoid damaging the softened area, and it should not be walked on until it is completely dried out. The Mirabond finish, unlike the surface of most other resilient floorings, will be softened by alcohol.

PRICE VARIATIONS IN FLOORING MATERIALS

Resilient floorings are manufactured in several types and gauges to meet various service requirements. In many cases, each type is made in a number of stylings to permit greater freedom of selection. These factors affect cost:

Type and style of the resilient flooring—Type of backing—Gauge or thickness of the material—Color and graining—Standard or special sizes.

One of the items often omitted from resilient flooring specifications is the naming of the particular flooring style and color group. This part of the specification is a very important factor in figuring costs. For example, sheet Vinyl Corlon falls into several price groupings according to gauge, style, and backing.

One of the clearest ways to specify resilient floorings is to indicate the manufacturer's name and color number. When this is not possible, or if a floor design cannot be selected in advance, it is important that a clear understanding be given of the percentage of each material to be used.

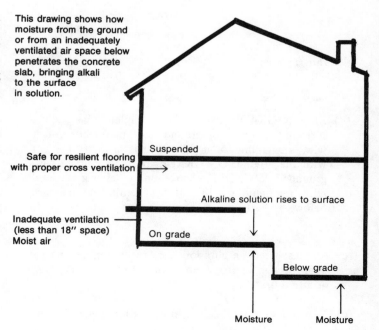

This drawing shows how moisture from the ground or from an inadequately ventilated air space below penetrates the concrete slab, bringing alkali to the surface in solution.

Suspended

Safe for resilient flooring with proper cross ventilation →

Alkaline solution rises to surface

Inadequate ventilation (less than 18" space) Moist air

On grade

Below grade

Moisture   Moisture

PRODUCT		weights oz./sq. yd.	standard sizes	description
CUSHION-AIRE® SUPREME "120" (Blue) **ROYAL CUSHION-AIRE®** (Purple) **CUSHION-AIRE® DELUXE** (Red) — Waffle type. Available in fire retardant FHA quality at nominal additional cost.		SUPREME 120 oz. .540 ga. ROYAL 100 oz. .500 ga. DELUXE 90 oz. .440 ga.	Seamless Widths: 36in., 54in., 9ft. Lengths: Supreme and Royal 50ft. Deluxe 60ft.	**CUSHION-AIRE®**, available in the three qualities: Supreme, Royal, and Deluxe, is luxury unsurpassed. Judged the finest underlay that money can buy for extra heavy duty commercial and luxury installations. Reinforced with heavy fabric backing. For use on or above grade; conventional or radiant heating.
CHAMPION (Blue) **CLASSIC** (Gold) **WHITEHALL** (White) — Waffle type. Available in fire retardant FHA quality at nominal additional cost.		CHAMPION 100 oz. .500 ga. CLASSIC 80 oz. .440 ga. WHITEHALL 72 oz. .440 ga.	Seamless Widths: 36in., 54in., 9ft. Lengths: Champion 50ft. Classic and Whitehall 60ft.	**CHAMPION, CLASSIC, WHITEHALL** are sponge rubber products for use where luxury is the goal, but, economy is a consideration. Spunbonded polyester Wundabac backing. For use on or above grade; conventional or radiant heating.
CONTOUR® DELUXE (White) — Waffle type. Available in fire retardant FHA quality at nominal additional cost.		CONTOUR DELUXE 68 oz. .440 ga.	Seamless Widths: 36in., 54in., 9ft. Lengths: 75ft.	**CONTOUR® DELUXE** is a permanently resilient cushion with a high density pattern face. Spunbonded polyester Wundabac backing. For use on or above grade; conventional or radiant heating.
VANGUARD (Green) **CHALLENGE** (Orange) — Waffle type. Available in fire retardant FHA quality at nominal additional cost.		VANGUARD 64 oz. .440 ga. CHALLENGE 56-60 oz. .420 ga.	Seamless Widths: 36in., 54in., 9ft. Lengths: 75ft.	**VANGUARD, CHALLENGE** are medium-priced sponge rubber cushions. Spunbonded polyester Wundabac backing. For use on or above grade; conventional or radiant heating.
COMET (Pink) **CORSAIR** (Copper Gold) — Waffle type. Only COMET available in fire retardant FHA quality at nominal additional cost.		COMET 48 oz. .410 ga. CORSAIR 42 oz. .400 ga.	Seamless Widths: 36in., 54in., 9ft. Lengths: 100ft.	**COMET, CORSAIR** are economy priced sponge rubber cushions. Spunbonded polyester Wundabac backing. For use on or above grade; conventional or radiant heating.
AIRLITE SUPREME (White) **AIRLITE DELUXE** (Red) — FLAT type. Available in fire retardant FHA (Pill Test) or Steiner Tunnel test qualities at nominal additional cost.		AIRLITE SUPREME 95 oz. .375 ga. AIRLITE DELUXE 72 oz. .310 ga.	Seamless Widths: 36in., 54in., 9ft. Lengths: 60ft.	**AIRLITE** is our premium quality FLAT type sponge rubber cushion. Spunbonded polyester Wundabac backing. Recommended for heaviest commercial installations. For use on or above grade; conventional or radiant heating.
PALISADE (Blue) — FLAT type. Available in fire retardant FHA (Pill Test) or Steiner Tunnel test qualities at nominal additional cost.		PALISADE 56 oz. .300 ga.	Seamless Widths: 36in., 54in., 9ft. Lengths: 75ft.	**PALISADE** is our medium grade FLAT sponge rubber cushion. Spunbonded polyester. Recommended for commercial installation. For use on or above grade; conventional or radiant heating.

PRODUCT		weights oz./sq. yd.	standard sizes	description
RUBBER-EASE conventional hair and India fiber cushion. Designed rubberized back for added strength and resiliency. Meets Fire Retardant Requirements as set forth in ASTM E84, Surface Burning Characteristics of Building Materials.		50 56 64	Widths: 27in., 36in., 6ft., 12ft. Lengths: 60ft. (64oz.—30ft.)	**RUBBER-EASE** is a double waffle carpet cushion, composed of an all animal hair top, free from dye, with a specially selected fiber center. It is reinforced with a designed rubberized application on the back. U.S. Testing Co. wear tests prove this product to be superior in minimizing carpet wear. **RUBBER-EASE** is proved best for sound absorption by the acoustical consultants for the Carpet & Rug Institute. Specifically designed for schools, commercial installations, and wherever maximum wear and resilience are required. RUBBER-EASE will double the life of your carpet selection.
PRINCETON OR SILVER-STEP India fiber with rubberized designed surfaces. Meets all FHA requirements, including flammability test ASTM E84.		32 40 50 54 64	Widths: 27in., 36in., 6ft., 12ft. Lengths: 60ft. (64oz.—30ft.)	**PRINCETON OR SILVER STEP CARPET CUSHIONS** contain a blend of animal hair and India fibers. The fiber center core is secured by a rubberized process on both surfaces. Princeton and Silver-Step meet or exceed the requirements of FHA Specification DDD-C-001023, in FHA Bulletin UM-44b. For application above, on, or below grade. Treated for moth protection. PRINCETON—colorfast Cocoa Brown; SILVER STEP—colorfast Silver.
CAMBRIDGE India fiber with rubberized designed surfaces.		32 40 50 54 64	Widths: 27in., 36in., 6ft., 12ft. Lengths: 60ft. (64oz.—30ft.)	**CAMBRIDGE CARPET CUSHION** contains a blend of selected India fibers. This fiber center core is secured by rubberized process on both surfaces. All materials are new, clean and tested for moth protection. For application above, on, or below grade. CAMBRIDGE—colorfast Cocoa Brown.
RUBBER-STEP the ultimate in commercial type rubberized carpet cushion. Conforms to specifications of the U. S. Public Health Service. Meets all FHA requirements, including flammability test ASTM E84.		52 56	Widths: 27in., 36in., 6ft., 12ft. Lengths: 60ft.	**RUBBER-STEP CARPET CUSHION** is a blend of specially selected India fibers. This fiber center core is held secure by rubberized process on both surfaces. Waffle pattern on floor side surface improves cushioning and adhesion to carpet and floor. For application above, on, or below grade. Applicable for conventional heated floors. Treated for moth protection. Colorfast Green.
ALL-HAIR 100% animal hair waffle top. Meets all FHA requirements.		40 50 64	Widths: 27in., 36in., 6ft., 12ft. Lengths: 60ft. (64oz.—30ft.)	**ALL-HAIR CARPET CUSHION** contains 100% all new and clean animal hair and is made with non-woven, high-tensile strength interliner. It is suitable for application above, on, or below grade. It is applicable to conventional or radiant heated floors. ALL-HAIR is BROWN in color. FREE FROM DYE, and it is treated for moth protection.
SPRING-STEP animal hair, waffle top, India fiber back.		32 40 50 54 64	Widths: 27in., 36in., 6ft., 12ft. Lengths: 60ft. (64oz.—30ft.)	**SPRING-STEP CARPET CUSHION** is a blend of all new and clean animal hair and India jute fiber. Waffle top face is animal hair free from dye. Back is reinforced India jute fiber. It is applicable to conventional or radiant heated floors. It is BROWN in color and treated for moth protection.

CARPET CONSTRUCTION

Carpet made by inserting face yarn or tufts through pre-manufactured backing by use of needles, similar in principle to a sewing machine. Yarns are held in place by coating back with latex and secondary back is applied to add body and stability. A variety of textures is possible. Represents approximately 87% of contract carpet used today.

A woven carpet will be either Velvet, Axminster or Wilton. The face and back are formed by the interweaving of the warp and weft yarns. The warp yarns run lengthwise and usually consist of chain, stuffer and pile yarns. The weft yarns or "shot" run across the width. The weft yarns bind in the pile and weave in the stuffer and chain yarns which form the carpet back.

The simplest of all carpet weaves. Pile is formed as loom loops warp yarns over wires inserted across loom. Pile height is determined by height of wire inserted. Velvets are traditionally known for smooth cut pile plush or loop pile textures, but can also create hi-lo loop or cut-uncut textures. Usually carpet is solid, moresque or striped in color. Represents approximately 7% of commercial carpet used today.

The Wilton loom operates basically the same as a velvet loom with the addition of a Jacquard mechanism with up to 6 colors or frames. Due to one color being utilized in surface at a time, other yarns remain buried in the body of the carpet until utilized. Wilton looms can produce cut pile, level loop, multi-level or carved textures. Represents approximately 3% of commercial carpet used today.

The Axminister loom is highly specialized and nearly as versatile as hand weaving. Color combinations and designs are limited only by the number of tufts in the carpet. Almost all the yarn appears on the surface and characteristic of this weave is a heavy ribbed back allowing carpet to be rolled length-wise only. Axministers produce single level cut pile textures. Represent less than 1% of commercial carpet used today.

Process produces complete carpet by imbedding pile yarns and adhering backing to a viscous vinyl paste which hardens after curing carpet. Has superior tuft bind and practically eliminates backing delamination. Over 90% of yarn is in the face. Fusion bonded process produces very dense cut pile or level loop fabrics in solid or moresque colors. Represents approximately 1% of commercial carpet used today.

The knitted process resembles weaving in that the face and back are made simultaneously. Backing and pile yarns are looped together with a stitching yarn on machines with 3 sets of needles. Knitted carpets are usually solid or tweed in color with a level loop pile texture. Represents less than 1% of the commercial carpet used today.

In tufted carpet, gauge is the spacing of needles across the width of the tufting machine expressed in fractions of an inch: 1/8 gauge = 8 ends or needles/inch.

The calculation by multiplying the number of ends across the width (gauge or pitch) by the number of tufts lengthwise (stitches or rows) per inch.

The height of the loop or tuft from the surface of the backing to the top of the pile is measured in fractions or decimals of an inch.

The total weight of pile yarns in the carpet measured in ox/yd.^{2} This excludes backing yarns or fabric.

A calculation used to measure the compactness of face yarns in a carpet. Increased density generally results in better performance.

Cotton Count: The number of 840 yard lengths per pound. Thus, a 1.00 cc has 840 yards/lb., etc. The higher the cotton count number the finer the yarn. Acrylic's, acrylic blends, polyester and spun nylon are usually referred to by cotton count. Examples: 2.14 cc. 2.65 cc. Other counts used are worsted count and woolen run.

Denier: The unit of weight for the size of a single filament yarn. The higher the denier number the heavier the yarn. Denier is equivalent to the number of grams per 9,000 meters. Examples: 1300 denier, 2600 denier. BCF nylon and polpropylene are expressed in denier.

Ply: the number of single ends of yarn twisted together to form a heavier, larger yarn. Ply is not a measure of quality. Example: 1300/3 (3 ends of 1300 denier yarn plied together).

Density Formula
$$D = \frac{36W}{H}$$

W= Average Pile Yarn Weight in ounces per square yard.
H= Average Pile Height in inches.
EXAMPLE: W= Carpet containing 40 oz. of pile yarn
H= Pile Height of .250 (8/32")

$$D = \frac{36W}{H} = \frac{36 \times 40}{.250} = 5760$$

The foundation construction which supports the pile yarns. Primary Backing: In tufted carpet, a woven or non-woven fabric into which pile yarns are attached; usually jute or polypropylene. In woven carpets backing yarns are usually kraftcord, cotton, polyester, jute or rayon.

Secondary Backing: An extra layer of material laminated to the underside of the carpet for additional dimensional stability and body. Usually latex, jute, H.D. foam, sponge rubber or vinyl.

CARPET CONSTRUCTION CHARACTERISTICS

A carpet construction specification prescribes how a carpet is to be manufactured without reference to its end use or performance. Here are the construction criteria you will look at most closely.

Magnification continuous filament yarn

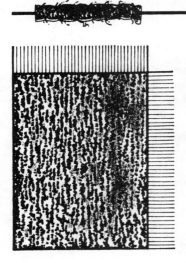

Number of tufts per sq. inch is determined by multiplying needles corresponding to a particular pitch or gauge by rows or stitches per inch. Example: 1/8 gauge, 8 needles times 8 stitches per inch equals 64 tufts per square inch.

PILE HEIGHT

.187

.218

.250

WIRE HEIGHT

.187

.218

.250

GAUGE (Tufted Fabric)

The distance between two needle points expressed in fractions of an inch.

 1/8"    1/10"    5/64"

STITCHES

The number of lengthwise yarn tufts in one inch of carpet.

 8

 10

 12.8

PITCH (Woven Fabric)

The number of single ends per 27 inches of width.

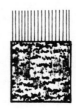 216   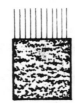 230    346

ROWS

The number of lengthwise yarn tufts in one inch of carpet.

 8

 10

 12.8

Pitch to Gauge Conversions

Pitch	108	143.9	172.8	180	189	216	243	252	256	270	346
Needles	4	5.3	6.4	6.6	7	8	9	9.3	9.5	10	12.8
Gauge	1/4	3/16	5/32		9/64	1/8	1/9			1/10	5/64

—Face Yarn
—Primary Backing
—Latex
—Secondary Backing

FACE FIBER

"the face yarn of carpet shall be pile of 100% 'Ultron' advanced generation nylon" or "the face yarn shall be advanced generation soil hiding, static resistant nylon fiber."

Pile Weight per Square Yard

Pile weight is measured in ounces per square yard. It is the amount of yarn used in the pile of the carpet, excluding the primary backing.

Total Weight
Pile weight + Latex + Backing = Total Weight

YARN PLY

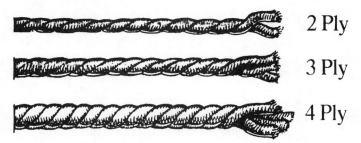

2 Ply

3 Ply

4 Ply

CONSTRUCTION METHODS

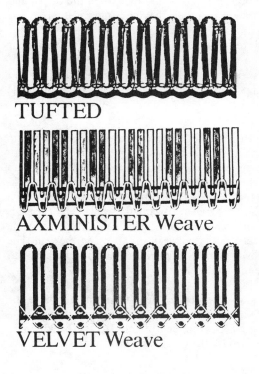

TUFTED

AXMINISTER Weave

VELVET Weave

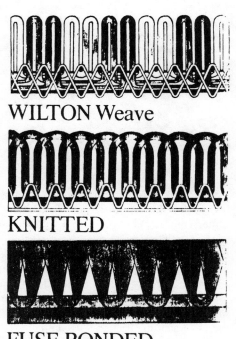

WILTON Weave

KNITTED

FUSE-BONDED

TILE

Under the heading of tile, we will include Ceramic Mosaic Tile, Slate, Blue Stone, Flagstone, Quarry Tile and Terrazzo. Terrazzo is nothing more than a concrete mix with marble chips mixed in. After setting, the entire floor is ground with a grinding machine for a smooth, even, colorful finish. Quarry Tile is installed the same as Ceramic Tile. (See Wall Finishes/Ceramic Tile) Slate, Bluestone and Flagstone must be pre-fitted before installation over a concrete base. Be sure to use the non-slip type Ceramic Mosaic Tile on floors.

CARPET

You cannot afford to purchase a cheap carpet. The cost of installation for expensive or inexpensive carpeting is the same. The second time around will cost you as much as, if not more than, a good quality carpet the first time. There is no surface that gets more abuse or wear than a floor. In the course of a few years, a carpet will be trampled by millions of feet, stained by gallons of liquid, have tons of dirt rubbed into its fibers and be subjected to hundreds of scrubbings, no carpet can take it all and not all carpets can take it. The secret----vacuum, vacuum, vacuum and soak up spills immediately.

Sun will fade carpets, especially dyed fibers. The carpet industry has a standard for lightfastness in dyed carpets by continuous exposure of 80 hours of Xenon lamp. Carpets in low humidity or inside air-conditioned buildings can build up static electricity, at best, a nuisance, at worst, a hazard. The level of human sensitivity to static electricity is 2.5 to 3 kilovolts. Before buying carpets check the static electricity build-up factor otherwise you will keep getting a shock everytime you touch a light switch or plug in your appliances, or turn a doorknob.

Your choice of carpet fiber is an important part of carpet performance:

DENSITY—- is weight of fiber per unit of volume. It varies with the denier of the yarn and the closeness of tufts and inversely with the pile height. The heavier the traffic the higher the density should be.

CONSTRUCTION—high traffic areas call for low pile-low traffic area a high pile will not jeopardize the carpet performance.

COLOR—should vary according to nature of soiling: beige in a sandy area, grey or blue where there is industrial soot, red or tan where soil is predominantly clay. That way carpets will hide dirt better and reduce cost of maintenance.

TESTS

1. Crush test measures resiliency and luxuriousness.

2. Pile test measures spot ignition of a carpet.

3. Tabor abrasion test measures the resistance to wear.

4. Tuft withdrawal tensometer measures how strongly the tufts are bonded to the backing.

5. Delamination test makes sure that when the carpet and backing are put together, they will stay together.

6. Tetrapod test puts 100,000 footsteps worth of wear and soil on the carpet to tell what effect the amount of traffic has on a carpet in terms of fuzzing, crushing and general appearance.

The tackless strip method should have a detached cushion or backing underneath, a tackless strip is a wood strip with two or more rows of rust resistance pins embeded, point up at an angle. These strips are nailed to the floor, carpet thickness away from the walls around the entire perimeter of the room with the pins angled toward the walls. The carpet is stretched in all directions and locked or hooked onto the pins, then forced down between the strip and the wall. The direct glue-down method involves glueing the carpet with adhesive, directly to the floor.

Any carpet, glue-down or tackless strip will not have the same wear life of the same carpet installed over a pad. Some carpets have a cushion bonded directly to the backing and is usually installed by the glue-down method.

Maintenance of a carpet plays an important part on the wear. The best and least expensive method of caring is preventative maintenance. Frequent vacuuming will make routine maintenance and cleaning easier and more effective. The grit below the surface of the pile causes an abrasive effect wearing down the fibers. These are removed or lessended by frequent vacuuming. The single most difficult problem in carpet maintenance is that of spilling and stains. Immediate action following a spill can work wonders on stains. If allowed to dry it may become difficult or impossible to remove completely. If the carpet cannot be removed for cleaning, good results can be obtained through rotary shampooing, steam extraction or dry foam cleaning. Do not overwet the carpet during cleaning.

In patching carpet to remove burned or permanently stained areas, cut out as small a piece as possible using square or rectangular cuts, cutting between the rows and minimizing cutting of tufts. Care should be taken to make sure the plug or patch has the same pile direction as the field of material and material from the same run should be used for the plug. When carpet is installed, save the excess for patching.

In selecting carpet cushion or backing, use caution. A soft cushion is squashed by each foot step stretching the carpet until it breaks. A firm cushion is best for long carpet life. Cushion is the reason for long life. Tests have shown a carpet will last 20% longer with a cushion or backing. The secret is to select a cushion or backing with enough give to absorb impact shock and with enough firmness to keep supporting the carpet back to its resting position.

Following are guidelines for selecting carpet:

A. Know your budget for carpet including installation. Buy the best you can afford.

B. Be aware of types of traffic loads, potential pivot and funnel traffic flow-moderate-heavy-extra heavy.

C. Know the maximum life expectancy.

D. Make certain that maintenance levels will be maintained to achieve fair, good or excellent appearance for life expectancy required.

E. Make certain that the colors, textures or patterns under consideration will be compatible for the types of soiling, stains and wear that varies with the area of installation.

F. Know the type of surface textures that will be required.

G. Select the right gauge or pitch.

H. Will the carpet:
   a. Eliminate static shock?
   b. Have sufficient tuft bind strength?
   c. Meet flammability requirements?
   d. Have piling and fuzzing resistance?
   e. Have proper bond strength to prevent separation from the backing?
   f. Have crush and wear resistance?
   g. Have adequate resistance to fading or sunlight?

Proper carpet installation is of prime importance in ensuring maximum wear and appearance. A faulty installation can result in rippling, bubbling, split and open seams, buckling, creasing or folding, and baseboard climbing. There are two principal methods of installing carpet: the TACKLESS STRIP method and the DIRECT GLUE-DOWN method.

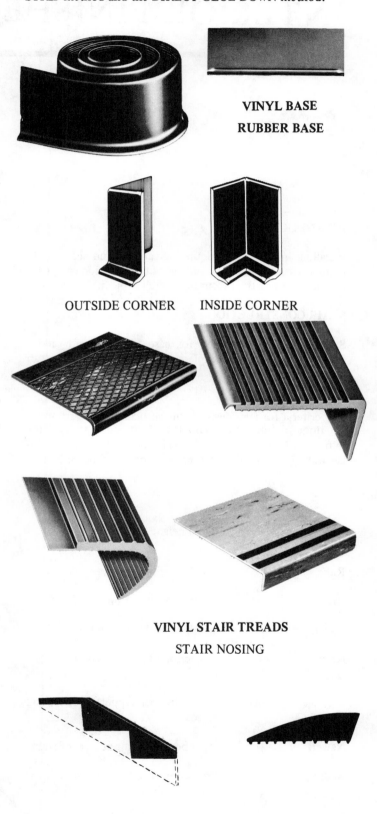

VINYL BASE
RUBBER BASE

OUTSIDE CORNER   INSIDE CORNER

VINYL STAIR TREADS
STAIR NOSING

STAIR MATERIAL   CARPET REDUCER

INTERIOR FINISHES

35

INTRODUCTION

Installing interior trim requires great care and accuracy in mating parts together. This phase of construction can greatly enhance or distract from the overall project.

STAIR CONSTRUCTION

Stairs should be designed for ease, comfort and safety. Stock stair parts for complete staircases of excellence can be selected from manufacturers catalogs and purchased from lumber dealers.

The criteria for stair design is the vertical distance from finish floor to finish floor and the width of the stairs. Minimum width should be 3'–6" wide from finish wall to finish wall. Terms used in stair construction may be defined as follows:

Rise:	Total height from floor to floor.
Run:	Total length of stairs.
Riser:	Vertical height of one step.
Tread:	Width of horizontal step.
Nosing:	Projection of tread beyond face of riser.
Carriage or Stringer:	Rough lumber supporting risers and treads.
Newel:	Main post of railing at start of stairs.
Railing:	Projection of open stair or wall for hand grasping.
Baluster:	Vertical member of railing supporting hand rail.
Winders:	Radiating or turns at stairs.
Landing:	Floor at top or bottom between stair endings of runs or flights.
Platform:	Intermediate landings between two parts of stairs.
Bullnose:	The first step which extends out forming a semi-circle after receiving the newel post.

The dimensions of treads and risers were established during the planning stage in order to prepare the rough stair opening. The total distance from floor to floor is divided by the number of risers to reach that distance. Risers should not exceed 8" in height. Between 7" and 8" is a comfortable height. The stair treads should not be less than 9" or more than 12". The total number of treads multiplied by the width or dimension of the tread will equal the stair run.

Stairs are made up of stringers cut from 2" x 12" with one on each side or wall and one in the center. Careful planning and cutting is necessary; if the risers are too high, the climb will strain the muscles and heart, if too low, the discomfort will be just as severe because of the multiple repetition of movement. If the tread is too short, the stair will be too steep and if too long will result in fatigue and waste of space. Experience has proven that a riser between 7" and 7-1/2" high offers the best comfort. Good stair ratio can be provided by using one of the following formulas: One tread plus two risers equal 24 or 25. One riser and one tread equal 17 or 18. One tread multiplied by one riser equal 70 to 75. The natural path or line of travel in climbing stairs which have a hand rail is taken at a distance of 1'–8" to 2'–0" from the rail. The minimum head room required at any point or part of overhead structures is 6'–6" measured vertically from the face of the riser. Try to avoid winders because the tread depth is decreased under the normal path of travel making the stairs potentially dangerous. Also, try to avoid a single step to sunken rooms because the likelihood of tripping is greater than with several steps.

Spiral or disappearing stairs are best obtained as a package from several manufacturers.

Referring to the model plans in Chapter 4, two flights of stairs will be necessary: basement to first floor and first floor to second floor. The vertical distance from basement to first floor is 8'—0" or 96", if the risers were 8", each divided by 96", will require 12 risers. There is always one tread less than the number of risers. 11 treads multiplied by 10" each will require 110" or a run of 9'—2".The distance from the first floor to second floor is 8'—4" or 100" divided by 13 risers will give us about 7—11/16" for each riser. 12 treads multiplied by 10" for each tread, will result in a run of 10'—0". With this information, the stringers can now be cut from 3 pieces of 2" x 12". All risers and treads should be of the same dimension for the same run. Be sure they are long enough to provide for the entire run without piecing

together more than one stringer,except at winders. In laying out the stair stringers, first make a template from 1" stock and use it as a model. Beginning at the top of the stairs,use the carpenters square by drawing the lines along the blades of the square set at the dimensions of the risers and treads. Repeat the process until all risers and treads are layed out-similar to roof rafters. Extreme accuracy is necessary in stringer layout because the stairs will be no better than the stringers. Use a sharp pencil and cut on the lines. Before the stringer is cut, substract from the first riser the thickness of the tread and the top riser will be shortened by the same thickness. Tread thickness is usally 1-1/8" oak, if exposed, and 2" (1-5/8") framing lumber if covered. Riser thickness is 3/4" stock. Don't forget the nosing which is generally about 1" more or less. If the stairway is enclosed, the stringers are nailed to the stud wall and if open stairs, they must be supported by 2" x 4", 16" apart under the stringers.

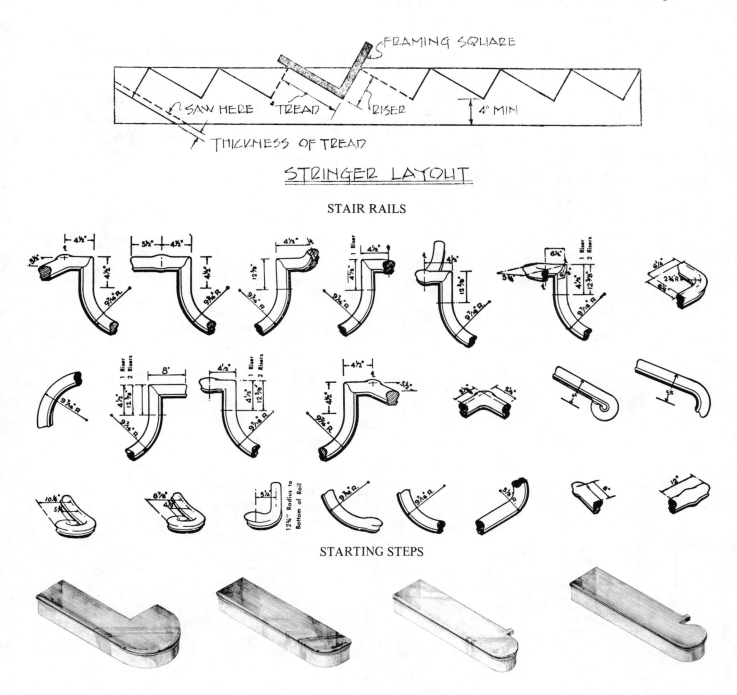

STRINGER LAYOUT

STAIR RAILS

STARTING STEPS

377

BALUSTERS

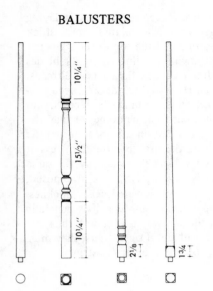

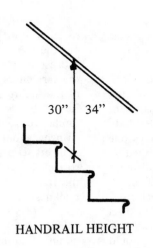

HANDRAIL HEIGHT

30"   34"

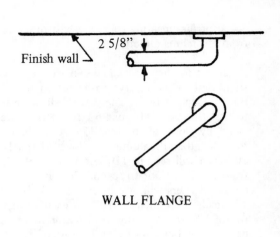

2 5/8"

Finish wall

WALL FLANGE

FOLDING–DISAPPEARING STAIRS

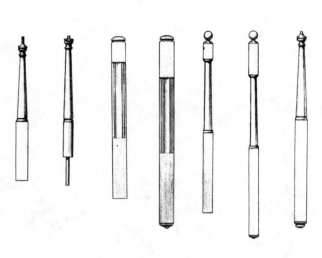

NEWEL POSTS

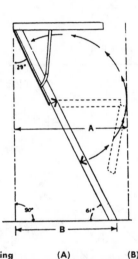

Ceiling Height	(A) Projection	(B) Landing Space
8'-5"	5'-0"	4'-10½"
8'-9"	5'-6"	5'-5"
10'-0"	6'-7"	6'-1"

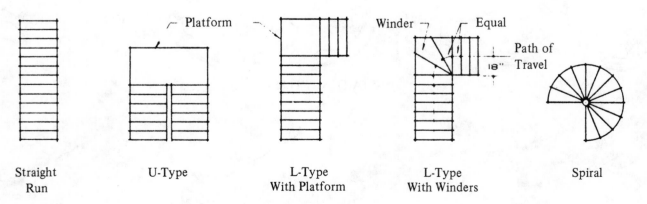

Platform

Winder   Equal

Path of Travel

18"

Straight Run   U-Type   L-Type With Platform   L-Type With Winders   Spiral

STAIR TYPES

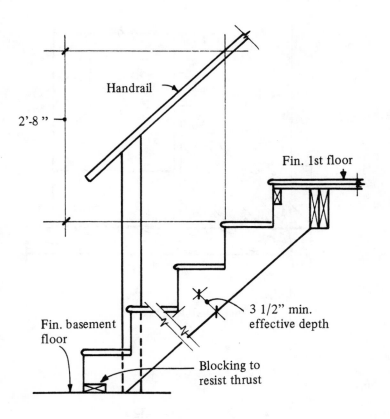

Handrail

2'-8"

Fin. 1st floor

Fin. basement floor

3 1/2" min. effective depth

Blocking to resist thrust

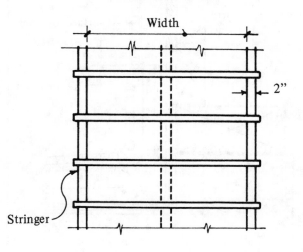

Width

2"

Stringer

Width - max. 30 in. for nominal 5/4 in. tread.
Factory-built stairs with wedged and glued treads and risers may be 3'-6" wide.

Provide an additional stringer when width exceeds the above figures.

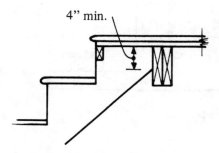

4" min.

OPEN-RISER BASEMENT STAIR FRAMING

Provide 4 inches (min.) solid bearing at header joists as shown at "A" or by other adequate methods of anchorage.

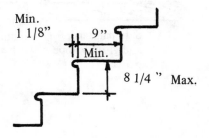

Min. 1 1/8"

9" Min.

8 1/4" Max.

HANDRAIL AND RAILING DETAILS

Handrails should be placed on the right side of stairs, descending. Horizontal dimension of handrail (grip) should not exceed 2 5/8". Handrails should return to wall or floor, or terminate in a post, scroll or loop (mandatory for housing for elderly or handicapped). Mounting height for stairs handrails should be 30" to 34". Railing height for stoops, porches, etc. should be at least 30"

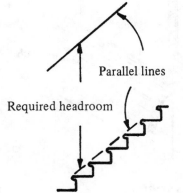

Parallel lines

Required headroom

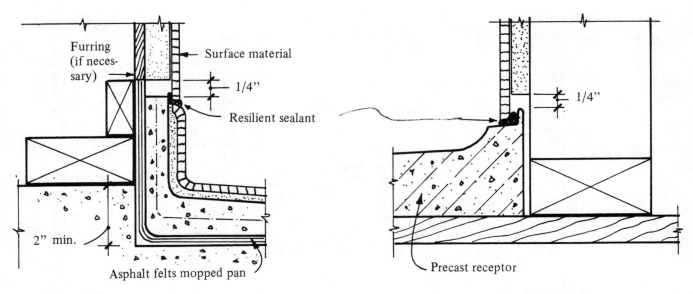

Furring (if necessary)

Surface material

1/4"

Resilient sealant

2" min.

Asphalt felts mopped pan

RECEPTOR ON CONCRETE SLAB

1/4"

Precast receptor

PRECAST RECEPTOR

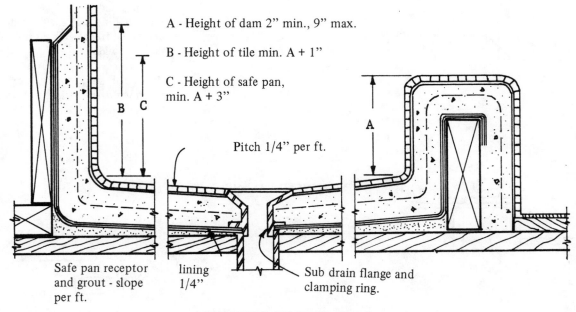

A - Height of dam 2" min., 9" max.

B - Height of tile min. A + 1"

C - Height of safe pan, min. A + 3"

B   C

Pitch 1/4" per ft.

A

Safe pan receptor and grout - slope per ft.

lining 1/4"

Sub drain flange and clamping ring.

RECEPTOR ON WOOD FLOOR

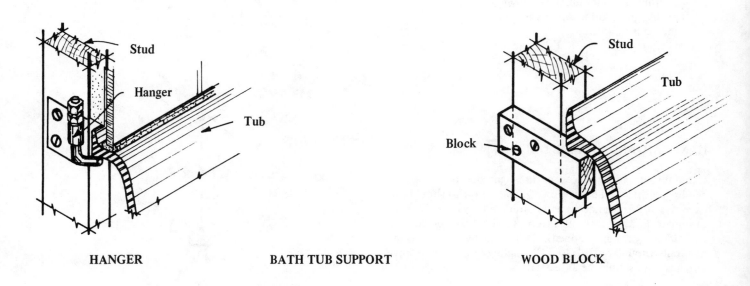

Stud

Hanger

Tub

HANGER

BATH TUB SUPPORT

Stud

Tub

Block

WOOD BLOCK

380

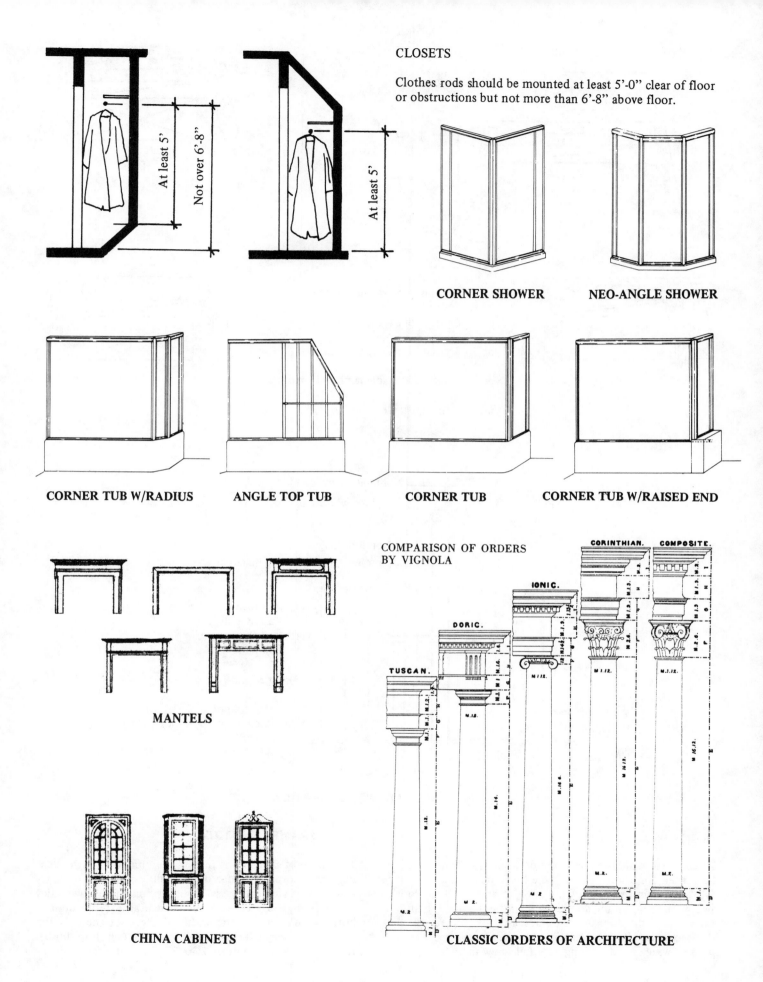

CLOSETS

Clothes rods should be mounted at least 5'-0" clear of floor or obstructions but not more than 6'-8" above floor.

At least 5'

Not over 6'-8"

At least 5'

CORNER SHOWER

NEO-ANGLE SHOWER

CORNER TUB W/RADIUS

ANGLE TOP TUB

CORNER TUB

CORNER TUB W/RAISED END

MANTELS

COMPARISON OF ORDERS BY VIGNOLA

TUSCAN.

DORIC.

IONIC.

CORINTHIAN.

COMPOSITE.

CHINA CABINETS

CLASSIC ORDERS OF ARCHITECTURE

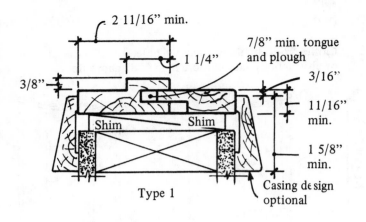

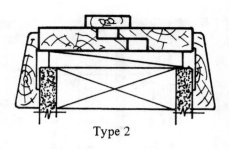

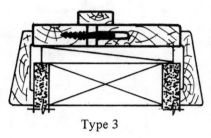

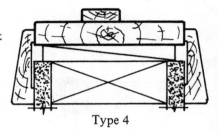

DOOR JAMBS

Wood door jambs are available in four basic types:

Type 1 - 2 piece adjustable jamb unit

Type 2 - 3 piece adjustable jamb unit

Type 3 - 3 piece adjustable jamb unit with pin

Type 4 - Non-adjustable jamb unit

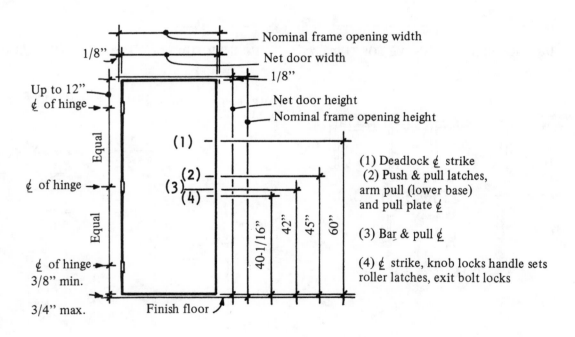

(1) Deadlock ₵ strike

(2) Push & pull latches, arm pull (lower base) and pull plate ₵

(3) Bar & pull ₵

(4) ₵ strike, knob locks handle sets roller latches, exit bolt locks

DOOR HARDWARE LOCATION

Hinges

When installing hinges, both the door and the jamb should be routed for a flush fit with the hinge pin center at least 1/2 inch from the edge of the jamb to afford a 180° door swing. The rout on the door edge should not extend the full thickness of the door but leave at least 1/4" of material on the back edge. Each hinge should have at least three screws per side which are 3/4" long with full screw threads.

DOOR FRAMES AND TRIM

The frame of the door is the lining around the rough opening which covers the edge of the wall opening and provides a means of supporting the door. It consists of two sides called jamb, a top called a head and if an exterior door, a bottom called a sill. The width of the door frame is the same dimension as the total wall thickness (finish to finish). If the stud wall is built of 2" x 3" studs, the frame thick-

OPENING: Check finish opening for PROPER WIDTH and HEIGHT as shown (see Special Note)

To obtain proper finish opening WIDTH:
    2 Door Unit . . . add ½″ to total width of 2 doors
    4 Door Unit . . . add ¾″ to total width of 4 doors

To obtain proper finish of opening HEIGHT:
    2 or 4 Door Unit . . . add 1⅞″ to total height of
    doors (plus additional for carpet thickness)

TRACK MOUNTING SURFACE OF HEADER MUST BE LEVEL
FOUR DOOR INSTALLATION   TWO DOOR INSTALLATION

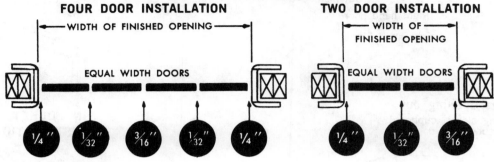

SPECIAL NOTE
If trimming of door WIDTH is necessary:
    a. Slight trimming — trim along pivot edge
    b. Major trimming — trim along hinge edge
If trimming of door HEIGHT is necessary:
    Trim at top of doors

ness will be less than a wall built of 2" x 4" studs. The clear dimension between the sides or jambs is the same dimension as the door width, and the distance between the finish floor and the top inside of the frame is the same as the door height. Door frames are usually delivered KD (knocked down) and must be assembled. When assembling the frame, be sure it is square and kept square by nailing a temporary diagonal brace across the top and a spreader across the bottom until the frame is secure and nailed in place. Some frames are pre-assembled including the door hardware and trim; one is called a split frame (halved), in the center, vertically) and the other type is installed by removing the trim from one side only, and replacing the trim after the frame is installed. Before installing the door frame, check the rough opening to be sure the frame will fit. There should be about 1/2" clearance on the back side of the frame, and the top, to allow enough clearance for leveling and trueing. Place the frame in the opening being sure the door side of the frame is on the correct side of the partition. Center the frame in the rough opening and secure on side with wood wedges. Wood shingles are an excellent source for wedges. Be sure the wedges are placed on both sides of the frame, otherwise the frame will not be square with the wall. Slide the wedges from the thin part together until the space between the

frame and the wall is filled, nail the frame through the wedges. Secure one side only with at least three wedges in the height of the frame. Be sure the one side is true, straight and level. Use a straight edge for checking accuracy. Repeat the process on the other side. Do not drive all nails home until all blocking or wedging is adjusted and the frame is straight, true and level. Break off or cut off the portion of the shingles or wedges that protrude beyond the frame thickness. When the door frame is secured, casing or trim is installed around the perimeter of the door frame on both sides of the frame. Any one of several stock patterns are available. Do not join the trim in line. Each piece must be full length from floor to top of frame. The trim should be about 3/8"back from the inner edge of the door frame with the same dimension on both sides and top. Square cut the floor end of the trim and mark the length of the casing or trim for a mitre cut at the top. Cut the mitre at a 45° angle with a fine saw, hand or power. Temporarily nail the jamb or side trim to the frame and cut and trim the top piece for a perfect joint at the miters. Use 4d finish, nails along the face frame and 8d finish nails into the studs. Repeat the operation on the other side of the frame. Use 8d finish nails for securing the frame.

SLIDING DOORS

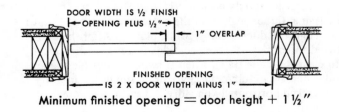

FOLDING DOORS

FOLDING DOORS

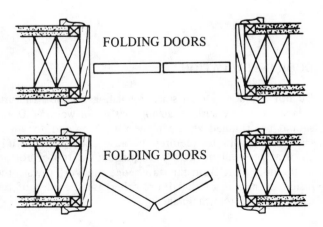

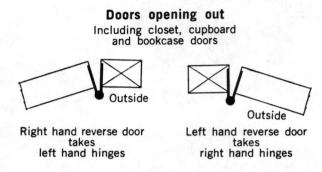

Doors opening in

Outside

Left hand door takes left hand hinges

Outside

Right hand door takes right hand hinges

Doors opening out

Including closet, cupboard and bookcase doors

Outside

Right hand reverse door takes left hand hinges

Outside

Left hand reverse door takes right hand hinges

HINGE DESIGNATION

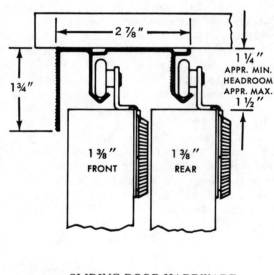

2 7/8"

1 3/4"

1 1/4" APPR. MIN. HEADROOM APPR. MAX. 1 1/2"

1 3/8" FRONT

1 3/8" REAR

SLIDING DOOR HARDWARE

OUTSIDE WALL INSTALLATIONS

Single Door

Bi-Parting Doors

IN POCKET INSTALLATIONS

Single Door

Bi-Parting Doors

BY-PASSING DOOR INSTALLATIONS

Two Doors

Three Doors

Four Doors

DOOR INSTALLATION

Do not cut doors to fit smaller openings or the structural balance may be disturbed causing twisting or warping. Doors should be trimmed with a plane for fitting and not much trimming should be required because doors are carefully sized at the mill or factory. In planing the top or bottom of the door start from the outer edge and work toward the inside or middle of the door, otherwise the edge of the door will tear from the plane.

Door clearances should be about 1/16" to 1/36" free of the door frame. Cut enough from the bottom to clear the finish floor. Hold the door securely while planing. After the door is fitted to correct size, the backside must have a slight bevel to clear the door frame when it swings about the frame. Handle doors carefully and any storing should be in a dry place stacked horizontally on a dry flat surface, covered.

The installation of hinges called butts, presents no special problem. The thickness of the butt metal is called the gain. The gain of the butt is cut into the door and frame to make a flush application. Separate the two parts of the but by removing the pin holding the two parts together. Position the butt on the door with one butt 7" down from the top being sure that the portion of the butt which receives the pin is facing the direction of the door swing. Mark the shape of the butt on the door with a sharp pencil leaving about 3/16" from the edge of the door. This is not to expose the edge of the butt when the door is in a closed position. Cut along the mark into the door the thickness of the butt or the butt gain. Try for size. When properly fitted, repeat the same procedure for the other butt 11" up from the bottom. 1-3/8" thick doors require two butts or a pair of butts, 1-3/4" thick doors require a pair and half or three butts. The third one is mid-point between the top and bottom. When the butts are cut and fitted into the door put in only two screws in each butt, place the door into the frame in the correct position and transfer the location of the butts onto the frame and repeat the same proccess with the other half of the butt cut into the door frame. When this has been completed, again install two screws in each butt and try the door for size making any adjustment necessary for proper fit. When the fitting and adjusting is completed, install the rest of the screws and pins and the job is completed. If slight adjustment is necessary in relocating the butts, plug the old screw holes with a wooden match. If the gain is too deep, adjustments can be made by using cardboard shims behind the butt.

If in-wall sliding doors are used, the frame is preassembled and installed as part of the wall during the installation of the studs. This is a packaged frame and the only requirement is to install the hanging hardware onto the top of the door and put the door in position. The hardware can be adjusted for ease of operation. The doors are standard size doors and are not special.

By-pass sliding doors have a track overhead and a guide at the floor. They act in much the same manner as the in-wall sliding door except the track is doubled to accommodate two doors. Folding doors consist of two or more doors hinged together operating from an overhead track. There is another type door called an accordian door which is a package unit complete with hardware.

WINDOW TRIM

The windows are already in place and require only to be finished off with the same trim or casing as the door frames. Use the same procedure as with door frames. Sometimes the trim is prefitted with the window and needs only to be installed. There are additional parts of the window trim which must be installed called the stool and apron. The stool is the horizontal shelf on the bottom of the window on the inside and the apron is installed under the sill against the wall.The length of the sill extends about 3/4" beyond the back side of the trim on both sides of the window. Place the sill in position and mark the inside finish of the window onto the sill on both sides. Allow the sill to come to within

1/16" of the window sash (the operating part of the window). Measure the depth of the cut at the jambs so that the sill comes up to the wall on both ends. Cut, fit, refit and sand smooth the cut edges. Secure the sill with 6d finish nails and install the casing resting with a square cut on top of the sill. The apron is of the same moulding as the casing and is as long as the distance from back to back of the jamb trim or casing. The ends of the apron have the same profile as the face of the casing. Sand smooth and nail with 6d finish nails.

DOOR JAMBS

SIZE	Thickness	Width	Rabbet	
2-8 x 6-8	1¼	3⅜	1⅜	Sgle
2-8 x 6-8	1¼	4⅜	1⅜	Sgle-Dble
2-8 x 6-8	1¼	4⅝	1⅜	Sgle-Dble
2-8 x 6-8	1¼	5⅜	1⅜	Sgle-Dble
3-0 x 7-0	1¼	4⅜	1⅜	Sgle
3-0 x 7-0	1¼	5⅜	1⅜	Sgle
3-0 x 7-0	1¼	4⅝	1¾	Sgle
3-0 x 7-0	1¼	5⅜	1¾	Sgle-Dble
3-0 x 7-0	1½	5⅜	1¾	Sgle

Side Jambs Dadoed to Receive Head Jamb

OAK INSIDE THRESHOLDS

SIZES
¾" x 3½" x 3'-0"
¾" x 4½" x 3'-0"
¾" x 4½" x 6'-0"
¾" x 5½" x 3'-0"
¾" x 5½" x 6'-0"

KITCHEN CABINETS

Three types of Cabinets are available for kitchens: built on job, custom built in a shop and stock or mass produced cabinets, selected to fit the allocated space. For the person not experienced in cabinetmaking, stock units offer the most economical and best choice.

All dimensions are standard with the base unit being 36" high and 24" deep, 15" to 18" from counter top to under side of upper cabinets, upper shelves 12" deep, distance from floor to upper most cabinet should be door height, usually 6'-8" above floor, the space between the upper cabinets and the ceiling is filled in with what is called a soffit to seal off the space. The soffit can be part of the wall design or an accent strip. The lower or base cabinet has a toe space 2" deep and 4" high. The toe space is necessary because without it working at the counter will be very uncomfortable because you could not get close enough to the counter for working comfort.

The built on job parts are built from 3/4" lumber core plywood with a choice or veneer. The parts are cut, sanded and assembled, or built to the wall piece by piece attached to the wall and floor. The vertical members are called stiles and the horizontal members are called rails.

WALL CABINET SPECIFICATIONS

All Wall Cabinets are 12″ deep. All single door Wall Cabinets invert to reverse the doors.

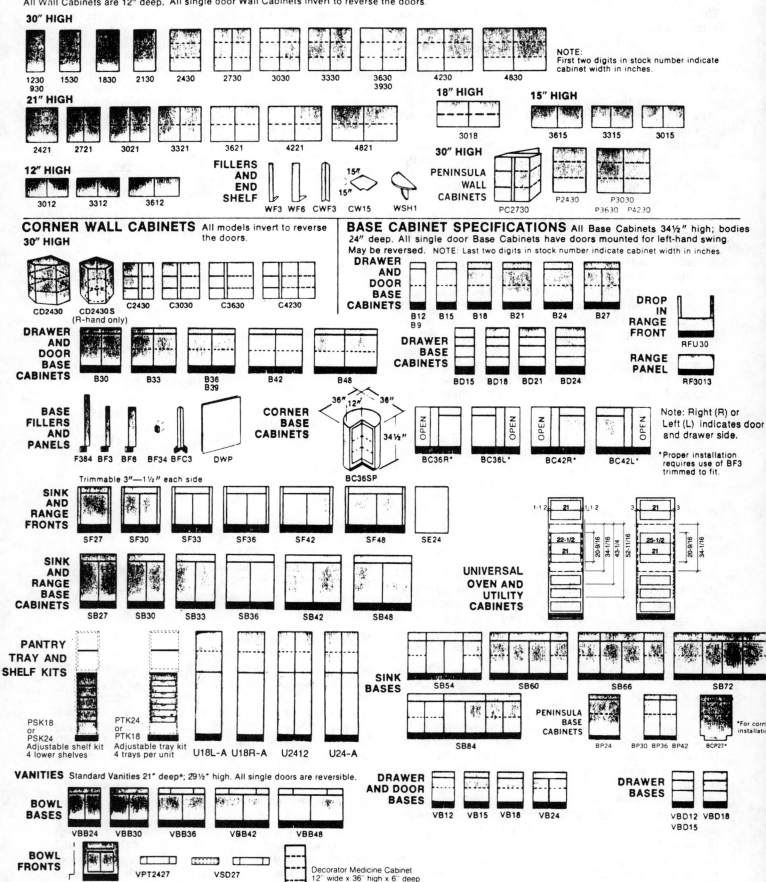

30″ HIGH

1230 930 · 1530 · 1830 · 2130 · 2430 · 2730 · 3030 · 3330 · 3630 3930 · 4230 · 4830

NOTE: First two digits in stock number indicate cabinet width in inches.

21″ HIGH

2421 · 2721 · 3021 · 3321 · 3621 · 4221 · 4821

18″ HIGH 3018

15″ HIGH 3615 · 3315 · 3015

12″ HIGH 3012 · 3312 · 3612

FILLERS AND END SHELF WF3 · WF6 · CWF3 · CW15 · WSH1 15″ 15″

PENINSULA WALL CABINETS 30″ HIGH PC2730 · P2430 P3630 · P3030 P4230

CORNER WALL CABINETS
All models invert to reverse the doors.

30″ HIGH

CD2430 · CD2430S (R-hand only) · C2430 · C3030 · C3630 · C4230

DRAWER AND DOOR BASE CABINETS B30 · B33 · B36 B39 · B42 · B48

BASE FILLERS AND PANELS F384 · BF3 · BF6 · BF34 · BFC3 · DWP

Trimmable 3″—1½″ each side

CORNER BASE CABINETS 36″ 12″ 36″ 34½″ BC36SP

SINK AND RANGE FRONTS SF27 · SF30 · SF33 · SF36 · SF42 · SF48 · SE24

SINK AND RANGE BASE CABINETS SB27 · SB30 · SB33 · SB36 · SB42 · SB48

PANTRY TRAY AND SHELF KITS
PSK18 or PSK24 Adjustable shelf kit 4 lower shelves
PTK24 or PTK18 Adjustable tray kit 4 trays per unit
U18L-A · U18R-A · U2412 · U24-A

BASE CABINET SPECIFICATIONS
All Base Cabinets 34½″ high; bodies 24″ deep. All single door Base Cabinets have doors mounted for left-hand swing. May be reversed. NOTE: Last two digits in stock number indicate cabinet width in inches.

DRAWER AND DOOR BASE CABINETS B12 B9 · B15 · B18 · B21 · B24 · B27

DROP IN RANGE FRONT RFU30

RANGE PANEL RF3013

DRAWER BASE CABINETS BD15 · BD18 · BD21 · BD24

OPEN · OPEN · OPEN · OPEN
BC36R* · BC36L* · BC42R* · BC42L*

Note: Right (R) or Left (L) indicates door and drawer side.

*Proper installation requires use of BF3 trimmed to fit.

UNIVERSAL OVEN AND UTILITY CABINETS
1-1 2 · 21 · 1-1 2 · 3 · 21 · 3
22-1/2 · 21 · 25-1/2 · 21
20-9/16 · 34-1/4 · 43-1/4 · 52-11/16 · 20-9/16 · 34-1/4

SINK BASES SB54 · SB60 · SB66 · SB72 · SB84

PENINSULA BASE CABINETS BP24 · BP30 · BP36 · BP42 · BCP27*
*For corn installati

DRAWER AND DOOR BASES VB12 · VB15 · VB18 · VB24

DRAWER BASES VBD12 · VBD15 · VBD18

VANITIES
Standard Vanities 21″ deep*; 29½″ high. All single doors are reversible.

BOWL BASES VBB24 · VBB30 · VBB36 · VBB42 · VBB48

BOWL FRONTS VFF27 · VPT2427 · VSD27

*VBB 2418 and VBB 3018 are 18″ deep.

Decorator Medicine Cabinet 12″ wide x 36″ high x 6″ deep 3 adjustable glass shelves
MC 1236

Construct the base first using 2" x 4" on edge for the toe space and secure the base shelf to the 2" x 4". Cut the stiles and rails about 1-1/2" wide being sure that the wood grain is running in the same direction for all the stiles and all the rails (the stiles and rails are not run in the same direction—stiles are vertical run and rails are horizontal run). Nail and glue the rails to the base shelf providing spacing for doors and drawers. Secure the rails to the stiles. Install a 1" x 3" wood furring to the wall to support the back of the counter top. Be sure the furring is nailed to the studs. The counter top can be 1/2" or 5/8" thick plywood nailed to the cabinet frame. After the counter top is installed, cut out for the sink. The upper cabinets are constructed in much the same manner as the lower or base unit. Manufacturers will supply the dimensions for built-in appliances. Nails need not be exposed in building cabinets on job. After the pieces have been cut and sanded, join the stiles and rails together from the back side, with a piece of 1/4" plywood glued and secured with small nails called brads. The 1/4" plywood should be a little narrower than the width of the stile and rail. Doors and drawers can be flush faced or lipped. Lip construction has a recess cut along the perimeter of the back of the door about 3/8" wide and 3/8" deep which means that the doors and drawers are 3/4" larger than the opening. This will cover the openings allowing greater freedom for fitting.

If plastic laminate (formica) is used for the counter top finish, contact cement must be used. When using contact cement, follow directions printed on label carefully and make certain the room is well ventilated. Contact is applied with a brush or special knotched metal trowel applied to both surfaces. Allow to dry thoroughly. Test dry the surfaces with a piece of paper. If the paper does not stick to the surface, the cement is dry and ready for bonding. Bring the two surfaces together in the exact position because once contact is made, no adjustment is possible. When joining large surfaces together, place a sheet of heavy paper between the two layers or contact surfaces, position the laminated plastic and slide the paper out for permanent bond. Apply pressure to the top surface for good contact. The parts of laminated plastic should be fitted before contacting. Trimming and finishing edges can be accomplished with a plane or file and finished with fine sandpaper.

After the cabinets have been completed, cabinet hardware should be installed. Select the proper style and size for drawers and doors. Carefully drill holes in proper location for hardware installation. Factory built cabinets are pre-finished, pre-assembled, including hardware. A variety of units are available to fit any space. Manufacturers provide detail instructions for installations. If the walls and floors are not level, straight and plumb, shimming may be necessary to prevent the cabinets from racking or twisting. Screws should penetrate the hanging strips and the studs. If studs are inaccessible, use toggle bolts. The counter is secured inside the cabinets after the units are in place.

BASEBOARD

This stock moulding is attached to the wall at floor level before the finish floor is installed. It is one of the last pieces of trim installed. Baseboards run around the entire perimeter of the room and stop against the door casing. Exterior corners are mitered and interior corners are coped. If joining baseboards is necessary, locate the joint over a stud. The location of the studs should be known before the baseboard is installed. If the stud location is not known or has not been recorded, drive a nail into the wall behind the baseboard location until a stud is located and simply measure 16" spacing from that point in both directions to locate the remainder of the studs. In applying the first piece of baseboard, cut to make a tight square fit against the adjacent wall. Run the adjoining piece forming an interior angle by coping the joint. To cope a joint, cut the end on a 45° angle exposing the profile or face of the moulding, cut along the profile with a coping saw forming an end cut the exact shape and profile as the face. Continue in the same manner until the entire room is completed. Use 8d finish nails to penetrate the studs.

FIREPLACE/CHIMNEY

The design of the chimney depends upon the number of flues contained within the chimney. The top of the chimney should extend at least 2'-0" above the highest point of the roof. The flue sizes are determined by the units attached. Normally heating units will require a 9" x 13" flue lining and fireplaces should be 1/10 the area of the firebox. Gas fired hot water domestic heaters may require 6" dia. flue linings. Check with manufacturers equipment before building a chimney. Flue linings are clay units surrounded by brick or stone constituting one chimney. There may be several flue linings in one chimney. A separate flue lining is required for each apparatus or fire. If more than one unit is attached to a common flue lining, there may be draft interference. Flues must have a minimum of 8" brick wall surrounding the flue and a minimum of 4" brick between the flues. Chimneys must be built completely divorced from the house and self-supporting. No part of the structure must be supported by the chimney. All frame work must be at least 2" clear of the chimney.

In fireplace design, the sides and back of the firebox should slope outward from the rear to front to direct the heat into the room and the smoke to the throat. A smoke shelf is necessary behind the damper to stop back drafts. To prevent smoke and gases from entering the room, proper sloping of sides and back, proper smoke chamber, flue, throat and damper are essential. A hinged cast iron damper is installed in the throat to regulate the draft. There are two kinds of dampers available: Rotary and Poker type. The rotary type is adjusted by a knob or handle on the face of the fireplace. This has a worm gear action mechanism operated by turning the knob. The poker type has no gears and is operated or adjusted by reaching under the throat with a poker. The hearth should extend about 1'-8" in front of the firebox and is used to catch burning embers. It should be built of a fireproof material such as brick, tile, marble or concrete, raised or flush with the floor. No woodwork should be placed within 8" of the sides of the firebox.

The chimney should be located to contain all the flue linings for the equipment or the equipment should be located near the chimney to avoid more than one chimney. The face of the fireplace may be constructed of brick, marble, or tile, with or without a mantel. The masonry above the firebox is supported by a steel L shaped member called a lintel. An ash dump is built into the fireplace floor with a 5" x 8" cast iron door directing the ashes into a pit at the base of the chimney which is cleaned out through a 12" x 8" cleanout cast iron door built into the masonry. The firebox is constructed of a special brick called fire brick with fireclay mortar. The chimney may be offset but this also may inhibit the efficiency of the chimney. This offset is called corbeling and is restricted to 1" projection in each brick course with a maximum height of the center of the flue lining not falling beyond the center of the wall below. In constructing the chimney, use face brick or stone only in areas where the chimney will be exposed to view. Surfaces not requiring a finish can be concrete block or common brick. Laying of brick, stone or block is similar to brick or stone veneer. Install the flue linings first and build around them. Be sure to seal the joints of flue linings with mortar. Other fireplace accessories are becoming popular called pre-fabricated metal circulators. Metal takes the place of the firebrick and is packaged with throat and damper. Face brick surrounds the front of the metal firebox. Some building codes may allow insulated metal chimneys instead of brick. These units are twist locked together in lengths of 24" or 30" with special through roof, through floor, and flashing and roof caps fittings.

FACTORY-BUILT CHIMNEYS

Anchor chimney to the building in such a manner that settling of the building or of the chimney, will not cause opening of the joints between chimney sections.

Join chimney sections to provide an integral flue structure with joints arranged to prevent condensation from penetrating into the interior of the chimney construction. Joint cement compounds, where used, must be resistant to acid and high temperatures.

Insulation must be impervious to high temperatures, protected from mechanical damage and should extend at least two feet above the highest point of the opening in the roof through which the chimney passes.

The chimney flue liner should extend up to the underside of the top of the chimney roof housing in a smokeproof and sparkproof joint, or should extend through the top of the housing. When liner is of clay tile, it should be at least 5/8" inch thick.

Dampers are used in all fireplaces. They are located in the forward part of the fireplace to allow for a smoke shelf They should be no less than 6" to 8" above the top of the fireplace opening. When fully opened they are required to stand vertically at least 1/2" to the room side of the vertical projection of the inner face of the flue. When fully opened, damper openings should be not less than 90% of the required flue area.

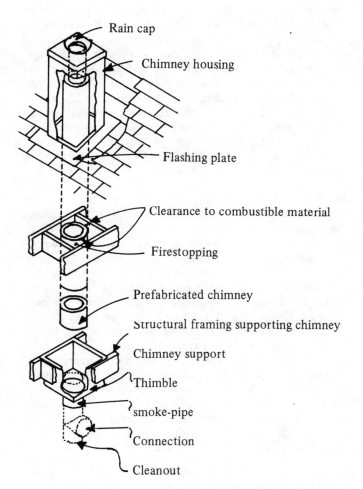

Rain cap
Chimney housing
Flashing plate
Clearance to combustible material
Firestopping
Prefabricated chimney
Structural framing supporting chimney
Chimney support
Thimble
smoke-pipe
Connection
Cleanout

FACTORY-BUILT CHIMNEYS

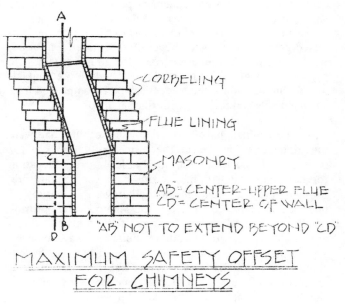

A
CORBELING
FLUE LINING
MASONRY
AB = CENTER-UPPER FLUE
CD = CENTER OF WALL
C
D
B
"AB" NOT TO EXTEND BEYOND "CD"

MAXIMUM SAFETY OFFSET FOR CHIMNEYS

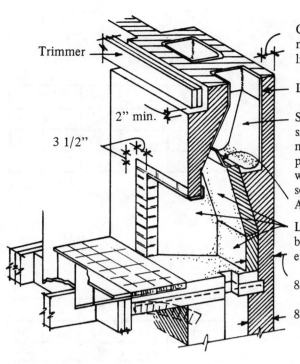

Trimmer

2" min.

3 1/2"

Chimney 4" solid masonry (min.) if liner is used.

Liner

Support flue-liner parge smoke chamber w/fire-clay mortar (refractory mortar) parging may be omitted if wall thickness is 8" solid masonry. Adjustable damper

Lining of fire-brick (may be laid 2" away) should extend full width of throat.

8" min. total thickness.

8" min. foundation wall.

CUT-AWAY SECTION OF TYPICAL FIREPLACE

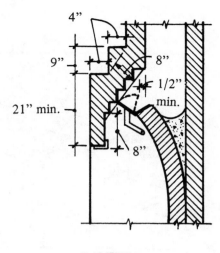

4"

9"

21" min.

8"

1/2" min.

8"

DAMPER

SINGLE FACED

FLUSH

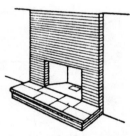

RAISED HEARTH

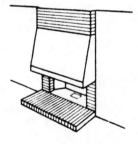

COPPER HOOD

DOUBLE FACED INTERIOR CORNER

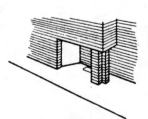

DOUBLE FACED PROJECTING CORNER

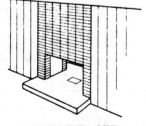

DOUBLE FACED OPPOSITE RIDGES

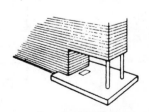

THREE-FACED

FREE-STANDING

389

FLUE AREAS FOR FIREPLACES HAVING 2 OR MORE OPENINGS (FACES)

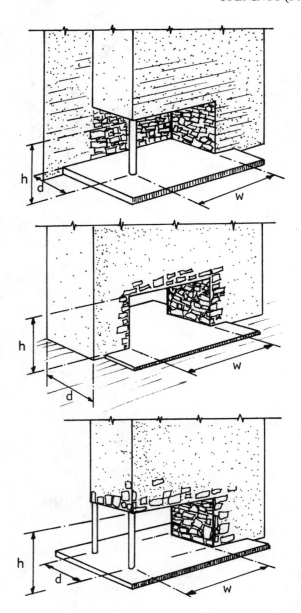

w	d	h	flue
30	30	36	16 x 16
34	20	30	12 x 16
42	24	42	16 x 20

Two faces adjacent

w	d	h	flue
30	24	42	16 x 20
34	28	30	16 x 16
38	28	36	16 x 20

Two faces opposite

w	d	h	flue
34	24	24	16 x 16
38	28	30	16 x 20
38	28	36	20 x 24

Three faces

CONCRETE CHIMNEY CAP

FLUE LINING

CUT-AWAY VIEW

BRICK

CHIMNEY CAP

CLAY FLUE LINER SIZES

NEW SIZES	ROUND (DIA.)	OLD SIZES
8 x 12	8	8 1/2 x 8 1/2
12 x 12	10	8 1/2 x 13
12 x 16	12	13 x 13
16 x 16	15	13 x 18
16 x 20	18	18 x 18
20 x 20	20	20 x 20
20 x 24	22	24 x 24

390

DAMPER SPECIFICATIONS

CAST IRON DAMPERS

WIDTH OF FIREPLACE IN INCHES	DAMPER DIMENSIONS IN INCHES				
	A	B	C	D	E
24 TO 26	28	21	13 1/2	24	10
27 TO 31	34	26 3/4	13 1/2	30	10
31 TO 34	37	29 3/4	13 1/2	33	10
35 TO 38	40	32 3/4	13 1/2	36	10
39 TO 42	46	38 3/4	13 1/2	48	10
43 TO 46	52	44 3/4	13 1/2	48	10
47 TO 50	57 1/2	50 1/2	13 1/2	54	10
51 TO 54	64	56 1/2	14 1/2	60	11 1/2
57 TO 60	76	58	14 1/2	72	11 1/2

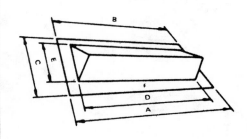

Mouldings

MOULDINGS

Wood and plastics are used to form mouldings for the final step before painting in construction. These are precision buildings products manufactured to national standards as trim material. To "trim out" a house means to install and finish the mouldings. Literally, mouldings are strips of wood or plastic up to 16' long and milled into about 30 different stock patterns, or profiles, continuous throughout their length. Each profile is designed for a primary use and some have a large number of secondary uses as well.

Tools required for working with mouldings are a miter box, cross cut saw, nailset, fine sandpaper, white woodworking glue and a ruler or tape measure. Most moulding joints are set at a 45° angle by setting the miter box accordingly, and trim each of the two pieces to be mated at opposite angles.

For tight joints, use both glue and nails. When measuring mouldings to be mitered add the width of the mouldings to the length of each miter. In joining or splicing moulding, orient the moulding flat on its back side in the miter box. Miter the ends to be joined at identical 45° angles. For interior corners, joints should be coped. Set the moulding in the miter box as it will be installed on the wall, upright against the back plate of the miter box and turn at 45° angle. The cut will expose the profile of the moulding to use a guide or template in cutting. Follow this profile with a coping saw to cut away the end at an angle resulting in a duplication of the same pattern which will fit over the adjoining moulding. Fill all nail holes with wood putty and use

#00 fine sandpaper in the direction of the grain. Prefinished mouldings are also available to match the paneling. Mouldings are available in lengths of 3 to 16 feet and are sold in specified or random lengths—which are less expensive. Order in pieces, pairs or sets on a hundred lineal feet basis.

PICTURE

11/16" x 1¾"
11/16" x 1⅜"

QUARTER ROUND

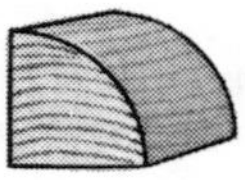

¼" x ¼"
⅜" x ⅜"
½" x ½"
⅝" x ⅝"
¾" x ¾"
⅞" x ⅞"

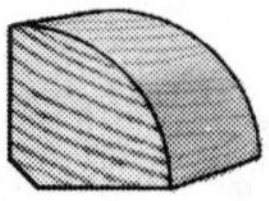

11/16" x 1⅜"

SCOTIA (See Cove—Scotia)

SCREEN MOULDINGS

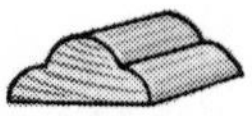

5/16" x ⅝"
⅜" x ¾"

¼" x ¾"

¼" x ¾"

SCREEN STOCK

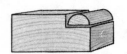

$\frac{11}{16}'' \times 1\frac{3}{4}''$
$1\frac{1}{16}'' \times 1\frac{3}{4}''$

$\frac{11}{16}'' \times 1\frac{3}{4}''$

CLOSET POLE

$1\frac{1}{8}''$
$1\frac{1}{16}''$
$1\frac{5}{16}''$
$1\frac{5}{8}''$

SHELF CLEAT

$\frac{11}{16}'' \times 1\frac{1}{2}''$

STAFF BEAD

B691 $1\frac{3}{8}'' \times 1\frac{5}{8}''$

$1\frac{1}{4}'' \times 2''$
$1\frac{1}{4}'' \times 2''$

CORNER BEAD

$1\frac{1}{16}'' \times 1\frac{1}{16}''$
$1\frac{5}{16}'' \times 1\frac{5}{16}''$
$\frac{3}{4}'' \times \frac{3}{4}''$

$1\frac{3}{16}'' \times 2\frac{1}{8}''$

INSIDE CORNER

$\frac{5}{16}'' \times 1''$

CORNICE

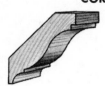

$\frac{9}{16}'' \times 1\frac{3}{4}''$
$\frac{9}{16}'' \times 3\frac{1}{4}''$
$\frac{9}{16}'' \times 2\frac{1}{4}''$

COVE—SCOTIA

$\frac{9}{16}'' \times 1\frac{3}{4}''$
$\frac{11}{16}'' \times 2\frac{1}{4}''$
$\frac{11}{16}'' \times 2\frac{3}{4}''$

$\frac{1}{2}'' \times \frac{7}{8}''$
$\frac{1}{2}'' \times \frac{1}{2}''$
$\frac{11}{16}'' \times \frac{7}{8}''$
$\frac{11}{16}'' \times 1\frac{1}{8}''$
$\frac{5}{8}'' \times \frac{3}{4}''$

CROWN

$\frac{9}{16}'' \times 3\frac{1}{4}''$
$\frac{9}{16}'' \times 3\frac{5}{8}''$
$\frac{9}{16}'' \times 2\frac{3}{4}''$
$\frac{11}{16}'' \times 5\frac{1}{4}''$
$\frac{11}{16}'' \times 4\frac{5}{8}''$
$\frac{11}{16}'' \times 4\frac{1}{4}''$

$\frac{9}{16}'' \times 3\frac{5}{8}''$
$\frac{9}{16}'' \times 2\frac{3}{4}''$
$\frac{11}{16}'' \times 4\frac{5}{8}''$

$1\frac{1}{16}'' \times 2\frac{1}{2}''$

CASING SETS FOR DOOR TRIM

$\frac{11}{16}'' \times 2\frac{1}{2}''$
$\frac{11}{16}'' \times 3\frac{1}{2}''$

$\frac{11}{16}'' \times 2\frac{1}{2}''$
$1\frac{1}{16}'' \times 3\frac{1}{2}''$

$\frac{11}{16}'' \times 2\frac{1}{2}''$

$\frac{11}{16}'' \times 2\frac{1}{2}''$
$\frac{11}{16}'' \times 3\frac{1}{2}''$

CASINGS 7'-0" LENGTHS

$\frac{11}{16}'' \times 2\frac{1}{2}''$
$\frac{11}{16}'' \times 2\frac{1}{2}''$
$\frac{11}{16}'' \times 3\frac{1}{2}''$
$\frac{11}{16}'' \times 2\frac{1}{2}''$
$\frac{11}{16}'' \times 3\frac{1}{2}''$

DRIP CAP

$\frac{3}{4}'' \times 1\frac{3}{4}''$

EXTENSION JAMB

$\frac{3}{4}'' \times \frac{3}{4}''$

FENCE CAP

$1\frac{1}{8}'' \times 1\frac{3}{4}''$

GLASS BEADS

$\frac{1}{4}'' \times \frac{11}{16}''$

$\frac{3}{8}'' \times \frac{7}{8}''$

$\frac{3}{8}'' \times \frac{1}{2}''$

CHAIR RAIL AND HOOK STRIP

$\frac{5}{8}'' \times 3\frac{1}{2}''$

$\frac{5}{8}'' \times 3\frac{1}{2}''$
$\frac{5}{16}'' \times \frac{3}{8}''$

$\frac{5}{8}'' \times 2\frac{1}{2}''$

S4S STRIPS

$\frac{11}{16}'' \times 1\frac{3}{4}''$
$\frac{11}{16}'' \times 2\frac{3}{4}''$
$1\frac{1}{16}'' \times 1\frac{3}{4}''$

CASING (MULLION)

$\frac{5}{16}'' \times 2''$

HALF ROUND

¼″ × ½″
5/16″ × 5/8″
3/8″ × 11/16″
½″ × 1″
5/8″ × 1¼″
11/16″ × 15/8″

HAND RAIL

1½″ × 1¾″

1½″ × 2½″

1¾″ × 19/16″

LATTICE S4S

¼″ × 11/8″
¼″ × 15/16″
¼″ × 1¾″

3/8″ × 1¾″
3/8″ × 2¼″

NOSING

3/8″ × ½″

11/16″ × 1¾″

SUB SILL

11/16″ × 4¼″

WALL

5/8″ × 7/8″

STOPS — Continued

3/8″ × 15/8″

3/8″ × 15/16″
3/8″ × 15/8″
3/8″ × 7/8″
3/8″ × 11/16″

PANEL, WALLBOARD, AND TILEBOARD

11/16″ × 7/8″

3/8″ × 1¾″
5/8″ × 2¼″

3/8″ × 1″

7/16″ × 11/8″

½″ × 9/16″

PANEL STOCK S4S

7/16″ × 2½″
7/16″ × 3½″
7/16″ × 4½″
7/16″ × 5½″
7/16″ × 7½″

PARTING BEAD

½″ × ¾″
3/8″ × ¾″

OFFSET PARTING BEAD

½″ × 13/16″

STOPS SETS FOR DOOR TRIM

3/8″ × 15/16″

3/8″ × 15/16″

CASING (TRANSOM)

½″ × 1¼″

STOPS

3/8″ × 15/8″
3/8″ × 15/16″
3/8″ × 11/16″
3/8″ × 7/8″
3/8″ × 1¾″
3/8″ × 35/8″

3/8″ × 2½″
3/8″ × 4¼″
3/8″ × 35/8″
3/8″ × 15/8″
3/8″ × 15/16″

STOOL CAP

11/16″ × 3¼″

¾″ × 4¼″

11/16″ × 3½″

11/16″ × 2¼″

11/16″ × 4¼″

15/16″ × 3¼″

APRON

5/8″ × 3½″

9/16″ × 2½″

5/8″ × 2″

5/8″ × 2½″

ASTRAGAL

11/16″ × 1¾″

393

BASE MOULDING

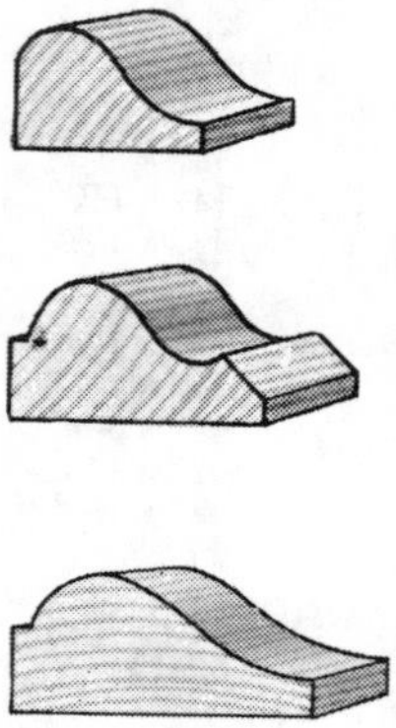

½″ x ¾″

⁹⁄₁₆″ x 1″
¹¹⁄₁₆″ x 1⅛″
¹¹⁄₁₆″ x 1⅜″

¹¹⁄₁₆″ x 1½″

BASE SHOE

¾″ x 1″

BED

⁹⁄₁₆″ x 1¾″
⁹⁄₁₆″ x 1½″
⁹⁄₁₆″ x 2¼″
⁹⁄₁₆″ x 2¾″
⁹⁄₁₆″ x 2″

CAP

¹¹⁄₁₆″ x 1⅜″

¹¹⁄₁₆″ x 1⅛″

¾″ x ¾″

ATTIC MOULDING

½″ x 1½″

BACK BAND

¹¹⁄₁₆″ x 1¹⁄₁₆″

BALUSTER STOCK

1¹⁄₁₆″
1⁵⁄₁₆″
1⅝″

CARPET STRIP

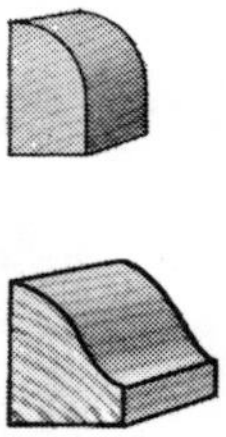

⁷⁄₁₆″ x ¾″

½″ x ¾″
⅝″ x ¾″

CASING

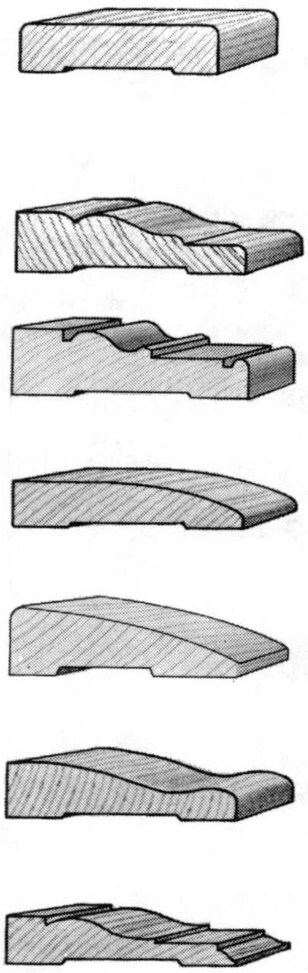

¹¹⁄₁₆″ x 3½″

¹¹⁄₁₆″ x 2½″
¹¹⁄₁₆″ x 3½″

¹¹⁄₁₆″ x 2½″

¹¹⁄₁₆″ x 2½″
¹¹⁄₁₆″ x 3½″

¹¹⁄₁₆″ x 2¼″

¹¹⁄₁₆″ x 2½″

¹¹⁄₁₆″ x 2½″
¹¹⁄₁₆″ x 3½″

BAND

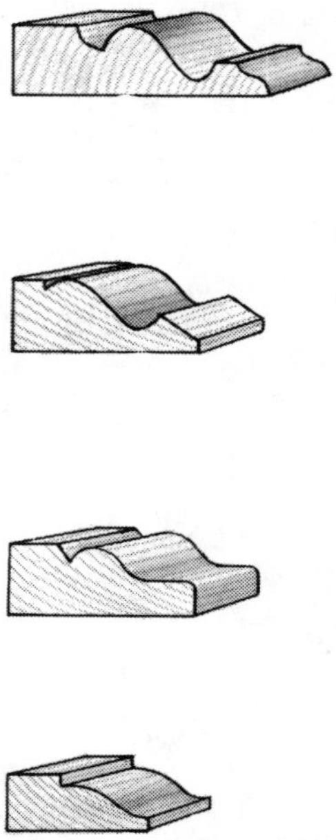

¹¹⁄₁₆″ x 2½″

¹¹⁄₁₆″ x 1⅛″
¹¹⁄₁₆″ x 1½″
¹¹⁄₁₆″ x 1¾″

¹¹⁄₁₆″ x 1¾″
¹¹⁄₁₆″ x 1½″
¹¹⁄₁₆″ x 1¼″

⁷⁄₁₆″ x 1¹⁄₁₆″

BASE

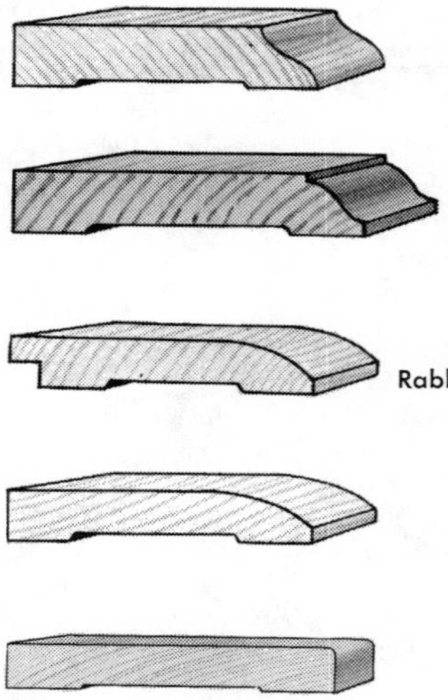

⁹⁄₁₆″ x 3½″

⁹⁄₁₆″ x 4½″

⁹⁄₁₆″ x 3½″

⁹⁄₁₆″ x 3½″
Rabbet ⁵⁄₁₆″ x ⅜″

⁹⁄₁₆″ x 3½″

⁹⁄₁₆″ x 4½″

⁹⁄₁₆″ x 4¼″

Ironing Board Cabinet Units

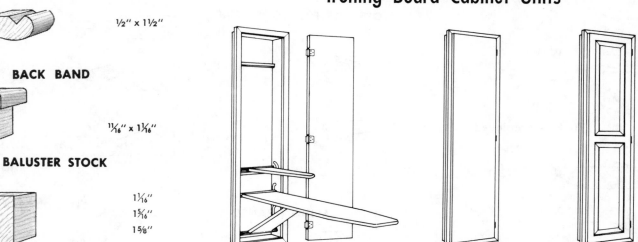

"HOW TO" WITH WOOD MOULDINGS

MOULDING CRAFTSMANSHIP

MITERING A MOULDING

This is a basic operation in working with moulding. Set your miter box saw at 45°, as shown in Figure 1. Trim each of the two mitering members in opposite cuts so together they form a tight, right angle (Figure 7). For tight miter joints, nail and glue at joint as shown. Make sure nails are countersunk below the surface. If you don't own a miter box, check the equipment rentals.

COPING A MOULDING

Set moulding in miter box as it is to be installed on wall, upright against backplate (Figure 2). Trim at 45° angle. Remaining profile serves as guide line for coping saw, used to trim away wedge at another 45° angle (Figure 5). Fit profile against face of adjoining moulding (Figure 6).

MAKING A JIG (Figure 3)

Many projects - require "picture framing" techniques of extreme accuracy. A jig is actually a "mold" in which frames are made more rapidly, accurately, and uniform in size. The inside dimensions of the jig equal the outside dimensions of the frame. The jig consists of stock pieces of lumber nailed to any flat, nailable surface. Blocks can be used (as shown) where necessary to straighten mouldings against side of jig.

MOULDING TOOLS

Miter box and saw	Carpenter's rule
Jig	Coping saw
White woodworking glue	(Figure 4)
Finishing nails	Fine sandpaper

Mouldings are available in a variety of lengths from 6 to 16 feet long.

When measuring moulding lengths for your materials list, always round off your measurement to the next highest foot. It is far wiser to come out long than short.

Make a list of your moulding needs by noting the number of pieces required by length in each pattern. From his stock, your lumber or millwork dealer will furnish random standard lengths. Many times shorter lengths are your best buy, so don't overlook specifying these when they are needed. Measuring mouldings to be mitered, add the width of the mouldings to the length for each miter. If your moulding is 3 inches wide and you have two miters, add 6 inches, then round off to the next highest foot.

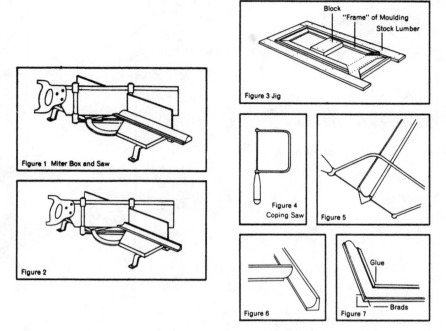

Figure 1 Miter Box and Saw

Figure 2

Figure 3 Jig

Figure 4 Coping Saw

Figure 5

Figure 6

Figure 7

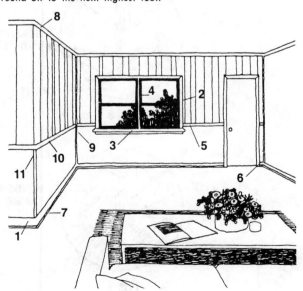

TYPES OF MOULDINGS

Standard moulding patterns and their uses are shown below and in room illustration.

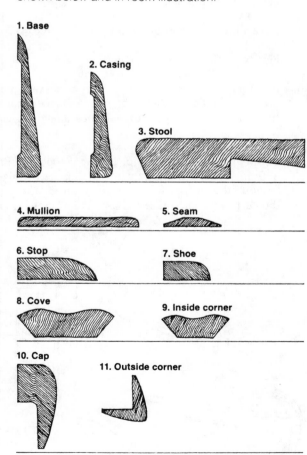

1. Base
2. Casing
3. Stool
4. Mullion
5. Seam
6. Stop
7. Shoe
8. Cove
9. Inside corner
10. Cap
11. Outside corner

395

REPLACE A BROKEN WINDOW

YOUR PROBLEM

A window is broken

Heat is lost around window panes where putty is missing or dried out.

WHAT YOU NEED

Window glass—correct size

Putty or glazing compound

Putty knife

Hammer

Pliers

Glazier points

HOW-TO

1. Work from the outside of the frame. (Fig. 1)

2. Remove the broken glass with pliers to avoid cutting your fingers. (Fig. 2)

3. Remove old putty and glazier points. Pliers will be helpful to do this. (Fig. 3)

4. Place a thin ribbon of putty in the frame. (Fig. 4)

5. Place glass firmly against the putty. (Fig. 5)

6. Insert glazier points. Tap in carefully to prevent breaking the glass. Points should be placed near the corners first, and then every 4 to 6 inches along the glass. (Fig. 6)

7. Fill the groove with putty or glazing compound. Press it firmly against the glass with putty knife or fingers. Smooth the surface with the putty knife. The putty should form a smooth seal around the window. (Fig.7)

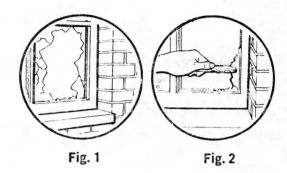

Fig. 1   Fig. 2

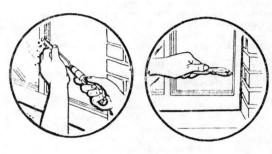

Fig. 3

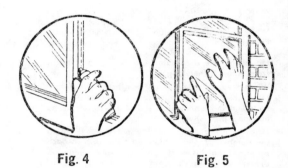

Fig. 4   Fig. 5

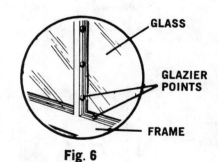

Fig. 6

Fig. 7

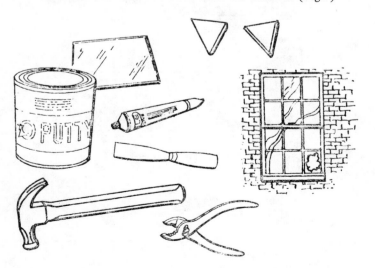

REPAIRING DRAWERS

YOUR PROBLEM

Drawers stick.

Drawers come apart.

Handles or knobs are loose or broken.

WHAT YOU NEED

Screwdriver

Sandpaper

Candle wax or paraffin

HOW-TO

FOR HANDLES AND KNOBS:

1. Tighten handles or knobs with screwdriver from the inside of the drawer. (Fig. 1)

2. You can buy knobs, or use small spools to replace lost knobs.

FOR STICKING DRAWERS:

1. Remove the drawer. Look for shiny places on top or bottom edges or on the sides. (Fig. 2)

2. Sand down these shiny areas. Try drawer to see if it moves more easily. Repeat sanding if it still sticks. (Fig. 3)

3. Rub the drawer and the frame, where they touch, with candle wax, paraffin, or soap. This makes drawers glide easier. This is important if drawers are usually filled with heavy items. (Fig. 4)

4. If glides are badly worn, the drawer may not close all the way. The drawer front stikes the frame. The drawer needs to be lifted. Remove it and insert two or three large smooth-head thumbtacks along the front of each glide. (Fig. 5)

5. Do drawers stick only in damp weather? When weather is dry, and drawers are not sticking, coat the unfinished wood with a penetrating sealer or with wax. (Fig. 6)

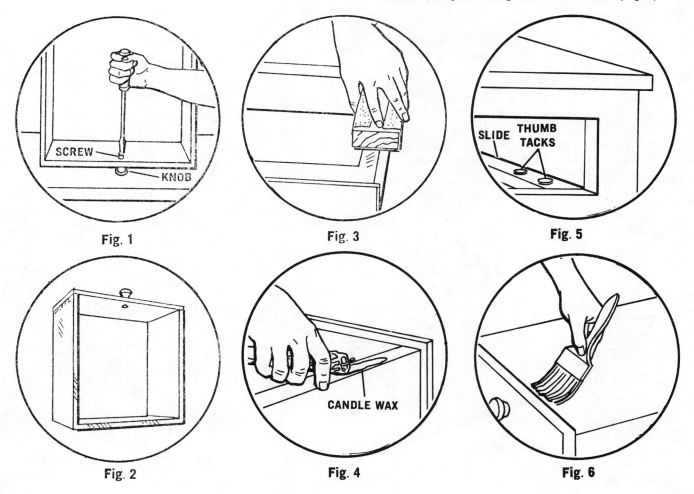

Fig. 1

Fig. 3

Fig. 5

Fig. 2

Fig. 4

Fig. 6

REPAIRING SCREENS

YOUR PROBLEM

Insects come in through holes in screens.

Small holes tend to become larger.

New screens cost money.

Help is hard to get

WHAT YOU NEED

Screening or ready-cut screen patches

Shears

A ruler or small block of wood with a straight edge.

Fine wire, or nylon thread.

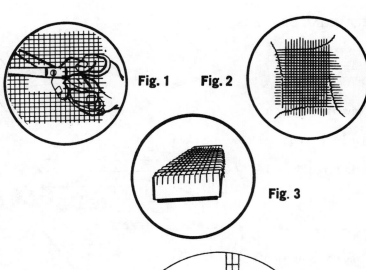

Fig. 1   Fig. 2

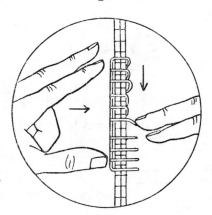

Fig. 3

HOW-TO

1. Trim the hole in the screen to make smooth edges. (Fig. 1.)

2. Cut a rectangular patch an inch larger than the hole.

3. Remove the three outside wires on all fours sides of the patch. (Fig. 2)

4. Bend the ends of the wires. An easy way is to bend them over a block or edge of a ruler. (Fig. 3)

5. Put the patch over the hole from the outside. Hold it tight against the screen so that the small, bent wire ends go through the screen. (Fig. 4)

6. From inside, bend down the ends of the wires toward the center of the hole. You may need someone outside to press against the patch while you do this. (Fig. 5)

MENDING—You can mend small holes by stitching back and forth with a fine wire or a nylon thread. Use a matching color. (Fig. 6)

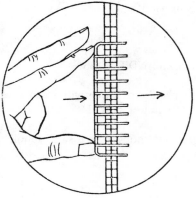

Fig. 4

Fig. 5

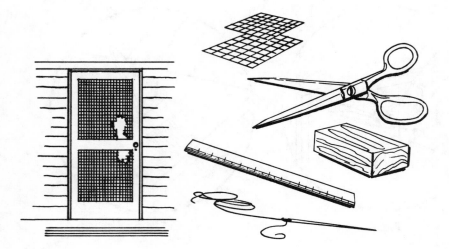

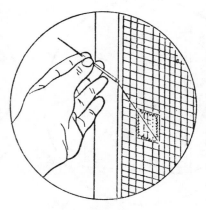

Fig. 6

FILL THE CRACK AROUND BATHTUB OR SHOWER

YOUR PROBLEM

There's a crack between the bathtub and wall. It should be filled to keep water out. Water can damage the walls and house frame. The crack catches dirt and looks bad.

WHAT YOU NEED

There are two types of waterproof crack filler. Choose one:

1. Waterproof grout

2. Plastic sealer

GROUT comes in powder form. It must be mixed with water. You can mix it in small amounts at a time. Grout costs less than plastic sealers.

PLASTIC SEALER comes in a tube. It looks like toothpaste. It is easier to use than grout, but costs more. Read directions on the package before you begin your project.

HOW-TO
PREPARE THE SURFACE

1. Remove the old crack filler from the crack. (Fig. 1)

2. Wash the surface to remove soap, grease, and dirt. (Fig. 2)

3. Dry the surface well before you make repairs. (Fig. 3)

USING GROUT

Put a small amount of grout in a bowl. (Fig. 4). Slowly add water and mix until you have a thick paste. Put this mixture in the crack with a putty knife. (Fig. 5) Press in to fill the crack. (Fig. 6) Smooth the surface. (Fig. 7)

Wipe excess grout from the wall and tub before it gets dry and hard. Let the grout dry well before anyone uses the tub.

Empty any left-over grout mixture. (Not down the drain!) Wash your bowl and knife before grout dries on them.

USING PLASTIC SEALER

You can squeeze plastic sealer from the tube in a ribbon along the crack. Use a putty knife or spatula to press it down and fill the crack. Smooth the surface. Work fast! Plastic sealer dries in a very few minutes. Keep the cap on the tube when you're not using it. (Fig. 8)

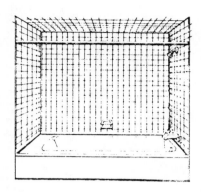

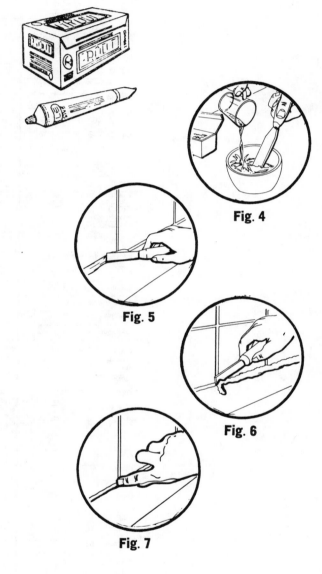

Fig. 4

Fig. 5

Fig. 6

Fig. 7

Fig. 1

Fig. 2

Fig. 3

Fig. 8

WOOD CHARACTERISTIC TABLE

SPECIES	PRINCIPAL USES Exterior	Interior	APPEARANCE Color	Figure	Grain	RELATIVE COSTS Lumber	Plywood
ASH, White		Trim, Frames, Panelling, Cabinets	Creamy White to Light Brown	High	Open	100	165
AVODIRE		Solid Trim Incidental to Veneered Panelling	Creamy Yellow	High	Closed	400	350
BEECH		Semi-Exposed Cabinet Parts	White to Reddish Brown	Low	Closed	80	Not Ge Availab
BIRCH, Yellow — "Natural"		Trim, Frames, Panelling, Cabinets	White to Dark Red	Medium	Closed	100	100
BIRCH, Yellow — "Select Red" (Heartwood)		Trim, Frames, Panelling, Cabinets	Dark Red	Medium	Closed	145	130
BIRCH, Yellow — "Select White" (Sapwood)		Trim, Frames, Panelling, Cabinets	Creamy White	Medium	Closed	130	120
BUTTERNUT		Trim, Frames, Panelling, Cabinets	Pale Brown	High	Open	200	210
CHERRY		Trim, Frames, Panelling, Cabinets	Reddish Brown	High	Closed	160	185
CHESTNUT — Wormy		Panelling and Trim	Greyish Brown	High	Open With Worm Holes	200	350
CYPRESS	Trim, Frames, Special Siding	Panelling and Trim	Slightly Red to Yellowish Brown	High	Closed	100	Not Ge Availab
FIR, Douglas — Flat Grain	Trim, Frames	Trim, Frames, Panelling	Reddish Tan	High	Closed	75	50
FIR, Douglas — Vertical Grain	Trim, Frames, Doors, Special Siding	Trim, Frames, Panelling	Reddish Tan	Low	Closed	80	115
GUM — Natural		Trim, Semi-Exposed Cabinet Parts	White to Greenish Tan With Mineral Streaks	Low	Closed	90	110
GUM — Quarter Sawn Red		Trim, Frames, Panelling, Cabinets	Reddish Brown With Dark Streaks	High	Closed	170	155
LAUAN, "Light Philippine Mahogany"	Trim, Frames, Doors, Special Siding	Trim, Frames, Panelling, Cabinets	Light to Reddish Brown	Low	Open	115	100
LIMBA		Trim, Frames, Panelling, Cabinets	Pale Yellow	Medium	Open	160	170
MAHOGANY, African — Plain Sawn	Trim, Frames, Doors, Sash, Special Siding	Trim, Frames, Panelling, Cabinets	Light to Dark Reddish Brown	Medium	Open	120	150
MAHOGANY, African — Quarter Sawn		Trim, Frames, Panelling, Cabinets	Reddish Brown	Low	Open	130	150
MAHOGANY, Tropical American- "Honduras"	Trim, Frames, Doors, Sash, Special Siding	Trim, Frames, Panelling, Cabinets, Bar Tops	Rich Golden Brown	Medium	Open	170	200
MAPLE, Hard — Natural		Trim, Frames, Panelling, Cabinets	White to Reddish Brown	Medium	Closed	100	100
MAPLE, Hard — Select White (Sapwood)		Trim, Frames, Panelling, Cabinets	White	Medium	Closed	130	140
MAPLE, Soft — Natural		Trim, Semi-Exposed Cabinet Parts	White to Reddish Brown	Low	Closed	85	Not Ge Availab
OAK, Red — Plain Sawn		Trim, Frames, Panelling, Cabinets	Reddish Tan to Brown	High	Open	85	145
OAK, Red — Rift Sawn		Trim, Frames, Panelling, Cabinets	Reddish Tan to Brown	Low	Open	130	180
OAK, White — Plain Sawn	Doors, Sills, Door Frames	Trim, Frames, Panelling, Cabinets	Greyish Tan	High	Open	120	165
OAK, White — Rift Sawn		Trim, Frames, Panelling, Cabinets	Greyish Tan	Low	Open	185	180
OAK, White — Quarter Sawn		Trim, Frames, Panelling, Cabinets	Greyish Tan	Low Figure Accented With Flakes	Open	185	250
OBECHE		Trim, Frames	Creamy White	Low	Open	130	Not Ge Availab
PECAN		Trim, Frames, Panelling	Reddish Brown With Dark Brown Stripes	High	Open	150	180
PINE, Idaho	Trim, Frames, Doors, Sash, Special Siding	Trim, Frames, Panelling, Cabinets	Creamy White	Low	Closed	80	Not Ge Availab
PINE, Northern	Trim, Frames, Doors, Sash, Special Siding	Trim, Frames, Panelling, Cabinets	Creamy White to Pink	Medium	Closed	80	Not Ge Availab
PINE, Ponderosa	Trim, Frames, Doors, Sash, Special Siding	Trim, Frames, Panelling, Cabinets	Light to Medium Pink	Medium	Closed	75	90
PINE, Sugar	Trim, Frames, Doors, Sash, Special Siding	Trim, Frames, Panelling, Cabinets	Creamy White	Low	Closed	80	Not Ge Availab
PINE, Yellow — Shortleaf	Trim, Frames, Special Siding	Trim, Frames, Panelling, Cabinet Parts	Pale Yellow	High	Closed	65	Not Ge Availab
POPLAR		Trim, Frames, Panelling, Cabinets	Pale Yellow to Brown With Green Cast	Medium	Closed	85	125
PRIMA VERA		Solid Trim Incidental to Veneered Panelling	Creamy Yellow	High	Open	350	325
RED CEDAR, Western	Trim, Window Frames, Special Siding	Trim, Panelling	Light to Dark Red	Medium	Closed	90	140
REDWOOD — Flat Grain (Heartwood)	Trim, Window Frames, Sash, Special Siding	Trim, Frames, Panelling	Deep Red	High	Closed	85	120
REDWOOD — Vertical Grain (Heartwood)	Trim, Window Frames, Special Siding	Trim, Frames, Panelling	Deep Red	Low	Closed	90	125
ROSEWOOD, Brazilian		Solid Trim Incidental to Veneered Panelling	Intermingled Reds, Browns, and Blacks	High	Open	535	780
SPRUCE, Sitka	Trim, Frames	Trim, Frames	Light Yellowish Tan	Low	Closed	75	90
TANGUILE — "Dark Philippine Mahogany" — Plain Sawn	Trim, Frames, Doors, Special Siding	Trim, Frames, Panelling, Cabinets	Light to Dark Red	Medium	Open	120	105
TANGUILE — "Dark Philippine Mahogany" — Quarter Sawn	Trim, Frames, Doors, Special Siding	Trim, Frames, Panelling, Cabinets	Dark Red	Low	Open	135	120
TEAK, East Indian	Trim, Frames, Doors, Special Siding	Trim, Frames, Panelling, Cabinets	Tawny Yellow to Dark Brown	High	Open	430	445
WALNUT		Trim, Frames, Panelling, Cabinets	Sapwood — Creamy White Heartwood — Medium to Dark Purplish Brown	High	Open	325	250

Note: Regional distribution differences may affect availability and cost relationship.

*Rated from 1 to 4 as follows:
1. In warehouse stock in good quantities and fair assortment of thickness lengths.

PRACTICAL SIZE LIMITATIONS			AVAILABILITY OF MATCHING PLYWOOD *	HARDNESS	DIMENSIONAL STABILITY **	FINISHING		REMARKS
Max. Prac. Thickness Without Lem.	Max. Prac. Width	Max. Prac. Length				Paint	Transparent	
1⅝″	7½″	12′	2	Very Hard	10/64″	Not Normally Used	Excellent	Bold grain, very strong
¾″	5½″	12′	3	Medium	9/64″	Not Normally Used	Excellent	Fine architectural veneer, solid lumber in limited supply
1⅝″	7½″	12′	4	Very Hard	14/64″	Excellent	Good	Low cost, low stability
1⅝″	7½″	12′	1	Hard	12/64″	Excellent	Good	Widely used
1⅝″	5½″	11′	2	Hard	12/64″	Not Normally Used	Excellent	Rich color
1⅝″	5″	11′	2	Hard	12/64″	Not Normally Used	Excellent	Uniform appearance
1 1/16″	5½″	9′	3	Medium	8/64″	Not Normally Used	Excellent	Rich appearance, limited supply
1⅝″	5½″	10′	2	Hard	9/64″	Not Normally Used	Excellent	Rich appearance
1⅝″	7½″	10′	3	Medium	9/64″	Not Normally Used	Excellent	Unique decorative wood
1¾″	9½″	16′	4	Medium	8/64″	Good	Good	Traditional exterior wood, has become scarce
2¾″	11″	16′	1	Soft	10/64″	Fair	Fair	Low cost, tendency to splinter and grain raise
1⅝″	11″	16′	2	Soft	6/64″	Good	Good	Good stability
1 1/16″	7½″	12′	2	Hard	10/64″	Excellent	Fair	Subject to regional usage
¾″	5½″	10′	3	Hard	6/64″	Not Normally Used	Excellent	Subject to regional usage
1¾″	11″	16′	2	Soft	10/64″	Fair	Good	Limited application for architectural woodwork
1 1/16″	9½″	12′	3	Medium	9/64″	Not Normally Used	Excellent	Very attractive natural blond wood
2¾″	11½″	16′	3	Medium	7/64″	Good	Excellent	Moderately priced, wide range of exterior and interior uses
2¾″	7½″	16′	2	Medium	5/64″	Not Normally Used	Excellent	Primarily used for architectural veneered products
2¾″	11½″	16′	3	Medium	6/64″	Not Normally Used	Excellent	Excellent architectural wood for all uses
2⅝″	7½″	12′	3	Very Hard	12/64″	Excellent	Good	Extremely hard
1⅝″	5½″	12′	2	Very Hard	12/64″	Not Normally Used	Excellent	Uniform appearance, extremely hard
1 1/16″	9½″	12′	4	Medium	9/64″	Excellent	Not Normally Used	Not widely used
1⅝″	9½″	14′	1	Hard	11/64″	Not Normally Used	Excellent	Excellent architectural wood, low cost, widely used
1 1/16″	5½″	12′	3	Hard	5/64″	Not Normally Used	Excellent	Excellent architectural wood, limited supply
1⅝″	7½″	12′	2	Hard	11/64″	Not Normally Used	Excellent	Wide range of grain patterns and color
¾″	4½″	10′	2	Hard	7/64″	Not Normally Used	Excellent	Limited availability
¾″	5½″	10′	3	Hard	7/64″	Not Normally Used	Excellent	Pronounced flake, very limited use and supply
¾″	9½″	14′	4	Medium	9/64″	Not Normally Used	Good	Economical blond wood
1 1/16″	7½″	12′	3	Hard	11/64″	Not Normally Used	Excellent	Subject to regional availability, attractive
2¾″	11″	16′	4	Soft	8/64″	Excellent	Good	True white pine, wide range of applications for general usage
2¾″	11″	16′	4	Soft	8/64″	Excellent	Good	True white pine, wide range of applications for general usage
2¾″	11″	16′	2	Soft	8/64″	Excellent	Good	Most widely used pine, wide range of applications for general usage
2¾″	11″	16′	4	Soft	7/64″	Excellent	Good	True white pine, wide range of applications for general usage
2¾″	11″	16′	4	Medium	10/64″	Good	Good	An economical hard pine
1⅝″	11″	12′	3	Medium	9/64″	Excellent	Good	Ideal interior hardwood, excellent paintability
¾″	5″	10′	3	Medium	10/64″	Not Normally Used	Excellent	Generally used for fine architectural veneer
1⅝″	11″	16′	3	Soft	6/64″	Good	Good	High natural decay resistance, limited availability
2¾″	11″	20′	2	Soft	6/64″	Good	Good	Superior exterior wood, high natural decay resistance
2¾″	11″	20′	2	Soft	3/64″	Excellent	Excellent	Superior exterior wood, high natural decay resistance
1 1/16″	3″	8′	3	Very Hard	7/64″	Not Normally Used	Excellent	Exotic figure, high cost
1¾″	11″	16′	3	Soft	10/64″	Good	Good	Limited general availability
2¾″	11″	16′	3	Medium	12/64″	Good	Good	Moderately priced attractive hardwood
2¾″	7½″	16′	2	Medium	8/64″	Not Normally Used	Good	Moderately priced attractive hardwood
2⅝″	9½″	14′	2	Very Hard	6/64″	Not Normally Used	Excellent	Outstanding wood for most applications, high cost
1⅝″	4½″	8′	1	Hard	10/64″	Not Normally Used	Excellent	Fine domestic hardwood, extremely limited widths and lengths, more readily available in veneer form, high cost

In warehouse stock in fair quantity but not in thicknesses other than ¼″ and ¾″; or sizes other than 4′-0″ x 8′-0″.
Produced on a special order only.
Not generally available.

**These figures represent possible width change in a 12″ board when moisture content is reduced from 10% to 5%. Figures are for plain sawn unless indicated otherwise in species column.

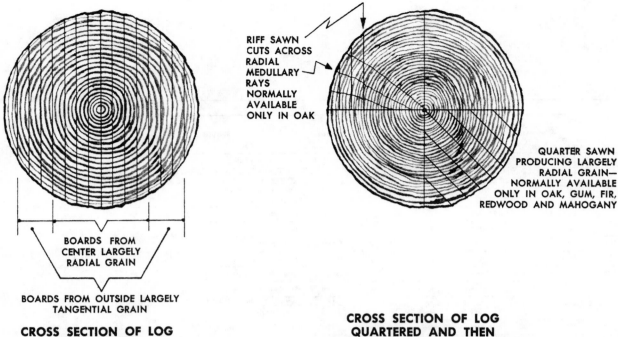

RIFF SAWN
CUTS ACROSS
RADIAL
MEDULLARY
RAYS
NORMALLY
AVAILABLE
ONLY IN OAK

QUARTER SAWN
PRODUCING LARGELY
RADIAL GRAIN—
NORMALLY AVAILABLE
ONLY IN OAK, GUM, FIR,
REDWOOD AND MAHOGANY

BOARDS FROM
CENTER LARGELY
RADIAL GRAIN

BOARDS FROM OUTSIDE LARGELY
TANGENTIAL GRAIN

**CROSS SECTION OF LOG
PLAIN SAWN**

Note: Relatively Wide Boards

**CROSS SECTION OF LOG
QUARTERED AND THEN
QUARTER SAWN OR RIFF SAWN**

Note: Relatively Narrow Boards

Below is shown exaggerated characteristic shrinkage distortion which is greatest in wide members. This plus superior appearance available in veneers is the reason for recommendation for use of relatively stable plywood for wide members.

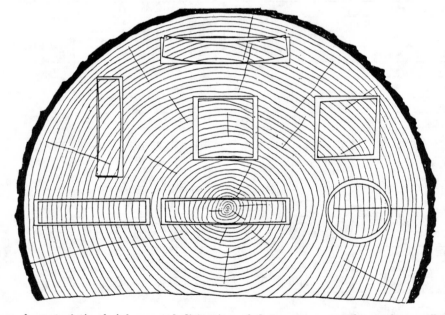

From characteristic shrinkage and distortion of flats, squares, and rounds as affected by the direction of the annual rings. Tangential shrinkage is about twice as great as radial.

HOW TO WORK PLYWOOD

LAYING OUT/CUTTING

Do this with care—to avoid waste and simplify your work. When many pieces are to be cut from one large full-size panel, you'll find it easiest to sketch the arrangement on a piece of paper before marking the plywood for cutting.

Be sure to allow for a saw kerf between adjacent pieces.

Try to work it out so that your first cuts reduce the panel to pieces small enough for easy handling, and most important, watch in planning your sequence of operations so as to cut all mating or matching parts with the same saw setting.

TYPES OF VENEER CUTS

The manner in which veneers are cut is an important factor in producing the various visual effects obtained. Two woods of the same species, but with their veneers cut differently, will have entirely different visual character even though their color values are similar.

In plywood manufacture, six principal methods of cutting veneers are used, depending on the type of veneer required, (whether for face, crossband, or core) the nature of the log and the veneer figure desired. Primarily the veneer slicer and veneer lathe are the equipment employed. The six methods are:

ROTARY

The log is mounted centrally in the lathe and turned against a razor sharp blade, like unwinding a roll of paper. Since this cut follows the log's annular growth rings a bold variegated grain marking is produced. Rotary cut veneer is exceptionally wide.

ALMOST ALL SOFTWOOD PLYWOOD IS CUT THIS WAY. LENGTHS IN ALMOST ALL HARDWOOD ARE LIMITED TO 8'-0".

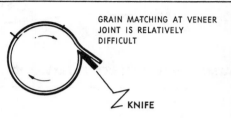

GRAIN MATCHING AT VENEER JOINT IS RELATIVELY DIFFICULT

KNIFE

PLAIN SLICING (OR FLAT SLICING)

The half log, or flitch, is mounted with the heart side flat against the guide plate of the slicer and the slicing is done parallel to a line through the center of the log. This produces a variegated figure.

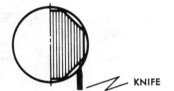

KNIFE

PLAIN SLICING

TYPICAL LARGE GRAIN CATHEDRALS

LARGE CATHEDRALS AT OUTSIDE OF LOG BECOMING SMALLER TOWARD CENTER.

QUARTER SLICING

The quarter log or flitch is mounted on the guide plate so that the growth rings of the log strike the knife at approximately right angles, producing a series of stripes, straight in some woods, varied in others.

KNIFE

QUARTER SLICING

UNIFORMLY SMALL GRAIN CATHEDRALS AND RELATIVELY NARROW PIECES.

HALF-ROUND SLICING

A variation of rotary cutting in which segments or flitches of the log are mounted off center in the lathe. This results in a cut slightly across the annular growth rings, and visually shows modified characteristics of both rotary and plain sliced veneers.

OFTEN USED ON RED OAK

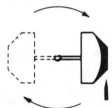

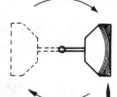

HALF-ROUND SLICING

KNIFE

FIGURE RESEMBLES ROTARY CUT.

BACK-CUT

The flitch is mounted as in half-round cutting except that the bark side faces in towards the lathe center. The veneers so cut are characterized by an enhanced striped figure and the inclusion of sapwood along the edges.

LESS OFTEN USED

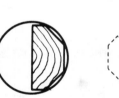

BACK-CUT

KNIFE

FIGURE SLIGHTLY SMALLER THAN OUTSIDE PORTION OF PLAIN SLICED.

RIFT-CUT

Rift cut veneer is produced in the various species of Oak. Oak has medullary ray cells which radiate from the center of the log like the curved spokes of a wheel. The rift or comb grain effect is obtained by cutting perpendicularly to these medullary rays either on the lathe or slicer.

NORMALLY LIMITED TO OAK

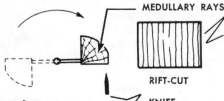

MEDULLARY RAYS

RIFT-CUT

KNIFE

FAIRLY UNIFORM GRAIN. RELATIVELY NARROW PIECES.

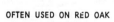

VENEER CORE

All plies are veneer — less than ¼" thick. Middle ply is called the "center". Plies on either side of the center, but beneath the outer plies, are called "crossbandings". Outer plies are called "faces" and "backs". Thickness varies from ⅛" to ¾" or more — odd number of plies from 3 to 11 or more.

CENTER

FACE VENEER

CROSSBANDING

BACK VENEER

ALMOST ALL SOFTWOOD PLYWOOD HAS VENEER CORE

LUMBER CORE

Center ply, called the "core" is composed of strips of lumber edge-glued into a solid slab. This type is usually 5-ply, ¾" thick but other thicknesses from ½" to 1⅛" are manufactured for special uses. There are three main core types:

a. **Staved** — all strips random length, butt-joined.
b. **Full-Length** — all strips one-piece.
c. **Banded** — outside strips full-length, others random length. Banding may be same type of lumber as rest of core but is usually a different species. Banding may include all four edges. Banded plywood is almost always produced for special uses — furniture, desk tops, and cupboard doors.

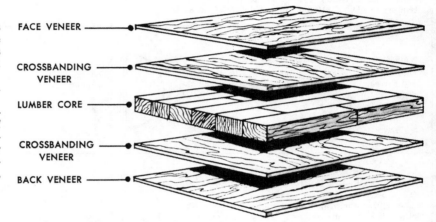

FACE VENEER

CROSSBANDING VENEER

LUMBER CORE

CROSSBANDING VENEER

BACK VENEER

NORMALLY LIMITED TO HARDWOOD PLYWOOD

CHIPS OR SHAVINGS BOARD CORE

Medium density boards made from wood particles and called variously "chip board" "particle board" or "shavings board" are being used more and more to replace lumber core in plywood. Developed from a need to increase the utilization of our remaining timber reserves, these boards stand on their own merits against solid lumber in all products where they are used interchangeably.

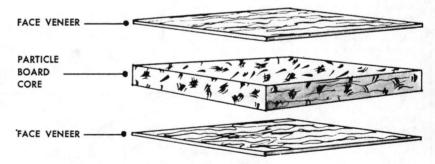

FACE VENEER

PARTICLE BOARD CORE

FACE VENEER

NORMALLY LIMITED TO HARDWOOD PLYWOOD

Note face grain direction. Except where indicated otherwise in the plan, you'll want this to run the long way of the piece. Mark the better face unless you are going to cut with a portable power saw; in that case, mark it on the back.

1. WHEN HAND-SAWING, place plywood with good face up. Use a saw having 10 to 15 points to the inch. Support the panel firmly so it won't sag. You can reduce splitting

out of the underside by putting a piece of scrap lumber under it and sawing it along with the plywood. It also helps to hold the saw at a low angle as shown. Most important of all: use a sharp saw.

2.   POWER SAWING on a radial or table saw should be done with good face of plywood up. Use a sharp combination blade or a fine—tooth one without much set. Let the blade protrude above the plywood just the height of the teeth. You'll find handling large panels an easier one-man job if you build an extension support with a roller. It can have a base of its own or may be clamped to a saw horse.

3.   PORTABLE POWER SAW should be used with a good face of the plywood down. Tack a strip of scrap lumber to the top of each saw horse and you can saw right through it without damaging the horse. Keep your saw blade sharp.

SABRE SAW allows cutting of irregular curves and shapes. If you place the front of the sabre saw platform against the face of the panel and tilt the blade downward to scratch the panel surface, you can work a saw slot into the panel for interior cuts without having to drill a pilot hole. Pay special attention to selection of sabre saw baldes: Use the finest tooth possible to get a smooth, even cut for the highest quality finish.

4.   PLANING PLYWOOD EDGES with plane or jointer won't be necessary if you make your cuts with a sharp saw blade. For very smooth edges that won't even require sanding, use a hollow-ground blade. If you do any planing, work from both ends of the edge toward the center to avoid tearing out plies at the end of the cut. Use a plane with a sharp blade; take very shallow cuts.

5.   SANDING before sealer or prime coat is applied should be confined to edges. Most appearance grade plywood is sanded smooth in manufacture—one of the big timesavers in its use—and further sanding of the surfaces will merely remove soft grain. After sealing, sand in direction of grain only. A sanding block, one type of which is shown, will prevent gouging.

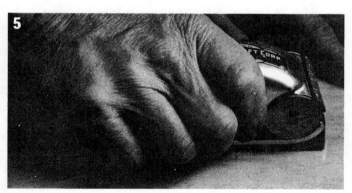

CONSTRUCTION JOINTS

6.   BUTT JOINTS, like the one indicated in the picture, are simplest to make, suitable for 3/4" plywood. For thinner panels, use a reinforcing block, or nailing strip to make a stronger joint. In both cases, glue will make the joint many times stronger than if it were made with nails or screws alone.

7.   FRAME CONSTRUCTION makes it possible to reduce weight by using thinner plywood, since it has amazing strength. Glue as recommended.

8.   RABBET JOINTS like this one are neat and strong, easy to make with power tools. You'll find this an ideal joint for drawers, buffets, chests, or cupboards. Miter joints (not shown) are the least noticeable and are easily finished. They do, however, require precision machining and careful fastening. (See No. 15 under Plywood Fasteners and clamping method under Assembling.)

9. DADO JOINTS, quickly made with a power saw, produce neat shelves. Use a dado head with blades shimmed out to produce these grooves in a single cut.

PLYWOOD FASTENERS

10. NAIL SIZE is determined primarily by the thickness of the plywood you're using. Used with glue, all nails shown here will produce strong joints. For 3/4" plywood, 6d casing nails or 8d finish nails. For 5/8", 6d or 8d. For 1/2", 4d or 6d. For 3/8", 3d or 4d. For 1/4", use 3/4" or 1" brads, 3d finish nails, or (for backs where there is no objection to heads showing) 1" blue lath nails. Substitute casing for finish nails wherever you want a heavier nail.

11. PRE-DRILLING is occasionally called for in careful work where nails must be very close to an edge. As indicated here, drill bit should be slightly smaller in diameter than the nail to be used.

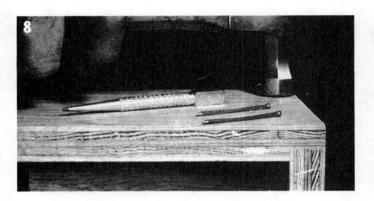

12. SPACE NAILS about 6" apart for most work. Closer spacing is necessary only with thin plywood where there may be slight buckling between nails. Nails and glue work together to produce a strong, durable joint.

13. FLAT-HEAD WOOD SCREWS are useful where nails will not provide adequate holding power. Glue should also be used if possible.

14. SCREWS AND NAILS should be countersunk and the holes filled with wood dough or surfacing putty. Apply filler so it is slightly higher than the plywood, then sanded level when dry. Lubricate screws with soap if hard to drive.

15. CORRUGATED FASTENERS can reinforce miter joints in 3/4" plywood and hold joints together while glue sets. For some jobs, sheet-metal screws are valuable; they have more holding power than wood screws, but come only in short lengths and do not have flat heads. Bolts and washers are good for fastening sectional units together and for installing legs, hinges or other hardware when great strength is required.

GLUING

16. Choose your glue from the chart snown. Before applying it, make sure of a good fit by testing the joint facing For lasting strength, both pieces should make contact at all points.

17. Apply glue with brush or stick. End grain absorbs glue so quickly that it is best to apply a preliminary coat. Allow to soak in for a few minutes, then apply another coat before joining the parts. Avoid excess glue when project is to be finished with stain or varnish.

18. Clamp the joints tightly with clamps as shown or with nails, screw, or other fasteners. Use blocks of wood under the jaws of the clamps to avoid damage to plywood. Since some glues will stain or seal wood and make it difficult to achieve a good finish, quickly wipe any excess, and sand the area after drying. Test for squareness, then allow glue to set.

ASSEMBLING

19. PLANNING pays off in assembly steps, just as in cutting parts. Frequently, your easiest solution is to break down complicated projects into sub-assemblies. They are simpler to handle and make joints more accessible, as shown by these partitioned shelves. Apply clamps with full jaw length in contact. When jaws are not parallel, as at right in picture, pressure is applied to only part of the joint.

20. A HANDY, little-known trick for clamping miter joints in cabinets is shown here. With paper sandwiched between, to permit easy removal, glue triangular blocks to the ends of each mitered piece.. Let glue set. Apply glue to mitered ends and pull together in alignment with clamps. Remove clamps after glue has set, pry blocks away and sand off paper.

21. SPECIAL CLAMPS frequently save work, help you do a better job. Here are various types of edge-clamps, used to glue wood or plastic edging to plywood. Bar clamps or quick C clamps grip the panel which is protected by scrap wood. Then edge clamping fixtures are inserted to bear against the edge-banding material while glue sets.

INSTALLING

22. FRAME WALLS permit hanging cabinets by use of long wood screws through the cabinet backs. Screws must be driven into wall studs to secure good holding power. Locate the first stud by tapping the wall, then measure off 16" intervals to find the other studs.

23. HOLLOW MASONRY WALLS call for use of toggle bolts or "Molly" fasteners (shown here). First drill hole with star drill or carbide-tipped bit, then insert "Molly" and tighten. After that you can remove he bolt and use it to hang the cabinet. For gypsum board walls, "Molly" bolts can be used where stud fastening is not possible, provided loads are relatively light.

24. CONCRETE, STONE or other solid masonry walls call for anchor bolts like this one. Fasten the base to the wall with black mastic, letting it squeeze through the holes. Hang plywood unit after mastic has set, using washers. Toggle bolts in expansion shields also may be used.

DRAWER CONSTRUCTION

25. THIS DRAWER, shown upside down, is easily made with saw and hammer. Butt joints are glued and nailed. The bottom should be 3/8" or 1/2" plywood for rigidity. The drawer front extends down to cover the front edge of the bottom.

26. ADDITIONAL STRIP of wood, glued and nailed to front panel, reinforces the bottom of this second type of drawer made with hand tools. Reinforcing permits use of economical 1/4" plywood for drawer bottoms.

27. POWER TOOLS make sturdy drawers easy to build. The picture shows one side (dadoed on outer face for drawer guide) being put into place. Rabbet drawer front (at right) to take sides; dado sides to fit drawer back. All four parts are grooved to take 1/4" plywood bottom.

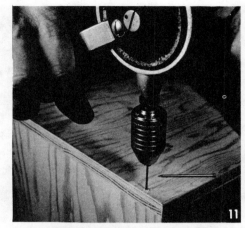

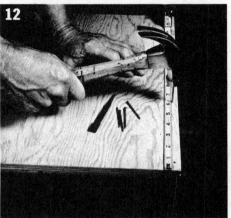

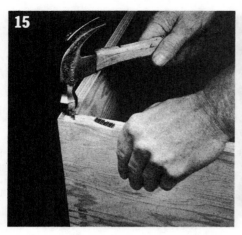

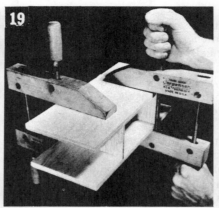

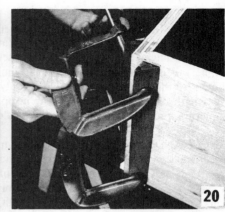

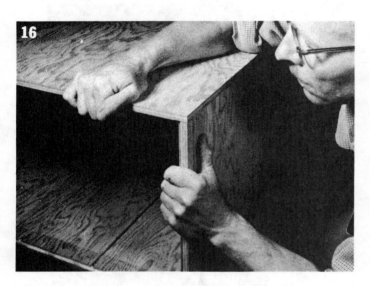

28/29. TWO TYPES OF GUIDES calling for use of power tools are shown in these two photographs. As recommended, the drawer side has been plowed before assembly to fit over a strip glued to the side of the cabinet. Procedure is reversed for the right panel.. Here the cabinet side has been dadoed before assembly. A matching strip is glued to the side of the drawer. Even heavy drawers slide easily on guides like these if waxed or lubricated with paraffin after finishing.

30. HAND TOOLS ONLY are required to make this drawer. The secret is its bottom, made of 3/8" or 1/2" plywood. This bottom extends 3/8" beyond the sides of the drawer to form a lip. Ease edges and apply paraffin for easy operation.

31. EXTENDED BOTTOM of drawer at left fits into slots formed by gluing pieces of 3/8" plywood to the inner surface of each side of the cabinet. Gap just wide enough to take the lip is left between the pieces.

32. POWER TOOLS will permit making a simpler and lighter version of the same drawer. The photograph shows details of construction. Bottom is 1/4" plywood cut 3/8" wider than the drawer on each side.

33. THIS DRAWER slides in slots dadoes into the 3/4" plywood sides of the cabinet. When power tools are used, this is one of the simplest of all methods of drawer-and-guide construction.

SLIDING DOORS

34. CLOSE-FITTING plywood sliding doors are made by rabbeting top and bottom edges of each door. Rabbet back of front door, front of back door. This lets doors almost touch, leaving little gap for dust and increases the effective depth of the cabinet. For 3/8" plywood doors rabbeted half their thickness, plow two grooves in top and bottom of cabinet 1/2" apart. With all plywood doors, seal all edges and give backs same paint treatment as front to maintain plywood's balanced construction.

35. FOR REMOVABLE DOORS, plow bottom grooves 3/16" deep, top grooves 3/8" deep. After finishing (see photo shown), insert door by pushing up into excess space in top groove, then dropping into bottom. Plowing can be eliminated by use of a fiber track made for sliding doors of this type.

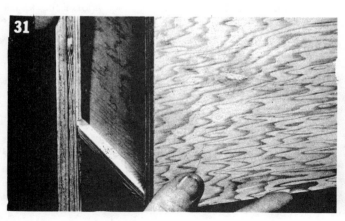

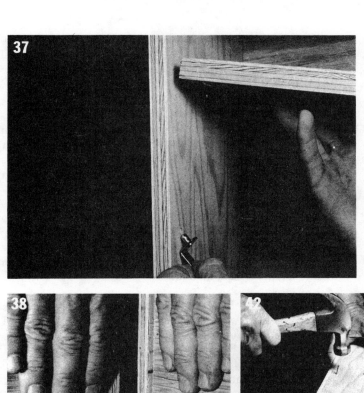

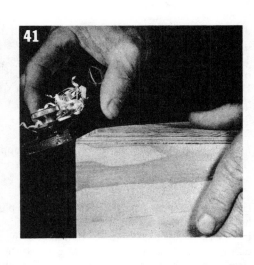

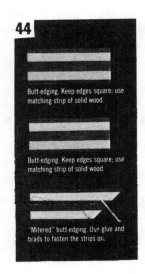

Butt-edging. Keep edges square; use matching strip of solid wood.

Butt-edging. Keep edges square; use matching strip of solid wood.

"Mitered" butt-edging. Use glue and brads to fasten the strips on.

EDGE FILLER

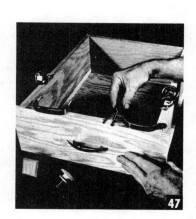

36. ONLY HAND TOOLS are required when this version of the sliding door is used. Front and back strips are stock 1/4" quarter-round molding. The strip between is 1/4" quarter-round molding. The strip between is 1/4" square. Use glue and brads or finish nails to fasten strips securely. Sliding door cabinet track also may be used.

37. The neatest and strongest way to hang a shelf is by making a dado joint or using metal shelf supports. A dado requires power tools and does not permit changing shelf height.

Here are inexpensive shelf supports that plug into blind holes 3/8" deep drilled in the plywood sides of the cabinet. Drill additional holes to permit moving shelves when desired. Another device is the use of slotted metal shelf strips into which shelf supports may be plugged at any height. For a better fit, set shelf strips flush in a dado cut, or cut out shelves around shelf strips.

38. STANDARD METHOD of applying backs to cabinets and other storage units calls for rabbeting sides. Cabinet as demonstrated here has rabbet just deep enough to take plywood back. For large units that must fit against walls that may not be perfectly smooth or plumb, the version shown in this photograph is better. This rabbet is made 1/2" or even 3/4" deep. The lip that remains after back has been inserted may be easily trimmed wherever necessary to get a good fit between plywood unit and house wall.

39. WHEN HAND TOOLS are used, attach strips of 1/4" quarter-round molding for the back to rest against. Glue and nail back to molding.

40. SHOWN HERE are two methods of applying cabinet backs without rabbets or moldings. One by nailing the back flush with outside edge. Second by setting the back 1/2" to 7/8" away from edges. The back becomes inconspicuous when cabinet is against the wall.

41. BEVEL cabinet backs that must be applied without a rabbet to make them less conspicuous. Install 3/8" plywood back flush with the edges of the cabinet, then bevel with light strokes of a block plane.

42. NAIL CABINET BACK into rabbet by driving nails at a slight angle, as indicated here. Use 1" brads or 4d finish nails. Where back will not be seen, 1" blue lath nails may be used.

43. TWO-HAND STAPLERS like this one are excellent for nailing cabinet backs. They drive long staples, setting them below the surface if desired, and greatly speed up the work. They are sometimes available on loan or rental.

EDGE TREATMENTS

44. THERE ARE many ways to finish plywood edges. You can achieve handsome, solid results by cutting a V groove and inserting a matching wood strip, but this method is comparatively difficult. Other suggested edge treatments are shown here.

Thin strips of real wood edge-banding now are available, already coated with pressure sensitive adhesive. Simply peel off backing paper and apply to plywood edges according to the manufacturer's recommendations.

45. LAMINATED PLASTIC surfacing materials may be applied to edges of tables with same contact cement used in applying to table tops. Apply to edges first, then to counter or table top. A thicker, more massive effect can be secured by nailing a 1" or 1-1/4" strip all around the underneath edge.

46. TO FILL END GRAIN on plywood edges that are to be painted, several varieties of wood putty are available; either powdered, to be mixed with water, or prepared, ready for use. Plaster spackling also works well. Sand smooth when thoroughly dry and then finish.

47. DRAWER PULLS and door handles of the types shown here are widely available. Use them in metal or wood to style your product. They come in a variety of traditional and "ranch" styles as well as in many modern designs.

48. SLIDING and rolling doors are most easily equipped with finger cups that you simply force into round holes. For large doors, use the rectangular cups or large round ones that are fastened in with screws. Round pulls at top are suitable where clearance is adequate, or you can make simple rectangular grips from wood.

49. SIMPLEST DRAWER PULL of all is a notch cut into the top of the drawer front. It may be rectangular, V shaped, or half-round. You can omit the notch from every other drawer, opening it by means of the notch in the drawer below, as shown. By sloping drawer fronts, the drawer may be pulled out by grasping the projecting bottom edge.

50. CATCHES come in many varieties besides the conventional friction type shown at extreme right in this picture. Touch type, being installed here, lets door open at a touch. Magnetic catch has no moving parts to break. Roller catches and the new ones made of polyethelyne are smoother and more durable than plan steel friction catches.

51. SURFACE HINGES are quickly mounted. They require no mortising, add an ornamental touch and come in many styles. A pair of H or H-L hinges will do for most doors; for larger doors or to add rigidity to smaller ones, use a pair of H-L plus one H (as shown here) or use three of the H type. Tee or strap hinges help prevent sag in large doors. On tall doors, one or two added hinges between those at top and bottom help prevent sag in large doors. On tall doors, one or two added hinges between those at top and bottom help to minimize warping.

52. OVERLAPPING (lipped) doors are neatly hung with semi-concealed hinges. They are excellent for plywood since screws go into flat grain. These have 1/2" inset, are made for doors of 3/4" plywood rabbeted to leave 1/4" lip. Such hinges are made in many styles and finishes, semi-concealed or full-surface.

53. CONCEALED PIN HINGES give a neat modern appearance to flush doors. They mount directly onto the cabinet side. Construction is simplified, because no face frame is necessary. Only the pivot is visible from the front when the door is closed. Use a pair for small doors, three (called "a pair and one-half") for larger doors.

Note: Doors are easier to hang if at least one side of the hinge mounts from the front, so that you can see what you are doing.

54. SEMI-CONCEALED loose-pin hinges like these offer the same appearance when door is closed as ordinary butt hinges, since only the barrel shows. They're much better, though, for flush plywood doors because screws go into flat plywood grain. A variation called a chest hinge may be used in the same way.

55. TWO METAL BRACKETS fasten to the top of each door with a pair of screws. Nylon wheels with ball bearings roll in a double-lipped track that is fastened to the door frame with screws. (Single-lipped track is also made, for single doors.) Installation is simple, with no mortising required.

Miscellaneous

"Shop." A non-grade stamp plywood panel that is usually marked as "shop." This economical grade may be used for various projects around the home where appearance or structural considerations are not a significant factor.

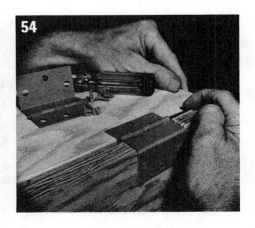

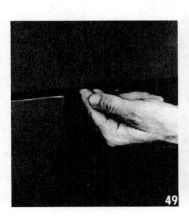

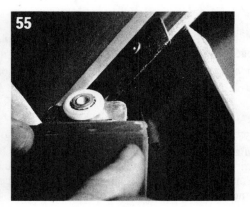

PLYWOOD THICKNESS	SCREW LENGTH	SCREW SIZE	DRILL SIZE FOR SHANK	DRILL SIZE FOR ROOT OF THREAD*
3/4" 5/8"	1½" 1¼"	#8	11/64"	1/8"
1/2" 3/8"	1¼"	#6	9/64"	3/32"
1/4"	1	#4	7/64"	1/16"

*If splitting is a problem (as in edges) make hole for threaded portion 1/64" larger (9/64", 7/64", and 5/64" respectively).

TYPE OF GLUE	DESCRIPTION	RECOMMENDED USE	PRECAUTIONS	HOW TO USE
UREA RESIN GLUE	Comes as powder to be mixed with water and used within 4 hours. Light colored. Very strong if well fitted.	Good for general wood gluing. First choice for work that must stand some exposure to dampness.	Needs well-fitted joints. tight clamping, and room temperature 70° or warmer.	Make sure joint fits tightly. Mix glue and apply thin coat. Allow 16 hours drying time.
LIQUID RESIN (WHITE) GLUE	Comes ready to use at any temperature. Clean-working, quick-setting. Strong enough for most work, though not quite so tough as urea resin glue	Good for indoor furniture and cabinetwork. First choice for small jobs where tight clamping or good fit may be difficult.	Not sufficiently resistant to moisture for outdoor furniture or outdoor storage units. Thoroughly clean up squeeze-out in areas to receive stain finish	Use at any temperature but preferably above 60°. Spread on both surfaces, clamp at once. Sets in 1½ hours.
RESORCINOL (WATERPROOF) GLUE	Comes as powder plus liquid, must be mixed each time used. Dark colored, very strong, completely waterproof.	This is the glue to use with Exterior type plywood for work to be exposed to extreme dampness.	Expense, trouble to mix and dark color make it unsuited to jobs where waterproof glue is not required. Needs good fit, tight clamping.	Use within 8 hours after mixing. Work at temperature above 70°. Apply thin coat to both surfaces; allow 16 hours drying time.

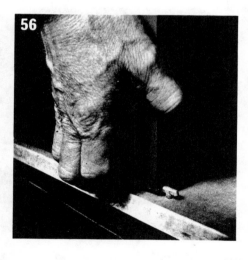

56. DOOR BOTTOM is kept in line by a simple T guide for each door. Two strips of 1/4" quarter-round molding, with 1/4" space between, will form slot if power tools are not available for making the slot.

57. ROLLING DOORS for closets and large storage units may have rollers mounted at either top or bottom. Top-mount hardware, shown in these three pictures, usually is smoother in operation, particularly when the door is tall and narrow.

TYPES AND USES

Plywood comes in two basic types, interior and exterior, the principal differences being that more of the lower veneer grades are permitted in the interior type, and the interior glueline does not have to be waterproof. The rule is simple: Interior plywood should not be exposed to the weather. Each type is available in a number of appearance grades (A, B, C, D) used for the face and back of each panel, determined by the veneer grade. Unsanded engineered grades are also available for wall and roof sheathing, subfloors, and structural/industrial uses.

Plywood is also classified by group based on the strength of the species used to make it. Group 1, the strongest, is made up largely of Douglas fir and southern pine plywood.

Interior

A-D. For interior applications where the appearance of only one side is important—paneling, built-ins, cabinet shelving.

B-D. Utility panel with one smooth, paintable side, for backing, sides of built-ins, utility shelving.

Decorative B-D. Rough sawn, brushed, grooved, or striated faces for paneling, accent walls, counter facing, displays.

Exterior

A-C. For applications where the appearance of only one side is important—sidings, soffits, fencing.

B-C. Outdoor utility panel with one smooth paintable side, for farm and work buildings, truck lining, containers, base for exterior coatings.

Engineered

Standard C-D. The interior unsanded sheathing grade , CDX also available (exterior glue).

Underlayment. The interior unsanded grade for underlayment used under resilient floor coverings and carpet. Available with exterior glue.

THE PRODUCT

Softwood plywood is a flat panel made of a number of thin sheets of wood veneer applied under pressure with the grain of each sheet perpendicular to the grain of the adjacent sheets. This cross-bonding produces great strength in both directions, and the glueline forms a bond that is stronger than the wood itself.

Split-proof puncture-proof, unique, pound for pound, a plywood panel is one of the strongest building materials made. Rigid, stable, and weighting far less than most metals, lumber, or hardboard of equivalent strength, it is easily worked, nailed, glued, and finished. Available everywhere building materials are sold, the most popular plywood panels are four feet wide, eight feet long, and from 1/4" to 3/4" thick.

HOW TO BUY AND SPECIFY

There is a tendency to overbuy plywood most often by substituting exterior for interior work on the theory that if exterior will stand up the the weather it will do even better indoors. Except where moisture or humidity is present, as in bathrooms and kitchens, this is not true; interior plywood will perform just as well in the controlled enviornment of the home and it costs less. Almost all plywood produced in the U.S. is inspected and certified by the American Plywood Association or other certifying agency and bears the agency grade stamp. Plywood is one product you can buy with confidence that it will perform as specified.

OVERLAID PLYWOOD is Exterior type plywood permanently protected with resin treated wood of either Medium or High Density. Both types can be worked in the same manner as regular plywood with these exceptions:

Sawing and drilling of overlaid plywood should always be done with the cutting edge of the tool entering the face of the panel. Tools should always be sharp and fed easily into the wood. Any chipping at the point of tool exit can be minimized by using a piece of scrap wood as a backup, or, in the case of sawing, by stripping tape along the line of the cut. Before surface-gluing HDO plywood, it is important to roughen the surface by a light sanding.

SAUNA

36

Saunas should have an upper and lower slatted wood bench constructed of 1" x 4" heartwood redwood slats. The bench should be 19" wide and 20" from the floor for the lower bench and stepped on the upper bench. Interior finish can be 1" x 4" redwood or cedar in a natural finish.

No plumbing is required for Saunas. Place the heater as low as possible to the floor. The ceiling must also be insulated and finished the same as the walls. Floor can be concrete or ceramic non-slip tile with removable wood buck boards in walking areas. Elderly and physically ill people suffering from heart disease or high blood pressure should consult a physician before entering a Sauna.

Saunas are built to specific requirements with a minimum of 3'—0" wide x 4'—0" long and a ceiling height of 7'—0" for one person only. If constructed as a separate building, follow the procedure as outlined for house construction. A Sauna differs only in the amount of insulation required which should be a minimum of R11 with foil face inward. Two fresh air vents, each 4" x 8", one placed no more than 12" above the floor and the other not less than 12" from the ceiling, should be installed of rustproof material preferably wood.

The heater must be mounted securely to the floor and all electric wiring should be #6AGW. (Check local code.) Do not install any electrical receptacles in a Sauna. If any windows are installed, they must be of insulating glass. No metallic or plastic materials should be used for interior finish. Nails, staples, etc., must be countersunk.

Most woods develop high surface temperatures which become uncomfortable to touch except heartwood redwood which insures a most comfortable temperature of any Sauna wood. No locking devices should be permitted on doors and the doors should be constructed of wood and opened outward with wood handles and controlled by a friction roller latch. A guard fence should be placed around the heater to prevent accidental burning. There should be no interior finish, such as paint or stain. The redwood must be left natural.

Steam is provided by a special igneous rock which provides a more even temperature. By pouring water over the rocks, a sudden hot moisture will be released in the room. This vapor striking the skin gives a brief mild burning sensation called "steam shock". Electric temperature controls are installed to heat the rock which are automatic on a timing device. Gas heaters are also available. If the Sauna is built in as part of the house, the steam produced by throwing water over the hot rocks is burned up by the heat and it will not damage the rest of the house.

Good Sauna design is a matter of three requirements:

1. Properly designed Sauna stove with adequate rocks.

2. Proper ventilation so the Sauna can breathe.

3. Proper woods for insulation against accident burns.

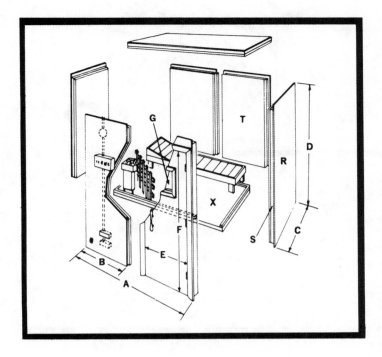

dimensions, in inches		
width, outside	A	72
width, minus door	B	44
depth, outside	C	48
height, outside	D	78
door width	E	22¾
door height	F	71¾
door window	G	9 x 18
wall and ceiling panels:		
exterior (mahogany)	R	¼
core (polyurethane)	S	1¾
interior (redwood)	T	⅜
floor panel:		
surface (redwood)	X	1

heater: 4 kw
220/240 volts/1 phase/60 cycle/
16 amp

floor area: 24 square feet
capacity: three persons sitting or one reclining

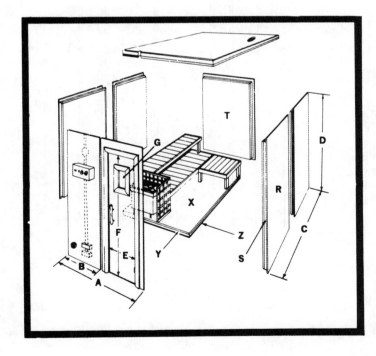

dimensions, in inches		
width, outside	A	60
width, minus door	B	33
depth, outside	C	96
height, outside	D	84
door width	E	22¾
door height	F	74¾
door window	G	9 x 18
wall and ceiling panels:		
exterior (mahogany)	R	¼
core (polyurethane)	S	1¾
interior (redwood)	T	⅜
floor panel:		
surface (redwood)	X	1
core (polyurethane)	Y	1¾
sub-base (marine plywood)	Z	¼

heater: 5 kw
220/240 volts/1 phase/60 cycle/
20 amp

floor area: 40 square feet
capacity: five persons sitting or two reclining

SITE WORK

37

One of the last segments of work to be done to complete the project is site work. This includes patios, walks, stairs, retaining walls, areaways, driveways, catch basins, final grading, recreational facilities, landscaping, fences etc.

AUTOMATIC LAWN SPRINKLERS

Underground lawn sprinklers work on a pre-programmed schedule to operate on or off, day or night, automatically. This is accomplished by an electrically operated control panel. The water service line may have to be increased if such a system is installed or planned. Special sprinkler heads are available for shrubs and borders, flower gardens, special unique areas, and large lawn areas.

TENNIS COURT

The surface of a tennis court will vary in material, control, comfort and price. The selection of surface material is judged on the best needs of the players. Consideration must be given to comfort, playability, appearance, longevity, maintenance and repair. Clay type courts are moderate in cost with a high maintenance factor. The ball has a high bounce and is slow playing. This type surface is easy on the feet. Hard courts are for sluggers and are moderate in cost to install. The ball has a medium bounce and is fast playing. This court is hard on the feet. Provisions should be made for proper drainage of all sub-surface and surface water. Perforated pipe laid in a bed of 6" gravel is recommended.

The guide specifications published by the U.S. Tennis Court and Track Builders Association describe the slope as: "All excavating, filling, compacting, grading and leveling work required hereunder shall be performed so that the finished court surface slopes one inch (1") in each 20 feet (20') on a true plane from side to side, end to end, or corner to corner for pervious construction."

For impervious construction, the slope is one inch (1") in each 10 feet (10') on a true plane from side to side, end to end, or corner to corner.

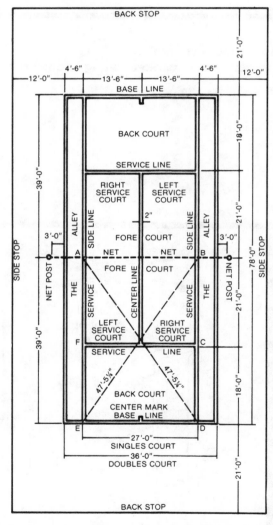

The base should be compacted before finish pavement and weed killer is recommended treatment over the gravel. The base course should be constructed of crushed stone or aggregate, hot-laid bituminous asphaltic concrete or a penetration macadam installed over the sub-base. The material should be spread and compacted so as to provide a uniform

418

thickness and density. Compaction should be performed with a powered steel wheel roller rated not less than 8 tons and not more than 10 tons. The surface of the base course should not vary more than 1/2" in any direction of 10'–0" over the base. A hot plant bituminous asphalt mix leveling course should be installed with 3/8" to 3/4" aggregate size. The compaction thickness should be about 1". The leveling course should be compacted with a steel roller of two to six tons capacity. This course after compaction should not vary more than 1/8" in 10'–0". The entire surface then should receive a coating of sealant in colors of green, red, or sand. All lines should be striped with white line paint in widths of 2in. 4"of clay or reinforced concrete can also be used as a playing surface, following the same directions for drainage and slope as the bituminous court.

The fence ususally is chain link type 8'–0", 10'–0" or 12'–0" high available in aluminum, galvanized steel or vinyl coated. This type fence is best installed by professionals because special tools are required to stretch the chain link attached to posts, which are spaced about 10'–0" apart.

All tennis courts should face north and south.

WALKS AND STEPS

Major walks should be 4'–0" wide and secondary walks be 2'–0" wide. Climatic conditions will determine which material to use for walks. In cold climates about the only practical material is concrete with a wood float finish. (Wood float leaves a rough finish, steel float leaves a smooth finish). Any other material can create problems because water will find its way in the joints or cracks of brick or stone, freeze and damage the material or force it out of position creating a hazard. Concrete should be 4" thick reinforced with wire mesh poured over a 6" gravel base. The tool marks in the concrete walks or sidewalks marking off squares of 4'–0" is designed for the concrete to crack along the tool marks or grooves making it easier to replace the damaged square without notice.

Rails for steps should be 1-1/2" dia. aluminum or 1" x 3" wood. Wrought iron will rust, if not properly maintained, leaving a rust streak along the route of travel. In preparing steps for a rail, simply insert a glass bottle upside down into the wet concrete at the position of the rail post. When the concrete is set and ready for the rail, simply break the bottle and insert the rail using a special compound mix available in hardware stores. Pitch all concrete walks and steps away from the house and install rails on both sides of stairs. Outside treads should be 12" wide and the number of risers will depend upon the distance from the finish grade to the floor not to exceed 8" for risers. Install a platform at least 4'–0" wide one step below the floor. Asphalt concrete or blacktop may be substituted for walks instead of concrete. Use 2" x 4" for forming the edges of walks. If the walk is serpentine in shape, use 1" x 3" wood furring for forms to make the bends. Be sure to order concrete with pea stone aggregate for walks.

Brick can also be used with a variety of design. They can be laid dry without mortar over a cushion of sand for a base or

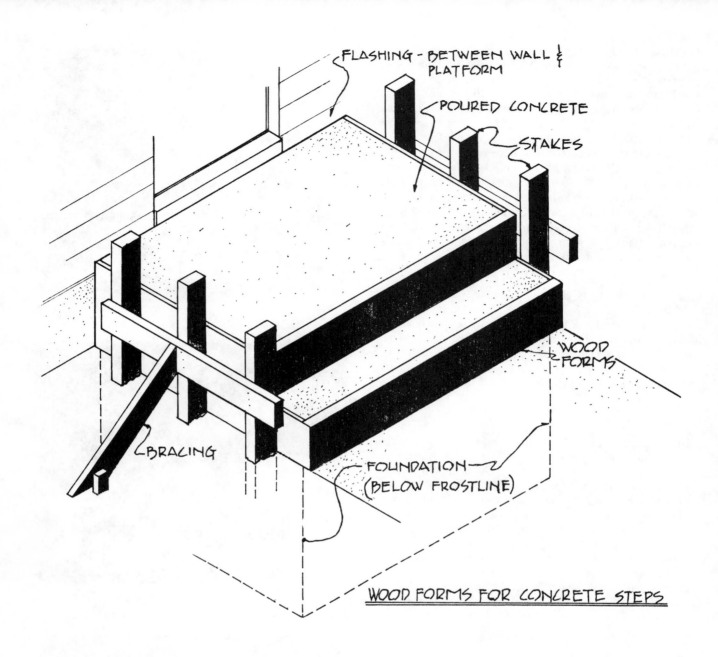

FLASHING - BETWEEN WALL & PLATFORM

POURED CONCRETE

STAKES

WOOD FORMS

BRACING

FOUNDATION (BELOW FROSTLINE)

WOOD FORMS FOR CONCRETE STEPS

they can be laid over a concrete base imbedded in mortar. Preformed asphalt block is another material used for walks. Marble chips scattered over wet concrete makes a very attractive walk if there is no snow to shovel. Flagstone, bluestone or slate is also popular for walks or steps. If used for walks a 4" concrete base is installed as a foundation to receive the stone which is set in mortar or the stone may be installed dry over a sand bed. Concrete foundations for stairs should have walls   8" thick extending below the frost line.

FLATWORK CONCRETE

Thoroughly mix the ingredients of concrete until it is uniform in appearance and all materials are distributed. If a mechanical mixer is used, about one minute will be required in the mixer for up to one cu. yd. with about 15 seconds for each additional 1/2 cu. yd. Do not overload the rating of the mechanical mixer. Mix the dry ingredients first, then add the water, slowly, pouring just enough to make a working consistency. When the concrete is placed into the forms, spread to an even thickness with a flat shovel or rake, to the height of the forms, then use a straightedge, usually a piece of 1" x 6" and run it along the top of the forms (be sure the straight edge is longer than the width of the forms) for a more level surface; this will fill the low spots and cut the high spots. If the width of the concrete is too wide for a straight edge, work sections using stakes driven into the ground set at proper height to conform with height of forms one at a time. This is called screeding. These stakes can be removed after screeding. A darby is then used to float the concrete surface immediately after it has been screeded. This process allows the water in the mix to surface, making it easier to work the surface in preparation for the next step. The darby will eliminate any high or low ridges left by the straightedge. The next step is called troweling. This is a hand tool made up of wood or metal about 12" long and 4" wide. This tool is used in a rotating motion over the surface of the concrete to allow a dense smooth finish. The wood trowel will give a rough finish and the steel trowel will give a smooth finish. The surface is then "tooled" with an edger to produce a smooth even edge along the slab for not only appearance but also to reduce the risk of possible damage to the edge. A joiner or groover is used to section off the concrete into panels. This sectioning, also called construction, or control joints which provide location of any possible cracks. All of the described operations must be done before the concrete begins to set. Work only a small section at a time.

Curing the concrete is one of the most important operations and most often neglected. Concrete should be protected so that little or no moisture is lost during early stages of hardening. Do not allow the concrete to dry too fast, especially during hot sunny days or drying winds. For at least three days after hardening, sprinkle with a garden hose.

Following are precautions to be used in hot weather concreting:

1. Have all material and tools ready before any work is started. Start late in the afternoon and schedule work with the least delay.

2. Soak the ground with water where concrete is to be placed.

3. Once concrete has been thoroughly mixed, place it immediately and strike it off and darby it at once.

4. Place temporary burlap water soaked covering over slab, finish a small section at a time and recover.

5. Start curing as soon as the surface is hard enough to resist marring or damage. Keep constantly wet to avoid alternate wetting and drying during the curing stage and continue curing for at least 7 days.

It is best not to do any concreting during cold weather but if you must, adhere to the following precautions:

1. Have materials ready before cold weather arrives.

2. Use heaters, insulating material and enclosures.

3. Do not place concrete on frozen ground. Protect excavations with straw or other insulating materials to prevent the ground from freezing.

4. Temperature of concrete should be between 50° and 70° when poured. When temperature is below 30°, the water should be heated.

5. No frozen aggregate lumps should be used.

6. Remove all frost from forms and reinforcing.

7. Use 1 lb. of calcium chloride per sack of cement to allow for quick hardening. Do not use admixtures to prevent concrete from freezing.

8. Maintain concrete temperature at 70° for 3 days and 50° for 5 days and do not allow concrete to freeze during next 4 days. Covering of concrete with straw will prevent freezing.

There are many special surface finishes which can be applied to concrete finishes. Coloring can be added for special effect around swimming pools or gardens. Sprinkling the surface with colored aggregates (stone) before hardening will produce an attractive rough surface. (Not recommended in areas subjected to snow.) These can be evenly spread by hand and patted into the surface with a darby or trowel. Geometric designs can be achieved with the use of the jointer tool. Leaf impressions add a highly decorative design, interest and excitement to the surface of the concrete. Leaves are taken from local trees and immediately after the concrete has been troweled, press the leaves carefully, stem side face down into the fresh surface. The leaves should be imbedded that they may be troweled over without dislodging them. Do not deposit any concrete over the leaf. The leaves can be removed after the concrete has hardened or left for time to remove. Circles of different sizes can be integrated into the surface design by using empty food cans. By lightly scoring the surface with a soft bristle broom will create an interesting effect.

Construction joints are placed in slabs where the concreting operations are concluded for the day, generally in conformity with a predetermined joint layout. If the concreting is interrupted long enough at any time for the placed concrete to harden, a construction joint is used. If possible, construction joints should not be located less than 5 feet from any other parallel joint.

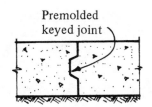

Premolded keyed joint

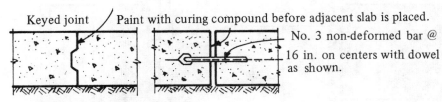

Keyed joint   Paint with curing compound before adjacent slab is placed.

No. 3 non-deformed bar @ 16 in. on centers with dowel as shown.

FORMWORK AND JOINTS

PORCH OR ENTRANCE SLAB

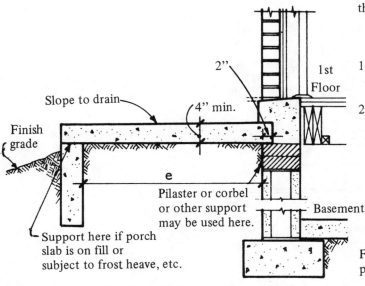

Slope to drain

Finish grade

2"

4" min.

1st Floor

e

Pilaster or corbel or other support may be used here.

Basement

Support here if porch slab is on fill or subject to frost heave, etc.

Note: if e = 3'-6", reinforce as required.

FORMWORK AND JOINTS

Isolation (Expansion) Joints (contd.)

Slab-on-ground isolation joints should be used where a concrete slab meets another slab or another construction, such as:

Sidewalk or driveway adjacent to foundation wall.
Between slabs at grade and surrounding foundation wall.
Between slabs and fixtures, such as drains, hydrants, lamp posts, columns, and other fixed equipment or structures.
Between garage slab (or apron) and driveway.
Between driveway and sidewalk and roadway.
Between driveway or sidewalk and steps, patio, planter, and similar constructions.

Control (Contraction) Joints, Sidewalks and Driveways

Slab-on-ground control (contraction) joints provide for horizontal movement of the adjacent slabs but do not allow differential vertical movement. Control joints allow for contraction caused by drying shrinkage and eliminate random cracking due to thermal volume changes. Control joints should occur at not over 5 ft. spacing in sidewalk slabs-on-ground and at not over 15 ft. spacing in driveway slabs-on-ground.

Following is a list of concrete surface defects, causes and remedies.

SCALING

When the surface of hardened concrete breaks away from the slab.

CAUSE	REMEDY
1. Early cycle of freezing and thawing.	Concrete temperature should be 50° or above when poured and maintained for 5 days.
2. Faulty workmanship caused by screeding, floating or finishing performed while bleed water is on surface and left to remain on surface.	Work freewater back into the slab or allow to evaporate before any finishing is performed.

CRAZING

Fine hair cracks on the surface of concrete forming a pattern similar to crushed eggshells.

CAUSE	REMEDY
1. Rapid surface drying caused by hot sun or drying winds.	Apply fog spray or cover with wet burlap after finishing and keep damp while curing for several days.
2. Premature floating and troweling due to excess amount of surface water.	Remove excess surface water by evaporation before finishing.

DUSTING

The appearance of powdered material on the surface is called dusting.

CAUSE	REMEDY
1. Excess of clay or silt in the mix.	Use clean and well graded aggregates.
2. Premature floating and troweling with excess water.	Remove excess water before finishing.
3. No curing or inadequate curing.	Proper time in curing is essential.

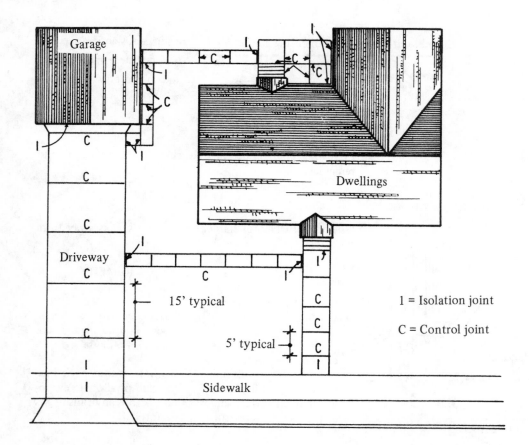

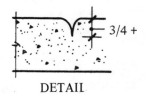

Tooled joint
for slab-on-
ground control
joint

3/4 +

DETAIL

1 = Isolation joint

C = Control joint

15' typical

5' typical

JOINTING OF RESIDENTIAL CONCRETE   SLABS-ON-GROUND

DRIVEWAYS

Gravel, asphalt, concrete, crushed stone or crushed shellfish shells provide an excellent driveway surface. Follow the same procedure as walks.

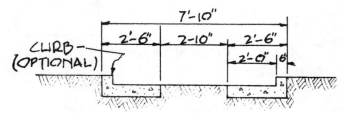

CONCRETE DRIVEWAY STRIPS

7'-10"

2'-6"   2'-10"   2'-6"

2'-0"   6"

CURB (OPTIONAL)

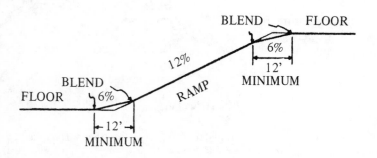

BLEND   FLOOR

6%

12%

12'
MINIMUM

RAMP

BLEND
FLOOR

6%

12'
MINIMUM

TRANSITION GRADES FOR RAMP ENDS

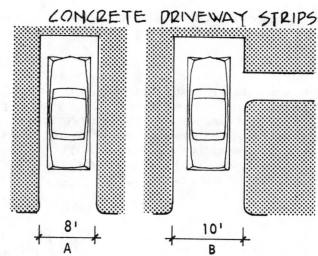

8'

A

10'

B

DRIVEWAY WIDTHS

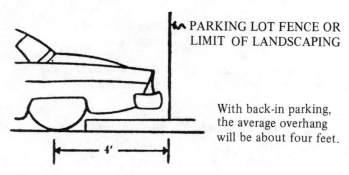

PARKING LOT FENCE OR
LIMIT OF LANDSCAPING

4'

With back-in parking, the average overhang will be about four feet.

Entering the car in illustration A above requires walking on the grass with resulting wear and possible erosion. The width shown in illustration B allows pedestrians to walk on pavement entering the car or using adjoining walks.

424

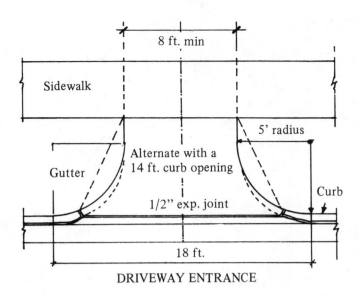

DRIVEWAY ENTRANCE

8 ft. min

Sidewalk

5' radius

Gutter

Alternate with a 14 ft. curb opening

Curb

1/2" exp. joint

18 ft.

Where driveways are not hardsurfaced the maximum gradient should be limited to 7 percent.

Alignment should be convenient for backing a car out of a drive or adequate turning space should be provided.

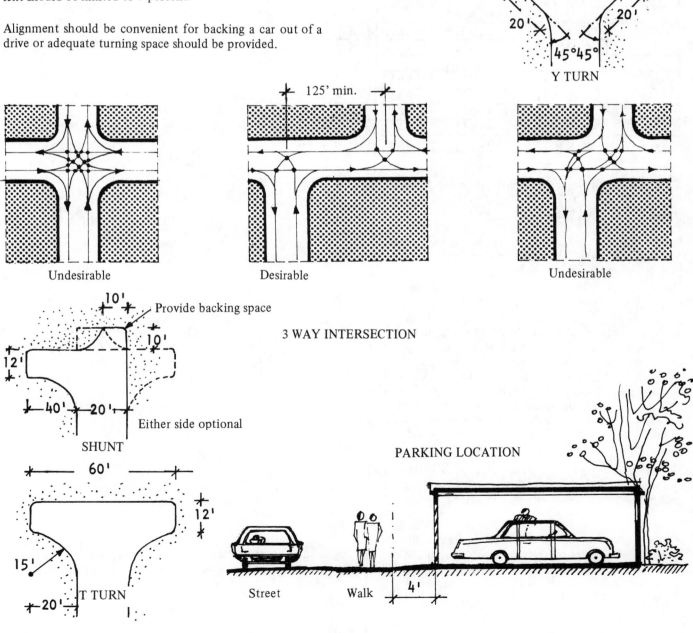

40'

20'

20'

CIRCLE WITHOUT PARKING

12' 12'

20' 20'

45° 45°

Y TURN

125' min.

Undesirable

Desirable

Undesirable

3 WAY INTERSECTION

10'

Provide backing space

10'

12'

40' 20'

Either side optional

SHUNT

60'

12'

15'

20'

T TURN

PARKING LOCATION

Street

Walk

4'

A	B	C	D	E	F	Per (X)
Parallel	8.0	8.0'	22'			
30°	8.0'	15.9'	16.0'	4.0'	11.0'	6.0
	8.5'	16.4'	17.0'	4.3'	11.0'	5.7
	9.0'	16.8'	18.0'	4.5	11.0'	5.4
	9.5'	17.2'	19.0'	4.8'	11.0'	5.2
	10.0'	17.7'	20.0'	5.0'	11.0'	5.0
45°	8.0'	18.4'	11.3'	5.5'	14.0'	8.2
	8.5'	18.7'	12.0'	5.7'	13.5'	7.8
	9.0'	19.1'	12.7'	6.2'	13.0'	7.4
	9.5'	19.4'	13.4'	6.6'	13.0'	7.0
	10.0'	19.8'	14.1'	7.0'	13.0'	6.7
60°	8.0'	19.6'	9.2'	6.9'	19.0'	10.1
	8.5'	19.8'	9.8'	7.4'	18.5'	9.5
	9.0'	20.1'	10.4'	7.8'	18.0'	9.0
	9.5'	20.3'	11.0'	8.2'	18.0'	8.5
	10.0'	20.6'	11.5'	8.7'	18.0'	8.1
90°	8.0'	18'	8.0'	0'	26'	12.5
	8.5'	18'	8.5'	0'	25'	11.8
	9.0'	18'	9.0'	0'	24'	11.1
	9.5'	18'	9.5'	0'	24'	10.5
	10.0	18'	10.0'	0'	24'	10.0

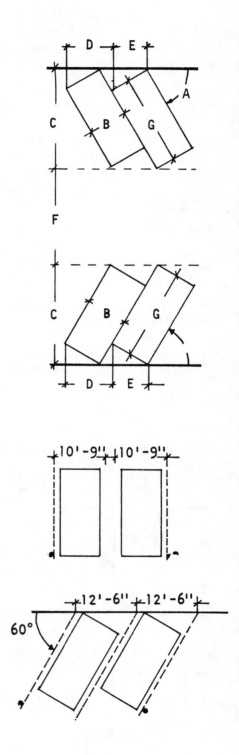

Street intersections should be at right angles. Intersections of more than two streets and off-sets at junctions of less than 125 feet should be avoided.

Where consistent with good traffic design and circulation, 3-way intersections and with only three collision points should be provided rather than the far more hazardous 4-way intersections which have sixteen collision points. See the 3 Way Intersection illustration.

Street intersections should be located away from both horizontal and vertical street curves that limit the range of vision. The space interval between the intersection and curve should be sufficient to assure safe sight distance, considering the design speed of the streets, see 305-1 of MAP reference "Geometric Design Guide for Local Roads and Streets" for suggested minimum sight distance in relation to design speed.

The design of a parking court should provide turning space in no parking area. The use of the wings of a shunt or "T" turn for parking space or driveway should be avoided.

Turning space for cars and service trucks should be provided for all parking courts, culs-de-sac or dead-end streets, where the alternative would be a long (150 feet or more) distance or where backing out would be dangerous.

4 ft. is the desirable minimum between pedestrian ways or traffic lanes and rear of parking spaces where vision is clear.

8 ft. is needed between pedestrian ways or traffic lanes and the rear of parking spaces where solid vision barriers such as garage walls exist.

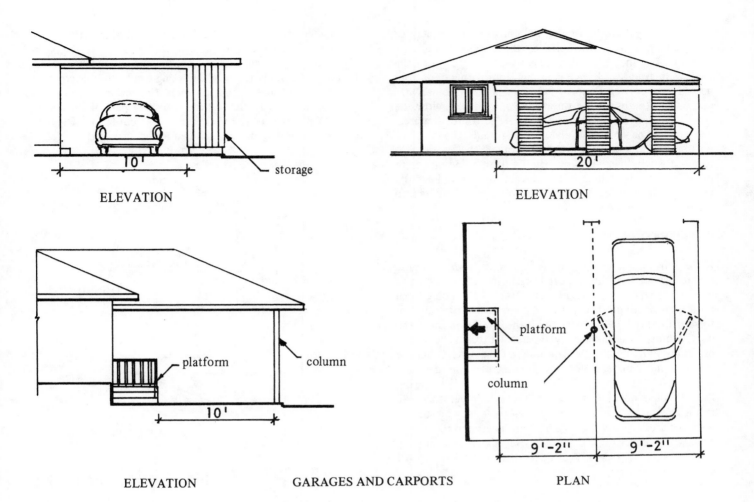

ELEVATION

ELEVATION

ELEVATION

PLAN

GARAGES AND CARPORTS

Width of a carport or garage is measured as the distance between obstructions such as posts, walls, storage or appliances.

Length of carport or garage is measured as the length of the roofed area.

	1 car	2 cars
Width	10'-0"	18'-4"
Length	20'-0"	20'-0"

The minimum outside radius for a turning circle with no parking, exclusive of space for a walk or utilities should be 40 feet.

The inside radius of a turning circle should be adequate for trucks and fire equipment, generally at least 20 feet.

Elderly and Handicapped

In housing for the elderly or handicapped, a parking space for a person in a wheelchair, on crutches or on braces should be 12 ft. wide and should permit alighting from a car onto a level surface suitable for wheeling and walking.

All right angle turning corners should have a minimum radius of 15 feet.

RETAINING WALLS

Where there is a sharp difference in finish grade, a retaining wall becomes necessary to hold back the higher ground. These walls can be built of brick, stone, concrete or wood railroad ties. The face wall should be tapered or slanted toward the high grade and should extend below the frost line. The thickness will depend upon the engineering loads to support the force, but generally the walls are 18" thick at the ground and taper up to about 12" at the top, reinforced with steel rods if built of concrete. Be sure to insert through the wall 3" or 4" pipe called weeps to relieve the pressure and drainage. These weeps are placed about every 4'-0" apart about 1/4 distance up from the bottom of the wall. Stone can be laid dry or in mortar, either of which will require a concrete foundation below the frost line to support the wall. The foundation or footing can be about 12" deep and 24" wide reinforced with steel rods. Railroad ties should have a header (insert tie with end exposed) every third course to lock the wall together. Be sure the wood ties are sealed against rot. A rail should be installed on top of all retaining walls.

AREAWAYS

If the bottom of the basement windows are below the finished grade, areaways are necessary to hold back the ground and to provide light and ventilation to the basement. These areaways must be secured to the foundation wall. Semi-circular, corrugated steel sheets are sometimes used for this purpose. They have flanges on the ends to secure them to the foundation wall with bolts. 8" thick concrete walls are also used but they are more expensive. The bottom of the well or areaway can have a concrete floor with a drain connected to a drywell or storm sewer or it can have a 2'-0" gravel base to absorb the water into a drain tile below the ground leading away from the house. The top of the areaway should be about 6" above the ground. The floor or bottom of the areaway should be about 8" below the bottom of the windows. A grating should be installed on top to prevent injury by falling into the well. Be sure to keep the areaways clean of leaves to prevent water from leaking into the basement windows.

CATCH BASINS

If the finish grade cannot be pitched away from the house to run off surface water, a catch basin must be installed to collect the water and divert it away from the building to an outlet, storm drain or drywell. The grade must be pitched toward the catch basin cover and if the cover is in the driveway, it must be a heavy duty type to withstand the weight of vehicles driving over it. The walls of the catch basin can be of stone, concrete block or pre-cast concrete designed for that use. If a series of catch basins are used in unison, the inlet pipe must be higher than the outlet pipe. If the soil is porous and will hold water, a catch basin may be substituted for a dry well, which is a hole in the ground filled with rock with a cover on top at grade level. Catch basins or dry wells must be kept clean so as not to restrict the drainage of water.

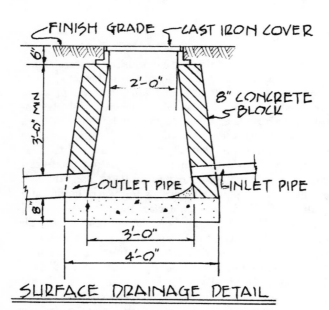

SURFACE DRAINAGE DETAIL

GREENHOUSE

Foundations for greenhouses are similar to residential construction. Check manufacturers catalog for a model before any foundation work is started. Generally they are constructed of tubular steel or aluminum frame, packaged, requiring only to be assembled after the foundation is completed. They can be free standing or attached to a building in a variety of sizes, styles and configurations. The type of mechanical connections is a matter of choice and may be

extended from the residence to the greenhouse without any concern for overloading the system. Be careful of the package you buy because it may not include any mechanical facilities or foundation work. Glazing can be double strength glass or translucent plastic panels. Collection of condensation discharged to the outside is usually part of the assembly or package as well as side and roof ventilation. The benches may or may not be included in the package.

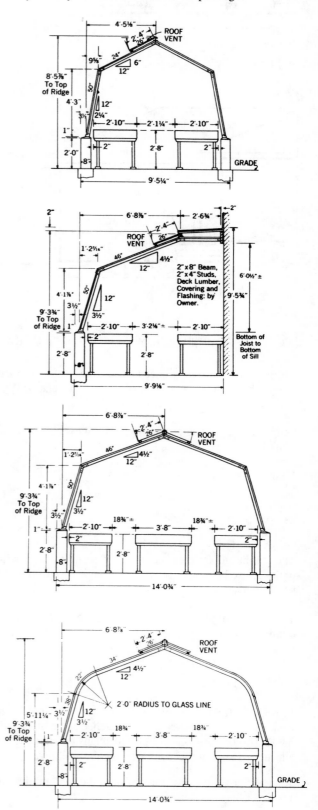

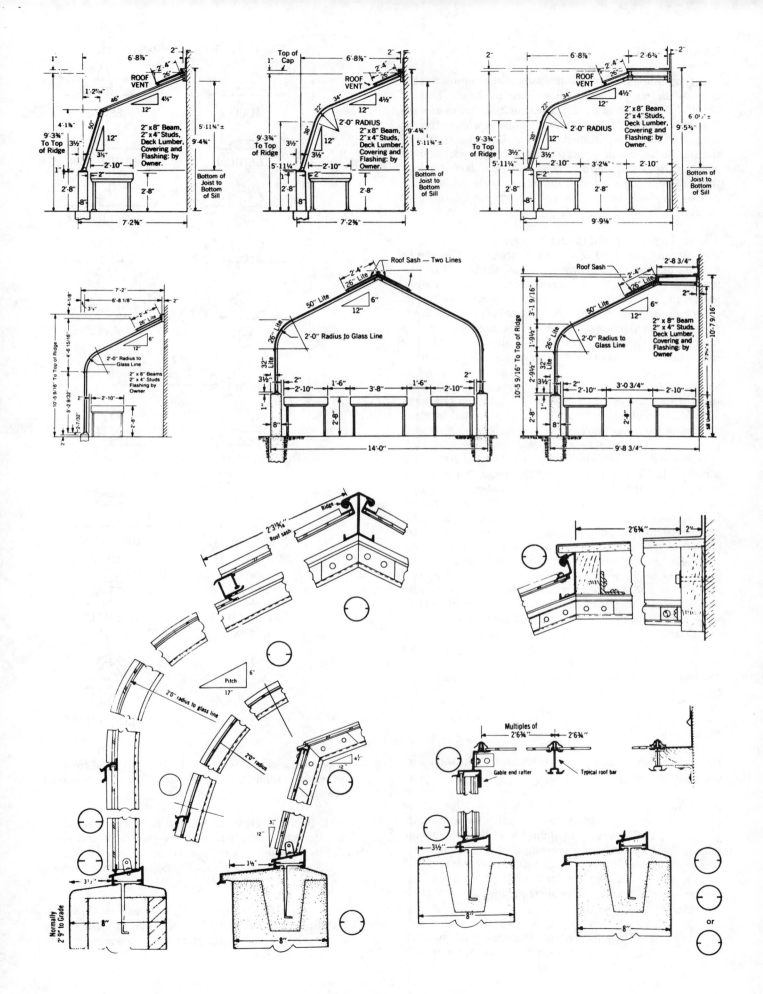

LANDSCAPING

The condition and chemical makeup of the topsoil will determine the results of growth of grass or shrubs. The soil should be tested to make this determination and treated accordingly. Normally this testing is done free of charge by local Agronomy Department of State. Collect a sample of the soil, at random, in a pint container for chemical analysis and a quart container for mechanical analysis and deliver them to the testing laboratory. When the tests are completed, they will make recommendations for treatment of the soil.

The grading of top soil should be a minimum of 3" thick after firming. The kind of area to be seeded will determine the mix of grass seed. Sunny turf areas, shady turf area or multi-use turf areas. One of the quickest ways to develop a lawn is to plant Turfgrass sod. Be sure to prepare the soil receiving the sod. Be careful in buying sod. It must meet the following specifications: Sod should be machine cut at a uniform soil thickness of 1/2", plus or minus 1/4". The pad size should be of standard length and width with no more than 5% deviation. Sod sections should be strong enough to support their own weight and retain their size and shape when suspended vertically from a firm grasp on the upper 10% of the section. Sod should not be harvested or transplanted when moisture content (excessively dry or wet) may adversely affect its survival. Sod should be harvested, delivered and installed within 36 hours. The first row of sod should be laid in a straight line with subsequent rows placed parallel to and tightly against each other. Lateral joint should be staggered to promote more uniform growth and strength. Care should be exercised to insure that the sod is not stretched or overlapped and that all joints are butted tight in order to prevent voids which would cause air drying of the roots. On sloping areas where erosion may be a problem, sod should be laid with staggered joints and secured by pegging. Water sod immediately after installation to prevent drying during progress of the work. Watering should be performed daily during the first week during the heat of the day to help prevent wilting. The first mowing should not be attempted until the sod is firmly rooted and secured in place and not more than 1/3 of the grass leaf should be removed by the initial cutting. Grass height should be maintained between 1-1/2" and 2-1/2".

NEW PLANT MATERIAL

Size — The selection of plant size characteristics should include the following considerations.

Initial Size — New trees and shrubs should be large enough to perform the first stages of their intended function. (Suggest 1 1/2" to 2" caliper minimum for shade trees, a minimum of 4'-5" height for evergreen trees, a minimum of 3 years growth for fast growing shrubs and a minimum of 5 years growth for slower growing shrubs). Often a few large specimens of new plant material are justified and preferable to a large number of smaller plants.

Ultimate Size— The ultimate size of selected plant materials should match the planned size requirements for the specific

TREE & SHRUB FORMS

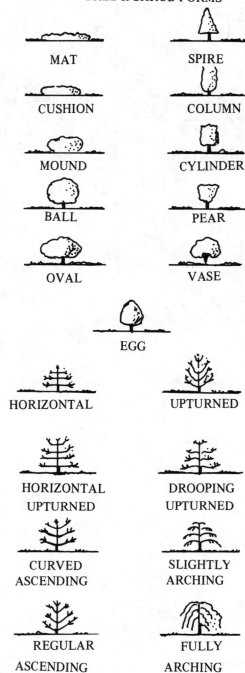

location as closely as possible. Plants which need frequent or expensive pruning to satisfy size requirements should not be used.

Growth Habits — Plants should not be placed where their normal growth habits will interfere with light and air at windows, block doors, grow over walks, obscure night lighting, or reach sizes totally out of scale with their surroundings.

Growth Rate — Plant materials with extremeley slow rates of growth which will not fulfill functional requirements for several years or with unpleasant rank suckering growth habits should be avoided.

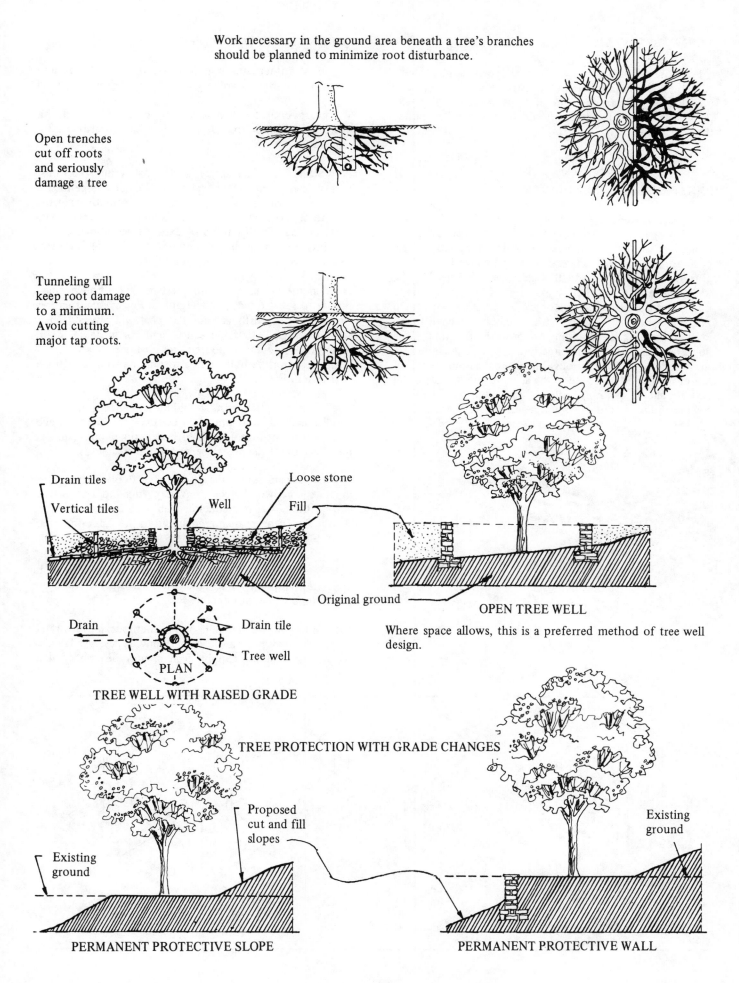

Work necessary in the ground area beneath a tree's branches should be planned to minimize root disturbance.

Open trenches cut off roots and seriously damage a tree

Tunneling will keep root damage to a minimum. Avoid cutting major tap roots.

Drain tiles

Vertical tiles

Well

Loose stone

Fill

Drain

Drain tile

Tree well

PLAN

TREE WELL WITH RAISED GRADE

Original ground

OPEN TREE WELL

Where space allows, this is a preferred method of tree well design.

TREE PROTECTION WITH GRADE CHANGES

Proposed cut and fill slopes

Existing ground

Existing ground

PERMANENT PROTECTIVE SLOPE

PERMANENT PROTECTIVE WALL

431

TREE PRESERVATION

Trees close to planned structures which cannot be protected should be removed before construction is started. Removal after construction usually involves increased expense. Good existing trees should be transplanted rather than destroyed.

BUILDING A GARDEN SHELTER

Most garden shelters are of post and beam design. Posts, properly spaced to provide adequate support, are set in the ground or securely connected to a firm foundation. The posts support horiozontal beams (plates) which in turn support the roof rafters at right angles to the beams (Fig. 1). Some shelters are attached to existing buildings and a modification of the basic post and beam construction is used. On the left of Figure 1 a ledger strip is shown attached to the existing building. The building performs the function of the posts, and the rafters rest directly on, and are anchored to, the ledger strip. The various dimensional requirements of the different parts as listed in the accompanying figures and text should be carefully noted. Check your local building code regarding permits, fees and regulations.

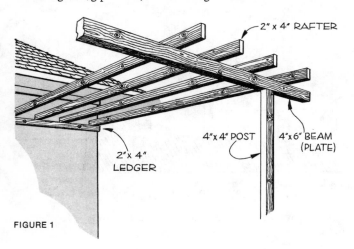

2" x 4" RAFTER

2" x 4" LEDGER

4"x 4" POST

4"x 6" BEAM (PLATE)

FIGURE 1

SETTING POSTS FOR SUPPORT

For posts or other structural members in or near the ground, Construction Heart garden grade redwood should be used.

The heartwood of redwood contains natural chemicals that protect the wood from decay and make it possible to use redwood in the ground.

Post Sizes. For most garden shelters, 4x4 and 4x6 Construction Heart redwood posts are sufficiently large in size. On larger structures, bigger posts are sometimes necessary to support heavier roof loads and still maintain wide post spacing. Two-by-fours or 2x6s are sometimes used in tandem, with spacer blocks between them at 24" intervals, to form a column instead of a solid post.

Posts in the Ground. The simplest method of anchoring a post is to set it directly in the ground.For many structures, firmly tamped earth around the post will give sufficient stability (Fig. 2A). If the soil is sandy or unstable, a concrete collar should be poured around the post after it has been placed in the hole and earth tamped around the base, as shown in Figure 2B.

The depth to which posts should be set depends on the soil conditions and wind pressure. Twenty-four inches is adequate for most 8- to 10-foot-high structures, but it may be necessary to set the posts deeper for higher shelters.

When posts are set in the ground, the floor of the shelter may be a redwood deck, gravel, paving blocks, grass or earth. Ordinarily, if a concrete slab is to be poured as the shelter floor, the posts are anchored to the slab rather than set in the ground.

Posts should be carefully plumbed with a level. When set in concrete, temporary bracing is often necessary to hold the post plumb while the concrete sets.

Posts on Concrete. Three common methods are illustrated here. Patented post anchors of many types, available at most local building supply dealers, may be imbedded in

POST FOOTINGS

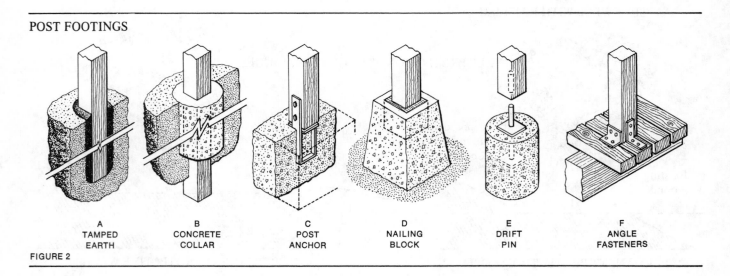

| A TAMPED EARTH | B CONCRETE COLLAR | C POST ANCHOR | D NAILING BLOCK | E DRIFT PIN | F ANGLE FASTENERS |

FIGURE 2

concrete as in Figure 2C. These provide positive anchorage of posts to concrete. Figure 2D shows the nailing block method, where the post is toenailed to a redwood block set in concrete. The nailing block is usually less secure, however, than a metal anchor bolted through the post.

When a concealed anchorage is desired, the drift pin (Fig. 2E) is often used. A small space should be left between the bottom of the post and the concrete surface to avoid the accumulation of moisture and dirt. A washer is good for this purpose.

Where the shelter is to be built above an existing redwood deck, the posts may be placed over the existing support members of the deck. The posts should be firmly anchored with angle fasteners as in Figure 2F.

All metal parts used in connection with redwood must be corrosion resistant to avoid iron staining.

CONNECTING POSTS AND BEAMS

The beams support the roof rafters and tie the posts together, giving rigidity to the structure. To perform these functions properly, the beams must be adequately connected to the posts. Where design permits, the best bearing is achieved when the beam is placed directly on top of the post.

Several methods of connection are possible. A patented post cap (Fig. 3A) is useful where the beam is the same width as the post. Many models are commercially available. A wood cleat (Fig. 3B) can also be used in connecting beams to posts. When the beam is smaller than the width of the post, it may be bolted to the post singly (Fig. 3C), or in pairs (Fig. 3D). When building a column, using 2-inch dimension redwood in tandem with redwood blocks spaced apart, a 2-inch-thick horizontal member may be bolted between the two parts of the column (Fig. 3E).

INSTALLING THE RAFTERS

The method of installing rafters varies with the manner in which they connect with the beam. Most common is to have the rafters resting on top of the supporting member and toenailed or anchored to it by some other conventional method (Fig. 4A right). Rafters may also be notched for design purposes or to lower the roof height, Fig. 4A shown. It should be noted, however, that this considerably weakens the structural strength of the rafter at notched points and thus decreases the weight load the beam and rafters can carry

Rafters for either a flat or sloping roof which are to be flush with the top of the beam may be attached in one of several ways: a patented metal rafter hanger, Fig. 4B, shown, a wood ledger strip nailed under the rafter for support, or the rafter can be toenailed and nailed from the reverse side of the beam (Fig. 4B,).

When rafters extend from an existing building, they may be attached either flush or on top of a ledger strip fastened to the building (Fig. 1). It is important that the ledger strip be bolted or securely fastened to the existing structure if it is to give the necessary support to the rafters.

Some roofing materials or methods require cross supports between rafters. This may be achieved by nailing blocking between the members.

REDWOOD FOR GARDEN USES

Knowing a few simple facts about redwood lumber will help you get the best performance from a garden structure at the most economical cost. Selecting the right grade is one of the most important steps.

Use only a heartwood grade of redwood (Select Heart, Construction Heart or Clear All Heart) for posts, ground-hugging skirtboards, and any framework that comes within 6 inches of the ground, or where the wood will come into contact with soil and alternate cycles of wetting and drying. Natural chemicals in the reddish-brown heartwood protect it from decay and insect attack. For other structural members, grades of redwood containing cream-colored sapwood (Select, Construction Common and Clear) are not only

BEAM CONNECTIONS

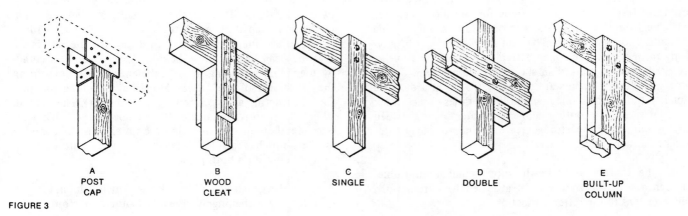

A
POST
CAP

B
WOOD
CLEAT

C
SINGLE

D
DOUBLE

E
BUILT-UP
COLUMN

FIGURE 3

structurally sound but visually very attractive. Clear redwood and redwood plywood provide greater weather tightness for garden shelter storage units.

MOUNTING RAFTERS

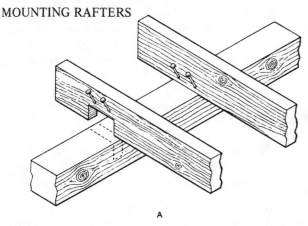

A

FIGURE 4

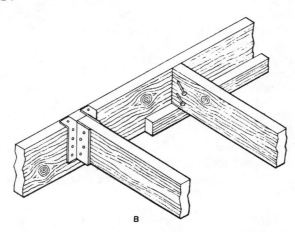

B

BLOCKING EGGCRATE

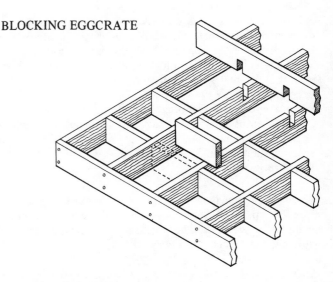

BLOCKING STAGGERED

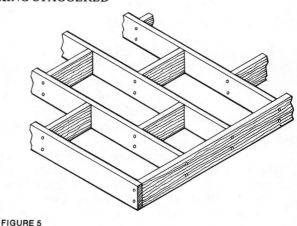

FIGURE 5

The garden grades of redwood, which contain knots and are usually more highly figured and patterned than the top grades, offer redwood's unique natural beauty and workability at a lower cost. And their characteristically natural look and texture make them ideal for garden shelters.

ROOFING POSSIBILITIES

A wide variety of materials can be used for the roof. Many are redwood or in combination with a redwood framework. Shingles or shakes, reed fencing, bamboo, window screening, lath, louvers, canvas, glass or plastic can be used. Recommended application instructions for most products are available from the suppliers. In most instances, only nailing is required for installation. The roof members might be anything from a slim ½ x 3-inch batten to a 2-inch-thick piece. Generally widths more than six inches are not used on the roof. The roof members are generally spaced at a distance equal to the width of one member. Sometimes 2-inch-thick material is used as roofing, allowing greater spans between rafters but requiring stronger rafters due to the greater weight on each rafter.

It may be desirable to make the roof members removable. In such a situation they can be attached to a framework which fastens to the rafters in sections.

One very popular type of overhead shelter is the eggcrate. The eggcrate is composed of horizontal roof supports at right angles to one another, with equal spacing in both directions. Normally the rafters in each direction are the same depth and thickness and are flush on the underside. Three methods of constructing the eggcrate are shown in Figure 5.

In the first method (Fig. 5, top left) rafters are placed in one direction and blocking nailed between them to form a straight line. The best method for proper alignment of the blocking is to measure and mark the spacing desired on the two end rafters. Then stretch a chalk line between the marks and snap it to mark the rest of the rafters. With a square, draw lines down the vertical faces of the rafters so that they can be seen from below. Blocking can be secured by toenailing or nailing through the ends of the block from the other side of the rafters. Mortising is another method for constructing an eggcrate (Fig. 5, top right). This is used where the span is not large or the members are of sufficient size. Members in one direction are notched to fit complementary notches in the cross-members. The resulting joints should be flush on both planes.

A third design choice of blocking, which eliminates the need for any toenailing, is shown in Figure 5, bottom.

Both the eggcrate and lath overheads may be covered over with another material, such as canvas, plastic or matting for more shade or protection from the elements.

Some landscaping situations suggest a trellis or colonnade instead of a regular rectangular shelter. Posts are placed in a single line, either straight or curved, and crossbars to support the trellis are fastened to the posts at right angles in the same manner as beams (Fig. 3A to 3E). In this type of construction it is highly recommended that the posts be set in the ground for the stability which this method of anchoring offers. Diagonal bracing of the crossbars to the posts is recommended for added stability.

WALLS FOR SHELTER

For sufficient stability lateral or diagonal bracing may be necessary. In areas where winds are strong, bracing or walls in a shelter provide strength against racking. If walls are not desired in spite of prevalent winds, diagonal bracing or shear panels should be used at corners.

FLOORS

A redwood deck makes a fast-draining, easily maintained floor and can extend beyond the limits of the shelter. Posts for the shelter can also serve as supports for the deck framing. And on a site that is not level, a redwood deck eliminates the necessity of grading.

SUGGESTED SPAN ALLOWANCES

The following suggested spans for non-stress-graded redwood lumber are for home or other informal use. Where more exacting requirements or engineering design are required by local codes, it is recommended that the STRUCTURAL GRADES of redwood lumber be used. The allowable spans may be calculated based upon the recommended design values listed for each structural grade in Standard Specifications for Grades of California Redwood Lumber, published by the Redwood Inspection Service.

The following tables are based on non-stress-graded redwood used in a single span with a live load of 40 lbs. per sq. ft. and a dead load of 10 lbs. per sq. ft.

SUGGESTED BEAM SPANS

BEAM SIZE	GRADE	WIDTH OF DECK			
		6'	8'	10'	12'
		Span	Span	Span	Span
4x6	Construction Heart Construction Common	4'-6"	4'-0"	3'-6"	3'-0"
4x8	Construction Heart Construction Common	6'-0"	5'-0"	4'-6"	4'-0"
4x10	Construction Heart Construction Common	7'-6"	6'-6"	6'-0"	5'-6"

Deflection limited to L/360

SUGGESTED DECKING SPANS

SIZE	GRADE	SPAN
2x4	Construction Heart, and Construction Common	24"
2x6	Construction Heart, and Construction Common	36"

SUGGESTED JOIST SPANS

JOIST SIZE	SPACING	CONSTRUCTION HEART AND CONSTRUCTION COMMON
2x6	16"	6'-0"
	24"	5'-0"
	36"	4'-0"
2x8	16"	9'-0"
	24"	7'-6"
	36"	6'-0"
2x10	16"	13'-0"
	24"	11'-0"
	36"	9'-0"

Deflection limited to L/240

NAILS AND HARDWARE

It is important to use corrosion resistant nails and other fastenings in the construction of your garden shelter. Use only stainless steel, aluminum alloy, or top quality hot-dipped galvanized fastenings. Common iron and steel fastenings or those galvanized by some other process are likely to corrode on exposure to weather, causing unattractive stains and loss of strength or holding power.

FINISHING REDWOOD

Redwood itself is far more durable than any finish yet developed. This means that selection of an exterior finish for redwood can be made on the basis of appearance, cost, and the durability of the finish itself. A redwood shelter can be left unfinished, to weather naturally from exposure to the elements.

Redwood can be treated with a water repellent for extra protection. This will modify the weathering process and stabilize redwood's color at a soft, buckskin tan, providing a re-application is made every two or three years. Redwood can be bleached chemically to a driftwood gray. A wide range of colors can be achieved with pigmented stains.

LUMBER SIZES

The table below gives the rough and surfaced sizes for garden grades of redwood. A 2x4, for example, measures approximately 2 by 4 inches unsurfaced, or rough. After surfacing, the same unseasoned 2x4 would measure 1 5/8 by 3-9/16 inches. Depending upon the requirements of your job, your lumber dealer can supply either rough or surfaced boards.

UNSEASONED BOARDS, STRIPS, DIMENSIONS

THICKNESSES

Rough (Approx. sizes)	¾	1	1¼	1½	2	3	4	6
Surfaced S1S or S2S	11/16	25/32*	11/16	15/16	1⅝	2⁹/16	3⁹/16	5⅝

WIDTHS

Rough (Approx. sizes)	3	4	6	8	10	12
Surfaced	2⁹/16	3⁹/16	5⅝	7½	9½	11½

*This item is frequently manufactured at ¾ inch net which is under the ALS minimum.

A GARDEN SHELTER CHECK LIST

The following are some considerations for planning a garden shelter:

Regulations. Check your local building authorities regarding codes, permits, fees.

Site Plan. Draw a plan of your property, preferably to scale, showing structures, plantings, walks, etc.

Use. Location and design are determined by use. You may want to think of uses according to generations: adults (relaxing, outdoor dining, gardening, entertaining) and children (sleepingbag bunkhouse, playhouse, playpen, depending on their ages).

Storage. Allow for ample storage and specifc items, especially larger ones. Adjustable shelves for smaller items offer greater adaptability.

Landscape. Relationship of shelter to neighboring structures, landscaping, and view are all-important. A shelter can screen off an inferior view or service area, focus attention on a pleasant vista, and/or act as a focal point of garden or lawn.

Topography. Sloping sites sometimes require more intricate construction, but they may also offer increased views and added design interest. On a level site a multi-level shelter can achieve the same two goals. A shelter floor flush with the ground means fewer steps, and is a great convenience to the elderly or handicapped.

Flooring. A redwood deck makes a fast-draining, easily maintained floor and can extend the limits of the shelter.

Privacy. Orient shelter away from too-close neighbors, and from noise and visibility from street and walks. Protect storage with some locked spaces. Perhaps entire structure is designed to be closed up during longer unused periods.

Nature. Take into account direction of prevailing breezes, and sun's path throughout the year. Most shelters have at least one wall, either solid or louvered, for protection against the weather. A line of cabinets and shelves can also fulfill this function. The amount of sun and rain will determine open or solid roof or combination of both. Sliding solid panels or removable sections of lattice offer light control and allow for seasonal adjustments. A lath or slat roof of redwood creates shadows while letting light penetrate, and breaks the wind without stopping vertical air circulation.

Utilities. You may want a telephone extension, or have an outside bell installed on your house. Some shelters are almost second homes with running water, electricity, and plumbing. The more independent a shelter, the further it can be from the house; otherwise, carefully consider the distance it will be necessary to carry things.

Design. Most shelters are essentially rectangular in plan. Many variations are possible involving the same basic construction elements. Where a more intricate design,

such as a hexagonal plan, is contemplated, it is wise to seek professional assistance. Flat and shed roofs are by far the most commonly employed in garden shelter design. Gable and pyramid roofs are somewhat more complicated for the do-it-yourselfer to undertake, but they are basic roof designs and most building contractors can handle them with ease.

WOOD DECK DETAILS

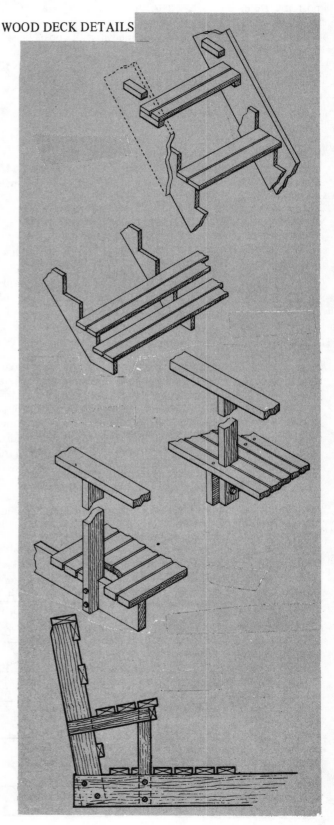

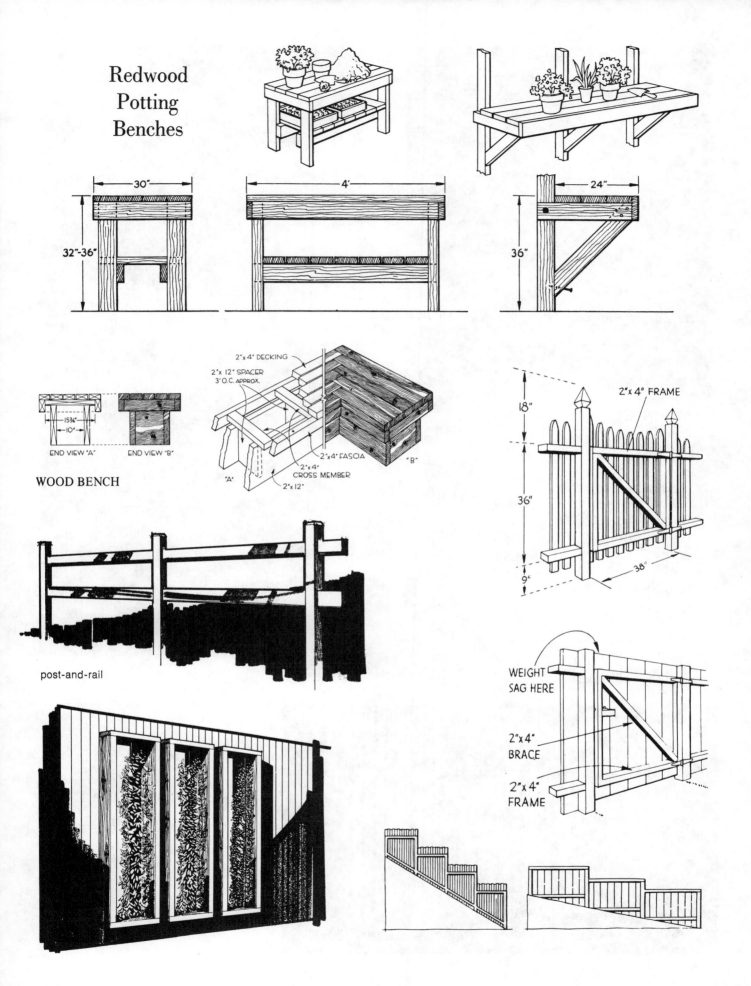

Redwood Potting Benches

30"

32"-36"

4'

24"

36"

2" x 4" DECKING

2" x 12" SPACER
3' O.C. APPROX.

2" x 4" FASCIA

"B"

2" x 4"
CROSS MEMBER

"A"

2" x 12"

END VIEW "A"   END VIEW "B"

15¾"

10"

WOOD BENCH

18"

2" x 4" FRAME

36"

9"

38"

post-and-rail

WEIGHT
SAG HERE

2" x 4"
BRACE

2" x 4"
FRAME

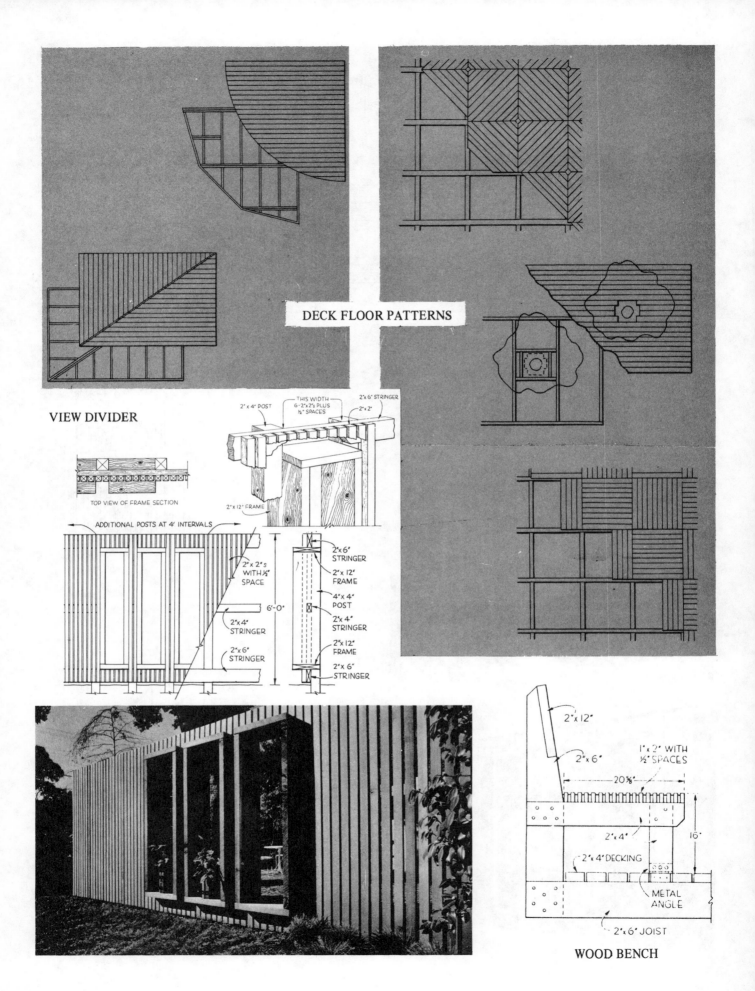

DECK FLOOR PATTERNS

VIEW DIVIDER

TOP VIEW OF FRAME SECTION

ADDITIONAL POSTS AT 4' INTERVALS

2" x 4" POST

THIS WIDTH
6-2"x 2"s PLUS
½" SPACES

2"x 6" STRINGER

2"x 2"

2" x 12" FRAME

2" x 2"s
WITH ½"
SPACE

6'-0"

2"x 4"
STRINGER

2"x 6"
STRINGER

2"x 6"
STRINGER

2"x 12"
FRAME

4"x 4"
POST

2"x 4"
STRINGER

2"x 12"
FRAME

2"x 6"
STRINGER

WOOD BENCH

2"x 12"

2"x 6"

1"x 2" WITH
½" SPACES

20⅝"

2"x 4"

16"

2"x 4" DECKING

METAL
ANGLE

2"x 6" JOIST

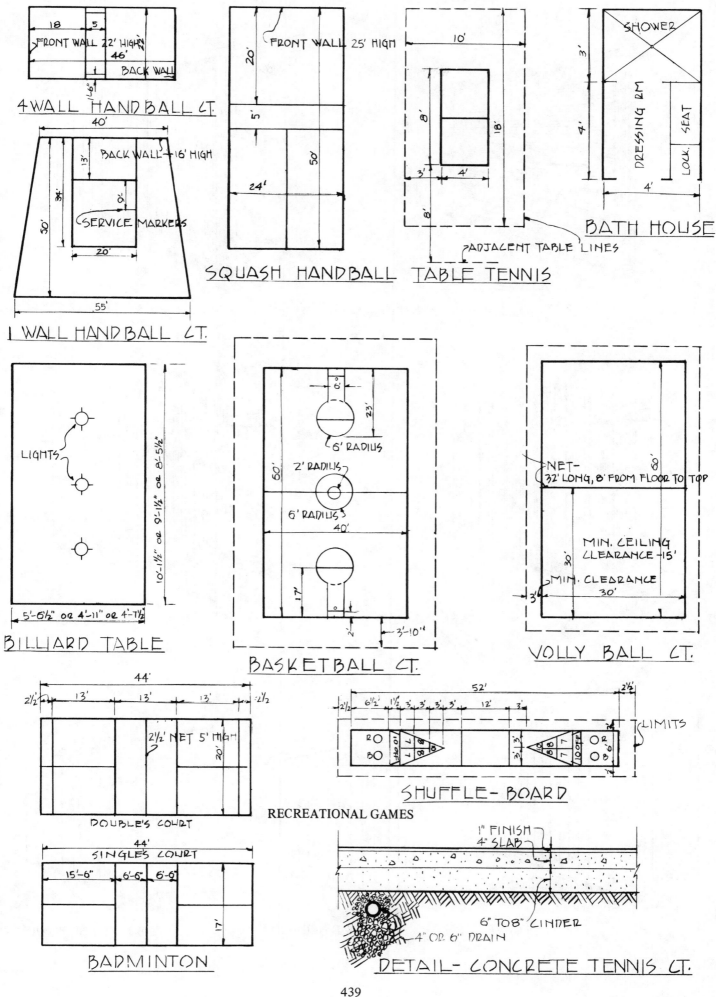

4 WALL HANDBALL CT.

FRONT WALL 22' HIGH
18 5
46'
BACK WALL

I WALL HANDBALL CT.

40'
BACK WALL - 16' HIGH
13'
34'
50'
SERVICE MARKERS
9'
20'
55'

SQUASH HANDBALL

FRONT WALL 25' HIGH
20'
5'
24'
50'

TABLE TENNIS

10'
8'
18'
3' 4'
8'
ADJACENT TABLE LINES

BATH HOUSE

SHOWER
3'
4'
DRESSING RM
LOK. SEAT
4'

BILLIARD TABLE

LIGHTS
10'-1½" OR 9'-1½" OR 8'-5½"
5'-6½" OR 4'-11" OR 4'-7½"

BASKETBALL CT.

6'
23'
6' RADIUS
2' RADIUS
50'
6' RADIUS
40'
17'
2'
3'-10"

VOLLY BALL CT.

NET-
32' LONG, 8' FROM FLOOR TO TOP
60'
MIN. CEILING CLEARANCE -15'
20'
MIN. CLEARANCE
30'
3'

BADMINTON

44'
2½' 13' 13' 13' 2½'
2½' NET 5' HIGH
20'
DOUBLE'S COURT

44'
SINGLE'S COURT
15'-6" 6'-6" 6'-6"
17'

RECREATIONAL GAMES

SHUFFLE-BOARD

52'
2½' 6½' 1½' 3' 3' 3' 3' 12' 3' 2½'
LIMITS
10 OFF 7 8 10 8 7 10 OFF

DETAIL - CONCRETE TENNIS CT.

1" FINISH
4" SLAB
6" TO 8" CINDER
4" OR 6" DRAIN

439

WOOD FENCES

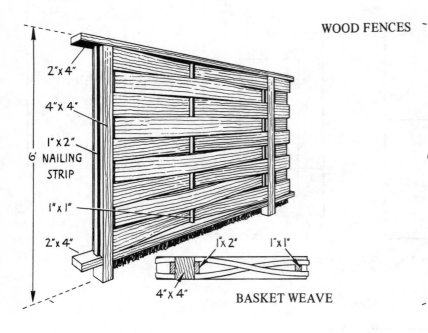

2" x 4"

4" x 4"

1" x 2" NAILING STRIP

6'

1" x 1"

2" x 4"

1" x 2"   1" x 1"

4" x 4"

BASKET WEAVE

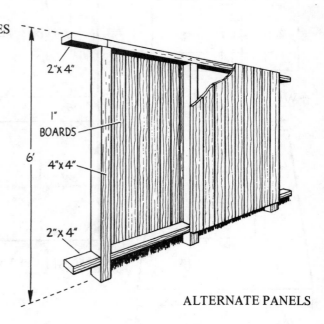

2" x 4"

1" BOARDS

4" x 4"

6'

2" x 4"

ALTERNATE PANELS

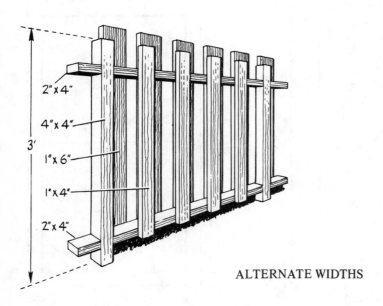

2" x 4"

4" x 4"

1" x 6"

3'

1" x 4"

2" x 4"

ALTERNATE WIDTHS

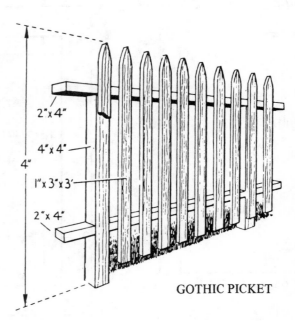

2" x 4"

4" x 4"

1" x 3" x 3'

4"

2" x 4"

GOTHIC PICKET

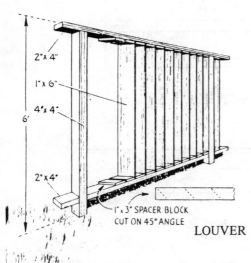

2" x 4"

1" x 6"

4" x 4"

6'

2" x 4"

1" x 3" SPACER BLOCK CUT ON 45° ANGLE

LOUVER

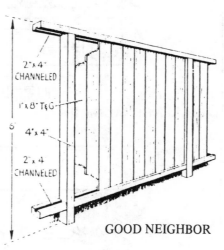

2" x 4" CHANNELED

1" x 8" T&G

4" x 4"

6'

2" x 4" CHANNELED

GOOD NEIGHBOR

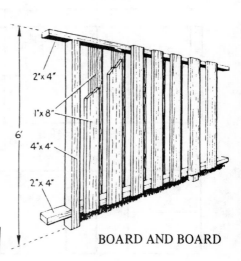

2" x 4"

1" x 8"

4" x 4"

6'

2" x 4"

BOARD AND BOARD

440

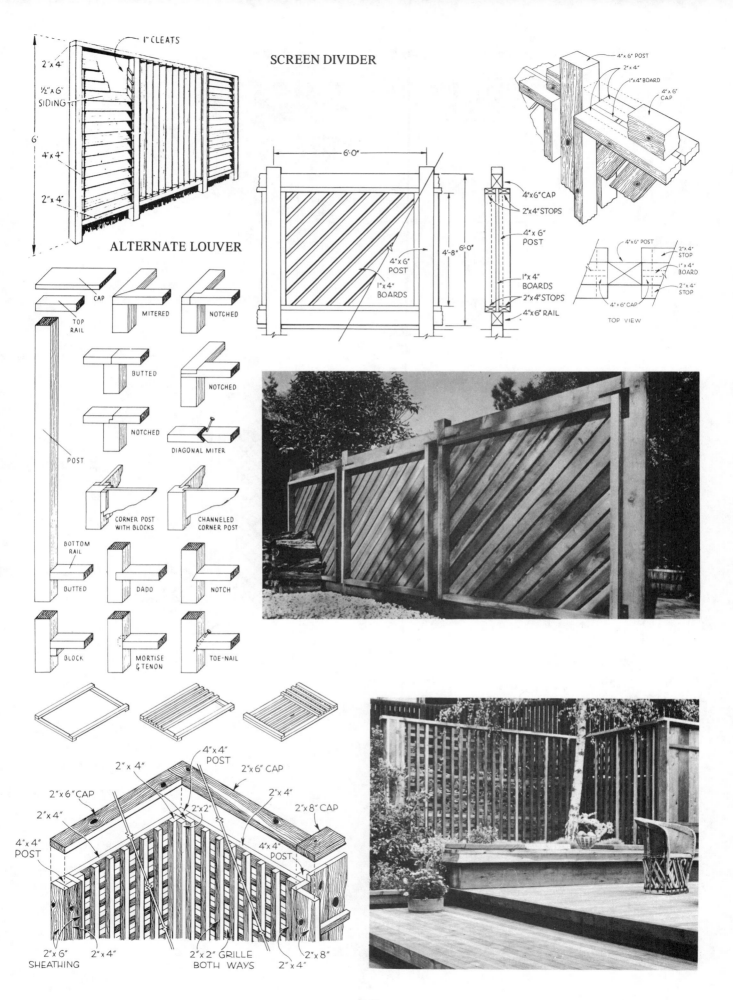

SCREEN DIVIDER

ALTERNATE LOUVER

1" CLEATS

2"x 4"

½"x 6" SIDING

6'

4"x 4"

2"x 4"

CAP

TOP RAIL

MITERED

NOTCHED

BUTTED

NOTCHED

POST

BUTTED

NOTCHED

NOTCHED

DIAGONAL MITER

CORNER POST WITH BLOCKS

CHANNELED CORNER POST

BOTTOM RAIL

BUTTED

DADO

NOTCH

BLOCK

MORTISE & TENON

TOE-NAIL

6'-0"

4'-8" 6'-0"

4"x 6" POST

1"x 4" BOARDS

4"x 6" CAP

2"x 4" STOPS

4"x 6" POST

1"x 4" BOARDS

2"x 4" STOPS

4"x 6" RAIL

4"x 6" POST

2"x 4"

1"x 4" BOARD

4"x 6" CAP

4"x 6" POST

2"x 4" STOP

1"x 4" BOARD

2"x 4" STOP

4"x 6" CAP

TOP VIEW

4"x 4" POST

2"x 6" CAP

2"x 4"

2"x 6" CAP

2"x 4"

2"x 2"

2"x 4"

4"x 4" POST

4"x 4" POST

2"x 8" CAP

4"x 4" POST

2"x 6" SHEATHING

2"x 4"

2"x 2" GRILLE BOTH WAYS

2"x 8"

2"x 4"

441

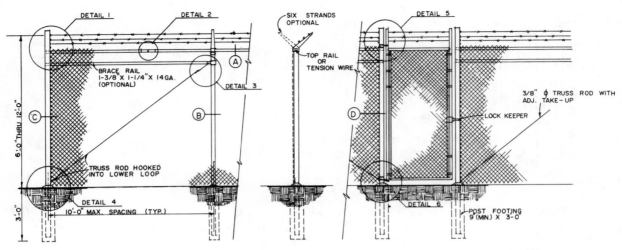

CORNER POST   LINE POST   GATE POST

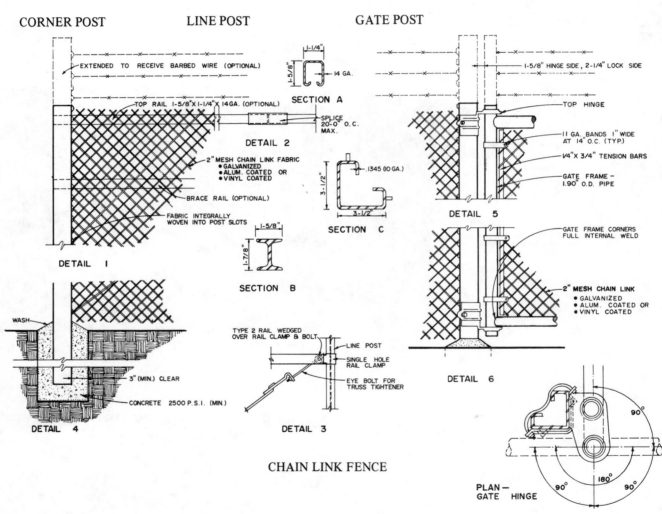

CHAIN LINK FENCE

HIGH COST OF
CHEAP CONSTRUCTION

38

No home can be successful unless it combines four basic essentials: good design, efficient plan, right material and sound construction. A home may be large or small, elaborate or inexpensive. It may boast of every modern convenience and labor saving device, yet without all four of these essentials it can never be a permanent, substantial and satisfactory home. The purpose of this Chapter is to treat in simple terms the construction principles and practices that will help to make your house a substantial home. It will show you the means of judging the construction of your home as it is being built; assist you in avoiding endless annoyances and excessive maintenance costs. This Chapter will equip you to identify good construction and help you to protect your interest. While details of construction vary in different areas, the principles are the same.

Saving a few nails at the cost of squeaking floors, saving a little labor and material at the expense of excessive fuel bills and repair costs, is an expensive economy. With the understanding of good construction and by insisting upon it, anyone may enjoy the comforts of a permanent, economical home. The chief breeder of shoddy structures, unwarranted repair bills and short lived houses, is the lack of appreciation of the value of right construction in house building. The manner in which the house is built is apparently of little interest to some. The completed house must look good. Aside from that, anybody's construction standards will do as long as they will give him the house he wants in the shortest possible time and at the least cost. Here is the biggest purchase of a lifetime—the one which he knows least about, the one which undoubtedly means most to him, the one that will be with him the longest—treated as an insignificant article on the bargain counter.

Little wonder that there is a class of home owners with low prices their principal stock in trade—with construction standards of questionable merit. It is not the intention to imply that the lavish spending of money is necessary to insure the owner a satisfactory home. There are economies that can be and should be practices in house building. It is the purpose of this Chapter to learn these economies and know how to apply them.

It is good for the prospective home owner to bear in mind that the history of a house is written not only on the first purchase price but also on future maintenance costs. Fifty dollars saved today by cheapening the construction of a house may cost five times that much in repair bills in a short time. This Chapter is presented to assist you in recognizing good construction and in obtaining permanent satisfaction.

THE IMPORTANCE OF GOOD CONSTRUCTION IN HOUSE BUILDING

The layman who views a half-finished house is often confused with its maze of framing and scaffolding. House building is not difficult to understand. A house has comparatively few main parts, and its erection is not complicated. Consider this simple grouping of the principal parts of a house frame: the foundation; the floor frame work, consisting of bearing posts, girders and joists; the walls and partitions built of studding; and the roof. All other framing members are incidental to one or another of these parts.

On the following pages, you will find examples of proved construction methods with engineering data for correct house building. You will find also some illustrations of poor building practices. An inspection of these illustrations will point out the importance of building correctly.

THE FOUNDATION

The purpose of the foundation is to support the house. This statement may seem superfluous, perhaps ridiculous.

Yet there are many houses in which defects are traceable to foundations that have failed to perform their full duty. It still holds true that a house is no stronger than its foundation.

Concrete blocks, poured concrete, brick and stone are the materials used for foundations; all are satisfactory when properly used.

Concrete, however, is not a synonym for permanency; there is good concrete and there is bad concrete. The strength of concrete for foundations is dependent upon the use of well-washed sand and gravel, mixed in proper proportions with cement and water. It is important that concrete should be prepared and applied under experienced supervision.

There has been a tendency to cheapen foundation walls by making them thinner than they should be.

Proper thickness of foundation walls is a matter usually governed by local building codes. These codes, and likewise good practice, require walls at least eight inches thick, and in the case of stone or brick walls, sixteen inches thick.

FOOTINGS

Foundation walls are enlarged at their base in order to furnish a larger bearing surface against the soil beneath. This enlarged base is termed "footing." One can readily see that the footings are an important part of the foundation, and particular attention should be paid to their size and shape. In the house where cheapness is the paramount issue, the footings are frequently slighted. It is apparent to the reader that these footings, which must bear most of the weight of the structure, should be carried down to firm ground and below the frost line. The folly of placing them on frozen ground is likewise readily seen.

No end of house ills and annoyances result from improper footings. Poor footings cause uneven settling of the foundation walls, and this in turn is transmitted to the whole house, throwing it out of plumb. The damage is visible inside the house in the form of cracked basement walls, cracked plaster on the upper floor walls, binding doors and windows and sloping floors. Joints in the woodwork will be forced open both inside and outside the house. Nor are these all the evils that can be ascribed to faulty footings and uneven settling of the walls. The pitch of the gutters may be altered, causing water to back up instead of flowing off. This water will overflow the gutters and may back up under the roofing, ruining the housewife's disposition by marring and straining interior decorations. Considerable expense may be involved in redecorating. This annoyance will continue with every thaw or heavy rain until the gutters are repaired or rebuilt. Proper precautions will forestall the house weaknesses described above and provide a firm base for the superstructure.

Often footings that are correct in every way are undermined to permit the entrance of service connections and rain leaders. This weakens the footings at this spot and may result in some of the house ills just mentioned. At the places where it is necessary to undermine footings, they should be either enlarged or, better still, reinforced with steel rods.

THE FOUNDATION

The importance of the footings under the foundation wall and bearing posts is apparent in the accompanying illustration. Properly designed footings are shown at points A and B. Note the broad, flat bearing surfaces of these footings.

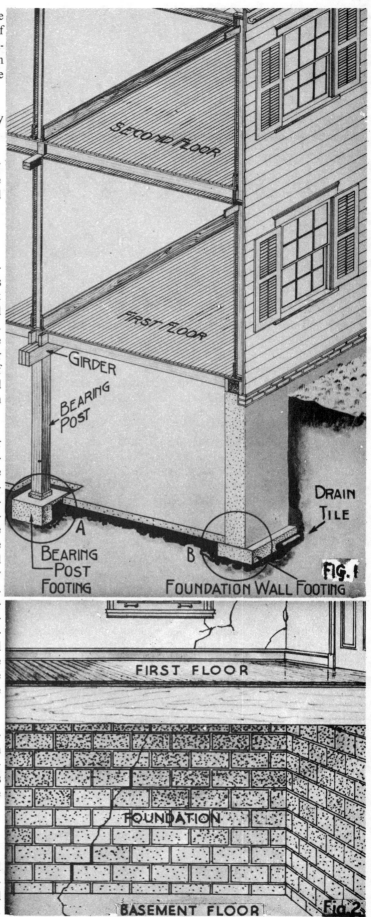

444

To support the weight of the structure above, all footings should rest upon firm ground.

With so many sizes and weights of houses and with such a disparity in the bearing power of various soils, it stands to reason that one size of footing is not suitable for all conditions.

However, it has been found that for the small house with average soil conditions the foundation wall footings (Point B) should extend at least four inches beyond the wall on both sides and should be at least eight inches deep. Likewise, it is a good rule to make the bearing post footings (Point A) from eight to twelve inches deep and from eighteen to twenty-four inches square, depending on the load to be carried and soil condition.

When the foundation is built in damp soil, the site should be drained with four-inch drain tile around the outside of the footings. This should be connected with the sewer or other drainage system.

In excessively damp soil, if a dry basement is to be assured, it is well to waterproof the outside of the foundation wall.

This illustration shows the inevitable result of inadequate footings under the foundation wall, a construction fault common in many houses.

Sagging porches like the one here shown are the result of insufficient support, again a matter of improper footing. Sometimes very good porch piers settle when service connection trenches are dug too close to them and are not properly refilled. The condition shown in this picture is by no means uncommon. It can easily be avoided by proper attention to footings at the time a house is being built. In a completed house, it is difficult and expensive to remedy.

To avoid the heaving action of the frost, porch foundations should be well footed and should be run down below the frost line.

As a business proposition, it is cheaper to build a good house than a poor one. The slight additional cost of building a house right is made up many times over by lower repair costs and higher resale value.

BEARING POST FOOTINGS

The foundation supports the outside walls and the weight of about half of the floor area. The remainder of the weight of the house is dependent upon the bearing posts for support. The bearing post footings should, therefore, not be neglected. Care should be exercised to see that trenches for water and sewer pipes are not dug close to these footings, as this will have a weakening effect on them.

When bearing posts settle unduly, the effect is apparent throughout the house. Plaster cracks appear on the inside walls, doors and windows become balky, and floors settle at the inner walls. The annoyances that result from uneven floors are familiar to everybody.

PORCH PIERS

Workmen who would not slight the footings under the foundation walls or those under the bearing posts sometimes fail to realize the importance of the porch piers and their footings. The porch piers are put in for the very practical purpose of supporting the porch; a sagging porch will surely result if the piers are not properly "rooted." Probably no one thing gives a house such a run-down, "hang -dog" look as a "sway back" porch. And appearance, it must be remembered, has a direct effect on the resale value of the house.

The importance of proper foundations, bearing posts, porch piers and their footings cannot be too strongly emphasized, for any settling must of necessity affect the entire superstructure of the house.

TYPES OF FRAMING

The framework of the house has aptly been termed its skeleton, and its purpose obviously is to give strength and rigidity to the structure. It is not necessary that the prospective builder know all of the details of the various types of framing or, for that matter, the method of constructing the one type he chooses, but the owner will find an acquaintance with house framing invaluable in his effort to secure a good house.

There are many types of house framing in use in various sections of the country, but for practical purposes, they may be grouped into four classes—the Braced Timber Frame, Modern Braced Frame, Balloon Frame, and Platform Frame.

THE BRACED TIMBER FRAME

The Braced Timber Frame is the oldest type and originated in New England. The early colonists brought with them a tradition of heavy, European half-timber construction, and this was nourished by the abundance of standing timber directly at hand. Nails had to be made by hand; therefore, the early craftsmen used them sparingly, devising methods of fastening that consisted of mortises and tenons held together by wooden dowel pins.

The principal framing members of the old New England houses were often hewn out of the trees nearest at hand and were ordinarily of much larger dimensions than were required to give the necessary strength. The time required in those days to prepare the timbers necessary for the building of a house, as well as the time required for its building permitted the timbers and framing members to dry out thoroughly before the building was completed. And under these conditions the old Braced Timber Frame resulted in a practically faultless house of which hundreds of old houses still standing in the eastern states today bear evidence.

THE MODERN BRACED FRAME

In those sections of the country where many of the old Braced Timber Frame houses still stand, a modern adaptation of the old Braced Timber Frame has been developed. This type of frame is sometimes called the "Combination Frame." Corner posts and girts built up of two or three pieces of two-inch lumber take the place of the solid timbers formerly used. Nails largely replace mortises, tenons, and dowel pins for fastening. With the elimination of the heavy timber girts the intermediate posts formerly required to support them have been done away with, and the studs, in addition to furnishing bearing surfaces for the inside and outside walls, are utilized for support as well. The corner bracing, however, is retained as in most cases, the solid sill.

This Modern Braced Frame is in every way adaptable to modern building needs, yet to be thoroughly efficient should not be slighted in its construction. This method of framing is shown (see diagram) in one case complete as it should be built and in the other case only partially developed at the sacrifice of much of its efficiency.

THE BALLOON FRAME

The Balloon Frame is another modern and accepted type of framing applicable to the building of substantial houses in all parts of the country. As is the case in the Modern Braced Frame, it is built almost entirely of two-inch lumber. Nails are also used for fastening in place of mortises and tenons. The distinguishing feature of the so-called Balloon Frame, however, is that the wall studs are made to extend up two stories high with the ends of the second floor joists spiked to their sides and resting upon a false girt or "ribband board" which is notched into them on the inside. A box sill is ordinarily used with this type of framing. The elimination of the girts in the walls has required the fitting of fire-stops between the studs to prevent the circulation of air throughout the walls. Floor headers and fire-stops between the joists accomplish a similar purpose. The sub-floors are laid diagonally with the joists. The bearing partition studs rests upon the girders. Corner bracing is also required unless the sheathing is applied diagonally.

The Balloon Frame offers the advantages of speed and economy. It also possesses excellent rigidity. Properly constructed, it is in every way to be recommended.

It is unfortunate that so logical a type of framing should be so grossly abused by careless builders in their over-zealous quest for speed and cheapness. It seems to have developed in two diametrically opposite directions. In the one case it has been improved to the point where it meets successfully all the demands of efficient building practice. In the other case it has been cheapened through harmful "corner-cutting" into a flimsy, short-lived structure. That you may appreciate the good points in the properly constructed Balloon Frame and, at the same time, guard against the construction abuses to which it is often subjected, it is shown in both its good and bad forms.

THE PLATFORM FRAME

With the advent of kiln-dried framing lumber, the more recently developed Platform Frame has been gaining preference rapidly. This type of framing is unquestionably the fastest and the safest form of good construction. Interior and exterior walls are framed exactly alike, thereby assuring balanced shrinkage or settling if any occurs. Each floor is framed separately, with the sub-floor in place before the wall and partition studs are raised. All studding may be the same length. This permits the specification and use of precision manufactured, exact length, ready-to-use lumber products with consequent labor and waste saving on the job. Braced with diagonal sheathing, let-in bracing or steel strapping, the Platform Frame is adequately rigid to withstand severe windstorm conditions.

SUPPORTING TIMBERS

Few indeed are the houses whose supporting timbers are not sufficient to carry even heavier loads than they will ever be called upon to bear.

"Why, then," the prospective builder is quick to ask, "must I interest myself in the supporting timbers in my new home?"

The answer is simple. Many house annoyances are caused by cheapening the house through the use of undersized supporting members.

The function of the supporting timbers is not merely to prevent the house from tumbling down. Many a house is cheapened by the use of undersized or too few supporting timbers and yet has strength enough to support any ordinary load. But the floors of these houses lack stiffness. And stiffness is vital to the satisfactory house.

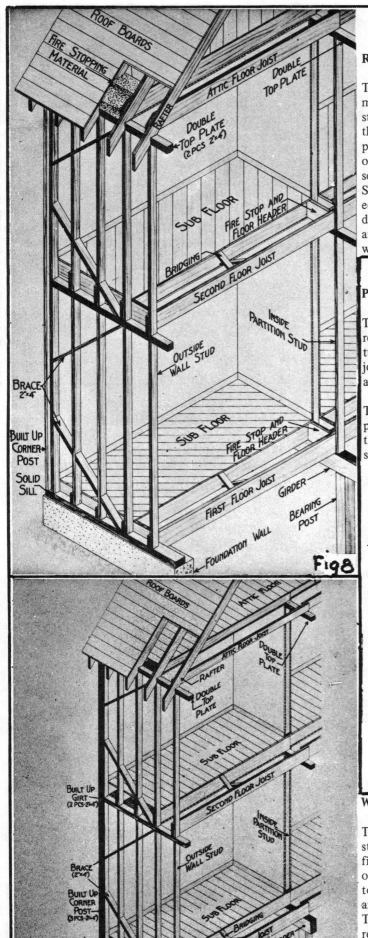

Labels on upper figure (Fig 8): ROOF BOARDS, FIRE STOPPING MATERIAL, RAFTER, ATTIC FLOOR JOIST, DOUBLE TOP PLATE, DOUBLE TOP PLATE (2 PCS 2"×4"), SUB FLOOR, FIRE STOP AND FLOOR HEADER, BRIDGING, SECOND FLOOR JOIST, INSIDE PARTITION STUD, OUTSIDE WALL STUD, BRACE 2"×4", BUILT UP CORNER POST, SOLID SILL, SUB FLOOR, FIRE STOP AND FLOOR HEADER, FIRST FLOOR JOIST, GIRDER, BEARING POST, FOUNDATION WALL, Fig8

Labels on lower figure (Fig 9): ROOF BOARDS, ATTIC FLOOR, RAFTER, DOUBLE TOP PLATE, ATTIC FLOOR JOIST, DOUBLE TOP PLATE, SUB FLOOR, SECOND FLOOR JOIST, INSIDE PARTITION STUD, OUTSIDE WALL STUD, BUILT UP GIRT (2 PCS 2"×4"), BRACE (2"×4"), BUILT UP CORNER POST (3 PCS 2"×4"), SOLID SILL, SUB FLOOR, BRIDGING, FIRST FLOOR JOIST, GIRDER, BEARING POST, FOUNDATION WALL, Fig9

RIGHT

The modern Braced Frame, constructed in this manner, makes an entirely satisfactory and efficient frame. The fire-stops or floor headers of two-inch lumber placed between the floor joists make this frame fire-resistant and vermin-proof, and also make it possible to lay the sub-floor diagonally with the joists, a very important consideration from several standpoints.

Stops to the passage of fire and heat in the walls are afforded by the girts. Note, too, that the partition studs rest directly upon the girder, a further consideration of importance in eliminating settling due to unequal shrinkage in the walls and bearing partitions.

POSTS AND GIRDERS

The outer ends of the joists which support the first floor rest directly upon the foundation wall, or on a sill which, in turn, rests upon the foundation wall. The inner ends of these joists rest upon girders which are supported by bearing posts as illustrated in Figure 13.

These girders and bearing posts support the main bearing partitions as well as a part of the weight of the floors and the contents of the house. They should, therefore, be of a size sufficient to support this weight.

SILLS

The sill furnishes a means of securing the superstructure to the foundation and provides a nailing surface for the joists. There are several types of sills in use which have the approval of good builders; three of these are shown in Figures 8, 10 and 12.

If a house is to be firmly anchored to the foundation (and it surely should be for a number or reasons), the sill must be more than merely set on the foundation. The solid or timber sill should be anchored by means of bolts and the box sill by concrete, known in this use as "beam-filling." This beam-filling also seals the joint between the framework and the foundation. When a solid sill or a combination sill is used, the joint between it and the foundation should be sealed by placing the sill, or the plate, on a bed of mortar.

WRONG

This illustration shows some common abuses in the construction of the Modern Braced Frame. Floor headers and fire stopping between the joists have been omitted. For lack of these headers the sub-floor has been laid at right angles to the joists at the expense of the rigidity of the structure and the success of the finished floor to be laid above it. The bearing partitions also rest upon the sub-floor with the result that these inside walls will settle as the joists, sub-floor boards and plates dry out and shrink under the artificial heat inside the house.

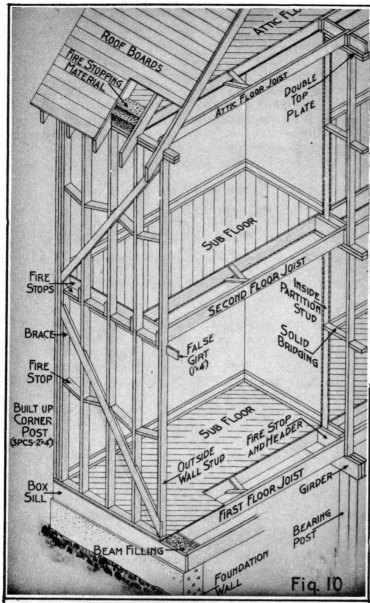

Labels in Fig. 10:
ROOF BOARDS
FIRE STOPPING MATERIAL
ATTIC FLOOR JOIST
DOUBLE TOP PLATE
SUB FLOOR
FIRE STOPS
INSIDE PARTITION STUD
BRACE
SECOND FLOOR JOIST
FALSE GIRT (1"×4")
SOLID BRIDGING
FIRE STOP
BUILT UP CORNER POST (3 PCS-2"×4")
SUB FLOOR
OUTSIDE WALL STUD
FIRE STOP AND HEADER
BOX SILL
FIRST FLOOR JOIST
GIRDER
BEARING POST
BEAM FILLING
FOUNDATION WALL
Fig. 10

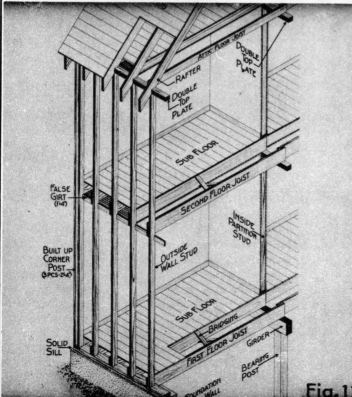

Labels in Fig. 11:
ATTIC FLOOR JOIST
DOUBLE TOP PLATE
RAFTER
DOUBLE TOP PLATE
SUB FLOOR
FALSE GIRT (1"×4")
SECOND FLOOR JOIST
INSIDE PARTITION STUD
BUILT UP CORNER POST (3 PCS-2"×4")
OUTSIDE WALL STUD
SUB FLOOR
BRIDGING
SOLID SILL
FIRST FLOOR JOIST
GIRDER
BEARING POST
FOUNDATION WALL
Fig. 11

BALLOON FRAME

RIGHT

Because the Balloon Frame has qualities and advantages that cannot be found in other types, conscientious builders everywhere have striven to build 100 per cent efficiency into this type of framing, with the result that today it is an eminently satisfactory frame from every standpoint.

Wall and corner studs, continuous from sill to plate, make for stiffness, corner braces and fire-stopping in the walls and floors for rigidity and fire-resistance, while by reducing as well as equalizing as far as possible the amount of cross sectional lumber subject to shrinkage in the inside and outside walls, the problem of plaster cracks and other ills traceable to shrinkage is largely solved.

Nor are these improvements of the kind that add greatly to the cost, in either time or material. In fact, the difference in the cost of a good Balloon Frame over that of a poor one is so small, when compared to the added efficiency, that it is surprising to find it so grossly misused.

In the hurry-up kind of construction this anchoring and sealing is often neglected or done in such a haphazard manner as to be of little value. Good workmanship in such places as this costs no more, and you will find it worth while to see that you get it. With good foundations and footings and with the primary supporting members of the house properly taken care of, you have a good start on a substantial house.

JOISTS

The joists furnish the support for the floors. Joist sizes, like girder sizes, are dependent upon the length of the span they bridge and upon the load they are required to carry. Failure to use joists of sufficient size is sometimes the cause of sagging, squeaking floors that seem insecure under foot, rattling light fixtures and cracked plaster in the ceilings underneath.

BRIDGING FLOOR JOISTS

By bridging is meant those small braces that extend crosswise from the top of one joist to the bottom of the next and in a straight, continuous line the length of the house. A trip to your basement will, or should, reveal one or more rows of bridging. It may be difficult to realize the

WRONG

This illustration shows how even the best method of framing a house may be reduced to total inefficiency by cutting the corners and cheapening its construction. Unfortunately, many so-called Balloon Frame houses are constructed in this manner. The elimination of corner braces robs the structure of much of its rigidity. The ready circulation of air between walls and floors is also responsible for serious heat losses in the finished house. A prediction of plaster cracks, squeaking floors and numerous other house ills is apparent in this cheapened frame.

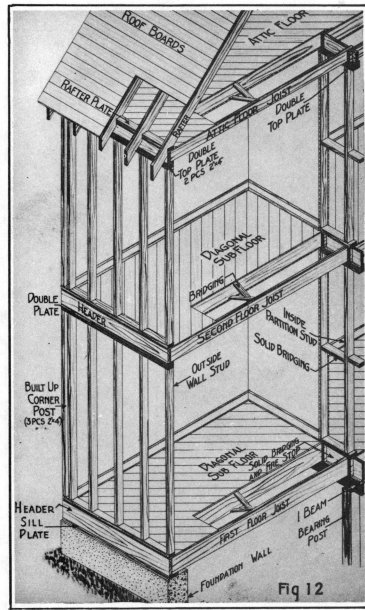

Fig 12

Labels on figure:
ROOF BOARDS
ATTIC FLOOR
RAFTER PLATE
RAFTER
ATTIC FLOOR JOIST
DOUBLE TOP PLATE
DOUBLE TOP PLATE 2 PCS 2"x4"
DIAGONAL SUB-FLOOR
BRIDGING
SECOND FLOOR JOIST
INSIDE PARTITION STUD
SOLID BRIDGING
DOUBLE PLATE
HEADER
OUTSIDE WALL STUD
BUILT UP CORNER POST (3 PCS 2"x4")
DIAGONAL SUB FLOOR
SOLID BRIDGING AND FIRE STOP
HEADER
SILL
PLATE
FIRST FLOOR JOIST
I BEAM
BEARING POST
FOUNDATION WALL

PLATFORM FRAME

In this type of frame the first floor is built on top of the foundation walls as though it were a platform. The outer ends of the floor joists rest on a sill, of combination type, while the inner ends rest on an I-beam upon which has been placed a two-inch plank. On the floor joists is nailed the sub-floor, laid diagonally.

The wall and partition framing is then run up another story to support another platform for the second floor. Again, the third or attic floor consists of a third platform built upon the second floor wall and partition framing, thus making the whole a series of platforms each supported by independent partitions.

The platform feature of this frame automatically firestops the walls and partitions at each floor level. The diagonal sub-flooring may be readily laid on each platform before any studs are raised, thereby speeding up the sub-flooring operation and assuring the workmen a safe sound floor on which to work.

With the increasing use of kiln-dried framing, the Platform Frame will continue to gain in popularity.

SUB-FLOORS

The sub-floor is the rough under-floor which is nailed to the joists and over which the finish floor is laid.

The sub-floor, if laid diagonally over the joists, gives a better foundation for the finish floor, and especially on the upper floors, also adds considerable stiffness to the structure.

The importance of properly nailing the floors can hardly be overstated. Many people are surprised to learn that it is the working up and down of the nails in their sockets that causes the annoying creaking and squeaking of floors when they are walked over. Bulging, humpy floors are also often the result of too few nails or of improper nailing. A nailing schedule for the laying of sub-floors require:

> For 4 and 6-inch boards—Use 2 nails per board per joist.

A recent development which saves considerable time and material is 1x6 End-Matched Douglas Fir. The end-matching eliminates the necessity for making joints over the joists, thereby reducing the sawing to a minimum and speeding up the laying of the sub-floor. End-Matched sub-flooring provides a sound, tight, squeak-eliminating base for the finished floor and is adequately strong for any form of residential construction.

PORCH FLOORS

No flooring receives harder wear than that on the porch. Attention to the following points will add materially to its life.

1. The porch floor should have a slight pitch so that water will run off quickly. Substantial piers and footings are necessary to assure an even floor year after year.

value of these small braces, but their importance can hardly be over-emphasized.

The purpose of bridging is to keep the joists in alignment and to distribute to all of the joists any exceptionally heavy, concentrated loads or sudden jolts that may be applied directly above one or two of them. Tests have shown that it requires three times as much weight to cause a certain amount of deflection in a bridged beam as it does to cause the same deflection in one that is not bridged. Figure 15 illustrates one good method of doing this bracing. Bridging is just as necessary between the second floor joists, though, of course, it is not visible in the completed house.

It is difficult to remedy defects due to poor bridging, or lack of bridging, once the house is built, but a simple matter to check during construction.

FLOORS

Despite the fact that precautions are employed to assure proper floor support, attention must also be given to correct methods of laying the sub-floor and finish floor.

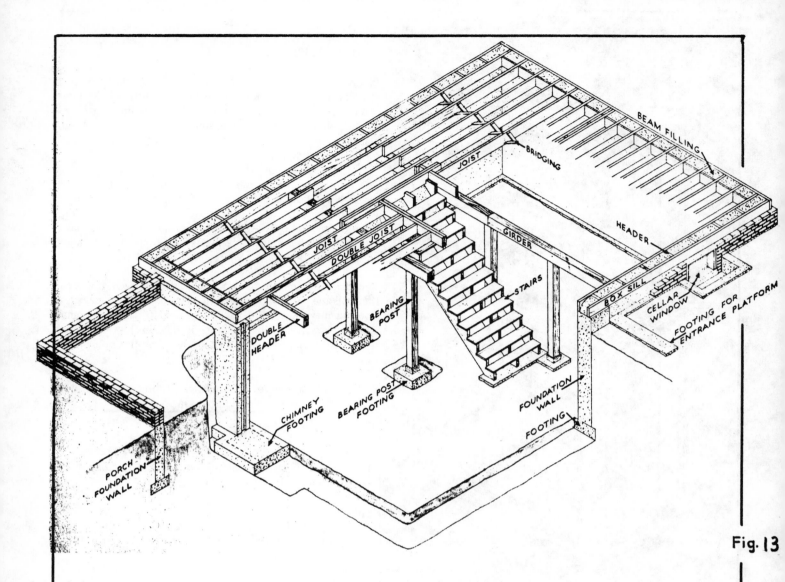

Fig. 13

In the building of this house, as has been pointed out, the improved Balloon method of framing has been used. The method of procedure is usually as follows:

After excavating for the basement, trenches are dug for all footings and piers. The footings, foundation walls, bearing post footings, chimney footings and porch piers are then put in, in the order mentioned. As the foundation wall is built up, the cellar window frames are set in place. The carpenters then place the girders and girder posts, after which the box sills are laid out and the floor joists put in place. All openinings through the floor for cellar stairs, chimney and clothes chutes, if any, are then framed.

The joists around these openings are doubled, as are the joists under all partitions set parallel to the joists. If beam-filling is used, as in this case, the one-inch boards which hold it in place and the joist headers are now put in and the beam-filling placed.

Bridging (See following sketches) is fitted in between the joists in the middle of the span and nailed to the joists. The rough stair horses for the cellar stairs are then cut and put in place.

Floor joists are often seriously weakened by mechanics when they are installing the plumbing and heating systems. It is highly important that the carpenters, who are familiar with the requirements of these framing members, do whatever cutting and notching of framing members necessary in this connection. It also becomes necessary to cut away joists for stairways, chimneys and other floor openings. This obviously weakens the floor structure and this lost strength must be regained. Just how it is done is illustrated in Figure 16.

2. Porch flooring should be dry when laid.
3. The joints of the porch flooring should be given a coat of white lead and oil just before the flooring is laid, and the whole floor, particularly under columns, should be painted immediately after being laid. A fresh coat of paint each year will greatly increase the life of the floor.
4. Circulation of air under the porch should be provided.

BUILDING AGAINST SHRINKAGE

Shrinkage is the natural result of the drying of wood. While certain difficulties in many houses are traceable directly to it, it does not follow that these defects need to be a part of the wood house.

This illustration shows the result of using floor joists of insufficient depth to have the required stiffness. Hence the sagging and the cracked plaster. Too small joists are often used merely because it is known that they will support the floor. These overworked joists invariably sag, however, when loads are applied, and cracked ceiling plaster and unsatisfactory floors are the result. Sometimes, when sagging floors are not noticeable to the eye, overworked joists are indicated by the feeling of insecurity when the floor is walked on.

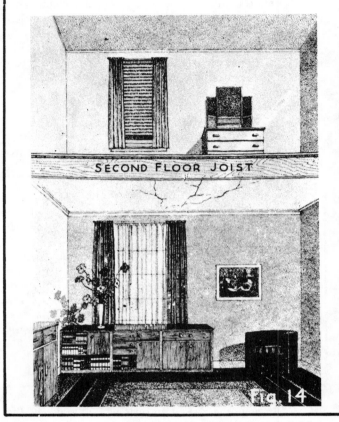

Shrinkage may be minimized by the use of seasoned lumber and a few simple construction methods sometimes overlooked by the builder.

Water exists in wood in two conditions: as free water contained within the cell cavities and as water absorbed in the cell walls. Removal of the free water merely reduces the weight of the wood; shrinkage begins with the removal of the absorbed water, and the amount of shrinkage that will take place in a piece of wood is directly proportionate to the amount of moisture which the cell walls have absorbed.

Therefore, since green lumber with a moisture content of 25 to 30 percent will shrink much more than lumber with a moisture content of only 15 per cent, the wisdom of using seasoned lumber in the framework of a house is immediately apparent. The development of modern dry kilns at all of the reputable West Coast mills makes it possible, in most sections, to buy correctly seasoned framing lumber at no greater cost than green unseasoned stock.

Shrinkage of wood, however, like the expansion and contraction of steel, cannot be entirely eliminated. Just as steel expands under heat and contracts when cooled, so

lumber, unprotected by paint, takes on and gives off moisture according to the variations in the humidity of the surrounding atmosphere. As a house ages, the lumber in its framework, subjected to the dry artificial heat in a winter, may, over a period of years, dry to a moisture content as low as 6 or 8 per cent. It is not practical to use framing lumber in the building of a house with as low a moisture content as this since, even though the lumber was dried to this state in the beginning, it would, during its process of building, absorb enough atmospheric moisture to bring it back to air-dry condition.

This additional shrinkage must, therefore, be taken care of in the manner in which the house is built. And this is rendered easy by the fact that lumber in drying shrinks mostly across the grain (in cross section) and only infinitesimally lengthwise (with the grain). making it necessary in designing the frame of a house merely to minimize and equalize as far as possible the amount of horizontal framing lumber appearing in cross section in the outside walls and bearing partitions.

In the properly designed house frame, then, the horizontal framing members in the outside walls and partitions—which are the only members in which wood in cross section is used, and so the only members subject to shrinkage—are minimized and equalized so far as it is possible without sacrificing the strength and rigidity of the structure. This may sound a bit complicated and involved, but reference to Figures 20 and 21 will clarify the matter.

In these illustrations proper and improper methods of providing for shrinkage in the improved Balloon Frame are shown. The same principle can, however, be applied to other types of frames.

Good builders everywhere are recognizing how easy it is to build against shrinkage and so are avoiding the numerous house ills that might otherwise result from the uneven settling of walls and partitions. Here again we have an illustration of how simple it is to see that one's house is substantially built if one will take the trouble to study the working plans and then check up the various details as the house is being built.

WALL AND PARTITION FRAMING

Obviously, the first essentials of wall framing are strength and rigidity, since the walls are required not only to carry a large part of the weight of the house, but must, as well, resist pressure from occasional high winds.

Wall and partition framing consists of studs, usually 2x4's, top and bottom plates and the necessary bracing and fire-stopping. Careful cutting, fitting, nailing, bracing, and fire-stopping are all essential to sound, substantial walls and partitions.

There are two kinds of walls and partitions, bearing and non-bearing. A bearing partition or wall is one which runs at right angles to and supports the ends of the joists. In other words, a bearing wall or partition is one which bears or supports a load from above. A non-bearing wall or partition acts only as a screen or enclosure.

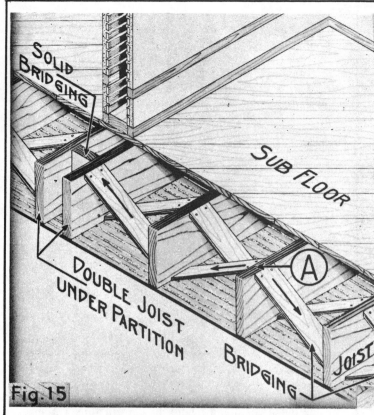

SOLID BRIDGING

SUB FLOOR

DOUBLE JOIST UNDER PARTITION

BRIDGING

JOIST

A

Fig.15

This drawing illustrates the proper bridging of floor joists so essential to good house construction. It is an item overlooked or only superficially taken care of in many houses where correct construction is sacrificed for speed and cheapness.

A load suddenly applied to a properly bridged floor joist is transmitted through the bridging to the neighboring joists and thus absorbed without damage.

Bridging tends to hold all floor joists in equal alignment but to be effective must be properly fitted and securely nailed.

Wherever joist spans exceed eight feet, bridging should be used. Exceptionally long joist spans should be bridged every six feet. Where a bearing partition runs parallel to the joists, the double joists beneath it should be braced with solid bridging.

To get the best foundation upon which to lay the finished floor and to stiffen the framework, the sub-floor boards should be laid diagonally with the joists.

As has been pointed out, non-bearing partitions should be supported by double bridged joists (see Figure 15). The studs which support the framing around stairways should also be doubled, as shown in Figure 16. Bearing partitions require special support, as pointed out in Figure 19, when these partitions do not occur directly over the partition below. In such a case, the studs in the bearing partition below, which support this off side bearing partition, should be reinforced with two rows of bridging. (This is also shown in Figure 19.)

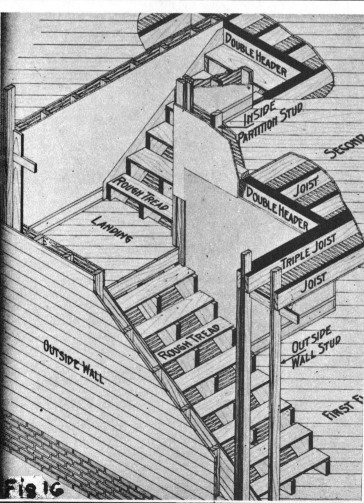

DOUBLE HEADER

INSIDE PARTITION STUD

SECOND

ROUGH TREAD

DOUBLE HEADER

JOIST

LANDING

TRIPLE JOIST

JOIST

ROUGH TREAD

OUTSIDE WALL STUD

OUTSIDE WALL

FIRST F

Fig 16

When it becomes necessary to cut away one or more of the floor joists, as in the case of an opening for a stairway, the strength lost in cutting off these joists must be regained.

Good practice calls for framing around floor openings similar to that shown here. The loose ends of the joists cut away are secured to a header composed of two pieces of lumber of the same dimensions as the joists.

These headers are, in turn, supported by double or triple joists, depending upon the amount of material it is necessary to add in order to return the strength of the joists that have been cut away. The framework around the opening is thus again tied together and the lost strength is regained.

Where headers longer than six feet are necessary, they should be fastened to their supporting joists by means of stirrup irons or joists hangers.

This illustration brings out very clearly those members which need reinforcing. The amount of added material required has in each case been designated.

Observance of these suggestions will insure construction in and around the stairway that will prove satisfactory in every way.

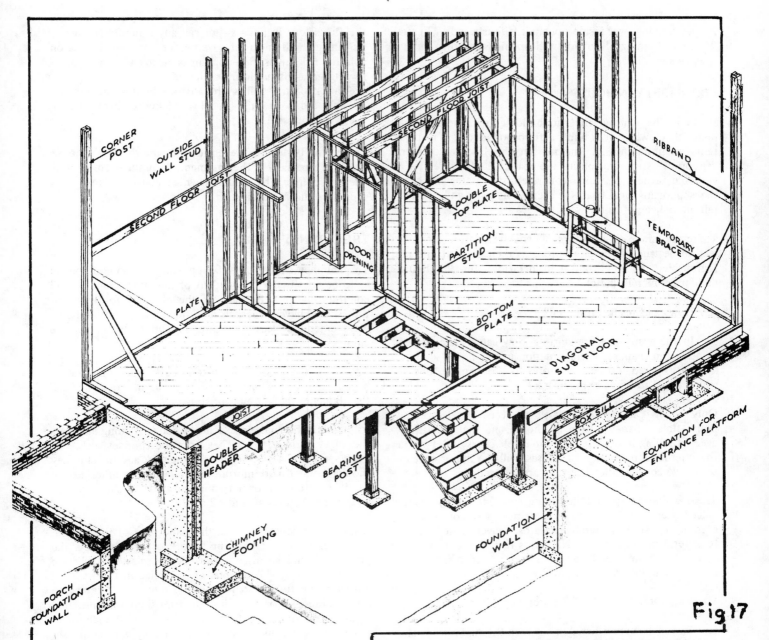

CORNER POST

OUTSIDE WALL STUD

SECOND FLOOR JOIST

SECOND FLOOR JOIST

DOUBLE TOP PLATE

PARTITION STUD

RIBBAND

TEMPORARY BRACE

DOOR OPENING

PLATE

BOTTOM PLATE

DIAGONAL SUB FLOOR

JOIST

DOUBLE HEADER

BEARING POST

BOX SILL

FOUNDATION FOR ENTRANCE PLATFORM

CHIMNEY FOOTING

FOUNDATION WALL

PORCH FOUNDATION WALL

Fig 17

For the sake of simplifying the illustrations in this series of drawings, the inside bearing partitions are shown resting on plates set on top of the sub-floor. In actual practice it would be better to run these bearing partition studs down between the joists and rest them directly upon the girders below, as suggested in Figure 20.

The studs and top plates for the first floor bearing partitions are cut and nailed together and the door openings in these partitions are framed before they are raised and braced in place.

The top and bottom plates and the ribband boards for the outside walls are then cut to exact length and the position of the outside wall studs is marked on each; also the position of all window and door openings. The outside wall studs are cut to proper length and notched out to receive the ribband board. The corner studs are then framed, raised and braced in place. The ribband board and remaining studs are next put in place.

When a partition supports more than the weight of the roof and two floors, as in the case of a bearing partition in the basement of a two-story house, the studs in this bearing partition which, in such a case, replace the main bearing posts, should be not less than 2x6 or 3x4 inches.

In all cases bearing partitions should have double top plates and should be braced with solid bridging not less than two inches in thickness and not less than the full width of the studs. (See Figure 19.)

WINDOW AND DOOR OPENINGS

It becomes necessary in the construction of the house to cut away part of the framing in the outside walls for door and window openings, and in the inside walls, or partitions, for door openings. Naturally this weakens the framework as a whole and the lost strength must be regained by reinforcing the framework around these openings.

453

Proper framing over inside openings is illustrated in Figure 25, while framing of outside wall openings is shown in Figures 29 and 30.

FIRE SAFETY IN HOUSES

It should be realized that no building, regardless of the materials of which it is built, is fireproof so long as its contents are inflammable. The masonry walls of a so-called "fireproof" structure confine the heat of the fire, creating a veritable furnace in which concrete disintegrates and even the supporting steel beams and columns twist and fail and fall into a heap of ruins.

Therefore, since all buildings of whatever nature are subject to destruction by fire as long as their contents are inflammable, the important considerations for the house builder are merely these:

1. How can fires be prevented?

2. In the event of a fire starting, how can it be confined through the manner of construction in a building so as to make its spread difficult and so as to allow ample time in which to get to it and extinguish it?

Only when it is realized that 96 per cent of all dwelling house fires originate inside the house and that practically every dwelling house fire is due to carelessness or defects in the internal construction of houses, will the importance of these two considerations be fully appreciated.

The installation of electric wiring and fixtures by experienced electricians under competent supervision and according to Underwriters' standards, leaves little chance for fires from this source. Neither is it difficult to so construct the chimney and the framing around it so as to eliminate the chimney as a cause of fire.

There are three methods of fire-stopping:

1. Two-inch lumber fitted in between the studs and joists.
2. The vital points boxed in with one-inch boards and the boxes filled with incombustible material such as loose mortar concrete, mineral wool, etc.
3. Metal lath, bent and nailed into place between the studs and joists. The lath is then plastered and the box thus formed filled with incombustible material.

Fire-stops are put into a building to pevent the passage of flames, hot air and gases. All joints should be tight; otherwise, hot gases will pass through them and ignite the wood above. Poorly fitted fire-stops are little better than none.

The slight additional expense involved in fire-stopping a house cannot rightfully be charged to fire prevention alone, since much of it serves as bracing in the frame of the house. Fire-stopping more than pays for itself in the additional strength and rigidity it gives to the entire structure. Figure 37 shows how this fire-stopping should be installed.

Thus, it is seen that next to the elimination of the causes of fire, right construction is of first importance in increasing the fire safety in houses—nor can any house, regardless of its outside wall and roof covering, be considered a reasonable fire risk, unless fire-stopping is made an integral part of its internal construction. On the other hand, by proper appreciation of the points brought out in this chapter, it is possible today to build an all-wood house that will be in every way fire-safe.

There is no better fire prevention measure than good housekeeping, especially in the basement. Accumulations of trash piles of combustible material which collect in any house should be guarded against.

THE CHIMNEY

The chimney should be self-supporting and so constructed as to be absolutely independent of the house framing. Soil conditions govern the size of the chimney footings, but they should never be less than 12 inches deep and should always extend at least 6 inches beyond each face of the chimney.

The walls of a chimney with terra cotta flue lining, should be not less than 4 inches thick if built of brick, nor less than 8 inches thick if built of stone.

All combustible materials such as wooden framing members should be at least two inches from the chimney wall. The open spaces between the floor framework and the chimney should be filled with mortar, mineral wool, or other incombustible material. Proper framing around the chimney is illustrated in Figures 40 and 42.

While it is permissible, from the standpoint of fire hazard, to plaster directly on the brickwork of the chimney, the practice should be discouraged because plaster cracks are certain to develop. When plaster is applied in this manner, however, the furring strips placed around the chimney to support the base or other interior trim should be insulated from the masonry by asbestos paper at least 1/8-inch thick. A better practice is to box in the chimney with studs, set two inches away from the brickwork, and on these to apply the lath and plaster.

The chimney should be capped with stone, terra cotta, concrete or cast iron and should extend at least three feet above a flat roof or two feet above a ridge roof. This assures a good draft for the heating plant.

Any increase in the wall thickness of the chimney should be made at least 12 inches below the rafters and not be made above the roof except for capping.

The proper construction of fireplaces is fully described and illustrated in Figure 45.

THE ROOF

Roof Pitch. Insufficient pitch probably causes more troublesome roofs than any other single factor, especially in climates where there is considerable snow. It is difficult to build

Fig. 18

a tight roof of low pitch in these localities. In climates where deep snows are customary, will also do well to hold to simple, straight roof lines.

RAFTERS

The roof rafters, the framing members of the roof, must be of sufficient size and strength to support the weight of the roof, to carry the snow load and to resist the wind pressure without sagging. If the rafters are undersized or spaced too far apart, they will sag. This sagging will split and loosen the shingles and cause a leaky roof.

ROOF SHEATHING

Roof sheathing boards give best results when laid tight. As the roof boards are depended upon for some bracing effect as well as to furnish the foundation for the roof covering, the joints should be staggered. All roof boards should be nailed with at least two 8-penny nails at each rafter. Boards wider than six inches require at least three nails. If the third floor of the house is to be occupied, the roof should be in-

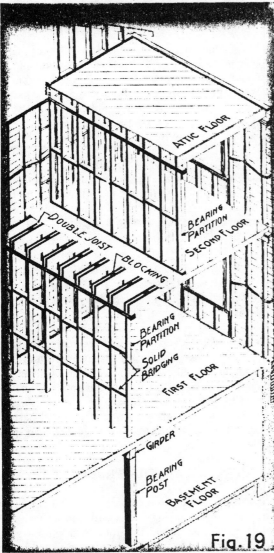

Fig. 19

This shows what happens to plastering on an inside wall when partition settles.

In addition to the cracked plaster in the corner, which is going to demand expensive repairing of plaster and premature redecorating, an unsightly crack has developed under the baseboard.

The condition noted in this picture is a result of one or more of the following causes:

1. Faulty footings under bearing posts.
2. Too small girders or too few posts.
3. A wide opening in a wall below this one improperly framed.
4. Joists under partition not doubled.
5. Joists of insufficient size.

Here is shown a condition not uncommon in house construction, i.e., a second floor bearing partition not directly over the bearing partition of the first floor but near the middle of the joist span. This condition calls for additional strength in the second floor joists which, in this case, has been secured by doubling the joists.

Note the blocking between the double joists and also that solid bridging has been added between the supporting studs in the main bearing partition.

This drawing also illustrates the economy in so planning a house as to have all bearing partitions directly over one another and directly above the supporting girders; thus avoiding the necessity for this extra reinforcing.

While the drawing shows a correct method of meeting the situation it illustrates, it is not necessarily the exact practice that should be followed in all cases. As pointed out in the text, it is more economical, where possible, to have bearing partitions on all floors directly over the bearing posts and girders in the basement.

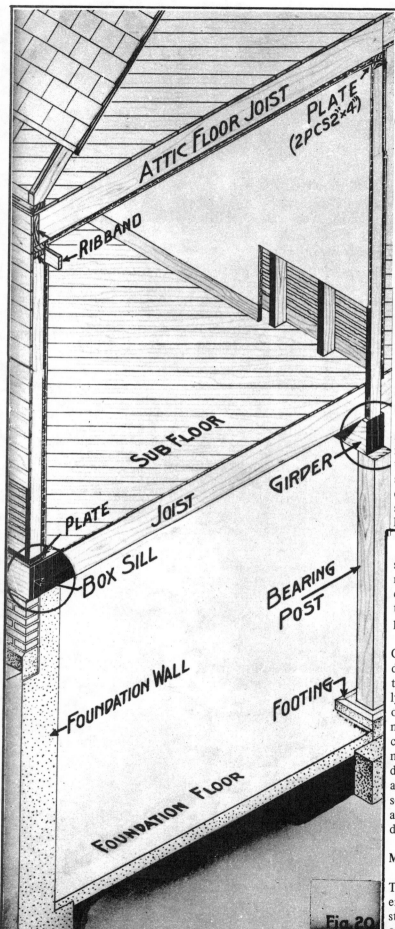

Fig. 20

RIGHT

This illustration shows one method of building against shrinkage by equalizing and minimizing, as far as possible, in both the outside walls and inside bearing partitions, the amount of lumber the shrinkage of which would cause settlement.

The members which are involved in this consideration appear in solid black within the circles.

In the outside wall any settlement which might occur due to shrinkage in the box sill and plate would be offset by an approximately equal amount of shrinkage in the girder under the inside bearing partition.

The slight additional settlement which might occur, due to shrinkage in the plates, upon which the second floor joists rest, would be so slight as to be negligible.

In contrast to Figure 21, note that the first floor bearing partition studs are brought down between the joists to rest directly upon the girder. Note also that the second floor bearing partition studs rest directly upon the top plates of the first floor partition.

Figure 21, in contrast to this one, shows a form of construction in which the shrinkage problem is ignored.

Any shrinkage that might occur in the top plates just beneath the attic floor joists, in both this drawing and Figure 21, would affect the attic floor only and would not be serious, due to the fact that the thickness of these plates is exactly the same in both the inside and outside walls. Any settlement of the attic floor would be so slight as to be negligible and would also be uniform.

sulated. Oven-like attics are the result of the hot summer rays of the sun beating down upon an uninsulated roof and can be avoided at slight cost. The dollars wasted in heat lost through the average roof in winter would, in a short time, pay for the cost of insulation.

GUTTERS. A well built gutter or eaves trough of proper design is essential to the tight roof. It is vitally important that the gutter be of sufficient size to carry water off rapidly and that it be so designed that it permits snow to slide off over it. In addition it must be constructed of durable material which will be relatively unaffected by the acids carried in smoke laden air. No other gutter, regardless of material, will answer these qualifications as well as kiln dried Douglas Fir gutter. Douglas Fir is immune to the ravages of rust and corrosion which have been responsible for so many gutter failures. Any one of the standard patterns and sizes of kiln dried Douglas Fir gutter will give splendid service when properly applied.

MAKING THE WALLS WEATHERPROOF

The making of a weatherproof house, no matter what material is used for wall covering, starts with proper wall construction. If the joints around the doors and windows and other points are not tight, good construction in the rest of

WRONG

This illustration of a common method of framing shows the shrinkage problem unsolved. The solid black within the circles indicates the relative amounts of lumber, the shrinkage of which would cause settlement in the outside and inside walls.

In the outside wall, settlement due to shrinkage in the 3-1/2 inch sill would be so slight as to be negligible—not over .08 of an inch if the sill were air-dry.

In the inside bearing partition, however, note that both the first and second story partition studs rest upon plates that are set on top of the joists and sub-floors. Any shrinkage in the cross section dimensions of the girders, first and second floor joists, sub-floor boards and plates will, therefore, cause settlement in this inside wall.

To solve correctly this problem of shrinkage, the house frame should be so constructed as to minimize and equalize, as far as possible, the amount of lumber appearing in cross section within the bearing walls and partitions.

Note in Figure 20 how easy it is through a slight variation in manner of construction to eliminate uneven settlement of this character.

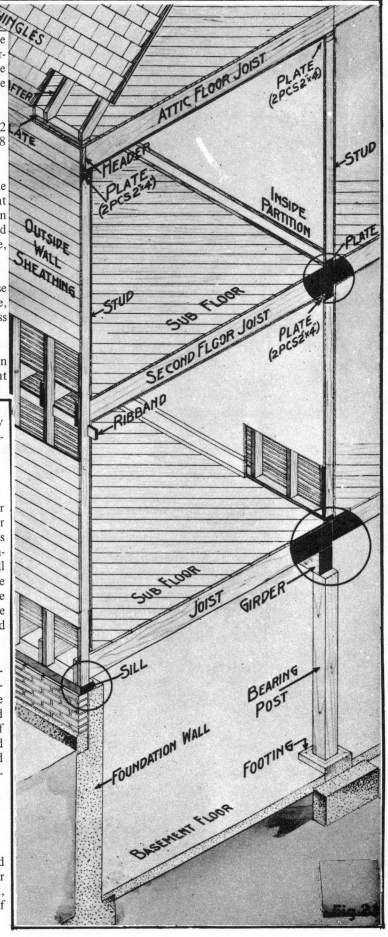

the wall will not make the house cool in summer nor easy to keep warm in winter. A number of these points are discussed in Figures 30, 31 and 49.

THE BREATHING WALL

Humidifying systems in modern homes increase the vapor pressure tending to force water vapor through the interior wall covering and into the wall construction. If the wall is insulated, but has no barrier against the passage of this vapor, then the inside surface of the sheathing frequently will be below the dew point temperature. In this case moisture would condense on the inside of the sheathing to form ice in very cold weather, and upon melting may enter the sheathing and framing directly causing paint failures and other construction troubles.

Wood sheathing permits the wall to breathe. The cell structure of wood permits the taking on and giving off of excessive moisture. With vapor proof sealing paper inside of the studs, or with a vapor barrier insulating blanket suspended in the stud space and a wind-proof paper on the outside of the sheathing, a safe, dry breathing wall is created. A good tight three-quarter inch tongued and grooved or shiplapped wood sheathing with a wind-proof building paper will provide adequate sidewall protection.

INTERIOR WALL COVERINGS

Plaster is not elastic, and regardless of the type of lath used with it, it will crack if there is any decided settlement or movement in the framing that holds it. The first essential, then, to a successful job of plastering is that the frame of the house be rigid.

457

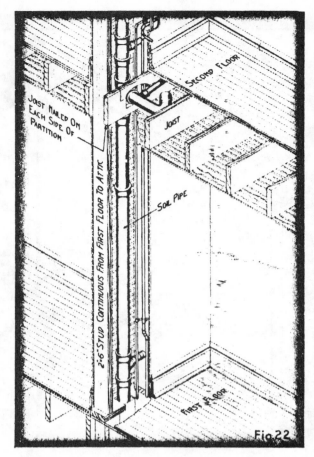

Fig. 22

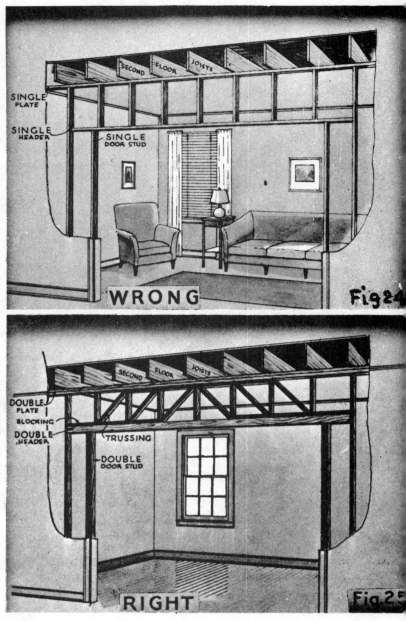

Fig 24

Fig 25

Lack of proper framing of the bathroom floor joists and the partitions in which the plumbing and heating pipes are to be located and careless cutting and notching of frame work to permit the passage of pipes, are responsible for many unsatisfactory bathroom floors and walls.

The above illustration shows one method of building a strong partiton for carrying these pipes and one which is not weakened by the necessary cutting and notching.

In this case, the 2x6 inch partition studs are made continuous from first floor to attic. This allows ample room for all pipes and makes a partition which loses no strength in the installation of plumbing and heating systems.

The joists at each side of the partition are nailed to each stud, thus assuring ample support for the floor. The joist notched out for the pipe should be cut in the manner shown and the piece replaced to provide nailing surface for the floor.

Fig. 23

Here is a condition common in many short-life houses. Figure 23 shows the result of improper framing around large openings in bearing partitions. In addition to the large jagged cracks running up from the opening, note the disfiguring crevice at the ceiling line. Also note that the trim or woodwork over the opening has sagged considerably.

The above illustration, Figure 24, shows the same cased opening with part of the plaster removed to show the cause of the condition picutred above. The framing around this opening is insufficient. The single plate and the single header were unable to carry the overhead load without giving somewhat. Hence the sagging noted in these members.

Figure 25 at the bottom illustrates how, with a little additional time and materials, the condition noted in the first illustration could have been avoided and with it the expense and annoyance involved in replastering and redecorating over this opening cure or cover up all of the evils occasioned by this faulty framing. The floor and the partition directly above will have sagged and the plaster on both sides of the partition will have cracked.

458

Note in the Fig. 25 illustration that the headers have been doubled and set on edge. The plate has been doubled also, as have the door studs. The 2x4 inch truss members and blocking have been added to give additional strength and rigidity to the framing. While other methods of meeting this situation might have been designed, the one here shown will illustrate how easily the condition shown in Figure 23 may be avoided.

At the left are shown two methods of applying the outside wall sheathing. Diagonal sheathing shown in Figure 27 adds materially to the stiffness and strength of the house.

The use of Endless lumber eliminates the usual added waste, because it is not necessary to make joints on studs.

With the sheathing laid horizontally, Figure 28, corner bracing should be used to give additional stiffness to the structure. The sheathing should be tongued and grooved or otherwise matched and the boards tightly driven together and nailed to each stud with at least two 8-penny nails in each board.

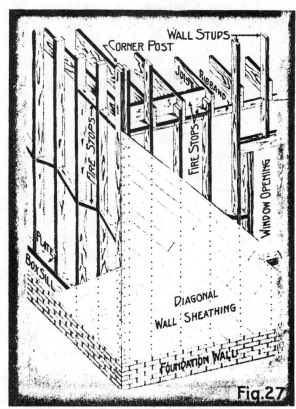

Fig.27

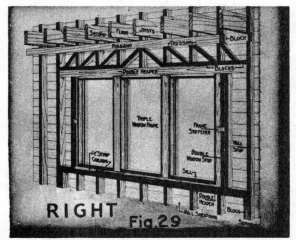

RIGHT Fig.29

This illustration shows the correct method of framing around a large opening in an outside wall—in this case for a triple window. The construction is very similar to that in Figure 25, for the same principles are involved. Note the adequate trussing and blocking, the double-header above and below and at the sides of the opening, also the frame stiffener and caulking, more clearly shown and explained below.

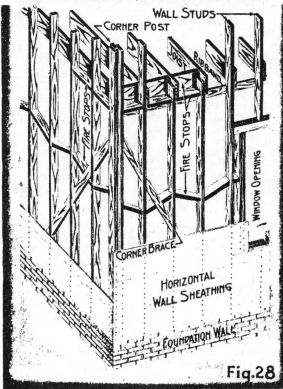

Fig.28

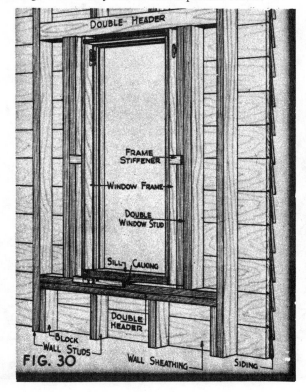

FIG. 30

RIGHT

Figure 30   shows the proper framing around window openings. Note the frame stiffeners. These help to keep the window frame straight and eliminate one cause of binding windows. As a general rule, all framing members around window (and door) openings should be doubled.

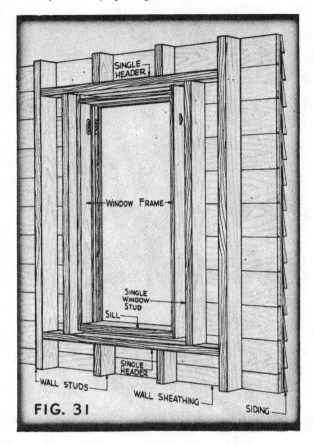

FIG. 31

WRONG

In the above illustration single framing members have been used. They do not replace the strength lost in cutting away the studs to make the opening. No caulking is shown. Failure to caulk allows free passage of air into the house.

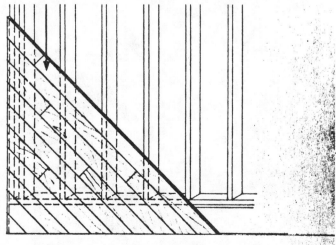

DIAGONAL SHEATHING Fig 32

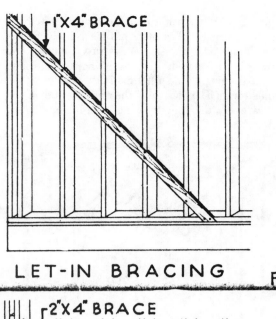

LET-IN BRACING Fig.33

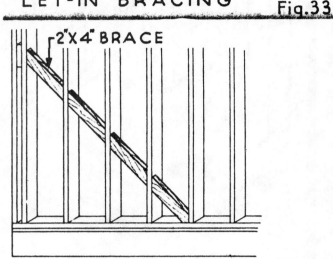

CUT-IN BRACING Fig.34

One of the four methods of bracing shown on this page should be used on all well constructed houses.

In Figure 32 bracing of the frame is accomplished by placing the sheathing at a 45° angle. Tests prove this method of bracing increases the rigidity of the house from two to seven times, depending on the number of openings which must be left for doors and window frames. This illustration shows the use of end-matched sheathing which may be used without making the joints on the studs. When ordinary sheathing is used, joints should be made only at the studs.

Some good builders prefer to brace the house frame with let-in bracing shown in Figure 33. This is accomplished by notching the studs to receive a continuous piece of 1x4 which is securely nailed to each stud. This type of bracing must be installed prior to the placing of the sheathing.

Another popular method of bracing the house frame and the one used in the house illustrated is the cut-in type. This consists of 2x4 members carefully cut and fitted between the studs after the sheathing has been nailed in place, Figure 34.

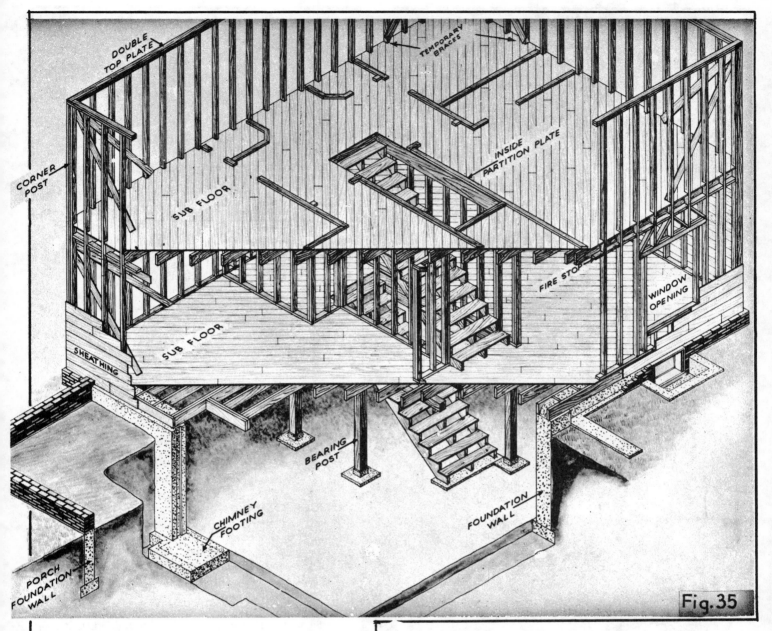

DOUBLE TOP PLATE

TEMPORARY BRACES

CORNER POST

SUB FLOOR

INSIDE PARTITION PLATE

SHEATHING

SUB FLOOR

FIRE STOP

WINDOW OPENING

BEARING POST

CHIMNEY FOOTING

FOUNDATION WALL

PORCH FOUNDATION WALL

Fig. 35

As the second floor joists are laid after the manner described in Figure 17, all openings in the floor for chimney, stairs, etc., are framed as in Figure 16. Joists are also doubled under any partitions that are to run parallel to them.

The outside wall studs are then capped with double top plates and another set of temporary braces put in as shown.

All necessary cutting, doubling and trussing, in the outside wall for the first floor window and outside doors and the fire-stopping at the second floor line is then done, after which the wall sheathing is put on up to the second floor line. The outside walls are straightened and the bridging is then put in between the second floor joists as in Figure 15. Headers between the joists are also put in.

To simplify this drawing, the cut-in bracing is not shown. Cut-in bracing will be installed after the sheathing has been applied.

No joints should occur directly over the corner of an opening. Lath should not run over or behind any partition; studs or well-braced backing strips should be arranged so that lath can be firmly nailed at each corner.

Ground strips of substantial material should be set straight and firmly nailed around all openings; these strips set the gauge for the thickness of the plaster. They are of assistance in getting a straight wall and are also valuable in securing an even, straight surface for the trim. Metal corner beads should be used on all projecting corners.

A simple understanding of the various reasons for cracked plaster in a house will go far towards enabling the home-builder to protect against it.

461

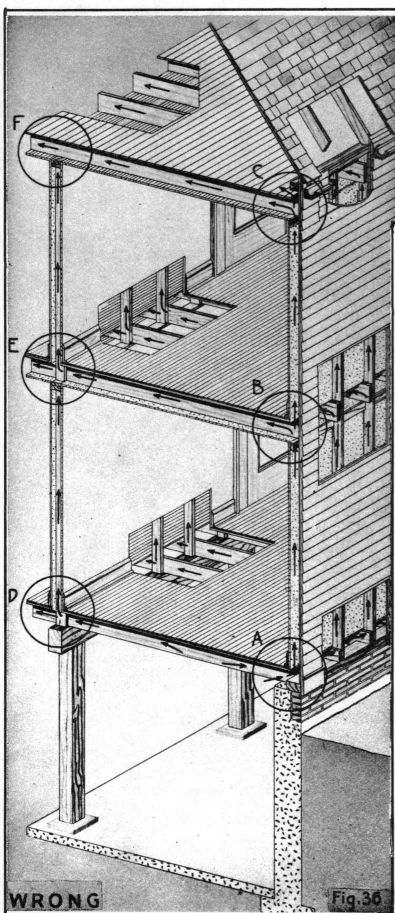

WRONG

Fig. 36

One glance at the accompanying illustration, showing a house without fire-stopping, should be sufficient to bring out the importance of closer attention to this important detail in the construction of a house. There are no fire-stops in this house. The arrows indicate the free circulation of air between the floor joists and between the wall studs.

Properly constructed and tightly-fitted fire-stops in the walls and floors, however, would confine the fire to one or two compartments and afford ample time to reach it and extinguish it without serious loss or damage.

The circles "A," "B," "C," "D," "E," and "F" indicate the vital points at which fire-stopping should have been used.

INTERIOR TRIM AND FINISH FLOORS

The pleasing appearance of interior woodwork and the satisfaction of having it "stay put" year in and year out depend so largely upon its treatment and the method of applying it as to merit consideration here.

Since the purpose of trim is to beautify, it should be well joined and pleasingly and appropriately finished. Satisfactory interior finish, like good plaster work, starts at the foundation footings. Uneven settling, due to those structural defects now familiar to the reader, is the greatest cause of unsightly openings and cracks in woodwork. A good job, however, is also dependent on the care the material receives before applying and the workmanship in placing it.

INTERIOR TRIM

Interior trim (including the lumber used for base boards, picture and cornice mouldings, door and window casings, etc.) is seasoned and kiln dried before it leaves the factory and should be protected from water and moisture until it is in place. It should not be allowed to stand out in the open after being delivered on the job, nor should it be brought into the house until after the plaster has dried. If it is allowed to absorb moisture, it will swell and warp, and if nailed when wet, unsightly cracks will develop as it dries out.

It is especially necessary to have a tight joint between the window stool and the sill in order to keep rain and cold from entering. To effect this tight joint, the under side of the stool and top of the sill, where they meet, should have a coating of good paint.

DOORS

The care of doors before they are hung is just as important as the care of interior trim, and the same precautions apply to both. Furthermore, if troublesome doors would be avoided, the top and bottom edge of each door should receive two coats of paint as the doors are hung. This prevents, to a large extent, the absorption of moisture that otherwise would cause the door to swell and bind.

This shows a method of fire-stopping in which boxes of one inch boards filled with incombustible material have been used throughout except at point "F," at which point a two-inch plank serves more effectively. Metal lath baskets carefully plastered after they are put in may be used in place of the inch boards.

It is important that when incombustible material is used, the space be filled to a point at least four inches above the floor level, to allow for settlement in the loose material.

A solid sill, although not recommended for the improved Balloon Frame, has been shown at point "A" to illustrate how fire-stopping should be done when this type of sill is used.

This drawing illustrates, in a very general way, the principles of fire-stopping. It does not show all of the different parts of a safe house, where fire-stops should be used. In the fire-safe house you will find fire-stops placed not only in the walls and beneath the floors, but in the stairways, around the clothes chutes and sliding door pockets. A number of other satisfactory methods of fire-stopping are also employed.

The slight additional cost of completely fire-stopping a house is more than offset by the added security it gives in return.

WINDOWS

There are several points in connection with the fitting of window sash that merit the attention of the home-builder. Balky windows that stick, first on one side and then the other, as one tries to open them, are often the result of loose fitting and present a situation difficult to remedy. Properly fitted windows in a new house, especially if they are in place during the time the plastering is being done, may bind a little until after the house has dried out, and until the woodwork has had time to adjust itself to the atmospheric condition in the completed house. If after a few months' time they continue to bind, this condition can then be quickly eliminated, provided, of course, that the construction around the window frame is not the cause of the trouble. Rattling windows are usually due to careless fitting of the window stops (the narrow strips which hold the lower sash in place). These stops should be held in place preferably by means of stop screws and washers, the holes in the stop being large enough to permit adjustment of the stop without entirely removing the screws.

Most of the difficulties may be overcome by the use of pre-fitted window units which come complete, ready to slip into place. These units are chemically treated to prevent decay.

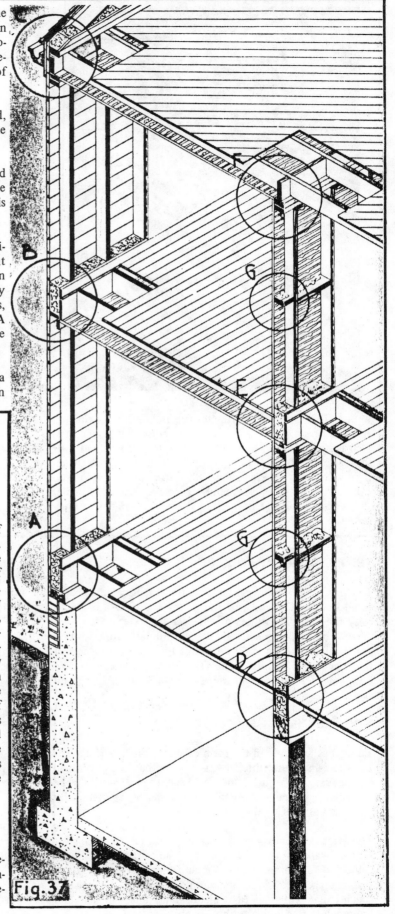

Fig. 37

Wrong. This construction invites fire and yet, in varying degrees, is not rare but quite common. Note that floor joists, boards and nailing blocks are built into the brickwork of the chimney. In addition to the fire hazard, this construction will result in cracked plaster. The settlement of the chimney will also cause members framed into it to settle. The correct method of framing around chimneys is illustrated in Figure 40.

Wrong. A chimney set on a bracket attached to a wall is a menace found in many houses even today. Note how the sagging of the bracket has opened the joints in the brickwork. In addition to this, the rafters and floor joists have been framed tight against the chimney, which has only a 4-inch wall without flue lining. A proper foundation for a chimney is shown in Figure 35.

THE EXTERIOR OF YOUR HOUSE

The principles of correct construction practice apply alike to all houses. The construction of the framework is practically the same, regardless of whether the exterior is wood, stucco, or brick veneer. Upon good lumber properly used and accurate workmanship depends the ultimate success of the completed building. The selection of the exterior covering of your house will depend upon your architectural style.

WOOD SIDING

Lumber is available in the form of siding cut to various patterns and in several thicknesses and widths. Siding is made in sizes ranging from 1/2-inch by 4 inches to 3/4-inch by 12 inches and is available in the correct species at practically any retail lumber yard.

The proper selection of the kind and grade of siding for outside wall covering is important. The outside of a house, subjected to sun and wind, rain and snow, receives its most severe usage. Exterior wood should be of a decay-resisting species that will hold tight at the joints and will take and hold paint. It should be thoroughly seasoned.

In applying siding, all joints around window frames and corner boards or at mitred corners should be carefully fitted. Spliced joints should be absolutely tight to prevent the infiltration of moisture.

Siding and all other exposed woodwork should be given a coat of paint (called the priming coat) as soon as it is in place. If it has been rained upon after application, it should be permitted to dry out before any paint is applied. It is highly important that a good grade of paint be used.

THE RIGHT LUMBER TO USE
IN HOUSE CONSTRUCTION

In the construction of a house, from the placing of the foundation footings, to the nailing of the last piece of interior trim, good workmanship and good materials are absolute essentials for a satisfactory job.

For the sills of a house, or any member placed near the ground, only heartwood or chemically preserved lumber should be used.

464

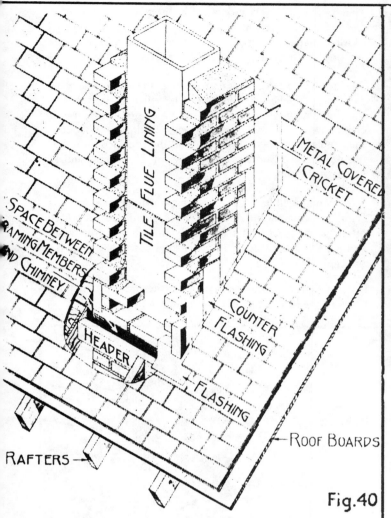

RAFTERS →

Fig.40

Fig.41

This is a familiar sight where snow and ice are the rule during the winter and early spring.

The valley formed by a gable on the side of the main roof becomes filled with drifting snow. Mild days and the heat lost through the roof causes the snow to melt and when followed by a drop in temperature at night, the downspout becomes clogged with ice.

When the water from the next day's thaw freezes, the entire gutter becomes filled with ice. Unless the gutters are of proper design, the valley will next become filled with ice and the water from further melting of the snow will, in its downward course, back up under the shingles and damage is done.

Having read that all combustible material should be at least two inches away from the chimney wall unless the brickwork is eight inches in thickness—the reader naturally wonders how it is possible to make a tight joint around the chimney at the roof.

This is accomplished by the use of what is called "flashing" and "counter flashing."

The term "flashing" is applied to the pieces of metal—tin, copper or lead—that are nailed onto the roof along with the shingles and bent up against the chimney wall, while "counter flashing" means the pieces of metal set into the brickwork and bent down over the flashing to form a water-tight joint.

The flashings should be arranged to overlap generously and allow for any movement that may occur in the chimney or roof.

What is called a "metal covered cricket" or "chimney saddle" is used to shed the water from behind the chimney.

This illustration also shows what is meant by tile or terra cotta flue lining and how the chimney is made weatherproof with a cement cap. The mortar joints of the flue lining should be well made and struck smooth on the inside.

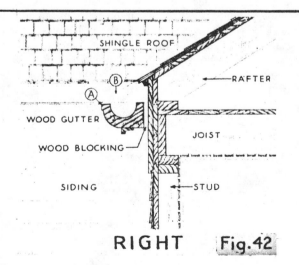

RIGHT **Fig.42**

The above illustration shows the correct method of installing a wood gutter. Note the blocks, spaced three feet apart, behind the gutter which provide openings for overflow in case the downspouts become clogged.

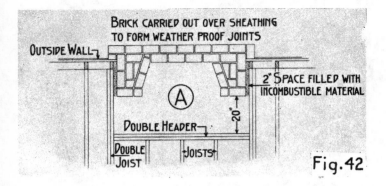

Fig. 42

These drawings show the method of floor framing around fireplaces built under the following conditions:

Figure 42—Fireplace partly exposed on outside of building.

Figure 43—Fireplace built against ouside wall but not exposed.

Figure 44—Fireplace inside of house having wood floor framing on all sides.

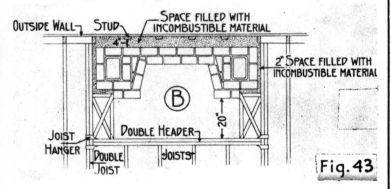

Fig. 43

The principle applied in each case is the same. All framing members on the sides of the fireplace should be at least 2 inches away from brick or masonry wall, unless protected by 8 or more inches of brickwork or 12 inches or more of masonry. The intervening space should be filled with incombustible material such as mineral wool, concrete or mortar.

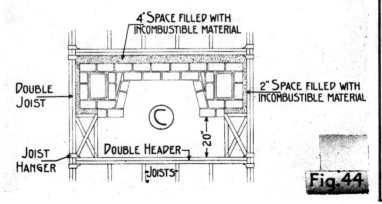

Fig. 44

The framing at back should be at least four inches away, and the intervening space at each floor filled with incombustible material. The back should be at least 8 inches thick and lined with fire brick.

The header-joists or beam supporting the trimmer arch in front of a fireplace should be not less than 20 inches from the chimney breast. The hearth should be not less than 4 inches thick and should extend at least 20 inches in front of the fireplace. The woodwork around the fireplace should be not nearer than 8 inches at the sides of the opening and 12 inches at the top.

The incombustible material used for filling between the framing members and the brickwork should be supported by strips of sheet metal or metal lath set into brickwork and nailed to the joists with a buckle joint to allow for the settling of the chimney.

Note in Figure 42 the method of weatherproofing the joint between the brickwork and the frame wall.

Fig 51

The use of building paper between the outside window casing and the wall sheathing, careful fitting of the sheathing around the opening and a well made window frame would have prevented the wind and dust from coming in at the sides of the window.

The water stains below the window could have been avoided if the construction was like that shown in Figure 47 or 48. Figure 49 shows faulty construction.

466

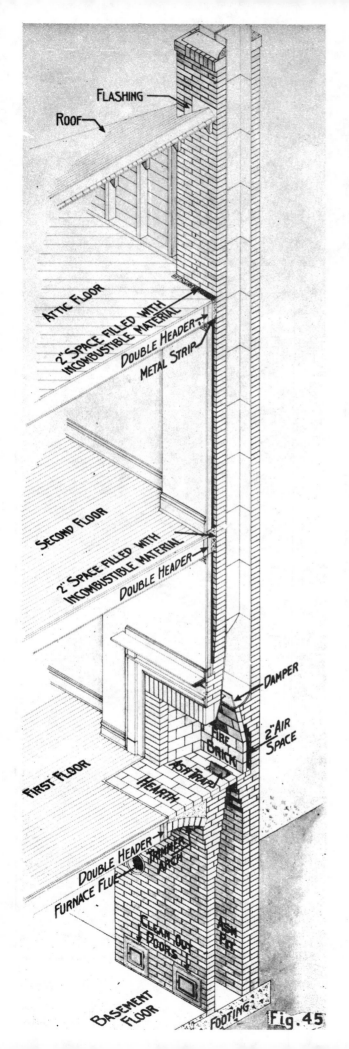

FLASHING

ROOF

ATTIC FLOOR

2" SPACE FILLED WITH INCOMBUSTIBLE MATERIAL

DOUBLE HEADER

METAL STRIP

SECOND FLOOR

2" SPACE FILLED WITH INCOMBUSTIBLE MATERIAL

DOUBLE HEADER

DAMPER

FIRE BRICK

2" AIR SPACE

FIRST FLOOR

ASH TRAP

HEARTH

DOUBLE HEADER

TRIMMER ARCH

FURNACE FLUE

CLEAN OUT DOORS

ASH PIT

BASEMENT FLOOR

FOOTING

Fig. 45

This illustration shows a properly-built fireplace and chimney. The chimney has two flues, one for the fireplace and one for the furnace. Note that the chimney stands practically independent of the framing around it. The following points are essential to the construction of a successful fireplace and chimney:

First—a good footing. This should have a projection of at least six inches and a depth of 12 inches. Do not use the foundation wall as one of the walls of the ash pit.

Second—the width, height and depth of the fireplace opening should be of proper proportion to each other and to the size of the room.

A fireplace opening about three feet wide and two feet high is large enough for the average living room. The depth should never be less than 16 inches, nor more than 24 inches. The height, except for very large fireplaces, should not be over two feet six inches and should never exceed the width. The area of the cross-section of the smoke flue should never be less than one-tenth to one-ninth the area of the fireplace opening.

Third—it should reflect heat into the room. This is accomplished by making the back two-thirds the width of the front, and by sloping the back and splaying the sides, as shown in the illustration. The sides and back of the fireplace should be built of good fire brick set in fire clay.

Fourth—the iron throat and damper should be of proper size and correctly located. The throat and damper should extend over the entire width of the fireplace.

Fifth—a properly constructed smoke shelf and smoke chamber should be provided.

The smoke shelf is formed by setting back the brickwork at top of the throat. It should be the full width of the throat and not less than 4 inches wide. Eight to 12 inches is still better. Its purpose is to deflect the down draft.

The smoke chamber is the space from the top of the throat to the bottom of the flue. This space is necessary to hold the smoke temporarily when a gust of wind across the top of the chimney momentarily cuts off the draft. Otherwise, the smoke would be forced into the room. The walls of the smoke chamber should be plastered smooth.

Sixth—the chimney should be carried high enough above the house to insure a good draft.

467

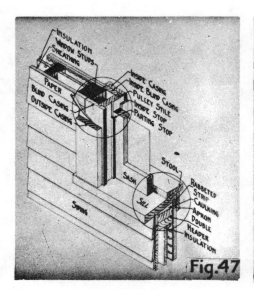

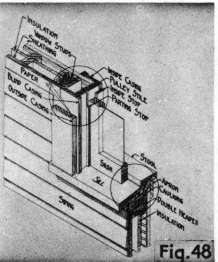

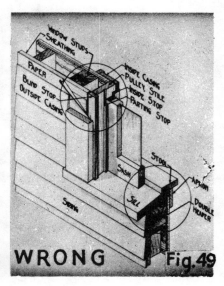

Above are shown three methods of constructing and fitting window frames. The point to be stressed is that of sealing up the joints around the window frame.

Figure 47 shows the type of window frame that permits of sealing up these joints most effectively. Here blind casings are used at the sides and top on both the outside and inside of the frame. These casings are nailed to the window studs at the top of the opening. The wall sheathing butts against the edge of the outside blind casing, and the joint between the two is sealed by means of the building paper and outside finish casing. The inside blind casing acts as a gauge for the plaster which is worked up to it, the joint between the two being concealed by the inside finish casing.

The space between the sill and the header is filled with caulking material and further closed up with a strip plowed into the sill. The top of the sill is rabbeted to receive the sash and the siding is let into a groove in the under side.

It is also important that the joint between the drip caps (the moulding across the top of the frame) and the siding be made absolutely tight. This is accomplished by the use of flashing nailed to the drip cap and bent to extend up behind the siding.

Figure 48 shows the same frame except for the inside blind casing and the strip under the sill, both of which have been omitted. It is not as efficient as the method shown above but can be made very effective if put in with care.

Figure 49 illustrates the most common type of frame and the one that is responsible for the condition shown in Figure 51.

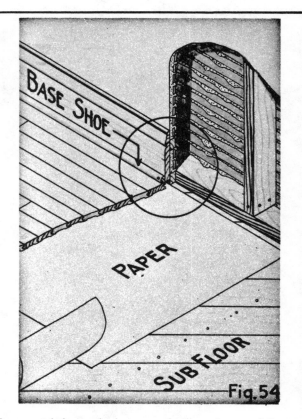

Often unsightly cracks between the base shoe and floor or between the base shoe and the base board are noticed. These cracks are due to shrinkage of the floor members or the base board and can be avoided if the base shoe is nailed to the sub-floor instead of to the base board or finish floor.

To permit doing this, the finish floor boards should be kept the thickness of the base board away from the plastered wall on all sides of the room.

Long nails should be used for nailing the base shoe in place. The drawing within the large circle shows proper placing of finish floor boards at the walls and proper nailing of base shoe.

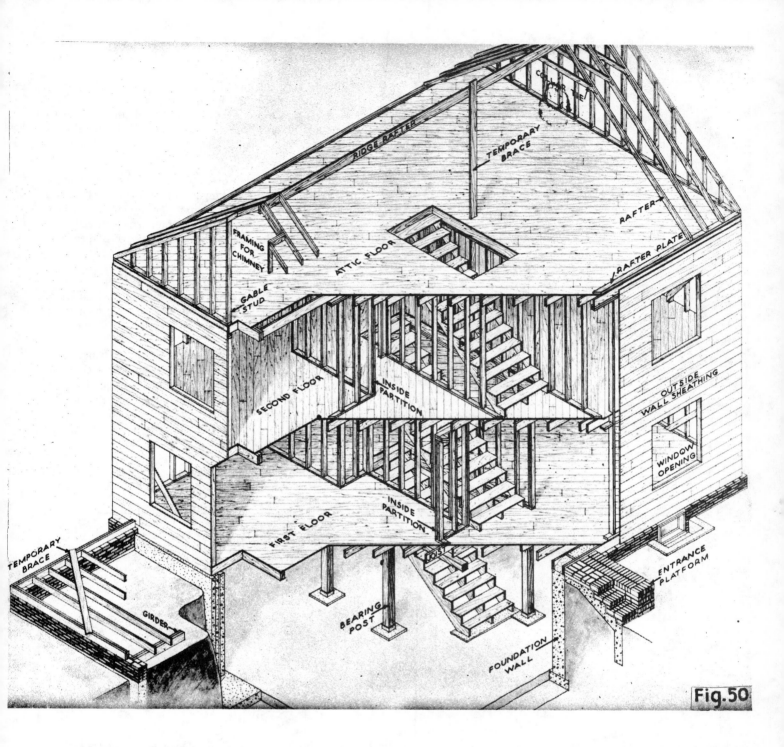

Fig. 50

When this frame is used, a hole is cut in the wall sheathing large enough to allow the frame to fit loosely. This leaves an opening the full height of the window on both sides, varying in width from one-half inch to an inch and with nothing but the joint between the outside casing and blind stops to protect it.

The sill is not rabbeted to receive the sash. The space between the sill and the header in the haphazard type of construction is usually not caulked but is left open to the ready passage of cold air and dust.

While these illustrations show frames for ordinary, double-hung sash, the same general principles apply to the construction and fitting of frames for stationary or casement sash.

The ridge rafter and roof rafters are laid out and cut to the required length, after which the ridge rafter and a pair of rafters are set up. The gable studs at each end of the building are next fitted into place. The balance of the rafters are then put in and the opening cut for the chimney is usually built before the roof boards are put on. Next, the rough framing for the porches is done.

469

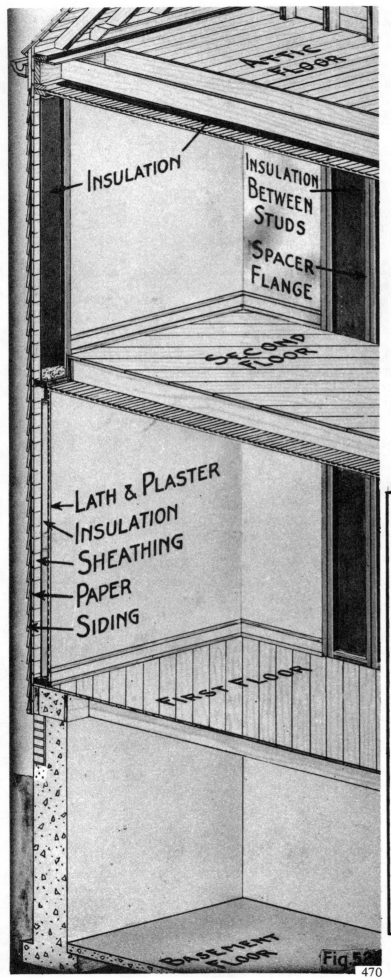

INSULATION

INSULATION
BETWEEN
STUDS

SPACER
FLANGE

ATTIC
FLOOR

SECOND
FLOOR

LATH & PLASTER
INSULATION
SHEATHING
PAPER
SIDING

FIRST FLOOR

BASEMENT FLOOR

Fig. 52

The method of applying insulating material between the studs is illustrated in this drawing.

The insulating blanket is formed with a flange along each edge which laps over and is nailed to the studding. A fibre cleat is used at top and bottom to attach the blanket to headers and plates. A specially designed stapling hammer is available for speedy installation.

Note how the insulation divides each wall compartment into two air spaces, thus making it more difficult for heat and cold to penetrate the walls. More important still, the insulating material itself contains innumerable small air cells that further increase the resistance to the passage of heat and cold.

On the second floor, where the flooring and joists make it difficult to fasten securely the lower ends of the insulation, insulating scrap should be packed in, as shown, to insure a good joint.

While this drawing shows the insulation applied beneath the attic floors, this is not the proper application for all cases. Where the third floor is to be used for living quarters, the insulation should be run up the studs, applied either between them or nailed to the inside faces and over the ceiling joists of the rooms finished off. The same principle applies in insulating the story-and-a-half house.

It is apparent from this drawing that the construction which makes a house fire-safe also makes thorough insulation easier.

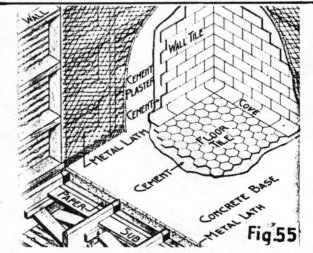

WALL

WALL TILE

CEMENT
PLASTER

CEMENT

COVE

METAL LATH

FLOOR
TILE

CEMENT

PAPER

SUB

CONCRETE BASE

METAL LATH

Fig. 55

This picture illustrates one method of securing a substantial foundation for tiled floors and walls. The top of each joist is beveled off or chamfered. Boards are set between the joists, as shown, with a 1/8-inch space between them to allow for swelling.

This layer of boards should be covered with a good grade of waterproof building paper.

The joists should be braced every six feet with bridging. The concrete should be at least 2 1/2 inches thick, reinforced with metal lath, and should extend not less than 3/4 inch above the tops of the joists, as shown.

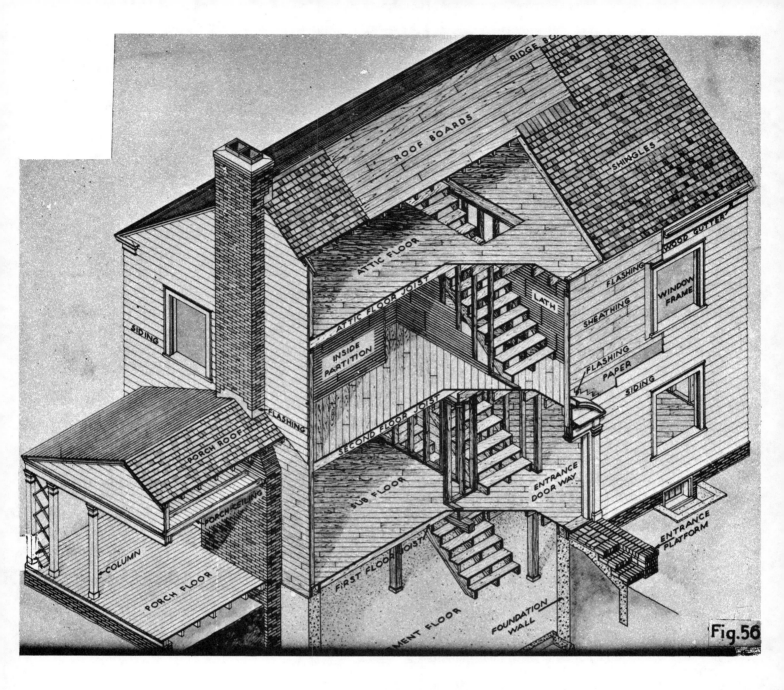

Fig.56

This is the last of the series of illustrations showing a Balloon Frame house in various stages of construction.

After the work mentioned in Figure 50, as shown is finished, the roof boards for the main and porch roofs are put on and the shingles laid.

While this is being done, the plumbers and heating men are busy installing the pipes for this equipment.

The window and outside door frames are then set in, and the balance of the outside finish such as base, corner boards, if any, and frieze boards and siding are put on.

The interior of the house is next made ready to receive the lath and plaster. This includes nailing blocks and baking for

lath and all interior finish, plaster grounds for interior trim, fire-stops between the studs and other places not already provided for, and insulation between wall studs and ceiling joists. Lath is then applied after which the plastering is done.

While the lathers are at work inside, the carpenters usually finish up the work on the porches. This consists of laying the floors, finishing the porch beams, railings, columns, lattice work, and putting in the ceiling.

After the plastering has thoroughly dried, the interior finish lumber is taken into the building, filled and stained by the painter, and applied by the carpenter. The finish floors are laid last. This work completed, the trim hardware is put on, and finish coats of paint and varnish are applied inside and out.

471

The essential requirements of lumber for the framework of a building are strength and proper seasoning. With modern lumber mills producing lumber in many kinds and grades, home builders have a wide variety of suitable framing woods from which to choose.

While some sections of the country have local woods from which good house frames may be built, the premier framing lumber species today are Douglas Fir and West Coast Hemlock.

Douglas Fir is the strongest framing wood, pound for pound, on the market. It is easily dried, and because of the enormous size of the logs, the amount of sapwood in that portion of the log used for framing is small. Douglas Fir machines well, does not warp or twist, and has little tendency to check or split when properly dried.

THE ENGINEERED HOUSE

To say that the fine old houses of our country, many having served as homes for hundreds of years, were properly engineered, may sound trite, but this is the fact. The artisans who built them, many of whom were ships' carpenters, followed sound engineering principles and while they may not have known it, they were leaving for us a priceless heritage of building artistry in design, sound construction, lasting value and a demonstration of the correct use of building materials.

The fine examples of the builder's art, expressed in a new method of house construction, were among the dozens of new things taking shape in the new country. New modes of living, new methods of self government, new patterns in the arts were in the process of development. These new principles of house construction were possible because here, wood was plentiful, here the right species for each use was available at low cost and what examples of good building they left as a monument to themselves and to their craft!

It was in 1854 that house building as we now know it was first used. No one knows who was the first builder to employ the modern method of using joists, studs and rafters in house construction but we do know that the methods in use today are the result of countless hours of thought and the application of sound engineering principles to the task of building a house that will stand against the rigors of time at a cost commensurate with best values.

Since the making of lumber is carried on by one of the most progressive industries in the country, refinements in manufacture and advancements in its use followed as a natural sequence. Constant improvements were being made such as square cutting to exact length, end-matching, improved seasoning, better surfacing and even more exact standards of manufacture gave further impetus to more and better building. This improved lumber lent itself ideally to the new and latest framing method called "platform or western framing" and the use of exact length studs, joists and other framing members contributed toward a reduction in house building costs and still gave sound long-lived buildings to the smartest of all home builders, the American citizen.

472

CONSTRUCTION FORMS

39

and CONTRACTS

THE AMERICAN INSTITUTE OF ARCHITECTS

AIA Document A310

Bid Bond

KNOW ALL MEN BY THESE PRESENTS, that we

as Principal, hereinafter called the Principal, and

a corporation duly organized under the laws of the State of
as Surety, hereinafter called the Surety, are held and firmly bound unto

as Obligee, hereinafter called the Obligee, in the sum of

Dollars ($),
for the payment of which sum well and truly to be made, the said Principal and the said Surety, bind ourselves, our heirs, executors, administrators, successors and assigns, jointly and severally, firmly by these presents.

WHEREAS, the Principal has submitted a bid for

NOW, THEREFORE, if the Obligee shall accept the bid of the Principal and the Principal shall enter into a Contract with the Obligee in accordance with the terms of such bid, and give such bond or bonds as may be specified in the bidding or Contract Documents with good and sufficient surety for the faithful performance of such Contract and for the prompt payment of labor and material furnished in the prosecution thereof, or in the event of the failure of the Principal to enter such Contract and give such bond or bonds, if the Principal shall pay to the Obligee the difference not to exceed the penalty hereof between the amount specified in said bid and such larger amount for which the Obligee may in good faith contract with another party to perform the Work covered by said bid, then this obligation shall be null and void, otherwise to remain in full force and effect.

Signed and sealed this   day of   19

_____
(Witness)

(Principal)   (Seal)

_____
(Title)

_____
(Witness)

(Surety)   (Seal)

_____
(Title)

1

THE AMERICAN INSTITUTE OF ARCHITECTS

AIA Document A111

Standard Form of Agreement Between Owner and Contractor

where the basis of payment is the

COST OF THE WORK PLUS A FEE

1978 EDITION

THIS DOCUMENT HAS IMPORTANT LEGAL CONSEQUENCES; CONSULTATION WITH
AN ATTORNEY IS ENCOURAGED WITH RESPECT TO ITS COMPLETION OR MODIFICATION

Use only with the 1976 Edition of AIA Document A201, General Conditions of the Contract for Construction.

This document has been approved and endorsed by The Associated General Contactors of America

---

AGREEMENT

made as of the   day of   in the year of Nineteen
Hundred and

BETWEEN the Owner:

and the Contractor:

the Project:

the Architect:

The Owner and the Contractor agree as set forth below.

1

ARTICLE 1

THE CONTRACT DOCUMENTS

1.1   The Contract Documents consist of this Agreement, the Conditions of the Contract (General, Supplementary and other Conditions), the Drawings, the Specifications, all Addenda issued prior to and all Modifications issued after execution of this Agreement. These form the Contract, and all are as fully a part of the Contract as if attached to this Agreement or repeated herein. An enumeration of the Contract Documents appears in Article 16. If anything in the Contract Documents is inconsistent with this Agreement, the Agreement shall govern.

ARTICLE 2

THE WORK

2.1   The Contractor shall perform all the Work required by the Contract Documents for

(Here insert the caption descriptive of the Work as used on other Contract Documents.)

ARTICLE 3

THE CONTRACTOR'S DUTIES AND STATUS

3.1   The Contractor accepts the relationship of trust and confidence established between him and the Owner by this Agreement. He covenants with the Owner to furnish his best skill and judgment and to cooperate with the Architect in furthering the interests of the Owner. He agrees to furnish efficient business administration and superintendence and to use his best efforts to furnish at all times an adequate supply of workmen and materials, and to perform the Work in the best way and in the most expeditious and economical manner consistent with the interests of the Owner.

ARTICLE 4

TIME OF COMMENCEMENT AND SUBSTANTIAL COMPLETION

4.1   The Work to be performed under this Contract shall be commenced

and, subject to authorized adjustments,

Substantial Completion shall be achieved not later than

(Here insert any special provisions for liquidated damages relating to failure to complete on time.)

2

ARTICLE 5

COST OF THE WORK AND GUARANTEED MAXIMUM COST

5.1   The Owner agrees to reimburse the Contractor for the Cost of the Work as defined in Article 8. Such reimbursement shall be in addition to the Contractor's Fee stipulated in Article 6.

5.2   The maximum cost to the Owner, including the Cost of the Work and the Contractor's Fee, is guaranteed not to exceed the sum of   dollars ($); such Guaranteed Maximum Cost shall be increased or decreased for Changes in the Work as provided in Article 7.

(Here insert any provision for distribution of any savings. Delete Paragraph 5.2 if there is no Guaranteed Maximum Cost.)

ARTICLE 6

CONTRACTOR'S FEE

6.1   In consideration of the performance of the Contract, the Owner agrees to pay the Contractor in current funds as compensation for his services a Contractor's Fee as follows:

6.2   For Changes in the Work, the Contractor's Fee shall be adjusted as follows:

6.3   The Contractor shall be paid   percent (%) of the proportional amount of his Fee with each progress payment, and the balance of his Fee shall be paid at the time of final payment.

3

477

ARTICLE 7

CHANGES IN THE WORK

7.1 The Owner may make Changes in the Work as provided in the Contract Documents. The Contractor shall be reimbursed for Changes in the Work on the basis of Cost of the Work as defined in Article 8.

7.2 The Contractor's Fee for Changes in the Work shall be as set forth in Paragraph 6.2, or in the absence of specific provisions therein, shall be adjusted by negotiation on the basis of the Fee established for the original Work.

ARTICLE 8

COSTS TO BE REIMBURSED

8.1 The term Cost of the Work shall mean costs necessarily incurred in the proper performance of the Work and paid by the Contractor. Such costs shall be at rates not higher than the standard paid in the locality of the Work except with prior consent of the Owner, and shall include the items set forth below in this Article 8.

8.1.1 Wages paid for labor in the direct employ of the Contractor in the performance of the Work under applicable collective bargaining agreements, or under a salary or wage schedule agreed upon by the Owner and Contractor, and including such welfare or other benefits, if any, as may be payable with respect thereto.

8.1.2 Salaries of Contractor's personnel when stationed at the field office, in whatever capacity employed. Personnel engaged, at shops or on the road, in expediting the production or transportation of materials or equipment, shall be considered as stationed at the field office and their salaries paid for that portion of their time spent on this Work.

8.1.3 Cost of contributions, assessments or taxes incurred during the performance of the Work for such items as unemployment compensation and social security, insofar as such cost is based on wages, salaries, or other remuneration paid to employees of the Contractor and included in the Cost of the Work under Subparagraphs 8.1.1 and 8.1.2.

8.1.4 The portion of reasonable travel and subsistence expenses of the Contractor or of his officers or employees incurred while traveling in discharge of duties connected with the Work.

8.1.5 Cost of all materials, supplies and equipment incorporated in the Work, including costs of transportation thereof.

8.1.6 Payments made by the Contractor to Subcontractors for Work performed pursuant to subcontracts under this Agreement.

8.1.7 Cost, including transportation and maintenance, of all materials, supplies, equipment, temporary facilities and hand tools not owned by the workers, which are consumed in the performance of the Work, and cost less salvage value on such items used but not consumed which remain the property of the Contractor.

8.1.8 Rental charges of all necessary machinery and equipment, exclusive of hand tools, used at the site of the Work, whether rented from the Contractor or others, including installation, minor repairs and replacements, dismantling, removal, transportation and delivery costs thereof, at rental changes consistent with those prevailing in the area.

8.1.9 Cost of premiums for all bonds and insurance which the Contractor is required by the Contract Documents to purchase and maintain.

8.1.10 Sales, use or similar taxes related to the Work and for which the Contractor is liable imposed by any governmental authority.

8.1.11 Permit fees, royalties, damages for infringement of patents and costs of defending suits therefor, and deposits lost for causes other than the Contractor's negligence.

8.1.12 Losses and expenses, not compensated by insurance or otherwise, sustained by the Contractor in connection with the Work, provided they have resulted from causes other than the fault or neglect of the Contractor. Such losses shall include settlements made with the written consent and approval of the Owner. No such losses and expenses shall be included in the Cost of the Work for the purpose of determining the Contractor's Fee. If, however, such loss requires reconstruction and the Contractor is placed in charge thereof, he shall be paid for his services a Fee proportionate to that stated in Paragraph 6.1.

8.1.13 Minor expenses such as telegrams, long distance telephone calls, telephone service at the site, expressage, and similar petty cash items in connection with the Work.

8.1.14 Cost of removal of all debris.

4

8.1.15 Costs incurred due to an emergency affecting the safety of persons and property.

8.1.16 Other costs incurred in the performance of the Work if and to the extent approved in advance in writing by the Owner.

(Here insert modifications or limitations to any of the above Subparagraphs, such as equipment rental charges and small tool charges applicable to the Work.)

ARTICLE 9

COSTS NOT TO BE REIMBURSED

9.1   The term Cost of the Work shall not include any of the items set forth below in this Article 9.

9.1.1   Salaries or other compensation of the Contractor's personnel at the Contractor's principal office and branch offices.

9.1.2   Expenses of the Contractor's principal and branch offices other than the field office.

9.1.3   Any part of the Contractor's capital expenses, including interest on the Contractor's capital employed for the Work.

9.1.4   Except as specifically provided for in Subparagraph 8.1.8 or in modifications thereto, rental costs of machinery and equipment.

9.1.5   Overhead or general expenses of any kind, except as may be expressly included in Article 8.

9.1.6   Costs due to the negligence of the Contractor, any Subcontractor, anyone directly or indirectly employed by any of them, or for whose acts any of them may be liable, including but not limited to the correction of defective or nonconforming Work, disposal of materials and equipment wrongly supplied, or making good any damage to property.

9.1.7   The cost of any item not specifically and expressly included in the items described in Article 8.

9.1.8   Costs in excess of the Guaranteed Maximum Cost, if any, as set forth in Article 5 and adjusted pursuant to Article 7.

ARTICLE 10

DISCOUNTS, REBATES AND REFUNDS

10.1   All cash discounts shall accrue to the Contractor unless the Owner deposits funds with the Contractor with which to make payments, in which case the cash discounts shall accrue to the Owner. All trade discounts, rebates and refunds, and all returns from sale of surplus materials and equipment shall accrue to the Owner, and the Contractor shall make provisions so that they can be secured.

(Here insert any provisions relating to deposits by the Owner to permit the Contractor to obtain cash discounts.)

ARTICLE 11

SUBCONTRACTS AND OTHER AGREEMENTS

11.1   All portions of the Work that the Contractor's organization does not perform shall be performed under Sub-contracts or by other appropriate agreement with the Contractor. The Contractor shall request bids from Sub-contractors and shall deliver such bids to the Architect. The Owner will then determine, with the advice of the Contractor and subject to the reasonable objection of the Architect, which bids will be accepted.

11.2   All Subcontracts shall conform to the requirements of the Contract Documents. Subcontracts awarded on the basis of the cost of such work plus a fee shall also be subject to the provisions of this Agreement insofar as applicable.

ARTICLE 12

ACCOUNTING RECORDS

12.1   The Contractor shall check all materials, equipment and labor entering into the Work and shall keep such full and detailed accounts as may be necessary for proper financial management under this Agreement, and the system shall be satisfactory to the Owner. The Owner shall be afforded access to all the Contractor's records, books, correspondence, instructions, drawings, receipts, vouchers, memoranda and similar data relating to this Contract, and the Contractor shall preserve all such records for a period of three years, or for such longer period as may be required by law, after the final payment.

ARTICLE 13

APPLICATIONS FOR PAYMENT

13.1   The Contractor shall, at least ten days before each payment falls due, deliver to the Architect an itemized statement, notarized if required, showing in complete detail all moneys paid out or costs incurred by him on account of the Cost of the Work during the previous month for which he is to be reimbursed under Article 5 and the amount of the Contractor's Fee due as provided in Article 6, together with payrolls for all labor and such other data supporting the Contractor's right to payment for Subcontracts or materials as the Owner or the Architect may require.

ARTICLE 14

PAYMENTS TO THE CONTRACTOR

14.1 The Architect will review the Contractor's Applications for Payment and will promptly take appropriate action thereon as provided in the Contract Documents. Such amount as he may recommend for payment shall be payable by the Owner not later than the   day of the month.

14.1.1 In taking action on the Contractor's Applications for Payment, the Architect shall be entitled to rely on the accuracy and completeness of the information furnished by the Contractor and shall not be deemed to represent that he has made audits of the supporting data, exhaustive or continuous on-site inspections or that he has made any examination to ascertain how or for what purposes the Contractor has used the moneys previously paid on account of the Contract.

14.2 Final payment, constituting the entire unpaid balance of the Cost of the Work and of the Contractor's Fee, shall be paid by the Owner to the Contractor   days after Substantial Completion of the Work unless otherwise stipulated in the Certificate of Substantial Completion, provided the Work has been completed, the Contract fully performed, and final payment has been recommended by the Architect.

14.3 Payments due and unpaid under the Contract Documents shall bear interest from the date payment is due at the rate entered below, or in the absence thereof, at the legal rate prevailing at the place of the Project.

(Here insert any rate of interest agreed upon.)

(Usury laws and requirements under the Federal Truth in Lending Act, similar state and local consumer credit laws and other regulations at the Owner's and Contractor's principal places of business, the location of the Project and elsewhere may affect the validity of this provision. Specific legal advice should be obtained with respect to deletion, modification, or other requirements such as written disclosures or waivers.)

ARTICLE 15

TERMINATION OF CONTRACT

15.1 The Contract may be terminated by the Contractor as provided in the Contract Documents.

15.2 If the Owner terminates the Contract as provided in the Contract Documents, he shall reimburse the Contractor for any unpaid Cost of the Work due him under Article 5, plus (1) the unpaid balance of the Fee computed upon the Cost of the Work to the date of termination at the rate of the percentage named in Article 6, or (2) if the Contractor's Fee be stated as a fixed sum, such an amount as will increase the payments on account of his Fee to a sum which bears the same ratio to the said fixed sum as the Cost of the Work at the time of termination bears to the adjusted Guaranteed Maximum Cost, if any, otherwise to a reasonable estimated Cost of the Work when completed. The Owner shall also pay to the Contractor fair compensation, either by purchase or rental at the election of the Owner, for any equipment retained. In case of such termination of the Contract the Owner shall further assume and become liable for obligations, commitments and unsettled claims that the Contractor has previously undertaken or incurred in good faith in connection with said Work. The Contractor shall, as a condition of receiving the payments referred to in this Article 15, execute and deliver all such papers and take all such steps, including the legal assignment of his contractual rights, as the Owner may require for the purpose of fully vesting in himself the rights and benefits of the Contractor under such obligations or commitments.

ARTICLE 16

MISCELLANEOUS PROVISIONS

16.1 Terms used in this Agreement which are defined in the Contract Documents shall have the meanings designated in those Contract Documents.

16.2 The Contract Documents, which constitute the entire agreement between the Owner and the Contractor, are listed in Article 1 and, except for Modifications issued after execution of this Agreement, are enumerated as follows:

(List below the Agreement, the Conditions of the Contract, General, Supplementary, and other Conditions, the Drawings, the Specifications, and any Addenda and accepted Alternates, showing page or sheet numbers in all cases and dates where applicable.)

This Agreement entered into as of the day and year first written above.

OWNER   CONTRACTOR

_____   _____

_____   _____

_____   _____

8

THE AMERICAN INSTITUTE OF ARCHITECTS

AIA Document A305

Contractor's Qualification Statement

Required in advance of consideration of application to bid or as a qualification statement in advance of award of contract. Approved and recommended by The American Institute of Architects and The Associated General Contractors of America.

The Undersigned certifies under oath the truth and correctness of all statements and of all answers to questions made hereinafter.

SUBMITTED TO:

	Corporation ☐
	Partnership ☐
	Individual ☐
SUBMITTED BY:	Joint Venture ☐
NAME:	Other
ADDRESS:	
PRINCIPAL OFFICE:	

(Note: Attach Separate Sheets As Required)

1.0 How many years has your organization been in business as a general contractor?
2.0 How many years has your organization been in business under its present business name?
3.0 If a corporation answer the following:
    3.1 Date of incorporation:
    3.2 State of incorporation:
    3.3 President's name:
    3.4 Vice-president's name(s):

    3.5 Secy's or Clerk's name:
    3.6 Treasurer's name:

1

4.0 If individual or partnership answer the following:
  4.1 Date of organization:
  4.2 Name and address of all partners. (State whether general or limited partnership.):

5.0 If other than corporation or partnership, describe organization and name principals:

6.0 We normally perform   % of the work with our own forces. List trades below:

7.0 Have you ever failed to complete any work awarded to you? If so, note when, where, and why:

2

8.0 Has any officer or partner of your organization ever been an officer or partner of another organization that failed to complete a construction contract? If so, state circumstances:

9.0 List name of project, owner, architect, contract amount, percent complete and scheduled completion of the major construction projects your organization has in process on this date:

10.0 List the name of project, owner, architect, contract amount, date of completion, percent of work with own forces of the major projects your organization has completed in the past five years:

3

11.0 List the construction experience of the principal individuals of your organization:

12.0 List states and categories in which your organization is legally qualified to do business:

13.0 Trade References:

14.0 Bank References:

15.0 Name of Bonding Company and name and address of agent:

16.0 Attach Statement of Financial Conditions, including Contractor's latest regular dated financial statement or balance sheet which must contain the following items:

Current Assets: (Cash, joint venture accounts, accounts receivable, notes receivable, accrued interest on notes, deposits, and materials and prepaid expenses), net fixed assets and other assets.

Current Liabilities: (Accounts payable, notes payable, accrued interest on notes, provision for income taxes, advances received from owners, accrued salaries, accrued payroll taxes), other liabilities, and capital (capital stock, authorized and outstanding shares par values, earned surplus).

Date of statement or balance sheet:

Name of firm preparing statement:

5

17.0 Dated at

this   day of   19

Name of Organization:

                    By:
                    Title:

18.0

M   being duly sworn deposes and says that he (she) is

the   of   Contractor(s)

and that answers to the foregoing questions and all statements therein contained are true and correct.

Subscribed and sworn before me this   day of   19

Notary Public:

My Commission Expires:

_____

OWNER'S INSTRUCTIONS FOR BONDS AND INSURANCE

AIA DOCUMENT G610

PROJECT: DATE:

OWNER: PROJECT NO:

TO: (ARCHITECT)

```
┌                                              ┐




└                                              ┘
```

Attention:

You are hereby instructed that the insurance coverage specified in the General Conditions, AIA Document A201, to be provided by the CONTRACTOR, and any other insurance described below, shall be furnished with the following minimum limits:

A. WORKMEN'S COMPENSATION (Clause 11.1.1.1)

Applicable Federal, State .... $_____

    Railroad required   (yes) (no) .... $_____

    Maritime required   (yes) (no) .... $_____

Employers' Liability .... $_____

B. CONTRACTOR'S LIABILITY INSURANCE (Clauses 11.1.1.2,.3,.4) including CONTRACTUAL LIABILITY (Subparagraph 11.1.2)

Form of insurance shall be:
(SELECT ONE)
- ☐ Comprehensive General Liability
- ☐ Comprehensive Automobile Liability

(1) BODILY INJURY

Each Occurrence .... $_____

Aggregate .... $_____

(2) PROPERTY DAMAGE
Including Completed Operations Broad Form   (yes) (no)

Each Occurrence .... $_____

Aggregate .... $_____

(3) PERSONAL INJURY

Each Person Aggregate .... $_____

General Aggregate .... $_____

(4) AUTOMOBILE LIABILITY — Owned, Non-owned and Hired

Bodily Injury Each Person .... $_____

Bodily Injury Each Occurrence .... $_____

Property Damage Each Occurrence .... $_____

1

The CONTRACTOR shall carry insurance in addition to that specifically named by the General Conditions as follows:

C. COMPLETED OPERATIONS AND PRODUCTS LIABILITY

Maintain for   (   ) years after final payment
Additionally named insureds:

D. XCU COVERAGE — Remove exclusion   (yes)   (no)

E. ELEVATOR LIABILITY (yes) (no)

(NOTE: This coverage is automatic in the Comprehensive General Liability Policy.)

F. AIRCRAFT LIABILITY — Owned and Non-owned (yes) (no)

Bodily Injury Each Person .... $_____
Bodily Injury Each Occurrence .... $_____
Property Damage Each Occurrence .... $_____

G. OTHER INSURANCE

            COVERAGE   AMOUNT

You are further instructed with regard to Bonds:

H. BID SECURITY will be required in Instructions to Bidders   (yes)   (no)

Bid security in the form of a Bid Bond (AIA Document A310) for _____%   (yes)   (no)

Other security   (yes)   (no) _____ (type) $_____

I. PERFORMANCE BOND AND LABOR AND MATERIAL PAYMENT BOND (AIA Document A311)   (yes)   (no)

For _____% of the Contract Sum

2

You are hereby instructed that the insurance coverage specified in the General Conditions, AIA Document A201, to be provided by the OWNER, and any other insurance described below, shall be furnished in accordance with the selected options. Limits are to be as indicated below:

(SELECT ONE OPTION ONLY)

☐ OPTION ONE — The Insurance Coverage described below will be furnished by the OWNER as provided for in the General Conditions.

☐ OPTION TWO — The Insurance Coverage described below shall be furnished by the CONTRACTOR.

☐ OPTION THREE — The Insurance Coverage described below shall be furnished by the OWNER and CONTRACTOR as follows:

A.	Owner's Liability	(Owner)	(Contractor)
B.	Property Insurance	(Owner)	(Contractor)
C.	Steam Boiler and Machinery	(Owner)	(Contractor)
D.	Loss of Use	(Owner)	(Contractor)
E.	Other Insurance		

Insurance Coverage shall be for the following minimum limits:

A. OWNER'S LIABILITY (Subparagraph 11.2.1)

(1) BODILY INJURY

Each Occurrence .... $_____
Aggregate .... $_____

(2) PROPERTY DAMAGE

Each Occurrence .... $_____
Aggregate .... $_____

(3) PERSONAL INJURY

Each Occurrence .... $_____
General Aggregate .... $_____

B. PROPERTY INSURANCE (Paragraph 11.3)
(SELECT ONE)
☐ Fire, Extended Coverage, Vandalism and Malicious Mischief
☐ All-risk

On the following form
(SELECT ONE)
☐ Completed value
☐ Reporting

In the names of the Owner and Contractor as their interests may appear with limits as follows:
(SELECT ONE)
☐ Full insurable value of the Work
☐ Amount equal to the Contract Sum for the Work

3

C. STEAM BOILER AND MACHINERY (Subparagraph 11.3.2)

    (1) Limit .... $_____

    (2) Objects to be insured (list Objects)

D. LOSS OF USE (Paragraph 11.4) .... $_____

E. OTHER INSURANCE

           COVERAGE   AMOUNT

BY: _____ DATE_____
(Owner)

_____

4

SOIL INVESTIGATION AND ENGINEERING SERVICES AGREEMENT

AIA DOCUMENT G602

PROJECT: DATE:

OWNER: ARCHITECT'S PROJECT NO:
(name, address)
                                                                 ARCHITECT:

TO (SOIL ENGINEER)

┌   ┐

                                                                 ATTENTION
                                                                 (in Architect's Office):

└   ┘

---

1. The Owner requests the Soil Engineer to submit a proposal for providing soil investigation and engineering services for the proposed Project at the Property described below. The information resulting from this investigation is to be used for engineering purposes, including foundation design, in connection with the Project described below. All work shall be performed by qualified personnel under the supervision of a Registered Professional Engineer, and the report(s) submitted shall bear his certification to that effect and his seal.

   The Soil Engineer shall submit this proposal by attaching hereto (and identifying in Article 16) a statement defining the scope of the procedures and services he proposes and their related costs and returning three signed copies to the Owner. If the proposal is accepted by the Owner, he will sign and return one copy to the Soil Engineer and one copy to the Architect.

   The Soil Engineer shall identify the ASTM or other recognized standard test methods and classifications used in preparing his report(s) and shall provide a detailed description of the test methods when requested by the Architect.

   The Soil Engineer shall, if requested by the Architect, notify the Architect before drilling equipment is removed from the site and advise him as to the field description of soil conditions encountered. The Owner authorizes the Soil Engineer to perform such additional borings or other exploration at that time as the Architect may require.

2. PROPERTY DESCRIPTION:
   (name, address)

   ☐ The Owner has title to this property and the right of entry for this subsurface investigation.

   ☐ The Owner has secured permission from the present owner and tenant for entry to the property for this subsurface investigation, subject to the following conditions:

   Present (owner) (tenant) is:

   Contact at the property:

1

3. PROJECT INFORMATION:

  Occupancy/Use:

  Type of Structure:

  Approximate column spacing:

  Approximate column loads:

  Approximate wall footing loads:

  Approximate main floor elevation:

  Number of stories and approximate highest elevation:

  Approximate elevation of lowest floor:

  Special problems:

4. BENCH MARK:

  ☐ Bench mark elevation   feet, located at

   shall be used as reference for ground elevation.

  ☐ Soil Engineer shall establish a bench mark at the site, record its location, and reference its elevation to either U.S.C. & G.S. or local datum.

5. BORING LOCATIONS, DEPTHS AND METHODS:

   The minimum number of borings required and their locations and depths are shown on the attached drawing(s). If it is found necessary to change the location or depth of any of these specified borings the Architect shall be notified and a new location or depth shall be agreed upon between Architect and Soil Engineer.

   If unusual conditions, including unanticipated rock, are encountered, the Soil Engineer shall immediately consult with the Architect as to further procedure.

   The Soil Engineer shall advise the Architect as to any further exploration and testing required to obtain information requisite to his professional interpretation of subsoil conditions at the building site and shall perform such additional work as the Architect authorizes. The extent of exploration undertaken shall be consistent with the scope of the project indicated by the information given above and any drawings attached hereto.

6. TIME: The specified investigation shall be completed and the logs and report(s) delivered to the Owner and Architect within (   ) days after authorization to proceed.

7. COST: The cost of the soil investigation and engineering services (including the furnishing of all materials, apparatus, labor and required insurance), for soil boring and other exploration procedures, sampling, field and laboratory testing, and preparing and submitting boring logs and reports shall be based upon: (select one)

  ☐ a. A lump sum for mobilization and demobilization including travel and per diem expenses, plus footage prices for field borings in soil and rock and unit prices for field laboratory tests, plus a lump sum for engineering reports and evaluation.

  ☐ b. Charges computed in accordance with Soil Engineer's current rate schedule.

  ☐ c.

8. BILLING FOR THE INVESTIGATION shall be:

  ☐ to the Owner at his address above, with copy to the Architect.

  ☐ to the Owner in care of the Architect, in duplicate, at Architect's office address.

9. INSURANCE: The Soil Engineer shall effect and maintain insurance to protect himself from claims under workmen's compensation acts; claims for damages because of bodily injury including personal injury, sickness or disease, or death of any of his employees or of any person other than his employees; and from claims for damages because of injury to or destruction of tangible property including loss of use resulting therefrom; and from claims arising out of the performance of professional services caused by any errors, omissions or negligent acts for which he is legally liable.

10. PROTECTION OF PROPERTY: The Soil Engineer shall take all reasonable precautions to prevent damage to property and any underground lines and shall restore the site to the condition existing prior to his entry, including backfilling of borings and patching of slabs and pavements.

2

11. SAMPLES: Unless otherwise stipulated, drilling and sampling will be performed in accordance with ASTM Methods D1586, D1587 and D2113. Samples of soil shall be taken at the ground surface, at 2 feet below existing grade and at each change in soil stratification or soil consistency, but not further apart than five feet in each of the borings unless otherwise specified on boring drawing(s). Where clayey cohesive soils are encountered, thin-walled tube samples shall be taken of representative strata. Split-spoon samples shall be placed in sealed glass jars labeled with the following information: (1) boring number, (2) sample number, (3) sample depth, (4) blows per foot required to drive sample, (5) date, (6) Project name, and (7) Soil Engineer's name.

Rock cores shall be not less than 1⅜" in diameter, and shall be placed in core boxes properly labeled as indicated above.

After all laboratory tests have been completed, and when requested to do so, samples shall be shipped to the Architect's office or other location as directed.

12. FIELD AND LABORATORY REPORTS: All data required to be recorded by the ASTM or other standard test methods employed shall be obtained, recorded in the field and referenced to boring numbers; soil shall be classified in the field logs in accordance with ASTM D2488, but the classification for final logs shall be based on the field information, plus results of tests, plus further inspection of samples in the laboratory by the Project Soil Engineer preparing the report. A chart illustrating the soil classification criteria and the terminology and symbols used on the boring logs shall be included with the report.

Vertical sections for each boring shall be plotted and graphically presented showing number of borings, date of start and finish, surface elevations, description of soil and thickness of each layer, depth to loss or gain of drilling fluid, number of blows per foot (N value), and, where applicable, depth to wet cave-in, depth to artesian head, ground water elevation and time when water reading was made (repeat observation after 24 hours), and presence of gases. Location of strata containing organic materials, wet materials or other inconsistencies that might affect engineering conclusions shall be noted.

Report all laboratory determinations of soil properties.

The Soil Engineer shall deliver one copy of soil reports and logs to the owner and (   ) copies to the Architect.

The Owner or the Architect may make and distribute copies of the reports and boring logs.

13. FOUNDATION ENGINEERING EVALUATION AND RECOMMENDATIONS

The Soil Engineer shall, based upon his analysis of information developed by his investigation or available to him, and based upon his consultation with the Architect on the design requirements of the Project, submit his professional evaluation or recommendation on each of the subjects checked below:

☐ Foundation support of the structure and slabs.

☐ Anticipation of and management of groundwater.

☐ Lateral earth pressures for design of walls below grade, including backfill, compaction and subdrainage requirements.

☐ Soil material and compaction requirements for support of structures and pavements.

☐ Pavement design.

☐ Design criteria for temporary excavation, sheet piling, underpinning and dewatering systems.

☐ Stability of slopes.

☐ Seismic activity.

☐ Frost penetration depth and effect.

☐ Analysis of soils to ascertain presence of potentially expansive, deleterious, chemically active or corrosive materials or conditions, or presence of gas.

☐ Specification clauses for foundation support, earthwork or subdrainage systems and the inspection and testing thereof.

☐

Recommendations or opinions on these subjects shall, if so directed by the Architect, be submitted as a separate report in one copy to the Owner and (   ) copies to the Architect.

The Soil Engineer shall include in his statement of costs the compensation for his services on the subjects checked.

3

14. ADDITIONAL INFORMATION:

15. ATTACHMENTS by Owner: (identify attached drawings and any other documents)

16. ATTACHMENTS by Soil Engineer: (Identify attached Cost Proposal and any other documents)

_____   _____
Accepted by Owner   Soil Engineer

_____   _____
Date: Date:

4

LAND SURVEY REQUISITION

AIA DOCUMENT G601

SURVEYOR ☐
OWNER ☐
ARCHITECT ☐
☐

PROJECT:

DATE:

OWNER:
(name, address)

ARCHITECT'S PROJECT NO:

ARCHITECT:

To (SURVEYOR)

⌐　　　　　　　　　　　　　　　　　　　¬

ATTENTION
(in Architect's Office):

L　　　　　　　　　　　　　　　　　　　⌟

☐ Please submit a proposal for

☐ The OWNER hereby authorizes you to make, for his account,

a Land Survey of the PROPERTY described below and to furnish to the ARCHITECT one reproducible transparency and three prints of each drawing. Each drawing shall bear the certification of the Licensed or Registered Land Surveyor doing the survey that all information thereon is true and is accurately shown.

TIME: The survey shall be completed and delivered to the Architect by:

USE OF DRAWINGS: It is understood that the Owner, or the Architect in his behalf, may reproduce the drawings and distribute the prints in connection with the use of or disposition of the property without incurring obligation for further payment.

COST: The cost of the survey including the drawings, establishment of site benchmark(s), and placing of property corner markers as required shall be:
    ☐ the sum of $
    ☐ as determined by application of rates in the attached Schedule.
    ☐

BILLING FOR THE SURVEY shall be:
    ☐ to the Owner at his address above, with copy to the Architect.
    ☐ to the Owner in care of the Architect, in duplicate, at Architect's office address.

DESCRIPTION OF PROPERTY TO BE SURVEYED:
    LEGAL:

    COMMON:

    ☐ See attached sketch ☐ See attached   ; return to Owner.

DRAWING REQUIREMENTS:
    Drawing sheets shall be trim size ___ " x ___ " with ___ " left binding edge and ___ " borders.
    Use scale 1" = ___ ' unless otherwise authorized by Architect. Include graphic scale.

    Show NORTH arrow and locate North at top of sheet ☐, or ☐ _____.
    Include legend of symbols and abbreviations used on drawing.
    Spot elevations on paving or other hard surfaces shall be to nearest .05' (or ½"), otherwise to the nearest .10' (or 1").
    Boundary and topographic information, where both are required, shall be on same drawing unless otherwise requested by Architect.
    State elevation datum on drawing. ☐ Use U.S.C. & G.S. datum; give location of benchmark used; or ☐ use assumed elevation ___ at ___ or ☐ _____.

SEE REVERSE SIDE FOR SPECIFICATION OF INFORMATION REQUIRED ON THIS SURVEY

Authorized by OWNER:	Accepted by LAND SURVEYOR:

NOTE: Check boxes for required items of information.

Precision of 1/500, corresponding to chain or stadia measurement, may be suitable for farm or woodland survey; 1/5000, requiring use of steel tape and attention to pull, plumbing and error in length of tape, is suitable for highway, urban property and most construction surveys; 1/10,000 to 1/30,000, requiring measurement of and compensation for tape tension and temperature, is required for surveys of high value city land. Other details of survey technique proportionately precise.

LAND (BOUNDARY) SURVEY REQUIREMENTS: Property dimensions in both U.S.Std. and District Std.

Error of closure of perimeter of property shall not exceed ☐ 1/5000 or ☐ _____

☐ 1. Boundary lines, giving length and bearing on each straight line; interior angles; radius, point of tangency, and length of curved lines. Set iron pin (monument) at property corners where none exists; drive pin 18" into ground, mark with wood stake; state on drawing whether corners were found or set and describe each.

☐ 2. Legal description, including measurements in recorded deeds for comparison with observed.

☐ 3. Area in square feet if less than one acre, in acres (to .001 acre) if over one acre.

☐ 4. Identity, jurisdiction and width of adjoining street and highways, width and how paved. Identity of landmarks.

☐ 5. Plotted location of structures on the property and on adjacent property within _____ feet. Dimension perimeters in ☐ feet and inches to nearest ½" ☐ feet and decimals to .05'. State character and number of stories. Dimension to property lines and other buildings. Vacant parcels shall be noted VACANT.

☐ 6. Encroachments, including cornices, belt courses, etc., either way across property lines.

☐ 7 Fences and walls; describe. Identify party walls and locate with respect to property lines.

☐ 8. Recorded or otherwise known easements and rights-of-way; state owner of right.

☐ 9. Possibilities of prescriptive rights-of-way and nature of each.

☐ 10. Anticipated street widenings.

☐ 11. Individual lot lines and lot and block numbers. ☐ Street numbers of buildings.

☐ 12. Zoning of property; if more than one zone, extent of each. ☐ Zoning of adjacent property and property across street or highway.

☐ 13. Building line and setback requirements, if any.

☐ 14. Names of owners of adjacent property.

☐ 15. Reconciliation or explanation of any discrepancies between survey and recorded legal description.

TOPOGRAPHICAL SURVEY REQUIREMENTS: All lines of levels shall be checked by separate check level lines or on previous turning points or benchmarks.

☐ 16. Minimum of one permanent benchmark on site for each four acres; description and elevation to nearest .01'.

☐ 17. Contours at _____ foot intervals; error shall not exceed one-half contour interval.

☐ 18. Spot elevations at each intersection of a _____ foot square grid covering the property and if possible _____ grid interval(s) beyond.

☐ 19. Spot elevations at street intersections and at _____ feet on center on curb, sidewalk, and edge of paving including far side of paving. If elevations vary from established grades, state established grades also.

☐ 20. Plotted location of structures, man-made and natural features; floor elevations and elevations at each entrance of buildings on property.

☐ 21. Location, size, depth and pressure of water and gas mains, central steam, and other utilities serving or on the property.

☐ 22. Location of fire hydrants available to property and size of main serving each.

☐ 23. Location of electric and telephone services and characteristics of service available.

☐ 24. Location, size, depth and direction of flow of sanitary sewers, combination sewers, storm drains and culverts serving or on property; location of catchbasins and manholes and inverts of pipe at each.

☐ 25. Name of operating authority of each utility.

☐ 26. Mean elevation of water in any excavation, well or nearby body; flood level of streams.

☐ 27. Extent of watershed onto property. ☐ Probability of freshets overrunning the site.

☐ 28. Locations of test borings if ascertainable and elevation of top of holes.

☐ 29. Trees of _____" and over (caliper 3' above ground) locate within 1' tolerance and give species.

☐ 30. Specimen trees flagged by Owner or Architect (_____ in number): locate to center within 6" tolerance, give species and caliper and ground elevation on upper slope side.

☐ 31. Perimeter outline only of thickly wooded areas unless otherwise directed.

☐ 32.

THE AMERICAN INSTITUTE OF ARCHITECTS

AIA Document A311

Performance Bond

KNOW ALL MEN BY THESE PRESENTS: that

(Here insert full name and address or legal title of Contractor)

as Principal, hereinafter called Contractor, and,

(Here insert full name and address or legal title of Surety)

as Surety, hereinafter called Surety, are held and firmly bound unto

(Here insert full name and address or legal title of Owner)

as Obligee, hereinafter called Owner, in the amount of

Dollars ($),

for the payment whereof Contractor and Surety bind themselves, their heirs, executors, administrators, successors and assigns, jointly and severally, firmly by these presents.

WHEREAS,

Contractor has by written agreement dated   19   , entered into a contract with Owner for
(Here insert full name, address and description of project)

in accordance with Drawings and Specifications prepared by

(Here insert full name and address or legal title of Architect)

which contract is by reference made a part hereof, and is hereinafter referred to as the Contract.

1

PERFORMANCE BOND

NOW, THEREFORE, THE CONDITION OF THIS OBLIGATION is such that, if Contractor shall promptly and faithfully perform said Contract, then this obligation shall be null and void; otherwise it shall remain in full force and effect.

The Surety hereby waives notice of any alteration or extension of time made by the Owner.

Whenever Contractor shall be, and declared by Owner to be in default under the Contract, the Owner having performed Owner's obligations thereunder, the Surety may promptly remedy the default, or shall promptly

1) Complete the Contract in accordance with its terms and conditions, or

2) Obtain a bid or bids for completing the Contract in accordance with its terms and conditions, and upon determination by Surety of the lowest responsible bidder, or, if the Owner elects, upon determination by the Owner and the Surety jointly of the lowest responsible bidder, arrange for a contract between such bidder and Owner, and make available as Work progresses (even though there should be a default or a succession of

defaults under the contract or contracts of completion arranged under this paragraph) sufficient funds to pay the cost of completion less the balance of the contract price; but not exceeding, including other costs and damages for which the Surety may be liable hereunder, the amount set forth in the first paragraph hereof. The term "balance of the contract price," as used in this paragraph, shall mean the total amount payable by Owner to Contractor under the Contract and any amendments thereto, less the amount properly paid by Owner to Contractor.

Any suit under this bond must be instituted before the expiration of two (2) years from the date on which final payment under the Contract falls due.

No right of action shall accrue on this bond to or for the use of any person or corporation other than the Owner named herein or the heirs, executors, administrators or successors of the Owner.

Signed and sealed this   day of   19

_____
(witness)

$\Big\{$

_____ (Seal)
(Principal)

_____
(Title)

_____
(Witness)

$\Big\{$

_____ (Seal)
(Surety)

_____
(Title)

2

THE AMERICAN INSTITUTE OF ARCHITECTS

AIA Document A311

Labor and Material Payment Bond

THIS BOND IS ISSUED SIMULTANEOUSLY WITH PERFORMANCE BOND IN FAVOR OF THE
OWNER CONDITIONED ON THE FULL AND FAITHFUL PERFORMANCE OF THE CONTRACT

KNOW ALL MEN BY THESE PRESENTS: that

(Here insert full name and address or legal title of Contractor)

as Principal, hereinafter called Principal, and,

(Here insert full name and address or legal title of Surety)

as Surety, hereinafter called Surety, are held and firmly bound unto

(Here insert full name and address or legal title of Owner)

as Obligee, hereinafter called Owner, for the use and benefit of claimants as hereinbelow defined, in the

amount of

(Here insert a sum equal to at least one-half of the contract price)   Dollars ($),

for the payment whereof Principal and Surety bind themselves, their heirs, executors, administrators, successors and assigns, jointly and severally, firmly by these presents.

WHEREAS,

Principal has by written agreement dated   19   , entered into a contract with Owner for
(Here insert full name, address and description of project)

in accordance with Drawings and Specifications prepared by

(Here insert full name and address or legal title of Architect)

which contract is by reference made a part hereof, and is hereinafter referred to as the Contract.

3

LABOR AND MATERIAL PAYMENT BOND

NOW, THEREFORE, THE CONDITION OF THIS OBLIGATION is such that, if Principal shall promptly make payment to all claimants as hereinafter defined, for all labor and material used or reasonably required for use in the performance of the Contract, then this obligation shall be void; otherwise it shall remain in full force and effect, subject, however, to the following conditions:

1. A claimant is defined as one having a direct contract with the Principal or with a Subcontractor of the Principal for labor, material, or both, used or reasonably required for use in the performance of the Contract, labor and material being construed to include that part of water, gas, power, light, heat, oil, gasoline, telephone service or rental of equipment directly applicable to the Contract.

2. The above named Principal and Surety hereby jointly and severally agree with the Owner that every claimant as herein defined, who has not been paid in full before the expiration of a period of ninety (90) days after the date on which the last of such claimant's work or labor was done or performed, or materials were furnished by such claimant, may sue on this bond for the use of such claimant, prosecute the suit to final judgment for such sum or sums as may be justly due claimant, and have execution thereon. The Owner shall not be liable for the payment of any costs or expenses of any such suit.

3. No suit or action shall be commenced hereunder by any claimant:

a) Unless claimant, other than one having a direct contract with the Principal, shall have given written notice to any two of the following: the Principal, the Owner, or the Surety above named, within ninety (90) days after such claimant did or performed the last of the work or labor, or furnished the last of the materials for which said claim is made, stating with substantial accuracy the amount claimed and the name of the party to whom the materials were furnished, or for whom the work or labor was done or performed. Such notice shall be served by mailing the same by registered mail or certified mail, postage prepaid, in an envelope addressed to the Principal, Owner or Surety, at any place where an office is regularly maintained for the transaction of business, or served in any manner in which legal process may be served in the state in which the aforesaid project is located, save that such service need not be made by a public officer.

b) After the expiration of one (1) year following the date on which Principal ceased Work on said Contract, it being understood, however, that if any limitation embodied in this bond is prohibited by any law controlling the construction hereof such limitation shall be deemed to be amended so as to be equal to the minimum period of limitation permitted by such law.

c) Other than in a state court of competent jurisdiction in and for the county or other political subdivision of the state in which the Project, or any part thereof, is situated, or in the United States District Court for the district in which the Project, or any part thereof, is situated, and not elsewhere.

4. The amount of this bond shall be reduced by and to the extent of any payment or payments made in good faith hereunder, inclusive of the payment by Surety of mechanics' liens which may be filed of record against said improvement, whether or not claim for the amount of such lien be presented under and against this bond.

Signed and sealed this   day of   19

_____
(Witness)

                 (Principal)   (Seal)

                 (Title)

_____
(Witness)

                 (Surety)   (Seal)

                 (Title)

4

THE AMERICAN INSTITUTE OF ARCHITECTS

AIA Document B141

Standard Form of Agreement Between Owner and Architect

1977 EDITION

THIS DOCUMENT HAS IMPORTANT LEGAL CONSEQUENCES; CONSULTATION WITH
AN ATTORNEY IS ENCOURAGED WITH RESPECT TO ITS COMPLETION OR MODIFICATION

AGREEMENT

made as of the   day of   in the year of Nineteen
Hundred and

BETWEEN the Owner:

and the Architect:

For the following Project:
(Include detailed description of Project location and scope.)

The Owner and the Architect agree as set forth below.

ARTICLE 1

ARCHITECT'S SERVICES AND RESPONSIBILITIES

BASIC SERVICES

The Architect's Basic Services consist of the five phases described in Paragraphs 1.1 through 1.5 and include normal structural, mechanical and electrical engineering services and any other services included in Article 15 as part of Basic Services.

1.1 SCHEMATIC DESIGN PHASE

1.1.1 The Architect shall review the program furnished by the Owner to ascertain the requirements of the Project and shall review the understanding of such requirements with the Owner.

1.1.2 The Architect shall provide a preliminary evaluation of the program and the Project budget requirements, each in terms of the other, subject to the limitations set forth in Subparagraph 3.2.1.

1.1.3 The Architect shall review with the Owner alternative approaches to design and construction of the Project.

1.1.4 Based on the mutually agreed upon program and Project budget requirements, the Architect shall prepare, for approval by the Owner, Schematic Design Documents consisting of drawings and other documents illustrating the scale and relationship of Project components.

1.1.5 The Architect shall submit to the Owner a Statement of Probable Construction Cost based on current area, volume or other unit costs.

1.2 DESIGN DEVELOPMENT PHASE

1.2.1 Based on the approved Schematic Design Documents and any adjustments authorized by the Owner in the program or Project budget, the Architect shall prepare, for approval by the Owner, Design Development Documents consisting of drawings and other documents to fix and describe the size and character of the entire Project as to architectural, structural, mechanical and electrical systems, materials and such other elements as may be appropriate.

1.2.2 The Architect shall submit to the Owner a further Statement of Probable Construction Cost.

1.3 CONSTRUCTION DOCUMENTS PHASE

1.3.1 Based on the approved Design Development Documents and any further adjustments in the scope or quality of the Project or in the Project budget authorized by the Owner, the Architect shall prepare, for approval by the Owner, Construction Documents consisting of Drawings and Specifications setting forth in detail the requirements for the construction of the Project.

1.3.2 The Architect shall assist the Owner in the preparation of the necessary bidding information, bidding forms, the Conditions of the Contract, and the form of Agreement between the Owner and the Contractor.

1.3.3 The Architect shall advise the Owner of any adjust-ments to previous Statements of Probable Construction Cost indicated by changes in requirements or general market conditions.

1.3.4 The Architect shall assist the Owner in connection with the Owner's responsibility for filing documents required for the approval of governmental authorities having jurisdiction over the Project.

1.4 BIDDING OR NEGOTIATION PHASE

1.4.1 The Architect, following the Owner's approval of the Construction Documents and of the latest Statement of Probable Construction Cost, shall assist the Owner in obtaining bids or negotiated proposals, and assist in awarding and preparing contracts for construction.

1.5 CONSTRUCTION PHASE—ADMINISTRATION OF THE CONSTRUCTION CONTRACT

1.5.1 The Construction Phase will commence with the award of the Contract for Construction and, together with the Architect's obligation to provide Basic Services under this Agreement, will terminate when final payment to the Contractor is due, or in the absence of a final Certificate for Payment or of such due date, sixty days after the Date of Substantial Completion of the Work, whichever occurs first.

1.5.2 Unless otherwise provided in this Agreement and incorporated in the Contract Documents, the Architect shall provide administration of the Contract for Construction as set forth below and in the edition of AIA Document A201, General Conditions of the Contract for Construction, current as of the date of this Agreement.

1.5.3 The Architect shall be a representative of the Owner during the Construction Phase, and shall advise and consult with the Owner. Instructions to the Contractor shall be forwarded through the Architect. The Architect shall have authority to act on behalf of the Owner only to the extent provided in the Contract Documents unless otherwise modified by written instrument in accordance with Subparagraph 1.5.16.

1.5.4 The Architect shall visit the site at intervals appropriate to the stage of construction or as otherwise agreed by the Architect in writing to become generally familiar with the progress and quality of the Work and to determine in general if the Work is proceeding in accordance with the Contract Documents. However, the Architect shall not be required to make exhaustive or continuous on-site inspections to check the quality or quantity of the Work. On the basis of such on-site observations as an architect, the Architect shall keep the Owner informed of the progress and quality of the Work, and shall endeavor to guard the Owner against defects and deficiencies in the Work of the Contractor.

1.5.5 The Architect shall not have control or charge of and shall not be responsible for construction means, methods, techniques, sequences or procedures, or for safety precautions and programs in connection with the Work, for the acts or omissions of the Contractor, Sub-

3

contractors or any other persons performing any of the Work, or for the failure of any of them to carry out the Work in accordance with the Contract Documents.

1.5.6 The Architect shall at all times have access to the Work wherever it is in preparation or progress.

1.5.7 The Architect shall determine the amounts owing to the Contractor based on observations at the site and on evaluations of the Contractor's Applications for Payment, and shall issue Certificates for Payment in such amounts, as provided in the Contract Documents.

1.5.8 The issuance of a Certificate for Payment shall constitute a representation by the Architect to the Owner, based on the Architect's observations at the site as provided in Subparagraph 1.5.4 and on the data comprising the Contractor's Application for Payment, that the Work has progressed to the point indicated; that, to the best of the Architect's knowledge, information and belief, the quality of the Work is in accordance with the Contract Documents (subject to an evaluation of the Work for conformance with the Contract Documents upon Substantial Completion, to the results of any subsequent tests required by or performed under the Contract Documents, to minor deviations from the Contract Documents correctable prior to completion, and to any specific qualifications stated in the Certificate for Payment); and that the Contractor is entitled to payment in the amount certified. However, the issuance of a Certificate for Payment shall not be a representation that the Architect has made any examination to ascertain how and for what purpose the Contractor has used the moneys paid on account of the Contract Sum.

1.5.9 The Architect shall be the interpreter of the requirements of the Contract Documents and the judge of the performance thereunder by both the Owner and Contractor. The Architect shall render interpretations necessary for the proper execution or progress of the Work with reasonable promptness on written request of either the Owner or the Contractor, and shall render written decisions, within a reasonable time, on all claims, disputes and other matters in question between the Owner and the Contractor relating to the execution or progress of the Work or the interpretation of the Contract Documents.

1.5.10 Interpretations and decisions of the Architect shall be consistent with the intent of and reasonably inferable from the Contract Documents and shall be in written or graphic form. In the capacity of interpreter and judge, the Architect shall endeavor to secure faithful performance by both the Owner and the Contractor, shall not show partiality to either, and shall not be liable for the result of any interpretation or decision rendered in good faith in such capacity.

1.5.11 The Architect's decisions in matters relating to artistic effect shall be final if consistent with the intent of the Contract Documents. The Architect's decisions on any other claims, disputes or other matters, including those in question between the Owner and the Contractor, shall be subject to arbitration as provided in this Agreement and in the Contract Documents.

1.5.12 The Architect shall have authority to reject Work which does not conform to the Contract Documents. Whenever, in the Architect's reasonable opinion, it is

necessary or advisable for the implementation of the intent of the Contract Documents, the Architect will have authority to require special inspection or testing of the Work in accordance with the provisions of the Contract Documents, whether or not such Work be then fabricated, installed or completed.

1.5.13 The Architect shall review and approve or take other appropriate action upon the Contractor's submittals such as Shop Drawings, Product Data and Samples, but only for conformance with the design concept of the Work and with the information given in the Contract Documents. Such action shall be taken with reasonable promptness so as to cause no delay. The Architect's approval of a specific item shall not indicate approval of an assembly of which the item is a component.

1.5.14 The Architect shall prepare Change Orders for the Owner's approval and execution in accordance with the Contract Documents, and shall have authority to order minor changes in the Work not involving an adjustment in the Contract Sum or an extension of the Contract Time which are not inconsistent with the intent of the Contract Documents.

1.5.15 The Architect shall conduct inspections to determine the Dates of Substantial Completion and final completion, shall receive and forward to the Owner for the Owner's review written warranties and related documents required by the Contract Documents and assembled by the Contractor, and shall issue a final Certificate for Payment.

1.5.16 The extent of the duties, responsibilities and limitations of authority of the Architect as the Owner's representative during construction shall not be modified or extended without written consent of the Owner, the Contractor and the Architect.

1.6 PROJECT REPRESENTATION BEYOND BASIC SERVICES

1.6.1 If the Owner and Architect agree that more extensive representation at the site than is described in Paragraph 1.5 shall be provided, the Architect shall provide one or more Project Representatives to assist the Architect in carrying out such responsibilities at the site.

1.6.2 Such Project Representatives shall be selected, employed and directed by the Architect, and the Architect shall be compensated therefor as mutually agreed between the Owner and the Architect as set forth in an exhibit appended to this Agreement, which shall describe the duties, responsibilities and limitations of authority of such Project Representatives.

1.6.3 Through the observations by such Project Representatives, the Architect shall endeavor to provide further protection for the Owner against defects and deficiencies in the Work, but the furnishing of such project representation shall not modify the rights, responsibilities or obligations of the Architect as described in Paragraph 1.5.

1.7 ADDITIONAL SERVICES

The following Services are not included in Basic Services unless so identified in Article 15. They shall be provided if authorized or confirmed in writing by the Owner, and they shall be paid for by the Owner as provided in this Agreement, in addition to the compensation for Basic Services.

4

1.7.1 Providing analyses of the Owner's needs, and programming the requirements of the Project.

1.7.2 Providing financial feasibility or other special studies.

1.7.3 Providing planning surveys, site evaluations, environmental studies or comparative studies of prospective sites, and preparing special surveys, studies and submissions required for approvals of governmental authorities or others having jurisdiction over the Project.

1.7.4 Providing services relative to future facilities, systems and equipment which are not intended to be constructed during the Construction Phase.

1.7.5 Providing services to investigate existing conditions or facilities or to make measured drawings thereof, or to verify the accuracy of drawings or other information furnished by the Owner.

1.7.6 Preparing documents of alternate, separate or sequential bids or providing extra services in connection with bidding, negotiation or construction prior to the completion of the Construction Documents Phase, when requested by the Owner.

1.7.7 Providing coordination of Work performed by separate contractors or by the Owner's own forces.

1.7.8 Providing services in connection with the work of a construction manager or separate consultants retained by the Owner.

1.7.9 Providing Detailed Estimates of Construction Cost, analyses of owning and operating costs, or detailed quantity surveys or inventories of material, equipment and labor.

1.7.10 Providing interior design and other similar services required for or in connection with the selection, procurement or installation of furniture, furnishings and related equipment.

1.7.11 Providing services for planning tenant or rental spaces.

1.7.12 Making revisions in Drawings, Specifications or other documents when such revisions are inconsistent with written approvals or instructions previously given, are required by the enactment or revision of codes, laws or regulations subsequent to the preparation of such documents or are due to other causes not solely within the control of the Architect.

1.7.13 Preparing Drawings, Specifications and supporting data and providing other services in connection with Change Orders to the extent that the adjustment in the Basic Compensation resulting from the adjusted Construction Cost is not commensurate with the services required of the Architect, provided such Change Orders are required by causes not solely within the control of the Architect.

1.7.14 Making investigations, surveys, valuations, inventories or detailed appraisals of existing facilities, and services required in connection with construction performed by the Owner.

1.7.15 Providing consultation concerning replacement of any Work damaged by fire or other cause during con-

struction, and furnishing services as may be required in connection with the replacement of such Work.

1.7.16 Providing services made necessary by the default of the Contractor, or by major defects or deficiencies in the Work of the Contractor, or by failure of performance of either the Owner or Contractor under the Contract for Construction.

1.7.17 Preparing a set of reproducible record drawings showing significant changes in the Work made during construction based on marked-up prints, drawings and other data furnished by the Contractor to the Architect.

1.7.18 Providing extensive assistance in the utilization of any equipment or system such as initial start-up or testing, adjusting and balancing, preparation of operation and maintenance manuals, training personnel for operation and maintenance, and consultation during operation.

1.7.19 Providing services after issuance to the Owner of the final Certificate for Payment, or in the absence of a final Certificate for Payment, more than sixty days after the Date of Substantial Completion of the Work.

1.7.20 Preparing to serve or serving as an expert witness in connection with any public hearing, arbitration proceeding or legal proceeding.

1.7.21 Providing services of consultants for other than the normal architectural, structural, mechanical and electrical engineering services for the Project.

1.7.22 Providing any other services not otherwise included in this Agreement or not customarily furnished in accordance with generally accepted architectural practice.

1.8 TIME

1.8.1 The Architect shall perform Basic and Additional Services as expeditiously as is consistent with professional skill and care and the orderly progress of the Work. Upon request of the Owner, the Architect shall submit for the Owner's approval, a schedule for the performance of the Architect's services which shall be adjusted as required as the Project proceeds, and shall include allowances for periods of time required for the Owner's review and approval of submissions and for approvals of authorities having jurisdiction over the Project. This schedule, when approved by the Owner, shall not, except for reasonable cause, be exceeded by the Architect.

ARTICLE 2

THE OWNER'S RESPONSIBILITIES

2.1 The Owner shall provide full information regarding requirements for the Project including a program, which shall set forth the Owner's design objectives, constraints and criteria, including space requirements and relationships, flexibility and expandability, special equipment and systems and site requirements.

2.2 If the Owner provides a budget for the Project it shall include contingencies for bidding, changes in the Work during construction, and other costs which are the responsibility of the Owner, including those described in this Article 2 and in Subparagraph 3.1.2. The Owner shall, at the request of the Architect, provide a statement of funds available for the Project, and their source.

5

2.3 The Owner shall designate, when necessary, a representative authorized to act in the Owner's behalf with respect to the Project. The Owner or such authorized representative shall examine the documents submitted by the Architect and shall render decisions pertaining thereto promptly, to avoid unreasonable delay in the progress of the Architect's services.

2.4 The Owner shall furnish a legal description and a certified land survey of the site, giving, as applicable, grades and lines of streets, alleys, pavements and adjoining property; rights-of-way, restrictions, easements, encroachments, zoning, deed restrictions, boundaries and contours of the site; locations, dimensions and complete data pertaining to existing buildings, other improvements and trees; and full information concerning available service and utility lines both public and private, above and below grade, including inverts and depths.

2.5 The Owner shall furnish the services of soil engineers or other consultants when such services are deemed necessary by the Architect. Such services shall include test borings, test pits, soil bearing values, percolation tests, air and water pollution tests, ground corrosion and resistivity tests, including necessary operations for determining subsoil, air and water conditions, with reports and appropriate professional recommendations.

2.6 The Owner shall furnish structural, mechanical, chemical and other laboratory tests, inspections and reports as required by law or the Contract Documents.

2.7 The Owner shall furnish all legal, accounting and insurance counseling services as may be necessary at any time for the Project, including such auditing services as the Owner may require to verify the Contractor's Applications for Payment or to ascertain how or for what purposes the Contractor uses the moneys paid by or on behalf of the Owner.

2.8 The services, information, surveys and reports required by Paragraphs 2.4 through 2.7 inclusive shall be furnished at the Owner's expense, and the Architect shall be entitled to rely upon the accuracy and completeness thereof.

2.9 If the Owner observes or otherwise becomes aware of any fault or defect in the Project or nonconformance with the Contract Documents, prompt written notice thereof shall be given by the Owner to the Architect.

2.10 The Owner shall furnish required information and services and shall render approvals and decisions as expeditiously as necessary for the orderly progress of the Architect's services and of the Work.

ARTICLE 3

CONSTRUCTION COST

3.1 DEFINITION

3.1.1 The Construction Cost shall be the total cost or estimated cost to the Owner of all elements of the Project designed or specified by the Architect.

3.1.2 The Construction Cost shall include at current market rates, including a reasonable allowance for overhead and profit, the cost of labor and materials furnished by the Owner and any equipment which has been designed, specified, selected or specially provided for by the Architect.

3.1.3 Construction Cost does not include the compensation of the Architect and the Architect's consultants, the cost of the land, rights-of-way, or other costs which are the responsibility of the Owner as provided in Article 2.

3.2 RESPONSIBILITY FOR CONSTRUCTION COST

3.2.1 Evaluations of the Owner's Project budget, Statements of Probable Construction Cost and Detailed Estimates of Construction Cost, if any, prepared by the Architect, represent the Architect's best judgment as a design professional familiar with the construction industry. It is recognized, however, that neither the Architect nor the Owner has control over the cost of labor, materials or equipment, over the Contractor's methods of determining bid prices, or over competitive bidding, market or negotiating conditions. Accordingly, the Architect cannot and does not warrant or represent that bids or negotiated prices will not vary from the Project budget proposed, established or approved by the Owner, if any, or from any Statement of Probable Construction Cost or other cost estimate or evaluation prepared by the Architect.

3.2.2 No fixed limit of Construction Cost shall be established as a condition of this Agreement by the furnishing, proposal or establishment of a Project budget under Subparagraph 1.1.2 or Paragraph 2.2 or otherwise, unless such fixed limit has been agreed upon in writing and signed by the parties hereto. If such a fixed limit has been established, the Architect shall be permitted to include contingencies for design, bidding and price escalation, to determine what materials, equipment, component systems and types of construction are to be included in the Contract Documents, to make reasonable adjustments in the scope of the Project and to include in the Contract Documents alternate bids to adjust the Construction Cost to the fixed limit. Any such fixed limit shall be increased in the amount of any increase in the Contract Sum occurring after execution of the Contract for Construction.

3.2.3 If the Bidding or Negotiation Phase has not commenced within three months after the Architect submits the Construction Documents to the Owner, any Project budget or fixed limit of Construction Cost shall be adjusted to reflect any change in the general level of prices in the construction industry between the date of submission of the Construction Documents to the Owner and the date on which proposals are sought.

3.2.4 If a Project budget or fixed limit of Construction Cost (adjusted as provided in Subparagraph 3.2.3) is exceeded by the lowest bona fide bid or negotiated proposal, the Owner shall (1) give written approval of an increase in such fixed limit, (2) authorize rebidding or renegotiating of the Project within a reasonable time, (3) if the Project is abandoned, terminate in accordance with Paragraph 10.2, or (4) cooperate in revising the Project scope and quality as required to reduce the Construction Cost. In the case of (4), provided a fixed limit of Construction Cost has been established as a condition of this Agreement, the Architect, without additional charge, shall modify the Drawings and Specifications as necessary to comply with the fixed limit. The providing of such service shall be the limit of the Architect's responsibility arising from the establishment of such fixed limit, and having done so, the Architect shall be entitled to compensation for all services performed, in accordance with this Agreement, whether or not the Construction Phase is commenced.

ARTICLE 4

DIRECT PERSONNEL EXPENSE

4.1 Direct Personnel Expense is defined as the direct salaries of all the Architect's personnel engaged on the Project, and the portion of the cost of their mandatory and customary contributions and benefits related thereto, such as employment taxes and other statutory employee benefits, insurance, sick leave, holidays, vacations, pensions and similar contributions and benefits.

ARTICLE 5

REIMBURSABLE EXPENSES

5.1 Reimbursable Expenses are in addition to the Compensation for Basic and Additional Services and include actual expenditures made by the Architect and the Architect's employees and consultants in the interest of the Project for the expenses listed in the following Subparagraphs:

5.1.1 Expense of transportation in connection with the Project; living expenses in connection with out-of-town travel; long distance communications, and fees paid for securing approval of authorities having jurisdiction over the Project.

5.1.2 Expense of reproductions, postage and handling of Drawings, Specifications and other documents, excluding reproductions for the office use of the Architect and the Architect's consultants.

5.1.3 Expense of data processing and photographic production techniques when used in connection with Additional Services.

5.1.4 If authorized in advance by the Owner, expense of overtime work requiring higher than regular rates.

5.1.5 Expense of renderings, models and mock-ups requested by the Owner.

5.1.6 Expense of any additional insurance coverage or limits, including professional liability insurance, requested by the Owner in excess of that normally carried by the Architect and the Architect's consultants.

ARTICLE 6

PAYMENTS TO THE ARCHITECT

6.1 PAYMENTS ON ACCOUNT OF BASIC SERVICES

6.1.1 An initial payment as set forth in Paragraph 14.1 is the minimum payment under this Agreement.

6.1.2 Subsequent payments for Basic Services shall be made monthly and shall be in proportion to services performed within each Phase of services, on the basis set forth in Article 14.

6.1.3 If and to the extent that the Contract Time initially established in the Contract for Construction is exceeded

or extended through no fault of the Architect, compensation for any Basic Services required for such extended period of Administration of the Construction Contract shall be computed as set forth in Paragraph 14.4 for Additional Services.

6.1.4 When compensation is based on a percentage of Construction Cost, and any portions of the Project are deleted or otherwise not constructed, compensation for such portions of the Project shall be payable to the extent services are performed on such portions, in accordance with the schedule set forth in Subparagraph 14.2.2, based on (1) the lowest bona fide bid or negotiated proposal or, (2) if no such bid or proposal is received, the most recent Statement of Probable Construction Cost or Detailed Estimate of Construction Cost for such portions of the Project.

6.2 PAYMENTS ON ACCOUNT OF ADDITIONAL SERVICES

6.2.1 Payments on account of the Architect's Additional Services as defined in Paragraph 1.7 and for Reimbursable Expenses as defined in Article 5 shall be made monthly upon presentation of the Architect's statement of services rendered or expenses incurred.

6.3 PAYMENTS WITHHELD

6.3.1 No deductions shall be made from the Architect's compensation on account of penalty, liquidated damages or other sums withheld from payments to contractors, or on account of the cost of changes in the Work other than those for which the Architect is held legally liable.

6.4 PROJECT SUSPENSION OR TERMINATION

6.4.1 If the Project is suspended or abandoned in whole or in part for more than three months, the Architect shall be compensated for all services performed prior to receipt of written notice from the Owner of such suspension or abandonment, together with Reimbursable Expenses then due and all Termination Expenses as defined in Paragraph 10.4. If the Project is resumed after being suspended for more than three months, the Architect's compensation shall be equitably adjusted.

ARTICLE 7

ARCHITECT'S ACCOUNTING RECORDS

7.1 Records of Reimbursable Expenses and expenses pertaining to Additional Services and services performed on the basis of a Multiple of Direct Personnel Expense shall be kept on the basis of generally accepted accounting principles and shall be available to the Owner or the Owner's authorized representative at mutually convenient times.

ARTICLE 8

OWNERSHIP AND USE OF DOCUMENTS

8.1 Drawings and Specifications as instruments of service are and shall remain the property of the Architect whether the Project for which they are made is executed or not. The Owner shall be permitted to retain copies, including reproducible copies, of Drawings and Specifications for information and reference in connection with the Owner's use and occupancy of the Project. The Drawings and Specifications shall not be used by the Owner on other projects, for additions to this Project, or for completion of this Project by others provided the Architect is not in default under this Agreement, except by agreement in writing and with appropriate compensation to the Architect.

8.2 Submission or distribution to meet official regulatory requirements or for other purposes in connection with the Project is not to be construed as publication in derogation of the Architect's rights.

ARTICLE 9

ARBITRATION

9.1 All claims, disputes and other matters in question between the parties to this Agreement, arising out of or relating to this Agreement or the breach thereof, shall be decided by arbitration in accordance with the Construction Industry Arbitration Rules of the American Arbitration Association then obtaining unless the parties mutually agree otherwise. No arbitration, arising out of or relating to this Agreement, shall include, by consolidation, joinder or in any other manner, any additional person not a party to this Agreement except by written consent containing a specific reference to this Agreement and signed by the Architect, the Owner, and any other person sought to be joined. Any consent to arbitration involving an additional person or persons shall not constitute consent to arbitration of any dispute not described therein or with any person not named or described therein. This Agreement to arbitrate and any agreement to arbitrate with an additional person or persons duly consented to by the parties to this Agreement shall be specifically enforceable under the prevailing arbitration law.

9.2 Notice of the demand for arbitration shall be filed in writing with the other party to this Agreement and with the American Arbitration Association. The demand shall be made within a reasonable time after the claim, dispute or other matter in question has arisen. In no event shall the demand for arbitration be made after the date when institution of legal or equitable proceedings based on such claim, dispute or other matter in question would be barred by the applicable statute of limitations.

9.3 The award rendered by the arbitrators shall be final, and judgment may be entered upon it in accordance with applicable law in any court having jurisdiction thereof.

ARTICLE 10

TERMINATION OF AGREEMENT

10.1 This Agreement may be terminated by either party upon seven days' written notice should the other party fail substantially to perform in accordance with its terms through no fault of the party initiating the termination.

10.2 This Agreement may be terminated by the Owner upon at least seven days' written notice to the Architect in the event that the Project is permanently abandoned.

10.3 In the event of termination not the fault of the Architect, the Architect shall be compensated for all services performed to termination date, together with Reimbursable Expenses then due and all Termination Expenses as defined in Paragraph 10.4.

10.4 Termination Expenses include expenses directly attributable to termination for which the Architect is not otherwise compensated, plus an amount computed as a percentage of the total Basic and Additional Compensation earned to the time of termination, as follows:

.1 20 percent if termination occurs during the Schematic Design Phase; or

.2 10 percent if termination occurs during the Design Development Phase; or

.3 5 percent if termination occurs during any subsequent phase.

ARTICLE 11

MISCELLANEOUS PROVISIONS

11.1 Unless otherwise specified, this Agreement shall be governed by the law of the principal place of business of the Architect.

11.2 Terms in this Agreement shall have the same meaning as those in AIA Document A201, General Conditions of the Contract for Construction, current as of the date of this Agreement.

11.3 As between the parties to this Agreement: as to all acts or failures to act by either party to this Agreement, any applicable statute of limitations shall commence to run and any alleged cause of action shall be deemed to have accrued in any and all events not later than the relevant Date of Substantial Completion of the Work, and as to any acts or failures to act occurring after the relevant Date of Substantial Completion, not later than the date of issuance of the final Certificate for Payment.

11.4 The Owner and the Architect waive all rights against each other and against the contractors, consultants, agents and employees of the other for damages covered by any property insurance during construction as set forth in the edition of AIA Document A201, General Conditions, current as of the date of this Agreement. The Owner and the Architect each shall require appropriate similar waivers from their contractors, consultants and agents.

ARTICLE 12

SUCCESSORS AND ASSIGNS

12.1 The Owner and the Architect, respectively, bind themselves, their partners, successors, assigns and legal representatives to the other party to this Agreement and to the partners, successors, assigns and legal representatives of such other party with respect to all covenants of this Agreement. Neither the Owner nor the Architect shall assign, sublet or transfer any interest in this Agreement without the written consent of the other.

ARTICLE 13

EXTENT OF AGREEMENT

13.1 This Agreement represents the entire and integrated agreement between the Owner and the Architect and supersedes all prior negotiations, representations or agreements, either written or oral. This Agreement may be amended only by written instrument signed by both Owner and Architect.

8

ARTICLE 14
BASIS OF COMPENSATION

The Owner shall compensate the Architect for the Scope of Services provided, in accordance with Article 6, Payments to the Architect, and the other Terms and Conditions of this Agreement, as follows:

14.1 AN INITIAL PAYMENT of   dollars ($)

shall be made upon execution of this Agreement and credited to the Owner's account as follows:

14.2 BASIC COMPENSATION

14.2.1 FOR BASIC SERVICES, as described in Paragraphs 1.1 through 1.5, and any other services included in Article 15 as part of Basic Services, Basic Compensation shall be computed as follows:

(Here insert basis of compensation, including fixed amounts, multiples or percentages, and identify Phases to which particular methods of compensation apply, if necessary.)

14.2.2 Where compensation is based on a Stipulated Sum or Percentage of Construction Cost, payments for Basic Services shall be made as provided in Subparagraph 6.1.2, so that Basic Compensation for each Phase shall equal the following percentages of the total Basic Compensation payable:

(Include any additional Phases as appropriate.)

Schematic Design Phase:	percent (%)
Design Development Phase:	percent (%)
Construction Documents Phase:	percent (%)
Bidding or Negotiation Phase:	percent (%)
Construction Phase:	percent (%)

14.3 FOR PROJECT REPRESENTATION BEYOND BASIC SERVICES, as described in Paragraph 1.6, Compensation shall be computed separately in accordance with Subparagraph 1.6.2.

9

14.4 COMPENSATION FOR ADDITIONAL SERVICES

14.4.1 FOR ADDITIONAL SERVICES OF THE ARCHITECT, as described in Paragraph 1.7, and any other services included in Article 15 as part of Additional Services, but excluding Additional Services of consultants, Compensation shall be computed as follows:

(Here insert basis of compensation, including rates and/or multiples of Direct Personnel Expense for Principals and employees, and identify Principals and classify employees, if required. Identify specific services to which particular methods of compensation apply, if necessary.)

14.4.2 FOR ADDITIONAL SERVICES OF CONSULTANTS, including additional structural, mechanical and electrical engineering services and those provided under Subparagraph 1.7.21 or identified in Article 15 as part of Additional Services, a multiple of ( ) times the amounts billed to the Architect for such services.

(Identify specific types of consultants in Article 15, if required.)

14.5 FOR REIMBURSABLE EXPENSES, as described in Article 5, and any other items included in Article 15 as Reimbursable Expenses, a multiple of ( ) times the amounts expended by the Architect, the Architect's employees and consultants in the interest of the Project.

14.6 Payments due the Architect and unpaid under this Agreement shall bear interest from the date payment is due at the rate entered below, or in the absence thereof, at the legal rate prevailing at the principal place of business of the Architect.

(Here insert any rate of interest agreed upon.)

(Usury laws and requirements under the Federal Truth in Lending Act, similar state and local consumer credit laws and other regulations at the Owner's and Architect's principal places of business, the location of the Project and elsewhere may affect the validity of this provision. Specific legal advice should be obtained with respect to deletion, modification, or other requirements such as written disclosures or waivers.)

14.7 The Owner and the Architect agree in accordance with the Terms and Conditions of this Agreement that:

14.7.1 IF THE SCOPE of the Project or of the Architect's Services is changed materially, the amounts of compensation shall be equitably adjusted.

14.7.2 IF THE SERVICES covered by this Agreement have not been completed within

( ) months of the date hereof, through no fault of the Architect, the amounts of compensation, rates and multiples set forth herein shall be equitably adjusted.

10

ARTICLE 15
OTHER CONDITIONS OR SERVICES

This Agreement entered into as of the day and year first written above.

OWNER

ARCHITECT

_____   _____

_____   _____

_____   _____

BY_____   BY_____

CHANGE ORDER

AIA DOCUMENT G701

OWNER ☐
ARCHITECT ☐
CONTRACTOR ☐
FIELD ☐
OTHER

PROJECT:
(name, address)

CHANGE ORDER NUMBER:

TO (Contractor)

ARCHITECT'S PROJECT NO:

CONTRACT FOR:

CONTRACT DATE:

You are directed to make the following changes in this Contract:

The original Contract Sum was . . . . $.

Net change by previous Change Orders . . . . $.

The Contract Sum prior to this Change Order was . . . . $.

The Contract Sum will be (increased) (decreased) (unchanged) by this Change Order . . . $.

The new Contract Sum including this Change Order will be . . . . $.

The Contract Time will be (increased) (decreased) (unchanged) by   (   ) Days.

The Date of Completion as of the date of this Change Order therefore is

ARCHITECT	CONTRACTOR	OWNER
Address	Address	Address
BY	BY	BY
DATE	DATE	DATE

ONE PAGE

THE AMERICAN INSTITUTE OF ARCHITECTS

AIA Document A107

Abbreviated Form of Agreement Between Owner and Contractor

For CONSTRUCTION PROJECTS OF LIMITED SCOPE where
the Basis of Payment is a STIPULATED SUM

1978 EDITION

*THIS DOCUMENT HAS IMPORTANT LEGAL CONSEQUENCES; CONSULTATION WITH
AN ATTORNEY IS ENCOURAGED WITH RESPECT TO ITS COMPLETION OR MODIFICATION*

This document includes abbreviated General Conditions and should not be used with other General Conditions.
It has been approved and endorsed by The Associated General Contractors of America.

AGREEMENT

made as of the   day of   in the year of Nineteen
Hundred and

BETWEEN the Owner:

and the Contractor:

the Project:

the Architect:

The Owner and the Contractor agree as set forth below.

1

ARTICLE 1
THE WORK

1.1   The Contractor shall perform all the Work required by the Contract Documents for

(Here insert the caption descriptive of the Work as used on other Contract Documents.)

ARTICLE 2
TIME OF COMMENCEMENT AND SUBSTANTIAL COMPLETION

2.1   The Work to be performed under this Contract shall be commenced

and, subject to authorized adjustments, Substantial Completion shall be achieved not later than

(Here insert any special provisions for liquidated damages relating to failure to complete on time.)

ARTICLE 3
CONTRACT SUM

3.1   The Owner shall pay the Contractor in current funds for the performance of the Work, subject to additions and deductions by Change Order as provided in the Contract Documents, the Contract Sum of

3.2   The Contract Sum is determined as follows:

(State here the base bid or other lump sum amount, accepted alternates, and unit prices, as applicable.)

ARTICLE 4
PROGRESS PAYMENTS

4.1 Based upon Applications for Payment submitted to the Architect by the Contractor and Certificates for Payment issued by the Architect, the Owner shall make progress payments on account of the Contract Sum to the Contractor as provided in the Contract Documents for the period ending the   day of the month as follows:

(Here insert payment procedures and provision for retainage, if any.)

4.2 Payments due and unpaid under the Contract Documents shall bear interest from the date payment is due at the rate entered below, or in the absence thereof, at the legal rate prevailing at the place of the Project.

(Here insert any rate of interest agreed upon.)

(Usury laws and requirements under the Federal Truth in Lending Act, similar state and local consumer credit laws and other regulations at the Owner's and Contractor's principal places of business, the location of the Project and elsewhere may affect the validity of this provision. Specific legal advice should be obtained with respect to deletion, modification, or other requirements such as written disclosure or waivers.)

ARTICLE 5
FINAL PAYMENT

5.1 Final payment, constituting the entire unpaid balance of the Contract Sum, shall be paid by the Owner to the Contractor when the Work has been completed, the Contract fully performed, and a final Certificate for Payment has been issued by the Architect.

ARTICLE 6
ENUMERATION OF CONTRACT DOCUMENTS

6.1 The Contract Documents, which constitute the entire agreement between the Owner and the Contractor, are listed in Article 7 and, except for Modifications issued after execution of this Agreement, are enumerated as follows:

(List below the Agreement, the Conditions of the Contract (General, Supplementary, and other Conditions), the Drawings, the Specifications, and any Addenda and accepted alternates, showing page or sheet numbers in all cases and dates where applicable.)

3

ARTICLE 7
CONTRACT DOCUMENTS

7.1 The Contract Documents consist of this Agreement with General Conditions, Supplementary and other Conditions, the Drawings, the Specifications, all Addenda issued prior to the execution of this Agreement, and all Modifications issued by the Architect after execution of the Contract such as Change Orders, written interpretations and written orders for minor changes in the Work. The intent of the Contract Documents is to include all items necessary for the proper execution and completion of the Work. The Contract Documents are complementary, and what is required by any one shall be as binding as if required by all. Work not covered in the Contract Documents will not be required unless it is consistent therewith and reasonably inferable therefrom as being necessary to produce the intended results.

7.2 Nothing contained in the Contract Documents shall create any contractual relationship between the Owner or the Architect and any Subcontractor or Sub-subcontractor.

7.3 By executing the Contract, the Contractor represents that he has visited the site and familiarized himself with the local conditions under which the Work is to be performed.

7.4 The Work comprises the completed construction required by the Contract Documents and includes all labor necessary to produce such construction, and all materials and equipment incorporated or to be incorporated in such construction.

ARTICLE 8
ARCHITECT

8.1 The Architect will provide administration of the Contract and will be the Owner's representative during construction and until final payment is due.

8.2 The Architect shall at all times have access to the Work wherever it is in preparation and progress.

8.3 The Architect will visit the site at intervals appropriate to the stage of construction to familiarize himself generally with the progress and quality of the Work and to determine in general if the Work is proceeding in accordance with the Contract Documents. However, the Architect will not be required to make exhaustive or continuous on-site inspections to check the quality or quantity of the Work. On the basis of his on-site observations as an architect, he will keep the Owner informed of the progress of the Work, and will endeavor to guard the Owner against defects and deficiencies in the Work of the Contractor. The Architect will not have control or charge of and will not be responsible for construction means, methods, techniques, sequences or procedures, or for safety precautions and programs in connection with the Work, and he will not be responsible for the Contractor's failure to carry out the Work in accordance with the Contract Documents.

8.4 Based on the Architect's observations and an evalua-

tion of the Contractor's Applications for Payment, the Architect will determine the amounts owing to the Contractor and will issue Certificates for Payment in accordance with Article 15.

8.5 The Architect will be the interpreter of the requirements of the Contract Documents. He will make decisions on all claims, disputes or other matters in question between the Contractor and the Owner, but he will not be liable for the results of any interpretation or decision rendered in good faith. The Architect's decisions in matters relating to artistic effect will be final if consistent with the intent of the Contract Documents. All other decisions of the Architect, except those which have been waived by the making or acceptance of final payment, shall be subject to arbitration upon the written demand of either party.

8.6 The Architect will have authority to reject Work which does not conform to the Contract Documents.

8.7 The Architect will review and approve or take other appropriate action upon the Contractor's submittals such as Shop Drawings, Product Data and Samples, but only for conformance with the design concept of the Work and with the information given in the Contract Documents.

ARTICLE 9
OWNER

9.1 The Owner shall furnish all surveys and a legal description of the site.

9.2 Except as provided in Paragraph 10.5, the Owner shall secure and pay for necessary approvals, easements, assessments and charges required for the construction, use or occupancy of permanent structures or permanent changes in existing facilities.

9.3 The Owner shall forward all instructions to the Contractor through the Architect.

9.4 If the Contractor fails to correct defective Work or persistently fails to carry out the Work in accordance with the Contract Documents, the Owner, by a written order, may order the Contractor to stop the Work, or any portion thereof, until the cause for such order has been eliminated; however, this right of the Owner to stop the Work shall not give rise to any duty on the part of the Owner to exercise this right for the benefit of the Contractor or any other person or entity.

ARTICLE 10
CONTRACTOR

10.1 The Contractor shall supervise and direct the Work, using his best skill and attention and he shall be solely responsible for all construction means, methods, techniques, sequences and procedures and for coordinating all portions of the Work under the Contract.

10.2 Unless otherwise specifically provided in the Contract Documents, the Contractor shall provide and pay for all labor, materials, equipment, tools, construction equipment and machinery, water, heat, utilities, transportation, and other facilities and services necessary for the proper

4

execution and completion of the Work, whether temporary or permanent and whether or not incorporated or to be incorporated in the Work.

10.3 The Contractor shall at all times enforce strict discipline and good order among his employees and shall not employ on the Work any unfit person or anyone not skilled in the task assigned to him.

10.4 The Contractor warrants to the Owner and the Architect that all materials and equipment incorporated in the Work will be new unless otherwise specified, and th. all Work will be of good quality, free from faults and defects and in conformance with the Contract Documents. All Work not conforming to these requirements may be considered defective.

10.5 Unless otherwise provided in the Contract Documents, the Contractor shall pay all sales, consumer, use and other similar taxes which are legally enacted at the time bids are received, and shall secure and pay for the building permit and for all other permits and governmental fees, licenses and inspections necessary for the proper execution and completion of the Work.

10.6 The Contractor shall give all notices and comply with all laws, ordinances, rules, regulations, and lawful orders of any public authority bearing on the performance of the Work, and shall promptly notify the Architect if the Drawings and Specifications are at variance therewith.

10.7 The Contractor shall be responsible to the Owner for the acts and omissions of his employees, Subcontractors and their agents and employees, and other persons performing any of the Work under a contract with the Contractor.

10.8 The Contractor shall review, approve and submit all Shop Drawings, Product Data and Samples required by the Contract Documents. The Work shall be in accordance with approved submittals.

10.9 The Contractor at all times shall keep the premises free from accumulation of waste materials or rubbish caused by his operations. At the completion of the Work he shall remove all his waste materials and rubbish from and about the Project as well as his tools, construction equipment, machinery and surplus materials.

10.10 The Contractor shall pay all royalties and license fees. He shall defend all suits or claims for infringement of any patent rights and shall save the Owner harmless from loss on account thereof.

10.11 To the fullest extent permitted by law, the Contractor shall indemnify and hold harmless the Owner and the Architect and their agents and employees from and against all claims, damages, losses and expenses, including but not limited to attorneys' fees arising out of or resulting from the performance of the Work, provided that any such claim, damage, loss or expense (1) is attributable to bodily injury, sickness, disease or death, or to injury to or destruction of tangible property (other than the Work itself) including the loss of use resulting therefrom, and (2) is caused in whole or in part by any negligent act or omission of the Contractor, any Subcontractor, anyone directly or indirectly employed by any of them or anyone for whose acts any of them may be liable, regardless of whether or not it is caused in part by a party indemnified hereunder. Such obligation shall not be construed to negate, abridge, or otherwise reduce any other right or

obligation of indemnity which would otherwise exist as to any party or person described in this Paragraph 10.11. In any and all claims against the Owner or the Architect or any of their agents or employees by any employee of the Contractor, any Subcontractor, anyone directly or indirectly employed by any of them or anyone for whose acts any of them may be liable, the indemnification obligation under this Paragraph 10.11 shall not be limited in any way by any limitation on the amount or type of damages, compensation or benefits payable by or for the Contractor or any Subcontractor under workers' or workmen's compensation acts, disability benefit acts or other employee benefit acts. The obligations of the Contractor under this Paragraph 10.11 shall not extend to the liability of the Architect, his agents or employees, arising out of (1) the preparation or approval of maps, drawings, opinions, reports, surveys, change orders, designs or specifications, or (2) the giving of or the failure to give directions or instructions by the Architect, his agents or employees provided such giving or failure to give is the primary cause of the injury or damage.

ARTICLE 11
SUBCONTRACTS

11.1 A Subcontractor is a person or entity who has a direct contract with the Contractor to perform any of the Work at the site.

11.2 Unless otherwise required by the Contract Documents or in the Bidding Documents, the Contractor, as soon as practicable after the award of the Contract, shall furnish to the Architect in writing the names of Subcontractors for each of the principal portions of the Work. The Contractor shall not employ any Subcontractor to whom the Architect or the Owner may have a reasonable objection. The Contractor shall not be required to contract with anyone to whom he has a reasonable objection. Contracts between the Contractor and the Subcontractors shall (1) require each Subcontractor, to the extent of the Work to be performed by the Subcontractor, to be bound to the Contractor by the terms of the Contract Documents, and to assume toward the Contractor all the obligations and responsibilities which the Contractor, by these Documents, assumes toward the Owner and the Architect, and (2) allow to the Subcontractor the benefit of all rights, remedies and redress afforded to the Contractor by these Contract Documents.

ARTICLE 12
WORK BY OWNER OR BY
SEPARATE CONTRACTORS

12.1 The Owner reserves the right to perform work related to the Project with his own forces, and to award separate contracts in connection with other portions of the Project or other work on the site under these or similar Conditions of the Contract. If the Contractor claims that delay or additional cost is involved because of such action by the Owner, he shall make such claim as provided elsewhere in the Contract Documents.

12.2 The Contractor shall afford the Owner and separate contractors reasonable opportunity for the introduction and storage of their materials and equipment and the execution of their work, and shall connect and coordinate his Work with theirs as required by the Contract Documents.

5

12.3 Any costs caused by defective or ill-timed work shall be borne by the party responsible therefor.

ARTICLE 13
MISCELLANEOUS PROVISIONS

13.1 The Contract shall be governed by the law of the place where the Project is located.

13.2 All claims or disputes between the Contractor and the Owner arising out of, or relating to, the Contract Documents or the breach thereof shall be decided by arbitration in accordance with the Construction Industry Arbitration Rules of the American Arbitration Association then obtaining unless the parties mutually agree otherwise. Notice of the demand for arbitration shall be filed in writing with the other party to the Owner-Contractor Agreement and with the American Arbitration Association and shall be made within a reasonable time after the dispute has arisen. The award rendered by the arbitrators shall be final, and judgment may be entered upon it in accordance with applicable law in any court having jurisdiction thereof. Except by written consent of the person or entity sought to be joined, no arbitration arising out of or relating to the Contract Documents shall include, by consolidation, joinder or in any other manner, any person or entity not a party to the agreement under which such arbitration arises, unless it is shown at the time the demand for arbitration is filed that (1) such person or entity is substantially involved in a common question of fact or law, (2) the presence of such person or entity is required if complete relief is to be accorded in the arbitration, (3) the interest or responsibility of such person or entity in the matter is not insubstantial, and (4) such person or entity is not the Architect or any of his employees or consultants. The agreement herein among the parties to the Agreement and any other written agreement to arbitrate referred to herein shall be specifically enforceable under the prevailing arbitration law.

ARTICLE 14
TIME

14.1 All time limits stated in the Contract Documents are of the essence of the Contract. The Contractor shall expedite the Work and achieve Substantial Completion within the Contract Time.

14.2 The Date of Substantial Completion of the Work is the date certified by the Architect when construction is sufficiently complete so that the Owner can occupy or utilize the Work for the use for which it is intended.

14.3 If the Contractor is delayed at any time in the progress of the Work by changes ordered in the Work, by labor disputes, fire, unusual delay in transportation, adverse weather conditions not reasonably anticipatable, unavoidable casualties, or any causes beyond the Contractor's control, or by any other cause which the Architect determines may justify the delay, then the Contract Time shall be extended by Change Order for such reasonable time as the Architect may determine.

ARTICLE 15
PAYMENTS AND COMPLETION

15.1 Payments shall be made as provided in Article 4 and Article 5 of this Agreement.

15.2 Payments may be withheld on account of (1) defective work not remedied, (2) claims filed, (3) failure of the Contractor to make payments properly to Subcontractors or for labor, materials, or equipment, (4) damage to the Owner or another contractor, or (5) persistent failure to carry out the Work in accordance with the Contract Documents.

15.3 When the Architect agrees that the Work is substantially complete, he will issue a Certificate of Substantial Completion.

15.4 Final payment shall not be due until the Contractor has delivered to the Owner a complete release of all liens arising out of this Contract or receipts in full covering all labor, materials and equipment for which a lien could be filed, or a bond satisfactory to the Owner indemnifying him against any lien. If any lien remains unsatisfied after all payments are made, the Contractor shall refund to the Owner all moneys the latter may be compelled to pay in discharging such lien, including all costs and reasonable attorneys' fees.

15.5 The making of final payments shall constitute a waiver of all claims by the Owner except those arising from (1) unsettled liens, (2) faulty or defective Work appearing after Substantial Completion, (3) failure of the Work to comply with the requirements of the Contract Documents, or (4) terms of any special warranties required by the Contract Documents. The acceptance of final payment shall constitute a waiver of all claims by the Contractor except those previously made in writing and identified by the Contractor as unsettled at the time of the final Application for Payment.

ARTICLE 16
PROTECTION OF PERSONS AND PROPERTY

16.1 The Contractor shall be responsible for initiating, maintaining, and supervising all safety precautions and programs in connection with the Work. He shall take all reasonable precautions for the safety of, and shall provide all reasonable protection to prevent damage, injury or loss to (1) all employees on the Work and other persons who may be affected thereby, (2) all the Work and all materials and equipment to be incorporated therein, and (3) other property at the site or adjacent thereto. He shall give all notices and comply with all applicable laws, ordinances, rules, regulations and orders of any public authority bearing on the safety of persons and property and their protection from damage, injury or loss. The Contractor shall promptly remedy all damage or loss to any property caused in whole or in part by the Contractor, any Subcontractor, any Sub-subcontractor, or anyone directly or indirectly employed by any of them, or by anyone for whose acts any of them may be liable, except damage or loss attributable to the acts or omissions of the Owner or Architect or anyone directly or indirectly employed by either of them or by anyone for whose acts either of them may be liable, and not attributable to the fault or negligence of the Contractor. The foregoing obligations of the Contractor are in addition to his obligations under Paragraph 10.11.

ARTICLE 17
INSURANCE

17.1 Contractor's liability insurance shall be purchased and maintained by the Contractor to protect him from claims under workers' or workmen's compensation acts and other employee benefit acts, claims for damages because of bodily injury, including death, and from claims for damages, other than to the Work itself, to property which may arise out of or result from the Contractor's operations under this Contract, whether such operations be by himself or by any Subcontractor or anyone directly or indirectly employed by any of them. This insurance shall be written for not less than any limits of liability specified in the Contract Documents, or required by law, whichever is the greater, and shall include contractual liability insurance applicable to the Contractor's obligations under Paragraph 10.11. Certificates of such insurance shall be filed with the Owner prior to the commencement of the Work.

17.2 The Owner shall be responsible for purchasing and maintaining his own liability insurance and, at his option, may maintain such insurance as will protect him against claims which may arise from operations under the Contract.

17.3 Unless otherwise provided, the Owner shall purchase and maintain property insurance upon the entire Work at the site to the full insurable value thereof. This insurance shall include the interests of the Owner, the Contractor, Subcontractors and Sub-subcontractors in the Work and shall insure against the perils of fire and extended coverage and shall include "all risk" insurance for physical loss or damage including, without duplication of coverage, theft, vandalism, and malicious mischief.

17.4 Any loss insured under Paragraph 17.3 is to be adjusted with the Owner and made payable to the Owner as trustee for the insureds, as their interests may appear, subject to the requirements of any mortgagee clause.

17.5 The Owner shall file a copy of all policies with the Contractor before an exposure to loss may occur.

17.6 The Owner and Contractor waive all rights against each other for damages caused by fire or other perils to the extent covered by insurance obtained pursuant to this Article or any other property insurance applicable to the Work, except such rights as they may have to the proceeds of such insurance held by the Owner as trustee. The Contractor shall require similar waivers in favor of the Owner and the Contractor by Subcontractors and Sub-subcontractors.

ARTICLE 18
CHANGES IN THE WORK

18.1 The Owner, without invalidating the Contract, may order Changes in the Work consisting of additions, deletions, or modifications, the Contract Sum and the Contract Time being adjusted accordingly. All such changes in the Work shall be authorized by written Change Order signed by the Owner and the Architect.

18.2 The Contract Sum and the Contract Time may be changed only by Change Order.

18.3 The cost or credit to the Owner from a change in the Work shall be determined by mutual agreement.

ARTICLE 19
CORRECTION OF WORK

19.1 The Contractor shall promptly correct any Work rejected by the Architect as defective or as failing to conform to the Contract Documents whether observed before or after Substantial Completion and whether or not fabricated, installed or completed, and shall correct any Work found to be defective or nonconforming within a period of one year from the Date of Substantial Completion of the Contract or within such longer period of time as may be prescribed by law or by the terms of any applicable special warranty required by the Contract Documents. The provisions of this Article 19 apply to Work done by Subcontractors as well as to Work done by direct employees of the Contractor.

ARTICLE 20
TERMINATION OF THE CONTRACT

20.1 If the Architect fails to issue a Certificate for Payment for a period of thirty days through no fault of the Contractor, or if the Owner fails to make payment thereon for a period of thirty days, the Contractor may, upon seven additional days' written notice to the Owner and the Architect, terminate the Contract and recover from the Owner payment for all Work executed and for any proven loss sustained upon any materials, equipment, tools, and construction equipment and machinery, including reasonable profit and damages applicable to the Project.

20.2 If the Contractor defaults or persistently fails or neglects to carry out the Work in accordance with the Contract Documents or fails to perform any provision of the Contract, the Owner may, after seven days' written notice to the Contractor and without prejudice to any other remedy he may have, make good such deficiencies and may deduct the cost thereof, including compensation for the Architect's additional services made necessary thereby, from the payment then or thereafter due the Contractor or, at his option, and upon certification by the Architect that sufficient cause exists to justify such action, may terminate the Contract and take possession of the site and of all materials, equipment, tools, and construction equipment and machinery thereon owned by the Contractor and may finish the Work by whatever method he may deem expedient, and if the unpaid balance of the Contract Sum exceeds the expense of finishing the Work, such excess shall be paid to the Contractor, but if such expense exceeds such unpaid balance, the Contractor shall pay the difference to the Owner.

ARTICLE 21
OTHER CONDITIONS OR PROVISIONS

This Agreement entered into as of the day and year first written above.

OWNER   CONTRACTOR

_____   _____

_____   _____

_____

8

CONTRACTOR'S AFFIDAVIT OF RELEASE OF LIENS

OWNER ☐
ARCHITECT ☐
CONTRACTOR ☐
SURETY ☐
OTHER

AIA DOCUMENT G706A

TO (Owner)

ARCHITECT'S PROJECT NO:

CONTRACT FOR:

CONTRACT DATE:

PROJECT:
(name, address)

State of:

County of:

The undersigned, pursuant to Article 9 of the General Conditions of the Contract for Construction, AIA Document A201, hereby certifies that to the best of his knowledge, information and belief, except as listed below, the Releases or Waivers of Lien attached hereto include the Contractor, all Subcontractors, all suppliers of materials and equipment, and all performers of Work, labor or services who have or may have liens against any property of the Owner arising in any manner out of the performance of the Contract referenced above.

EXCEPTIONS: (If none, write "None". If required by the Owner, the Contractor shall furnish bond satisfactory to the Owner for each exception.)

SUPPORTING DOCUMENTS ATTACHED HERETO:

1. Contractor's Release or Waiver of Liens, conditional upon receipt of final payment.

2. Separate Releases or Waivers of Liens from Subcontractors and material and equipment suppliers, to the extent required by the Owner, accompanied by a list thereof.

CONTRACTOR:

Address:

BY:

Subscribed and sworn to before me this
day of   19

Notary Public:

My Commission Expires:

ONE PAGE

CERTIFICATE OF SUBSTANTIAL COMPLETION

AIA DOCUMENT G704

Distribution to:
OWNER ☐
ARCHITECT ☐
CONTRACTOR ☐
FIELD ☐
OTHER ☐

PROJECT:
(name, address)

TO (Owner):

⌐ ⌐

∟ ⌡

DATE OF ISSUANCE:

ARCHITECT:

ARCHITECT'S PROJECT NUMBER:

CONTRACTOR:

CONTRACT FOR:

CONTRACT DATE:

PROJECT OR DESIGNATED PORTION SHALL INCLUDE:

The Work performed under this Contract has been reviewed and found to be substantially complete. The Date of Substantial Completion of the Project or portion thereof designated above is hereby established as

which is also the date of commencement of applicable warranties required by the Contract Documents, except as stated below.

DEFINITION OF DATE OF SUBSTANTIAL COMPLETION

The Date of Substantial Completion of the Work or designated portion thereof is the Date certified by the Architect when construction is sufficiently complete, in accordance with the Contract Documents, so the Owner can occupy or utilize the Work or designated portion thereof for the use for which it is intended, as expressed in the Contract Documents.

A list of items to be completed or corrected, prepared by the Contractor and verified and amended by the Architect, is attached hereto. The failure to include any items on such list does not alter the responsibility of the Contractor to complete all Work in accordance with the Contract Documents. The date of commencement of warranties for items on the attached list will be the date of final payment unless otherwise agreed to in writing.

_____   BY _____   DATE _____
ARCHITECT

The Contractor will complete or correct the Work on the list of items attached hereto within   days from the above Date of Substantial Completion.

_____   BY _____   DATE _____
CONTRACTOR

The Owner accepts the Work or designated portion thereof as substantially complete and will assume full possession thereof at   (time) on   (date).

_____   BY _____   DATE _____
OWNER

The responsibilities of the Owner and the Contractor for security, maintenance, heat, utilities, damage to the Work and insurance shall be as follows:

(Note—Owner's and Contractor's legal and insurance counsel should determine and review insurance requirements and coverage; Contractor shall secure consent of surety company, if any.)

APPLICATION AND CERTIFICATE FOR PAYMENT

AIA DOCUMENT G702

TO (Owner):

PROJECT:

ATTENTION:

APPLICATION NO:

PERIOD FROM:
          TO:

ARCHITECT'S
PROJECT NO:

CONTRACT DATE:

CONTRACT FOR:

CONTRACTOR'S APPLICATION FOR PAYMENT

Application is made for Payment, as shown below, in connection with the Contract.
Continuation Sheet, AIA Document G703, is attached.

The present status of the account for this Contract is as follows:

ORIGINAL CONTRACT SUM .... $ _____

Net change by Change Orders .... $ _____

CONTRACT SUM TO DATE .... $ _____

TOTAL COMPLETED & STORED TO DATE .... $ _____
(Column G on G703)

RETAINAGE _____ % _____
or total in Column I on G703

TOTAL EARNED LESS RETAINAGE .... $ _____

LESS PREVIOUS CERTIFICATES FOR PAYMENT .... $ _____

CURRENT PAYMENT DUE .... $ _____

State of: County of:
Subscribed and sworn to before me this   day of   , 19
Notary Public:
My Commission expires:

CHANGE ORDER SUMMARY

	ADDITIONS	DEDUCTIONS
Change Orders approved in previous months by Owner		
TOTAL		
Approved this Month		
Number	Date Approved		
TOTALS		
Net change by Change Orders		

The undersigned Contractor certifies that to the best of his knowledge, information and belief the Work covered by this Application for Payment has been completed in accordance with the Contract Documents, that all amounts have been paid by him for Work for which previous Certificates for Payment were issued and payments received from the Owner, and that current payment shown herein is now due.

CONTRACTOR:

By: _____   Date: _____

ARCHITECT'S CERTIFICATE FOR PAYMENT

In accordance with the Contract Documents, based on on-site observations and the data comprising the above application, the Architect certifies to the Owner that the Work has progressed to the point indicated; that to the best of his knowledge, information and belief, the quality of the Work is in accordance with the Contract Documents; and that the Contractor is entitled to payment of the AMOUNT CERTIFIED.

AMOUNT CERTIFIED .... $ _____
(Attach explanation if amount certified differs from the amount applied for.)
ARCHITECT:

By: _____   Date: _____

This Certificate is not negotiable. The AMOUNT CERTIFIED is payable only to the Contractor named herein. Issuance, payment and acceptance of payment are without prejudice to any rights of the Owner or Contractor under this Contract.

AIA DOCUMENT G702 • APPLICATION AND CERTIFICATE FOR PAYMENT • APRIL 1978 EDITION • AIA® • © 1978
THE AMERICAN INSTITUTE OF ARCHITECTS, 1735 NEW YORK AVENUE, N.W., WASHINGTON, D.C. 20006

G702 — 1978

CERTIFICATE OF INSURANCE

AIA DOCUMENT G705

This certifies to the Addressee shown below that the following described policies, subject to their terms, conditions and exclusions, have been issued to:

NAME & ADDRESS OF INSURED

COVERING (SHOW PROJECT NAME AND/OR NUMBER AND LOCATION)

Addressee:
(Owner)

Date

KIND OF INSURANCE	POLICY NUMBER	Inception/Expiration Date	LIMITS OF LIABILITY	
1. (a) Workmen's Comp.			$ ///////////	Statutory Workmen's Compensation
(b) Employers' Liability			$	One Accident and Aggregate Disease
2. Comprehensive General Liability			$	Each Occurrence—Premises and Operations
			$	Each Occurrence—Independent Contractors
			$	Each Occurrence—COMPLETED OPERATIONS AND PRODUCTS
(a) Bodily Injury			$	Each Occurrence—Contractual
			$	Aggregate— COMPLETED OPERATIONS AND PRODUCTS
(b) Personal Injury			$	Each Person Aggregate
			$	General Aggregate
			$	Each Occurrence—Premises—Operations
			$	Each Occurrence—INDEPENDENT CONTRACTOR
(c) Property Damage			$	Each Occurrence—COMPLETED OPERATIONS AND PRODUCTS
			$	Each Occurrence—Contractual
			$	Aggregate—
			$	Aggregate— OPERATIONS, INDEPENDENT CONTRACTOR, PRODUCTS AND CONTRACTUAL
3. Comprehensive Automobile Liability				
(a) Bodily Injury			$	Each Person—
			$	Each Occurrence—
(b) Property Damage			$	Each Occurrence—
4. (Other)				

UNDER GENERAL LIABILITY POLICY OR POLICIES

Yes   No

1. Does Property Damage Liability Insurance shown include coverage for XC and U hazards? ....———— ————
2. Is Occurrence Basis Coverage provided under Property Damage Liability? ....———— ————
3. Is Broad Form Property Damage Coverage provided for this Project? ....———— ————
4. Does Personal Injury Liability Insurance include coverage for personal injury sustained by any person as a result of an offense directly or indirectly related to the employment of such person by the Insured? ....———— ————
5. Is coverage provided for Contractual Liability (including indemnification provision) assumed by Insured? ....———— ————

UNDER AUTOMOBILE LIABILITY POLICY OR POLICIES

1. Does coverage above apply to non-owned and hired automobiles? ....———— ————
2. Is Occurrence Basis Coverage provided under Property Damage Liability? ....———— ————

CANCELLATION OR NON-RENEWAL
In the event of cancellation or non-renewal of any of the foregoing, fifteen (15) days written notice shall be given to the party to whom this certificate is addressed.

EXTENT OF CERTIFICATION
This certificate is issued as a matter of information only and confers no rights upon the holder. By its issuance the company does not alter, change, modify or extend any of the provisions of the above policies.

NAME OF INSURANCE COMPANY

ADDRESS

SIGNATURE OF AUTHORIZED REPRESENTATIVE

ONE PAGE

REGISTER OF
BID DOCUMENTS

AIA DOCUMENT G804

PROJECT:

OWNER:

CONTRACT:

NOTICE FOR BIDS DATE:

☐ INVITED LIST   ☐ OPEN   ☐ PREQUALIFICATION

BIDS DUE DATE: _____ AM / PM _____ TIME ZONE

AT:

ADDENDA DATES: 1._____   2._____   3._____   4._____   5._____

PROJECT NO: _____

REFUNDABLE
DEPOSIT $_____
FOR_____ SETS

NON-REFUNDABLE CHARGES:

$_____ COMPLETE SET

$_____ SHEET OF DRAWINGS

$_____ PAGE OF SPECIFICATIONS

ADDENDA					RECIPIENT			DEPOSIT OR CHARGE					DOCUMENTS			
1	2	3	4	5	NAME	ADDRESS	PHONE	DATE REC'D	AMOUNT	CHECK	CASH	DATE REFUND	DATE ISSUED	SET NOS. ISSUED	DATE RET'D	PARTIAL SETS DESCRIPTION
✓	✓	✓	✓	✓						✓	✓					

CONTRACTOR'S AFFIDAVIT OF PAYMENT OF DEBTS AND CLAIMS

OWNER ☐
ARCHITECT ☐
CONTRACTOR ☐
SURETY ☐
OTHER

AIA Document G706

TO (Owner)

⌐   ⌐

⌐ ARCHITECT'S PROJECT NO:

CONTRACT FOR:

L   ⌐ CONTRACT DATE:

PROJECT:
(name, address)

State of:

County of:

The undersigned, pursuant to Article 9 of the General Conditions of the Contract for Construction, AIA Document A201, hereby certifies that, except as listed below, he has paid in full or has otherwise satisfied all obligations for all materials and equipment furnished, for all work, labor, and services performed, and for all known indebtedness and claims against the Contractor for damages arising in any manner in connection with the performance of the Contract referenced above for which the Owner or his property might in any way be held responsible.

EXCEPTIONS: (If none, write "None". If required by the Owner, the Contractor shall furnish bond satisfactory to the Owner for each exception.)

SUPPORTING DOCUMENTS ATTACHED HERETO:

1. Consent of Surety to Final Payment. Whenever Surety is involved, Consent of Surety is required. AIA DOCUMENT G707, CONSENT OF SURETY, may be used for this purpose.
   Indicate attachment: (yes   ) (no   ).

The following supporting documents should be attached hereto if required by the Owner:

1. Contractor's Release or Waiver of Liens, conditional upon receipt of final payment.

2. Separate Releases or Waivers of Liens from Subcontractors and material and equipment suppliers, to the extent required by the Owner, accompanied by a list thereof.

3. Contractor's Affidavit of Release of Liens (AIA DOCUMENT G706A).

CONTRACTOR:

Address:

BY:

Subscribed and sworn to before me this
                    day of   19

Notary Public:

My Commission Expires:

ONE PAGE

CONSENT OF SURETY COMPANY TO FINAL PAYMENT

OWNER ☐
ARCHITECT
CONTRACTOR ☐
SURETY ☐
OTHER

AIA DOCUMENT G707

PROJECT:
(name, address)

TO (Owner)

⌐

⌐ ARCHITECT'S PROJECT NO:

CONTRACT FOR:

∟

∟ CONTRACT DATE:

CONTRACTOR:

In accordance with the provisions of the Contract between the Owner and the Contractor as indicated above, the
(here insert name and address of Surety Company)

, SURETY COMPANY,

on bond of (here insert name and address of Contractor)

, CONTRACTOR,

hereby approves of the final payment to the Contractor, and agrees that final payment to the Contractor shall not relieve the Surety Company of any of its obligations to (here insert name and address of Owner)

, OWNER,

as set forth in the said Surety Company's bond.

IN WITNESS WHEREOF,
the Surety Company has hereunto set its hand this   day of   19

_____
Surety Company

_____
Signature of Authorized Representative

Attest:
(Seal):

_____
Title

NOTE: This form is to be used as a companion document to AIA DOCUMENT G706, CONTRACTOR'S AFFIDAVIT OF PAYMENT OF DEBTS AND CLAIMS, Current Edition

ONE PAGE

THE AMERICAN INSTITUTE OF ARCHITECTS

AIA Document A201

General Conditions of the Contract for Construction

*THIS DOCUMENT HAS IMPORTANT LEGAL CONSEQUENCES; CONSULTATION
WITH AN ATTORNEY IS ENCOURAGED WITH RESPECT TO ITS MODIFICATION*

TABLE OF ARTICLES

This document has been approved and endorsed by The Associated General Contractors of America.

1

ARTICLE 1

CONTRACT DOCUMENTS

1.1 DEFINITIONS

1.1.1 THE CONTRACT DOCUMENTS

The Contract Documents consist of the Owner-Contractor Agreement, the Conditions of the Contract (General, Supplementary and other Conditions), the Drawings, the Specifications, and all Addenda issued prior to and all Modifications issued after execution of the Contract. A Modification is (1) a written amendment to the Contract signed by both parties, (2) a Change Order, (3) a written interpretation issued by the Architect pursuant to Subparagraph 2.2.8, or (4) a written order for a minor change in the Work issued by the Architect pursuant to Paragraph 12.3. The Contract Documents do not include Bidding Documents such as the Advertisement or Invitation to Bid, the Instructions to Bidders, sample forms, the Contractor's Bid or portions of Addenda relating to any of these, or any other documents, unless specifically enumerated in the Owner-Contractor Agreement.

1.1.2 THE CONTRACT

The Contract Documents form the Contract for Construction. This Contract represents the entire and integrated agreement between the parties hereto and supersedes all prior negotiations, representations, or agreements, either written or oral. The Contract may be amended or modified only by a Modification as defined in Subparagraph 1.1.1. The Contract Documents shall not be construed to create any contractual relationship of any kind between the Architect and the Contractor, but the Architect shall be entitled to performance of obligations intended for his benefit, and to enforcement thereof. Nothing contained in the Contract Documents shall create any contractual relationship between the Owner or the Architect and any Subcontractor or Sub-subcontractor.

1.1.3 THE WORK

The Work comprises the completed construction required by the Contract Documents and includes all labor necessary to produce such construction, and all materials and equipment incorporated or to be incorporated in such construction.

1.1.4 THE PROJECT

The Project is the total construction of which the Work performed under the Contract Documents may be the whole or a part.

1.2 EXECUTION, CORRELATION AND INTENT

1.2.1 The Contract Documents shall be signed in not less than triplicate by the Owner and Contractor. If either the Owner or the Contractor or both do not sign the Conditions of the Contract, Drawings, Specifications, or any of the other Contract Documents, the Architect shall identify such Documents.

1.2.2 By executing the Contract, the Contractor represents that he has visited the site, familiarized himself with the local conditions under which the Work is to be performed, and correlated his observations with the requirements of the Contract Documents.

1.2.3 The intent of the Contract Documents is to include all items necessary for the proper execution and completion of the Work. The Contract Documents are complementary, and what is required by any one shall be as binding as if required by all. Work not covered in the Contract Documents will not be required unless it is consistent therewith and is reasonably inferable therefrom as being necessary to produce the intended results. Words and abbreviations which have well-known technical or trade meanings are used in the Contract Documents in accordance with such recognized meanings.

1.2.4 The organization of the Specifications into divisions, sections and articles, and the arrangement of Drawings shall not control the Contractor in dividing the Work among Subcontractors or in establishing the extent of Work to be performed by any trade.

1.3 OWNERSHIP AND USE OF DOCUMENTS

1.3.1 All Drawings, Specifications and copies thereof furnished by the Architect are and shall remain his property. They are to be used only with respect to this Project and are not to be used on any other project. With the exception of one contract set for each party to the Contract, such documents are to be returned or suitably accounted for to the Architect on request at the completion of the Work. Submission or distribution to meet official regulatory requirements or for other purposes in connection with the Project is not to be construed as publication in derogation of the Architect's common law copyright or other reserved rights.

ARTICLE 2

ARCHITECT

2.1 DEFINITION

2.1.1 The Architect is the person lawfully licensed to practice architecture, or an entity lawfully practicing architecture identified as such in the Owner-Contractor Agreement, and is referred to throughout the Contract Documents as if singular in number and masculine in gender. The term Architect means the Architect or his authorized representative.

2.2 ADMINISTRATION OF THE CONTRACT

2.2.1 The Architect will provide administration of the Contract as hereinafter described.

2.2.2 The Architect will be the Owner's representative during construction and until final payment is due. The Architect will advise and consult with the Owner. The Owner's instructions to the Contractor shall be forwarded

2

through the Architect. The Architect will have authority to act on behalf of the Owner only to the extent provided in the Contract Documents, unless otherwise modified by written instrument in accordance with Subparagraph 2.2.18.

2.2.3 The Architect will visit the site at intervals appropriate to the stage of construction to familiarize himself generally with the progress and quality of the Work and to determine in general if the Work is proceeding in accordance with the Contract Documents. However, the Architect will not be required to make exhaustive or continuous on-site inspections to check the quality or quantity of the Work. On the basis of his on-site observations as an architect, he will keep the Owner informed of the progress of the Work, and will endeavor to guard the Owner against defects and deficiencies in the Work of the Contractor.

2.2.4 The Architect will not be responsible for and will not have control or charge of construction means, methods, techniques, sequences or procedures, or for safety precautions and programs in connection with the Work, and he will not be responsible for the Contractor's failure to carry out the Work in accordance with the Contract Documents. The Architect will not be responsible for or have control or charge over the acts or omissions of the Contractor, Subcontractors, or any of their agents or employees, or any other persons performing any of the Work.

2.2.5 The Architect shall at all times have access to the Work wherever it is in preparation and progress. The Contractor shall provide facilities for such access so the Architect may perform his functions under the Contract Documents.

2.2.6 Based on the Architect's observations and an evaluation of the Contractor's Applications for Payment, the Architect will determine the amounts owing to the Contractor and will issue Certificates for Payment in such amounts, as provided in Paragraph 9.4.

2.2.7 The Architect will be the interpreter of the requirements of the Contract Documents and the judge of the performance thereunder by both the Owner and Contractor.

2.2.8 The Architect will render interpretations necessary for the proper execution or progress of the Work, with reasonable promptness and in accordance with any time limit agreed upon. Either party to the Contract may make written request to the Architect for such interpretations.

2.2.9 Claims, disputes and other matters in question between the Contractor and the Owner relating to the execution or progress of the Work or the interpretation of the Contract Documents shall be referred initially to the Architect for decision which he will render in writing within a reasonable time.

2.2.10 All interpretations and decisions of the Architect shall be consistent with the intent of and reasonably inferable from the Contract Documents and will be in writing or in the form of drawings. In his capacity as interpreter and judge, he will endeavor to secure faithful performance by both the Owner and the Contractor, will not

show partiality to either, and will not be liable for the result of any interpretation or decision rendered in good faith in such capacity.

2.2.11 The Architect's decisions in matters relating to artistic effect will be final if consistent with the intent of the Contract Documents.

2.2.12 Any claim, dispute or other matter in question between the Contractor and the Owner referred to the Architect, except those relating to artistic effect as provided in Subparagraph 2.2.11 and except those which have been waived by the making or acceptance of final payment as provided in Subparagraphs 9.9.4 and 9.9.5, shall be subject to arbitration upon the written demand of either party. However, no demand for arbitration of any such claim, dispute or other matter may be made until the earlier of (1) the date on which the Architect has rendered a written decision, or (2) the tenth day after the parties have presented their evidence to the Architect or have been given a reasonable opportunity to do so, if the Architect has not rendered his written decision by that date. When such a written decision of the Architect states (1) that the decision is final but subject to appeal, and (2) that any demand for arbitration of a claim, dispute or other matter covered by such decision must be made within thirty days after the date on which the party making the demand receives the written decision, failure to demand arbitration within said thirty days' period will result in the Architect's decision becoming final and binding upon the Owner and the Contractor. If the Architect renders a decision after arbitration proceedings have been initiated, such decision may be entered as evidence but will not supersede any arbitration proceedings unless the decision is acceptable to all parties concerned.

2.2.13 The Architect will have authority to reject Work which does not conform to the Contract Documents. Whenever, in his opinion, he considers it necessary or advisable for the implementation of the intent of the Contract Documents, he will have authority to require special inspection or testing of the Work in accordance with Subparagraph 7.7.2 whether or not such Work be then fabricated, installed or completed. However, neither the Architect's authority to act under this Subparagraph 2.2.13, nor any decision made by him in good faith either to exercise or not to exercise such authority, shall give rise to any duty or responsibility of the Architect to the Contractor, any Subcontractor, any of their agents or employees, or any other person performing any of the Work.

2.2.14 The Architect will review and approve or take other appropriate action upon Contractor's submittals such as Shop Drawings, Product Data and Samples, but only for conformance with the design concept of the Work and with the information given in the Contract Documents. Such action shall be taken with reasonable promptness so as to cause no delay. The Architect's approval of a specific item shall not indicate approval of an assembly of which the item is a component.

2.2.15 The Architect will prepare Change Orders in accordance with Article 12, and will have authority to order minor changes in the Work as provided in Subparagraph 12.4.1.

3

2.2.16 The Architect will conduct inspections to determine the dates of Substantial Completion and final completion, will receive and forward to the Owner for the Owner's review written warranties and related documents required by the Contract and assembled by the Contractor, and will issue a final Certificate for Payment upon compliance with the requirements of Paragraph 9.9.

2.2.17 If the Owner and Architect agree, the Architect will provide one or more Project Representatives to assist the Architect in carrying out his responsibilities at the site. The duties, responsibilities and limitations of authority of any such Project Representative shall be as set forth in an exhibit to be incorporated in the Contract Documents.

2.2.18 The duties, responsibilities and limitations of authority of the Architect as the Owner's representative during construction as set forth in the Contract Documents will not be modified or extended without written consent of the Owner, the Contractor and the Architect.

2.2.19 In case of the termination of the employment of the Architect, the Owner shall appoint an architect against whom the Contractor makes no reasonable objection whose status under the Contract Documents shall be that of the former architect. Any dispute in connection with such appointment shall be subject to arbitration.

ARTICLE 3

OWNER

3.1 DEFINITION

3.1.1 The Owner is the person or entity identified as such in the Owner-Contractor Agreement and is referred to throughout the Contract Documents as if singular in number and masculine in gender. The term Owner means the Owner or his authorized representative.

3.2 INFORMATION AND SERVICES REQUIRED OF THE OWNER

3.2.1 The Owner shall, at the request of the Contractor, at the time of execution of the Owner-Contractor Agreement, furnish to the Contractor reasonable evidence that he has made financial arrangements to fulfill his obligations under the Contract. Unless such reasonable evidence is furnished, the Contractor is not required to execute the Owner-Contractor Agreement or to commence the Work.

3.2.2 The Owner shall furnish all surveys describing the physical characteristics, legal limitations and utility locations for the site of the Project, and a legal description of the site.

3.2.3 Except as provided in Subparagraph 4.7.1, the Owner shall secure and pay for necessary approvals, easements, assessments and charges required for the construction, use or occupancy of permanent structures or for permanent changes in existing facilities.

3.2.4 Information or services under the Owner's control shall be furnished by the Owner with reasonable promptness to avoid delay in the orderly progress of the Work.

3.2.5 Unless otherwise provided in the Contract Documents, the Contractor will be furnished, free of charge, all copies of Drawings and Specifications reasonably necessary for the execution of the Work.

3.2.6 The Owner shall forward all instructions to the Contractor through the Architect.

3.2.7 The foregoing are in addition to other duties and responsibilities of the Owner enumerated herein and especially those in respect to Work by Owner or by Separate Contractors, Payments and Completion, and Insurance in Articles 6, 9 and 11 respectively.

3.3 OWNER'S RIGHT TO STOP THE WORK

3.3.1 If the Contractor fails to correct defective Work as required by Paragraph 13.2 or persistently fails to carry out the Work in accordance with the Contract Documents, the Owner, by a written order signed personally or by an agent specifically so empowered by the Owner in writing, may order the Contractor to stop the Work, or any portion thereof, until the cause for such order has been eliminated; however, this right of the Owner to stop the Work shall not give rise to any duty on the part of the Owner to exercise this right for the benefit of the Contractor or any other person or entity, except to the extent required by Subparagraph 6.1.3.

3.4 OWNER'S RIGHT TO CARRY OUT THE WORK

3.4.1 If the Contractor defaults or neglects to carry out the Work in accordance with the Contract Documents and fails within seven days after receipt of written notice from the Owner to commence and continue correction of such default or neglect with diligence and promptness, the Owner may, after seven days following receipt by the Contractor of an additional written notice and without prejudice to any other remedy he may have, make good such deficiencies. In such case an appropriate Change Order shall be issued deducting from the payments then or thereafter due the Contractor the cost of correcting such deficiencies, including compensation for the Architect's additional services made necessary by such default, neglect or failure. Such action by the Owner and the amount charged to the Contractor are both subject to the prior approval of the Architect. If the payments then or thereafter due the Contractor are not sufficient to cover such amount, the Contractor shall pay the difference to the Owner.

ARTICLE 4

CONTRACTOR

4.1 DEFINITION

4.1.1 The Contractor is the person or entity identified as such in the Owner-Contractor Agreement and is referred to throughout the Contract Documents as if singular in number and masculine in gender. The term Contractor means the Contractor or his authorized representative.

4.2 REVIEW OF CONTRACT DOCUMENTS

4.2.1 The Contractor shall carefully study and compare the Contract Documents and shall at once report to the Architect any error, inconsistency or omission he may discover. The Contractor shall not be liable to the Owner or the Architect for any damage resulting from any such errors, inconsistencies or omissions in the Contract Documents. The Contractor shall perform no portion of the Work at any time without Contract Documents or, where required, approved Shop Drawings, Product Data or Samples for such portion of the Work.

4.3 SUPERVISION AND CONSTRUCTION PROCEDURES

4.3.1 The Contractor shall supervise and direct the Work, using his best skill and attention. He shall be solely responsible for all construction means, methods, techniques, sequences and procedures and for coordinating all portions of the Work under the Contract.

4.3.2 The Contractor shall be responsible to the Owner for the acts and omissions of his employees, Subcontractors and their agents and employees, and other persons performing any of the Work under a contract with the Contractor.

4.3.3 The Contractor shall not be relieved from his obligations to perform the Work in accordance with the Contract Documents either by the activities or duties of the Architect in his administration of the Contract, or by inspections, tests or approvals required or performed under Paragraph 7.7 by persons other than the Contractor.

4.4 LABOR AND MATERIALS

4.4.1 Unless otherwise provided in the Contract Documents, the Contractor shall provide and pay for all labor, materials, equipment, tools, construction equipment and machinery, water, heat, utilities, transportation, and other facilities and services necessary for the proper execution and completion of the Work, whether temporary or permanent and whether or not incorporated or to be incorporated in the Work.

4.4.2 The Contractor shall at all times enforce strict discipline and good order among his employees and shall not employ on the Work any unfit person or anyone not skilled in the task assigned to him.

4.5 WARRANTY

4.5.1 The Contractor warrants to the Owner and the Architect that all materials and equipment furnished under this Contract will be new unless otherwise specified, and that all Work will be of good quality, free from faults and defects and in conformance with the Contract Documents. All Work not conforming to these requirements, including substitutions not properly approved and authorized, may be considered defective. If required by the Architect, the Contractor shall furnish satisfactory evidence as to the kind and quality of materials and equipment. This warranty is not limited by the provisions of Paragraph 13.2.

4.6 TAXES

4.6.1 The Contractor shall pay all sales, consumer, use and other similar taxes for the Work or portions thereof provided by the Contractor which are legally enacted at the time bids are received, whether or not yet effective.

4.7 PERMITS, FEES AND NOTICES

4.7.1 Unless otherwise provided in the Contract Documents, the Contractor shall secure and pay for the building permit and for all other permits and governmental fees, licenses and inspections necessary for the proper execution and completion of the Work which are customarily secured after execution of the Contract and which are legally required at the time the bids are received.

4.7.2 The Contractor shall give all notices and comply with all laws, ordinances, rules, regulations and lawful orders of any public authority bearing on the performance of the Work.

4.7.3 It is not the responsibility of the Contractor to make certain that the Contract Documents are in accordance with applicable laws, statutes, building codes and regulations. If the Contractor observes that any of the Contract Documents are at variance therewith in any respect, he shall promptly notify the Architect in writing, and any necessary changes shall be accomplished by appropriate Modification.

4.7.4 If the Contractor performs any Work knowing it to be contrary to such laws, ordinances, rules and regulations, and without such notice to the Architect, he shall assume full responsibility therefor and shall bear all costs attributable thereto.

4.8 ALLOWANCES

4.8.1 The Contractor shall include in the Contract Sum all allowances stated in the Contract Documents. Items covered by these allowances shall be supplied for such amounts and by such persons as the Owner may direct, but the Contractor will not be required to employ persons against whom he makes a reasonable objection.

4.8.2 Unless otherwise provided in the Contract Documents:

  .1 these allowances shall cover the cost to the Contractor, less any applicable trade discount, of the materials and equipment required by the allowance delivered at the site, and all applicable taxes;

  .2 the Contractor's costs for unloading and handling on the site, labor, installation costs, overhead, profit and other expenses contemplated for the original allowance shall be included in the Contract Sum and not in the allowance;

  .3 whenever the cost is more than or less than the allowance, the Contract Sum shall be adjusted accordingly by Change Order, the amount of which will recognize changes, if any, in handling costs on the site, labor, installation costs, overhead, profit and other expenses.

4.9 SUPERINTENDENT

4.9.1 The Contractor shall employ a competent superintendent and necessary assistants who shall be in attendance at the Project site during the progress of the Work. The superintendent shall represent the Contractor and all communications given to the superintendent shall be as binding as if given to the Contractor. Important communications shall be confirmed in writing. Other communications shall be so confirmed on written request in each case.

4.10 PROGRESS SCHEDULE

4.10.1 The Contractor, immediately after being awarded the Contract, shall prepare and submit for the Owner's and Architect's information an estimated progress schedule for the Work. The progress schedule shall be related to the entire Project to the extent required by the Contract Documents, and shall provide for expeditious and practicable execution of the Work.

4.11 DOCUMENTS AND SAMPLES AT THE SITE

4.11.1 The Contractor shall maintain at the site for the Owner one record copy of all Drawings, Specifications, Addenda, Change Orders and other Modifications, in good order and marked currently to record all changes made during construction, and approved Shop Drawings, Product Data and Samples. These shall be available to the Architect and shall be delivered to him for the Owner upon completion of the Work.

4.12 SHOP DRAWINGS, PRODUCT DATA AND SAMPLES

4.12.1 Shop Drawings are drawings, diagrams, schedules and other data specially prepared for the Work by the Contractor or any Subcontractor, manufacturer, supplier or distributor to illustrate some portion of the Work.

4.12.2 Product Data are illustrations, standard schedules, performance charts, instructions, brochures, diagrams and other information furnished by the Contractor to illustrate a material, product or system for some portion of the Work.

4.12.3 Samples are physical examples which illustrate materials, equipment or workmanship and establish standards by which the Work will be judged.

4.12.4 The Contractor shall review, approve and submit, with reasonable promptness and in such sequence as to cause no delay in the Work or in the work of the Owner or any separate contractor, all Shop Drawings, Product Data and Samples required by the Contract Documents.

4.12.5 By approving and submitting Shop Drawings, Product Data and Samples, the Contractor represents that he has determined and verified all materials, field measurements, and field construction criteria related thereto, or will do so, and that he has checked and coordinated the information contained within such submittals with the requirements of the Work and of the Contract Documents.

4.12.6 The Contractor shall not be relieved of responsibility for any deviation from the requirements of the Contract Documents by the Architect's approval of Shop Drawings, Product Data or Samples under Subparagraph 2.2.14 unless the Contractor has specifically informed the Architect in writing of such deviation at the time of submission and the Architect has given written approval to the specific deviation. The Contractor shall not be relieved from responsibility for errors or omissions in the Shop Drawings, Product Data or Samples by the Architect's approval thereof.

4.12.7 The Contractor shall direct specific attention, in writing or on resubmitted Shop Drawings, Product Data or Samples, to revisions other than those requested by the Architect on previous submittals.

4.12.8 No portion of the Work requiring submission of a Shop Drawing, Product Data or Sample shall be commenced until the submittal has been approved by the Architect as provided in Subparagraph 2.2.14. All such

portions of the Work shall be in accordance with approved submittals.

4.13 USE OF SITE

4.13.1 The Contractor shall confine operations at the site to areas permitted by law, ordinances, permits and the Contract Documents and shall not unreasonably encumber the site with any materials or equipment.

4.14 CUTTING AND PATCHING OF WORK

4.14.1 The Contractor shall be responsible for all cutting, fitting or patching that may be required to complete the Work or to make its several parts fit together properly.

4.14.2 The Contractor shall not damage or endanger any portion of the Work or the work of the Owner or any separate contractors by cutting, patching or otherwise altering any work, or by excavation. The Contractor shall not cut or otherwise alter the work of the Owner or any separate contractor except with the written consent of the Owner and of such separate contractor. The Contractor shall not unreasonably withhold from the Owner or any separate contractor his consent to cutting or otherwise altering the Work.

4.15 CLEANING UP

4.15.1 The Contractor at all times shall keep the premises free from accumulation of waste materials or rubbish caused by his operations. At the completion of the Work he shall remove all his waste materials and rubbish from and about the Project as well as all his tools, construction equipment, machinery and surplus materials.

4.15.2 If the Contractor fails to clean up at the completion of the Work, the Owner may do so as provided in Paragraph 3.4 and the cost thereof shall be charged to the Contractor.

4.16 COMMUNICATIONS

4.16.1 The Contractor shall forward all communications to the Owner through the Architect.

4.17 ROYALTIES AND PATENTS

4.17.1 The Contractor shall pay all royalties and license fees. He shall defend all suits or claims for infringement of any patent rights and shall save the Owner harmless from loss on account thereof, except that the Owner shall be responsible for all such loss when a particular design, process or the product of a particular manufacturer or manufacturers is specified, but if the Contractor has reason to believe that the design, process or product specified is an infringement of a patent, he shall be responsible for such loss unless he promptly gives such information to the Architect.

4.18 INDEMNIFICATION

4.18.1 To the fullest extent permitted by law, the Contractor shall indemnify and hold harmless the Owner and the Architect and their agents and employees from and against all claims, damages, losses and expenses, including but not limited to attorneys' fees, arising out of or resulting from the performance of the Work, provided that any such claim, damage, loss or expense (1) is attributable to bodily injury, sickness, disease or death, or to injury to or destruction of tangible property (other than the Work itself) including the loss of use resulting therefrom,

6

and (2) is caused in whole or in part by any negligent act or omission of the Contractor, any Subcontractor, anyone directly or indirectly employed by any of them or anyone for whose acts any of them may be liable, regardless of whether or not it is caused in part by a party indemnified hereunder. Such obligation shall not be construed to negate, abridge, or otherwise reduce any other right or obligation of indemnity which would otherwise exist as to any party or person described in this Paragraph 4.18.

4.18.2 In any and all claims against the Owner or the Architect or any of their agents or employees by any employee of the Contractor, any Subcontractor, anyone directly or indirectly employed by any of them or anyone for whose acts any of them may be liable, the indemnification obligation under this Paragraph 4.18 shall not be limited in any way by any limitation on the amount or type of damages, compensation or benefits payable by or for the Contractor or any Subcontractor under workers' or workmen's compensation acts, disability benefit acts or other employee benefit acts.

4.18.3 The obligations of the Contractor under this Paragraph 4.18 shall not extend to the liability of the Architect, his agents or employees, arising out of (1) the preparation or approval of maps, drawings, opinions, reports, surveys, change orders, designs or specifications, or (2) the giving of or the failure to give directions or instructions by the Architect, his agents or employees providing such giving or failure to give is the primary cause of the injury or damage.

ARTICLE 5

SUBCONTRACTORS

5.1 DEFINITION

5.1.1 A Subcontractor is a person or entity who has a direct contract with the Contractor to perform any of the Work at the site. The term Subcontractor is referred to throughout the Contract Documents as if singular in number and masculine in gender and means a Subcontractor or his authorized representative. The term Subcontractor does not include any separate contractor or his subcontractors.

5.1.2 A Sub-subcontractor is a person or entity who has a direct or indirect contract with a Subcontractor to perform any of the Work at the site. The term Sub-subcontractor is referred to throughout the Contract Documents as if singular in number and masculine in gender and means a Sub-subcontractor or an authorized representative thereof.

5.2 AWARD OF SUBCONTRACTS AND OTHER CONTRACTS FOR PORTIONS OF THE WORK

5.2.1 Unless otherwise required by the Contract Documents or the Bidding Documents, the Contractor, as soon as practicable after the award of the Contract, shall furnish to the Owner and the Architect in writing the names of the persons or entities (including those who are to furnish materials or equipment fabricated to a special design) proposed for each of the principal portions of the Work. The Architect will promptly reply to the Contractor in writing stating whether or not the Owner or the Architect, after due investigation, has reasonable objection to any such proposed person or entity. Failure of the Owner or Architect to reply promptly shall constitute notice of no reasonable objection.

5.2.2 The Contractor shall not contract with any such proposed person or entity to whom the Owner or the Architect has made reasonable objection under the provisions of Subparagraph 5.2.1. The Contractor shall not be required to contract with anyone to whom he has a reasonable objection.

5.2.3 If the Owner or the Architect has reasonable objection to any such proposed person or entity, the Contractor shall submit a substitute to whom the Owner or the Architect has no reasonable objection, and the Contract Sum shall be increased or decreased by the difference in cost occasioned by such substitution and an appropriate Change Order shall be issued; however, no increase in the Contract Sum shall be allowed for any such substitution unless the Contractor has acted promptly and responsively in submitting names as required by Subparagraph 5.2.1.

5.2.4 The Contractor shall make no substitution for any Subcontractor, person or entity previously selected if the Owner or Architect makes reasonable objection to such substitution.

5.3 SUBCONTRACTUAL RELATIONS

5.3.1 By an appropriate agreement, written where legally required for validity, the Contractor shall require each Subcontractor, to the extent of the Work to be performed by the Subcontractor, to be bound to the Contractor by the terms of the Contract Documents, and to assume toward the Contractor all the obligations and responsibilities which the Contractor, by these Documents, assumes toward the Owner and the Architect. Said agreement shall preserve and protect the rights of the Owner and the Architect under the Contract Documents with respect to the Work to be performed by the Subcontractor so that the subcontracting thereof will not prejudice such rights, and shall allow to the Subcontractor, unless specifically provided otherwise in the Contractor-Subcontractor agreement, the benefit of all rights, remedies and redress against the Contractor that the Contractor, by these Documents, has against the Owner. Where appropriate, the Contractor shall require each Subcontractor to enter into similar agreements with his Sub-subcontractors. The Contractor shall make available to each proposed Subcontractor, prior to the execution of the Subcontract, copies of the Contract Documents to which the Subcontractor will be bound by this Paragraph 5.3, and identify to the Subcontractor any terms and conditions of the proposed Subcontract which may be at variance with the Contract Documents. Each Subcontractor shall similarly make copies of such Documents available to his Sub-subcontractors.

ARTICLE 6

WORK BY OWNER OR BY SEPARATE CONTRACTORS

6.1 OWNER'S RIGHT TO PERFORM WORK AND TO AWARD SEPARATE CONTRACTS

6.1.1 The Owner reserves the right to perform work related to the Project with his own forces, and to award

7

536

separate contracts in connection with other portions of the Project or other work on the site under these or similar Conditions of the Contract. If the Contractor claims that delay or additional cost is involved because of such action by the Owner, he shall make such claim as provided elsewhere in the Contract Documents.

6.1.2 When separate contracts are awarded for different portions of the Project or other work on the site, the term Contractor in the Contract Documents in each case shall mean the Contractor who executes each separate Owner-Contractor Agreement.

6.1.3 The Owner will provide for the coordination of the work of his own forces and of each separate contractor with the Work of the Contractor, who shall cooperate therewith as provided in Paragraph 6.2.

6.2 MUTUAL RESPONSIBILITY

6.2.1 The Contractor shall afford the Owner and separate contractors reasonable opportunity for the introduction and storage of their materials and equipment and the execution of their work, and shall connect and coordinate his Work with theirs as required by the Contract Documents.

6.2.2 If any part of the Contractor's Work depends for proper execution or results upon the work of the Owner or any separate contractor, the Contractor shall, prior to proceeding with the Work, promptly report to the Architect any apparent discrepancies or defects in such other work that render it unsuitable for such proper execution and results. Failure of the Contractor so to report shall constitute an acceptance of the Owner's or separate contractors' work as fit and proper to receive his Work, except as to defects which may subsequently become apparent in such work by others.

6.2.3 Any costs caused by defective or ill-timed work shall be borne by the party responsible therefor.

6.2.4 Should the Contractor wrongfully cause damage to the work or property of the Owner, or to other work on the site, the Contractor shall promptly remedy such damage as provided in Subparagraph 10.2.5.

6.2.5 Should the Contractor wrongfully cause damage to the work or property of any separate contractor, the Contractor shall upon due notice promptly attempt to settle with such other contractor by agreement, or otherwise to resolve the dispute. If such separate contractor sues or initiates an arbitration proceeding against the Owner on account of any damage alleged to have been caused by the Contractor, the Owner shall notify the Contractor who shall defend such proceedings at the Owner's expense, and if any judgment or award against the Owner arises therefrom the Contractor shall pay or satisfy it and shall reimburse the Owner for all attorneys' fees and court or arbitration costs which the Owner has incurred.

6.3 OWNER'S RIGHT TO CLEAN UP

6.3.1 If a dispute arises between the Contractor and separate contractors as to their responsibility for cleaning up as required by Paragraph 4.15, the Owner may clean up and charge the cost thereof to the contractors responsible therefor as the Architect shall determine to be just.

ARTICLE 7

MISCELLANEOUS PROVISIONS

7.1 GOVERNING LAW

7.1.1 The Contract shall be governed by the law of the place where the Project is located.

7.2 SUCCESSORS AND ASSIGNS

7.2.1 The Owner and the Contractor each binds himself, his partners, successors, assigns and legal representatives to the other party hereto and to the partners, successors, assigns and legal representatives of such other party in respect to all covenants, agreements and obligations contained in the Contract Documents. Neither party to the Contract shall assign the Contract or sublet it as a whole without the written consent of the other, nor shall the Contractor assign any moneys due or to become due to him hereunder, without the previous written consent of the Owner.

7.3 WRITTEN NOTICE

7.3.1 Written notice shall be deemed to have been duly served if delivered in person to the individual or member of the firm or entity or to an officer of the corporation for whom it was intended, or if delivered at or sent by registered or certified mail to the last business address known to him who gives the notice.

7.4 CLAIMS FOR DAMAGES

7.4.1 Should either party to the Contract suffer injury or damage to person or property because of any act or omission of the other party or of any of his employees, agents or others for whose acts he is legally liable, claim shall be made in writing to such other party within a reasonable time after the first observance of such injury or damage.

7.5 PERFORMANCE BOND AND LABOR AND MATERIAL PAYMENT BOND

7.5.1 The Owner shall have the right to require the Contractor to furnish bonds covering the faithful performance of the Contract and the payment of all obligations arising thereunder if and as required in the Bidding Documents or in the Contract Documents.

7.6 RIGHTS AND REMEDIES

7.6.1 The duties and obligations imposed by the Contract Documents and the rights and remedies available thereunder shall be in addition to and not a limitation of any duties, obligations, rights and remedies otherwise imposed or available by law.

7.6.2 No action or failure to act by the Owner, Architect or Contractor shall constitute a waiver of any right or duty afforded any of them under the Contract, nor shall any such action or failure to act constitute an approval of or acquiescence in any breach thereunder, except as may be specifically agreed in writing.

8

7.7 TESTS

7.7.1 If the Contract Documents, laws, ordinances, rules, regulations or orders of any public authority having jurisdiction require any portion of the Work to be inspected, tested or approved, the Contractor shall give the Architect timely notice of its readiness so the Architect may observe such inspection, testing or approval. The Contractor shall bear all costs of such inspections, tests or approvals conducted by public authorities. Unless otherwise provided, the Owner shall bear all costs of other inspections, tests or approvals.

7.7.2 If the Architect determines that any Work requires special inspection, testing, or approval which Subparagraph 7.7.1 does not include, he will, upon written authorization from the Owner, instruct the Contractor to order such special inspection, testing or approval, and the Contractor shall give notice as provided in Subparagraph 7.7.1. If such special inspection or testing reveals a failure of the Work to comply with the requirements of the Contract Documents, the Contractor shall bear all costs thereof, including compensation for the Architect's additional services made necessary by such failure; otherwise the Owner shall bear such costs, and an appropriate Change Order shall be issued.

7.7.3 Required certificates of inspection, testing or approval shall be secured by the Contractor and promptly delivered by him to the Architect.

7.7.4 If the Architect is to observe the inspections, tests or approvals required by the Contract Documents, he will do so promptly and, where practicable, at the source of supply.

7.8 INTEREST

7.8.1 Payments due and unpaid under the Contract Documents shall bear interest from the date payment is due at such rate as the parties may agree upon in writing or, in the absence thereof, at the legal rate prevailing at the place of the Project.

7.9 ARBITRATION

7.9.1 All claims, disputes and other matters in question between the Contractor and the Owner arising out of, or relating to, the Contract Documents or the breach thereof, except as provided in Subparagraph 2.2.11 with respect to the Architect's decisions on matters relating to artistic effect, and except for claims which have been waived by the making or acceptance of final payment as provided by Subparagraphs 9.9.4 and 9.9.5, shall be decided by arbitration in accordance with the Construction Industry Arbitration Rules of the American Arbitration Association then obtaining unless the parties mutually agree otherwise. No arbitration arising out of or relating to the Contract Documents shall include, by consolidation, joinder or in any other manner, the Architect, his employees or consultants except by written consent containing a specific reference to the Owner-Contractor Agreement and signed by the Architect, the Owner, the Contractor and any other person sought to be joined. No arbitration shall include by consolidation, joinder or in any other manner, parties other than the Owner, the Contractor and any other persons substantially involved in a common question of fact or law, whose presence is required if complete relief is to be accorded in the arbitration. No person other than the Owner or Contractor shall be included as an original third party or additional third party to an arbitration whose interest or responsibility is insubstantial. Any consent to arbitration involving an additional person or persons shall not constitute consent to arbitration of any dispute not described therein or with any person not named or described therein. The foregoing agreement to arbitrate and any other agreement to arbitrate with an additional person or persons duly consented to by the parties to the Owner-Contractor Agreement shall be specifically enforceable under the prevailing arbitration law. The award rendered by the arbitrators shall be final, and judgment may be entered upon it in accordance with applicable law in any court having jurisdiction thereof.

7.9.2 Notice of the demand for arbitration shall be filed in writing with the other party to the Owner-Contractor Agreement and with the American Arbitration Association, and a copy shall be filed with the Architect. The demand for arbitration shall be made within the time limits specified in Subparagraph 2.2.12 where applicable, and in all other cases within a reasonable time after the claim, dispute or other matter in question has arisen, and in no event shall it be made after the date when institution of legal or equitable proceedings based on such claim, dispute or other matter in question would be barred by the applicable statute of limitations.

7.9.3 Unless otherwise agreed in writing, the Contractor shall carry on the Work and maintain its progress during any arbitration proceedings, and the Owner shall continue to make payments to the Contractor in accordance with the Contract Documents.

ARTICLE 8

TIME

8.1 DEFINITIONS

8.1.1 Unless otherwise provided, the Contract Time is the period of time allotted in the Contract Documents for Substantial Completion of the Work as defined in Subparagraph 8.1.3, including authorized adjustments thereto.

8.1.2 The date of commencement of the Work is the date established in a notice to proceed. If there is no notice to proceed, it shall be the date of the Owner-Contractor Agreement or such other date as may be established therein.

8.1.3 The Date of Substantial Completion of the Work or designated portion thereof is the Date certified by the Architect when construction is sufficiently complete, in accordance with the Contract Documents, so the Owner can occupy or utilize the Work or designated portion thereof for the use for which it is intended.

8.1.4 The term day as used in the Contract Documents shall mean calendar day unless otherwise specifically designated.

8.2 PROGRESS AND COMPLETION

8.2.1 All time limits stated in the Contract Documents are of the essence of the Contract.

9

8.2.2 The Contractor shall begin the Work on the date of commencement as defined in Subparagraph 8.1.2. He shall carry the Work forward expeditiously with adequate forces and shall achieve Substantial Completion within the Contract Time.

8.3 DELAYS AND EXTENSIONS OF TIME

8.3.1 If the Contractor is delayed at any time in the progress of the Work by any act or neglect of the Owner or the Architect, or by any employee of either, or by any separate contractor employed by the Owner, or by changes ordered in the Work, or by labor disputes, fire, unusual delay in transportation, adverse weather conditions not reasonably anticipatable, unavoidable casualties, or any causes beyond the Contractor's control, or by delay authorized by the Owner pending arbitration, or by any other cause which the Architect determines may justify the delay, then the Contract Time shall be extended by Change Order for such reasonable time as the Architect may determine.

8.3.2 Any claim for extension of time shall be made in writing to the Architect not more than twenty days after the commencement of the delay; otherwise it shall be waived. In the case of a continuing delay only one claim is necessary. The Contractor shall provide an estimate of the probable effect of such delay on the progress of the Work.

8.3.3 If no agreement is made stating the dates upon which interpretations as provided in Subparagraph 2.2.8 shall be furnished, then no claim for delay shall be allowed on account of failure to furnish such interpretations until fifteen days after written request is made for them, and not then unless such claim is reasonable.

8.3.4 This Paragraph 8.3 does not exclude the recovery of damages for delay by either party under other provisions of the Contract Documents.

ARTICLE 9

PAYMENTS AND COMPLETION

9.1 CONTRACT SUM

9.1.1 The Contract Sum is stated in the Owner-Contractor Agreement and, including authorized adjustments thereto, is the total amount payable by the Owner to the Contractor for the performance of the Work under the Contract Documents.

9.2 SCHEDULE OF VALUES

9.2.1 Before the first Application for Payment, the Contractor shall submit to the Architect a schedule of values allocated to the various portions of the Work, prepared in such form and supported by such data to substantiate its accuracy as the Architect may require. This schedule, unless objected to by the Architect, shall be used only as a basis for the Contractor's Applications for Payment.

9.3 APPLICATIONS FOR PAYMENT

9.3.1 At least ten days before the date for each progress payment established in the Owner-Contractor Agreement, the Contractor shall submit to the Architect an itemized Application for Payment, notarized if required, supported

by such data substantiating the Contractor's right to payment as the Owner or the Architect may require, and reflecting retainage, if any, as provided elsewhere in the Contract Documents.

9.3.2 Unless otherwise provided in the Contract Documents, payments will be made on account of materials or equipment not incorporated in the Work but delivered and suitably stored at the site and, if approved in advance by the Owner, payments may similarly be made for materials or equipment suitably stored at some other location agreed upon in writing. Payments for materials or equipment stored on or off the site shall be conditioned upon submission by the Contractor of bills of sale or such other procedures satisfactory to the Owner to establish the Owner's title to such materials or equipment or otherwise protect the Owner's interest, including applicable insurance and transportation to the site for those materials and equipment stored off the site.

9.3.3 The Contractor warrants that title to all Work, materials and equipment covered by an Application for Payment will pass to the Owner either by incorporation in the construction or upon the receipt of payment by the Contractor, whichever occurs first, free and clear of all liens, claims, security interests or encumbrances, hereinafter referred to in this Article 9 as "liens"; and that no Work, materials or equipment covered by an Application for Payment will have been acquired by the Contractor, or by any other person performing Work at the site or furnishing materials and equipment for the Project, subject to an agreement under which an interest therein or an encumbrance thereon is retained by the seller or otherwise imposed by the Contractor or such other person.

9.4 CERTIFICATES FOR PAYMENT

9.4.1 The Architect will, within seven days after the receipt of the Contractor's Application for Payment, either issue a Certificate for Payment to the Owner, with a copy to the Contractor, for such amount as the Architect determines is properly due, or notify the Contractor in writing his reasons for withholding a Certificate as provided in Subparagraph 9.6.1.

9.4.2 The issuance of a Certificate for Payment will constitute a representation by the Architect to the Owner, based on his observations at the site as provided in Subparagraph 2.2.3 and the data comprising the Application for Payment, that the Work has progressed to the point indicated; that, to the best of his knowledge, information and belief, the quality of the Work is in accordance with the Contract Documents (subject to an evaluation of the Work for conformance with the Contract Documents upon Substantial Completion, to the results of any subsequent tests required by or performed under the Contract Documents, to minor deviations from the Contract Documents correctable prior to completion, and to any specific qualifications stated in his Certificate); and that the Contractor is entitled to payment in the amount certified. However, by issuing a Certificate for Payment, the Architect shall not thereby be deemed to represent that he has made exhaustive or continuous on-site inspections to check the quality or quantity of the Work or that he has reviewed the construction means, methods, techniques, sequences or procedures, or that he has made any examination to ascertain how or for what purpose the Contractor has used the moneys previously paid on account of the Contract Sum.

9.5 PROGRESS PAYMENTS

9.5.1 After the Architect has issued a Certificate for Payment, the Owner shall make payment in the manner and within the time provided in the Contract Documents.

9.5.2 The Contractor shall promptly pay each Subcontractor, upon receipt of payment from the Owner, out of the amount paid to the Contractor on account of such Subcontractor's Work, the amount to which said Subcontractor is entitled, reflecting the percentage actually retained, if any, from payments to the Contractor on account of such Subcontractor's Work. The Contractor shall, by an appropriate agreement with each Subcontractor, require each Subcontractor to make payments to his Subsubcontractors in similar manner.

9.5.3 The Architect may, on request and at his discretion, furnish to any Subcontractor, if practicable, information regarding the percentages of completion or the amounts applied for by the Contractor and the action taken thereon by the Architect on account of Work done by such Subcontractor.

9.5.4 Neither the Owner nor the Architect shall have any obligation to pay or to see to the payment of any moneys to any Subcontractor except as may otherwise be required by law.

9.5.5 No Certificate for a progress payment, nor any progress payment, nor any partial or entire use or occupancy of the Project by the Owner, shall constitute an acceptance of any Work not in accordance with the Contract Documents.

9.6 PAYMENTS WITHHELD

9.6.1 The Architect may decline to certify payment and may withhold his Certificate in whole or in part, to the extent necessary reasonably to protect the Owner, if in his opinion he is unable to make representations to the Owner as provided in Subparagraph 9.4.2. If the Architect is unable to make representations to the Owner as provided in Subparagraph 9.4.2 and to certify payment in the amount of the Application, he will notify the Contractor as provided in Subparagraph 9.4.1. If the Contractor and the Architect cannot agree on a revised amount, the Architect will promptly issue a Certificate for Payment for the amount for which he is able to make such representations to the Owner. The Architect may also decline to certify payment or, because of subsequently discovered evidence or subsequent observations, he may nullify the whole or any part of any Certificate for Payment previously issued, to such extent as may be necessary in his opinion to protect the Owner from loss because of:

.1 defective work not remedied,

.2 third party claims filed or reasonable evidence indicating probable filing of such claims,

.3 failure of the Contractor to make payments properly to Subcontractors or for labor, materials or equipment,

.4 reasonable evidence that the Work cannot be completed for the unpaid balance of the Contract Sum,

.5 damage to the Owner or another contractor,

.6 reasonable evidence that the Work will not be completed within the Contract Time, or

.7 persistent failure to carry out the Work in accordance with the Contract Documents.

9.6.2 When the above grounds in Subparagraph 9.6.1 are removed, payment shall be made for amounts withheld because of them.

9.7 FAILURE OF PAYMENT

9.7.1 If the Architect does not issue a Certificate for Payment, through no fault of the Contractor, within seven days after receipt of the Contractor's Application for Payment, or if the Owner does not pay the Contractor within seven days after the date established in the Contract Documents any amount certified by the Architect or awarded by arbitration, then the Contractor may, upon seven additional days' written notice to the Owner and the Architect, stop the Work until payment of the amount owing has been received. The Contract Sum shall be increased by the amount of the Contractor's reasonable costs of shut-down, delay and start-up, which shall be effected by appropriate Change Order in accordance with Paragraph 12.3.

9.8 SUBSTANTIAL COMPLETION

9.8.1 When the Contractor considers that the Work, or a designated portion thereof which is acceptable to the Owner, is substantially complete as defined in Subparagraph 8.1.3, the Contractor shall prepare for submission to the Architect a list of items to be completed or corrected. The failure to include any items on such list does not alter the responsibility of the Contractor to complete all Work in accordance with the Contract Documents. When the Architect on the basis of an inspection determines that the Work or designated portion thereof is substantially complete, he will then prepare a Certificate of Substantial Completion which shall establish the Date of Substantial Completion, shall state the responsibilities of the Owner and the Contractor for security, maintenance, heat, utilities, damage to the Work, and insurance, and shall fix the time within which the Contractor shall complete the items listed therein. Warranties required by the Contract Documents shall commence on the Date of Substantial Completion of the Work or designated portion thereof unless otherwise provided in the Certificate of Substantial Completion. The Certificate of Substantial Completion shall be submitted to the Owner and the Contractor for their written acceptance of the responsibilities assigned to them in such Certificate.

9.8.2 Upon Substantial Completion of the Work or designated portion thereof and upon application by the Contractor and certification by the Architect, the Owner shall make payment, reflecting adjustment in retainage, if any, for such Work or portion thereof, as provided in the Contract Documents.

9.9 FINAL COMPLETION AND FINAL PAYMENT

9.9.1 Upon receipt of written notice that the Work is ready for final inspection and acceptance and upon receipt of a final Application for Payment, the Architect will promptly make such inspection and, when he finds the Work acceptable under the Contract Documents and the Contract fully performed, he will promptly issue a final Certificate for Payment stating that to the best of his knowledge, information and belief, and on the basis of his observations and inspections, the Work has been completed in accordance with the terms and conditions of the Contract Documents and that the entire balance found to be due the Contractor, and noted in said final Certificate, is due and payable. The Architect's final Certificate for Payment will constitute a further representation that the conditions precedent to the Contractor's being entitled to final payment as set forth in Subparagraph 9.9.2 have been fulfilled.

9.9.2 Neither the final payment nor the remaining retained percentage shall become due until the Contractor submits to the Architect (1) an affidavit that all payrolls, bills for materials and equipment, and other indebtedness connected with the Work for which the Owner or his property might in any way be responsible, have been paid or otherwise satisfied, (2) consent of surety, if any, to final payment and (3), if required by the Owner, other data establishing payment or satisfaction of all such obligations, such as receipts, releases and waivers of liens arising out of the Contract, to the extent and in such form as may be designated by the Owner. If any Subcontractor refuses to furnish a release or waiver required by the Owner, the Contractor may furnish a bond satisfactory to the Owner to indemnify him against any such lien. If any such lien remains unsatisfied after all payments are made, the Contractor shall refund to the Owner all moneys that the latter may be compelled to pay in discharging such lien, including all costs and reasonable attorneys' fees.

9.9.3 If, after Substantial Completion of the Work, final completion thereof is materially delayed through no fault of the Contractor or by the issuance of Change Orders affecting final completion, and the Architect so confirms, the Owner shall, upon application by the Contractor and certification by the Architect, and without terminating the Contract, make payment of the balance due for that portion of the Work fully completed and accepted. If the remaining balance for Work not fully completed or corrected is less than the retainage stipulated in the Contract Documents, and if bonds have been furnished as provided in Paragraph 7.5, the written consent of the surety to the payment of the balance due for that portion of the Work fully completed and accepted shall be submitted by the Contractor to the Architect prior to certification of such payment. Such payment shall be made under the terms and conditions governing final payment, except that it shall not constitute a waiver of claims.

9.9.4 The making of final payment shall constitute a waiver of all claims by the Owner except those arising from:

.1 unsettled liens,
.2 faulty or defective Work appearing after Substantial Completion,
.3 failure of the Work to comply with the requirements of the Contract Documents, or
.4 terms of any special warranties required by the Contract Documents.

9.9.5 The acceptance of final payment shall constitute a waiver of all claims by the Contractor except those previously made in writing and identified by the Contractor as unsettled at the time of the final Application for Payment.

ARTICLE 10

PROTECTION OF PERSONS AND PROPERTY

10.1 SAFETY PRECAUTIONS AND PROGRAMS

10.1.1 The Contractor shall be responsible for initiating, maintaining and supervising all safety precautions and programs in connection with the Work.

10.2 SAFETY OF PERSONS AND PROPERTY

10.2.1 The Contractor shall take all reasonable precautions for the safety of, and shall provide all reasonable protection to prevent damage, injury or loss to:

.1 all employees on the Work and all other persons who may be affected thereby;
.2 all the Work and all materials and equipment to be incorporated therein, whether in storage on or off the site, under the care, custody or control of the Contractor or any of his Subcontractors or Sub-subcontractors; and
.3 other property at the site or adjacent thereto, including trees, shrubs, lawns, walks, pavements, roadways, structures and utilities not designated for removal, relocation or replacement in the course of construction.

10.2.2 The Contractor shall give all notices and comply with all applicable laws, ordinances, rules, regulations and lawful orders of any public authority bearing on the safety of persons or property or their protection from damage, injury or loss.

10.2.3 The Contractor shall erect and maintain, as required by existing conditions and progress of the Work, all reasonable safeguards for safety and protection, including posting danger signs and other warnings against hazards, promulgating safety regulations and notifying owners and users of adjacent utilities.

10.2.4 When the use or storage of explosives or other hazardous materials or equipment is necessary for the execution of the Work, the Contractor shall exercise the utmost care and shall carry on such activities under the supervision of properly qualified personnel.

10.2.5 The Contractor shall promptly remedy all damage or loss (other than damage or loss insured under Paragraph 11.3) to any property referred to in Clauses 10.2.1.2 and 10.2.1.3 caused in whole or in part by the Contractor, any Subcontractor, any Sub-subcontractor, or anyone directly or indirectly employed by any of them, or by anyone for whose acts any of them may be liable and for which the Contractor is responsible under Clauses 10.2.1.2 and 10.2.1.3, except damage or loss attributable to the acts or omissions of the Owner or Architect or anyone directly or indirectly employed by either of them, or by anyone for whose acts either of them may be liable, and not attributable to the fault or negligence of the Contractor. The foregoing obligations of the Contractor are in addition to his obligations under Paragraph 4.18.

10.2.6 The Contractor shall designate a responsible member of his organization at the site whose duty shall be the prevention of accidents. This person shall be the Contractor's superintendent unless otherwise designated by the Contractor in writing to the Owner and the Architect.

10.2.7 The Contractor shall not load or permit any part of the Work to be loaded so as to endanger its safety.

10.3   EMERGENCIES

10.3.1 In any emergency affecting the safety of persons or property, the Contractor shall act, at his discretion, to prevent threatened damage, injury or loss. Any additional compensation or extension of time claimed by the Contractor on account of emergency work shall be determined as provided in Article 12 for Changes in the Work.

ARTICLE 11

INSURANCE

11.1   CONTRACTOR'S LIABILITY INSURANCE

11.1.1 The Contractor shall purchase and maintain such insurance as will protect him from claims set forth below which may arise out of or result from the Contractor's operations under the Contract, whether such operations be by himself or by any Subcontractor or by anyone directly or indirectly employed by any of them, or by anyone for whose acts any of them may be liable:

  .1 claims under workers' or workmen's compensation, disability benefit and other similar employee benefit acts;

  .2 claims for damages because of bodily injury, occupational sickness or disease, or death of his employees;

  .3 claims for damages because of bodily injury, sickness or disease, or death of any person other than his employees;

  .4 claims for damages insured by usual personal injury liability coverage which are sustained (1) by any person as a result of an offense directly or indirectly related to the employment of such person by the Contractor, or (2) by any other person;

  .5 claims for damages, other than to the Work itself, because of injury to or destruction of tangible property, including loss of use resulting therefrom; and

  .6 claims for damages because of bodily injury or death of any person or property damage arising out of the ownership, maintenance or use of any motor vehicle.

11.1.2 The issuance required by Subparagraph 11.1.1 shall be written for not less than any limits of liability specified in the Contract Documents, or required by law, whichever is greater.

11.1.3 The insurance required by Subparagraph 11.1.1 shall include contractual liability insurance applicable to the Contractor's obligations under Paragraph 4.18.

11.1.4 Certificates of Insurance acceptable to the Owner shall be filed with the Owner prior to commencement of the Work. These Certificates shall contain a provision that coverages afforded under the policies will not be cancelled until at least thirty days' prior written notice has been given to the Owner.

11.2   OWNER'S LIABILITY INSURANCE

11.2.1 The Owner shall be responsible for purchasing and maintaining his own liability insurance and, at his option, may purchase and maintain such insurance as will protect him against claims which may arise from operations under the Contract.

11.3   PROPERTY INSURANCE

11.3.1 Unless otherwise provided, the Owner shall purchase and maintain property insurance upon the entire Work at the site to the full insurable value thereof. This insurance shall include the interests of the Owner, the Contractor, Subcontractors and Sub-subcontractors in the Work and shall insure against the perils of fire and extended coverage and shall include "all risk" insurance for physical loss or damage including, without duplication of coverage, theft, vandalism and malicious mischief. If the Owner does not intend to purchase such insurance for the full insurable value of the entire Work, he shall inform the Contractor in writing prior to commencement of the Work. The Contractor may then effect insurance which will protect the interests of himself, his Subcontractors and the Sub-subcontractors in the Work, and by appropriate Change Order the cost thereof shall be charged to the Owner. If the Contractor is damaged by failure of the Owner to purchase or maintain such insurance and to so notify the Contractor, then the Owner shall bear all reasonable costs properly attributable thereto. If not covered under the all risk insurance or otherwise provided in the Contract Documents, the Contractor shall effect and maintain similar property insurance on portions of the Work stored off the site or in transit when such portions of the Work are to be included in an Application for Payment under Subparagraph 9.3.2.

11.3.2 The Owner shall purchase and maintain such boiler and machinery insurance as may be required by the Contract Documents or by law. This insurance shall include the interests of the Owner, the Contractor, Subcontractors and Sub-subcontractors in the Work.

11.3.3 Any loss insured under Subparagraph 11.3.1 is to be adjusted with the Owner and made payable to the Owner as trustee for the insureds, as their interests may appear, subject to the requirements of any applicable mortgagee clause and of Subparagraph 11.3.8. The Contractor shall pay each Subcontractor a just share of any insurance moneys received by the Contractor, and by appropriate agreement, written where legally required for validity, shall require each Subcontractor to make payments to his Sub-subcontractors in similar manner.

11.3.4 The Owner shall file a copy of all policies with the Contractor before an exposure to loss may occur.

11.3.5 If the Contractor requests in writing that insurance for risks other than those described in Subparagraphs 11.3.1 and 11.3.2 or other special hazards be included in the property insurance policy, the Owner shall, if possible, include such insurance, and the cost thereof shall be charged to the Contractor by appropriate Change Order.

11.3.6 The Owner and Contractor waive all rights against (1) each other and the Subcontractors, Sub-subcontractors, agents and employees each of the other, and (2) the Architect and separate contractors, if any, and their subcontractors, sub-subcontractors, agents and employees, for damages caused by fire or other perils to the extent covered by insurance obtained pursuant to this Paragraph 11.3 or any other property insurance applicable to the Work, except such rights as they may have to the proceeds of such insurance held by the Owner as trustee. The foregoing waiver afforded the Architect, his agents and employees shall not extend to the liability imposed by Subparagraph 4.18.3. The Owner or the Contractor, as appropriate, shall require of the Architect, separate contractors, Subcontractors and Sub-subcontractors by appropriate agreements, written where legally required for validity, similar waivers each in favor of all other parties enumerated in this Subparagraph 11.3.6.

11.3.7 If required in writing by any party in interest, the Owner as trustee shall, upon the occurrence of an insured loss, give bond for the proper performance of his duties. He shall deposit in a separate account any money so received, and he shall distribute it in accordance with such agreement as the parties in interest may reach, or in accordance with an award by arbitration in which case the procedure shall be as provided in Paragraph 7.9. If after such loss no other special agreement is made, replacement of damaged work shall be covered by an appropriate Change Order.

11.3.8 The Owner as trustee shall have power to adjust and settle any loss with the insurers unless one of the parties in interest shall object in writing within five days after the occurrence of loss to the Owner's exercise of this power, and if such objection be made, arbitrators shall be chosen as provided in Paragraph 7.9. The Owner as trustee shall, in that case, make settlement with the insurers in accordance with the directions of such arbitrators. If distribution of the insurance proceeds by arbitration is required, the arbitrators will direct such distribution.

11.3.9 If the Owner finds it necessary to occupy or use a portion or portions of the Work prior to Substantial Completion thereof, such occupancy shall not commence prior to a time mutually agreed to by the Owner and Contractor and to which the insurance company or companies providing the property insurance have consented by endorsement to the policy or policies. This insurance shall not be cancelled or lapsed on account of such partial occupancy. Consent of the Contractor and of the insurance company or companies to such occupancy or use shall not be unreasonably withheld.

11.4 LOSS OF USE INSURANCE

11.4.1 The Owner, at his option, may purchase and maintain such insurance as will insure him against loss of use of his property due to fire or other hazards, however caused. The Owner waives all rights of action against the Contractor for loss of use of his property, including consequential losses due to fire or other hazards however caused, to the extent covered by insurance under this Paragraph 11.4.

ARTICLE 12

CHANGES IN THE WORK

12.1 CHANGE ORDERS

12.1.1 A Change Order is a written order to the Contractor signed by the Owner and the Architect, issued after execution of the Contract, authorizing a change in the Work or an adjustment in the Contract Sum or the Contract Time. The Contract Sum and the Contract Time may be changed only by Change Order. A Change Order signed by the Contractor indicates his agreement therewith, including the adjustment in the Contract Sum or the Contract Time.

12.1.2 The Owner, without invalidating the Contract, may order changes in the Work within the general scope of the Contract consisting of additions, deletions or other revisions, the Contract Sum and the Contract Time being adjusted accordingly. All such changes in the Work shall be authorized by Change Order, and shall be performed under the applicable conditions of the Contract Documents.

12.1.3 The cost or credit to the Owner resulting from a change in the Work shall be determined in one or more of the following ways:

.1 by mutual acceptance of a lump sum properly itemized and supported by sufficient substantiating data to permit evaluation;

.2 by unit prices stated in the Contract Documents or subsequently agreed upon;

.3 by cost to be determined in a manner agreed upon by the parties and a mutually acceptable fixed or percentage fee; or

.4 by the method provided in Subparagraph 12.1.4.

12.1.4 If none of the methods set forth in Clauses 12.1.3.1, 12.1.3.2 or 12.1.3.3 is agreed upon, the Contractor, provided he receives a written order signed by the Owner, shall promptly proceed with the Work involved. The cost of such Work shall then be determined by the Architect on the basis of the reasonable expenditures and savings of those performing the Work attributable to the change, including, in the case of an increase in the Contract Sum, a reasonable allowance for overhead and profit. In such case, and also under Clauses 12.1.3.3 and 12.1.3.4 above, the Contractor shall keep and present, in such form as the Architect may prescribe, an itemized accounting together with appropriate supporting data for inclusion in a Change Order. Unless otherwise provided in the Contract Documents, cost shall be limited to the following: cost of materials, including sales tax and cost of delivery; cost of labor, including social security, old age and unemployment insurance, and fringe benefits required by agreement or custom; workers' or workmen's compensation insurance; bond premiums; rental value of equipment and machinery; and the additional costs of supervision and field office personnel directly attributable to the change. Pending final determination of cost to the Owner, payments on account shall be made on the Architect's Certificate for Payment. The amount of credit to be allowed by the Contractor to the Owner for any deletion or change which results in a net decrease in the Contract Sum will be the amount of the actual net cost as confirmed by the Architect. When both additions and credits covering related Work or substitutions are involved in any one change, the allowance for overhead and profit shall be figured on the basis of the net increase, if any, with respect to that change.

12.1.5 If unit prices are stated in the Contract Documents or subsequently agreed upon, and if the quantities originally contemplated are so changed in a proposed Change Order that application of the agreed unit prices to the quantities of Work proposed will cause substantial inequity to the Owner or the Contractor, the applicable unit prices shall be equitably adjusted.

12.2   CONCEALED CONDITIONS

12.2.1 Should concealed conditions encountered in the performance of the Work below the surface of the ground or should concealed or unknown conditions in an existing structure be at variance with the conditions indicated by the Contract Documents, or should unknown physical conditions below the surface of the ground or should concealed or unknown conditions in an existing structure of an unusual nature, differing materially from those ordinarily encountered and generally recognized as inherent in work of the character provided for in this Contract, be encountered, the Contract Sum shall be equitably adjusted by Change Order upon claim by either party made within twenty days after the first observance of the conditions.

12.3   CLAIMS FOR ADDITIONAL COST

12.3.1 If the Contractor wishes to make a claim for an increase in the Contract Sum, he shall give the Architect written notice thereof within twenty days after the occurrence of the event giving rise to such claim. This notice shall be given by the Contractor before proceeding to execute the Work, except in an emergency endangering life or property in which case the Contractor shall proceed in accordance with Paragraph 10.3. No such claim shall be valid unless so made. If the Owner and the Contractor cannot agree on the amount of the adjustment in the Contract Sum, it shall be determined by the Architect. Any change in the Contract Sum resulting from such claim shall be authorized by Change Order.

12.3.2 If the Contractor claims that additional cost is involved because of, but not limited to, (1) any written interpretation pursuant to Subparagraph 2.2.8, (2) any order by the Owner to stop the Work pursuant to Paragraph 3.3 where the Contractor was not at fault, (3) any written order for a minor change in the Work issued pursuant to Paragraph 12.4, or (4) failure of payment by the Owner pursuant to Paragraph 9.7, the Contractor shall make such claim as provided in Subparagraph 12.3.1.

12.4   MINOR CHANGES IN THE WORK

12.4.1 The Architect will have authority to order minor changes in the Work not involving an adjustment in the Contract Sum or an extension of the Contract Time and not inconsistent with the intent of the Contract Documents. Such changes shall be effected by written order, and shall be binding on the Owner and the Contractor.

The Contractor shall carry out such written orders promptly.

ARTICLE 13

UNCOVERING AND CORRECTION OF WORK

13.1   UNCOVERING OF WORK

13.1.1 If any portion of the Work should be covered contrary to the request of the Architect or to requirements specifically expressed in the Contract Documents, it must, if required in writing by the Architect, be uncovered for his observation and shall be replaced at the Contractor's expense.

13.1.2 If any other portion of the Work has been covered which the Architect has not specifically requested to observe prior to being covered, the Architect may request to see such Work and it shall be uncovered by the Contractor. If such Work be found in accordance with the Contract Documents, the cost of uncovering and replacement shall, by appropriate Change Order, be charged to the Owner. If such Work be found not in accordance with the Contract Documents, the Contractor shall pay such costs unless it be found that this condition was caused by the Owner or a separate contractor as provided in Article 6, in which event the Owner shall be responsible for the payment of such costs.

13.2   CORRECTION OF WORK

13.2.1 The Contractor shall promptly correct all Work rejected by the Architect as defective or as failing to conform to the Contract Documents whether observed before or after Substantial Completion and whether or not fabricated, installed or completed. The Contractor shall bear all costs of correcting such rejected Work, including compensation for the Architect's additional services made necessary thereby.

13.2.2 If, within one year after the Date of Substantial Completion of the Work or designated portion thereof or within one year after acceptance by the Owner of designated equipment or within such longer period of time as may be prescribed by law or by the terms of any applicable special warranty required by the Contract Documents, any of the Work is found to be defective or not in accordance with the Contract Documents, the Contractor shall correct it promptly after receipt of a written notice from the Owner to do so unless the Owner has previously given the Contractor a written acceptance of such condition. This obligation shall survive termination of the Contract. The Owner shall give such notice promptly after discovery of the condition.

13.2.3 The Contractor shall remove from the site all portions of the Work which are defective or nonconforming and which have not been corrected under Subparagraphs 4.5.1, 13.2.1 and 13.2.2, unless removal is waived by the Owner.

13.2.4 If the Contractor fails to correct defective or nonconforming Work as provided in Subparagraphs 4.5.1, 13.2.1 and 13.2.2, the Owner may correct it in accordance with Paragraph 3.4.

13.2.5 If the Contractor does not proceed with the correction of such defective or non-conforming Work within a reasonable time fixed by written notice from the Architect, the Owner may remove it and may store the materials or equipment at the expense of the Contractor. If the Contractor does not pay the cost of such removal and storage within ten days thereafter, the Owner may upon ten additional days' written notice sell such Work at auction or at private sale and shall account for the net proceeds thereof, after deducting all the costs that should have been borne by the Contractor, including compensation for the Architect's additional services made necessary thereby. If such proceeds of sale do not cover all costs which the Contractor should have borne, the difference shall be charged to the Contractor and an appropriate Change Order shall be issued. If the payments then or thereafter due the Contractor are not sufficient to cover such amount, the Contractor shall pay the difference to the Owner.

13.2.6 The Contractor shall bear the cost of making good all work of the Owner or separate contractors destroyed or damaged by such correction or removal.

13.2.7 Nothing contained in this Paragraph 13.2 shall be construed to establish a period of limitation with respect to any other obligation which the Contractor might have under the Contract Documents, including Paragraph 4.5 hereof. The establishment of the time period of one year after the Date of Substantial Completion or such longer period of time as may be prescribed by law or by the terms of any warranty required by the Contract Documents relates only to the specific obligation of the Contractor to correct the Work, and has no relationship to the time within which his obligation to comply with the Contract Documents may be sought to be enforced, nor to the time within which proceedings may be commenced to establish the Contractor's liability with respect to his obligations other than specifically to correct the Work.

13.3 ACCEPTANCE OF DEFECTIVE OR NON-CONFORMING WORK

13.3.1 If the Owner prefers to accept defective or non-conforming Work, he may do so instead of requiring its removal and correction, in which case a Change Order will be issued to reflect a reduction in the Contract Sum where appropriate and equitable. Such adjustment shall be effected whether or not final payment has been made.

ARTICLE 14

TERMINATION OF THE CONTRACT

14.1 TERMINATION BY THE CONTRACTOR

14.1.1 If the Work is stopped for a period of thirty days under an order of any court or other public authority having jurisdiction, or as a result of an act of government, such as a declaration of a national emergency making materials unavailable, through no act or fault of the Contractor or a Subcontractor or their agents or employees or any other persons performing any of the Work under a contract with the Contractor, or if the Work should be stopped for a period of thirty days by the Contractor because the Architect has not issued a Certificate for Payment as provided in Paragraph 9.7 or because the Owner has not made payment thereon as provided in Paragraph 9.7, then the Contractor may, upon seven additional days' written notice to the Owner and the Architect, terminate the Contract and recover from the Owner payment for all Work executed and for any proven loss sustained upon any materials, equipment, tools, construction equipment and machinery, including reasonable profit and damages.

14.2 TERMINATION BY THE OWNER

14.2.1 If the Contractor is adjudged a bankrupt, or if he makes a general assignment for the benefit of his creditors, or if a receiver is appointed on account of his insolvency, or if he persistently or repeatedly refuses or fails, except in cases for which extension of time is provided, to supply enough properly skilled workmen or proper materials, or if he fails to make prompt payment to Subcontractors or for materials or labor, or persistently disregards laws, ordinances, rules, regulations or orders of any public authority having jurisdiction, or otherwise is guilty of a substantial violation of a provision of the Contract Documents, then the Owner, upon certification by the Architect that sufficient cause exists to justify such action, may, without prejudice to any right or remedy and after giving the Contractor and his surety, if any, seven days' written notice, terminate the employment of the Contractor and take possession of the site and of all materials, equipment, tools, construction equipment and machinery thereon owned by the Contractor and may finish the Work by whatever method he may deem expedient. In such case the Contractor shall not be entitled to receive any further payment until the Work is finished.

14.2.2 If the unpaid balance of the Contract Sum exceeds the costs of finishing the Work, including compensation for the Architect's additional services made necessary thereby, such excess shall be paid to the Contractor. If such costs exceed the unpaid balance, the Contractor shall pay the difference to the Owner. The amount to be paid to the Contractor or to the Owner, as the case may be, shall be certified by the Architect, upon application, in the manner provided in Paragraph 9.4, and this obligation for payment shall survive the termination of the Contract.

appendix

BRICK AND BLOCK COURSES

BLOCK NO. OF COURSES	BRICK NO. OF COURSES	HEIGHT OF COURSE	BLOCK NO. OF COURSES	BRICK NO. OF COURSES	HEIGHT OF COURSE
	1	0' – 2 5/8"		37	8' – 2 5/8"
	2	0' – 5 3/8"		38	8' – 5 3/8"
1	3	0' – 8"	13	39	8' – 8"
	4	0' – 10 5/8"		40	8' – 10 5/8"
	5	1' – 1 3/8"		41	9' – 1 3/8"
2	6	1' – 4"	14	42	9' – 4"
	7	1' – 6 5/8"		43	9' – 6 5/8"
	8	1' – 9 3/8"		44	9' – 9 3/8"
3	9	2' – 0"	15	45	10' – 0"
	10	2' – 2 5/8"		46	10' – 2 5/8"
	11	2' – 5 3/8"		47	10' – 5 3/8"
4	12	2' – 8"	16	48	10' – 8"
	13	2' – 10 5/8"		49	10' – 10 3/8"
	14	3' – 1 3/8"		50	11' – 1 3/8"
5	15	3' – 4"	17	51	11' – 4"
	16	3' – 6 5/8"		52	11' – 6 5/8"
	17	3' – 9 3/8"		53	11' – 9 3/8"
6	18	4' – 0"	18	54	12' – 0"
	19	4' – 2 5/8"		55	12' – 2 5/8"
	20	4' – 5 3/8"		56	12' – 5 3/8"
7	21	4' – 8"	19	57	12' – 8"
	22	4' – 10 5/8"		58	12' – 10 5/8"
	23	5' – 1 3/8"		59	13' – 1 3/8"
8	24	5' – 4"	20	60	13' – 4"
	25	5' – 6 5/8"		61	13' – 6 5/8"
	26	5' – 9 3/8"		62	13' – 9 3/8"
9	27	6' – 0"	21	63	14' – 0"
	28	6' – 2 5/8"		64	14' – 2 5/8"
	29	6' – 5 3/8"		65	14' – 5 3/8"
10	30	6' – 8"	22	66	14' – 8"
	31	6' – 10 5/8"		67	14' – 10 5/8"
	32	7' – 1 3/8"		68	15' – 1 3/8"
11	33	7' – 4"	23	69	15' – 4"
	34	7' – 6 5/8"		70	15' – 6 5/8"
	35	7' – 9 3/8"		71	15' – 9 3/8"
12	36	8' – 0"	24	72	16' – 0"

MORTAR JOINT IS 3/8"

BOARD FEET CONTENT

LENGTH IN FEET

Size in Inches	8	10	12	14	16	18	20	22	24
1 x 2	1-1/3	1-2/3	2	2-1/3	2-2/3	3	3-1/3	3-2/3	4
1 x 3	2	2-1/2	3	3-1/2	4	4-1/2	5	5-1/2	6
1 x 4	2-2/3	3-1/3	4	4-2/3	5-1/3	6	6-2/3	7-1/3	8
1 x 5	3-1/3	4-1/6	5	5-5/6	6-2/3	7-1/2	8-1/3	9-1/6	10
1 x 6	4	5	6	7	8	9	10	11	12
1 x 8	5-1/3	6-2/3	8	9-1/3	10-2/3	12	13-1/3	14-2/3	16
1 x 10	6-2/3	8-1/3	10	11-2/3	13-1/3	15	16-2/3	18-1/3	20
1 x 12	8	10	12	14	16	18	20	22	24
1 x 14	9-1/3	11-2/3	14	16-1/3	18-2/3	21	23-1/3	25-2/3	28
1 x 16	10-2/3	13-1/3	16	18-2/3	21-1/3	24	26-2/3	29-1/3	32
5/4 x 4	3-1/3	4-1/6	5	5-5/6	6-2/3	7-1/2	8-1/3	9-1/6	10
5/4 x 6	5	6-1/4	7-1/2	8-3/4	10	11-1/4	12-1/2	13-3/4	15
5/4 x 8	6-2/3	8-1/3	10	11-2/3	13-1/3	15	16-2/3	18-1/3	20
5/4 x 10	8-1/3	10-5/12	12-1/2	14-7/12	16-2/3	18-3/4	20-5/6	22-11/13	25
5/4 x 12	10	12-1/2	15	17-1/2	20	22-1/2	25	27-1/2	30
6/4 x 4	4	5	6	7	8	9	10	11	12
6/4 x 6	6	7-1/2	9	10-1/2	12	13-1/2	15	16-1/2	18
6/4 x 8	8	10	12	14	16	18	20	22	24
6/4 x 10	10	12-1/2	15	17-1/2	20	22-1/2	25	27-1/2	30
6/4 x 12	12	15	18	21	24	27	30	33	36
2 x 4	5-1/3	6-2/3	8	9-1/3	10-2/3	12	13-1/3	14-2/3	16
2 x 6	8	10	12	14	16	18	20	22	24
2 x 8	10-2/3	13-1/3	16	18-2/3	21-1/3	24	26-2/3	29-1/3	32
2 x 10	13-1/3	16-2/3	20	23-1/3	26-2/3	30	33-1/3	36-2/3	40
2 x 12	16	20	24	28	32	36	40	44	48
2 x 14	18-2/3	23-1/3	28	32-2/3	37-1/3	42	46-2/3	51-2/3	56
2 x 16	21-1/3	26-2/3	32	37-1/3	42-2/3	48	53-1/3	58-2/3	64
3 x 4	8	10	12	14	16	18	20	22	24
3 x 6	12	15	18	21	24	27	30	33	36
3 x 8	16	20	24	28	32	36	40	44	48
3 x 10	20	25	30	35	40	45	50	55	60
3 x 12	24	30	36	42	48	54	60	66	72
3 x 14	28	35	42	49	56	63	70	77	84
3 x 16	32	40	48	56	64	72	80	88	96
4 x 4	10-2/3	13-1/3	16	18-2/3	21-1/3	24	26-2/3	29-1/3	32
4 x 6	16	20	24	28	32	36	40	44	48
4 x 8	21-1/3	26-2/3	32	37-1/3	42-2/3	48	53-1/3	58-2/3	64
4 x 10	26-2/3	33-1/3	40	46-2/3	53-1/3	60	66-2/3	73-1/3	80
4 x 12	32	40	48	56	64	72	80	88	96
4 x 14	37-1/3	46-2/3	56	65-1/3	74-2/3	84	93-1/3	102-2/3	112
4 x 16	42-2/3	53-1/3	64	74-2/3	85-1/3	96	106-2/3	117-1/3	128
6 x 6	24	30	36	42	48	54	60	66	72
6 x 8	32	40	48	56	64	72	80	88	96
6 x 10	40	50	60	70	80	90	100	110	120
6 x 12	48	60	72	84	96	108	120	132	144
6 x 14	56	70	84	98	112	126	140	154	168
6 x 16	64	80	96	112	128	144	160	176	192
8 x 8	42-2/3	53-1/3	64	74-2/3	85-1/3	96	106-2/3	117-1/3	128
8 x 10	53-1/3	66-2/3	80	93-1/3	106-2/3	120	133-1/3	146-2/3	160
8 x 12	64	80	96	112	128	144	160	176	192

	Aluminum		Copper	Galv. Iron or Steel		Sheet Lead	Stainless Steel	Terne Plate	Zinc-Copper Alloy
	Minimum		Minimum Thickness	Minimum Gage		Minimum Weight	Minimum Thickness	Min. Gage	Minimum Thickness
USE	Thickness	Tensile Strength		1.25 oz.	1.50 oz.				
	in.	psi	in.	ga.	ga.	psf	in.	ga.	in.
Areaways	---	---	---	16	18	---	---	---	---
Flashing									
exposed	.019	16,000	.020	26	28	2.5	.015	30	.020
concealed	.015	14,000	.012	28	30	1.5	.010	30	.012
head	.024	16,000	.020	28	28	---	.015	30	.020
Gutters	.027	16,000	.020	26	26	---	.015	---	.025
Downspouts	.020	14,000	.020	26	28	---	.015	---	.025
Roofing	.019	19,000	.020	26	28	3.0	.015	---	.020
Siding	---	---	---	26(6)	26	---	---	---	---
Roof Valley	.019	16,000	.020	26	28	2.5	.015	30	.020
Gravel Stops (fascias)	.024	19,000	.020	26	28	---	.015	---	.020
Ventilators	.027	16,000	---	26	28	---	---	---	---
Ductwork		16,000	---			---	---	---	---
Shower Pans	---	---	.015	---	---	4.0	---	---	---

WEIGHTS OF BUILDING MATERIALS

MATERIAL	WEIGHT
CONCRETE	
With stone reinforced	150 pcf
With stone plain	144 pcf
With cinders, reinforced	110 pcf
Light concrete (Aerocrete)	65 pcf
(Perlite)	45 pcf
(Vermiculite)	40 pcf
METAL AND PLASTER	
Masonry mortar	116 pcf
Gypsum and sand plaster	112 pcf
BRICK AND BLOCK MASONRY (INCLUDING MORTAR)	
4" brick wall	35 psf
8" brick wall	74 psf
8" concrete block wall	100 psf
12" concrete block wall	150 psf
4" brick veneer over 4" concrete block	65 psf
WOOD CONSTRUCTION	
Frame wall, lath and plaster	20 psf
Frame wall, 1/2" gypsum board	12 psf
Floor, 1/2" subfloor + 3/4" finished	6 psf
Floor, 1/2" subfloor and ceramic tile	16 psf
Roof, joist and 1/2" sheathing	3 psf
Roof, 2" plank and beam	5 psf
Roof, built-up	7 psf

MATERIAL	WEIGHT
WOOD CONSTRUCTION (CONTINUED)	
Ceiling, joist and plaster	10 psf
Ceiling, joist and 1/2" gypsum board	7 psf
Ceiling, joist and acoustic tile	5 psf
Wood shingles	3 psf
Spanish tile	15 psf
Copper sheet	2 psf
Tar and gravel	6 psf
STONE	
Sandstone	147 pcf
Slate	175 pcf
Limestone	165 pcf
Granite	175 pcf
Marble	165 pcf
GLASS	
1/4" plate glass	3.28 psf
1/8" double strength	1.63 psf
1/8" insulating glass with air space	3.25 psf
4" block glass	20.00 psf
INSULATION	
Cork board 1" thick	.58 psf
Rigid foam insulation 2" thick	.3 psf
Blanket or bat 2" thick	.1 psf

SIZES AND DIMENSIONS FOR REINFORCING BARS

WEIGHT LB. PER FT.	NOMINAL DIAMETER INCHES	SIZE	NUMBER	NOMINAL CROSS SECT. AREA SQ. IN.	NOMINAL PERIMETER
.376	.375	3/8	3	.11	1.178
.668	.500	1/2	4	.20	1.571
1.043	.625	5/8	5	.31	1.963
1.502	.750	3/4	6	.44	2.356
2.044	.875	7/8	7	.60	2.749
2.670	1.000	1	8	.79	3.142
3.400	1.128	1*	9	1.00	3.544
4.303	1.270	1-1/8*	10	1.27	3.990
5.313	1.410	1-1/4*	11	1.56	4.430
7.650	1.693	1-1/2*	14	2.25	5.320
13.600	2.257	2*	18	4.00	7.090

*These sizes rolled in rounds equivalent to square cross section area.

RECOMMENDED STYLES OF WELDED WIRE FABRIC REINFORCEMENT FOR CONCRETE

TYPE OF CONSTRUCTION	RECOMMENDED STYLE	REMARKS
Barbecue Foundation Slab	6x6-8/8 to 4x4-6/6	Use heavier style fabric for heavy, massive fireplaces or barbecue pits.
Basement Floors	6x6-10/10, 6x6-8/8 or 6x6-6/6	For small areas (15-foot maximum side dimension) use 6x6-10/10. As a rule of thumb, the larger the area or the poorer the sub-soil, the heavier the gauge.
Driveways	6x6-6/6	Continuous reinforcement between 25- to 30-foot contraction joints.
Foundation Slabs (Residential only)	6x6-10/10	Use heavier gauge over poorly drained sub-soil, or when maximum dimension is greater than 15 feet.
Garage Floors	6x6-6/6	Position at midpoint of 5- or 6-inch thick slab.
Patios and Terraces	6x6-10/10	Use 6x6-8/8 if sub-soil is poorly drained.
Porch Floor a. 6-inch thick slab up to 6-foot span b. 6-inch thick slab up to 8-foot span	6x6-6/6	Position 1 inch from bottom form to resist tensile stresses.
Sidewalks	6x6-10/10 6x6-8/8	Use heavier gauge over poorly drained sub-soil. Construct 25- to 30-foot slabs as for driveways.
Steps (Free span)	6x6-6/6	Use heavier style if more than five risers. Position fabric 1 inch from bottom form.
Steps (On ground)	6x6-8/8	Use 6x6-6/6 for unstable sub-soil.

ESTABLISHING ELEVATIONS WITH A BUILDER'S LEVEL

Set up the instrument where locations for which elevations are to be determined may be seen through the telescope. Level up the instrument and take a reading on the measuring rod by means of the horizontal cross hair in the telescope. The rod is then moved to the second point to be established. Then the rod is raised or lowered until the reading is the same as the original. The bottom of the rod is then at the same elevation as the original point.

MEASURING DIFFERENCE IN ELEVATION

To obtain the difference in elevation between two points, such as A and B in Fig. 25, set up and level the instrument at an intermediate point C. With the measuring rod held on point A note the reading where the horizontal cross hair in the telescope crosses the graduation marks on the rod. Then with the rod held on point B, sight on the rod and note where the horizontal cross hair cuts the graduations on the rod. The difference

between the reading at A (5 ft.) and the reading at B (5½ ft.) is the difference in elevation between A and B. Thus point B is 1/2 ft. lower than point A.

When, for any reason such as irregularity of the ground or a large difference in elevation, the two points whose difference in elevation is to be determined cannot be sighted from a single point, intermediate points must be used for setting up the instrument, as shown in Fig. 26.

ESTABLISHING POINTS ON A LINE WITH A TRANSIT

Level the instrument and center it accurately over a point on the line by means of a plumb bob. Then sight the telescope on the most distant visible known point of that line. Lock the horizontal motion clamp screw to keep the telescope on line, and place the vertical cross hair exactly on the distant point with the tangent screw. Then, by rotating the telescope in the vertical plane, the exact location of any number of stakes on that same line may be determined (Fig. 27).

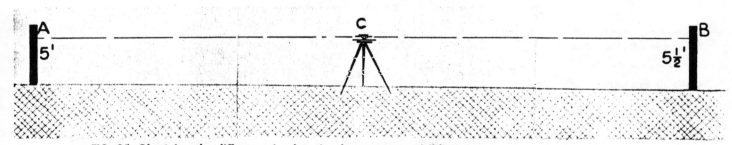

FIG. 25. Obtaining the difference in elevation between two visible points.

FIG. 26. Obtaining the difference in elevation between two points not visible to each other.

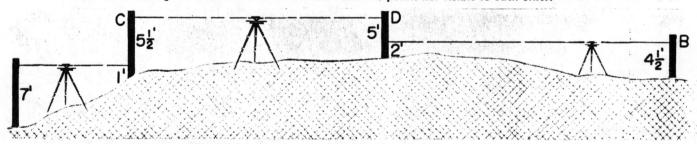

FIG. 27. Establishing points on a line with a transit.

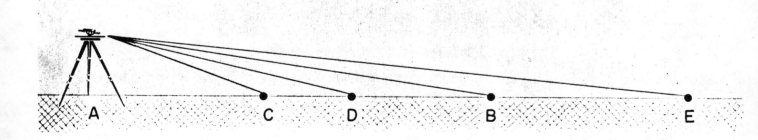

550

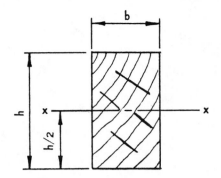

PROPERTIES of SECTIONS
for
CERTAIN STANDARD DIMENSION and TIMBER

Dressed (S4S) Sizes

Moment of Inertia and Section Modulus are given with respect to x---x axis with dimensions b and h as shown on sketch.

Nominal Size b h	Standard Dressed Size S4S b h	Area of Section $A = bh$	Moment of Inertia $I = \dfrac{bh^3}{12}$	Section Modulus $S = \dfrac{bh^2}{6}$	Board Feet Per Linear Foot of Piece
2 X 4	1-5/8 X 3-5/8	5.89	6.45	3.56	2/3
2 X 6	1-5/8 X 5-1/2	8.93	22.53	8.19	1
2 X 8	1-5/8 X 7-1/2	12.19	57.13	15.23	1-1/3
2 X 10	1-5/8 X 9-1/2	15.44	116.10	24.44	1-2/3
2 X 12	1-5/8 X 11-1/2	18.69	205.95	35.82	2
3 X 4	2-5/8 X 3-5/8	9.52	10.42	5.75	1
3 X 6	2-5/8 X 5-1/2	14.43	36.40	13.23	1-1/2
3 X 8	2-5/8 X 7-1/2	19.69	92.29	24.61	2
3 X 10	2-5/8 X 9-1/2	24.94	187.55	39.48	2-1/2
3 X 12	2-5/8 X 11-1/2	30.19	332.69	57.86	3
4 X 6	3-5/8 X 5-1/2	19.95	50.25	18.28	2
4 X 8	3-5/8 X 7-1/2	27.19	127.44	33.98	2-2/3
4 X 10	3-5/8 X 9-1/2	34.44	259.00	54.53	3-1/3
4 X 12	3-5/8 X 11-1/2	41.69	459.43	79.90	4
4 X 14	3-5/8 X 13-1/2	48.94	743.24	110.11	4-2/3
4 X 16	3-5/8 X 15-1/2	56.19	1,124.92	145.15	5-1/3
6 X 6	5-1/2 X 5-1/2	30.25	76.26	27.73	3
6 X 8	5-1/2 X 7-1/2	41.25	193.36	51.56	4
6 X 10	5-1/2 X 9-1/2	52.25	392.96	82.73	5
6 X 12	5-1/2 X 11-1/2	63.25	697.07	121.23	6
6 X 14	5-1/2 X 13-1/2	74.25	1,127.67	167.06	7
6 X 16	5-1/2 X 15-1/2	85.25	1,706.78	220.23	8
6 X 18	5-1/2 X 17-1/2	96.25	2,456.38	280.73	9
8 X 8	7-1/2 X 7-1/2	56.25	263.67	70.31	5-1/3
8 X 10	7-1/2 X 9-1/2	71.25	535.86	112.81	6-2/3
8 X 12	7-1/2 X 11-1/2	86.25	950.55	165.31	8
8 X 14	7-1/2 X 13-1/2	101.25	1,537.73	227.81	9-1/3
8 X 16	7-1/2 X 15-1/2	116.25	2,327.42	300.31	10-2/3
8 X 18	7-1/2 X 17-1/2	131.25	3,349.61	382.81	12
8 X 20	7-1/2 X 19-1/2	146.25	4,625.00	475.00	13-1/3
10 X 10	9-1/2 X 9-1/2	90.25	678.76	142.90	8-1/3
10 X 12	9-1/2 X 11-1/2	109.25	1,204.03	209.40	10
10 X 14	9-1/2 X 13-1/2	128.25	1,947.80	288.56	11-2/3
10 X 16	9-1/2 X 15-1/2	147.25	2,948.07	380.40	13-1/3
10 X 18	9-1/2 X 17-1/2	166.25	4,242.84	484.90	15
10 X 20	9-1/2 X 19-1/2	185.25	5,870.11	602.06	16-2/3
12 X 12	11-1/2 X 11-1/2	132.25	1,457.51	253.48	12
12 X 14	11-1/2 X 13-1/2	155.25	2,357.86	349.31	14
12 X 16	11-1/2 X 15-1/2	178.25	3,568.71	460.48	16
12 X 18	11-1/2 X 17-1/2	201.25	5,136.07	586.98	18
12 X 20	11-1/2 X 19-1/2	224.25	7,105.92	728.81	20
12 X 22	11-1/2 X 21-1/2	247.25	9,530.00	887.50	22
12 X 24	11-1/2 X 23-1/2	270.25	12,435.00	1,057.50	24
Decking - (Based on strip one foot wide and of thickness indicated)					
1'-0 X 2	12 X 1-5/8	19.50	4.29	5.28	2
1'-0 X 3	12 X 2-5/8	31.50	18.00	13.76	3
1'-0 X 4	12 X 3-1/2	42.00	42.88	24.50	4

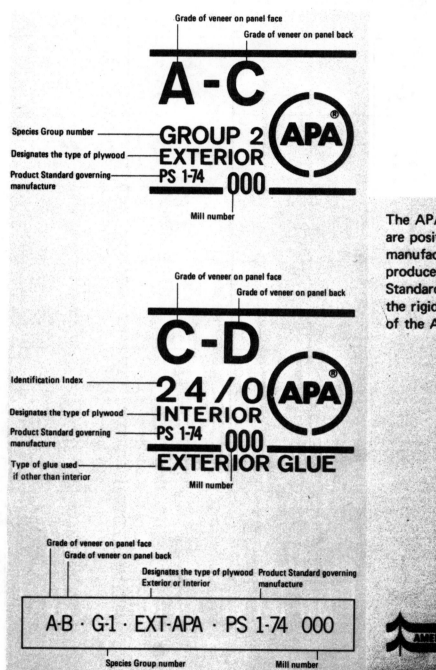

Grade of veneer on panel face
Grade of veneer on panel back

A-C

Species Group number —— **GROUP 2**
Designates the type of plywood —— **EXTERIOR** **APA**®
Product Standard governing —— **PS 1-74**
manufacture
000

Mill number

Grade of veneer on panel face
Grade of veneer on panel back

C-D

Identification Index —— **24/0** **APA**®
Designates the type of plywood —— **INTERIOR**
Product Standard governing —— **PS 1-74**
manufacture
000
Type of glue used —— **EXTERIOR GLUE**
if other than interior

Mill number

Grade of veneer on panel face
Grade of veneer on panel back
Designates the type of plywood   Product Standard governing
Exterior or Interior   manufacture

A-B · G-1 · EXT-APA · PS 1-74 000

Species Group number   Mill number

The APA grade-trademarks on plywood are positive identification by the manufacturer that the plywood has been produced in accordance with U.S. Product Standard PS 1 and has been subject to the rigid inspection and testing program of the American Plywood Association.

Guide to engineered grades of plywood

SPECIFIC GRADES AND THICKNESSES MAY BE IN LOCALLY LIMITED SUPPLY.
SEE YOUR DEALER FOR AVAILABILITY BEFORE SPECIFYING.

	Grade Designation	Description and Most Common Use	Typical Grade-trademarks	Face	Back	Inner Plies	Most Common Thicknesses (inch) (1)
Interior Type	C-D INT-APA	For wall and roof sheathing, subflooring, industrial uses such as pallets. Also available with intermediate glue or exterior glue. Specify intermediate glue for moderate construction delays; exterior glue for better durability in somewhat longer construction delays, and for treated wood foundations. (2) (10)	C-D 32/16 INTERIOR PS 1-74 000 (APA)	C	D	D	5/16 3/8 1/2 5/8 3/4
	STRUCTURAL I C-D INT-APA and STRUCTURAL II C-D INT-APA	Unsanded structural grades where plywood strength properties are of maximum importance: structural diaphragms, box beams, gusset plates, stressed-skin panels, containers, pallet bins. Made only with exterior glue.	STRUCTURAL I C-D 24/0 INTERIOR PS 1-74 000 EXTERIOR GLUE (APA)	C[6]	D[7]	D[7]	5/16 3/8 1/2 5/8 3/4
	UNDERLAYMENT INT-APA	For underlayment or combination subfloor-underlayment under resilient floor coverings, carpeting in homes, apartments, mobile homes. Specify exterior glue where moisture may be present, such as bathrooms, utility rooms. Touch-sanded. Also available in tongue and groove. (2) (3) (9)	UNDERLAYMENT GROUP 1 INTERIOR PS 1-74 000 (APA)	C Plugged	D	C[8] & D	1/4 3/8 1/2 5/8 3/4
	C-D PLUGGED INT-APA	For built-ins, wall and ceiling tile backing, cable reels, walkways, separator boards. Not a substitute for UNDERLAYMENT as it lacks UNDERLAYMENT's indentation resistance. Touch-sanded. (2) (3) (9)	C-D PLUGGED GROUP 2 INTERIOR PS 1-74 000 (APA)	C Plugged	D	D	5/16 3/8 1/2 5/8 3/4
	2·4·1 INT-APA	Combination subfloor-underlayment. Quality base for resilient floor coverings, carpeting, wood strip flooring. Use 2·4·1 with exterior glue in areas subject to moisture. Unsanded or touch-sanded as specified. (2) (5) (11)	2·4·1 GROUP 1 INTERIOR PS 1-74 000 (APA)	C Plugged	D	C & D	1-1/8"
Exterior Type	C-C EXT-APA	Unsanded grade with waterproof bond for subflooring and roof decking, siding on service and farm buildings, crating, pallets, pallet bins, cable reels. (10)	C-C 42/20 EXTERIOR PS 1-74 000 (APA)	C	C	C	5/16 3/8 1/2 5/8 3/4
	STRUCTURAL I C-C EXT-APA and STRUCTURAL II C-C EXT-APA	For engineered applications in construction and industry where full Exterior type panels are required. Unsanded. See (9) for species group requirements.	STRUCTURAL I C-C 32/16 EXTERIOR PS 1-74 000 (APA)	C	C	C	5/16 3/8 1/2 5/8 3/4
	UNDERLAYMENT C-C Plugged EXT-APA / C-C PLUGGED EXT-APA	For underlayment or combination subfloor-underlayment under resilient floor coverings where severe moisture conditions may be present, as in balcony decks. Use for tile backing where severe moisture conditions exist. For refrigerated or controlled atmosphere rooms, pallets, fruit pallet bins, reusable cargo containers, tanks and boxcar and truck floors and linings. Touch-sanded. Also available in tongue and groove. (3) (9)	UNDERLAYMENT C-C PLUGGED GROUP 2 EXTERIOR PS 1-74 000 (APA) / C-C PLUGGED GROUP 3 EXTERIOR PS 1-74 000 (APA)	C Plugged	C	C[8]	1/4 3/8 1/2 5/8 3/4
	B-B PLYFORM CLASS I & CLASS II EXT-APA	Concrete form grades with high re-use factor. Sanded both sides. Mill-oiled unless otherwise specified. Special restrictions on species. Also available in HDO. (4)	B-B PLYFORM CLASS I EXTERIOR PS 1-74 000 (APA)	B	B	C	5/8 3/4

(1) Panels are standard 4x8-foot size. Other sizes available.
(2) Also made with exterior or intermediate glue.
(3) Available in Group 1, 2, 3, 4, or 5.
(4) Also available in STRUCTURAL I.
(5) Made only in woods of certain species to conform to APA specifications.
(6) Special improved C grade for structural panels.
(7) Special improved D grade for structural panels.
(8) Special construction to resist indentation from concentrated loads.
(9) Also available in STRUCTURAL I (all plies limited to Group 1 species) and STRUCTURAL II (all plies limited to Group 1, 2, or 3 species).
(10) Made in many different species combinations. Specify by Identification Index.
(11) Can be special ordered in Exterior type for porches and patio decks, roof overhangs, and exterior balconies.

Veneer Grades

N — Smooth surface "natural finish" veneer. Select, all heartwood or all sapwood. Free of open defects. Allows not more than 6 repairs, wood only, per 4x8 panel, made parallel to grain and well matched for grain and color.

A — Smooth, paintable. Not more than 18 neatly made repairs, boat, sled, or router type, and parallel to grain, permitted. May be used for natural finish in less demanding applications.

B — Solid surface. Shims, circular repair plugs and tight knots to 1 inch across grain permitted. Some minor splits permitted.

C Plugged — Improved C veneer with splits limited to 1/8 inch width and knotholes and borer holes limited to 1/4 x 1/2 inch. Admits some broken grain. Synthetic repairs permitted.

C — Tight knots to 1-1/2 inch. Knotholes to 1 inch across grain and some to 1-1/2 inch if total width of knots and knotholes is within specified limits. Synthetic or wood repairs. Discoloration and sanding defects that do not impair strength permitted. Limited splits allowed.

D — Knots and knotholes to 2-1/2 inch width across grain and 1/2 inch larger within specified limits. Limited splits are permitted. Limited to Interior grades of plywood.

Guide to appearance grades of plywood

	Grade Designation [2]	Description and Most Common Uses	Typical Grade-trademarks	Face	Back	Inner Plies	Most Common Thicknesses (inch) [3]					
							1/4	5/16	3/8	1/2	5/8	3/4
Interior Type	N-N, N-A, N-B INT-APA	Cabinet quality. For natural finish furniture, cabinet doors, built-ins, etc. Special order items.	NN G1 INT APA PS1 74 / NA G2 INT APA PS1 74	N	N,A, or B	C						3/4
	N-D-INT-APA	For natural finish paneling. Special order item.	ND G3 INT APA PS1 74	N	D	D	1/4					
	A-A INT-APA	For applications with both sides on view. Built-ins, cabinets, furniture and partitions. Smooth face; suitable for painting.	AA G4 INT APA PS1 74	A	A	D	1/4		3/8	1/2	5/8	3/4
	A-B INT-APA	Use where appearance of one side is less important but two smooth solid surfaces are necessary.	AB G4 INT APA PS1 74	A	B	D	1/4		3/8	1/2	5/8	3/4
	A-D INT-APA	Use where appearance of only one side is important. Paneling, built-ins, shelving, partitions, and flow racks.	A-D GROUP 1 INTERIOR PS1 74 000 (APA)	A	D	D	1/4		3/8	1/2	5/8	3/4
	B-B INT-APA	Utility panel with two smooth sides. Permits circular plugs.	BB G3 INT APA PS1 74	B	B	D	1/4		3/8	1/2	5/8	3/4
	B-D INT-APA	Utility panel with one smooth side. Good for backing, sides of built-ins. Industry: shelving, slip sheets, separator boards and bins.	B-D GROUP 3 INTERIOR PS1 74 000 (APA)	B	D	D	1/4		3/8	1/2	5/8	3/4
	DECORATIVE PANELS—APA	Rough-sawn, brushed, grooved, or striated faces. For paneling, interior accent walls, built-ins, counter facing, displays, and exhibits.	DECORATIVE BD G1 INT APA PS1 74	C or btr.	D	D		5/16	3/8	1/2	5/8	
	PLYRON INT-APA	Hardboard face on both sides. For counter tops, shelving, cabinet doors, flooring. Faces tempered, untempered, smooth, or screened.	PLYRON INT APA PS1 74		C & D					1/2	5/8	3/4
Exterior Type [7]	A-A EXT-APA	Use where appearance of both sides is important. Fences, built-ins, signs, boats, cabinets, commercial refrigerators, shipping containers, tote boxes, tanks, and ducts. (4)	AA G3 EXT APA PS1 74	A	A	C	1/4		3/8	1/2	5/8	3/4
	A-B EXT-APA	Use where the appearance of one side is less important. (4)	AB G1 EXT APA PS1 74	A	B	C	1/4		3/8	1/2	5/8	3/4
	A-C EXT-APA	Use where the appearance of only one side is important. Soffits, fences, structural uses, boxcar and truck lining, farm buildings. Tanks, trays, commercial refrigerators. (4)	A-C GROUP 1 EXTERIOR PS1 74 000 (APA)	A	C	C	1/4		3/8	1/2	5/8	3/4
	B-B EXT-APA	Utility panel with solid faces. (4)	BB G1 EXT APA PS1 74	B	B	C	1/4		3/8	1/2	5/8	3/4
	B-C EXT-APA	Utility panel for farm service and work buildings, boxcar and truck lining, containers, tanks, agricultural equipment. Also as base for exterior coatings for walls, roofs. (4)	B-C GROUP 2 EXTERIOR PS1 74 000 (APA)	B	C	C	1/4		3/8	1/2	5/8	3/4
	HDO EXT-APA	High Density Overlay plywood. Has a hard, semi-opaque resin-fiber overlay both faces. Abrasion resistant. For concrete forms, cabinets, counter tops, signs and tanks. (4)	HDO·60/60 BB PLYFORM I·EXT APA·PS1 74	A or B	A or B	C or C plgd		5/16	3/8	1/2	5/8	3/4
	MDO EXT-APA	Medium Density Overlay with smooth, opaque, resin-fiber overlay one or both panel faces. Highly recommended for siding and other outdoor applications, built-ins, signs, and displays. Ideal base for paint. (4)	MDO BB G4 EXT APA PS1 74	B	B or C	C		5/16	3/8	1/2	5/8	3/4
	303 SIDING EXT-APA	Proprietary plywood products for exterior siding, fencing, etc. Special surface treatment such as V-groove, channel groove, striated, brushed, rough-sawn. (6)	303 SIDING 16 oc GROUP 1 EXTERIOR PS1 74 000 (APA)	(5)	C	C			3/8	1/2	5/8	
	T 1-11 EXT-APA	Special 303 panel having grooves 1/4" deep, 3/8" wide, spaced 4" or 8" o.c. Other spacing optional. Edges shiplapped. Available unsanded, textured, and MDO. (6)	303 SIDING 16 oc T-1-11 GROUP 1 EXTERIOR PS1 74 000 (APA)	C or btr.	C	C					5/8	
	PLYRON EXT-APA	Hardboard faces both sides, tempered, smooth or screened.	PLYRON EXT APA PS1 74		C					1/2	5/8	3/4
	MARINE EXT-APA	Ideal for boat hulls. Made only with Douglas fir or western larch. Special solid jointed core construction. Subject to special limitations on core gaps and number of face repairs. Also available with HDO or MDO faces.	MARINE AA EXT APA PS1 74	A or B	A or B	B	1/4		3/8	1/2	5/8	3/4

(1) Sanded both sides except where decorative or other surfaces specified.
(2) Available in Group 1, 2, 3, 4, or 5 unless otherwise noted.
(3) Standard 4x8 panel sizes, other sizes available.
(4) Also available in Structural I (all plies limited to Group 1 species) and Structural II (all plies limited to Group 1, 2, or 3 species).
(5) C or better for 5 plies; C Plugged or better for 3-ply panels.
(6) Stud spacing is shown on grade stamp.
(7) For finishing recommendations, see form V307.
(8) For strength properties of appearance grades, refer to "Plywood Design Specification," form Y510.

Guide to Identification Index on Engineered Grades

Thickness (inch)	C-D INT - APA C-C EXT - APA			NOTES:
	Group 1 & Structural I	Group 2* or 3 & Structural II*	Group 4**	
5/16	20/0	16/0	12/0	
3/8	24/0	20/0	16/0	
1/2	32/16	24/0	24/0	
5/8	42/20	32/16	30/12†	
3/4	48/24	42/20	36/16†	
7/8	--------	48/24	42/20	

NOTES:

* Panels with Group 2 outer plies and special thickness and construction requirements, or STRUCTURAL II panels with Group 1 faces, may carry the Identification Index numbers shown for Group 1 panels.

** Panels made with Group 4 outer plies may carry the Identification Index numbers shown for Group 3 panels when they conform to special thickness and construction requirements detailed in PS 1.

† Check local availability.

Key Definitions:

Type:

Plywood is manufactured in two types: Exterior type with 100% waterproof glueline and Interior type with highly moisture-resistant glueline. Interior type plywood may be bonded with exterior, intermediate, or interior glue. Specify Exterior type plywood for all permanent outdoor applications and those subject to continuing moist conditions or extreme high humidity. For other applications, Interior type may be used.

Group:

Wood from more than 70 species of varying strength may be used in plywood manufacture. The species are grouped on the basis of stiffness and strength, and divided into five classifications—Groups 1 through 5. Stiffest and strongest woods are in Group 1. The group number in the American Plywood Association grade-trademark refers to the weakest species used in face and back, except in decorative and sanded panels 3/8 inch thick or less. These are identified by the face species group. PS 1 lists species in all groups.

Appearance Grades:

Within each type of plywood are grade designations based on an appearance grading system for the veneer. Grades are N, A, B, C, and D, with N and A veneers the best looking. Panel grades are generally designated by veneer grade of panel face and back and by glue line (i.e., interior or exterior). PS 1 details allowable characteristics and repairs.

Engineered Grades:

Engineered grades are designed for demanding construction applications where properties such as nail bearing, shear, compression, tension, etc., are of maximum importance and appearance is secondary to strength.

C-D INTERIOR and C-D INTERIOR WITH EXTERIOR GLUE (CDX) are Interior type panels for uses such as sheathing. They will withstand considerable exposure to outdoor moisture conditions during construction, but must not be mistaken for Exterior plywood. STRUCTURAL I C-D is limited to Group 1 species throughout. STRUCTURAL II C-D permits Group 1, 2, or 3 species. Both are bonded with exterior glue.

Identification Index:

The basic unsanded grades of plywood—C-D sheathing, C-C Exterior, and STRUCTURAL I and II C-C and C-D carry an Identification Index of two numbers in the American Plywood Association grade-trademark, for example 24/0 or 32/16. The left-hand number refers to maximum recommended spacing of roof framing in inches when the panel is used as roof sheathing. The right-hand number refers to maximum spacing of floor framing when the panel is used for subflooring. In each case, face grain is across supports and panel is continuous across two or more spans.

IMPORTANT NOTE: The spans referred to in the Index numbers are accepted by most major building codes. Local interpretations may vary, however. So make sure your specifications comply with the local code under which you are building.

Class I, Class II:

Applies only to Plyform grade for concrete form plywood. Indicates species mix permitted. Plyform Class I is limited to Group 1 faces, Group 1 or 2 crossbands, and Group 1, 2, 3, or 4 center ply. Plyform Class II is limited to Group 1 or 2 faces (Group 3 under certain conditions) and Group 1, 2, 3, or 4 inner plies.

Method of Ordering:

Appearance grades: Designate the species group, number of pieces, width, length, type, grade, finished thickness and agency certification of quality:
"Group 2 plywood: 100 pcs., 48" x 96", Interior type, A-D grade, sanded 2 sides to 1/4" thickness, APA grade-trademarked".

Engineered grades: Designate grade, Identification Index, number of pieces, width, length, thickness, and agency certification of quality:
"C-D, 24/0, 100 pcs., 48" x 96", 3/8" thick. APA grade-trademarked. (If exterior glue or intermediate glue are desired, note 'exterior glue' or 'intermediate glue'.)"

Concrete form: Designate the Class, number of pieces, width, length, thickness, grade, and agency certification of quality. Concrete form panels are mill-oiled, unless otherwise specified:
"Plyform, Class I, 100 pcs., 48" x 96", 5/8" thick, B-B Exterior type, APA grade-trademarked.

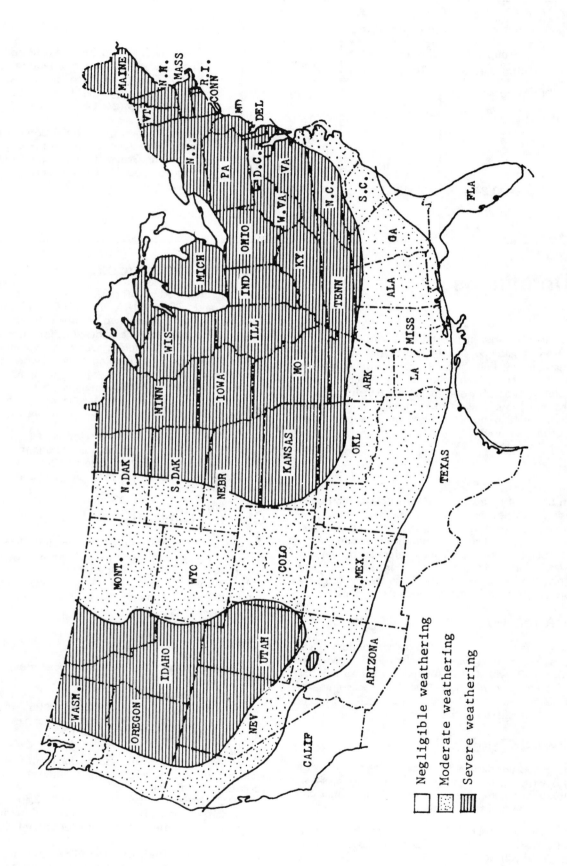

WEATHERING AREAS

Negligible weathering
Moderate weathering
Severe weathering

556

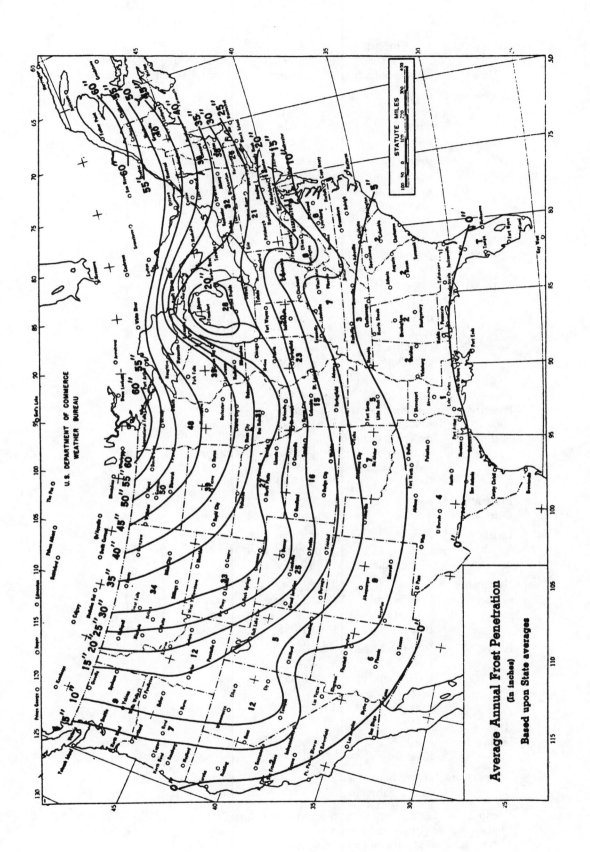

U. S. DEPARTMENT OF COMMERCE
WEATHER BUREAU

STATUTE MILES

Average Annual Frost Penetration
(In inches)
Based upon State averages

557

metric

Unit	Current U.S. term (multiply factor)	Conversion Factor*	SI term (divide factor)	SI Symbol
Length	inch	25.400	millimeter	mm
	foot	0.305	meter	m
	yard	0.914	meter	m
	mile	1.609	kilometer	km
Area	square inch	645.2	square millimeter	mm^2
	square foot	0.093	square meter	m^2
	square yard	0.836	square meter	m^2
	square mile	2.590	square kilometer	km^2
	acre	0.405	hectare	ha
Mass (weight)**	ounce	28.350	gram	g
	pound	0.454	kilogram	kg
	ton (2000 pounds)	0.907	metric ton	t
Volume	fluid ounce	29.574	milliliter	ml
	pint	0.473	liter	L
	quart	0.946	liter	L
	gallon	3.785	liter	L
	cubic foot	0.028	cubic meter	m^3
	cubic yard	0.765	cubic meter	m^3
	barrel (petroleum)	0.159	cubic meter	m^3
Force Pressure and Stress	pound force	4.448	newton	N
	psi (pounds per square inch)	6.895	kilopascal	kPa
	psf (pounds per square foot)	.048	kilopascal	kPa
	ton per square foot	95.760	kilopascal	kPa
Electric Current†	ampere	no conversion	ampere	A
Light	lumen	no conversion	lumen	lm
	candela	no conversion	candela	cd
	foot candle	10.76	lux	lx
Heat, work or energy	Foot pound	1.356	joule	J
	kilowatt hour	3.600	megajoule	MJ
	BTU	1.055	kilojoule	kJ
Power	foot pound per second	1.355	watt	W
	BTU/hour	0.293	watt	W
	horse power	0.746	kilowatt	kW
	tons (refrigeration)	3.517	kilowatt	kW
Heat factors	U value	5.679	metric U value	undecided
	K value	1.730	metric K value	undecided
Temperature	degree Fahrenheit	††	degree Celcius	°C
	degree Fahrenheit	††	Kelvin	K

* conversion factors have been rounded to the third decimal place.

** mass and weight are not synonymous.

† electric terms already in common use.

†† to convert °F to °C subtract 32 and multiply by 1.8; to convert °F to K add 459.67 and multiply by 1.8

THE METRIC SYSTEM

LINEAR MEASURE

10 millimeters	= 1 centimeter
10 centimeters	= 1 decimeter
10 decimeters	= 1 meter
10 meters	= 1 decameter
10 decameters	= 1 hectometer
10 hectometers	= 1 kilometer

SQUARE MEASURE

100 sq. millimeters	= 1 sq. centimeter
100 sq. centimeters	= 1 sq. decimeter
100 sq. decimeters	= 1 sq. meter
100 sq. meters	= 1 sq. decameter
100 sq. decameters	= 1 sq. hectometer
100 sq. hectometers	= 1 sq. kilometer

CUBIC MEASURE

1000 cu. millimeters	= 1 cu. centimeter
1000 cu. centimeters	= 1 cu. decimeter
1000 cu. decimeters	= 1 cu. meter

LIQUID MEASURE

10 milliliters	= 1 centiliter
10 centiliters	= 1 deciliter
10 deciliters	= 1 liter
10 liters	= 1 decaliter
10 decaliters	= 1 hectoliter
10 hectoliters	= 1 kiloliter

WEIGHTS

10 milligrams	= 1 centigram
10 centigrams	= 1 decigram
10 decigrams	= 1 gram
10 grams	= 1 decagram
10 decagrams	= 1 hectogram
10 hectograms	= 1 kilogram
100 kilograms	= 1 quintal
10 quintals	= 1 ton

LINEAR MEASURE

1 inch	=	= 2.54 centimeters
1 foot	= 12 inches	= 0.3048 meter
1 yard	= 3 feet	= 0.9144 meter
1 rod	= 5 1/2 yds. or 16 1/2 ft.	= 5.029 meters
1 furlong	= 40 rods	= 201.17 meters
1 mile (statute)	= 5280 ft. or 1760 yds.	= 1609.3 meters
1 league (land)	= 3 miles	= 4.83 kilometers

SQUARE MEASURE

1 sq. inch	=	= 6.452 sq. centimeters
1 sq. foot	= 144 sq. inches	= 929 sq. centimeters
1 sq. yard	= 9 sq. feet	= 0.8361 sq. meter
1 sq. rod	= 30 1/4 sq. yards	= 25.29 sq. meters
1 acre	= 43,560 sq. feet or 160 sq. yds.	= 0.4047 hectare
1 sq. mile	= 640 acres	= 259 hectares or 2.59 sq. kilometers

CUBIC MEASURE

1 cu. inch	=	= 16.387 cu. centimeters
1 cu. foot	= 1728 cu. inches	= 0.0283 cu. meter
1 cu. yard	= 27 cu. feet	= 0.7646 cu. meter

ANGULAR AND CIRCULAR MEASURE

1 minute	=	60 seconds
1 degree	=	60 minutes
1 right angle	=	90 degrees
1 straight angle	=	180 degrees
1 circle	=	360 degrees

SPAN OF JOISTS

Span Calculations provide for carrying the live loads shown and the additional weight of the joists and double flooring.

Size	Spacing	20# L.L. Plaster Clg.	30# Live Load Plaster Clg.	30# Live Load No Plaster	40# Live Load Plaster Clg.	40# Live Load No Plaster	50# Live Load Plaster Clg.	50# Live Load No Plaster	60# Live Load Plaster Clg.	60# Live Load No Plaster
2×4	12"	7'-8"								
2×4	16"	7'-0"								
2×4	24"	6'-1"								
2×6	12"	11'-9"	11'-6"	13'-4"	10'-8"	12'-0"	10'-0"	10'-11"	9'-6"	10'-1"
2×6	16"	10'-9"	10'-6"	11'-11"	9'-8"	10'-6"	9'-1"	9'-6"	8'-7"	8'-9"
2×6	24"	9'-6"	9'-3"	9'-6"	8'-6"	8'-7"	7'-10"	7'-10"	7'-2"	7'-2"
2×8	12"	15'-7"	15'-3"	17'-9"	14'-1"	15'-10"	13'-3"	14'-5"	12'-7"	13'-4"
2×8	16"	14'-3"	13'-11"	15'-5"	12'-11"	13'-10"	12'-1"	12'-7"	11'-5"	11'-8"
2×8	24"	12'-7"	12'-3"	12'-5"	11'-4"	11'-5"	10'-4"	10'-4"	9'-7"	9'-7"
2×10	12"	19'-7"	19'-2"	22'-2"	17'-9"	19'-11"	16'-8"	18'-2"	15'-10"	16'-10"
2×10	16"	17'-11"	17'-6"	19'-5"	16'-3"	17'-5"	15'-3"	15'-10"	14'-6"	14'-8"
2×10	24"	15'-10"	15'-6"	16'-0"	14'-3"	14'-5"	13'-1"	13'-1"	12'-1"	12'-1"
2×12	12"	23'-6"	23'-0"	26'-7"	21'-4"	23'-11"	20'-1"	21'-10"	19'-1"	20'-2"
2×12	16"	21'-7"	21'-1"	23'-7"	19'-7"	21'-0"	18'-5"	19'-1"	17'-5"	17'-8"
2×12	24"	19'-1"	18'-8"	19'-3"	17'-3"	17'-4"	15'-9"	15'-9"	14'-7"	14'-7"
3×8	12"	17'-10"	17'-7"	22'-0"	16'-4"	19'-9"	15'-4"	18'-0"	14'-7"	16'-9"
3×8	16"	16'-3"	16'-1"	19'-4"	14'-11"	17'-4"	14'-1"	15'-10"	13'-4"	14'-7"
3×8	24"	14'-5"	14'-3"	16'-4"	13'-2"	14'-4"	12'-4"	13'-1"	11'-9"	12'-1"
3×10	12"	22'-4"	22'-0"	27'-2"	20'-6"	24'-8"	19'-3"	22'-7"	18'-4"	21'-0"
3×10	16"	20'-6"	20'-3"	24'-0"	18'-10"	21'-9"	17'-8"	19'-10"	16'-10"	18'-4"
3×10	24"	18'-2"	17'-11"	20'-3"	16'-7"	18'-1"	15'-7"	16'-5"	14'-10"	15'-2"

SPAN OF RAFTERS

Span Calculations provide for carrying the live loads shown and the additional weight of the rafters, sheathing and wood shingles.

Size	Spacing	15# L.L. No Plaster	15# L.L. Plaster	20# L.L. No Plaster	20# L.L. Plaster	30# L.L. No Plaster	30# L.L. Plaster	40# L.L. No Plaster	40# L.L. Plaster
2×4	12"	11'-6"	8'-11"	10'-4"	8'-4"	8'-10"	7'-6"	7'-10"	6'-11"
2×4	16"	10'-0"	8'-2"	9'-0"	7'-7"	7'-8"	6'-10"	6'-10"	6'-3"
2×4	24"	8'-3"	7'-1"	7'-5"	6'-8"	6'-4"	6'-0"	5'-7"	5'-6"
2×6	12"	17'-6"	13'-8"	15'-9"	12'-9"	13'-6"	11'-6"	12'-0"	10'-8"
2×6	16"	15'-4"	12'-6"	13'-10"	11'-8"	11'-9"	10'-6"	10'-6"	9'-8"
2×6	24"	12'-8"	11'-0"	11'-5"	10'-3"	9'-9"	9'-3"	8'-7"	8'-6"
2×8	12"	22'-10"	17'-11"	20'-9"	16'-10"	17'-10"	15'-3"	15'-10"	14'-1"
2×8	16"	20'-1"	16'-4"	18'-2"	15'-5"	15'-7"	13'-11"	13'-11"	11'-8"
2×8	24"	16'-9"	14'-7"	15'-1"	13'-8"	12'-11"	12'-3"	11'-5"	11'-4"

GIRDERS

Safe Load in lbs. for Spans from 6 to 10 feet.

SIZE	6 ft.	7 ft.	8 ft.	9 ft.	10 ft.
6×8 SOLID	6,874	5,891	5,148	4,584	4,124
6×8 BUILT UP	6,090	4,220	4,560	4,062	3,654
6×10 SOLID	11,029	9,451	8,260	7,355	6,618
6×10 BUILT UP	9,774	8,376	7,320	6,519	5,865
8×8 SOLID	9,373	8,033	7,020	6,251	5,624
8×8 BUILT UP	8,120	6,960	6,080	5,416	4,872
8×10 SOLID	15,038	12,887	11,262	10,027	9,023
8×10 BUILT UP	13,032	11,168	9,760	8,692	7,820

DECIMAL EQUIVALENTS

DECIMAL OF A FOOT						DECIMAL OF AN INCH	
FRACTION	DECIMAL	FRACTION	DECIMAL	FRACTION	DECIMAL	FRACTION	DECIMAL
1/16	0.0052	4-1/16	0.3385	8-1/16	0.6719	1/64	0.015625
1/8	0.0104	4-1/8	0.3438	8-1/8	0.6771	1/32	0.03125
3/16	0.0156	4-3/16	0.3490	8-3/16	0.6823	3/64	0.046875
1/4	0.0208	4-1/4	0.3542	8-1/4	0.6875	1/16	0.0625
5/16	0.0260	4-5/16	0.3594	8-5/16	0.6927	5/64	0.078125
3/8	0.0313	4-3/8	0.3646	8-3/8	0.6979	3/32	0.09375
7/16	0.0365	4-7/16	0.3698	8-7/16	0.7031	7/64	0.109375
1/2	0.0417	4-1/2	0.3750	8-1/2	0.7083	1/8	0.125
9/16	0.0459	4-9/16	0.3802	8-9/16	0.7135	9/64	0.140625
5/8	0.0521	4-5/8	0.3854	8-5/8	0.7188	5/32	0.15625
11/16	0.0573	4-11/16	0.3906	8-11/16	0.7240	11/64	0.171875
3/4	0.0625	4-3/4	0.3958	8-3/4	0.7292	3/16	0.1875
13/16	0.0677	4-13/16	0.4010	8-13/16	0.7344	13/64	0.203125
7/8	0.0729	4-7/8	0.4063	8-7/8	0.7396	7/32	0.21875
15/16	0.0781	4-15/16	0.4115	8-15/16	0.7448	15/64	0.234375
1-	0.0833	5-	0.4167	9-	0.7500	1/4	0.250
1-1/16	0.0885	5-1/16	0.4219	9-1/16	0.7552	17/64	0.265625
1-1/8	0.0938	5-1/8	0.4271	9-1/8	0.7604	9/32	0.28125
1-3/16	0.0990	5-3/16	0.4323	9-3/16	0.7656	19/64	0.296875
1-1/4	0.1042	5-1/4	0.4375	9-1/4	0.7708	5/16	0.3125
1-5/16	0.1094	5-5/16	0.4427	9-5/16	0.7760	21/64	0.328125
1-3/8	0.1146	5-3/8	0.4479	9-3/8	0.7813	11/32	0.34375
1-7/16	0.1198	5-7/16	0.4531	9-7/16	0.7865	23/64	0.359375
1-1/2	0.1250	5-1/2	0.4583	9-1/2	0.7917	3/8	0.375
1-9/16	0.1302	5-9/16	0.4635	9-9/16	0.7969	25/64	0.390625
1-5/8	0.1354	5-5/8	0.4688	9-5/8	0.8021	13/32	0.40625
1-11/16	0.1406	5-11/16	0.4740	9-11/16	0.8073	27/64	0.421875
1-3/4	0.1458	5-3/4	0.4792	9-3/4	0.8125	7/16	0.4375
1-13/16	0.1510	5-13/16	0.4844	9-13/16	0.8177	29/64	0.453125
1-7/8	0.1563	5-7/8	0.4896	9-7/8	0.8229	15/32	0.46875
1-15/16	0.1615	5-15/16	0.4948	9-15/16	0.8281	31/64	0.484375
2-	0.1667	6-	0.5000	10-	0.8333	1/2	0.500
2-1/16	0.1719	6-1/16	0.5052	10-1/16	0.8385	33/64	0.515625
2-1/8	0.1771	6-1/8	0.5104	10-1/8	0.8438	17/32	0.53125
2-3/16	0.1823	6-3/16	0.5156	10-3/16	0.8490	35/64	0.546875
2-1/4	0.1875	6-1/4	0.5208	10-1/4	0.8542	9/16	0.5625
2-5/16	0.1927	6-5/16	0.5260	10-5/16	0.8594	37/64	0.578125
2-3/8	0.1979	6-3/8	0.5313	10-3/8	0.8646	19/32	0.59375
2-7/16	0.2031	6-7/16	0.5365	10-7/16	0.8698	39/64	0.609375
2-1/2	0.2083	6-1/2	0.5417	10-1/2	0.8750	5/8	0.625
2-9/16	0.2135	6-9/16	0.5469	10-9/16	0.8802	41/64	0.640625
2-5/8	0.2188	6-5/8	0.5521	10-5/8	0.8854	21/32	0.65625
2-11/16	0.2240	6-11/16	0.5573	10-11/16	0.8906	43/64	0.671875
2-3/4	0.2292	6-3/4	0.5625	10-3/4	0.8958	11/16	0.6875
2-13/16	0.2344	6-13/16	0.5677	10-13/16	0.9010	45/64	0.703125
2-7/8	0.2396	6-7/8	0.5729	10-7/8	0.9063	23/32	0.71875
2-15/16	0.2448	6-15/16	0.5781	10-15/16	0.9115	47/64	0.734375
3-	0.2500	7-	0.5833	11-	0.9167	3/4	0.750
3-1/16	0.2552	7-1/16	0.5885	11-1/16	0.9219	49/64	0.765625
3-1/8	0.2604	7-1/8	0.5938	11-1/8	0.9271	25/32	0.78125
3-3/16	0.2656	7-3/16	0.5990	11-3/16	0.9323	51/64	0.796875
3-1/4	0.2708	7-1/4	0.6042	11-1/4	0.9375	13/16	0.8125
3-5/16	0.2760	7-5/16	0.6094	11-5/16	0.9427	53/64	0.828125
3-3/8	0.2813	7-3/8	0.6146	11-3/8	0.9479	27/32	0.84375
3-7/16	0.2865	7-7/16	0.6198	11-7/16	0.9531	55/64	0.859375
3-1/2	0.2917	7-1/2	0.6250	11-1/2	0.9583	7/8	0.875
3-9/16	0.2969	7-9/16	0.6302	11-9/16	0.9635	57/64	0.890625
3-5/8	0.3021	7-5/8	0.6354	11-5/8	0.9688	29/32	0.90625
3-11/16	0.3073	7-11/16	0.6406	11-11/16	0.9740	59/64	0.921875
3-3/4	0.3125	7-3/4	0.6458	11-3/4	0.9792	15/16	0.9375
3-13/16	0.3177	7-13/16	0.6510	11-13/16	0.9844	61/64	0.953125
3-7/8	0.3229	7-7/8	0.6563	11-7/8	0.9896	31/32	0.96875
3-15/16	0.3281	7-15/16	0.6615	11-15/16	0.9948	63/64	0.984375
4-	0.3333	8-	0.6667	12-	1.0000	1-	1.000

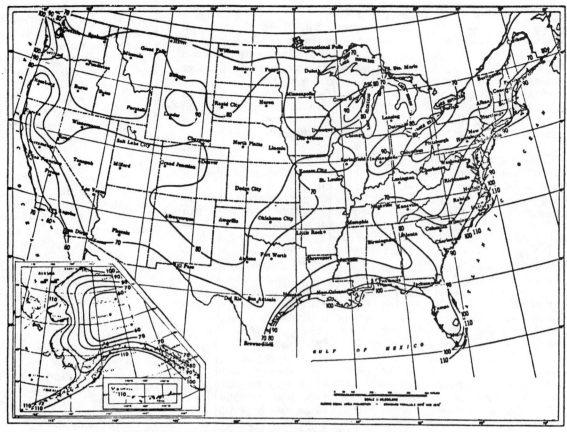

BASIC WIND SPEED IN MILES PER HOUR. ANNUAL EXTREME-MILE
30 FT ABOVE GROUND, 50-YR. MEAN RECURRENCE INTERVAL.

BASIC WIND SPEED

SAFE LOADS IN LBS. PER SQUARE FOOT ON DIFFERENT TYPES OF SOIL	
MATERIAL	Safe Load Lbs. Sq. Ft.
Soft, wet clay or soft clay and wet sand mixed	2,000
Sand and clay—Firm clay or wet sand	4,000
Dry solid clay or firm dry sand	5,000
Hard clay—Firm coarse sand—Gravel	8,000
Firm coarse sand and gravel mixed	12,000
Hard Pan	20,000

MATERIALS FOR SETTING CERAMIC TILE

Introduction:

The following are the most widely used materials for setting ceramic tile. Each possesses specific qualities that make it suitable for installing tile over certain backings or under a given set of conditions.

The conventional portland cement mortar method (including the one coat method)—is the only recognized thick-bed method—all others are thin-bed methods and are covered by existing trade jurisdictional decisions of record. Thin-bed bonding materials, including Dry-Set mortars and latex-portland cement mortars, can be used to bond ceramic tile to a cement mortar bed, as is customary when a neat cement bond coat is used. The neat cement bond coat can be used only when cement mortar bed is still plastic. Dry-Set mortars can be used, according to ANSI A108.5, on a cured bed. Under normal job conditions, a minimum of 24 hours cure is adequate, but longer mortar bed cures up to 10 days are desirable. When the bed to receive the tile is still plastic, Dry-Set mortar can be used as a 1/16'' thick bond coat. When organic adhesives are used, the mortar setting bed must be dry.

To insure practical and satisfactory installations, the cement mortar bed to receive the tile, whether left plastic or allowed to harden is to be applied by the tile contractor who must necessarily establish all the finished dimensions, at the time this bed is applied.

Non-cement setting materials such as epoxies and furans offer properties not possible with cement-based mortar. However, special skills on the part of the tile setter are required. *These materials can be appreciably greater in cost than cement-based mortars.*

Portland Cement Mortar:

A mixture of portland cement and sand, roughly in proportions of 1:6 on floors and of portland cement, sand and hydrated lime in proportions of 1:5:1/2 to 1:7:1 for walls.

Portland Cement mortar is used in the conventional method for setting ceramic tile. It is suitable for most surfaces and ordinary types of installation. The thick bed, 3/4'' to 1'' on walls and 3/4'' to 1 1/4'' on floors, facilitates accurate slopes or planes in the finished tile work.

Portland Cement mortars can be reinforced with metal lath or mesh, can be backed with membranes and can be applied over open studding on walls or on rough floors. They are structurally strong, are not affected by prolonged contact with water, and can be used to plumb and square surfaces installed by others. Suitable backings when properly prepared are: brick or cement masonry, concrete, wood frame, rough wood floors, plywood floors, foam insulation board, gypsum board, portland cement, and gypsum plaster. The one-coat method may be used over masonry, plaster or other solid backing that provides firm anchorage for metal lath.

Use of neat cement bond coat on cement mortar requires soaking of wall tile.

Complete installation specifications are contained in ANSI A108.1,2 and 3.

Dry-Set Mortar:

A mixture of portland cement with sand and additives imparting water retentivity which is used as a bond coat for setting tile.

Dry-Set mortar is suitable for use over a variety of surfaces. It is used in one layer, as thin as 3/32'', after tile are beat in, has excellent water and impact resistance, is water cleanable, non-flammable, good for exterior work, and requires no pre-soaking of tile.

Dry-Set mortar is available as an unsanded mortar and as a factory-sanded mortar. Presanded mortars, to which only water need be added, are strongly recommended. Dry-Set mortar is not affected by prolonged contact with water but does not form a water barrier. It is not a setting bed and is not intended to be used in truing or leveling the work of others.

Suitable backings when properly prepared include plumb and true masonry, concrete, cut-cell expanded polystyrene or rigid closed-cell urethane insulation board, gypsum board, concrete glass fiber reinforced backer board, lean portland cement mortar and cured conventional wall and floor setting beds, brick, ceramic tile, and marble.

Complete installation specifications and material specifications are contained in ANSI A108.5, ANSI A118.1 and, for conductive Dry-Set mortar, in ANSI A108.7 and ANSI A118.2.

Latex-Portland Cement Mortar:

A mixture of portland cement, sand and special latex additive which is used as a bond coat for setting tile.

The uses of latex-portland cement mortar are similar to those of Dry-Set mortar. It is somewhat more flexible than portland cement mortar. Since latices vary, follow manufacturer's directions carefully.

When latex-portland cement mortar is used to install ceramic tile in an area that will be immersed in water (e.g. swimming pools), it is recommended that the completed installation shall be cured a minimum of 14 days and be allowed to *thoroughly dry out* before exposure to water. Early immersion inhibits full development of the strength of the latex mortar and increases water sensitivity.

Complete installation specifications and material specifications are contained in ANSI A108.5 and ANSI A118.4.

Epoxy Mortar:

A mortar system employing epoxy resin and epoxy hardener portions.

Epoxy mortar is suitable for use where chemical resistance of floors, high bond strength and high impact resistance are important considerations. Acceptable sub-floors when properly prepared include concrete, wood and plywood, steel plate, and ceramic tile. Application is made in one thin layer. Pot life, adhesion, water-cleanability before cure, and chemical resistance vary with manufacturer. Complete installation and material specifications are contained in ANSI A108.6 and ANSI A118.3

Epoxy grout is also available. See section on grouts.

Epoxy Adhesive:

An adhesive system employing epoxy resin and epoxy hardener portions.

Epoxy adhesive is formulated for thin-setting of tile on floors, walls, and counters with epoxy as the major binder. It is designed primarily for economical high bond strength and ease of application and not for optimum chemical resistance. However, its chemical and solvent resistance tends to be better than that of organic adhesives.

There is no nationally recognized specification for use of epoxy adhesives in tile work.

Furan Mortar:

A mortar system consisting of furan resin and furan hardener portions.

Furan mortar is suitable for use where chemical resistance of floors is an important consideration. Acceptable sub-floors when properly prepared include concrete, wood and plywood, steel plate, and ceramic tile.

Properties vary with manufacturer. There is no nationally recognized specification for use of furans in tile work.

Furan grouts are also available. See section on grouts.

Organic Adhesive:

A prepared organic material, ready to use with no further addition of liquid or powder, which cures or sets by evaporation.

Organic adhesives are suitable for installing tile on floors, walls and counters where surfaces are appropriate and properly prepared—in accordance with adhesive manufacturers' directions. Such surfaces are concrete, gypsum board, portland cement, gypsum plaster, cement asbestos board, wood and plywood, brick, ceramic tile, and marble.

Adhesives are applied in one thin layer with notched trowel. Where leveling or truing is required an underlayment is used.

Adhesives obviate soaking of tile. They are not generally suitable for swimming pools or exteriors. They supply some flexibility to the tile facing. Bond strength varies greatly among numerous brands available. Solvents in some adhesives are irritating to some persons and some adhesives are flammable.

Adherence to ANSI A136.1-1967 is the minimum criterion for selecting an organic adhesive, Type I for prolonged water resistance and Type II for intermittent water resistance. Complete installation specifications are contained in ANSI A108.4.

Special Tile-Setting Mortars:

In connection with other tile-setting materials, instructions for use and installation specifications should be obtained from the manufacturer and followed carefully.

Thresholds:

By acting as a transitional piece between two different finished floor levels, thresholds permit the use of the conventional mortar method in rooms where it would not otherwise be possible. They also can be used with thin-set methods.

SPECIAL PRODUCTS
Pregrouted Ceramic Tile Sheets:

Individual ceramic tiles factory assembled into pregrouted sheets of various sizes for various interior floor and wall installations. Such sheets, which also may be components of an installation system, are generally grouted with an elastomeric material such as silicone, urethane, or polyvinyl chloride (PVC) rubber, each of which is engineered for its intended use. The perimeter of these factory pre-grouted sheets may include the entire, or part of the grout between sheets, or none at all. Field applied perimeter grouting shall be of the same elastomeric material as used in the factory pregrouted sheets or as recommended by the manufacturer.

Factory pregrouted ceramic tile sheets offer flexibility, good tile alignment, over-all dimensional uniformity and grouts that resist stains, mildew, shrinkage, and cracking. Factory pregrouted sheets tend to reduce total installation time where the requirement of returning a room to service or the allotted time for ceramic tile installation (as on an assembly line) is critical.

Special Purpose Tile:

Special purpose tile are either glazed or unglazed and made to meet or to have special physical design or appearance characteristics.

They are not required to meet all requirements of TCA 137.1 Consult the manufacturer's specifications. They are sometimes manufactured to create an architectural effect toward the casual. These tiles vary in size one tile from the other. Variations in plane may be expected. Larger tiles will develop greater variations in joint width.

Concrete, Glass Fiber Reinforced Backer Board:

A backer board designed for use with ceramic tile in wet areas. Available in various sizes and thicknesses, this material can be nailed or screwed in place over wood studs. Ceramic tile can be bonded to it with either dry-set or latex-portland cement mortars. It can be used in place of metal lath, portland cement scratch coat and mortar bed.

MATERIALS FOR GROUTING CERAMIC TILE

Introduction:

Grouting materials for ceramic tile are available in many forms to meet the requirements of the different kinds of tile and types of exposures. Portland cement is the base for most grouts and is modified to provide specific qualities such as whiteness, uniformity, hardness, flexibility and water retentivity. Non-cement based grouts such as epoxies and furans offer properties not possible with cement grouts. However, special skills on the part of the tile setter are required. *These materials can be appreciably greater in cost than cement-based grouts.* See ANSI specifications for grouting details and follow grout manufacturers' instructions.

Commercial Portland Cement Grout:

A mixture of Portland Cement and other ingredients to produce a water resistant, dense, uniformly colored material.

Wall type, usually white in color, is designed for conventional mortar installations with a very fine variety of aggregate. Soaking of wall tile is necessary. Floor type, usually gray, is designed for use with ceramic mosaics, quarry and paver tiles on both walls and floors.

Damp curing is required for both wall and floor types.

Sand-Portland Cement Grout:

An on-the-job mixture of 1 part portland cement to 1 part fine graded sand is used for joints up to 1/8 inch wide; 1:2 for joints up to 1/2 inch wide; and 1:3 for joints over 1/2 inch wide. Up to 1/5 part lime may be added.

Sand-portland cement grout is used with ceramic mosaic tile, quarry and paver tile on floors and walls. Damp curing is necessary.

Dry-Set Grout:

A mixture of portland cement and additives providing water retentivity.

Dry-Set grout has the same characteristics as Dry-Set mortar (See Dry-Set Mortar section). It is suitable for grouting all walls and floors subject to ordinary use.

This grout obviates soaking of wall tile, although dampening is sometimes required under very dry conditions. Damp curing may develop greater strength in portland cement grouts.

Latex-Portland Cement Grout:

A mixture of any one of the three preceding grouts with special latex additive.

Latex-portland cement grout is suitable for all installations subject to ordinary use (See section on Latex-Portland Cement Mortar).

It is less rigid and less permeable than regular cement grout.

Mastic Grout:

A one part grouting composition that is used directly from the container.

Mastic grout hardens by coalescence and does not require damp curing as do portland cement based grouts. It is more flexible and stain resistant than regular cement grout.

ACRI-FIL® is the trademark for mastic grout prepared under license of the Tile Council of America, Inc.

Furan Resin Grout for Quarry Tile, Packing House Tile, and Paver Tile:

A grout system consisting of a furan resin and hardener portions.

Furan grout is used in industrial areas requiring chemical resistance. Use of this grout involves extra costs and special installation skills. Architects should select the type of furan grout applicable to the specified exposure.

Epoxy Grout for Quarry Tile, Packing House Tile, Ceramic Mosaic Tile and Paver Tile:

A grout system employing epoxy resin and hardener portions, often containing coarse silica filler, especially formulated for industrial and commercial installations where chemical resistance is of paramount importance.

These grouts also provide high bond strength and impact resistance. They impart structural qualities to the tile when used both as a mortar and grout, especially over wood subfloors. Their use involves extra costs and special installation skills.

Architects should select the type of epoxy grout applicable to the specified exposure. Complete installation and material specifications are contained in ANSI A108.6 and A118.3.

Silicone Rubber Grout:

An engineered elastomeric grout system for interior use employing a single component nonslumping silicone rubber which upon curing is resistant to staining, moisture, mildew, cracking, crazing and shrinking.

This grout adheres tenaciously to ceramic tile, cures rapidly, withstands prolonged exposures to both hot and subfreezing temperatures as well as hot cooking oils, free steam, oxygen, and prolonged exposure to hot, humid conditions.

Use of this grout may involve extra costs.

WALL TILING INSTALLATION GUIDE

Simplest methods are indicated; those for heavier services are acceptable. Some very large or heavy tile may require special setting methods. Consult ceramic tile manufacturer.

SERVICE REQUIREMENTS	WALL TYPE (numbers refer to Handbook Method numbers)					
	Masonary or Concrete	Page	Wood Studs	Page	Metal Studs	Page
Heavy Service—Dry or limited water exposure: dairies, breweries, commercial kitchens, toilet rooms.	W212-76 W221-76*	16 17	W223-76 W231-76	17 18	W241-76 W242-76	18 18
Heavy Service—Wet: gang showers, commercial tubs, showers, laundries.	W211-76 W212-76 W221-76*(1)	16 16 17	W231-76 W512-76 W514-76	18 22 23	W241-76 W512-76 W514-76	18 22 23
Light Service—Dry or limited water exposure: residential kitchens and toilet rooms, commercial dry area interiors and decoration.	W212-76 W221-76* W223-76	16 17 17	W223-76 W243-76	17 19	W242-76 W243-76	18 19
Light Service—Wet: residential tub enclosures and showers.	W211-76 W212-76	16 16	W222-76 W223-76 B513-76 B515-76	17 17 23 23	W241-76 B513-76 B515-76	18 23 23
Exterior	W251-76 W252-76	19 19	W231-76	18		

*Use Detail W221 where there may be dimensional instability, possible cracks developing in or foreign coating (paint. etc.) on structural wall which includes clevage membrane (15 lb. felt or polyethylene) between wall surface and tile installation.
(1) Use over masonry backing.

GROUT SPECIFICATION GUIDE

Printed through the courtesy of the Mortar Manufacturers Standards Association. A rubber trowel should be used when grouting glazed tile with sanded grout.		GROUT TYPE See p. 6 for complete description									
		Commercial Portland Cement		Sand Port-land Cem-ent	Dry-Set		Latex (3)	Mastic (3)	Epoxy (1)	Furan (1)	Silicone or Ure-thane (2)
		Wall	Floor		Wall	Floor					
TILE TYPE	WALL TILE	●			●		●	●			●
TILE TYPE	CERAMIC MOSAICS		●	●	●	●	●		●		●
TILE TYPE	QUARRY, PAVER, & PACKING HOUSE TILE		●	●		●	●		●	●	
AREAS OF USE	Dry and intermittently wet areas	●	●	●	●	●	●	●	●	●	●
AREAS OF USE	Areas subject to prolonged wetting	●	●	●	●	●	●		●	●	●
AREAS OF USE	Exteriors		●	●	●	●	● (4)				
PERFORMANCE	Stain Resistance (5)	D	C	E	D	C	B	A	A	A	A
PERFORMANCE	Crack Resistance (5)	D	D	E	D	D	C	C	B	C	A
PERFORMANCE	Colorability (5)	B	B	C	B	B	B	A	B	Black Only	Restricted

(1) Mainly used for chemical resistant properties. Consult manufacturer when installation will be exposed to prolonged service temperature above 140 F.
(2) Special tools needed for proper application. Silicone, urethane and modified polyvinylchloride used in pregrouted ceramic tile sheets.
(3) Special cleaning procedures and materials recommended.
(4) Follow manufacturer's directions.
(5) Five performance ratings—Best to Minimal (A B C D E)

FLOORS
INSTALLATION PERFORMANCE LEVELS

Performance-Level Requirement Guide

Use this guide to find the performance level required, then consult the selection table to the right and choose an installation which meets or exceeds that performance level. For example: Method F113-76, rated Heavy, can also be used in any area requiring a lower performance level.

GENERAL AREA DESCRIPTIONS		RECOMMENDED PERFORMANCE-LEVEL RATING
Office Space Commercial Reception Areas	a) General	Light
Public Space in Restaurants and Stores, Corridors, Shopping Malls	a) General	Moderate
Kitchens	a) Residential b) Commercial c) Institutional	Residential or light Heavy Extra Heavy
Toilets, Bathrooms	a) Residential b) Commercial c) Institutional	Residential Light or Moderate Moderate or Heavy
Hospitals	a) General b) Kitchens c) Operating Rooms	Moderate Extra Heavy Heavy—use Method F122-76
Food Plants, Bottling Plants, Breweries, Dairies	a) General	Extra Heavy
Exterior Decks	a) Roof Decks b) Walkways and Decks on Grade	Extra Heavy—use Method F153-76 Heavy, Extra Heavy—use Method F151-76 or F152-76
Light Work Areas, Laboratories, Light Receiving and Shipping, etc.	a) General	Moderate or Heavy

Notes:
Consideration must also be given to (1) the tile selected with respect to the wear properties of the surface, (2) fire resistance properties of the installation and its backing, (3) acoustical properties, especially Impact Noise Rating of the entire floor, i.e., floor structure, tile installation, and ceiling below considered as an entity, (4) slip-resistance.

The tile used in the test of installations listed in the Selection Table were all unglazed unless otherwise noted. Unglazed tile of Standard Grade will give satisfactory wear, or abrasion resistance in all the installations listed. If, however, a decorative glazed tile or an especially soft body decorative unglazed tile is used, care must be taken to have the manufacturer approve the tile for the intended use. Color, pattern, surface texture, and glaze hardness all must be considered in determining whether the tile will be acceptable on a particular floor.

For waterproof floors (to prevent seepage to substrate or story below), refer to Method F121-76 and also specify particular setting method desired.

Selection Table

Maximum Performance Level

RESIDENTIAL:
Normal residential foot traffic and occasional 300 pound loads on soft (70 or less Shore A Durometer) rubber wheels. (Equivalent to passing test cycles 1 thru 3 of ASTM Test Method C 627-70.)

LIGHT:
Light commercial and better residential use, 200 pound loads on hard (100 or less Shore A Durometer) rubber wheels. (Equivalent to passing test cycles 1 thru 6 of ASTM Test Method C 627-70).

MODERATE:
Normal commercial and light institutional use, 300 pound loads on rubber wheels and occasional 100 pound loads on steel wheels. (Equivalent to passing test cycles 1 thru 10 of ASTM Test Method C 627-70.)

HEAVY:
Heavy commercial use, 200 pound loads on steel wheels, 300 pound loads on rubber wheels. (Equivalent to passing test cycles 1 thru 12 of ASTM Test Method C 627-70.)

EXTRA HEAVY:
Extra heavy commercial use, high impact service; meat packing areas, institutional kitchen, industrial work areas, 300 pound loads on steel wheels. (Equivalent to passing test cycles 1 thru 14 of ASTM Test Method C 627-70.)

Tests, from which the Performance Levels in this table were determined, utilized representative products meeting recognized industry standards. Dry-

Specification must include Handbook Method Number, grout, setting method and tile description as tabulated to achieve the intended performance level.

Handbook Method Number	page	Description	Grout	Comments On Use
F116-76	11	Organic adhesive on concrete Ceramic mosaic or glazed floor tile	Wet cured* 1 pc: 1 sand	Dry-Set or Latex-portland cement mortar preferred
F142-76	14	Organic adhesive on wood Ceramic mosaic or quarry tile	Latex-portland cement	Residential, low cost, bathroom, foyer
F143-76	14	Epoxy mortar on wood Ceramic mosaic tile	Wet cured* 1 pc: 1 sand	High bond strength in residential use
TR713-76	27	Epoxy adhesive over existing resilient tile Ceramic mosaic or quarry tile	Latex-portland cement	Residential renovation
F141-76	14	Portland cement mortar on wood Ceramic mosaic tile	1 pc: 1 sand	Depressed wood subfloor in residence
F143-76	14	Epoxy mortar on wood Ceramic mosaic tile	ANSI A118.3 epoxy	Best for wood subfloors
F113-76	10	Dry-Set mortar on concrete Ceramic mosaic tile	Wet cured* 1 pc: 1 sand	Economy for smooth surface
F113-76	10	Dry-Set mortar on concrete Ceramic mosaic tile	Latex-portland cement	Economy
F113-76 F114-76	10 11	Dry-Set mortar on concrete** Ceramic mosaic tile	ANSI A118.3 epoxy	Mild chemical resistance
F122-76	12	Conductive Dry-Set mortar** Conductive tile	ANSI A118.3 epoxy	Hospital operating rooms, other special
F111-76 F112-76	10 10	Portland cement mortar Ceramic mosaic tile	1 pc: 1 sand	Smoothest floor surface
F113-76 F152-76	10 15	Dry-Set mortar Quarry Tile	Wet cured* 1 pc: 2 sand	Economy for smooth surface
F113-76	10	Dry-Set mortar on concrete Ceramic mosaic tile	Wet cured* 1 pc: 1 sand	Best general thin-set method
F122-76	12	Conductive Dry-Set mortar Conductive tile	Wet cured* 1 pc: 1 sand	Hospital operating rooms, other special
F111-76 F112-76 F151-76	10 10 15	Portland cement mortar Quarry tile or Packing house tile	1 pc: 2 sand	Smooth, hard service best ceramic tile floor
F113-76	10	Dry-Set mortar on concrete Quarry tile or packing house tile	Wet cured* 1 pc: 2 sand	Best general thin-set method
F113-76 F114-76 F115-76	10 11 11	Dry-Set mortar on concrete Quarry tile or Packing house tile	ANSI A118.3 epoxy	General, on concrete, for mild chemical resistance
F143-76	14	Epoxy mortar on wood Quarry tile or packing house tile	ANSI A118.3 epoxy	Hard service on wood subfloor, chemical resistance
F131-76 F132-76	12 13	Epoxy mortar on concrete Quarry tile or packing house tile	ANSI A118.3 epoxy	Chemical resistance
F134-76	13	Chemical resistant mortar on acid proof membrane Packing house tile***	Furan or ANSI A118.3 epoxy	For continuous or severe chemical exposure

Set mortar—TCA formula 759; Epoxy mortar and grout—TCA formula AAR-II; and Epoxy adhesive—TCA formula C-150.

*Floor covered after grouting with polyethylene sheeting for three days. Water added to entire surface on second day and sheeting replaced.

**Rates "Heavy" if Dry-Set is wet cured for three days before grouting.
***Floor may show surface wear under constant steel wheel traffic.

FLOORS, INTERIOR

Concrete Subfloor

| Cement Mortar, Cleavage Membrane | F111-76 | Cement Mortar, Bonded | F112-76 | Dry-Set Mortar or Latex-Portland Cement Mortar | F113-76 |

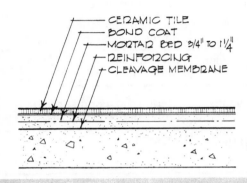

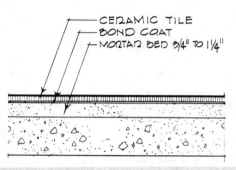

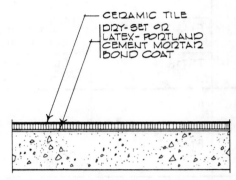

Recommended Uses:
- over structural floors subject to bending and deflection.

Requirements:
- reinforcing mesh mandatory.
- mortar bed thickness to be uniform.
- nominal 1 1/4" thick.

Materials:
- portland cement—ASTM C-150 Type I.
- sand—ASTM C-144.
- mortar—1 part portland cement, 6 parts damp sand by volume.
- reinforcing—2" x 2" x 16/16 gauge welded wire mesh or equivalent.
- cleavage membrane—15 lb. roofing felt or 4 mil polyethylene film. (May be omitted over waterproof membranes and pans, by other trades. See Method F121-76).
- bond coat—portland cement paste on a plastic bed, or Dry-Set mortar on a cured bed or latex-p.c. mortar on a cured bed.
- expansion joints (see Page 20).
- grout—specify type (see Pages 6 & 7).

Preparation by Other Trades:
- slab depression to be accurate with float finish.
- slope, when required, to be in subfloor.
- max. variation in the slab shall not exceed 1/4" in 10' - 0" from the required plane.

Expansion Joint (when specified, shall be detailed by the architect):
- where tile work abuts restraining surfaces such as perimeter walls, curbs, columns, pipes, etc.
- directly over joints in structural floors including construction joints or cold joints.
- 24' to 36' each way in large areas.
- expansion joints mandatory with quarry tile, recommended with other tile.

Installation Specifications:
- glazed wall tile—ANSI A108.1-1967 (glazed tile with extra duty glaze on light duty floors only).
- ceramic mosaics—ANSI A108.2-1967.
- quarry tile and paver tile—ANSI A108.3-1967.

Recommended Uses:
- on slab-on-grade construction where no bending stresses occur.
- on properly cured structural slabs of limited area.

Limitations:
- on precast concrete floor systems use cleavage membrane, follow Method F111-76.

Requirements:
- mortar bed thickness to be uniform.
- nominal 1 1/4" thick.

Materials:
- portland cement—ASTM C-150 Type 1.
- sand—ASTM C-144.
- mortar—1 part portland cement, 6 parts damp sand by volume.
- bond coat—portland cement paste on a plastic bed, or Dry-Set mortar on a cured bed or latex-p.c. mortar on a cured bed.
- expansion joints (see Page 20).
- grout—specify type (see Pages 6 & 7).

Preparation by Other Trades:
- slab depression to be accurate with screeded finish and free of cracks, waxy or oily films, and curing compounds.
- slope when required, to be in subfloor.
- max. variation in the slab shall not exceed 1/4" in 10' - 0" from the required plane.

Expansion Joint (when specified, shall be detailed by the architect):
- where tile work abuts restraining surfaces such as perimeter walls, curbs, columns, pipes, etc.
- directly over joints in structural floor including construction joints or cold joints.
- 24' to 36' each way in large areas.
- expansion joints mandatory with quarry tile; recommended with other tile.

Installation Specifications:
- glazed wall tile—ANSI A108.1-1967 (glazed tile with extra duty glaze on light duty floors only).
- ceramic mosaics—ANSI A108.2-1967.
- quarry tile and paver tile—ANSI A108.3-1967.

Recommended Uses:
- on plane, clean concrete.

Limitations:
- use Method F111-76 over precast concrete floor systems.

Requirements:
- slab to be well cured, dimensionally stable and free of cracks, waxy or oily films, and curing compounds.
- mortar bond coat 3/32" min.

Materials:
- Dry-Set mortar—conform with ANSI A118.1-1967.
- latex-portland cement mortar—conform with ANSI A118.4-1973.
- expansion joints (see Page 20).
- grout—specify type (see Pages 6 & 7).

Preparation by Other Trades:
- slab to have steel trowel and fine broom finish with no curing compounds used.
- slope, when required, to be in subfloor.
- max. variation in the slab shall not exceed 1/8" in 10'-0" from the required plane.

Expansion Joint (when specified, shall be detailed by the architect):
- where tile work abuts restraining surfaces such as perimeter walls, curbs, columns, pipes, etc.
- directly over joints in structural floor including construction joints or cold joints.
- expansion joints mandatory with quarry tile, recommended with other tile.

Installation Specifications:
- ANSI A108.5-1967.

All specifications for ceramic tile installations must conform to local building codes, ordinances, trade practices and climatic conditions.

FLOORS, INTERIOR

Concrete Subfloor

Cement Mortar, F114-76	Dry-Set Mortar, F115-76	Adhesive, Organic F116-76
Epoxy or Furan Grout	Epoxy or Furan Grout	

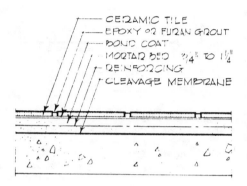

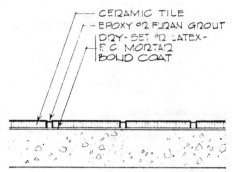

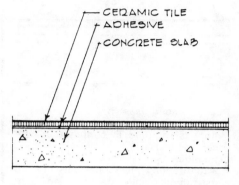

Recommended Uses:
- with tile set by Method F111-76 requiring good stain resistance and resistance to erosion caused by occasional contact with mild chemicals such as found in commercial dining areas, photographic dark rooms, public toilets, public foyers, etc.
- for use with quarry tile and paver tile.

Requirements:
- tile surface must be waxed before grouting with furan resin.

Materials:
- epoxy grout—ANSI A118.3-1969.
- furan resins—certified by manufacturer as suitable for intended use.

Published Specifications:
- tile installation—ANSI A108.3-1967.
- epoxy grout—ANSI A108.6-1969.
- furan grout—manufacturer's literature.

Tile Installation:
- follow Method F111-76.

Recommended Uses:
- with tile set by Method F112-76 or Method F113-76 requiring good stain resistance and resistance to erosion caused by occasional contact with mild chemicals such as found in commercial dining areas, photographic dark rooms, public toilets, public foyers, etc.
- for use with quarry tile and paver tile.

Requirements:
- tile surface must be waxed before grouting with furan resin.

Materials:
- epoxy grout—ANSI A118.3-1969.
- furan resins—certified by manufacturer as suitable for intended use.

Published Specifications:
- tile installation—ANSI A108.5-1967.
- epoxy grout—ANSI A108.6-1969.
- furan grout—manufacturer's literature.

Tile Installation:
- follow Method F112-76 or F113-76.

Recommended Uses:
- for use over concrete floors in residential construction only. For heavier service selected Method F113-76.

Limitations:
- will not withstand high impact or wheel loads.
- consult adhesive manufacturer for installation over floors with radiant heating.

Requirements:
- slab to be well cured, dimensionally stable and free of cracks, waxy or oily films, and curing compounds.

Materials:
- organic adhesive—floor type conforming to ANSI A136.1-1967.
- grout—specify type (See pages 6 & 7).

Preparation by Other Trades:
- slab to have steel trowel finish, with no curing compounds used.
- max. variation in the slab shall not exceed 1/16'' in 3' - 0'' from the required plane.

Expansion Joint (when specified shall be detailed by the architect):
- optional except in large areas.
- directly over joints in structural floor including construction joints or cold joints.
- expansion joints mandatory with quarry tile abutting rigid surfaces.

Installation Specifications:
- ANSI A108.4-1968.

FLOORS, INTERIOR Con't.

All specifications for ceramic tile installations must conform to local building codes, ordinances, trade practices and climatic conditions.

Concrete Subfloor

Waterproofing Membrane   F121-76

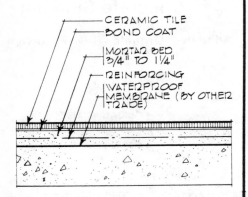

CERAMIC TILE
BOND COAT
MORTAR BED 3/4" TO 1 1/4"
REINFORCING
WATERPROOF MEMBRANE (BY OTHER TRADE)

CONDUCTIVE

Cement Mortar Bed   F122-76

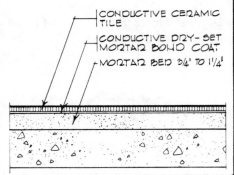

CONDUCTIVE CERAMIC TILE
CONDUCTIVE DRY-SET MORTAR BOND COAT
MORTAR BED 3/4" TO 1 1/4"

CHEMICAL RESISTANT

Epoxy Grout and Mortar   F131-76

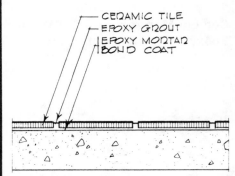

CERAMIC TILE
EPOXY GROUT
EPOXY MORTAR
BOND COAT

Recommended Uses:
- wherever a positively waterproof interior floor is required in conjunction with ceramic tile.

Limitations:
- waterproofing membrane must not be used directly under tile set by any thin-bed method.
- not recommended for severe chemical exposure.

Requirements:
- waterproofing membrane must be covered by a nominal 1 1/4'' thick mortar bed. The membrane must be flexible and free from the subfloor beneath it so that cracks or movement in the subfloor will not tear the membrane.
- depressed subfloor is mandatory when required to maintain floor elevation.

Preparation by Other Trades:
- max. variation in the slab shall not exceed 1/4'' in 10' - 0'' from the required plane.
- slope subfloor to drain.
- max. variation in the mortar bed shall not exceed 1/8'' in 10' - 0'' from the required plane.

Specifications:
- waterproofing membrane is installed by other trades and is separate from tile work. Specify type of waterproofing, i.e.: built-up roofing lead pan, synthetic rubber, or other proprietary type.

Expansion Joints:
- none in subfloor beneath membrane unless special installation method is designed to accommodate them.

NOTE: To be used with Method F111-76.

Recommended Uses:
- preferred method of installing conductive tile in new construction.
- in hospital operating rooms, certain laboratories, etc.
- where leveling of subfloor is required.

Limitations:
- perimeter expansion joints recommended.

Materials:
- portland cement—ASTM C-150 Type 1.
- sand—ASTM C-144.
- mortar—1 part portland cement, 4 to 5 parts damp sand by volume.
- conductive Dry-Set mortar—ANSI A118.2-1967.
- expansion joints (see Page 20).
- grout—specify type (see Pages 6 & 7). Conductive mortar shall not be used as grout.

Preparation by Other Trades:
- slab depression to be accurate with screed finish.
- max. variation in the slab shall not exceed 1/4'' in 10' - 0'' from the required plane.

Preparation by Tile Trade:
- mortar bed to be installed and damp cured for three days under vaporproof membrane and then allowed to dry for at least four additional days before installing tile.
- max. variation in the mortar bed shall not exceed 1/8'' in 10' - 0'' from the required plane.

Expansion Joint (when specified, shall be detailed by the architect):
- where tile work abuts restraining surfaces such as perimeter walls, curbs, columns, pipes, etc.
- directly over joints in structural floor including construction joints or cold joints.
- 24' to 36' each way in large areas.

Installation Specifications:
- ANSI A108.7-1967.
- NFPA NO. 56A

NOTE: Thin-bed method directly on concrete slab suitable only over sound, smooth, well cured subfloors of existing concrete, existing ceramic tile or terrazzo.

Recommended Uses:
- for setting and grouting ceramic mosaics, quarry tile and paver tile.
- where moderate chemical exposure and severe cleaning methods are used, such as in commercial kitchens, dairies, breweries, food processing plants, etc.

Limitations:
- for severe chemical exposures and where complete protection is needed, refer to Method F134-76.

Requirements:
- structurally sound subfloor, carefully finished to proper elevation and slope.
- surfaces to receive epoxy mortar must be free of sealers, curing compounds, oil, dirt and dust, and must be dry.

Materials:
- epoxy mortar and grout—ANSI A118.3-1969.

Preparation by Other Trades:
- slab to have steel trowel and fine broom finish.
- slope, when required, to be in subfloor.
- max. variation in the slab shall not exceed 1/8'' in 10' - 0'' from the required plane.

Expansion Joints:
- expansion joint not required except over joints in structural floor.

Installation Specifications:
- ANSI—A108.6-1969.

NOTE: Extreme heat or improper steam cleaning will soften epoxy grouts and wash them out of joints. Architect should consult resin manufacturer for special precautions when chemical exposure is severe, or at high temperature.

All specifications for ceramic tile installations must conform to local building codes, ordinances, trade practices and climatic conditions.

FLOORS, INTERIOR
CHEMICAL RESISTANT
Concrete Subfloor

Epoxy Grout and Mortar F132-76   Furan Resin   F133-76   Epoxy Grout and Mortar F134-76 or Furan Resin

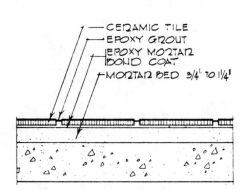

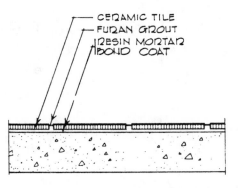

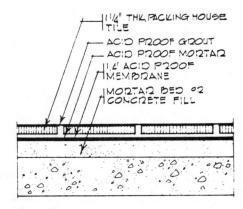

Epoxy Grout and Mortar F132-76

Recommended Uses:
- where leveling of subfloor is required.
- for setting and grouting ceramic mosaics, quarry tile and pavers tile.
- where moderate chemical exposure and severe cleaning methods are used, such as in commercial kitchens, dairies, breweries, food processing plants, etc.

Limitations:
- for severe chemical exposures and where complete protection is needed, refer to Method F134-76.

Requirements:
- surfaces to receive epoxy mortar must be free of sealers, curing compounds, coatings, oil, dirt and dust and must be dry.
- over structural floors subject to bending and deflection use cleavage membrane under mortar bed, see Method F111-76.

Materials:
- epoxy mortar and grout—ANSI A118.3-1969.

Preparation by Tile Trade:
- follow Method F112-76 for mortar bed over slab-on-grade.
- follow Method F111-76 for mortar bed over structural floors subject to bending and deflection.

Installation Specifications:
- tile installation—ANSI A108.6-1969

NOTES: Extreme heat or improper steam cleaning will soften epoxy grouts and wash them out of joints. Architect should consult resin manufacturer for special precautions when chemical exposure is severe, or at high temperature.

Joints must be completely filled with epoxy. Partial filling with sand or mortar is unacceptable.

Furan Resin F133-76

Recommended Uses:
- for setting and grouting quarry tile and paver tile.
- in kitchens, chemical plants, etc.

Limitations:
- for severe chemical exposures and where complete protection is needed, refer to Method F134-76.

Requirements:
- structurally sound subfloor, carefully finished to proper elevation.

Materials:
- furan resins — certified by manufacturer as suitable for intended use.
- resin mortar bed as recommended by grout manufacturer.

Preparation by Other Trades:
- slab to have steel trowel and fine broom finish.
- slope, when required, to be in subfloor.
- max. permissible variation in slab 1/4'' in 10' - 0'' from required plane.

Expansion Joint (when specified, shall be detailed by the architect):
- where tile work abuts restraining surfaces such as perimeter walls, curbs, columns, pipes, etc.
- directly over joints in structural floor including construction joints or cold joints.
- 16' to 24' each way in large areas, or as recommended by resin manufacturer.

Installation Specifications:
- manufacturer's literature.

Installation:
- warm resin and floor when floor temperature is below 50 F.
- pot life and working time is shortened by high temperature (95 to 100F).
- apply with notched trowel recommended by manufacturer.
- surface of slab must be neutralized with an acid solution and thoroughly dried before resin is applied.
- tile surface must be waxed.

Grouting:
- after tile is set, apply furan grout taking care not to remove wax coating on tile.
- 24 hours after grout is applied clean tile surface with steam or boiling water.

NOTE: Architect should consult resin manufacturer for special precautions when chemical exposure is severe, or at high temperature.

Epoxy Grout and Mortar F134-76 or Furan Resin

Recommended Uses:
- for setting 1 1/4'' thick packing house tile in areas of continuous or severe chemical exposure where special protection against leakage or damage to concrete subfloor is required.

Requirements:
- requires acid-proof membrane.
- structurally sound subfloor, carefully finished to proper elevation and slope.
- for epoxy installation follow Method F131-76.
- for furan installation follow Method F133-76.

Preparation by Other Trades:
- max. variation in the concrete fill or mortar bed shall not exceed 1/8'' in 10' - 0'' from the required plane.
- acid-proof membrane may be installed by other trades separate from tile work.

Expansion Joint:
- none in subfloor beneath continuous membrane unless special installation method is designed to accommodate them.

Specifications:
- acid-proof membrane—manufacturer's literature.

NOTES: The entire floor system is usually installed by a specialty ceramic tile flooring contractor and should be so specified.

Architect should consult resin manufacturer for special precautions when chemical exposure is severe, or at high temperature.

Joints must be clean and completely filled with epoxy or furan. Partial filling with sand or mortar is unacceptable.

FLOORS, INTERIOR con't.

Wood Subfloor

| **Cement Mortar** | F141-76 | **Adhesive, Organic** | F142-76 | **Epoxy Mortar** | F143-76 |

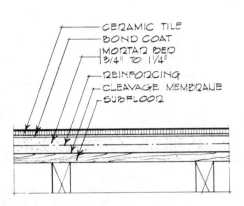

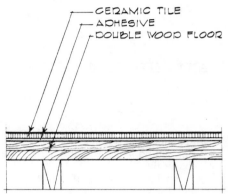

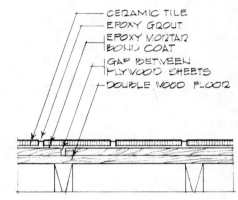

Recommended Uses:
- over all wood floors that are structurally sound.

Requirements:
- cleavage membrane required.
- reinforcing mandatory.
- deflection not to exceed 1/360 of span, including live and dead load.

Materials:
- portland cement—ASTM C-150 Type 1.
- sand—ASTM C-144.
- mortar—1 part portland cement, 6 parts damp sand by volume.
- bond coat—portland cement paste on a plastic bed, or Dry-Set mortar on a cured bed, or latex-p.c. mortar on a cured bed.
- reinforcing—2'' x 2'' x 16/16 gauge welded wire mesh or equivalent. Metal lath or other acceptable wire reinforcing nailed to the floor may be used in small residential bathrooms. Do not use ribbed lath.
- cleavage membrane—15 lb. roofing felt or 4 mil polyethylene film (may be omitted over waterproof membranes and pans).
- expansion joints (see Page 20).
- grout—specify type (see Pages 6 & 7).

Preparation by Other Trades:
- subfloor—5/8'' plywood or 1'' nominal boards when on joists 16'' o.c.
- depressing floor between joists on ledger strips permissible in residential use.

Expansion Joint (when specified, shall be detailed by the architect):
- optional except in large areas.
- expansion joints mandatory with quarry tile abutting rigid surfaces.

Installation Specifications:
- glazed wall tile—ANSI A108.1-1967 (glazed tile with extra duty glaze on light duty floors only).
- ceramic mosaics—ANSI A108.2-1967.
- quarry tile and paver tile—ANSI A108.3-1967.

Recommended Uses:
- over wood floors exposed to residential traffic only. For heavier service select Methods F141-76 or F143-76.

Limitations:
- will not withstand high impact or wheel loads.
- not recommended in wet areas.

Requirements:
- deflection not to exceed 1/360 of span, including live and dead load.
- double wood floor required.
- special grout required.

Materials:
- organic adhesive—floor type conforming to ANSI A136.1-1967.
- expansion joints (see Page 20).
- grout—specify latex-p.c. or epoxy (see Pages 6 & 7).

Preparation by Other Trades:
- subfloor—5/8'' plywood or 1'' nominal boards when on joists 16'' o.c.
- overlay—3/8'' min. exterior plywood with 1/8'' gap between sheets.
- max. variation in the plywood surface shall not exceed 1/16'' in 3'-0'' from the required plane. Adjacent edges of plywood sheets shall not be more than 1/32'' above or below each other.

Expansion Joint (when specified, shall be detailed by the architect):
- optional except in large areas.
- expansion joints mandatory with quarry tile abutting rigid surfaces.

Installation Specifications:
- ANSI A108.4-1968.

Recommended Uses:
- over wood floors where resistance to foot traffic in better residential, normal commercial and light institutional use is desired with thin-bed construction.
- where water, chemical and stain resistance is desired.

Requirements:
- deflection not to exceed 1/360 of span, including live and dead load.
- double wood floor required except in some residential uses.
- gap in top layer of exterior grade plywood required.
- gap between exterior grade plywood sheets to be filled with epoxy when it is spread for setting tile.
- with single floors in residential use, solid blocking required under all end joints of plywood.

Materials:
- epoxy mortar and grout—ANSI A118.3-1969.

Preparation by Other Trades:
- subfloor—5/8'' plywood or 1'' nominal boards when on joists 16'' o.c.
- overlay—5/8'' exterior grade plywood with gap of 1/4'' between sheets.
- residential use—overlay of 1/2'' exterior grade plywood or single layer of 5/8'' exterior grade plywood permissible. Maintain 1/4'' gap between sheets and provide solid blocking under single floor.
- max. variation in the plywood surface shall not exceed 1/8'' in 10'-0'' from the required plane. Adjacent edges of plywood sheets shall not be more than 1/32'' above or below each other.

Expansion Joint (when specified, shall be detailed by the architect):
- required over structural joints.

Installation Specifications:
- ANSI A108.6-1969.

FLOORS, EXTERIOR

PATIOS and WALKWAYS

Roof Deck, Membrane

Cement Mortar, Bonded F151-76

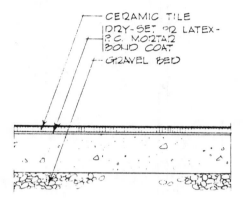

Dry-Set Mortar or F152-76
Latex-Portland Cement Mortar

Cement Mortar F153-76

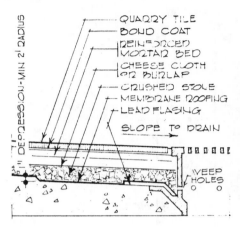

Recommended Uses:
- exterior floors, decks or patios where membrane is not used and where positive drainage below slab is provided.

Requirements:
- sloped slab required to provide complete surface drainage.
- gravel bed or other means of drainage below slab, is required.
- expansion joints are mandatory.
- cover completed tile work and keep damp for 7 days.

Materials:
- portland cement—ASTM C-150 type 1.
- sand—ASTM C-144.
- mortar—1 part portland cement, 6 parts damp sand by volume.
- expansion joints (see Page 20).
- grout—specify type (see Pages 6 & 7).

Preparation by Other Trades:
- provide subsurface drainage.
- slope slab for complete drainage.
- float finish slab, max. variation in the slab shall not exceed 1/4'' in 10' - 0'' from the required plane.

Expansion Joint (when specified, shall be detailed by the architect):
- where tile work abuts restraining surfaces such as walls, curbs, parapets, columns, pipes, drains, etc.
- directly over joints in structural floor including construction joints or cold joints.
- 12' to 16' each way in deck; do not exceed 16' between joints.

Installation Specifications:
- ceramic mosaics—ANSI A108.2-1967.
- quarry tile—ANSI A108.3-1967.

Recommended Uses:
- exterior floors, decks or patios where membrane is not used and where positive drainage below slab is provided.

Requirements:
- slab same as Method F113-76.
- sloped slab required to provide complete surface drainage.
- gravel bed or other means of drainage below slab is required.
- expansion joints are mandatory.
- mortar bond coat 3/32'' min.
- cover completed tile work and keep damp for 7 days.

Materials:
- Dry-Set mortar—conform with ANSI A118.1-1967.
- latex-portland cement mortar—conform with ANSI A118.4-1973.
- expansion joints (see Page 20).
- grout—specify type (see Pages 6 & 7).

Preparation by Other Trades:
- provide subsurface drainage.
- slope slab for complete drainage.
- steel trowel and fine broom finish slab; max. variation in the slab shall not exceed 1/8'' in 10' - 0'' from the required plane.

Expansion Joint (when specified, shall be detailed by the architect):
- where tile work abuts restraining surfaces such as walls, curbs, parapets, columns, pipes, drains, etc.
- directly over joints in structural floor including construction joints or cold joints.

Installation Specifications:
- ANSI A108.5-1967.

Recommended Uses:
- exterior roofs or decks of concrete, steel or wood where a waterproof roof membrane is used.

Limitations:
- although this is the best known method of installation for a quarry tile roof deck, it is not reliable in areas where the mortar bed will be subjected to frequent freeze-thaw cycles. The best insurance against eventual tile damage from stresses imposed by freezing is to assume the use of strong, dense, red quarry tile by specifying an average water absorption below 1/2 percent.

Requirements:
- roof drains by other trades must provide complete drainage at membrane level by use of weep holes as shown or other methods. Tile over flat deck with poor or no drainage will not stand up.
- reinforcing mesh mandatory.
- expansion joints are mandatory.
- surround roof drain with broken pieces of quarry tile to prevent stone or mortar from blocking weep holes.
- cover completed tile work and keep damp for 7 days.

Materials:
- portland cement—ASTM C-150 Type 1.
- sand—ASTM C-144.
- mortar—1 part portland cement, 5 parts damp sand.
- mortar bed thickness 1'' to 1 1/4''.
- dense quarry tile as approved by manufacturer.
- crushed stone max. size 1/2''. Slope stone bed to obtain pitch to drain.
- crushed stone bed 1'' min.
- burlap—cheesecloth may be used. This layer is to keep the mortar bed from entering the stone bed without inhibiting the drainage of moisture from the mortar bed to the stone.
- expansion joints (see Page 20).
- grout—specify type (see Pages 6 & 7).

Expansion Joint (shall be detailed by the architect):
- where tile work abuts restraining surfaces such as walls, curbs, parapets, columns, pipes, drains, etc.
- 12' to 16' each way in deck; do not exceed 16' between joints.
- expansion joints should not go through the gravel bed; they should extend only to the bottom of the setting bed.

Installation Specifications:
- quarry tile—ANSI A108.3-1967.

NOTE: Methods F111, F112, F113 and F142 are also suitable for exterior use when appropriate precautions are taken, including expansion joint placement and consideration for the particular climatic conditions and exposure.

WALLS, INTERIOR

Masonry or Concrete

Cement Mortar Bonded   W211-76

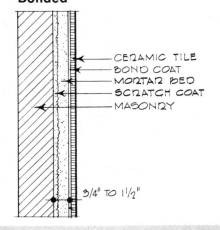

CERAMIC TILE
BOND COAT
MORTAR BED
SCRATCH COAT
MASONRY

3/4" TO 1 1/2"

Dry-Set Mortar or Latex-Portland Cement Mortar   W212-76

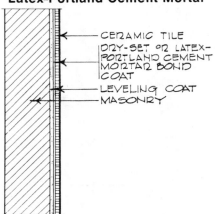

CERAMIC TILE
DRY-SET OR LATEX-PORTLAND CEMENT MORTAR BOND COAT
LEVELING COAT
MASONRY

Dry-Set Mortar or Latex-Portland Cement Mortar   W213-76

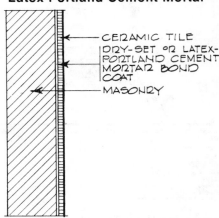

CERAMIC TILE
DRY-SET OR LATEX-PORTLAND CEMENT MORTAR BOND COAT
MASONRY

Recommended Uses:
- over clean, sound, dimensionally stable masonry or concrete.

Limitations:
- do not use over cracked or coated surfaces. Select Method W221-76 or W222-76 for such surfaces.

Requirements:
- require leveling coat if surface is irregular or if mortar bed would otherwise exceed 3/4'' in thickness.
- scratch coat is not necessary over concrete block walls and a mortar bed, not to exceed 3/4'' in thickness, may be used directly over a properly dampened block surface.

Materials:
- portland cement—ASTM C-150 Type 1.
- hydrated lime—ASTM C-206 Type S or ASTM C-207 Type S.
- sand—ASTM C-144.
- scratch coat—1 part portland cement, 1/2 part lime, and 4 parts dry sand to 5 parts damp sand or 1 part portland cement, 3 parts dry sand to 4 parts damp sand.
- mortar bed—1 part portland cement, 1/2 part hydrated lime and 5 parts damp sand *to* 1 part portland cement, 1 part hydrated lime and 7 parts damp sand, by volume.
- bond coat—portland cement paste. Dry-Set or latex-p.c. mortar permissible with wall tile. (For Dry-Set or latex-p.c. mortar on a *cured* bed, follow Method W213-76).
- expansion joints (see Page 20).
- grout—specify type (see Pages 6 & 7).

Preparation by Other Trades:
- max. variation in the masonry surface shall not exceed 1/4'' in 8' - 0'' from the required plane.

Preparation by Tile Trade:
- surface must be free of coatings, oil, wax, and be roughened to permit scratch coat to bond.
- max. variation in the scratch coat shall not exceed 1/4'' in 8'-0'' from the required plane.

Expansion Joint (when specified, shall be detailed by the architect):
- directly over all masonry control joints, changes in materials and 24' to 36' elsewhere.

Installation Specifications:
- glazed wall tile—ANSI A108.1-1967.
- ceramic mosaics—ANSI A108.2-1967.
- quarry tile and paver tile—ANSI A108.3-1967.

Recommended Uses:
- over clean, sound, dimensionally stable masonry, concrete or cured portland cement mortar when variation in surface exceeds 1/4'' in 8' - 0''.

Limitations:
- do not use over cracked or coated surfaces. Select Method W221-76 or W222-76 for such surfaces.

Requirements:
- concrete surfaces to be free of oil, coatings or wax and be roughened to permit bonding of leveling coat.
- max. variation in the surface of leveling coat shall not exceed 1/8'' in 8' - 0'' from the required plane.
- provide expansion joints directly over expansion or control joints in backing.
- leveling coat shall be cured at least 24 hours before tile is applied.

Materials:
- leveling coats or spot patching 1/4'' thick or less—Dry-Set mortar which is suitable for use with vitreous tile or latex-portland cement mortar; or Dry-Set mortar to which an equal volume of a mixture of 1 part portland cement and 1 1/2 parts sand has been added.
- leveling coats thicker than 1/4''—a minimum of 1/2'' thick mortar bed of 1 part portland cement, 1/2 part hydrated lime and 5 parts damp sand *to* 1 part portland cement, 1 part hydrated lime and 7 parts damp sand, by volume.

Tile Installation:
- follow Method W213-76.

Recommended Uses:
- over clean, sound, dimensionally stable masonry, concrete or concrete glass fiber reinforced backer board.

Limitations:
- do not use over cracked or coated surfaces. Select Method W221-76 or W222-76 for such surfaces.

Requirements:
- surface must be free of coatings, oil and wax.
- max. variation in the masonry surface shall not exceed 1/8'' in 8' - 0'' from the required plane.

Materials:
- Dry-Set mortar—conform with ANSI A118.1-1967.
- latex-portland cement mortar—conform with ANSI A118.4-1973.
- mortar bed min. thickness 3/32''.
- expansion joints (see Page 20).
- grout—specify type (see Pages 6 & 7).

Expansion Joint (when specified, shall be detailed by the architect):
- directly over all masonry control joints and changes in back-up materials.

Installation Specifications:
- ANSI A108.5-1967.

All specifications for ceramic tile installations must conform to local building codes, ordinances, trade practices and climatic conditions.

WALLS, INTERIOR

Solid Backing

Cement Mortar   W221-76

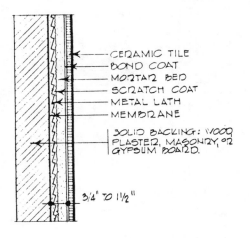

CERAMIC TILE
BOND COAT
MORTAR BED
SCRATCH COAT
METAL LATH
MEMBRANE

SOLID BACKING: WOOD PLASTER, MASONRY, OR GYPSUM BOARD.

3/4" TO 1½"

Recommended Uses:
- over masonry, plaster or other solid backing that provides firm anchorage for metal lath.
- ideal for remodeling or on surfaces that present bonding problems.

Requirements:
- require a leveling coat if variation in scratch coat exceeds 1/4'' in 8' - 0'' from the required plane or if thickness of mortar bed would exceed 3/4''.
- apply membrane, metal lath (self-furring lath preferred) and scratch coat.
- cut lath at all expansion joints.

Materials:
- membrane—15 lb. roofing felt or 4 mil polyethylene film.
- portland cement—ASTM C-150 Type 1
- hydrated lime—ASTM C-206 Type S or ASTM C-207 Type S.
- sand—ASTM C-144.
- scratch coat—1 part portland cement, 1/2 part lime, and 4 parts dry sand to 5 parts damp sand or 1 part portland cement, 3 parts dry sand to 4 parts damp sand.
- mortar bed—1 part portland cement, 1/2 part hydrated lime and 5 parts damp sand *to* 1 part portland cement, 1 part hydrated lime and 7 parts damp sand, by volume.
- bond coat—portland cement paste. Dry-Set or latex-p.c. mortar permissible with wall tile. (For Dry-Set or latex-p.c. mortar on a *cured* bed, follow Method W213-76.
- expansion joints (see Page 20).
- grout—specify type (see Pages 6 & 7).

Expansion Joint (when specified, shall be detailed by the architect):
- directly over control joints and 24' to 36' elsewhere.

Installation Specifications:
- glazed wall tile—ANSI A108.1-1967.
- ceramic mosaics—ANSI A108.2-1967.
- quarry tile and paver tile—ANSI A108.3-1967.

NOTE: Use furring strips (Method W231-76) if lath attachment cannot be made directly to backing.

One Coat Method   W222-76

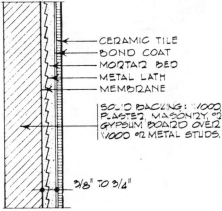

CERAMIC TILE
BOND COAT
MORTAR BED
METAL LATH
MEMBRANE

SOLID BACKING: WOOD PLASTER, OR GYPSUM BOARD OVER WOOD OR METAL STUDS.

3/8" TO 3/4"

Recommended Uses:
- over masonry, plaster or other solid backing that provides firm anchorage for metal lath.
- ideal for remodeling or on surfaces that present bonding problems.
- ideal for remodeling where space limitations exist.
- preferred method of applying tile over gypsum plaster or gypsum board in showers and tub enclosures.

Requirements:
- max. variation in the backing surface shall not exceed 1/4'' in 8' - 0'' from the required plane.
- apply membrane and metal lath.
- cut lath at all expansion joints.

Materials:
- membrane—15 lb. roofing felt or 4 mil polyethylene film.
- metal lath—galvanized or painted expanded metal lath or other approved wire reinforcing.
- portland cement—ASTM C-150 Type 1.
- hydrated lime—ASTM C-206 Type S or ASTM C-207 Type S.
- sand—ASTM C-144.
- mortar bed—1 part portland cement, 1/2 part hydrated lime and 5 parts damp sand *to* 1 part portland cement, 1 part hydrated lime and 7 parts damp sand, by volume.
- bond coat—portland cement paste. Dry-Set or latex-p.c. mortar permissible with wall tile. (For Dry-Set or latex-p.c. mortar on a *cured* bed, follow Method W213-76).
- expansion joints (see Page 20).
- grout—specify type (see Pages 6 & 7).

Expansion Joint (when specified, shall be detailed by the architect):
- directly over control joints and 24' to 36' elsewhere.

Installation Specifications:
- glazed wall tile—ANSI A108.1-1967.
- ceramic mosaics—ANSI A108.2-1967.
- quarry tile and paver tile—ANSI A108.3-1967.

NOTE: Use furring strips (Method W231-76). if lath attachment cannot be made directly to backing.

NOTE: For sound transmission rated construction see Method RW261-76.

Organic Adhesives   W223-76

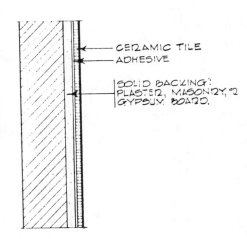

CERAMIC TILE
ADHESIVE

SOLID BACKING: PLASTER, MASONRY, OR GYPSUM BOARD.

Recommended Uses:
- interiors over gypsum board, plaster. exterior plywood or other smooth surfaces.

Materials:
- organic adhesives—ANSI A136.1-1967. Type I for prolonged water resistance and Type II for intermittent water resistance.
- water resistant gypsum backing board ASTM C630-74. (Required in wet areas).
- gypsum board—ASTM C36-75 (suitable for dry areas only).
- expansion joints (see Page 20).
- grout—specify type (see Pages 6 & 7).

Preparation by Other Trades:
- max. variation in the backing surface shall not exceed 1/8'' in 8' - 0'' from the required plane.

Preparation by Tile Trade:
- prime surface before applying adhesive when recommended by adhesive manufacturer.
- allow minimum of 24 hours after tile is set for solvent evaporation before grouting.

Installation Specifications:
- ANSI A108.4-1968.

NOTE: In wet areas such as tub enclosures and shower stalls use water-resistant gypsum backing board conforming to ASTM C630-74 with all openings carefully sealed or use Method W222-76 or W231-76.

575

WALLS, INTERIOR Con't.

All specifications for ceramic tile installations must conform to local building codes, ordinances, trade practices and climatic conditions.

Wood Studs or Furring

Cement Mortar W231-76

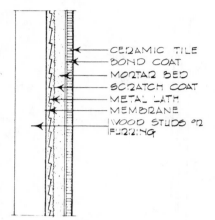

Recommended Uses:
- over dry, well braced wood studs or furring.
- preferred method of installation over wood studs in showers and tub enclosures.

Requirements:
- wood studs or furring must be protected from moisture by building felt, or polyethylene film.
- apply membrane, metal lath and scratch coat.
- require a leveling coat if variation in scratch coat exceeds 1/4" in 8'-0" from the required plane or if thickness of mortar bed would exceed 3/4".
- concrete glass fiber reinforced backer board may be used in place of metal lath scratch coat and mortar bed; follow manufacturer's directions. Set tile in Dry-Set mortar or latex portland cement mortar.

Materials:
- membrane—15 lb. roofing felt or 4 mil polyethylene film.
- portland cement—ASTM C-150 Type 1.
- hydrated lime—ASTM C-206 Type S or ASTM C-207 Type S.
- sand—ASTM C-144.
- scratch coat—1 part portland cement, 1/2 part lime, and 4 parts dry sand to 5 parts damp sand or 1 part portland cement, 3 parts dry sand to 4 parts damp sand.
- mortar bed—1 part portland cement, 1/2 part hydrated lime and 5 parts damp sand *to* 1 part portland cement, 1 part hydrated lime and 7 parts damp sand, by volume.
- bond coat—portland cement paste. Dry-Set or latex-p.c. mortar permissible with wall tile. (For Dry-Set or latex-p.c. mortar on a *cured* bed, follow Method W213-76).
- grout—specify type (see Pages 6 & 7).

Installation Specifications:
- glazed wall tile—ANSI A108.1-1967.
- ceramic mosaics—ANSI A108.2-1967.
- quarry tile and paver tile—ANSI A108.3-1967.

Metal Studs

Cement Mortar W241-76

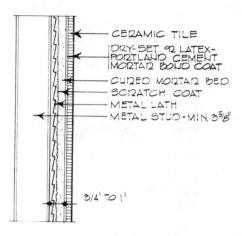

3/4" TO 1"

Recommended Uses:
- over metal studs.

Requirements:
- set tile in Dry-Set or latex-p.c. mortar on a cured mortar bed.
- scratch coat and mortar bed must not be richer than specified below.
- do not exceed 1" total thickness of mortar and scratch coat.
- stud spacing not to exceed 16" o.c.
- minimum recommended stud width is 3 5/8".
- studs shall be 20 gauge or heavier.

Materials:
- membrane—15 lb. roofing felt or 4 mil polyethylene film (required in wet areas).
- portland cement—ASTM C-150 Type 1.
- hydrated lime—ASTM C-206 Type S or ASTM C-207 Type S.
- sand—ASTM C-144.
- scratch coat—1 part portland cement, 1/2 part lime, and 4 parts dry sand to 5 parts damp sand or 1 part portland cement, 3 parts dry sand to 4 parts damp sand.
- mortar bed — 1 part portland cement, 1/2 part hydrated lime and 5 parts damp sand *to* 1 part portland cement, 1 part hydrated lime and 7 parts damp sand by volume.
- Dry-Set mortar—conform with ANSI A118.1-1967.
- latex-portland cement mortar—conform with ANSI A118.4-1973.
- metal lath—galvanized or painted expanded metal lath 3.4 lbs./sq. yd. or sheet lath 4.5 lbs./sq. yd. Do not use rib lath.
- metal studs—ASTM C645-74.
- expansion joints (see Page 20).
- grout—specify type (see Pages 6 & 7).

Preparation:
- apply metal lath and scratch coat.

Expansion Joint (when specified, shall be detailed by the architect):
- refer to ANSI installation specification.

Installation Specifications:
- ANSI A108.5-1967.

Gypsum Board Organic Adhesives W242-76

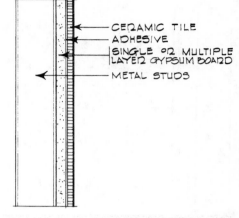

Recommended Uses:
- over gypsum board screwed to metal studs, single or double layer installed in accordance with GA-216-75.
- where a gypsum board, non-load bearing partition is desired with durable, low-maintenance finish.
- for fire-resistant, sound-insulated, ceramic-tiled walls. (Fire-resistance and sound-insulation ratings calculated on partitions before tiling.)
- for dry areas in schools, institutions and commercial buildings.

Requirements:
- minimum recommended stud width for 16" o.c. spacing is 2 1/2", for 24", o.c. spacing is 3 5/8".
- in tub enclosures and shower stalls use water-resistant gypsum backing board with all openings carefully sealed, or use Method W222-76 or W231-76.
- minimum recommended single layer gypsum board thickness is 1/2".
- studs shall be 25 gauge or heavier.

Materials:
- organic adhesive—ANSI A136.1-1967. Type I for prolonged water resistance and Type II for intermittent water resistance.
- metal studs—ASTM C645-74.
- water-resistant gypsum backing board ASTM C630-74.
- gypsum board—ASTM C36-75 (suitable for dry areas only).
- expansion joints—none required, except over discontinuity in backing (see Page 20).
- grout—specify latex-p.c. grout or mastic grout (ACRI-FIL®) (see Pages 6 & 7).

Preparation by Other Trades:
- max. variation in the gypsum board surface shall not exceed 1/8" in 8'-0" from the required plane nor more than 1/16" per foot. Corners, door jambs, etc. must be plumb within 1/8" in 8'-0".

Preparation by Tile Trade:
- prime surface before applying adhesive when recommended by adhesive manufacturer.
- allow minimum of 24 hrs. after tile is set for solvent evaporation before grouting.

Installation Specifications:
- tile—ANSI A108.4-1968.
- gypsum board—GA-216-75.

576

WALLS, INTERIOR

Wood or Metal Studs

WALLS, EXTERIOR

Masonry

Gypsum Board Dry-Set Mortar	W243-76

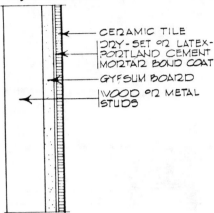

Cement Mortar	W251-76

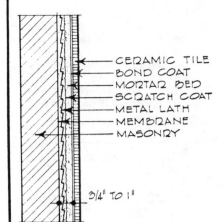

Dry-Set Mortar or Latex Portland Cement Mortar	W252-76

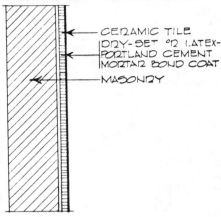

Recommended Uses:
- dry interiors over gypsum board. In wet areas such as tub enclosures and shower stalls use Method W222-76.
- for dry areas in schools, institutions and commercial buildings.

Limitations:
- do not use over water-resistant gypsum backing board.

Requirements:
- latex-portland cement or mastic (ACRI-FIL®) grout over metal studs.

Materials:
- gypsum board—ASTM C36-73.
- Dry-Set mortar—conform with ANSI A118.1-1967.
- latex-portland cement mortar—conform with ANSI A118.4-1973.
- grout—specify type (see Pages 6 & 7).

Preparation by Other Trades:
- max. variation in the gypsum board surface shall not exceed 1/8'' in 8' - 0'' from the required plane.

Installation Specifications:
- tile—ANSI A108.5-1967.
- gypsum board—GA-216-75.

Recommended Uses:
- over masonry or concrete on exteriors.

Requirements:
- flashing and membrane necessary to exclude moisture from mortar bed.
- apply membrane, metal lath (self-furring lath preferred) and scratch coat.
- expansion joints mandatory.
- cut lath at all expansion joints.
- require a leveling coat if variation in scratch coat exceeds 1/4'' in 8' - 0'' from the required plane or if thickness of mortar bed would exceed 3/4''

Materials:
- membrane—15 lb. roofing felt or 4 mil polyethylene film.
- portland cement—ASTM C-150 Type 1.
- hydrated lime—ASTM C-206 Type S or ASTM C-207 Type S.
- sand—ASTM C-144.
- scratch coat—1 part portland cement, 1/2 part lime, and 4 parts dry sand to 5 parts damp sand or 1 part portland cement, 3 parts dry sand to 4 parts damp sand.
- mortar bed—1 part portland cement, 1/2 part hydrated lime and 5 parts damp sand *to* 1 part portland cement, 1 part hydrated lime and 7 parts damp sand, by volume.
- bond coat—portland cement paste. Dry-Set or latex-p.c. mortar permissible with wall tile. (For Dry-Set or latex-p.c. mortar on a *cured* bed, follow Method W213-76).
- expansion joints (see Page 20).
- grout—specify type (see Pages 6 & 7).

Expansion Joint (when specified, shall be detailed by the architect):
- directly over masonry control joints.
- where tile abuts other materials, elsewhere 12' to 16' vertically and horizontally.

Installation Specifications:
- glazed wall tile—ANSI A108.1-1967.
- ceramic mosaics—ANSI A108.2-1967
- quarry tile and paver tile—ANSI A108.3-1967.

Recommended Uses:
- over clean, sound, dimensionally stable masonry or concrete.

Limitations:
- do not use over cracked or coated surfaces. Select Method W251-76.

Materials:
- Dry-Set mortar—conform with ANSI A118.1-1967.
- latex-portland cement mortar—conform with ANSI A118.4-1973.
- expansion joints (see Page 20).
- grout—specify type (see Pages 6 & 7).

Preparation:
- surface must be free of coatings, oil, wax.
- all concrete should be bush-hammered or heavily sand-blasted.
- max. variation in the masonry surface shall not exceed 1/8'' in 8' - 0'' from the required plane.

Expansion Joint (when specified, shall be detailed by the architect):
- directly over masonry control joints.
- where tile abuts other materials.

Installation Specifications:
- ANSI A108.5-1967.

NOTE: Methods W211, W212, W213, and W231 are also suitable for exterior use when appropriate precautions are taken including flashing, expansion joint placement, and consideration for the particular climatic conditions and exposure.

WALLS, SOUND-RATED
Metal Studs

One Coat Method   **RW261-76**

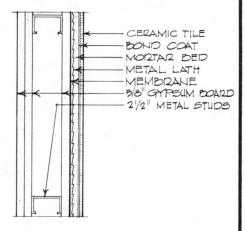

- CERAMIC TILE
- BOND COAT
- MORTAR BED
- METAL LATH
- MEMBRANE
- 5/8" GYPSUM BOARD
- 2½" METAL STUDS

Recommended Uses:
- I for Sound Transmission Class (STC) rating of 48
- II for Sound Transmission Class (STC) rating of 53

Requirements I:
- 2 1/2", 25 gauge, galvanized steel screw studs spaced 16" o.c.
- double layer of 5/8" type X gypsum board applied parallel to studs with staggered joints to one side and 1 layer of type X gypsum board applied parallel to studs under tile work on other side.
- membrane required in wet areas.
- ceramic tile installed by method W222-76 on 3/4" setting bed.

Requirements II:
- same as I above with 2" thick mineral wool having a density of 4.5 pounds per cubic foot inserted between the studs.

Materials:
- metal studs—ASTM C645-74.
- gypsum board—ASTM C36-73, Type X.
- membrane—4 mil polyethylene film.
- metal lath—self-furring, galvanized or painted expanded metal lath 3.4 lbs/sq. yd.
- mortar bed—1 part portland cement, 1 part hydrated lime and 6 parts dry sand.
- tile—glazed wall tile 9/32" thick.

Installation Specifications:
- glazed wall tile—See Method W222-76.
- gypsum board—GA-214-75.

NOTE: Recognizing the increasing demand for sound control by occupants, mortgage lending institutions and building code authorities, three industry groups, the Ceramic Tile Institute, Northern California Ceramic Tile Industry and the Tile Council of America, Inc. have undertaken a program to determine sound transmission loss classes for various ceramic tiled wall assemblies. Since STC ratings vary with the construction of the wall, the above ratings are valid only for the walls described. Tests were performed according to ASTM E90-70, "Recommended Practice for Laboratory Measurement of Airborne Sound Transmission Loss of Building Partitions." STC ratings determined by ASTM 413-70T.

EXPANSION JOINTS

All specifications for ceramic tile installations must conform to local building codes, ordinances, trade practices and climatic conditions.

Also Use These Details for Control, Contraction, and Isolation Joints.

    EJ411-76

Note: Preparation of openings left by the tile contractor and installation of back-up strip and sealant should be specified in the Caulking and Sealant section of the job specification.

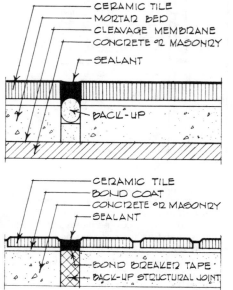

- CERAMIC TILE
- MORTAR BED
- CLEAVAGE MEMBRANE
- CONCRETE OR MASONRY
- SEALANT
- BACK-UP

- CERAMIC TILE
- BOND COAT
- CONCRETE OR MASONRY
- SEALANT
- BOND BREAKER TAPE
- BACK-UP STRUCTURAL JOINT

Joint Design Essentials

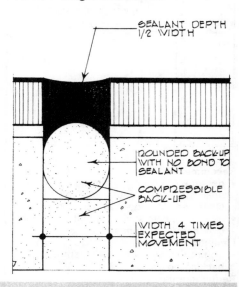

- SEALANT DEPTH ½ WIDTH
- ROUNDED BACK-UP WITH NO BOND TO SEALANT
- COMPRESSIBLE BACK-UP
- WIDTH 4 TIMES EXPECTED MOVEMENT

Expansion Joint Widths:
- exterior (all tile)—minimum 3/8" for joints 12' on center, minimum 1/2" for joints 16' on center. Minimum widths must be increased 1/16" for each 15 F of the actual temperature range greater than 100 F between summer high and winter low. (Decks exposed to the sky in northern U.S.A. usually require 3/4" wide joints on 12' centers.)
- interior for quarry tile and paver tile —same as grout joint, but not less than 1/4".
- interior for ceramic mosaic tile and glazed wall tile—preferred not less than 1/4", but never less than 1/8".
- joints through tile and mortar directly over any structural joints in the backing must never be narrower than the structural joint.

Preparation:
- tile edges to which the sealant will bond must be clean and dry. Sanding or grinding of these edges is recommended to obtain optimum sealant bond.
- primer on these tile edges is mandatory when recommended by the sealant manufacturer. Care must be taken to keep primer off tile faces.

Installation:
- set compressible back-up strip when mortar is placed or utilize removable wood strip to provide space for back-up after mortar has cured.
- install sealant after tile work and grout are dry. Follow sealant manufacturer's recommendations.
- refer to sealant section in ANSI tile installation specification.

Materials:
- single-component sealant (not trafficked areas) shall be a non-sag type complying with Federal Specification TT-S-001543 or TT-S-00230c.
- two-component sealant shall comply with Federal Specification TT-S-00227e; use Type II (non-sag) for joints in vertical surfaces and Type I (self-leveling) for joints in horizontal surfaces.
- back-up strip shall be a flexible and compressible type of closed-cell foam polyethylene or butyl rubber, rounded at surface to contact sealant, as shown in details above, and as recommended by sealant manufacturers. It must fit neatly into the joint without compacting and to such a height to allow a sealant depth of 1/2 the width of the joint. Sealant must not bond to the back-up material.

NOTES: In very small rooms (less than 12' wide) and also along the sides of narrow corridors (less than 12') expansion joints are not needed.

The performance requirements of certain special locations, such as exterior swimming pools, dairies, food plants, etc., may exceed the minimum requirements of the sealant specifications given above. Therefore, follow recommendations of experienced manufacturers as to specific sealants suitable in the job environment. In some severe environments a program for regular maintenance of sealant in joints may be required.

All specifications for ceramic tile installations must conform to local building codes, ordinances, trade practices and climatic conditions.

SWIMMING POOLS

NCAA and AAU Recommendations

Cement Mortar P431-76

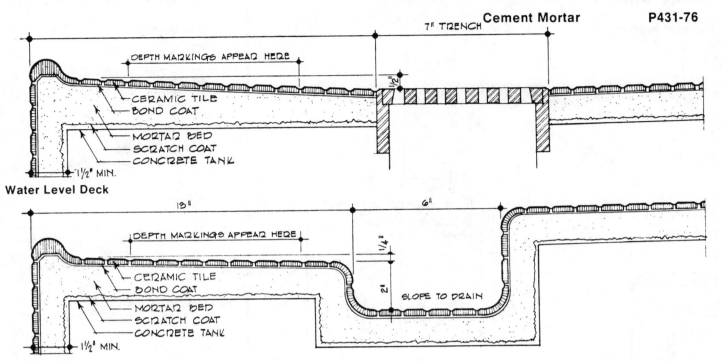

Water Level Deck

Roll Out Rim

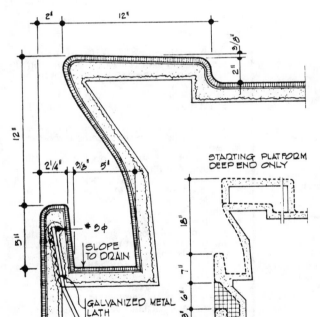

Gutter Detail

Recommended Uses:
- all interior and exterior pools.

Requirements:
- concrete tank must be water tight.

Materials:
- tile—Standard Grade conforming with TCA 137.1.
- special ceramic gutter shapes are available.
- portland cement—ASTM C-150 Type 1.
- sand—ASTM C-144.
- hydrated lime—ASTM C-206 Type S or ASTM C-207 Type S.
- waterproofing—use a commercially prepared waterproof portland cement or an approved waterproofing admixture.
- mortar bed (pool bottom)—1 part portland cement, 4 parts damp sand by volume.
- scratch coat and mortar bed (pool walls and gutter)—1 part portland cement, 1/2 part lime, and 4 parts dry sand to 5 parts damp sand or 1 part portland cement, 3 parts dry sand to 4 parts damp sand.
- bond coat—portland cement paste.
  Alternate: Dry-Set mortar on a cured bed (7 day cure recommended before Dry-Setting; 100% coverage of the back of the tile or tile sheet required).
- grout—1 part portland cement, 1 part 30 mesh sand by volume.
- metal lath (gutter reinforcing)—3.4 lb. galvanized diamond mesh tied to reinforcing rods.

Preparation by Other Trades:
- concrete tank to be finished with medium-rough bush-hammer finish or with aggregate exposed.
- deviations from dimensions, contours, slopes must not exceed 1/2'' nor encroach on the 1 1/2'' minimum thickness of tile work in order to provide exact dimensional requirements in length and width and specified tolerances of NCAA, AAU, YMCA or other.
- provide 3/8'' d. rods for handrails as detailed.
- concrete tank shall be watertight. Before tile work is started test by filling with water. No appreciable drop in water level will be permitted.

Preparation by Tile Trade:
- inspect tank for requirements included in Preparation by Other Trades above.
- check dimensions before starting tile work.
- report any defects to architect in writing.
- submit shop drawing for all details, lettering and markings.
- after approval of the concrete tank, wash with hose under high pressure and sweep with a stiff broom. Surface to be free of grease, oil, wax or other coatings.

Expansion Joint (when specified, shall be detailed by the architect):
- directly over any joints in the concrete tank.
- exterior pools require expansion joints in tile work on 12' to 16' centers.
NOTE: Pool plans and elevations are available and were printed in 1968 Handbook.

TILE TUBS

All specifications for ceramic tile installations must conform to local building codes, ordinances, trade practices and climatic conditions.

Membrane

Cement Mortar   B511-76

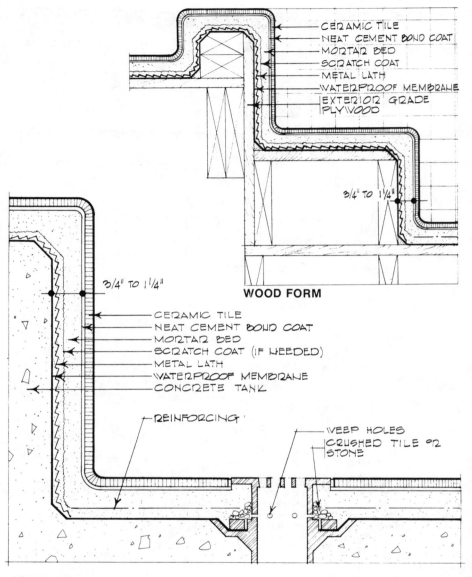

WOOD FORM

CONCRETE TANK
(Preferred)

Requirements:
- waterproof membrane required except in slab-on-grade installations where membrane may be omitted.
- slope tank so that membrane will slope to the drain.
- flange drain with weep holes required.
- wood framing, if used, should be pressure treated and designed to resist deflection and movement.

Preparation by Other Trades:
- test tank, membrane and drainage fittings for leaks before starting tile work.

Installation Methods:
- attach metal lath only above water line.
- follow Method F121-76.

BATHTUB WALLS

Wood or Metal Studs

Cement Mortar   B512-76

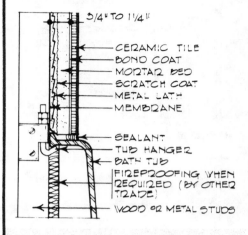

Recommended Uses:
- over dry, well braced wood studs, furring or metal studs.
- preferred method of installation over wood studs for bathtubs.

Requirements:
- wood studs or furring must be protected from moisture by roofing felt, or polyethylene film.
- over metal studs: see Method W241-76.
- apply membrane, metal lath and scratch coat.
- require a leveling coat if variation in scratch coat exceeds 1/4'' in 8' - 0'' from the required plane or if thickness of mortar bed would exceed 3/4''.
- concrete glass fiber reinforced backer board may be used in place of metal lath scratch coat and mortar bed; follow manufacturer's directions. Set tile in Dry-Set mortar or latex-portland cement mortar.

Materials:
- membrane—15 lb. roofing felt or 4 mil polyethylene film.
- portland cement—ASTM C-150 Type 1.
- hydrated lime—ASTM C-206 Type S or ASTM C-207 Type S.
- sand—ASTM C-144.
- scratch coat—1 part portland cement, 1/2 part lime, and 4 parts dry sand to 5 parts damp sand or 1 part portland cement, 3 parts dry sand to 4 parts damp sand.
- mortar bed—1 part portland cement, 1/2 part hydrated lime and 5 parts damp sand to 1 part portland cement, 1 part hydrated lime and 7 parts damp sand, by volume.
- bond coat—portland cement paste, Dry-Set or latex-p.c. mortar.
- grout—specify type (see Pages 6 & 7).
- elastomeric caulking—after tile work and grout is dry.
- metal studs—ASTM C645-70.

Preparation by Other Trades:
- over metal studs see Method W241-76.
- studs square and plumb, opening for recessed bathtubs not to exceed 1/2'' more than total length of tub.
- bathtub installed level and supported with metal hangers or on end grain wood blocks.
- fireproofing behind tub when required.

Installation Specifications:
- glazed wall tile—ANSI A108.1-1967.
- ceramic mosaics—ANSI A108.2-1967.
- quarry tile and paver tile—ANSI A108.3-1967.

All specifications for ceramic tile installations must conform to local building codes, ordinances, trade practices and climatic conditions.

SHOWER RECEPTORS, WALLS

Wood or Metal Studs

Gypsum Board   B513-76
Organic Adhesives

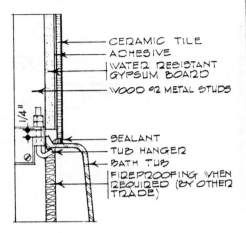

Recommended Uses:
- in tub enclosures and tub-showers over water-resistant gypsum backing board on wood or metal studs.

Requirements:
- to be used in conjunction with Methods W223-76 or W242-76.
- water resistant gypsum backing board single layer thickness shall be minimum 1/2'' thick over studs spaced at maximum 16'' o.c.
- water resistant gypsum backing board shall be applied horizontally with the factory paperbound edge spaced a minimum of 1/4'' above the lip of the tub.

Materials:
- see Methods W223-76 or W242-76.

Preparation by Other Trades:
- all openings cut in backing board for plumbing and all cut joints between adjoining pieces shall be sealed with adhesive or other materials recommended by manufacturer of backing board.

Preparation by Tile Trade:
- prime surface before applying adhesive when recommended by adhesive manufacturer.
- allow minimum of 24 hrs. after tile is set for solvent evaporation before grouting.

Installation Specifications:
- see Methods W223-76 or W242-76.

Cement Mortar   B514-76

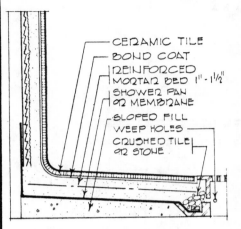

Recommended Uses:
- over wood or concrete subfloors.

Requirements:
- slope required in pan or membrane 1/4'' per ft. to weep holes in drain.
- membrane or pan to turn up wall at least 5'' above high point of shower floor.

Materials:
- portland cement—ASTM C-150 Type 1.
- sand—ASTM C-144.
- mortar—1 part portland cement, 4 parts damp sand by volume. (Use waterproof cement or a waterproofing admixture).
- reinforcing—2'' x 2'' x 16/16 gauge wire mesh or equivalent.
- grout—specify type (see Pages 6 & 7).
- lead, copper or composition pan as installed by others.

Preparation by Other Trades:
- form slope for membrane with cement mortar or preformed liners.

Preparation by Tile Trade:
- surround drain with broken pieces of tile or crushed stone to prevent mortar from blocking weep holes.

Installation Specifications:
- glazed wall tile—ANSI A108.1-1967 (use extra duty glazed tile on floor).
- ceramic mosaics—ANSI A108.2-1967.
- quarry tile and paver tile—ANSI A108.3-1967.

Gypsum Board   B515-76
Organic Adhesives

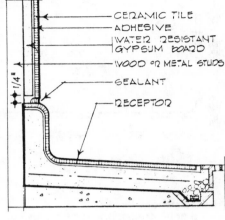

Recommended Uses:
- in showers over water-resistant gypsum backing board on wood or metal studs.

Requirements:
- to be used in conjunction with Methods W223-76 or W242-76.
- water resistant gypsum backing board single layer thickness shall be minimum 1/2'' thick over studs spaced at maximum 16'' o.c.
- water resistant gypsum backing board shall be applied horizontally with the factory paperbound edge spaced a minimum of 1/4'' above the lip of the receptor or sub-pan.

Materials:
- see Methods W223-76 or W242-76.

Preparation by Other Trades:
- all openings cut in backing board for plumbing and all cut joints between adjoining pieces shall be sealed with adhesive or other materials recommended by manufacturer of backing board.
- see Methods W223-76 or W242-76 for additional preparations.

Preparation by Tile Trade:
- prime surface before applying adhesive when recommended by adhesive manufacturer.
- allow minimum of 24 hrs. after tile is set for solvent evaporation before grouting.

Installation Specifications:
- see Methods W-223-76 or W242-76.

COUNTERTOPS

STAIRS, INTERIOR

Wood Base

Cement Mortar   C611-76

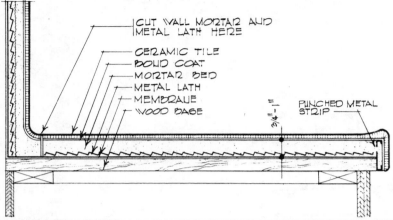

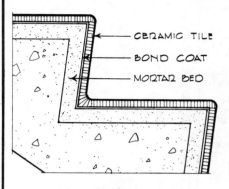

Cement Mortar   S631-76

CONCRETE STAIRS

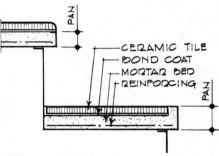

METAL STAIRS

Recommended Uses:
- on countertops, drainboards, lavatory tops, etc.
- preferred method where sink or lavatory is to be recessed.

Requirements:
- the bottom edge of the countertop trim must be set the proper distance above the finish floor material to allow clearance for dishwashers, compactors, etc.
- cut lath off at corner as shown.
- use extra-duty glazed tile or unglazed tile.

Materials:
- membrane—15 lb. roofing felt, 4 mil polyethylene film or duplex type reinforced asphalt paper.
- portland cement—ASTM C-150 Type 1.
- sand—ASTM C-144.
- mortar—1 part portland cement, 6 parts damp sand by volume.
- reinforcing—3.4 lb. metal lath, 2 x 2

welded wire mesh or other approved wire mesh.
- grout—specify type (see Pages 6 & 7).

Preparation by Other Trades:
- base to be 1'' x 6'' boards with 1/4'' gap between boards or 3/4'' exterior plywood with dot and dash saw cuts 6'' to 8'' on center through the length of the plywood board to prevent warping.

Preparation by Tile Trade:
- a punched metal strip attached to the front edge of the cabinet is used in some geographical areas as a screed and support for the countertop trim. It is filled with wall mortar.

Installation Specifications:
- glazed wall tile—ANSI A108.1-1967. (glazed tile with extra-duty glaze).
- ceramic mosaics—ANSI A108.2-1967.
- quarry tile and paver tile—ANSI A108.3-1967.

Concrete Stairs:
- concrete to be finished with medium-rough bush-hammer finish and be free of cracks, waxy or oily films and curing compounds.

Metal Stairs:
- reinforcing mesh mandatory. Attach to metal by tack welds or other means.
- metal stair riser may be tiled. Cut mortar bed and reinforcing at juncture of tread and riser.

Design Considerations:
- use cove tile at junction of riser and tread for easy maintenance. Quarry or paver tile cove can be set horizontally or vertically to facilitate lay out.
- finished step nosings are available in specially shaped quarry and paver tile pieces.
- use full radius ceramic mosaic bullnose tile for nosings.
- slip-resistant tile should be specified on stair treads.

Tile Installation:
- metal stairs—Method F111-76. Membrane not required.
- concrete stairs—Method F112-76.

Thin-Set   C612-76

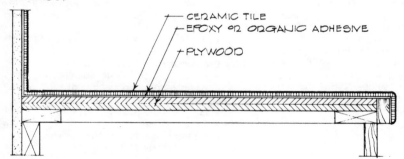

Recommended Uses:
- on countertops where thin-set method is desired.

Requirements:
- 3/4'' exterior plywood base required.
- the bottom edge of the countertop trim must be set the proper distance above the finish floor material to allow clearance for dishwashers, compactors, etc.

Materials:
- epoxy mortar—ANSI A118.3-1969.
- organic adhesive—ANSI A136.1-1967. Type I for prolonged water resistance.
- grout—specify type (see Pages 6 & 7).

Preparation by Other Trades:
- when tile is set with epoxy leave 1/4'' gap between sheets of plywood. Apply batten to under side of sheets to cover gap.

Preparation by Tile Trade:
- when tile is set with epoxy completely fill gap between sheets of plywood with epoxy.
- prime surface before applying organic adhesive when recommended by adhesive manufacturer.

Installation Specifications:
- adhesive—ANSI A108.4-1968.
- epoxy—ANSI A108.6-1969.

REFRIGERATOR ROOMS

All specifications for ceramic tile installations must conform to local building codes, ordinances, trade practices and climatic conditions.

STEAM ROOMS

Insulation

Cement Mortar or Dry-Set Mortar

R651-76

Membrane

Cement Mortar

SR652-76

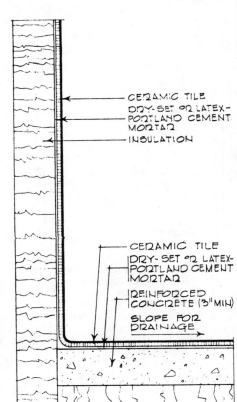

- CERAMIC TILE
- BOND COAT
- MORTAR BED 3/4"-1"
- SCRATCH COAT
- METAL LATH
- INSULATION
- TIE WIRES

- CERAMIC TILE
- BOND COAT
- MORTAR BED 3/4"-1 1/4"
- REINFORCED CONCRETE (3"MIN)
- SLOPE FOR DRAINAGE

- CERAMIC TILE
- DRY-SET OR LATEX-PORTLAND CEMENT MORTAR
- INSULATION

- CERAMIC TILE
- DRY-SET OR LATEX-PORTLAND CEMENT MORTAR
- REINFORCED CONCRETE (3"MIN)
- SLOPE FOR DRAINAGE

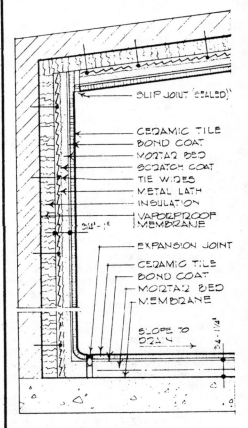

- SLIP JOINT (SEALED)
- CERAMIC TILE
- BOND COAT
- MORTAR BED
- SCRATCH COAT
- TIE WIRES
- METAL LATH
- INSULATION
- VAPORPROOF MEMBRANE
- EXPANSION JOINT
- CERAMIC TILE
- BOND COAT
- MORTAR BED
- MEMBRANE
- SLOPE TO DRAIN

Requirements:

- use tile designated as frostproof by the manufacturer in all rooms subject to freezing temperatures.
- reinforced concrete slab must be provided over floor insulation to resist wheel load of hand and mechanical trucks. (3" minimum; 4" or more for fork lift trucks.)

Tile Installation:

- wall and ceiling tile may be applied directly to cut-cell polystyrene, rigid closed-cell urethane or foam glass insulation with Dry-Set mortar where impact resistance is not required.
- on walls and ceilings with other types of insulation and when impact resistance is required, attach metal lath and follow Method W222-76 or install on a mortar bed meeting the requirements of Method W241-76.
- floors may be installed in accordance to Method F112-76 (cement mortar). F113-76 (Dry-Set mortar or latex-portland cement mortar), or F131-76 (epoxy grout and mortar).

Requirements:

- steam rooms require a continuous waterproof membrane on all surfaces to prevent moisture from penetrating adjoining spaces.
- most membranes will require insulation on walls and ceilings to protect them from excessive heat. Insulation must be capable of withstanding 240 F.
- install open slip joints in all corners between walls, and ceilings and to divide areas that exceed 16' - 0" in length.
- anchor galvanized metal lath to walls and ceilings with monel or stainless steel wire extending through insulation to supporting members.
- slope ceilings (2" per ft. minimum) to avoid condensation from dripping onto occupants, (sometimes sloped to center to minimize run-down on walls).

Tile Installation:

- floors—follow Method F121-76.
- walls and ceiling—follow Method W221-76 with waterproof membrane.

THRESHOLDS, SADDLES

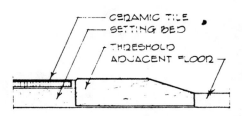

- CERAMIC TILE
- SETTING BED
- THRESHOLD
- ADJACENT FLOOR

TH 421-76

Notes: *Thresholds adjust between adjacent floors. Commercial and residential types are available in marble, stone, slate, etc. Thresholds can be made in virtually any size or shaped to fit special conditions.*

Use 100% coverage of bonding material between threshold and floor.

583

RENOVATION

Tile Over Tile

Interior Walls

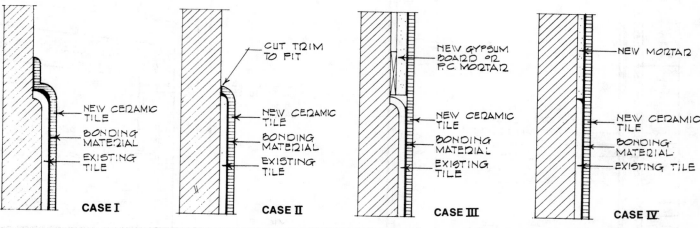

Recommended Uses:
- for alteration of ceramic-tiled areas where modernization or a change of design is desired in residences, motels and hotels, restaurants, public rest rooms, etc.
- also applicable to smooth walls of marble, stone, slate, etc.

Requirements:
- existing installation must be sound, well bonded, and without major structural cracks.

NOTE: If installation is not sound, Methods W221-76 and W222-76 may be applicable.

Materials, Grouting, Expansion Joints, Installation Specifications:
- for organic adhesive installation see Method W223-76.
- for Dry-Set or latex-portland cement mortar installation see Method W213-76.
- for epoxy mortar installation refer to ANSI A108.6-1969.
- for epoxy adhesive installation refer to manufacturer's literature.

Preparation:
- remove soap scum, wax, coatings, oil, etc. from existing tile surfaces. Mechanical abrasion with a Carborundum disk followed by a clear water wash is recommended. Other cleaning methods involve use of soapless detergents, commercial tile cleaners, and, in special cases, solvents or acid. Solvents and acids should be used with care and only when necessary because of their hazardous nature.
- installation must be thoroughly dry before setting the new tile.
- Case I—prepare wall above tile to receive trim tile as shown above.
- Case II—cut trim tile to fit over existing trim.
- Cases III & IV—apply new gypsum board above existing wainscot tile to prepare for full wall tiling.
  Use portland cement mortar, water-resistant gypsum backing board or concrete glass fiber reinforced backer board in tub enclosures and shower stalls.
  In wet areas the application of gypsum board over any base which causes a vapor barrier to exist, such as old tile or paint shown in Cases III and IV will lead to failure unless such barrier is vented.

Tile Over Tile

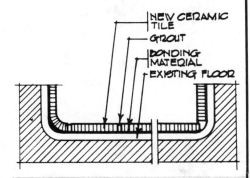

Recommended Uses:
- for alteration of ceramic-tiled areas where modernization or a change of design is desired in residences, motels and hotels, restaurants, public rest rooms, etc.
- also applicable to smooth floors of terrazzo, stone, slate, etc.

Requirements:
- existing installation must be sound, well bonded, and without structural cracks.
- when possible, floor-mounted plumbing and heating fixtures should be removed before beginning work.
- threshold required to adjust between adjacent floors (see Method TH421-76).

Preparation:
- remove soap scum, wax, coatings, oil, etc. from existing tile surfaces. Mechanical abrasion with a Carborundum disk followed by a clear water wash is recommended. Other cleaning methods involve use of soapless detergents, commercial tile cleaners, and, in special cases, solvents or acid. Solvents and acids should be used with care and only when necessary because of their hazardous nature.
- installation must be thoroughly dry before setting the new tile.

Materials, Grouting, Expansion Joints, Installation Specifications:
- for epoxy mortar installation refer to ANSI A108.6-1969.
- for Dry-Set mortar or latex-portland cement mortar installation see Method F113-76.
- for organic adhesive installation refer to ANSI A108.4-1967 and follow manufacturer's directions.
- require current certification that adhesive conforms with ANSI A136.1-1967 from adhesive manufacturer.

NOTES: Use Ceramic Tile floor Performance-Level Requirement Guide, Pages 8 & 9, to select adequate installation method.

If installation is not sound, Methods F111-76 and F141-76 may be applicable.

Tile Over Other Surfacing Materials

Ceramic tile may be considered as a surfacing material over existing wall finishes such as paint, wood paneling, cold glazes (sprayed on plastic), plastic laminates and steel plate, or existing floor surfacing such as epoxy coatings, paint, vinyl or asphalt tile, seamless flooring, exposed concrete, hardwood flooring and steel plate. Ideally, existing finishes should be completely removed so that the tile work can be placed on the substructure following Handbook Methods in the F, W, B and C series. However, this is not always practical. The following, therefore, is intended as a general guide for renovation with ceramic tile. In all cases consult the setting material manufacturer or his literature before starting the work. Consideration should be given to covering the existing surface with a more suitable base. For example: badly cracked or irregular walls should be overlayed with firmly attached gypsum board, concrete glass fiber reinforced backer board or plywood to provide a sound tile-setting base.

WARNING: Special installation precautions are necessary when installing thin-set tile over old concrete floors in bakeries, kitchens and meat processing areas. Fats and greases penetrate into concrete floors and cannot be completely neutralized. Note preparation sections below.

Organic Adhesives

Suitable Backings:
- smooth walls of all types including plaster, gypsum board, plywood, and masonry.
- smooth floors of all types including wood, concrete and terrazzo in residences or areas of equivalent light performance requirements (see Pages 8 and 9).
- new gypsum board nailed or glued over existing walls.
- plastic laminate counter tops & walls.

Requirements:
- the backing surface must be sound, clean and dry.
- max. variation in backing surface shall not exceed 1/8'' in 8' - 0'' from the required plane.
- abrupt irregularities such as trowel marks, ridges and grains shall be less than 1/32'' above adjacent area.

Preparation:
- roughen surfaces which are glossy, painted or which have loose surface material by sanding or scarifying.
- surface material must be removed if non-compatible with adhesive.
- use primer when recommended by the adhesive manufacturer as proper for the particular backing.
- clean thoroughly to remove all oil, dirt and dust.
- apply underlayment as needed according to manufacturer's directions.

Tile Installation:
- follow ANSI A108.4-1968.

Dry-Set or Latex-Portland Cement Mortar

Suitable Backings:
- prepared portland cement plaster, concrete, concrete masonry, structural clay tile, brick or concrete glass fiber reinforced backer board nailed over existing walls.
- new gypsum board nailed or glued over existing walls.

Requirements:
- the backing surface must be sound, clean and dry.
- maximum permissible variation in floor surfaces, 1/8'' in 10' - 0''; in wall surfaces 1/8'' in 8' - 0'' from the required plane.

Preparation:
- roughen concrete or masonry walls and floors which are glossy, painted or effloresced, or which have loose surface material. This should be accomplished by sand-blasting, chipping or scarifying.
- clean thoroughly to remove all sealers, coatings, oil, dirt and dust to expose masonry surface.

Tile Installation:
- follow ANSI A108.5-1967 for Dry-Set mortar, and latex-portland cement mortar.

Tile-Setting Epoxy and Epoxy Adhesive

Suitable Backings:
- generally all sound wall and floor finishes.
- especially valuable for setting tile floors over non-masonry surfaces where moderate performance level is required.
- suitable for speedy installation where down time must be kept to a minimum.

Requirements:
- backing surface must be sound, clean and dry.
- maximum permissible variation in floor surfaces, 1/8'' in 10' - 0''; in wall surfaces, 1/8'' in 8' - 0'' from the required plane.

Preparation:
- roughen surfaces which are glossy, painted or effloresced, or which have loose surface material, by sanding or scarifying.
- clean thoroughly to remove all waxes, oil, dirt and dust.
- with epoxy adhesives, use primer when recommended by the manufacturer as proper for the particular backing.

Tile Installation:
- follow ANSI A108.6-1969 for tile-setting epoxy, and manufacturer's specifications for epoxy adhesive.
- epoxy formulations vary with respect to chemical resistance and use on vertical surfaces. Consult manufacturer's specifications.

A variety of techniques can be used to control traffic noise in residential developments.

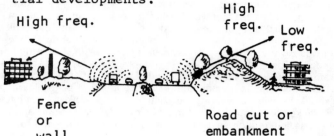

High freq.

High freq.

Low freq.

Fence or wall

Road cut or embankment

Office

Apartment

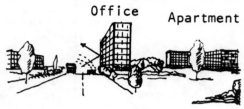

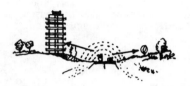

Buildings located in open areas are less noisy than in congested areas.

Traffic arteries between tall buildings are quite noisy.

Hollows or depressions are generally noisier than flat open land.

Wind direction

Noise path

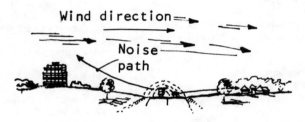

Upwind building locations are less noisy than downwind locations.

Buildings located at intersections of major traffic arteries are extremely noisy due to accelerating, decelerating, and braking

Buildings located on the crests of hilly traffic arteries are very noisy due to low gear acceleration noise.

586

glossary

ABUT . . . . Joining the end of building material
ACCELERATION . . . A mixture to booster setting of concrete or plaster
ACOUSTICAL . . . . Sound absorbing material
ACRE . . . . 43,560 square feet of land area
ADHESIVE . . . . Substance used to hold materials together
AGGREGATE . . . . Material used to make concrete such as stone
ALCOVE . . . . Recessed space off a larger room
ALKYD RESIN . . . . . . Material used to make paint and stain
ANCHOR BOLT . Threaded rod inserted in wall to anchor sill plate
ANGLE IRON . . . Steel L shaped bar used for supporting brick or block
APRON . . . . Trim under window stool
ARCH . . . . Building material used to form a curve
AREAWAY . Open recessed space in basement window for light and ventilation
ASBESTOS . . . . Fireproof building material
ASH PIT . . . . Area below fireplace to collect ashes
ASPHALT . . . . Insoluble waterproofing material
ASTRAGAL Small moulding or bead used on one of a pair of doors
ATRIUM . . . . Interior outdoor court
ATTIC . . . . Space between roof and ceiling
AWNING WINDOW . . . Outswinging window horizontally hinged
BACKFILL . . . . Earth used to fill around foundation
BALLON FRAME . Type of building with studs extending from sill to top of wall uninterrupted
BALLUSTER . . Small vertical member between stairs and top rail
BANNISTER . . . . Stair rail
BASEBOARD . . . . Wall covering at intersection of floor and wall
BASECOAT . . . . First coat of plaster
BATTEN . . . . Strip of wood covering joint
BATTER BOARD . . . Horizontal boards used to lay out building
BAY WINDOW . . . . Outward from wall projecting window
BEAD . . . . Narrow rounded moulding
BEAM . . . . . Horizontal structural member supporting loads
BEARING PARTITION . . . . Wall for supporting loads
BEARING PLATE . . Support member used to distribute load over wide area
BENCH MARK . . . . Permanent mark on ground used in surveying
BEVEL SIDING . . . Exterior finish thicker at bottom than at top
BIBB . . . . Threaded hose connection
BIRD'S MOUTH-OR HEEL . . . . . . End of rafter resting on plate
BLIND NAILING . . . . Concealed nails
BLOCKING . . . . Wood Filler
BOARD FOOT . . . Unit for measuring lumber 1" thick, 12" wide and 12" long
BOND . . . . . Arrangement of masonry units in a wall to lock wall
BRICK VENEER . . . . Brick facing
BRIDGING . . . . Cross bracing between joists and studs
BROWN COAT . . . . Second coat of plaster
BTU . . . . British Thermal Unit used to measure heat
BUILT-UP BEAM Beam constructed of small members put together
BUILT-UP ROOF . . . . Several layers of felt and asphalt
BULKHEAD . . . . Entrance from basement floor
BUTT . . . . Door hinge
CANT . . . . . . Angular roof board to eliminate sharp right angles

CANTILEVER . . . . . A beam fixed on one end free of the other
CASEMENT WINDOW . . . . . . Window opening similar to door
CASING . . . . Frame around door or window opening
CATCH BASIN . . . . Receptacle for collecting water underground
CAULKING . . . . . Waterproof material to seal joints and cracks
CEMENT PLASTER . . . . . . Plaster containing portland cement
CENTER TO CENTER . . . Measurement center of one member to center of another
CHAIR RAIL . . Rail along wall to prevent chair from marring wall
CHASE . . Vertical space containing mechanical piping and wiring
CHORD . . . . . . Horizontal member of truss connecting corners
CIRCUIT . . . . Path for electrical current
CIRCUIT BREAKER . . . . Opening and closing a circuit
CLAPBOARD . . . . Exterior siding thicker at one edge
CLEAT . . . . Wood strip holding two units together
COLLAR BEAM . . Horizontal member tieing two opposite rafters together
COMMON NAILS . . . . Large headed nails
CONDUCTOR . . . . Pipe to lead water from roof
CONDUIT . . . . Pipe carrying electric wires
CONVECTOR . . . . Heat transfer surface
COPE . . . . Cut end of moulded wood same contour as face
CORBEL . . . . To extend outward to carry superincumbent load
CORNER BEAD . . . . Metal bead at external corners
CORNICE . . . . Roof projection beyond wall
COUNTER FLASHING . . . . Flashing under exposed flashing
COUNTERSUNK . . . . Recessed head of nail or screw
COVE . . . . Inside curve (concave) shape to mate with right angle moulding
CRAWL SPACE . . . . . Shallow space between ground and floor
CRICKET . . . . . . Pitched roof behind chimney to divert water
CROSS BRACING . . . . Diagonal boards
CROWN MOULDING . . . Decorative moulding used at ceiling and under roof overhang
CUPOLA . Small structure on top of roof usually holding weather-vane
CURTAIN WALL . Wall used for separation only non-load bearing
DADO . . . . Groove across grain of board
DAMPER . . . . Movable steel plate to regulate draft
DARBY . . . . Flat tool used for plastering
DEAD LOAD . . . . Motionless load such as wind, snow, etc.
DECIBEL . . . . Measurement of sound
DIAMOND MESH . . . . Metal lath
DIMENSION . . . . Lumber framing 2" thick
DOOR CASING . . . . Trim around door opening
DOOR FRAME . . . . Enclosure for supporting door
DOOR JAMB . . . . Vertical pieces of door frame
DOOR SILL . . . . Bottom of door frame (threshold)
DOOR STOP . . . . Wood strip stopping door at frame
DORMER . . . . Structure projecting from roof
DOUBLE HEADER . Two pieces of framing lumber nailed together
DOUBLE HUNG . . . . Window moving up and down
DOVETAIL JOINT . . . . Wedge shaped wood joint
DOWN SPOUT . . . . . Vertical pipe carrying rain water from roof
DRAIN . . . . Pipe carrying waste water
DRIP CAP Metal used to prevent water from running down window or door

DRY ROT . . . . Wood decay
DRY WALL . . . Interior use of paper covered plaster in large sheets
DRY WELL . . . . Shallow well for rain water disposal
DUCT . . . . Sheet metal shaft for air distribution
DUPLEX OUTLET . . . . Electrical plug
DUTCHMAN . . . . Wood piece to cover error
EAVE . . . . Lower portion of roof extended beyond wall
EFFLORESCENSE . . White fleecy surface deposit found on brick wall
ELBOW . . . . L shaped pipe fitting
ELEVATION . . . . Vertical side projection
ESCUTCHEON Decorative plate around door lock and pipe passing through floor or wall
EXCAVATION . . . . Hole formed by removing earth
EXPANDED METAL . . . . Diamond shaped slit sheet metal
EXPANSION JOINT . Bituminous filler used to prevent crakcing of floor and wall through expansion due to temperature change
FACADE . . . . Front or face of building
FACE BRICK . . . . Finish brick
FACE NAIL . . . . Nail driven through face of material
FASCIA . . . . Horizontal member on edge of roof
FELT PAPER . . . Thin sheet paper used for roofing and sheathing
FENESTRATION . . . . Windows and doors
FIBERBOARD . . . . Building board of fiberous material
FILL . . . . Raise subgrade
FIRE BRICK . . . . Brick to withstand high temperatures
FIRE DOOR . . . . Door to resist fire
FIRE STOP . . . . Obstruction of passage to prevent spread of fire
FIRE WALL . . . . Resist spread of fire
FLASHING . . . . Seal to prevent leaks
FLOAT . . . . . . Tool used for finishing concrete or plaster
FLUE . . . . Chimney passage for smoke and gases
FLUE LINING . . . . Terra-cotta or clay flue in chimney
FOOTING . . . . Foundation base of concrete
FRIEZE . . . . Wall directly under roof overhang
FURRING . . . . . . Wood strips fastened to wall or ceiling
FUSE . . . . Electric current cut-off
GABLE . . . . Triangular portion at end of roof
GALVANIZED . . . . Zinc coated metal
GAMBREL . . . . Two plained roof surface or slope
GIRDER . . . . Horizontal structural member
GLAZING . . . . Placing glass in windows or frame
GRADE . . . . Level of ground
GRAIN . . . . Arrangement of wood fibers
GRAVEL STOP . . . . . . Metal strip around edge of roof
GROUND . . . . Wood plaster stop
GROUT . . . . Plaster like material to seal joints
GUTTER . . . . Trough to carry water from roof
GYPSUM BOARD . . . . . Plaster sandwich with paper covering
HALF TIMBER . . . Boards geometrically placed-space filled with stucco or masonry
HANGER . . . . Iron strap to support joists
HEADER . . . . Small beam
HEARTH . . . . Fireproof front of fireplace
HEARTWOOD . . . . Between pitch and sapwood of tree
HIP RAFTER . . . . Rafter from plate to ridge intersecting roof pitch
HIP ROOF . . . . Pitched on all sides
HOSE BIBB . . . . Threaded water pipe connection for hose
I BEAM . . . . steel beam I shaped
INCANDESCENT LAMP . . Bulb with filament wire used for light from electricity
INTERIOR TRIM . . . . All inside finish
JACK RAFTER . . . . Short rafter between wall and ridge
JALOUSIE . . . . Long narrow glass slats in windows
JAMB . . . . Vertical frame of door or window
JOIST . . . . Member supporting floor or ceiling
JOURNEYMAN . . . . Skilled tradesman
KALAMEIN . . . . Metal covered wood door used for fire door
KD . . . . Knocked down must be assembled
KILN . . . . Oven for drying lumber
KIP . . . . 1,000 lbs
KNEE WALL . . . . Low wall on 1½ story house
KNOT . . . . Cross section of tree branch
LAG SCREW . . . . Square headed wood screw
LALLY COLUMN . . . . Steel column to support beam
LAMINATE . . . . Several layers of material bonded together

LATH . . . . Base used for plaster
LAVATORY . . . . Wash basin
LEADER . . . . Vertical pipe carrying rain water
LEDGER . . . . Wood strip for joist bearing
LINEAL FOOT . . . . Measure on straight line
LINTEL . . . . Horizontal wall opening supporting load
LIVE LOAD . . . . . .Movable articles such as furniture, people, etc.
LOAD BEARING WALL . . . . Wall carrying load
LOOKOUT . . . . . . Short lumber supporting projected cornice
M . . . . 1,000 Units
MAIN RUNNERS . . . . Heaviest supporting member of suspended ceiling
MANHOLE . . . . Sewer cover
MANSARD . . . . Two planed roof
MANTEL . . . . Fireplace shelf
MASTIC . . . . Waterproofing material to seal cracks
MATCHED LUMBER . . . . . . Tongue and grooved edge lumber
MECHANICAL EQUIPMENT . Plumbing, heating, ventilating, air-conditioning and electrical
MEETING RAIL . . . . . Horizontal rail of double hung window
MEMBRANE . . . . Waterproofing
MESH . . . . Crossing of parallel wires forming a grid
METAL LATH . . . . Plaster base
MILLWORK . . . . Finish wood products
MITRE . . . . Beveled cut
MODULAR . . . . Fixed repeated divisional units
MONOLITHIC . . . . Concrete cast in one unit
MORTAR . . . . Mixture of sand cement and water
MORTISE . . . . Recessed cut into surface
MOSAIC . . . . Small colored glass or tile
MOTIF . . . . Design theme
MOULDING . . . . Finish trim
MULLION . . . Vertical bar section separating two or more doors or windows
MUNTIN . . . . Bar separating or dividing glass
NAIL SET . . . . Small tool used to recess nails
NEWEL . . . . Main post of stair rail
NOMINAL . . . . Lumber size before drying
NON-BEARING PARTITION . . . . Divider wall non-load bearing
NOSING . . . . Projected stair tread edge
ON CENTER-O.C. . Center to center measurement of one member to another
OUTLET . . . . Electrical wire connections
OVERHANG . . . . Projection beyond wall or roof
PALLETS . . . . Portable
PANEL . . . . Flat surface framed by thicker material
PANELBOARD . . . . Electric circuit control center
PARAPET . . . . Wall projecting above roof
PARGE . . . . To coat surface with plaster or mortar
PARQUET . . . . Patterned wood flooring
PARTICLE BOARD . . . . . Flat composition board of wood chips
PARTITION . . . . Dividing wall
PENNY . . . . A term used for length and weight of nails
PERSPECTIVE . . . . Pictorial drawing
PICTURE MOULD . . . . Moulding to hang pictures
PILASTER . . . . Built in column against wall
PILE . . . . Heavy structural column forced into earth
PITCH . . . . Roof slope
PLAIN SAWED . . . . . . Lumber cut on a tangent to growth rings
PLANCHER . . . . Underside of cornice
PLANK . . . . Lumber 2" thick or more
PLATE . . . . . . Horizontal member for supporting floor or roof
PLENUM . Forced chamber of air connected to distribution ducts
PLINTH . . . . Projecting band at bottom of casing
PLUMB . . . . Level vertically
PLYWOOD . . . Three or more layers of flat sheets of wood joined together
POINTING . . . . Filling joints in masonry wall
PORTLAND CEMENT . . . Powdered rock used to make concrete
POST & BEAM . . . Type of construction using column and beam
PRE-CAST . . . Concrete units made in shop delivered for erection
PRE-FABRICATED . . . . Built in sections
PRIME COAT . . . . First coat of paint
PUMICE . . . . Crushed volcanic lava used for polishing
PURLIN . . . . Structural member
QUARTER ROUND . . . . Small moulding
QUARTER SAWED . . . . Lumber cut 90° to annual rings

QUARTER TILE . . . . Unglazed floor tile
QUOINS . . . . Wall projection at corners
RABBET . . . . Grooved edge to receive another piece
RADIANT HEAT . . . . Concealed in floor or ceiling
RAFTER . . . . Roof supporting member
RAKE . . . . Trim parallel to roof slope
READY MIX CONCRETE . . . . Pre-mixed at plant
REFLECTIVE INSULATION . . . . . Surfaced to reduce heat loss
REINFORCED CONCRETE . . Concrete embedded with steel rods
RESILIENT . . . . . Ability of material to withstand original shape
RETAINING WALL . . . . Lateral pressure support for earth
RETARDER . . . . Reduce evaporation rate
REVEAL . . . . Visible part of door or window jamb
RIBBON . . . . Narrow wood strip to support joists
RIDGE . . . . Top edge of roof
RIP RAP . . . . Stone placed to reduce erosion
RISER . . . . Vertical part of step
ROCK LATH . . . . Plaster base
ROLL ROOFING . . . . Roof covering material
ROOF SHEATHING . . . . Covering of roof rafters
ROTARY CUT . . . . Shaving log on lathe
ROUGH OPENING . . . . Unfinished opening
RUN . . . . Horizontal distance of stairs
SADDLE . . . . Small pitched roof behind chimney to divert water
SASH . . . . A frame for holding panes of glass in a window
SASH CORD . . . . . . Rope to counterbalance double hung sash
SCAFFOLD . . . . Temporary platform
SCRATCH COAT . . . . First coat plaster
SCRIBE . . . . Fitting to an irregular surface
SCUTTLE . . . . Opening in roof for access
SEASONING . . . . Removing moisture from wood
SEPTIC TANK . . . . Sewage settling tank
SHAKE . . . . Hand split shingles
SHEATHING . . . . Covering over studs or rafters
SHED ROOF . . . . Single pitched roof
SHIM . . . . Wedge
SHINGLE . . . . Exterior wall or roof covering
SHIPLAP . . . . Joint between two wood pieces
SHOE MOULD . . . . . Small moulding against baseboard at floor
SHORING . . . . . Bracing to support structure during construction
SIDING . . . . Finished outside surface
SILL . . . . . . Wood member on top of foundation-wood member
across window or door bottom
SKIM COAT . . . . Finish coat usually plaster
SLEEPER . . . . . Wood piece on or in concrete to nail wood floor
SOFFIT . . . . Underside of overhang
SOFT WOOD . . . . From tree having needles
SOIL STACK . . . . Vertical plumbing waste discharge pipe
SOLE . . . . Horizontal member under studs
SOLID BRIDGING . . Full size members placed between framing
SPACKLE . . . . Plaster used to cover wall board joints
SPECIFICATIONS . . . . Written detail of building products
SPLASH BLOCK Masonry block to spread water from roof drain at
ground
STAGGER . . . . Alternate intervals
STAKE . . . . Wedge shaped stick driven in ground
STILE . . . . Vertical member of door
STIRRUP . . . . Heavy metal strap to support framing
STOOL . . . . Shelf on bottom of window inside
STOOP . . . . Small platform
STOP BEAD . . . . Moulding used to stop door in frame
STORY POLE . . . . Rod or stick used for measuring units
STRAIGHT EDGE . . . . True edge piece used for accuracy
STRETCHER . . . . Long side of brick exposed
STRINGER . . . . Stair supports
STUCCO . . . . Outside finish plaster
STUDS . . . . Vertical wall framing members
SUB FLOOR . . . . Rough floor under finish floor
SUSPENDED CEILING . . . . Hanging ceiling
TAIL BEAM . . . . Short framing member
TEE BEAM . . . . Frame member
TENSILE STRENGTH . . . . Strength of building material to
support load
TERMITE SHIELD . . . . Metal used to prevent termite damage to
building
TERRA COTTA . . . . Sand and clay baked building material

TERRAZZO . Marble chips and conc. surface ground smooth floor
THRESHOLD . . . . Sill on bottom of door frame
THROAT . . . . Smoke passage above fireplace
TOE NAIL . . . . Nail driven at angle
TOE SPACE . . . . Recessed space at floor under counter
TONGUE . . . . Projection bead of board
TRANSOM . . . . Panel opening above door
TRAP . . . . U-shaped pipe below plumbing fixture
TREAD . . . . Horizontal part of stairs
TRIM . . . . Finish wood work
TROWEL . . . . . Tool used for finishing plaster or concrete
TRUSS . . . . No column roof support
UNDERLAYMENT . . . . Material under floor
UPRIGHT . . . . Timber support rafters
VALLEY . . . . Trough formed at roof intersecting slopes
VALLEY RAFTER . . . . . Diagonal rafter intersecting roof slopes
VALVE . . . . Fluid or liquid flow regulator
VAPOR BARRIER Water tight material to prevent passage of vapor
VENEER . . . . Thin faced covering
VENT . . . . Vertical pipe used to ventilate plumbing
WAINSCOT . . . . Lower part of two part wall
WATERTABLE Extend around building at bottom of exterior wall
WEATHERSTRIP . . . . Sealing of doors and windows
WEEP HOLE . . . . . Opening at bottom of wall for water drainage
WELL OPENING . . . . Floor opening for stairs
WINDER . . . . Turning of stairs
WIRE GLASS . . . . Wire mesh in glass
WYTHE . . . . .Single width of masonry wall

abbreviations

Acoustic	ACST	Building	BLDG
Acoustical Plaster	ACST PL	Building Line	BL
Addition	ADD	Built In	BLT IN
Adhesive	ADH	Bulkhead	BLKHD
Aggregate	AGGR	Bulletin Board	BB
Air Conditioning	AIR COND. OR A.C	Buzzer	BZ
Alternate	ALT	By	2"x4" (example)
Alternating Current	AC	Cabinet	CAB
Aluminum	ALUM	Candlepower	CP
American Institute of Architects	A.I.A.	Carpenter	CARP
American Institute of Steel Construction	A.I.S.C.	Casing	CSG
American Society of Heating, Ventilating Engineers	A.S.H.V.E.	Cast Iron	CI
American Society of Testing Materials	A.S.T.M.	Catch Basin	CB
American Wire Gauge	AWG	Caulking	CLKG
Amount	AMT	Ceiling	CLG
Ampere	AMP	Cellar	CEL
Anchor Bolt	AB	Cement	CEM
Angle	L	Cement Mortar	CEMT ' MR
Apartment	APT	Cement Plastic	CMT ' PL
Approval	APP	Center to Center	CC or OC or C
Approximate	APPROX	Ceramic Tile	CT
Architect	ARCH	Cesspool	CP
Architectural Terra Cotta	ATC	Channel	C
Area	A	Circuit	CIR
Asbestos	ASB	Circuit Breaker	CKT' BR
Asphalt	ASPH	Cleanout	CO
Asphalt Tile	AT	Closet	CLO
Assemble	ASSEM	Clothes Dryer	CL'D
Assembly	ASSBY	Coefficient	COEF
Associate	ASSOC	Cold Water	CW
At	@	Combination	COMB
Automatic Pressure	ATM PRESS	Composition	COMP
Automobile	AUTO	Concrete	CONC
Avenue	AVE.	Concrete Block	CB
Average	AVG	Concrete Floor	CON FL
Balcony	BLCNY	Concrete Masonry Unit	CMU
Basement	BSMT	Construction	CONST
Bathroom	B	Construction Specification Institute	C.S.I.
Beam	BM	Contractor	CONTR
Bedroom	BR	Copper	CPR
Bench Mark	BM	Counter	CNTR
Between	BET	Countersunk	CSNK
Bevel	BEV	Courses	C
Blocking	BLKG	Cover	COV
Board	BD	Cross Section	X SECT
Board Feet	BD FT	Cubic	CU
Board Measure	BM	Cubic Feet	CU FT
Book Shelves	BK SH	Cubic Feet Minute	CFM
Bottom	BOT	Cubic Inch	CU IN
Boulevard	BLVD	Cubic Yard	CU YD
Bracket	BRKT	Damper	DMPR
Brass	BR	Dampproofing	DMPRF
British Thermal Unit	BTU	Decibel	DB
Bronze	BRZ	Decorative	DEC
Broom Closet	BC	Degree Fahrenheit	0° F

Detail	DET	Glass Block	GL BL
Diagram	DIA	Government	GOVT
Diameter	DIA. OR ∅	Grade	GR
Dimension	DIM	Granite	GR
Dining Room	DR	Grating	GRTG
Direct Current	D. C.	Grease Trap	GT
Dishwasher	DW	Gypsum	GYP
Distance	DIST	Hall	H
Ditto	DO	Hardware	HDW
Divide	DIV	Hardwood	HDWD
Door	DR	Head	HD
Double Hung Window	DH W	Heater	HTR
Double Strength Glass Grade A	DSA	Height	HT
Double Strength Glass Grade B	DSB	Hexagon	HEX
Dowel	DWL	Hollow Metal	HM
Down	DN	Horizontal	HORIZ
Downspout	DS	Horse Power	HP
Drain	DR	Hose Bibb	HB
Drainboard	DB	Hot Water	HW
Drawing	DWG	Hour	HR
Dressed and Matched Four Sides	D&M4S	House	HSE
Drinking Fountain	DF	Hundred	C
Dryer	D	I Beam	I
Drywall	DW	Inches	" OR IN
Dry Well	DW	Information	INFO
Each	EA	Inside Diameter	ID
East	E	Insulation	INSUL
Edge Grain	EG	Interior	INT
Elbow	ELL	Joint	JT
Electric	ELEC	Joist	JST
Elevator	ELEV	Kalamein	KAL
Emergency	EMERGCY	Kiln Dried	KD
Enclosure	ENCL	Kilowatt	KW
Engineer	ENG	Kitchen	KIT
Entrance	ENT	Kitchen Cabinet	KIT CAB
Equipment	EQUIP	Kitchen Sink	KIT S
Estimate	EST	Knocked Down	KD
Excavate	EXC	Laboratory	LAB
Expansion Joint	EX JT	Ladder	LAD
Extension	EXT	Laminated	LAM
Exterior	EXT	Landing	L
Extra Heavy	XH	Latitude	LAT
Fabricate	FAB	Laundry	L
Face to Face	F to F	Laundry Chute	LC
Facing Tile	FT	Lavatory	LAV
Fahrenheit	F	Leader	LDR
Family Room	FAM R	Left	L
Federal Housing Administration	FHA	Length	LGTH
Feet	FT	Level	LEV
Feet Per Minute	FPM	Library	LIB
Feet Per Second	FPS	Light	LT
Figure	FIG	Light Weight Concrete	LWC
Finish	FIN	Limestone	LS
Finish Floor	FIN FL	Lineal Feet	LF
Fire Brick	FB	Linen Closet	L CL
Fire Extinguisher	FX	Lining	LNG
Fire Hose	FH	Linoleum	LINO
Fireproof	FP	Living Room	LR
Fitting	FITG	Long	LG
Fixture	FIXT	Louver	LVR
Flange	FLG	Lumber	LBR
Flashing	FL	Machine	MACH
Floor	FL	Manufacturer	MFG
Floor Drain	FD	Marble	MBL
Fluorescent	FLUOR	Mark	MK
Foot Board Measure	FBM	Masonry Opening	MO
Footing	FTG	Material	MAT
Foundation	FDN	Maximum	MAX
Frame	FR	Mechanical	MECH
Fresh Air Intake	FAI	Medicine Cabinet	MED C
Front	FR	Medium	MED
Full Size	FS	Metal	MET
Furred Ceiling	F CLG	Millemeter	m
Gallon	GAL	Minimum	MIN
Galvanized	GALV	Miscellaneous	MISC
Gauge	GA	Model	MOD

Modular	MOD	Saddle	S
Moulding	MLDG	Schedule	SCH
National	NAT	Screen	SCR
National Board of Fire Underwriters	N.B.F.U.	Second	SEC
National Electrical Code	N.E.C.	Section	SECT
National Lumber Manufacturers Association	N.L.M.A.	Self Closing	SC
Nominal	NOM	Service	SERV
North	N	Sewer	SEW
Not In Contract	N.I.C.	Sheathing	SHTNG
Number	NO. OR #	Sheet Metal	SM
Octogan	OCT	Shelves	SH
Office	OFF	Shower	SH
On Center	OC	Siding	SDG
Opening	OPNG	Sill Cock	SC
Opposite	OPP	Single Strength Grade A Glass	SAS
Ornament	ORN	Single Strength Grade B Glass	SBS
Ounce	OZ	Sink	S
Outside Diameter	OD	Slop Sink	SS
Overhead	OVHD	Socket	SOC
Page	PG	Soil Pipe	SP
Painted	PTD	South	S
Pair	PR	Specifications	SPEC
Panel	PNL	Square Feet	SQ FT OR ⊡
Parallel	PAR	Stairs	ST
Partition	PTN	Standard	STD
Passage	PASS	Stand Pipe	STP
Pedestal	PED	Station	STA
Penny	d	Steel	ST
Percent	%	Steel Plate	SP
Perforated	PERF	Stirrup	STIR
Perpendicular	PERP	Stock	STK
Piece	PC	Stone	ST
Plaster	PLAS	Street	ST
Plate	P	String	STR
Plate Glass	P GL	Structural	STR
Platform	PLTFM	Substitute	SUB
Plumbing	PLMB	Supersede	SUPSD
Point	P	Supplement	SUPP
Polish	POL	Supply	SUP
Polyvinyl Chloride	PVC	Surface	SUR
Position	POS	Surface 2 Sides	S2S
Pounds	LB OR #	Surface 4 sides	S4S
Poured Concrete	P/C	Suspended Ceiling	SUS CLG
Precast	PRCST	Switch	SW
Prefabricate	PREFAB	Symbol	SYM
Property	PROP	System	SYS
Push Button	PB	Tar & Gravel	T & G
Quantity	QTY	Technical	TECH
Quart	QT	Tee	T
Radiator	RAD	Telephone	TEL
Radius	R	Television	TV
Random length and width	RL&W	Temperature	TEMP
Rang	R	Terra-Cotta	TC
Receptacle	RECP	Terrazzo	TER
Recessed	REC	Thermostat	THERMO
Rectangle	RECT	Thickness	THK
Redwood	RDWD	Thousand	M
Reference	REF	Thread	THD
Refrigerator	REFG	Tongue and Groove	T & G
Register	REG	Tread	T
Reinforced Concrete	REINF	Typical	TYP
Required	REQ	Ultimate	ULT
Return	RET	Unfinished	UNFIN
Revision	REV	United States Gauge	USG
Revolution Per Minute	RPM	Urinal	UR
Right	R	Vanity	VAN
Right Hand	RH	Vent	V
Riser	R	Vertical	VERT
Road	RD	Vestibule	VEST
Roof	RF	Volts	V
Roof Drain	RD	Volume	VOL
Roofing	RFG	Wall Cabinet	W/CAB
Room	RM	Wall Vent	WV
Rough	RGH	Water	W
Round	RD	Water Closet	WC
Rubber	R	Waterproof	WP

Watts	W	Window	WDH
Weatherstrip	WS	Wire Glass	W GL
Weephole	WH	With	W/
Weight	WT	Without	WO/
West	W	Wood	WD
Wide Flange Beam	WF	Wrought Iron	WI
Width	WTH	Yards	YD

Zinc . . . . Z OR ZN

bibliography

EXPLORING WOODWORKING, Fred W. Zimmerman, The Goodheart-Wilcox Co., Inc.

ARCHITECTS' AND BUILDERS' HANDBOOK, Kidder-Parker, John Wiley & Sons

SIMPLIFIED ENGINEERING FOR ARCHITECTS AND BUILDERS, Harry Parker, John Wiley & Sons, Inc.

MANUAL OF STEEL CONSTRUCTION, American Institute of Steel Construction, Inc.

TIME SAVER STANDARDS, F. W. Dodge Corporation

MECHANICAL AND ELECTRICAL EQUIPMENT FOR BUILDINGS, Gay-Fawcett-McGuiness, John Wiley & Sons, Inc.

HOW TO PLAN A HOUSE, Townsend-Dalzell, American Technical Society

HEATING, VENTILATING AND AIR CONDITIONING GUIDE, American Society of Heating and Ventilating Engineers

ARCHITECTURAL RESIDENTIAL DRAWING AND DESIGN, Clois E. Kicklighter, The Goodheart-Wilcox Company, Inc.

THE COMPLETE BOOK OF INTERIOR DECORATING, Mary Derieux, Isabelle Stevenson, Greystone Press

MANUAL OF LATHING AND PLASTERING, John R. Diehl, Mac Publishers Association

ARCHITECTURAL GRAPHIC STANDARDS, Charles George Ramsey, Harold Reeve Sleeper, John Wiley & Sons, Inc.

WHEN YOU BUILD, Edited by Marshall Reid, Robert M. Mcbride & Company

ARCHITECTURAL DRAWING AND LIGHT CONSTRUCTION, Edward J. Muller, Prentice-Hall, Inc.

ARCHITECTURAL DRAFTING AND DESIGN, Ernest R. Weidhass, Allyn & Bacon, Inc.

MODERN CARPENTRY, Willis H. Wagner, The Goodheart-Willcox Co., Inc.

STRENGTH OF HOUSES, U. S. Department of Commerce

CARPENTRY AND JOINERY WORK, Nelson Burbank, Simmons-Broadman Publishing Corporation

DON GRAF'S DATA SHEETS, Don Graph, Reinhold Publishing Corporation

ARCHITECTURAL DETAILS, Louis Roullion, Charles Ramsey, John Wiley & Sons, Inc.

TIMBER CONSTRUCTION MANUAL, John Wiley & Sons, Inc.

CONCRETE REINFORCING STEEL INSTITUTE DESIGN HANDBOOK, Concrete Reinforcing Steel Institute

MATERIALS AND METHODS OF ARCHITECTURAL CONSTRUCTION, Gay and Parker, John Wiley & Sons, Inc.

AUDELS HANDBOOK OF PRACTICAL ELECTRICITY, Frank Grahm, Theo. Audel & Company

MODERN WOODWORKING, Willis H. Wagner, The Goodheart-Wilcox Co., Inc.

ARCHITECTURAL DRAFTING AND DESIGN, Hepler & Wallach, McGraw Hill Book Company

ARCHITECTURAL DRAFTING, William J. Hornung, Prentice-Hall, Inc.

ENGINEERING MANUAL, International Truss Plate Corporation

TYPICAL DESIGNS OF TIMER STRUCTURES, Timber Engineering Company

WOOD STRUCTURAL DESIGN DATA, National Lumber Manufacturers Association

WOOD STRUCTURAL DESIGN DATA, National Forest Products Association

BUILDING CONSTRUCTION COST DATA, Robert Means Co., Inc.

HUD MINIMUM PROPERTY STANDARDS 4900.1, U. S. Dept. of Housing and Urban Development

MANUAL OF ACCEPTABLE PRACTICES 4930.1, U. S. Dept. of Housing and Urban Development

index